THE PILLAR NEW TESTAMENT COMMENTARY

General Editor

D. A. CARSON

Paul's Letter to the
ROMANS

Colin G. Kruse

WILLIAM B. EERDMANS PUBLISHING COMPANY
GRAND RAPIDS, MICHIGAN / CAMBRIDGE, U.K.

APOLLOS
NOTTINGHAM, ENGLAND

Published 2012 by

Wm. B. Eerdmans Publishing Co.

2140 Oak Industrial Drive N.E., Grand Rapids, Michigan 49505 /
P.O. Box 163, Cambridge CB3 9PU U.K.

www.eerdmans.com

and in the United Kingdom by

APOLLOS

Norton Street, Nottingham,
England NG7 3HR

Printed in the United States of America

28 27 26 25 24 23 22   7 6 5 4 3 2

Library of Congress Cataloging-in-Publication Data

Kruse, Colin G.

Paul's letter to the Romans / Colin G. Kruse.

pages   cm   — (The Pillar New Testament commentary)

Includes bibliographical references and index.

ISBN 978-0-8028-3743-1 (cloth: alk. paper)

1. Bible. N.T. Romans — Commentaries.   I. Title.

BS2665.53.K78   2012

227'.1077 — dc23

2012006677

British Library Cataloguing in Publication Data

A catalogue record for this book is available from the British Library.

ISBN 978-1-84474-582-1

Dedicated to my beloved wife of fifty years,

Rosemary,

and to my esteemed colleagues in the three institutions

in which I have had the privilege of teaching:

Satya Wacana Christian University, Indonesia,

Ridley Melbourne,

and

the Melbourne School of Theology

Contents

COMMENTARY

INDEXES

Editor's Preface

Commentaries have specific aims, and this series is no exception. Designed for serious pastors and teachers of the Bible, the Pillar commentaries seek above all to make clear the text of Scripture as we have it. The scholars writing these volumes interact with the most important informed contemporary debate, but avoid getting mired in undue technical detail. Their ideal is a blend of rigorous exegesis and exposition, with an eye alert both to biblical theology and to the contemporary relevance of the Bible, without confusing the commentary and the sermon.

The rationale for this approach is that the vision of "objective scholarship" (a vain chimera) may actually be profane. God stands over against us; we do not stand in judgment of him. When God speaks to us through his Word, those who profess to know him must respond in an appropriate way, and that is certainly different from a stance in which the scholar projects an image of autonomous distance. Yet this is no surreptitious appeal for uncontrolled subjectivity. The writers of this series aim for an even-handed openness to the text that is the best kind of "objectivity" of all.

If the text is God's Word, it is appropriate that we respond with reverence, a certain fear, a holy joy, a questing obedience. These values should be reflected in the way Christians write. With these values in place, the Pillar commentaries will be warmly welcomed not only by pastors, teachers, and students, but by general readers as well.

*   *   *

Especially since Reformation times (though in fact even earlier), Paul's letter to the Romans has played an extraordinary role in shaping the understanding and life of Christians. To mention only four passages: How we think about natural revelation is hugely indebted to Romans 1–2; Luther called Romans 3:21-26 the center of the entire Bible; Romans 11 wrestles with the relationship between Israel and the church; and Romans 8 has been called the most important chapter in the Bible, unfolding the entire plan of salvation from justification to glorification, all grounded in the matchless love of God for his people. Moreover, in recent decades (to go back no further), Romans has called forth a disturbingly large array of interpretations. That means a good commentary must not only provide a reliable unpacking of the text, but it must also be a useful guide to the plethora of books and essays that swirl around this letter. Enter Colin Kruse. Readers of The Pillar New Testament Commentary will know him for the clarity and good sense in his commentary on John's letters in the PNTC series. Here his skills come to the fore again: clarity of thought and writing, independent judgment, deep reverence for what the text actually says, and uncommon wisdom in sorting through the vast secondary literature without getting bogged down. It is a pleasure to commend this commentary and include it in the series.

D. A. CARSON

Author's Preface

To be invited to produce a commentary on Paul's Letter to the Romans for inclusion in the Pillar New Testament Commentary series is a special privilege, and one for which I am grateful to both the editor of the series, Professor Don Carson, and the William B. Eerdmans Publishing Company. This commentary replaces an earlier volume written by Dr. Leon Morris, who was the principal of Ridley College when I joined the faculty there back in 1979. It is my hope that this book of mine will prove to be a worthy successor to his work.

This commentary is based upon the text of the New International Version (NIV 2011). Unless otherwise indicated, all quotations from the Scriptures of the Old and New Testaments are from the NIV 2011. Quotations from the Apocrypha are taken from the New Revised Standard Version (NRSV). Included in the commentary are additional notes on matters of special interest or importance. If these were included in the actual commentary, readers might lose track of Paul's developing argument. Some may prefer, therefore, on a first reading of the commentary on a particular portion of text, to skip over the additional notes and come back to them later on.

The Letter to the Romans is arguably the apostle Paul's most important piece of writing. While it addresses issues of crucial importance for first-century believers, in particular those of the Christian congregations in Rome, in doing so it also addresses matters of great importance for believers of all times. Romans is essentially an exposition and defense of the gospel of God concerning his Son, Jesus Christ, a gospel in which the righteousness of God is revealed for the salvation of all who believe in his Son. This exposition and defense is carried out against the background of God's sovereign action as creator, judge, and redeemer of the world.

The Letter includes important statements about the person and work of God the Father, Jesus Christ the Son, and the Holy Spirit. In addition, it addresses such major theological themes as the righteousness of God, the atonement, justification, predestination, faith, hope, the role of the Mosaic law, and believers' freedom from it as a regulatory norm, the renewal of the creation, and the place of Israel in the purposes of God. It also deals with practical matters such as ministry in the Christian congregation, believers' relation to the state, and attitudes to be adopted by the 'weak' and the 'strong' in the Christian community, and it refers to Paul's many associates and ministerial colleagues, including many notable women.

Work on this commentary has occupied the greater part of my discretionary time over the last eight years. Much of that work has, by necessity, been of a solitary nature, but happily it was enhanced by three months spent in the scholarly Christian community at Tyndale House, Cambridge. I am very grateful for the interaction I enjoyed with members of the staff and other researchers working there at the time. I also appreciated very much the encouragement of my colleagues at the Melbourne School of Theology, and in particular of Dr. Greg Forbes and Dr. Ted Woods, fellow lecturers in the Biblical Studies Department. I also valued the advice of General Editor of the Pillar New Testament Commentary series, Professor Don Carson, during the period of my work on this project and his insightful comments on the completed manuscript. I am grateful to Milton Essenburg of William B. Eerdmans Publishing Company for his understanding and willingness to accommodate me when I had to ask for extensions to the date of submission of the manuscript, and for his subsequent editorial work on the manuscript.

Colin G. Kruse

Abbreviations

1, 2, 3 Enoch	Ethiopic, Slavonic, Hebrew *Enoch*
2, 3 Apoc. Bar.	Syriac, Greek *Apocalypse of Baruch*
AB	Anchor Bible
ABD	*Anchor Bible Dictionary*
ABR	*Australian Biblical Review*
ACCSR	Gerald Bray, ed., *Ancient Christian Commentary on Scripture: New Testament, VI: Romans*
AnglTheolRev	*Anglican Theological Review*
Apoc. Mos.	*Apocalypse of Moses*
AsiaJT	*Asia Journal of Theology*
AUSS	*Andrews University Seminary Studies*
BAGD/BGD	W. Bauer, *A Greek-English Lexicon of the New Testament and Other Early Christian Literature*
BBR	*Bulletin of Biblical Research*
BECNT	Baker Exegetical Commentary on the New Testament
B.G.U.	*Berliner Griechische Urkunden*
Bib	*Biblica*
Bib. Ant.	Ps.-Philo, *Biblical Antiquities*
BibInt	*Biblical Interpretation*
BibToday	*Bible Today*
BibTrans	*Bible Translator*
Bijdr	*Bijdragen*
BJRL	*Bulletin of the John Rylands Library*
BN	*Biblische Notizen*
BR	*Biblical Research*
BSac	*Bibliotheca Sacra*
BTB	*Biblical Theology Bulletin*
BZ	*Biblische Zeitschrift*
BZNW	Beihefte zur ZNW
CalvTheolJourn	*Calvin Theological Journal*
CBQ	*Catholic Biblical Quarterly*

ConBNT	Coniectanea biblica, New Testament
CurrTheolMiss	*Currents in Theology and Mission*
Dead Sea Scrolls	
1QH	*Thanksgiving Hymns*
1QIsª	The complete Isaiah scroll
1QS	*Rule of the Community*
1QSa	*Rule of the Congregation* (Appendix a to 1QS)
1QSb	*Rule of the Blessings* (Appendix b to 1QS)
4Q161	*Commentary on Isaiah*
4Q246	*Apocryphon of Daniel* (known as the 'Son of God fragment')
4Q285	*Sefer-ha-Milhamah*
4QFlor	*Florilegium* (or *Eschatological Midrashim*)
1QpHab	*Pesher Habakkuk*
4QpIsaª	*Pesher Isaiah*
4QpGenª	*Pesher Genesis*
4QpPs	*Pesher Psalms*
4QTest	*Testimonia*
CD	*Damascus Document*
DNTB	*Dictionary of New Testament Background*
DPL	*Dictionary of Paul and His Letters*
DSS	Dead Sea Scrolls
EKKNT	Evangelisch-katholischer Kommentar zum Neuen Testament
Epictetus	
Diatr.	*Diatribai (Discourses)*
ERT	*Evangelical Review of Theology*
ET	English translation
ETL	*Ephemerides theologicae lovanienses*
EvQ	*Evangelical Quarterly*
EvTh	*Evangelische Theologie*
ExpTim	*Expository Times*
FilolNT	*Filologia Neotestamentaria*
FoiVie	*Foi et Vie*
Greg	*Gregorianum*
HeyJ	*Heythrop Journal*
HorBibTheol	*Horizons in Biblical Theology*
HR	*History of Religions*
HTR	*Harvard Theological Review*
IBS	*Irish Biblical Studies*
ICC	International Critical Commentary
IDB	*Interpreter's Dictionary of the Bible*
IDB Sup	*Interpreter's Dictionary of the Bible* Supplement
Ign. *Eph.*	Ignatius, *Letter to the Ephesians*
Instit. Or.	Quintilian, *Institutio Oratoria*
Int	*Interpretation*
Irenaeus	
Adv. Haer.	*Adversus haereses*
JAAR	*Journal of the American Academy of Religion*

JB	Jerusalem Bible
JBL	*Journal of Biblical Literature*
JETS	*Journal of the Evangelical Theological Society*
Josephus	
Ag. Ap.	*Against Apion*
Ant.	*Antiquities of the Jews*
Wars	*Jewish Wars*
JPT	*Journal of Pentecostal Theology*
JSNT	*Journal for the Study of the New Testament*
JSNTSup	*Journal for the Study of the New Testament* Supplement Series
JTS	*Journal of Theological Studies*
Jub.	*Jubilees*
Judaica	*Judaica: Beiträge zum Verständnis . . .*
KJV	King James Version
KJVS	King James Version with Strong's Numbers
LBS	Library of Biblical Studies
LCL	Loeb Classical Library
lit.	literally
LNTS	Library of New Testament Studies
LS	*Louvain Studies*
LSJ	Liddell–Scott–Jones, *Greek-English Lexicon*
LTJ	*Lutheran Theological Journal*
LXX	Septuagint
MM	J. H. Moulton and G. Milligan, *The Vocabulary of the Greek Testament*
MT	Massoretic Text
NA²⁷	*Novum Testamentum Graece,* 27th rev. ed.
NASB	New American Standard Bible
NEB	New English Bible
Neot	*Neotestamentica*
NIBC	New International Biblical Commentary
NICNT	New International Commentary on the New Testament
NIDNTT	*New International Dictionary of New Testament Theology*
NIV	New International Version
NJB	New Jerusalem Bible
NotesTrans	*Notes on Translation*
NovT	*Novum Testamentum*
NRSV	New Revised Standard Version
NT	New Testament
NTS	*New Testament Studies*
Odes Sol.	*Odes of Solomon*
OT	Old Testament
Paed.	Clement of Alexandria, *Paedagogus*
P. Lond.	*Greek Papyrii in the British Museum*
Philo	
Abr.	*De Abrahamo*
Cong.	*De congressu eruditionis gratia*

Decal.	*De decalogo*
Mig.	*De migratione Abrahami*
Opif.	*De opificio mundi*
Praem.	*De praemiis et poenis*
Spec. Leg.	*De specialibus legibus*
Virt.	*De virtutibus*
Vit. Mos.	*De vita Moses*
PNTC	Pillar New Testament Commentary
Pol.	Aristotle, *Politica*
Ps.-Phoc.	*Pseudo-Phocylides*
PSB	*Princeton Seminary Bulletin*
PSB Sup	*Princeton Seminary Bulletin* Supplement
Pss. Sol.	*Psalms of Solomon*
Rabbinic Literature	
b. Sanh.	Babylonian Talmud *Sanhedrin*
m. 'Abot	Mishnah tractate *'Abot*
m. Giṭṭin	Mishnah tractate *Giṭṭin*
m. Makk.	Mishnah tractate *Makkoth*
m. Sanh.	Mishnah tractate *Sanhedrin*
Exod. Rab.	*Exodus Rabbah*
RB	*Revue biblique*
RelSRev	*Religious Studies Review*
ResQ	*Restoration Quarterly*
RevScRel	*Revue des sciences religieuses*
RSV	Revised Standard Version
RTR	Reformed Theological Review
SB (or Str-B)	(H. Strack and) P. Billerbeck, *Kommentar zum Neuen Testament*
SBB	Stuttgarter biblische Beiträge
SBLDS	Society of Biblical Literature Dissertation Series
SBT	Studies in Biblical Theology
Seneca	
Clem.	*De clementia*
Ep.	*Epistulae morales*
Frag.	*Fragmenta*
Ira	*De ira*
Vit. beat.	*De vita beata*
SH	Sanday and Headlam, *The Epistle to the Romans*
Sib. Or.	*Sibylline Oracles*
Sir	Ecclesiasticus (Wisdom of Jesus the Son of Sirach)
SJT	*Scottish Journal of Theology*
SNTSMS	Society for New Testament Studies Monograph Series
SR	*Studies in Religion/Sciences religieuses*
ST	*Studia Theologica*
Str-B (or SB)	(H. Strack and) P. Billerbeck, *Kommentar zum Neuen Testament*
StudBib	*Studia Biblica*
Tacitus	
Ann.	*Annales*

T. Benj.	*Testament of Benjamin*
T. Dan	*Testament of Dan*
T. Gad	*Testament of Gad*
T. Job	*Testament of Job*
T. Naph.	*Testament of Naphtali*
TBei	*Theologische Beiträge*
TDNT	*Theological Dictionary of the New Testament*
TEV	Today's English Version
TLG	*Thesaurus linguae Graecae*
TNTC	Tyndale New Testament Commentaries
TrinJ	*Trinity Journal*
TTZ	*Trierer theologische Zeitschrift*
TynBul	*Tyndale Bulletin*
TZ	*Theologische Zeitschrift*
VoxRef	*Vox Reformata*
WTJ	*Westminster Theological Journal*
WUNT	Wissenschaftliche Untersuchngen zum Neuen Testament
ZNW	*Zeitschrift für die neutestamentliche Wissenschaft*
ZTK	*Zeitschrift für Theologie und Kirche*

Bibliography

Aageson, J. W., 'Typology, Correspondence, and the Application of Scripture in Romans 9–11', *JSNT* 31 (1987) 51-72.

Abasciano, Brian J., 'Corporate Election in Romans 9: A Reply to Thomas Schreiner', *JETS* 49 (2006) 351-71.

———, *Paul's Use of the Old Testament in Romans 9.1-9: An Intertextual and Theological Exegesis* (Library of New Testament Studies 301; London/New York: T&T Clark, 2006).

Achtemeier, P. J., 'Righteousness in the N.T.', *IDB* 4, 91-99.

———, 'Romans 3:1-8: Structure and Argument', *AnglTheolRev* Sup. 11 (1990) 77-87.

———, '"Some Things in Them Hard to Understand": Reflections on an Approach to Paul', *Int* 38 (1984) 254-67.

———, *Romans* (Atlanta: John Knox, 1985).

Adams, Edward, 'Abraham's Faith and Gentile Disobedience: Textual Links between Romans 1 and 4', *JSNT* 65 (1997) 47-66.

Aletti, Jean-Noël, 'Rm 1,18–3,20: Incohérence ou cohérence de l'argumentation paulinienne?' *Bib* 69 (1988) 47-62.

———, 'Rm 7.7-25 encore une fois: Enjeux et propositions', *NTS* 48 (2002) 358-76.

———, 'Romains 4 et Genèse 17: Quelle énigme et quelle solution?' *Bib* 84 (2003) 305-25.

Anchor Bible Dictionary (ABD) (New Haven: Yale University Press, 1992).

Anderson, Chip, 'Romans 1:1-5 and the Occasion of the Letter: The Solution to the Two-Congregation Problem in Rome', *TrinJ* 14 (1993) 25-40.

Arichea, Daniel C., Jr., 'Who Was Phoebe? Translating *Diakonos* in Romans 16.1', *BibTrans* 39 (1988) 401-9.

Atallah, Ramez, 'The Objective Witness to Conscience: An Egyptian Parallel to Romans 2:15', *ERT* 18 (1994) 204-13.

Badenas, Robert, *Christ the End of the Law: Romans 10.4 in Pauline Perspective* (Sheffield: JSOT Press, 1985).

Badke, William B., 'Baptised into Moses — Baptised into Christ: A Study in Doctrinal Development', *EvQ* 60 (1988) 23-29.

Bailey, Jon Nelson, 'Paul's Political Paraenesis in Romans 13:1-7', *ResQ* 46 (2004) 11-28.

Baker, Bruce A., 'Romans 1:18-21 and Presuppositional Apologetics', *BSac* 155 (1998) 280-98.

Baker, Murray, 'Paul and the Salvation of Israel: Paul's Ministry, the Motif of Jealousy, and Israel's Yes', *CBQ* 67 (2005) 469-84.

Balch, David L., 'Romans 1:24-27, Science, and Homosexuality', *CurrTheolMiss* 25 (1998) 433-40.

Bammel, C. P., 'Patristic Exegesis of Romans 5:7', *JTS* 47 (1996) 532-42.

Banks, Robert, 'Romans 7.25a: An Eschatological Thanksgiving?' *ABR* 26 (1978) 34-42.

Barclay, John M. G., 'Paul and Philo on Circumcision: Romans 2:25-29 in Social and Cultural Context', *NTS* 44 (1998) 536-56.

Barrett, C. K., *A Commentary on the Epistle to the Romans* (London: Adam & Charles Black, 1957).

————, *The New Testament Background: Selected Documents* (London: SPCK, 1961).

Barth, Karl, *A Shorter Commentary on Romans* (London: SCM, 1959).

Bassler, Jouette M., 'Divine Impartiality in Paul's Letter to the Romans', *NovT* 26 (1984) 43-58.

Baxter, A. G., and J. A. Ziesler, 'Paul and Arboriculture: Romans 11.17-24', *JSNT* 24 (1985) 25-32.

Bayes, J. F., 'The Translation of Romans 8:3', *ExpTim* 111 (1999) 14-16.

Beale, G. K., and D. A. Carson, eds., *Commentary on the New Testament Use of the Old Testament* (Grand Rapids: Baker, 2007).

Bechtler, Steven Richard, 'Christ, the *Telos* of the Law: The Goal of Romans 10:4', *CBQ* 56 (1994) 288-308.

Beker, J. C., 'The Faithfulness of God and the Priority of Israel in Paul's Letter to the Romans', *HTR* 79 (1986) 10-16.

Bell, Richard H., 'Rom 5.18-19 and Universal Salvation', *NTS* 48 (2002) 417-32.

————, *The Irrevocable Call of God: An Inquiry into Paul's Theology of Israel* (WUNT 184; Tübingen: Mohr Siebeck, 2005).

————, *No One Seeks for God: An Exegetical and Theological Study of Romans 1:18–3:20* (WUNT 106; Tübingen: Mohr Siebeck, 1998).

Belleville, Linda, '*Iounian . . . episēmoi en tois apostolois*: A Re-examination of Romans 16.7 in Light of Primary Source Materials', *NTS* 51 (2005) 231-49.

Benware, Wilbur A., 'Romans 1.17 and Cognitive Grammar', *BibTrans* 51 (2000) 330-40.

Berding, Kenneth, 'Romans 12.4-8: One Sentence or Two?' *NTS* 52 (2006) 433-39.

Berkley, Timothy W., *From a Broken Covenant to Circumcision of the Heart: Pauline Intertextual Exegesis in Romans 2:17-29* (SBLDS 175; Atlanta: Society of Biblical Literature, 2000).

Bertone, John A., 'The Function of the Spirit in the Dialectic between God's Soteriological Plan Enacted but Not Yet Culminated: Romans 8.1-27', *JPT* 15 (1999) 75-97.

Bird, Michael, '"Raised for Our Justification": A Fresh Look at Romans 4:25', *Colloquium* 35 (2003) 31-46.

Black, David A., 'The Pauline Love Command: Structure, Style, and Ethics in Romans 12:9-21', *FilolNT* 2 (1989) 3-22.

Bligh, John, 'Baptismal Transformation of the Gentile World', *HeyJ* 37 (1996) 371-81.

Boers, Hendrikus, 'The Structure and Meaning of Romans 6:1-14', *CBQ* 63 (2001) 664-82.

Boismard, Marie-Émile, 'Rm 16,17-20: Vocabulaire et style', *RB* 107 (2000) 548-57.

————, *L'énigme de la letter aux Éphésiens* (Études bibliques N.S. 39; Paris: Gabalda, 1999).

Bolt, John, 'The Relation between Creation and Redemption in Romans 8:18-27', *CalvTheolJourn* 30 (1995) 34-51.

Bornkamm, Gunther, 'The Letter to the Romans as Paul's Last Will and Testament', in *The Romans Debate: Revised* (ed. Karl P. Donfried; Peabody, Mass.: Hendrickson, 1991), 16-28.

Bowsher, Herbert, 'To Whom Does the Law Speak? Romans 3:19 and the Works of the Law Debate', *WTJ* 68 (2006) 295-303.

Branick, Vincent P., 'The Sinful Flesh of the Son of God (Rom 8:3): A Key Image of Pauline Theology', *CBQ* 47 (1985) 246-62.

Bray, Gerald, 'Adam and Christ (Romans 5:12-21)', *Evangel* 18 (2000) 4-8.

————, ed., *Ancient Christian Commentary on Scripture: New Testament, VI: Romans* (ACCSR) (Downers Grove, Ill.: InterVarsity Press, 1998).

Bridger, Francis, 'Entropy, Sexuality and Politics: A Reply to Michael Williams', *Anvil* 10 (1993) 111-23.

Brindle, Wayne A., '"To the Jew First": Rhetoric, Strategy, History, or Theology?' *BSac* 159 (2002) 221-33.

Brooks, E. W., *Joseph and Asenath: The Confession and Prayer of Asenath, Daughter of Pentephres the Priest* (London: SPCK, 1918).

Brown, Michael Joseph, 'Paul's Use of *doulos Christou Iēsou* in Romans 1:1', *JBL* 120 (2001) 723-37.

Bruce, F. F., *The Epistle to the Romans* (TNTC; Leicester: Inter-Varsity Press, 1963).

Bultmann, Rudolf, 'Glossen im Romerbrief', in *Exegetica: Aufsatze zur Erforschung des Neuen Testaments* (Tübingen: Mohr Siebeck, 1967), 278-84.

————, *Theology of the New Testament*, I (London: SCM, 1952).

Burer, Michael H., and Daniel B. Wallace, 'Was Junia Really an Apostle? A Re-examination of Rom 16.7', *NTS* 47 (2001) 76-91.

Burke, Trevor J., 'Adoption and the Spirit in Romans 8', *EvQ* 70 (1998) 311-24.

————, 'Pauline Adoption: A Sociological Approach', *EvQ* 73 (2001) 119-34.

Busch, Austin, 'The Figure of Eve in Romans 7:5-25', *BibInt* 12 (2004) 1-36.

Byrne, Brendan, '"Rather Boldly" (Rom 15,15): Paul's Prophetic Bid to Win the Allegiance of the Christians in Rome', *Bib* 74 (1993) 83-96.

————, *Romans* (Sacra Pagina 6; Collegeville, Minn.: Liturgical Press, 1996).

Byrskog, Samuel, 'Epistolography, Rhetoric and Letter Prescript: Romans 1.1-7 as a Test Case', *JSNT* 65 (1997) 27-46.

Calvert-Koyzis, N., 'Abraham: New Testament', in *The IVP Dictionary of the New Testament*, ed. Daniel G. Reid (Downers Grove/Leicester: InterVarsity Press, 2004), 1-16.

Campbell, Douglas A., 'False Presuppositions in the *Pistis Christou* Debate: A Response to Brian Dodd', *JBL* 116 (1997) 713-19.

————, 'Natural Theology in Paul? Reading Romans 1.19-20', *International Journal of Systematic Theology* 1 (1999) 231-52.

————, 'Romans 1:17 — A Crux Interpretum for the *PISTIS CHRISTOU* Debate', *JBL* 113 (1994) 265-85.

————, *The Rhetoric of Righteousness in Romans 3.21-26,* JSNTSup 65 (Sheffield: JSOT Press, 1992).

Campbell, W. S., 'Christ, the End of the Law: Romans 10:4', in *Studia Biblica 1978: III. Papers on Paul and Other New Testament Authors. Sixth International Congress on Biblical Studies* (ed. E. A. Livingstone; JSNTSup 3; Sheffield: JSOT Press, 1980), 77-78.

————, 'Romans III as a Key to the Structure and Thought of the Letter', *NovT* 23 (1981) 37-39.

Capes, David B., 'YHWH and His Messiah: Pauline Exegesis and the Divine Christ', *HorBibTheol* 16 (1994) 121-43.

Caragounis, Chrys C., 'Romans 5.15-16 in the Context of 5.12-21: Contrast or Comparison?' *NTS* 31 (1985) 143-48.

Carras, George P., 'Romans 2,1-29: A Dialogue on Jewish Ideals', *Bib* 73 (1992) 183-207.

Carson, D. A., 'Why Trust a Cross? Reflections on Romans 3:21-26', *ERT* 28 (2004) 345-62.

Carson, D. A., Peter T. O'Brien, Mark A. Seifrid, eds., *Justification and Variegated Nomism,* Vol. 1 — *The Complexities of Second Temple Judaism* (Tübingen: Mohr Siebeck/Grand Rapids: Baker Academic, 2001).

————, eds., *Justification and Variegated Nomism,* Vol. II — *The Paradoxes of Paul* (Tübingen: Mohr Siebeck/Grand Rapids: Baker Academic, 2004).

Carter, T. L., 'The Irony of Romans 13', *NovT* 46, no. 3 (2004) 209-28.

Cavallin, H. C. C., '"The Righteous Shall Live by Faith": A Decisive Argument for the Traditional Interpretation', *ST* 32 (1978) 40-43.

Cervin, Richard S., 'A Note regarding the Name "Junia(s)" in Romans 16.7', *NTS* 40 (1994) 464-70.

Chang, Hae-Kyung, '*(apo)karadokia* bei Paulus und Aquila', *ZNW* 93 (2002) 268-78.

Charlesworth, James H., ed., *The Old Testament Pseudepigrapha,* Vol. 1: *Apocalyptic Literature and Testaments* (New York: Doubleday, 1983).

————, ed., *The Old Testament and Pseudepigrapha,* Vol. 2: *Expansions of the "Old Testament" and Legends, Wisdom and Philosophical Literature, Prayers, Psalms, and Odes, Fragments of Lost Judeo-Hellenistic Works* (New York: Doubleday, 1985).

Choi, P. Richard, 'The Problem of Translating *en tō autou haimati* in Romans 3:25a', *AUSS* 38 (2000) 199-201.

Christoffersson, Olle, *The Earnest Expectation of the Creature: The Flood-Tradition as Matrix of Romans 8:18-27* (ConBNT 23; Stockholm: Almqvist & Wiksell, 1990).

Clarke, Andrew D., 'Another Corinthian Erastus Inscription', *TynBul* 42 (1991) 146-51.

————, 'The Good and the Just in Romans 5:7', *TynBul* 41 (1990) 128-42.

Cohn-Sherbok, Rabbi Dan, 'Some Reflections on James Dunn's "The Incident at Antioch (Gal. 2.11-18)"', *JSNT* 18 (1983) 68-74.

Coleman, Thomas M., 'Binding Obligations in Romans 13:7: A Semantic Field and Social Context', *TynBul* 48 (1997) 307-27.

Collins, Nina L., 'The Jewish Source of Rom 5:17, 16, 10, and 9: The Verses of Paul in Relation to a Comment in the Mishnah at *m. Makk* 3.15', *RB* 112 (2005) 27-45.

Cook, John G., 'The Logic and Language of Romans 1,20', *Bib* 75 (1994) 494-517.

Cosgrove, Charles H., 'What If Some Have Not Believed? The Occasion and Thrust of Romans 3 1-8', *ZNW* 78 (1987) 90-105.

Coxhead, Steven R., 'Deuteronomy 30:11-14 as a Prophecy of the New Covenant in Christ', *WTJ* 68 (2006) 305-20.

Cranfield, C. E. B., 'Romans 6:1-14 Revisited', *ExpTim* 106 (1994-95) 40-43.

———, '"The Works of the Law" in the Epistle to the Romans', *JSNT* 43 (1991) 89-101.

———, *The Epistle to the Romans*, I (ICC; Edinburgh: T&T Clark, 1975).

———, *The Epistle to the Romans*, II (ICC; Edinburgh: T&T Clark, 1979).

Cranford, Michael, 'Abraham in Romans 4: The Father of All Who Believe', *NTS* 41 (1995) 71-88.

———, 'Election and Ethnicity: Paul's View of Israel in Romans 9.1-13', *JSNT* 50 (1993) 27-41.

Croft, Steve, 'Text Messages: The Ministry of Women and Romans 16', *Anvil* 21 (2004) 87-94.

Cuvillier, Elian, 'Evangile et traditions chez Paul: Lecture de Romains 6,1-14', *Hokhma* 45 (1990) 3-16.

———, 'Soumission aux autorités et liberté chrétienne: Exégèse de Romains 13,1-7', *Hokhma* 50 (1992) 29-47.

Dahl, N. A., 'The Future of Israel', in *Studies in Paul: Theology for the Early Christian Mission* (Minneapolis: Augsburg, 1977).

———, and Samuel Sandmel, 'Review of *Paul and Palestinian Judaism: Comparison of Patterns of Religion* by E. P. Sanders', *RelSRev* 4 (1978) 153-60.

Danby, Herbert, *The Mishnah Translated from the Hebrew with Introductions and Brief Explanatory Notes* (Oxford: Oxford University Press, 1933).

Das, A. Andrew, *Paul, the Law, and the Covenant* (Peabody, Mass.: Hendrickson, 2001).

Davies, Glen N., *Faith and Obedience in Romans: A Study in Romans 1–4* (JSNTSup 39; Sheffield: JSOT Press, 1990).

Davies, Margaret, 'New Testament Ethics and Ours: Homosexuality and Sexuality in Romans 1:26-27', *BibInt* 3 (1995) 315-31.

Day, John N., '"Coals of Fire" in Romans 12:19-20', *BSac* 160 (2003) 414-20.

Derrett, J. Duncan M., 'You Abominate False Gods; but Do You Rob Shrines?' *NTS* 40 (1994) 558-71.

deSilva, D. A., 'Honor and Shame', *DNTB* 518-22.

De Young, James B., 'The Meaning of "Nature" in Romans 1 and Its Implications for Biblical Proscriptions of Homosexual Behavior', *JETS* 31 (1988) 429-41.

Dillon, Richard J., 'The Spirit as Taskmaster and Troublemaker in Romans', *CBQ* 60 (1998) 682-702.

Dodd, Brian, 'Romans 1:17 — A Crux Interpretum for the *Pistis Christou* Debate?' *JBL* 114 (1995) 470-73.

Dodd, C. H., 'HILASKESTHAI, Its Cognates, Derivatives, and Synonyms, in the Septuagint', *JTS* 32 (1931) 352-60.

———, *The Epistle of Paul to the Romans* (London: Fontana, 1959).

Donaldson, Terence L., ' "Riches for the Gentiles" (Rom 11:12): Israel's Rejection and
    Paul's Gentile Mission', *JBL* 112 (1993) 81-98.
Donfried, Karl P., ed., *The Romans Debate: Revised and Expanded Edition* (Peabody,
    Mass.: Hendrickson, 1991).
Downs, David J., ' "The Offering of the Gentiles" in Romans 15.16', *JSNT* 29 (2006)
    173-86.
du Toit, A. B., ' "God's Beloved in Rome" (Rm 1:7): The Genesis and Socio-Economic
    Situation of the First-Generation Christian Community in Rome', *Neot* 32, no.
    2 (1998) 367-88.
————, 'Persuasion in Romans 1:1-17', *BZ* 33 (1989) 192-209.
Dunn, James D. G., 'Works of the Law and the Curse of the Law (Galatians 3.10-14)',
    in *The New Perspective on Paul, Revised Edition* (Grand Rapids: Eerdmans, 2005)
    121-40.
————, *Jesus, Paul and the Law: Studies in Mark and Galatians* (Louisville: Westminster
    John Knox, 1990).
————, *Romans 1–8* (WBC 38A; Dallas: Word Books, 1988).
————, *Romans 9–16* (WBC 38B; Dallas: Word Books, 1988).
————, *The Theology of Paul the Apostle* (Edinburgh: T&T Clark, 1998).
Earnshaw, John D., 'Reconsidering Paul's Marriage Analogy in Romans 7.1-4', *NTS*
    40 (1994) 68-88.
Eastman, Susan, 'Whose Apocalypse? The Identity of the Sons of God in Romans
    8:19', *JBL* 121 (2002) 263-77.
Eckstein, Hans-Joachim, ' "Denn Gottes Zorn wird vom Himmel her offenbar
    werden." Exegetische Erwägungen zu Röm 1 18', *ZNW* 78 (1987) 74-89.
————, ' "Nahe ist dir das Wort": Exegetische Erwägungen zu Röm 10 8', *ZNW* 79
    (1988) 204-20.
Édart, Jean-Baptiste, 'De la nécessité d'un sauveur: Rhétorique et théologie de Rm
    7,7-25', *RB* 105 (1998) 359-96.
Efferin, Henry, 'A Study on General Revelation: Romans 1:18-32; 2:12-16', *Stulos
    Theological Journal* 4 (1996) 147-55.
Elliott, Neil, *The Rhetoric of Romans: Argumentative Constraint and Strategy and Paul's
    Dialogue with Judaism* (JSNTSup 45; Sheffield: JSOT Press, 1990).
Elmer, Ian J., 'I, Tertius: Secretary or Co-author of Romans', *ABR* 56 (2008) 45-60.
Engberg-Pedersen, Troels, 'Paul's Stoicizing Politics in Romans 12-13: The Role of
    13:1-10 in the Argument', *JSNT* 29 (2006) 163-72.
————, *Paul and the Stoics* (Edinburgh: T&T Clark, 2000).
Epp, Eldon Jay, *Junia: The First Woman Apostle* (Minneapolis: Fortress, 2005).
Epstein, I., trans., *The Babylonian Talmud* (London: Soncino, 1936).
Esler, Philip F., 'Ancient Oleiculture and Ethnic Differentiation: The Meaning of the
    Olive-Tree Image in Romans 11', *JSNT* 26 (2003) 103-24.
————, 'Paul and Stoicism: Romans 12 as a Test Case', *NTS* 50 (2004) 106-24.
————, 'The Sodom Tradition in Romans 1:18-32', *BTB* 34 (2004) 4-16.
————, *Conflict and Identity in Romans: The Social Setting of Paul's Letter* (Minneapolis:
    Fortress, 2003).
Evans, C. A., 'Son of God Text (4Q246)', *DNTB* 1134-37.
Fitzmyer, Joseph A., 'The Consecutive Meaning of *eph' hō* in Romans 5.12', *NTS* 39
    (1993) 321-39.

————. *Romans* (AB; New York: Doubleday, 1993).

Flebbe, Jochen, *Solus Deus: Untersuchungen zur Rede von Gott im Brief des Paulus und die Römer* (BZNW 158; Berlin: de Gruyter, 2008).

Flusser, David, '"Durch das Gesetz dem Gesetz gestorben" (Gal 2,19)', *Judaica* 43 (1987) 30-46.

Forsyth, P. T., *The Cruciality of the Cross* (2nd ed.; London: Independent Press, 1948).

Frary, Stephen W., 'Who Will Deliver Me? An Exegesis of Rom. 7:24–8:11', *Faith & Mission* 17 (2000) 17-29.

Fryer, Nico S. L., 'The Meaning and Translation of *Hilastērion* in Romans 3:25', *EvQ* 59 (1987) 99-116.

Führer, Werner, '"Herr ist Jesus": Die Rezeption der urchristlichen Kyrios-Akklamation durch Paulus Römer 10,9', *KD* 33 (1987) 137-49.

Fuller, Daniel P., *Gospel and Law: Contrast or Continuum?* (Grand Rapids: Eerdmans, 1980).

Fung, Ronald Y.-K., *The Epistle to the Galatians* (NICNT; Grand Rapids: Eerdmans, 1988).

Gagnon, Robert A. J., 'Heart of Wax and a Teaching That Stamps: *Typos Didachs* (Rom 6:17b) Once More', *JBL* 112 (1993) 667-87.

————, 'The Meaning of *hymōn to agathon* in Romans 14:16', *JBL* 117 (1998) 675-689.

Garlington, D. B., '*HIEROSYLEIN* and the Idolatry of Israel (Romans 2.22)', *NTS* 36 (1990) 142-51.

————, 'The Obedience of Faith in the Letter to the Romans, Part I: The Meaning of *hypakoē pisteōs* (Rom 1:5; 16:26)', *WTJ* 52 (1990) 201-24.

————, 'The Obedience of Faith in the Letter to the Romans, Part II: The Obedience of Faith and Judgment by Works', *WTJ* 53 (1991) 47-72.

————, 'Romans 7:14-25 and the Creation Theology of Paul', *TrinJ* 11 (1990) 197-235.

Gaston, Lloyd, *Paul and the Torah* (Vancouver: University of British Columbia Press, 1987).

Gathercole, Simon J., 'A Law unto Themselves: The Gentiles in Romans 2.14-15 Revisited', *JSNT* 85 (2002) 27-49.

————, 'Romans 3.25-26: An Exegetical Study' (Atonement Conference, London School of Theology, July 2005, on EAUK website).

————, *Where Is Boasting? Early Jewish Soteriology and Paul's Response in Romans 1–5* (Grand Rapids: Eerdmans, 2002).

Getty, Mary Ann, 'Paul and the Salvation of Israel: A Perspective on Romans 9–11', *CBQ* 50 (1988) 456-69.

————, 'Paul on the Covenants and the Future of Israel', *BTB* 17 (1987) 92-99.

Gieniusz, Andrzej, 'Rom 7,1-6: Lack of Imagination? Function of the Passage in the Argumentation of Rom 6,1–7,6', *Bib* 74 (1993) 389-400.

Giesen, Heinz, 'Das heilige Gesetz — missbraucht durch die Sünde (Röm 7)', *TTZ* 114 (2005) 202-21.

Gignilliat, Mark S., 'Working Together with Whom? Text-Critical, Contextual, and Theological Analysis of *synergei* in Romans 8,28', *Bib* 87 (2006) 511-15.

Gill, David W. J., 'Erastus the Aedile', *TynBul* 40 (1989) 293-301.

Gillman, Florence Morgan, 'Another Look at Romans 8:3: "In the Likeness of Sinful Flesh"', *CBQ* 49 (1987) 597-604.

Given, Mark D., 'Restoring the Inheritance in Romans 11:1', *JBL* 118 (1999) 89-96.

Glenny, W. Edward, 'The "People of God" in Romans 9:25-26', *BSac* 152 (1995) 42-59.

Gordon, David, 'Why Israel Did Not Obtain Torah-Righteousness: A Translation Note on Rom 9:32', *WTJ* 54 (1992) 163-66.

Grappe, Christian, 'Qui me délivera de ce corps de mort? L'esprit de vie! *Romains* 7,24 et 8,2 comme éléments de typologie adamique', *Bib* 83 (2002) 472-92.

Greene, M. Dwaine, 'A Note on Romans 8:3', *BZ* 35 (1991) 103-6.

Greenlee, J. Harold, 'Some "Called" People: Romans 1:1, 6-7', *NotesTrans* 11 (1997) 49-51.

Grindheim, Sigurd, *The Crux of Election: Paul's Critique of Jewish Confidence in the Election of Israel* (WUNT 2/202; Tübingen: Mohr Siebeck, 2005).

Guerra, Anthony J., 'Romans 4 as Apologetic Theology', *HTR* 81 (1988) 251-70.

Gundry, Robert H., 'The Moral Frustration of Paul before His Conversion: Sexual Lust in Romans 7:7-25', in *Pauline Studies*, Festschrift for F. F. Bruce, ed. Donald A. Hagner and Murray J. Harris (Exeter: Paternoster, 1980), 228-45.

Haacker, Klaus, 'Die Geschichtstheologie von Röm 9–11 im Lichte philonischer Schriftauslegung', *NTS* 43 (1997) 209-22.

Hafemann, Scott, 'Eschatology and Ethics: The Future of Israel and the Nations in Romans 15:1-13', *TynBul* 51 (2000) 161-92.

Hagner, Donald, 'Paul and Judaism: Testing the New Perspective', in Peter Stuhlmacher, *A Challenge to the New Perspective: Revisiting Paul's Doctrine of Justification — With an Essay by Donald A. Hagner* (Downers Grove, Ill.: InterVarsity Press, 2001), 75-105.

Hahne, Harry Alan, *The Corruption and Redemption of Creation: Nature in Romans 8.19-22 and Jewish Apocalyptic Literature* (LNTS 336; London/New York: T&T Clark, 2006).

Harder, G., 'Nature', in *New International Dictionary of New Testament Theology*, ed. C. Brown (4 vols.; Grand Rapids: Zondervan, 1975-1985), II, 656-61.

Harding, Mark, 'The Salvation of Israel and the Logic of Romans 11:11-36', *ABR* 46 (1998) 55-69.

Harrison, J. R., 'Paul, Eschatology and the Augustan Age of Grace', *TynBul* 50 (1999) 79-91.

Hartung, Matthias, 'Die kultische bzw. Agrartechnisch-biologische Logik der Gleichnisse von der Teighebe und vom Ölbaum in Röm 11.16-24 und die sich daraus ergebenden theologischen Konsequenzen', *NTS* 45 (1999) 127-40.

Hassold, William J., '"Avoid Them": Another Look at Romans 16:17-20', *CurrTheolMiss* 27 (2000) 196-208.

Hays, Richard B., '"Have We Found Abraham to Be Our Forefather according to the Flesh?" A Reconsideration of Rom 4:1', *NovT* 27 (1985) 76-98.

———, 'PISTIS and Pauline Christology: What Is at Stake?' in *Pauline Theology*, Vol. IV: *Looking Back, Pressing On*, ed. E. Johnson and D. M. Hay (Atlanta: Scholars Press, 1997), 35-60.

———, *The Faith of Jesus Christ: An Investigation of the Narrative Substructure of Galatians 3.1–4.11* (SBLDS 56; Chico, Calif.: Scholars Press, 1983).

Heard, Warren J., Jr., 'Spain', *ABD*, VI, 176.

Heil, John Paul, 'Christ, the Termination of the Law (Romans 9:30–10:8)', *CBQ* 63 (2001) 484-98.

————, 'From Remnant to Seed of Hope for Israel: Romans 9:27-29', *CBQ* 64 (2002) 703-20.

Heiligenthal, Roman, 'Soziologische Implikationen der paulinischen Rechtferti-gungslehre im Galaterbrief am Beispiel der "Werke des Gesetzes": Beobach-tungen zur Identitätsfindung einer frühchristlichen Gemeinde', *Kairos* 26 (1984) 38-53.

Hiebert, D. Edmond, 'Romans 8:28-29 and the Assurance of the Believer', *BSac* 148 (1991) 170-83.

Hill, David, *Greek Words and Hebrew Meanings: Studies in the Semantics of Soteriological Terms* (Cambridge: Cambridge University Press, 1967).

Hills, Julian V., ' "Christ Was the Goal of the Law . . ." (Romans 10:4)', *JTS* 44 (1993) 585-92.

Hofius, Otfried, ' "All Israel Will Be Saved": Divine Salvation and Israel's Deliver-ance in Romans 9–11', *PSB* Sup. 1 (1990) 19-39.

————, 'Das Gesetz des Mose und das Gesetz Christi', *ZTK* 80 (1983) 262-86.

Holst, Richard, 'The Meaning of "Abraham Believed God" in Romans 4:3', *WTJ* 59 (1997) 319-26.

Hommel, Hildebrecht, 'Denen, die Gott lieben . . . Erwägungen zu Römer 8,28', *ZNW* 80 (1989) 126-29.

Hooker, M. D., 'Adam in Romans I', *NTS* 6 (1960) 300-301.

————, 'Interchange in Christ', *JTS* n.s. 22 (1971) 349-61.

Hübner, Hans, *Law in Paul's Thought* (Edinburgh: T&T Clark, 1984).

Huggins, Ronald V., 'Alleged Classical Parallels to Paul's "What I want to do I do not do, but what I hate, that I do" (Rom 7:15)', *WTJ* 54 (1992) 153-61.

Hvalvik, Reidar, 'A "Sonderweg" for Israel: A Critical Examination of a Current In-terpretation of Romans 11.25-27', *JSNT* 38 (1990) 88-107.

Isaak, Jon, 'The Christian Community and Political Responsibility: Romans 13:1-7', *Direction* 32 (2003) 32-46.

Ito, Akio, '*Nomos (tōn) ergōn* and *nomos pisteōs:* The Pauline Rhetoric and Theology of *Nomos*', *NovT* 45 (2003) 237-59.

————, 'Romans 2: A Deuteronomistic Reading', *JSNT* 59 (1995) 21-37.

————, 'The Written Torah and the Oral Gospel: Romans 10:5-13 in the Dynamic Tension between Orality and Literacy', *NovT* 48 (2006) 234-60.

Jegher-Bucher, Verena, 'Erwählung und Verwerfung im Römerbrief? Eine Untersuchung von Röm 11,11-15', *TZ* 47 (1991) 326-36.

Jervell, Jacob, 'The Letter to Jerusalem', in *The Romans Debate: Revised,* ed. Karl P. Donfried (above), 53-64.

Jervis, L. Anne, 'Reading Romans 7 in Conversation with Post-Colonial Theory: Paul's Struggle toward a Christian Identity of Hybridity', *Theoforum* 35 (2004) 173-93.

————, *The Purpose of Romans: A Comparative Letter Structure Investigation* (JSNTSup 55; Sheffield: JSOT Press, 1991).

Jewett, Robert, 'The God of Peace in Romans: Reflections on Crucial Lutheran Texts', *CurrTheolMiss* 25 (1998) 186-94.

————, 'The Law and the Co-existence of Jews and Gentiles in Romans', *Int* 39 (1985) 341-56.

————, 'Romans as an Ambassadorial Letter', *Int* 36 (1982) 5-20.

————, *Romans: A Commentary* (Hermeneia; Minneapolis: Fortress, 2007).

Johnson, Dan G., 'The Structure and Meaning of Romans 11', *CBQ* 46 (1984) 91-103.

Johnson, S. Lewis, Jr., 'Paul and the Knowledge of God', *BSac* 129 (1972) 61-74.

Judant, D., 'A propos de la destinée d'Israel: Remarques concernant un verset de l'épître aux Romains XI,31', *Divinitas* 23 (1979) 108-25.

Junker, Günther H., '"Children of Promise": Spiritual Paternity and Patriarch Typology in Galatians and Romans', *BBR* 17 (2007) 131-60.

Kammler, Hans-Christian, 'Die Prädication Jesu Christi als "Gott" und die paulinische Christologie: Erwägungen zur Exegese von Röm 9,5b', *ZNW* 94 (2003) 164-80.

Käsemann, Ernst, 'The "Righteousness of God" in Paul', in *New Testament Questions of Today* (Grand Rapids: Eerdmans/London: SCM, 1969), 168-82.

————, *Commentary on Romans* (Grand Rapids: Eerdmans/London: SCM, 1980).

Kearsley, R. A., 'Women in Public Life in the Roman East: Iunia Theodora, Claudia Metrodora and Phoebe, Benefactress of Paul', *TynBul* 50 (1999) 189-211.

Keesmaat, Sylvia C., 'Exodus and the Intertextual Transformation of Tradition in Romans 8.14-30', *JSNT* 54 (1994) 29-56.

Keller, Winfrid, *Gottes Treue — Israels Heil: Röm 11,25-27. Die These vom "Sonderweg" in der Diskussion* (Stuttgarter biblische Beiträge 40; Stuttgart: Katholisches Bibelwerk, 1998).

Kim, Johann D., *God, Israel, and the Gentiles: Rhetoric and Situation in Romans 9–11* (SBLDS 176; Atlanta: Society of Biblical Literature, 2000).

Kio, S. Hre, 'What Does "YOU WILL HEAP BURNING COALS UPON HIS HEAD" Mean in Romans 12.20?' *BibTrans* 51 (2000) 418-24.

Kirk, J. R. Daniel, 'Reconsidering *Dikaiōma* in Romans 5:16', *JBL* 126 (2007) 787-92.

Kiuchi, Nobuyoshi, 'Living like the Azazel-Goat in Romans 12:1b', *TynBul* 57 (2006) 251-61.

Klassen, William, 'Kiss (NT)', in *ABD*, IV, 91.

Klein, Günter, 'Paul's Purpose in Writing the Epistle to the Romans', in *The Romans Debate Revised*, ed. Karl P. Donfried (above), 29-43.

————, 'Righteousness in the N.T.', *IDB* Sup, 750-52.

Kline, Meredith G., 'Gospel until the Law: Rom 5:13-14 and the Old Covenant', *JETS* 34 (1991) 433-46.

Klumbies, Paul-Gerhard, 'Der eine Gott des Paulus: Röm 3,21-31 als Brennpunkt paulinischer Theologie', *ZNW* 85 (1994) 192-206.

Koch, Dietrich-Alex, 'Der Text von Hab 2 4b in der Septuaginta und im Neuen Testament', *ZNW* 76 (1985) 68-85.

Krentz, Edgar, 'The Name of God in Disrepute: Romans 2:17-29 [22-23]', *CurrTheolMiss* 17 (1990) 429-39.

Kreuzer, Siegfried, '"Der den Gottlosen rechtfertigt" (Röm 4,5): Die frühjüdische Einordnung von Genesis 15 als Hintergrund für das Abrahambild und die Rechtfertigungslehre des Paulus', *TBei* 33 (2002) 208-19.

Kroger, Daniel, 'Paul and the Civil Authorities: An Exegesis of Romans 13:1-7', *AsiaJT* 7 (1993) 344-66.

Kruger, M. A., '*TINA KARPON*, "Some Fruit" in Romans 1:13', *WTJ* 49 (1987) 167-73.

Kruse, C. G., 'Call/Calling', in *The Dictionary of Paul and His Letters*, ed. Gerald F.

Hawthorne, Ralph P. Martin, and Daniel G. Reid (Downers Grove, Ill.: InterVarsity Press, 1993) 84-85.

———, 'The Price Paid for a Ministry among Gentiles: Paul's Persecution at the Hands of the Jews', in *Worship, Theology and Ministry in the Early Church: Essays in Honor of Ralph P. Martin*, ed. Michael J. Wilkins and Terence Paige (JSNTSup 87; Sheffield: Sheffield Academic Press, 1992), 260-72.

———, *New Testament Models for Ministry: Jesus and Paul* (Nashville: Thomas Nelson, 1983).

———, *Paul, the Law and Justification* (Leicester: Apollos/Inter-Varsity Press, 1996).

———, *The Second Epistle of Paul to the Corinthians* (TNTC 8; Leicester: Inter-Varsity Press/Grand Rapids: Eerdmans, 1987).

Kümmel, Werner, G. *Römer 7 und die Bekehrung des Paulus* (Munich: Kaiser, 1974).

Kyrychenko, Alexander, 'The Consistency of Romans 9–11', *ResQ* 45 (2003) 215-27.

Lambrecht, Jan, 'The Caesura between Romans 9.30-33 and 10.1-4', *NTS* 45 (1999) 141-47.

———, 'Grammar and Reasoning in Romans 11,27', *ETL* 79 (2003) 179-83.

———, 'Grammar and Reasoning in Romans 7,12 and 7,13-14', *ETL* 80 (2004) 470-74.

———, 'Paul's Logic in Romans 3:29-30', *JBL* 119 (2000) 526-28.

———, 'The Implied Exhortation in Romans 8,5-8', *Greg* 81 (2000) 441-51.

———, *The Wretched "I" and Its Liberation: Paul in Romans 7 and 8* (Louvain Theological and Pastoral Monographs 14; Louvain: Peeters, 1992).

Lamp, Jeffrey S., 'Paul, the Law, Jews, and Gentiles: A Contextual and Exegetical Reading of Romans 2:12-16', *JETS* 42 (1999) 37-51.

Lampe, Peter, 'The Roman Christians of Romans 16', in *The Romans Debate Revised*, ed. Karl P. Donfried (above), 216-30.

Leenhardt, F. J., *L'épître de St Paul aux Romains* (Commentaire du Nouveau Testament VI; Neuchâtel: Delachaux et Niestlé, 1957).

Légasse, Simon, 'Être baptisé dans la mort du Christ: Étude de Romains 6,1-14', *RB* 98 (1991) 544-59.

Levison, John R., 'Adam and Eve in Romans 1.18-25 and the Greek *Life of Adam and Eve*', *NTS* 50 (2004) 519-34.

Lichtenberger, Hermann, 'Der Beginn der Auslegungsgeschichte von Römer 7: Röm 7,25b', *ZNW* 88 (1997) 284-95.

Lightfoot, J. B., *Saint Paul's Epistle to the Philippians* (New York: Macmillan, 1903).

Lindars, Barnabas, 'The Old Testament and Universalism in Paul', *BJRL* 69 (1987) 511-27.

Linss, Wilhelm C., 'Exegesis of *telos* in Romans 10:4', *BR* 33 (1988) 5-12.

Little, Joyce A., 'Paul's Use of Analogy: A Structural Analysis of Romans 7:1-6', *CBQ* 46 (1984) 82-90.

Löfstedt, Bengt, 'Notes on St Paul's Letter to the Romans', *FilolNT* 1 (1988) 209-10.

Longenecker, Bruce W., 'Different Answers to Different Issues: Israel, the Gentiles and Salvation History in Romans 9–11', *JSNT* 36 (1989) 95-123.

———, '*Pistis* in Romans 3.25: Neglected Evidence for the "Faithfulness of Christ"?' *NTS* 39 (1993) 478-80.

Longenecker, Richard, *Biblical Exegesis in the Apostolic Period* (Carlisle: Paternoster, 1995; first published by Eerdmans, 1975).

Loughlin, Gerard, 'Pauline Conversations: Rereading Romans 1 in Christ', *Theology and Sexuality* 11 (2004) 72-102.

Lowe, Bruce A., 'Oh *dia!* How Is Romans 4:25 to Be Understood?' *JTS* 57 (2006) 149-57.

Lowe, Chuck, '"There Is No Condemnation" (Romans 8:1): But Why Not?' *JETS* 42 (1999) 231-50.

MacLeod, David J., 'Eternal Son, Davidic Son, Messianic Son: An Exposition of Romans 1:1-7', *BSac* 162 (2005) 76-94.

Malick, David E., 'The Condemnation of Homosexuality in Romans 1:26-27', *BSac* 150 (1993) 327-40.

Malina, Bruce J., 'The Received View and What It Cannot Do, III: John and Hospitality', *Semeia* 35 (1986) 171-89.

Manson, T. W., 'St. Paul's Letter to the Romans — and Others', in *The Romans Debate: Revised*, ed. Karl P. Donfried (above), 3-15.

———, *On Paul and John: Some Selected Themes*, ed. Matthew Black (SBT 38; London: SCM, 1963).

Marcus, Joel, '"Let God Arise and End the Reign of Sin!" A Contribution to the Study of Pauline Parenesis', *Bib* 69 (1988) 386-95.

Marshall, I. H., *New Testament Theology: Many Witnesses, One Gospel* (Downers Grove, Ill.: InterVarsity Press, 2004).

Martens, John W., 'Romans 2.14-16: A Stoic Reading', *NTS* (40 (1994) 55-67.

Martin, Brice L., 'Some Reflections on the Identity of *egō* in Rom. 7:14-25', *SJT* 34 (1981) 39-47.

Martin, Troy W., 'The Good as God (Romans 5.7)', *JSNT* 25 (2002) 555-70.

Mathewson, Dave, 'Verbal Aspect in Imperatival Constructions in Pauline Ethical Injunctions', *FilolNT* 9 (1996) 21-36.

Mathewson, Mark D., 'Moral Intuitionism and the Law Inscribed on Our Hearts', *JETS* 42 (1999) 629-43.

Matlock, R. Barry, 'The Rhetoric of *pistis* in Paul: Galatians 2.16; 3.22; Romans 3.22, and Philippians 3.9', *JSNT* 30 (2007) 173-203.

Maurer, Christian, '*Synoida/syneidēsis*', in *Theological Dictionary of the New Testament (TDNT)* (Grand Rapids: Eerdmans, 1970), VII, 898-919.

McCruden, Kevin B., 'Judgment and Life for the Lord: Occasion and Theology of Romans 14,1–15,13', *Bib* 86 (2005) 229-44.

McDonald, J. I. H., 'Romans 13.1-7: A Test Case for New Testament Interpretation', *NTS* 35 (1989) 540-49.

McDonald, Patricia M., 'Romans 5.1-11 as a Rhetorical Bridge', *JSNT* 40 (1990) 81-96.

McFadden, K. W., 'The Fulfillment of the Law's *Dikaiōma*: Another Look at Romans 8:1-4', *JETS* 52 (2009) 483-97.

Meggitt, Justin J., 'The Social Status of Erastus (Rom. 16:23)', *NovT* 38 (1996) 218-23.

Meile, Eva, 'Isaaks Opferung: Eine Note an Nils Alstrup Dahl', *ST* 34 (1980) 111-28.

Merkle, Ben L., 'Romans 11 and the Future of Ethnic Israel', *JETS* 43 (2000) 709-21.

Metzger, Bruce M., ed., *A Textual Commentary on the Greek New Testament* (2nd ed.; Stuttgart: Deutsche Bibelgesellschaft/German Bible Society, 1994).

Miller, James E., 'Pederasty and Romans 1:27: A Response to Mark Smith', *JAAR* 65 (1997) 861-66.

————, 'The Practices of Romans 1:26: Homosexual or Heterosexual?' *NovT* 37 (1995) 1-11.

Miller, Robert W., 'The Text of Rom 11:31', *Faith & Mission* 23 (2006) 37-53.

Milne, D. J. W., 'Genesis 3 in the Letter to the Romans', *RTR* 39 (1980) 10-18.

————, 'Romans 7:7-12, Paul's Pre-conversion Experience', *RTR* 43 (1984) 9-17.

Moiser, Jeremy, 'Rethinking Romans 12–15', *NTS* 36 (1990) 571-82.

Montefiore, C. G., 'The Genesis of the Religion of St. Paul', in *Judaism and St Paul: Two Essays* (London: Max Goschen, 1914), 1-129.

Moo, Douglas J., *The Epistle to the Romans* (NICNT; Grand Rapids: Eerdmans, 1996).

Moo, Jonathan, 'Romans 8.19-22 and Isaiah's Cosmic Covenant', *NTS* 54 (2008) 74-89.

Moody, R. M., 'The Habakkuk Quotation in Romans 1:17', *ExpTim* 92 (1981) 205-8.

Moore, George Foot, 'Christian Writers on Judaism', *HTR* 14 (1921) 197-254.

Mora, Vincent, 'Romains 16,17-20 et la lettre aux Éphesiens', *RB* 107 (2000) 541-47.

Morris, Leon, *The Apostolic Preaching of the Cross* (3rd ed.; Grand Rapids: Eerdmans/ London: Tyndale, 1965).

————, *The Epistle to the Romans* (PNTC; Grand Rapids: Eerdmans, 1988).

Morrison, Bruce, and John Woodhouse, 'The Coherence of Romans 7:1–8:8', *RTR* 47 (1988) 8-16.

Moyise, Steve, 'The *Catena* of Romans 3:10-18', *ExpTim* 106 (1994-95) 367-70.

Munck, Johannes, *Paul and the Salvation of Mankind* (London: SCM, 1959).

Murphy-O'Connor, Jerome, 'The Pauline Network', *BibToday* 42 (2004) 219-23.

Murray, John, *The Epistle to the Romans: The English Text with Introduction, Exposition, and Notes* (Grand Rapids: Eerdmans, 1965).

Mussner, Franz, 'Heil für alle: Der Grundgedanke des Römerbriefs', *Kairos* 23 (1981) 207-14.

Nanos, Mark D., *The Mystery of Romans: The Jewish Context of Paul's Letter* (Philadelphia: Fortress, 1996).

Napier, Daniel, 'Paul's Analysis of Sin and Torah in Romans 7:7-25', *ResQ* 44 (2002) 15-32.

Neufeld, Matthew G. 'Submission to Governing Authorities: A Study of Romans 13:1-7', *Direction* 23 (1994) 90-97.

Ng, Esther Yue L., 'Phoebe as *Prostatis*', *TrinJ* 25 (2004) 3-13.

Nickle, Keith F., *The Collection: A Study in Paul's Strategy* (SBT 48; London, SCM, 1966).

O'Brien, Peter, 'Romans 8:26, 27: A Revolutionary Approach to Prayer?' *RTR* 46 (1987) 65-73.

————, 'Was Paul a Covenantal Nomist?' in D. A. Carson, Peter T. O'Brien, and Mark A. Seifrid, eds., *Justification and Variegated Nomism*, Vol. II — *The Paradoxes of Paul* (Tübingen: Mohr Siebeck/Grand Rapids: Baker Academic, 2004), 249-96.

————, *The Epistle to the Philippians: A Commentary on the Greek Text* (NIGTC; Grand Rapids: Eerdmans, 1991).

O'Neill, J. C., *Paul's Letter to the Romans* (Baltimore: Penguin Books, 1975).

Obeng, E. A., '"Abba, Father": The Prayer of the Sons of God', *ExpTim* 99 (1988) 363-66.

Oden, Thomas C., 'Without Excuse: Classic Christian Exegesis of General Revelation', *JETS* 41 (1998) 55-68.

Osborne, William L., 'The Old Testament Background of Paul's "All Israel" in Romans 11:26a', *AsiaJT* 2 (1988) 282-93.

Oss, Douglas A., 'The Interpretation of the "Stone" Passages by Peter and Paul: A Comparative Study', *JETS* 32 (1989) 181-200.

Oster, Richard E., Jr., '"Congregations of the Gentiles" (Rom 16:4): A Culture-based Ecclesiology in the Letters of Paul', *ResQ* 40 (1998) 39-52.

Owen, Paul L., 'The "Works of the Law" in Romans and Galatians: A New Defense of the Subjective Genitive', *JBL* 126 (2007) 553-77.

Packer, James I., 'Le "malheureux" de Romains 7', *Hokhma* 55 (1994) 19-25.

Paffenroth, Kim, 'Romans 12:9-21 — A Brief Summary of the Problems of Translation and Interpretation', *IBS* 14 (1992) 89-99.

Parlier, Isabelle, 'La folle justice de Dieu: Romains 8,31-39', *FoiVie* 91 (1992) 103-10.

Peng, Kuo-Wei, *Hate the Evil, Hold Fast to the Good: Structuring Romans 12:1–15:1* (LNTS 300; London/New York: T&T Clark, 2006).

Peterman, G. W., 'Romans 15.26: Make a Contribution or Establish Fellowship?' *NTS* 40 (1994) 457-63.

Petersen, Anders Klostergaard, 'Shedding New Light on Paul's Understanding of Baptism: A Ritual-Theoretical Approach to Romans 6', *ST* 3-28 (1998) 3-28.

Peterson, David, 'Worship and Ethics in Romans 12', *TynBul* 44 (1993) 271-88.

Phipps, William E., 'Paul on "Unnatural" Sex', *CurrTheolMiss* 29 (2002) 128-31.

Pierce, C. A., *Conscience in the New Testament* (SBT; London: SCM, 1955).

Piper, John, 'The Demonstration of the Righteousness of God in Romans 3:25, 26', *JSNT* (1980) 2-32.

Plisch, U.-K., 'Die Apostelin Junia: Das exegetische Problem in Röm 16.7 im Licht von Nestle-Aland[27] und der sahidischen Überlieferung', *NTS* 42 (1996) 477-78.

Poirier, John C., 'Romans 5:13-14 and the Universality of Law', *NovT* 38 (1996) 344-58.

Porcher, Marie-Jo, 'Quelques considérations sur l'usage du Psaume 32 dans l'épître aux Romains (Rm 4,1-12)', *RevScRel* 77, no. 4 (2003) 552-64.

Porter, Calvin L., 'Romans 1.18-32: Its Role in the Developing Argument', *NTS* 40 (1994) 210-28.

Porter, Stanley, 'The Argument of Romans 5: Can a Rhetorical Question Make a Difference?' *JBL* 110 (1991) 662-65.

———, 'Diatribe', in *DNTB*, 296-98.

———, 'Romans 13:1-7 as Pauline Political Rhetoric', *FilolNT* 3 (1990) 115-39.

———, *Verbal Aspect in the Greek of the New Testament, with Reference to Tense and Mood* (New York: Peter Lang, 1993).

Poythress, Vern S., 'Is Romans 1[3-4] a *Pauline* Confession after All?' *ExpTim* 87 (1975-76) 180-83.

Quarles, Charles L., 'From Faith to Faith: A Fresh Examination of the Prepositional Series in Romans 1.17', *NovT* 45 (2003) 1-21.

Räisänen, Heikki, 'Galatians 2.16 and Paul's Break with Judaism', *NTS* 31 (1985) 543-53.

———, *Paul and the Law* (Philadelphia: Fortress, 1986).

Rapinchuk, Mark, 'Universal Sin and Salvation in Romans 5:12-21', *JETS* 42 (1999) 427-41.

Rastoin, Marc, 'Une bien étrange greffe (Rm 11,17): Correspondances rabbiniques d'une expression paulinienne', *RB* 114 (2007) 73-79.

Reasoner, Mark, *The Strong and the Weak: Romans 14.1–15.13 in Context* (SNTSMS 103; Cambridge: Cambridge University Press, 1999).

Reed, Jeffrey T., 'Indicative and Imperative in Rom 6,21-22: The Rhetoric of Punctuation', *Bib* 74 (1993) 244-57.

Refoulé, François, 'Cohérence ou incohérence de Paul en Romains 9–11?' *RB* 98 (1991) 51-79.

——, 'Note sur Romains IX,30-33', *RB* 92 (1985) 161-86.

Rehmann, Luzia Sutter, 'The Doorway into Freedom: The Case of the "Suspected Wife" in Romans 7.1-6', *JSNT* 79 (2000) 91-104.

Reichrath, Hans L., 'Juden und Christen — Eine Frage von "Ökumene?" Was uns Römer 15,7-13 dazu lehrt', *Judaica* 47 (1991) 22-30.

Reid, Marty L., 'A Consideration of the Function of Rom 1:8-15 in Light of Greco-Roman Rhetoric', *JETS* 38 (1995) 181-91.

Reinbold, Wolfgang, 'Israel und das Evangelium: Zur Exegese von Römer 10,19-21', *ZNW* 86 (1995) 122-29.

——, 'Paulus und das Gesetz: Zur Exegese von Röm 9,30-33', *BZ* 38 (1994) 253-64.

Rhyne, C. Thomas, '*Nomos Dikaiosynēs* and the Meaning of Romans 10:4', *CBQ* 47 (1985) 486-99.

Rimbach, James A., '"All Creation Groans": Theology/Ecology in St. Paul', *AsiaJT* 1 (1987) 379-91.

Robinson, D. W. B., 'The Salvation of Israel in Romans 9–11', *RTR* 26 (1967) 81-96.

Rodgers, Peter R., 'The Text of Romans 8:28', *JTS* 46 (1995) 547-50.

Romanello, Stefano, 'Rom 7,7-25 and the Impotence of the Law: A Fresh Look at a Much Debated Topic Using Literary-Rhetorical Analysis', *Bib* 84 (2003) 510-30.

Romaniuk, Kazimierz, 'Was Phoebe in Romans 16,1 a Deaconess?' *ZNW* 81 (1990) 132-34.

Romerowski, Sylvain, 'Israël dans le plan de Dieu', *La revue réformée* 51 (2000) 51-68.

Rowe, C. Kavin, 'Romans 10:13: What Is the Name of the Lord?' *HorBibTheol* 22 (2000) 135-73.

Russell, Walt, 'Insights from Postmodernism's Emphasis on Interpretive Communities in the Interpretation of Romans 7', *JETS* 37 (1994) 511-27.

Sabou, Sorin, 'A Note on Romans 6:5: The Representation *(homoiōma)* of His Death', *TynBul* 55 (2004) 219-29.

Sanday, William, and Arthur C. Headlam, *The Epistle to the Romans* (ICC; Edinburgh: T&T Clark, 1895).

Sanders, E. P., *Paul and Palestinian Judaism: A Comparison of Patterns of Religion* (London: SCM, 1977).

——, *Paul, the Law, and the Jewish People* (London: SCM, 1985).

Sandt, H. W. M. van de, 'Research into Rom. 8:4a: The Legal Claim of the Law', *Bijdr* 37 (1976) 252-69.

Sass, Gerhard, 'Röm 15,7-13 — als Summe des Römerbriefs gelesen', *EvTh* 53 (1993) 510-27.

Satran, F. David, 'Paul among the Rabbis and the Fathers: Exegetical Reflections', *PSB* Sup 1 (1990) 90-105.

Schoeps, H. J., *Paul: The Theology of the Apostle in the Light of Jewish Religious History* (London: Lutterworth, 1961).

Schreiber, Stefan, 'Arbeit mit der Gemeinde (Röm 16.6, 12): Zur versunkenen Möglichkeit der Gemeindeleitung durch Frauen', *NTS* 46 (2000) 204-26.

Schreiner, Thomas R., 'Corporate and Individual Election in Romans 9: A Response to Brian Abasciano', *JETS* 49 (2006) 373-86.

———, 'Did Paul Believe in Justification by Works? Another Look at Romans 2', *BBR* 3 (1993) 131-55.

———, 'Does Romans 9 Teach Individual Election unto Salvation? Some Exegetical and Theological Reflections', *JETS* 36 (1993) 25-40.

———, 'Israel's Failure to Attain Righteousness in Romans 9:30–10:3', *TrinJ* 12 (1991) 209-20.

———, 'Paul's View of the Law in Romans 10:4-5', *WTJ* 55 (1993) 113-35.

———, '"Works of Law" in Paul', *NovT* 33 (1991) 217-44.

———, *The Law and Its Fulfilment: A Pauline Theology of Law* (Grand Rapids: Baker, 1993).

———, *Romans* (BECNT 6; Grand Rapids: Baker, 1998).

Scroggs, R., *The New Testament and Homosexuality: Contextual Background for Contemporary Debate* (Philadelphia: Fortress, 1983).

Seewann, Maria-Irma, 'Semantische Untersuchung zu *pōrōsis*, veranlasst durch Röm 11,25', *FilolNT* 10, nos. 19-20 (1997) 139-56.

Segal, Alan F., 'Paul's Experience and Romans 9–11', *PSB* Sup 1 (1990) 56-70.

———, 'Romans 7 and Jewish Dietary Law', *SR* 15 (1986) 361-74.

Seifrid, Mark A., 'Natural Revelation and the Purpose of the Law in Romans', *TynBul* 49 (1998) 115-29.

———, 'Paul's Approach to the Old Testament in Rom 10:6-8', *TrinJ* 6 (1985) 3-37.

———, 'The Subject of Rom 7:14-25', *NovT* 34 (1992) 313-33.

———, *Justification by Faith: The Origin and Development of a Central Pauline Theme* (Leiden: Brill, 1992).

Seitz, Erich, 'Korrigiert sich Paulus? Zu Röm 5,6-8', *ZNW* 91 (2000) 279-87.

———, '*Logon syntemnōn* — Eine Gerichtsankündigung? (Zu Römer 9,27/28)', *BN* 109 (2001) 56-82.

Sevenster, J. N., *Paul and Seneca* (Leiden: Brill, 1961).

Shogren, Gary Steven, '"Is the Kingdom of God about Eating and Drinking or Isn't It?" (Romans 14:17)', *NovT* 42 (2000) 238-56.

———, 'The "Wretched Man" of Romans 7:14-25 as *Reductio ad absurdum*', *EvQ* 72 (2000) 119-34.

Smiga, George, 'Romans 12:1-2 and 15:30-32 and the Occasion of the Letter to the Romans', *CBQ* 53 (1991) 257-73.

Smiles, Vincent M., 'The Concept of "Zeal" in Second-Temple Judaism and Paul's Critique of It in Romans 10:2', *CBQ* 64 (2002) 282-99.

Smit, Peter-Ben, 'A Symposium in Rom. 14:17? A Note on Paul's Terminology', *NovT* 49 (2007) 40-53.

Smith, Geoffrey, 'The Function of "Likewise" (*hōsautos*) in Romans 8:26', *TynBul* 49 (1998) 29-38.

Smith, Mark D., 'Ancient Bisexuality and the Interpretation of Romans 1:26-27', *JAAR* 64 (1996) 223-56.

Snodgrass, Klyne R., 'Justification by Grace — To the Doers: An Analysis of the Place of Romans 2 in the Theology of Paul', *NTS* 34 (1988) 72-93.

Snyman, A. H., 'Style and Rhetorical Situation of Romans 8.31-39', *NTS* 34 (1988) 218-31.

Stanley, Christopher D., 'The Significance of Romans 11:3-4 for the Text History of the LXX Book of Kingdoms', *JBL* 112 (1993) 43-54.

Stein, Robert H., 'The Argument of Romans 13:1-7', *NovT* 31 (1989) 323-43.

Stendahl, Krister, 'Paul and the Introspective Conscience of the West', in *Paul Among Jews and Gentiles and Other Essays* (London: SCM, 1977), 78-96.

Stowers, Stanley K., '*Ek pisteōs* and *dia tēs pisteōs* in Romans 3:30', *JBL* 108 (1989) 665-74.

———, *Letter Writing in Greco-Roman Antiquity* (Philadelphia: Westminster, 1986).

———, *A Rereading of Romans: Justice, Jews, and Gentiles* (New Haven: Yale University Press, 1994).

Strauss, Steve, 'Missions Theology in Romans 15:14-33', *BSac* 160 (2003) 457-74.

Strecker, Georg, *The Johannine Letters* (Hermeneia; Philadelphia: Fortress, 1996).

Strelan, G., 'A Note on the Old Testament Background of Romans 7:7', *LTJ* 15 (1981) 23-25.

Stuhlmacher, Peter, 'Der Abfassungszweck des Römerbriefes', *ZNW* 77 (1986) 180-93.

Swart, Gerald, 'Why without Excuse? An Inquiry into the Syntactic and Semantic Relations of Romans 1:18-21', *Neot* 39 (2005) 389-407.

Tannehill, Robert C., *Dying and Rising with Christ: A Study in Pauline Theology* (Berlin: Töpelmann, 1966).

Tanner, J. Paul, 'The New Covenant and Paul's Quotations from Hosea in Romans 9:25-26', *BSac* 162 (2005) 95-110.

Taylor, John W., 'From Faith to Faith: Romans 1.17 in the Light of Greek Idiom', *NTS* 50 (2004) 337-48.

Taylor, N. H., 'Dying with Christ in Baptism: Issues in the Translation and Interpretation of Romans 6.3-4', *BibTrans* 59 (2008) 38-49.

Thielman, Frank, 'Unexpected Mercy: Echoes of a Biblical Motif in Romans 9–11', *SJT* 47 (1994) 169-81.

———, *From Plight to Solution: A Jewish Framework for Understanding Paul's View of the Law in Galatians and Romans* (Leiden: E. J. Brill, 1989).

———, *Paul and the Law: A Contextual Approach* (Downers Grove, Ill.: InterVarsity Press, 1994).

Thompson, Richard W., 'The Alleged Rabbinic Background of Rom 3,31', *ETL* 63 (1987) 136-48.

———, 'How Is the Law Fulfilled in Us? An Interpretation of Rom 8:4', *LS* 11 (1986) 31-40.

———, 'The Inclusion of the Gentiles in Rom 3,27-30', *Bib* 69 (1988) 543-46.

———, 'Paul's Double Critique of Jewish Boasting', *Bib* 67 (1986) 520-31.

Thorley, John, 'Junia, a Woman Apostle', *NovT* 38 (1996) 18-29.

Thornton, T. C. G., 'Propitiation or Expiation?' *ExpTim* 80 (1968-69) 53-55.

Thorsteinsson, Runar M., 'Paul and Roman Stoicism: Romans 12 and Contemporary Stoic Ethics', *JSNT* 29 (2006) 139-61.

———, 'Paul's Missionary Duty towards Gentiles in Rome: A Note on the Punctuation and Syntax of Rom 1.13-15', *NTS* 48 (2002) 531-47.

Thrall, M. E., 'The Pauline Use of *syneidēsis*', *NTS* 14 (1967-68) 118-25.

Tobin, Thomas H., 'The Jewish Context of Rom 5:12-14', *Studia Philonica Annual* 13 (2001) 159-75.

———, 'What Shall We Say That Abraham Found? The Controversy behind Romans 4', *HTR* 88 (1995) 437-52.

Tomson, Peter J., 'What Did Paul Mean by "Those Who Know the Law"? (Rom 7.1)', *NTS* 49 (2003) 573-81.

Trocmé, Etienne, 'From "I" to "We": Christian Life according to Romans, Chapters 7 and 8', *ABR* 35 (1987) 73-76.

Trudinger, Paul, 'An Autobiographical Digression? A Note on Romans 7:7-25', *ExpTim* 107 (1996) 173-74.

Tsumura, D. T., 'An OT Background to Rom 8.22', *NTS* 40 (1994) 620-21.

Van der Horst, Peter W., '"Only Then Will All Israel Be Saved": A Short Note on the Meaning of *kai houtōs* in Romans 11:26', *JBL* 119 (2000) 521-25.

Vasholz, Robert, 'The Character of Israel's Future in Light of the Abrahamic and Mosaic Covenants', *TrinJ* 25 n.s. (2004) 39-59.

Vermes, G., *The Complete Dead Sea Scrolls in English* (London: Penguin, 1998).

Viard, Jean-Sébastien, 'Loi, chair et liberation: Une solution structurelle au problème de Romains 7,1-6', *Theoforum* 36 (2005) 155-73.

Vickers, Brian, 'Grammar and Theology in the Interpretation of Rom 5:12', *TrinJ* 27 (2006) 271-88.

Voorwinde, Stephen, 'Rethinking Israel: An Exposition of Romans 11:25-27', *VoxRef* 68 (2003) 4-48.

———, 'Who Is the "Wretched Man" in Romans 7:24?' *VoxRef* 54 (1990) 11-26.

Vos, J. S., 'Die hermeneutische Antinome bei Paulus (Galater 3.11-12; Römer 10.5-10)', *NTS* 38 (1992) 254-70.

Wagner, J. Ross, 'The Christ, Servant of Jew and Gentile: A Fresh Approach to Romans 15:8-9', *JBL* 116 (1997) 473-85.

Walker, William O., Jr., 'Romans 1.18–2.29: A Non-Pauline Interpolation?' *NTS* 45 (1999) 533-52.

Wallace, Daniel B., *Greek Grammar beyond the Basics: An Exegetical Syntax of the New Testament* (Grand Rapids: Zondervan, 1996).

Wasserman, Emma, 'The Death of the Soul in Romans 7: Revisiting Paul's Anthropology in Light of Hellenistic Moral Psychology', *JBL* 126 (2007), 793-816.

Watson, Nigel M., '"And if children, then heirs" (Rom 8:17) — Why Not Sons?' *ABR* 49 (2001) 53-56.

———, 'Justified by Faith: Judged by Works — An Antinomy', *NTS* 29 (1983) 209-21.

Watson, N. W., 'Review Article', *NTS* 20 (1974) 217-28.

Wedderburn, A. J. M., *Baptism and Resurrection: Studies in Pauline Theology against Its Graeco-Roman Background* (WUNT 44; Tübingen: Mohr Siebeck, 1987).

———, *The Reasons for Romans* (Edinburgh: T&T Clark, 1988).

Weder, Hans, 'Gesetz und Sunde: Gedanken zu einen qualitativen Sprung im Denken des Paulus', *NTS* 31 (1985) 357-76.

Weiss, Herold, 'Paul and the Judging of Days', *ZNW* 86 (1995) 137-53.

Westerholm, Stephen, *Israel's Law and the Church's Faith: Paul and His Recent Interpreters* (Grand Rapids: Eerdmans, 1988).

———, *Perspectives Old and New on Paul: The "Lutheran" Paul and His Critics* (Grand Rapids: Eerdmans, 2004).

Whelan, Caroline F., '*Amica Pauli:* The Role of Phoebe in the Early Church', *JSNT* 49 (1993) 67-85.

Whitsett, Christopher G., 'Son of God, Seed of David: Paul's Messianic Exegesis in Romans 2:3-4 *(sic)*', *JBL* 119 (2000) 661-81.

Wiefel, Wolfgang, 'The Jewish Community in Ancient Rome and the Origins of Roman Christianity', in *The Romans Debate, Revised,* ed. Karl P. Donfried (above), 85-101.

Wilckens, Ulrich, *Der Brief an die Römer,* 1. Teilband (EKKNT 6/1; Zurich, Einsiedeln, Koln/Neukirchen-Vluyn: Benziger Verlag/Neukirchener Verlag, 1978).

Williams, Michael, 'Romans 1: Entropy, Sexuality and Politics', *Anvil* 10 (1993) 105-10.

Williams, S. K., 'The "Righteousness of God" in Romans', *JBL* 99 (1980) 241-90.

Winandy, Jacques, 'La mort de Jésus: Une morte au péché?' *ETL* 76 (2000) 433-34.

Winter, Bruce W., 'The Public Honouring of Christian Benefactors: Romans 13.3-4 and 1 Peter 2.14-15', *JSNT* 34 (1988) 87-103.

———, 'Roman Law and Society in Romans 12–15', in *Rome in the Bible and the Early Church,* ed. P. Oakes (Grand Rapids: Baker, 2002), 67-102.

Witherington, Ben, III, with Darlene Hyatt, *Paul's Letter to the Romans: A Socio-Rhetorical Commentary* (Grand Rapids: Eerdmans, 2004).

Woyke, Johannes, '"Einst" und "Jetzt" in Röm 1–3? Zur Bedeutung von *nyni de* in Röm 3,21', *ZNW* 92 (2001) 206.

Wright, Christopher J. H., *Deuteronomy* (NIBC; Peabody, Mass.: Hendrickson, 1996).

Wright, N. T., 'A Fresh Perspective on Paul?' *BJRL* 83 (2001) 21-39.

———, 'The Law in Romans 2', in *Paul and the Mosaic Law,* ed. James D. G. Dunn (Grand Rapids: Eerdmans, 2001), 131-50.

———, 'The Letter to the Romans: Introduction, Commentary, and Reflections', in *The New Interpreter's Bible,* X (Nashville: Abingdon, 2002) 395-770.

———, 'New Perspectives on Paul', in *Justification in Perspective: Historical Developments and Contemporary Challenges,* ed. Bruce L. McCormack (Grand Rapids: Baker/Edinburgh: Rutherford House, 2006), 243-64.

———, *The Climax of the Covenant: Christ and the Law in Pauline Theology* (Edinburgh: T&T Clark, 1991).

———, *Justification: God's Plan and Paul's Vision* (London: SPCK, 2009).

———, *What Saint Paul Really Said* (Oxford: Lion, 1997).

Wu, Julie L., 'The Spirit's Intercession in Romans 8:26-27: An Exegetical Note', *ExpTim* 105 (1993-94) 13.

Yates, J. C., 'The Judgement of the Heathen: The Interpretation of Article XVIII and Romans 2:12-16', *Churchman* 100 (1986) 220-30.

Yinger, Kent L., 'Romans 12:14-21 and Nonretaliation in Second Temple Judaism: Addressing Persecution within the Community', *CBQ* 60 (1998) 74-96.

Young, Richard Alan, 'The Knowledge of God in Romans 1:18-32: Exegetical and Theological Reflections', *JETS* 43 (2000) 695-707.

Ziesler, John A., 'The Just Requirement of the Law (Romans 8.4)', *ABR* 35 (1987) 77-82.

————, 'The Role of the Tenth Commandment in Romans 7', *JSNT* 33 (1988) 41-56.

————, *Paul's Letter to the Romans* (London: SCM/Philadelphia: Trinity Press International, 1989).

Zorn, Walter, 'The Messianic Use of Habakkuk 2:4a in Romans', *Stone-Campbell Journal* 1 (1998) 213-30.

Introduction

I. ROME AND ITS POPULATION

When Paul wrote Romans, the empire was under the rule of Nero Claudius Caesar, the fourth of the Julio-Claudian dynasty (Tiberius [14-37], Caligula [37-41], Claudius [41-54], and Nero [54-68]). Nero's early reign was regarded as the best period since the death of Octavian (Caesar Augustus). Nero had not yet become the murderous tyrant of his later years. As capital of the empire, Rome attracted peoples from all over the Mediterranean region. It is estimated that in the mid to late 50s Rome had a population of about 400,000 made up of 'slaves (30%) and freed men and women (30%), and freeborn (40%)'.[1] It is also estimated that about 10 percent of the population were Jews.

In A.D. 41 the emperor Claudius extended Jewish rights throughout the empire, but in the same year, according to Dio Cassius, he ordered the Jews, 'while continuing their traditional mode of life, not to hold meetings' (*Hist. Rom.* 60.6.6). Several years later, according to Acts 18:2, Claudius ordered all the Jews to leave Rome, an order believed to have been issued in A.D. 49. The Roman historian Suetonius (b. ca. A.D. 70; d. ca. A.D. 130) says, 'since the Jews constantly made disturbances at the instigation of Chrestus, he [Claudius] expelled them from Rome' (*De Vita Claudii* 25.4). This is believed to be a reference to the same event mentioned in Acts 18:2. Questions have been raised about how these accounts of the expulsion of Jews should be understood. In particular, it has been argued that Luke's account should be regarded as hyperbole because later in Acts, where Paul's meeting with Jews in Rome is described (Acts 28:16-24), there is no indication that they were aware of the expulsion, an event that must have been traumatic for the Jewish community at the time. There is no indication either of the ani-

---

1. Peter Lampe, 'The Roman Christians of Romans 16', in *The Romans Debate, Revised and Expanded Edition*, ed. Karl P. Donfried (Peabody, Mass.: Hendrickson, 1991), 230.

1

mosity between Jews and Christians that one would expect if the expulsion had been triggered by disputes about the Christ.[2] However, the edict of Claudius lapsed when he died in A.D. 54 and by A.D. 58, when Paul wrote Romans, many Jews, including Priscilla and Aquila, had returned to Rome. By the time Paul arrived there in ca. A.D. 60, some eleven years would have passed since the issuing of the edict of expulsion, and some six years since Jews had begun returning to Rome. Sufficient time had elapsed to explain why the event might not be at the forefront of the minds of the Jews with whom Paul met in Rome. In any case, whether every last Jew or only a majority of them had been expelled, there is no good reason to doubt the fundamental accuracy of the reports of Luke and Suetonius.

II. CHRISTIANS IN ROME

The Christian community in Rome probably owed its foundation to the work of Christian travelers, immigrants, and merchants, some of whom may have been present in Jerusalem on the Day of Pentecost (cf. Acts 2:10) and were therefore either Jews or proselytes. Accordingly, the earliest Christian community in Rome would have been Jewish in character. However, following the edict of Claudius promulgated in A.D. 49 when Jews were expelled from the capital, it would have been comprised mainly of Gentiles. When in A.D. 54 Claudius died and this edict lapsed, Jews began to trickle back into Rome, and Jewish believers again became part of the Christian community.

Nevertheless some have argued that the implied audience of Romans is entirely Gentile.[3] In 11:13 Paul does say: 'I am talking to you Gentiles', and it could be argued that when he says in 7:1: 'I am speaking to those who know the law', this does not necessarily refer to Jews. It could refer to Gentiles who have some background in the synagogue. However, it is significant that 50 percent of the names the apostle mentions in chapter 16 are Jewish, and it is highly unlikely that he would have written the letter without having them in mind as well (see 'Additional Note: The Twenty-Six Named Individuals in Romans 16:3-15', 574-75). We should think, then, of an audience comprised of a Gentile majority and a Jewish minority.

According to the Acts of the Apostles, there were Christian communities in Puteoli (situated about 180 km. southeast of Rome) as well as in Rome itself (Acts 28:13-15). Most Christians in Rome lived in the Transtiberium region (Trastevere) and along the Appian Way, the poorer

---

2. Johann D. Kim, *God, Israel, and the Gentiles: Rhetoric and Situation in Romans 9–11* (SBLDS 176; Atlanta: Society of Biblical Literature, 2000), 54-56.

3. Cf., e.g., Stanley K. Stowers, *A Rereading of Romans: Justice, Jews, and Gentiles* (New Haven: Yale University Press, 1994), 21-33; Mark D. Nanos, *The Mystery of Romans: The Jewish Context of Paul's Letter* (Minneapolis: Fortress, 1996), 75-84.

parts of Rome. A small number lived in the better parts, especially those who were slaves in well-to-do households. Those in the poorer parts lived in *insulae*, flimsy, overcrowded apartment blocks often of wooden construction and therefore terrible firetraps.[4] Most Christians were either freed-[wo]men or slaves. As many as 60 percent of them were of slave origin. In this respect the Roman Christian community differed from other Pauline congregations, for example, Corinth, which, according to Malherbe and Meeks, represented a fair cross section of their urban societies.[5] There are indications that some of Paul's audience at least had been exposed to persecution (12:14, 17-21).[6]

III. PAUL'S SITUATION: A SCENARIO

Paul's encounter with the risen Christ on the Damascus Road involved a conversion *to* Christ (not *from* Judaism) and a call to be an apostle to the Gentiles. As such, his life was marked by several interlocking motivations, the most fundamental of which was his aim to please God (2 Cor 5:9; 1 Thess 2:4).[7] Connected with this was his sense of obligation to preach the gospel (1:14; 1 Cor 9:16), free of charge (1 Cor 9:18; 2 Cor 11:7), in places where Christ had not been named (15:20; 2 Cor 10:16). He did all in his power to ensure that believers were strengthened and grew to maturity in their faith (Col 1:28) so that they would not fall prey to those who would turn them away from their pure devotion to Christ (2 Cor 11:2-3). He felt a deep sense of responsibility for Gentile believers especially, both those who were the fruit of his own apostolic ministry and those who were not (1:14-15; Gal 4:19).

His ambition to go on preaching where Christ was not already known was constrained by the needs of, and threats to, existing believing communities for which he was responsible. So, for instance, he wrote to the Corinthians: 'Our hope is that, as your faith continues to grow, our sphere of activity among you will greatly expand, so that we can preach the gospel in the regions beyond you' (2 Cor 10:15-16). When Paul wrote this, he was involved in a life-and-death struggle to ensure that the Corinthians' faith was not subverted by false apostles (2 Corinthians 11–13). It was only when this matter had been dealt with that he would feel free to

---

4. A. B. du Toit, '"God's Beloved in Rome" (Rm 1:7). The Genesis and Socio-Economic Situation of the First-Generation Christian Community in Rome', *Neot* 32 (1998) 367-88, provides a detailed description of living conditions in the Transtiberium.

5. Cf. du Toit, '"God's Beloved in Rome" (Rm 1:7)', 386-87.

6. Joseph A. Fitzmyer, *Romans* (AB; New York: Doubleday, 1993), 25-39, provides an excellent account of 'Rome and the Roman Christians'.

7. Prior to his conversion Paul also sought to please God, but in a way that proved to be misguided.

pursue further his ambition to preach in 'regions beyond' where Christ had not been named.

This casts some light on the provenance of Romans. As apostle to the Gentiles, Paul felt under obligation to the believers in Rome (1:14-15). He had long wanted to fulfill this obligation (1:13-14), but his ministry, both evangelistic and pastoral, in the eastern Mediterranean meant that he had to defer doing so (15:20-24). But once he had completed that ministry, his mind turned first to the need to exercise a ministry among the Romans believers, and having done that, to pursue his ambition to preach in the western Mediterranean, in Spain. However, before he could do either of these things, he had another obligation to fulfill: he had to convey to Jerusalem the collection for the poor saints taken up among the Gentile churches of Galatia, Macedonia, and Achaia (15:25-28). As it turned out, events in Jerusalem meant further unwelcome delays in carrying out his plans, and his eventual arrival in Rome was as a prisoner, and that curtailed his freedom of movement.

IV. ROMANS: A SUMMARY OF THE CONTENT

In 1:1-7 Paul introduces himself to the Roman believers as an apostle set apart for the gospel of God, a gospel concerning God's Son, born as the seed of David and therefore the Jewish Messiah, and appointed Son of God with power and therefore Lord of the Gentiles as well as the Jews. Of this gospel Paul has been appointed an apostle to the Gentiles, and the Roman believers, being predominantly Gentiles, are numbered among these and therefore are included among those for whom he is responsible.

1:8-17 the apostle seeks to establish good rapport with his audience by referring to their faith, which is being 'reported all over the world', and saying that they feature constantly in his prayers, not least his prayer that he might succeed at last in coming to visit them, something he has been hindered from doing until now. He says that he is eager to preach the gospel to them because he is under obligation to all people, including his audience in Rome. He insists that he is not ashamed of this gospel, for it is the power of God for salvation for all who believe because in it the righteousness of God is revealed. This revelation of the righteousness of God in the gospel is in fact the major theme of the letter.

In 1:18–11:31 Paul expounds and defends the gospel, showing how the righteousness of God is revealed in it. This involves a number of steps. First, he explains that such a revelation of God's saving righteousness is needed because humanity otherwise stands exposed to the wrath of God because of its sin (1:18-32). Those who take the high moral ground because they know better, including Jewish people who have the law but do not keep it, have no immunity (2:1-29). The apostle's insistence that the Jews are not immune does not constitute a denial of the advantages they have as God's people, in particular their possession of the law (3:1-8). However, these advantages do not mean that they are better off than the Gentiles, for even their law testifies to their sinfulness, and so, like the Gentiles, they stand accountable before God.

Paul takes the second step in his exposition and defense of the gospel in 3:21–5:21. Here he shows how God has set forth his own Son as the atoning sacrifice for sins so that people may be justified through the redemption he has provided in Christ, and by so doing he has shown that he is just when he justifies sinners who have faith in Jesus. Because both Jews and Gentiles are justified through faith without reference to the law, all grounds of illegitimate boasting on the part of Jewish people have been removed. The one God justifies the circumcised and the uncircumcised in the same way: through faith. At this point Paul introduces the case of Abraham to show that, contrary to some current Jewish belief, he was justified by faith without works and while uncircumcised. He emphasizes that what was written about Abraham was written not only for his sake but also for the sake of all those who believe, to whom God will likewise credit righteousness. There follows a brief pastoral application that spells out the blessings of justification (5:1-11), before Paul portrays the saving action of God in Christ and its blessed effect for all who believe by comparing and contrasting it with Adam's sinful act which had disastrous results for all humanity.

The third step in Paul's exposition in 6:1–8:39 involves showing that salvation by grace through faith does not promote moral anarchy, as some of his detractors had alleged. Rather, believers as those who have died to sin and now serve their new master, Christ, cannot continue in sin. It involves showing also that while believers need to be free from the law so as to bear fruit for God, this is not to say that there is anything wrong with the law. On the contrary, the law is good, but having been laid under tribute by sin, it has become part of the problem, not part of the solution. It also involves showing that those who are in Christ are empowered by the Spirit, enabling them to live in a way that the law promoted but was unable to effect because of human sin. Paul also shows that believers, who have the firstfruits of the Spirit, experience suffering and frustration as they await their inheritance as children of God. The creation itself likewise endures frustration as it awaits liberation. Even in this time of waiting the Spirit helps believers in their weakness, and God himself works all things together for good for those who love him and are called according to his purpose. Therefore, nothing can separate them from the love of God in Christ Jesus.

In the fourth step of his exposition and defense of the gospel in 9:1–11:36 Paul deals with the pressing problem of Israel's rejection of the gospel. Can it be said that the righteousness of God is revealed in the gospel if the majority of the Jewish people, to whose ancestors God's promises were originally made, do not experience his promised blessings? Has the word of God failed? In response Paul first stresses his own agony over the majority of his kinsfolk who, despite their many God-given privileges, still will not believe. He explains that God's promises have not failed, for God has always chosen some rather than others as he has the right as creator to do, and he has always maintained a remnant of believing Jews of which Paul himself is a part. Next he explains that it is not only God's choice that is operating, but that unbelieving Israelites also bear responsibility. They have refused to submit to God's righteousness, insisting upon their own way of establishing righteousness by the law. Finally, lest his Gentile audience become arrogant in their attitude towards unbelieving Jews, the apostle insists that God will remain faithful to his promises and show himself righteous by bringing 'all Israel' to salvation.

Following his exposition and defense of the gospel, Paul spells out for his audience in 12:1–15:13 certain important behavioral implications. There are implications for their life in the Christian community, in the wider world, and in particular in relationships between Jewish and Gentile believers within their community.

Paul concludes the body of his letter in 15:14-33 by explaining why he has written so boldly: as apostle to the Gentiles who in the 'priestly duty of proclaiming the gospel' presides over the self-offering of the Gentiles to God, he reminds them of certain things so that their offering may be acceptable, sanctified by the Holy Spirit. He then speaks of his desire to visit them and spend time with them on his way to Spain, after he has delivered the collection to the saints in Jerusalem. He expresses his hope that they will help facilitate his mission. He also solicits his audience's prayers for the trip to Jerusalem, so that he may be delivered from the machinations of unbelievers there and that the collection will be graciously received by the saints.

In the final chapter, 16:1-27, Paul commends Phoebe, who probably carried his letter to Rome, greets acquaintances who are now (back) in Rome, warns his audience about those who cause divisions, and finally conveys greetings to the Roman believers from those presently with him (in Corinth), before concluding with an ascription of praise and glory to God.

V. THE PURPOSE OF ROMANS

The purpose for which Paul wrote Romans has been the subject of extensive debate. Part of the problem presented by the letter is that in 1:1-15 and 15:14–16:27 Paul implies that he was writing to prepare the way for his visit to Rome and a subsequent mission to Spain, while seeking prayer support for his impending visit to Jerusalem with the collection. However, such a purpose does not seem sufficient to explain the long theological and ethical sections of the letter (1:16–11:36; 12:1–15:13). Any satisfying solution to the problem of purpose, therefore, must show how the theological and ethical sections of the letter relate to the purpose implied in Paul's statements at the beginning and end of the letter. Put another way, the argument running through 1:16–15:13 has to be understood first, and then related to the implied purpose found in 1:1-15 and 15:14–16:27. It is important to attempt first of all, then, a brief statement of the argument of 1:16–15:13.

Paul states his basic thesis in 1:16-17: 'For I am not ashamed of the gospel, because it is the power of God that brings salvation to everyone who believes: first to the Jew, then to the Gentile. For in the gospel the righteousness of God is revealed — a righteousness that is by faith from first to last; just as it is written, "The one righteous will live by faith"'. Essentially, then, Paul's thesis is that the power of God is revealed through the gospel for all who have faith. In succeeding sections of the letter he argues the case for this thesis, defends it against possible objections, and spells out some of its ethical implications. He begins by arguing in 1:18–3:20 that God acts righteously in making no distinctions between Jews and Gentiles in the matter of sin, and therefore none in the matter of judgment either. In 3:21–5:21 he goes on to argue that, just as God reveals his righteousness in making no distinctions in the matter of sin and judgment, so too he reveals his righteousness in making no distinctions in the matter of salvation either. Jews and Gentiles alike are to be justified by the grace of God through faith in Jesus Christ, and that apart from works of the law. Such a thesis was open to a number of objections. Paul responds to some of these objections as he goes along, but in chapters 6–8 he deals specifically and at length with objections concerning moral standards and the nature and role of the law. In chapters 9–11 he deals with objections concerning the place of Israel in the saving purposes of God, maintaining that God has been righteous in his dealings with Israel and will not fail to act in faithfulness to his covenant with her. Having argued the case for his thesis, and having dealt with some of the objections that could be raised against it, in 12:1–15:13 Paul proceeds to draw out the ethical implications of the gospel in respect to such matters as ministry in the church, submission to rulers, love of fellow believers, life in the light of an imminent end, and toleration of other believers.

If the brief description of the overall argument of Romans outlined above is accepted, it must then be asked what Paul's purpose was in arguing along those lines. We could answer, at one level, that his purpose was to explain and defend his gospel of justification by grace through faith for Jews and Gentiles without distinction. That is probably true. If so, we must then ask: Why did he feel he had to give this explanation and make this defense when writing Romans, and how is it all to be related to the implied purpose for writing found in the opening and closing sections of the letter? In other words, what was Paul's overall purpose in writing Romans? Numerous suggestions have been made in response to this question, though not all of them succeed in explaining the overall purpose. Broadly speaking, these suggestions may be grouped into three main categories: those which explain it in terms of (a) a situation existing in the Roman congregations; (b) a stage in Paul's apostolic career; and (c) a combination of these.[8] A representative selection of the different suggestions is provided below.

(a) A Situation Existing in the Roman Congregations. Various identifications of this situation have been put forward. These include: (i) The Roman church lacked apostolic foundation, and Paul wrote Romans to provide the church with an apostolic presentation of the gospel, something he says he intended to do in person when he made his visit to Rome.[9] (ii) When the Christian Jews who had been expelled from Rome by Claudius were allowed to return, they found that the Christian house churches in Rome had developed a form of organization quite different from the synagogal form they had when they left. They also found themselves as a small Jewish Christian minority within a Gentile Christian majority. Paul wrote Romans to urge the Gentile Christian majority to live harmoniously with the Jewish Christian minority.[10] (iii) There was conflict in the Roman church between law-observant Christian Jews and law-free Gentile Christians. It was in response to this situation that Paul wrote Romans.[11] (iv) There was conflict between strong and weak *Gentile* believers over the matter of law observance. Paul dealt with this problem by applying the conclusions he had reached in his debate with the synagogue concerning what had become a central issue in the Christian church.[12] (v) Paul wrote Romans as an attempt to 'evangelize' by letter those whom he had so far been unable to 'evangelize' in person in order to elicit a proper response to the gospel on the part of his Roman readers (15:15-16).[13] (vi) The main function of Romans was to allow the Christians at Rome to hear the gospel from Paul so that they might be drawn into his apostolic orbit, and so that they too might become part of that offering of the Gentiles which, by Paul's priestly ministry of the gospel, would become acceptable to God.[14]

(b) A Stage in Paul's Apostolic Career. The following are some of the

---

8. Karl P. Donfried, ed., *The Romans Debate, Revised and Expanded Edition* (Peabody, Mass.: Hendrickson, 1991), brings together many of the contributions to this debate.

9. Günter Klein, 'Paul's Purpose in Writing the Epistle to the Romans', in *The Romans Debate, Revised,* 29-43.

10. Wolfgang Wiefel, 'The Jewish Community in Ancient Rome and the Origins of Roman Christianity', in *The Romans Debate, Revised,* 85-101. Cf. also W. S. Campbell, 'Romans III as a Key to the Structure and Thought of the Letter', *NovT* 23 (1981) 37-39, who also identifies anti-Judaism on the part of Gentile Christians as a cause of division in the Christian community in Rome.

11. A. J. M. Wedderburn, *The Reasons for Romans* (Edinburgh: T&T Clark, 1988), 64-65.

12. Ulrich Wilckens, *Der Brief an die Römer,* 1. Teilband (EKKNT 6/1; Zurich, Einsiedeln, Köln/Neukirchen-Vluyn: Benziger Verlag/Neukirchener Verlag, 1978), 39-42.

13. Neil Elliott, *The Rhetoric of Romans: Argumentative Constraint and Strategy and Paul's Dialogue with Judaism* (JSNTSup 45; Sheffield: JSOT Press, 1990), 69-104.

14. L. Anne Jervis, *The Purpose of Romans: A Comparative Letter Structure Investigation* (JSNTSup 55; Sheffield: JSOT, 1991), 163-64.

suggestions relating the purpose of Romans to a stage in his apostolic career: (i) Paul wrote his letter to the Romans at the close of a period of bitter controversy over matters affecting the churches of Galatia, Corinth, and possibly Macedonia. It sums up the positions he reached as a result of engagement in these controversies, and it constitutes a 'manifesto' setting forth his deepest convictions on central issues; a manifesto that he sought to give the widest publicity.[15] (ii) Paul wrote Romans on the eve of his departure for Jerusalem with the collection. In the core of the letter (1:18–11:36) he sets out for his Roman readers the content of the 'collection speech' he intended to give in Jerusalem so as to elicit their support and intercession for him when he went to Jerusalem.[16] (iii) Paul wrote Romans as an 'ambassadorial' letter to advocate a cooperative mission to evangelize Spain. He needed the assistance of the Roman Christians to provide contacts in Spain because of the lack of Jewish population there that could provide him with a base of operations. Also, Greek was not widely spoken, and Paul would need the help of those in Rome who could assist with translation. But he needed to ensure that those who assisted him would not discredit the mission by carrying with them a sub-Christian Roman system of honor that would be resisted by the barbarians of Spain and so his mission be jeopardized. The exposition of the gospel that shows that God honors sinners of all cultures impartially through Christ was thus intended to serve the cause of Paul's Spanish mission.[17] (iv) Paul addresses Gentile believers who still associated with the Jewish synagogues in Rome, stressing the importance of 'the obedience of faith'. It is incumbent upon Gentile Christians to obey the *halakhot* applicable to 'righteous Gentiles', and this means submitting to the synagogue authorities. His purpose for doing so was so that when he arrived in Rome and began by preaching the gospel to Jews, the behavior of Gentile Christians in the synagogue would not prove to be a stumbling block to them.[18]

(c) *A Combination of the Above*. It is not surprising that many scholars understand the purpose of Romans as a combination of matters related to situations in the Roman churches and Paul's apostolic career: (i) When Paul wrote Romans he had two concerns. The first was to prepare for his visit to Rome and subsequent Spanish mission, while seeking prayer support for his visit to Jerusalem. The second was to respond to certain prob-

---

15. T. W. Manson, 'St. Paul's Letter to the Romans — and Others', in *The Romans Debate, Revised*, 3-15. Gunther Bornkamm, 'The Letter to the Romans as Paul's Last Will and Testament', in *The Romans Debate, Revised*, 16-28, takes up and extends Manson's approach by suggesting that in Romans we have a statement of Paul's 'realizations' about the gospel; realizations which he now wanted to defend in Jerusalem. Bornkamm believes that Romans is the last of the authentic letters of Paul, and as such it has become in fact the historical 'testament of Paul'.

16. Jacob Jervell, 'The Letter to Jerusalem', *The Romans Debate, Revised*, 53-64.

17. Robert Jewett, 'Romans as an Ambassadorial Letter', *Int* 36 (1982) 5-20; Robert Jewett, *Romans: A Commentary* (Hermeneia; Minneapolis: Fortress, 2007), 87-88.

18. Nanos, *The Mystery of Romans*, 289-334.

lems in the Roman church about which he had been acquainted.[19] (ii) 'The
Jewish question' Paul had to deal with previously was emerging as a
problem once more as he contemplated his impending visit to Jerusalem.
It was also threatening disunity in the Roman Christian community. These
things compelled Paul to write about the relationship between Judaism
and Christianity in Romans.[20] (iii) Among the Jews returning to Rome after their expulsion by Claudius were Jewish Christians who had heard
about the conflicts in which Paul had been engaged in Galatia, Philippi,
and Corinth. They opposed Paul and his gospel, and their criticisms are
reflected in the rhetorical questions of 3:7; 4:1; 6:1, 15; 7:7, 12, 14. Paul
wrote Romans to overcome these criticisms so as to prepare the way for
his planned visit to Rome and so that he might secure the help of the
church there for his Spanish mission.[21] (iv) A significant section of the Roman church was still clinging to the law as the means of obtaining justification at the coming judgment. Paul wrote urging them to let go of the law
for the sake of unity, for the sake of his grand vision — one eschatological
people made up of Jews and Gentiles (15:6) — and to bring the church
within the scope of his own authority as apostle to the Gentiles.[22] (v) The
Roman Christian community consisted of two main groups, Judean and
Gentile Christ followers. Paul's aim in Romans was to bring about unity in
the church by highlighting his readers' new identity as followers of Christ
(without denying the importance of their ethnic identity). This he sought
to do, not only for the sake of the Roman Christ-followers themselves, but
also so that they would not 'get in the way' of his preparation for the missionary journey to Spain, and to secure their prayer support for his visit to
Jerusalem with the collection.[23]

A Working Hypothesis. Early in Romans Paul indicates that members
of his audience were included among those for whom he feels responsible
(1:5-6), and that he wants to exercise a ministry among them, as he had
done among other Gentiles (1:13-15). However, another obligation prevented him from doing so straightaway. He had to travel to Jerusalem with
the collection for poor believers taken up among churches of Galatia, Macedonia, and Achaia. It would appear that, being obliged to delay his trip to
Rome, Paul wrote a letter so as to exercise a ministry by letter as a forerun-
ner to his ministry in person when he finally reached Rome. This is consis-

19. John Ziesler, *Paul's Letter to the Romans* (London/Philadelphia: SCM/Trinity, 1989), 15-16.
20. J. C. Beker, 'The Faithfulness of God and the Priority of Israel in Paul's Letter to the Romans', *HTR* 79 (1986) 12.
21. Peter Stuhlmacher, 'Der Abfassungszweck des Römerbriefes', *ZNW* 77 (1986) 186-91.
22. Brendan Byrne, '"Rather Boldly" (Rom 15,15): Paul's Prophetic Bid to Win the Allegiance of the Christians in Rome', *Bib* 74 (1993) 85-86.
23. Philip E. Esler, *Conflict and Identity in Romans: The Social Setting of Paul's Letter* (Minneapolis: Fortress, 2003), 359.

tent with the only *explicit* statement the apostle makes about his purpose for writing found in 15:15-16:

> Yet I have written to you quite boldly on some points to remind you of them again, because of the grace God gave me, to be a minister of Christ Jesus to the Gentiles. He gave me the priestly duty of proclaiming the gospel of God, so that the Gentiles might be an offering acceptable to God, sanctified by the Holy Spirit.

This confirms that Paul's *primary* purpose in writing Romans was to minister to the believers in Rome for whom he had an apostolic responsibility. He wanted to ensure that their understanding of the gospel was such that they would constitute an acceptable sacrifice to God, consecrated by the Holy Spirit. If this was Paul's primary purpose, we can understand why it was necessary for him to provide such a comprehensive statement and defense of his gospel, for as people are exposed to and embrace the truth of the gospel, the Holy Spirit works in their lives producing sanctification. Consistent with this primary purpose is the apostle's attempt to deal with divisions within the Roman Christian community (11:13-32; 14:1–15:13) and to answer the objections to his gospel (3:1, 9; 4:1; 6:1, 15; 7:7, 13; 9:6, 14, 30; 11:1, 11) that were being voiced in Rome (16:17-18), which, if left unanswered, would hinder his audience from fully embracing his gospel. If Paul's *primary* purpose is identified in this way, it does not rule out such *secondary* purposes as preparing the way for his visit to Rome and subsequent mission in Spain, and soliciting the Roman Christians' prayers for his impending 'collection visit' to Jerusalem (15:22-32).

VI. RHETORICAL MATTERS

Paul's Letter to the Romans is not easily classified in terms of the contemporary literary conventions. The opening and closing sections of the letter resemble those of an occasional personal letter. The opening identifies the sender and recipients, includes a greeting, and is followed by a thanksgiving section. The closing section relates the apostle's present situation and future plans and includes a request for support, before concluding with greetings, a warning, and a doxology. However, the body of the letter is not at all like a personal letter. It constitutes an extended theological treatise, one that expounds and defends the gospel, and is followed by a long ethical section spelling out important practical implications of the gospel.

However, the letter *as a whole* cannot be categorized as a theological treatise or letter-essay because this does not properly account for the opening and closing sections, and also because letter-essays were generally supplementary to other writings.[24] Nor can the letter as a whole be described as epideictic (i.e., reinforcing and celebrating commonly held values), even though there are certainly significant epideictic sections in the letter (5:1-2, 11, 21; 8:1-2, 10, 31-39; 11:33-36) because it contains significant deliberative (exhortatory) sections as well (6:11-13; 12:1–15:13). The suggestion that it should be read as an ambassadorial letter that seeks help for the Spanish mission does not adequately account for the extended theological section in the body of the letter, even though the view does find some support in the closing section of the letter. To regard the letter as essentially delibera- tive intended to persuade and dissuade and set in an epistolary framework does not do justice to the theological section. Romans, then, does not fit eas- ily into any of the single categories suggested and is best read as a letter that utilizes various forms. It is certainly an occasional letter with clear traits of a personal letter, but it also incorporates an extended letter-essay (treatise). It does reinforce and celebrate commonly held values, and it does include significant exhortatory sections as well.

In Romans Paul employs a number of rhetorical devices. For exam- ple, in chapter 2 he uses diatribe (in which an author engages a hypotheti- cal dialogue partner), in chapter 3 internal dialogue (whereby an author poses and responds to his/her own questions), and in chapter 7 speech-in- character (a device by which an author adopts a particular persona to artic- ulate the experience of particular persons). He makes use of creedal state- ments, hymns and benedictions, Scripture quotations, syllogisms, and midrashic argument. He makes extensive use also of well-known stylistic features, including parallelism, anaphora (repetition of initial words or syl- lables), homoioteleuton (similar-sounding endings), and chiasm (repetition of words or ideas in reverse sequence).[25]

VII. AUTHORSHIP, PLACE, AND DATE OF WRITING

The Pauline authorship of Romans has rarely been seriously questioned. The evidence indicates that Paul was in Corinth when he wrote the letter. Granted that chapter 16 is part of the original letter (see the discussion of 'The Integrity of Romans', 13-14 below), we have a reference to greetings sent by 'Gaius, whose hospitality I and the whole church here enjoy' (16:23), to the believers in Rome. He is most likely to be identified with the Gaius who was one of those in Corinth whom Paul baptized (1 Cor 1:14). We also have a reference to greetings sent by 'Erastus, who is the city's di- rector of public works' (16:23), to the Roman believers. There is a distinct

24. Cf. Brendan Byrne, S.J., *Romans* (Sacra Pagina 6; Collegeville, Minn.: Liturgical Press, 1996), 15.

25. Cf. Jewett, *Romans*, 24-28, 30-31.

possibility that he is to identified with the aedile of the inscription with the name Erastus that was discovered in 1929 east of the stage building of the theatre in Corinth (see a full discussion in the commentary on 16:23). Both of these references support the view that Romans was written while Paul was in Corinth. In 16:1 Paul commends 'our sister Phoebe, a servant of the church in Cenchreae' that was one of Corinth's two seaports, and as she is commended at the beginning of the long list of people to whom Paul wants his greetings extended, this suggests that Phoebe was the courier who carried Paul's letter to Rome. This, too, suggests that the apostle was situated in (or around) Corinth when he wrote the letter. Finally, according to Acts 20:3 Paul spent three months in Greece towards the end of his third missionary journey prior to his departure for Jerusalem with the collection. In Greece he would have been most likely to stay in Corinth in fellowship with the church he had founded there.

In chapter 15 there are certain pointers that indicate the date Paul wrote his Romans: He had completed his mission in the eastern Mediterranean (15:23); the churches of Macedonia and Achaia had made their contributions to the collection for the poor believers in Jerusalem (15:26-27), which places the writing of Romans after that of 2 Corinthians 8–9; and Paul is about to embark on his trip to Jerusalem to convey the collection monies there (15:25). After that he hopes to visit Rome en route to Spain (15:28). While the date of writing can be confidently placed after the writing of 2 Corinthians 8–9 and just prior to Paul's departure for Jerusalem, there are differences of opinion concerning the allocation of an exact chronological date, generally put by scholars somewhere between A.D. 54 and 59.[26]

VIII. THE INTEGRITY OF ROMANS

The question of the integrity of Romans relates primarily to chapter 16 and its place in the letter. While the majority texts include this chapter as an integral part of Romans, there are variations in the textual tradition that have caused questions to be raised. In particular there is evidence for the placement of the doxology (located traditionally at 16:25-27) in six different locations listed by Metzger as: (a) 1:11–16:23 + doxology; (b) 1:1–14:23 + doxology + 15:1–16:23 + doxology; (c) 1:1–14:23 + doxology + 15:1–16:24; (d) 1:1–16:24; (e) 1:1–15:23 + doxology + 16:1-23; (f) 1:1–14:23 + 16:24 + doxology.[27] Different positions adopted by various scholars regarding this matter have

26. For detailed discussions see, e.g., C. E. B. Cranfield, *The Epistle to the Romans*, I (ICC; Edinburgh: T&T Clark, 1975), 12-16; Jewett, *Romans*, 18-21; Fitzmyer, *Romans*, 85-88.

27. Bruce M. Metzger, ed., *A Textual Commentary on the Greek New Testament* (2nd ed.; Stuttgart: Deutsche Bibelgesellschaft/German Bible Society, 1994), 471.

been repeatedly summarized and do not need to be rehearsed again here.[28] The majority acknowledge the authenticity of 16:1-23. Lampe provides the following reasons why chapter 16 should be regarded as an original part of Romans: (i) Paul never ends his letters with the formulation 'the God of peace be with all of you' (15:33); rather, such a formula usually precedes requests to pass on greetings — like those in chapter 16. (ii) There is no evidence in the textual tradition that any manuscript of Romans concludes with chapter 15. Both chapters 15 and 16 are either included or omitted together. (iii) The unique features of chapter 16 with its many greetings coincides with the fact that chapters 1–15 reveal that Paul is writing to a church which he did not found and has never visited, yet from which he seeks support for his mission. (iv) Romans 15:19-29 indicates that chapters 1–15 were written from Greece at the conclusion of Paul's third missionary journey. This coincides with the apostle's situation reflected in chapter 16: he wrote the letter from Greece, entrusted it to Phoebe of Cenchreae (one of Corinth's two seaports) for delivery; and among those who send greetings are Timothy, Sosipater, and Gaius, who are those one would expect to be with Paul at the end of his third missionary journey.[29] In the commentary that follows, chapter 16 is therefore treated as an integral part of Romans.

IX. THE INFLUENCE OF 'THE NEW PERSPECTIVE'

'The new perspective' is a term coined by James Dunn to represent a new approach to the interpretation of Paul's letters and is used in the Manson Memorial Lecture he delivered at the University of Manchester in 1982.[30] This new approach was sparked off by the publication in 1977 of E. P. Sanders' book, *Paul and Palestinian Judaism*,[31] a book that has proved to be a watershed in Pauline studies. Sanders' aim was to compare Palestinian Judaism and Pauline Christianity. The impact of his book and the ongoing debate to which it gave rise can be considered under the following headings.

A. Judaism

Sanders' examination of Palestinian Judaism was based on his study of Jewish sources dating from 200 B.C. to A.D. 200. These included early rab-

---

28. See, e.g., the detailed discussions in Cranfield, *Romans*, I, 2-11; Fitzmyer, *Romans*, 55-67; Jewett, *Romans*, 4-18.

29. Lampe, 'The Roman Christians', 217-21.

30. James D. G. Dunn, 'The New Perspective on Paul', *BJRL* 65 (1983) 95-122, now conveniently included in the collection, *The New Perspective on Paul, Revised Edition* (Grand Rapids: Eerdmans, 2005), 99-120, to which subsequent references are made.

31. E. P. Sanders, *Paul and Palestinian Judaism: A Comparison of Patterns of Religion* (London: SCM, 1977).

binic (Tannaitic) literature, the Dead Sea Scrolls, and a selection of works from the Apocrypha and Pseudepigrapha. As a result of this study he concluded that Palestinian Judaism is best described as 'covenantal nomism'. What is meant by this term is best described in his own words:

> The 'pattern' or 'structure' of covenantal nomism is this: (1) God has chosen Israel and (2) given the law. The law implies both (3) God's promise to maintain the election and (4) the requirement to obey. (5) God rewards obedience and punishes transgression. (6) The law provides for means of atonement, and atonement results in (7) maintenance or re-establishment of the covenantal relationship. (8) All those who are maintained in the covenant by obedience, atonement, and God's mercy belong to the group which will be saved. An important interpretation of the first and last points is that election and ultimately salvation are considered to be by God's mercy rather than human achievement.[32]

Sanders, while commended by many for the work he did on the Jewish sources and for correcting distorted views of first-century Judaism, has not been without his critics. His approach to the study of Judaism using the categories of 'getting in' and 'staying in' has been criticized as inappropriate because these categories emerged not from the Jewish documents themselves but were shaped by Pauline scholarship.[33] Jacob Neusner, a prolific Jewish author, is particularly critical of this aspect of Sanders' work. He says that 'in regard to Rabbinic Judaism, Sanders's book is so profoundly flawed as to be hopeless and, I regret to say it, useless in accomplishing its stated goals of systemic description and comparison'.[34] However, Neusner did commend Sanders for making an apologetic for rabbinic Judaism that combats the ignorance and malicious anti-Semitism of other accounts of it.

Westerholm argues that while it is misleading to characterize Judaism as a religion of 'works-salvation', nevertheless observance of the law may be regarded as Israel's path to life. He stresses that Paul not only implied that his opponents believed that the law serves a soteriological function, but that the apostle himself believed it was given for that purpose.[35] Schreiner, while endorsing Sanders' work insofar as it destroys the caricature of Judaism as a religion that has no theology of grace and is obsessed with earning merit, argues that it was legalistic because its soteriology was synergistic, that is, sal-

---

32. Sanders, *Paul and Palestinian Judaism*, 422.

33. Cf., e.g., Jacob Neusner, 'Comparing Judaisms', *HR* 18 (1978) 177-91; Thomas F. Best, 'The Apostle Paul and E. P. Sanders: The Significance of Paul and Palestinian Judaism', *ResQ* 25 (1982) 65-74; Nils A. Dahl and Samuel Sandmel, 'Review of *Paul and Palestinian Judaism: A Comparison of Patterns of Religion* by E. P. Sanders', *RelSRev* 4 (1978) 153-60; W. Horbury, 'Paul and Judaism', *ExpTim* 90 (1979) 116-18.

34. Neusner, 'Comparing Judaisms', 191.

35. Stephen Westerholm, *Israel's Law and the Church's Faith: Paul and His Recent Interpreters* (Grand Rapids: Eerdmans, 1988), 156.

vation was by God's grace *and* human works.[36] There was nothing wrong with legalism if the required works could be performed. The problem is that it rests upon the mistaken view that human beings are good and that their works can be sufficient.[37] Hagner says: 'In its best theology, Judaism *is* a religion of grace. Often, however, its gracious foundations are tacitly assumed and often the law takes a place of overwhelming priority. It is not surprising if a religion whose heart lies in praxis rather than theory (theology), a religion dominated by nomism, where the covenant is more presupposed than articulated, inadvertently produces followers who fall into a legalistic mode of existence. This may explain the "exception" of 4 Ezra (cf. 2 Baruch) with its clear legalism, which Sanders does not deny'.[38]

A comprehensive and critical response to Sanders' portrayal of first-century Judaism is the book edited by Carson, O'Brien, and Seifrid, intended to provide 'a fresh evaluation of the literature of Second Temple Judaism' and to test the applicability of 'covenantal nomism' as an appropriate description of Jewish beliefs in that period.[39] Distinguished specialists examined different types of literature from the period (including Prayers and Psalms; the Pseudepigrapha; Jewish Apocalypses; Testaments; Wisdom literature; the writings of Josephus; Tannaitic literature; the Targums, the writings of Philo, and Qumran literature). Summarizing the results, Carson notes: (i) Parts of the literature examined did reflect 'covenantal nomism' so that it may be said that Sanders is not wrong everywhere, 'but he is wrong when he tries to establish his category is right everywhere'. (ii) Covenantal nomism is a reductionist category because 'all its inspiration is found in one kind of biblical ideas, while complementary biblical ideas are completely ignored'.[40] (iii) Covenantal nomism as a category proves to be not only reductionist but misleading because it 'cannot itself accomplish what Sanders wants it to accomplish, viz. serve as an explanatory bulwark against all suggestions that some of this literature embraces works-righteousness and merit theology precisely because covenantal nomism embraces the same phenomena. Sanders has to some extent constructed a "heads I win, tails you lose" argument: it is rhetorically effective, but not a fair reflection of the diverse literature'.[41] Carson concludes his summary: 'Examination of Sanders's covenantal nomism leads one to the conclusion that the New Testament documents, not least Paul, must not be

36. Thomas R. Schreiner, *The Law and Its Fulfillment: A Pauline Theology of Law* (Grand Rapids: Baker, 1993), 94.
37. Schreiner, *The Law and Its Fulfilment*, 98.
38. Donald Hagner, 'Paul and Judaism: Testing the New Perspective', in Peter Stuhlmacher, *A Challenge to the New Perspective: Revisiting Paul's Doctrine of Justification — With an Essay by Donald A. Hagner* (Downers Grove: InterVarsity Press, 2001), 87-88.
39. D. A. Carson, Peter T. O'Brien, and Mark A. Seifrid, eds., *Justification and Variegated Nomism*, Vol. I — *The Complexities of Second Temple Judaism* (Tübingen: Mohr Siebeck/ Grand Rapids: Baker Academic, 2001).
40. Carson, O'Brien, and Seifrid, *Justification and Variegated Nomism*, I, 543.
41. Carson, O'Brien, and Seifrid, *Justification and Variegated Nomism*, I, 545.

read *exclusively* against this background. It is too doctrinaire, too unsupported by the sources themselves, too reductionistic, too monopolistic'.[42]

B. Pauline Religion

After his study of Palestinian Judaism Sanders turned his attention to a study of Paul's religion. To do this, he undertook an investigation of the seven letters of Paul whose authenticity is unquestioned (Romans, 1 and 2 Corinthians, Galatians, Philippians, 1 Thessalonians, and Philemon). This investigation led him to conclude that Paul's religion is best understood as 'participationist eschatology'. Sanders says:

> The heart of Paul's thought is not that one ratifies and agrees to a covenant offered by God, becoming a member of a group with a covenantal relation with God and remaining in it on the condition of proper behavior; but that one dies with Christ, obtaining new life and the initial transformation which leads to the resurrection and ultimate transformation, that one is a member of the body of Christ and one Spirit with him, and that one remains so unless one breaks the participatory union by forming another.[43]

What distinguishes Palestinian Judaism from Pauline Christianity is not to be found in the matter of grace and works but in Paul's understanding of righteousness. Once again we let Sanders speak for himself:

> To be righteous in Jewish literature means to obey the Torah and to repent of transgression, but in Paul it means to be saved by Christ. Most succinctly, righteousness in Judaism is a term which implies the maintenance of status among the group of the elect; in Paul it is a transfer term. In Judaism, that is, commitment to the covenant puts one 'in', while obedience (righteousness) subsequently keeps one in. In Paul's usage, 'be made righteous' ('be justified') is a term indicating getting in, not staying in the body of the saved. Thus when Paul says one cannot be made righteous by works of law, he means that one cannot, by works of law, 'transfer to the body of the saved'. When Judaism said that one is righteous who obeys the law, the meaning is that one thereby stays in the covenant. The debate about righteousness by faith or by works of law thus turns out to result from the different usage of the 'righteous' word group.[44]

For Sanders, then, as far as Paul is concerned, what is wrong with Judaism is not its zeal for the law or that it promotes a quest for self-

---

42. Carson, O'Brien, and Seifrid, *Justification and Variegated Nomism*, I, 548.
43. Sanders, *Paul and Palestinian Judaism*, 514.
44. Sanders, *Paul and Palestinian Judaism*, 544.

righteousness based on the works of the law, but rather that it is unenlightened. In Sanders' oft-quoted words: 'In short, *this is what Paul finds wrong in Judaism: it is not Christianity*'.[45] The overall effect of Sanders' work has been to call into question both the way first-century Judaism has been depicted as a religion of works-righteousness and the way the letters of Paul have been interpreted. Those who embrace Sanders' conclusions tend to be critical of traditional Protestant exegesis heavily influenced by the Reformation emphasis upon the doctrine of justification by faith.

C. The Works of the Law

In an essay that marked his first foray into the debate, Dunn acknowledges his indebtedness to Sanders for correcting a distorted image of first-century Judaism.[46] However, he says Sanders failed to take the opportunity his work provided to explore the extent to which Paul's theology could be explained in terms of Judaism's covenantal nomism.[47] Dunn argued that when Paul speaks of the 'works of the law', he has in mind circumcision, food laws, and Sabbath, the characteristic marks of faithful Jews that distinguished them from Gentiles. 'When Paul denied the possibility of "being justified by works of the law" it is precisely this basic Jewish self-understanding which he is attacking — the idea that God's acknowledgment of covenant status is bound up with, even dependent upon, observance of these particular regulations'.[48]

Dunn's initial description of Paul's understanding of the works of the law in terms of the Jewish identity markers, circumcision, food laws, and Sabbath observance, has been subject to criticism on two counts. First, this was not the way the works of the law were understood by Jewish people. For them the works of the law were not just circumcision, obeying food laws, and observing the Sabbath, but obedience to all that the law requires,[49] something they practiced simply because this was required under the terms of the Mosaic covenant.[50] Second, in Romans, when Paul concluded that no one will be justified by works of the law (3:20), this was because even the Jews who had the law failed to observe its requirements,

45. Sanders, *Paul and Palestinian Judaism*, 552.

46. Dunn, 'The New Perspective on Paul', 99-120.

47. Dunn, 'The New Perspective on Paul', 103.

48. Dunn, 'The New Perspective on Paul', 111. A similar approach is adopted by Roman Heiligenthal, 'Soziologische Implikationen der paulinischen Rechtfertigungslehre im Galaterbrief am Beispiel der "Werke des Gesetzes": Beobachtungen zur Identitätsfindung einer frühchristlichen Gemeinde', *Kairos* 26 (1984) 38-53.

49. Cf. David Flusser, '"Durch das Gesetz dem Gesetz gestorben" (Gal 2,19)', *Judaica* 43 (1987) 34; Heikki Räisänen, *Paul and the Law* (Philadelphia: Fortress, 1986), 177; Thomas Schreiner, '"Works of Law" in Paul', *NovT* 33 (1991) 232-44.

50. Cf. Rabbi Dan Cohn-Sherbok, 'Some Reflections on James Dunn's "The Incident at Antioch (Gal. 2.11-18)"', *JSNT* 18 (1983) 70.

and it was not their failure to practice circumcision, to obey food laws, or observe the Sabbath that he had in mind. The failure he highlighted was their failure in the moral area.

In later work Dunn acknowledges that he failed to explain that the '"works of the law" do not mean *only* circumcision, food laws and Sabbath, but the requirements of the law in general'.[51] Nevertheless, he continued to insist that the works of the law do refer *particularly* to 'those requirements which bring to sharp focus the distinctiveness of Israel's identity'.[52] He claims that recognition of the social function of the law goes a long way towards resolving the tensions and contradictions in Paul's thought. In particular, he says, it resolves the problem of the tension between Paul's negative and positive statements about the law. It is the social function of the law that Paul criticizes even while he affirms its positive role, one fulfilled in the love of one's neighbor.[53] For further discussion, see 'Additional Note: The Works of the Law', 173-76.

D. Paul's Critique of Judaism

Dunn says that Sanders' work goes much further in making sense of Paul in his Jewish context than Sanders himself realized.[54] But while stressing that first-century Judaism was not legalistic and that Jewish people were not seeking to amass merit by works of righteousness, he failed to recognize the sociological significance of the works of the law, that is, he failed to recognize that for Jews the works of the law functioned as identity markers of the covenant people. Recognizing this, Dunn argues that Paul was critical of Judaism, not because it was legalistic but because of its exclusivism. Only those who submitted to circumcision and took upon themselves the yoke of the law could be included in the people of God.

It is true that Paul was critical of Judaism because of its exclusivism, its ethnocentrism. This is reflected in his argument in 2:1-29 and implied in 3:27-30. However, his major criticism was that, as he did prior to his conversion (Phil 3:2-9), some Jewish people were seeking to establish their own righteousness by works of the law rather than submitting to God's righteousness (9:30–10:4).[55] To carry out the works of the law is in itself a good thing, but to do so believing it to be grounds for ultimate justification is mistaken, and sets aside the way to justification provided by God.

---

51. James D. G. Dunn, *Jesus, Paul and the Law: Studies in Mark and Galatians* (Louisville: Westminster John Knox, 1990), 4.

52. James D. G. Dunn, 'Works of the Law' (Galatians 3.10-14)', *The New Perspective on Paul, Revised Edition* (Grand Rapids: Eerdmans, 2005), 130.

53. Dunn, 'Works of the Law', 131.

54. Dunn, 'The New Perspective on Paul', 105.

55. Cf. Hagner, 'Paul and Judaism', 100.

E. Justification

Those influenced by the new perspective emphasize that Paul's doctrine of justification is to be understood in the context of his mission to the Gentiles. It is those who believe in Jesus Christ, be they Jews or Gentile, whom God justifies. Those who believe in Christ may be said to have been justified (5:1). Justification, then, is not a term Paul uses to refer to the *means* by which people are 'saved' and so included in the people of God; rather, it is something that may be predicated of those who are *already* saved. They are saved by God's grace through what he has done in Christ so that their sins have been forgiven, and now they are numbered among God's people. On this basis, Wright argues: 'Justification . . . is not a matter of *how someone enters the community of the true people of God,* but of *how you tell who belongs to that community,* not least in the period of time before the eschatological event itself, when the matter will become public knowledge'.[56] If justification is related only to the question, 'Who are included among the people of God?' it becomes an ecclesiological, not a soteriological, term.

It is not surprising that this emphasis by some of those who embrace the new perspective has attracted criticism. O'Brien claims that this approach diminishes the human predicament — exposure to the wrath of God because of rebellion and sin. It also marginalizes what is prominent in Paul's teaching, that is, that justification brings present and future pardon and acquittal. He claims that justification is an essential element of the gospel.[57] Westerholm says that in the new perspective the charge of legalism leveled against Judaism has been substituted for the charge of ethnocentrism. He finds in Paul's writings evidence for both among some Jews, and insists that the primary reason Paul saw for their failure to achieve the righteousness they sought was reliance upon deeds of righteousness.[58] Hagner quotes J. Gresham Machen: 'Paul was not devoted to the doctrine of justification by faith because of the Gentile mission; he was devoted to the Gentile mission because of the doctrine of justification by faith'.[59] He argues that Dunn's emphasis upon national righteousness, rather than legalism, as the main thrust of Paul's criticism of Judaism 'pushes justification by faith very much to the periphery, making it pertinent only to the Gentiles. The problem is a bigger one than simply holding the two emphases in balance. Despite Dunn's claim, I do not see how his approach can do anything but take all vitality out of the doctrine'.[60]

---

56. Tom Wright, *What Saint Paul Really Said* (Oxford: Lion, 1997), 119.

57. Peter T. O'Brien, 'Was Paul a Covenantal Nomist?' in D. A. Carson, Peter T. O'Brien, and Mark A. Seifrid, eds., *Justification and Variegated Nomism,* Vol. II — *The Paradoxes of Paul* (Tübingen: Mohr Siebeck/Grand Rapids: Baker Academic, 2004), 296.

58. Stephen Westerholm, *Perspectives Old and New on Paul: The "Lutheran" Paul and His Critics* (Grand Rapids: Eerdmans, 2004), 444-45.

59. Hagner, 'Paul and Judaism', 90.

60. Hagner, 'Paul and Judaism', 104-5.

However, as the debate about the significance of the new perspective for an understanding of justification has proceeded, both Dunn and Wright have clarified their positions, seeking to show that they do not negate the insights of the Reformation. Dunn, while maintaining that Paul's doctrine of justification by faith was hammered out in the context of the Gentile mission, asserts that 'justification by faith alone needs to be reasserted as strongly as ever it was by Paul or by Augustine or by Luther — against all attempts to add anything extra'.[61] Both Dunn and Wright insist that their emphasis upon the ecclesiological nature of justification by faith should not be interpreted to mean that they minimize the importance of the individual's need for salvation. However, the emphasis upon the ecclesiological implications of justification, important as they may be to correct previous neglect, does seem to have resulted in moving the truth of justification as the acquittal of guilty sinners based upon the forgiveness of their sins from the centre to the periphery. At least this is the impression with which many of their readers have been left. In a recent publication Wright seeks to correct this impression. He affirms the insights of the Reformation, insisting that it is not his purpose to do away with them, but rather to locate them in the wider context of covenant theology.[62] He describes justification as 'the declaration (a) that someone is in the right (his or her sins having been forgiven through the death of Jesus) and (b) that this person is a member of the true covenant family'. However, while the justification of believers does lead on to their being incorporated into the people of God, that would appear to be a by-product of rather than intrinsic to justification itself.

F. Summing Up . . .

(i) The literature of Second Temple Judaism reveals a Judaism that is more complex than what may be portrayed simply as covenantal nomism. In places it does reflect a Judaism that may be described as covenantal nomism, but in other places it reflects legalism. (ii) The early interpretation of the 'works of the law' as the sociological identity markers of circumcision, keeping food laws, and Sabbath observance has given way to the recognition that the 'works of the law' denote all that the law requires. (iii) While it is true that ethnocentrism and exclusivism were aspects of the Judaism that Paul criticized, he was equally if not more critical of the legalistic tendencies found among some of his fellow Jews. (iv) Paul's teaching on justification by faith was articulated in the context of his mission to the Gentiles as part of his defense of the incorporation of Gentile believers into

---

61. James D. G. Dunn, 'The New Perspective: Whence, What and Whither?', in *The New Perspective on Paul, Revised Edition* (Grand Rapids: Eerdmans, 2005), 96.

62. Tom Wright, *Justification: God's Plan and Paul's Vision* (London: SPCK, 2009), 222.

the people of God without having to submit to circumcision or take upon themselves the yoke of the law. At its heart, however, this doctrine has to do with God's gracious acquittal of guilty sinners, both Jews and Gentiles. (v) Justification is God's declaration in favor of believers — he will accept no charges brought against them (8:33); a declaration effective for them in the present time (5:1, 9; 8:1) and to be confirmed on the last day. (vi) The doctrine of justification by faith is not itself the gospel message — the gospel is the good news of what God as done through his Son's atoning death and resurrection to deal with the effects of the fall upon individuals, society, and ultimately the cosmos.

X. THEOLOGICAL THEMES

At various places in the commentary and in the additional notes I discuss important themes in Romans. What is offered below brings together material related to a number of the more pervasive themes with brief comments. This is not intended to be in any way a full discussion of these matters, but, hopefully, it will serve to alert readers to some important theological features of Romans.

A. God the Father

Romans is a profoundly theological document in the sense that who God is, what he is like, and what he does constitute the main subject matter.[63] God is 'one' (3:30), 'the God and Father of our Lord Jesus Christ' (15:6), immortal (1:23), eternal (16:26), and 'the only wise God' (16:27). His wisdom and knowledge are unfathomable (11:33). He exercises the divine prerogatives of giving life (4:17) and executing judgment (2:16; 3:6, 19; 14:10-12). He has made known his eternal power and divine nature through what he has made (1:19-20).

The righteousness of God is a major theme. His decrees are righteous (1:32). He is righteous when he passes judgment upon sinners (2:2, 5), including Jewish sinners (3:4-5). His wrath is 'revealed from heaven against all the godlessness and wickedness of men' (1:18). He hands people over to the consequences of their sin (1:24, 26, 28). But while 'the riches of his kindness, forbearance and patience' are intended to lead people to repentance (2:4), those who refuse to repent store up wrath for themselves on the day of God's wrath (2:5). He does not show favoritism, but rewards all people according to their works (2:6-11). The righteousness of God is especially re-

---

63. Cf. Jochen Flebbe, *Solus Deus: Untersuchungen zur Rede von Gott im Brief des Paulus und die Römer* (BZNW 158; Berlin: de Gruyter, 2008).

vealed in the gospel, that is, his saving righteousness whereby he brings people into a right relationship with himself (1:17). This he reveals without reference to the Mosaic law and for the benefit of all who believe (3:21-22). There is no compromise of God's righteousness when he justifies sinners who believe, for by setting forth his Son as the atoning sacrifice for their sins he demonstrated his righteousness so that he can be both just and the justifier of those who have faith in Jesus (3:25-26).

The love of God is another important theme in Romans. God demonstrated his love for human beings in that while they were sinners Christ died for them (5:8). Into the hearts of those who believe God pours out his love by the Holy Spirit (5:5), and nothing whatever shall be able to separate them from the love of God in Christ Jesus (8:39). Believers are described as those who are loved by God (1:7), and even unbelieving Israelites, though they are enemies as far as the gospel is concerned, are, as far as election is concerned, loved by God on account of the patriarchs (11:28), for God's gifts and calling are irrevocable (11:29).

The sovereign will and purpose of God find repeated expression in Romans. Paul recognizes that his own movements are determined by the will of God (1:10; 15:32). God's will has been made known through the law given to Israel (2:18). Believers are transformed by the renewing of their minds so as to 'be able to test and approve what God's will is — his good, pleasing and perfect will' (12:2). Believers have been called according to God's purpose (8:28). God exercises his divine prerogative in showing mercy to whomever he will and hardening whomever he will (9:11-18). As a potter determines what he will do with the clay, so God determines those to whom he will show his wrath (those he has borne with great patience) and those to whom he will make known the riches of his glory (the objects of his mercy drawn from among both Jews and Gentiles) (9:19-24). Temporal authorities are established by God's decree (13:2) and function as his servants to punish wrongdoers and commend those who do right (13:3-6). Ultimately, God's sovereignty will be acknowledged by all when every knee will bow to him (14:11).

Not surprisingly in a letter that expounds and defends the gospel, the grace of God is a pervasive theme. Paul has his apostleship by the grace of God (1:5; 12:3; 15:15). Believers are justified by God's grace through faith (3:24; 5:2) as Abraham was (4:1-8, 23-25). God's grace and the gift of God that came through grace have far greater effects for good than the effects for evil that proceeded from Adam's trespass (5:15, 17), so it may said that 'where sin increased, grace increased all the more' (5:20). Just as sin reigned in death, so God's grace reigns through righteousness to eternal life through Jesus Christ (5:21). Because believers live under God's grace, not the law, sin shall not be their master (6:14). There is still a remnant of believing Jews chosen by grace (11:5-6). By God's grace believers receive different gifts for ministry (12:16). It is no wonder, then, that in greetings to his audience at the opening and closing of Romans Paul invokes God's grace upon them (1:7; 16:20)

The theological focus of Romans is very evident in the fact that God is the primary agent of salvation. He made known the gospel of his saving righteousness through the law and the prophets (1:2; 3:21). Through the preaching of the gospel his power for salvation is made known and released for the benefit of all who believe (1:16-17). This saving righteousness comes from God and is effected through the redemption in Jesus Christ (3:24). God set him forward as a sacrifice of atonement in order to demonstrate his justice, having passed over sins committed beforehand, so he can be both just and the justifier of sinners who have faith in Jesus (3:25-26). God credited righteousness to Abraham as a gracious gift when he believed (4:2-5). David speaks of the blessing of those to whom God credits righteousness: He forgives their sins and never counts them against them (4:6-8). What God did for Abraham he does for all who believe in him who raised Jesus from the dead (4:22-24). God delivered Christ over to death for our sins, and raised him to life for our justification (4:25). The death of Christ for sinners is the demonstration of God's love (5:8), and through it God has reconciled us to himself (5:10-11). God, faced with the powerlessness of the law to bring about the fulfillment of its own demands due to the weakness of human flesh, sent his Son to condemn sin in the flesh, so that the law's righteous requirement might be fulfilled in believers (8:3-4). God works in all things for the good of those who love him, those whom he called according to his purpose and whom he predestined to be conformed to the likeness of his Son (8:28-29). He predestined them, called them, justified them, and glorified them. He is 'for us' so that no one can be against us. Having not spared his own Son, he will along with him give us all things. He will entertain no charges brought against us (8:30-33). God is able to restore those of unbelieving Israel if they do not persist in unbelief, and by so doing ensure that 'all Israel' will be saved (11:23-26). Ultimately, God will crush Satan under the feet of believers (16:20).

God is uniquely the Father of our Lord Jesus Christ and he is uniquely his Son. Paul can speak of the people of Israel being adopted as God's sons (9:4), but more often he speaks of believers being adopted as God's sons and daughters. Being led by the Spirit, they show that they are his children (8:14). They have received the Spirit of adoption by whom they cry, 'Abba, Father' as the Spirit himself testifies with their spirits that they are God's children (8:15-16). Because believers are God's children, they are also God's heirs, joint heirs with Christ (8:17). Being God's children and having the 'firstfruits of the Spirit', believers eagerly await their adoption, the redemption of their bodies, the time when they enter into 'the glorious freedom of the children of God' (8:21-23). God has predestined them to be conformed to the likeness of his Son so that he becomes the firstborn (*prōtotokos*, the unique Son) among many brothers (and sisters) (8:29).

B. Jesus Christ the Son of God

While Romans is profoundly theological in the sense that God is the main active agent, it is also deeply Christological in that what God does he does 'through Christ'. So, on the last day God will judge men's secrets *through* Jesus Christ (2:16); believers are justified by God *through* the redemption in Christ Jesus (3:24); they have peace with God *through* our Lord Jesus Christ (5:1); *through* him they have reconciliation with God (5:11); God's grace reigns through righteousness to bring eternal life to believers *through* Jesus Christ our Lord (5:21); and the gift of God to believers is eternal life *through* Christ Jesus our Lord (6:23).

As far as the person of Christ is concerned, his human ancestry is traced from the Jewish people (9:5). He became a servant of the Jews to confirm the promises made to the patriarchs (15:8). He is the messianic Son of David according to his human nature, and declared to be the Son of God with power by his resurrection from the dead (1:3-4). Being raised from the dead he became the Lord of both the dead and the living (14:9). While in Romans Christ is frequently referred to as the Son of God (1:3, 4, 9; 5:10; 8:3, 29, 32), he is never simply equated with God. Paul reserves the title *theos* for God, and generally uses the title *kyrios* ('Lord') for Jesus (notwithstanding 9:5 — see the commentary).

The work of Christ emphasized in Romans is what he achieved through his death in obedience to God. His death was the sacrifice of atonement whereby redemption was won for believers (3:24-25). When he died for sinners (5:6, 8; 14:15), he removed the basis upon which anyone could condemn those who believe in him (8:1, 34). Through his death on their behalf, believers have 'died' to sin (6:2-7; 8:2) and to the law (7:4), and in this freedom they are able to bear fruit for God (7:6). Christ brought to an end the period of the law's jurisdiction (10:4). By the Spirit he now lives in those who believe (8:9-11), and though they are many and have differing gifts, they form one body in him (12:4-5). Being now raised from the dead, Christ is at God's right hand, where he intercedes for believers (8:34). He continues his ministry through Paul to bring Gentiles to the obedience of faith by the power of signs and miracles and the power of the Spirit (15:18-19).

C. The Holy Spirit

As noted above, Romans is both profoundly theological and deeply Christological, but it also has much to say about the Spirit, and in this way it reflects elements of the later doctrine of the Trinity. The Spirit is referred to as 'the Holy Spirit' five times (5:5; 9:1; 14:17; 15:13, 16), 'the Spirit of God' four times (8:9, 11 [2x], 14); 'the Spirit of Christ' once (8:9); 'the Spirit of holiness' once (1:4); 'the Spirit of adoption' once (8:15); and simply 'the Spirit' fifteen times (2:29; 7:6; 8:4, 5, 6, 9, 13, 14, 16, 23, 26, 27 [2x]; 15:19, 30). The ti-tles 'the Spirit of God' and 'the Spirit of Christ' indicate the intimate relationship between God the Father, the Son, and the Spirit.

The activity of the Holy Spirit occupies an important place in Romans. The first reference to this occurs in 1:4, where Paul says that Christ was appointed Son of God with power according to the Spirit of holiness by his resurrection from the dead. The second reference relates to true circumcision of the heart effected by the Spirit (2:29). All other references to the Spirit's activity relate to his ministry in the lives of believers: By the Spirit God pours his love into their hearts (5:5); the Spirit of life sets believers free from the law of sin and death (8:2) so that the just requirement of the law may be fulfilled in them as they live according to the Spirit (8:4); the Spirit lives in believers and will give life to their mortal bodies (8:11); by the Spirit believers are enabled to put to death the misdeeds of the body (8:13). Believers are led by the Spirit (8:14); the Spirit testifies to their spirits that they are children of God (8:15-16); they enjoy the firstfruits of the Spirit (8:23); the Spirit helps them in their weakness, and when they do not know how to pray, he intercedes for them (8:26-27). The Spirit generates hope in believers (15:13) and sanctifies them so that they become an acceptable offering to God (15:16). Finally, Paul says that he carried out his mission in the eastern Mediterranean 'through the power of the Spirit' (15:19).

D. The Righteousness of God

In 1:16-17 Paul describes the gospel as the power of God for salvation for all who believe, for in it the righteousness of God is revealed. In the major theological section of the letter, 1:18–11:36, the apostle expounds and defends this gospel, showing how the righteousness of God is revealed in it. Five aspects of the righteousness of God are evident or implied: (i) his distributive justice whereby God recompenses all people in accordance with their works; (ii) his covenant faithfulness whereby God always remains true to his promises — his word does not fail; (iii) his saving action whereby God reveals his righteousness in acting for the salvation of his people; (iv) his gift of righteousness, that is, the status of being declared righteous by God; and (v) the righteousness of life he requires of believers and is the outworking of his saving righteousness and the gift of righteousness he bestows upon them. Of these five aspects, God's saving action in Christ enabling the justification of sinners receives the major emphasis (see 'Additional Note: "The Righteousness of God"', 79-81).

E. The Atonement

As might be expected, in a letter in which Paul expounds the gospel, the subject of the atonement is addressed in several places. The key text is 3:24-

26, in which Paul says that believers have been justified by God's grace through the redemption that came by Jesus Christ, whom God presented as a sacrifice of atonement *(hilastērion)*. There has been extended debate concerning the meaning of *hilastērion,* a word that may carry three different meanings: expiation, the mercy seat, and propitiation. Expiation denotes the removal of sin, the mercy seat is the place where the blood of the sacrifice was applied on the great annual Day of Atonement, and propitiation denotes the removal of wrath. It is true that on the basis of Christ's death God wipes away sins, and therefore the atonement involves expiation. It is possible that there is an allusion to the mercy seat in this text. It cannot be denied that Christ's death also functions as propitiation. In Romans the wrath of God is revealed against all ungodliness and wickedness of humanity, and those who presume upon his grace while continuing in sin only store up wrath for themselves on the Day of Judgment. If people were to be reconciled to God, propitiation had to be effected through the atoning sacrifice of Christ (cf. 5:9-10). This must never be understood, however, in the pagan sense of human beings trying to appease the wrath of deities, for according to the gospel it was God himself who did not spare his own Son but gave him up for us, setting him forth as the atoning sacrifice for our sins (see 'Additional Note: *Hilastērion'*, 188-91).

F. Justification

Paul employed his doctrine of justification by grace through faith when he was defending the right of Gentiles to be included among God's people, but it was not simply 'a fighting doctrine' to counter the arguments of his opponents. He speaks of it in passages not concerned with the question of Gentile inclusion (cf. 8:29-30; 1 Cor 6:11; 2 Cor 3:9; Phil 3:9; Tit 3:7). At its heart justification has to do with God's gracious acquittal of guilty sinners, and it is in fact integral to the apostle's understanding of salvation.

Justification as understood by Paul is essentially forensic in character. It refers to God's decision as judge to justify sinners who believe in his Son, that is, to confer upon them the status of being righteous in his sight. To be able to do this without being unjust himself, God had to present Christ as a sacrifice of atonement to deal with the problem of their sins. Only then could he 'be just and the one who justifies those who have faith in Jesus' (3:26). Thus Paul says that Christ was put to death for our sins and raised for our justification (4:25), that justification comes through his blood (5:9), and that it was Christ's obedience (primarily his death) that effected justification for all who believe (5:16-19).

Justification, God's adjudication in favor of those who believe in his Son, becomes effective the moment a person puts their faith in Christ. It is a present status enjoyed by believers. So Paul can say, 'Therefore, since we have been justified through faith, we have peace with God through our

Lord Jesus Christ' (5:1). In 8:31-39 Paul celebrates the blessings of the justified: 'God is for us', and having given his Son for us, he will graciously give
us all things with him; God will entertain no charges against us, for he himself has justified us; there is no condemnation because Christ has died for
us and, having been raised to life, now intercedes for us; therefore, nothing
can separate us from the love of God that is in Christ Jesus our Lord. Our
present justification will by God's grace be confirmed on the Last Day.

G. Faith

As would be expected in a letter that expounds the gospel as 'the power of
God that brings salvation to everyone who believes' (1:6), faith is a crucial
theme. Paul describes himself as an apostle set apart for the gospel of God,
charged with the task of calling people to the obedience of faith, that is, the
obedience that consists in faith response to the gospel (1:1, 5). In this gospel
the righteousness of God is revealed from faith to faith, probably meaning
that God's saving righteousness elicits faith first among the Jews and then
among the Gentiles (1:17). The saving righteousness of God that brings justification for all who believe is appropriated by faith (3:22). For God to remain just while justifying those who have faith, it was necessary for him to
present his Son as a sacrifice of atonement (3:25-26). Both Jews and Gentiles
are justified by faith apart from observing the law (3:28-30). The fact that
God justified Abraham, that is, credited righteousness to him, as a gift in
recognition of his faith and not because of works that he performed, nor because he had then been circumcised, shows that on the human side all that
is required is faith (4:1-22). The conclusion Paul draws from his discussion
of Abraham is: 'The words "it was credited to him" were written not for
him alone, but also for us, to whom God will credit righteousness — for us
who believe in him who raised Jesus our Lord from the dead' (4:23-24). In
the process of his discussion of the significance of Abraham, Paul reveals
his understanding of the nature of faith through which people are justified.
Abraham 'did not waver through unbelief regarding the promise of God,
but was strengthened in his faith and gave glory to God, being fully persuaded that God had power to do what he had promised' (4:20-21). Faith is
acceptance of the word of God and the belief that he is able to and will do
what he has promised.

H. The Mosaic Law

As the apostle to the Gentiles, Paul had to defend the right of Gentiles to be
included in the people of God without having to undergo circumcision or
take upon themselves the yoke of the law. The gospel he proclaimed was a
gospel in which the righteousness of God was revealed apart from the law

and was therefore applicable to Gentiles as well as Jews. This fact, however, constituted no devaluation of the law. The receiving of the law was one of Israel's great privileges (9:4), one that enabled them to 'approve of what is superior', to be 'a guide for the blind, a light for those in the dark, an instructor of the foolish, a teacher of little children', because they 'have in the law the embodiment of knowledge and truth' (2:18-20). Their legitimate boast in having the law was only inappropriate when they failed to observe it.

Paul, however, saw another function of the law. He says that 'it was brought in so that the trespass might increase' (5:20). This statement has been variously interpreted (see the commentary on 5:20) but is best understood to mean that the law led to an increase in the number of trespasses in the sense that what were not known to be trespasses before the giving of the law were clearly recognized as such thereafter. This receives support from Paul's statement in 7:7: 'I would not have known what sin was had it not been for the law. For I would not have known what coveting really was if the law had not said, "You shall not covet"'. While Paul says that the law 'was brought in so that the trespass might increase', he also added, 'But where sin increased, grace increased all the more'.

While Paul recognized that receiving the law was one of the great privileges of Israel, he also recognized that the period of its role as a regulatory norm for the people of God came to an end with the death and resurrection of Christ. The clearest expression of this is found in 7:1-6, where, employing the image of a woman being freed from the law of marriage by the death of her husband, he says that as believers 'by dying to what once bound us, we have been released from the law so that we serve in the new way of the Spirit, and not in the old way of the written code' (7:6).

Believers, though released from the law as a regulatory norm, do not live sinful lives. In fact, paradoxically, it is precisely because they are no longer under the law, but under grace, that sin is not their master (6:14). In fact, the sort of life the law was unable to bring about in people is actually made possible for those who live according to the Spirit (8:3-4) and walk in the way of love (13:8-10). The law still has an educative role for believers (cf. 3:10-20; 4:1-25; 8:35-37; 9:6-17, 25-33; 10:5-13, 15-21; 11:2-4, 7-10, 25-27, 33-36; 14:10-12; 15:8-12). The Mosaic law is no longer their regulatory norm, but the OT still functions as Scripture for them. It testifies to the gospel (1:1-2; 3:21; 4:1-25; 16:25-26), and, interpreted paradigmatically in the light of Christ, it provides guidance for godly living (cf. 12:17-21; 13:8-10; 14:10-12; 15:2-4).

I. Israel in the Purposes of God

Paul argues that Jews and Gentiles are alike in the matter of sin and judgment (1:18-3:20) and also in the matter of salvation (3:21-31). In 11:32 he declares: 'God has bound everyone over to disobedience so that he may have mercy on them all'. It might seem, then, that Paul negates any special place for Israel in the purposes of God, but this is not the case. He acknowledges that there are many advantages in being a Jew (3:1-2; 9:4-5), even while insisting that they are no better off in the matter of sin and judgment (3:9). He argues that since there is one God, he will justify both the circumcised (Jews) and the uncircumcised (Gentiles) by faith, and that this excludes all Jewish boasting on mere ethnic grounds (3:28-30).

While Israel can claim no immunity in the matter of judgment, and no special privileges in the matter of salvation, this does not mean that they have no special place in the purposes of God. In 9:4-5 the apostle says of the people of Israel: 'Theirs is the adoption to sonship; theirs the divine glory, the covenants, the receiving of the law, the temple worship and the promises. Theirs are the patriarchs, and from them is traced the human ancestry of the Messiah, who is God over all, forever praised! Amen'. Yet despite these privileges many of the people of Israel had rejected the gospel and failed to experience its blessings, and this raises the question whether God's word has failed. In response Paul provides two explanations for this state of affairs. First, in 9:1-29 he argues that 'not all who are descended from Israel are Israel' (9:6). God said to Moses, 'I will have mercy on whom I have mercy, and I will have compassion on whom I have compassion' (9:15), and so Paul insists, 'God has mercy on whom he wants to have mercy, and he hardens whom he wants to harden' (9:18). Ultimately, therefore, the reason why some experience the blessings of the gospel while others do not is the effect of God's choice.

Second, in 9:30–10:21 Paul argues that the people of Israel themselves bear responsibility for their failure. They sought to establish their own righteousness and would not submit to God's righteousness (10:3). The problem was not that the gospel was remote from them; rather, it was near, and it was available to them as it was to everyone else, for as the Scripture says, 'Everyone who calls on the name of the Lord will be saved' (10:6-13). The problem was, as Isaiah said, that even though God held out his hands to Israel all day long, she remained 'a disobedient and obstinate people' (10:21).

However, this is not the end of the story, for even though Israel has rejected the gospel, God has not rejected his people. He has always maintained a remnant of faithful Israelites, as he did in the time of Elijah, and Paul himself is one of them (11:1-5). Paul notes that in the present time, when the majority of Israelites have stumbled, this has provided occasion for the gospel to be taken to the Gentiles, and many of them were responding positively. Israel's stumbling meant that salvation had come to the Gentiles. But Paul believes that there will yet be a turning on the part of Israel, and if their stumbling meant reconciliation for the world, their acceptance will mean life from the dead (11:11-15). Paul says to his audience: 'I do not want you to be ignorant of this mystery, brothers and sisters, so that you may not be conceited: Israel has experienced a hardening in part until the full number of the Gentiles has come in. And so all Israel will be saved. As it is written: "The deliverer will come from Zion; he will turn godlessness away from Jacob. This is my covenant with them when I take away their sins"' (11:25-27). What it means for 'all Israel' to be saved has been interpreted in different ways. The least problematic interpretation is that it refers to the salvation of the 'elect of Israel of all time' (see 'Additional Note: "All Israel Will Be Saved"', 448-51).

J. The Centrum Paulinum

By the *centrum Paulinum* is meant the center, heart, or organizing principle of Paul's theology. Because of the occasional nature of Paul's letters, it is difficult to determine what this is.[64] Nearly all of Paul's letters address particular pastoral or theological problems, and what they contain is directed to those concerns. The nearest thing we have to an articulation of Paul's theology is his Letter to the Romans, though even this, it may be argued, has an occasional character. His letters, then, do not contain an articulation of what he believes to be the center, heart, or organizing principle of his theology. While the *centrum Paulinum* cannot be said to be an important theme in Romans, a discussion of the matter is included here because Romans, more than Paul's other letters, provides clues as to what it might be.

Many suggestions have been put forward regarding the *centrum Paulinum*, and a number of these are described briefly below. From Reformation times until relatively recently, Protestant interpretation of Paul was dominated by the belief that the central feature of Paul's theology is justification by faith. This view was questioned by Wrede and Deissmann, who regarded Paul's teaching on justification as a polemically conditioned and isolated phase of his thought — introduced in his conflict with Judaizers and neglected thereafter. Schweitzer, in similar fashion, said that justification by faith was just a 'subsidiary crater' within the main rim of Pauline theology. He argued that union with Christ was the central theme of Pauline thought, something he understood as a 'quasi-physical' union with Christ that occurred through baptism. Sanders argues that the main theme of Paul's theology was the saving action of God in Jesus Christ that makes it possible for people to participate in that action by their union with him.

Cullmann believed that the idea of a linear succession of saving acts of God (central to which was the Christ event) is the key to understanding Paul's thought. Stendahl, who regarded justification by faith simply as a fighting doctrine introduced by Paul in his conflict with the Judaizers, like

---

64. By way of comparison we may note that in the Synoptic Gospels the center, heart, and organizing principle of Jesus' theology appears to be the kingdom of God: (i) it constituted his primary message when preaching to the crowds; (ii) a great many of his parables related to the kingdom; (iii) the miracles he performed were largely signs of the kingdom; and (iv) the Sermon on the Mount may be described as ethics for the children of the kingdom.

Cullmann regarded salvation history as the underlying theme of Paul's theology. Käsemann acknowledged the importance of salvation history for Paul but insisted that justification is at the heart of the apostle's theology. He contends: 'Justification and salvation-history belong together, but everything depends on the right co-ordination. Just as the church must not take precedence over Christ, so salvation-history must not take precedence over justification. It is its sphere. But justification remains the centre, the beginning and the end of salvation-history. Otherwise the cross of Jesus would also inevitably lose its central position'.

Ridderbos argues that the unifying center of Paul's theology is the work of Christ as the center of redemptive history. Paul's theology is the exposition of the new redemptive facts of the Christ event, understood against the background of the great redemptive-historical framework of salvation history. Ladd cites Ridderbos with approval. His own contribution is to apply his understanding of eschatology to the question about the *centrum Paulinum.* He believes that the inbreaking of the new age in Christ is the central feature of Pauline theology, and it offers a solution to the tension between justification and mysticism (or the new life in Christ). Both justification and the gift of the Spirit belong to the new age, and have now become matters of present experience.

Fitzmyer argues that the key to Paul's theology should be formulated in terms of what the apostle stated over and over in various ways. He draws attention, for example, to 1 Corinthians 1:23-24: 'we proclaim Christ crucified, a stumbling block to Jews and foolishness to Gentiles, but to those who are the called, both Jews and Greeks, Christ the power of God and the wisdom of God'. He says: 'This story of the cross thus puts Christ himself at the center of his soteriology (God's new mode of salvation) and all else in Paul's teaching has to be orientated to this christocentric soteriology'.

Martin holds that any model of the center of Pauline theology must: (i) respect the divine initiative in grace; (ii) speak to the cosmic and human predicament; (iii) preserve the centrality of the cross and the responsiveness of faith; (iv) lay a basis in the indicative for the imperative call to total commitment and decision, and (v), above all, take 'theo-logy' seriously as concerned with the story of God and the destiny of humankind. His own suggestion for the best 'omnibus' term to describe such a model in Pauline theology is reconciliation.

Beker argues that the triumph of God is the integrating theme of Paul's theology. He says that Paul is a theocentric theologian. While the Christ event is the turning point in time that announces the end time, all that Christ did and does is for the sake of the final triumph and glory of God. The triumph of God as the coherent center of Paul's theology, Beker says, is reflected in passages like 1 Corinthians 15:20-28 and Romans 8.

Dunn says that the 'fulcrum point' of Paul's theology is Christ. He is responsible for a realignment of Paul's heritage — God is now known through Christ; the righteousness of God is now related to Christ; Israel is expanded to incorporate all who believe in Christ; Christ is the key to understanding Scriptures (the veil is lifted when a person turns to Christ); Christianity is Christ — he is the thread running throughout; Christ inaugurates a whole new world; faith is now faith in Christ; salvation involves growing in conformity to Christ; and the church is the body of Christ.

The various suggestions that have been made concerning what constitutes the *centrum Paulinum* (justification, union with Christ, salvation history, Christ as the center of redemptive history, eschatology, reconciliation, the triumph of God) are, every one of them, important Pauline themes. Which of them should be adopted as the *centrum Paulinum* will no doubt continue to be debated. In respect to what may be deduced from Romans itself concerning this matter, note should be taken of the overwhelmingly theocentric nature of the letter (described in the section on 'God the Father' above). The gospel Paul expounds is the gospel of God in which the righteousness of God, the grace of God, and the love of God are revealed. God's sovereign will is determinative in the matter of salvation as he exercises his divine prerogative to have mercy upon whom he will have mercy. God himself is the primary agent of salvation, and he effects it through the redemptive activity of his Son whom he put forward as the atoning sacrifice for sins. Accordingly, the focus of Paul's exposition of God's saving activity is upon the work of the Son. Perhaps it may be said, then, that, as far as Romans is concerned, the center, heart, and organizing principle of Pauline theology is the action of God through the person and work of Jesus Christ to deal with the effects of human sin, individually, communally, and cosmically. In brief, as far as Romans is concerned, the *centrum Paulinum* is the gospel of God comprehensively conceived.

Commentary

I. LETTER INTRODUCTION, 1:1-17

The introduction to Paul's Letter to the Romans consists of two parts. The first part is the traditional greeting from the author to the recipients. In the case of Romans it is substantially longer than the greetings in Paul's other letters. The second part is the traditional thanksgiving section in which the apostle informs his audience of his prayers for them and his longing to visit them, a visit he wants to make in order that he might have some ministry among them.

A. Greetings, 1:1-7

> [1]Paul, a servant of Christ Jesus, called to be an apostle and set apart for the gospel of God — [2]the gospel he promised beforehand through his prophets in the Holy Scriptures [3]regarding his Son, who as to his earthly life was a descendant of David, [4]and who through the Spirit of holiness was appointed the Son of God in power by his resurrection from the dead: Jesus Christ our Lord. [5]Through him we received grace and apostleship to call all the Gentiles to the obedience that comes from faith for his name's sake. [6]And you also are among those Gentiles who are called to belong to Jesus Christ.
> [7]To all in Rome who are loved by God and called to be his holy people:
> Grace and peace to you from God our Father and from the Lord Jesus Christ.

The format of the opening greeting of a Greek letter (as evidenced by the many letters found among the papyri recovered in Egypt in the first half of the twentieth century) was normally quite brief: 'A to B, greeting'.[1]

---

1. Cf., e.g., *P. Lond.* 42, cited in C. K. Barrett, *The New Testament Background: Selected Documents* (London: SPCK, 1961), 27-28.

Appropriately, when writing for a largely Gentile audience, Paul adopts this Greek form for his greeting.[2] He employs the direct form of address (using the second person) in his greetings, which introduces a certain sense of intimacy. This is balanced, however, and especially so in Romans, by reference to his status ('a servant of Christ Jesus, called to be an apostle'), indicating that the letter is a more official and serious communication.

The greeting formulae in Paul's letters are generally enlarged and Christianized, as, for example, in 1 Thessalonians 1:1: 'Paul, Silas and Timothy, to the church of the Thessalonians in God the Father and the Lord Jesus Christ: Grace and peace to you'. Sometimes the content of the greeting provides hints of what might be expected in the body of the letter. For example, in his greeting in 1 Corinthians 1:1-3 Paul emphasizes that he was 'called to be an apostle . . . by the will of God' and addresses his letter 'to the church of God in Corinth, to those sanctified in Christ Jesus and called to be his holy people, together with all those everywhere who call on the name of our Lord Jesus Christ — their Lord and ours'. By doing so he foreshadows the fact that he will be defending his apostleship, while reminding the Corinthian believers that they are called to be holy and that they are but a part of a wider Christian community and therefore need to follow the rules Paul lays down for all his churches (cf. 1 Cor 7:17; 11:16; 14:33-34).

The greeting in Romans is much fuller than either that in 1 Thessalonians or 1 Corinthians and is unique among the greetings in Paul's letters, in particular because of its length and theological density. The content of the greeting can be set out as follows:

> A. *Paul, a servant of Christ Jesus,*
> > *called to be an apostle*
> > *and set apart for the gospel of God —*
> > > *the gospel he promised beforehand*
> > > *through his prophets*
> > > *in the Holy Scriptures*
> > *regarding his Son,*
> > > *who was a descendant of David,*
> > > > *as to his earthly life*
> > > *and who was appointed the Son of God in power*
> > > > *through the Spirit of holiness*
> > > > *by his resurrection from the dead:*
> > > *Jesus Christ our Lord.*
> > *Through him we received grace and apostleship*
> > > *to call to the obedience that comes from faith*
> > > *all the Gentiles.*
> > > *for his name's sake,*
> > *And you also are among those Gentiles who are called to belong to*
> > > *Jesus Christ.*

---

2. Cf. Cranfield, *Romans*, I, 45-46.

B. *To all in Rome who are loved by God and called to be his holy people:*

C. *Grace and peace to you*
    from God our Father
    and from the Lord Jesus Christ.

From this layout it can be seen that the greeting has the three basic elements of standard Greek epistolary greetings (A: 'Paul, a servant of Jesus Christ . . .'; B: 'to all in Rome who are loved by God . . .'; C: Greeting: 'grace and peace to you . . .'). The first element ('Paul, a servant of Jesus Christ . . .') is greatly expanded so that Paul can introduce himself as 'called to be an apostle' and 'set apart for the gospel of God'. This gospel God promised beforehand through his prophets and it concerns his Son. The Son is then described as a descendant of David (his human lineage) and the Son of God with power (by divine appointment). It is from the Son of God that Paul has received his call and the grace enabling him to be an apostle, in particular an apostle to the Gentiles. His Roman Gentile audience, he insists, are included among those for whom he has been appointed an apostle.

The second element of the greeting ('to all in Rome who are loved by God . . .') is brief and contains no expressions of endearment or honor often found in Greek letters (as, e.g., in Titus 1:4; Philem 1-2), nor any veiled rebuke (as in the case of 1 Cor 1:2). This can be accounted for by the fact that Paul is addressing many people whom he had not met before (cf. 1:8-13). The third element ('Grace and peace to you . . .') is quite brief, as is the case in most of Paul's letters (cf., e.g., 1 Cor 1:3; 2 Cor 1:2; Eph 1:2; Col 1:2; 1 Thess 1:1; 2 Thess 1:2; Philem 3), but not all (cf. Gal 1:3-5).

The original audience of Paul's letter might have wondered why the opening greeting (prescript) was so extraordinarily long. Those who had some knowledge of epistolary conventions and rhetorical strategies would sense that Paul was going to great lengths to introduce himself so as to secure a good hearing for what he was to write in the rest of the letter.[3] From the contents of the prescript an astute audience would also detect hints about what Paul intended to convey to them in his letter, but they would have to listen carefully to what was being read to discover exactly what that was.[4]

1:1 *Paul* was the apostle's Roman name. It was common for Jews in NT times to have a Gentile name alongside their Jewish name (in the apostle's case: Saul).[5] Using his Roman name probably helped to facilitate his

---

3. Cf. Byrne, *Romans*, 37-38.

4. Samuel Byrskog, 'Epistolography, Rhetoric and Letter Prescript: Romans 1.1-7 as a Test Case', *JSNT* 65 (1997) 27-46, provides a helpful discussion of these matters.

5. Cranfield, *Romans*, I, 49-50, says: 'Since Paul was a Roman citizen, the matter is rather more complicated. It is very probable that he possessed the three names characteristic of a Roman citizen, a *praenomen* or personal name, a *nomen* or clan name, and a *cognomen* or family name. It is probable that one of the two names given in Acts 13.9 ['Saul, who was

travels around the empire.[6]

Unusually, Paul does not associate any of his colleagues with him in the authorship of this letter, even though Timothy was with him when he composed the final greetings (16:21). Dunn suggests 'that Paul wanted to present himself in his own person to these largely unknown congregations, as (the) apostle to the Gentiles (cf. 11:13), and with the subsequent exposition of the gospel understood very much as his. . . . It was on their reaction to this very personal statement that the success or failure of this letter would hang'.[7]

Paul further introduces himself to his audience as *a servant of Christ Jesus*,[8] literally 'a slave of Christ Jesus'. He introduces himself in this way in only one other letter (Phil 1:1),[9] but he does speak of himself as a slave of Christ in Galatians 1:10. Elsewhere he refers to believers as 'slaves of Christ' (1 Cor 7:22; Eph 6:6; Col 4:12). In the LXX the title 'a servant/slave of the Lord' is used of Joshua (Josh 24:30; Judg 2:8), Moses (2 Kgs 18:12), and Jonah (Jon 1:9), and the title 'child/slave of God' is used of Shadrach, Meshach, and Abednego (Dan 3:26, LXX 3:93) and Moses (Dan 9:11). In referring to himself as a servant/slave of the Lord, Paul may have had in mind, in particular, the servant passage in Isaiah 49:1-7. In all these LXX references the expression appears to have honorific connotations: To be a servant/slave of the Lord is to have high status.[10] However, as Moo notes, 'the connotations of humility, devotion, and obedience are never absent from the OT phrase and are surely primary here [in 1:1] also'.[11]

For the first-century audience of Paul's letter the word 'slave' would have other connotations as well as connotations related to the institution of

---

also called Paul'] was one of Paul's official *tria nomina,* and the other a *signum* or *supernomen,* an unofficial, informal name, additional to the three official names, such as was common at this time in the east. "Saul" in a Latinized form could have been the apostle's *cognomen,* and "Paulus" his signum. But it is much more likely that it was the other way round, that "Paulus" was his *cognomen* and "Saul" in its Semitic form his *signum.* That in his work as a missionary among the Gentiles he should have preferred to use one of his Roman names is readily understandable'.

6. Cf. David J. MacLeod, 'Eternal Son, Davidic Son, Messianic Son: An Exposition of Romans 1:1-7', *BSac* 162 (2005) 77.

7. James D. G. Dunn, *Romans 1–8* (WBC 38A; Dallas: Word Books, 1988), 7.

8. Manuscript evidence at this point is fairly evenly balanced, some supporting [*doulos*] *Christou Iēsou* (followed by the NIV), others supporting [*doulos*] *Iēsou Christou* (followed by the NRSV). The former variant, followed by the NIV, treats 'Christ' as an official title ('Messiah'), whereas the latter, followed by the NRSV, treats 'Christ' as a proper name.

9. He does refer to himself as 'a slave of God' *(doulos theou)* in Tit 1:1.

10. Jewett, *Romans,* 100, draws attention to 'the local connotation of this expression [a slave of Christ Jesus], which makes perfect sense in a letter to Rome, where influential slaves in imperial service proudly bore the title "slave of Caesar". More than four thousand slaves and freedmen associated with Caesar's household, his personal staff, and the imperial bureaucracy have been identified through grave inscriptions with this kind of title'.

11. Douglas J. Moo, *The Epistle to the Romans* (NICNT; Grand Rapids: Eerdmans, 1996), 41.

slavery. For them, a slave was someone who belonged entirely to another and from whom absolute obedience could be expected. Paul would have been quite happy for his reference to himself as a slave of Christ Jesus to be understood in this way because he thought of himself, and in fact of all believers (1 Cor 7:22; Eph 6:6; Col 4:12), as slaves of Christ — people who belonged to Christ and owed him their full obedience (1 Cor 6:20).[12]

It is significant that here Paul refers to himself as a slave of 'Christ Jesus', not 'Jesus Christ'. In the latter 'Christ' might be regarded as a proper name, but in the former it clearly functions as a description of Jesus' status — he is the Messiah (*Christos* being the Greek equivalent of the Hebrew word for Messiah).[13]

Paul describes himself further as one *called to be an apostle* (lit. 'a called apostle').[14] This is the normal way he introduces himself in his letters (cf. 1 Cor 1:1; 2 Cor 1:1; Gal 1:1; Eph 1:1; Col 1:1; 1 Tim 1:1; 2 Tim 1:1; Tit 1:1). Paul's calling as an apostle was according to the purpose of God (1 Cor 1:1) and involved being set apart for, or wholly dedicated to, the preaching of the gospel (1:1). The key text for understanding Paul's calling is Galatians 1:15-16 (NRSV: 'But when God, who had set me apart before I was born and called me through his grace, was pleased to reveal his Son to me, so that I might proclaim him among the Gentiles, I did not confer with any human being'). This text reflects Paul's conviction that he was chosen by God for the task before he was born; that his calling came to him by revelation at a time determined by God himself; that it rested entirely upon God's grace, not upon anything deserving on Paul's part; that it involved a direct revelation of Jesus Christ to him involving no human mediation; and that the scope of his ministry was to be primarily among Gentile peoples.[15] Two things were fundamental to Paul's apostleship: he had seen the risen Lord (1 Cor 15:3-8), and he had been commissioned by him to preach the gospel to the Gentiles (1:1-5; 15:15-16; Gal 1:1, 15). By introducing himself as an apostle to his Roman audience, most of whom did not know him, Paul pro-

12. Michael Joseph Brown, 'Paul's Use of *doulos Christou Iēsou* in Romans 1:1', *JBL* 120 (2001) 724, 731-32, argues that Paul's reference to himself as a 'slave of Christ' *(doulos Christou)* was appropriate when writing to the Roman church, for it included within its membership imperial slaves belonging to Caesar's household *(familia Caesaris)*. These people were socially mobile, sometimes rising to positions of power and authority, but were despised by the aristocrats. By describing himself as a *doulos Christou* Paul was presenting himself as one who likewise suffered contempt (in his case as an apostle to the Gentiles), and would hope thereby to secure a better hearing from those in the Roman church who were the objects of contempt. However, as Origen observed: 'The reality of Paul's freedom [is not] compromised by this in any way. As he himself says: *Though I am free from all men, I have made myself a slave of all.* . . . For he serves Christ not in the spirit of slavery but in the spirit of adoption, for Christ's service is more noble than any freedom' ('Commentary on the Epistle to the Romans' [*ACCSR*, 17]).

13. Cf. N. T. Wright, 'The Letter to the Romans: Introduction, Commentary, and Reflections', in *The New Interpreter's Bible*, X (Nashville: Abingdon, 2002), 415.

14. Cf. Harold J. Greenlee, 'Some "Called" People', *NotesTrans* 11 (1997) 49-51.

15. For a fuller discussion of Paul's calling, see C. G. Kruse, 'Call/Calling', *DPL* 85.

vides them with a good reason to give their attention to the contents of his letter: he writes as one who has been called and commissioned by God. See 'Additional Note: Paul's Apostleship', 56-57.

Paul further describes himself as one *set apart for the gospel of God*. The word translated 'set apart' is often used to mean separating people from contact with others (as in Matt 25:32; Luke 6:22; 2 Cor 6:17; Gal 2:12), but here it means setting apart for a purpose (the proclamation of the gospel), something that was inherent in Paul's conversion/commissioning experience on the Damascus Road. Paul uses the same word in Galatians 1:15-16, where he says that he was 'set apart' from birth by God to preach Christ among the Gentiles. It is also used in Acts 13:2, where the Holy Spirit tells the prophets and teachers in Antioch to 'set apart' Paul and Barnabas for the work to which he has called them. Barrett comments: 'Paul had been a Pharisee (Phil. iii.5), supposing himself to be set apart from other men for the service of God; he now truly was what he had supposed himself to be — separated, not, however, by human exclusiveness but by God's grace and election'.[16]

As an apostle, Paul's primary function was to proclaim the gospel (cf. 1 Cor 1:17), one that he calls here 'the gospel of God', as he does frequently in his letters (Rom 15:16; 2 Cor 11:7; 1 Thess 2:2, 8, 9; 1 Tim 1:11).[17] The essential background to the word 'gospel' is found in the LXX. Although the noun 'gospel' itself *(euangelion)* is found there only once (in 2 Sam 4:10, where it means the reward given for good news), the cognate verb *(euangelizō)* is found twenty-three times, and uniformly means to bring or proclaim good news. Particularly relevant are passages where it is used in relation to proclaiming news of God's salvation (e.g., Ps 96:2 [LXX 95:2]; Nah 1:15 [LXX 2:1]; Isa 40:9; 52:7; 61:1). *Euangelion* was also used in the emperor cult to refer to important announcements (e.g., the birth of an heir, or the emperor's accession). It may be, as some scholars have suggested, that Paul's description of the gospel as 'the gospel of God' distinguishes it implicitly from all other 'gospels', in particular those of Roman emperors.[18]

1:2 Paul describes 'the gospel of God' as *the gospel he promised before-*

---

16. C. K. Barrett, *A Commentary on the Epistle to the Romans* (London: Adam & Charles Black, 1967), 17. Dunn, *Romans 1–8*, 9, however, believes that any such allusion would have been lost on the original audience.

17. Even more often Paul refers to his gospel as 'the gospel of Christ' (Rom 15:19; 1 Cor 9:12; 2 Cor 2:12; 4:4; 9:13; 10:14; Gal 1:7; Phil 1:27; 1 Thess 3:2). In 1:3-4 he will make clear that the content of the gospel concerns Christ (in this sense it may be called the 'gospel of Christ'), but it is essentially God's gospel. God the Father initiated the plan of salvation, which he accomplished through Christ (cf. 2 Cor 5:18-19).

18. Ben Witherington III, with Darlene Hyatt, *Paul's Letter to the Romans: A Socio-Rhetorical Commentary* (Grand Rapids: Eerdmans, 2004), 31-32, notes: 'In the light of the use of this term of emperors at their births or when they accomplished something dramatic, it is also clear that Paul intends an implicit anti-imperial sort of rhetoric. The one who really offers salvation and true Good News for human beings is the God who has sent Jesus and raised him from the dead'. Cf. Wright, 'Romans', 415-16; Cranfield, *Romans*, I, 55.

hand through his prophets in the Holy Scriptures. In 16:26 he describes the gospel in similar terms as that 'made known through the prophetic writings by the command of the eternal God'.[19] In 3:21 he insists that the law and the prophets testify to the righteousness made known through the gospel. In these ways he deliberately links the gospel he proclaims with God's promises to Israel in the OT. Besides such explicit statements, Paul's frequent quotations from the OT in Romans reflect implicitly his conviction that the gospel was 'promised beforehand' (1:17; 4:3, 7, 8, 9, 16-17, 22; 9:25-26; 10:6-8, 11, 13; 11:26-27; 15:9-12), as do quotations in his other letters (1 Cor 2:9; 15:27, 54-55; 2 Cor 6:2, 16-18; Gal 3:6, 8, 11, 13, 16; 4:27-28; Eph 4:7-8). An examination of all these references indicates that the OT Scriptures in which Paul found the gospel foreshadowed are Genesis, Deuteronomy, Psalms, Isaiah, Ezekiel, Hosea, Joel, and Habakkuk. For Paul, these books constitute (the law) and the prophets which proclaimed beforehand 'the gospel of God'.[20]

Paul frequently refers to the writings of the OT as 'the Scripture(s)' (4:3; 9:17; 10:11; 11:2; 15:4; 16:26; 1 Cor 15:3, 4; Gal 3:8, 22; 4:30; 1 Tim 5:18; 2 Tim 3:16), but only here as 'the *Holy* Scriptures'. This is, perhaps, to highlight their importance, and thereby the importance of the gospel promised beforehand in them, so that his audience will give their attention to what he is to write about it. In 1 Corinthians 15:3-4 Paul states explicitly that the core elements of the gospel are in accordance with the Scriptures: 'For what I received I passed on to you as of first importance: that Christ died for our sins according to the Scriptures, that he was buried, that he was raised on the third day according to the Scriptures'.

The way Paul refers to the gospel here, as something proclaimed beforehand, suggests that he has in mind not simply a message of good news, but the events which constitute the basis of that good news, that is, what God achieved through Christ — the manifestation of the righteousness of God. Moo comments appropriately, therefore, when he says that the gospel 'becomes functionally equivalent to "Christ" or God's intervention in Christ'.[21]

1:3-4 Here, citing, it seems, an early Christian creed, Paul describes the content of 'the gospel of God' mentioned in 1:2. Slightly rearranging the text, the content of the gospel may be set out as that:

---

19. Cf. Tit 1:2: 'the hope of eternal life, which God, who does not lie, promised before the beginning of time'.

20. Byrne, *Romans*, 43, says of the verb 'promised beforehand' (*proepēngeilato*) that, while it 'usually has the sense of "promise beforehand" (e.g., BAGD 705), the more basic sense of "announce beforehand" (cf. LSJ 1478) conveys more effectively Paul's sense of scripture as primarily addressed to the present (eschatological) age (cf. 15:4; 1 Cor 9:10). The prophets (writing) in the "holy scriptures" did not simply "promise" good news at a future date but actually made an anticipatory proclamation of the gospel, which is now being realized (cf. Gal 3:8) and "heard" when they are read'.

21. Moo, *Romans*, 43.

> *regarding his Son,*
>> *who was a descendant of David,*
>>> *as to his earthly life*
>> *who was appointed the Son of God in power*
>>> *through the Spirit of holiness*
>>> *by his resurrection from the dead:*
> *Jesus Christ our Lord.*

Several arguments have been put forward to support the view that these verses contain material from an early creed. Some of these are more cogent than others, and some are based upon particular exegeses of these verses that are still subject to debate. However, their cumulative effect is impressive and supports the view that Paul is incorporating credal material in 1:3-4 (see 'Additional Note: Paul's Use of Credal Material in 1:3-4', 47-49).

Turning to the actual content of 1:3-4, we notice first and foremost that Paul points out that the gospel is 'regarding *his* Son' (cf. 1:9). Paul was very conscious that God's own Son was at the heart of the gospel message. Accordingly, he says elsewhere that God sent *his Son* to redeem those under the law (Gal 4:5); that he did not spare *his own Son*, but gave him up for us all (8:32); and that he reconciled humanity to himself through *his Son* (5:10; cf. 2 Cor 5:18-21). 'His Son' in this context denotes a unique relationship. It is true that in the OT various figures are spoken of as God's sons, for example, Israel's king (2 Sam 7:14; Ps 2:7), Israel the nation (Exod 4:22-23; Jer 31:9), and angels (Gen 6:2; Job 1:6; 38:7; Dan 3:25), but here in 1:3-4 it becomes clear that 'his Son' means much more than these.

Paul employs two participial clauses to describe God's Son, the one describing what he is 'as to his earthly life' (lit. 'according to the flesh') and the other what he is 'through the Spirit of holiness' (lit. 'according to the Spirit of holiness'). Before we unpack these participial clauses, we should make a general comment on the distinction Paul makes about what God's Son is according to the flesh and according to the Spirit of holiness. Some have taken this to distinguish the human and divine natures of Christ, that is, his humanity and his deity, but this is unlikely. It probably refers to how Christ is to be understood in the period of his incarnation ('a descendant of David'), and how he is to be understood following his resurrection ('the Son of God in power').[22]

---

22. Cf. MacLeod, 'Eternal Son, Davidic Son, Messianic Son', 86. Byrne, *Romans*, 39, says: 'The credal formula which Paul cites to indicate this envisages what might be called the "messianic career" of Jesus in two stages. 1. In terms of his human origins ("according to the flesh"), Jesus fulfils a key requirement for messianic "candidacy" in the understanding of early Christianity and some Jewish circles: birth from the royal house of David. 2. As raised from the dead and entered thereby into the new age marked by the Spirit ("according to the Spirit of holiness")'. Cf. Witherington, *Romans*, 32: 'v. 3 does not focus on Jesus' human nature per se, but rather on his human lineage through David, and v. 4 is not about what Christ is according to his divine nature but rather about what happened to Jesus at the

In the first of the two participial clauses Paul calls God's Son the one 'who as to his earthly life [lit. 'according to the flesh']²³ was a descendant of David'. By describing him in this way Paul affirms his Jewish lineage, stretching back to King David. In the Gospel accounts Jesus' Davidic lineage is traced through Joseph (cf. Matt 1:16, 20; Luke 1:27; 2:4; 3:23), even though the Gospels affirm that Joseph was not his natural father (Matt 1:18-25; Luke 1:34). Cranfield suggests that 'the implication of the narratives is that Jesus' Davidic descent rests on Joseph's having accepted Him as his son and thereby legitimized Him'.²⁴

There is only one other place in the Pauline corpus where Jesus is described as 'a descendant of David' (2 Tim. 2:8), though this is implied in 15:12 (where he is described as 'the Root of Jesse' — David's father). By referring to him as 'a descendant of David' Paul alludes to promises of a Davidic Messiah found in the OT, the Pseudepigrapha, and the Qumran writings (2 Sam 7:12-13; Pss 89:3-4, 20-29; 132:11-12; Jer 23:5; Zech 3:8; 6:12-13; the *Psalms of Solomon* 17–18; 4 Ezra 12:31-32; *T. Jud.* 24:1-6; 1QM 11:1-18; 4QFlor 1:10-14), and echoes early Christian belief that Jesus was the long-awaited Davidic Messiah (Matt 1:1, 17; 9:27; 12:23; 15:22; 20:30-31; 21:9, 15; 22:42; Mark 10:47-48; 11:10; 12:35-37; Luke 1:32, 69; 3:31; 18:38-39; 20:41-42, 44; John 7:42; Acts 13:34; 15:16; Rev 5:5; 22:16).²⁵

In the second participial clause the apostle describes Jesus as the one 'who through the Spirit of holiness was appointed the Son of God in power by his resurrection from the dead: Jesus Christ our Lord'. A number of matters in this statement call for special comment. First, the expression 'the Spirit of holiness' is found only here in the NT.²⁶ It can be interpreted in two

---

resurrection, when God's Spirit raised him from the dead and designated or marked him out as Son of God in power'.

23. Paul uses the expression 'according to the flesh' *(kata sarka)* in two ways in his letters: (a) negatively, meaning 'according to the sinful human nature' (8:4-5, 12-13; 2 Cor 1:17; 5:16; 10:2; 11:18); and (b) neutrally, meaning 'in relation to human nature' or 'according to (mere) human standards' (4:1; 9:3, 5; 1 Cor 1:26; 10:18; 2 Cor 10:3; Gal 4:23, 29; Eph 6:5; Col 3:22). The use of *kata sarka* here in 1:3 is clearly of the second neutral type, indicating that, as far as his human nature was concerned, God's Son was of the lineage of King David.

24. Cranfield, *Romans,* I, 59.

25. Byrne, *Romans,* 44, comments: 'The complexity of Jewish messianic belief at the time of Jesus has been increasingly recognized. However, there were undoubtedly circles which interpreted the biblical oracles . . . as foretelling the rise of an anointed prince of David's line who would play a key role in bringing about the restoration of Israel's fortunes in both a political and religious sense. Qumran messianism certainly included expectation of such a Davidic prince, along with priestly and prophetic figures (1QSa 2:14; CD 7:18-20; 4QpGenᵃ 5:1-4; 4QFlor 1:11-13; 4QpIsaᵃ frags. 8-10, col. 3:10-18; 4QTest 9–13; cf. also *Pss. Sol.* 17:21-46; 18:5-9). It is not surprising, then, that descent from David should feature in an early Christian credal formula asserting the messianic status of Jesus (cf. esp. 2 Tim 2:8)'.

26. Byrne, *Romans,* 45, holds that *pneuma hagiōsynēs,* 'featuring the Semitic adjectival genitive, has a biblical anticipation in the Hebrew of Ps 51:11 (MT 51:13) and Isa 63:10-11 and parallels in Qumran literature (1QS 4:21; 8:16; 9:3; 1QH 7:6-7; 9:32). The Greek phrase

main ways: (a) as the 'Spirit of holiness'. Here Spirit has a capital 'S', indicating it is a reference to the Holy Spirit, the third person of the Trinity. In this case what Jesus is in respect of his human nature, a descendant of David, is contrasted with what he is in respect of the Holy Spirit, declared to be the Son of God. This is supported by the fact that Paul frequently contrasts what is 'according to the flesh' with what is 'according to the Spirit', where 'Spirit' refers to the Holy Spirit (cf. Rom 8:4, 5, 6, 9, 13; Gal 3:3; 4:29; 5:16, 17; 6:8; Phil 3:3; 1 Tim 3:16), the third person of the Trinity. In this case 'the Spirit of holiness' may be either equivalent to 'the Holy Spirit', or mean Spirit of sanctification, the Spirit who sanctifies.[27]

(b) The NRSV construes it as 'the spirit of holiness'. Here 'spirit' is spelled with a lower-case 's', which would allow 'the spirit of holiness' to be interpreted as the human spirit of Jesus, which is holy.[28] Such an interpretation receives some support from the fact that Paul does in a few places use 'flesh' and 'spirit' to refer to the physical body and the spirit of human beings respectively (1 Cor 5:5; 2 Cor 7:1; Col 2:5). Militating against this interpretation is the fact that elsewhere in Paul's writings the word 'spirit', when linked with the expression 'according to' as it is here, always refers to the Holy Spirit (cf. 8:4, 5; Gal 4:29).

If we take 'the Spirit of holiness' as a reference to the Holy Spirit, there is a second matter that demands attention. The NIV translation describes Jesus Christ as the one 'appointed Son of God'; however, many other English translations have, 'declared to be the Son of God'. These translations lessen the possibility of Paul's statement being interpreted in an adoptionist manner.[29] However, this runs counter to the use of the same verb elsewhere in the NT, where it never means 'to declare', but rather 'to

---

occurs in the *Testament of Levi*: ". . . and he (the eschatological Priest) will grant to the saints to eat of the tree of life. The spirit of holiness shall be upon them. And Beliar shall be bound by him, and he shall grant to his children the authority to trample on wicked spirits" (18:11-12). This is a significant parallel to the Christological statement in Rom 1:4 because it links possession or imparting of the spirit with authority and power to overcome forces hostile to God (cf. 1 Cor 15:25-28). In Rom 1:4 the reference is almost certainly to the Spirit of God. The risen Lord's imparting of the Spirit (1 Cor 15:45; 2 Cor 3:18; cf. John 20:19-23) indicates his own messianic status and the dawn of the new age. "Before" the resurrection, Jesus' messianic qualifications could only be based upon his "fleshly" descent from David; postresurrection, they are palpable in the shape of the Spirit'.

27. Dunn, *Romans 1–8*, 15, comments: 'The term is clearly Semitic in character, modeled on the Hebraic form (not the LXX) of Ps 51:11 and Isa 63:10-11. . . . It would almost certainly be understood by Paul and the first Christians as denoting the Holy Spirit, the Spirit which is characterized by holiness, partaker of God's holiness'.

28. So, e.g., Fitzmyer, *Romans*, 236.

29. However, adoptionist interpretations are ruled out by the fact that the one who is appointed Son of God with power is already described as 'his Son'. Cf. Thomas R. Schreiner, *Romans* (BECNT 6; Grand Rapids: Baker, 1998), 38-39, who says: 'The placement of the words *tou huiou autou* ['of his Son'] before the two participles suggests that the one who became the seed of David and was appointed God's Son in power at the resurrection was already the Son before these'.

determine', 'to decree', or 'to appoint' (Luke 22:22; Acts 2:23; 10:42; 11:29; 17:26, 31; Heb 4:7).[30] It is preferable then to stay with the translation 'appointed Son of God'.[31] In regard to the significance of this statement Moo's comment is apposite: 'In this passage, we must remember that the Son is the subject of the entire statement in vv. 3-4: It is the *Son* who is "appointed" Son. The tautologous nature of this statement reveals that being appointed Son has to do not with a change in essence — as if a person or human messiah becomes Son of God for the first time — but with a change in status or function'.[32]

The third matter to be explained is what the apostle means when describing Jesus Christ as 'appointed Son of God in power', implying that he is the one with power. Other translations render the text 'declared with power to be the Son of God', in which case 'with power' is linked with the participle 'declared/appointed', implying that the declaration that Jesus is the Son of God was made with power. Grammatically either translation is possible. However, Paul's statement in Philippians 2:6-11 that, following Jesus' willingness to humble himself even to death on a cross, God exalted him to the place of supreme authority, suggests that here in 1:4 it is better to think of Jesus being appointed to be the Son of God 'with power' rather than of being 'declared powerfully' to be the Son of God.[33] Wright com-

---

30. Cranfield, *Romans,* I, 61-62, observes: 'No clear example, either earlier than, or contemporary with, the NT, of its use in the sense "declare" or "show to be" has been adduced. This being so, it is probably right to conclude that the support for this interpretation afforded by various Greek Fathers is due to a doctrinal consideration rather than to their superior knowledge of Greek usage'.

31. But see Leon Morris, *The Epistle to the Romans* (PNTC; Grand Rapids: Eerdmans, 1988), 45, who says: 'K. L. Schmidt argues that there is no great urgency to decide between "declaration or decree" and "appointment and institution" because "a divine declaration is the same as a divine appointment: God's *verbum* is *efficax*. It would seem that *declared* is the better way to understand the expression, but that "appointed" is possible in a sense which safeguards the truth that Jesus was Son of God before as well as after the resurrection'. Chip Anderson, 'Romans 1:1-5 and the Occasion of the Letter: The Solution to the Two-Congregation Problem in Rome', *TrinJ* 14 N.S. (1993) 32, commenting on Paul's statement that Christ is 'appointed' Son of God, cites L. C. Allen, who argues: 'The *huiou theou* ("Son of God") in v. 4 is most likely derived from Ps 2:7, "You are my Son", the coronation "decree" of Yahweh. Thus Jesus was "decreed", in the plan and promises of God, to be his Son. This understanding of the declaration is confirmed by the fact that such terminology was already used in early Christian preaching concerning Jesus. In Acts 10:42 Peter declares that Jesus was *ho hōrismenos hypo tou theou* ("the one appointed by God") as Judge. And again, in Acts 17:31, Paul himself proclaims that God had fixed a day to judge the world *en andri hō hōrisen* ("through a man whom he appointed"; cf. Luke 22:22; Acts 2:23; 11:29; 17:26). Thus it seems likely that the background to Paul's statement is found in the promise announced in 2 Sam 7:5-16, where God foretold a future Davidic king, and in Psalm 2, where God decrees that an anointed Davidic king shall be called his "Son"'.

32. Moo, *Romans,* 48.

33. Dunn, *Romans 1–8,* 14, comments: '"In power" was presumably important to Paul. It indicated that Jesus' divine sonship (v 3) had been "upgraded" or "enhanced" by the resurrection, so that he shared more fully in the very power of God, not simply in status

bines both these alternatives when he says: 'Jesus was declared to be son of God "in power". This phrase seems to refer *both* to the power of God that raised Jesus from the dead (see 1 Cor 6:14; 15:24, 43; 2 Cor 13:4; Eph 1:19-20; Phil 2:10) *and* that thereby declared his identity as Messiah, and to the powerful nature of his sonship, through which he confronts all the powers of the world, up to and including death itself, with the news of a different and more effective type of power altogether' (italics added).[34]

Fourth, we need to ask in what sense it was 'by his resurrection from the dead' that Jesus Christ was appointed Son of God in power. This implies that Jesus, through the Spirit, was appointed to be the Son of God by means of his resurrection from the dead. This is possible (even though in Paul's writings the Holy Spirit is never the *agent* who raises Jesus from the dead) because in 8:11 Paul does speak of the Spirit as the *means* by which God raised Jesus from the dead. In this case we could interpret 1:4 to mean that through the Spirit, by the resurrection, God appointed Jesus to be the Son of God with power. The alternative translation is 'from the time of the resurrection'. In this case it is not 'by' the resurrection that Jesus is appointed to be the Son of God with power, but rather 'from the time of' the resurrection he has been appointed to be the Son of God with power. The difference between these two interpretations is in the end not great. If it was from the time of the resurrection that Jesus was appointed to be the Son of God in power, then it means that the resurrection was determinative for this appointment.[35]

Fifth, what is the significance here of the title 'Son of God'? This title is now known to have had messianic connotations in first-century Judaism. One of the Dead Sea Scrolls, 4QFlor 1:10-14 (dating from the first century B.C.), cites God's promise to David to establish the throne of his son (2 Samuel 7:12-13) and interprets it as a promise for the end time when the Branch of David will arise to save Israel.[36] At a minimum, therefore, being declared to be the Son of God means being declared to be the Messiah. This is remi-

---

at God's right hand . . . but in "executive authority", able to act on and through people in the way Paul implies elsewhere (e.g., 8:10; 1 Cor 15:45; Gal 2:20; Col 2:6-7)'. Interestingly, both [Pseudo-]Constantius and Augustine relate 'in power' to Christ being born of the Holy Spirit and the Virgin Mary (*ACCSR*, 10).

34. Wright, 'Romans', 418-19.

35. Wright, 'Romans', 419, says: 'The resurrection told Paul not only who Jesus was (the Messiah), but also what time it was (the start of the "age to come")'.

36. The text of 4QFlorilegium may be found in G. Vermes, *The Complete Dead Sea Scrolls in English* (London: Penguin, 1998), 493-96. Another fragment from Qumran, 4Q246, known as the 'Son of God fragment', refers to 'the son of God' and 'the son of the Most high', and speaks of an eternal kingdom, all of which is remarkably paralleled by what is found in Luke 1:32-35 ('he will be great and will be called the Son of the Most High'; 'be called the Son of God'; 'he will reign . . . his kingdom will never end'). This has led C. A. Evans, 'Son of God Text (4Q246)', *DNTB* 1134-37, to recognize messianic overtones in this fragment, but debate continues over the intended identity of 'the son of God' in the fragment (cf. discussion in Vermes, *Dead Sea Scrolls*, 576-77).

niscent of the early Christian preaching recorded in Acts 2:32-36 in which the resurrection was proclaimed as God's vindication of the crucified Jesus as the true Messiah (cf. Acts 2:36: 'Therefore let all Israel be assured of this: God has made this Jesus, whom you crucified, both Lord and Messiah').

Finally, God's Son, the message about whom constitutes the gospel, is now explicitly identified as 'Jesus Christ our Lord'. Expressions like this which combine the name Jesus and/or Christ with 'Lord' (e.g., 'the Lord Jesus Christ', 'Jesus our Lord', 'our Lord Jesus Christ', 'Christ Jesus our Lord', 'the Lord Jesus', 'our Lord Christ', 'our Lord Jesus') are Paul's favorite designations for Jesus in Romans (cf. 1:4, 7; 4:24; 5:1, 11, 21; 6:23; 7:25; 8:39; 13:14; 14:14; 15:6, 30; 16:18, 20). By referring to the Lord as 'Jesus *Christ*' Paul is implying that Jesus is the Jewish Messiah. By speaking of Jesus as *Lord,* Paul is not only acknowledging him as his master (cf. 1:1) but also underscoring his deity, for Paul unhesitatingly cites passages in the OT where the title 'Lord' refers to Yahweh and applies them to Jesus (10:13/Joel 2:32; 14:11/Isa 45:23).

The description of Jesus Christ our Lord *(kyrios)* as the one declared to be the Son of God with power, when heard by the believers in Rome, the imperial capital, would have very significant connotations. Caesar claimed to be the *kyrios* with political power, and those who acknowledged Jesus as *kyrios* were acknowledging a greater power. He was not only the Lord of individual believers, but also the one who would subdue all political as well as spiritual powers beneath his feet (cf. Phil 2:9-11: those 'in heaven and on earth and under the earth'), and indeed the one who would renew the whole created order (8:19-21).[37]

ADDITIONAL NOTE:
PAUL'S USE OF CREDAL MATERIAL IN 1:3-4

The arguments in support of the view that Paul employs creedal material in 1:3-4 have been listed conveniently by Poythress,[38] and can be described as follows: First, the parallelism of the two well-balanced participial phrases ('who . . . was a descendant of David' and 'who . . . was appointed the Son of God') is typical of credal formulae. Similar parallelism is found in two other places in the Pauline corpus:

> He appeared in the flesh,
>   was vindicated by the Spirit,
>   was seen by angels,
>   was preached among the nations,

---

37. Cf. N. T. Wright, 'A Fresh Perspective on Paul?' *BJRL* 83 (2001) 35-36.
38. Vern S. Poythress, 'Is Romans 1[3-4] a *Pauline* Confession after All?' *ExpTim* 87 (1975-76) 180.

was believed on in the world,
was taken up in glory.   (1 Tim 3:16)

Remember Jesus Christ,
    raised from the dead,
    descended from David.
This is my gospel.   (2 Tim 2:8)

Second, reference to Jesus' Davidic ancestry is rare in Paul's writings. The only other explicit reference is found in the credal statement of 2 Timothy 2:8,[39] and this suggests that Paul is drawing upon traditional credal material in 1:3-4 rather than engaging in his own free composition. Third, Paul's use of 'flesh' and 'spirit' in these verses is uncharacteristic, suggesting that he is using traditional credal material. Fourth, by saying that Jesus was appointed Son of God from the time of his resurrection implies an adoptionist Christology which is at variance with Christology elsewhere in Paul's letters, where preexistence and incarnation are implied (cf. Gal 4:4; Col 1:15-17; Rom 1:3-4; and possibly Phil 2:6-8). Fifth, if 1:3-4 is Paul's own statement of the content of the gospel, it would be striking in its failure to include any reference to the crucifixion, which was so central to the apostle's understanding of the gospel (cf. 1 Cor 1:13, 17-18, 23; 2:2; Gal 3:1; 5:11; 6:12, 14; Eph 2:16; Phil 2:8; 3:18; Col 1:20; 2:14). Sixth, the expressions 'appointed the Son of God' and 'Spirit of holiness' are rare in Paul's writings, also suggesting that he is drawing on other material here.

While points 3 and 4 are subject to criticism (Paul uses 'flesh' and 'spirit' to depict *both* the constituent parts of human nature *and* the contrast between human nature and the Holy Spirit; therefore, it is difficult to be dogmatic about what is uncharacteristic; we have already seen that adoptionist interpretations of 1:3-4 are unwarranted), the other points do make a reasonable case for saying that in 1:3-4 Paul is citing early Christian credal material. His purpose in doing so could well be to show his Roman audience that he holds orthodox Christian convictions, and so gain a better hearing for what is to follow in his letter. This is a widely held view among interpreters of Romans,[40] though it has been challenged again in recent times. Whitsett argues that, rather than drawing upon early Christian credal formulae, in 1:3-4 Paul is combining early Christian exegesis of 2 Samuel 7 and Psalm 2 to speak of Jesus' Davidic ancestry and his universal rule. Whitsett points to Romans 15:12 ('Isaiah says, "The Root of Jesse will spring up, one who will arise to rule over the nations; in him the Gentiles will hope"'), where these two themes are brought together again,

39. There is an allusion to Jesus' Davidic ancestry in Rom 15:12, where Paul cites Isa 11:10 and applies its reference to 'the Root of Jesse [David's father]' to Jesus.

40. So, e.g., Rudolf Bultmann, *Theology of the New Testament*, I (London: SCM, 1952), 49; Cranfield, *Romans*, I, 57-58; Dunn, *Romans 1–8*, 5; Ziesler, *Romans*, 60; Byrne, *Romans*, 43-45. Moo, *Romans*, 45-46.

to support his view that Paul reflected upon these passages and from his reflections composed 1:3-4.[41] There seems to be little doubt that Paul reflected upon these key passages and that this accounts for his appeal to the themes of Jesus' Davidic descent and his universal rule. However, what appears to be the credal form of 1:3-4 remains to be explained.

Poythress critiques the arguments put forward both in support of and against 1:3-4 being a citation of an early Christian creed. He argues that some compromise is required and concludes that 1:3-4 is Paul's own free composition, but that in composing it he has made use of traditional expressions and ideas that are also found in early creeds.[42] Wright's comment about this matter is deserving of attention: 'But it must be stressed, here and elsewhere, that the reason why Paul quoted things, if he did, was that they expressed exactly what he intended to say at the time. . . . Whether or not Paul wrote vv. 3-4 from scratch himself (and we must guard against assuming that a writer such as Paul was incapable of dictating an apparently formulaic statement off the top of his head, especially as he had had countless occasions to sum up his message orally before a wide variety of audiences), the passage as it stands offers a striking statement of that messianic view of Jesus that we shall discover at the heart of the letter'.[43]

1:5 Having defined the content of the gospel as that which concerns God's Son in 1:3-4, Paul proceeds to speak of his own apostleship: *Through him we received grace and apostleship to call all the Gentiles to the obedience that comes from faith for his name's sake.* Again a number of things call for comment. First, Paul indicates that it was 'through him' (lit. 'through whom'), meaning through Jesus Christ, God's Son, that he received grace and apostleship. It was on the Damascus Road that Paul was confronted by Christ and received his commission to be an apostle. Speaking of this event in Galatians 1:15-16, he says: 'God, who set me apart from my mother's womb and called me by his grace, was pleased to reveal his Son in me so that I might preach him among the Gentiles'. Paul's apostleship came 'through' Christ, but ultimately it came from God. It is not surprising, therefore, that Paul often speaks of himself as 'an apostle of Christ by the will of God' (cf. 1 Cor 1:1; 2 Cor 1:1; Eph 1:1; Col 1:1; 2 Tim 1:1) or 'an apostle of Christ Jesus by the command of God' (1 Tim 1:1), and that he says he is 'an apostle — sent not from men nor by man, but by Jesus Christ and God the Father' (Gal 1:1).

Second, Paul says, '*we* received grace and apostleship'. The reference to 'we' could be taken as a reference to Paul and his colleagues (he does not associate any of them with himself in the opening address [1:1], however,

---

41. Christopher G. Whitsett, 'Son of God, Seed of David: Paul's Messianic Exegesis in Romans 2:3-4 *(sic)*', *JBL* 119 (2000) 661-62.

42. Poythress, 'Is Romans 1³⁻⁴ a *Pauline* Confession after All?' 180-82.

43. Wright, 'Romans', 416-17.

although according to 16:21 Timothy was with him when he wrote). Alternatively, the 'we' could be a writer's literary plural. Käsemann regards the
plural 'we' as 'undoubtedly literary and gives an official emphasis', adding
that in this letter 'Paul approaches the Roman community as an individual,
and he does this consciously, since he intends to give an account of his own
message'.[44] Alternatively, Dunn writes: 'Somewhat unexpectedly (in view
of v 1) Paul links others with himself — *we* received. He does not regard
himself as the sole apostle to the Gentiles, which would in any case have
been a difficult position to maintain in writing to a largely Gentile church
which he had not founded'.[45] Jewett comments along similar lines: 'I infer
that Paul wishes to convey solidarity with the apostles whose emissaries
had established the house and tenement churches in Rome in the decades
before the writing of this letter. Whereas some of the twelve apostles restricted their mission to the land of Israel, remaining as leaders of the Jerusalem church, the missionaries who reached Rome obviously shared Paul's
calling to a Gentile mission. In 16:7, for example, Paul greets a married couple currently ministering in Rome by the name of Andronicus and Junia,
who are "prominent among the apostles"'.[46]

'Grace and apostleship' is a hendiadys, that is, an expression using
two words to convey one concept. Paul does not mean that he received
grace *and* apostleship, but rather that he received the grace *of* apostleship.
Thus in Ephesians 4:7, 10 Paul says that 'to each one of us grace has been
given as Christ apportioned it, . . . and it was he who gave some to be apostles', that is, he gave some the grace of apostleship. Commenting upon
'grace and apostleship', Origen says: 'For he [the Father] gives grace to his
apostles, by which those who are struggling may say: I worked harder than
any of them, though it was not I but the grace of God which is with me. . . .
It was only through the grace which had been given to the apostles that the
gentiles, who were strangers from the covenant of God and from the life of
Israel, could believe in the gospel'.[47]

Third, Paul says that he received grace and apostleship 'to call all the
Gentiles to the obedience that comes from faith' (lit. 'for obedience of faith
among all the Gentiles'). As an apostle he was to bring about 'obedience of
faith'. This phrase is susceptible to a number of translations/interpreta-
tions.[48] The two main alternatives are to construe 'of faith' as (i) a genitive

44. Ernst Käsemann, *Commentary on Romans* (Grand Rapids: Eerdmans/London:
SCM, 1980), 14.
45. Dunn, *Romans 1–8*, 16.
46. Jewett, *Romans*, 109.
47. 'Commentary on the Epistle to the Romans' (*ACCSR*, 11-12).
48. Cranfield, *Romans*, I, 66, lists the following seven alternatives: (i) 'obedience to the
faith' (i.e., to faith in the sense of *fides quae creditur*, the body of doctrine accepted); (ii) 'obedience to faith' (i.e., to the authority of faith); (iii) 'obedience to God's faithfulness attested
in the gospel'; (iv) 'the obedience which faith works'; (v) 'the obedience required by faith';
(vi) 'believing obedience'; (vii) 'the obedience which consists in faith'. Cranfield notes that
'the first three of these interpretations assume that the genitive is objective, the fourth and

of origin and interpret the phrase, as the NIV does, to mean 'obedience that comes from faith', or (ii) as a genitive of apposition and interpret it to mean 'obedience that consists in faith'. Both options receive support from statements Paul makes elsewhere. The first is supported by such passages as 6:16; Eph 6:1, 5; Phil 2:12; Col 3:20, 22; and 2 Thess 3:14, which presuppose that obedience to godly instruction should issue from faith in Christ. The second finds support in passages like 6:17; 10:16; 15:18-20; 16:25-26; and 2 Thess 1:8, which speak of obedience in terms of the call of the gospel to believe in God's Son, that is, obedience that consists in faith. The question is how should we interpret 'the obedience of faith' in 1:5.

We get some help by examining the only other use of the phrase 'obedience of faith' in Paul's writings — in the closing doxology of Romans: 'Now to him who is able to establish you in accordance with my gospel, the message I proclaim about Jesus Christ, in keeping with the revelation of the mystery hidden for long ages past, but now revealed and made known through the prophetic writings by the command of the eternal God, so that all the Gentiles might come to the obedience that comes from faith' [lit. 'for obedience of faith for all nations'] — to the only wise God be glory forever through Jesus Christ! Amen' (16:25-27). In the immediate context the 'obedience of faith' here is linked with Paul's gospel and the proclamation of Jesus Christ, suggesting that obedience of faith is primarily the obedience that consists in faith in the gospel. In 15:18-19, while not using the exact phrase 'obedience of faith', Paul can speak of what Christ accomplished through him 'in leading the Gentiles to obey God' (lit. 'for obedience of Gentiles') through his proclamation of the gospel of Christ. Again obedience appears to be acceptance of the gospel call to believe in Christ, that is, the obedience that consists in faith. Accordingly, the refusal of Paul's Jewish contemporaries to believe in Christ can be described as disobedience, or, as Paul puts in 10:2-3, a refusal to submit to God's righteousness: 'For I can testify about them that they are zealous for God, but their zeal is not based on knowledge. Since they did not know the righteousness of God and sought to establish their own, they did not submit to God's righteousness' — a righteousness that comes through faith in Christ. All this supports the view that 'the obedience of faith' is best understood to mean 'the obedience that consists in faith'.

In its immediate context the 'obedience of faith' in 1:5 is linked with the grace of apostleship that Paul received to proclaim the gospel, suggesting that the obedience of faith here is to be understood primarily as obedience to the gospel's call to believe in God's Son, that is, the obedience that consists in faith. This receives further support from the fact that Paul speaks apparently synonymously when he says, 'I thank my God through Jesus Christ for all of you, because your *faith* is being reported all over the

---

fifth that it is subjective, the sixth that it is adjectival, and the last that it is a genitive of apposition or definition'.

world' (1:8; italics added), and 'everyone has heard about your *obedience,* so I rejoice because of you' (16:19; italics added).

However, care must be taken not to assume that faith *consisting* in obedience can be separated from faith *expressing* itself in obedience. As noted above, there are many places in Paul's writings, not least in Romans, that indicate that obedience to godly instruction should issue from faith in Christ. It is not surprising, then, that a number of scholars adopt what may be described as a 'both and' interpretation of the obedience of faith. Garlington argues that Paul chose an ambiguous phrase so he could express two ideas at the same time. He contends that both 'obedience consisting in faith' and 'obedience issuing from faith' are too restrictive to convey Paul's meaning. He concludes that 'faith's obedience' or 'believing obedience' are better translations of this phrase and preserve the intended ambiguity.[49] Schreiner says: 'It is unlikely, though, that "the obedience of faith" should be confined to a single act of obedience that occurred when the gospel was first believed. Nor should faith and obedience be sundered as if Christians could have the former without the latter. . . . The belief first exercised upon conversion is validated as one continues to believe and obey (11:20-22)'.[50] Similarly, Dunn observes: 'The genitive construction is probably to be taken as embracing both the sense "response which is faith" and "obedience which stems from faith" — "interchangeable ideas"'.[51]

Fourth, Paul says that the purpose of his apostleship is to 'to call all the Gentiles to the obedience that comes from faith'. The word translated 'Gentiles' in the NIV can mean 'nations', 'peoples', or 'Gentiles'. Thus, on the face of it, the sphere of Paul's apostleship could either be all nations and peoples (including both Jews and Gentiles) or be limited to all Gentiles. When Paul uses the word elsewhere in Romans most frequently, it means Gentiles as distinct from Jews (1:13; 2:14, 24; 3:29; 9:24, 30; 10:19; 11:11-13, 25; 15:7-12, 16, 18, 27; 16:24), but in a couple of places it seems to include both Jews and Gentiles (4:17-18; 16:26). In the light of the meaning it most frequently carries, and the fact that Paul was called specifically to be an apostle to the Gentiles (cf. Gal 1:16; 2:6-9), we can safely conclude that here in 1:5 Paul is speaking of the scope of his apostleship as among Gentiles. This, of course, does not mean that he felt no responsibility for Jews, or that he did not minister among them. Romans 9:1-5; 10:1 reflect his intense concern for the salvation of his fellow Jews, Acts 13:14-46; 14:1; 17:1-4, 10-12, 17; 18:1-8, 19-20; 19:8-10 speaks of Paul's ministry in Jewish synagogues in one city after another, and 2 Corinthians 11:24 reflects the cost he paid for doing so.[52]

---

49. D. B. Garlington, 'The Obedience of Faith in the Letter to the Romans, Part I: The Meaning of *hypakoē pisteōs* (Rom 1:5; 16:26)', *WTJ* 52 (1990) 224.

50. Schreiner, *Romans,* 35.

51. Dunn, *Romans 1–8,* 17. Similarly Moo, *Romans,* 51-53.

52. Cf. Colin G. Kruse, 'The Price Paid for a Ministry among Gentiles: Paul's Persecution at the Hands of the Jews', in *Worship, Theology and Ministry in the Early Church: Essays in*

Fifth, the purpose of Paul's apostleship was to bring about the obedience of faith among all the Gentiles 'for his name's sake', that is, for the sake of Jesus Christ. It was through Jesus Christ that he received the grace of apostleship, and it was for the sake of Christ primarily that he carried out his apostolic ministry. Like the Jewish envoy/apostle (*šālîaḥ*) who carried out instructions for and on behalf of his principal, so Paul carried out his apostleship for and on behalf of Christ. From this we may infer that it was the desire of Jesus Christ himself to call Gentiles to the obedience of faith (cf. Matt 28:18-20; Luke 24:46-48; John 10:16; Acts 1:6-8), and this he effected through Paul.[53]

1:6 Having informed his audience about his calling as an apostle to bring about the obedience of faith among all the Gentiles, Paul immediately adds, *And you also are among those Gentiles who are called to belong to Jesus Christ* (lit. 'among whom you are also Jesus Christ's called ones').[54] Paul deliberately (the 'you' is emphatic) includes (the majority of) his audience among the Gentiles for whom he has apostolic responsibility, thereby paving the way for him to address them in this letter.[55] However, Paul recognizes that they are not just Gentiles, but Gentiles who, in response to the gospel, 'belong to Jesus Christ'.

1:7 After the first element of his greeting, the long self-introduction (1:1-6), Paul comes to the second element where he identifies, quite briefly, those whom he is addressing: *To all in Rome who are loved by God and called to be his holy people* (lit. 'to all who are in Rome, beloved of God, called ones, saints').[56] Paul has placed 'all' in the emphatic position, emphasizing that it is to 'all' the members of the Roman congregations that he addresses his letter. It was not just to the leaders who are named in chapter 16,[57] nor only

---

Honor of Ralph P. Martin, ed. Michael J. Wilkins and Terence Paige (JSNTSup 87; Sheffield: Sheffield Academic Press, 1992), 260-72.

53. Cranfield, *Romans,* I, 67, adopts a different view: *'hyper tou onomatos autou* is better understood as meaning "for the sake of His name" in the sense of "for the glory of His name" (i.e., in order that He Himself may be known and glorified). . . . It is a reminder that the true end of the preaching of the gospel and of the winning of men to faith is not just the good of those to whom the preaching is directed, but also — and above all — the glorification of Christ, of God'. Similarly, Schreiner, *Romans,* 35-36.

54. Cf. Greenlee, 'Some "Called" People', 49-51.

55. A. B. du Toit, 'Persuasion in Romans 1:1-17', *BZ* 33 (1989) 194, points out correctly that in 1:5-6 'Paul uses what classical logicians would call a syllogism, more specifically, an *enthymeme,* which is a syllogism with one premise omitted. The full syllogism would have been something like this:

  A. Paul has received the privileged task of preaching the gospel to the heathen nations.
  B. The inhabitants of Rome formed part of the heathen nations.
  C. Therefore it was also Paul's task to preach the gospel to the inhabitants of Rome'.

56. Cf. Greenlee, 'Some "Called" People', 49-51.
57. Cranfield, *Romans,* I, 68.

the Gentile majority but also the Jewish minority.[58] Dunn says that 'all' is 'given a place of emphasis, possibly suggesting a degree of factionalism (cf. 16:17-20), or at least that there was some tension among the different Christian groups in Rome'.[59]

The words 'in Rome' are missing here (and in 1:15) from a few manuscripts,[60] but are widely supported in other manuscripts, including early and reliable witnesses,[61] and should be regarded as original.[62] The fact that Paul says he wants to visit the members of his audience when en route from Jerusalem to Spain supports the view that the letter was addressed to the Christian community in Rome, and that therefore 'in Rome' should be regarded as original.

The brevity of Paul's address, devoid of any personal references, reflects the fact that the church in Rome was not one he founded or had previously visited. He knows that all who believe in Christ are dear to God and so addresses them as those 'loved by God' (lit. 'God's beloved'). He also knows that those who believe in Christ have been called and set apart for God, and so addresses them as those 'called to be his holy people' (lit. 'called saints' or 'saints [who are] called [by God]'). The one who calls believers (to be his holy people) is God himself (cf. Gal 1:6; 5:8). He issues his call though the preaching of the gospel (cf. 1 Thess 1:4-5; 2 Thess 2:14), using human agents. This call is according to the purpose and grace of God (cf. 2 Tim 1:9), and those whom he calls are those whom he has predestined for salvation (8:30). They include both Jews and Gentiles (9:24-26; 1 Cor 1:24) and for the most part are the lowly, not the exalted (cf. 1 Cor 1:26).[63]

Paul uses the expression 'holy people' or 'saints' extensively in his letters as a designation for believers.[64] Essentially it means people who are set apart for, or consecrated to, God. The idea of Christians being holy has its roots in the OT, where Israel is spoken of as holy, meaning set apart as God's special people. Paul expects believers to be 'holy' not only in the

---

58. Witherington, *Romans*, 36.

59. Dunn, *Romans 1-8*, 19.

60. G it[g] Origen[acc,to,1739]

61. P[10,26vid] ℵ A B C D[abs1] Ψ 6 33 81 104 256 263 424 436 459 1175 1241 1319 1506 1573 1739 1852 1881 1912[vid] 1962 2127 2200 2464 *Byz* [KLP] *Lect* it[ar,b,d,(mon),0] vg syr[p,h,pal] cop[(sa),boh] arm eth geo slav Origen[gr,lat] Chrysostom Theodoret Ambrosiaster Pelagius Augustine.

62. The Committee preparing the fourth revised edition of *The Greek New Testament* (UBS, 1983) suggests that the omission of *en Romē* in a few manuscripts can be explained 'either as the result of an accident in transcription, or, more probably, as a deliberate excision, made in order to show that the letter is of general, not local, application' (Metzger, ed., *A Textual Commentary, ad loc.*).

63. For a fuller discussion of the calling of believers, see Kruse, 'Call/Calling', *DPL*, 84-85.

64. Cf. Rom 1:7; 8:27; 12:13; 15:25-26, 31; 16:2, 15; 1 Cor 6:1-2; 14:33; 16:1, 15; 2 Cor 1:1; 8:4; 9:1, 12; Eph 1:1, 15, 18; 2:19; 3:8, 18; 4:12; 5:3; 6:18; Phil 1:1; 4:21-22; Col 1:2, 4, 12, 26; 1 Thess 3:13; 2 Thess 1:10; 1 Tim 5:10.

sense of being set apart but also in the sense of being pure and blameless (cf. Rom 12:1; 1 Cor 7:34; Eph 1:4; 5:3, 27; Col 1:22; 1 Thess 3:13).[65]

Following the second element of his greeting, the brief address (1:7a), Paul comes, in 1:7b, to the third and final element, the actual greeting itself: *Grace and peace to you from God our Father and from the Lord Jesus Christ*. In ancient Greco-Roman letters the actual greeting was simply *chairein* ('greetings'). Stowers points out that as Paul's word 'grace' *(charis)* is related to the traditional 'greeting' *(chairein)*, 'his salutation reads like a kind of Christian play on the standard formula'.[66] However, for Paul it would have been more than a play on words. The grace of God is a very rich concept in his writings, not least in Romans, having many different nuances of meaning depending upon the context in which it is used. It can mean a gracious deed carried out by God (5:20-21), divine favor shown to people (11:5-6), God's beneficence dispensed to people (12:3, 6), or a privileged status that people enjoy (5:2, 17).[67] In the context of 1:7 Paul is invoking the divine favor upon his audience.

Formulae like 'peace be with you' were used in the OT for greetings from God to human beings (Judg 6:22-23; Isa 57:19), as invocations of God's peace upon people/Israel (Pss 29:11; 125:5; 128:6), and for greetings between human beings (1 Chr 12:18; Ezra 5:7; Ps 122:7-8; Tob 12:17; 2 Macc 1:1). In Israel, the basic meaning of 'peace' was something like 'well-being', and it was thought of as social rather than individual well-being.[68] In the NT similar formulae were used by Jesus when greeting his disciples (Luke 24:36; John 20:19, 21, 26), and when giving instructions to his disciples concerning the way they were to approach people on their Galilean mission (Matt 10:12-13: 'As you enter the home, give it your greeting. If the home is deserving, let your peace rest on it; if it is not, let your peace return to you'). Here in 1:7, however, the traditional greeting is transformed into an invocation: 'Grace and peace to you from God our Father and from the Lord Jesus Christ'. Peace, like grace, is a very rich concept for the apostle Paul. God is

---

65. Morris, *Romans*, 53, comments: 'We should not overlook the plural. We sometimes speak of an individual man or woman as "a saint" or refer to "St. Peter", or "St. Mary", or the like. This is not a New Testament usage. The word is never used there of any individual believer. It is always plural when used of believers, and the plural points to believers as a group, a community set apart for God. Again, the term does not convey the idea of outstanding ethical achievement which we usually understand by "saintliness". While the importance of right living is insisted on and may even be implied with this very term, the main thrust is not there. It is rather in the notion of belonging to God'. Dunn, *Romans 1–8*, 20, asserts: 'To describe nonproselyte (= non–law-keeping) Gentiles as "saints" is indicative of the boldness of Paul's argument in the letter over against those more characteristically Jewish views. In more general terms the fact that Gentiles should count themselves *hagioi* ['saints', 'holy ones'] when they offered no sacrifices, called no man "priest", practiced no rite of circumcision, must have been puzzling to most pagans and offensive to most Jews'.

66. Stanley K. Stowers, *Letter Writing in Greco-Roman Antiquity* (Philadelphia: Westminster, 1986), 21.

67. BAGD, *ad loc*.

68. Cf. Dunn, *Romans 1–8*, 20.

described as 'the God of peace' (15:33; 16:20). The gospel itself was an offer of peace with God — an offer proclaimed by Christ through his apostles (Eph. 2:17: 'He came and preached peace to you who were far away and peace to those who were near'). Further, Paul says, God bestows glory, honor, and peace upon all who do good, both Jew and Gentile (2:10), those who are justified by faith enjoy 'peace with God' (5:1), and a person whose mind is controlled by the Spirit enjoys 'life and peace' (8:6). The kingdom of God is described as a matter of 'righteousness, peace and joy in the Holy Spirit' (14:17), and believers are to 'make every effort to do what leads to peace' (14:19). Towards the end of the letter Paul invokes God's peace again upon his audience with the words, 'May the God of hope fill you with all joy and peace as you trust in him, so that you may overflow with hope by the power of the Holy Spirit' (15:13).

It is significant that when Paul invokes grace and peace upon his audience, he does so nearly always in the form in which it is found here (cf. 1 Cor 1:3; 2 Cor 1:2; Gal 1:3; Eph 1:2; Phil 1:2; 2 Thess 1:2; Philem 3), and with only slight variations elsewhere (1 Thess 1:1; 1 Tim 1:2; 2 Tim 1:2). He invokes grace and peace from both God the Father and Jesus Christ our Lord, reflecting the fact that the grace and peace believers enjoy with God comes to them through, and only through, what God has done in Christ (cf. 2 Cor 5:18-21).

Fitzmyer suggests that Paul's 'grace and peace' 'echoes the priestly blessing pronounced by the sons of Aaron over the Israelites: 'The LORD bless you and keep you; the LORD make his face shine on you and be gracious to you; the LORD turn his face toward you and give you peace' (Num 6:24-26). He says: 'If Paul's greeting echoes this blessing, then "grace" would represent God's merciful bounty or covenantal favour . . . revealed in Christ Jesus, and "peace" would connote the fullness of prosperity and well-being characteristic of God's goodness to Israel of old. For all this Paul prays: that it may come to the Christians of Rome from God our Father and the Lord Jesus Christ as the sum of evangelical blessings'.[69]

ADDITIONAL NOTE: PAUL'S APOSTLESHIP

Information gleaned from uses of the word 'apostle' in other Pauline letters reveals more of his understanding of his status and role as an apostle: he was one who had 'seen Jesus our Lord' (1 Cor 9:1); who was included among those whom God had appointed first in the church (1 Cor 12:28); in whose ministry the 'marks of a true apostle' were being performed (2 Cor 12:12); who had been sent, 'not from men nor by man, but by Jesus Christ and God the Father' (Gal 1:1); who, with other apostles and prophets, and

---

69. Fitzmyer, *Romans*, 228.

with Christ Jesus himself, formed the very foundation of the church (Eph 2:20); one to whom the mystery of Christ, hidden for ages past, had now been revealed (Eph 3:3-5); and who had been appointed 'a true and faithful teacher of the Gentiles' (1 Tim 2:7).

Elsewhere I have explored in detail Paul's understanding of apostleship, noting his strong sense of divine calling understood after the fashion of the calling of the OT prophets. His apostleship involved both a delegated authority and responsibility to represent his Lord — he called himself an ambassador of Christ, charged with responsibility for the interests of Christ among people, especially Gentiles. The language he used concerning the representative character of his apostolate suggests that he understood it in terms not unlike those used in relation to the Jewish *šālîaḥ* concept — as an agent representing his principal, and functioning with the authority of the principal insofar as he was carrying out his principal's commission. Paul's apostleship involved proclamation of the gospel and a demonstration of the power of God by signs and wonders as Christ continued his own witness and ministry through him. In these respects Paul's apostolic ministry differs little from Jesus' own ministry as reflected in the Synoptic Gospels. However, in other respects Paul's understanding of apostleship went beyond what we know of Jesus' conception of it. For example, Paul came to regard his apostolate as an integral part of God's activity in Christ for the salvation of humankind: God reconciled people to himself through Christ; Paul besought people, on behalf of Christ, to be reconciled to God. He saw his ministry as an apostle as an indispensable part of God's plan, for through it what was lacking in the affliction of the Christ was filled up.[70]

B. Paul's Prayer and Purpose for Writing, 1:8-17

> [8]*First, I thank my God through Jesus Christ for all of you, because your faith is being reported all over the world.* [9]*God, whom I serve in my spirit in preaching the gospel of his Son, is my witness how constantly I remember you* [10]*in my prayers at all times; and I pray that now at last by God's will the way may be opened for me to come to you.*
>
> [11]*I long to see you so that I may impart to you some spiritual gift to make you strong —* [12]*that is, that you and I may be mutually encouraged by each other's faith.* [13]*I do not want you to be unaware, brothers and sisters, that I planned many times to come to you (but have been prevented from doing so until now) in order that I might have a harvest among you, just as I have had among the other Gentiles.*
>
> [14]*I am obligated both to Greeks and non-Greeks, both to the wise and the*

---

70. Colin G. Kruse, *New Testament Models for Ministry: Jesus and Paul* (Nashville: Thomas Nelson, 1983), 78-82, 90-93, 106-11, 126-28, 136-40, 145-51, 160-69, 177-79.

foolish. ¹⁵*That is why I am so eager to preach the gospel also to you who are in Rome.*

¹⁶*For I am not ashamed of the gospel, because it is the power of God that brings salvation to everyone who believes: first to the Jew, then to the Gentile.* ¹⁷*For in the gospel the righteousness of God is revealed — a righteousness that is by faith from first to last, just as it is written: 'The righteous will live by faith'.*

Following his expansive greeting (1:1-7), here in 1:8-17 Paul informs his audience of his prayers for them, both thanksgiving for their faith (1:8) and his request that a way might be opened for him to visit them (1:9-10). He says he wants to impart some spiritual gift to them but emphasizes that this sharing will be a mutual affair. He expects to be encouraged by his audience's faith just as he hopes to strengthen them by the impartation of some spiritual gift (1:11-12). He tells them that many times previously he had wanted to visit and have 'a harvest' among them as he has had among other Gentiles, but had so far been prevented from doing so (1:13). He wants to visit them because he is under obligation to preach the gospel to them (1:14-15). He is eager to do this, for he is not ashamed of this gospel because it is the power of God for the salvation for all who believe, Greeks as well as Jews, for in it the righteousness of God is revealed (1:16-17).

There is a striking similarity between the ideas expressed in 1:8-17 that precedes the body of the letter, and those expressed in 15:14-33 that follows it. In both places Paul: (a) affirms his audience, giving thanks for their faith, which is known 'all over the world' (1:8), and telling them that he is convinced that they are 'full of goodness, filled with knowledge and competent to instruct one another' (15:14); (b) speaks of his ministry of gospel preaching among the Gentiles (1:9, 16-17 par. 15:16); (c) tells of his prayerful longing to visit them in Rome (1:10) and announces that he hopes to do so after his visit to Jerusalem when en route to Spain (15:22-24); (d) assures them that his purpose for making a visit is for mutual encouragement/refreshment, both his and theirs (1:11-12 par. 15:24, 32); and (e) explains that hitherto he has been hindered from visiting them (1:13), prevented from doing so because of the demands of his mission in the eastern Mediterranean, but that this has now been completed, enabling him to make his way first to Jerusalem and then to Rome en route to Spain (15:22, 25, 28). The way these matters are expressed prior to and following the body of the letter, thus bracketing the theological argument (1:18–15:13), supports the view that 1:8-17 functions as a *propositio* setting out the purpose of the letter, and 15:14-33 functions as a *peroratio* summing up what has been the main thrust of the letter.

1:8   Adopting standard letter-writing practice, Paul establishes rapport with his audience by saying: *First, I thank my God through Jesus Christ for all of you, because your faith is being reported all over the world.* Traditionally this part of a letter was concerned with the health and well-being of the recipients, but in this case it is concerned with their faith. The 'first' has no corresponding 'second'. The NEB renders it, 'Let me begin'. . . .

It is noteworthy that Paul addresses his thanksgiving to '*my* God' (he does so also in 1 Cor 1:4; Phil 1:3), and in other places, too, he refers to God as '*my* God' (2 Cor 12:21; Phil 4:19). This reflects Paul's sense of intimacy with God.[1] Something similar is reflected in respect to Paul's relationship to the Lord Jesus Christ when he speaks of him as the one 'who loved *me* and gave himself for *me*' (Gal 2:20). When Paul gives thanks to his God, it is 'through Jesus Christ' (cf. 7:25). Such a relationship with God is possible only 'through Jesus Christ' — for he is the one through whom believers receive reconciliation with God (cf. 5:11).

Origen notes that Paul gives thanks 'for all of you', something the apostle does in letters when he has no grave faults in his audience to reprove; 'but where he criticizes people or reproves them he does not add to his thanksgiving that he gives thanks for them all — see, e.g., 1 Corinthians or Colossians. In Galatians he does not even give thanks at all, because he is surprised that they have so quickly abandoned the gospel that called them and chosen another one instead'.[2]

1:9-10   In these verses Paul assures his audience of his prayers for them. Such assurances of prayer are commonplace in the *exordia* of letters found among the ancient Greek papyri.[3] Their purpose was to establish rapport with the audience and engender a willingness on their part to give the letter a good hearing when it was read to them. Paul begins by saying, *[For] God . . . is my witness how constantly I remember you in my prayers at all times.* The conjunction 'for' is omitted by the NIV, obscuring somewhat the connection between 1:8 and 1:9 that Schreiner says 'signals that Paul's prayer of thanksgiving is linked with his desire to visit in verses 9-15 as an emissary of the gospel'.[4]

To assert something and call upon God as witness is tantamount to speaking under oath. Paul frequently uses oath formulae to stress the importance of something he wants to say (cf. 2 Cor 1:23; 1 Thess 2:5, 10; cf. Rom 9:1; 2 Cor 11:31; Gal 1:20), and for the most part he does so when speaking of what takes place in his inner life, for which there are no other witnesses. Käsemann says: 'it probably indicates that Paul did not know that Jesus prohibited oaths',[5] but it is more likely that Paul's use of oath formulae reflects the early church's understanding that Jesus' teaching was directed against inappropriate use of oaths rather constituting a blanket prohibition.

The God whom he calls as witness, Paul says, is the God *whom I serve*

---

1. Cf. Jewett, *Romans,* 119, who comments: 'the expression "my God" refers to the regent whom he serves. Far from claiming that God is Paul's possession, the "my" indicates the subordination of the servant to the master'.

2. 'Commentary on the Epistle to the Romans' (*ACCSR,* 16).

3. E.g., *P. Lond.* 42; *B.G.U.* 27, cited in Barrett, *New Testament Background,* 27-29.

4. Schreiner, *Romans,* 49.

5. Käsemann, *Romans,* 18.

in my spirit in preaching the gospel of his Son. This verb 'to serve' *(latreuō)* is used by Paul (1:9, 25; Phil 3:3; 2 Tim 1:3) and other NT writers (Matt 4:10; Luke 1:74; 2:37; 4:8; Acts 7:7, 42; 24:14; 26:7; 27:23; Heb 8:5; 9:9, 14; 10:2; 12:28; 13:10; Rev 7:15; 22:3), always in relation to the service or worship of God/gods. In the LXX too it is used almost exclusively in this way. Paul's use of this verb here in 1:9 indicates that he saw his apostolic ministry as a form of service to/worship of God.[6]

The NIV describes Paul's service as something carried out 'in my spirit'. In other places where Paul refers to 'my spirit' it signifies his own human spirit, not the Holy Spirit (cf. 1 Cor 14:14; 2 Cor 2:13), and therefore we should understand it in this way here also. Cranfield lists seven interpretations for 'in my spirit'[7] before concluding that when Paul says he serves God 'in my spirit', he is referring to his ministry of prayer. In the immediate context, where Paul is assuring his audience of his prayers for them, such a suggestion is feasible.[8] Fitzmyer comments: 'Paul does not mean he worships God only inwardly. His cultic service is manifested in his evangelical preaching; to proclaim Christ Jesus is for Paul an act of worship that he directs with his spirit to God himself (see 15:15-16). Yet Paul's very prayer for the Christians of Rome is an integral part of his worship of God'.[9] Ziesler adopts the view that spirit 'refers to the divine in-breathing, or else the human self as quickened by God (cf. Rom, 8:1-11). It thus has the sort of meaning we should indicate by giving the word a capital letter: Spirit/Pneuma. It is possible, therefore, that here Paul is saying that he serves God by means of God's own empowering'.[10]

Paul says that he serves God in his spirit 'in preaching the gospel of

6. In 15:15-16, in similar vein, Paul describes himself as 'a minister *(leitourgos)* of Christ Jesus to the Gentiles' whom God 'gave the priestly duty of proclaiming the gospel of God, so that the Gentiles might become an offering acceptable to God, sanctified by the Holy Spirit'. This description of Paul and his ministry is replete with cultic terminology. The word *leitourgos* is sometimes (though not always) used in the LXX and the NT to denote those who perform service to God (cf. Ezra 7:24; Neh 10:39; Pss 103:21; 104:4; Isa 61:6; Heb 1:7; 8:2). In 15:16, where Paul describes himself as a minister *(leitourgos)* exercising 'the priestly duty of proclaiming the gospel of God', it is clearly used in this way. This is further underlined when Paul describes this priestly duty as necessary to ensure that 'the Gentiles might become an offering acceptable to God'. Paul was, as it were, presiding as a priest over the offering of the Gentiles to God.

7. Cranfield, *Romans*, I, 76-77: '(i) the Spirit of God dwelling in Paul; (ii) spiritual as opposed to carnal service; (iii) wholehearted service; (iv) sincere service as opposed to mere outward appearance; (v) the organ of service, that is, Paul's spirit; (vi) the fact that Paul's whole person is involved in service; (vii) his ministry of prayer, the inward aspect of his apostolic service'.

8. Early church fathers interpreted *en tō pneumati mou* as 'not in body nor in soul but in the best part of him, i.e., in spirit' (Origen, 'Commentary on the Epistle to the Romans'), 'not in the circumcision made with hands, nor in new moons, nor in the sabbath or the choice of foods, but in the spirit, that is, in the mind' (Ambrosiaster, 'Commentary on Paul's Epistles'), both cited in *ACCSR*, 19-20.

9. Fitzmyer, *Romans*, 244.

10. Ziesler, *Romans*, 66.

his Son' (lit. 'in the gospel of his Son'). This should be understood to mean, not that it is God's Son's gospel that Paul preaches, but that the gospel he preaches is the gospel concerning God's Son. This is spelled out unambiguously in 1:1-3, where Paul describes himself as 'an apostle . . . set apart for the gospel of God . . . regarding his Son'. Fitzmyer argues that 'the gospel of his Son 'is to be understood in the active sense of the preaching of the gospel . . . as in Gal 2:7; Phil 4:3, 15; 1 Cor 9:14b, 18b; 2 Cor 2:12; 8:18. "Of his Son" is an objective gen.: in the preaching of the gospel about his Son'.[11]

Paul appeals to the God whom he serves as a witness to the truth of *how constantly I remember you in my prayers at all times.* As mentioned above, such affirmations of prayer for the recipients of one's letter served to establish rapport with them and ensure a sympathetic hearing when the letter was read. In Paul's case, this affirmation was more than mere adherence to letter writing convention. He was affirming the reality of his continual prayer for his audience, something he was willing to state under oath, calling upon God as his witness.

As he prays, one of Paul's petitions is *that now at last by God's will the way may be opened for me to come to you.* The NRSV rendering of Paul's request follows the original more closely: 'asking that by God's will I may somehow at last succeed in coming to you'.[12] Later in this letter Paul will explain that hitherto he has been prevented from visiting them because of his mission in the eastern Mediterranean. However, he has completed that work and now wants to preach to those in the western Mediterranean (Spain), and that will allow him to fulfill his desire to visit the believers in Rome on the way and enjoy their company (15:20-24). Paul, who insists that his calling to be an apostle is by the will of God (1 Cor 1:1; 2 Cor 1:1; Eph 1:1; Col 1:1; 2 Tim 1:1), recognizes here in 1:10, as he does in 15:32, that the progress of his life and ministry is determined by the will of God, not simply his own plans. It is noteworthy that Paul had his desires, but these were subordinated to God's will. He was content to allow God to order his mission according to his will. The Acts of the Apostles tells how Paul's plans were redirected by the Holy Spirit, resulting in his crossing over into Macedonia to begin evangelism on the European continent (Acts 16:6-10). By God's will the way was opened eventually for Paul to reach Rome and

---

11. Fitzmyer, *Romans*, 245. Morris, *Romans*, 58, adopts the opposite position: 'Paul speaks of his service of God as "in the gospel" (not in preaching the gospel; he says nothing about preaching, but simply that he serves in his spirit in the gospel). The gospel is central to the living out of the Christian life as Paul sees it; really to understand the gospel and accept it means a change in one's whole life. It is central to Paul's preaching, certainly (cf. 1 Cor 1:17). But that is not his point here'.

12. The verb *euodōthēsomai*, rendered as 'the way may be opened for me' by the NIV, while in the passive voice (as it is always in the NT and the LXX) regularly has the active sense 'to prosper' or 'succeed' (BAGD, *ad loc.*). However, Jewett, *Romans*, 122, says: 'what Paul has regularly petitioned is that he be granted "good passage" to Rome, whereby the literal meaning of *euodoō*, "be on a good path", seems more relevant than the metaphorical meaning, "have good success"'.

preach the gospel there, but not in the way the apostle might have planned (Acts 25:9-12) nor in circumstances he might have chosen (Acts 28:16-31).

1:11-12 In these verses Paul explains what he hopes to achieve when he comes to Rome: *I long to see you so that I may impart to you some spiritual gift.* Paul's reference to his longing to see the believers in Rome is repeated in 15:23 ('I have been longing for many years to see you'), underscoring the heartfelt connection the apostle had with fellow believers, even when he did not know many of them in person.[13]

There is some indefiniteness in the expression 'some spiritual gift' which, it has been argued, would be appropriate in the light of the fact that Paul had no firsthand acquaintance with most of the members of the Roman churches, and at the time of writing would not know what precise gift he would want to offer them. It is susceptible to two main interpretations: (i) It denotes some ministerial gift such as prophecy, teaching, or tongues.[14] This is most unlikely, for in Paul's writings the one who imparts such spiritual gifts is never Paul, or any other human being, but always God (the Holy Spirit) (cf. 12:6; 1 Cor 12:1-4, 7-11, 28).[15] (ii) It denotes the apostle's understanding of the gospel of Jesus Christ. This interpretation is supported by the fact that elsewhere Paul speaks of sowing 'spiritual seed' among people (1 Cor 9:11) where what is meant is the preaching of the gospel, and of the 'spiritual blessings', first promised to the Jews, being experienced by Gentiles through the preaching of the gospel (Rom 15:27). And if Paul's letter to the Romans foreshadows in writing the sort of spiritual gift he wanted to impart in person, then that gift is a reminder of the content of the gospel he proclaims (Rom 15:15-16).[16]

13. Witherington, *Romans*, 41, comments: "Quintilian stresses that appeals to emotions . . . are especially necessary in deliberative oratory" (*Instit. Or.* 3.8.12). . . . Paul readily displays emotions from the beginning of this document, stressing how he longs to see the Roman Christians, and later expressing great anxiety and pathos over his fellow Jews (chs. 9–11), and then exhorting the Roman Christians to love. He is following the rules of deliberative oratory. Emotion is especially to be displayed at the beginning and at the end of major portions of a deliberative discourse. We see this clearly at the end of the theological segment of the discourse in chs. 9–11, and then again at the end of the pragmatic portion of the discourse in ch. 15'.

14. So, e.g., Barrett, *Romans*, 24.

15. It is true that 1 Tim 4:14 and 2 Tim 1:6 speak of the gift *(charisma)* (of God) being given to Timothy through the laying on of Paul's hands (the context of 1 Tim 4:14 suggests that it was a gift of preaching and teaching that was imparted). However, even in these texts, the gift is God's gift, imparted *by* God, *through* the laying on of hands.

16. Jewett, *Romans*, 124, argues that the meaning of *charisma pneumatikos* must be left open: 'The unprecedented expression *charisma pneumatikon* sounds at first redundant, since early Christians considered the gifts of divine grace and individual grace-gifts to be spiritual. Paul obviously felt the need to communicate as a charismatic with charismatics, emphasizing the spiritual bond that linked all believers together with Christ who is "the Spirit" (2 Cor 3:17). It is therefore misleading to reduce *charisma pneumatikon* to the preaching of the gospel, the gift of tongues or of prophecy, the gift of the Spirit, or to the gift of grace, because the particle *ti* ("some, some kind of") leaves open the question of precisely what Paul seeks to contribute within the parameters of a charismatic gift'.

The purpose of imparting this gift, Paul says, is *to make you strong*. If the suggestion made above about the nature of the gift Paul wished to impart is correct, then he believed his explanation of the gospel, when understood by his audience, would make them strong in their faith.[17] And being so strengthened in faith, their self-offering to God would be 'acceptable to God, sanctified by the Holy Spirit' (cf. 15:16).

However, Paul does not want his audience to think that the benefits of his intended visit will flow in one direction only. Lest they gain the wrong impression from what he has just written, he adds — *that is, that you and I may be mutually encouraged by each other's faith [both yours and mine]*. The NIV omits the words 'both yours and mine', possibly because it is formally superfluous in the light of 'each other's faith'. However, it is Paul's way of stressing the fact that he will be looking for mutual encouragement, not just an opportunity to convey some spiritual gift to his audience. It was not only Paul's faith and his understanding of the gospel that would strengthen the relationship, but also his exposure to the faith of the Roman believers, a faith that he says was being spoken about 'all over the world' (1:8).[18] Paul says later in his letter that he is convinced that his audience is 'full of goodness, filled with knowledge and competent to instruct one another' (15:14). In the presence of such people of faith Paul expected that he would also be encouraged.[19]

17. Early church fathers, assuming that the apostle Peter proclaimed the gospel first in Rome, insist that Paul's point here is that he does not want to change what they have received, but rather to strengthen them. Thus, e.g., [Pseudo-]Constantius ('Holy Letter of St. Paul to the Romans'): 'Paul says that he wants to strengthen the Romans, who held their faith from the preaching of Peter, not because they had received something inferior from Peter but that their faith would be strengthened by the witness and teaching of both apostles'; Theodoret of Cyrrhus ('Interpretation of the Letter to the Romans'): 'Paul only wants to share what he has himself received. And because the great Peter was the first to have taught them, Paul adds that he merely wants to confirm them in the teaching which has already been given to them and to water the trees which have been planted' (both cited in *ACCSR*, 23-24).

18. Gennadius of Constantinople, who like other church fathers assumed that the apostle Peter was the first to preach the gospel in Rome, asserts: 'Paul says this for fear of tripping up his hearers, who might not have known what to say to the prospect of sharing in some spiritual gift. For what could have been lacking in the teaching of Peter? Paul might be accused of criticizing Peter's teaching . . . of thinking that he was a greater apostle than Peter, of claiming to be on closer terms with Christ and more beloved by Christ than Peter was. Fearing attacks of this kind, Paul first of all sets out the purpose of his coming, thereby sufficiently refuting the charge of presumption. Then he goes on to say not that he is giving them something but that he is going to share something with them, which is quite different. . . . Paul reassures them that he has no intention of preaching anything new to them but that he intends to confirm them in what they have already received from Peter' ('Commentary from the Greek Church', *ACCSR*, 24-25).

19. Marty L. Reid, 'A Consideration of the Function of Rom 1:8-15 in Light of Greco-Roman Rhetoric', *JETS* 38 (1995) 181-91, holds that in 1:8-15 Paul is using the 'rhetoric of mutuality' and that this provides a clue to the nature of his communication to the Romans: it is an endeavor to establish 'a mutual relationship between himself and the audience'

1:13-15 In these verses Paul assures his audience that his desire to visit them has been a long-standing one. He prefaces this assurance with the formula, *I do not want[20] you to be unaware, brothers and sisters,* a formula he uses often when wanting to impress upon his audience something he thinks is important for them to understand (cf. 11:25; 1 Cor 10:1; 12:1; 2 Cor 1:8; 1 Thess 4:13). In this case what he wants them to understand is *that I planned many times to come to you (but have been prevented from doing so until now).* Towards the end of the letter Paul mentions again how often his plans to visit them had been hindered, explaining that this was due to his ambition (and, we might add, his sense of obligation) to preach the gospel 'where Christ was not known'. Having discharged that duty in the eastern Mediterranean, he was 'now' in a position to fulfill his long-standing desire to visit the believers in Rome (15:20-24). In 1 Thessalonians 2:18 Paul speaks of how he was hindered from returning to Thessalonica by Satan, but here in 1:13 the hindrance is of a different nature. We may infer from 15:20-24 that it was his ambition and sense of obligation to preach the gospel in the eastern Mediterranean that hindered him from coming to Rome previously.

One of the purposes for his intended visit, Paul says, is *in order that I might have a harvest among you, just as I have had among the other Gentiles.* The expression 'a harvest' (lit. 'certain fruit') signals what Cranfield calls 'a certain reserve and circumspection felt to be appropriate in speaking of fruit to be obtained by him in a church he has not founded'.[21] By the time Paul wrote Romans he had been involved in ministry and had seen much fruit for his labors among Gentiles in the Roman provinces of Galatia, Macedonia, Achaia, and Asia. Now he looks forward to having fruitful ministry among the Gentiles of Rome as well. In Philippians 1:22 he uses the same word 'fruit' in reference to ongoing 'fruitful labor' (lit. 'fruit of work') he will have among the Philippian believers if his life is spared. In that instance the fruit he anticipated was their 'progress in joy and faith' (Phil 1:25-26). Paul hopes his visit with the believers in Rome will produce similar fruit.[22]

---

(183), so that he could then clarify matters of 'covenantal status, obligations and belief' (191). Cranfield, *Romans,* I, 80, quotes Calvin: 'Note how modestly he expresses what he feels by not refusing to seek strengthening from inexperienced beginners. He means what he says, too, for there is none so void of gifts in the Church of Christ who cannot in some measure contribute to our spiritual progress'.

20. The reading 'I do not want' *(ou thelō)* has strong manuscript support and is in accord with Paul's usage elsewhere. The variant reading, 'I do not suppose' *(ouk oiomai),* has little support. Cf. Metzger, ed., *A Textual Commentary,* 447.

21. Cranfield, *Romans,* I, 82.

22. M. A. Kruger, '*TINA KARPON,* "Some Fruit' in Romans 1:13', *WTJ* 49 (1987) 167-73, suggests that 'fruit' in 1:13 should be interpreted as contributions to the collection which Paul hoped to receive from the Romans. He argues that 'fruit' is not converts by showing that where the word is used elsewhere in Paul's writings it is not converts but the fruit borne in the life of those who believe (168-70). He recognizes that it is not clear that 'fruit'

The apostle continues: *I am obligated both to Greeks and non-Greeks, both to the wise and the foolish.*[23] Fitzmyer offers the following explanation of the words translated here as 'Greeks and non-Greeks' *(Hellēsin te kai barbarois):*

> As used by Paul, it [*Hellēnes*] would refer to the Greek-speaking people among the *ethnē* [Gentiles], and especially to the cultured people of the Greco-Roman world, particularly in the great cities. *Barbaroi*, however, would refer to non-Greek-speaking Gentiles. The adj. *barbaros* is formed

---

means donations to the collection in 1:13, but argues that by the time the audience hears 15:22-29 read, it will finally become clear to them that what he was hinting at in 1:13 was in fact a contribution to the collection. Kruger seeks to overcome the problem that Paul's reference to preaching 'the gospel also to you who are in Rome' in 1:15 represents an objection to his argument by saying that it involves a *dativus commodi* ('to preach the gospel "for you" not "to you" — indirect object). He will preach the gospel for the Romans in Spain as he preached the gospel for the Antiochenes in the eastern Mediterranean' (171).

Kruger is probably right when he says that 'fruit' does not mean converts in 1:13 (seeing that Paul is addressing those who are already believers). However, there are problems with Kruger's view that 'fruit' in 1:13 means contributions to the collection. The indications in Romans are that the collection had been completed. Paul was on his way to Jerusalem to present it to the believers there, and thereafter he hoped to make his way via Rome to Spain. There is no evidence that he intended to take up the matter of the collection with the Roman believers when he visited them, nor any suggestion that he intended to seek further contributions to be taken to Jerusalem. What he planned to do after the 'collection visit' to Jerusalem was the projected mission to Spain. In the light of the fact that 'fruit' in Phil 1:22 refers clearly to the 'progress of joy and faith' among the believers, it is probably better to understand fruit in Rom 1:13 along similar lines. It is the 'fruit' of mutual encouragement (cf. 1:12), or, as Phil 1:22 puts it, 'progress in joy and faith', theirs and his, that he is hoping for when he visits them.

Jewett, *Romans*, 130, suggests a different meaning for 'fruit': 'The use of the indefinite pronoun *tina* ("some, some kind of") signals that ordinary evangelistic fruit is not in view, that he does not intend to win converts in Rome as he had elsewhere, but that some other kind of fruit is in view. As 15:24 and 28 go on to detail, Paul hopes to gain logistical and tactical support from Rome for his mission to Spain'.

23. Many editions of the Greek text of Romans, and nearly all English translations, punctuate 1:13-15 as does the NIV, placing a period after the word 'Gentiles' at the end of 1:13 and regarding 1:14(-15) as a new sentence, thus providing the translation: 'I do not want you to be unaware, brothers and sisters, that I planned many times to come to you (but have been prevented from doing so until now) in order that I might have a harvest among you, just as I have had among the other Gentiles. I am obligated both to Greeks and non-Greeks, both to the wise and the foolish. That is why I am so eager to preach the gospel also to you who are in Rome'. However, Runar M. Thorsteinsson, 'Paul's Missionary Duty towards Gentiles in Rome: A Note on the Punctuation and Syntax of Rom 1.13-15', *NTS* 48 (2002) 531-47, makes a case for placing a comma after 'Gentiles', and the period after 'both to Greeks and non-Greeks, both to the wise and the foolish'. Punctuated in this way, the reference to 'Greeks and non-Greeks, wise and foolish' stands in apposition to 'the other Gentiles' rather than being part of a new sentence in which Paul says he is indebted to preach the gospel to all kinds of people. The text of 1:13-15 would then read: 'I do not want you to be unaware, brothers, that I planned many times to come to you (but have been prevented from doing so until now) in order that I might have a harvest among you, just as I have had among other Gentiles, both Greeks and non-Greeks, both the wise and the foolish. I am obligated, and so I am eager, to preach the gospel to you who are in Rome'.

onomatopoetically of reduplicated *bar*, which to ancient Greeks imitated the unintelligible sounds of foreign languages; they even likened them to the twittering of birds (Herodotus, *History* 2.57). See 1 Cor 14:11. The phrase, however, expresses more than a difference of language, because *barbaroi* for Greeks of the classical and Hellenistic periods connoted peoples less cultured, among whom they included national enemies such as the Persians and Egyptians. In the Roman period, Spaniards, Gauls, and Germans would have been included.[24]

Having spoken of his desire to have some 'harvest/fruit' among his audience, Paul continues: *I am obligated. . . . That is why I am so eager to preach the gospel also to you who are at Rome.* Paul's sense of obligation (he says, literally, 'I am a debtor') comes from his calling as an apostle, as one 'set apart for the gospel of God' (1:1). Paul's eagerness to preach the gospel to those 'in Rome',[25] who are clearly already believers, seems on first reading to be at odds with his stated desire in 15:20 'to preach the gospel where Christ was not known'. However, this would not be the case if Paul thought that his exposition of the gospel would enhance the existing faith of his audience.[26]

1:16-17 Technically and in context 1:16-17 continues and concludes the introduction to the letter and explains why Paul is keen to preach the gospel to his audience: he is not ashamed of the gospel because it is the power of God for the salvation of all who believe.[27]

However, while 1:16-17 is technically part of the introduction to the letter, it is also transitional, and provides a statement of the main theme of the letter. It functions as the *propositio*, that is, a statement of the proposition that will be argued and defended in the rest of the letter.[28] Thus 1:16-17 foreshadows major themes expounded later in the letter, such as salvation for all who believe, the place of the Jewish people in the plan of salvation, and the revelation of the righteousness God.

Paul, then, begins the explanation of his eagerness to preach to the

24. Fitzmyer, *Romans*, 250-51.

25. The words 'in Rome' *(en Rōmē)* are missing in a few manuscripts in 1:15, as they are in 1:7, omitted probably in an attempt to show that the letter is of general application (see the comments on 1:7).

26. Schreiner, *Romans*, 53, comments: 'One of the difficulties with Paul's longing to preach the gospel in Rome is resolved when we realize that preaching the gospel for Paul involved more than initial conversion. . . . His goal as an apostle was to bring about the obedience of faith among the Gentiles (Rom. 1:5; 16:26). The obedience of faith, which as 1:1-7 shows is part and parcel of the gospel, cannot be limited to the initial decision to join the Christian community'. du Toit, 'Persuasion in Romans 1:1-17', 208, offers an alternative interpretation: When Paul says he wants to preach the gospel to you *(hymin)* he does not mean the Roman Christians specifically, but he was using the plural in a broader geographic sense to denote the people of Rome in general.

27. du Toit, 'Persuasion in Romans 1:1-17', 197, correctly includes 1:13-17 as the third part of Paul's introduction.

28. Cf. Witherington, *Romans*, 47-48.

Romans by saying: *For I am not ashamed of the gospel.*[29] Byrne argues that Paul's assertion that he is not ashamed of the gospel 'represents a standard rhetorical device (litotes) in which an understatement couched as a double negative has the effect of placing even greater stress upon the corresponding positive affirmation. "I am not ashamed of the gospel" really amounts to a forceful "I am mighty proud of the gospel"'.[30] However, Jewett is closer to the mark when he says that interpretations like that of Byrne 'sidestep the precise social issues of shame or honor that orators sought to address in employing the "I am ashamed/not ashamed" formula. . . . There were deeply ingrained social reasons why Paul should have been ashamed to proclaim such a gospel [a gospel of Christ crucified]'. . . .[31] In a world in which matters of honor and shame were extremely important, Paul had to reject the shame heaped upon him by those who despised the gospel, by declaring that he was not ashamed of it.[32]

Paul refuses to accept shaming in respect of the gospel *because it is the power of God that brings salvation to everyone who believes.* By thus stating his firm conviction concerning the efficacy of the gospel, Paul also introduces the main thesis to be argued in his letter. In what follows he will expound and defend this understanding of the gospel as 'the power of God that brings salvation to everyone who believes'. In 1 Corinthians 1:18-25 Paul acknowledges that his gospel is regarded as 'foolishness' by those who reject it but insists that it is the power of God for those who are being saved. By the time Paul wrote Romans he had witnessed repeatedly the power of God released through the preaching of the gospel bringing salvation to those who believed. He had seen people turn from idols to serve the living and true God (1 Thess 1:5, 9; 2:13), and have their lives morally transformed. Paul's clearest description of the latter is found in 1 Corinthians 6:9-11:

> Or do you not know that wrongdoers will not inherit the kingdom of God? Do not be deceived: Neither the sexually immoral nor idolaters nor adulterers nor men who have sex with men nor thieves nor the

29. The expression 'to be ashamed' *(epaischynomai)* occurs again in 6:21 where Paul refers to practices from believers' pre-Christian past, practices of which they are now ashamed. The same verb is found three times in 2 Timothy, where Timothy is urged not to be ashamed of testifying about the Lord, or of Paul his prisoner (2 Tim 1:8); where Paul asserts that as an apostle and teacher of the gospel he is not ashamed, despite his sufferings, because he knows whom he has trusted (2 Tim 1:11-12); and where he seeks mercy for his friend Onesiphorus because, being not ashamed of Paul's chains, he often refreshed him by his presence (2 Tim 1:16).

30. Byrne, *Romans*, 51.

31. Jewett, *Romans*, 136-37.

32. Richard J. Dillon, 'The Spirit as Taskmaster and Troublemaker in Romans 8', *CBQ* 60 (1998) 683-84, says (citing Wedderburn, *The Reasons for Romans*, 104) that Paul's statement, 'I am not ashamed of the gospel', '"makes far better sense if some in Rome in fact claimed that he ought to be ashamed of his gospel", which they found to be "in some way discredited and disgraceful"'.

greedy nor drunkards nor slanderers nor swindlers will inherit the kingdom of God. *And that is what some of you were. But you were washed, you were sanctified, you were justified in the name of the Lord Jesus Christ and by the Spirit of our God.* (italics added)

However, while the gospel was indeed the power of God that brings salvation resulting in moral transformation in this life, for Paul, and especially so in Romans, salvation involves much more. Negatively it involves escape from the wrath of God (5:9), and positively it brings a share in glory (8:30; cf. Phil 3:20-21).[33]

Paul asserts that this power of God brings salvation 'to everyone who believes'. It is important to note that salvation is for those who *believe*. It is not automatically bestowed upon everyone whether they believe in Jesus Christ or not, despite later texts in Romans (e.g., 5:18) that are sometimes (erroneously) interpreted in a universalistic way.[34] What Paul emphasizes at this point in the letter is simply that faith is the means by which everyone may access salvation. Later in the letter he will have more to say about the nature of faith, relating it explicitly to faith in Christ (3:21-26).

While the salvation mediated through the gospel is for everyone who believes, Paul says it is *first*[35] *to the Jew, then to the Gentile.*[36] There is no question that Paul believed the Jewish people had a special place in God's purposes. Here in 1:16 he says that the gospel is the power of God for salvation, 'first to the Jew, then for the Gentile', and in 2:10 he states that there will be honor and peace for everyone who does good, 'first for the Jew, then for the Gentile'. This last statement is balanced by the preceding statement in 2:9, which warns that there will be trouble and distress for those who do evil, 'first for the Jew, then for the Gentile'. Jewish privilege, Paul believed, carried with it a heightened responsibility. Paul's statements about Jewish priority here have a counterpart in Luke's presentation of Paul's mission in the Acts of the Apostles. His regular practice upon entering a city was to seek out the Jewish community first (usually in the local synagogue) and share the gospel with them (Acts 13:4-5, 14-44; 14:1; 16:13-15; 17:1-4, 10-12, 16-17; 18:1-4; 19:8; 28:16-24). On three occasions Luke reports that when the

33. Ambrosiaster comments on 'the power of God for salvation' as follows: 'It is the power of God which calls persons to faith and which gives salvation to all who believe, because it remits sins and justifies, so that one who has been marked with the mystery of the cross cannot be bound by the second death' ('Commentary on Paul's Epistles', *ACCSR*, 29).

34. Cf. Fitzmyer, *Romans*, 256, 'Paul realizes that human beings must react to the gospel, and such reaction is a human response, the condition without which God does not save. "Faith" in some form is used by Paul four times in these two verses, thus showing the importance that he puts on it'.

35. The word 'first' *(prōton)* is missing in a few manuscripts, the omission being thought to be due to Marcion, who found the idea of Jewish priority unacceptable.

36. 'For the Gentile' translates *Hellēni,* which, literally translated, would be 'for [the] Greek'. However, *Hellēn* can refer to either ethnic Greeks, or those more heavily influenced by Greek culture, so meaning non-Jews, i.e., Gentiles (cf. BAGD, *ad loc.*).

local Jewish community as a whole rejected the message, Paul informed them that he had first to preach the gospel to them, but seeing they had rejected it, he would turn to the Gentiles (Acts 13:46-47; 18:16; 28:24-29). Paul's practice was strategically effective. By seeking out the Jewish synagogues first he would find an immediate audience for his message, one that included not only Jews but also Gentiles well disposed towards Judaism (i.e., proselytes and God-fearers). Among those who accepted his message he would find people who would help further his mission.

However, more than strategy appears to be involved when Paul speaks of the gospel being 'first to the Jew, then to the Gentile'. We receive most help in understanding what this special place of the Jewish people meant for the apostle from statements later in Romans. In 3:1 he asks, 'What advantage, then, is there in being a Jew, or what value is there in circumcision?' He answers, 'Much in every way! First of all, the Jews have been entrusted with the very words of God' (3:2). In 9:4-5 he says of the Jewish people: 'Theirs is the adoption to sonship; theirs the divine glory, the covenants, the receiving of the law, the temple worship and the promises. Theirs are the patriarchs, and from them is traced the human ancestry of the Messiah, who is God over all, forever praised! Amen'. And in 11:28-29, acknowledging at the time that many of his kinsfolk had rejected the gospel, he says, 'As far as the gospel is concerned, they are enemies for your sake; but as far as election is concerned, they are loved on account of the patriarchs, for God's gifts and his call are irrevocable' (11:29). In the light of such texts as these it would appear that Paul's understanding of Jewish priority rests upon the place God himself had given them in his plan of salvation by his sovereign choice of the Jewish people, his covenants with them, his promises to them, and the way he was working out his purposes through them, culminating in the sending of Christ. Because of their special place in God's plans, Paul believed that he must offer the gospel first to the Jews, then to the Gentiles.[37]

Having declared that he is not ashamed of the gospel because it is the power of God that brings salvation to both Jews and Gentiles, Paul adds, *For in the gospel the righteousness of God is revealed.* In context, this statement functions as part of Paul's explanation of why he is not ashamed of the gospel. However, it also introduces for the first time the term 'righteousness', which occurs thirty-four times in twenty-nine verses in Romans. Of particular importance are those places where the 'righteousness *of God*' is mentioned (or implied),[38] including here in 1:17. 'The righteousness *of God*' can be construed as a genitive of source or origin, that is, Paul is saying that the gospel reveals a righteousness that comes from God (and is presumably bestowed by him upon those who believe). It is also possible to construe 'the

---

37. Cf. Wayne A. Brindle, '"To the Jew First": Rhetoric, Strategy, History, or Theology?' *BSac* 159 (2002) 221-33.
38. 1:17; 3:5, 21, 22, 25, 26; 10:3 (2x).

righteousness of God' as a possessive genitive (i.e., God's righteousness — "righteousness' being understood as a quality of God), or as a subjective genitive (i.e., God's righteousness understood as God-initiated righteous action). See 'Additional Note: The Righteousness of God', 79-81.

Cranfield makes a strong case for interpreting the righteousness of God in 1:17 as the status of righteousness that God bestows upon those who believe. He does so on the grounds that in 10:3 it is natural to interpret 'the righteousness of God' in this way because it is contrasted with 'their own [righteousness]', denoting a righteousness achieved by one's own efforts. This same idea is found in Philippians 3:9, where Paul contrasts 'a righteousness of my own that comes from the law' with 'that which is through faith'. For Cranfield the strongest reason for interpreting 'the righteousness of God' in 1:17 as the righteous status bestowed by God is the fact that it 'agrees better with the structure of the argument of the epistle' in which 1:18–4:25 expounds the words 'the man who is righteous by faith' and 5.1–8.39 expounds the promise that the man who is righteous by faith 'will live',[39] both of which are also found in 1:17.

However, a strong case can also be made for construing the genitive of 'the righteousness of God' in 1:17 as a subjective genitive and for interpreting the righteousness of God in 1:17 as his saving action on behalf of believers. It is noteworthy that in just three verses, 1:16-18, Paul speaks of the 'power of God', the 'righteousness of God', and the 'wrath of God', and their close juxtaposition suggests that they should all be understood along similar lines as those things expressed in God's actions. Further, the 'righteousness of God', Paul says, is revealed in the gospel (1:17), which he has just described as 'the power of God that brings salvation to everyone who believes' (1:16),[40] suggesting that 'the righteousness of God' involves the powerful saving action of God on behalf of all who believe. Such an understanding of the righteousness of God as saving action is found also in the following passages of the OT and the DSS:

> The LORD has made his salvation known and revealed his righteousness to the nations. He has remembered his love and his faithfulness to Israel; all the ends of the earth have seen the salvation of our God. (Ps 98:2-3)

> I am bringing my righteousness near, it is not far away; and my salvation will not be delayed. I will grant salvation to Zion, my splendor to Israel. (Isa 46:13)

---

39. Cranfield, *Romans*, I, 97-98.

40. In vv. 16-17 there is a series of epexegetic conjunctions where Paul explains why he is eager to preach the gospel to those in Rome: 'for (*gar*) I am not ashamed of the gospel, because (*gar*) it is the power of God that brings salvation. . . . For (*gar*) in the gospel the righteousness of God is revealed', indicating the connection between the righteousness of God and the power of God for salvation.

My righteousness draws near speedily, my salvation is on the way, and my arm will bring justice to the nations. The islands will look to me and wait in hope for my arm. (Isa 51:5)

Who is this coming from Edom, from Bozrah, with his garments stained crimson? Who is this, robed in splendor, striding forward in the greatness of his strength? It is I, proclaiming victory [lit. 'righteousness'], mighty to save. (Isa 63:1)

As for me, if I stumble, the mercies of God shall be my eternal salvation. If I stagger because of the sin of flesh, my justification shall be by the righteousness of God which endures forever. (1QS 11:12)[41]

These considerations support the view that 'the righteousness of God' in 1:17 does involve God's saving action on behalf of believers. The strong cases that can be made for both interpretations suggest that a 'both and' approach might be the best way forward. Accordingly, we could say that the righteousness of God is his saving action whereby he brings people into a right relationship with himself.[42]

We must next ask in what way the righteousness of God is revealed *in the gospel*. Is it revealed in the sense of a proclamation *about* the saving action of God? Or is the saving action of God actually *released* through the proclamation of the gospel for all who believe? Statements made by the apostle such as those below suggest that the latter as well as the former is involved:

My message and my preaching were not with wise and persuasive words, but with a demonstration of the Spirit's power, so that your faith might not rest on human wisdom, but on God's power. (1 Cor 2:4-5)

For we know, brothers and sisters loved by God, that he has chosen you, because our gospel came to you not simply with words but also with power, with the Holy Spirit and deep conviction. (1 Thess 1:4-5)

And we also thank God continually because, when you received the word of God, which you heard from us, you accepted it not as a human word, but as it actually is, the word of God, which is indeed at work in you who believe. (1 Thess 2:13)

Having said that the righteousness of God is revealed in the gospel, Paul adds that this was *a righteousness that is by faith from first to last*. 'By faith from first to last' is one of two traditional translations of the original (lit. 'from faith to faith') which construes the phrase as an idiom of emphasis meaning 'entirely by faith'.[43] Another translation, found in the NRSV,

---

41. Translation by Vermes, *Dead Sea Scrolls*, 116.
42. Cf. Moo, *Romans*, 74.
43. Cf., e.g., Byrne, *Romans*, 54, who argues that the expression 'from faith to faith' 'is

construes the phrase as 'through faith for faith', implying a purpose. Each of these translations interprets both the first and second references to 'faith' as the act of believing (or possibly what is believed).

In more recent times there has been a tendency to distinguish the first reference to 'faith' from the second. One such approach regards the first as a reference to faithfulness — either God's faithfulness to his covenant, or Christ's faithfulness in carrying out his role in God's redemptive plan. In these cases, 'from faith to faith' means that the faithfulness of God/Christ brings about the response of faith in believers.

The main drawback to this last approach is that it runs counter to the way the formula 'from A to A' is used consistently in ancient Greek literature, where the 'A' in both cases always denotes the same thing (e.g., 'from shore to shore', 'from strength to strength', 'from town to town', etc.) and where some movement between the two is implied. If we allow this to guide our understanding of 'from faith to faith', we would have to interpret it so that some movement between the two is implied. In context where Paul speaks of the gospel being the power of God for salvation for everyone who believes, 'first to the Jew, then to the Gentile' (1:16), the movement implied could be from the faith response of the Jews to a similar faith response among the Gentiles. (For a fuller discussion of the interpretation of this key phrase, see 'Additional Note: From Faith to Faith', 75-78.) However, no final decision can be reached about the meaning of the formula without first seeking to understand the force of the biblical quotation Paul provides to support his assertion that in the gospel 'the righteousness of God is revealed from faith to faith'.

Following his statement that in the gospel a righteousness of God is revealed 'from faith to faith', Paul adds, *just as it is written: 'The righteous will live by faith'*. The quotation is from Habakkuk 2:4, and any interpretation of 'from faith to faith' must find support in this quotation. So the way Paul's quotation is understood is crucial. To begin with, it is helpful to note the various forms in which this text appears in the MT and the LXX as reflected in the translations below:

MT   the righteous will live by *his* faith
LXX   the righteous shall live by *my* faithfulness

The MT text is unambiguous, and the faith involved is not the faithfulness of God but the faith(fullness) of the righteous person.[44] The LXX text differs

---

best understood in an intense sense underlying the centrality of faith. The righteousness revealed by the gospel, that which makes it a "power of God leading to salvation", is a righteousness entirely discerned and appropriated through faith. Perhaps we could best paraphrase Paul's phrase and intention by saying, "It is faith through and through, faith from beginning to end"'.

44. The commentary on Habakkuk found among the DSS provides an interpretation of the text of Hab 2:4 (though the text itself is missing due to damage to the scroll) which in-

from that of the MT, and is ambiguous. It may be rendered in one of three ways: (i) as shown above: 'the righteous shall live by my faithfulness', (ii) 'the righteous shall live by his faith in me', and (iii) 'my by-faith-righteous-one shall live'. The form of the quotation of Habakkuk 2:4 in 1:17 differs from the forms found in the MT and LXX, as do the forms of the quotation in the two other places where it is found in the NT:

Rom 1:17   the righteous will live by faith
Gal 3:11   the righteous will live by faith
Heb 10:38   my righteous one will live by faith

Paul's citation of Habakkuk 2:4 in both 1:17 and Galatians 3:11 lacks the 'his' of the MT, and the 'my' of the LXX. The citation of the text in Hebrews 10:38 lacks the 'his' of the MT, and has the 'my' qualifying 'righteous' instead of 'faithfulness' (as it does in the LXX).[45] Hebrews 10:38 is unambiguous and may be rendered: 'My righteous one shall live by faith'. Both 1:17 and Galatians 3:11 are ambiguous, the translation being determined by what 'by faith' is believed to qualify. If it qualifies 'righteous', then the text would be rendered: 'The one who is righteous through faith shall live', but if it qualifies 'will live', then it would be rendered: 'The righteous one will live by faith'. The translation of the Habakkuk quotation in Romans 1:17, then, cannot be decided grammatically, but must be decided upon other grounds, that is, comparison with other Pauline usage and its immediate context.

In respect to other Pauline usage, Paul's citation of Habakkuk 2:4 in Galatians 3:11 is crucial. There he points to Abraham as one who had righteousness credited to him (was justified) because of his faith in God, and says that Scripture foresaw that God would also justify the Gentiles by faith. This was announced beforehand to Abraham in the words, 'All nations shall be blessed through you'. By way of contrast, Paul says, those of the works of the law are under a curse. He concludes, 'Clearly no one is justified before God by the law, because, "The righteous will live by faith"' (Gal 3:11). In this context Paul's citation of Habakkuk 2:4 functions *generally* as a scriptural proof text that people are justified by faith. If we allow

---

dicates that the text was originally the same as that in the MT. The commentary reads: 'Interpreted this concerns all those who observe the Law in the House of Judah, whom God will deliver from the House of Judgement because of their suffering and because of their faith in the Teacher of righteousness' (1QpHab 8:1-3). In this case the faith is again that of the righteous person, even though it is interpreted as faith in the Teacher of Righteousness.

45. If Paul and the writer of Hebrews were working with a Greek text the same as that preserved in the preferred text of the LXX cited above, then it would appear that both of them modified the text to make it express the theological point they were making. Dietrich-Alex Koch, 'Der Text von Hab 2 4b in der Septuaginta und im Neuen Testament', *ZNW* 76 (1985) 84-85, argues that the preferred LXX text of Hab 2:4b is the original, all three NT readings of the text are secondary, and the variant readings of the LXX are the result of the later influence of the three NT readings.

Paul's use of Habakkuk 2:4 in Galatians 3:11 to influence our interpretation of Romans 1:17, there is a *prima facie* case for interpreting it in this context also as a proof text for justification by faith.[46] Paul would probably be mystified by our attempts to decide whether he intended 'by faith' to qualify 'righteous' or 'live'. Either would suit his purpose, which was to show that justification is not a reward for observing the law, but a declaration by God in favor of those who have faith in his Son.[47]

If, as argued above, 'from faith to faith' is an idiom of growth, so that both occurrences of 'faith' in this construction refer to the one sort of faith, and therefore cannot refer to the faithfulness of God on the one hand and the faith of believers on the other, then both must refer to human faith.[48]

---

46. Cf. Cranfield, *Romans*, I, 102, argues for the interpretation, 'the one made righteous by faith shall live' because the immediate context (which says nothing about living by faith) requires it, because the structure of the letter requires it (for 1:18–4:25 expounds the meaning of *ho dikaios ek pisteōs*), and because the connection between righteousness and faith is made explicitly in 5:1. Similarly, Morris, *Romans*, 72.

47. R. M. Moody, 'The Habakkuk Quotation in Romans 1:17', *ExpTim* 92 (1981) 205-8, argues that 'by faith' *(ek pisteōs)* qualifies both 'righteous' *(dikaios)* and 'shall live' *(zēsetai)* on the grounds that 1:16-17 is an introduction to the whole letter and the letter deals with more than faith in its initial role in respect to justification; it deals with the role of faith in the ongoing Christian life as well. He supports his argument with appeal to syntax and to the relationship of 1:17 to the rest of the letter, with a comparison of Paul's use of Hab. 2:4 in 1:17 and Gal. 3:11, and with a consideration of Paul's approach to Hab 2:4.

Dunn, *Romans 1–8*, 45-46, also suggests a 'both/and' approach, arguing that rules of interpretation current in Pharisaic circles in Paul's day were designed to draw out as much meaning as possible from a given text, and that this is probably what the apostle is doing in 1:17. He also takes the very inability of commentators to resolve the 'either/or' debate over 1:17 as evidence supporting a 'both/and' approach.

Glen N. Davies, *Faith and Obedience in Romans: A Study in Romans 1–4* (JSNTSup 39; Sheffield: JSOT Press, 1990), 41-42, opts for a 'both/and' approach as well, arguing that, while the primary reference is to the righteous who live by faith, there is a secondary reference to the fact that they are also made righteous by faith. In his view the citation from Hab 2:4 'bears witness to a justifying faith which produces a life characterized by faith' and this 'establishes a continuity of God's way of salvation before and after Christ. The same principle which was outlined by the prophet in the seventh century (and previously demonstrated in the life of Abraham) is operative now'.

H. C. C. Cavallin, '"The Righteous Shall Live by Faith": A Decisive Argument for the Traditional Interpretation', *ST* 32 (1978) 40-43, agrees that Rom 1:17 should be understood in the light of Gal 3:11. In his view, *ek pisteōs*, in the citation of Hab 2:4b, must be taken to qualify *zēsetai*, not *ho dikaios*, because in Gal 3:11-12 the logic is that 'where there is life there is also righteousness, and vice versa. What gives life — faith or law — also gives righteousness'. So too, essentially, Fitzmyer, *Romans*, 264-65; Byrne, *Romans*, 54; Witherington, *Romans*, 55-56.

48. Cf. Jewett, *Romans*, 139-45: 'In contrast to these various efforts to construe faith in Hab 2:4 as "faithfulness", it is clear that Paul translated Hab 2:4 in an independent manner that eliminates this option. The contexts of Rom 1:16-17 and Gal 3:6-14 and the deletion in each of the personal pronoun point indisputably in the direction of "faith" as a theological formula for participation in the Christ movement. As we have seen, the word *pistis* appears no less than six times in this short pericope prior to the citation of Hab 2:4, each time with the connotation of acceptance of the gospel and subsequent participation in the community

Accordingly, Paul's citation of Habakkuk 2:4 in 1:17 would function *generally* as a proof text supporting his assertion that the righteousness of God is revealed in the gospel, resulting in the growth of faith among Jews and Gentiles. This may possibly be understood, as Taylor suggests, as faith spreading from among Jews to among Gentiles[49] in line with Paul's earlier statement that the gospel is the power of God for salvation for everyone who believes, 'first to the Jew, then to the Gentile'. In the light, then, of both Paul's use of the Habakkuk 2:4 quotation in Galatians 3:11 and its context in 1:16-17, there is good reason to regard it here as a proof text for justification by faith, available to both Jews and Gentiles who believe. Thus we could paraphrase 1:15-17 as follows:

> So I am eager to preach the gospel to you also who are in Rome. For I am not ashamed of the gospel, for it is the power of God that brings salvation to everyone who believes, first to the Jew, then to the Gentile. For the righteousness of God is revealed in the gospel, and seen in the growth of faith in Christ, beginning with faith among the Jews and spreading to the Gentiles, as it is written, 'the righteous by faith will live'.[50]

While the main thrust of Paul's statement in 1:17 supported by the citation of Habakkuk 2:4 appears to support the view that the power of God for salvation mediated through the preaching of the gospel is to be received by faith, this does not mean that the apostle is contradicting the meaning that text had in its historical context. Authentic faith for Paul always involved obedience and faithfulness.[51]

ADDITIONAL NOTE: FROM FAITH TO FAITH

In a recent article, Quarles lists the following interpretations of the expression, 'from faith to faith': (i) from faith in the law to faith in the gospel

---

of believers. That *pistis* here refers to the faithfulness of God or Christ would more easily have been achieved by citing one of the LXX versions of Hab 2:4, which Paul obviously chose not to do'.

49. Taylor, 'From Faith to Faith', 348.

50. Walter Zorn, 'The Messianic Use of Habakkuk 2:4a in Romans', *Stone-Campbell Journal* 1 (1998) 227, argues for a quite different interpretation of Paul's quotation of Hab 2:4. He says: 'It is very possible that Paul understood Hab 2:4b to be "messianic", referring to Christ himself and he is "the righteous One" who shall live (resurrection?) by (*ek*, literally "out of") *pistis*. Thus, Paul could avoid the well-known "error" of the *emou*, highlight the "messianic" use by effectively using the "catch-phrase" *ek pisteōs* throughout his letter, and allow the *pistis* its nuances of "faith" or "faithfulness", depending on the initial use at Romans 1:17 for Christ and its later understanding for Christians incorporated "into Christ", i.e., "the one who is *ek pisteōs Christou*" = "the one who shares the faith[fulness] of Christ" (3:26)'.

51. Cf. Schreiner, *Romans*, 75; Dunn, *Romans 1–8*, 45-46.

(Tertullian); (ii) from faith in the prophets to faith in the gospel (Theodoret; similarly Origen); (iii) from the faith of OT saints to the faith of NT believers (Chrysostom); (iv) from the faith of the gospel preachers to the faith of those who respond to it (Augustine); (v) from God's faithfulness to man's faith (Ambrosiaster, adopted by Barth; similarly Dunn); (vi) either from present faith to future faith, or from faith in the unseen realities to faith in realities actually possessed (Aquinas); (vii) faith that advances and grows (Calvin; similarly Sanday and Headlam, Lagrange); (viii) by faith and faith alone, that is, regarding 'from faith to faith' as an idiom of emphasis (Lietzmann, Nygren, Cranfield, Ziesler, Moo, Byrne, Fitzmyer, Schreiner); (ix) by faith to those who believe (Cornely, Hill, Murray); (x) faith as the ground and goal (Lightfoot).[52] To these may be added the suggestion of Waetjen that 'from faith to faith' means out of the trust (fund) of Abraham into the trust (fund) of Christ, that is, the 'trust funds' established by God on the one hand by his covenant with Abraham and on the other hand by the new covenant in Christ.[53]

Quarles then conducts a review of the use of the formula 'from A to A' in extrabiblical Greek, using the *Thesaurus Linguae Graecae (TLG)* to scan texts from the Homeric period to A.D. 600, and says that in these texts (i) 'even in idiomatic usage, the prepositions of the construction retain their basic senses, "from" or "out of" and "to" respectively'; (ii) the object of the preposition 'to' in the construction is sometimes modified by the adjective 'another' and the adjective is frequently implied even when it is not stated; (iii) in some instances the construction expresses development or intensification.[54] Turning his attention to the LXX, Quarles notes that of the seventeen times the construction 'from A to A' occurs, in nine instances it has a temporal sense (denoting duration, progression, or repetition), and in seven instances it has a locative sense (denoting point of departure and destination). The remaining use of the construction found in Psalm 83:8 (E.T. 84:7: 'from strength to strength'), depending upon one's exegesis of the text in its context, denotes either 'physical movement from one place to another or progressive degrees of strength' (but not emphasis, as is sometimes claimed).[55] Finally, Quarles focuses upon the use of the construction in Paul's letters apart from Romans, that is, in 2 Corinthians 2:16; 3:18. He argues that in 2 Corinthians 2:16 ('To the one we are an aroma that brings

52. Charles L. Quarles, 'From Faith to Faith: A Fresh Examination of the Prepositional Series in Romans 1.17', *NovT* 45 (2003) 2-5.

53. Herman C. Waetjen, 'The Trust of Abraham and the Trust of Jesus Christ: Romans 1:17', *CurrTheolMiss* 30 (2003) 451. Waetjen explains it as follows: 'the *diathēkē* [covenant] was based on *pistis* [faith], the trust fund that God established with Abraham. But because its benefits were made available after the second testamentary heir, Jesus Christ, had fulfilled the conditions of the *diathēkē* [covenant], Paul can designate this trust fund "the trust of Jesus Christ", as he does in Gal 2:16'.

54. Quarles, 'From Faith to Faith', 5-8.

55. Quarles, 'From Faith to Faith', 9-11.

death; to the other, an aroma that brings life') the 'from A to A' construction is used to speak of 'the impact of Paul and his companions on those who embraced or rejected them', the prepositions retaining their common senses expressing source and result respectively. In respect to 2 Corinthians 3:18 he says that the construction is used to denote transformation of believers from one degree of glory to another.[56] Quarles's review of the use of the construction 'from A to A' in all this literature leads him to conclude: The 'from-to' prepositional series 'often expresses range, duration, repletion, source and destination, previous state and new state or progression. It does not appear to function as an idiom of emphasis'.[57] The weight of evidence, then, is against interpreting 'from faith to faith' in 1:17 to mean that the righteousness of God is received *entirely through faith* ('by faith from first to last'). Quarles's own conclusion is: 'The two most likely options are that a) the construction expresses that the revelation of the righteousness of God originated with the faithfulness of Christ and results in the faith of the believer[58] or that b) the revelation of the righteousness of God extends from the faith of the Old Testament believer to the faith of the New Testament believer'. The latter is Quarles's preferred option, and is the interpretation offered long ago by Chrysostom.[59]

More recently, Taylor has suggested another interpretation, arguing that the expression 'from A to A' denotes progression in faith.[60] Also on the basis of work done in the *TLG*, the LXX, and the NT, Taylor shows that the formula 'from A to A', when used in relation to places, denotes movement from one place to a similar place (e.g., Sir 36:26 [E.T. 36:31]: 'from town to town'), in relation to time it denotes 'repeated action over time': 'from generation to generation' (e.g., Lev 21:17) or 'from day to day', and in relation to abstract nouns it carries the sense of 'increase, progression, or movement from a lower to a higher plane' (e.g., Ps 83:8 [E.T. 84:8]: 'they go from strength to strength'; 2 Cor 2:16: to some an aroma of death to death, to some an aroma of life to life'; 2 Cor 3:18: 'being transformed from glory to glory'). In all cases, the first and second elements of the idiom, 'from A to

---

56. Quarles, 'From Faith to Faith', 11-13.

57. Quarles, 'From Faith to Faith', 13.

58. Douglas A. Campbell, 'Romans 1:17 — A Crux Interpretum for the *PISTIS CHRISTOU* Debate', *JBL* 113 (1994) 277-81, argues that this Christological interpretation gains support when Hab 2:4 is recognized as an early church messianic proof text. Brian Dodd, 'Romans 1:17 — A Crux Interpretum for the *Pistis Christou* Debate?' *JBL* 114 (1995) 470-73, believes that Campbell has made a convincing case for the Christological interpretation of *ek pisteōs* in 1:17b, while taking issue with his move to a 'global generalization about Paul's usage everywhere'. Douglas A. Campbell, 'False Presuppositions in the *Pistis Christou* Debate: A Response to Brian Dodd', *JBL* 116 (1997) 713-19, provides further clarification of his position in response to Dodd's critique.

59. Quarles, 'From Faith to Faith', 21.

60. John W. Taylor, 'From Faith to Faith: Romans 1.17 in the Light of Greek Idiom', *NTS* 50 (2004) 337-48. Taylor acknowledges the work of Quarles, 'From Faith to Faith', but seeks to take it a step further.

A', denote the same thing, and there is progression, movement, or growth between them.[61]

In the case of Romans 1:17, then, Taylor argues that *'from faith to faith'* denotes growth in the same faith. It is unlikely, therefore, that the first reference to faith is theological or Christological (i.e., God's faithfulness or Christ's faithfulness) while the second is anthropological (the faith or faithfulness of believers). On these grounds he rules out interpretations that speak of the righteousness of God being revealed through the gospel beginning with the faithfulness of either God or Christ and leading to faith or faithfulness in believers. Taking note of such OT passages as Psalm 98:2 (LXX 97:2); Isaiah 51:4-8; 52:10; 56:1 which speak of the revelation of God's righteousness for the salvation of Israel and it being witnessed by the nations, Taylor suggests that *'from faith to faith'* 'is Paul's excited report of the success of the gospel and the growing number of believers, and in particular of the advance or growth of faith among the Gentiles. . . . [Faith] in each case thus stands for a believing response to the gospel, but the increase in faith indicated by the idiom is not personal or individual growth in faith but the mounting number of converts that Paul has seen in his ministry'.[62] Taylor suggests further that it is possible to understand 1:17 in the following way: 'For in the gospel — the prophetic proclamation of salvation in Christ — the righteousness of God is now being revealed, starting from the faith of the Jews first, and now growing also among the Gentiles'.[63] This growth of faith is the evidence of the revelation of the righteousness of God through the preaching of the gospel. We might add to Taylor's suggestion that this growth of faith begins with the faith of the Jews and then spreads through Paul's ministry to the Gentiles is consistent with Paul's immediately preceding statement that the gospel 'is the power of God that brings salvation to everyone who believes: *first to the Jew, then to the Gentile'* (1:16).[64]

---

61. Cf. Wilbur A. Benware, 'Romans 1.17 and Cognitive Grammar', *BibTrans* 51 (2000) 338, who applies the principles of what he describes as 'cognitive grammar' to the question of the meaning of *ek pisteōs eis pistin*, and, recognizing the way the idiom is used in Greek literature, says: 'From the point of view of Cognitive Grammar, the asyndetic relation of the two prepositional phrases in Rom 1.17 leads to an interpretation whereby a TR [trajectory] *dikaiosynē theou* "moves" between a Source *(pistis)* and a Goal *(pistis)*. Since the Source and Goal are expressed by the identical noun, the idiom is best interpreted as "begins in faith(fullness) and ends in faith(fullness)", or "faith(fullness) from beginning to end". Parallel passages must be rendered similarly, for example 2 Cor 2.16: "death from beginning to end" and "life from beginning to end", consistent with the use of this idiom in Greek literature in general'.

62. Taylor, 'From Faith to Faith', 346. Zorn, 'The Messianic Use of Habakkuk 2:4a', 213-30, espouses a similar view, but argues that it is particularly the growth of faith among Gentiles that is the evidence of the revelation of the righteousness of God.

63. Taylor, 'From Faith to Faith', 348.

64. Cf. Jewett, *Romans*, 143-44: 'The parallels to this sequence of prepositions make clear that progression, transformation, or movement is intended. For example, Ps 83:8 promises that the faithful shall move forward "from strength to strength". . . . Paul uses

ADDITIONAL NOTE: THE RIGHTEOUSNESS OF GOD

Paul speaks of five different aspects of the righteousness of God in Romans. First, God's righteousness as *distributive justice* is implied in 1:18-32, where he says that God recompenses humanity in accordance with its response to his revelation, and also in 2:2-11, where he says that God renders to all people according to their works — those who with patience and well-doing seek immortality will be rewarded with eternal life, while those who are factious and do not obey the truth will be punished with wrath and fury. It is implied again in 3:1-20, where Paul defends God's righteousness by showing that God acts justly when he judges unfaithful Jews.

Second, God's righteousness as *covenant faithfulness* is defended in 3:3-9, where Paul argues that when God judges Israel it is not evidence of a failure of covenant loyalty on his part, but of sinfulness on Israel's part. In 9:1-29 God's covenant faithfulness is further defended when Paul rejects charges that God's word has failed (9:6), that there is injustice on God's part (9:14), and that God has no right to find fault with Israel (9:19). Paul argues that Israel has failed to obtain the blessing, not because God is unfaithful to his covenant with Israel, but because that blessing always depended on election and mercy, not on any inherent rights based on being born a Jew. God's covenant faithfulness is further defended in 11:1-10, where Paul argues that God has always maintained a remnant of Israel in whom his covenant promises are fulfilled.

Third, God's righteousness as *saving action* is expounded in 3:21-26. Here God's righteousness is manifested, apart from the law, by providing redemption through Christ's death, so making possible a righteousness (a right standing before God) to be received by faith.

Fourth, God's righteousness as *the gift of justification and a right relationship* with himself, already foreshadowed in 3:21-26, is expounded in terms of the experience of Abraham in 4:1-25. It is referred to again in 5:17 ('the gift of righteousness' received by believers as a result of Christ's obedience), and explained further in 9:30–10:4, where the apostle speaks of a

---

this formula several times, "from death to death . . . from life to life" (2 Cor 2:16; cf. 3:18) and the classical parallels contain the same progressive element. This rhetorical structure is violated by theologically motivated interpretations that define "faith" differently when following *ek* as compared with *eis,* or that take the expression as primarily decorative, and an emphatic expression of the doctrine of *sola fide,* or as meaninglessly redundant. In view of Paul's use of "faith" in 1:5, 8, 12, and 16 as appropriation of the gospel that allows cultural variations to stand side by side with equal validity, it is most likely that the progression in this verse refers to missionary expansion of the gospel, which relies on the contagion of faith. This also brings the expression into consistency with the following citation from Habakkuk, which is altered by Paul to make plain to his audience that faith refers to acceptance of the gospel'.

righteousness, not based on law (observance by Jews), but which comes from God, and is received by all those who believe.

Fifth, the righteousness of God (as a gift) which leads to *righteousness of life* in believers is expounded in 6:1-23 (esp. vv. 16-18), where Paul points out that those who are under [the] grace [of justification] are no longer slaves of sin but are slaves of righteousness. This aspect of the righteousness of God is also reflected in 8:4, where the purpose of Christ's death is to condemn sin in the flesh so that the just requirement of the law might be fulfilled in believers.

All these aspects of God's righteousness can be included under the one umbrella idea of *God acting in accordance with his own nature for the sake of his name*.[65] Understood in this way, it can include God's distributive justice, his covenant loyalty, his saving action, and his gift of justification leading to righteousness of life.

If there is evidence for all of these aspects of God's righteousness in Romans, the question is: Which of them corresponds most closely to Paul's intention in 1:17? This has been widely debated, and a number of approaches have been championed.[66] There are those who argue that 'the righteousness of God' in 1:17 should be construed as a genitive of origin and that it refers to the righteous status given by God to those who believe the gospel.[67] Others argue against this view, and in favor of construing it as 'God's own righteousness',[68] that it is best understood as a divine attribute — God's uprightness — which is expressed in his saving activity (and par-

65. John Piper, 'The Demonstration of the Righteousness of God in Romans 3:25, 26', *JSNT* (1980) 2-32, argues for this meaning of the righteousness of God in Rom 3:25-26.

66. Cf. discussions in K. L. Onesti and M. T. Brauch, 'Righteousness, Righteousness of God', *DPL*, 827-37; P. J. Achtemeier, 'Righteousness in the N.T.', *IDB*, IV, 91-99; Rudolf Bultmann, *Theology of the New Testament*, I, 270-85; E. Käsemann, 'The "Righteousness of God" in Paul', in *New Testament Questions of Today* (London: SCM 1969), 168-82; M. T. Brauch, 'Perspectives on "God's Righteousness" in Recent German Discussion', in E. P. Sanders, *Paul and Palestinian Judaism: A Comparison of Patterns of Religion* (London: SCM, 1977), 523-43; J. A. Ziesler, *The Meaning of Righteousness in Paul: A Linguistic and Theological Enquiry* (Cambridge: Cambridge University Press, 1972); N. W. Watson, 'Review Article', *NTS* 20 (1974) 217-28; G. Klein, 'Righteousness in the N.T.', *IDB* Sup, 750-52; Cranfield, *Romans*, I, 91-92; C. E. B. Cranfield, *The Epistle to the Romans*, II (ICC; Edinburgh: T&T Clark, 1979), 824-26; W. Sanday and A. C. Headlam, *The Epistle to the Romans* (Edinburgh: T&T Clark), 34-49; S. K. Williams, 'The "Righteousness of God" in Romans', *JBL* 99 (1980) 241-90; Piper, 'The Demonstration of the Righteousness of God in Rom 3:25-26', 2-32.

67. E.g., Cranfield, *Romans*, I, 98.

68. Wright, 'Romans', 425, says: 'It is important to note that the NIV translation ("righteousness from God is revealed") presupposes what I argued . . . to be the wrong understanding of the phrase. Instead of God's own righteousness, it suggests that Paul is referring here to the status that Christians have as a result of God's justifying action. Although this is a possible meaning of the Greek, there is no warrant for it in Paul's Jewish background; it makes the reading of 3:21-26 very problematic; and it effectively splits off other sections of Romans, notably chaps. 9–11, from the early chapters, since in 9–11 the questions Paul is addressing are precisely those summarized in Jewish literature by the notion of God's own righteousness'.

alleled in context by the attributes of 'God's wrath' and 'God's power').[69] Others scholars argue that 'the righteousness of God' should be construed as a subjective genitive and that it refers to God's saving activity in Christ, in which his power for salvation is revealed to provide salvation for those who believe.[70] Yet other scholars opt for the view that 'the righteousness of God' in 1:17, should be interpreted as God's covenant faithfulness — his faithfulness to his covenant promises to Israel expressed in the revelation of his power for salvation.[71] Still others opt for a 'both and' approach to the meaning of 'the righteousness of God' in 1:17, arguing that it should not be restricted to either a status given by God or his saving activity, but that it should be understood to include both.[72] It is this last interpretation of 'the righteousness of God' in 1:17 that is adopted in this commentary, that is, it is best understood to mean God's saving action in Christ whereby he brings people into a right relationship with himself.

II. EXPOSITION AND DEFENSE OF THE GOSPEL, 1:18–11:36

Paul's exposition of the gospel proceeds through several stages. First, he demonstrates that, apart from the gospel, all humanity is under the power of sin and exposed to the wrath of God (1:18–3:20). Second, he shows how God has provided salvation through the atoning death of Christ for all who believe the gospel, whether they are Jews or Gentiles, and that this is inde-

---

69. E.g., Fitzmyer, *Romans*, 262: 'In 1:16-17 the attribute sense of the subjective gen. is just as suitable as the gift idea; for God's uprightness even as an attribute can be the object of the gospel's revelation. In fact, it is more suitable than the gift idea, being immediately paralleled by not only "the power of God" (1:16b), but also "the wrath of God" (1:18), another attribute of divine activity'. . . .

70. So, e.g., Jewett, *Romans*, 142: 'The early Christian mission is thus viewed as a decisive phase in the revelation of God's righteousness, restoring individuals, establishing new communities of faith, and ultimately restoring the whole creation. This missional context makes it likely that *dikaiosynē theou* should be taken as a subjective genitive referring to God's activity in this process of global transformation, rather than as an objective genitive that would refer to the human righteousness bestowed by God. The fact that "God's power" in 1:16 and "God's wrath" in 1:18 are both subjective genitives renders it likely that "righteousness of God" should be taken in the same way, and commentators who believe that Paul intended both the subjective and objective genitive in 1:17 disregard this contextual and grammatical evidence'.

71. So, e.g., Dunn, *Romans 1–8*, 40-42.

72. So, e.g., Byrne, *Romans*, 53-54; Witherington, *Romans*, 52-53. Cf. Moo, *Romans*, 74-75: 'This more comprehensive interpretation of "righteousness of God" in 1:17 has several advantages. First, it is built on the most frequent meaning of the phrase in the OT, so that Paul's audience in Rome would have an immediate starting point for their understanding of Paul's language. Second, it does justice to the nuances of both divine activity and human receptivity that occur in the text, Third, it enables us to relate the phrase to Paul's broader use of "righteousness", where he frequently highlights the end result of the process of justification in the believer's status of righteousness'.

pendent of the Mosaic law. On the human side, only faith in Jesus Christ is required (3:21–5:21). Third, there follows a defense of this gospel against charges that it would lead to moral anarchy (6:1-23), or that it involves a denigration of the God's law (7:1–8:11), culminating with an explanation of the glorious liberty in store for the children of God and the whole creation (8:17-25). A great emotive climax follows (8:31-39) that paves the way for the final element of Paul's defense of his gospel in which he vigorously denies that it implies that God's promises to Israel have failed or that it nullifies her special place in God's purposes (9:1–11:36). This entire exposition is written to provide his audience with a clear presentation of the gospel, and to deal with criticisms of it that appear to have been aired in Rome, criticisms which might prevent them from embracing his gospel (and supporting his mission). He also writes to ensure that the believers in Rome, informed by the gospel, are sanctified by the Holy Spirit and become an offering acceptable to God (15:15-16).

A. Humanity under the Power of Sin
and Exposed to Wrath, 1:18–3:20

In this long section Paul begins his exposition of the gospel by establishing the culpability of all humanity, including both Jews and Gentiles. He focuses upon the Gentile world in 1:18-32 and then upon those who take the high moral ground, in particular Jewish people, in 2:1–3:20. He demonstrates that the whole world is held accountable to God, that all people are alike in the matter of sin and judgment.

1. Primary Focus on the Sins of the Gentile World, 1:18-32

The first step in Paul's demonstration that all humanity is exposed to the wrath of God because of sin is the assertion that all people are liable to judgment because of their idolatry, an assertion that is particularly applicable to the Gentile world (1:18-32).[1] However, this is definitely not intended

---

1. Cranfield, *Romans*, I, 105-6, says: 'That in this sub-section Paul has in mind primarily the Gentiles is no doubt true. But it may be doubted whether we shall do justice to his intention, if we assume — as many interpreters seem inclined to do — that these verses refer exclusively to them. In v. 18 he uses the general term "men", and nowhere in the sub-section does he use either "Gentiles" or Greek". In describing men's idolatry in v. 23 he echoes the language of Ps 106.20 and Jer 2.11, the former of which refers to Israel's worship of the golden calf and the latter to Israel's forsaking the Lord for other gods at a much later date. . . . The implication would seem to be that Paul himself reckoned that, by describing — as he certainly was doing in 1.18-32 — the obvious sinfulness of the heathen he was, as a matter of fact, describing the basic sinfulness of fallen man as such, the inner reality of the life of Israel no less than of that of the Gentiles. And the correctness of this view is confirmed by the fact that the "Wherefore" at the beginning of 2.1, which has proved so baffling

as a criticism of his largely Gentile audience, for they are people whom Paul describes as 'those Gentiles who are called to belong to Jesus Christ', those 'who are loved by God and called to be his holy people' (1:6-7), and those who 'are full of goodness, filled with knowledge and competent to instruct one another' (15:14).

Paul's devastating critique of the Gentile world in 1:18-32, then, appears to serve a rhetorical purpose. Being aware of Jewish criticisms of his gospel being aired in Rome (cf. 3:8; 6:1, 15), the apostle begins to engage a hypothetical Jewish opponent for the sake of his predominantly Gentile Christian audience. The critique of the Gentile world in 1:18-32 is typical of Jewish censure of Gentiles (cf., e.g., Wis 13–14), a critique that his hypothetical opponent who takes the high moral ground would readily endorse.

This sets a trap for the opponent, enabling Paul to take the second step in demonstration of the fact that all humanity is exposed to the wrath of God because of sin. Thus he goes on immediately to show that all those who take the high moral ground, while practicing the very things they condemn in others, are simply storing up wrath for themselves on the day of God's wrath, something he says that applies to the Jew first and also the Gentile (2:1-16).[2]

---

to commentators, becomes, on this assumption, perfectly intelligible: if 1.18-32 does indeed declare the truth about all men, then it really does follow from it that the man who sets himself up as a judge of his fellows is without excuse. So we understand these verses as the revelation of the gospel's judgment of all men, which lays bare not only the idolatry of ancient and modern paganism but also the idolatry ensconced in Israel'. . . .

But Fitzmyer, *Romans*, 270-71, argues: 'In vv 18-32, though Paul speaks only of "human beings" (*anthrōpoi*, 1:18) and never specifies "Gentiles" or "Greeks", it becomes clear from 2:1 on (or at least from 2:9) that he has been thinking in this first subsection of non-Jewish humanity. . . . Paul's allusions to Ps 106.20 and Jer 2:11 (which refer to incidents in Israel's history) do not mean that he envisages Jewish humanity as well in vv 18-32. He is simply extrapolating from such incidents in the history of the chosen people and applying the ideas to the pagan world'.

Similarly Moo, *Romans*, 97, who contends: 'Two considerations, in particular, favor a reference mainly to Gentiles. First, the passage is reminiscent of Jewish apologetic arguments in which Gentile idolatry was derided and the moral sins of the Gentile world were traced to that idolatry. Second, the knowledge of God rejected by those depicted in 1:18-32 comes solely through "natural revelation" — the evidences of God in creation and, perhaps, the conscience. The situation with Jews is, of course, wholly different, for Paul holds them responsible for the special revelation they have been given in the law (cf. 2:12-13, 17-29)'.

2. Cf. Douglas A. Campbell, 'Natural Theology in Paul? Reading Romans 1.19-20', *International Journal of Systematic Theology* 1 (1999) 244-47, 251-52, who argues that 1:19–3:20 should be understood as an *ad hominem* strategy whereby Paul 'savages' the position he spells out in 1:19-32. The depiction of Gentiles in 1:19-32 is that held by Paul's opposing Jewish teachers, and he will show in 2:1–3:20 that such a position regarding Gentiles is unacceptable, and in fact would mean the Jewish teachers themselves would stand condemned under such a theology of salvation. Cf. also Byrne, *Romans*, 63: 'Moreover, the opening section, 1:18-32, which at first sight appears to target the alienation of the Gentile world, has its own rhetorical role to play within the wider block, 1:18–3:20. It catches the Jewish dialogue partner in a rhetorical "trap" (2:1-3; cf. Gal 2:15-16) designed to drive home more effectively the thesis that there is no righteousness to be had on the basis of the law. Recognition of these rhetorical

In the third step, having his hypothetical Jewish opponent particularly in mind, Paul insists that possession of the law and circumcision will not provide him with immunity from God's judgment if he does not obey the law and in that way shows that he is circumcised in heart as well as in the flesh (2:17-29).[3]

Finally, Paul shows that there is no compromise of God's righteousness involved when God pronounces judgment upon the Jewish people despite their privilege of possessing the 'the very words of God' (3:1-20). All peoples, apart from God's grace in Christ, stand exposed to his judgment. By so doing, Paul makes clear to his largely Gentile Christian audience in Rome that Jews who criticize his gospel have no right to claim the higher moral ground.[4]

"roles within roles" played by the various sections is vital to interpretation. No single element in the running argument can be taken simply in isolation and given independent value. This caution is particularly important in the case of the first element, 1:18-32'.

3. J. C. O'Neill, *Paul's Letter to the Romans* (Baltimore: Penguin Books, 1975), 53, and, more recently, William O. Walker Jr., 'Romans 1.18–2.29: A Non-Pauline Interpolation?' *NTS* 45 (1999) 533-52, have argued that 1:18-32 is part of a non-Pauline interpolation (1:18–2:29), without which Paul's argument would flow easily from 1:17 directly to 3:1. Their argument is based upon considerations of language ('almost a third of the nouns, adjectives, and verbs in Rom 1.18-32 — a total of 34 words or 31.9 percent — appear nowhere else in the authentic Pauline letters'), context (there is an abrupt change of subject matter at 1:18 — it is 'no longer *the gospel as the revelation of God's saving righteousness;* now it is *the wrath of God* that is revealed against wicked people'), and theological content (much of the theological content appears to be un-Pauline or even anti-Pauline — e.g., those who practice the law will be justified).

However, arguments based on language are always difficult to sustain because one has to allow for an author to change his style of expression to suit his purpose. Questions of context and theological emphases are important, but in this case both these things can be shown to be consistent with Paul's purpose if 1:18–2:29 is regarded as an integral part of the letter. For example, Paul's statement in 1:16 that the gospel is 'the power of God for the salvation of everyone who believes: first for the Jew, then for the Gentile', implies that all peoples, Jews and Gentiles alike, have sinned and are equally exposed to the judgment of God and therefore need that salvation. It was to show his audience that this is not without foundation in Jewish tradition, being rooted in the OT, that Paul interposed 1:18–2:29.

4. Calvin L. Porter, 'Romans 1.18-32: Its Role in the Developing Argument', *NTS* 40 (1994) 210-28, adopts a different approach to 1:18-32. In a two-step process he argues: (i) This passage contains arguments similar to those found in Hellenistic Jewish discourse (e.g., the Wisdom of Solomon) that are used to strengthen the boundaries between Jews and Gentiles. (ii) Paul's purpose in Romans, and in particular in 2:1-16, is to argue against such a use of this sort of discourse because it hinders the progress of his Gentile mission. Put another way, Paul is setting forth the well-known Jewish polemic against Gentiles in 1:18-32 only to demonstrate the following point: 'No one can speak the exclusionary discourse of Rom 1.18-32. Every mouth is silenced' (228).

The difference between Porter's view of the function of 1:18-32 and that set out above and adopted in this commentary is that for Porter 1:18-32 is a discourse that Paul wants his Roman audience to eschew, rather than one functioning as part of his argument showing that all humanity, Jews as well as Gentiles, stand exposed to the judgment of God. There is very little in the immediate context to suggest that Paul thought his audience needed to be rebuked for indulging in such 'exclusionary discourse'. It is better to read 2:1-16 as a dia-

Before turning to the detailed exegesis of 1:18-32, it will be helpful to comment on two general matters affecting our approach to the whole. First is the matter of the structure of this passage. As has often been noted,[5] there is a threefold repetition of a pattern of human rebellion and divine retribution, as may be seen in the following:

> People *exchanged* the glory of the immortal God for images. . . . Therefore God *gave them over* in the sinful desires of their hearts. (1:21-24)

> They *exchanged* the truth of God for a lie. . . . Because of this, God *gave them over* to shameful lusts. (1:25-26a)

> Even their women *exchanged* natural relations for unnatural ones. In the same way the men also abandoned natural relations with women. . . . He [God] *gave them over* to a depraved mind, so that they do what ought not to be done. (1:26b-31)

Second, there may be an Adamic allusion in 1:18-32. M. D. Hooker (among others) suggests this:

> Of Adam it is supremely true that God manifested to him that which can be known of him (v. 19); that from the creation onwards, God's attributes were clearly discernible to him in the things which had been made, and that he was thus without excuse (v. 20). Adam, above and before all men, knew God, but failed to honour him as God, and grew vain in his thinking and allowed his heart to be darkened (v. 20). Adam's fall was the result of his desire to be as God, to attain knowledge of good and evil (Gen. iii.5), so that claiming to be wise, he in fact became a fool (v. 21). Thus he not only failed to give glory to God but, according to rabbinic tradition, himself lost the glory of God which was reflected in his face (v. 23). In believing the serpent's lie that his action would not lead to death (Gen. iii.4) he turned his back on the truth of God, and he obeyed, and thus gave his allegiance to a creature, the serpent, rather than to the Creator (v. 25). Adam, certainly, knew God's *dikaiōma* ['righteous requirement'] (cf. Rom. vv. 12-14); by eating the forbidden fruit he not only broke that *dikaiōma* ['righteous requirement'], but also consented with the action of Eve, who had already taken the fruit (v. 32).[6]

However, caution is needed before adopting this view too quickly, for, as Fitzmyer points out, the case is not as strong as it first seems:

---

tribe in which Paul engages a hypothetical Jewish opponent in a dialogue for the benefit of his Gentile Christian audience.

5. Cf., e.g., Dunn, *Romans 1–8*, 53; Moo, *Romans*, 96; Wright, 'Romans', 431.

6. M. D. Hooker, 'Adam in Romans 1', *NTS* 6 (1960) 300-301. Cf. also D. J. W. Milne, 'Genesis 3 in the Letter to the Romans', *RTR* 39 (1980) 10-12; Dunn, *Romans 1–8*, 53.

This interpretation reads too much of Genesis into the text. What allusions are alleged to be there are to Genesis 1, not to Genesis 2–3. To invoke 'rabbinic tradition', as does Hooker ('Adam', 301), is to invoke literature dating from many centuries later than Paul, especially when it comes from the Babylonian Talmud and *Bereshit Rabbah*. . . . Hooker (ibid.) recognizes, indeed, that the vbs. *exapesteilen*, 'he sent forth', and *exebalen*, 'he cast out' (Gen 3:23-24), are 'different' from *paredōken*, 'he delivered over' (1:24, 26, 28); but, if so, where is the allusion to Genesis? The parallelism between vv. 23, 25, 28 and vv. 24, 26-27, may be there (Hooker, 'A Further Note'), but that still fails to show any influence of 'the account of Adam's fall in Genesis' on the Pauline discussion. By way of contrast, see Wis 10:1, where Adam *is* referred to as 'the first-formed father of the world, when he alone had been created'. Yet Paul has nothing that echoes such a reference to Adam, even though he otherwise alludes to passages in this part of the Book of Wisdom (chaps. 10–19) in his argument. The alleged echoes of the Adam stories in Genesis are simply nonexistent.[7]

a. Humanity's Rejection of the Revelation of God in Nature, 1:18-23

[18]*The wrath of God is being revealed from heaven against all the godlessness and wickedness of people, who suppress the truth by their wickedness,* [19]*since what may be known about God is plain to them, because God has made it plain to them.* [20]*For since the creation of the world God's invisible qualities — his eternal power and divine nature — have been clearly seen, being understood from what has been made, so that people are without excuse.*

[21]*For although they knew God, they neither glorified him as God nor gave thanks to him, but their thinking became futile and their foolish hearts were darkened.* [22]*Although they claimed to be wise, they became fools* [23]*and exchanged the glory of the immortal God for images made to look like a mortal human being and birds and animals and reptiles.*

1:18-19 The revelation of God's righteousness through the gospel is needed, Paul says, [because] *the wrath of God is being revealed from heaven against all the godlessness and wickedness of people.*[8] The conjunction 'because' is omitted in the NIV translation, thus obscuring the connection between 1:17 and 1:18 and making it difficult for modern readers to recognize that it is humanity's sinfulness and consequent exposure to the wrath of God that made the revelation of God's righteousness through the gospel necessary.[9]

---

7. Fitzmyer, *Romans*, 274.

8. Mark A. Seifrid, 'Natural Revelation and the Purpose of the Law in Romans', *TynBul* 49 (1998) 117, notes correctly that in Rom 1:18-32 Paul has in mind God's wrath upon those who worship idols, whereas in 2:1-11 it is those who assume the role of judge that he has in mind.

9. Cf. Richard H. Bell, *No One Seeks for God: An Exegetical and Theological Study of Romans 1:18–3.20* (WUNT 106; Tübingen: Mohr Siebeck, 1998), 255.

When the apostle says the wrath of God is being revealed 'from heaven', he may be alluding to the Sodom tradition, a tradition developed and persisting in Jewish oral culture (and therefore known not only by Paul but also many of the illiterate Christians with a synagogue background who heard his letter read). In the Sodom tradition God rained down fire and brimstone 'from heaven' upon a godless and wicked city.[10] Manson offers the following explanation of the nature of God's wrath:

> The relation of man to God being one of hostility *(echthra)*, the corresponding relation of God to man is also described in one word — wrath *(orgē)*. This is not an affective condition in God corresponding to what we should call 'anger' or 'rage'. It is rather to be defined with Schlatter as the will of God as opposed to evil. But though the Anger of God *(orgē theou)* is not to be regarded as bad temper, we must not blind ourselves to the fact that for Paul it was a very serious thing. This inflexible resistance of God to evil, his determination to extirpate it in every shape or form, means that man's condition as subject, slave, and instrument of sin is one that can only end in calamity for himself. The natural man is travelling as fast as his two feet will carry him to perdition *(apōleia)*.[11]

Our understanding of the revelation of the wrath of God in 1:18 will depend in part upon the way we interpret the expression 'is being revealed'. Paul uses the present tense of the verb here, and this has led some interpreters to say that Paul envisages God's wrath being presently poured out. The wrath of God can then be interpreted in terms of God's handing people over to the natural outworking of their sinful behavior in the present time, as described in 1:24, 26, and 28. Moo, one who adopts this view, quotes Schiller's famous aphorism: 'The history of the world is the judgment of the world'.[12]

There are, however, other ways of interpreting the revelation of God's wrath. Barth taught that the revelation of God's wrath, like the revelation of his righteousness, occurs in the preaching of the gospel, which at its heart is the preaching of the cross which makes known both the seriousness of sin that calls forth God's wrath, and the abundant grace of God in providing salvation.[13] However, it seems clear that the revelation of God's righteousness in 1:17 is more than the provision of information; it mediates God's power for salvation. If we recognize the parallelism existing between the revelations of 1:17 and 1:18, the revelation of God's wrath will involve

10. Cf. Philip F. Esler, 'The Sodom Tradition in Romans 1:18-32', *BTB* 34 (2004) 9-10.

11. T. W. Manson, *On Paul and John: Some Selected Themes*, ed. Matthew Black (SBT 38; London: SCM, 1963), 41-42.

12. Moo, *Romans*, 101.

13. Karl Barth, *A Shorter Commentary on Romans* (London: SCM, 1959), 25-26. Cranfield, *Romans*, I, 110, adopts a similar view.

more than information; it will have concrete expression in history and at
the close of the age (1:21-32; 2:5).[14]

Another suggestion is that Paul is using the present tense here to depict the pouring out of God's wrath in the future. The following arguments
have been advanced for this view: (i) The revelation of God's wrath is said
to be 'from heaven', and where this expression is used elsewhere in Paul's
letters it refers to a future event — the revelation of Jesus Christ on the Last
Day (1 Thess 4:16; 2 Thess 1:7); (ii) At the end of this passage Paul says that
those who are guilty of this wickedness know that they 'deserve death' —
suggesting that the punishment is still in the future; (iii) in the next chapter
he speaks explicitly of people storing up wrath for themselves 'for the day
of God's wrath, when his righteous judgment will be revealed' (2:5).[15] The
weakness of this view is that it fails to account for the implied parallelism
of the revelations of God's righteousness for salvation and the revelation of
his wrath.

There is another view that seeks to combine both the present and future interpretations. For example, Dunn says: 'God's final judgment is simply the end of a process already in train (cf. particularly 1 *Enoch* 84.4; 91.7-
9)! The clear implication [of 1:17-18] is that the two heavenly revelations are
happening concurrently, as well as divine righteousness, so also divine
wrath; to take the second *apokalyptetai* ['is revealed'] as future (Eckstein) destroys the parallel and draws an unnecessary distinction between God's
wrath and the divine action in "he handed over" in *paredōken* (vv 24, 26,
28)'.[16] To see the future judgment as the culmination of the present revelation of God's wrath towards human wickedness is an attractive way of
bringing together the various emphases the apostle makes in regard to the
revelation of the wrath of God — that which is presently being revealed
(1:18), and that which is being stored up for the day of wrath (2:5).

What attracts God's wrath is the 'godlessness and wickedness of people'. The terms 'godlessness and wickedness' denote, on the one hand, lack
of reverence for the deity ('godlessness'), and on the other a violation of human rights ('wickedness').[17] Paul spells out in some detail the nature of the
'godlessness and wickedness', which he believes will attract God's wrath
(see the commentary on 1:19-32 below). Briefly stated, this involves, on the
one hand, knowing God but not glorifying him as God nor giving thanks to
him, becoming futile in one's thinking and exchanging the glory of the immortal God for images of mere creatures, and exchanging the truth of God
for a lie and worshipping the creature rather than the Creator. On the other

14. Cf. Moo, *Romans*, 100-101.
15. Cf. Hans-Joachim Eckstein, '"Denn Gottes Zorn wird vom Himmel her offenbar
werden": Exegetische Erwägungen zu Röm 1 18', *ZNW* 78 (1987) 74-89, who argues, in the
light of its context in 1:18-32, that the term *apokalyptetai* ['is revealed], used in relation to the
revelation of God's wrath in 1:18, can only be understood in a future, eschatological sense.
16. Dunn, *Romans 1-8*, 54.
17. Cf. BAGD, *ad loc.*

hand, it involves abandoning natural sexual relations for unnatural ones, practicing every kind of wickedness, and not only doing so but also approving the behavior of others who do the same while knowing that those who practice such things deserve death.[18]

The fundamental reason why God's wrath will be revealed against such people is that they *suppress the truth by their wickedness*.[19] The word translated 'suppress' in this context may be construed in one of two ways: (i) to mean 'suppress' (as in the NIV) so that Paul is saying that these people are suppressing or rejecting the truth they know; (ii) to mean 'hold on to' so that Paul would be saying that the people are holding the truth they know, but nevertheless behaving in a way that is entirely inconsistent with that claim.[20] The latter translation would be in accord with what Paul later accuses his hypothetical dialogue partner of doing (cf. 2:1, 17-24). Baker comments aptly: 'The two possibilities are complementary, not contradictory. If the unsaved possess the truth in an unrighteous state, they are actually suppressing it. Likewise, the suppression of truth seems to presuppose the possession of it'.[21]

Paul says that people are culpable *since what may be known about God is plain to them, because God has made it plain to them*. The phrase translated 'what may be known about God', taken by itself, is ambiguous. It could mean either as 'what *is* known about God' (so, e.g., NASB) or 'what *may* be known about God' (so, e.g., NIV). The word translated 'known' is found only here in Paul's writings but fourteen times elsewhere in the NT, and in every case it refers to something that is known or being made known, not something that may be known.[22] This would support the translation of

18. Cranfield, *Roman*, I, 112, comments: 'in view of the fact that the single *pasan* ['all'] embraces both *asebeian* ['godlessness'] and *adikian* ['wickedness'], and the fact that in the participial clause *adikia* ['wickedness'] by itself is apparently meant to represent the double expression, it is more probable that they are here used as two names for the same thing combined in order to afford a more rounded description of it than either gives by itself (*asebeia* ['godlessness'] focusing attention on the fact that all sin is an attack on the majesty of God, *adikia* ['wickedness'] on the fact that it is a violation of God's just order'.

19. John R. Levison, 'Adam and Eve in Romans 1.18-25 and the Greek *Life of Adam and Eve*', *NTS* 50 (2004) 525-28, suggests a parallel between the suppression of the truth in Rom 1:18 and Eve's suppression of the truth when she urges Adam to eat the forbidden fruit by hiding from him the consequences in the Greek *Life of Adam and Eve* 21:1-6.

20. Cf. BAGD, *ad loc*.

21. Bruce A. Baker, 'Romans 1:18-21 and Presuppositional Apologetics', *BSac* 155 (1998) 285.

22. Luke 2:44; 23:49; John 18:15, 16; Acts 1:19; 2:14; 4:10, 16; 9:42; 13:38; 15:18; 19:17; 28:22, 28. *Contra* Cranfield, *Romans*, I, 113, who says: 'While elsewhere in the NT (in which, apart from its use here and twice in John, its occurrences are confined to Luke and Acts) *gnōstos* always means "known", in classical Greek and also in the LXX it sometimes has the meaning "knowable"; and there is little doubt that this is its sense here, since, if it meant "known", the sentence would scarcely be regarded as anything but a tautologism. The phrase as a whole must mean "that which is knowable (to man) of God", i.e., "God, in so far as He is knowable (to man)"'. Cf. Fitzmyer, *Romans*, 279; Käsemann, *Romans*, 39; Byrne, *Romans*, 66-73.

1:19a as 'what is known about God'. The reason why what is known about God 'is plain to them' is that God himself 'has made it plain to them'.[23] What the apostle means by this is spelled out in 1:20.

ADDITIONAL NOTE: THE WRATH OF GOD

The word translated 'wrath' occurs 298 times (in 284 verses) in the LXX, and in 223 of these occurrences it refers to the wrath of God (the others refer to human anger). References to the wrath of God in the LXX more often denote temporal punishments imposed or threatened because of the sins of Israel (most frequently) or the nations (less frequently). However, in the prophetic writings there are a significant number of references to the pouring out of God's wrath on the great coming 'day of the LORD'. In the Pauline corpus the word 'wrath' occurs twenty-one times (in 19 verses), and of these eighteen refer to God's wrath. Of the references to the wrath of God eleven refer to his wrath to be revealed on the Last Day (Rom 2:5 [2x], 8; 5:9; 9:22 [2x]; 12:19; Eph 5:6; Col 3:6; 1 Thess 1:10; 5:9), two clearly refer to temporal punishments (Rom 13:4, 5), three are general statements (Rom 3:5; 4:15; Eph 2:3), and what the last two denote is not immediately clear (Rom 1:18; 1 Thess 2:16). Elsewhere in the NT the word 'wrath' occurs fifteen times (in 15 verses), and of these twelve refer to the wrath of God (the other three to human anger). Of those which refer to God's wrath, nine are references to God's wrath poured out on the Last Day (Matt 3:7; Luke 3:7; 21:23; Rev 6:16, 17; 11:18; 14:10; 16:19; 19:15), two are temporal expressions of God's wrath (Heb 3:11; 4:3), and one is a reference to God's wrath abiding upon those who reject his Son (John 3:36).

It is evident from these references to God's wrath in both the LXX and the NT that it denotes his personal indignation towards human sinfulness. This is now recognized widely by modern interpreters of Paul so that the older liberal view championed by C. H. Dodd according to which God's wrath was reduced to 'an inevitable process of cause and effect in a moral universe'[24] is generally rejected.[25] Byrne says: 'The sense of divine wrath is bound up with the biblical conception of a personal God whose dealings with humankind are attended by an intense moral will. The wrath of God

---

23. Witherington, *Romans*, 66, says that 'vv. 21, 28 and 32 suggest that Paul is not just talking about God making himself objectively known, so that it was possible for a pagan to know God to some degree. Rather, Paul is saying that in some sense they actually do subjectively know God. Otherwise, they could not have exchanged this truth for a lie or suppressed this knowledge'.

24. C. H. Dodd, *The Epistle of Paul to the Romans* (London: Fontana, 1959), 50.

25. Cf., e.g., Wright, 'Romans', 431; Cranfield, *Romans*, I, 108-9; Dunn, *Romans 1–8*, 54-55; Byrne, *Romans*, 72-73.

blazes out when that will, and specifically the love that lies behind it, is thwarted by human pride, rebellion, obstinacy or disloyalty'. . . .[26]

1:20 In this verse Paul spells out what is known about God, and how God has made it known: *For since the creation of the world God's invisible qualities — his eternal power and divine nature — have been clearly seen, being understood from what has been made, so that people are without excuse.*[27] Paul's statement here echoes the words of Psalm 19:1-4:

> The heavens declare the glory of God;
>   the skies proclaim the work of his hands.
> Day after day they pour forth speech;
>   night after night they reveal knowledge.
> They have no speech, they use no words;
>   No sound is heard from them.
> Yet their voice goes out into all the earth,
>   their words to the ends of the world.

Paul's claim that 'God's invisible qualities' are revealed through creation, and that people are culpable for their failure to appreciate this, has a parallel in the Wisdom of Solomon (believed to have been written by a Hellenistic Jew, probably in Alexandria, in the latter part of the first century B.C.):

> For all people who were ignorant of God were foolish by nature; and they were unable from the good things that are seen to know the one who exists, nor did they recognize the artisan while paying heed to his works; but they supposed that either fire or wind or swift air, or the circle of the stars, or turbulent water, or the luminaries of heaven were the gods that rule the world. If through delight in the beauty of these things people assumed them to be gods, let them know how much better than these is their Lord, for the author of beauty created them. And if people were amazed at their power and working, let them perceive from them how much more powerful is the one who formed them. For from the greatness and beauty of created things comes a corresponding perception of their Creator. (13:1-5 NRSV)

---

26. Byrne, *Romans*, 72-73.

27. Cf. Chrysostom: 'Will the heathen say at the judgment that they were ignorant of God? Did they not hear the heaven sending forth a voice while the well ordered-harmony of all things spoke out more clearly than a trumpet? Did you not see the hours of night and day remaining constantly unmoved, the good order of winter, spring and the other seasons remaining both fixed and unmoved? . . . Yet God did not set so great a system of teaching before the heathen in order to deprive them of any excuse but so that they might come to know him. It was by their failure to recognize him that they deprived themselves of every excuse' ('Homilies on Romans 3' [*ACCSR*, 39]).

From the earliest Christian centuries the following three steps in Paul's argument in 1:20 have been identified: (i) since the creation of the world God's nature has been clearly seen; (ii) it is to be understood through what he has made; and (iii) this is the reason humanity is without excuse for its failure to honor God as God.[28] Instead of honoring God, Paul goes on to explain, they gave themselves over to idolatry (1:21-23).

Paul's reference to God's 'invisible qualities' (lit. 'his invisible things') echoes the witness of Scripture to God's invisibility (Exod 33:19-20; John 1:18; 6:46; Heb 11:27), and corresponds with his own statements elsewhere (Col 1:15-16; 1 Tim 1:17). God's invisible qualities evident through creation are described here as 'his eternal power and divine nature'. God's 'eternal power' is seen in the work of creation, and perhaps this eternal power is the aspect of his 'divine nature' to which Paul refers. Baker identifies three attributes of God implied by this verse: personal, eternal, and dynamic. He adds: 'The fact that God is eternal and powerful was common to Judaism and Greek philosophy. But the idea of a personal God, while natural to Judaism, would have been foreign to Greek philosophy, which believed in a nonpersonal origin of the universe'.[29]

The word Paul uses to denote God's 'divine nature' is found only here in the NT and only once in the LXX — in Wisdom 18:9: 'For in secret the holy children of good people offered sacrifices, and with one accord agreed to the divine law (lit. 'the law of the deity')'. It denotes the quality or characteristic(s) pertaining to deity, divinity, divine nature, divineness.[30]

'God's invisible qualities — his eternal power and divine nature', the apostle explains, 'have been clearly seen, being understood from what has been made'. The verb translated 'clearly seen' is found only here in the NT, and eight times in the LXX, of which seven places denote seeing with the eyes (Exod 10:5; Num 24:2; Deut 26:15; Jdt 6:19; Job 10:4; 39:26; Bar 2:16), and only one denotes 'considering' with the mind (3 Macc 3:11). Being guided by the predominant usage, we should probably recognize that Paul intended his audience to conclude that God's invisible qualities are to be understood, in the first instance, by seeing with their eyes what he has created, and then by considering its significance.[31]

---

28. Cf. Thomas C. Oden, 'Without Excuse: Classic Christian Exegesis of General Revelation', *JETS* 41 (1998) 55-68. John G. Cook, 'The Logic and Language of Romans 1,20', *Bib* 75 (1994) 497, describes 1:20 as an enthymeme with the following form: 'Minor premise: The invisible things of God (God's eternal power and divinity) are perceived through the understanding from the creation of the world in God's works. Conclusion: Therefore human beings are without excuse (for not honoring God). The unstated major premise is something like the following: If people are aware of truth about God and suppress it by not honoring God, then they are without excuse (for not honoring God)'.

29. Baker, 'Romans 1:18-21', 289, 'First the term *aidios* shows the eternality of God; second, that God is powerful is shown in the word *dynamis*; and third, that God is personal is seen in the use of the pronoun *autou* ['his'] here and in the preceding phrase'.

30. BAGD, *ad loc.*

31. Baker, 'Romans 1:18-21', 292, remarks: 'Taking into consideration the Hellenistic

Cook notes that there are parallels to Paul's language in 1:20 in the works of the Hellenistic philosophers Ps.-Aristotle, Stobaeus, Themistius, and the Hellenistic Jewish historian Josephus.[32] In addition, he cites extensively from the *Thesaurus Linguae Graecae (TLG)* to show how key words used by Paul in 1:20 ('understood', 'seen', 'the invisible things', 'eternal power and deity') all appear in philosophical contexts, and also individually in Hellenistic Jewish authors.[33] He concludes that Paul was willing 'to use tools of the dominant culture, including thoughts about God and philosophical terminology, in order to communicate to the Roman church', that his 'argument shows his departure from the dominant Hellenistic culture of his time. His countercultural condemnation of image worship was a rejection of a norm that united the dominant culture'.[34]

ADDITIONAL NOTE: NATURAL THEOLOGY

Paul's statements in 1:19-20 raise the question of natural theology. Did the apostle believe that knowledge of God was available to humankind through creation, and, if so, in what way?

Käsemann, while acknowledging an appeal to natural theology in Acts 14:15-17; 17:22-29, questions its existence in Paul's letters: 'Characteristic of Paul is what he does not adopt and the great restraint shown in what he does adopt. In contrast to Acts, for example, creation is not an independent doctrine in the authentic Pauline epistles'. . . .[35] Cranfield rejects any notion of natural theology, if by that is meant that people can come unaided to a knowledge of God through creation: 'The result of God's self-manifestation in His creation is not a natural knowledge of God on men's

---

backdrop for Paul's argument in this section, it becomes clear why Paul chose both words to express this thought. If he had used only *kathoratai* [seen'], the phrase would have been ambiguous. One could argue that the reality and nature of God may be seen with the eye but not understood with the mind. On the other hand, if the apostle had written *nooumena* ['understood'] without *kathoratai* ['seen'], he would have left the interpretive door open to the Hellenistic notions that revelation is merely internal or mystical. The use of both terms, however, avoids both ambiguity and philosophical confusion. "By allowing the meaning of the verb to be determined by the participle, Paul clearly affirmed the epistemological truism that knowledge (even of God) occurs through the conjunction of reflection and sensation"'. Cf. Byrne, *Romans,* 73: 'The Greek sentence contains an oxymoron (*aorato . . . kathoratai* ['invisible . . . seen']) that seems designed to bring out the paradox that the visible things made by God enable a spiritual "seeing" ("perception" — cf. the qualifying participial phrase *nooumena*) of the invisible divine attributes. The Pauline text here has a remarkable parallel from the Greek philosophical tradition in Ps.-Aristotle, *De Mundo* 399b.20: "though by nature invisible to every mortal being, he (God) is seen through his works"'.

32. Cook, 'The Logic and Language of Romans 1,20', 498-500.

33. Cook, 'The Logic and Language of Romans 1,20', 501-13.

34. Cook, 'The Logic and Language of Romans 1,20', 514-16.

35. Käsemann, *Romans,* 40.

part independent of God's self-revelation in His Word, a valid though limited knowledge, but simply the excuselessness of men in their ignorance. A real self-disclosure of God has indeed taken place and is always occurring, and men ought to have recognized, but in fact have not recognized, Him. . . . Barrett is surely correct over against a great many interpretations of this passage when he declares: "it is not Paul's intention" in these verses "to establish a natural theology; nor does he create one unintentionally"'.[36]

Other scholars espouse more positive approaches to the matter, albeit with various qualifications. Young lists three different approaches: (i) a knowledge of God available to human beings by the application of reason to the evidence available in creation; (ii) a direct revelation from God to every person through creation; (iii) a vague awareness of God shared by all by virtue of their very existence in the world he created.[37] Having scanned 'Paul's symbolic world' (Greco-Roman and Jewish literature) to locate influences that might have affected the apostle's understanding of these things, Young concludes that the texts surveyed reflect the fact that human beings confronted with God's creation have an 'unthematic awareness' of the Creator. He defines this 'unthematic awareness' as:

> A passive and spontaneous mental activity based on observation. It is not a deliberate rational process. When one is thrown into a den of lions, there is an immediate awareness that this is a dangerous situation from which one must escape. In a similar way when one is 'thrown' into the created world, one becomes aware of his or her creaturely finitude, and, as Wolfhart Pannenberg says, becomes aware of "a vague sense of infinitude". The human mind perceives that whatever lies beyond must be the Creator, who alone should be worshipped.[38]

Other scholars adopt a similar attitude, though they do not articulate it as clearly as Young does. Wright says: 'Paul clearly does believe that when humans look at creation *they are aware, at some level*, of the power and divinity of the creator' (italics added).[39] Schreiner says: 'God has stitched into the fabric of the human mind his existence and power, so that *they are instinctively recognized* when one views the created world' (italics added).[40]

Then there are scholars who argue that Paul believed that some knowledge of God is discernible through creation when people engage in rational contemplation. Fitzmyer says: 'Although God cannot be seen with

36. Cranfield, *Romans*, I, 116.

37. Cf. Richard Alan Young, 'The Knowledge of God in Romans 1:18-32: Exegetical and Theological Reflections', *JETS* 43 (2000) 695-96.

38. Young, 'The Knowledge of God in Romans 1:18-32', 706. Henry Efferin, 'A Study on General Revelation: Romans 1:18-32; 2:12-16', *STJ* 4 (1996) 153, after reviewing Rom 1:18-32; 2:12-16, comes to the conclusion that 'the most consistent view, according to the Bible, should be that *there is general revelation but no natural theology*'.

39. Wright, 'Romans', 432.

40. Schreiner, *Romans*, 86.

human senses, he is perceived in his works *by the human mind. . . .* In the *contemplation* of the created world and in *reflection* on it, a human being perceives the great "Unseen" behind it all — the omnipotence and divine character of its Maker' (italics added)'.[41] Dunn's approach is similar: 'It is scarcely possible that Paul did not intend his audience to think in terms of *some kind of rational perception* of the fuller reality in and behind the created cosmos' (italics added).[42]

There are others who argue against this view. So, for example, Schreiner: 'Neither is Paul suggesting that knowledge of God's existence and power is the result of careful deduction and reasoning, so that the text can be used to encourage sophisticated rational argumentation as an apologetic for God's existence. . . . Instead, this knowledge of God is a reality for all people, not simply for those who possess unusually logical minds. They come to a knowledge of God through the created world because "God made it manifest to them"'.[43]

The majority of scholars, even those who discern a 'natural theology' of some sort in 1:19-20, emphasize that it was not Paul's purpose to provide one, nor that he thought such knowledge would be saving,[44] but rather they insist that he employed it to highlight human culpability — that human beings 'are without excuse'.[45]

1:21 People's godlessness is an affront to God, *for although they knew God, they neither glorified him as God nor gave thanks to him.* This statement may imply temporality — the knowing preceding the failure to glorify God or give thanks to him (i.e., rendering the text: 'when they knew God, they neither glorified him as God nor gave thanks').[46] If so, Johnson's comment would be appropriate: 'The apostle is writing of historical events and interpreting the story of man after the fall. The result is that the words provide the reader with an interesting insight into the biblical interpretation of the spiritual history of man'.[47] However, if a verbal aspect approach is adopted to the tenses in the whole section (1:18-21), it becomes a passage made up of timeless statements — 'the present-tense verbs setting the stage and providing the conclusion and the aorist verbs specifying the details'.[48]

Paul's reference to the fact that people 'knew God' raises the question

41. Fitzmyer, *Romans,* 280.
42. Dunn, *Romans 1–8,* 58.
43. Schreiner, *Romans,* 86-87.
44. Cf. Wright, 'Romans', 432; Witherington, *Romans,* 68; Schreiner, *Romans,* 86.
45. Byrne, *Romans,* 67; Witherington, *Romans,* 68.
46. The aorist participle *gnontes* and the aorist indicatives *edoxasan* and *eucharistēsan* would then refer to historical events.
47. S. Lewis Johnson Jr., "Paul and the Knowledge of God', *BSac* 129 (1972) 72-73, cited by Baker, 'Romans 1:18-21', 293.
48. Stanley E. Porter, *Verbal Aspect in the Greek of the New Testament, with Reference to Tense and Mood* (New York: Peter Lang, 1993), 236, cited by Baker, 'Romans 1:18-21', 293-94.

of his understanding of the nature of that knowledge. As suggested in 'Additional Note: Natural Theology' above, this knowledge was discernible through creation, probably intuitively, and perhaps also as a result of contemplation of the created order. Such knowledge was clearly limited — it was not saving, and, as far as Paul was concerned, rendered humanity 'without excuse'.

Paul emphasizes two aspects of human sinfulness that render people 'without excuse': the failure to glorify God and to give him thanks.[49] Neither of these fundamental responses is forthcoming from those who suppress the truth by their wickedness.[50] Instead, Paul says, *their thinking became futile and their foolish hearts were darkened.*[51] When the apostle asserts that their thinking became futile', he appears to be alluding to Psalm 94:11 (LXX 93:11): 'The LORD knows all human plans; he knows that they are futile', a text he cites in 1 Corinthians 3:20 ('The Lord knows that the thoughts of the wise are futile'). What this entails is spelled out in 1:22-23.[52]

1:22-23   Paul describes the outcome of their futile thinking: *although they claimed to be wise, they became fools and exchanged the glory of the immortal God for images made to look like a mortal human being and birds and animals and reptiles.* Some scholars see in Paul's reference to people claiming to be wise but becoming fools an allusion to Genesis 3:1-7, where the primeval pair accepted the serpent's false promise and disobeyed God, expecting to gain wisdom, but in fact descended into folly.[53] However, Fitzmyer may be closer to the mark when he says: 'Paul echoes Ps 106:20, "they exchanged their glory

49. Jewett, *Romans*, 157, comments: 'It was generally assumed that the reception of a gift imposed the obligation of giving thanks. Epictetus follows Plato in maintaining the need for every civilized person to have a "sense of gratitude" *(to euchariston)* and recommends that "we should be giving thanks to God for those things for which we ought to give Him thanks. . . . Particularly eloquent is Epictetus's arguments that to be consistent with the nature of humankind, one must praise God: "If, indeed, I were a nightingale, I should be singing as a nightingale; if a swan, as a swan. But as it is, I am a rational being; therefore I must be singing hymns of praise to God"'.

50. It has been frequently noted that Paul's reference to the Gentiles' failure to glorify God here in 1:21 stands in contrast to his comment in 4:20 that Abraham gave glory to God. The failure of the Gentiles can be seen as a negative foil for Abraham's faith. Cf. Edward Adams, 'Abraham's Faith and Gentile Disobedience: Textual Links between Romans 1 and 4', *JSNT* 65 (1997) 47, and references there.

51. [Pseudo-]Constantius says: 'This applies to Pythagoras, Socrates, Plato, Aristotle, Democritus, Epicurus and all the philosophers who considered themselves wise' ('The Holy Letter of St. Paul to the Romans' [*ACCSR*, 41]).

52. Cranfield, *Romans*, I, 118, comments: 'It is important to understand the significance of this statement correctly. It implies no contempt for reason (those Christians who disparage the intellect and the processes of rational thought have no right at all to claim Paul as a supporter). But it is a sober acknowledgment of the fact that the *kardia* as the inner self of man shares fully in the fallenness of the whole man, that the intellect is not a part of human nature somehow exempted from the general corruption, not something which can be appealed to as an impartial arbiter capable of standing outside the influence of the ego and returning a perfectly objective judgment'.

53. Cf. Dunn, *Romans 1–8*, 60-61; Wright, 'Romans', 433.

for the image of a grass-eating bullock", which alludes to the worship of the golden calf at Sinai (Exod 32:1-34). This rather clear allusion to the golden calf makes highly unlikely an implicit allusion to the Adam narratives'.[54]

In any case there is a tragic irony here: 'the glory of the immortal God' is exchanged for mere 'images made to look like a human being'.[55] The prophet Isaiah parodies the folly of those who do these things: 'The carpenter measures with a line and makes an outline with a marker; he roughs it out with chisels and marks it with compasses. He shapes it in human form, human form in all its glory, that it may dwell in a shrine' (Isa 44:13). Ambrosiaster is more scathing:

> So blinded were their hearts that they altered the majesty of the invisible God, which they knew from the things which he had made, not into men but, what is worse and is an inexcusable offense, into the image of men, so that the form of a corruptible man was called a God by them, i.e., a depiction of a man. Moreover, they did not dare honor living people with this name but elevated the images of dead men to the glory of God! What great idiocy, what great stupidity, in that they knew they were calling them to their damnation, among whom an image was more powerful than the truth, and the dead were mightier than the living! Turning away from the living God they preferred dead men, among whose number they found themselves.[56]

More ridiculous than exchanging 'the glory of the immortal God for images made to look like a mortal human being' is to exchange his glory for the images of 'birds and animals and reptiles'. Human beings do reflect the glory of God being created in his image (Gen 1:26-27), even though that image is tarnished by sin, but the same cannot be said for birds, animals, and reptiles.[57] In referring to the images of 'birds and animals and reptiles', Paul may be alluding to Psalm 106:20 (LXX 105:20), where Israel's folly in the matter of the golden calf (cf. Exod 32:1-6) is described: 'They exchanged their glorious God for an image of a bull, which eats grass'. Paul could also be alluding to Deuteronomy 4:15-18:

> You saw no form of any kind the day the LORD spoke to you at Horeb out of the fire. Therefore watch yourselves very carefully, so that you do not become corrupt and make for yourselves an idol, an image of any shape, whether formed like a man or a woman, or like any animal on

54. Fitzmyer, *Romans*, 283.

55. Levison, 'Adam and Eve', 525-28, suggests that there are parallels in the Greek *Life of Adam and Eve* 14:2; 20:2; 21:5 which speak of the loss of the glory of immortality, it being exchanged for 'God's rage and human mortality'.

56. 'Commentary on Paul's Epistles' (*ACCSR*, 42).

57. Cf. Wis 13:10: 'But miserable, with their hopes set on dead things, are those who give the name "gods" to the works of human hands, gold and silver fashioned with skill, and likenesses of animals, or a useless stone, the work of an ancient hand'.

earth or any bird that flies in the air, or like any creature that moves along the ground or any fish in the waters below.

Ambrosiaster castigates those who worship images of men and animals:

They so diminished the majesty and glory of God that they gave the title of 'god' to the images of things which were small and tiny. For the Babylonians were the first to deify a notion of Bel, who was portrayed as a dead man, who supposedly had once been one of their kings. They also worshiped the dragon serpent, which Daniel the man of God killed and of which they had an image. The Egyptians also worshiped a quadruped which they called Apis and which was in the form of a bull. Jeroboam copied this evil by setting up calves in Samaria, to which the Jews were expected to offer sacrifices. . . . By doing this, those who knew the invisible God did not honor him.[58]

b. The Divine Reaction to Human Rejection, 1:24-32

[24]*Therefore God gave them over in the sinful desires of their hearts to sexual impurity for the degrading of their bodies with one another.* [25]*They exchanged the truth about God for a lie, and worshiped and served created things rather than the Creator — who is forever praised. Amen.*
[26]*Because of this, God gave them over to shameful lusts. Even their women exchanged natural sexual relations for unnatural ones.* [27]*In the same way the men also abandoned natural relations with women and were inflamed with lust for one another. Men committed shameful acts with other men, and received in themselves the due penalty for their error.*
[28]*Furthermore, just as they did not think it worthwhile to retain the knowledge of God, so God gave them over to a depraved mind, so that they do what ought not to be done.* [29]*They have become filled with every kind of wickedness, evil, greed and depravity. They are full of envy, murder, strife, deceit and malice. They are gossips,* [30]*slanderers, God-haters, insolent, arrogant and boastful; they invent ways of doing evil; they disobey their parents;* [31]*they have no understanding, no fidelity, no love, no mercy.* [32]*Although they know God's righteous decree that those who do such things deserve death, they not only continue to do these very things but also approve of those who practice them.*

1:24-25 Because people chose to turn away from worshipping God, he gave them over to become slaves to their sin.[59] In 1:24-32 Paul says three

---

58. 'Commentary on Paul's Epistles' (*ACCSR*, 42-43).
59. Later in this letter Paul writes: 'Don't you know that when you offer yourselves to someone as obedient slaves, you are slaves to the one whom you obey — whether you are slaves to sin, which leads to death, or to obedience, which leads to righteousness?' (6:16; cf. John 8:34).

times that God gave people over to captivity: captivity to their sinful desires, shameful lusts, and depraved minds (1:24, 26, 28). In the first of his three references to people being handed over to captivity because they chose to turn away from God, Paul says: *Therefore God gave them over in the sinful desires of their hearts.* Handing people over in the bondage of their sinful desires is God's response to their refusal to honor him or give him thanks and exchanging the glory of the immortal God for images. The word the apostle uses when saying God 'gave over' to captivity those who turned away from him is used extensively in the LXX when God is said to hand people over to their enemies or to deliver people's enemies into their hands (cf., e.g., Gen 14:20; Exod 23:31; Lev 26:25; Num 21:34; Deut 1:27; 21:10; Josh 7:7; Judg 13:1; 1 Sam 14:10; 1 Kgs 8:46; 2 Chr 13:16; Isa 19:4; 36:15; Jer 21:10; Ezek 11:9). In the NT the word is likewise used of people being given into the hands of other powers (cf., e.g., Matt 5:25; 10:17; 17:22; 24:9; Mark 14:41; Luke 20:20; Acts 3:13; 1 Cor 5:5; 2 Cor 4:11; 1 Tim 1:20). Here in 1:24-32 Paul implies that more is involved than the natural outworking of people's choices when they turn away from God. God himself consigns them to captivity in their sins. As repeatedly indicated in both the OT and the NT, God effects his judgments in conjunction with human choices, but never simply dependent upon those choices. Contrary to what some of the early church fathers wrote,[60] this handing over is not equivalent to passive abandonment, but involves an active consignment on God's part.[61] The nature of this cap-

---

60. Ambrosiaster comments: 'They were given over, not so that they could do what they did not want to do, but so that they could carry out exactly what they desired. And this is the goodness of God' ('Commentary on Paul's Epistles'). Commenting on the same text, Chrysostom says: *'God gave them up* means simply that he left them to their own concoctions. For as an army commander if forced to retreat abandons his deserting soldiers to the enemy, he does not thereby actively push them into the enemy camp but passively withdraws his own protection over them. In the same way, God left those who were not ready to receive what comes from him but were the first to desert him, even though he had fully done his part' ('Homilies on Romans'). [Pseudo-]Constantius says: 'In saying that God gave them up to their own lusts, Paul is not claiming that God is the direct cause of this but merely that since God did not bring vengeance on them after much longsuffering and patience, he allowed them to act according to their own desires. He did this, wanting them to be converted to repentance' ('The Holy Letter of St. Paul to the Romans'). (all three quotations are cited in *ACCSR*, 44). Cf. Dunn, *Romans 1-8*, 62-63: 'Paul would see the act of handing over as punitive, but not as spiteful or vengeful. For him it is simply the case that man apart from God regresses to a lower level of animality. God has handed them over in the sense that he has accepted the fact of man's rebellious desire to be free of God (in terms of Gen 3, to be "as God"), and has let go of the control which restrained them from their baser instincts. The rationale is, presumably, that God does not retain control over those who do not desire it; he who wants to be on his own is granted his wish'.

61. Cf. Jewett, *Romans*, 166-67: 'When *paredōken* ['he handed over'] is followed by a dative expression and then by an *eis* ['to'] clause indicating the purpose, it is a technical expression for the police or courts in turning someone over to official custody for the purpose of punishment. This semantic field supports the translation with a formal expression such as "he consigned"'; Cranfield, *Romans*, I, 121: 'Paul's meaning is neither that these men fell out of the hands of God, as Dodd seems to think, nor that God washed His hands of them;

tivity to which God consigns people Paul first describes as bondage *to sexual impurity for the degrading of their bodies with one another*. What this involves is spelled out in 1:26-27 — see commentary on those verses below.

The apostle explains again (cf. 1:23) that those whom God handed over to this captivity were the people who *exchanged the truth about God for a lie, and worshiped and served created things rather than the Creator — who is forever praised. Amen*. There may be an allusion here to Genesis 3, where Adam and Eve believed the lie of the serpent instead of the truth of God and in effect worshipped the creature (the serpent) instead of the Creator (God). If this is the case, while Paul may not have been intentionally describing the sin of Adam and Eve, he saw in Genesis 1–3 something that aptly depicted the state of the Gentile world of his own day.[62] Chrysostom comments: 'Look how strong his condemnation is, for he does not say merely that they served the creature but that they did so more than the creator, thereby giving fresh force to the charge against them and removing any plea for mitigation'.[63] It is noteworthy that in 1 Thessalonians 1:9 Paul describes people's response to the gospel in opposite terms: 'you turned to God from idols to serve the living and true God'.

Paul describes the Creator as the one 'who is forever praised' (lit. 'blessed forever') an expression he uses elsewhere (9:5; 2 Cor 11:31). In 2 Corinthians 1:3; Ephesians 1:3 he extols God with the words, 'Praise be to the God and Father of our Lord Jesus Christ'. Both these expressions reflect typical Jewish/biblical ways of referring to God.[64]

1:26 In 1:24-25 Paul said that those who exchanged the truth of God for a lie were handed over by God to their sinful desires . . . to the degrading of their bodies. In 1:26 Paul reiterates this when he says, *Because of this,*

---

but rather that this delivering them up was a deliberate act of judgment and mercy on the part of the God who smites in order to heal (Isa 19.22), and that throughout the time of their God-forsakenness God is still concerned with them and dealing with them'; Moo, *Romans*, 110-11: 'Paul's purpose in this verse is to highlight the divine side of the cycle of sin; but it must be balanced with the human side, presented in Eph. 4:19, where Paul says that Gentiles "gave themselves up" to licentiousness, leading to all kinds of "uncleanness". God does not simply let the boat go — he gives it a push downstream. Like a judge who hands over a prisoner to the punishment his crime has earned, God hands over the sinner to the terrible cycle of ever-increasing sin'.

62. Levison, 'Adam and Eve', 525-33, identifies several parallels between Rom 1:18-25 and the Greek *Life of Adam and Eve*. In particular he draws attention to (i) the suppression of the truth (cf. Rom 1:18) by Eve when she urges Adam to eat the forbidden fruit by hiding from him the consequences, the loss of the glory of God (*Life* 21–22); and (ii) the forfeiture by humans of their right of dominion over the animals and the animals instead exercising dominion over Eve so that people serve the creature rather than the Creator (cf. Rom 1:25) (*Life* 10–12).

63. 'Homilies on Romans' (*ACCSR*, 45).

64. The expression 'blessed be God' or the like is used extensively in the LXX (more than 50 times; cf., e.g., Gen 9:26; Exod 18:10; Ruth 4:14; 1 Sam 25:32; 2 Sam 6:21; 1 Kgs 1:48; 1 Chr 29:10; 2 Chr 2:12; Ezra 7:27; Ps 18:46; 89:52; Zech 11:5; Dan 3:28; 1 Esdr 4:40; Jdt 13:17; Tob 3:11; 1 Macc 4:30; 2 Macc 1:17).

God gave them over to shameful lusts, explaining that *even their women ex-changed natural relations for unnatural ones.* When people exchanged the truth of God for a lie, God in turn 'gave them over' to a further exchange, that of 'natural relations' for 'unnatural ones'. The word translated 'rela-tions' here *(chrēsis)*, although found only in 1:26-27 in the NT, was used fre-quently in extrabiblical literature to denote sexual intercourse.[65] We are as-sisted in understanding what Paul meant by 'natural' and 'unnatural' in this context by observing the occurrences of the 'nature/natural' *(physis/ physikos)* word group elsewhere in the Pauline corpus. It can connote what people are by birth or character:

> We who are Jews by birth *(physei,* lit. 'by nature') and not sinful Gentiles. (Gal 2:15)

> All of us also lived among them at one time, gratifying the cravings of our flesh and following its desires and thoughts. Like the rest, we were by nature *(physei)* deserving of wrath. (Eph 2:3)

In other places it connotes the natural order of things:

> For if God did not spare the natural *(kata physin)* branches, he will not spare you either. . . . After all, if you were cut out of an olive tree that is wild by nature *(kata physin),* and contrary to nature *(para physin)* were grafted into a cultivated olive tree, how much more readily will these, the natural *(kata physin)* branches, be grafted into their own olive tree! (Rom 11:21, 24)

> Does not the very nature of things *(hē physis autē,* lit. 'nature itself') teach you that if a man has long hair, it is a disgrace to him. (1 Cor 11:14)

> Formerly, when you did not know God, you were slaves to those who by nature *(physei)* are not gods. (Gal 4:8)

In 1:26 Paul uses *physis/physikos* to denote natural and unnatural rela-tions, that is, those consistent with human nature *(kata physin)* or contrary to human nature *(para physin),* a usage consistent with what is found in both Greek and Jewish literature.[66] For example, Plato condemns pederasty and marriage between men as 'contrary to nature';[67] *T. Naph.* 3:4-5 charges people: 'Do not become like Sodom, which departed from the order of na-

---

65. Cf. BDAG, *ad loc.*

66. Cf. James B. de Young, 'The Meaning of "Nature" in Romans 1 and Its implica-tions for Biblical Proscriptions of Homosexual Behavior', *JETS* 31 (1988) 429-41.

67. Plato, *Laws* 636a-b: 'The gymnasia and common meals corrupt the pleasures of love which are natural not to man only but also natural to beasts'; 636c: 'Pleasure in mating is due to nature *(kata physin)* when male unites with female, but contrary to nature *(para physin)* when male unites with male *(arrenōn)* or female with female *(thēleiōn)'.*

ture'; Philo combines the Greek notion of things contrary to nature with the
Jewish idea of things contrary to law, and regards sexual aberrations as vio-
lations of 'the law of nature' (*Abr.* 135–136); Josephus speaks of women's
menstruation and the union of a man and wife as 'according to nature' (*Ag.
Ap.* 2.199), while he describes sodomy as 'unnatural' (*Ag. Ap.* 2.275); Seneca
condemned homosexual exploitation (*Ep.* 47.7-8), and Plutarch regarded
homosexual practice as 'contrary to nature' (*The Dialogue on Love* 751c-e;
752b-c).[68] The early church fathers interpreted Paul's statement in 1:26 that
their 'women [lit. 'females']'[69] exchanged natural relations for unnatural
ones' as female homosexual practice. For example, Ambrosiaster says:
'Paul tells us that these things came about, that a woman should lust after
another woman, because God was angry at the human race because of its
idolatry',[70] and Chrysostom maintains: 'But when God abandons a person
to his own devices, then everything is turned upside down. Thus not only
was their doctrine satanic, but their life was too. . . . How disgraceful it is
when even the women sought after these things, when they ought to have a
greater sense of shame than men have'.[71]

Paul's statement in 1:26 has generally been assumed to be a reference
to female homosexuality, an assumption based on the following verse
(1:27), which says that the men 'in the same way' abandoned natural relations with women, being inflamed with lust for one another. However,
Miller argues that while there are a few references to female homosexuality
in ancient literature,[72] there are frequent references to unnatural heterosex-

68. Cf. De Young, 'The Meaning of "Nature" in Romans 1', 431-34, 436. Cranfield,
Romans, I, 125-26, comments: 'By *physikos* (here used to describe that which is *kata physin*)
and *para physin* Paul clearly means "in accordance with the intention of the Creator" and
"contrary to the intention of the Creator", respectively'.

69. Cranfield, *Romans*, I, 125, says: 'The use of the adjectives meaning "female"
[*thēlys*] and "male" [*arsēn*] rather than the words *gynē* ['woman/wife'] and *anēr* ['man/hus-
band'] is appropriate here, since it is the sexual differentiation as such on which attention is
specially concentrated (cf. Gen 1.27; Mt 19.4 = Mk 10.6; Gal 3,28)'.

70. 'Commentary on Paul's Epistles' (*ACCSR*, 46).

71. 'Homilies on Romans' (*ACCSR*, 47). Cf. Jewett, *Romans*, 173: 'To substantiate the
claim in v. 26a concerning dishonourable passions, Paul introduces with *gar* ("for") the example of perverse sexual relations. The *exemplum* ("example") is a widely used means of
proof in Greco-Roman rhetoric, particularly suited for the epideictic genre that concerns itself with praise and blame of various types of behavior. The most effective examples are
drawn from everyday experience and derive their argumentative force from shared opinion
or prejudice. Here we have the most egregious instance Paul can find to demonstrate his
thesis about human distortion, the arena of sexual perversity that created wide revulsion in
the Jewish and early Christian communities of his time. . . . The depiction of a particularly
unpopular example for the sake of an effective argument leads Paul to highly prejudicial
language, particularly to the modern ear. It should be clear from the outset, however, that
Paul's aim is not to prove the evils of perverse sexual behavior; that is simply assumed. The
aim is to develop a thesis about the manifestation of divine wrath in the human experience
of Paul's time. In contrast to traditional moralizing based on this passage, sexual perversion
is in Paul's view "the result of God's wrath, not the reason for it"'.

72. James E. Miller, 'The Practices of Romans 1:26; Homosexual or Heterosexual?'

ual intercourse involving women who accepted oral or anal penetration instead of normal sexual intercourse. This they did sometimes to avoid disturbing a pregnancy and at other times as a means of contraception. When women accept anal or oral penetration, they are adopting practices similar to those of male homosexuals, hence Paul can begin 1:27, 'in the same way the men'. . . .[73] Fitzmyer rejects the view, saying: 'Only modern eisegesis could read these words of Paul and understand them as referring to female contraception'.[74] Jewett concurs: 'In the light of these parallels, it is clear that Paul has in mind female homoeroticism in this verse, rather than women's engaging in oral or anal intercourse with males, or heterosexual women committing homoerotic acts. There is a strikingly egalitarian note in Paul's treating same-sex intercourse among females as an issue in its own right and holding women to the same level of accountability as men. It is nevertheless clear that Paul's choice and description of the lesbian example reflect confidence that his audience, shaped by a similar philosophical and religious heritage, "will share his negative judgment"'.[75]

1:27   Adding to his statement about women exchanging natural relations for unnatural relations, Paul says: *In the same way the men also abandoned natural relations with women and were inflamed with lust for one another.* The expression 'in the same way' indicates that male homosexual practice is intended here[76] just as female homosexual practice was intended in 1:26. Jewett comments:

> Paul turns next to the example of male homoeroticism, the weaker case in his cultural setting because of its positive evaluation by some Greco-Roman writers and its popularisation among the Roman ruling class, including Emperor Nero. This weakness is treated rhetorically by presenting male perversion as similar to the more disreputable female perversion. . . . The link between the two sentences clarifies that both male and female homoeroticism are seen as evidence of the same *pathē atimias* ('passions of dishonor'). . . . The rest of v. 27 continues the rhetorical effort to buttress the case about the despicable quality of homosexuality. To be 'inflamed with their lust for one another' . . . is rare and derogatory language in the NT, but heat and flame are typically associated with sexual passion in Greco-Roman sources.[77]

NovT 37 (1995) 4-8, provides an exhaustive list of classical references: Plato, *Symposium* 189d-91e; Phaedrus, *Fables* 4.16; Ovid, *Metamorphoses* 9.720-97; Lucian, *Dialogue of the Courtesans* 5 (289-92) and *Amores* 28; three of Martial's epigrams (1.90; 7.67, 70); the Elder Seneca, *Controversies* 1.2.23; C. Aurelianus (*Carantella*, 169); Plutarch, *Lycurgus* 18.

73. Miller, 'The Practices of Romans 1:26', 8-11.

74. Fitzmyer, *Romans*, 287.

75. Jewett, *Romans*, 176.

76. A practice condemned in Lev 18:22: 'Do not have sexual relations with a man as one does with a woman; that is detestable'; and in Lev 20:13: 'If a man has sexual relations with a man as one does with a woman, both of them have done what is detestable'

77. Jewett, *Romans*, 178.

'Natural relations with women' were abandoned as men became 'inflamed with lust for one another'. This is made even more explicit when Paul adds: *Men committed shameful acts with other men.* 'Shameful acts' refers to behavior that elicits disgrace.[78] Paul does not spell out the nature of these 'shameful acts', but noncoital intercourse is surely implied.[79] However, he does spell out the consequences of the 'shameful acts': the men *received in themselves the due penalty for their error.* They were handed over (by God) to the tyranny of their own lusts as a due 'penalty' for their 'perversion'.[80]

The word translated 'error' carries the idea of 'a thoroughly serious going astray from the truth in thought and/or in conduct'.[81] Throughout Scripture homosexual practice is universally condemned as 'a serious going astray' (see 'Additional Note: The Nature of Homosexual Practice Condemned by Paul', 109-15). The apostle emphasizes that the penalty for people practicing this perversion was received 'in themselves': God handed them over to the tyranny of their sinful practices and the outworking of those in the baleful effects upon individuals and in their relationships with one another.[82]

Jewett, who recognizes that Paul condemns all forms of homosexual activity, suggests that the apostle included this in his letter to the Romans in order to encourage slaves who were being sexually exploited by their masters:

> While the Jewish background of Paul's heterosexual preference has been frequently cited as decisive by previous researchers, little attention has been given to the correlation between homosexuality and slavery. The right of masters to demand sexual services from slaves and

78. Cf. BAGD, *aschēmosynē, ad loc.*

79. Both anal and oral intercourse were known in antiquity. Cf. Miller, 'The Practices of Romans 1:26', 8-11.

80. The word translated 'penalty' here is *antimisthia*. It can denote positively 'reward' or negatively 'penalty'. In this context it is used negatively denoting penalty, a 'requital based upon what one deserves'; cf. BAGD, *ad loc.*

81. Cf. Cranfield, *Romans,* I, 127.

82. David E. Malick, 'The Condemnation of Homosexuality in Romans 1:26-27', *BSac* 150 (1993) 332-33, rejects the suggestion that in Rom 1:26-27 Paul is imposing Jewish customs and rules, pointing out that: *'hai thēleiai autōn* ("their women", v. 26) and *hoi arsenes* ("the men", v. 27) are terms chosen by Paul to highlight the created order of male and female rather than other connotations which might be communicated through *gynē* and *anēr.* It is significant that the Septuagint uses *arsēn* and *thēlys* in referring to the creation of humankind as "male" and "female". When Jesus discussed divorce, He spoke of God's created order in Genesis 1:27, and both Matthew 19:4 and Mark 10:6 use *arsēn* and *thēlys* to refer to male and female. Also in Paul's first epistle, he used these terms to define men and women as polar opposites in the race (Gal 3:28). Therefore these words for men and women do not refer to the cultural heritage of marriage but to the "natural" expression of mankind as seen in God's creation. This, as well as the use of other terms and concepts in 1:23, 26, shows that Paul's discussion was based not Jewish customs and rules but on the Hebrew creation account'.

freedmen is an important factor in grasping the impact of Paul's rhetoric, because slavery was so prominent a feature of the social background of most of Paul's audience in Rome. . . . I suggest that Paul's rhetoric may provide entrée into the similarly unhappy experience of Christian slaves and former slaves who had experienced and resented sexual exploitation, both for themselves and for their children, in a culture marked by aggressive bisexuality. . . . For those members of the Roman congregation still subject to sexual exploitation by slave owners or former slave owners who are now functioning as patrons, the moral condemnation of same-sex and extra-marital relations of all kinds would confirm the damnation of their exploiters and thus raise the status of the exploited above that of helpless victims with no prospect of retribution.[83]

1:28 Paul speaks now for a third time (cf. 1:24, 26) of God handing people over to experience the tyranny of their own sinful behavior: *Furthermore, just as they did not think it worthwhile to retain the knowledge of God, so God gave them over to a depraved mind, so that they do what ought not to be done.* Once again Paul says that God 'gave them over' to the bondage of sin, this time to a depraved mind, because they rejected the knowledge of God made available to them through creation (cf. 1:21-24, 24-27). Paul makes a play on words here. He says that since people did not think it *worthwhile* to acknowledge God, he gave them over into the tyranny of a mind that was *not worthwhile/depraved*,[84] a mind that Cranfield describes as 'so debilitated and corrupted as to be a quite untrustworthy guide in moral decisions'.[85] As a result of their refusal to retain the knowledge of God, God gave them up and they proceeded to do 'what ought not to be done' (lit. 'things that are not proper or fitting'). What these things are Paul describes in 1:29-31.

1:29-31 Paul describes here what he means by things that 'ought not to be done'. First he expresses it in general terms: *They have become filled with every kind of wickedness,[86] evil, greed and depravity.* Then he describes these things in more detail: *They are full of envy, murder, strife, deceit and malice. They are gossips, slanderers, God-haters, insolent, arrogant and boastful; they invent ways of doing evil; they disobey their parents; they have no understanding, no fidelity, no love,[87] no mercy.*[88] Most of these descriptors are self-explanatory.

---

83. Jewett, *Romans,* 180-81.

84. The play on words is obvious in the original. Paul says that because people did not think it worthwhile *(ou edokimasan)* to acknowledge God, he gave them over to the tyranny of a mind that was not worthwhile *(adokimon).*

85. Cranfield, *Romans,* I, 128.

86. The Textus Receptus includes 'fornication' *(porneia)* before 'evil' *(ponēria)* here, probably an unintentional addition to the text on the part of a weary scribe.

87. Some manuscripts insert either before or after 'heartless' *(astorgous)* the word 'unforgiving' *(aspondos),* possibly influenced by its inclusion in a similar list in 2 Tim 3:3.

88. Cranfield, *Romans,* I, 129, notes that 1:29-31 'comprise a list of vices arranged in three distinct groups: (i) four abstract nouns in the dative singular all qualified by *pasē* ['ev-

Some call for extra comment. Commenting on 'gossips' and 'slanderers', Cranfield says: 'Both words denote people who go about to destroy other people's reputations by misrepresentation'. He distinguishes the gossip from the slanderer: 'the former denoted specifically one who whispers his slanders in his listener's ear, whereas the latter means a slanderer quite generally, irrespective of whether he whispers his calumnies or proclaims them from the house-tops', adding that the one who whispers slander 'is, of course, the more vicious and dangerous kind, inasmuch as he is one against whom there is virtually no human defense'.[89]

The word translated 'God haters' was used in earlier times only in the passive voice to mean 'god-detested' or 'god-forsaken'. However, in this context it is better translated as 'God-hater (the cognate noun, meaning 'hatred/enmity toward God', is found in *1 Clem.* 35:5).[90]

The word translated 'insolent' (lit. 'insolent persons') is found elsewhere in the NT only in 1 Timothy 1:13, where Paul says: 'I was once a blasphemer and a persecutor and *a violent man*' (italics added). The apostle uses the cognate verb in 1 Thessalonians 2:2: 'We had previously suffered and been *treated outrageously* in Philippi' (italics added). Cranfield says: 'It is best understood here as signifying the man who, in his confidence in his own superior power, wealth, social status, physical strength, intellectual or other ability, treats his fellow men with insolent contemptuousness and thereby affronts the majesty of God'.[91]

Jewett notes that those who disobeyed their parents were 'perceived by ancient Jews and Romans as profoundly dangerous. Deut 21:18-21 prescribed the death penalty for children who are disobedient to their mothers and fathers. While there are no indications that this law was enforced among Jews of the first century, there was frequent stress "on the honour and respect due to parents". Roman law was even more severe, as Seneca the Elder reminded his audience of the ancient practice: "Remember, fathers expected absolute obedience from their children and could punish re-

---

ery kind of'] and dependent on the participle *peplērōmenous* [filled'], which stands in apposition to *autous* ['them'] in v. 28; (ii) five nouns in the genitive singular all depending on the adjective *mestous* ['full'], which is also in apposition to *autous* ['them']; (iii) a series of twelve items all of which are directly in apposition to *autous* ['them'], the first seven of them being positive and the last five negative. Within these groupings a tendency to a further grouping in pairs according to rhetorical rather than substantial considerations is noticeable (thus *phthonou* and *phonou*, *asynetous* and *asynthetous* feature assonance; *epheuretas kakōn* and *goneusin apeitheis* are a pair of two-word phrases; and the last two items both have the privative *a-* besides having a certain relatedness of meaning)'.

A number of these words used by Paul to describe people's sinful behavior are found only here in the NT (*kakoētheia*, malice or meanness; *psithyristēs*, gossiper; *katalalos*, slanderer; *theostygēs*, God-hating; *epheuretēs*, inventor; *asynthetos*, faithless/covenant breaker; *aneleēmōn*, ruthless/unmerciful).

89. Cranfield, *Romans*, I, 130-31.
90. Cf. BAGD, *ad loc.*
91. Cranfield, *Romans*, I, 131.

calcitrant children even with death". . . . Such authority was still an important factor in Roman family and political life in the first century'.[92] The word translated 'faithless' means reneging on one's word, or possibly breaking a formal agreement, thus 'covenant breaking'.[93]

Commenting on the last four elements in Paul's list of vices, 'they have no understanding, no fidelity, no love, no mercy', Jewett says: 'The rhetorical highpoint of the 21 vices and evil persons comes with four rhyming words that begin with the alpha negative, translated here as "without".[94] The impression is that under the pervasiveness of the "unfit mind", the whole world is lacking in four of the attributes viewed as essential for humanity by Greco-Romans and Jewish thinkers. . . . The pithy translation of the NJB captures the matter with appropriate rhetorical force: "without brains, honor, love or pity"'.[95]

1:32 In this final verse of the section 1:18-32, Paul takes his description of the sin of humanity one step further, heightening people's culpability: *Although they know God's righteous decree that those who do such things deserve death, they not only continue to do these very things but also approve of those who practice them.* Paul uses the expression 'righteous decree/requirement' again in 2:26 in relation to the Gentile world when he asks: 'If those who are not circumcised keep the law's *requirements,* will they not be regarded as though they were circumcised?' (italics added) and in 8:4, where he says that the purpose of Christ's death was 'that the righteous *requirement* of the law might be fully met in us, who do not live according to the flesh but according to the Spirit' (italics added). It is significant that in these two other cases it is the requirements of *the law* that Paul speaks of — something which was known only by Jews, whereas here in 1:32 he speaks of 'God's righteous decree' — something known to Gentiles as well. What he means by the latter is explained further in 2:14-15: 'Indeed, when Gentiles, who do not have the law, do by nature things required by the law, they are a law for themselves, even though they do not have the law. They show that the requirements of the law [lit. 'the work of the law'] are written on their hearts' (see the commentary on this text below).

The apostle says that not only do people know God's 'righteous decree'; they also know that those who ignore or reject it 'deserve death'. The term 'deserving of death' elsewhere in the NT refers to capital punishment (Luke 23:15; Acts 23:29; 25:11, 25; 26:31). While some of the offenses listed by Paul here did attract the death penalty under Roman and Jewish law (e.g., murder, disobedience to parents), clearly not all of them did. Dunn suggests that Paul was alluding to the Genesis 2–3 narrative of Adam's rebellion and the penalty attached ('you must not eat from the tree of the

---

92. Jewett, *Romans,* 188.
93. Cf. BAGD, *ad loc.*
94. *Asynetous, asynthetous, astorgous, aneleēmonas.*
95. Jewett, *Romans,* 189.

knowledge of good and evil, for when you eat of it you will certainly die'), where death denotes Adam's 'standing under the primeval sentence of death' (Gen 2:16).[96] In the context of Romans 1–2, where Paul says 'the wrath of God is being revealed from heaven against all the godlessness and wickedness of people' (1:18) and 'because of your stubbornness and your unrepentant heart, you are storing up wrath against yourself for the day of God's wrath' (2:5), 'deserving death' could well refer to the final condemnation of the wicked.

Paul heightens people's culpability when he adds: 'they not only continue to do these very things but also approve of those who practice them'. This would appear to be the ultimate act of rejecting what they know of God. They not only do what they know is wrong, but they encourage others to do so by their approval. In so doing they usurp God's prerogative of defining good and evil, denying that what he says is evil is in fact evil. Ambrosiaster comments:

> Those who knew by the law of nature that God requires righteousness realized that these things were displeasing to God, but they did not want to think about it, because those who do such things are worthy of death, and not only those who do them but those who allow them to be done, for consent is participation. Their wickedness is double, for those who do such things but prevent others are not so bad, because they realize that these things are evil and do not justify them. But the worst people are those who do these things and approve of others doing them as well, not fearing God but desiring the increase of evil. They do not seek to justify them either, but in their case it is because they want to persuade people that there is nothing wrong in doing them.[97]

Paul's depiction of the sin of the Gentiles is reminiscent of Jewish polemic (cf., e.g., Wisdom 13–14), and those with any Jewish background would recognize this depiction of the Gentile world and assent to the view that it was guilty of the sins of idolatry and immorality and therefore liable to judgment.[98] But in the next chapter Paul will address a hypothetical dialogue partner who takes the high moral ground, in particular the Jewish person, and insist that he too will be liable to judgment if, despite his Jewish privileges, he is guilty of similar practices. All this the apostle demon-

---

96. Dunn, *Romans 1–8*, 69.

97. 'Commentary on Paul's Epistles' (*ACCSR*, 50).

98. Byrne, *Romans*, 72, remarks: 'Paul, presumably, is not unaware that the Gentile world contained religious teachers and philosophers (one thinks, for example, of Paul's contemporary, Seneca) who did *not* approve of dissolute behavior and who, in an enlightened and uplifting way, condemned much of the behaviour listed. . . . In rhetorical terms, then, Paul would have hoped by the close of this section of his letter, to have created in his audience a *pathos* of horror and revulsion. But the concluding allusion to those who "approve" of the evil-doing has subtly introduced the notion of sitting in judgment upon the actions of others. Those who judge and approve are evidently condemned'.

strates for the benefit of his largely Gentile Christian audience, providing them with an exposition of the gospel and mounting his defense against its Jewish detractors.

ADDITIONAL NOTE: THE NATURE OF THE HOMOSEXUAL PRACTICE CONDEMNED BY PAUL

Paul's references to homosexual practice have given rise to widely differing opinions concerning exactly what it was he condemned. Did he condemn all forms of homosexual practice or only certain expressions of it? Crucial to this discussion is what he meant by 'nature' *(physis)* in this context, and in particular what he understood to be 'contrary to nature' *(para physin)*.

In Greek literature *physis* denotes 'natural condition, quality or state'. Thus Aristotle can say that 'Man is, by virtue of his natural make-up, "a political creature"'.[99] In the LXX *physis* is found in Wisdom (e.g., 13:1: 'For all people who were ignorant of God were foolish by nature [*physei*]'; 19:20: 'Fire even in water retained its normal power, and water forgot its fire-quenching nature [*physeōs*]') and 3 and 4 Maccabees (e.g., 4 Macc 5:8-9: 'When nature [*dia . . . physeōs*] has granted it to us, why should you abhor eating the very excellent meat of this animal? It is senseless not to enjoy delicious things that are not shameful, and wrong to spurn the gifts of nature [*ta tēs physeōs charitas*]') where it denotes what people and things are by nature. For Philo *physis* denotes 'the work of God', the created world, including the nature of human beings themselves.[100] For Josephus *physis* denotes the condition of animals and humans, the natural qualities of living things and places, the regular order of nature and the whole created world.[101]

Physis is found nine times in the Pauline letters. In 2:14, 17 it is used to describe Gentiles who by nature *(ek physeōs)* do not have the law and who by nature *(ek physeōs)* are uncircumcised. In Romans 11:21, 24 it is used to denote the natural branches *(tōn kata physin kladōn)* of a cultivated olive tree as distinct from branches that contrary to nature *(para physin)* are grafted into a cultivated live tree. In Galatians 2:15 the apostle speaks of 'we who are Jews by birth' *(physei)*, and in Galatians 4:8 he speaks of 'those who by nature *(physei)* are not gods'. In Ephesians he describes both himself and his audience as those who were, prior to their conversion, 'by nature *(physei)* deserving of wrath'.[102]

---

99. Aristotle, *Pol.* 1253ª 3, cited in G. Harder, 'Nature', *NIDNTT*, II, 657.
100. Harder, 'Nature', *NIDNTT*, II, 659.
101. Harder, 'Nature', *NIDNTT*, II, 659-60.
102. The one use of *physis* by Paul which does not fit this pattern is found in 1 Cor 11:14, where he says that 'the very nature of things' *(physis)* teaches 'that if a man has long hair, it is a disgrace to him', where 'the very nature of things' refers to cultural custom.

What Paul means by 'contrary to nature' *(para physin)* is the subject of different interpretations. Some argue for a restricted meaning of 'contrary to nature', interpreting it as 'what is contrary to my personal nature'. Those who adopt such a meaning are then able to deny that all homosexual relations are 'contrary to nature', claiming that it only applies to heterosexuals who act like homosexuals and are thus guilty of perversion. They deny that it applies to those believed to be born as homosexuals (inverts). Loughlin argues that what Paul says does not apply to homosexuality in the modern sense but to what was regarded as shameful in his own day, that is, to males adopting a passive position (being penetrated like a female) or a female adopting the active rather than the passive position in the sexual act.[103] However, there is nothing in either the OT or the Pauline letters to suggest that Paul approved homosexual relations of any type, or that he distinguished perverts from inverts.

Others argue that what Paul considered 'contrary to nature' was pederasty, that is, adult male sexual exploitation of boys.[104] However, such a view fails to account for the fact that Paul condemns sexual relations between male and male (in parallel to sexual relations between female and female), not between men and boys. De Young comments: 'The terms "toward one another", "men with men", "in themselves" and "their error" all argue for adult reciprocal mutuality and mutual culpability, which would not characterize pederasty. As the error is mutual, so is the recompense. The idea of "exchanged . . . abandoned the natural function" suggests that adult sexual relations are intended'.[105] Smith, after reviewing the evidence for the nature of ancient pederasty, nonpederastic homosexual practices, and female homosexuality, concludes (*contra* the views of John Boswell [*Christianity, Social Tolerance, and Homosexuality*] and Robin Scroggs [*The New Testament and Homosexuality*]): 'Paul probably did know at least several different types of homosexual practices among both men and women. He used general language in Rom. 1 because he intended his proscription to apply in a general way to all homosexual behavior, as he understood it'.[106]

Balch suggests that Paul was critical of unbridled eros which, being insatiable, is 'contrary to nature', and that he was possibly criticizing homosexual activity that was insatiable and therefore shameful, and not same-sex relations per se. However, he does allow that the apostle may

---

103. Cf. Gerard Loughlin, 'Pauline Conversations: Rereading Romans 1 in Christ', *Theology and Sexuality* 11 (2004) 92-93; David L. Balch, 'Romans 1:24-27, Science, and Homosexuality', *CurrTheolMiss* 25 (1998) 439-40.

104. Cf. R. Scroggs, *The New Testament and Homosexuality: Contextual Background for Contemporary Debate* (Philadelphia: Fortress, 1983), 116; James E. Miller, 'Pederasty and Romans 1:27: A Response to Mark Smith', *JAAR* 65 (1997) 861-64.

105. De Young, 'The Meaning of "Nature" in Romans 1', 440; cf. Byrne, *Romans*, 77; Dunn, *Romans 1–8*, 65.

106. Mark D. Smith, 'Ancient Bisexuality and the Interpretation of Romans 1:26-27', *JAAR* 64 (1996) 246.

have assumed that all homosexual activity was itself shameful and 'contrary to nature'.[107]

Phipps relativizes Paul's condemnation of homosexual activity in 1:26-27 by treating it as *descriptive* of the sexism of his culture, arguing that we should turn to 12:10, 16 to discover what the apostle saw as *prescriptive* for sexual ethics — that people should love one another and live in harmony.[108] Others are prepared to recognize that Paul condemned all homosexual activity as he knew of it in his day, but argue that he did not know about homosexual orientation as it is understood by some today,[109] and for this reason his modern readers need not accept his views. Davies acknowledges that Romans 1:26-27 'unambiguously condemns homosexual practice, including both passive and active participants and female as well as male practitioners',[110] but regards Paul's condemnation of homosexual practice as 'an anomalous emotional blind spot in an otherwise radical transformation of tradition'.[111]

The majority of modern interpreters of Paul, however, agree that the plain language of 1:26-27 involves condemnation of all homosexual practice.[112] Fitzmyer, citing Hays, argues that those who deny that Paul saw homosexual practice as morally reprehensible ignore '"the plain sense of the text, which places its explicit reference" to homosexual activity "in direct parallelism with the 'base mind and improper conduct' which the vice list of 1:29-31 elaborates"'.[113] Fitzmyer himself draws attention to *T. Naph.* 3:2-4, whose reference to deviant homosexual conduct as contrary to the order of creation, he says, underlies Paul's thinking:

> The sun, moon, and stars do not change their order; so you must not change the law of God by the disorder of your deeds. Gentiles, in going astray and forsaking the Lord, have changed their order and gone after stones and wooden objects, led away by spirits of error. But not so (will) you (be), my children. You have recognized in the heaven's vault, in the earth, in the sea, and in all created things the Lord who made them all, so that you should not become like Sodom, which changed the order of its nature.[114]

---

107. Balch, 'Romans 1:24-27', 437.

108. William E. Phipps, 'Paul on "Unnatural" Sex', *CurrTheolMiss* 29 (2002) 131.

109. Cf. Michael Williams, 'Romans 1: Entropy, Sexuality and Politics', *Anvil* 10 (1993) 108-9; Byrne, *Romans*, 70.

110. Margaret Davies, 'New Testament Ethics and Ours: Homosexuality and Sexuality in Romans 1:26-27', *BibInt* 3 (1995) 315-16.

111. Davies, 'New Testament Ethics and Ours', 318.

112. Cf., e.g., Cranfield, *Romans*, I, 127; Francis Bridger, 'Entropy, Sexuality and Politics: A Reply to Michael Williams', *Anvil* 10 (1993) 116-17; Witherington, *Romans*, 69; Dunn, *Romans 1–8*, 65-66; Schreiner, *Romans*, 96-97; De Young, 'The Meaning of "Nature" in Romans 1', 438-40; Barrett, *Romans*, 39; Byrne, *Romans*, 77.

113. Fitzmyer, *Romans*, 286.

114. Fitzmyer, *Romans*, 276.

Malick rejects the view that Paul did not regard homosexuality as a sin in itself, but as a punishment for sin, that is, idolatry, noting that 'each person need not be an idolater for this passage to have relevance to him. Also, all idolaters need not experience this particular form of judgment; many other consequences are listed in verses 28-20'.[115] Malick concludes his study of 1:26-27 as follows:

> A contextual and exegetical examination of Romans 1:26-27 reveals that attempts by some contemporary writers to do away with Paul's prohibitions against present-day same-sex relations are false. Paul did not impose Jewish customs and rules on his audience; instead he addressed same-sex relations from the transcultural perspective of God's created order. Nor was homosexuality simply a sin practiced by idolaters in Paul's day; it was a distorting consequence of the fall of the human race in the Garden of Eden. Neither did Paul describe homosexual acts by heterosexuals. Instead he wrote that homosexual activity was an exchange of the created order (heterosexuality) for a talionic perversion (homosexuality), which is never presented in Scripture as an acceptable norm for sexuality. Also, Hellenistic pederasty does not fully account for the terms and logic of Romans 1:26-27, which refers to adult-adult mutuality. Therefore it is clear that in Romans 1:26-27 Paul condemned homosexuality as a perversion of God's design for human sexual relations.[116]

By way of conclusion we may cite De Young's succinct summary of the evidence for homosexual practice in the ancient world and Jewish and Christian attitudes towards it:

> Homosexuality seems to have existed more widely among the ancient Greeks than among any other people. The predominant form was pederasty.... Examples of lesbianism as well as male adult-adult homosexuality are found. The Greeks recognized the difference between what is natural and unnatural (cf. Plato, *Laws* 636a-c; 836a-c; 838; 841d-e). Greek religion gave significant support to homosexuality.... Philo and Josephus condemned homosexuality in general, not only pederasty, in the strongest terms. . . . Seneca condemns homosexual exploitation (*Moral Epistles* 47.7-8) that forces an adult slave to dress, be beardless, and behave as a woman.... Other evidence of the prevalence and form of homosexuality during Paul's day comes from Roman legislation. As early as 226 B.C. the *Lex Scantinia* penalized homosexual practices. Cicero refers to subsequent application of it in 50 B.C., and other references are made to it by Suetonius (applied under Domition), Juvenal and others (including Tertullian). The *Lex Julia de adulteris coercendis* (about 17 B.C.), initially concerned with sexual offenses against a virgin

---

115. Malick, 'The Condemnation of Homosexuality', 333-35.
116. Malick, 'The Condemnation of Homosexuality', 340.

or widow *(stuprum)*, came to be applied to sexual acts committed with boys (third century) and then to homosexual acts between adults (fourth century). Justinian's *Codex* (sixth century) applied *Lex Julia* to homosexuality further and set the legal tradition in western civilization. Another evidence of homosexuality comes from the poets, satirists and historians of the day. Juvenal and Martial wrote of formal marriage unions of homosexuals. Historians and others viewed the second century B.C. as the turning point in Roman history. With military conquests achieved, Rome underwent 'a moral crisis from which she never recovered'. It came about from the direct influx into Rome of 'Asiatic luxury and Greek manners' that included homosexuality and other debauchery. . . . Throughout Scripture, adult homosexuality is assumed. This is apparent in the record of Sodom (Genesis 19: 'men' of the city desired 'men'), Gibeah (Judges 19), and other condemnations of sodomy (Deut 23:17-18; Lev 18:22; 20:13). This is the case with the intertestamental literature also. Only in *T. Levi* 17:11 is pederasty specifically cited. Throughout Scripture the condemnation is universal and absolute. It is never contemplated that one specific form of homosexuality is condemned while others are tolerated or accepted, whether this be homosexual rape (claimed for Genesis 19; Judges 19), male prostitution (claimed for Deuteronomy 23; 2 Kgs 23:7; 1 Kgs 14:24; 15:12; 22:46; Leviticus 18; 20; 1 Cor 6:9-11; 1 Tim 1:8-10), pederasty (claimed for the NT, esp. Rom 1:26-27), or perversion — that is, abandoning one's 'natural' orientation for another (claimed for Romans 1). In Paul the passive *(malakoi)* and active *(arsenokoitai)* partners are outside the kingdom of God (1 Cor 6:9).[117]

De Young concludes his detailed discussion of the subject as follows:

If these observations are correct, then the view of those who see *physis* as meaning 'what is natural to me' and thus try to justify inversion or orientation is wrong. Never does the term have such meaning in Greek literature or Biblical contexts. . . . In regard to the nature of homosexuality, for Scroggs to claim that Paul 'must have had, *could only have had*, pederasty in mind' is untenable. First, this assumes 'that Greco-Roman culture decisively influenced New Testament statements about homosexuality' and that 'Paul is dependent for his judgement that it is against nature ultimately on Greek, not Jewish sources . . . not on some doctrine of creation'. This overlooks the context and Paul's dependency on OT concepts, as shown above. Second, Paul's words themselves contradict this view and support a much more general idea of homosexuality, which would include adult-adult mutuality. Several terms bear this out. Paul writes literally 'males with males' committing indecent acts; he does not say 'men with boys' (as Plato is capable of saying: *Laws*

117. De Young, 'The Meaning of "Nature" in Romans 1', 435-37.

836a-c). This phrase appears to be unique to Paul. He compares ('likewise') lesbianism with male perversion. As lesbianism was usually between adults in mutuality, so the force of the comparative argues for male adult-adult mutuality. The phrase 'natural use' or 'function' argues for activity or 'relations' (NIV) of adults, not adult-child behavior, and not an orientation alone nor a Platonic relationship. 'Degrading passions' (v 26) and 'burned in their desire' argue that this is not Platonic nor morally neutral, whether referring to propensity or orientation or activity. The terms 'toward one another', 'men with men', 'in themselves' and 'their error' all argue for adult reciprocal mutuality and mutual culpability, which would not characterize pederasty. As the error is mutual, so is the recompense. The idea of 'exchanged . . . abandoned the natural function' suggests that adult sexual relations are intended. If the 'model' of homosexuality makes a difference regarding acceptability or culpability, why is Scripture silent on the matter? Why is there no explicit debate over the matter in Philo or Josephus or among the Greeks? . . . The only model of sexual expression contemplated in Scripture is that which is patterned after the creation model of Genesis 1–2. This is the pattern that our Lord (Matthew 5:19) and his disciples taught or commanded.[118]

Dunn provides another helpful summary of the evidence for homosexual practice in the ancient world, and the attitudes of those in the Greco-Roman and Jewish world to it:

In the Greco-Roman world homosexuality was quite common and even highly regarded, as is evident from Plato's *Symposium* and Plutarch's *Lycurgus.* It was a feature of social life, indulged in not least by the gods (e.g., Zeus' attraction to Ganymede) and emperors (e.g., Nero's seduction of free-born boys was soon to become notorious). The homosexual reputations of the women of Lesbos was well established long before Lucian made it the theme of his fifth *Dialogue of the Courtesans* (second century A.D.). But Jewish reaction to it as a perversion, a pagan abomination, is consistent throughout the OT (Lev 18:22; 20:13; 1 Kgs 14:24; 15:12; 22:46; 2 Kgs 23:7), with the sin of Sodom often recalled as a terrible warning (e.g., Gen 18:1-28; Deut 23:18; Isa 1:9-10; 3:9; Jer 23:14; Lam 4:6; Ezek 16:43-58). In the period of early Judaism, abhorrence of homosexuality is not just part of the reaction against Greek mores, since we find it also in those most influenced by Greek thought (Wis Sol 14:26; *Ep. Arist.* 152; Philo, *Abr.* 135–37; *Spec. Leg.* 3.37-42; *Sib. Or.* 3:184-86, 764; *Ps. Phoc.* 3, 190–92, 213–14; Josephus, *Ap.* 2.273-75); note also the sustained polemic against homosexual promiscuity and homosexuality in *T. 12 Patr.* (particularly *T. Lev.* 14.6; 17:11; *T. Naph.* 4.1) and in *Sib. Or.* (e.g., 3:185-87, 594-600, 763). . . . In other words, antipathy to homosexu-

118. De Young, 'The Meaning of "Nature" in Romans 1', 438-40.

ality remains a consistent and distinctive feature of Jewish understanding of what man's createdness involves and requires. That homosexuality is of a piece with idolatry is taken for granted (as several of the same passages show), both understood as demeaning of the people who indulge in them. The link between man's fall (Gen 3) and sexual perversity (as here) is also typically Jewish, since Gen 6:1-4 also played a considerable part in Jewish attempts to account for the origin of sin (*Jub.* 4.22; 5:1-10; 7.21; 1 *Enoch* 6–11; 86; *T. Reub.* 5; *T. Naph.* 3; CD 2:18-21; etc.). Elsewhere in the NT see 1 Cor 6:9; 1 Tim 1:10; 2 Pet 2; Jude 7.[119]

ADDITIONAL NOTE:
PAUL'S DEPICTION OF THE GENTILE WORLD

It has been often said that Paul's unflattering depiction of the Gentile world of the first century is based on traditional Jewish polemic against Gentiles, and should not be taken as either his own understanding of the state of affairs or a true representation of the Gentile world. A couple of comments can be made: (i) Clearly Paul knew of Gentile people of goodwill and of moral standards in the Gentile world that were not all bad (cf. 2:14-15). (ii) Nevertheless, it is instructive that the references he makes to his Gentile converts' lives before they became Christians include depictions of the Gentile world that are not far removed from what we find stated, albeit in general terms, in Romans 1:18-32. For example, note the following texts:

> Or do you not know that wrongdoers will not inherit the kingdom of God? Do not be deceived: Neither the sexually immoral nor idolaters nor adulterers nor men who have sex with men nor thieves nor the greedy nor drunkards nor slanderers nor swindlers will inherit the kingdom of God. And that is what some of you were. But you were washed, you were sanctified, you were justified in the name of the Lord Jesus Christ and by the Spirit of our God. (1 Cor 6:9-11)

> You know that when you were pagans, somehow or other you were influenced and led astray to mute idols. Therefore I want you to know that no one who is speaking by the Spirit of God says, 'Jesus be cursed', and no one can say, 'Jesus is Lord', except by the Holy Spirit. (1 Cor 12:2-3)

> So I tell you this, and insist on it in the Lord, that you must no longer live as the Gentiles do, in the futility of their thinking. They are darkened in their understanding and separated from the life of God because

---

119. Dunn, *Romans 1–8*, 65-66.

of the ignorance that is in them due to the hardening of their hearts. Having lost all sensitivity, they have given themselves over to sensuality so as to indulge in every kind of impurity, and they are full of greed. (Eph 4:17-19)

Put to death, therefore, whatever belongs to your earthly nature: sexual immorality, impurity, lust, evil desires and greed, which is idolatry. Because of these, the wrath of God is coming. You used to walk in these ways, in the life you once lived. But now you must also rid yourselves of all such things as these: anger, rage, malice, slander, and filthy language from your lips. Do not lie to each other, since you have taken off your old self with its practices and have put on the new self, which is being renewed in knowledge in the image of its Creator. (Col 3:5-10)

At one time we too were foolish, disobedient, deceived and enslaved by all kinds of passions and pleasures. We lived in malice and envy, being hated and hating one another. (Tit 3:3)

Similarly, the sins and temptations his converts continued to struggle with and sometimes succumbed to point in the same direction:

It is actually reported that there is sexual immorality among you, and of a kind that even pagans do not tolerate: A man is sleeping with his father's wife. And you are proud! Shouldn't you rather have gone into mourning and have put out of your fellowship the man who has been doing this? (1 Cor 5:1-2)

The very fact that you have lawsuits among you means you have been completely defeated already. Why not rather be wronged? Why not rather be cheated? Instead, you yourselves cheat and do wrong, and you do this to your brothers and sisters. (1 Cor 6:7-8)

It is God's will that you should be sanctified: that you should avoid sexual immorality; that each of you should learn to control your own body in a way that is holy and honorable, not in passionate lust like the pagans, who do not know God; and that in this matter no one should wrong or take advantage of a brother or sister. The Lord will punish all those who commit such sins, as we told you and warned you before. (1 Thess 4:3-6)

Again the implications of the apostle's general teaching flows along similar lines:

We know that the law is good if one uses it properly. We also know that the law is made not for the righteous but for lawbreakers and rebels, the ungodly and sinful, the unholy and irreligious, for those who kill their fathers or mothers, for murderers, for the sexually immoral, for those practicing homosexuality, for slave traders and liars and perjurers — and for whatever else is contrary to the sound doctrine that conforms to the gospel concerning the glory of the blessed God, which he entrusted to me. (1 Tim 1:8-11)

But mark this: There will be terrible times in the last days. People will be lovers of themselves, lovers of money, boastful, proud, abusive, disobedient to their parents, ungrateful, unholy, without love, unforgiving, slanderous, without self-control, brutal, not lovers of the good, treacherous, rash, conceited, lovers of pleasure rather than lovers of God — having a form of godliness but denying its power. Have nothing to do with such people. (2 Tim 3:1-5)

We may add to Paul's statements the witness of other NT writers:

For you have spent enough time in the past doing what pagans choose to do — living in debauchery, lust, drunkenness, orgies, carousing and detestable idolatry. They are surprised that you do not join them in their reckless, wild living, and they heap abuse on you. (1 Pet 4:3-4)

His divine power has given us everything we need for a godly life through our knowledge of him who called us by his own glory and goodness. Through these he has given us his very great and precious promises, so that through them you may participate in the divine nature, having escaped the corruption in the world caused by evil desires. (2 Pet 1:3-4)

2. Primary Focus on the Sins of the Jewish World, 2:1–3:20

Having established the culpability of humanity in 1:18-32, in this section of the letter Paul proceeds to show that those who take the high moral ground, in particular the Jewish people, are also culpable, and have no special immunity when it comes to the judgment of God.

a. God Shows No Favoritism, 2:1-16

¹You, therefore, have no excuse, you who pass judgment on someone else, for at whatever point you judge another, you are condemning yourself, because you who pass judgment do the same things. ²Now we know that God's judgment against those who do such things is based on truth. ³So when you, a mere human being, pass judgment on them and yet do the same things, do you think you will escape God's judgment? ⁴Or do you show contempt for the riches of his kindness, forbearance and patience, not realizing that God's kindness is intended to lead you to repentance?

⁵But because of your stubbornness and your unrepentant heart, you are storing up wrath against yourself for the day of God's wrath, when his righteous judgment will be revealed. ⁶God "will repay each person according to what they have done". ⁷To those who by persistence in doing good seek glory, honor and immortality, he will give eternal life. ⁸But for those who are self-seeking and who reject the truth and follow evil, there will be wrath and anger. ⁹There will be trouble and distress for every human being who does evil: first for the Jew, then for the Gentile; ¹⁰but glory, honor and peace for everyone who does good: first for the Jew, then for the Gentile. ¹¹For God does not show favoritism.

¹²All who sin apart from the law will also perish apart from the law, and all who sin under the law will be judged by the law. ¹³For it is not those who hear the law who are righteous in God's sight, but it is those who obey the law who will be declared righteous. ¹⁴(Indeed, when Gentiles, who do not have the law, do by nature things required by the law, they are a law for themselves, even though they do not have the law. ¹⁵They show that the requirements of the law are written on their hearts, their consciences also bearing witness, and their thoughts sometimes accusing them and at other times even defending them.) ¹⁶This will take place on the day when God judges people's secrets through Jesus Christ, as my gospel declares.

In 1:18-32 Paul spoke of the wrath of God revealed against all human wickedness, depicted in terms of the sins of the Gentile world. This depiction was something those with a Jewish background in the church at Rome would recognize as reminiscent of Jewish anti-Gentile polemic, and something to which they would assent. Paul's depiction of the sins of humanity culminates in 1:32 with the indictment: 'Although they know God's righteous decree that those who do such things deserve death, they not only continue to do these very things but also approve of those who practice them'. In 2:1-16 Paul further develops the theme of practicing evil, declaring that those who condemn others for the evil they practice, while practicing the same things themselves, will in no way escape the judgment of God.[120] The key text in this passage is 2:11: 'For God does not show favoritism'. God holds all peoples accountable. Those who sin 'apart from the law' (Gentiles) will be judged apart from the law, while those who sin 'under the law' (Jews) will be judged by the law (2:12). God will reward or punish all people according to their deeds. Paul applies what he says to all who take the high moral ground and judge others while being guilty of the same evil practices, particularly those of his Jewish kinspeople — 'first for the Jew' (2:9-10).[121]

120. The threefold use of the verb 'to practice' *(prassō)* found in 2:1-3 connects the passage 2:1-16 back to 1:32: 'You who pass judgment do the same things *(ta auta prasseis)'* (2:1); 'God's judgment against those who do such things *(ta toiauta prassontas)* is based on truth' (2:2); 'So when you . . . pass judgment on them and yet do the same things *(ta toiauta prassontas)* . . .' (2:3).

121. Cf. Jouette M. Bassler, 'Divine Impartiality in Paul's Letter to the Romans', *NovT* 26 (1984) 54.

In 1:18-32 Paul used the third person plural ('they') when depicting the sins of humanity. But in 2:1ff., where he exposes the hypocrisy and impending judgment of those who take the high moral ground in relation to those who practice evil, the apostle uses the second person singular ('you'). (The use of the second person is dropped in 2:2, 6-16, but resumed again in 2:17ff.) It is a mistake to think that Paul's use of the second person singular indicates that he is addressing directly one of his Roman Christian audiences or even all of them — elsewhere in the letter he makes quite clear that he has a high opinion of their Christian standing (cf. 1:8; 15:14). It is better to regard his use of the second person singular as an application of the rhetorical device known as the diatribe. Using this device, an orator/author does not address his audience directly, but instead engages a hypothetical dialogue partner. The dialogue between orator/author and the hypothetical dialogue partner is intended to be heard by the audience and to be a vehicle for their instruction.[122] In the case of 2:1-16 Paul is explaining for the benefit of his audience that people who know what God requires but do not carry it out are left exposed to the righteous judgment of God. While he does not state it explicitly, Paul has unrepentant Jewish people in mind ('first for the Jew'), pointing out that (Christian) Gentiles fulfill the law that the unrepentant Jews do not.[123]

2:1 Continuing, then, the theme of judgment found in 1:18-32, Paul says: *You, therefore, have no excuse, you who pass judgment on someone else, for at whatever point you judge another, you are condemning yourself, because you who pass judgment do the same things.* Literally rendered, the first part of this verse would read: 'Therefore, you are without excuse, O man, every one who judges'. The NIV has omitted the words 'O man'[124] and 'every one', and added the words, 'on someone else'.

The connection between 2:1-16 and 1:32 is established by the conjunction 'therefore' as well as the repeated use of the verb 'to practice' mentioned above. The similar factor found in 1:32 and 2:1 is that people know what God requires. The difference is that in the first instance they know

---

122. S. E. Porter, 'Diatribe', *DNTB*, 296-98, provides a helpful description of the nature and use of the diatribe in the Greco-Roman world, and in the NT.

123. Surprisingly, Witherington, *Romans*, 78, says of Paul's intention in 2:1-16: 'Paul may seem on the surface to be speaking here about human beings in general, but in fact he is focusing on Gentiles. *He provides a strong critique of those in his audience* [italics added] who might have the tendency to see themselves as morally superior to their fellow Gentiles, and indeed to their fellow Christians as well. One might well ask what sort of Roman Gentile might reflect such attitudes as we find critiqued here. There are at least two: God-fearers who had already imbibed the usual Jewish critique of pagan idolatry and immorality before becoming Christians, and Romans who had absorbed the philosophy of self-mastery reflected in the letters of Seneca and the writings of Epictetus'.

124. Paul uses the expression *ō anthrōpe* ('O man') three times in Romans (2:1, 3; 9:20), and in each case in a confrontational way. The only other places it is found in the NT are 1 Tim 6:11 (where it is used positively: *Sy de ō anthrōpe theou* ('You, man of God') and in Jas 2:20 (where again it is used confrontationally: *ō anthrōpe kene* ('you foolish person').

what God requires but continue to do the opposite and give their approval to others who do the same, whereas in the second instance, knowing what God requires, they condemn the evil actions of others while doing the same things themselves.[125]

When Paul claims that such people 'have no excuse', he uses an expression also found is 1:20, where he says that humanity is 'without excuse' for practicing idolatry because from the creation of the world God has revealed his eternal power and deity to them through the things he has made. Thus, as far as accountability before God is concerned, Paul implies that those (primarily Jewish people) who know enough of what God requires to pronounce judgment upon others while being guilty of the same things themselves, are no better than the rest of humanity; no better than idolaters.

There is a play on words in 2:1, where Paul says, 'at whatever point you *judge* another, you are *judging/condemning* yourself'. The NIV's 'at whatever point' translated literally is 'in that which', which is more specific than 'at whatever point'. Paul is implying that his hypothetical dialogue partner is guilty of precisely the same transgressions for which he pronounces judgment upon another, and so his judgment of the other is tantamount to condemnation of himself. But in what sense are those whom Paul's dialogue partner represents as guilty of 'the same things' as those indicted in 1:18-32? Dunn says that the things Paul has in mind 'are the sort of things listed in 1:29-31. . . . The prominence given in that list to sins of pride and presumption . . . may well already have had the Jewish interlocutor in mind, since it is precisely Jewish presumption regarding their favored status as the people of God which underlay so much Jewish disparagement of Gentile religion'.[126]

2:2-3   In 2:2 Paul adopts the first person plural address ('we') to include his audience with himself when he says: *Now we know that God's judgment against those who do such things is based on truth* (lit. 'according to truth'). Paul assumes his audience agrees that God's judgment against those who practice evil is 'based on truth' (i.e., on a true assessment of their behavior) and therefore fully deserved. Then, reverting to the second person singular address of the diatribe, he asks his dialogue partner: *So when you, a mere human being, pass judgment on them and yet do the same things, do*

---

125. Jewett, *Romans*, 196, comments on the connection between 1:32 and 2:1: 'The first word is the inferential conjunction *dio* ("therefore"), which we should understand in the full logical sense, drawing the inference from the preceding argument. The reduction of the conjunction to a nonlogical transition rests on a misperception of 1:18-32 as pertaining only to Gentiles, whereas it includes "*all* impiety and unrighteousness of humans who by unrighteousness are suppressing the truth" (1:18)'. Dunn, *Romans 1–8*, 79, comments on *dio* ('therefore'): 'The unexpected conclusion takes the form of a challenge to anyone who thought himself exempt from the preceding indictment, with something of the force of Nathan's conclusion to David: "You are the man" (2 Sam 12:7)'.

126. Dunn, *Romans 1–8*, 80.

you think you will escape God's judgment?' Paul addresses his dialogue partner as 'a mere human being' (lit. 'O man', the same address used in 2:1).
Here again it is used in a confrontational way: When you [O man] pass
judgment on them . . . do you think you (emphatic) will escape God's judgment when you do the same things as those whom you condemn?[127] Later,
in 2:17-24, Paul will accuse a Jewish dialogue partner of breaking the very
law that he is so proud of knowing.

2:4-5 Paul presses home his point by asking a further question: *Or
do you show contempt for the riches of his kindness, forbearance and patience, not
realizing that God's kindness is intended to lead you to repentance?* If the dialogue partner thinks he will escape judgment because of God's 'kindness,
forbearance and patience', he is deeply mistaken. When the apostle uses
the word 'kindness' in relation to God, he does so usually in connection
with the salvation of those who believe (11:22; Eph 2:7; Tit 3:4), and he uses
the words 'forbearance' and 'patience' in connection with God's forbearance of sinners (3:25-26; 9:22; 1 Tim 1:16). In a similar way in 11:22 Paul
speaks of 'the kindness and sternness of God' — kindness shown to those
who respond positively to the gospel, and sternness towards those who do
not. This same kindness is mentioned in Ephesians 2:7 ('the incomparable
riches of his grace, expressed in his kindness to us in Christ Jesus') and Titus 3:4 ('when the kindness and love of God our Savior appeared'). Here in
2:4, however, 'kindness' is linked with 'forbearance and patience',[128] and it
is expressed in his forbearance towards sinners, providing opportunity for
and leading them toward repentance.[129]

The terminology of repentance does not feature largely in Paul's
writings. The noun 'repentance' is found in only three other places and the
verb 'to repent' only once in the Pauline corpus.[130] Moo suggests that this
is the case 'because the coming of Christ had revealed to Paul that accep-

127. Moo, *Romans*, 132, notes: 'This is just the attitude revealed in . . . *The Psalms of
Solomon,* where the author asserts that "those who do lawlessness will not escape the judgement of the Lord" (15:8)'.

128. Origen distinguishes 'forbearance' (NIV: 'tolerance') and patience: 'Forbearance
differs from patience in that it applies more to those who sin because of their weakness and
not deliberately, whereas patience is brought to bear in the case of those who sin deliberately, as if to glory in their wrongdoing' ('Commentary on the Epistle to the Romans'
[*ACCSR,* 55]).

129. A similar point is made in 2 Pet 3:3-9, esp. 3:9: 'The Lord is not slow in keeping
his promise, as some understand slowness. Instead he is patient with you, not wanting anyone to perish, but everyone to come to repentance'.

130. Cf. 2 Cor 7:9-10: 'Yet now I am happy, not because you were made sorry, but because your sorrow led you to *repentance.* For you became sorrowful as God intended and so
were not harmed in any way by us. Godly sorrow brings *repentance* that leads to salvation
and leaves no regret, but worldly sorrow brings death'; 2 Tim 2:25: 'Opponents must be
gently instructed, in the hope that God will grant them *repentance* leading to a knowledge of the truth'; 2 Cor 12:21: 'I am afraid that when I come again my God will humble me
before you, and I will be grieved over many who have sinned earlier and have not *repented*
of the impurity, sexual sin and debauchery in which they have indulged' (italics added).

tance with God requires a stronger action than the word "repentance" often connoted'.[131]

Those who continue unrepentant, Paul declares, 'show contempt for the riches of his [God's] kindness'. Paul uses the verb 'to show contempt' in contexts where looking down on or failing to show respect for others is involved.[132] Those who do not repent of their sins in the light of God's kindness fail to show respect to God and to honor him as they should (cf. 1:21), and therefore invite his judgment upon themselves. To 'show contempt for' is much stronger than to 'presume upon' God's kindness, an attitude that is reflected in the following passage found in the Wisdom of Solomon, a passage of which Paul was probably aware:

> But you, our God, are kind and true, patient, and ruling all things in mercy. For even if we sin we are yours, knowing your power; but we will not sin, because we know that you acknowledge us as yours. For to know you is complete righteousness, and to know your power is the root of immortality. (15:1-3)

Paul, of course, knows that God is kind, true, and patient. What he cannot accept is the presumption on the part of those who take the high moral ground and assume that that they will be judged more leniently than others. For the apostle this is not only presumptuous, but actually shows contempt for God's kindness.

Paul goes on to spell out very clearly the implications of this contempt: *But because of your stubbornness and your unrepentant heart, you are storing up wrath against yourself for the day of God's wrath, when his righteous judgment will be revealed.* Far from escaping the judgment of God because he knows what God requires and can pass judgment on others, Paul tells his dialogue partner that, by his failure to repent, he is actually 'storing up wrath' against himself. Paul uses the verb 'to store up' in an unusual way here. Almost everywhere else in the NT it is used of storing up treasure for one reason or another (Matt 6:19-20; Luke 12:21; 1 Cor 16:2; 2 Cor 12:14; Jas 5:3). The only exceptions are found in 2 Peter 3:7 and here in 2:5, where it is used metaphorically to speak of God's judgment/wrath stored up against the ungodly.[133] Chrysostom says: 'The true originator of wrath is the one

---

131. Moo, *Romans*, 133-34. Witherington, *Romans*, 81, notes that: '*Metanoia,* "repentance", was a word familiar to Gentiles. It usually conveyed the sense of a change of mind in Stoic thought, or sometimes even remorse for something done in the past. The Hebrew equivalent is *shub,* which means to turn back or return. In Christian contexts the term is virtually equivalent to "convert". . . . If we ask how Paul's largely Gentile audience would have heard the term, they may have focused on the concept of "change of mind" and so of lifestyle'.

132. In 1 Cor 11:22 the wealthy are guilty of showing contempt for the church of God by humiliating the poor; in 1 Tim 4:12 Paul tells Timothy not to let people 'look down' on him because of his youth; and in 1 Tim 6:2 Paul tells Timothy to charge believing slaves who have believing masters not to show less respect for them because they are brothers.

133. Cranfield, *Romans*, I, 145, comments: 'The use of *thēsaurizein* ['to store up'] is

who has stored it up, not the one who is judged, as Paul makes plain. For he says, *you are storing up wrath for yourself, not God is storing up wrath for you*.[134] While it is true that human sin is what attracts God's wrath and to that extent people may be said to be storing up wrath for themselves by their sinful deeds, it is also the case that God's decision to defer judgment to provide opportunity for repentance is tantamount to his storing up wrath for those who refuse to repent.

Paul says that his dialogue partner is storing up wrath against himself 'for the day of God's wrath'. Paul nowhere else speaks of 'the day of God's wrath', but he does speak of 'the day', 'the day of our Lord Jesus', 'the day of redemption', 'the day of Christ Jesus', 'the day of Christ', 'the day of the Lord', 'this day', 'the day he comes', and 'that day' (2:16; 1 Cor 1:8; 3:13; 5:5; 2 Cor 1:14; Eph 4:30; Phil 1:6, 10; 2:16; 1 Thess 5:2, 4; 2 Thess 1:10; 2:2; 2 Tim 1:12, 18). On that day judgment will be declared and God's wrath on the wicked revealed (cf. 2:16; 1 Cor 3:13; 2 Thess 1:5-10). See 'Additional Note: The Wrath of God', 90-91.

Paul speaks of the day of God's wrath as the day of the revelation of God's 'righteous judgment'. The expression is found only here in the NT, but Paul does use an equivalent expression in 2 Thessalonians 1:5 where he speaks of the 'evidence that God's judgment is righteous'. In that context God's judgment is seen to be righteous as he pays back those who have persecuted his people.[135] What Paul means by the revelation of God's righteous judgment here in 2:5 is spelled out in the verses that follow (2:6-11).

2:6 Beginning with this verse, and continuing through until v. 11, Paul ceases to address his dialogue partner (using the second person, 'you'), and adopts the third person as he describes more objectively the impartial judgment of God. Moo identifies the following chiastic structure:

A God will judge everyone equitably	v. 6
B Those who do good will attain eternal life	v. 7
C Those who do evil will suffer wrath	v. 8
C' Wrath for those who do evil	v. 9
B' Glory for those who do good	v. 10
A' God judges impartially	v. 11

He comments: 'Unlike some chiastically structured paragraphs, the main point of vv. 6-11 occurs not at the center but at the beginning and the end

---

ironical. Compare LXX Prov 1.18. The metaphor is elsewhere used of storing up something desirable, as in Mt 6.20'.

134. 'Homilies on Romans' (*ACCSR*, 58).

135. In 2 Thess 1:9-10 Paul describes the nature of that judgment: 'They will be punished with everlasting destruction and shut out from the presence of the Lord and from the glory of his might on the day he comes to be glorified in his holy people and to be marveled at among all those who have believed'.

(vv. 6, 11): God will judge every person impartially, assessing each according to the same standard — works'.[136]

The apostle cites almost exactly the LXX version of Proverbs 24:12 when he writes: God *'will repay each person according to what they have done'.*[137] That God judges all people in accordance with their works is a pervasive theme in the OT (cf., e.g., Ps 62:12; Prov 24:12; Isa 3:10; Jer 17:10; Hos 12:2; Eccl 12:14), the teaching of Jesus (Matt 16:27; 25:31-46; John 5:28-29), the writings of Paul (cf., e.g., 2 Cor 5:10; 11:15; Gal 6:7-9; Eph 6:8; Col 3:24-25 2 Tim 4:14), and other NT letters (cf., e.g., 1 Pet 1:17; Rev 2:23; 20:12-13; 22:12). It is also a fundamental assumption in later writings of Judaism.[138] What Paul means by 'works' here is made clear in what follows (2:7-10).

2:7 In this verse Paul begins to explain what he means by saying that God pays people back 'according to what they have done'.[139] First he says that *to those who by persistence in doing good seek glory, honor and immortality, he will give eternal life.* Where Paul speaks elsewhere of 'good works' he does not mean by it careful observance of the Mosaic law so as to merit salvation. 'Good works' elsewhere in Paul's writings relates to the behavior expected of followers of Christ, those who are already saved.[140] On first reading the way 'doing good' is used here in 2:7 appears to be an exception to the rule because it is linked to receiving eternal life, but closer inspection reveals that this is not the case, especially when compared with its opposite in 2:8 (see the commentary below).

Commenting upon Paul's reference to 'persistence in doing good', Garlington says that 'the bottom line then is that the obedience of faith which finally justifies is perseverance, motivated by love', adding that 'the passage from present justification by faith alone to future justification by the obedience of faith is both natural and to be expected, given the broader purview — and especially the creation character — of Paul's theology of faith and obedience'.[141] To allay the fears of Christian people, Garlington contin-

---

136. Moo, *Romans*, 135-36.

137. Cf. Rom 2:6: *hos apodōsei hekastō kata ta erga autou,* and Prov 24:12: *hos apodidōsin hekastō kata ta erga autou.* Cf. LXX Ps 61:13 (ET 62:13): *sy apodōseis hekastō kata ta erga autou* ('you repay to each one according to his works').

138. See documentation in Klyne R. Snodgrass, 'Justification by Grace — To the Doers: An Analysis of the Place of Romans 2 in the Theology of Paul', *NTS* 34 (1988) 90, n. 38.

139. Akio Ito, 'Romans 2: A Deuteronomistic Reading', *JSNT* 59 (1995) 25-26, argues that there is a Deuteronomistic background to 2:7-10, noting that 2:7, 10 promise blessings to those who do good and 2:8-9 pronounce judgment upon those who do evil, just as is the case in Deuteronomy 27-30.

140. Cf. 13:3; 2 Cor 9:8; Eph 2:10; Col 1:10; 2 Thess 2:17; 1 Tim 2:10; 5:10; 2 Tim 2:21; 3:17; Tit 1:16; 3:1. Typical are 2 Cor 9:8 ('God is able to bless you abundantly, so that in all things at all times, having all that you need, you will abound in every good work') and Col 1:9-10 ('We have not stopped praying for you . . . so that you may live a life worthy of the Lord and please him in every way: bearing fruit in every good work, growing in the knowledge of God').

141. D. B. Garlington, 'The Obedience of Faith in the Letter to the Romans, Part II: The Obedience of Faith and Judgment by Works', *WTJ* 53 (1991) 68-69.

ues, 'although the obedience in question entails specific and concrete acts of a lifestyle pleasing to God (e.g., Matt 25:31-46)', it must be remembered that 'the future justification of God's people is not made to hinge on, say, 51% (or more!) of law-keeping, because obedience itself is the product of faith; and where true faith and love exist, there must be ultimate justification'.[142]

Paul speaks often about the 'glory' in store for believers in Romans (2:7, 10; 5:2; 8:18, 21; 9:23), as he does elsewhere (1 Cor 2:7; 15:43; 2 Cor 3:18; 4:17; Eph 1:18; Phil 3:21; Col 1:27; 3:4; 1 Thess 2:12; 2 Thess 2:14; 2 Tim 2:10). In fact it is quite surprising how great a place this theme occupies in his thinking. While he does not explain in detail what this glory involves, it is a pervasive theme in his writings. See 'Additional Note: The Glory in Store for Believers', 228-29.

In the ancient Greco-Roman world to receive honor was to be publicly acknowledged or praised for one's worth. It was something much sought after, and its opposite, to be exposed to shame, was to be avoided at all costs.[143] It is quite unusual for Paul to speak of people seeking honor from God. In fact, it is only here in 2:7 and 2:10 that he does so.[144] Elsewhere in the NT only Christ is said to receive honor from God (cf. Heb 2:7, 9; 2 Pet 1:17). In 2 Peter 1:17 Jesus Christ receives honor when God publicly acknowledges him as his Son: 'He received honor and glory from God the Father when the voice came to him from the Majestic Glory, saying, "This is my Son, whom I love; with him I am well pleased"'. In the OT there is one place where God promises to honor those who honor him (1 Sam 2:30).

When Paul speaks of 'immortality' elsewhere (cf. 1 Cor 15:42, 50, 53, 54; 2 Tim 1:10), he does not mean by it the immortality of the soul (ongoing life as a disembodied spirit), but rather in terms of resurrection to immortality. In 1 Corinthians 15:42, 50, 53, 54 he speaks explicitly of the resurrection body as immortal/imperishable, and the same is implied in the case of 2 Timothy 1:10. It is reasonable, therefore, to assume that the word has the same meaning here in 2:7.[145]

To those who persist in doing good and so seek glory, honor, and immortality God gives 'eternal life'. In several places Paul speaks of the 'life' from God that believers experience in the present time (6:4; 8:6, 10; 2 Cor 2:16; 4:10-12; Col 3:3-4),[146] but where he speaks of 'eternal life', as he does

142. Garlington, 'The Obedience of Faith in the Letter to the Romans, Part II', 70.

143. Cf. D. A. de Silva, 'Honor and Shame', *DNTB*, 518-22.

144. He speaks frequently of the honor that believers should show to God (1 Cor 6:20; 1 Tim 1:17; 1 Tim 6:16) and to other people, including parents (Eph 6:2), genuine widows (1 Tim 5:3), fellow believers (Rom 12:10; 1 Cor 12:23-24), elders (1 Tim 5:17), masters (1 Tim 6:1), and the governing authorities (Rom 13:7).

145. In the LXX *aphtharsia* (immortality') is found only in 4 Macc 17:12 ('For on that day virtue gave the awards and tested them for their endurance. The prize was immortality [*aphtharsia*] in endless life') and Wis 2:23 ('For God created us for incorruption [*aphtharsia*], and made us in the image of his own eternity').

146. The word *zōē* ('life') on its own can sometimes also be used to denote 'eternal life' in the sense of future reward (cf. 11:15; 2 Cor 5:4; 1 Tim 4:8; 6:19; 2 Tim 1:1, 10).

here in 2:7, the context always indicates that he has in mind the future reward for, and final outcome of, belief in Jesus Christ (2:7; 5:21; 6:22-23; Gal
6:8; 1 Tim 1:16; 6:12; Tit 1:2; 3:7). Paul does not spell out in detail the nature
of 'eternal life'. However, it clearly involves life in a resurrection body
(2 Cor 5:4; cf. Rom 8:23) and sharing in Christ's glory (Col 2:4; cf. Rom 8:17-
21). In other places, while not explicitly speaking of eternal life, the apostle
indicates that believers will reign with Christ (2 Tim 2:12) and share in his
judgment of the world and of angels (1 Cor 6:1-3).[147]

2:8 In 2:7 Paul described the reward in store for those who 'do
good'. Here in 2:8 he outlines what is in store for those who do the opposite: *But for those who are self-seeking and who reject the truth and follow evil,
there will be wrath and anger.* Before commenting on this verse in detail, it's
worth noting that if these things constitute the opposite of 'doing good',
then by implication 'doing good' may be understood as seeking God, accepting the truth of his revelation, and eschewing evil practices — the opposite of self-seeking, rejecting the truth, and following evil.[148]

Paul contrasts those who by 'doing good seek glory, honor and immortality' with those who 'are self-seeking and who reject the truth and follow evil'. The word translated 'self-seeking' is found only in the writings of
Aristotle prior to NT times. There it 'denotes a self-seeking pursuit of political office by unfair means'.[149] While the meaning of the word in the NT is
debatable, translations such as 'selfishness' and 'selfish ambition' make
good sense in each of the contexts in which they occur (2:8; 2 Cor 12:20; Gal

---

147. Cranfield, *Romans*, I, 157, says that Paul is referring 'to goodness of life, not however as meriting God's favor but as the expression of faith. It is to be noted that Paul speaks
of those who seek (*zētousin*) glory, honour and incorruption, not of those who deserve them.
Doxa, timē and *aphtharsia* ['glory', 'honour' and 'immortality'] here denote eschatological
gifts of God already firmly associated in Jewish thought with the resurrection life of the
blessed'.

148. Wright, 'Romans', 439-40, comments: 'The attitude of the two groups is not described in moralistic terms. Paul does not, as a rabbi might have done, produce a list of
things that will qualify or disqualify for "the age to come". Rather, the one group, by "patience in well doing", *seeks for* glory, honor, and immortality. Paul does not say that they
earn them or grasp them; merely that they are seeking them. The other group, seeking their
own selfish gain, does "not obey the truth, but obeys injustice". . . . The first group is defined in terms of that for which they seek and the means by which that quest is pursued; the
second, in terms of that which is obeyed and not obeyed. We are left to fill in the gaps and to
presume that the former do obey the truth and that the latter do not patiently seek for
glory'.

Dunn, *Romans 1–8*, 86, says: '"Patient persistence in good work" is possible only for
those who recognize their creaturely dependence on God, and who live their lives out of a
spirit of gratitude and worship. . . . And that open and complete trust in God he finds only
possible through Jesus Christ. But here is the broadly stated principle which is in view — a
principle all would accept, even if they fail to recognize that the ideal cannot be achieved
apart from such faith. The underlying claim is that the narrower Jewish interpretation of the
principle in fact fails to appreciate the breadth of its applicability, whereas his [Paul's] own
is open to Jew and Gentile alike on the same terms'.

149. Cf. BAGD, *ad loc.*

5:20; Phil 1:17; 2:3; Jas 3:14, 16). It would appear, then, that Paul is saying that those who disobey the truth are motivated by 'self-seeking'.

The truth they 'reject' is God's truth, something made clear by the fact that where Paul uses the word translated 'reject' elsewhere it always carries the idea of disobeying God or rejecting his revelation (2:8; 10:21; 11:30-31; 15:31). This is also the case where the word is used in other books of the NT (John 3:36; Acts 14:2; 19:9; Heb 3:18; 11:31; 1 Pet 2:8; 3:1, 20; 4:17). There is a sad irony involved here in 2:8; for those who reject the truth, Paul says, follow evil. 'Self-seeking' here in 2:8, then, involves pursuing evil for one's own purposes instead of obeying God's revelation.

Paul adds that for those who follow evil, there will be 'wrath and anger'. Only here does he use the expression 'wrath and anger', but he speaks frequently of God's 'wrath' elsewhere in Romans (1:18; 2:5, 8; 3:5; 4:15; 5:9; 9:22; 12:19; 13:4-5) as well as in his other writings (Eph 2:3; 5:6; Col 3:6; 1 Thess 1:10; 2:16; 5:9). (See 'Additional Note: The Wrath of God', 90-91.) In Romans he says that 'the wrath of God is being revealed from heaven against all godlessness and wickedness of people' (1:18), that it is being stored up against the unrepentant and self-seeking (2:5, 8), but that those who are justified by Christ's blood will be saved from God's wrath (5:9). In other letters the apostle reminds his audience that because of sinful behavior God's wrath is coming on those who are disobedient (Eph 5:3-6; Col 3:5-8; 1 Thess 2:16), and that prior to conversion, 'like the rest, we were by nature deserving of wrath' (Eph 2:3), but that we have been rescued from the wrath of God through the Lord Jesus Christ (1 Thess 1:10; 5:9). Probably Paul's clearest statement of what the wrath of God entails is to be found in 2 Thessalonians 1:6-9:

> God is just: He will pay back trouble to those who trouble you. . . . This will happen when the Lord Jesus is revealed from heaven in blazing fire with his powerful angels. He will punish those who do not know God and do not obey the gospel of our Lord Jesus. They will be punished with everlasting destruction and shut out from the presence of the Lord and from the glory of his might.

2:9-11 Restating what he said in 2:2-8 in slightly different terms, Paul says here: *There will be trouble and distress for every human being who does evil: first for the Jew, then for the Gentile; but glory, honor and peace for everyone who does good: first for the Jew, then for the Gentile. For God does not show favoritism.* When the apostle uses the word translated 'trouble' elsewhere, it denotes persecution or troubles that believers experience in this life. Only here in 2:9 and in 2 Thessalonians 1:6 ('God is just: He will pay back trouble to those who trouble you') does he use it to refer to God's retribution for those who do evil. Likewise, the word translated 'distress' is normally used by Paul to denote the hardships of this life, especially those borne by him in carrying out his apostolic ministry (8:35; 2 Cor 6:4;

12:10). Its use here in 2:9 to denote God's punishment of evildoers is the only exception.

In 2:7 Paul said that God rewards with the gift of eternal life those who 'by persistence in doing good seek glory, honor and immortality'. In 2:10 the reward itself is glory, honor, and peace'. In 2:10 'peace' replaces the 'immortality' sought by those who persist in doing good in 2:7. Paul asserts that both the reward for those who do good and the retribution for those who do evil will be 'first for the Jew, then for the Gentile'. In 1:16 he spoke of the gospel as the power of God for salvation 'first to the Jew, then to the Gentile', a statement reflecting Paul's belief in Israel's priority in God's salvation plan (see the commentary on 1:16). But here in 2:9-10 the priority of Israel in the matter of blessing when they do good is balanced by their priority in judgment when they do evil. Greater privilege brings greater accountability.[150] Moo stresses: 'In contrast to the Jews' tendency to regard their election as a guarantee that they would be "first" in salvation and "last" in judgment, Paul insists that their priority be applied equally to both'.[151]

In this context the formula, 'first for the Jew, then for the Gentile', carries the idea that there will be no special considerations for the Jewish people when it comes to judgment. This is made explicit here when Paul adds: 'For God does not show favoritism'. The word 'favoritism' (prosōpolēmpsia) denotes the sin of partiality — something never found in God. In Deuteronomy 10:17 we read: 'For the LORD your God is God of gods and Lord of lords, the great God, mighty and awesome, who shows no partiality and accepts no bribes'. Cf. Testament of Job 43:13: 'Righteous is the Lord, true are his judgments. With him there is no favoritism. He will judge us all together'.[152] Paul always uses the word 'favoritism' in connection with God's impartiality in matters of judgment (2:11; Eph 6:9; Col 3:25).[153] The words, 'God does not show favoritism', could stand as the heading over the whole of 2:1-16, and what Paul means by it is spelled out further in the verses that follow (2:12-16). Paul's emphasis here upon the fact that God does not show favoritism reflects the fact that his hypothetical dialogue partner in 2:1-16 is indeed a representative Jew, one who would expect to receive favorable treatment from God because he is a Jew.

2:12-13   These verses open with the words, [For] all who sin apart from the law will also perish apart from the law, and all who sin under the law will be

150. Jewett, Romans, 208, says: 'That the word "Jew" comes first in this formula, following a traditional biblical concept, should not be taken to mean that Jews in particular are under attack here. . . . Paul is making a case that God will treat Jews and Greeks "equally and not on the basis of membership in one group or another", as Stowers shows [Diatribe, 113]'.

151. Moo, Romans, 139.

152. James H. Charlesworth, ed., The Old Testament Pseudepigrapha, Vol. 1: Apocalyptic Literature and Testaments (New York: Doubleday, 1983), 862.

153. Luke uses the cognate noun prosōpolēmptēs ('one who shows partiality') in Acts 10:34 when he reports Peter's statement to Cornelius: 'I now realize how true it is that God does not show favoritism' (hoti ouk estin prosōpolēmptēs para tō theō [BAGD: 'he is not one to show partiality']).

judged by the law. The NIV omits the conjunction 'for', obscuring the fact that what Paul says in 2:12-13 explains God's impartiality in judgment stressed in the previous verse. God will judge with an even hand both those who sin apart from the law (Gentiles) and those who sin under the law (Jews). Living 'under the law' was one of the chief factors, if not the chief factor, that distinguished Jews from Gentiles. Paul says that Gentile people who sin apart from the law will 'perish' without reference to the law.[154] While God shows no favoritism when he judges, he does nevertheless take into account the revelation people have received. Therefore, when speaking of the Jewish people the apostle says, 'all who sin under the law will be judged by the law'.[155]

Those who are privileged to have the law will be judged in accordance with that law. And there will be no immunity for them simply because they know the law. Paul explains: *For it is not those who hear the law* [lit. 'hearers of the law'] *who are righteous in God's sight, but it is those who obey the law* [lit. 'doers of the law'] *who will be declared righteous.*[156] Paul's point here is that being a 'hearer' of the law does not guarantee righteousness in God's sight. One must be a 'doer' of the law as well.[157] His purpose is to show that Jewish knowledge of the law is no ground for being 'declared righteous' by God.[158] Jewish people will be judged in accordance with their obedience to the law. And shortly Paul will argue that his Jewish dialogue partner and those whom he represents are guilty of disobedience to the law, despite their possession and knowledge of it (2:17-24).[159] When Paul says that 'it those who obey the law who will be declared righteous', he employs the future tense, suggesting that it is future justification that he has in mind (cf. 2:16).

---

154. Normally when the apostle Paul refers to those who are 'perishing' he has in mind those who reject the gospel (1 Cor 1:18; 2 Cor 2:15; 4:3; 2 Thess 2:9-12), though that is not explicit here.

155. Jewett, *Romans,* 211, observes: 'The passive form of the verb *krithēsontai* ("they will be judged by the law") clearly implies that God is the source of judgment'.

156. Jeffrey S. Lamp, 'Paul, the Law, Jews, and Gentiles: A Contextual and Exegetical Reading of Romans 2:12-16', *JETS* 42 (1999) 43, notes that Jewish sources also stress the importance of doing as well as hearing the law, but also that the concept of hearing the law 'had a more positive connotation', as evident in the *Shema* (Deut 6:4).

157. James 1:23-35, in a different context, stresses the need for people to be 'doers' *(poiētai),* not just hearers *(akroatai),* of 'the word', pointing out that the blessing comes with the doing, a point made by Jesus himself in John 13:17: 'Now that you know these things, you will be blessed if you do them'.

158. A similar point is made in Jer 8:8: 'How can you say, "We are wise, for we have the law of the LORD", when actually the lying pen of the scribes has handled it falsely?'

159. Garlington, 'The Obedience of Faith in the Letter to the Romans, Part II', 63-64, argues that 'Paul, in a very un-Jewish manner, pits "hearing" against "doing" for the purpose of remonstrating with Israel that her particular hearing and doing are unacceptable to God in the final judgment'. Basing his comments upon 10:14-21, he explains this by saying that 'Israel has heard — but she has not heard. Because she has not heard with "the hearing of faith", i.e., faith directed toward the gospel, she is incapable of "the obedience of faith", which grows out of the gospel'.

When Paul speaks of those who will be 'declared righteous' here, he uses for the first time a verb found in fifteen places in Romans. Many of the instances of Paul's use of this verb relate to those who are 'justified by faith', that is, those who are declared to be righteous by God on the basis of the redemption provided through his Son and because of their faith in him (3:24, 26, 28, 30; 4:2, 5; 5:1, 9; 8:30, 33). In 3:20 the apostle will emphasize that 'no one will be declared righteous in God's sight by the works of the law; rather, through the law we become conscious of our sin'. Therefore, Paul's statement here in 2:13 that 'it is those who obey the law who will be declared righteous' appears to run counter to, or even contradict, what he says in the rest of the letter. However, this is not actually the case, as becomes clear when each text is read first in its own context. For a discussion of the apparent contradiction see the commentary on 3:20 below.[160]

2:14-16   These verses explain how Gentiles who do not possess the law of Moses as do the Jews may nevertheless still be judged on the principle of performance, as will the Jews. They constitute one long sentence in the original, which the NIV renders as two sentences, and the first of which (2:14-15) is interpreted as a parenthesis: *(Indeed, when Gentiles, who do not have the law, do by nature things required by the law, they are a law for themselves, even though they do not have the law. They show that the requirements of the law are written on their hearts, their consciences also bearing witness, and their thoughts sometimes accusing them and at other times even defending them.) This will take place on the day when God will judge people's secrets through Jesus Christ,*[161] *as my gospel declares.* A better translation that preserves the flow of the original (reflecting exegetical decisions to be taken and admittedly rather stilted) would read:

> For[162] when Gentiles who by nature [as Gentiles] do not have the law do what the law requires, these, though not having [the] law, are a law to themselves, who show the work of the law written in their hearts, their consciences confirming [what the law says] and their thoughts among themselves accusing or even excusing on the day when God judges men's secrets according to my gospel through Jesus Christ.

---

160. Cranfield, *Romans*, I, 154-55, comments: 'That doing what the law commands is the decisive thing, and not just hearing it and knowing about it, was a truth familiar to the Rabbis; but, though Paul takes up a Rabbinic doctrine, he is giving it fresh content. In its context in Romans this sentence can hardly be intended to imply that there are some who are doers of the law in the sense that they so fulfil it as to earn God's justification. Rather is Paul thinking of that beginning of grateful obedience to be found in those who believe in Christ, which, though very weak and faltering and in no way deserving God's favour, is, as the expression of humble trust in God, well-pleasing in His sight'.

161. Manuscript evidence is fairly evenly balanced in support of 'Jesus Christ' (NIV, NRSV) and 'Christ Jesus' (NASB).

162. The verses 2:14-16 are connected with the preceding verses (2:12-13) with the conjunction *gar* ('for', rendered 'indeed' by the NIV and omitted altogether by the NRSV).

These verses present the interpreter with several problems. First, the NIV's translation, 'Gentiles, who do not have the law, do by nature things required by the law', is open to question. What is the significance of 'by nature' in this clause? Does it qualify the verb 'do', thus yielding a translation like that of the NIV: 'Gentiles, who do not have the law, *do by nature things required by the law*'. Or does it qualify 'Gentiles', thus yielding a translation like 'Gentiles, *who by nature do not have the law*, do the things required by the law'. There are good reasons for adopting the latter option, including the fact that when Paul uses 'by nature' elsewhere it always qualifies a state of being, never an action, and the fact that in 2:12 he speaks of those 'who sin apart from the law' (Gentiles) perishing 'apart from the law' and so characterizing the Gentiles as those who do not have the law by virtue of being Gentiles. In 2:14, then, it is better to see 'by nature' qualifying what the Gentiles *are* (those who do not have the law) than what they *do* (the things required by the law). So Paul's point is that these Gentiles who, as Gentiles, do not have the privilege of possessing the law nevertheless do what the law requires.

A second problem is the meaning of the 'things required by the law' (lit. 'the things of the law') that the Gentiles carry out. Those who say that the Gentiles of 2:14 are pagans argue that 'the things required by the law' can refer only vaguely to some of the things the law requires, and that it cannot have any comprehensive sense. However, Gathercole rightly points out that while the scope of the phrase 'the things of' is general in its NT usage, it is also nearly always inclusive and comprehensive in meaning. Thus, for example, the contrast between 'the concerns [lit. 'things'] of God' and 'the concerns [lit. 'things'] of men' referred to in Matthew 16:23/Mark 8:33 is comprehensive in meaning. Even when a contrast is not implied Paul uses such phrases in a comprehensive way (cf. 14:19; 1 Cor 13:11; 2 Cor 11:30). There is, then, nothing to suggest that the meaning of 'the things required by the law' is anything but comprehensive here in 2:14,[163] and that it therefore should be understood to denote generally the demands of the Mosaic law.[164]

The third problem is: if 'the things required by the law' refers generally to the demands of the Mosaic law, who then are the Gentiles who do the 'things required by the law'? They are unlikely to be, as some have suggested, either pagans who unknowingly observe some of the things demanded by the Mosaic law or pre-Christian Gentiles (like Ruth) who lived godly lives. They are more likely to be Christian Gentiles[165] upon whose hearts the law has been written by the Spirit, those in whom the new cov-

---

163. S. J. Gathercole, 'A Law unto Themselves: The Gentiles in Romans 2.14-15 Revisited', *JSNT* 85 (2002) 34. Simon J. Gathercole, *Where Is Boasting? Early Jewish Soteriology and Paul's Response in Romans 1–5* (Grand Rapids: Eerdmans, 2002), 126-27.

164. *Ta tou nomou* ('the things of the law') then is best construed as an objective genitive ('those things prescribed by the law').

165. Jewett, *Romans*, 213, notes: 'It is significant that Paul refers here to *ethnē* ("Gentiles") without the article, implying that some but not all Gentiles are in view'.

enant promise to Israel finds fulfillment (Jer 31:33: ' "This is the covenant I will make with the people of Israel after that time", declares the LORD. "I will put my law in their minds and write it on their hearts" '). Paul certainly believed that the law is 'fulfilled' (though not observed in all its detail) by those who believe in Jesus Christ and walk in the Spirit (8:3-4; 13:10; Gal 5:13-25). This is the interpretation adopted in this commentary. For a more detailed discussion of the debate surrounding this problem see 'Additional Note: Gentiles Who Do the Things Required by the Law', 136-40.

A fourth issue is the interpretation of Paul's statement regarding the Gentiles, 'they are a law for themselves, even though they do not have the law', and his explanation of this with the additional statement, 'they show that the requirements of the law [lit. 'the work of the law'] are written on their hearts'. A likely explanation of those whom Paul has in mind is that they are Gentile Christians on whose hearts God has written his law according to the new covenant promise found in Jeremiah 31:33. Lamp argues against an allusion to Jeremiah 31:33 here on the grounds that in 2:15 Paul speaks of '*the work of* the law' being written on their hearts, not 'the law', as in Jeremiah 31:33,[166] but this appears to be a splitting of hairs. Mathewson also argues against an allusion to Jeremiah 31:33, suggesting instead that Paul has in mind 'a moderate moral intuitionism', a 'natural ability of the mind to grasp immediately God's moral demands in an a priori manner', adding: 'We are born with the capacities to apprehend immediately and directly and non-inferentially know the created order around us'.[167] However, there seem to be more reasons to see an allusion here to Jeremiah 31:33, where there is a reference to the work of the law being written on the heart, than there is to adopt a reference to moral intuitionism when there are no indications in the text that this is what the apostle intended (for a fuller discussion see 'Additional Note: Gentiles Who Do the Things Required by the Law', 136-40).

A fifth matter needing explanation is the significance of the words, 'their consciences also bearing witness, and their thoughts sometimes accusing them and at other times even defending them'. There is no word in the original corresponding to the NIV's 'also'. Its inclusion by the NIV (and NRSV) skews the meaning of 2:15b so that it implies there are three witnesses: the work of the law, the consciences of the Gentiles, and their thoughts. In fact there are only two witnesses, the consciences of the Gentiles and their thoughts, and these confirm 'the work of the law written on their hearts'.

The verb translated 'bear witness' *(symmartyreō)* is found only three times in the NT, all of which are in Romans: here and in 8:16 and 9:1. While

---

166. Lamp, 'Paul, the Law, Jews, and Gentiles', 47. Cf. Dunn, *Romans*, I, 105; Byrne, *Romans*, 105.

167. Mark D. Mathewson, 'Moral Intuitionism and the Law Inscribed on Our Hearts', *JETS* 42 (1999) 633.

etymologically it might be argued that it means 'to bear witness with or alongside of', its use elsewhere indicates that it should be construed more generally to mean 'to confirm'. In 8:16 Paul says, 'The Spirit himself *testifies* with our spirit that we are God's children' (italics added). In this case the Holy Spirit and the believers' spirits are not joint witnesses, but rather the Holy Spirit bears witness to the human spirits of believers, confirming that they are children of God. In 9:1 Paul says, 'I speak the truth in Christ — I am not lying, my conscience *confirms* it through the Holy Spirit' (italics added). In this case Paul's conscience confirms to him that he is speaking the truth in Christ.[168] Here in 2:15 the consciences of the Gentiles bear witness to them, confirming the effects of 'the work of the law' in their hearts (see 'Additional Note: Conscience', 91).

As their consciences confirm the effect of 'the work of the law' written on their hearts, Paul says there is another witness: 'their thoughts sometimes accusing them and at other times even defending them'.[169] This clause is not easy to translate. A literal rendering would be: 'and the thoughts among themselves accusing or even excusing' (cf. NRSV, 'and their conflicting thoughts will accuse or perhaps excuse them').[170] The context implies that the witness of the Gentiles' thoughts takes place in the future when it says, 'This will take place on the day when God judges people's secrets through Jesus Christ, as my gospel declares'. Paul appears to be saying here that, while the Gentiles' consciences are confirming the law written on their hearts in the present, their thoughts may either accuse or excuse them on the day of judgment in the future.[171] Schreiner objects to this view on the grounds that if Gentile Christians are meant it is odd that Paul speaks of their thoughts bringing accusations on the Day of Judgment.[172] Wright re-

---

168. Cf. BAGD, *symmartyreō*.

169. The verb 'to accuse' *(katēgoreō)* is found frequently in the NT — twenty-three times in twenty-two verses (Matt 12:10; 27:12; Mark 3:2; 15:3, 4; Luke 6:7; 23:2, 10, 14; John 5:45 [2x]; 8:6; Acts 22:30; 24:2, 8, 13, 19; 25:5, 11, 16; 28:19; Rom 2:15; Rev 12:10). In every case except here in 2:15 it denotes a charge brought by one person against another, and carries legal overtones. Only in 2:15, containing Paul's only use of the word, does it refer to people's own thoughts accusing them. The verb 'to defend' *(apologeomai)* is found ten times in the NT (Luke 12:11; 21:14; Acts 19:33; 24:10; 25:8; 26:1, 2, 24; Rom 2:15; 2 Cor 12:19). In all cases but one it denotes a legal defense against charges brought by one person against another. The exception is again here in 2:15, where it refers to people's thoughts defending themselves.

170. *Allēlōn* refers to *logismoi*, not to *ethnē*. Fitzmyer, *Romans*, 311, comments: 'The prep. phrase *metaxy allēlōn*, "between one another", is not easily interpreted. It is best understood as referring to the mutual debate of inward thoughts in the Gentile conscience; the debate would concern the pros and cons of conduct'.

171. *Contra* Cranfield, *Romans*, I, 161, who says: 'the suggestion that the witness of conscience belongs to the present and the debate of the *logismoi* to the time of the last judgment is very much less likely than the view that these two genitive absolute formulations must be taken closely together, the second being understood as clarifying the first. On this view there can be no difference of time between them'.

172. Thomas Schreiner, 'Did Paul Believe in Justification by Works? Another Look at Romans 2', *BBR* 3 (1993) 147-52.

sponds: 'The Jewish law, which is now in some sense or other written on their hearts, and which in some sense they "do", nevertheless has a sufficiently ambiguous relation to them for them still to be concerned that the eventual issue might be in doubt. Hence as judgment day approaches, they may well find inner conflict as they reflect on their situation. They would not have this inner conflict were they not Christians'.[173] We might add that Paul's statement in 2 Corinthians 5:10 ('For we must all appear before the judgment seat of Christ, so that each of us may receive what is due us for the things done while in the body, whether good or bad') is sufficient to cause even believers to approach the Day of Judgment with some apprehension.

The accusing or excusing of the thoughts of the Gentiles, Paul says, 'will take place on the day when God will judges[174] people's secrets'. Already Paul has spoken about 'the day of God's wrath, when his righteous judgment will be revealed' against those with stubborn and unrepentant hearts (2:5).[175] Here he says that the thoughts of the Gentiles will accuse or defend them when God himself pronounces judgment. When Paul says that on that day 'God will judge people's secrets', he probably has in mind the revelation of God's judgment concerning even their secret thoughts and motives. That the apostle thought in these terms is confirmed by 1 Corinthians 4:5, where he says, 'He [God] will bring to light what is hidden in darkness and will expose the motives of the heart. At that time each will receive their praise from God'. Here 'what is hidden in darkness' stands in apposition to 'the motives of the heart'. It is noteworthy that when Paul speaks about the judgment of believers in 1 Corinthians 4:5, he says that this will also include appropriate commendation ('at that time each will receive his praise from God').

Paul affirms that God will judge men's secrets 'through Jesus Christ'. That God has entrusted judgment to his Son, Jesus Christ, is stated explicitly in only one other place in the Pauline letters, that is, in 2 Timothy 4:1, where the apostle issues his charge to Timothy 'in the presence of God and of Christ Jesus, who will judge the living and the dead'. Here in 2:16 Paul

173. N. T. Wright, 'The Law in Romans 2', in *Paul and the Mosaic Law,* ed. James D. G. Dunn (Eerdmans: Grand Rapids, 2001), 146.

174. The Greek original *krinei* may be accented either as *krineí* or as *kríne,* the former denoting the future tense, the latter the present tense. The NIV rendering of *krinei* as a future tense verb is preferable in this context where the apostle is referring to the future judgment day. Cf. Cranfield, *Romans,* I, 162.

175. Ramez Atallah, 'The Objective Witness to Conscience: An Egyptian Parallel to Romans 2:15', *ERT* 18 (1994) 204-13, also argues that the role of conscience Paul portrays here operates on the Day of Judgment. He notes that, based on the judgment scene in the Osiris myth, 'it can be said that the Egyptians came to think of judgment after death as a weighing of the heart, which represented a man's conscience, against truth, personified as *Maat.* A man's conscience could excuse or accuse him on the day of judgment. The basis of judgment was the quality of life of the deceased. There was an implied standard to which he had to measure up'. Atallah argues that the Osiris Myth provides useful background information for interpreting 2:15-16. While this is an interesting parallel, it is doubtful that Paul's thinking would have been influenced by the Osiris myth.

asserts that God will exercise judgment 'through Jesus Christ', 'as my gospel declares' (lit. 'according to my gospel'). God's judgment of humankind through his Son, Jesus Christ, Paul claims, is part of his gospel message. This may be illustrated by Luke's account of Paul's preaching in Acts 17:31: 'For he has set a day when he will judge the world with justice by the man he has appointed. He has given proof of this to everyone by raising him from the dead'. In two other places the apostle refers to important truths that are 'according to my gospel',[176] but it is only here in 2:16 that he refers to God's judgment being according to his gospel.

Paul's main point in 2:14-16 is not to praise the Gentiles but to remind his dialogue partner of God's impartiality. The Jews cannot boast simply because they possess the law, for it can be shown that Gentile Christians who do not possess the law exhibit such good behavior that they put the Jews, represented by his dialogue partner, to shame. Summing up, it can be said that in 2:1-16 Paul does indeed speak of impartial judgment according to people's works, but that this must not be equated with judgment based upon works of the law. The works upon which people are judged are to be understood as the way they respond to the goodness of God that they have experienced.[177] In all cases this is meant to lead people to repentance and so to the experience of forgiveness and justification. Failure to respond to the goodness of God, no matter what form the experience of his goodness may take, renders people liable to wrath on the day of wrath. In particular the Jews cannot boast about their possession of the law as if that puts them in a better position as far as the judgment of God is concerned. Indeed, Paul says that (Christian) Gentiles 'who do not have the law' fulfill it in a way that puts to shame those (unbelieving Jews) who have the law but do not obey it.

ADDITIONAL NOTE: THE USE OF *PHYSEI* IN 2:14

Paul uses the dative *physei* in three other places in his letters that may throw some light on its use here in 2:14. In each case *physei* is used to denote what people or gods *are* by nature (Gal 2:15: 'We who are Jews by birth [*hēmeis physei Ioudaioi*] and not 'Gentile sinners'; Gal 4:8: 'Formerly . . . you were slaves to those who by nature are not gods [*tois physei mē ousin theois*]';

---

176. Rom 16:25: 'Now to him who is able to establish you in accordance with my gospel (*kata to euangelion mou*, lit. 'according to my gospel')'; 2 Tim 2:8: 'Remember Jesus Christ, raised from the dead, descended from David. This is my gospel (*kata to euangelion mou*, lit. 'according to my gospel')'.

177. Snodgrass, 'Justification by Grace — To the Doers', 81, comments: 'Those people who have seen Romans 2 as a description of circumstances prior to the coming of the gospel are correct. They are incorrect, however, if they conclude that the coming of the gospel negated or reversed the basic structure of what preceded. The issue after the coming of Christ, as before, is an obedient response to the amount of light received so that God is honoured as God and a relationship with him is established'.

Eph 2:3: 'Like the rest, we were by nature deserving of wrath [*tekna physei orgēs*]'). If we allow this other usage to determine our approach to 2:14, we would interpret it to mean, 'Gentiles by nature do not have the law'.[178] Dunn has argued against this approach on the grounds that in the other three cases *physei* is used within the phrase it qualifies (see transliterations of Gal 2:15; 4:8 and Eph 2:3 above), not after it as here in 2:14 *(ethnē to mē nomon echonta physei)*.[179] However, it must be noted that it is not found within the following phrase *(ta tou nomou poiōsin* ['they perform the things of the law']) either, and so neither interpretation can be supported by the position occupied by *physei*.[180] The choice between the two alternatives must be made on other grounds.

The view that *physei* qualifies the preceding phrase *(ethnē ta mē nomon echonta* ['Gentiles who do not have the law']) is argued by Gathercole on several grounds, including the following: (i) When Paul uses *physei* elsewhere, it always qualifies a state of being, never an action. Thus in 2:14 it is better to see it qualifying what the Gentiles *are* by nature (those who do not have the law) than what they *do* by nature (the things required by the law). (ii) In 2:27 Paul says that those 'not circumcised physically' obey the law, and this is similar to the statement in 2:14 that Gentiles who by birth do not have the law, do the things required by the law. (iii) Paul nowhere else suggests that Gentiles spontaneously observe even some aspects of the law (and 1 Cor 5:1 and Phil 4:8-9 are no exceptions to this rule).[181] In addition, the flow of Paul's thought in 2:12-16 supports this view. In 2:12 he speaks of those 'who sin apart from the law' (Gentiles) perishing 'apart from the law'. Thus he is already characterizing Gentiles as those who do not have the law by virtue of being Gentiles.[182]

ADDITIONAL NOTE:
GENTILES WHO DO THE THINGS REQUIRED BY THE LAW

There appear to be essentially three different identifications of the Gentiles who do the things required by the law: (i) pagan Gentiles who observe

178. A number of scholars have adopted this interpretation; cf. discussion in Cranfield, *Romans*, I, 156-57; Paul J. Achtemeier, '"Some Things in Them Hard to Understand": Reflections on an Approach to Paul', *Int* 38 (1984) 257-58.

179. Cf. Dunn, *Romans 1–8*, 98. Similarly, Fitzmyer, *Romans*, 310; Byrne, *Romans*, 92; Barrett, *Romans*, 51-52.

180. Gathercole, 'A Law unto Themselves', 36, notes other examples in which *physei* occurs at the end of the phrase it qualifies (cf. Wis 13:1a; Ign., *Eph.* 1:1; Josephus, *Ant.* 8.152).

181. Gathercole, 'A Law unto Themselves', 36-37.

182. Wright, 'The Law in Romans 2', 145, also argues that *physei* must be taken with what precedes, and therefore Paul is speaking of Gentiles who by nature do not have the law. Jewett, *Romans*, 214, reaches the same conclusion.

some of the moral precepts of the Mosaic law without being acquainted with the law itself; (ii) godly Gentiles referred to in the OT upon whose hearts the work of the law had been written by the Spirit of God; and (iii) Christian Gentiles on whose hearts the law of God has been written in accordance with the new covenant promise of Jeremiah 31:33. We will look at each of these in turn.

(1) Pagan Gentiles Who Observe Some of the Moral Precepts of the Mosaic Law

Origen, writing in the early third century, is typical of those early church fathers who speak of Gentiles who have the moral law written on their hearts. He says: 'The Gentiles need not keep the Sabbaths or the new moons or the sacrifices which are written down in the law. For this law is not what is written in the hearts of the Gentiles. Rather it is that which can be discerned naturally, e.g., that they should not kill or commit adultery, that they should not steal nor bear false witness, that they should honor father and mother, etc. It may well be that since God is the one Creator of all, these things are written on the hearts of the Gentiles. . . . For the natural law may agree with the law of Moses in the spirit, if not in the letter. For how would anyone understand by nature that a child should be circumcised on the eighth day?'[183]

In similar vein Yates argues that all Paul was saying in this passage is that, as a matter of fact, we find pagans conforming formally and externally to the moral precepts of the law about which they are unaware.[184] Byrne's approach is similar: 'Paul points to the performance on the part of some Gentiles of deeds corresponding to the dictates of the Mosaic law. In so far as they are human beings they find in their very nature . . . a moral order corresponding to what the law prescribes. Paul need not have more than a few outstanding individuals in mind (so that what is stated here does not really counter the pessimistic judgment of the Gentile world as a whole formulated earlier on [1:19-32; cf. 3:9, 23]). Nor does he mean that these few "righteous Gentiles" carry out the law in its entirety. The point is that their exceptional pattern of life overthrows any exaggerated claims made for the law as sole moral guide and criterion of judgment'.[185] Witherington says: 'Paul assumes that sometimes some Gentiles fulfil some of the requirements of the Law, just as Jews do. This does not mean they always do so, or

183. 'Commentary on the Epistle to the Romans' (*ACCSR*, 67).

184. J. C. Yates, 'The Judgement of the Heathen: The Interpretation of Article XVIII and Romans 2:12-16', *Churchman* 100 (1986) 225. Similarly, Dunn, *Romans 1–8*, 98-99; Moo, *Romans*, 148-50. J. Achtemeier, *Romans* (Atlanta: John Knox, 1985) 45, argues that the passage in no way indicates that the Gentiles, who had the 'natural law', have achieved what the Jews, who had the written law, could not achieve.

185. Byrne, *Romans*, 89.

do so perfectly, for Paul will go on to call all sinners. It does mean that there is some obedience to the will or Law of God among those who are not Christians, with Gentiles in focus here'.[186] Schreiner comments: 'Paul . . . is describing non-Christian Gentiles who have written on their hearts the moral norms of the law. Occasionally they obey these moral norms, although they usually fail to keep the law, and thus their consciences will accuse them on the eschatological judgment day'.[187]

Martens' approach falls generally into the category of those who argue that Paul is referring to pagan Gentiles who observe some of the moral precepts of the Mosaic law. However, he argues specifically that when Paul speaks of 'doing the law by nature' he is dependent upon the Stoic theory of the law of nature, according to which only sages could understand it and so be in a position to perform it. He also argues that both Paul and his audience would have known that the Stoics believed that there were only a few sages, if any, who had ever managed to do so. Martens concludes that Paul adopts the Stoic view, according to which it is theoretically possible to keep the law of nature, but practically it is out of the question.[188]

(2) Godly Gentiles Referred to in the Old Testament

Davies argues that Paul does view the status of some Gentiles in a positive light, that the apostle seeks to show that God's impartiality has always extended to the Gentiles, and that God saves those upon whose hearts has been written the work of the law (he points to such OT figures as the citizens of Nineveh, Job, Melchizedek, Rahab, Ruth, and Naaman as examples). Davies' conclusion is that 2:12-16 refers to 'pre-Christian Gentiles, who are not only doers of the law but who are also justified before God'.[189]

(3) Christian Gentiles on Whose Hearts the Law of God Has Been Written

If there is an allusion to Jeremiah 31:33 in 2:14-16, then 'the law written on their hearts' means much more than an innate moral sense. It means a godly moral disposition. What is implied by Jeremiah 31:33 is expressed more fully by Ezekiel 36:26-27: 'I will give you a new heart and put a new spirit in you; I will remove from you your heart of stone and give you a heart of flesh. And I will put my Spirit in you and move you to follow my decrees and be careful to keep my laws'. Wright emphatically supports this

---

186. Witherington, *Romans*, 83.
187. Schreiner, 'Did Paul Believe in Justification by Works?' 147.
188. John W. Martens, 'Romans 2.14-16: A Stoic Reading', *NTS* 40 (1994) 66-67.
189. Davies, *Faith and Obedience in Romans*, 60-67.

view: 'I find it next to impossible that Paul could have written this phrase, with its overtones of Jeremiah's new covenant promise, simply to refer to pagans who happen by accident to share some of Israel's moral teaching. More likely by a million miles that he is hinting quietly, and proleptically, at what he will say far more fully later on: that Gentile Christians belong within the new covenant'.[190]

Gathercole also argues in favor of the view that the Gentiles here are in fact Christian Gentiles. He rejects the claim made by others that 'the antithesis between Jews and Christian Gentiles [implied in these verses] is never found elsewhere in Paul', pointing out that 9:30 and 11:11-14 contain that very antithesis. He also notes that the language of 2:14 has a close parallel in 9:30, where believing Gentiles are contrasted with unbelieving Jews,[191] and therefore claims that there is no reason in principle why the Gentiles of 2:14 may not be understood to be Christian Gentiles.[192]

This view is also supported by Jewett: 'The most likely of these views from a rhetorical point of view is that Paul is here describing the status of converted Gentiles. Having assented that wrath is already evident among unconverted Gentiles (1:18-31) and that Jews are not exempt from God's impartial judgment (2:1-13), the audience, consisting mainly of converted Gentiles, would assume that their current situation is described in these verses which provide a preliminary form of Paul's strategy of touting Gentile conversion in order to provoke Jewish conversion through jealousy (11:11-14). The alleged contradiction between these verses and chap. 3 is removed if one takes the latter as claiming that all unconverted Gentiles and Jews have sinned and fallen short of the glory of God, and that salvation is by grace alone for Jews as well as Gentiles'.[193]

There are, however, scholars who put forward reasons to reject this view. Witherington contends: 'Paul does not speak here of the Law written on pagans' hearts, but rather of the effect of the Law written on their hearts, so Jer. 31.33 is not in view here, any more than Gentile Christians are'.[194] Byrne says: 'It is hard to see, however, how Paul could say of Gentile Christians that, lacking the law of Moses as a moral guide, they attain such guidance by the enlightenment of "nature"; for Paul, those "in Christ" find moral guidance and capacity through the Spirit, which creates in them the "mind" or attitude of Christ (cf. 8:1-13; 12:1-2; 13:8-10; cf. 6:17; Phil 2:5). The

---

190. Wright, 'The Law in Romans 2', 147. Wright adds: 'In short, if 2.25-9 is an anticipation of fuller statements, within the letter, of Paul's belief that Christian Gentiles do indeed fulfill the law even though they do not possess it, 2.13-14 looks as though it is a still earlier statement of very nearly the same point'.

191. 9:30: *ethnē ta mē diōkonta dikaiosynēn katelaben dikaiosynēn*

2:14: *ethnē ta mē nomon exonta physei to tou nomou poiōsin*

192. Gathercole, 'A Law unto Themselves', 31-32. *Where Is Boasting?* 128-29. Ito, 'Romans 2: A Deuteronomistic Reading', 28-35, also argues for the Gentile Christian view, noting especially the *pneuma-gramma* contrast in 2:29.

193. Jewett, *Romans*, 213.

194. Witherington, *Romans*, 83.

tension is best resolved when seemingly inconsistent statements across Romans 1–3 are not played off against one another in a systematizing way but seen as individual stages in a total rhetorical construction. Paul's passing endorsement of the possibility that some Gentiles fulfill the law's requirement is designed to highlight the failure on the Jewish side'.[195]

Schreiner, who regards 2:14-15 as an aside,[196] rejects the Gentile Christian interpretation of these verses on the grounds that (i) Paul holds that the Gentiles who do not have the law 'are a law to themselves' — an odd way of describing the law of God that Jeremiah 31:33 says is written on people's hearts under the new covenant, and (ii) if Gentile Christians are meant, it is also odd that Paul speaks of their thoughts bringing accusations on the day of judgment.[197] However, Schreiner does argue that Paul has Gentile Christians in mind in 2:7, 10, 26-29, on several grounds, chief among which is that in 2:26-29 uncircumcised Gentiles will be regarded as if they were circumcised because true circumcision is not outward and physical but inward and 'by the Spirit, not by the written code', and that only Christians have the Holy Spirit and are thus able to fulfill the law (cf. 8:3-4), and that this is in line with Jeremiah 31:33.[198]

Summing up, we may say that for Paul's argument to stand he must have believed that some Gentiles at least did observe something of what the law demands; therefore, the hypothetical approach is unsatisfactory. The view that Paul adopts a Stoic view is also unsatisfactory, for to enable Paul's argument to stand it is not enough to say that he implies that, while it is theoretically possible to obey the law, it is practically impossible. The view that Paul was expressing, that some pagans conform formally and externally to the moral precepts of the law of which they are unaware, is unlikely in the light of Paul's previous statements about the Gentile world in 1:18-32. Davies suggestion that Paul has in mind 'pre-Christian Gentiles, who are not only doers of the law but who are also justified before God' is feasible but is not an argument Paul advances anywhere else in his writings, nor are there any clues in the context which point in this direction. However, the view that the Gentiles who do the things required by the law are Gentile Christians in whose hearts the law had been written finds support in the promise of Jeremiah 31:33 despite the pedantic objection that 2:15 speaks of 'the work of the law' written on people's hearts, rather than the law itself, as in the case of Jeremiah 31:33.

195. Byrne, *Romans*, 91.

196. Schreiner, 'Did Paul Believe in Justification by Works?' 144.

197. Wright, 'The Law in Romans 2', 146, counters this view, saying: 'They are not simply lawless Gentiles; but the Jewish law, which is now in some sense or other written on their hearts, and which in some sense they "do", nevertheless has a sufficiently ambiguous relation to them for them still to be concerned that the eventual issue might be in doubt'.

198. Schreiner, 'Did Paul Believe in Justification by Works?' 147-52.

ADDITIONAL NOTE: CONSCIENCE

The word 'conscience' is found more often in the Pauline corpus than in the rest of the books of the NT put together. Unlike the Stoics,[199] Paul did not regard conscience as the voice of God within, nor did he restrict its function to a person's past acts (usually the bad ones), as was the case in the secular Greek world of his day.[200] For Paul the conscience was a human faculty whereby a person either approves or disapproves his or her actions (whether already performed or only intended) and those of others.[201] The conscience is not to be equated with the voice of God or the moral law; rather, it is a human faculty which adjudicates upon human action in the light of the highest standard a person perceives.[202] Seeing that all of human nature has been affected by sin, both a person's perception of the standard of action required and the function of the conscience itself (as a constituent part of human nature) are affected by sin. For this reason conscience can never be accorded the position of ultimate judge of one's behavior. It is possible that the conscience may excuse one for what God will not excuse, and, conversely, it is equally possible that conscience may condemn a person for what God allows. The final judgment, therefore, belongs only to God (cf. 1 Cor 4:2-5). Nevertheless, to reject the voice of conscience is to court spiritual disaster (cf. 1 Tim 1:19). We cannot reject the voice of conscience with impunity, but we can modify the highest standard to which it relates by gaining for ourselves a greater understanding of the truth.

---

199. C. A. Pierce, *Conscience in the New Testament* (SBT; London: SCM, 1955), 13-20, has demonstrated that a Stoic background for Paul's concept of conscience is highly improbable, and that it is dependent rather upon 'popular philosophy' reflected in vernacular speech in Hellenistic Greek.

200. Cf. J. N. Sevenster, *Paul and Seneca* (Leiden: Brill, 1961), 84-102; C. Maurer, '*Synoida/syneidēsis*', *TDNT* 7 (1971) 899-907.

201. Cf. M. E. Thrall, 'The Pauline Use of *syneidēsis*', *NTS* 14 (1967-68) 118-25. Robert H. Stein, 'The Argument of Romans 13:1-7', *NovT* 31 (1989) 337, says: 'Pierce and Jewett have argued that in Paul conscience always refers retrospectively to acts already committed, i.e., "to the pain a man suffers when he has done wrong", and not prospectively to the future. Yet in 13:5 the command "one must be subject [to the authorities, not only because of possible punishment but also because of conscience]" is clearly based on future considerations'.

202. Origen comments: 'Conscience is the spirit which the apostle says is *with* the soul, according to which we have been instructed in the higher things. This spirit or conscience is linked to the soul as a teacher and guide to point out what things are best and to reprove and condemn faults. The apostle was speaking of it when he said: *What person knows a man's thoughts except the spirit of the man which is in him?*' ('Commentary on the Epistle to the Romans' [*ACCSR*, 68]).

ADDITIONAL NOTE: JUSTIFICATION FOR THE DOERS

On first reading 2:1-16 seems to contradict the basic thrust of Romans[203] that no one will be justified by works of the law, but only by grace through faith. However, in this passage Paul maintains that God 'will repay each person according to what they have done' (v. 6); 'there will be trouble and distress for every human being who does evil' (v. 9), 'but glory and honor and peace for everyone who does good' (v. 10), and that doers of the law will be declared righteous (2:13).[204] In addition to these surprising statements, Paul says in 2:14-15: 'Indeed, when Gentiles, who do not have the law, do by nature things required by the law, they are a law for themselves, even though they do not have the law. They show that the requirements of the law are written on their hearts'.

Snodgrass claims that more often than not scholars who discuss these texts spend more time explaining them *away* than explaining them. He lists the following 'common ways of evading the text':

1. Paul is speaking only hypothetically *as if* the law could be fulfilled and *as if* the gospel had not come. What Paul really believes one finds in 3.9f. and 3.20f.
2. Paul was speaking of Gentile Christians who fulfill the law through faith in Christ and a life in the Spirit.
3. This section (like other texts which speak of judgment) is an unexpurgated and unnecessary fragment from Paul's Jewish past.
4. This chapter is merely a contradiction in Paul's thought which must be allowed to stand.
5. Paul only means to say in 2.14-15 that Gentiles have a law and therefore are responsible and will be judged. There is only one outcome for both Jews and Gentiles on the basis of works, and it is negative.[205]

If these are all evasions of what the text really says, how should it be explained properly? Did Paul really teach that God's judgment of human beings is based upon their works? And did he really mean to say that, whereas Jews who have the law did not keep it, the Gentiles who did not

203. So much so that E. P. Sanders, *Paul, the Law, and the Jewish People* (London: SCM, 1985), 123, says that in the whole section 1:18–2:29 Paul has taken over homiletic material from Diaspora Judaism, and his treatment of the law here cannot be harmonized with what he says about it elsewhere.

204. Paul speaks elsewhere, hypothetically at least, of the possibility of people being declared righteous if they do what the law requires. In 10:5 he says, 'Moses writes this about the righteousness that is by the law: "The person who does these things will live by them"'. And in Gal 3:12 he says, 'The law is not based on faith; on the contrary, it says, "The person who does these things will live by them"'.

205. Snodgrass, 'Justification by Grace — To the Doers', 73. In addition to the above, Snodgrass lists the more radical suggestion made by J. C. O'Neill that Romans 2 was a Hellenistic Jewish tract that was added to Paul's letter by a later hand.

have the law practiced what the law demanded? It must be recognized that Paul *did* say that God judges all people according to their works (2:6-10). It must also be realized that the point Paul emphasized in saying this was that God's judgment is entirely impartial. This is in line with his overall purpose in 1:18–3:20, which is to show that the Jews have no special immunity where God's judgment is concerned. Modern interpreters have no problem with impartiality in judgment. The problem is how to relate this impartial judgment on the basis of works to Paul's doctrine of justification by faith. The difficulty is exacerbated because it is often assumed that the basis of judgment is to be human success or otherwise in fulfilling the demands of the law.[206]

However, it is evident from Paul's emphasis upon repentance in this passage that he did not have in mind judgment according to human success in fulfilling the demands of the law. Paul says that it is by their hard, impenitent hearts that those who judged others while excusing themselves are storing up wrath for themselves on the day of God's wrath. They do not realize that the goodness of God is intended to lead them to repentance, and so to forgiveness according to his grace (vv. 4-5).[207] God judges people impartially according to their works when out of his kindness and forbearance he gives eternal life to the repentant who seek glory and immortality by persistence in well-doing (vv. 7, 10). He also judges people impartially according to their works when he repays with wrath and anger the unrepentant who reject the truth and follow evil (vv. 8-9).

The residual problem of this approach is that it still seems to leave justification dependent upon persistence in well-doing.[208] But the problem is more apparent than real. No one would want to say, for instance, that Paul thought that there was justification for those who persist in doing evil. The fact of the matter is that, while Paul believed that justification is for those who receive the gospel by faith, independently of works of the law, he strenuously resisted the blasphemous suggestion that those who are so justified would persist in evil-doing (cf. 3:8). On the contrary, they would

---

206. This problem arises when interpreters import the notion of justification by works of the law that Paul mentions in 3:20 into chap. 2. Cf. Snodgrass, 'Justification by Grace — To the Doers', 82-84.

207. Nigel M. Watson, 'Justified by Faith: Judged by Works — An Antinomy', *NTS* 29 (1983) 217, 220, correctly observes that Paul's warnings of judgment are directed primarily to those who are puffed up, whereas his assurances of justification are for the penitent. He concludes: 'The message of judgment is the valid word of God, not for those whose sins have found them out, but for those who are presuming on God's grace'.

208. Bassler, 'Divine Impartiality', 58, recognizes that 'the simultaneous affirmation of the two doctrines, judgment according to works and justification by grace, does give rise to a certain degree of logical tension, especially if one seeks in Paul a perfectly consistent and coherent system. Paul himself, however, does not seem to recognize this tension. The reason for this is probably that in both cases the point Paul stresses is the same. Whether justifying on the basis of faith or judging on the basis of performance, God makes no distinction between Jew and Gentile. In both cases he shows no partiality'.

persist in doing good (yielding their members instruments of righteousness; cf. 6:11-14).[209]

It is evident from Paul's writings that those who are justified by faith
will also be judged according to their works, something the apostle implies
in 1 Corinthians 3:12-15 and makes abundantly clear in 2 Corinthians 5:10:
'For we must all appear before the judgment seat of Christ, that each of us
may receive what is due us for the things done while in the body, whether
good or bad'. The question is how these two things are related to each
other. The answer appears to be that Paul expected those who were justified by faith, as a result of the Spirit's activity in their lives, to produce the
fruit of good works and be judged by these on the last day. Käsemann says:
'The decisive thing is that the doctrine of judgment according to works not
be ranked above justification but conversely be understood in the light of it
. . . although this perspective is not yet apparent here. Again, the difficulties
in exposition are largely connected with a failure to pay due regard to the
power-character even of the righteousness of God received as a gift, since
this involves a radical separation of gift and Giver, and of Giver and Judge.
If the gift is finally the sign and content of Christ's lordship in earth, we can
no longer live by our own will and right but constantly stand in responsibility and accountability. . . . To this degree the last day does not differ from
each earthly day'.[210] Similar conclusions are reached by a number of modern interpreters of Paul.[211]

---

b. Having the Law and Circumcision Provides No Immunity, 2:17-29

In 2:1-16 Paul, using the rhetoric of the diatribe and addressing a hypothetical dialogue partner, warned him and those he represented of the judgment
of God stored up against those who take the high moral ground; those who
judge others for the evil they practice while practicing the same things
themselves. Though what he said applies to all who take the high moral
ground, the apostle had in mind primarily fellow Jews who were guilty of
these things (2:10: 'first for the Jew'). What is implied in 2:1-16 becomes explicit in 2:17-29, where Paul clearly addresses a Jewish dialogue partner,
and accuses him of failing to live in a way that is consistent with the great
privileges he enjoys as a Jew — notably having the law and circumcision
yet failing to obey that law and manifest true circumcision of heart and by

---

209. Cf. Snodgrass, 'Justification by Grace — To the Doers', 86. Davies, *Faith and Obedience in Romans*, 53-71, esp. 70, says, for Paul: 'Where there is no obedience, there is no faith;
where there is true faith, there is also obedience'; cf. Cranfield, *Romans*, I, 153. Cf. also my
discussion of this passage in Colin G. Kruse, *Paul, the Law and Justification* (Leicester:
Apollos/Inter-Varsity Press, 1996), 175-78.

210. Käsemann, *Romans*, 58.

211. Cf., e.g., Fitzmyer, *Romans*, 297-98; Witherington, *Romans*, 81; Moo, *Romans*, 143;
Wright, *Justification*, 158-68.

so doing bringing into disrepute the name of God.[212] It is important to remember that Paul is engaging this hypothetical dialogue partner as a rhetorical device in his overall presentation of the gospel and humanity's need for it. He does so for the benefit of his audience for whom he has high regard (1:8; 15:14). He is not implying that they are guilty of the presumption he ascribes to his dialogue partner. Carras describes 2:1-29 as 'an "inner Jewish debate" where Paul and his objector are debating points regarding the essential nature of the view that what Paul found wrong with the Jewish religion (as perceived through the "critic") was that the Jew violated central tenets of his own religion by claiming a criterion of judgement for himself different from all others'.[213]

The passage 2:17-29 falls into two sections. In the first, 2:17-24, Paul takes his Jewish dialogue partner to task for bragging about his possession of the law while disobeying it. In the second, 2:25-29, the apostle reminds his dialogue partner that circumcision is of no value if one is a lawbreaker, and that true circumcision is a matter of the heart and effected by the Spirit.

(i) Bragging about the law while failing to obey it, 2:17-24

[17]*Now you, if you call yourself a Jew; if you rely on the law and boast in God;* [18]*if you know his will and approve of what is superior because you are instructed by the law;* [19]*if you are convinced that you are a guide for the blind, a light for those who are in the dark,* [20]*an instructor of the foolish, a teacher of little children, because you have in the law the embodiment of knowledge and truth —* [21]*you, then, who teach others, do you not teach yourself? You who preach against stealing, do you steal?* [22]*You who say that people should not commit adultery, do you commit adultery? You who abhor idols, do you rob temples?* [23]*You who boast in the law, do you dishonor God by breaking the law?* [24]*As it is written: 'God's name is blasphemed among the Gentiles because of you'.*

Paul has structured 2:17-24 quite carefully. In 2:17-18 he lists five privileges that the one who calls himself a Jew claims to enjoy; he relies upon the law; he brags about his relationship with God; he knows God's will; he is able to approve what is superior; and he is instructed by the law. In 2:19-20 he lists the things the Jew claims he can do because of these privileges: he can guide the blind; act as a light for those in darkness; instruct the foolish, and teach infants, all because he has in the law 'the embodiment of knowledge and truth'. Next, in 2:21-23, Paul points out the dissonance between these privileges and what the Jew claims he can do on the one hand,

---

212. Jewett, *Romans,* 221, comments: 'In an elegant manner that Paul's audience would have enjoyed, Paul augments the previous depiction of the pretentious bigot with a series of boasts that exaggerate well-known Jewish claims'.

213. George P. Carras, 'Romans 2,1-29: A Dialogue on Jewish Ideals', *Bib* 73 (1992) 206.

and his actual behavior on the other hand. Then in 2:24 Paul brings this section to an end with a scriptural quotation to show that such behavior dishonors God.

2:17-18   Paul opens his address to his dialogue partner by reciting in these verses five Jewish privileges of which he could be legitimately proud if only his behavior was consistent with his claims. He begins: *Now you, if you call yourself a Jew.* The address is in the singular number: 'if you [sing.] call yourself a Jew'.[214] The word translated 'Jew' can mean 'Judean' and denote those whose identity is tied up with their land of origin (Judea) even if they do not presently live in Judea.[215] It can also denote those whose identity is defined by adherence to the Mosaic law.[216] Obviously these two things are not mutually exclusive. However, as Paul continues his argument, it becomes clear that his use of the term 'Jew' here denotes one whose identity is defined by the Mosaic law: *if you rely on the law and boast in God.* The Jewish privileges alluded to here are possession of the law and a special relationship with God. To rely upon[217] the law and God's revelation through it was both legitimate and praiseworthy for the people of Israel to do. Jewish delight in the law is expressed in Psalm 19:7-10: 'The law of the LORD is perfect, refreshing the soul. The statutes of the LORD are trustworthy, making wise the simple. The precepts of the LORD are right, giving joy to the heart. The commands of the LORD are radiant, giving light to the eyes. The fear of the LORD is pure, enduring forever. The decrees of the LORD are firm, and all of them are righteous. They are more precious than gold, than much pure gold; they are sweeter than honey, than honey from the honeycomb'. Even more fulsome is Psalm 119, which celebrates at length the glories of God's law. Jewish reliance upon the law is reflected in 2 *Apoc. Bar.* 48:22-24:

> In your law we have put our trust, because, behold, your Law is with us, and we know that we do not fall as long as we keep your statutes. We shall always be blessed; at least, we did not mingle with the nations. For we are all a people of the Name; we, who received one Law for the

214. Origen asserts 'that Paul does not say that the person he is rhetorically addressing is a Jew; only that he calls himself one, which is not at all the same thing. For Paul goes on to teach that the true Jew is the one who is circumcised in secret, i.e., in the heart, who keeps the law in spirit and not according to the letter, whose praise is not from men but from God' ('Commentary on the Epistle to the Romans' [*ACCSR*, 71]).

215. Cf. Esler, *Conflict and Identity in Romans*, 12, 62-74.

216. Fitzmyer, *Romans*, 315-16, says: '*Ioudaios* ['Jew'] was the common contemporary name for a member of the people of Israel, an adherent of OT monotheism, especially in the Diaspora. From Maccabean times on it came to be used by Jews themselves instead of the older names "Hebrew" or "Israelite"'. Jewett, *Romans*, 22, cites Schürer: 'The Jew is "one who identifies with beliefs, rites, and customs of adherents of Israel's Mosaic and prophetic tradition"'.

217. The verb rendered 'rely on' is *epanapauomai,* which means 'to find rest, comfort or support in'; cf. BAGD, *ad loc.*

One. And that Law that is among us will help us, and that excellent wisdom which is in us will support us.[218]

'To boast in God' is to celebrate another of Israel's great privileges: that the Creator of the world is her God, and Israel is his people. To boast in God is not only legitimate but is something that Israel was exhorted to do. The prophet Jeremiah charged the people of Israel: 'This is what the LORD says: "Let not the wise boast of their wisdom or the strong boast of their strength or the rich boast of their riches, but let the one who boasts boast about this: that they have the understanding to know me, that I am the LORD, who exercises kindness, justice and righteousness on earth, for in these I delight", declares the LORD' (Jer 9:23-24). Paul does not criticize his dialogue partner for relying on the law or boasting of his relationship with God but, as we will see, only for doing so while he disobeys the law and dishonors God by his behavior. Moses reminded Israel of their privileges in his address to the nation on the plains of Moab: 'What other nation is so great as to have their gods near them the way the LORD our God is near us whenever we pray to him? And what other nation is so great as to have such righteous decrees and laws as this body of laws I am setting before you today?' (Deut 4:7-8).

Paul continues to rehearse the privileges of the Jew: *if you know his will and approve of what is superior because you are instructed by the law.* Jewett notes: 'There are many examples of the formula "to do your will" or "to do God's will", but nowhere can I find a precise parallel to "knowing" God's will. Although pious Jews could exclaim, "Happy are we, Israel, because we know what is pleasing to God" (Bar 4:4; see also Wis 15:2-3), it is quite a different manner *(sic)* to claim knowledge of God's inscrutable will'.[219] While there are many things about God's 'inscrutable will' that we cannot know, the point Paul is making here is that by possession of the law and the instruction it provides Jews can know God's will in relation to the way they should live. The law was a lamp to their feet and a light for their path (cf. Ps 119:105).

Paul further underscores the privileges of Israel when he refers to his dialogue partner's ability 'to approve' of what is superior because he has received instruction by the law.[220] The verb translated 'approve' carries the sense of 'approval following testing'. Later in the letter Paul informs his audience that they 'will be able to test and approve what God's will is' as they

218. Charlesworth, ed., *The Old Testament Pseudepigrapha*, I, 636.

219. Jewett, *Romans*, 223.

220. The ability of the Jew to approve what is superior is based on his being 'instructed by the law'. The verb 'instruct' *(katēcheō)* is used by Paul to denote religious instruction also in 1 Cor 14:19 ('But in the church I would rather speak five intelligible words to instruct others than ten thousand words in a tongue') and Gal 6:6 ('The one who receives instruction in the word should share all good things with their instructor'), and it used in the same way in Luke 1:4; Acts 1:25; 21:21, 24.

allow themselves to 'be transformed by the renewing of your mind' (12:2).
A similar idea is expressed in Paul's letter to the Philippian believers: 'And
this is my prayer: that your love may abound more and more in knowledge
and depth of insight, so that you may be able to discern what is best and
may be pure and blameless for the day of Christ', where it also denotes
things that are superior or the best (Phil. 1:9-10).[221] In the context of 2:18-20
'what is superior' is the knowledge of God's will in terms of moral instruction that Jews have access to through the law and therefore could pass on to
others.

2:19-20   In 2:17-18 Paul listed five privileges Israel enjoys; here in
2:19-20 he lists things his dialogue partner and those whom he represents
claim they can do because of these privileges: *if you are convinced that you are
a guide for the blind, a light for those who are in the dark,*[222] *an instructor of the
foolish, a teacher of little children, because you have in the law the embodiment of
knowledge and truth.* Here the apostle describes the basis upon which his dialogue partner, as a Jew, can teach others. He can be (i) 'a guide for the
blind' — those who do not know the law; (ii) 'a light for those who are in
the dark' — a role that Israel was intended to have vis-à-vis the Gentiles (cf.
Isa 42:6; 49:6);[223] (iii) 'an instructor of the foolish' — one who not only
informs but disciplines and corrects (cf. Heb 12:9);[224] and (iv) 'a teacher of
little children', all because he has 'in the law the embodiment[225] of knowledge and truth'.[226] Certainly Jews had the potential to do these things because of their possession of the law. Nowhere is this more clearly affirmed
than in Psalm 119, which describes the function of the law in providing understanding and guidance for living, perhaps best summed up in the

221. Jewett, *Romans*, 223-24, comments: 'The concept of approval through testing was
a hallmark of popular moral philosophy; for example, Epictetus *Diss.* 1.7.6; 1.7.8 refers to
the inherent "power of discernment" *(dynamis dokimastikē)* and regularly calls his followers
to discern what is true or false (e.g., *Diss.* 1.27.7; 2.12.20; 2.18.25; 2.23.7-8). Hellenistic Jewish
authors employed *dokimazō* in the same manner to describe public testing of what is true or
false, for example, Josephus's description of the testing of Abraham (*Ant.* 1.223.3)'.

222. Dunn, *Romans 1–8*, 112, comments on the phrases, 'a guide for the blind, and a
light for those in the dark': 'None of these phrases necessarily implies an actively outgoing
missionary concern (despite, e.g., Bassler, *Divine Impartiality*, 150), more a sense of superior
privilege . . . and readiness to accept those who acknowledge their blindness and come for
light and teaching'.

223. It is noteworthy that while Paul will deny this role to his dialogue partner because he disobeys the law, the Paul of Acts claims it for himself. Cf. Acts 13:47: 'For this is
what the Lord has commanded us: "I have made you a light for the Gentiles, that you may
bring salvation to the ends of the earth"'.

224. Cf. Sir 37:19: 'Some people may be clever enough to teach many, and yet be useless to themselves'.

225. The only other place 'embodiment' *(morphōsis)* is found in the NT is 2 Tim 3:5:
'having a form *(morphōsin)* of godliness but denying its power'.

226. Cf. Sir 24:25-27, where it is said of the law: 'It overflows, like the Pishon, with
wisdom, and like the Tigris at the time of the first fruits. It runs over, like the Euphrates,
with understanding, and like the Jordan at harvest time. It pours forth instruction like the
Nile, like the Gihon at the time of vintage'.

words, 'The unfolding of your words gives light; it gives understanding to the simple' (Ps 119:130).[227]

2:21-24 In 2:17-20 Paul listed those things of which his dialogue partner could be legitimately proud, if only his behavior was consistent with what he claimed. In 2:21-24 Paul exposes the hypocrisy of his dialogue partner insofar as he taught others but did not teach himself, and bragged about the law, but by disobeying it dishonored the God who gave it. As Moo notes: 'Such a charge was certainly not new. The OT (cf. Ps. 50:16-21), Judaism (cf. *'Abot R. Nat.* 29[8a]), and Jesus (e.g., Matt. 23:3) made similar accusations'.[228]

Paul begins by attacking the hypocrisy of his dialogue partner. In 2:21-23 he asks five questions: *You, then, who teach others, do you not teach yourself? You who preach against stealing, do you steal? You who say that people should not commit adultery, do you commit adultery? You who abhor idols, do you rob temples? You who boast in the law, do you dishonor God by breaking the law?*[229] Paul's depiction of his dialogue partner's hypocrisy with the rhetorical questions, 'Do you steal?' 'Do you commit adultery?' 'Do you rob temples?' presents problems. Are they to be taken literally or metaphorically? If they are taken metaphorically, Paul would be speaking like the prophets of the OT who accused Israel of robbing God of what was due to him, of acting like adulterers when they went after other gods, and, we might add, robbing temples when they did not bring in their tithes. Whether Paul would expect his predominantly Gentile audience in Rome to understand such allusions to the teaching of the prophets is doubtful. It is more likely that he would expect what he said to be taken literally.

Particularly problematic is the question, 'Do you rob temples?' Attempts have been made to interpret this metaphorically. For example, Garlington argues for a metaphorical interpretation of robbing temples by noting that the one Paul accuses of perpetrating this act is one who boasts in the law. For Paul, then, the new idol is the Torah, and the sacrilege to which Paul was referring is 'Israel's idolatrous attachment to the law itself'.[230] An-

---

227. Ambrosiaster writes: 'The teacher of the law is right to glory in these things, because he is teaching the form of truth. But if the teacher does not accept the Expected One whom the law has promised, he glories in vain in the law, to which he is doing harm as long as he rejects the Christ who is promised in the law. In that case he is no more learned than the fools, nor is he a teacher of children, nor is he a light to those who are in the darkness, but rather he is leading all of these into perdition' ('Commentary on Paul's Epistles' [*ACCSR*, 72]).

228. Moo, *Romans*, 163.

229. Dunn, *Romans 1–8*, 113, says: 'Each of the clauses in vv 21-23 could be punctuated either as statements or as questions (so most; otherwise Zeller). The rhetorical style suggests that the four sentences of vv 21-22 are intended as questions, whereas the scriptural proof (v 24) attached to the fifth clause (v 23) indicates that it should be taken as a statement, indeed as the explicit conclusion to what had been implied in the preceding verses (so, e.g., SH, Lagrange, Lietzmann, Cranfield, NEB, NJB; against RSV, NIV)'.

230. D. B. Garlington, '*HIEROSYLEIN* and the Idolatry of Israel (Romans 2.22)', *NTS* 36 (1990) 148. Similarly, Fitzmyer, *Romans*, 318.

other way of interpreting 'to rob temples' metaphorically is to interpret it as withholding the temple tax that Jews were obliged to send to the Jerusalem temple.[231] Josephus records a particular instance of this kind of temple robbery, the so-called Fulvia scandal:

> There was a man who was a Jew, but had been driven away from his own country by an accusation laid against him for transgressing their laws, and by the fear he was under of punishment for the same; but in all respects a wicked man: — he then living at Rome, professed to instruct men in the wisdom of the laws of Moses. He procured also three other men, entirely of the same character with himself, to be his partners. These men persuaded Fulvia, a woman of great dignity, and one that had embraced the Jewish religion, to send purple and gold to the temple at Jerusalem; and when they had gotten them, they employed them for their own uses, and spent the money themselves; on which account it was that they at first required it of her. Whereupon Tiberius, who had been informed of the thing by Saturninus, the husband of Fulvia, who desired inquiry might be made about it, ordered all the Jews to be banished out of Rome. (*Ant.* 18.3.5)[232]

To interpret Paul's reference to temple robbery literally and as a failure of his Jewish dialogue partner and those whom he represents also raises particular problems. The practice of actual temple robbery was well known in the ancient world.[233] What is puzzling is Paul's indictment of Jews for this offense when the practice of idolatry was absent in Israel at the time he wrote. Several approaches have been adopted to explain this. Krentz draws attention to the extensive use of the verb 'to rob temples' in vice lists of Greek authors prior to A.D. 200, where it always carries the literal sense of robbing temples, and argues that its use here in 2:22 should be understood in the same way.[234] Chrysostom writes: 'It was strictly forbidden for Jews to touch any of the treasures deposited in heathen temples, because they would be defiled. But Paul claims here that the tyranny of greed has persuaded them to disregard the law at this point'.[235] Derrett argues that '"temple robbery" includes profiting in any way from a heathen religious endowment's assets, whether directly or indirectly'. Opportunities

---

231. Cf. Moo, *Romans 1–8*, 161.

232. Cited from *Josephus: Complete Works*, trans. William Whiston (6th ed.; Grand Rapids: Kregel, 1969).

233. When Paul and his associates had accusation brought against them before the city clerk of Ephesus (Acts 19:37-38), the latter said to complainants: 'You have brought these men here, though they have neither robbed temples nor blasphemed the goddess. If, then, Demetrius and his fellow craftsmen have a grievance against anybody, the courts are open and there are proconsuls'.

234. Edgar Krentz, 'The Name of God in Disrepute: Romans 2:17-29 [22-23]', *CurrTheolMiss* 17 (1990) 433, n. 22.

235. 'Homilies on Romans' (*ACCSR*, 74).

for such profiting occurred, he says, when, due to negligence, dishonesty, mishaps, or war, stolen items from pagan shrines entered the market, and then Jewish businessmen took the commercial opportunities this presented to them.[236] Cranfield adopts a similar approach when he says: 'Paul would presumably be referring to . . . the use by Jews of articles stolen (whether by themselves or others) from idol-shrines and the casuistry of Rabbis who invented various exceptions to the categorical prohibitions of Deut 7.25f — and probably also to still more subtle forms of complicity in idolatry'.[237]

Other scholars who take the literal approach insist that Paul's statement about robbing temples is not an indictment of all Jews but that the apostle is speaking rhetorically.[238] Byrne says: 'There were undoubtedly Jews who stole and Jews who failed in sexual morality. Less easily understandable in a literal sense is the charge of robbing temples. . . . But Paul is not asserting that all Jews failed in the areas suggested or that the vices were characteristic of the nation as a whole. Within an established rhetorical pattern, he is attempting to drive home the point that possession of the law has not prevented Jews from failing to abide by its key moral precepts as formulated in the Decalogue'.[239] While it is difficult to be certain about the precise meaning of Paul's reference to robbing temples, the overall purpose of 2:21-22 is clear enough. It highlights the hypocrisy of his dialogue partner and those whom he represents, that is, Jews who teach others but do not practice what they preach.

The NIV's translation, 'You who boast in the law, do you dishonor God by breaking the law?' could also be translated as a statement: 'You who boast in the law dishonor God by breaking the law',[240] and this would seem to be preferable in the light of the change in sentence structure (the switch from the use of participles in the preceding questions to the relative pronoun and the finite verb here), and the fact that this statement and the quotation from Isaiah in 2:24 flow together.[241]

Possession of the law was a legitimate ground for boasting in the good sense because such boasting was rejoicing in the great gift of God to Israel (cf. Deut 4:7-8). Paul is saying that his dialogue partner's boasting is reprehensible because he was not obeying the law in which he boasted. More than that, his disobedience dishonored God. Paul explains what this means

---

236. J. Duncan M. Derrett, 'You Abominate False Gods; but Do You Rob Shrines?' *NTS* 40 (1994) 570, 564-65. Similarly, Käsemann, *Romans,* 71.

237. Cranfield, *Romans,* I, 169.

238. So, e.g., Dunn, *Romans 1–8,* 113; similarly Schreiner, *Romans,* 134.

239. Byrne, *Romans,* 98.

240. So Moo, *Romans,* 165: 'This verse, which is probably a statement (NA[27], NEB, JB) rather than another rhetorical question (KJV, NASB, RSV, NIV, TEV), brings home to Paul's Jewish addressee the accusation developed in vv. 17-22. Whereas v. 17 spoke of the Jew "relying on" the law, this verse heightens the sense by speaking of the Jew as "boasting" in it'.

241. Cf. Timothy W. Berkley, *From a Broken Covenant to Circumcision of the Heart: Pauline Intertextual Exegesis in Romans 2:17-29* (SBLDS 175; Atlanta: Society of Biblical Literature, 2000), 137.

with a scriptural quotation: *As it is written: 'God's name is blasphemed among the Gentiles because of you'*. He is citing Isaiah 52:5 (LXX): 'The Lord says, "Because of you my name is always blasphemed among the Gentiles"'. Isaiah was speaking of the Jews' Babylonian captivity, during which time God's name had been blasphemed among the Gentiles. As his people were punished for their disobedience to his law, it provided occasion for God's name to be profaned among the Gentiles.[242] Paul implies that his dialogue partner's failure to obey the law is likewise bringing God's name into dispute. Possession of the law is of no value unless one obeys it.[243]

(ii) True circumcision, 2:25-29

> [25]*Circumcision has value if you observe the law, but if you break the law, you have become as though you had not been circumcised.* [26]*So then, if those who are not circumcised keep the law's requirements, will they not be regarded as though they were circumcised?* [27]*The one who is not circumcised physically and yet obeys the law will condemn you who, even though you have the written code and circumcision, are a lawbreaker.*
>
> [28]*A person is not a Jew who is one only outwardly, nor is circumcision merely outward and physical.* [29]*No, a person is a Jew who is one inwardly; and circumcision is circumcision of the heart, by the Spirit, not by the written code. Such a person's praise is not from other people, but from God.*

In this section Paul reminds his dialogue partner that physical circumcision is of no value if one is a lawbreaker, and that true circumcision is a matter of the heart and effected by the Spirit. By so doing he removes another basis of unacceptable Jewish boasting over against Gentiles and a false basis of confidence about acceptability before God.

2:25   In 2:23-24 Paul stated the effect of his dialogue partner's disobedience to the law — it brought dishonor to God's name. Here in 2:25 he states that disobedience also invalidates Jewish circumcision. *Circumcision has value if you observe the law, but if you break the law, you have become as though you had not been circumcised.* That Paul states that circumcision has value for people who obey the law is noteworthy in the light of his relativizing its importance in both Romans and Galatians. The importance

---

242. The prophet Ezekiel makes a similar point: 'And wherever they went among the nations they profaned my holy name, for it was said of them, "These are the LORD's people, and yet they had to leave his land"' (Ezek 36:20). Ito, 'Romans 2: A Deuteronomistic Reading', 25-27, argues for a Deuteronomistic background for 2:24 because of the parallel allusions to God's name being brought into disrepute because of Jewish disobedience in 2:24 and Deut 29:24

243. Wright, 'Romans', 447, comments on 2:23-24: 'The real problem is Israel's failure to bring God worldwide honor. That was the purpose for which Torah had been given. What Israel has done with Torah has instead brought dishonor; the pagan nations scorn the true God on the basis of the behavior of the covenant people. Breaking Torah nullifies boasting in Torah'.

of circumcision as the mark of covenant relationship with God is spelled out clearly in Genesis 17:9-14:

> Then God said to Abraham, 'As for you, you must keep my covenant, you and your descendants after you for the generations to come. This is my covenant with you and your descendants after you, the covenant you are to keep: Every male among you shall be circumcised. You are to undergo circumcision, and it will be the sign of the covenant between me and you. For the generations to come every male among you who is eight days old must be circumcised, including those born in your household or bought with money from a foreigner — those who are not your offspring. Whether born in your household or bought with your money, they must be circumcised. My covenant in your flesh is to be an everlasting covenant. Any uncircumcised male, who has not been circumcised in the flesh, will be cut off from his people; he has broken my covenant'.

However, if Jewish people disobeyed the law, Paul says, the physical mark of circumcision was emptied of its significance for them. They became as if they 'had not been circumcised' (lit. 'your circumcision as become uncircumcision').[244] For Paul to say that the circumcision of Jews who disobeyed the law had become uncircumcision was tantamount to saying that they were no better than pagan Gentiles.[245]

2:26-27 In 2:25 Paul implied that Jewish people who were circumcised but disobeyed the law were no better than pagan Gentiles. In 2:26-27 he asks his dialogue partner: *So then, if those who are not circumcised keep the law's requirements, will they not be regarded as though they were circumcised?*[246] If disobedience on the part of Jewish people means their circumcision is regarded uncircumcision, then obedience to the law on the part of Gentile people will mean that their uncircumcision will be regarded by God as circumcision. For the uncircumcision of the Gentiles to be regarded as circumcision means that in God's sight they are counted as members of the covenant people.[247] The law's 'requirements' are the demands of the Mosaic law as indicated by the extensive use of the term translated as such with this meaning in the LXX. However, Paul's understanding of Gentiles keeping of the law's requirements was quite different from that of Rabbinic Judaism of his day. Barrett states it well:

---

244. 'Circumcision *(peritomē)* and 'uncircumcision' *(akrobystia)* were nicknames, even terms of abuse, used by Jews and Gentiles for one another.

245. Ambrosiaster asks: 'So why did Paul prohibit what he shows to be of value if the law is observed? Paul answers by saying that if the law is not kept, the Jew effectively becomes a Gentile' ('Commentary on Paul's Epistles' [ACCSR, 76]).

246. When the Greek text *(ean oun hē akrobystia ta dikaiōmata tou nomou phylassē, ouch hē akrobystia autou eis peritomēn logisthēsetai)* is translated literally, it yields: 'If therefore the uncircumcision keeps the requirements of the law, his uncircumcision will be reckoned as circumcision, won't it?'

247. Cf. Cranfield, *Romans*, I, 173.

Paul makes clear beyond doubt what he means by keeping, and by transgressing, the law. It is possible to neglect so weighty a command as circumcision — and fulfil the law; it is possible to observe the letter of the law, including circumcision — and transgress the law. This is not Rabbinic Judaism, or any other orthodox kind of Judaism. Paul's new Christian conviction, that Jesus, whom the law had cast out, crucified, and cursed, was the risen Lord in heaven, led him to a revaluation of religion, and in particular of the law, the basis of his own national religion, far more radical than is often perceived. He not merely had new faith, and a new theology; in the light of these he came to the conclusion that the old faith — the Old Testament and Judaism — meant something different from what he had thought. It was not a closed system, complete in itself, requiring only strict and unimaginative obedience; for those who had eyes to see it pointed forward to Christ, and the Gospel which was the power of God unto salvation — for everyone who had faith.[248]

The fact that Paul's question, 'will they not be regarded as though they were circumcised? (lit. 'will not his uncircumcision be reckoned as circumcision?'), employs the future passive tense of the verb ('will . . . be reckoned') suggests that the reckoning will be a future determination by God. As Byrne comments: 'The "reckoning" in question is that of God (cf. 4:4-6), the divine assessment set to be given at the great judgment'.[249]

To drive home his point, Paul writes: *The one who is not circumcised physically and yet obeys the law will condemn you.* 'The one who is not circumcised physically' (lit. 'the uncircumcision by nature') is of course the Gentile.[250] This person, Paul says to his dialogue partner, will condemn you (sing.) *who, even though you have the written code[251] and circumcision, are a lawbreaker.*[252] This is the first of three references to the Mosaic law as 'the written code' found in Romans (2:27, 29; 7:6). In 2:13-16 Paul implied that the Gentiles who do what the law requires put to shame Jewish people who do not obey their law. Here in 2:27 Paul makes an even more drastic statement: the obedient Gentile will condemn the Jew who, though privileged to have the written code (the law) and to bear the mark of the covenant in his flesh (circumcision), is nevertheless a 'lawbreaker'. The apostle has in mind not

---

248. Barrett, *Romans*, 59.

249. Byrne, *Romans*, 102. Cf. Jewett, *Romans*, 233.

250. Paul uses again here the word *physis* ('by nature', translated here as 'physically') found in 2:14, but this time not to describe those who by their birth as Gentiles do not have the law, but one who by virtue of being a Gentile is not circumcised.

251. The word translated 'written code' *(gramma)* is also used with this meaning in 2 Cor 3:6, 7; 2 Tim 3:15, but with its literal meaning 'letter' (of the alphabet) in Gal 6:11.

252. 'Even though you have the written code and circumcision' translates *dia grammatos kai peritomēs* in which *dia* indicates attendant or prevailing circumstance. BAGD translates 2:27b as follows: 'you who, (though provided) with the written code and circumcision, are a transgressor/violator of the law'.

so much Gentiles acting as judges but rather as witnesses for the prosecution. Their obedience to the law will constitute the 'evidence of what the Jew ought to have been and could have been'.[253]

This text raises the question of which Gentiles Paul believes will condemn lawbreaking Jews.[254] Some argue that Paul is speaking without reference to the gospel and that he is referring to Gentiles who carry out some aspects of the law.[255] Others argue that the apostle has in mind Gentile Christians, those on whose hearts the law has been written by the Spirit according to the promise of the new covenant.[256] Given the context, in particular what the apostle says about true circumcision being a matter 'of the heart, by the Spirit, not by the written code' in the following verses, the latter option (that the Gentiles in mind are Gentile Christians) seems preferable. (see 'Additional Note: Gentiles Who Do the Things Required by the Law', 136-40).

2:28-29 To drive home his point further, Paul tells his dialogue partner what is involved in being a 'true' Jew and what constitutes 'true' circumcision.[257] Stating his point negatively, Paul insists: [*For*] *a person is not a Jew who is one only outwardly, nor is circumcision merely outward and physical. No, a person is a Jew who is one inwardly; and circumcision is circumcision of the heart, by the Spirit, not by the written code.* The NIV omits the conjunction 'for', obscuring somewhat the fact that this verse provides an explanation as to *why* the law-keeping Gentile will judge the law-breaking Jew. The behavior of the law-abiding Gentile will throw into bold relief the reprehensible behavior of the law-breaking Jew, and thereby function as a witness for the prosecution in condemning the law-breaking Jew. To make his point about the 'true' Jew and 'true' circumcision Paul employs three antitheses: outward/inward, of the flesh/of the heart, and by the written code/by the Spirit.[258] By so doing, he contrasts what we might call the 'nominal' Jew and the 'true' Jew. The 'nominal' Jew is described as a Jew 'who is one outwardly', that is, one who is seen to observe those practices that characterize

253. Cf. Cranfield, *Romans,* I, 174; Moo, *Romans,* 172.

254. Paul may have in mind the condemnation of the disobedient on the Day of Judgment (cf. 2:16), when Christians (including Christian Gentiles) will participate, in association with Christ, in the judgment of the world (cf. 1 Cor 6:2).

255. Cf. Moo, *Romans,* 171; Fitzmyer, *Romans,* 322.

256. So Cranfield, *Romans,* I, 174; Schreiner, *Romans,* 139-41.

257. But cf. Wright, 'Romans', 449, who says: 'We should note that he [Paul] does not say, as the NEB and others do, the "true" Jew, the "true" circumcision. His point is more stark. The name "Jew", and the attribute "circumcision", belong to the secret/heart/spirit people, not to the visibility/flesh/letter people (cf. Phil 3:3, where a closely accurate translation might be "the 'circumcision' means us"). It is as shocking as that. As if to emphasize that he really means it, Paul will at once go on to challenge himself on the point and to think through what follows'.

258. Cf. John M. G. Barclay, 'Paul and Philo on Circumcision: Romans 2:25-9 in Social and Cultural Context', *NTS* 44 (1998), 551-55, who notes that while Paul speaks of the evident and hidden Jew, when it comes to circumcision he refers only to evident circumcision. However, he argues, correctly, that the context implies an evident/hidden antithesis.

a Jewish person. The true Jew, however, is described as a Jew 'who is one inwardly' (lit. 'the one in secret'), that is, one who receives the approval of God, who knows the secrets of people's hearts.[259] The NIV's translation 'inwardly' could be misleading. What is implied is not a Platonic contrast between what is visible and invisible, but between what is seen by human beings and what is seen by God.[260] God sees the secrets of human hearts.[261]

Circumcision in the flesh is described as 'outward', while true circumcision is described as 'circumcision of the heart', effected 'by the Spirit' and 'not by the written code'. In the previous verse (2:27) Paul referred to the law as the 'written code', and elsewhere he contrasts life and ministry in the Spirit with life and ministry under 'the written code' (cf. 7:6; 2 Cor 3:6-7). Therefore, to say that circumcision of the heart is 'by the Spirit, not by the written code' is to say that it is something that only the Spirit can bring about in the heart of a person, in contrast physical circumcision in obedience to the law.

When speaking about circumcision of the heart, Paul is reiterating well-known teaching of the law and the prophets. The prophet Jeremiah accused Israel of being 'uncircumcised in heart': 'Egypt, Judah, Edom, Ammon, Moab and all who live in the wilderness in distant places. For all these nations are really uncircumcised, and even the whole house of Israel is uncircumcised in heart' (Jer 9:26).[262] The same prophet exhorted the Judeans to circumcise their hearts: 'Circumcise yourselves to the LORD, circumcise your hearts, you people of Judah and inhabitants of Jerusalem' (Jer 4:4). And Moses exhorted the Israelites: 'Circumcise your hearts, therefore, and do not be stiff-necked any longer' (Deut 10:16), and even promised that God himself will circumcise their hearts: 'The LORD your God will circumcise your hearts and the hearts of your descendants, so that you may love him with all your heart and with all your soul, and live' (Deut 30:6).[263] Jeremiah complained of the uncircumcised ears of his hearers, expressed in their unwillingness to obey the word of the Lord (Jer 6:10). The same teach-

---

259. A distinction between those who are 'true' Jews and those who are not is implied in 9:6-8: 'It is not as though God's word had failed. For not all who are descended from Israel are Israel. Nor because they are his descendants are they all Abraham's children. On the contrary, "It is through Isaac that your offspring will be reckoned". In other words, it is not the children by physical descent who are God's children, but it is the children of the promise who are regarded as Abraham's offspring'.

260. Cf. Barclay, 'Paul and Philo on Circumcision', 554.

261. Cf. 2:16; 1 Cor 4:5; 14:25.

262. The prophet Ezekiel also speaks of Gentiles as those with uncircumcised hearts: 'In addition to all your other detestable practices, you brought foreigners uncircumcised in heart and flesh into my sanctuary' (Ezek 44:7); 'This is what the Sovereign LORD says: No foreigner uncircumcised in heart and flesh is to enter my sanctuary, not even the foreigners who live among the Israelites' (Ezek 44:9).

263. Ito, 'Romans 2: A Deuteronomistic Reading', 25-27, argues for a Deuteronomic background for 2:29 because of the parallel references to the circumcision of the heart in 2:29 and Deut 30:6.

ing is found in the Qumran literature (1QS 5:5; 1QH 2:18; 1QpHab 11:13), the Pseudepigrapha (*Jub.* 1:23; *Odes Sol.* 11:1-3), and Philo (*Spec. Leg.* 1.305; cf. *Mig.* 92).[264]

This material from the OT and postbiblical Jewish literature identifies those with uncircumcised hearts as those who resist the word of the Lord, and those with circumcised hearts as those who are obedient to it. It was appropriate, then, for Paul to rebuke his Jewish dialogue partner for bragging about the law while he disobeyed it, and to remind him that true circumcision is a matter of the heart and effected by the Spirit. In the light of the overall stance adopted by the apostle in this passage, it is evident that for him the 'true' Jew is the Jewish Christian believer. It is also evident that he relativizes the importance of physical circumcision, even for Jews.[265]

Paul's final comment concerning the 'true' Jew, the one who is circumcised in heart, is that *such a person's praise is not from other people, but from God.*[266] By addressing such a comment to his dialogue partner Paul implies that those who brag about the law and put their confidence in being circumcised physically are seeking praise from other people, but not from God, and by so doing show that their hearts have not been circumcised by the Spirit. Those who adopt Paul's radical definition of a 'true' Jew and 'true' circumcision would, as Barclay says, 'have to reckon on getting his praise from God, not from fellow Jews'.[267]

c. God's Faithfulness Is Not Nullified by Jewish Unbelief, 3:1-20

In 2:17-29, employing the rhetoric of the diatribe, Paul upbraided his dialogue partner for calling himself a Jew while not obeying the law, and insisted that true circumcision is circumcision of the heart by the Spirit, not in the flesh. This raises the question whether God's promises to Israel and her election as God's people have been abrogated. In 3:1-20 Paul will argue that this is not the case, even though he insists that Jews, like Gentiles, are all 'under the power of sin'.

In 3:1-9 the apostle continues to use the rhetoric of the diatribe to instruct his audience.[268] This time, however, he does so by posing questions

264. Cf. Byrne, *Romans*, 104.

265. Käsemann, *Romans*, 73, says: 'Neither OT prophecy nor the apologetics and propaganda of the Diaspora synagogue dismissed circumcision as irrelevant because of circumcision of the heart, whereas this is precisely what Paul does'.

266. Jesus criticized the Pharisees and teachers of the law because they sought the praise of men (Matt 23:6; Mark 12:39; Luke 20:46). The Fourth Evangelist criticized Jewish leaders who were not prepared to confess Christ because 'they loved human praise more than praise from God' (John 12:42-43).

267. Barclay, 'Paul and Philo on Circumcision', 550.

268. Dillon, 'The Spirit as Taskmaster', 685, argues that 3:1-8 'shows that the author is a man "with his back to the wall", clustering in the space of eight verses the potentially devastating objections against his message which could have doomed his mission and cast him adrift as a lonely pariah. The battery of rhetorical questions articulates three basic com-

and providing the answers himself.[269] The questions he poses are not merely hypothetical but reflect real objections to his gospel to which he must respond. Thus his strategy in 3:1-9 is to raise questions that might prove to be problematic for his audience (3:1, 3, 5, 7-8a, 9a), provide emphatic responses (3:2a, 4a, 6a, 8b, 9b) and then offer reasons for those responses (3:2b, 4b, 6b, 9c).[270] In the process of doing so, the apostle will show that it is not only when God provides salvation for Israel but also when he brings judgment upon her that he is acting in faithfulness to his word. He follows all this up with a series of quotations from the 'law' highlighting the sinfulness of humanity, arguing that what the 'law' says applies to those under the law (i.e., the Jews), and so declares that no one will be declared righteous in God's sight by observing the law.

(i) Five rhetorical questions, 3:1-9

[1]What advantage, then, is there in being a Jew, or what value is there in circumcision? [2]Much in every way! First of all, the Jews have been entrusted with the very words of God.

[3]What if some were unfaithful? Will their unfaithfulness nullify God's faithfulness? [4]Not at all! Let God be true, and every human being a liar. As it is written: "So that you may be proved right when you speak and prevail when you judge".

[5]But if our unrighteousness brings out God's righteousness more clearly, what shall we say? That God is unjust in bringing his wrath on us? (I am using a human argument.) [6]Certainly not! If that were so, how could God judge the world? [7]Someone might argue, "If my falsehood enhances God's truthfulness and so increases his glory, why am I still condemned as a sinner?" [8]Why not say — as some slanderously claim that we say — "Let us do evil that good may result"? Their condemnation is just!

---

plaints: (1) that Paul denies Israel's historic privilege, and so (2) that he proclaims an unfaithful God who has no right to judge people, and (3) that his law-*free* gospel is, in fact, a "law-*less*" gospel, a license for self-indulgence and immorality. Of the three complaints, Paul hastens to answer the second one first (in 3:21–4:25); he then gathers all his weaponry to demolish the third (in chaps. 5–8), whereupon he can finally lay the first to rest (in chaps. 9–11). These challenges, and the *challengers* as well, must have been *real* menaces to Paul's reception in (Jerusalem and) Rome (15:30-32), not merely rhetorical stratagems for advancing the exposition of his doctrine'.

269. It is possible that Paul's use of first person pronouns ('I', 'we', 'us') could be understood to include a dialogue partner, and some scholars do interpret 3:1-8(9) as a dialogue between Paul and an interlocutor. So, e.g., Stowers, *A Rereading of Romans,* 165-66; Byrne, *Romans,* 106-7; Jewett, *Romans,* 242. Moo, *Romans,* 178, notes the influence of the diatribe in 3:1-9 but says that 'few solid exegetical results come from this identification, not least because the diatribe style itself is quite amorphous and variable; and as Stowers notes, Paul shows evidence of having adapted it rather considerably'.

270. Cf. P. J. Achtemeier, 'Romans 3:1-8: Structure and Argument', *AnglTheolRev* Sup. 11 (1990) 77-87.

⁹What shall we conclude then? Do we have any advantage? Not at all!
For we have already made the charge that Jews and Gentiles alike are all un-
der the power of sin.

3:1-2 The diatribe of 2:17-29 concluded with the radical statement:
'No, a person is a Jew who is one inwardly; and circumcision is circumcision of the heart, by the Spirit, not by the written code' (2:29). It would
seem that Paul was implying that there is no more advantage in being a Jew
or in physical circumcision than there is in being a Gentile and
uncircumcised. Confirming just how radical a statement this was is the fact
that Paul felt it necessary to deal with the question that would cause problems for his audience, especially for those who were Jews or who had some
previous involvement in the synagogue: *What advantage, then, is there in be-*
ing a Jew, or what value is there in circumcision? Barrett comments: 'If negative
answers were returned to these questions the result would be offensive not
only (as is often supposed) to Jewish national sentiment but to theology. . . .
God did choose the Jews out of all mankind and did bestow special privileges upon them. To reduce them therefore to the level of other nations is
either to accuse the Old Testament of falsehood, or to accuse God of failure
to carry out his plans. It is this theological objection to his thesis that Paul is
bound to meet'.[271]

The apostle responds to these questions emphatically when he says:
Much in every way! Later in the letter Paul will provide a comprehensive list
of the many ways in which the Jews are advantaged,[272] but here, offering a
reason for his response, he focuses upon one of the most important of these
advantages: *First of all, the Jews have been entrusted with the very words of God.*
The word translated 'first of all' can mean either the 'first in a sequence' or
'of first importance'. Those who opt for 'first in a sequence' suggest that
Paul had in mind a list of Israel's privileges, as, for example, listed in 9:4-5,
but in his haste to make his point about 'the very words of God' he omitted
to complete his list. If we opt for the second alternative, 'of first importance', it would mean that Paul was not necessarily intending to provide a
comprehensive list of Israel's privileges but rather was highlighting what
was most important: Israel's privilege in having received the words of God.
This second alternative seems preferable because it functions as a launch-
ing place for Paul's defense of God's faithfulness to his word, despite Israel's unfaithfulness.[273] To be a Jew is to be a member of Israel, the nation

271. Barrett, *Romans*, 62.
272. Cf. 9:4-5: 'Theirs is the adoption to sonship; theirs the divine glory, the covenants, the receiving of the law, the temple worship and the promises. Theirs are the patriarchs, and from them is traced the human ancestry of the Messiah'.
273. Jewett, *Romans*, 243, points out: 'Many commentators state that Paul's listing of
the oracles of God with *prōton* ("in the first place, above all, chiefly") indicates that he intended a further enumeration, but breaks off in a distracted manner and postpones the further listing of Jewish advantages until 9:3-5. The enumeration theory overlooks how

entrusted with 'the very words of God'.[274] For Paul, pre-eminent among the 'words of God' entrusted to the Jewish people would have been the preaching of the gospel by Jesus Christ himself and continued by Paul and the other apostles.

3:3-4 Knowing that many Jews did not heed the 'words of God', Paul deals with a second question he thinks would trouble some in his audience: *What if some were unfaithful? Will their unfaithfulness nullify God's faithfulness?* Paul's reference to 'some' who were unfaithful implies that some were faithful; those who like the apostle himself and early Jewish Christians responded positively to the gospel. Moo says: 'Paul's use of "some" to designate the unfaithful Jews must be motivated partially by a desire to lessen the offense, since Rom 9–11 shows that he regarded most Jews as having failed to respond appropriately to God's word'.[275]

To be unfaithful, or to refuse to believe, is here equivalent to rejecting God's word, and in Paul's mind this is primarily so when people reject the gospel. In 11:20 he speaks of Jewish people being excluded from the blessings of the gospel, like branches broken off from an olive tree, because of their unbelief. However, their not having faith will not nullify the faithfulness of God. His faithfulness, despite Israel's lack of faith, will be seen in two ways. First, and this is what Paul stresses in the immediate context, God remains faithful to the terms of his covenant with Israel when he imposes judgment upon Israel for her faithlessness (this is the point of 3:4-6). Second, God will be faithful to his covenant by grafting those 'branches' broken off back into the 'olive tree' of Israel 'if they do not persist in unbelief' (11:23), something that had already occurred in the life of the apostle himself (cf. 1 Tim 1:13: 'Even though I was once a blasphemer and a persecutor and a violent man, I was shown mercy because I acted in ignorance and unbelief'). The form of Paul's question, 'Will their unfaithfulness nullify God's faithfulness?'[276] indicates that the expected answer is 'no', and this is confirmed by what follows in 3:4, where Paul insists that God remains true to his word.[277]

ēpisteuthēsan ("were believed, entrusted") defines and delimits the sense of *ta logia tou theou* ("the oracles of God"), which in other sources can refer to the messianic promises, the promises to Abraham and the patriarchs, the commandments of the Torah, or even the whole of Scripture'. . . .

274. 'The very words of God' translates *ta logia tou theou*. The word *logion* is found in only three other places in the NT (Acts 7:38; Heb 5:12; 1 Pet 4:11), and in each case it is used to denote the word of God as it does here. It is used frequently in the OT, notably in the Psalms (and especially in Psalm 119) in the same way, sometimes meaning God's law, other times his word through the prophets, and other times his promises to his people.

275. Moo, *Romans*, 184. Fitzmyer, *Romans*, 327, notes that the 'some' will become 'all' in v. 9.

276. *mē hē apistia autōn tēn pistin tou theou katargēsei?*

277. Charles H. Cosgrove, 'What If Some Have Not Believed? The Occasion and Thrust of Romans 3 1-8', *ZNW* 78 (1987) 98, says: 'Where the opponent will have spoken of God's unfaithfulness to torah-faithful Israel as an implication of Paul's gospel, the apostle

Responding to the question, 'Will their unfaithfulness nullify God's faithfulness?' Paul exclaims: *Not at all!* — his first use of this strong denial formula.[278] Having thus emphatically rejected the suggestion that human unfaithfulness nullifies God's faithfulness, Paul offers the reason for this response by declaring: *Let God be true, and every human being a liar.* God will be true to his word, faithful to all he has said or promised, and this fact must be maintained even if it were to mean that every human being is shown to be a liar. God is true to his word, not only when he blesses his people in accordance with his promises, but also when he visits judgment upon them for their disobedience (cf. Neh 9:32-33, in which the Levites acknowledge in respect to the hardships they have experienced that 'in all that has happened to us, you [the great and awesome God, who keeps his covenant of love] have remained righteous; you have acted faithfully, while we acted wickedly').

In support of this declaration, Paul cites almost word for word Psalm 51:4 (LXX 50:6): *As it is written: 'So that you may be proved right when you speak and prevail when you judge'.*[279] In Psalm 51 David confesses his sin and acknowledges that God is right in what he says and justified in his judgment of his servant before asking to be cleansed from his sin. The NRSV translates Psalm 51:4 as follows: 'Against you, you alone, have I sinned, and done what is evil in your sight, so that you are justified in your sentence and blameless when you pass judgment'. The inference Paul appears to draw from this quotation is that God is 'blameless' in his judgments, that is, no faithlessness on the part of human beings will cause him to be anything but blameless in his judgments. It is probably the final judgment that Paul has in mind. Chrysostom asks: 'What does the word *justified* mean? It means that if there were a trial and an examination of the things which God had done for the Jews and also of what they had done to him, the victory would be with God, and all the right would be on his side'.[280]

---

speaks of God's faithfulness over against Jewish unfaithfulness *(apistia).* Where the opponent will have objected to the seeming arbitrariness in God's rejection of Israel as Paul conceives it, the apostle stresses the commensurability of that rejection with Israel's "falsehood" in rejecting the Messiah'.

278. 'Not at all' translates *mē genoito,* an expression denoting strong denial, used for the first time here in Romans but found frequently both later in this letter and in other letters of Paul where the apostle expresses strong disagreement (cf. 3:6, 31; 6:2, 15; 7:7, 13; 9:14; 11:1, 11; 1 Cor 6:15; Gal 2:17; 3:21; 6:14).

279. *Hopōs an dikaiōthēs en tois logois sou kai nikēseis en tō krinesthai se;* LXX: *hopōs an dikaiōthēs en tois logois sou kai nikēsēs en tō krinesthai se* — the only difference being the use of the future active indicative of *nikaō* in Rom 3:4 instead of the aorist active subjunctive in the LXX). The NIV correctly construes *krinesthai* as present middle ('judge'), not as present passive ('are judged'), as do some other translations, e.g., NASB, KJV, KJVS. Cf. Bengt Löfstedt, 'Notes on St Paul's Letter to the Romans', *FilolNT* 1 (1988) 209. Byrne, *Romans,* 113, says: 'Since *nikān* is used as a technical term for winning a legal suit . . . the sense of "prevail when going to court" seems most appropriate for both the LXX and Paul's quotation'.

280. 'Homilies on Romans' *(ACCSR,* 84).

3:5-6 Continuing in the diatribe style, Paul deals with a third question for the benefit of his audience: *But if our unrighteousness brings out God's righteousness more clearly, what shall we say? That God is unjust in bringing his wrath on us? (I am using a human argument.)* In this question the 'unrighteousness' of human beings is the antithesis of God's righteousness. In this context the righteousness of God denotes the justness of his character. The question appears to pick up on the quotation from Psalm 51 in the previous verse, where God is said to be blameless when he passes judgment. But it also calls into question the justice of God in bringing down his wrath upon people for their unrighteousness when their unrighteousness puts into bold relief the righteousness of God. Paul realizes that such a question is out of order, so he adds in parentheses: 'I am using a human argument', apologizing, as it were, for even asking such a blasphemous question.

To this blasphemous question Paul responds emphatically: *Certainly not! —* a second use of the strong denial formula. The reason Paul offers for his emphatic response is in the form of a question: *If that were so, how could God judge the world?* Paul's point appears to be that if God were said to be unjust in bringing his wrath upon unrighteous Jews, the corollary would be that he could not judge the (Gentile) world either. It is, however, a *sine qua non* that God is the judge of the whole world (cf., e.g., Pss 7:6; 9:7; Isa 2:4; 34:8). It is also a given in the OT that the judge of all the earth will do right (cf. Gen 18:25).

3:7-8 These two verses contain the next step in Paul's diatribe, and it has similarities with what is found in the previous two verses. There the premise of his question was that human unrighteousness puts into bold relief God's righteousness, while the premise for the question here in 3:7-8 is that human falsehood puts into bold relief God's truthfulness. Paul's fourth question then is: *Someone might argue, 'If my falsehood enhances God's truthfulness and so increases his glory, why am I still condemned as a sinner?'*[281] This question is equally as inappropriate as the previous one, but Paul responds differently. He does not employ an emphatic denial. Rather, he responds with another question that reveals he has in mind serious allegations made about his own ministry: *Why not say — as some slanderously claim that we say — 'Let us do evil that good may result'?* Clearly there were those who accused Paul of encouraging people to 'do evil that good may result'. It seems the sort of teaching found later in the letter, that 'where sin increased, grace increased all the more' (5:20), was taken to imply that it was legitimate to 'do evil that good may result'. Paul alludes to such distortions of his teaching again in chapter 6,[282] and in that context he refutes them at length. Rather than provide any reasoned response here, Paul dismisses the

---

281. Moo, *Romans*, 194, regards the use of the first person singular here as a 'rhetorical variant of the first person plural in v. 5', adding that 'Paul is speaking more in the person of the objector himself than he was in v. 5'.

282. 'What shall we say, then? Shall we go on sinning so that grace may increase?' (6:1); 'What then? Shall we sin because we are not under law but under grace?' (6:15).

allegation of his opponents with the words: *Their condemnation is just!* In Paul's mind those who distort the truth of the gospel will have to answer to God himself and deserve condemnation for the harm they cause God's people (cf. 1 Cor 3:10-15; 2 Cor 11:13-15; Gal 1:6-9; 5:7-10).[283]

3:9 Bringing this part of his diatribe to a conclusion with a fifth question, Paul asks: *What shall we conclude then? Do we have any advantage?* To this question he supplies another emphatic negative response: *Not at all!* The NIV's 'Do we have any advantage?' translates a verb found only here in the NT, and the form in which it is found may be construed either as a present middle or a present passive indicative. Regarded as a present middle it has the active meaning, 'to have an advantage'.[284] If it is construed as a present passive, it could mean 'to be excelled', 'to lose the advantage', or 'to be worse off'. Paul's question would then be, 'Are we worse off?'[285] making the meaning of the question the very opposite to what it is when the verb is construed as a present middle with active meaning. Grammatically either translation is possible. The issue, then, must be determined by the context.[286]

The immediate context does not allow us to decide the issue one way or another because the reason Paul gives for responding negatively to the question could make sense irrespective of how the question is construed. So, for example, if the question is, 'Do we [Jews] have any advantage?' the denial, 'Not at all', would be supported by the fact that 'Jews and Gentiles alike are all under sin'. Similarly, if the question is, 'Are we [Jews] any worse off?' the denial, 'Not at all', would be equally supported by the fact that 'Jews and Gentiles alike are all under sin'. However, the wider context supports the view that the question is to be construed as, 'Do we have any advantage?' Following the question, answer, and reason for that answer given in 3:9, Paul provides a series of quotations from 'the law' (= OT) illustrating the sinfulness of humanity, and concludes: 'Now we know that whatever the law says, it says to those who are under the law, so that every mouth may be silenced and the whole world held accountable to God' (3:19). Those under the law are the Jewish people. Paul's purpose in listing

---

283. Byrne, *Romans*, 110, comments: 'the charge that surfaces here is clearly one that dogged the preaching of the Pauline gospel — one which he perhaps anticipated rising in the Roman community as his letter was being read'.

284. Cf. Moo, *Romans*, 200-201.

285. Cf. Fitzmyer, *Romans*, 331: '. . . the passive meaning of *proechometha* is to be preferred: "Are we (Jews) excelled (by others)? Not at all!" Such a meaning is not inappropriate after the argument in vv 1-8; in fact, it supplies the climactic question to Paul's dialogue with the Jewish interlocutor, enabling him to assert what he writes in v 9b'. Jewett, *Romans*, 257, opts for the following rendition: 'Are we excelled? i.e. are we in a worse position (than they)?' and says: 'I therefore conclude that in response to the interlocutor's question, "Are we [Jews] at a disadvantage?" Paul's reply, "Not at all!" advances his case that all groups have sinned and no group has an inherent superiority before God. In Colenso's words, "there is no favouritism"'.

286. See discussion in BAGD, *ad loc.*

the quotations from 'the law' is to silence the boasting of those under the law, that is, the Jews, so that the whole world, Jews as well as Gentiles, may be held accountable to God for their sins. In other words, what Paul is doing in 3:9-20 is to counter any claims by Jewish people that they 'have any advantage'. Thus it is better to construe the verb as a present middle with an active meaning, 'to have an advantage'.

The question, 'Do we have any advantage?' receives a very strong denial: 'Not at all!', a denial found in this particular form in only one other place in the NT.[287] Paul supports this strong denial by adding: *For we have already made the charge that Jews and Gentiles alike are all under the power of sin* (cf. 1:18-32; 2:1-29).[288] Paul speaks in similar terms of people being 'under the power of sin' in 7:14, where he says that those outside of Christ are sold as slaves 'to sin', and in Galatians 3:22, where he says, 'Scripture has locked up everything under the control of sin [lit. 'under sin']'. In other places Paul describes what life is like under sin (see 'Additional Note: Life under Sin', below), but here he will go on to quote extensively from the OT (3:10-18) to support his claim that Jews and Gentiles alike are under the power of sin'.[289] He quotes mainly from the Psalms but also from Ecclesiastes, Proverbs, and Isaiah.

ADDITIONAL NOTE: LIFE UNDER SIN

Paul describes what it means to be under sin in several different ways in his letters. In 6:14-22 he speaks of pre-Christian existence as slavery to sin that leads to death, a state in which people are 'free from the control of righteousness'. In 7:5 he describes it as a state in which 'sinful passions aroused by the law' are 'at work in us'. In 7:14-24 he depicts it as the moral frustration of the person who knows what is right but is unable to carry it out. In

---

287. In 1 Cor 5:10, where Paul strongly rejects the idea that he encouraged believers not to associate with 'the people of this world who are immoral, or the greedy and swindlers, or idolaters', explaining: 'not at all *(ou pantōs)* meaning the people of this world who are immoral, or the greedy and swindlers, or idolaters. In that case you would have to leave this world'.

288. Wright, 'Romans', 457, says: 'Paul now begins a lawcourt metaphor, which he will develop further in vv. 19-20. He has already laid a charge, like a plaintiff in a case; a charge against both Jews and Greeks ("Greeks" here, as usual, is a metonym for "Gentiles in general"). . . . By "already charged" he is referring back, obviously, to the argument that began in 1:18'.

289. Wright, 'Romans', 457, comments: 'In Paul's usage, "sin" refers not just to individual human acts of "sin", of missing the mark (the basic meaning of the word) as regards the divine intention for full human flourishing and fulfillment. "Sin" takes on a malevolent life of its own, exercising power over persons and communities. It is almost as though by "sin" Paul is referring to what in some other parts of the Bible is meant by "Satan" (though Paul can use that language too; e.g., 16:20); this is particularly striking in 7:7-25'.

1 Corinthians 6:9-11 Paul describes the members of the Corinthian church prior to their conversion as sexually immoral, idolaters, adulterers, male prostitutes, homosexual offenders, thieves, the greedy, drunkards, slanderers, and swindlers. In 1 Corinthians 12:2 Paul reminds his audience: 'You know that when you were pagans, somehow or other you were influenced and led astray to mute idols'. In Galatians 4:8 Gentiles prior to their conversion are described as 'slaves to those who by nature are not gods'. In Ephesians 2:1-3 Paul reminds his audience of their bondage under sin prior to their conversion: 'As for you, you were dead in your transgressions and sins, in which you used to live when you followed the ways of this world and of the ruler of the kingdom of the air, the spirit who is now at work in those who are disobedient. All of us also lived among them at one time, gratifying the cravings of our flesh and following its desires and thoughts. Like the rest, we were by nature deserving of wrath'. Their lives were then marked by futility in thinking and darkened understanding; they were alienated from God, insensitive, sensual, and impure (Eph 4:17-20). Colossians speaks in a similar way, describing the pre-Christian state of the audience as alienated from God and his enemies in their minds because of evil behavior (Col 1:21). Their previous lives were marked by sexual immorality, impurity, lust, evil desires and greed, which is idolatry, anger, rage, malice, slander, and filthy language and lying (Col 3:5-9). Titus 3:3 runs along similar lines in describing the lives of believers prior to conversion as 'foolish, disobedient, deceived and enslaved by all kinds of passions and pleasures . . . lived in malice and envy, being hated and hating one another'.

(ii) Scriptural support, 3:10-18

[10]As it is written: 'There is no one righteous, not even one; [11]there is no one who understands; there is no one who seeks God. [12]All have turned away, they have together become worthless; there is no one who does good, not even one'. [13]'Their throats are open graves; their tongues practice deceit'. 'The poison of vipers is on their lips'. [14]'Their mouths are full of cursing and bitterness'. [15]'Their feet are swift to shed blood; [16]ruin and misery mark their ways, [17]and the way of peace they do not know'. [18]'There is no fear of God before their eyes'.

To support his claim that Jews and Gentiles alike are under the power of sin, Paul provides a catena of OT quotations.[290] He begins his quotations

290. Whether this is, as Fitzmyer, *Romans,* 334, indicates, a reproduction of a preexistent list derived from a liturgical setting (as the parallel in Justin Martyr, *Dialogue with Trypho* 27.3, suggests) or an *ad hoc* composition by Paul himself is difficult to determine. Moo, *Romans,* 202, identifies the following structure in Paul's catena: 'The first line (v. 10) is the heading of what follows, with the last line (v. 18) coming back to the same themes in an inclusio. Verses 11-12 develop the first line with a series of five generally synonymous repe-

in support of his claim as follows: *As it is written: 'There is no one righteous, not even one; there is no one who understands; there is no one who seeks God. All have turned away, they have together become worthless; there is no one who does good,*[291] *not even one'.* The statement, 'there is no one righteous', comes from Ecclesiastes 7:20: 'Indeed, there is no one on earth who is righteous; no one who does what is right and never sins', and the claim that 'there is no one who understands, there is no one who seeks God' draws upon Psalm 14:2 (LXX 13:2): 'The Lord looks down from heaven on all mankind to see if there are any who understand, any who seek God', and Psalm 53:2 (LXX 52:3): 'God looks down from heaven on all mankind to see if there are any who understand, any who seek God', while the quotation, 'All have turned away, they have together become worthless; there is no one who does good, not even one', comes from Psalm 14:3 (LXX 13:3): 'All have turned away, all have become corrupt; there is no one who does good, not even one', and Psalm 53:3 (LXX 52:4): 'Everyone has turned away, all have become corrupt; there is no one who does good, not even one'.

Paul then adds further quotations: *'Their throats are open graves; their tongues practice deceit'. 'The poison of vipers is on their lips'. 'Their mouths are full of cursing and bitterness'.* These are taken from Psalm 5:9 (LXX 5:10): 'Their throat is an open grave;[292] with their tongue they tell lies', Psalm 140:3 (LXX 139:4): 'the poison of vipers is on their lips', and Psalm 10:7: 'His mouth is full of lies and threats'.

Paul concludes his quotations with the following: *'Their feet are swift to shed blood; ruin and misery mark their ways, and the way of peace they do not know'. 'There is no fear of God before their eyes'.* These are taken from Proverbs 1:16: 'For their feet rush into evil, they are swift to shed blood', Isaiah 59:7-8: 'Their feet rush into sin; they are swift to shed innocent blood. They pursue evil schemes; acts of violence mark their ways. The way of peace they

---

titions of the theme "there is no one righteous", all introduced with "there is no", and with a reference to "all people" breaking them up in the middle (v. 12a). The next four lines (vv. 13-14) describe sins of speech, each line referring to a different organ of speech. Verses 15-17, on the other hand, focus on sins of violence against others'.

291. Many manuscripts include here a second *ouk estin* ('there is not'), which is found in the LXX. It may have been omitted by some manuscripts as superfluous.

292. Origen comments: 'Every grave contains the uncleanness of the dead body inside. This is why our Lord said in the Gospel that the scribes and Pharisees were whited sepulchres. On the outside they appear to be beautiful, but on the inside they are full of all sorts of uncleanness. But in this passage Paul seems to be revealing something more than this about the sins of those whom he is talking about, because he says that they are an *open* grave, not one which is shut and covered up. Those who were called a closed sepulchre had enough sense of shame not to reveal their sins to the public. But these people are called an open grave because they have their uncleanness and impurity on display, and they are so accustomed to evil that . . . whenever they open their mouth, instead of speaking the Word of God, the word of life, they open their throat and speak the word of death, the word of the devil, not from the heart but from the grave. Whenever you see a man cursing and swearing, you may be sure that he is one of this type' ('Commentary on the Epistle to the Romans' [*ACCSR*, 91]).

do not know', and Psalm 36:1 (LXX 35:2): 'I have a message from God in my heart concerning the sinfulness of the wicked: There is no fear of God before his eyes'.

ADDITIONAL NOTE:
PAUL'S USE OF SCRIPTURE IN THE CATENA

The quotations that Paul uses in his catena, read in their original contexts, do not say there are no righteous persons at all. Ecclesiastes 7:20 is found in a passage (Eccl 7:15-22) in which the preacher comments upon the fate of both the righteous and the wicked. The wider context of Psalm 14:2, 3 speaks of evildoers being overwhelmed with dread while 'God is present in the company of the righteous' (Ps 14:4-5). Similarly, Psalm 53:3, while saying 'there is no one who does good, not even one', contrasts these evildoers with God's own people — those for whom the psalmist longs to see fortunes restored by God (Ps 53:4-6). Such is the case also with Psalm 5:9, which says, 'Their throat is an open grave; with their tongue they tell lies', for the context of this verse makes it clear that the psalmist is speaking about the wicked, but the righteous will find refuge in the Lord. The same is true of Psalm 140:3, for it is of the wicked that it is said, 'the poison of vipers is on their lips', but the psalmist seeks protection from the Lord against such evildoers, and is confident that 'the righteous will praise your name, and the upright will live in your presence' (Ps 140:13). The same pattern emerges when Proverbs 1:16 is examined in its context. It speaks of those whose feet rush into sin and who are swift to shed blood. Solomon warns his son against such people, assuring him that whoever listens to the Lord 'will live in safety and be at ease, without fear of harm' (Prov 1:33). Isaiah 59:7-8 adds: 'Their feet rush into sin; they are swift to shed innocent blood. They pursue evil schemes; acts of violence mark their ways. The way of peace they do not know'. However, the context shows that the prophet is assuring God's people that 'the arm of the Lord is not too short to save, nor his ear too dull to hear' (Isa 59:1) — rather, it is their sins that have at that time separated them from their God — and promising that 'the Redeemer will come to Zion, to those in Jacob who repent of their sins' (Isa 59:20). Finally, while Psalm 36:1 speaks of 'the sinfulness of the wicked' of whom it is said, 'there is no fear of God before his eyes', this is in the context of a celebration of the faithfulness of God and his righteousness towards 'the upright in heart' (Ps 36:5-10).[293]

Paul would have been well aware that the texts he quoted do in fact distinguish righteous individuals from the unrighteous. He quotes these texts to show that the Jewish people as a nation cannot claim to be any

---

293. Cf. Steve Moyise, 'The Catena of Romans 3:10-18', *ExpTim* 106 (1994-95) 368.

better morally than other nations (something he argued for in chapter 2 — they had the law but did not obey it), for their own Scriptures testify to the moral failure of many. It is towards this conclusion that the apostle is working, as the next verse makes clear: 'Now we know that whatever the law says, it says to those who are under the law, so that every mouth may be silenced and the whole world held accountable to God'. It is important to recognize that Paul is speaking as a Jew about the Jewish people. There is no anti-Semitism here.

Origen seeks to come to terms with Paul's use of these scriptures: 'That no one has done good, not even one, is a hard saying and difficult to understand. How is it possible that no one, Jew or Greek, has ever done anything good? Are we supposed to believe that nobody has ever shown hospitality, fed the hungry, clothed the naked, delivered the innocent from the hands of the powerful or done anything similar? It does not seem possible to me that Paul was intending to assert anything as incredible as that. I think that what he meant must be understood as follows. If someone lays the foundation for a house and puts up one or two walls or transports some building material to the site, can he be said to have built the house, just because he has set to work on it? The man who will be said to have built the house is the one who has finished off each and every part of it. So I think that here the apostle is saying that no one has done good in the sense that no one has brought goodness to perfection and completion'.[294]

Others have sought to explain Paul's use of scripture in different ways. Moo asserts: 'The fact that many of these quotations denounce only the wicked or unrighteous within Israel — and hence do not seem to fit Paul's universalistic intention — has been taken as indication that Paul's intention is not to condemn *all* people. But Paul's actual intention is probably more subtle; by citing texts that denounce the unrighteous and applying them, implicitly, to all people, including all Jews, he underscores the argument of 2:1–3:8 that, in fact, not even faithful Jews can claim to be righteous'.[295]

Byrne says: 'Paul's judgment here is one that few Torah-observant Jews would accept and one that all, with few exceptions, have found and continue to find deeply offensive. Harsh as the verdict may be, however, in applying the accusatory scriptural catena to the Jews, Paul remains true to the original reference of the texts cited, all of which assert or complain about the infidelity in Israel. Similar pessimistic verdicts appear in later books of the Old Testament (e.g., Isa 59:12-15; 64:5-12; Ezra 9:6-15; Neh 9:16-38; Dan 9:4-19; Tob 3:1-6) and in the literature of apocalyptic Judaism (e.g., *Jub.* 23:16-21; 4 *Ezra* 7:22-24, 46, 62-74, 116-26; 8:35; 1QH 1:25-27; 29-31; 6:18-22; 9:14; 12:30-31; 1QS 11:9). Such texts provide some context within which to set Paul's otherwise singular accusation. Speaking as a Jew, from within Israel (cf. the "we" of v 9a), Paul externalizes the self-judgment that

---

294. 'Commentary on the Epistle to the Romans' (*ACCSR*, 90).
295. Moo, *Romans*, 202-3.

had been an essential element of his own conversion (cf. Gal 2:15-16) and which led him to see in a new light the "law-righteousness" in which he had been "blameless" (Phil 3:6)'.[296]

Dunn comments: 'Once again it needs to be stressed that the point of the catena is not simply to demonstrate that scripture condemns all humankind, but more precisely to demonstrate that scriptures which had been read from the presupposition of a clear distinction between the righteous and the unrighteous (cf. *Jub.* 21.21-22; and see further on 1:17, *dikaios*) in fact condemned all humankind as soon as that clear distinction was undermined'.[297]

On the function of Paul's catena Jewett comments: 'The catena declares a complete betrayal of Israel's religious heritage on the part of those who should be the first to embody it. Since the catena was probably created by Jewish sectarians, and was intended to buttress their claims against other groups whom they considered to be heretics, Paul has taken this weapon out of their hands and turned it back on its creators. With Paul's elimination of the distinction between the righteous and fools, the catena relegates all Jews along with all Gentiles to the category of sinners and traitors, placing them on [the] same level as enemies of God'.[298]

Moyise cites Edgar with approval: 'The verses Paul adduces in Rom. iii to prove the universality of sin do not in their original context refer to all men, but in most cases to the wicked, the enemies of Israel'. He adds that his own examination of the texts Paul cites (Eccl 7:20; Pss 5:9; 10:7; 14:1-3; 36:1; 53:2-3; 140:3; Prov 1:16; Isa 59:7-8) in their own contexts reveals that while two have wicked Jews in mind (Ps 5:9; Isa 59:7-8) and the two texts from the wisdom literature appear to be quite general (Eccl 7:20; Prov 1:16), the others are nonspecific (Pss 10:7; 14:1-3; 36:1; 53:2-3; 140:3) and may be understood to refer to the wicked among the Jewish people.[299]

Paul's purpose in listing these quotations is to say that as a people Jews are no better than Gentiles. Paul would certainly know of the many righteous persons spoken of in the OT, not least Abraham, to whom he refers in the next chapter (4:1-25). However, it must be said that such 'righteous' persons are not the morally flawless, but those who have responded with repentance to the goodness of God. Not one of them would have been declared righteous by God because of their peerless behavior. Thus Paul's conclusion that follows in the next verse stands.[300]

---

296. Byrne, *Romans*, 118.

297. Dunn, *Romans 1-8*, 149.

298. Jewett, *Romans*, 263-64.

299. Moyise, 'The Catena of Romans 3:10-18', citing S. L. Edgar, 'Respect for Context in Quotations from the Old Testament', *NTS* 9 (1962-63) 56.

300. Moyise, 'The Catena of Romans 3:10-18', 370, concludes that 'Paul's interpretative comments in Romans 3:9, 19 steer the reader towards the conclusion that all need the gospel, but the old context adds a second voice that God has always been with the righteous and against the wicked'.

(iii) Concluding statement, 3:19-20

19Now we know that whatever the law says, it says to those who are under the law, so that every mouth may be silenced and the whole world held accountable to God. 20Therefore no one will be declared righteous in God's sight by the works of the law; rather, through the law we become conscious of our sin.

3:19   Paul draws the following conclusion from his catena of quotations: *Now we know that whatever the law says, it says to those who are under the law, so that every mouth may be silenced and the whole world held accountable to God.* Paul refers to his catena of quotations as what 'the law' says, using the word 'law' with its widest connotation to include the law, the prophets, and the writings, that is, the entire OT. In fact, none of Paul's quotations are drawn from the Pentateuch, only from Isaiah, Ecclesiastes, Proverbs, and the Psalms (i.e., the prophets and the writings). The 'law', Paul says, is addressed to 'those who are under the law' (lit. 'those [with]in the law'), that is, to Jewish people,[301] and he implies it accuses them of being sinful, 'so that every mouth may be silenced and the whole world held accountable to God'.[302] The verb translated 'to silence' here has the literal meaning 'to shut or close'. When used in relation to a person speaking it means 'to silence' (cf. 1 Macc 9:55; 2 Cor 11:10). In 3:19 the imagery is that of the lawcourt. To stop one's mouth by placing a hand over it signified that one had no more to say in one's defense. If a person who was judged to be clearly guilty continued speaking, the court might order their mouths to be stopped (cf. Acts 23:2: 'At this the high priest Ananias ordered those standing near Paul to strike him on the mouth'). Paul's point is that the Jewish law, by condemning Jewish failures, silences all claims by Jews to be superior to Gentiles.

Once Jewish mouths are silenced and the Jewish people are seen to be no better than Gentiles, then the whole world stands accountable before God and liable to punishment for their evil deeds. Thus, any claim Jewish

301. Herbert Bowsher, 'To Whom Does the Law Speak? Romans 3:19 and the Works of the Law Debate', *WTJ* 68 (2006) 297, is virtually on his own when he argues in respect to 'those who are under the law' in 3:19 that 'it is all mankind that is within the scope of the law', that 'this law is restricted to something very close to the moral law as has been traditionally understood. The ceremonial/restorative law is not in view here', and that 'the indictment of v. 19 includes all mankind, both Jew and Gentile, which dissolves any boundary line between them'.

302. Jewett, *Romans*, 264, comments: 'One thinks of the scene in Nehemiah when Ezra reads the law aloud and "all the people wept when they heard the words of the law" (Neh 8:9, see also 13:3). There was thought to be a responsibility to "hear" the law as it directed its message to individuals: "If one turns away his ear from hearing the law, even his prayer is an abomination" (Prov 28:9). . . . This catena is therefore binding on Jewish people who are "within the law" as well as to all others. In view of the references to "every mouth, "all the world", and "all flesh" in vv. 19-20, Paul's formulation allows no evasions to stand'.

people might make to be more righteous than Gentile people is negated by their own law.

3:20 Following Paul's applicatory conclusion to the scriptural quotations, 'whatever the law says, it says to those who are under the law, so that every mouth may be silenced and the whole world held accountable to God', he draws his general conclusion to the whole of 1:18–3:20: *Therefore no one will be declared righteous in God's sight by the works of the law.*[303] This appears to be an adaptation of Psalm 143:2 ('Do not bring your servant into judgment, for no one living is righteous before you'), to which Paul has added 'by works of law'. Paul's statement, if translated literally, would read, 'all flesh will not be justified before him by works of the law'. The phrase 'all flesh' is used regularly in both the LXX and the NT to denote humankind,[304] and this is most likely the case here as well. If so, Paul is not speaking of individuals but of humankind in general: neither Jewish people nor Gentile people will be declared righteous in God's sight by observing the law.[305]

The verb translated 'to declare righteous' can have four different shades of meaning: (i) to take up a legal cause (e.g., Isa 1:17 LXX), (ii) to render a favorable verdict (e.g., Rom 2:13), (iii) to cause someone to be released from a claim (e.g., Acts 13:38), and (iv) to prove that someone is in the right (Rom 3:4).[306] This verb is found fifteen times in Romans with three of the four shades of meaning listed above. Most frequently it is used to denote a 'favorable verdict' made by God (2:13; 3:20, 24, 26, 28, 30; 4:2, 5; 5:1, 9; 8:30 [2x], 33). Once it is used in reference to being 'set free'/'justified' from sin (6:7), and once in reference to God's being 'proved right' in what he says (3:4). Clearly in 3:20 it is used to denote a favorable verdict by God, something that Paul says is impossible for those who seek it by observing the law. Paul employs the future tense of the verb here, probably indicating that he is thinking of the declaration of God's favorable verdict on the last day.

303. The statement, 'no one will be declared righteous in his sight by the works of the law', translates *ex ergōn nomou ou dikaiōthēsetai pasa sarx enōpion autou*. This is closely paralleled in Galatians 2:16: *ex ergōn nomou ou dikaiōthēsetai pasa sarx*, 'by the works of the law no one will be justified'.

304. Gen 6:12; 7:21; 8:17; 9:11; Pss 65:2; 145:21; Prov 26:10; Job 34:15; Sir 13:16; 14:17; 44:18; Zech 2:13; Isa 40:5; 40:6; 49:26; 66:16, 23; Ezek 20:48; 21:5, 7; Matt 24:22; Mark 13:20; Luke 3:6; 1 Cor 1:29; 15:39; 1 Pet 1:24.

305. Dunn, *Romans 1–8*, 158-59, says: 'In itself the psalm provides a substantial and clinching reference to round off the preceding catena: the psalmist confesses his own liability to judgment because he, like all the rest of humankind, can make no assumption that he will be acquitted or vindicated by God. But Paul makes the point doubly applicable by using a modified text. First, he adds, as again also in Gal 2:16, "by works of law". . . . As a second modification of Ps 143:2, Paul reads "no flesh" instead of "no one living", the point being no doubt that "flesh" denotes man in his weakness and corruptibility, man in his dependence on this world. It is precisely man in his independence from God . . . who can have no hope of acquittal on the day of judgment'.

306. BAGD, *ad loc*.

The expression 'works of law' here in 3:20 is the first of only eight occurrences in Paul's writings (3:20, 28; Gal 2:16 [3x]; 3:2, 5, 10). It is found in no other NT documents or in the LXX. It is a concept that has been variously interpreted: (i) In earlier Protestant exegesis it was understood as obedience to the law carried out by Jewish people with a view to amassing merit that would ensure a favorable verdict from God. (ii) Another view is that 'the works of the law' refers to the observance of the requirements of the law by Jewish people (especially circumcision, Sabbath observance, and the food laws) that distinguished them from the Gentiles, so that being declared righteous in God's sight by observing the law is equivalent to being declared righteous in God's sight because of membership in the Jewish race. (iii) Another alternative is that 'the works of the law' refers to the fulfillment of the law's demands by Jewish people, not in order to secure a favorable verdict from God, but simply because that is what God required of them as his covenant people. In each case 'the works of the law' denotes obedience to the law's requirements, the difference lying in the motive for or the significance of that obedience. In the first case obedience is motivated by the desire to amass merit to secure a favorable verdict from God. It is likely that some Jews adopted this attitude, and Paul's response would then be that no one is able to amass sufficient merit to earn a favorable verdict from God. In the second case obedience has the significance of distinguishing Jews from Gentiles. Again it is likely that some Jews relied upon the fact that they were Jews, God's covenant people, to secure a favorable verdict from God on the last day. Paul's response would then be that Jewish ethnic identity is not enough to guarantee a favorable verdict from God. In the third case obedience is the response of the Jewish people to their covenant God. They obey God's commands simply because they are the commands of their God. Paul's only reservation about this third approach would be that it can easily degenerate into one or other of the other two approaches, as it appears to have done in his own case (cf. Phil 3:3-9). See the discussion in 'Additional Note: The Works of the Law', 173-76.

Paul explains why no one will be declared righteous in God's sight when he adds: *rather, through the law we become conscious of sin* (lit. 'for through law [comes] knowledge of sin'). That observance of the law's requirements should be a means of securing God's favorable verdict (justification) was never intended. In fact, one of the functions of the law was to do the opposite — to make people conscious of their sin. In 7:7 Paul says, 'I would not have known what sin was had it not been for the law. For I would not have known what coveting really was if the law had not said, "You shall not covet"'.[307]

---

307. Clement of Alexandria: 'The law did not create sin; it revealed it' ('Stromata' [*ACCSR*, 95]). Dunn, *Romans 1-8*, 160, holds that the primary function of 3:20b 'is as a criticism of Paul's fellow Jews for their failure to recognize the role of the law as demonstrated in 3:10-18. If they had properly understood the law they would have realized it was not intended to provide a ground of confidence or boasting (2:17, 23), but rather to eliminate such

One problem thrown up by 3:20 is that in it Paul appears to contradict what he said previously. The apparent contradiction is obvious when the two relevant texts are placed one after the other: 'those who obey the law who will be declared righteous' (2:13), 'no one will be declared righteous in God's sight by the works of the law' (3:20). However, the contradiction is more apparent than real. The important thing is to read each text in its own context. In the case of 2:13 Paul is addressing Jewish people who are presuming upon the grace of God while disobeying the law he gave them, whereas that grace of God shown to them should lead to their repentance expressed in obedience to the law. Paul's point is that the mark of Jewish people who are the recipients of God's grace is obedience to his law. Where there is no obedience, there has been no genuine experience of grace. In the case of 3:20 Paul is arguing that no Jewish person will hear God's favorable declaration on the last day because they obey his law. In fact, the law exposes their sin.[308]

ADDITIONAL NOTE: THE WORKS OF THE LAW

Traditionally, Protestant exegesis since the Reformation has understood 'the works of the law' in Paul's writings to denote works by which Jews attempted to amass merit before God in order to be justified. Bultmann suggested that the very attitude behind such an attempt was wrong. Even if people could carry out all that the law demanded, they would not be justified because the underlying attitude itself was sinful.[309]

In the twentieth century there were protests, especially on the part of Jewish scholars (which went unheeded for a long time), against this portrayal of first-century Jewish beliefs.[310] More recently a significant number of NT scholars have conceded that first-century Judaism was not, in principle at least, a religion in which salvation was based upon works of the law. Now efforts are being made to exegete Paul's references to 'works of the law' in new ways.

---

confidence or boasting (cf. 1 Cor 1:29, 31); it was addressed to the covenant people to make them conscious of sin, aware of being under the power of sin even as members of the covenant people (3:9, 19)'.

308. Jean-Noël Aletti, 'Rm 1,18–3,20. Incohérence ou cohérence de l'argumentation paulinienne?' *Bib* 69 (1988) 62, comments: 'In Rom 1:18–3:20 Paul's aim is not to defend divine justice, nor to show that men are culpable and under wrath, but to dismiss all objections to equal retribution for Jew and Greek: the legal framework is of utmost importance. In doing so, Paul can (Rom 3:21 ff) return to the proposition: if we admit that there is no exception with regard to wrath, do we not do the same for the gift of justification?'

309. Bultmann, *Theology of the New Testament*, I, 264. Schreiner, '"Works of Law" in Paul', 219-20, documents the many scholars who have followed Bultmann in this respect.

310. Outstanding among the earlier protesters were Montefiore, Moore, Schoeps, Davies, Stendahl, and Sandmel.

Owen suggests a quite different understanding of 'the works of the law'. He argues that the genitive phrase 'the works of the law' is best taken in a subjective sense: 'The phrase would therefore denote the effects of the Law's activity among humankind since the time of the giving of the Law to Israel. . . . The emphasis in this turn of phrase would then lie not so much on human failure to fully obey the Law (though that is implied) as on the Law's own inability (owing to the gripping power of sin) to produce in people a righteousness that can survive before the bar of God's judgment. The issue is precisely whether the Jewish people are right to place their confidence in the righteousness provided by the Law (Rom 2:17-18; Phil 3:9; cf. Bar 4:4; 2 *Bar.* 48:22)'.[311] While it is true that Paul does speak of the inability of the law to produce righteousness (cf., e.g., Rom 8:3-4; Gal 2:21), that is not the point he is making in either Galatians or Romans when he refers to 'the works of the law'.

Dunn draws attention to the social function of the law for the Jewish people. Their observance of the law distinguished them from the Gentiles, and in particular those aspects of the law that were more obvious: circumcision, Sabbath observance, and dietary rules. These functioned as Jewish identity-markers. Paul did not attack the law as such, nor the observance of the law by Jewish people. What he did attack was the Jewish insistence upon 'the works of the law' in a way that meant that righteousness was defined exclusively in Jewish terms, and so excluded Gentiles.[312] Dunn argues that Paul 'has the devout Jew in view, but not as a type of the universal *homo religiosus* who thinks that his piety somehow puts God in his debt. . . . His target was rather the devout Jew in his presupposition that as a member of the covenant people he could expect God's righteousness to be put forth in his favor because he was "within the law". Nor is Paul attacking a general human presumption that by good works one can earn God's favor, that starting from scratch, as it were, one can achieve God's recognition by hard work. . . . His target was rather the devout Jew who reckoned himself already a member of the covenant people and as such already accepted by God'.[313]

Arguing along similar lines, Wright says: 'The "works" that were regarded in Paul's day as particularly demonstrating covenant membership were, of course, those things that marked out the Jews from their pagan neighbors, not least in the Diaspora: the Sabbath, the food laws, and circumcision. A strong case can therefore be made for seeing "works of the law", in Romans and Galatians, as highlighting these elements in particular. This case rests on the larger thrust of Paul's argument, in which "the

311. Paul L. Owen, 'The "Works of the Law" in Romans and Galatians: A New Defense of the Subjective Genitive', *JBL* 126 (2007) 553-54.
312. Dunn, 'The New Perspective on Paul', 107-11. See his further development of the idea in 'Works of Law', 219-25. A similar approach is adopted by Heiligenthal, 'Soziologische Implikationen der paulinischen Rechtfertigungslehre', 38-53.
313. Dunn, *Romans 1–8*, 154-55.

Jew" is appealing not to perfect performance of every last commandment, but to possession of Torah as the badge of being God's special people. Special they are, but also sinning; and sin means that the specialness is of no ultimate avail'.[314]

The strength of the approach adopted by Dunn and Wright is that it takes note of the fact that 'the works of the law' in view in Galatians in particular involved at least circumcision, calendrical rules (including Sabbaths), and possibly dietary rules as well. It was these things, the Judaizers insisted, that must be observed if the Galatians wished to be true children of Abraham and inheritors of God's promises. What is open to question, however, is whether Paul's critique of the Judaizers' teaching begins and ends with an attack on this sort of understanding of 'the works of the law'. The evidence of Galatians seems to indicate that Paul's critique of the law was far more thoroughgoing than this. It was not restricted to a mere misuse of the law.[315] He believed that the coming of Christ had put an end to the role of the law as a restraining force as far as believers were concerned. In Galatians 3:23-25 Paul speaks about the time before faith came, when 'we' were under the law's guardianship, but when faith came 'we' were no longer under it. The guardianship of the law involved the restraint of the Jewish people in a wide range of religious, moral, and ethical matters, as well as requiring circumcision and the observance of Sabbaths and food laws. When Paul referred to 'the works of the law', then, he had something more than Jewish identity markers in mind. 'The works of the law' is the carrying out of all those things that the law requires.[316] This would seem to be the implication of Paul's words in Galatians 3:10: 'For all who rely on the works of the law are under a curse; for it is written, "Cursed is everyone who does not observe and obey all the things written in the book of the law"'.

In Romans the expression, 'the works of the law', is found only twice: (i) in 3:20 as an addition to Paul's allusion to Psalm 143, and (ii) in 3:28 in the statement, 'For we maintain that a person is justified by faith apart from the works of the law'. When Paul concludes that no flesh would be justified by the works of the law (3:20), it was because even the Jews who had the law failed to observe it. What the apostle had in mind was not their failure to practice circumcision or to observe the special days and seasons laid down in the law. The Jews whom Paul accuses of breaking the law had

314. Wright, 'Romans', 461.

315. Heikki Räisänen, 'Galatians 2.16 and Paul's Break with Judaism', *NTS* 31 (1985) 543-53, argues that 'Paul's critique of the law is more radical than Dunn allows' (544). He points out that just a few verses later Paul spoke of dying to the law that he might live to God (2:19), a statement whose meaning can hardly be exhausted in the notion of a change of attitude to the law as an identity-marker (548).

316. David Flusser, '"Durch das Gesetz dem Gesetz gestorben" (Gal 2,19)', *Judaica* 43 (1987) 34, holds that in Judaism the works of the law belong organically and inseparably with the law itself, and the law is actualized only when its demands are carried out. In other words, the 'works of the law' is the carrying out of the demands of the law. So also Räisänen, *Paul and the Law*, 177; Schreiner, '"Works of Law" in Paul', 232-44.

been circumcised (2:27); their failure in respect of the works of the law was in the moral area:

> You, then, who teach others, do you not teach yourself? You who preach against stealing, do you steal? You who say that people should not commit adultery, do you commit adultery? You who abhor idols, do you rob temples? You who boast in the law, do you dishonor God by breaking the law? (2:21-23)

When Paul says in Romans that 'no one will be declared righteous in God's sight by the works of the law', he means that no one will be justified on account of his/her moral achievements. For even the Jews who were best placed to do this, being instructed by the law so that they knew God's will and could approve what was excellent, failed to perform God's will or practice what was morally excellent. Thus we may conclude that 'the works of the law' in Romans, while not excluding those aspects of the law highlighted in Galatians (circumcision and observance of special days and seasons), denotes primarily the moral demands of the law.[317]

B. God's Saving Righteousness Revealed, 3:21–4:25

Having argued in 1:18–3:20 that the whole world is accountable to God and that no one will be justified by works of the law, in 3:21–4:25 Paul shows that God has revealed his righteousness apart from the law for the salvation of all who believe. God will justify both Jews and Gentiles by grace through faith, thus removing all grounds of illegitimate boasting. He then shows that Abraham was justified by faith and not by any works he performed nor because he was circumcised. The statement that Abraham's faith was credited to him for righteousness was made not for his benefit alone but also for the benefit of all who believe in him who raised Jesus from the dead.

1. The Righteousness of God Revealed, 3:21-31

Paul began his extended theological exposition of the gospel (1:18–11:36) by showing that, apart from the gospel, Jew and Gentile alike are under the

---

317. *Contra* Dunn, 'Works of the Law', 223, who puts it the other way around: '"works of the law" refer not exclusively but particularly to those requirements which bring to sharp focus the distinctiveness of Israel's identity'. More satisfactory is the conclusion reached by Westerholm, *Perspectives Old and New on Paul*, 321: 'We are thus left with the view that the "works of the law" are the deeds demanded by the Sinaitic law code, a law that rests on works'. Cf. C. E. B. Cranfield, '"The Works of the Law" in the Epistle to the Romans', *JSNT* 43 (1991) 93-95; Moo, *Romans*, 207-17; Mark A. Seifrid, *Christ, Our Righteousness: Paul's Theology of Justification* (Downers Grove: InterVarsity Press, 2000), 99-105.

power of sin, accountable to God and exposed to the wrath of God (1:18–3:20). The next step in his exposition is to show that God has revealed his righteousness in providing salvation through the atoning death of Christ for all who believe the gospel, whether they are Jews or Gentiles, that this is independent of the Mosaic law, and that on the human side only faith in Jesus Christ is required (3:21–5:21). Central to this part of Paul's theological exposition is 3:21-26, a passage that expresses the very heart of the gospel, as he understood it. In the original language it is one long sentence, despite the fact that, probably for ease of reading, the NIV has rendered it as five distinct sentences.

It is worth noting that 3:21-26, and indeed 3:27-31 also, is dominated by the theme of the righteousness of God. Paul says that now, apart from the law, the *righteousness of God* has been made known (3:21), a *righteousness of God* given through faith in Jesus Christ to all who believe (3:22). For just as there is no distinction between Jews and Gentiles in the matter of sin and judgment, for all have sinned and lack the glory of God, so both will be *justified/declared righteous* freely by God's grace (3:23-24). This necessitated God's presenting Christ as an atoning sacrifice (3:25a) so as to demonstrate *his righteousness* in the present time, seeing that previously he left sins unpunished (3:25b), and so that he could be both *just/righteous* and the one who *declares righteous* sinners who have faith in Jesus (3:26). Paul insists that Jewish boasting is excluded because all people are *justified/declared righteous* by faith (3:28) and because God will *justify/declare righteous* both Jews and Gentiles by faith (3:30). This extended exposition of how the righteousness of God is revealed in the gospel is, of course, what Romans is all about, and what the apostle stated at the outset: in 1:16-17.[1]

a. The Heart of the Gospel, 3:21-26

> [21]*But now apart from the law the righteousness of God has been made known, to which the Law and the Prophets testify.* [22]*This righteousness is given through faith in Jesus Christ to all who believe. There is no difference between Jew and Gentile,* [23]*for all have sinned and fall short of the glory of God,* [24]*and all are justified freely by his grace through the redemption that came by Christ Jesus.* [25]*God presented Christ as a sacrifice of atonement, through the shedding of his blood — to be received by faith. He did this to demonstrate his righteousness, because in his forbearance he had left the sins committed beforehand unpunished —* [26]*he did it to demonstrate his righteousness at the present time, so as to be just and the one who justifies those who have faith in Jesus.*

1. Wright, 'Romans', 465, commenting on 3:21-25, says: 'The main subject Paul expounds in this section is God's creation of a single worldwide family composed of believing Jews and believing Gentiles alike. Since the main thing standing in the way of this achievement is human sin, the central focus of the paragraph describing how God has done it is the way God has dealt with sin through the death of Jesus'.

It is possible that in 3:21-26 Paul is utilizing an early Christian creed. The passage contains a number of words[2] and concepts[3] not found elsewhere in Paul's letters. However, it is equally possible that Paul penned the words himself, reflecting early Christian understanding of Jesus' death, one that is found also in Hebrews 9–10.

3:21 Having concluded the previous section of his exposition with the statement, 'Therefore no one will be declared righteous in God's sight by the works of the law; rather, through the law we become conscious of sin' (3:20), Paul opens this next section with the words, *But now apart from the law the righteousness of God has been made known, to which the Law and the Prophets testify.* 'But now' is an expression used fourteen times in Paul's letters, sometimes to mark the next step in his argument (7:17; 1 Cor 12:18; 15:20), but most frequently as a temporal marker signaling that what is to follow relates to the present time or situation, in contrast to what pertained in the past (3:21; 6:22; 7:6; 15:23, 25; 1 Cor 13:13; 2 Cor 8:11, 22; Eph 2:13; Col 1:22; 3:8).[4] Here in 3:21 'but now' has been variously interpreted: (i) temporally to denote a new stage in salvation history; (ii) temporally to denote the eschatological present; and (iii) rhetorically to pick up what the apostle foreshadowed in 1:16-17.

Woyke interprets 'but now' here in an exclusively rhetorical manner, arguing that it marks a break with 1:18–3:20 and connects Paul's developing argument back to 1:16-17.[5] There does appear to be a deliberate rhetorical connection back to 1:16-17,[6] but it is best not to see this as exclusively rhetorical.[7] That 'but now' has a temporal function in 3:21 is confirmed by the apostle's use of the fuller expression, 'at the present time', in 3:26, where he speaks again of the demonstration of God's righteousness.[8] What the apostle is affirming is that with the coming of Jesus Christ, his death, resurrection, and the sending of the Spirit, a new age has begun in which the righteousness of God is being revealed apart from the law.[9] This distinguishes it from OT times when the revelation of the righteousness of God was connected to the giving of the law and carried with it the demand of obedience to the law.

The 'righteousness of God' that is 'now' revealed is his saving righteousness, his saving action in Jesus Christ by which human sin is atoned

---

2. *hilastērion* ('atoning sacrifice'), *paresis* ('pardon'), and *proginomai* ('to be past').

3. E.g., the depiction of Christ's death in terms of the great Day of Atonement ritual.

4. Cf. BAGD, *ad loc.*

5. Johannes Woyke, '"Einst" und "Jetzt" in Röm 1–3? Zur Bedeutung von *nyni de* in Röm 3,21', *ZNW* 92 (2001) 206.

6. Compare 1:17: *dikaiosynē gar theou* . . . *apokalyptetai* and 3:21: *dikaiosynē theou pephanerōtai.*

7. Cf. Käsemann, *Romans*, 92; Barrett, *Romans*, 72-73.

8. Cf. Byrne, *Romans*, 123; Moo, *Romans*, 221-22; Cranfield, *Romans*, I, 201; Witherington, *Romans*, 101.

9. Taking *chōris nomou* ('apart from law') to be related to *pephanerōtai* ('revealed'), not with *dikaiosynē theou* ('righteousness of God').

for so that humanity's broken relationship with God may be restored.[10] What this involves is spelled out in the following verses (3:22-26). However, the righteousness of God as his saving activity is only one aspect, albeit a very important one, of the many aspects of the righteousness of God Paul refers to in Romans (see 'Additional Note: The Righteousness of God', 78-81, and the commentary on 1:16-17).

When Paul says that a righteousness of God 'has been made known', he employs the perfect tense of the verb. The perfect tense is employed to denote a state of affairs brought about by the action of the verb. In this case the new state of affairs is that in which the righteousness of God has now been made known;[11] made known when God's saving action in Jesus Christ was revealed.

This revelation of the righteousness of God has been made known 'apart from the law', something which Paul emphasizes by placing 'apart from the law' in the initial position of the sentence. The primary sense of this statement is that God's righteousness has been manifested apart from, that is, without reference to the system of the Mosaic law. As Moo observes correctly, 'it is not the manner in which God's righteousness is *received* that Paul is talking about here, but the manner in which it is *manifested* — the divine side of the "process" by which people are made right with God'.[12] However, the corollary, as Paul will emphasize, is that Gentiles may also enjoy the benefits of God's saving action without having to take on all the obligations of the Mosaic law. That this is implied by Paul's use of 'apart from the law' is confirmed by the use of a similar expression in 3:28, where he says, 'we maintain that a man is justified by faith apart from the works of the law' (lit. 'without works of law').

While the righteousness of God is revealed apart from the law, this does not mean that it is opposed to the law. On the contrary, Paul says, the law and the prophets 'testify' to it. In several other places in Romans the apostle makes this clear. In 1:2 he speaks of 'the gospel he [God] promised beforehand through his prophets in the Holy Scriptures'. In 1:17 he states that 'in the gospel the righteousness of God is revealed — a righteousness that is by faith from first to last' and supports this by a quotation from the prophet Habakkuk: 'The righteous will live by faith' (Hab 2:4). In 4:1-5 Paul appeals to the account of Abraham in the law to show that the faith of the

10. Cf. Fitzmyer, *Romans*, 344, who points out that the righteousness of God here is 'The divine attribute, of which Paul wrote in 1:17 . . . and to which he referred in 3:5' and that 'has now been made known in the eschatological and salvific mission of Jesus Christ. It is God's bounteous and powerful uprightness whereby he acquits his sinful people in a just judgment'. *Contra* Cranfield, *Romans*, I, 202, who interprets 'the righteousness of God' here 'as meaning a status of righteousness before God which is God's gift'.

11. Chrysostom says: 'Paul does not say that the righteousness of God has been *given* but that it has been *manifested*, thus destroying the accusation that it is something new. For what is manifested is old but previously concealed. He reinforces this point by going on to mention that the Law and the Prophets had foretold it' ('Homilies on Romans' [*ACCSR*, 99]).

12. Moo, *Romans*, 223.

Jewish patriarch was credited to him for righteousness without works, stating that 'to the one who does not work but trusts God who justifies the ungodly, their faith is credited as righteousness' (4:5). In 10:6-13 Paul appeals to the law to show that Moses described both 'the righteousness that is by the law' (10:5) and 'the righteousness that is by faith' (10:6).

3:22 Paul further describes the righteousness of God that has now been revealed when he says, *This righteousness is given through faith in Jesus Christ to all who believe.* In the original there is no equivalent for the NIV's 'this', and there is no sentence break between 3:21 and 3:22, the latter being an expansion of Paul's description of the righteousness of God found in the former. The 'righteousness of God' is his saving righteousness (manifested in the sending of his Son) that makes possible his accounting righteous, that is, justification of 'all who believe'. However, this understanding of the text has been called into question.

The NIV's 'through faith in Jesus Christ' translates a phrase that can also be rendered 'through the faithfulness of Jesus Christ'.[13] Both these translations are legitimate renderings of the original, for the Greek noun *pistis* can mean either faith/belief or faithfulness/loyalty. In support of the NIV translation it can be noted that what Paul says in 3:22 expands what he said in 3:21: that the righteousness of God has been revealed 'apart from the law', that is, apart from the obligations laid upon people by the Mosaic law. This is consistent with the translation 'through faith in Jesus Christ', which then indicates the means by which both Jew and Gentile may become recipients of the righteousness (a right relationship with God) made available by God's saving righteousness 'apart from the law'.

In support of the alternate rendition ('through the faithfulness of Jesus Christ') it can be noted that in 3:24 the apostle tells how justification comes through 'the redemption that came by Christ Jesus', and in 5:18-19 he explains that it was through the one act of righteousness, the obedience of one man, that many were made righteous. Thus it could be said that the saving action of God of which the apostle speaks in 3:21-22 is to be seen in the faithfulness of Jesus Christ's obedience to the will of the Father in giving himself as the atoning sacrifice for sin. The second option would not negate Paul's emphasis upon the importance of faith in Jesus Christ, because having said that 'this righteousness is given through the faithfulness of Jesus Christ', he adds immediately that this is 'to all who believe'. The second option has been taken up and defended by a number of influential interpreters of Paul in recent years, interpreters who argue that if the first option ('faith in Jesus Christ' — objective genitive) is adopted, the words that follow, 'to all who believe', would be redundant.[14]

---

13. The inclusion of the article *tēs* in the expression *dia* [*tēs*] *pisteōs Iēsou Christou* ('through [the] faith of Jesus Christ') in some manuscripts is consistent with this rendering, as its omission in other manuscripts is consistent with the previous rendering, though neither is decisive.

14. So, e.g., Wright, 'Romans', 470; Richard B. Hays, *The Faith of Jesus Christ: An Inves-*

However, defenders of the first option respond by pointing out that what we have in 3:22 is not a redundancy but repetitive emphasis. Carson argues that the redundancy disappears once it is recognized that 'there is a profound reason for this repetition, viz. the prepositional phrase "for all". The point may be demonstrated by the somewhat paraphrastic rendering, "This righteousness from God comes through faith in Jesus Christ — to *all* who have faith in him"'.[15] A growing number of scholars support this option.[16] This has been argued at length by Matlock who claims, in the light of the fact that 3:22 is an amplification of 3:21, that the repetition is not out of place.[17] It is this approach that is adopted in this commentary, especially because it is consistent with Paul's overall purpose in 1:18–4:25 to expound what it means to be accounted righteous, by faith.

What Paul means by 'all who believe' is made clear by what he says next: [*for*] *there is no difference between Jew and Gentile*. Unfortunately the NIV makes a new sentence of this, omitting the coordinating conjunction 'for'. Paul's point is that this righteousness from God through faith is for all who believe, both Jews and Gentiles, because there is no distinction between them in the crucial matter of their standing before God (cf. 1:16). A similar point is made in 10:12: 'For there is no difference between Jew and Gentile — the same Lord is Lord of all and richly blesses all who call on him'.

3:23-24   These verses continue Paul's thought from 3:22, there being no sentence break at the end of the verse 'there is no difference between Jew and Gentile, *for all have sinned and fall short of the glory of God*'. There is no difference in the matter of sin and judgment between Jews and Gentiles because 'all have sinned'. That 'all' have sinned is something Paul has already established — in respect to humanity in general, particularly

---

tigation of the Narrative Substructure of Galatians 3.1–4.11 (SBLDS 56; Chico, Calif.: Scholars Press, 1983), 171; 'PISTIS and Pauline Christology: What Is at Stake?', in *Pauline Theology, IV: Looking Back, Pressing On*, ed. Elizabeth Johnson and David M. Hay (Atlanta: Scholars Press, 1997), 46; Stowers, *A Rereading of Romans*, 353 n. 4; Douglas A. Campbell, *The Rhetoric of Righteousness in Romans 3.21-26* (JSNTSup 65; Sheffield, UK: JSOT Press, 1992), 62-63; Witherington, *Romans*, 101.

15. Donald A. Carson, 'Why Trust a Cross? Reflections on Romans 3:21-26', *ERT* 28 (2004) 351.

16. So, e.g., Fitzmyer, *Romans*, 345; Dunn, *Romans 1–8*, 166-67; Moo, *Romans*, 225; Byrne, *Romans*, 124-25; Jewett, *Romans*, 275.

17. R. Barry Matlock, 'The Rhetoric of *pistis* in Paul: Galatians 2.16; 3.22, Romans 3.22, and Philippians 3.9', *JSNT* 30 (2007) 184, notes that 'not only is *pas*, in its own right, a thematic word in Romans (1.5, 16; 2.9-10; 3.9, 19-20, 22-23; 4.11, 16; 5.12, 18; 10.4, 11-13; 11.26, 32 . . .); it also keeps some interesting company with *pisteuō*: in addition to *eis pantas tous pisteuontas* in Rom. 3.22, we have *panti tō pisteuonti* (1.16), *pantōn tōn pisteuontōn* (4.11) and *pas ho pisteuōn* (10.11). But more than just this general emphasis on "all" in Romans, and more even than the repeated combination of *pas* and *ho pisteuōn*, is the matter of Paul's emphasis at this precise point: *ou gar estin diastolē, pantes gar hēmarton kai hysterountai tēs doxēs tou theou*, "for there is no distinction, since all have sinned and fall short of the glory of God" (3.23, the fifth repetition of *pas* in as many verses). In addition to all this, Rom. 3.22 is formally an amplification of v. 21, in which case repetition might not be thought out of place'.

Gentiles, in 1:18-32, and in respect to those who take the high moral ground, particularly Jews, in 2:1–3:19.

Not only have all sinned, but all 'fall short of the glory of God' as well. 'Fall short' is the present passive form (with active meaning) of a verb Paul uses seven times elsewhere in his letters to indicate either a lack of something (1 Cor 1:7; 8:8; 2 Cor 11:9; Phil 4:12) or to be inferior to something or someone (1 Cor 12:24; 2 Cor 11:5; 12:11). In 3:23 he uses it to mean 'lack something', in this case to say that human beings lack the glory of God, by which Paul means that they lack the original glory that they had being created in the image of God. The *Apocalypse of Moses* (the Greek translation of the *Life of Adam and Eve,* dating from the first century A.D.) depicts Eve crying in despair to the serpent that tempted her to eat the forbidden fruit in the Garden of Eden: 'And I wept saying, "Why have you done this to me, that I have been estranged from my glory with which I was clothed?"' (*Apoc. Mos.* 20:2-3), and it also depicts Adam reproaching Eve for giving him the same fruit to eat: 'O evil woman! Why have you wrought destruction among us? You have estranged me from the glory of God' (*Apoc. Mos.* 21:6).[18] Humanity's lost glory, Paul believes, will be restored in the future. He speaks in 5:2 of believers boasting in their 'hope of the glory of God', in 1 Corinthians 2:7 of the wisdom of God 'destined for our glory before time began', and in Colossians 1:27 of Christ in the Gentiles as their 'hope of glory', and, finally, in 1 Thessalonians 2:12 he reminds believers that God calls them 'into his kingdom and glory'. It would appear, then, that the status humanity enjoyed, being created in 'the image and glory of God', was marred by sin so that Paul can say, 'all have sinned and fall short of the glory of God'. But in the case of believers this status is in process of being restored as they are being transformed from one degree of glory to another (2 Cor 3:18), and it will be restored fully when their hope of sharing in the glory of God reaches its consummation in the new age (8:18-21, 30; cf. 1 John 3:2-3).

Having insisted that there is no distinction between Jews and Gentiles in the matter of sin — they have all sinned and all fall short of the glory of God — Paul adds that there is likewise no distinction in the matter of salvation: *and all are justified freely by his grace through the redemption that came by Christ Jesus.* In 3:20 Paul concluded that 'no one will be declared righteous in God's sight by the works of the law', but now he declares that a righteousness of God has been made known apart from the law so that he can say that all (both Jews and Gentiles) 'are justified freely by his grace'. Here in 3:24 the verb 'to justify' means to render a favorable verdict. It is by God's grace that he justifies/renders a favorable verdict for all who put their faith in his Son, Christ Jesus.[19] Later in the letter (5:1-11; 8:28-39) Paul

18. Citations from James H. Charlesworth, ed., *The Old Testament and Pseudepigrapha,* Vol. 2 (New York: Doubleday, 1985), 281.

19. By describing God's Son as 'Christ Jesus' (rather than 'Jesus Christ') Paul emphasizes that it is through 'the *Messiah,* Jesus' that redemption was effected.

will spell out in more detail what it means to be justified by God's grace (see the commentary on these passages below).

Justification properly belongs to the last judgment. It is then that God will render his final verdict upon human beings. In the case of those who have believed in his Son it will be a favorable verdict. While it is on the Last Day that God's 'righteous judgment will be revealed' (2:5), Paul notes that for believers this is anticipated in the present. Accordingly, he can say in 5:1-2a: 'Therefore, since we have been justified through faith, we have peace with God through our Lord Jesus Christ, through whom we have gained access by faith into this grace in which we now stand'.[20] Marshall describes what it means to be justified as being 'put into a right relationship with God, in which the sins that persons have committed are no longer counted against them and consequently they can enter into a relationship with God characterized by peace and not by wrath'.[21]

Paul maintains that believers are justified 'freely'. The apostle uses the adverb 'freely' normally to mean without cost or without payment (cf. 2 Cor 11:7; 2 Thess 3:8). In the present context, where he is emphasizing that a righteousness of God is revealed 'apart from law', to be justified 'freely' means to be justified without the added demand to observe the law of Moses.

When Paul adds that believers are justified 'by his grace', he introduces one of his favorite theological concepts. He speaks of God's grace in many different connections (see 'Additional Note: Grace [*Charis*]', 185-86), but here in 3:24 the context makes clear that he has in mind God's grace manifested 'through the redemption that came by Christ Jesus'. The word translated 'redemption' is found ten times in the NT (Luke 21:28; Rom 3:24; 8:23; 1 Cor 1:30; Eph 1:7, 14; 4:30; Col 1:14; Heb 9:15; 11:35) and only once in the LXX (Dan 4:34). The LXX uses cognates of redemption quite extensively,[22] and these provide important background information for his un-

---

20. Cf. Wright, 'Romans', 471. Barrett, *Romans*, 75-76, rejects the popular notion that to justify means to treat people as righteous, first, because 'it ignores the fact that behind Paul's Greek verb there lies a Hebrew verb, to which the Greek of the LXX points. This Hebrew verb *(hitzdiq)* is in the Hiph'il form, which is regularly causative in meaning; it cannot possibly be weakened so far as to mean 'to treat as righteous'. Second, because doctrinally, 'it may be said that this account of justification must lead either to Pelagianism (since faith itself will be treated as a righteous work, or at least as righteousness in germ), or to the kind of legal fiction which men feel instinctively is not legitimate even for God, if he be a moral being. Not even he may pretend that black is white'. Instead, he says, 'It is far better, and more in harmony with Paul's teaching as a whole, to suppose that "to justify" *(dikaioun)* does mean "to make righteous", but at the same time to recognize that "righteous" does not mean "virtuous", but "right", "clear", "acquitted" in God's court. Justification then means no legal fiction but an act of forgiveness on God's part, described in terms of the proceedings of a law court. Far from being a legal fiction, this is a creative act in the field of divine-human relations'.

21. I. H. Marshall, *New Testament Theology: Many Witnesses, One Gospel* (Downers Grove, Ill.: InterVarsity Press, 2004), 310.

22. The following cognate words are found frequently in the LXX: *lytron*/redemption — twenty times; *lytrōsis*/redemption — twelve times; *lytrōtēs*/redeemer — four times, and

derstanding of redemption. This includes the redemption of the firstborn by the payment of the redemption price, an individual's redemption from slavery also by the payment of a redemption price, as well as Israel's redemption from slavery in Egypt and her exile in Assyria and Babylon. More important for our purposes, however, is what may be gleaned from the contexts in which Paul uses the verb 'to redeem' and the noun 'redemption'. He uses the verb 'to redeem' when speaking of people being delivered 'from all wickedness' (Tit 2:14). In its context here it appears to mean deliverance from the power of sin, from slavery to sin.[23] He uses the noun 'redemption' in two places where he equates redemption with the forgiveness of sins (Eph 1:7; Col 1:14),[24] which implies that believers are redeemed from the effects of their sins, namely God's condemnation. In three places redemption is spoken of as taking place on the last day (Rom 8:23; Eph 1:14; 4:30) and involves the 'redemption of our bodies' (Rom 8:23).[25] Because, as the apostle affirms here in 3:24, this redemption 'came by Jesus Christ', he

---

lytroō/to redeem — 108 times. The idea of redemption found in the use of the *lytr-* word group in the LXX can be described as follows: (i) *lytrōtēs* (redeemer) is used twice of God himself as Redeemer of David and of Israel, and twice of the Levites who have the rights as redeemers of their houses in the year of jubilee; (ii) the nouns *lytron/lytrōsis/apolytrōsis* (redemption) are used four times for the redemption price for a person's life, seven times for the redemption price of the firstborn's life, four times for the redemption price of slaves, three times for the redemption price of houses or land, four times for the redemption of Israel by God, once for the redemption price of the tithe, twice to deny the possibility of accepting a redemption price for a murderer, once to warn that a man will not accept a redemption price from someone who has committed adultery with his wife, once to say that Cyrus will release the exiles without a redemption price being paid, and once to refer to the time of Nebuchadnezzar's restoration; (iii) the verb *lytroō*/to redeem is used fifty-two times in relation to God as the redeemer of Israel (especially from Egyptian bondage), twice for the redemption of the firstborn sons, six times for the redemption of animals, four times for the redemption of slaves, six times for the redemption of houses and land, twice for the redemption of devoted things, once for the redemption of a tithe, fourteen times for the redemption of individuals from trouble or their enemies, once of Nebuchadnezzar being exhorted to deliver the oppressed, and once of the impossibility of a person redeeming the life of another or giving God a ransom for him. Paul uses only one of these cognates *(lytroō)*, and that only once (Tit 2:14).

23. Moo, *Romans*, 229-30, comments: 'in the second and first centuries B.C., "redemption" often refers to the "ransoming" of prisoners of war, slaves, and condemned criminals. If "redemption" has this connotation here, then Paul would be presenting Christ's death as a "ransom", a "payment" that takes the place of the penalty for sins "owed" by all people to God. . . . While it is not clear whether Paul was thinking specifically of slave manumissions when he applied the word to Christian salvation, it is likely that Paul views sin as that power from which we need to be liberated (cf. 3:9)'.

24. Heb 9:15 also speaks of redemption in terms of forgiveness of sins: 'For this reason Christ is the mediator of a new covenant, that those who are called may receive the promised eternal inheritance — now that he has died as a ransom *(apolytrōsin)* to set them free from the sins committed under the first covenant'.

25. In Luke 21:28 Jesus also speaks of redemption as a future event: 'When these things begin to take place, stand up and lift up your heads, because your redemption is drawing near'.

can also say that Christ 'has become for us wisdom from God — that is, our righteousness, holiness and redemption' (1 Cor 1:30).[26]

Summing up, we can say that Paul's understanding of redemption is primarily freedom from sin's penalty (= forgiveness) and power, and this in the present time. While redemption is experienced to a certain extent in the present time, it will be fully realized on the last day and will include the 'redemption of our bodies', that is, resurrection to immortality. There was a price paid for this redemption, as Paul will explain in the next verse (3:25): God had to set forth his own Son as an atoning sacrifice.

ADDITIONAL NOTE: GRACE *(CHARIS)*

The word *charis* is used extensively also in the LXX (132 times in 128 verses). Most frequently (70 times in 68 verses) it translates the Hebrew word *ḥēn*, meaning 'favor', and it is often found in expressions such as 'to find favor in someone's eyes'. When people found favor, it usually meant that the one showing favor would act to meet their needs or deliver them from their troubles (cf., e.g., Gen 6:8; 39:4; Exod 12:36; Num 11:15; 32:5; 1 Sam 20:29; Jer 31:2).

The word *charis* is found one hundred times (in 95 verses) in Paul's letters, signifying that it represented a most important theological concept for him. With only nine exceptions (where *charis* is used of the kindness shown by believers[27] or to express thanks),[28] it denotes the grace of God. It is found frequently in the opening and closing greetings of Paul's letters (e.g., in 1 Cor 1:3: 'Grace and peace to you from God our Father',[29] but most often to refer to God's goodwill expressed in action for the benefit of believers.[30]

Paul speaks of God's grace, God's goodwill expressed in action, in

---

26. Origen's comment on the meaning of redemption is as follows; '*Redemption* is the word used for what is given to enemies in order to ransom captives and restore them to their liberty. Therefore human beings were held in captivity by their enemies until the coming of the Son of God, who became for us not only the wisdom of God, and righteousness and sanctification, but also redemption. He gave himself as our redemption, that is, he surrendered himself to our enemies and poured out his blood on those who were thirsting for it. In this way redemption was obtained for believers' ('Commentary on the Epistle to the Romans' [*ACCSR*, 101]). The latter part of Origen's comment, that Christ 'surrendered himself to our enemies and poured out this blood on those who were thirsting for it', goes well beyond what Scripture says about Christ's death as a ransom.

27. 2 Cor 8:6, 7, 19; Col 4:6.

28. 1 Cor 15:57; 2 Cor 8:16; 9:15; 1 Tim 1:12; 2 Tim 1:3.

29. Cf. Rom 16:20; 1 Cor 16:23; 2 Cor 1:2; 13:14; Gal 1:3; 6:18; Eph 1:2; 6:24; Phil 1:2; 4:23; Col 1:2; 4:18; 1 Thess 1:1; 5:28; 2 Thess 1:2; 3:18; 1 Tim 1:2; 6:21; 2 Tim 1:2; 4:22; Tit 1:4; 3:15; Philem 3, 25.

30. Cf. Rom 1:5; 3:24; 4:16; 5:15, 17, 20, 21; 6:1, 14, 15; 11:5, 6; 12:3, 6; 15:15; 1 Cor 1:4; 3:10; 15:10; 2 Cor 1:12; 4:15; 6:1; 8:1, 9; 9:8, 14; 12:9; Gal 1:6, 15; 2:9, 21; 5:4; Eph 1:6, 7; 2:5, 7, 8; 3:2, 7, 8; 4:7; Phil 1:7; Col 1:6; 2 Thess 1:12; 2:16; 1 Tim 1:14; 2 Tim 1:9; 2:1; Tit 2:11; 3:7.

many different connections. He mentions it in relation to (i) his own calling and empowering to be an apostle (1:5; 12:3; 15:15; 1 Cor 3:10; 15:10; 2 Cor 1:12; 2:14; 12:9; Gal 2:9; Eph 3:2, 7-8; 1 Tim 1:14), (ii) the calling of believers to faith in Christ through the gospel (Gal 1:6); (iii) God's gift of salvation and justification (3:24; 5:15, 17; 2 Tim 1:9; Tit 2:11; 3:7); (iv) God's empowering of believers (2 Tim 2:1); (v) the fulfillment of God's promises and the hope he places before believers (4:16; 2 Thess 2:16); (vi) the standing believers have before God (5:2; 6:1, 14-15); (vii) God's redemptive activity through Christ (5:20-21; 2 Cor 4:15; 6:1; 8:9; Gal 2:21; 5:4; Eph 1:6-7; 2:5, 7-8; Phil 1:7; Col 1:6; 2 Thess 1:12); (viii) God's choice of the faithful remnant (Rom 11:5-6); (ix) God's gifts of ministry (Rom 12:6; Eph 4:7); and (x) God's work enabling generosity and concern for others in the lives of believers (2 Cor 8:1, 6-7, 16; 9:8, 14).[31]

3:25a For the sake of easy reading in English, the NIV renders 3:25a as a new sentence: *God presented Christ as a sacrifice of atonement, through the shedding of his blood — to be received by faith.* In fact, 3:25b is a continuation of the one long sentence, 3:21-26, and, literally translated, may be rendered: 'whom God put forward as an atoning sacrifice through faith in his blood'. In 3:24b Paul said that 'redemption came through Christ Jesus'. In 3:25a he emphasizes that the initiative for providing this redemption lay with God. He paid the redemption price. He it was who presented Christ as 'a sacrifice of atonement'. As P. T. Forsyth comments, 'The prime doer in Christ's cross was God. Christ was God reconciling. He was God doing the very best for man, and not man doing his very best before God'.[32]

The verb here translated 'presented' can mean either 'to set forth publicly' or 'to plan or purpose'. It is used with this latter sense in the two other places where it is found in Paul's writings (1:13; Eph 1:9), and it should probably be construed in this way here too, thus referring to God's eternal purpose rather than his setting something forth publicly.[33]

The word translated 'sacrifice of atonement' *(hilastērion)* is found only twice in the NT, in Hebrews 9:5 and here in 3:25. Its precise meaning is the subject of some debate. Possible meanings include: the removal of guilt and the purifying of the sinner (expiation),[34] the appeasing of God's wrath to-

---

31. BAGD, *ad loc.*, has the following comment regarding 'the practical application of God's goodwill': 'The context will show whether the emphasis is upon the *possession of divine favor* as a source of blessings for the believer, or upon a *store of favor* that is dispensed, or a *favored status* (i.e. standing in God's favor) that is brought about, or a *gracious deed* wrought by God in Christ, or a *gracious work* that grows fr. more to more'.

32. P. T. Forsyth, *The Cruciality of the Cross* (2nd ed.; London: Independent Press, 1948), 17.

33. Cf. Cranfield, *Romans*, I, 209.

34. So, e.g., C. H. Dodd, 'HILASKESTHAI, Its Cognates, Derivatives, and Synonyms, in the Septuagint', *JTS* 32 (1931) 360; T. C. G. Thornton, 'Propitiation or Expiation?' *ExpTim* 80 (1968-69) 54-55; Campbell, *The Rhetoric of Righteousness*, 188-89.

wards sinners (propitiation),[35] and as an allusion to the mercy seat in the tabernacle[36] (see 'Additional Note: *Hilastērion*', 188-91). It is certainly true that the death of Christ makes possible the removal of guilt and the purifying of sinners. However, in the context of Romans where Paul says that 'the wrath of God is being revealed from heaven against all the godlessness and wickedness of men' (1:18), and where he warns those who judge others for their sins while practicing the same things themselves that they are storing up wrath against themselves on the day God's wrath (2:5), the idea of propitiation cannot be excluded from Paul's use of *hilastērion* here in 3:25.[37] It must be stressed that the context makes clear that this must not be thought of in pagan terms to mean overcoming the wrath of a hostile god, for it is God himself who takes the initiative in providing his own Son as the atoning sacrifice for our sins.[38]

The apostle says that God presented his Son as a sacrifice of atonement 'through the shedding of his blood — to be received by faith', the literal translation of which is 'through faith in his blood'. Nowhere else in Paul's letters is the blood of Christ the object of faith, so this is unlikely to be what he intends here. There have been a number of suggestions for resolving the interpretive difficulties presented by this text:

(i) If 'faith' is removed, the phrase would be more straightforward, referring simply then to a sacrifice of atonement 'through his blood'. Käsemann argues that 'faith' is a rather clumsy insertion by Paul into the traditional formula he cites in 3:24-26 so as 'to relate salvation and faith to one another'.[39] However, if we are not prepared to account for the difficulty in terms of clumsiness on Paul's part, we need to look for other alternatives.

(ii) Bearing in mind that *pistis* can carry the meaning of either 'faith' or 'faithfulness', it has been suggested that the text be rendered as follows: God presented his Son as a sacrifice of atonement through the *faithfulness* of Christ in allowing his blood to be spilled.[40] This re-

---

35. So, e.g., Leon Morris, *The Apostolic Preaching of the Cross* (3rd ed.; London: Tyndale, 1965), 206; David Hill, *Greek Words and Hebrew Meanings: Studies in the Semantics of Soteriological Terms* (Cambridge: Cambridge University Press, 1967), 37-38.

36. So, e.g., Nico S. L. Fryer, 'The Meaning and Translation of *Hilastērion* in Romans 3:25', *EvQ* 59 (1987) 105-11.

37. To adopt this interpretation would not exclude allusions to the 'mercy seat', as in the OT it was on the mercy seat that the blood of the sacrifice was sprinkled on the great Day of Atonement (Lev 16:14-17).

38. Cf. Rom 8:32: 'He who did not spare his own Son, but gave him up for us all — how will he not also, along with him, graciously give us all things?" Carson, 'Why Trust a Cross?' 353-59, provides a helpful discussion of these matters.

39. Käsemann, *Romans*, 98. Similarly Byrne, *Romans*, 133; Cranfield, *Romans*, I, 210.

40. Cf. Bruce W. Longenecker, '*Pistis* in Romans 3.25: Neglected Evidence for the "Faithfulness of Christ"?' *NTS* 39 (1993), 479-80; Wright, 'Romans', 476-77. P. Richard Choi, 'The Problem of Translating *en tō autou haimati* in Romans 3:25a', *AUSS* 38 (2000) 201, adopts

moves the need to regard 'his blood' as the object of faith. The problem with this view is that it overlooks the fact that Paul's overall purpose in this passage is to stress that both Jews and Gentiles are on the same footing as far as justification is concerned — both are justified by faith in Jesus Christ.

(iii) If 'in his blood' is regarded as descriptive of the 'sacrifice of atonement' and 'through faith' as expressing the means by which people access its benefits, the NIV rendition of the text becomes possible: 'God presented Christ as a sacrifice of atonement, through the shedding of his blood — to be received by faith'.[41]

(iv) In similar fashion, but with a slight variation, 'in his blood' could be regarded as descriptive of the action of the verb 'presented', with 'through faith' again expressing the means by which people access the benefits. This is the view espoused by Fitzmyer, who offers the following translation: 'Through his blood God has presented him as a means of expiating sin for all who have faith'.[42]

Either the third or fourth alternative appears preferable to the first or second, because they are consistent with the overall thrust of 3:21-31, which is to stress that faith is the prerequisite for justification in the case of both Jews and Gentiles.

ADDITIONAL NOTE: *HILASTĒRION*

Formally, *hilastērion* is a neuter form of the adjective *hilastērios*, used in both the LXX and the NT always as a substantive, with only one exception found in the LXX, where it is used adjectivally.[43] *Hilastērion* is found twenty-eight times in the LXX, where it refers to the mercy seat in the tabernacle, the only exceptions being one reference in Amos (9:1) that the NIV translates as 'the tops of the pillars', and three in Ezekiel (43:14, 17, 20) that the NIV translates as 'ledge'. *Hilastērion* is found in only two places in the NT, here in 3:25 and in Hebrews 9:5, and in both places it functions as a substantive. In Hebrews 9:5 it denotes the mercy seat in the tabernacle (translated 'atonement cover' in the NIV).

---

a similar position, arguing that the phrase *en tō haimati* is best translated 'with his blood', resulting in the following rendition of 3:25a: 'whom God set forth as the mercy seat . . . with his blood (upon it)'. . . . Accordingly, the rendition "with his blood" would mean that we translate *dia [tēs] pisteōs* as "through (his) (covenant) faithfulness", which is also in keeping with the fragment's Jewish character'.

41. Cf. Moo, *Romans*, 236-37.
42. Fitzmyer, *Romans*, 341.
43. Exod 25:17: *poiēseis hilastērion epithema chrysiou* ('make an atonement cover of pure gold'). Cf. Fryer, 'The Meaning and Translation of *Hilastērion*', 100-104.

The cognate verb *hilaskomai* is found twelve times in the LXX, where it nearly always means to forgive (people their sins). It is found twice in the NT, once in Luke 18:13 where it means to forgive, and once in Hebrews 2:17 where it means to make atonement for sins.

The cognate verb, *exhilaskesthai* is not found in the NT, but it is found 105 times in the LXX in ninety-seven verses. These include several texts where *exhilaskesthai* denotes atonement that involves cleansing the sinner (e.g., Lev 12:7, 8; 14:18, 20, 29, 31, 53; 15:30; Num 8:21); many others where atonement effects forgiveness (e.g., Lev 4:20, 26, 31, 35; 5:10, 13, 16, 18; 6:7; 19:22; Num 15:28; Pss 65:3; 78:38; 79:9; Isa 22:14; Jer 18:23; Ezek 16:23); and several more where atonement means removal of wrath (Gen 32:20; Exod 30:12; 32:30; Num 8:19; 17:11 [E.T. 16:46]; 35:31; Prov 16:4; Isa 47:11).

The cognate *hilasmos* is found six times in the LXX, indicated by the italicized words in the descriptions of its use in the relevant texts which follow: Leviticus 25:9, referring to the Day of *Atonement;* Numbers 5:8, used in connection with the ram with which *atonement* is made for the wrongdoer; Psalm 129:4 (E.T. 130:4), where the psalmist rejoices that God does not keep a record of sins and that there is *forgiveness* with him; Amos 8:14, a strange use of the word in reference to those who swear by the *sin* of Samaria; Ezekiel 44:27, referring to the *sin offering* a priest must make for his own sins, and 2 Maccabees 3:33, referring to the high priest making the *offering of atonement.* In addition to these six occurrences of *hilasmos* there is one more in a variant reading of Daniel 9:9, which speaks of the mercies and *forgivenesses* of the Lord. It is found only twice in the NT, both in 1 John. The first is in 1 John 2:1-2: 'But if anybody does sin, we have an advocate with the Father — Jesus Christ, the Righteous One. He is the *atoning sacrifice* [*hilasmos*] for our sins'. In this context *hilasmos* is found in juxtaposition with the idea of advocacy. Jesus is the one who speaks to the Father in our defense when we sin. He is, as it were, pleading for mercy to be shown to us, and this suggests that his role as the atoning sacrifice is to secure that mercy; in other words, in this context *hilasmos* means propitiation.[44] Though 1 John 2:2 does support the idea of propitiation, this must not be thought of in pagan terms as the overcoming of the wrath of a hostile god because, as 1 John 4:10 makes clear, it was God himself who provided his Son as the atoning sacrifice for our sins.

The *hilastērion* cognates in both the LXX and the NT for the most part

---

44. Georg Strecker, *The Johannine Letters* (Hermeneia; Philadelphia: Fortress, 1996), 39, n. 17, argues that the idea of propitiation cannot be excluded in this context because 'it accords with the preceding argumentation', in particular the reference to the blood of Jesus (1:7) and purification (1:9). The idea of a life given for propitiation of the sins of others is also found in 4 Macc 6:26-29, where the dying martyr asks that his punishment might suffice for his people, that his blood might effect their purification, that his life might be accepted in exchange for theirs. There is, of course, a great difference between the death of the martyrs (who, though godly, were yet sinners themselves) and the death of Christ (who is described as the righteous one).

relate to atonement and forgiveness. In many cases they denote cleansing from or forgiveness of sins, and in a significant number of the uses of *exhilaskesthai* appeasing of wrath is clearly intended. The indications are that the notion of atonement in the OT is best understood comprehensively to include both the cleansing and forgiveness of the sinner, and the turning away of God's anger. All this suggests that neither the idea of expiation nor that of propitiation can be ruled out as possible meanings for *hilastērion* in 3:25. In determining the meaning of *hilastērion* in 3:25 it is to its immediate and wider context in Romans that we must appeal. As noted in the commentary on 3:25a above, the wider context forbids ruling out the notion of propitiation.

There has been widespread debate concerning whether *hilastērion* in 3:25 is best interpreted to mean propitiation or expiation or both. Byrne is one who denies the propitiatory sense, focusing instead upon the expiatory effect of Christ's death: 'From the outset it has to be said that such cannot be the meaning here since. . . . God is the subject of the action, and it makes no sense to speak of any personage, divine or human, appeasing his or her own wrath. The verb form, chiefly in the composite *exhilaskesthai*, appears frequently in the LXX as a translation of the Hebrew *kippēr* to express the removal or expiation of human sin on the part of God or God's accredited agent (the priest). . . . The most secure translation of the indeterminate *hilastērion* occurring in v. 25 is simply "a means of expiation". Nonetheless, echoes of the "Day of Atonement" ritual are almost certainly present. Paul . . . sees God as instituting in Christ the culminating exercise of the "Day of Atonement" expiation and renewal'.[45]

Dunn argues that both expiation and propitiation are included in Paul's reference to Christ as the *hilastērion* in 3:25: 'The older dispute as to whether *hilastērion* should be rendered "propitiation" or "expiation" . . . has also suffered from an unnecessary polarizing of alternatives. . . . Assuredly, the logic of Paul's exposition is that the wrath of God (expounded in 1:18–3:20) is somehow averted by Jesus' death (cf. 2 Macc 7:38), but the passage also portrays God as offerer of the sacrifice rather than its object'. . . .[46] Wright's view is essentially the same: 'You propitiate a person who is angry; you expiate a sin, crime, or stain on your character. Vehement rejection of the former idea in many quarters has led some to insist that only "expiation" is in view here. But the fact remains that in 1:18–3:20 Paul has declared that the wrath of God is revealed against all ungodliness and wickedness and that despite God's forbearance this will finally be meted out; that in 5:9, and in the whole promise of 8:1-30, those who are Christ's are rescued from wrath; and that the passage in which the reason for the change is stated is 3:25-26, where we find that God, though in forbearance allowing sins to go unpunished for a while, has now revealed that righ-

45. Byrne, *Romans*, 126-27.
46. Dunn, *Romans 1–8*, 171.

teousness, that saving justice, that causes people to be declared "righteous" even though they were sinners'.[47] Barrett's view ends up being similar: 'We can hardly doubt (since Paul says that God set forth Christ in this capacity) that expiation rather than propitiation is in his mind; though it would be wrong to neglect the fact that expiation has, as it were, the effect of propitiation: the sin that might justly have excited God's wrath is expiated (at God's will), and therefore no longer does so'.[48] Moo interprets 3:25 along similar lines: 'The OT frequently connects the "covering", or forgiving, of sins with the removal of God's wrath. It is precisely the basic connotation of "propitiate" that led the translators of the LXX to use the *hilask-* words for the Hebrew words denoting the covering of sins. This is not, however, to deny the connotation "expiation"; the OT cult serves to "wipe away" the guilt of sin at the same time as — and indeed, because — the wrath of God is being stayed. When to the linguistic evidence we add the evidence of the context of Rom. 1–3, where the wrath of God is an overarching theme (1:18; cf. 2:5), the conclusion that *hilastērion* includes reference to the turning away of God's wrath is inescapable'.[49] Cranfield and Witherington argue that the idea of propitiation is primary.[50] In the light of the overall argument of 1:18–3:26 that includes reference to the wrath of God, the idea of propitiation should be retained alongside that of expiation. Christ's atoning sacrifice is effective both in removing God's wrath towards sinners and in removing the stain of their sins.

3:25b Paul states that it was necessary for God to present his Son as an atoning sacrifice *to demonstrate his righteousness,* something necessitated

47. Wright, 'Romans', 476.
48. Barrett, *Romans*, 77-78.
49. Moo, *Romans*, 235.
50. Cranfield, *Romans*, I, 215-17; Witherington, *Romans*, 108-9. Jewett, *Romans*, 285-86, is on his own when he argues against all notions of atonement in 3:25, whether expiatory or propitiatory, preferring to speak of the effect of Christ's death in terms of cleansing: 'In view of the need for temple purification on the Day of Atonement when the "mercy seat" was approached by the high priest, it appears that a kind of renewed temple was thereby created. In a way parallel to the Qumran community, which hoped for an eschatological temple to replace the corrupt temple in Jerusalem, the hymn celebrates the death of Jesus as having established a new "place of atonement, epiphany, and the presence of God". This understanding of the hymn renders unnecessary elaborate theories about the typological, functional, or metaphorical interpretation of Christ as the mercy seat. Since blood had a cleansing rather than a directly atoning function with regard to the mercy seat, the long-standing debate about propitiation or expiation is largely irrelevant for the interpretation of this verse. The central claim in the hymn is that Christ provided a new means of access to God that reached beyond the sins of Israel. In view of Paul's other statements about atonement, moreover, it seems unlikely that he shared an expiatory theory, which concentrates so exclusively on the matter of forgiveness, a matter of decidedly secondary interest in his theology. Propitiation also seems far from Paul's intent'. Jewett's interpretation does not take sufficient account of Paul's emphasis upon the wrath of God, and therefore the need for propitiation.

because in his forbearance he had left the sins committed beforehand unpunished (lit. 'on account of the passing over of sins committed beforehand in the forbearance of God'). Already in 2:4 Paul has spoken of God's 'forbearance' in face of human sin: 'Or do you show contempt for the riches of his kindness, forbearance and patience, not realizing that God's kindness is intended to lead you to repentance?' Both there and here in 3:25b-26a God's forbearance is shown in the postponement of judgment, his leaving sin unpunished for the time being.

Presenting Christ as an atoning sacrifice was in part to demonstrate God's righteousness, his justice, in the light of the fact that he passed over sins committed beforehand, leaving them unpunished. The sins committed beforehand would appear to be those committed before the coming of Christ and before the atoning sacrifice was made. By passing over these sins God appears to have compromised his righteousness — any judge who passes over a person's offenses without punishment cannot be said to be righteous/just.[51]

There are a number of scholars who reject the view that God's righteousness here denotes his just/righteous character, arguing rather that it refers to his covenantal faithfulness. To sustain this view they argue that the word *(paresis)* found only here in the NT and translated as 'passing over' should be translated as 'forgiveness', so that what Paul is saying here is that God, to show faithfulness to his covenant, provided forgiveness for the sins committed under the old covenant.[52] However, as has been often pointed out,[53] there is no lexical support for construing paresis as forgiveness. The noun itself occurs only here in the NT; however, the cognate verb *(pariēmi)*, which can mean to avoid doing something, to let fall, or to be careless, lax in effort,[54] is found in Luke 11:42 where it means to neglect to do something, and in Hebrews 12:12 where it means to droop. Elsewhere it never means to forgive. In the light of this, it is very unlikely that the one occurrence of *paresis* in the NT here in 3:25 means forgiveness, and it should be interpreted to refer to God passing over sins in the sense of not punishing them.[55]

3:26 By presenting his Son as an atoning sacrifice God demonstrated that he has not compromised his righteousness. Paul asserts: *he did it to demonstrate his righteousness at the present time.* This is the second of two purpose clauses dependent upon the opening statement of 3:25: 'God pre-

---

51. Cranfield, *Romans*, I, 211, says: 'the reference to God's being righteous in the last part of v. 26 would seem to tell strongly in favor of understanding *dikaiosynē* in these two verses as referring to God's own righteousness, and *endeixis* as meaning 'proving'.

52. Cf. Ziesler, *Romans*, 115-16. Byrne, *Romans*, 133, appears to favor this view.

53. Cf., e.g., Simon Gathercole, 'Romans 3.25-26: An Exegetical Study' (Atonement Conference, London School of Theology, July 2005, on EAUK website); Moo, *Romans*, 238; Barrett, *Romans*, 79-80.

54. BDAG, *ad loc.*

55. Cf. Gathercole, 'Romans 3.25-26: An Exegetical Study'.

sented Christ as a sacrifice of atonement'). The first is 'to demonstrate his righteousness' in the light of having passed over sins committed beforehand, and the second here is 'to demonstrate his righteousness' at the present time when he justifies those who have faith in Jesus.

In the past God may have appeared to be unrighteous because he left sinners unpunished, but 'at the present time' he has put forward his Son as an atoning sacrifice 'to demonstrate his justice' (lit. 'for a demonstration of his righteousness'). Sins have not been merely 'passed over'. It is worth noting that the death of Christ is not only a demonstration of God's love for sinners (5:8) but also a demonstration of God's justice. Atonement has been made, hence God can *be just and the one who justifies those who have faith in Jesus.* There is no abrogation of his justice when he makes salvation available to 'those who have faith in Jesus'. When God justifies those who have faith in Jesus, it does not mean that he recognizes in them some ethical achievement or character that leads him to justify them. Rather, Paul says, employing the imagery of the lawcourt,[56] he rules in favor of repentant sinners 'who have faith in Jesus'[57] only because he has presented his Son as an atoning sacrifice for our sins.

b. Jewish Boasting Is Excluded, 3:27-31

[27]Where, then, is boasting? It is excluded. Because of what law? The law that requires works? No, because of the law that requires faith. [28]For we maintain that a person is justified by faith apart from the works of the law. [29]Or is God the God of Jews only? Is he not the God of Gentiles too? Yes, of Gentiles too, [30]since there is only one God, who will justify the circumcised by faith and the uncircumcised through that same faith. [31]Do we, then, nullify the law by this faith? Not at all! Rather, we uphold the law.

It is important to note that when Paul says that God 'justifies those who have faith in Jesus' (3:26), he implies that there are no distinctions between Jews and Gentiles in this matter.[58] Using the rhetoric of the diatribe

---

56. Cf. Wright, 'Romans', 473.

57. Byrne, *Romans*, 134, comments: 'The sense of the rather cryptic Greek phrase *tōn ek pisteōs* appearing here is illuminated by the similar expression *hoi ek pisteōs* occurring in Gal 3:7, 9 as a designation of those whose religious existence rests upon a basis of faith (contrast *hoi ek peritomēs*, Gal 4:12; *hoi ek nomou*, Rom 4:14, 16). In the rather similar construction in Rom 4:16 *(tō ek pisteōs Abraam)* the reference is clearly to Abraham's own faith. But despite the similarity in construction and the reference simply to "Jesus", this cannot confirm a subjective understanding ("faith of Jesus") in the present instance'.

58. Wright, 'Romans', 480, argues: 'The point here is that Paul is now ruling out the "boast" whereby "the Jew" maintained a status above that of the Gentiles. Paul is not addressing the more general "boast" of the moral legalist whose system of salvation is one of self-effort, but the ethnic pride of Israel according to the flesh, supported as it was by the possession of the Torah and the performance of those "works" that set Israel apart from the pagans'. However, as Moo, *Romans*, 244, comments: 'In 3:27–4:25, Paul expounds the great

again in 3:27-31 (cf. 2:17-29; 3:1-9), Paul poses a number of questions raised by his belief that there are no distinctions in the matter of justification (3:27a, 27c, 29a, 29b, 31) to which he himself provides the answers (3:27b, 29c, 31b).

3:27 That God 'justifies [all] those who have faith in Jesus' causes Paul to ask: *Where, then, is boasting?* If Jews and Gentiles are treated in the same way by God in the matter of justification, Jews might well ask what has become of their grounds for boasting. In Paul's letters there are both legitimate and illegitimate grounds for Jewish boasting.[59] The most comprehensive Pauline statement of Jewish privileges which constitute legitimate grounds for boasting is found in 9:4-5: 'Theirs is the adoption to sonship; theirs the divine glory, the covenants, the receiving of the law, the temple worship and the promises. Theirs are the patriarchs, and from them is traced the human ancestry of the Messiah'. However, while it is legitimate for Jews to boast about their possession of the law and their relationship to God (2:17), it is illegitimate to boast of their works as a basis of justification (cf. 4:2). The illegitimate boasting Paul has in mind does not appear to be restricted to Jewish boasting based on their covenantal privileges but also includes boasting in works done. In chapter 4, where Paul discusses the case of Abraham, he shows that the patriarch was not justified by the works he did but only through faith. His faith was credited to him as righteousness as a gift, not as wages due to him for works done (4:2-5). The contrast there is between faith and works, not faith and covenant privileges.[60]

---

theological thesis of 3:21-26. Or to be more accurate, he expounds one key element in that thesis. . . . Faith is contrasted with "works of the law" (3:28), "works" (4:1-8), circumcision (4:9-12), the law (4:13-16), and "sight" (4:17-22). With these contrasts Paul enunciates what has become a hallmark of the Reformation teaching" *sola fide* — that "faith alone" is the means by which a person can be brought into relation with the God of the Bible. *Sola fide,* Paul argues in this section, is necessary in order to maintain *sola gratia:* "by grace alone". But it is also necessary in order to ensure that Gentiles have equal access with Jews to the one God. . . . This concern with the inclusion of the Gentiles is thus also an important theme in this section; but, contrary to many contemporary scholars, who are reacting to what they perceive to be an excessive concern with the individual and his or her relationship to God in traditional theology, it is not the main theme'.

59. There are likewise legitimate and illegitimate grounds for boasting by believers. According to Paul, it is legitimate to boast/rejoice in the Lord (15:17; 1 Cor 1:31; 2 Cor 10:17; Phil 3:3); in the cross of Christ (Gal 6:14); in the hope of glory (5:2); in reconciliation (5:11); in making the gospel available free of charge (1 Cor 9:15; 2 Cor 11:10); in one's converts (1 Cor 15:31; 2 Cor 7:4, 14; 8:24; 9:2, 3; Phil 2:16; 1 Thess 2:19); in Paul himself (2 Cor 1:14; 5:12; Phil 1:26); in having a clear conscience (2 Cor 1:12); in one's authority as an apostle (2 Cor 10:8); in one's own good actions (Gal 6:4); and even in one's weaknesses and sufferings, knowing that God's grace is sufficient (5:3; 2 Cor 12:9). It is illegitimate to boast of one's own self (1 Cor 1:29; 4:7); in works to earn salvation (Eph 2:9); in one's exclusive relationship with Christian leaders (1 Cor 3:21); in working beyond the sphere assigned or in other people's work (2 Cor 10:13, 15, 16); in foolish claims about spiritual experiences (2 Cor 11:16, 17, 18, 30; 12:1); in claiming to work like Paul when actually not doing so (2 Cor 11:12); in compelling Gentiles to be circumcised (Gal 6:13); and in Christian 'liberty' that approves incest (1 Cor 5:6).

60. Cf. Moo, *Romans*, 246-47.

Paul's response to the question, 'Where, then, is boasting?' is: *It is excluded*. Already in 2:17-24 he took his hypothetical Jewish dialogue partner to task for boasting in the law (2:17, 23) because by his disobedience to the law (2:21-22) he dishonored God, causing God's name to be blasphemed among the Gentiles (2:23-24). In that case the boasting of Jewish people was excluded on the basis of their disobedience to the law. However, here in 3:27 Paul takes a different tack when he raises the question of the basis for the exclusion of boasting. He asks: *Because of what law? The law that requires works?* He answers: *No, because of the law that requires faith.* Jewish boasting is excluded, not only because of their failure to obey the law, but also because 'the law requires faith' (lit. '[the] law/principle of faith'), as the apostle will explain in the following verses (3:28-30).[61] (See 'Additional Note: *nomos* in 3:27', below, for a discussion of the question whether *nomos* here should be taken as a 'principle' or as a reference to the Torah.)

ADDITIONAL NOTE: *NOMOS* IN 3:27

The issue is the way *nomos tōn ergōn* ('law of works') and *nomos pisteōs* ('law of faith') ought to be understood. The word *nomos* itself may carry three different meanings. It is used frequently in Romans (74 times in 50 verses), predominantly denoting the law of Moses (2:12 [4x], 13 [2x], 14 [3x], 15, 17, 20, 23, 25 [2x], 26, 27 [2x]; 3:19 [2x], 20 [2x], 21 [2x], 27, 28, 31 [2x]; 4:13, 14, 15 [2x], 16; 5:13 [2x], 20; 6:14, 15; 7:1, 2 [2x], 3, 4, 5, 6, 7 [3x], 8, 9, 12, 14, 16, 22, 25a; 8:3, 4, 7; 9:31; 10:4, 5; 13:8, 10) or OT Scripture as a whole (7:1), but on seven other occasions it appears to denote a principle (7:21, 23 [3x], 25b; 8:2 [2x]), as it does here in 3:27.[62]

Not all commentators agree that *nomos* in 3:27 should be rendered 'principle' rather than 'law/Torah'. Some argue that Paul's use of *nomos* in Romans consistently denotes the law of Moses. Wright, for example, contends: 'Paul is thus distinguishing, not for the last time in the letter, between the Torah seen in two different ways. On the one hand, there is "the Torah of works" — this is Torah seen as that which defines Israel over against the nations, witnessed by the performance of the works that Torah prescribes — not only Sabbath, food-laws and circumcision, though these are the obvious things that, sociologically speaking, give substance to the theologically based separation. On the other hand, there is the new category Paul is forging here: "the Torah of faith", in a sense yet to be explained

61. Cf. Richard W. Thompson, 'Paul's Double Critique of Jewish Boasting', *Bib* 67 (1986) 520-31, esp. 531.

62. BAGD, *ad loc.*, notes three meanings for *nomos:* (i) 'a procedure or practice that has taken hold, *a custom, rule, principle, norm*', citing 3:27 as an example of this; (ii) 'constitutional or statutory legal system, *law*'; (iii) 'a collection of holy writings precious to God's people, *sacred ordinance*'.

(like many things in chap. 3)'.[63] Cranfield also interprets *nomos* as a reference to the law of the OT, describing it as 'God's law, not misunderstood as a law which directs men to seek justification as a reward for their works, but properly understood as summoning men to faith'.[64] Ito suggests that the deeper meaning of the *nomos tōn ergōn* is 'the part of the Torah which reveals the Jewish failure to live up to the standard demanded of them in the Torah', and *nomos pisteōs* denotes 'the part of the Torah that presents Abraham's faith'.[65]

Other scholars argue in favor of interpreting *nomos* in 3:27 as 'principle'. Fitzmyer and Byrne favor this view,[66] as does Witherington, who suggests that in Romans 'the principle of faith' *(nomos pisteōs)* is equivalent to 'the obedience of faith' *(hypakoē pisteōs)*.[67] Moo also supports the view that *nomos* in 3:27 should be understood as 'principle', arguing against the view that it consistently denotes the Mosaic law. He says:

> An even more serious objection to this interpretation [that *nomos* denotes the Mosaic law throughout] is the close relationship between the law of Moses and faith that it assumes. For such a positive relationship between these two contradicts both the movement of this passage and Paul's larger teaching about the law. In both 3:21-26 and 3:28, the faith that gains a standing with God is explicitly distanced from the Mosaic law ('apart from the law'; 'apart from works of the law'). . . . A second interpretation is, then, to be preferred: Paul is contrasting two different 'laws'. On this view, the word *nomos*, in both its actual occurrences in this verse, has a metaphorical sense: 'principle', or 'rule'. . . . Paul's question, while meant to have a general reference — 'what "rule" or "system of demands" excludes boasting?' — would naturally bring to mind the law, the torah. Paul then adds the contrasting modifiers to make clear his point: no, it is not through the torah, that law which demands works, through which boasting is excluded; it is through the 'rule' of faith, the 'ordinance' or 'demand' of God for faith as the basis for justification (v. 28).[68]

3:28-30   In these verses Paul explains how the principle of faith excludes Jewish boasting. To begin he says: *For*[69] *we maintain that a person is justified by faith apart from the works of the law.* By casting this statement in the

63. Wright, 'Romans', 480-81.

64. Cranfield, *Romans*, I, 220.

65. Akio Ito, '*Nomos (tōn) ergōn* and *nomos pisteōs*: The Pauline Rhetoric and Theology of *Nomos*', *NovT* 45 (2003) 256.

66. Fitzmyer, *Romans*, 363; Byrne, *Romans*, 136-37.

67. Witherington, *Romans*, 111.

68. Moo, *Romans*, 249.

69. In some manuscripts 'for' *(gar)* is replaced by 'therefore' *(oun)*; however, the former is to be preferred because in context 3:28 provides the basis for, not the conclusion to be drawn from, what precedes.

first person plural ('we') the apostle includes his readers among those who with him have accepted this view.[70] If God justifies those who believe in his Son without their having to observe the law, then Gentiles are placed on the same footing as Jews, and Jews can no longer claim possession of the law as a ground for boasting of superiority over Gentiles.[71]

To reinforce his point that Jewish boasting is excluded by the principle of faith, that all people may be justified by faith without the works of the law, Paul asks, *Or is God the God of Jews only? Is he not the God of Gentiles too?* The form of the latter question expects the answer which Paul himself then provides: *Yes, of Gentiles too.* There is only one God, and he is God of all creation and the entire human race, Gentiles as well as Jews. Despite the special place of Israel in salvation history (cf. 11:25-29), she cannot claim an exclusive relationship to God.[72]

To reinforce his point Paul adds, *since there is only one God, who will justify the circumcised by faith and the uncircumcised through that same faith.* Paul's 'since there is only one God' (lit. 'since God is one') reflects the fundamental belief of Judaism, encapsulated in the *Shema* of Deuteronomy 6:4: 'Hear, O Israel: The LORD our God, the LORD is one'.[73] Paul refers to the oneness of God also in 1 Corinthians 8:6 ('yet for us there is but one God, the Father,

---

70. Jewett, *Romans*, 298, says: 'It is noteworthy that only here in the Pauline letters is *logizomai* used in the first person plural, which suggests an appeal to "the common opinion among all the Christian communities'.

71. Luther introduced into his German translation of this verse the notion that it is by faith *alone* that a man is justified even though the word 'alone' *(monos)* does not appear in the original. It is noteworthy that recent Catholic scholars agree that this inclusion of 'alone' correctly expresses Paul's theology. So, e.g., Byrne, *Romans*, 137; Fitzmyer, *Romans*, 360-62. Wright, 'Romans', 482, says: 'There is no problem in adding the word "alone" to the word "faith" . . . as long as we recognize what it means: not that a person is "converted" by faith alone without moral effort (that is true, but it is not the truth that Paul is stressing here), nor that God's grace is always prior to human response (that is equally true, and equally not Paul's emphasis here), but that the badge of membership in God's people, the badge that enables all alike to stand on the same, flat ground at the foot of the cross, is faith'.

72. Moo, *Romans*, 251, notes: 'In Judaism, God was the God of Gentiles only by virtue of his creative work, while only the Jews enjoy any meaningful relationship with God; this is expressed in later Jewish text: "I am God over all that came into the world, but I have joined my name only with you [Israel]; I am not called the God of the idolaters, but the God of Israel" (*Exod. Rab.* 29 [88d]). Only by accepting the torah could Gentiles hope to become related to God in the same way as Jews'.

73. The Lord Jesus himself cites the *Shema* in Mark 12:29-31 when, in answer to a question about the greatest commandment, he says: 'The most important one . . . is this: "Hear, O Israel, the Lord our God, the Lord is one. Love the Lord your God with all your heart and with all your soul and with all your mind and with all your strength". The second is this: "Love your neighbor as yourself". There is no commandment greater than these'. The apostle Paul refers to the unity of God in other places as well (cf. 1 Cor 8:4, 6; Gal 3:20; Eph 4:6; 1 Tim. 2:5), and a similar reference is found in Jas 2:19. Paul-Gerhard Klumbies, 'Der Eine Gott des Paulus: Röm 3,21-31 als Brennpunkt paulinischer Theologie', *ZNW* 85 (1994) 205-6, says that the reason Paul only seldomly quotes the expression, 'God is one', is that his understanding of God is drawn more from what God has revealed and achieved through Christ than from his Jewish heritage.

from whom all things came and for whom we live'). Appealing to the fundamental belief that God is one, he argues that the one God will justify Jews ('the circumcised') and Gentiles ('the uncircumcised') in the one way — by faith.[74] Paul employs the future tense, 'will justify', here, reflecting the fact that justification belongs properly to the end time, the final day of judgment, when God will adjudicate in favor of all those who have put their faith in his Son.

There has been some debate concerning possible distinctions in meaning between the justification of the circumcised 'by faith' and the uncircumcised 'through faith'. Early church fathers were divided in their views about this matter. Theodore of Mopsuestia was of the opinion that 'Paul says *the ground of their faith* with respect to the Jews because, although they had other ways of seeking righteousness, they could not obtain it except through their faith. When speaking about the Gentiles, he says *through their faith* because this is the only claim to righteousness which they have'.[75] However, Augustine said: 'The difference of preposition *(on the ground of* versus *through)* does not indicate any difference of meaning but serves simply to vary the phrase'.[76] Most likely, these expressions are stylistic variations.[77]

3:31 If, as Paul argued in 3:28, people are justified by faith 'apart from the works of the law', then the question arises: *Do we, then, nullify the law by this faith?* The word Paul uses for 'nullify' has a range of meanings, but here means 'to invalidate'.[78] To this question, whether his teaching

---

74. Richard W. Thompson, 'The Inclusion of the Gentiles in Rom 3,27-30', *Bib* 69 (1988) 546, says: 'Those who understand v. 30 to mean that the oneness of God *causes* God to justify everyone on the same basis fail to realize that for Paul, it is not because God is one that he justifies on the basis of faith, but because faith is in Christ (see 3,21-26). In vv. 28-30 Paul is saying to his audience: From our Jewish faith we learn that God is one; from the new revelation in Christ we learn that God justifies all persons on the basis of faith. The oneness of this God, whom we *now* know (3,21: *nyni*) to justify by faith, becomes a reason for saying that this God is indeed the God of the Gentiles'. Similarly, Jan Lambrecht, 'Paul's Logic in Romans 3:29-30', *JBL* 119 (2000) 526-28. Dunn, *Romans 1–8*, 189, adds: 'Here in effect Paul does go behind Israel's salvation-history claim to have been specially chosen by God. God's Lordship as Creator is even more fundamental, and belongs to salvation history no less than his election of Israel'.

75. 'Pauline Commentary from the Greek Church' (*ACCSR*, 106-7).

76. 'On the Spirit and the Letter 50' (*ACCSR*, 107).

77. So, e.g., Barrett, *Romans*, 84; Byrne, *Romans*, 140. Stanley K. Stowers, 'Ek Pisteōs and dia tēs pisteōs in Romans 3:30', *JBL* 108 (1989) 674, argues, 'the phrases with *ek pisteōs* express the "vicarious" benefits of Abraham's and Jesus' heroic faithfulness toward God. From this perspective the emphasis is not so much God's plan and action as it is the merit of human agents who have gained God's favor for the peoples of the earth'. However, a check of the use of *ek pisteōs* elsewhere in Paul's letters reveals that it denotes overwhelmingly faith exercised by believers and never the merit of human agents as Stowers suggests.

78. Cf. BAGD, *ad loc.* Käsemann, *Romans*, 104, and Cranfield, *Romans*, I, 190, suggest that Paul's reference to nullifying (*katargeō*) and upholding (*histēmi/histanō*) the law has to do with rabbinic formulae, corresponding to the Hebrew/Aramaic *bṭl* and *qwm*, which, it is argued, when used in combination denote rabbinic technical terms for abolishing and fulfilling the law. Hans Hübner, *Law in Paul's Thought* (Edinburgh: T&T Clark, 1984), 141, de-

about justification by faith nullifies or invalidates the law, Paul responds emphatically: *Not at all!* This expression denoting strong denial, used here for the second time in Romans, is found frequently in this letter and in other letters of Paul where the apostle expresses strong disagreement (cf. 3:4, 6, 31; 6:2, 15; 7:7, 13; 9:14; 11:1, 11; 1 Cor 6:15; Gal 2:17; 3:21; 6:14). When introducing this whole section dealing with 'the righteousness given through faith in Jesus Christ to all who believe' (3:21-31), Paul insisted that it was something 'to which the Law and the Prophets testify' (3:21). This he foreshadowed also in the opening paragraph of his letter when he described the gospel of God that he was set apart to preach as 'the gospel he [God] promised beforehand through his prophets in the Holy Scriptures' (1:2). Clearly, then, Paul would not say that faith nullifies the law.

Having rejected emphatically the suggestion that the law is nullified by faith, Paul asserts, *Rather, we uphold the law.* There are two suggestions concerning the way Paul upholds the law by preaching that people are justified by faith without observing the law: (i) In 8:3-4 Paul writes: 'For what the law was powerless to do because it was weakened by the flesh, God did by sending his own Son in the likeness of sinful flesh to be a sin offering. And so he condemned sin in the flesh, in order that the righteous requirement of the law might be fully met in us, who do not live according to the flesh but according to the Spirit'. The apostle implies that, while people are justified without having to observe the law, nevertheless there is a sense in which the law is fulfilled in the lives of the justified who live according to the Spirit (see the commentary on 8:3-4 below).[79] (ii) In the very next chapter (4:1-25) Paul shows from the law that Abraham was justified by faith without works and argues that this will also be the case for all who have faith in Christ, for Gentiles as well as Jews. It may be best to say that in both these ways Paul's teaching about justification by faith upholds the law: it enables a fulfillment of what the law sought to bring about in human behavior, and it fulfils what is foreshadowed in the law's account of Abraham's justification.[80]

---

nies a rabbinic background for this view, but more recently it has been supported again by O. Hofius, 'Das Gesetz des Mose und das Gesetz Christi', *ZTK* 80 (1983) 262-86, 279 n. 57. However, Richard W. Thompson, 'The Alleged Rabbinic Background of Rom 3,31', *ETL* 63 (1987) 147-48, has argued convincingly against this view on the grounds that rabbinic texts that contain *bṭl* and *qwm* and appealed to in support of the view use the terms 'in such a variety of contexts that one could hardly speak of them as a "formula" with any specialized meaning', and that it is questionable 'whether *qwm* and *bṭl* were even the best equivalents for *histanō* and *katargeō*'.

79. Moo, *Romans*, 253-55, and Byrne, *Romans*, 140-41, favor this view. Chrysostom, 'Homilies on Romans' (*ACCSR*, 107), says: 'Paul's use of the word *uphold* shows that the law was failing. . . . The purpose of the law was to make man righteous, but it had no power to do that. But when faith come it achieved what the law could not do, for once a man believes he is immediately justified. Faith therefore established what the law intended and brought to fulfillment what its provisions aimed for. Consequently faith has not abolished the law but perfected it'.

80. Käsemann, *Romans*, 105, adopts this view.

Paul does not spell out here what is involved when he says that God 'justifies those who have faith in Jesus' (3:26). Later in the letter he will show that there is no condemnation for believers (8:1) because God justifies (i.e. adjudicates in favor of) those who believe in his Son and as a result will entertain no charges against them in God's presence (8:31-34). This adjudication belongs properly to the end time (cf. 3:30), but now with the death and resurrection of Christ it may be said that it has already been made in favor of believers (5:1; 8:1).

ADDITIONAL NOTE: JUSTIFICATION

Because the whole world is held accountable to God, and because no one will be justified by the works of the law (3:19-20), God has revealed his saving righteousness apart from the law. By his grace alone he justifies freely sinners who believe in his Son on the basis of the redemption effected through him (3:24). Redemption was made possible when God set forth Christ as the atoning sacrifice for sins, and by doing so demonstrated his justice, which would otherwise have been compromised when justifying sinners. By setting Christ forward as the atoning sacrifice, God could be both just and the justifier of those who have faith in Jesus (3:25-26). From all this it is clear that when Paul speaks about justification he is doing so in legal terms, in terms of the judge acting justly when declaring righteous those who believe in his Son. The doctrine of justification is itself not the gospel. The gospel is the message concerning what God has done through Christ to deal with the effects of human sin (cf. 1 Cor 15:1-4) and to liberate humanity and the whole creation from the effects of sin (cf. 8:19-24). Those who believe the gospel and give their allegiance to his Son God justifies, that is, he declares them to be in the right. They enjoy the status of those for whom God has made a favorable adjudication.

Sanday and Headlam agree that justification is essentially a judicial verdict but, because God treats sinners as though they were righteous, they argue that 'the Christian life is made to have its beginning in a fiction'.[81] However, to declare a person righteous, as God does in the case of sinners who believe in his Son, is no legal fiction, but 'a legal *reality* of the utmost significance'. It means that God has acquitted believers of all charges that could be brought against them for their sins. Paul says that this verdict of acquittal, understood in Jewish theology to be hoped for at the last judgment, is made when people believe.[82]

The apostle Paul employed the doctrine of justification by faith when defending the right of Gentiles to be numbered among the people of God

---

81. Sanday and Headlam, *Romans,* 36.
82. Cf. Moo, *Romans,* 227-28.

without the need to submit to circumcision or take upon themselves the yoke of the Mosaic law. Being justified by faith, as Abraham was, they are numbered among his children, and become inheritors of the promises God made to him, including the promise of the Spirit (Gal 3:6-9, 14). Though Paul used this doctrine against the Judaizers, those who would deny a place for Gentiles in the people of God unless they were circumcised and obeyed the Mosaic law, it was not for him simply a fighting doctrine that could be set aside when he was not involved in that dispute. This is indicated by the fact that he speaks of justification in passages that do not deal with the question of Gentile inclusion (cf. 8:29-30; 1 Cor 6:11; 2 Cor 3:9; Phil 3:9; Tit 3:7).

---

2. God's Dealings with Abraham, 4:1-25

Before examining 4:1-25 in detail, a few preliminary comments need to be made. First, it is important to recognize that 4:1-25 is a continuation of what Paul said in 3:29-31. Several considerations support this: (a) What Paul emphasizes in 3:29-30 (God justifies both the circumcision [Jews] and the uncircumcision [Gentiles] by faith) is also the main thrust of 4:9-12; (b) 4:2-8 is an exposition of the law (in particular the law's description of Abraham's being accounted righteous) which is part of Paul's demonstration that the principle of faith does not overturn the law but rather upholds it, which is what he asserted in 3:31.

Second, Paul's discussion of the case of Abraham is not intended primarily to provide an example of one who was justified by faith, though it does do that. His main purpose is to show that God makes no distinctions between Jews and Gentiles as far as salvation is concerned.[83]

Third, 4:1-25 functions as an apology in which the apostle appeals to the Scriptures to defend his gospel in the light of possible Jewish objections. To make this defense, Paul appeals to the experience of Abraham (and also David) to support his case. In addition, he draws attention to Abraham as a universal father figure, something used often in Jewish apologetics. What the apostle has to show is that, contrary to Jewish tradi-

---

83. A point made strongly, e.g., by Michael Cranford, 'Abraham in Romans 4: The Father of All Who Believe', *NTS* 41 (1995) 83, 87-88. Cf. Wright, 'Romans', 487-88, who notes: 'It [chap. 4] is not simply, as it has so often been labeled, a "proof from scripture", or even an "example", of Paul's "thesis" of justification by faith in 3:21-31. . . . The chapter is, in fact, a full-dress exposition of the covenant God made with Abraham in Genesis 15, showing at every point how God always intended and promised that the covenant family of Abraham would include Gentiles as well as Jews. Irrespective of what we might say about a systematic presentation of Paul's ideas, in his present argument this is the main topic, to which "justification by faith" makes a vital contribution, rather than the other way round. . . . Paul is arguing, then, that Abraham's faith is the sole badge of membership in God's people, and that therefore all those who share it are "justified"'.

tion,[84] Abraham was justified by his faith and not because of his meritorious obedience.

Finally, Paul defends his gospel by showing that it is consistent with God's previous acts in history, thereby emphasizing the continuity between the way God acted in the case of Abraham and the way he acts now in accordance with his gospel.[85]

The passage 4:1-25 may be analyzed as follows: After introducing the subject of Abraham (4:1) Paul shows that God justified Abraham apart from any 'works' that he had done (4:2-8). Next he shows that God credited righteousness to Abraham while he was still uncircumcised (4:9-12). Then he argues that God did not make Abraham the inheritor of the world because he lived by the law (4:13-17a). After that he explains the essential nature of Abraham's faith (4:17b-22). Finally, he brings out the relevance of God's dealings with Abraham for all believers, Gentiles as well as Jews (4:23-25).

a. God Justifies Abraham apart from Works, 4:1-8

> [1]*What then shall we say that Abraham, our forefather according to the flesh, discovered in this matter? [2]If, in fact, Abraham was justified by works, he had something to boast about — but not before God. [3]What does Scripture say? 'Abraham believed God, and it was credited to him as righteousness'. [4]Now to the one who works, wages are not credited as a gift but as an obligation. [5]However, to the one who does not work but trusts God who justifies the ungodly, their faith is credited as righteousness. [6]David says the same thing when he speaks of the blessedness of the one to whom God credits righteousness apart from works: [7]'Blessed are those whose transgressions are forgiven, whose sins are covered. [8]Blessed is the one whose sin the Lord will never count against them'.*

In this section Paul shows that if Abraham was justified on the basis of his works he would have grounds for boasting, but in fact this was not the case. He simply believed God, and that was counted to him as righteousness.

4:1   Paul asks: *What then shall we say that Abraham, our forefather ac-*

---

84. Cf. Ben Sirach 44:20-21; 1 Macc 2:50, 52; *Jub.* 15:1-10; 17:17-18; 23:10a; CD 3:1-3; *m. Kidd.* 4:14. Barrett, *Romans,* 86, comments on Jewish attitudes to Abraham: 'He was the father of the race (Isa. li. 1f.), and perfectly righteous (e.g. *Kiddushin,* iv. 14: We find that Abraham our father had performed the whole law before it was given, for it is written, Because that Abraham obeyed my voice and kept my charge, my commandments, my statutes, and my laws [Gen. xxvi. 5]). In particular, he was the type of absolute trust in God (e.g. *Aboth,* v. 3: With ten temptations was Abraham our father tempted, and he stood steadfast in them all). The Hellenistic synagogue pursued the same theme in its own way by representing Abraham as the fulfilment of all the (Greek) virtues (Philo, *Abraham,* 52ff.; Josephus, *Antiquities,* i.256)'.

85. Cf. Anthony J. Guerra, 'Romans 4 as Apologetic Theology', *HTR* 81 (1988) 258-65.

cording to the flesh,[86] *discovered in this matter?* With the word 'then' Paul connects what he is about to say about Abraham with what precedes (3:21-31), where he claimed that a righteousness of God comes through faith in Christ apart from the law. Now he addresses the case of Abraham to show that it does not invalidate his claim.

It is possible that the words, 'according to the flesh', relate not to 'our forefather' (yielding 'Abraham our forefather according to the flesh'), but to 'discovered' so that the text would read: 'What then shall we say Abraham has found according to the flesh?' The answer to this question would be 'nothing' of spiritual value, for 4:2-5 shows that he was not justified by works but by believing God's promise.

Where the expression 'what then shall we say?' is found elsewhere in the NT (and it is found only in Romans), it always stands as an independent question followed by another related question.[87] This leads Hays to suggest the following translation of 4:1: 'What shall we say? Have we found [on the basis of Scripture] that Abraham is our forefather according to the flesh?'[88] What is implied by this second question is something Paul proceeds to refute. Abraham cannot be claimed by Jews to be their true forefather simply on the basis of physical descent (according to the flesh), but only on the basis that they have faith in the promises of God as Abraham did.[89] This of course opens the door for the Gentiles to claim Abraham as their forefather as well, something that the apostle is at pains to show later in the chapter (4:9-12, 14-17).[90]

4:2   Paul begins his treatment of the case of Abraham by stating: *If, in fact, Abraham was justified by works, he had something to boast about — but*

---

86. The designation 'forefather' *(propatora)* is found only here in the NT. In some manuscripts it is replaced with 'father' *(patera)*, which is used frequently in reference to Abraham in the NT.

87. 6:1: 'What shall we say, then *(ti oun eroumen)?* Shall we go on sinning so that grace may increase?'; 7:7: 'What shall we say, then *(ti oun eroumen)?* Is the law sinful?'; 8:31: 'What, then, shall we say *(ti oun eroumen)* in response to these things? If God is for us, who can be against us?'; 9:14: 'What then shall we say *(ti oun eroumen)?* Is God unjust?'; 9:30: 'What then shall we say *(ti oun eroumen)?* That the Gentiles, who did not pursue righteousness, have obtained it, a righteousness that is by faith?'

88. Richard B. Hays, '"Have we found Abraham to be our forefather according to the flesh?" A Reconsideration of Rom 4:1', *NovT* 27 (1985) 79-80.

89. Hays, '"Have we found Abraham to be our forefather according to the flesh?"', 86-88. Cf. Wright, 'Romans', 489-90; Moo, *Romans*, 259-60.

90. Dunn, *Romans 1–8*, 198, says that when Paul asks what Abraham 'has found' *(heurēkenai)* he 'may well have intended to evoke the phrase which occurs quite frequently in the LXX, *heuriskein charin* (or *eleos*), "to find grace (or mercy)". It is prominent in Genesis (13 times), but also in Exod 33 (4 times), 1 Samuel (6 times), and Sirach (7 times). . . . Note particularly Gen 18:3 — Abraham himself speaks of "finding favor in God's sight". That the phrase was still in familiar usage in the first century in Jewish circles is indicated by Luke 1:30, Acts 7:46, Heb 4:16, and 4 Ezra 12.7. . . . Paul's purpose in evoking the phrase would probably be to prepare the ground for the following exposition in which *charis* features (vv 4, 16), by implying from the outset that Abraham's standing before God was an act of divine favor'.

not before God. This is a conditional sentence in which the protasis assumes something for the sake of argument ('if, in fact, Abraham was justified by works'). Paul is saying that if Abraham was justified by works, then he would have something to boast about, but he insists that Abraham had no grounds for boasting 'before God'. Abraham is no exception to the conclusion Paul reached in 3:20 that no one will be justified by 'works of the law'.

By saying this, Paul was also denying what his Jewish contemporaries asserted. Some believed that Abraham was a clear example of one who was justified by works, in particular by his obedience to God in being willing to offer up his son Isaac (Gen 22:1-18).[91] In Jewish writings of the time we find the exhortation: 'Remember the deeds of the ancestors, which they did in their generations; and you will receive great honor and an everlasting name. Was not Abraham found faithful when tested, and it was reckoned to him as righteousness? Joseph in the time of his distress kept the commandment, and became lord of Egypt' (1 Macc 2:51-53); 'For Abraham was perfect in all of his actions with the Lord and was pleasing through righteousness all of the days of his life' (*Jub.* 23:10);[92] 'He kept the law of the Most High, and entered into a covenant with him; he certified the covenant in his flesh, and when he was tested he proved faithful' (Sir 44:20); 'And we find that Abraham our father had performed the whole Law before it was given, for it is written, *Because Abraham obeyed my voice and kept my charge, my commandments, my statutes, and my laws*' (*m. Kidd.* 4.14)'.[93]

For his gospel to have credibility with those with a background in the synagogue, Paul had to show that Abraham was in fact justified by faith, not works — neither by his obedience in offering Isaac nor by observing the law before it was given. Paul does allude to the offering of Isaac (when in 8:32 he describes God as the one 'who did not spare his own Son, but gave him up for us all'), but when he wants to show that Abraham was accounted righteous by God he chooses an incident earlier in the patriarch's life: his believing response to the promise of God (Gen 15:6).[94]

When Paul says, 'If, in fact, Abraham was justified by works, he had something to boast about — *but not before God*' (italics added), it might be inferred that Paul is merely limiting the scope of boasting by saying that while Abraham did not have grounds for boasting before God, he did have

---

91. However, the Genesis 22 account of the offering of Isaac does not include any statement that Abraham was accounted righteous because of this obedience; only that God reconfirmed his covenant with him because of his obedience; a covenant that had been previously confirmed when Abraham was ninety-nine years old (cf. Gen 17:1-14). The covenant confirmed and reconfirmed was the one God made with Abraham when he believed God's promises, a belief that was credited to him as righteousness (Gen 15:1-21).

92. Cited from Charlesworth, ed., *The Old Testament and Pseudepigrapha,* II, 100.

93. Herbert Danby, *The Mishnah Translated from the Hebrew with Introductions and Brief Explanatory Notes* (Oxford: Oxford University Press, 1933), 329.

94. Cf. Eva Meile, 'Isaaks Opferung: Eine Note an Nils Alstrup Dahl', *ST* 34 (1980) 111-12.

grounds for boasting before human beings. But such an inference is ruled out by the fact that there are no hints of this in the text and it would not be relevant anyhow. The apostle is discussing the role of works in relation to justification, and that is something one has before God, not before human beings.

4:3 Paul then asks: *What does the Scripture say?* He answers his own question by quoting from Genesis 15:6: '*Abraham believed God, and it was credited to him as righteousness*'. It was essential for Paul to show from Scripture that God's dealings with Abraham are consistent with the gospel as he proclaimed it, for, as noted in the commentary on 4:2 above, they were interpreted quite differently in contemporary Jewish exegesis.

As has often been noted, in the text which Paul cites (Gen 15:6) the word 'believe' is found for the first time in the Scriptures, and that in relation to righteousness.[95] In the context of Genesis 15 Abraham was responding to the promise given him by God that he would grant him an heir (one coming from his own body) and that his descendants would ultimately be as numerous as the stars of the heavens. Abraham's faith was not a general belief in God, nor even a general belief in God's reliability, but rather belief in the promises God made to him. His faith had objective content as well as being subjective trust in God.[96] Abraham believed the promise, and the Scripture says that 'it was credited to him as righteousness'. Abraham had no righteousness of his own that would guarantee his acceptance by God. Prior to his call by God he had probably been a worshipper of the moon God, Nanna, in Ur of the Chaldees (cf. Josh 24:2-3: 'Long ago your ancestors, including Terah the father of Abraham and Nahor, lived beyond the River and worshiped other gods. But I took your father Abraham from the land beyond the Euphrates and led him throughout Canaan and gave him many descendants').[97] That his faith 'was credited as righteousness' was a

---

95. Cf., e.g., Jean-Noël Aletti, 'Romains 4 et Genèse 17: Quelle énigme et quelle solution?' *Bib* 84 (2003) 318; Moo, *Romans*, 261.

96. Something discussed by Richard Holst, 'The Meaning of "Abraham Believed God" in Romans 4:3', *WTJ* 59 (1997) 319-26. He cites N. T. Wright approvingly: 'The nature of that faith (not in the sense of an analysis of the act of believing but in the sense of an analysis of what is believed) is of vital importance'. Holst adds: 'The distinction is important — the knowledge of God is mediated through his word. Rom 4 makes clear that God's self-disclosure through the word of promise is the reason for Abraham's subjective faith, and that apart from it an analysis of his faith is impossible' (319-20). Käsemann, *Romans*, 107, asserts: 'In no sense, whether as *fides qua* or *fides quae* (the faith with which or the faith which we believe), can faith stand on its own apart from the word. By nature it is the relation of reception and preservation of the message of salvation. This emerges in the formula *pisteuein eis*, which not by chance in Paul is continually resolved by participial, relative, or *hoti* clauses. Faith is neither a virtue, a religious attitude, nor an experience. It is faith by hearing. It enters into the promise of salvation and becomes obedient to it'.

97. Cf. Kreuzer, '"Der den Gottlosen rechtfertigt" (Röm 4,5), 208-19, who, after considering early Jewish traditions regarding Abraham's stay in Mesopotamia, says that before his call Abraham was 'ungodly' not in the sense of being immoral but rather as a pagan living in a pagan environment.

matter of pure undeserved grace on God's part.[98] It is important to explain what Paul means when he says that Abraham's faith was 'credited' to him as righteousness. The verb 'to credit' is a bookkeeping term that can be applied metaphorically to human beings.[99] By crediting Abraham's faith as righteousness God was accepting him as one now fit for relationship with him and choosing to take no account of his sin, as the apostle will make clear in the following verses.

4:4-5 It must be noted that Abraham's faith did not *earn* him this right standing; it was granted him as a gift from God, as Paul immediately makes clear with a human analogy: *Now to the one who works, wages are not credited as a gift but as an obligation.* When people do a day's work, their employers are obliged to pay their wages. In no sense are these wages to be regarded as a gift. But the matter is different when God credits righteousness to sinners: *However, to the one who does not work but trusts God who justifies the ungodly, their faith is credited as righteousness.* When God justifies the wicked, he is like an employer who gives wages to those who do no work![100] It should, perhaps, be added that trusting God is definitely not to be regarded as a work performed by the righteous; rather, it is the only recourse of the wicked. Paul shows something of what this involves in the following verses (4:6-8). Origen comments: 'Faith relies on the grace of the justifier. Works rely on the justice of the rewarder'.[101]

The description of God as the one 'who justifies the ungodly' is on the surface quite shocking. In the OT the very opposite is emphasized. So, for example, Exodus 23:7: 'Have nothing to do with a false charge and do not put an innocent or honest person to death, for I will not acquit the guilty'; Proverbs 17:15: 'Acquitting the guilty and condemning the innocent — the LORD detests them both'. Yet God has always shown mercy and grace towards the repentant, while not acquitting those who are guilty and unrepentant (cf. Exod 34:6-7). However, God's acquittal of the wicked and repentant is based upon the fact that he has provided an atoning sacri-

---

98. The statement Paul cites from Gen 15:6 here in 4:3 is also found in Ps 106:31 in relation to Phinehas's dramatic action in killing the idolater Zimri and his Midianite mistress Cosbi (Num 25:6-9, 14-15), in response to which God ended the plague he had brought upon Israel. In this case it was Phinehas's deed that was reckoned to him as righteousness, something very different from the point the apostle Paul is making by citing Gen 15:6, where the same statement is made in relation to Abraham's faith. Fitzmyer, *Romans,* 374, notes that 'the contrast between Gen 15:6 and Ps 106:31 was hotly disputed in Reformation times'.

99. The apostle uses it in Philem 18 when he says of Onesimus: 'If he has done you any wrong or owes you anything, charge it to me [*touto emoi elloga*]'). Wright, 'Romans', 490-91, explains the significance of Paul's use of the metaphor: God, as it were, 'made an entry in Abraham's ledger writing "faith in the promise", in the column marked "righteousness"'.

100. Cranford, 'Abraham in Romans 4', 80, makes the following point: 'The key issue is not faith versus works, but reckoning according to obligation versus reckoning according to favour'.

101. 'Commentary on the Epistle to the Romans' (*ACCSR,* 111).

fice so that he can be both just and the justifier of those who have faith in Jesus (3:26).[102]

4:6-8 Appealing now to the testimony of another important OT figure, Paul writes: *David says the same thing when he speaks of the blessedness*[103] *of the one to whom God credits righteousness apart from works.*[104] Following the Jewish principle of establishing the truth from the mouth of two witnesses, Paul appeals to the words of David in Psalm 32:1 to confirm his argument.[105] The psalm affirms what the experience of Abraham exemplifies, that is, 'the blessedness of the one to whom God credits righteousness apart from works': *'Blessed are those whose transgressions are forgiven, whose sins are covered. Blessed is the one whose sin the Lord will never count against them'*. In appealing to this psalm Paul employs the rabbinic exegetical principle of *gezerah shawah* (verbal analogy based upon the same word applied to two different cases),[106] which enables him to connect Psalm 32:1 with Genesis 15:6 quoted in 4:3 because of the common use of the verb 'to count/reckon'. In 4:3 righteousness was credited to Abraham, and in 4:8 the man is blessed whose sin is never counted against him. However, it is not only the common use of the verb 'to count/reckon' that allows Paul to use Psalm 32 to expound the significance of Genesis 15:6, but also the correspondences existing between the two passages. Aletti notes the following correspondences: Abraham is uncircumcised, David is a sinner; Abraham and David are both without good works; Abraham has faith in the divine word and hope in its fulfillment, David has hope in divine mercy.[107]

Paul's quotation is a verbatim reproduction of the LXX text of Psalm 31:1-2 (E.T. Ps 32:1-2). The original context is instructive:

102. Westerholm, *Israel's Law and the Church's Faith*, 119, makes an important observation concerning the relevance of 4:4-5: 'Since the issue ("works of the law" *versus* "faith in Jesus Christ") permits restatement in terms of a general distinction between "works" and "faith", the point of attack cannot be limited to statutes in the Law which serve as Jewish "identity markers". While Paul certainly rejected the view that the works of the law were the essential identifying marks of the true people of God, he also rejected the view that works in general and fulfilment of the law's demands in particular were required of those to whom God will credit righteousness'.

103. The word 'blessedness' is used only three times in the NT, and only by Paul. Besides its use here in 4:6, it is also found in 4:9 ('Is this blessedness [God not counting people's sins against them] only for the circumcised') and in Gal 4:15 (lit. 'Where, then, is your blessedness?').

104. Paul does not develop the idea of righteousness credited 'without works' here, but in the light of 3:20-21 we can safely assume that he means righteousness credited without the performance of works required by the law *(ex ergōn nomou)*.

105. Byrne, *Romans*, 146-47, says: 'By citing a text from "the Law" (that is, the Pentateuch) in the shape of Gen 15:6 and from "the Prophets" in the shape of Ps 32:1-2 (David, the putative author of the Psalms, being reckoned as a prophet) Paul makes good his earlier claim that "the Law and the Prophets bear witness" to the righteousness of God that stands revealed "apart from the law" (3:21b)'.

106. Cf. Richard N. Longenecker, *Biblical Exegesis in the Apostolic Period* (Carlisle: Paternoster, 1995 [first published by Eerdmans, 1975]), 34.

107. Aletti, 'Romains 4 et Genèse 17', 322.

Blessed is the one whose transgressions are forgiven, whose sins are covered. Blessed is the one whose sin the Lᴏʀᴅ does not count against them and in whose spirit is no deceit. When I kept silent, my bones wasted away through my groaning all day long. For day and night your hand was heavy on me; my strength was sapped as in the heat of summer. Then I acknowledged my sin to you and did not cover up my iniquity. I said, 'I will confess my transgressions to the Lᴏʀᴅ'. And you forgave the guilt of my sin. (Ps 32:1-5, italics added)

The psalm portrays a person weighed down by a sense of sin, but who receives forgiveness from God and is assured that his sin will 'never'[108] be counted against him again, and this without any 'works' on the part of the person that might enable him to boast. Paul implies by this quotation that when God credits righteousness to people, it presupposes the forgiveness of their transgressions, the covering of their sins, and the decision on God's part never to count their sins against them.[109] This all serves to show that when faith is credited to people as righteousness, it is an undeserved gift of God. All that people contribute is their sin, for which they need forgiveness. Incidentally, Paul's quotation of the psalm provides some insight into what the apostle considered to be the nature of forgiveness: the decision to waive the right to demand satisfaction from those concerned for the wrong done, so that the wrong is no longer counted against them.[110]

b. God Credits Righteousness to Abraham without Circumcision, 4:9-12

[9]*Is this blessedness only for the circumcised, or also for the uncircumcised? We have been saying that Abraham's faith was credited to him as righteousness.* [10]*Under what circumstances was it credited? Was it after he was circumcised, or before? It was not after, but before!* [11]*And he received circumcision as a sign, a seal of the righteousness that he had by faith while he was still uncircumcised. So then, he is the father of all who believe but have not been circumcised, in order that righteousness might be credited to them.* [12]*And he is then also the father of the circumcised who not only are circum-*

---

108. The strong negative *ou mē* is used.

109. Moo, *Romans*, 266, comments: 'Two other implications follow from the association of these Psalm verses with Paul's exposition. First, it is clear that the forgiveness of sins is a basic component of justification. Second, Paul reveals again his strongly forensic understanding of justification. For he uses this quotation to compare justification to the non-accrediting or not "imputing" of sins to a person. This is an act that has nothing to do with moral transformation, but "changes" people only in the sense that their relationship to God is changed — they are "acquitted" rather than condemned'.

110. Marie-Jo Porcher, 'Quelques considérations sur l'usage du Psaume 32 dans l'épître aux Romains (Rm 4,1-12)', *RevScRel* 77, no. 4 (2003) 563, says that Paul seems to exclude every interpretation of the psalm that might limit the benediction of vv. 1-2 to a particular category of individuals, namely, the circumcised.

*cised but who also follow in the footsteps of the faith that our father Abraham
had before he was circumcised.*

Having described the blessedness of those to whom God credits righteousness apart from works and whose sins he forgives, in 4:9-12 Paul proceeds to make clear that this blessedness is available to all people. He begins by asking: *Is this blessedness only for the circumcised, or also for the uncircumcised?* In answer to this question Paul explains: *We have been saying that Abraham's faith was credited to him as righteousness.* It was not the fact that Abraham was circumcised that was credited to him as righteousness, but rather his faith. If so, it becomes important for Paul to ask: *Under what circumstances was it [his faith] credited? Was it after he was circumcised, or before?* He answers his own question: *It was not after, but before!* He bases this assertion upon the fact that Scripture says that God credited Abraham's faith to him as righteousness (Gen 15:6) well before it recounts God's command to him to be circumcised (Gen 17:9-14). Paul adds: *And he received circumcision as a sign, a seal of the righteousness that he had by faith while he was still uncircumcised.* Paul describes circumcision as a 'seal' of the righteousness he had by faith, and not as a 'sign' of covenant as it is described in Genesis 17:11. By describing circumcision as a seal of the righteousness Abraham had by faith, Paul is actually saying that circumcision functioned as confirmation of the righteousness Abraham had through faith.[111] As has often been noted, Paul appears to avoid calling circumcision a sign of the covenant because his Jewish contemporaries regarded it as a sign of the Mosaic covenant, something that distinguished Israel from the nations (cf. Judg 14:3; 1 Sam 14:6). By describing it as a sign of the righteousness Abraham already had by faith before he was circumcised, he shows that this righteousness is universally available.[112]

The fact that Abraham received the sign of circumcision as confirmation of the righteousness he had while he was uncircumcised has two important corollaries for Paul. The first is: *So then, he is the father[113] of all who believe but have not been circumcised, in order that righteousness might be credited to them.[114]* Just as faith was credited to Abraham as righteousness when he

111. Paul's use of the word 'seal' *(sphragis)* elsewhere confirms that he understood it as a confirmation (cf. 1 Cor 9:2: 'Even though I may not be an apostle to others, surely I am to you! For you are the seal *(sphragis)* of my apostleship in the Lord'; 2 Tim 2:19: 'Nevertheless, God's solid foundation stands firm, sealed with this inscription *(echōn tēn sphragida tautēn*, lit. 'having this seal'): "The Lord knows those who are his", and, "Everyone who confesses the name of the Lord must turn away from wickedness"'.

112. So, too, Dunn, *Romans 1–8*, 209; Moo, *Romans*, 268; Fitzmyer, *Romans,* 381; Byrne, *Romans,* 147; Barrett, *Romans,* 91-92.

113. Construing *eis to einai* as an articular infinitive with the preposition *eis* indicating result.

114. The articular infinitive with the preposition, *eis to logisthēnai,* indicating purpose. But cf. Cranfield, *Romans,* I, 237: 'The latter *eis* with the articular infinitive clause would seem to be rather better explained as consecutive than as final. It depends on *pisteuontōn'*.

was uncircumcised, so likewise faith may be credited as righteousness to others who are uncircumcised. In this sense it may be said that Abraham is the 'father' of all the uncircumcised who believe, that is, believing Gentiles.

The second corollary is: *And he is then also the father of the circumcised who not only are circumcised but who also follow in the footsteps of the faith that our father Abraham had before he was circumcised.* That Abraham received circumcision (as a sign of the faith he already had) means that he may be said to be the 'father' of the circumcised (Jews) also. But the apostle straight-away makes clear that this is not because they are circumcised but because they 'follow in the footsteps of the faith that our father Abraham had before he was circumcised'. Faith is crucial in every case, not circumcision (or ethnicity)! To follow in someone's footsteps is to act in the same way or to follow his/her example. Paul uses the expression again in 2 Corinthians 12:18: 'Did we not conduct ourselves with the same spirit? Did we not take the same steps' (NRSV)? A similar expression is found in 1 Peter 2:21: 'To this you were called, because Christ suffered for you, leaving you an example, that you should follow in his steps'. It is important to note that Paul says that the example to be followed is not that of Abraham's behavior generally but the example of his faith. Abraham is the father of Jewish people who walk in the footsteps of their father Abraham's *faith*, and as far as Paul is concerned, he is not the father of those Jews who do not walk in those footsteps.[115]

Dunn offers the following comment: 'Paul expresses his point very deliberately. Judaism could readily embrace the thought of Abraham as the father of Gentiles, by virtue of their becoming proselytes (Str-B, 3:211). But Paul argues that Gen 15:6 shows Abraham to be father of the uncircumcised *in their uncircumcision*, so long as they share his *faith*. It is thus precisely his own distinction between faith and works of the law which he finds validated by Gen 15:6'.[116] Barrett makes the following important observations:

> That Abraham is the father of the Jewish people is of course a commonplace (v. 1). He was so regarded by the Rabbis as the first proselyte, and thus as the father of proselytes (e.g. M*e*khilta Ex. xxii.20 (101a): Abraham called himself a proselyte *(ger)*, for it is written, I am a stranger *(ger)* and a sojourner with you (Gen. xxiii. 4). Paul's words thus bear a superficial similarity to those of the Rabbis; but the substance is completely different. (i) Abraham is not the father of Jews first, and then, in a derivative way, the father of Gentile proselytes also. He is first of all the father of believing Gentiles. (ii) He is their father not on the ground of their cir-

---

115. Ambrosiaster comments: 'Paul says this because Abraham by believing became the forefather of the circumcision, but of the heart, not only of those who descended from him but also of those who, from among the nations, believed in the way he did. He is the father of the Jews according to the flesh, but according to faith he is the father of all believers'. 'Commentary on Paul's Epistles' (*ACCSR*, 116).

116. Dunn, *Romans 1–8*, 210.

cumcision but on the ground of their faith. Not outward incorporation into the visible ranks of Israel 'after the flesh' by means of an ancient ceremony, but the trustful and obedient acceptance of God's word admits them to the family of God's people. (iii) In like manner, the privilege of descent from Abraham is accorded to Jews not in virtue of their birth and circumcision but in virtue of their faith (cf. ix.6-13). They must 'join the ranks' (the words translated 'follow in the footsteps' suggest the metaphor of soldiers walking in file) of faith; and faith is (as the example of Abraham shows) independent of circumcision.[117]

c. God Makes Abraham the Inheritor of the World without the Law, 4:13-17a

[13]*It was not through the law that Abraham and his offspring received the promise that he would be heir of the world, but through the righteousness that comes by faith.* [14]*For if those who depend on the law are heirs, faith means nothing and the promise is worthless,* [15]*because the law brings wrath. And where there is no law there is no transgression.*

[16]*Therefore, the promise comes by faith, so that it may be by grace and may be guaranteed to all Abraham's offspring — not only to those who are of the law but also to those who have the faith of Abraham. He is the father of us all.* [17]*As it is written: 'I have made you a father of many nations'.*

In this section Paul shows that Abraham did not receive the promise that he would inherit the world because he observed the law but through faith. And the promise will be fulfilled for all Abraham's offspring, Gentiles as well as Jews, who have the same faith as Abraham.

4:13-15a   Paul begins this section by offering further support for the view just expressed in 4:11-12 — that Abraham is the father of all who believe, both Gentiles and Jews. He explains: [*For*] *it was not through law that Abraham and his offspring received the promise that he would be heir of the world, but through the righteousness that comes by faith.* The omission of the word 'for' in the NIV obscures the connection Paul makes between 4:11-12 and 4:13ff., that is, that Abraham can be the father of both believing Gentiles and believing Jews because the promise was not received 'through the law'.[118]

---

117. Barrett, *Romans*, 90-91.

118. Dunn, *Romans 1–8*, 212, says: 'What is striking is the way in which when the concept "promise" emerges [in Jewish writings] it is subordinated to or its effects seen as mediated through the law; thus 2 Macc 2:17-18 speaks of God restoring the inheritance *(klēronomia)* "as promised through the law" *(kathōs epēngeilato dia tou nomou),* and Pss. Sol. 12:6 prays: "Let the Lord's pious ones inherit the promises of the Lord". . . . Whether Paul knows these specific passages we cannot tell, but he must certainly have been aware of such sentiments among his fellow Jews, since they are precisely what he denies: "not through the law"'. . . .

Paul argues that, just as circumcision was not decisive in the matter of having righteousness credited to people, so neither is living by the law decisive when it comes to receiving what God has promised. This was clearly the case with Abraham himself because the promise was made long before the law was given (the law was given 430 years[119] after the promise was made; cf. Gal 3:17), and more importantly because when God made the promise to Abraham and his offspring no mention was made of the law. On the contrary, the promise was connected only with 'the righteousness that comes by faith'. Abraham believed the promise, his faith in the promise of God was credited to him as righteousness, and this was the ground upon which God would fulfill the promises he made to him.

Paul indicates that the content of the promise was 'that he would be heir of the *world*'. There is no OT text that corresponds exactly with Paul's statement. According to Genesis God promised to give Abraham and his descendants the whole land of Canaan, 'from the wadi of Egypt to the great river, the Euphrates' (Gen 15:18-21), and that they would 'take possession of the cities of their enemies' (Gen 22:17). However, before Paul's time the promise of land had come to be understood to mean that they would inherit the world, as the following texts (among many others)[120] reveal:

> I shall give to your seed all of the land under heaven, and they will rule in all nations as they have desired. And after this all of the earth will be gathered together, and they will inherit it forever. (*Jub.* 32:19)

> To the elect there shall light, joy, and peace, and they shall inherit the earth. (*1 Enoch* 5:7)

> All this I have spoken before you, O Lord, because you have said that it was for us that you created the world. As for the other nations which have descended from Adam, you have said that they are nothing. . . . And now, O Lord, behold these nations, which are reputed as nothing, domineer over us and devour us. But we your people, whom you have called your first-born, only begotten, zealous for you, and most dear, have been given into their hands. If the world has indeed been created for us, why do we not possess our world as an inheritance? How long will this be so? (*4 Ezra* 6:55-59)

> Therefore the Lord assured him [Abraham] with an oath that the nations would be blessed through his offspring; that he would make him as numerous as the dust of the earth, and exalt his offspring like the

119. A figure that seems to be based upon Exod 12:40, where the Israelites' sojourn in Egypt is said to have been 430 years in duration. For a discussion of the chronological difficulties involved see Ronald Y.-K. Fung, *The Epistle to the Galatians* (NICNT; Grand Rapids: Eerdmans, 1988), 157, n. 26.

120. See also *Jub.* 19:21; 22:14; *2 Apoc. Bar.* 14:13; 44:12-13; 51:3; 57:1-3; Philo, *Vit. Mos* 1.155; *4 Ezra* 6:59; 7:9-11; *m. 'Abot* 2:7; 5:19.

stars, and give them an inheritance from sea to sea and from the Euphrates to the ends of the earth. (Sir 44:21)[121]

However, when the apostle spoke of Abraham inheriting 'the world', he was probably not simply adopting current Jewish beliefs, but rather saw the fulfillment of the promise to Abraham in the light of Christ and in terms of the coming kingdom, and all that God promises his people.[122]

Having said that it was through the righteousness that comes by faith and not through the law that Abraham received the promise, Paul draws a logical but astounding conclusion: *For if those who depend on the law are heirs, faith means nothing and the promise is worthless, because law brings wrath.* The precise meaning of those who depend on the law' (lit. 'those of the law') has been the subject of some debate. Is the NIV translation correct when it renders the text as 'those who depend on the law', allowing the interpretation that in the present context Paul is denying that any who rely on their observance of the law are the true heirs of the promise?[123] Or does it mean simply Jewish people, and is Paul here denying that ethnic identity, membership in the ancient covenant people of God, guarantees that Jews are heirs of the promise?[124] Or is it possible that 'those of the law' denotes those who are both Jews in the ethnic sense and who also seek righteousness by observance of the law's demands.[125] It is probably best to adopt the 'both and' approach — 'those of the law' refers to ethnic Jews who rely on their observance of the law for a share in the inheritance.[126]

121. Byrne, *Romans*, 157, n. 13, comments: 'Across a broad range of the representative literature, the content of the "promise" or "inheritance" undergoes notable "extension" to include, first, the whole world (cf. Sir 44:21; *Jub.* 19:21; Philo, *Vit. Mos.* 1.155; cf. *1 Enoch* 5:7b) and then, in an eschatological sense, the "world to come", the blessings of salvation (cf. *Pss. Sol.* 12:6; *Bib. Ant.* 32:3; *Sib. Or.* 3:768-69; *4 Ezra* 6:59; 7:9; *2 Apoc. Bar.* 14:13; 44:13; 51:3; 57:1-3; *m. 'Abot* 2:7; 5:19; further the rabbinic material in SB 3.209). In *Jub.* 22:14; 32:19 the patriarchal blessings specifically apply to Israel the lordship of the world conferred upon human beings (Adam) according to Gen 1:26-28 (cf. Ps 8:6-8) — a hope cherished also at Qumran: 4QpPs 37 3:1-2 ("... all the inheritance of Adam"); 1QH 17:15; 1QS 4:22-23; CD 3:20; cf. also *4 Ezra* 6:54). Here we see an intersection of what might be called the "Adamic" and the "Abrahamic" trajectories with respect to "promise", "inheritance" and the lordship of the world. Paul's view of the messianic lordship of the risen Jesus (Phil 2:9-11; 1 Cor 15:20-28; Phil 3:20-21) appears to presuppose this intersection (cf. esp. the "messianic" use of Psalm 8 in the latter of the two passages). Believers come into this "inheritance" through their existence in and conformity to the risen Lord: cf. 1 Cor 3:21b-23; 6:2-3; also Rom 5:17'.

122. Severian writes: 'Paul says that the righteous will inherit the world because the ungodly will be thrown out and handed over to punishment on the day of judgment, but the righteous will possess the universe which remains, and will have been renewed, and the good things of heaven and earth will be theirs'. 'Pauline Commentary from the Greek Church' (*ACCSR*, 118).

123. So, e.g., Moo, *Romans*, 275.

124. So, e.g., Dunn, *Romans 1–8*, 214.

125. Cf. Byrne, *Romans*, 158.

126. Jewett, *Romans*, 326, says: 'Since Gentile proselytes could also become "sons of

Paul says that if those who are Jews and live by the law are heirs of the promise, then 'faith means nothing' (lit. 'faith has been emptied')[127] because it is no longer the necessary condition for receiving the inheritance. In fact, the promise would be 'worthless' also because the promise that Abraham's descendants would inherit the land was made in response to Abraham's faith (Gen 15:1-21) — a promise that would be worthless if it depended on his observance of the law (which had not yet been given!). The apostle also implies that being people of the law cannot be the ground upon which God gives the inheritance because those who rely solely upon their ethnicity and their observance of the law to qualify them for a share in the inheritance are sadly mistaken. For if, as Paul has argued in chapters 2–3, they are in fact transgressors of the law, then upon them the law 'brings wrath'.

4:15b   It is not clear why Paul adds here the statement: *And where there is no law there is no transgression.* Is he saying something that was true in the case of Abraham, for he lived before the law was given, so he could not be a transgressor of the law (cf. 5:12-14; 7:7-13; Gal 2:18-20)?[128] Or, as seems more likely, is this verse parenthetical, prompted by the mention of the law in 4:13-15a, and, although expressing one of Paul's strong convictions, not logically connected to its immediate context?

4:16-17a   Having shown that the promised inheritance could not be obtained by Jewish people through observance of the law because that would render faith of no value and make the promise worthless, and because the law brings wrath, Paul explains: *Therefore, the promise comes by faith, so that it may be by grace and may be guaranteed to all Abraham's offspring.* The NIV's 'therefore' implies a reference back to what precedes. However, it appears preferable to see it pointing forward to what follows because of

---

the law", it is inappropriate to conclude that Paul's primary interest here is to overcome the ethnic prerogative with regard to the promise'.

127. Paul uses the verb 'to empty' *(kenoō)* in four other places in his letters: in 1 Cor 1:17, where he speaks of preaching the gospel 'not with wisdom and eloquence, lest the cross of Christ be emptied *(kenōthē)* of its power'; in 1 Cor 9:15, where he speaks of his determination to preach the gospel free of charge, saying 'I would rather die than allow anyone to deprive me of this boast' *(to kauchēma mou oudeis kenōsei,* lit. 'no one will empty my [ground of] boasting'); in 2 Cor 9:3, where he tells the Corinthians that he is sending 'the brothers' to them to ensure that they have their contribution to the collection ready when he arrives 'in order that our boasting about you in this matter should not prove hollow' *(hina mē to kauchēma hēmōn to hyper hymōn kenōthē en tō merei toutō,* lit. 'in order that our boasting about you in this matter may not [prove to] have been emptied'); and in Phil 2:7, where he says of Christ that 'he made himself nothing' *(heauton ekenōsen,* lit. 'emptied himself').

128. In order to argue that Abraham become an inheritor of the promise because of his observance of the law, Jewish scholars had to argue for the preexistence of the law, and that Abraham observed it even before it was promulgated on Sinai: he offered the firstfruits *(Jub.* 15:1-2); kept the feast of tabernacles *(Jub.* 16:20); and observed the law of the Most High (Sir 44:20). Cf. N. Calvert-Koyzis, 'Abraham: New Testament', in *The IVP Dictionary of the New Testament,* ed. Daniel G. Reid (Downers Grove/Leicester: InterVarsity Press, 2004), 1-16, esp. 2.

the purpose clause that it introduces, which could then be translated: 'For this reason [it is] by faith, so that [it may be] by grace'. Behind this stands the express purpose of God. He has determined that the fulfillment of the promise should come through faith 'so that it may be by grace' and so that it 'may be guaranteed to all Abraham's offspring' (lit. 'the seed'). It is God's intention that the realization of the promise be effected by his grace, and not be based on ethnicity and law observance, and so in this way it 'may be guaranteed to *all* Abraham's offspring', Gentile as well as Jewish believers.[129] This Paul underlines when he adds that the promise is guaranteed *not only to those who are of the law but also to those who have the faith of Abraham,* that is, not only believing Jews but all those who 'have the faith of Abraham', including believing Gentiles. 'Those who are of the law' (lit. 'the one of the law') here probably denotes the Jewish believer, and Paul is saying that the reason God made the reception of the promised inheritance dependent on being a person of faith like Abraham rather than simply a person of the law is so that the inheritance may be received by Gentile believers and not only by Jewish believers.

Because Gentile as well as Jewish believers may be said to be 'of the faith of Abraham', Paul can say that *he is the father of us all.* Offering scriptural support for this, the apostle adds: *As it is written: 'I have made you a father of many nations'.* 'Nations' here translates a word that can mean nations, peoples, or Gentiles, but in its original context it refers to the multitude of Abraham's physical descendants: 'As for me, this is my covenant with you: You will be the father of many nations. No longer will you be called Abram; your name will be Abraham, for *I have made you a father of many nations.* I will make you very fruitful; I will make nations of you, and kings will come from you' (Gen 17:4-6, italics added). Cranfield comments: 'In Genesis the thought may be simply of the Ishmaelites and Edomites and the descendants of Abraham and Keturah, though it is not impossible that a more far-reaching thought is already present. Among the Rabbis there were some who claimed on the basis of this Genesis verse that Abraham can be said to be the father of proselytes and even the father of all men'.[130] In any case, Paul clearly cites the text in support of his claim that believing Gentiles are numbered among the 'nations' of which Abraham is father. The apostle sees fulfillment of this promise, not simply in the multitude of Abraham's physical descendants but also, and more significantly, in the multitude of both Jews and Gentiles who walk in the footsteps of Abraham's faith and so have their own faith credited to them as righteousness. In this way they become 'heirs of the world', as God promised.

129. Thomas H. Tobin, 'What Shall We Say That Abraham Found? The Controversy behind Romans 4', *HTR* 88 (1995) 448-49, notes the different way Paul uses the idea of Abraham's offspring/seed *(sperma)* in Rom 4:16 and Gal 3:15-18. In the former *sperma* denotes all those, Gentiles as well as Jews, who share Abraham's faith, while in the latter *sperma* refers to Christ.

130. Cranfield, *Romans*, I, 243.

d. The Essential Nature of Abraham's Faith, 4:17b-22

17bHe is our father in the sight of God, in whom he believed — the God who gives life to the dead and calls into being things that were not. 18Against all hope, Abraham in hope believed and so became the father of many nations, just as it had been said to him, 'So shall your offspring be'. 19Without weakening in his faith, he faced the fact that his body was as good as dead — since he was about a hundred years old — and that Sarah's womb was also dead. 20Yet he did not waver through unbelief regarding the promise of God, but was strengthened in his faith and gave glory to God, 21being fully persuaded that God had power to do what he had promised. 22This is why 'it was credited to him as righteousness'.

In these verses Paul unpacks the nature of Abraham's faith, the faith counted to him as righteousness and by which he received the promise that he and his seed would inherit the world.

4:17b The apostle begins: *He is our father in the sight of God in whom he believed.* This is the NIV's rendition of a grammatically difficult clause that, translated literally, is 'before God in whom he believed', to which the NIV has added the words, 'he is our father', to construe it as the beginning of a new sentence.[131] While this clause introduces a new section dealing with the nature of Abraham's faith, it is also grammatically connected to what precedes. Literally translated, 4:17 as a whole reads: 'As it is written: "I have made you a father of many nations", before God in whom he believed'.[132] Having said that Abraham is 'our father in the sight of God', Paul adds that this is the God 'in whom he believed', that is, in whom Abraham believed. Paul then describes the God in whom Abraham believed as *the God who gives life to the dead.* For Paul, to give life is a distinctly divine prerogative (8:11; 1 Cor 15:22, 36, 45; 2 Cor 3:6) as it is in both the OT (Deut 32:39; 1 Sam 2:6; 2 Kgs 5:7; Neh 9:6; Ps 71:20) and elsewhere in the NT (John 5:21; 6:63). As the apostle's argument proceeds, it becomes clear that neither Abraham's age nor the 'deadness' of Sarah's womb was any obstacle to the God who gives life to 'the dead' when he acts to fulfill his promise to Abraham.

The apostle further describes this God as the one who *calls into being*

---

131. The NRSV provides a different rendering of this text, construing it as a subordinate clause (shown in italics below), and placing the latter part of 4:16 in parenthesis, so that 4:16-17 reads: 'For this reason it depends on faith, in order that the promise may rest on grace and be guaranteed to all his descendants, not only to the adherents of the law but also to those who share the faith of Abraham (for he is the father of all of us, as it is written, 'I have made you the father of many nations') — *in the presence of the God in whom he believed, who gives life to the dead and calls into existence the things that do not exist'.* In this case it would appear that those who share the faith of Abraham do so in the presence of God.

132. Cranfield, *Romans,* I, 243, says: '*katenanti hou episteusen theou* is equivalent to *katenanti tou theou hō episteusen.* The words are naturally connected with *hos estin patēr pantōn hēmōn,* v. 17a being a parenthesis'.

things that were not (cf. NRSV: 'calls into existence the things that do not exist').[133] This appears to imply *creatio ex nihilo*. There are numerous Jewish texts which express this idea: 'The one who in the beginning of the world called that which did not yet exist and they obeyed you' (*2 Apoc. Bar.* 21:4); 'And with a word you bring to life that which does not exist, and with great power you hold that which has not yet come' (*2 Apoc. Bar.* 48.8); 'He called the non-existent into existence' (Philo, *Spec. Leg.* 4.187); 'I beg you, my child, to look at the heaven and the earth and see everything that is in them, and recognize that God did not make them out of things that existed. And in the same way the human race came into being' (2 Macc 7:28); 'Before anything existed at all, from the very beginning, whatever exists I created from the non-existent, and from the invisible the visible' (*2 Enoch* 24.2).[134] It would seem on first reading that Paul is using this widespread notion here in 4:17b to describe God as the one who creates *ex nihilo*, a commonly held view.[135] As his argument proceeds, then, he would be implying that God calls into existence a child for Abraham, admittedly not *ex nihilo*, but certainly when otherwise there was no possibility at all that such a child would come into existence. Moo, however, sounds a cautionary note:

> There can be no doubt that Paul's language is quite close to this Jewish *creatio ex nihilo* tradition and that an allusion to either God's general creative power or his spiritual creative power would not be out of place in the context. However, if this were Paul's purpose, it is surprising that he speaks of God's calling things 'as though' they existed; we would have expected him to say 'calls things into being'. This leads us to conclude, somewhat hesitantly and reluctantly, that the clause cannot refer to God's creative power as such, whether general or spiritual. It is, then, the nature of God as 'speaking of' or 'summoning' that which does not yet exist as if it does that Paul must mean. And this interpretation fits the immediate context better than a reference to God's creative power, for it explains the assurance with which God can speak of the 'many nations' that will be descended from Abraham.[136]

4:18-22 In these verses Paul describes the nature of Abraham's faith in God. *Against all hope, Abraham in hope believed and so became the father of many nations* (lit. 'who against hope believed in hope so that he became the

133. The idea of calling things into existence is also found in Isa 48:13: 'My own hand laid the foundations of the earth, and my right hand spread out the heavens; when I summon them, they all stand up together'.

134. Paul uses the expressions *ta mē onta* and *ta onta* metaphorically in 1 Cor 1:28 when he says: 'God chose the lowly things of this world and the despised things — and the things that are not *(ta mē onta)* — to nullify the things that are *(ta onta)'*. In this context the expressions are used to refer to people who are 'nobodies' and others who are 'somebodies'.

135. So, e.g., Fitzmyer, *Romans*, 386; Cranfield, *Romans*, I, 244-45; Dunn, *Romans 1–8*, 218.

136. Moo, *Romans*, 282.

father of many nations'). The NIV substitutes 'Abraham' for 'who', thus construing the text, not as a relative clause, but as the beginning of a new sentence: This does not change the meaning and makes for easier reading. The essential point is that despite all those things that militated against the possibility of Abraham becoming a father of many nations — things that will be spelled out in 4:19 — he believed the promise of God, *just as it had been said to him, 'So shall your offspring be'.*[137] Paul's quotation is taken verbatim from Genesis 15:5 (LXX), which, when read in its context, reflects the magnitude of the promise and how impossible Abraham considered its fulfillment to be:

> But Abram said, 'Sovereign LORD, what can you give me since I remain childless and the one who will inherit my estate is Eliezer of Damascus?' And Abram said, 'You have given me no children; so a servant in my household will be my heir'. Then the word of the LORD came to him: 'This man will not be your heir, but a son who is your own flesh and blood will be your heir'. He took him outside and said, 'Look up at the sky and count the stars — if indeed you can count them'. Then he said to him, *'So shall your offspring be'*. Abram believed the LORD, and he credited it to him as righteousness. (Gen 15:2-6, italics added)

Paul proceeds to explain what it meant for Abraham to believe in hope against all hope. First, his faith involved no denial of the realities of his own situation: *Without weakening in his faith, he faced the fact*[138] *that his body was as good as dead — since he was about a hundred years old*[139] *— and that Sarah's womb was also dead.* Cranfield offers the following explanation for one of the puzzling elements in the story of Abraham: 'The difficulty of Abraham's subsequent marriage to Keturah and begetting of six sons by her (Gen 25.1f) need not worry us unduly. The difficulty concerns Gen 17.17 as much as Paul. Augustine, who drew attention to it, argued that it was only Sarah who was incapable of becoming a parent, while Calvin concluded that "When Abraham, who before had been like a dry, withered

137. Jewett, *Romans,* 336, notes: 'By introducing the following citation from Genesis with the words *kata to eirēmenon* ("as he had been told"), Paul again evokes the face-to-face encounter with God that we noted in v. 17b. Abraham's faith is a proper response to his encounter with God's promise'.

138. The NIV's 'he faced the fact' translates *katenoēsen,* 'he considered'. There is a variant reading, *ou katenoēsen,* 'he did not consider', that appears to say the very opposite. In context the two readings amount to the same thing. In the first case Abraham's strong faith was untroubled when he 'faced the fact' (NIV) of his body being as good as dead, and in the second case, his strong faith enabled him not to consider his body as good as dead as a hindrance to God's ability to do what he promised.

139. Oecumenius says: 'Paul was right to say: *about a hundred,* because Abraham was not a hundred but only ninety-nine years old'. 'Pauline Commentary from the Greek Church' (*ACCSR,* 123). Moo, *Romans,* 284, comments: 'Since Gen. 17:1 claims that Abraham was ninety-nine years old when the promise of offspring was renewed, Paul's is an acceptable approximation'.

tree, was revived by the heavenly blessing, he not only had the power to beget Isaac, but having been restored to the age of virility, was afterward able to produce other offspring"'.[140]

Second, Abraham's faith involved unwavering trust in God's promise: *Yet he did not waver through unbelief regarding the promise of God, but was strengthened in his faith and gave glory to God.*[141] Abraham did not allow the stubborn realities of his situation to cause his faith in the promise of God to waver; on the contrary, the apostle says that he 'was strengthened in his faith'. Paul's use of the passive voice of the verb implies that it was God who strengthened his faith. Moo comments: 'In what way did Abraham's faith "grow strong"? In the sense that anything gains strength in meeting and overcoming opposition — muscles when weights are raised; holiness when temptation is successfully resisted. So Abraham's faith gained strength from its victory over the hindrance created by the conflict between God's promise and the physical evidence'.[142]

Being strengthened in his faith, Paul adds, '[he] gave glory to God', that is, being strengthened in his faith [by God], he gave glory to God.[143] What is implied is that people's faith in God is what glorifies God — expressing their belief in his goodness, truthfulness, reliability, and, in particular, his promises. Abraham gave glory to God by steadfastly acknowledging the trustworthiness of his promise to him, *being fully persuaded that God had power to do what he had promised.* Abraham's faith included not only belief in God's trustworthiness, but also being 'fully persuaded'[144] that God had the power to perform what he promised. Paul concludes this section by quoting Genesis 15:6 once more, *This is why 'it was credited to him as righteousness'* (cf. 4:3). By so doing he emphasizes that it was Abraham's unwavering faith that God credited to him as righteousness, thus making him acceptable to God.

e. The Relevance of God's Dealings with Abraham for All Believers, 4:23-25

Having argued his case in respect of Abraham — that it was his faith that was credited to him as righteousness — Paul proceeds to explain the implications of this for his audience.

140. Cranfield, *Romans*, I, 247-48.

141. Wright, 'Romans', 500, comments: 'Paul pulls a veil over the various episodes such as Abraham's passing Sarah off as his sister and the whole matter of Hagar and Ishmael. . . . The feature of this faith to which Paul draws attention is its persistence in hoping for new life when Abraham's and Sarah's bodies were, in terms of potential childbearing, as good as dead because of their age'.

142. Moo, *Romans*, 285-86.

143. The expression 'to give glory to God' is used with several nuances of meaning in the NT. It can involve variously believing the promises of God (4:20); giving thanks (Luke 17:18); speaking the truth (John 9:24); acknowledging God (Acts 12:23; Rev 11:13; 16:9); and praising God (Rev 19:7).

144. *Plērophoreō* followed by *hoti* means 'to be fully convinced that . . .'. Cf. BAGD, *ad loc.*

²³The words 'it was credited to him' were written not for him alone, ²⁴but also for us, to whom God will credit righteousness — for us who believe in him who raised Jesus our Lord from the dead. ²⁵He was delivered over to death for our sins and was raised to life for our justification.

4:23-24   Addressing his audience directly,[145] Paul says: *The words 'it was credited to him' were written not for him alone, but also for us.* The statement, 'the words . . . were written not for his sake alone', implies that they were written in the first place for Abraham's sake. Generally this has been taken to mean that they were written to preserve the memory of Abraham,[146] though Jewett argues that earlier scholars understood them to mean 'written to his honor' — something he says that would have been self-evident in an honor-shame culture.[147]

When Paul states that 'the words . . . were written not for his sake alone, but also for us', he is affirming that Scripture not only had relevance for Abraham but is also relevant for his audience, and in fact for all believers. Paul believed that what is found in Scripture as a whole applies not only to those about whom or for whom it was originally written, but also to his audiences. In 15:4 he writes: 'For everything that was written in the past was written to teach us, so that through the endurance taught in the Scriptures and the encouragement they provide we might have hope', and in 1 Corinthians 10:11, referring to the exodus generation, he says to the Corinthian believers: 'These things happened to them as examples and were written down as warnings for us, on whom the culmination of the ages has come'. Consistent with this approach to Scripture, Paul here insists that, when Genesis 15:6 says that Abraham 'believed the LORD; and he credited it to him as righteousness', these words 'were written not for him alone, but also for us'. It has application for all who, like Abraham, believe the promise of God (and in this context that includes Gentile believers).

Accordingly, Paul adds, *to whom God will credit righteousness — for us who believe in him who raised Jesus our Lord from the dead.* All who believe in the one who raised Jesus from the dead will have their faith credited to them as righteousness. It is possible that when Paul says that God 'will credit righteousness', he has in mind God's declaration in favor of those who believe on the Day of Judgment. However, in the light of 5:1, 9, where Paul says that believers 'have (now) been justified', a reference to a pres-

---

145. Wright, 'Romans', 501, comments on the fact that in 4:23-25 Paul addresses his audience directly once more: 'He has not talked specifically about "us" (i.e., himself and his audience) since 1:5-15. Insofar as he has been addressing anyone, it has been the hypothetical debating partner within the "diatribe" style; for the rest, the argument has remained at a general level. Now at last he places his readers on the carefully drawn map; from here the next four chapters will develop, in which "we", and "our" status before God, are a major theme'.
146. Cf., e.g., Dunn, *Romans 1–8*, 222; Byrne, *Romans*, 161; Cranfield, *Romans*, I, 250.
147. Jewett, *Romans*, 340.

ent experience of justification (= the crediting of righteousness) cannot be ruled out.

Christian faith is here spoken of as faith 'in him who raised Jesus our Lord from the dead' (i.e., God). It is unusual, but not unique in Paul's letters, for God to be spoken of as the object of believers' faith (cf. 2 Tim 1:12; Tit 3:8). Typically Jesus Christ is the object of believers' faith (Rom 3:22; 9:33; 10:10-11, 14; Gal 2:16; 3:22; Eph 1:13; Phil 1:29: 1 Tim 1:16; 1 Tim 3:16).[148] A possible reason for the apostle's choosing to speak of God as the object of believers' faith here is to show how this corresponds to Abraham's faith that was also faith *in God.*

Paul describes God as the one 'who raised Jesus our Lord from the dead', a description he uses repeatedly (see also 8:11; 10:9; 1 Cor 6:14; 15:15; 2 Cor 4:14; Gal 1:1).[149] Christian faith here is depicted as belief in the one who raised Christ from the dead — similar, we might say, to the faith of Abraham, who, according to the writer to the Hebrews, when asked to sacrifice his son Isaac, believed that God 'could even raise the dead' (Heb 11:17-19).

4:25 Having spoken of 'Jesus our Lord' as the one whom God raised form the dead Paul adds: *He was delivered over to death for our sins and was raised to life for our justification.* The two clauses in this verse reveal an obvious parallelism:

> he   was delivered over   for our sins
> and   was raised   for our justification

This may reflect early Christian tradition based on Isaiah 53:12 LXX ('his soul was delivered over to death'). If so, Paul would have employed it because the text was familiar to his audience, and because it expressed what he wanted to say. It is significant that the two clauses make use of the passive voice ('was delivered over', 'was raised'), clearly functioning as 'divine passives', God himself delivered over his Son for our sakes, and God also is the one who raised him up.

The interpretation of the two occurrences of the preposition 'for' is debated. There are three main possibilities: (i) both are causal: he was handed over to death *because of* our sins, he was raised *because of* our justification — it is rather strange to say that Christ had to be raised because we were justified; (ii) the first is causal: he was handed over to death *because of*

148. Occasionally some gospel truth is described as the object of faith (Rom 6:8; 10:9; 1 Thess 4:14); and on numerous occasions faith is spoken of in an absolute sense, with no direct object (Rom 1:16; 4:11; 10:4; 13:11; 15:13; 1 Cor 1:21; 3:5; 15:2, 11; 2 Cor 4:13; Eph 1:19; 1 Thess 1:7; 2:10, 13; 2 Thess 1:10).

149. When the apostle speaks of Jesus' resurrection, he never says that Jesus *rose* from the dead, but says always, either implicitly (Rom 4:25; 6:9; 7:4; 8:34; 1 Cor 15:4, 12, 13, 14, 20; 2 Cor 5:15; 2 Tim 2:8) or explicitly (Rom 4:24; 6:4; 8:11; 10:9; 1 Cor 6:14; 15:15; 2 Cor 4:14; Gal 1:1; Eph 1:20; Col 2:12; 1 Thess 1:10), that he *was raised* by God.

our sins, but the second is prospective: he was raised *with a view to* our justification — the most likely: clearly Christ was handed over to death because
of our sins, and his vindication by resurrection (like the Servant) was not
for him only but also for those who have a share in his vindication and are
so justified;[150] (iii) both are prospective: he was handed over to death *with a
view to* [dealing with] our sins, he was raised *with a view to* our justification
— less likely in respect to the first preposition, seeing that it is necessary to
add 'dealing with' for it to make sense.[151]

In relation to Christ being handed over for our sins, we may say that
at one level it was Pilate who handed Jesus over to death, but at another
and far more important level it was God himself who handed him over.
Later, reflecting on one of the implications of such a costly action on God's
part, Paul says: 'He who did not spare his own Son, but gave him up for us
all — how will he not also, along with him, graciously give us all things?'
(8:32). The incredible fact that *Jesus our Lord* was handed over for *our* sins,
the ultimate expression of God's love for humanity, stands at the very heart
of Paul's gospel. When defining the gospel that he and the other early apostles preached, the apostle said: 'For what I received I passed on to you as of
first importance: that Christ died for our sins according to the Scriptures'
(1 Cor 15:3). Ephesians 1:7 expresses it more clearly: 'In him we have redemption through his blood, the forgiveness of sins, in accordance with the
riches of his grace'. The apostle states it with great profundity in 2 Corinthians 5:19-21: 'God was reconciling the world to himself in Christ, not counting people's sins against them. . . . God made him who had no sin to be sin
for us, so that in him we might become the righteousness of God'.[152]

---

150. BAGD, *ad loc.*: '*dia ta paraptōmata* on account of transgressions 4:25a (cp. Is 53:5;
PsSol 13:5); but *dia tēn dikaiōsin* in the interest of justification vs. 25b'. Cf. Moo, *Romans*, 289;
Cranfield, *Romans*, I, 252.

151. For a full discussion of the three alternatives, see Michael Bird, ' "Raised for Our
Justification": A Fresh Look at Romans 4:25', *Colloquium* 35 (2003) 39-44.

152. Various interpretations have been suggested for this profound statement:
(a) Christ was made a sinner, (b) Christ was made a sin offering, (c) Christ was made to bear
the consequences of our sins. The first interpretation is rightly rejected out of hand. The second can be supported by appeal to Paul's use of sacrificial terminology elsewhere to bring
out the significance of Christ's death (e.g., 3:25; 1 Cor 5:7). However, the third interpretation
is to be preferred, supported by the fact that in Gal 3:13 Paul interprets the work of Christ in
terms of his bearing the consequences of our sins: 'Christ redeemed us from the curse of the
law by becoming a curse for us, for it is written, "Cursed is every one who is hung on a
pole" '. This interpretation is further supported by the fact that the statement, 'God made
him who had no sin to be sin for us' (2 Cor 5:21a) is balanced in antithetical parallelism by
the words, 'so that in him we might become the righteousness of God' (2 Cor 5:21b). The
former must be construed in such a way that the latter is understood as its antithetical counterpart. If becoming the righteousness of God means that God has adjudicated in our favor
with all its resultant blessings, then to become sin, being the antithetical counterpart of that,
will mean that God has adjudicated against Christ because he took upon himself the burden
of our sins (cf. Isa 53:4-6, 12) with the result that his relationship with God was (momen-
tarily, but terribly beyond all human comprehension) severed. See the discussion in

While it is clear from Paul's writings what the apostle meant when he wrote that Christ 'was delivered over to death for our sins', it is not immediately clear what he meant when he wrote that Christ 'was raised to life for our justification'. This is the only place in Paul's letters where the resurrection of Christ is explicitly connected with justification.[153] Schreiner observes: 'To say that Jesus was raised because of our justification is to say that his resurrection authenticates and confirms that our justification has been secured. . . . The resurrection of Christ constitutes evidence that his work on our behalf has been completed'.[154]

Alternatively, the significance of Christ's being raised for our justification may be understood in terms of the present intercessory work of the risen Christ. Thus in 8:34 Paul asks: 'Who then is the one who condemns? No one. Christ Jesus, who died — more than that, who was raised to life — is at the right hand of God and is also interceding for us'. Here Christ's being raised to life is juxtaposed with his intercession for us. As the risen Christ, he intercedes for us, and in the light of that God graciously justifies us. While the focus of debate has been upon the significance of the parallel clauses, 'delivered over to death for our sins' and 'raised to life for our justification', Paul's main emphasis in this verse appears to have been overlooked. Lowe remarks: 'Paul's emphasis is that Christ's handing over was *for us,* and his resurrection was also *for us*'.[155]

In 5:18 Paul says that it was Christ's 'righteous act', that is, his death on the cross, that led to our justification. This should alert us to the fact that it was not Paul's intention in 4:25 to drive a wedge between the effects of Christ's death (securing forgiveness for our transgressions) and his resurrection (leading to our justification). Rather, it was the death and resurrection of Jesus as one great salvation event that secured both our forgiveness and our justification. While it is possible to speak separately about forgive-

---

Colin G. Kruse, *The Second Epistle of Paul to the Corinthians* (TNTC 8; Leicester: Inter-Varsity Press/Grand Rapids: Eerdmans, 1987), 128-30.

153. Though Bird, 'Raised for Our Justification', 31, suggests that it may be implied in 1 Cor 15:17; 1 Tim 3:16.

154. Schreiner, *Romans,* 244. Moo, *Romans,* 290, notes: 'We must still insist that Paul is affirming here a theological connection between Jesus' resurrection and our justification (cf. 5:10). As Jesus' death provides the necessary grounds on which God's justifying action can proceed, so his resurrection, by vindicating Christ and freeing him forever from the influence of sin (cf. 6:10), provides for the ongoing power over sins experienced by the believer in union with Christ'. Similarly Wright, 'Romans', 504: 'the resurrection of Jesus can at this level be seen as the declaration of justification. And this can perfectly well be expressed as "He was raised because of our justification"'.

155. Bruce A. Lowe, 'Oh *dia!* How Is Romans 4:25 to Be Understood?' *JTS* 57 (2006) 151-52. To further support his view Lowe draws attention to Isaiah 53 and says, 'If, as is argued, the LXX of Isa. 53:5 *(dia ta hamartias hēmōn)* is part of the source behind Rom. 4:25a, why is it not recognized that *hēmeis* is the word of emphasis in both expressions? Such an *echo* of the wider ideas of Isa. 53 has largely been passed over, but when noted provides strong support for the idea that the "for us" in 4:25 is the point of focus, even as it is in Rom. 4:23-4'.

ness and justification, they cannot be separated in fact. Those whose sins God forgives he also justifies.[156]

C. Justification Brings Freedom and Hope, 5:1–8:39

In this long section Paul spells out the blessings of salvation enjoyed by those whom God justifies. They have peace with God and rejoice in hope of sharing his glory. They are able to rejoice in suffering knowing that God uses even this to develop character. As his love is shed abroad in their hearts, their hope increases all the more. This love was demonstrated in Christ's death for them, whereby the effects of Adam's transgression are more than compensated in the lives of those who believe. Where sin abounded, grace abounds all the more. But this does not mean believers continue in sin, for they have died to sin and now live under the lordship of Christ, and no longer under the law of Moses. This does not mean there is anything wrong with the law itself; sin is the problem taking the opportunity the law provided to deepen people's bondage. For those who have been justified and freed from the law there is no longer any condemnation and, paradoxically, the requirement of the law is fulfilled in their lives as they walk in the Spirit. Even so, they experience sufferings in the present time, though these are not worth comparing with the glory to be revealed in them. The creation itself awaits this revelation, for then it too will be released from the futility to which it was subjected. In the meantime the Spirit helps believers in their weakness, while God ensures that all things work together for their good. The section concludes with a great emotive climax celebrating the love of God in Christ for all believers.

1. Justified by Faith, 5:1-11

At 5:1 a new section of the letter (5:1–8:39) begins. A number of factors indicate this to be the case: (i) The opening words, 'Therefore, since we have been justified through faith . . .', sum up the argument of 1:18–4:25 and prepare the way for what follows. (ii) Key words in 5:1-11 recur in 8:18-39 (love of God/Christ; justify; glory; peace; hope; tribulation; save; endurance). (iii) The exposition of Scripture in 1:18–4:25 gives way to Paul's own line of thought in 5:1–8:39. (iv) There is a noticeable change of style — the largely polemic style employed in 1:18–4:25 gives way to a more pastoral style in 5:1–8:39. Striking features of 5:1-11 include the prominent place given to the death of Christ and the introduction of the theme of the Holy Spirit.

There are several ways in which 5:1-11 has been analyzed, which are

---

156. So, too, Cranfield, *Romans*, I, 252.

often very similar with only minor variations.[1] The following analysis serves the exposition that follows: 5:1-2, the benefits of justification; 5:3-5, rejoicing even in suffering; 5:6-10, God's love demonstrated in Christ's death for us; and 5:11, rejoicing in God having received our reconciliation.

When expounding these things, the apostle includes his audience with himself as those who are recipients of these blessings. This he does by the repeated use of the first person plural ('we'), in contrast to the predominant use of the third person in the preceding chapters (1:16–4:25, except, of course, the use of the second singular in the diatribe of chap. 2). By so doing the apostle seeks to reinforce the relationship between himself and his Roman audience that he sought to establish in 1:1-15. There it was done diplomatically and in terms of his audience's status as (predominantly) Gentile believers and Paul's role as apostle to the Gentiles. Here in 5:1-11, however, the relationship is based upon their common share in the justifying grace of God.[2]

a. The Benefits of Justification, 5:1-2

[1]*Therefore, since we have been justified through faith, we have peace with God through our Lord Jesus Christ, [2]through whom we have gained access by faith into this grace in which we now stand. And we boast in the hope of the glory of God.*

In 4:22-25, where Paul argued that Scripture says that Abraham's faith 'was credited to him for righteousness', he also insisted that this was written 'not for him alone, but also for us, to whom God will credit righteousness — for us who believe in him who raised Jesus our Lord from the dead'. From this flow many blessings for believers, and in 5:1-2 the apostle expounds a number of them.

5:1 Paul begins: *Therefore, since we have been justified through faith, we have peace with God through our Lord Jesus Christ.* Paul uses an aorist participle of the verb 'to justify', thereby presenting justification as a completed act and, as the following verses show, a completed act that is the basis of other blessings experienced by believers in the present and that provides hope for the future. God justifies, in the here and now, those who believe in his Son, and this will be confirmed on the Day of Judgment. Then it will become clear that God has rejected any and all charges brought against those whom he justifies (cf. 8:33). On God's part justification is an act of sheer grace.

On the part of the human recipients it is faith alone that God recog-

---

1. Cf., e.g., Wright, 'Romans', 514; Byrne, *Romans*, 164-65.

2. Cf. Patricia M. McDonald, 'Romans 5.1-11 as a Rhetorical Bridge', *JSNT* 40 (1990) 82-91, esp. 81, says that 5:1-11 functions as 'a rhetorical bridge between the apostle and the Roman Christians'.

nizes as the prerequisite for justification. In chapter 4 Paul showed that Abraham's belief in the promises of God was reckoned to him as righteousness, and he emphasized that Scripture records this fact for the benefit of all who similarly believe. The faith of those whom God justifies is faith like that of Abraham; faith that takes God at his word, believing the gospel of God concerning his Son, and accepting his promise of salvation. This they do without claiming any merit of their own. They are the ones who 'have been justified through faith'.

The first benefit of justification that Paul mentions in 5:1 is that the enmity between human beings and God is ended, and 'we have peace with God'. So saying, he employs the present tense of the verb 'to have', thus depicting this peace as the ongoing experience of believers. There is a textual variant at this point that has the hortatory subjunctive, 'let us have' *(echōmen)*, instead of the present indicative 'we have' *(echomen)*, in which case the text would be urging people to have peace with God rather than declaring that they already have it.[3] The substitution of hortatory subjunctive for the present indicative, however, may be explained by auditory confusion on the part of copyists.[4] The indicative, indicating that believers have peace with God, suits the context better where the apostle is listing present benefits of justification. It is therefore to be preferred.[5]

We have this peace 'through our Lord Jesus Christ' because it was by his atoning sacrifice that our sins were dealt with so that they are no longer counted against us. This peace is both objective and subjective. It is objective in the sense that it is a peace established through Christ's atoning sacrifice (3:25) when he made peace by the blood of his cross (cf. Col 1:20). It is subjective in that we then have a sense of being at peace with God as the Holy Spirit bears witness with our spirits that we are children of God (cf. 8:15-16). This peace with God must of course manifest itself in harmonious relationships within the Christian community, something the apostle will stress in 12:1-15:13. It goes without saying that the peace won for us by Christ's death and resurrection differs fundamentally from the *Pax Romana* won and maintained by Romans emperors by the exercise of brutal force.

5:2 Explaining further the blessings we enjoy, Paul adds that Christ is the one *through whom we have gained access by faith*[6] *into this grace in which we now stand.* The word 'access' is found only in the Pauline corpus in the

---

3. Robert Jewett, 'The God of Peace in Romans: Reflections on Crucial Lutheran Texts', *CurrTheolMiss* 25 (1998) 187-88, supports this variant (citing the work of Stanley Porter, 'The Argument of Romans 5: Can a Rhetorical Question Make a Difference?' *JBL* 110 [1991] 662-65). Cf. Jewett, *Romans*, 348.

4. The hortatory subjunctive, 'let us have' *(echōmen)*, may, when read, sound very much like the present indicative 'we have' *(echomen)*. Cf. Fitzmyer, *Romans*, 395.

5. Cf. Wright, 'Romans', 515.

6. The words 'by faith' *(tē pistei)* are omitted in some manuscripts, though the evidence for their inclusion and omission is evenly balanced. In context, the sense of the passage is not materially altered either way.

NT (here and in Eph 2:18; 3:12).[7] In the Ephesians texts it refers to access to God himself, whereas here in 5:2 it is access into his grace. Where the word is used in extrabiblical texts in relation to persons (e.g., to Cyrus),[8] it implies that a certain standing in that person's presence has been granted.[9]

In this context, the 'grace' into which we have access is that of being justified by faith. When the apostle speaks of this grace as that 'in which we now stand', he uses the perfect tense, which focuses attention upon the status/standing of justified believers who have access to God.[10] The word 'now' in the phrase 'in which we *now* stand', though not found in the original, being added by the NIV translators, does reflect the fact that the status we enjoy is experienced in the here and now. The grace in which we stand is better understood as the justifying grace of God rather than our peace with God, something recognized by most scholars.[11]

Moving from the blessings we enjoy in the here and now, Paul refers to our future felicity when he says: *And we boast in the hope of the glory of God.* The verb 'to boast' is an unusual choice in this context. When used elsewhere by the apostle, it is most often in contexts where he contrasts legitimate with illegitimate boasting.[12] This suggests that Paul may not only be drawing out the blessings of justification for those who believe in Jesus Christ so that we can legitimately boast in hope of sharing the glory of God, but may have also at the back of his mind those whose boasting is illegitimate because it is not based on faith in Christ.

The 'glory of God' about which we rejoice/boast in hope is the restoration of the glory lost at the fall. The status humanity enjoyed, being created in the image and glory of God, was marred by sin. In the case of believers this is in process of being restored as we are 'being transformed into his image with ever-increasing glory' (2 Cor 3:18). It will be restored fully when our hope of sharing in the glory of God reaches its consummation in

7. Eph 2:18: 'For through him we both have access (*prosagōgēn*) to the Father by one Spirit'; Eph 3:12: 'in whom we have access (*prosagōgēn*) to God in boldness and confidence through faith in him' (NRSV).

8. Cf. BAGD, *ad loc.*

9. Fitzmyer, *Romans,* 396, comments: 'The peace that Christians experience is derived from being introduced into the sphere of divine favor by Christ, who has, as it were, escorted them into the royal audience-chamber of God's presence'.

10. Jewett, *Romans,* 350, suggests that the possible background to the concept of standing in grace is to be found in the LXX, where 'to stand' (*histēmi*) is employed in descriptions of the Levites' standing before God in the temple. Cf. 2 Chr 29:11: 'the LORD has chosen you to stand (*stēnai*) before him and serve him, to minister before him and to burn incense'.

11. Cranfield, *Romans,* I, 259, supports this view by noting that otherwise 'the whole relative clause *di' hou, k.t.l.* would be tautologous after *eirēnē echomen . . . dia tou kyriou hēmōn Iesou Christou'.* Moo, *Romans,* 301, describes 'this grace' as 'the realm in which "grace reigns" (5:21), a realm that is set in contrast to the realm or domain of the law (6:14, 15; the believer is not "under law" but "under grace"; cf. also Gal. 5:4)'.

12. Cf. 2:17, 23; 1 Cor 1:29, 31; 3:21; 4:7; 13:3; 2 Cor 5:12; 7:14; 9:2; 10:8, 13, 15-17; 11:12, 16, 18, 30; 12:1, 5-6, 9; Gal 6:13-14; Eph 2:9; Phil 3:3.

the new age (8:18-21, 30; cf. 1 John 3:2-3).[13] See 'Additional Note: The Glory in Store for Believers', below.

ADDITIONAL NOTE:
THE GLORY IN STORE FOR BELIEVERS

Paul's references to the glory in store for believers occur pervasively throughout his letters and are found in many differing contexts and employed for differing purposes:

1. *The Reward of a Good Life.* In 2:7, 10 Paul says that those who seek glory through persistence in doing good will be rewarded by God with glory, honor, and peace, and that this will be the case 'first for the Jew, then for the Gentile'.

2. *The Hope of Glory.* Believers have access to the grace of God, including their sure hope of participating in the glory of God, through their faith in Jesus Christ (5:1-2). This is made known to them through the preaching of the gospel of Christ (Col 1:27), through which they are also called into God's kingdom and glory (1 Thess 2:12; 2 Thess 2:14). Paul prays that the eyes of his converts' hearts may be opened to know the hope to which they are called, that is, the riches of his glorious inheritance (lit. 'the riches of the glory of his inheritance'). It is the presence of Christ in/among believers now that is their hope of glory (Col 1:27), a glory in which they will appear when Christ himself appears (Col 3:4). Our Lord himself described the future glory of believers when he said: 'Then the righteous will shine like the sun in the kingdom of their Father' (Matt 13:43).

3. *Suffering and Glory.* There is a connection between the sufferings experienced by believers in the present time and their participation in the glory yet to be revealed. Paul asserts that his present 'light and momentary' sufferings (in fact they were heavy and ongoing) are achieving (lit. 'are producing/working') for him an eternal glory that far outweighs his sufferings (2 Cor 4:17). He adds that the sufferings we endure now are not worth comparing with the glory to be revealed in us (8:18). He believed that his own sufferings made it possible for his converts to 'obtain the salvation that is in Christ Jesus, with eternal glory' (2 Tim 2:10).

4. *Resurrection Glory.* Believers' future glory includes a glorious resurrection body. The present mortal body will die, sown, as it were, in dis-

---

13. Wright, 'Romans', 516, comments: 'The content of the hope is "glory". This is an advance statement of the theme developed in 8:18, 21, 30 (cf. Col 1:27). Adam's lost glory (3:23) is regained in the Messiah: not simply dazzling beauty, but the status and task of being God's vicegerent over creation. That this is what Paul has in mind becomes clear in 8:18-27, where the revelation of God's children and their glory leads to the liberation of the whole created order. When humans are restored to be as they were intended to be, then the whole of creation will be renewed under their lordship'.

honor to be raised in glory (1 Cor 15:43; Rom 8:23), for when Christ appears he will 'transform our lowly bodies so that they will be like his glorious body' (Phil 3:21). At this time creation itself will be released from its bondage to decay and be brought into the freedom of the glory of the children of God (8:21).

5. *Prepared Beforehand for Glory*. Believers have been prepared beforehand and called from among both Jews and Gentiles to share in the glory of God, the glory that God has also prepared beforehand for them (1 Cor 2:9).

6. *Present Transformation to Ever-Increasing Glory*. As believers await the future glory prepared beforehand for them, they themselves 'are being transformed into his likeness with ever-increasing glory, which comes from the Lord, who is the Spirit' (2 Cor 3:18).

---

b. Rejoicing Even in Suffering, 5:3-5

In these verses Paul says, surprisingly, that as a result of God's grace we not only rejoice in hope of sharing the glory of God but also rejoice in our sufferings in the light of the beneficial effects they produce.

> *³Not only so, but we also glory in our sufferings, because we know that suffering produces perseverance; ⁴perseverance, character; and character, hope. ⁵And hope does not put us to shame, because God's love has been poured out into our hearts through the Holy Spirit, who has been given to us.*

5:3-5 Explaining why we can rejoice in sufferings and their beneficial effects, Paul says: *Not only so, but we also rejoice in our sufferings, because we know that suffering produces perseverance; perseverance, character; and character, hope.* The word used for 'sufferings' is one Paul usually employs to denote the afflictions or persecutions that he and the Roman believers encounter from without, from a hostile world.[14] He may also have in mind the tribulation of the last days that will usher in the messianic age. If so, it would give further reason for us to rejoice — the suffering we are experiencing is but the precursor of the coming glorious age.

'We glory' translates a verb whose essential meaning is 'to boast'. This is not the only place where the apostle speaks about boasting in sufferings — he does so notably in 2 Corinthians 11–12 when seeking to counter the illegitimate boasting of false apostles.[15] However, here in 5:3-4 the

---

14. Cf., e.g., 8:35; 2 Cor 1:4, 8; 2:4; 4:17; 6:4; 8:2; Eph 3:13; Col 1:24; 1 Thess 1:6; 3:3, 7; 2 Thess 1:4. Jewett, *Romans*, 353, suggests: 'Paul evidently has specific hardships in mind that are known to himself and the Roman congregation. These difficulties related to the expulsion of Jewish Christian leaders under Claudius and their return from exile after 54 C.E. would certainly be included along with whatever portion of Paul's own sufferings that were known in Rome'.

15. In 2 Corinthians Paul responds to the boasting of false apostles who made odious

boasting of which he speaks is not a boasting about the sufferings themselves but boasting because we know that God makes even our suffering
serve our good. Thus, under God's good hand, the suffering we experience
produces 'perseverance', the ability to endure difficulties with patience and
fortitude. Paul makes a similar point in 2 Corinthians 1:6 where he writes:
'If we are distressed, it is for your comfort and salvation; if we are com-
forted, it is for your comfort, which produces in you patient endurance of
the same sufferings we suffer'. Paul mentions endurance/perseverance frequently as a Christian virtue (cf. 2 Cor 6:4; 12:12; Col 1:11; 1 Thess 1:3, 4;
1 Tim 6:11; 2 Tim 3:10; Tit 2:2).[16]

Perseverance in turn, Paul says, '[produces] character'. The word
translated 'character' is found in the NT only in Paul's letters, where it carries the meaning of either the process of testing/an ordeal (2 Cor 2:9; 8:2) or
the outcome of testing (5:4; 2 Cor 9:13; 13:3; Phil 2:22), a tested and approved character, as it does here. Under God this is what is produced in us
by perseverance in suffering.[17]

Character developed through perseverance in its turn, Paul adds,
'[produces] hope'. While it is easy to understand how suffering produces
perseverance and how perseverance produces character, it is difficult to explain how character produces hope, and the apostle gives no indication of
the way he thinks this occurs. We might surmise that, if the character produced by perseverance includes a greater trust in God, this in turn
strengthens our hope of sharing the glory promised by God. The following
comment by Moo is pertinent: 'Sufferings, rather than threatening or weakening hope, as we might expect to be the case, will, instead, increase our

---

comparisons between their ministry and his. They boasted of their Jewish pedigree and piety, their rhetorical prowess, and the charismatic accompaniments to their ministry. Paul,
while letting it be known that in most of these matters he and his ministry were equal to or
better than theirs, proceeded to turn this whole matter of boasting on its head. He boasted
of his sufferings, for these were the marks of the genuine apostle of Christ. Far from being a
negation of genuine apostleship, suffering, weakness and persecution were the badges of
true apostleship, and in these the power of God was made perfect (2 Cor 11:18–12:10).

16. Byrne, *Romans*, 170, comments: '"Endurance" *(hypomonē)* is a strong word denoting persevering steadfastness in the face of suffering; it is a favored term of the Greek Stoics
and also features prominently in the "martyr" theology of Judaism, reflecting the double
sense of fortitude under suffering and trust in God for ultimate deliverance (cf. 4 Macc 1:11;
9:8, 30; 15:30; 17:4, 12, 17, 23); Job was regarded as a particular example of this quality'.

17. Paul probably drew his concept of God testing his people and the production
thereby of godly character from the OT (cf., e.g., Job 23:10: 'when he has tested me, I will
come forth as gold'; Prov 17:3: 'The crucible for silver and the furnace for gold, but the LORD
tests the heart'; Wis. 3:6: 'like gold in the furnace he tried them'). The apostle may also have
had in mind the testing of Abraham's faith in the matter of the binding of Isaac. Just possibly he had been informed of what Jesus said to Peter: 'Simon, Simon, Satan has asked to sift
you as wheat. But I have prayed for you, Simon, that your faith may not fail' (Luke 22:31-
32). In Jas 1:12 we read: 'Blessed is the one who perseveres under trial because, having stood
the test *(dokimos)*, that person will receive the crown of life that God has promised to those
who love him'.

certainty in that hope. Hope, like a muscle, will not be strong if it goes unused. It is in suffering that we must exercise with deliberation and fortitude our hope, and the constant reaffirmation of hope in the midst of apparently "hopeless" circumstances will bring ever-deeper conviction of the reality and certainty of that for which we hope (see Rom. 4:18-19)'.[18]

What the apostle wants to emphasize is that *hope does not put us to shame*. The verb 'to put to shame' he uses here is found in two other places in Romans, and in both cases within a quotation from Isaiah 28:16.[19] In both places also the quotation is used to show that those who put their trust in God will never be put to shame; their trust will never be shown to be in vain. What Paul is affirming here in 5:5 is that our hope in sharing the glory of God will never be a cause of shame for us, as will that of those who entertain vain hopes.[20]

The reason Paul gives for saying that this hope will not disappoint us is that *God's love has been poured out into our hearts through the Holy Spirit, who has been given to us*. It is because of 'God's love made palpable in the experience of the Spirit (v 5b)' that we have confidence and do not lose hope. This is the first reference to the love of God in Romans, and by speaking of it as being 'poured out' Paul emphasizes its lavish bestowal upon believers (cf. 8:35, 39; Eph 2:4-5; 3:18-19). When Paul says that 'God's love has been poured out . . . by the Holy Spirit', he may be alluding to the prophecy of Joel cited by the apostle Peter on the Day of Pentecost: '"In the last days", God says, "I will pour out my Spirit on all people. . . . Even on my servants, both men and women, I will pour out my Spirit in those days, and they will prophesy"' (Acts 2:17-18 [italics added]; cf. Joel 2:28-29, LXX 3:1-2).[21]

The NIV's 'God's love' may also be translated as 'the love of God', and this may be understood in two ways. First, as our 'love for God' — the presence of the Holy Spirit then creating in us a love for God.[22] Second, it

---

18. Moo, *Romans*, 303-4.

19. 9:33: 'As it is written: "See, I lay in Zion a stone that causes people to stumble and a rock that makes them fall, and the one who believes in him will never be put to shame *(kataischynthēsetai)*"'. 10:11: 'As the Scripture says, "Anyone who believes in him will never be put to shame *(kataischynthēsetai)*"'.

20. Witherington, *Romans*, 136, says: 'In an honor-shame culture such as Paul lived in, to have believed in a false God, to have placed one's hope in a hoax, and for this to become public knowledge was one of the ultimate forms of humiliation (see Ps. 22:5; 25:3, 20)'.

21. Dunn, *Romans 1–8*, 253, says: 'Here it is important to recall that in prophetic expectation the outpouring of the Spirit was looked for as the mark of the new age (see particularly Isa 32:15; 34:16; 44:3; Ezek 11:19; 36:26-27; 37:4-14; Joel 2:28-32). Together with the echo of Jer 31:31-34 and Joel 2:28-29 in the preceding phrase, Paul effectively brings to clear expression what had been more implicit throughout his argument from 3:21 onwards: That with Christ's death and resurrection the new age of Jewish expectation had already dawned. Within contemporary Judaism the only real parallel is the sect at Qumran (see particularly 1QH 7.6-7; 12.11-12; 14.13; 16.11-12; 17.26); but Qumran's outworking of that experience in increased devotion to the covenant, as marked by an intensification of the works of the law, was radically different from Paul's'.

22. Wright, 'Romans', 517, says: 'It is possible . . . preferable, to read "the love of God"

could be understood as 'God's love for us' — the Holy Spirit filling us with a sense of God's love for us. Two considerations support the latter: (i) In the immediate context Paul goes on to describe the outstanding nature of God's love for us (5:6-11, esp. 5:8: 'God demonstrates his own love for us in this: While we were still sinners, Christ died for us'); (ii) In 8:15-16 Paul says, 'The Spirit you received does not make you slaves, so that you live in fear again; rather, the Spirit you received brought about your adoption to sonship. And by him we cry, "*Abba,* Father". The Spirit himself testifies with our spirit that we are God's children'. In this case the Holy Spirit creates within believers a sense of their filial relationship with God, a sense of God's love for them as his children.

Paul states that 'God's love has been poured out into our hearts', prompting the question when this outpouring was received by believers. Käsemann says: 'The [perfect] tense [of the verb] suggests an ongoing state established by a once-for-all act. What is in mind is probably the baptismal event in which the Spirit is imparted, according to the common view of primitive Christianity'.[23] Even though more recent grammatical studies have revised this understanding of the perfect tense, Käsemann is probably correct in saying that the pouring out of the love of God by the Spirit into the hearts of believers is something that occurs at baptism. This may be accepted so long as we understand that in the early church baptism was the focal point of the conversion-initiation experience when human beings expressed their repentance and faith by submission to baptism and when God forgave them their sins and bestowed upon them his Spirit.

Paul's belief that the Holy Spirit has been given to believers is expressed more fully elsewhere. He indicates that God bestows his Holy Spirit upon believers as a guarantee in the present of their full participation in salvation in the future. He uses two metaphors to express this truth. First, he depicts the Holy Spirit as the 'firstfruits' of the 'full harvest' of salvation (8:23: 'we ourselves, who have the firstfruits of the Spirit, groan inwardly as we wait eagerly for our adoption to sonship, the redemption of our bodies'). Second he speaks of the Holy Spirit as the deposit or down payment given by God in the present guaranteeing provision of full salvation in the future (2 Cor 5:5: 'Now the one who has fashioned us for this very purpose is God, who has given us the Spirit as a deposit guaranteeing what is to come'; Eph 1:13-14: 'When you believed, you were marked in him with a seal, the promised Holy Spirit, who is a deposit guaranteeing our inheritance until the redemption of those who are God's possession').

---

in 5:5 as a[n] . . . allusion to the *Shema,* and to take it therefore as the objective genitive: our love for God. This then links up with two previous programmatic passages in the letter: 1:5, where Paul speaks of "the obedience of faith" as the result of the gospel, and 3:30, where the monotheism of the *Shema* undergirds justification itself'.

23. Käsemann, *Romans,* 135.

c. God's Love Demonstrated in Christ's Death for Us, 5:6-11

⁶You see, at just the right time, when we were still powerless, Christ died for the ungodly. ⁷Very rarely will anyone die for a righteous person, though for a good person someone might possibly dare to die. ⁸But God demonstrates his own love for us in this: While we were still sinners, Christ died for us.

⁹Since we have now been justified by his blood, how much more shall we be saved from God's wrath through him! ¹⁰For if, while we were God's enemies, we were reconciled to him through the death of his Son, how much more, having been reconciled, shall we be saved through his life! ¹¹Not only is this so, but we also boast in God through our Lord Jesus Christ, through whom we have now received reconciliation.

In these verses Paul explains the extent of God's love for believers, the sense of which is shed abroad in their hearts by the Holy Spirit. It is a love that is demonstrated in the death of God's own Son for us.

5:6 He begins: [*For*] *you see, at just the right time, when we were still powerless,*[24] *Christ died for the ungodly.* The preposition 'for', omitted by the NIV, connects the explanation of the nature of God's love in these verses with the previous statement about God's love being poured into our hearts by the Holy Spirit. Literally rendered, 5:6 would read: 'For while we were still weak/powerless, at the right time Christ died for the ungodly'. 'At the right time' designates the time appointed by God to effect the work of salvation. In Galatians 4:4-6, a passage that has significant affinity with 5:5-6, the apostle expresses the same idea, albeit using different words: 'But when the set time had fully come, God sent his Son, born of a woman, born under law, to redeem those under law'. . . . Here in 5:6 the time is further defined as 'when we were still powerless (lit. 'weak')', usually construed as morally weak because of the context where Paul immediately refers to Christ's death for the *ungodly.*[25]

It was at this time, so defined, that 'Christ died for the ungodly'. As Byrne points out: 'This is the language used earlier to designate the wickedness of the unredeemed world against which God's wrath is revealed

24. 'You see, at just the right time, when we were still powerless, Christ died for the ungodly' translates *eti gar Christos ontōn hēmōn asthenōn eti kata kairon hyper asebōn apethanen.* The repetition of *eti* here is awkward, but has very strong manuscript support. Its omission in some manuscripts probably represents attempts to improve the text.

25. But cf. Dunn, *Romans 1–8*, 254, who says: 'The *asthenēs* does not have any particular theological overtones here (despite BGD, "morally weak"); Paul uses it and related words simply in a general sense to characterize the human condition as such in contrast to the power of God (as in 8:26; 1 Cor 15:43; cf. Wisd Sol 9:5 . . .). . . . The argument that "'weak' is far too mild a word to represent the state of those for whom Christ died" (O'Neill) misses the point that Paul begins a crescendo here (weak, ungodly, sinners, enemies — vv 6, 8, 10); the obvious place to begin is with the weakness of the creature over against the omnipotence of the Creator (cf. 1:20; 4:21)'.

(1:18; cf. also 4:5). "We" were part of that world alienated from God and it was precisely for us as part of that world that Christ died'.[26]

What distinguishes the love of God for humanity more than anything else is that 'Christ died for the ungodly', those who actually violate God's expectations of humanity,[27] those whom Paul will shortly describe as God's 'enemies' (5:10). It was not unknown in the ancient world that someone might lay down his/her life for a friend,[28] but to do so for one's enemy was unheard of. Within the Jewish context it was well known that one might die out of loyalty to the law (2 Macc 7:9; 8:21) or on behalf of the nation (John 18:14), but to die for the ungodly, those whose wickedness attracts the wrath of God (1:18), was unthinkable. Sirach 12:4-7 reads:

> Give to the devout, but do not help the sinner. Do good to the humble, but do not give to the ungodly; hold back their bread, and do not give it to them, for by means of it they might subdue you; then you will receive twice as much evil for all the good you have done to them. For the Most High also hates sinners and will inflict punishment on the ungodly. Give to the one who is good, but do not help the sinner.[29]

5:7 To highlight the extraordinary nature of God's love, the apostle first points out by way of comparison that *very rarely will anyone die for a righteous person, though for a good person someone might possibly dare to die.* 'A righteous person' is the NIV's rendering of the anarthrous substantive adjective 'righteous', and 'a good person' is its rendering of the articular substantive adjective 'the good'. The addition of 'person' in both cases is interpretive. Most commentators agree that the 'righteous' indeed denotes 'a

---

26. Byrne, *Romans*, 167.

27. The word 'ungodly' *(asebēs)* is used also in 1 Tim 1:9-11, a passage that lists being ungodly *(asebēs)* with a number of other sins and thereby throws light upon its significance: 'We also know that law is made not for the righteous but for lawbreakers and rebels, the ungodly *(asebesi)* and sinful, the unholy and irreligious; for those who kill their fathers or mothers, for murderers, for the sexually immoral, for those practicing homosexuality, for slave traders and liars and perjurers — and for whatever else is contrary to the sound doctrine that conforms to the gospel concerning the glory of the blessed God, which he entrusted to me'.

28. In the ancient world friendship was very important, and operated at a number of levels: political friendship in which certain people were known as friends of the king (friends of Caesar); benefactor-client friendship in which a wealthy person would become the patron of someone less-well-off; and mutual friendship among equals. Especially in this last category friendship involved sharing of confidences, possessions, and in the extreme case laying down one's life for one's friend.

29. Witherington, *Romans*, 137, comments: 'How different is the logic here compared to Sirach 12:1-7, which advises to recognize whom you are doing good to and "give to the godly person but do not help the sinner". Seneca advised giving help to those who deserved it (*De beneficiis* 4.27.5), and Aristotle (*Ethics* 9.8.1169a) speaks of doing good for one's friends. Paul's logic runs counter to the normal conventions of the day. He stresses that God's action in Christ is without human analogy'.

righteous person'; however, there has been debate concerning the way 'the good' should be construed.

Some scholars argue that 'righteous' and 'the good' are synonymous.[30] However, the early church fathers tended to interpret 'the good' as a reference to God or to Christ for whom martyrs were prepared to die.[31] Recently Martin has defended this view by citing extensively from ancient authors to show that the articular substantive adjective 'the good' is frequently used of deity.[32] Others interpret 'the good' as a reference to a generous benefactor. While it is rare indeed for people to lay down their lives for the morally upright, it is not inconceivable that they might do so for their benefactors. Clarke reviews the six principal interpretations offered for the 'righteous' and 'the good' in 5:7 before concurring with Cranfield that the 'good person' is best understood as a benefactor. In the client-benefactor relationship clients were under obligation towards their benefactors. Andrews concludes: 'The obligations which were owed to one's benefactor were socially binding, and it would not have been unthinkable for a man to lay down his life for such an honourable person'.[33]

5:8 In contrast to the point he made about those for whom human beings might dare to die, Paul begins by saying: *But God demonstrates his own love for us in this: While we were still sinners, Christ died for us.* Elsewhere Paul speaks of the death of Christ as a proof of *Christ's* love for him (cf. Gal 2:20: 'I live by faith in the Son of God, who loved me and gave himself for me'), but here Christ's death is the demonstration of *God's* love for humanity. The apostle has already said that God, by presenting his Son 'as a sacrifice of atonement', demonstrated his justice while justifying sinners (3:25-

30. So, e.g., Erich Seitz, 'Korrigiert sich Paulus? Zu Röm 5,6-8', *ZNW* 91 (2000) 279-87.

31. So, e.g., Origen, 'Commentary on the Epistle to the Romans' (*ACCSR*, 131); [Pseudo-] Constantius, 'The Holy Letter of St. Paul to the Romans (*ACCSR*, 132). C. P. Bammel, 'Patristic Exegesis of Romans 5:7', *JTS* 47 (1996) 532-42, reports patristic discussions of 5:7 in which early church fathers (in particular Rufinus, Jerome, and Origen) reject the heretical interpretation that the righteous for whom one will scarcely die is 'the just God of the law and prophets' and for whom there were few martyrs, and that the good for whom one would dare to die is 'the good Christ or Father of Christ' for whom there were many martyrs. Bammel concludes that, according to Origen, 'Christ is to be described as both just and good, but also that the Old Testament prophets risked martyrdom on his behalf. Thus there is no distinction to be made between Old Testament martyrdom and New Testament martyrdom — both are *pro bono*, i.e. for Christ' (539).

32. Troy W. Martin, '*The Good* as God (Romans 5.7)', *JSNT* 25 (2002) 59-65, argues that construing it this way overcomes several otherwise difficult exegetical problems: (i) 'The definite article, which occurs with *agathou* but not with *dikaiou* in v. 7, supports a divine reference by removing the grammatical congruence of *agathou* and *dikaiou*'. . . . (ii) 'Accepting God as the referent for *tou agathou* resolves the first exegetical issue of Rom. 5.7 by removing the need to distinguish between a righteous and a good person. The anarthrous *dikaiou* in the former half of this verse refers to any human being who is righteous, while the articular *agathou* in the latter half refers to God from whom all goodness derives'.

33. Andrew D. Clarke, 'The Good and the Just in Romans 5:7', *TynBul* 41 (1990) 128-42. Cf. also Bruce W. Winter, 'The Public Honouring of Christian Benefactors: Romans 13.3-4 and 1 Peter 2.14-15', *JSNT* (1988) 93; Wright, 'Romans', 519.

26). Now he stresses that this action was at the same time a demonstration of God's love for sinners. And this demonstration of God's love was made while the objects of that love were still at enmity with him (cf. 5:10).

5:9 Because Christ has died for us sinners, certain amazing things follow. First: *Since we have now been justified by his blood, how much more shall we be saved from God's wrath through him!* This 'how much more' argument is one the apostle uses four times in this chapter (5:9, 10, 15, 17). It is the argument from the greater to the lesser. In this case Paul argues that believers, having '*now* been justified by his blood' (the greater), may be sure that they *will* 'be saved from God's wrath through him (the lesser)'. The ultimate threat confronting sinners is neither sin itself, nor the power of Satan, nor even death, but the wrath of God (see 'Additional Note: The Wrath of God', 90-91), and we are saved from that only through the death of Christ. Käsemann insists: 'There is not the slightest reason, for fear of anthropomorphism, to make of this an objective principle (Dodd) or impersonal process (Hanson, *Wrath*, 89) or even to relate wrath to the sufferings of vv 3f. What is meant is the consuming power of the World-Judge which according to 1:18ff. has already announced itself in hidden form in earthly history'.[34]

The apostle can speak variously of our being justified by God's grace 'through the redemption that came by Christ Jesus' (3:24), 'through faith' in Christ (5:1), and here 'by his blood' (5:9). All these are aspects of God's justifying grace. He can adjudicate in favor of those who believe in his Son because he has given him as the atoning sacrifice for their sins, something effected through the blood of his Son — his death in their place. Other references to Christ's blood in Paul's letters are found in 3:25; 1 Corinthians 10:16; 11:25, 27; Ephesians 1:7; 2:13; Colossians 1:20.

5:10 The second outcome of Christ's death for believers that Paul stresses here is that they are 'saved by his life': *For if, while we were God's enemies, we were reconciled to him through the death of his Son, how much more, having been reconciled, shall we be saved through his life!* Before we explore what it means to be 'saved through his life', we need to comment on a couple of other matters mentioned in this verse.

First, prior to their conversion believers were 'God's enemies'. This is not the only place where Paul speaks of unbelievers being God's enemies. In 11:28 he says that his unbelieving Jewish kinsfolk were, as far as the gospel is concerned, enemies on your (the Gentiles') account. In Philippians 3:18 Paul mentions, 'even with tears', that 'many live as enemies of the cross of Christ'. And in Colossians 1:21 he reminds his audience that 'once you were alienated from God and were enemies in your minds because of your evil behavior'. The question arises whether here Paul intends to say that the enmity is found on the human side or on God's side. That Paul was convinced that there is enmity towards God on the human side is implied in 1:30 ('God haters') and 8:7 ('the mind governed by the flesh is hostile to

---

34. Käsemann, *Romans*, 138.

God'), and in Colossians 1:21 ('once you were alienated from God and were enemies in your minds'). But in the previous verse (5:9) Paul has just said that believers have been saved from 'God's wrath' through Christ, and this indicates that there was also hostility on God's side towards sinners. Wright's comment is very helpful: 'We should not, I think, cut the knot and suggest that the enmity was on our side only. God's settled and sorrowful opposition to all that is evil included enmity against sinners. The fact that God's rescuing love has found a way of deliverance and reconciliation is part of the wonder of the gospel'.[35]

Second, Paul says that believers, who were once enemies of God, have been 'reconciled to him through the death of his Son'. If the relationship between God and humanity was one of mutual enmity and if the relationship was to be restored, reconciliation would have to be effected. The initiative for this reconciliation was taken, not, as one might expect, by those who were alienated from God, but by God himself. Reconciliation with God, though not a major theme in Paul's letters, is nevertheless an important one. Apart from his references to reconciliation here in 5:10-11, it is implied in 5:1 ('since we have been justified through faith, we have peace with God') and spoken of explicitly in 11:15 ('For if their [unbelieving Jews'] rejection brought reconciliation of the world, what will their acceptance be but life from the dead?) and 2 Corinthians 5:18-19 ('All this is from God, who reconciled us to himself through Christ and gave us the ministry of reconciliation: that God was reconciling the world to himself in Christ, not counting men's sins against them').[36]

35. Wright, 'Romans', 520. Jewett, *Romans,* 364, rejects this approach. He argues: 'In his most explicit discussion of human enmity and reconciliation, Paul appeals to human volition, "We beseech you, in behalf of Christ, be reconciled to God" (2 Cor 5:20); this passage opens with the appeal: "let us have peace with God" (Rom 5:1). The atoning death of Christ did not aim at assuaging divine wrath, since "God was in Christ reconciling the world to himself, not counting their trespasses against them" (2 Cor 5:10), a viewpoint echoed throughout this pericope: Christ died "on our behalf" (Rom 5:8), for "the ungodly" (5:6), to demonstrate "God's love" (5:6, 8), not to prompt a transformation of divine wrath into love. To turn this into a drama of assuaging God's anger or counterbalancing divine justice is to impose later theories of the atonement onto a passage where they do not belong'.

36. The concept of reconciliation with God was not unknown in Judaism. Cf. 2 Macc 1:5: 'May he hear your prayers and be reconciled to you, and may he not forsake you in time of evil'; 2 Macc 5:20: 'What was forsaken in the wrath of the Almighty was restored again in all its glory when the great Lord became reconciled'; 2 Macc 7:33: 'And if our living Lord is angry for a little while, to rebuke and discipline us, he will again be reconciled with his own servants'; 2 Macc 8:29: 'When they had done this, they made common supplication and implored the merciful Lord to be wholly reconciled with his servants'. Dunn, *Romans 1–8,* 260, notes: 'The idea of reconciliation through a mediator was familiar — particularly in the case of Moses turning away God's wrath from Israel (Ps 106:23; Josephus *Ant.* 3.315), but also Aaron (Wisd Sol 18:20-25) and Phineas (Sir 45:23 . . .)'. Jewett, *Romans,* 365-66, comments: 'Victors claim to be able to impose reconciliation, as illustrated by Alexander the Great's grandiose claim to be *diallaktēs tōn holōn* ("reconciler for the whole world", Plutarch *Mor.* 329c). This background has led Martin Hengel and Ferdinand Hahn to suggest that the Greco-Roman ruler cult was a source of Paul's concept of reconciliation. . . . Seyoon Kim ar-

The juxtaposition of justification (5:9) and reconciliation (5:10) is noteworthy, and raises the question of distinctions between the two concepts. As used by Paul, the terms are very close but nevertheless distinct. Justification is essentially a legal term relating to decisions in a court of law, whereas reconciliation is a personal term relating to the restoration of relationships. But Paul's understanding of God as the justifier of sinners cannot be separated from his understanding of God as reconciler. For Paul God is not the detached judge dispensing judgment, but the lover of sinners desiring reconciliation with them.

We come back now to the question of what the apostle means by 'be saved through his life'. It has been suggested that Paul's meaning is not so much that we are saved 'through his life' but rather that we are saved 'in his life'? If the phrase were interpreted in this way, the apostle would be implying that our full salvation comes about by sharing in his risen life.[37] While there is some truth in this suggestion, it has little support in the immediate context. The context (cf. 5:9) suggests that to be saved by his life involves being 'saved through him from the wrath of God'. In this case Paul could have in mind the intercessory role of the risen Christ mentioned in 8:34 ('Christ Jesus who died . . . is at the right hand of God and is also interceding for us') and in other NT writings (Heb 7:25: 'he is able to save completely those who come to God through him, because he always lives to intercede for them'; 1 John 2:1-2: 'But if anyone does sin, we have an advocate with the Father — Jesus Christ, the Righteous One. He is the atoning sacrifice for our sins'). This latter alternative is preferable because it has contextual support as well as support in other NT documents that the first alternative lacks.

5:11 Paul concludes this section (5:1-11) of his letter by adding, *Not only is this so, but we also boast in God through our Lord Jesus Christ, through whom we have now received reconciliation.* 'We boast' is something the apostle has already said we do in the hope of the glory of God (5:2) and even in our sufferings because God uses them to benefit us (5:3-4). Here he points out that we boast because we have even *now* received reconciliation. Paul began this section of his letter by listing the benefits for believers of having *now* been justified by faith (5:1-5), and in 5:11 he concludes it by saying that we can boast in having *now* received reconciliation. Justification and reconciliation are closely related in Paul's thought. Believers are both justified and reconciled by the death of Christ ('by his blood'/'through the death of his Son'), and, being justified/reconciled, they shall be saved by him on the last day ('saved through him from the wrath of God'/'saved by his life'). While justification and reconciliation are closely related, they are not identical concepts. Justification highlights the forensic aspect and reconciliation the rela-

---

gues that Paul's conversion provides the likely location for the development of the concept of reconciliation. Paul's former enmity against God was transformed by divine love, and he thereupon took up the task of bearing a reconciling gospel to the hated Gentiles'.

37. So, e.g., Wright, 'Romans', 520. Similarly Moo, *Romans*, 312; Dunn, *Romans 1–8*, 260; Fitzmyer, *Romans*, 401.

tional aspect of the salvation made possible through Christ's death, though, of course, justification cannot be said to be without its relational significance, and reconciliation presupposes a resolution of the forensic problem.[38]

2. The Humanity-Wide Effects of the Actions of Adam and Christ, 5:12-21

[12]*Therefore, just as sin entered the world through one man, and death through sin, and in this way death came to all people, because all sinned —*

[13]*To be sure, sin was in the world before the law was given, but sin is not charged against anyone's account where there is no law.* [14]*Nevertheless, death reigned from the time of Adam to the time of Moses, even over those who did not sin by breaking a command, as did Adam, who is a pattern of the one to come.*

[15]*But the gift is not like the trespass. For if the many died by the trespass of the one man, how much more did God's grace and the gift that came by the grace of the one man, Jesus Christ, overflow to the many!* [16]*Nor can the gift of God be compared with the result of one man's sin: The judgment followed one sin and brought condemnation, but the gift followed many trespasses and brought justification.* [17]*For if, by the trespass of the one man, death reigned through that one man, how much more will those who receive God's abundant provision of grace and of the gift of righteousness reign in life through the one man, Jesus Christ!*

[18]*Consequently, just as one trespass resulted in condemnation for all people, so also one righteous act resulted in justification and life for all people.* [19]*For just as through the disobedience of the one man the many were made sinners, so also through the obedience of the one man the many will be made righteous.*

[20]*The law was brought in so that the trespass might increase. But where sin increased, grace increased all the more,* [21]*so that, just as sin reigned in death, so also grace might reign through righteousness to bring eternal life through Jesus Christ our Lord.*

In 5:1-11 Paul explained the many blessings that flow from justification by faith. Following this explanation, in 5:12-21 he picks up again the main theme running through 3:21–5:21, that is, that there are no distinctions between Jews and Gentiles in the matter of salvation, or, more precisely as far as 5:12-21 is concerned, that Christ's death has humanity-wide implications. To do so the apostle further explains what God has done 'through our Lord Jesus Christ' by contrasting the glorious effects of Christ's action with the damning effects of Adam's action. The only similarity between the act of Adam and the act of Christ is the humanity-wide

---

38. Cf. Kruse, *Paul, the Law and Justification*, 200.

effects of each, the one (Adam's) being for evil, the other (Christ's) being for good. The effect of the 'one' in both cases had consequences for 'all/the many'. Paul places great emphasis on this, as can be seen from the repeated use of 'the one' (12x) and 'all/the many' (9x) in this passage.

Before exploring in detail Paul's exposition of what God did through Christ in 5:12-21, it is necessary to identify the overall structure and the movement of thought in this passage. It opens with what proves to be the first half of a comparison of the effects of Adam's action and Christ's action: 'just as sin entered the world through one man . . .' (5:12). Before completing the comparison the apostle explains how sin could be in the world before the law that defined sin was given (5:13-14). Next he highlights the differences between the effects of Adam's action and Christ's action (5:15-17). Only then in 5:18-19 does he state (and restate) the full comparison he has in mind, in which he highlights the dire consequences for humanity of Adam's action and the blessed result for all (believers) of Christ's action (5:18-19). Finally, because the consequences of both these acts come into effect without reference to the law, Paul explains why the law was introduced: to increase the trespass (5:20a), only to add that where sin abounded, God's grace abounded all the more through Jesus Christ (5:20b-21).[39]

5:12 Paul opens his exposition with the words, *Therefore, just as sin entered the world through one man.* Normally, Paul employs the expression translated 'therefore' to bring out the implications of something he has just said.[40] In this case, however, its antecedent is not obvious. Here it appears to function, uncharacteristically, as a transitional phrase.[41] Paul uses 'just as'

---

39. This is how structure of the passage has been understood by most recent interpreters. So, e.g., Cranfield, *Romans*, I, 272-73; Wright, 'Romans', 523; cf. also Hans Weder, 'Gesetz und Sunde: Gedanken zu einen qualitativen Sprung im Denken des Paulus', *NTS* 31 (1985) 363. However, Chrys C. Caragounis, 'Romans 5.15-16 in the Context of 5.12-21: Contrast or Comparison?' *NTS* 31 (1985) 143-46, argues that if vv. 15-17 are regarded as contrasts made before the comparison is drawn, and then v. 18 is taken as a mere repetition of v. 12 without any arguments to support it, Paul would be asserting what he needed to prove. Caragounis argues that, in fact, vv. 15-17 are integral to Paul's argument, supplying the ground upon which the great conclusion of v. 18 stands.

40. He uses *dia touto* ('therefore') in this way, e.g., in 1:26; 4:16; 13:6; 15:19; 1 Cor 4:17; 11:10, 30; 2 Cor 4:1; 13:10; Eph 5:17; 6:13; Col 1:9; 1 Thess 3:5, 7; 2 Thess 2:11; 1 Tim 1:16; 2 Tim 2:10.

41. The exact significance of *dia touto* has been variously described. Cranfield, *Romans*, I, 271, says: 'The point of *dia touto* is that Paul is now going on to indicate in vv. 12-21 the conclusion to be drawn from what has been said in vv. 1-11'. Wright, 'Romans', 523, contends: 'The opening *dia touto* . . . should thus be read not simply as "therefore", but "so it comes about that": not a new point to be deduced, but a summary, a conclusion that can be drawn because of what has been said briefly, in advance, in 5:1-11'. Dunn, *Romans 1–8*, 271-72, argues: 'The *dia touto* does not signify a conclusion drawn simply from an immediately preceding argument; v 11 had already effectively rounded off the preceding train of thought. Its function is rather to indicate that vv 12-21 serve as a conclusion to the complete argument from 1:18–5:11'. Jewett, *Romans*, 372, notes: 'The formula *dia touto* ("on this account") is commonplace in Paul (Rom 1:26; 4:16; 13:6; 15:9, etc.) but never otherwise appears in combination with the comparative conjunction *hōsper* ("just as")'.

frequently to introduce comparisons,[42] and this is implied here, even though the reader has to wait until 5:18-19 to see the comparison stated in full.[43]

When Paul says, 'sin entered the world through one man', he is alluding to Genesis 3 and Adam's disobedience in eating forbidden fruit from the tree of the knowledge of good and evil. It was through Adam ('one man') that 'sin entered the world'. The apostle is saying more than that Adam's one sinful act was sin entering the world. What he writes elsewhere implies that Adam's one sinful act released into the world a new baleful power, called sin.[44] This is implied in numerous places in Paul's letters, predominantly in Romans,[45] particularly in those texts that speak of people being slaves to sin (6:6-7, 17-18, 20; cf. Gal 3:22). It is also implied in those places where Paul speaks of sin seizing opportunity to deceive and entrap people (7:8-9, 11) and as a force operating within people and rendering their wills powerless to resist it (7:17, 20, 23, 25), a force which could be overcome only by the action of God in Christ (8:2-3).

While sin entered the world through one man, that was not the end of the matter. Paul adds: *and death through sin*, that is, 'and death entered the world through sin'. This refers to the divine punishment for sin Adam and Eve were warned about in Genesis 2:17: 'You must not eat from the tree of the knowledge of good and evil, for when you eat from it you will certainly die'. However, what Paul focuses on in 5:12-21 is not the entry of sin as such, but what followed — the reign of death. When the apostle speaks of death entering the world through sin, he is not thinking of the result of sin in respect to Adam only, but of the power of death unleashed into the world as a result of his sin, a power that afflicts all people: *in this way death came to all people*. This, Paul asserts, is *because all sinned*. These words translate *eph' hō pantes hēmarton*, a clause that has been translated and interpreted in a number of different ways. Crucial for understanding it is the meaning of the expression *eph' hō*, which can connote different things.[46] The main alternatives for its meaning in 5:12 are as follows.

42. Cf., e.g., the use of *hōsper* ('just as') in 5:19, 21; 6:4, 19; 11:31-32; 1 Cor 11:12; 15:22; 2 Cor 8:7; Gal 4:29.

43. Thomas H. Tobin, 'The Jewish Context of Rom 5:12-14', *Studia Philonica Annual* 13 (2001) 170, offers the following translation of 5:12: 'Therefore, just as *(hōsper)* sin entered the world through one human being, and through sin death, even so *(kai houtōs)* did death spread to all human beings, with the result that *(eph' hō)* all sinned'.

44. Origen writes: 'Perhaps someone will object that the woman sinned before the man and even that the serpent sinned before her . . . and elsewhere the apostle says: *Adam was not deceived, but the woman was deceived.* . . . How is it then that sin seems to have come in through one man rather than through one woman? . . . Here the apostle sticks to the order of nature, and thus when he speaks about sin, because of which death has passed to all men, he attributes the line of human descent, which has succumbed to this death because of sin, not to the woman but to the man' ('Commentary on the Epistle to the Romans' [*ACCSR*, 135]).

45. See 5:21; 6:6-7, 10-13, 17-18, 20, 22-23; 7:8-9, 11, 13-14, 17, 20, 23, 25; 8:2-3; 1 Cor 15:56; Gal 3:22.

46. It is found in only five places in the NT. In Acts 7:33 it carries its literal sense, 'upon which' ('Take off your sandals; the place where [*upon which*] you are standing is holy

The NIV construes it as 'because', thus yielding the translation 'death came to all people, *because* all sinned'. In this case individuals are subject to death because they all have sinned in their own persons.[47] If it is translated 'in whom', we get the translation: 'sin entered the world through one man, *in whom* all sinned, and death through sin, and in this way death came to all people'. In this case, people are subject to death, not because of their own sin but because of Adam's sin.[48] Ambrosiaster says: 'For it is clear that all have sinned in Adam as though in a lump. For, being corrupted by sin himself, all those whom he fathered were born under sin.[49] Others construe it differently again — in one case to indicate the result of Adam's sin was that death passed to all,[50] and in another to indicate the realm in which the effect of Adam's sin occurs — that is, in the world.[51]

There is now a tendency among a number of scholars, no matter how precisely they construe *eph' hō*, to identify a primary and a secondary cause for human beings becoming subject to death. The primary cause is Adam's disobedience, through which death first entered the world, and the secondary cause is the sin of disobedience of all human beings, who likewise bring death upon themselves.[52]

ADDITIONAL NOTE: THE NATURE OF DEATH THAT ENTERED THE WORLD THROUGH SIN

What Paul means by 'death' when he says 'sin entered the world . . . and death through sin' has been variously interpreted. In the past it was understood to refer to physical death only, but in more recent times scholars have opted for either spiritual death alone, or both physical and spiritual death. Bray argues that it refers only to spiritual death:

---

ground'). In Paul's letters elsewhere it can mean 'because' (2 Cor 5:4: 'For while we are in this tent, we groan and are burdened, *because* we do not wish to be unclothed but to be clothed with our heavenly dwelling'); 'for which' (Phil 3:12: 'I press on to take hold of that *for which* Christ Jesus took hold of me'); and 'for me' (Phil 4:10: 'you were concerned [*for me*], but had no opportunity to show it' [NRSV]). Fitzmyer, *Romans,* 413-17, lists a total of eleven possible meanings of *eph' hō.*

47. So, e.g., Dunn, *Romans 1–8,* 273; Byrne, *Romans,* 177. Weder, 'Gesetz und Sunde', 364-68, argues that the effect of Adam's sin is based upon the fact that his disobedience is repeated, but the effect of grace upon the many is based upon the fact that they allow the act of Christ to bring good. In the one case sinners are imitators, in the other recipients.

48. So, e.g., Milne, 'Genesis 3 in the Letter to the Romans', 13-15; Moo, *Romans,* 327.

49. 'Commentary on Paul's Epistles' (*ACCSR,* 136).

50. Treating *eph' hō* as equivalent to *hōste.* So, e.g., Joseph A. Fitzmyer, 'The Consecutive Meaning of *eph' hō* in Romans 5.12', *NTS* 39 (1993) 321-38; Brian Vickers, 'Grammar and Theology in the Interpretation of Rom 5:12', *TrinJ* 27 (2006) 272.

51. Jewett, *Romans,* 376.

52. So, e.g., Cranfield, *Romans,* I, 274-79; Byrne, *Romans,* 177; Fitzmyer, *Romans,* 416; Dunn, *Romans 1–8,* 274; Wright, 'Romans', 527.

However, there is no evidence that the death which sin brought into the world involved any fundamental change in human nature. As far as we can tell from Scripture, Adam was created as a mortal being, with a human life-cycle which, in the natural course of events, would have begun and ended, just like the life-cycle of animals or plants. It can be argued, with considerable plausibility, that in the Garden of Eden, Adam and Eve were protected from things which would cause their death, but that is not the same thing as saying that they were immortal by nature. When they were expelled from the Garden, the protection was removed, but in physical terms, Adam and Eve remained the same beings as before. . . . The death which is referred to here is spiritual death, the state of being cut off from God, and this spiritual death has now spread to the entire human race. It is a broken relationship with the creator which is passed on from one generation to the next.[53]

Wright adopts a similar approach:

One potentially helpful way of understanding the entry of death into the world through the first human sin is to see 'death' here as more than simply the natural decay and corruption of all the created order. The good creation was nevertheless transient; evening and morning, the decay and new life of autumn and spring, pointed on to a future, a purpose, which Genesis implies it was the job of the human race to bring about. All that lived in God's original would decay and perish, but 'death' in that sense carried no sting. The primal pair were, however, threatened with a different sort of thing altogether: a 'death' that would result from sin and involve expulsion from the garden (Gen 2:17). This death is a darker force, opposed to creation itself, unmaking that which was good, always threatening to drag the world back to chaos. Thus, when humans turned away in sin from the creator as the one whose image they were called to bear, what might have been a natural sleep acquired a sense of shame and threat'.[54]

Attractive though this view is on first reading, it would seem to run aground in the light of Genesis 3:22: 'And the LORD God said, "The man has now become like one of us, knowing good and evil. He must not be allowed to reach out his hand and take also from the tree of life and eat, *and live forever*"' (italics added). This seems to imply that had Adam not sinned he would have lived forever.

More commonly held than the view that spiritual death alone is what Paul had in mind is the view that death here includes both physical and spiritual death, and this view is to be preferred because it accounts best for the scriptural evidence. Thus Dunn says: 'As in the broader sweep of Jew-

53. Gerald Bray, 'Adam and Christ (Romans 5:12-21)', *Evangel* 18 (2000) 5-6.
54. Wright, 'Romans', 526.

ish thought also, there is no suggestion of a distinction between "spiritual" and "physical" death: human weakness (5:6), the corruptibility of the flesh (see on 1:3 and 7:5), and death are all of a piece in that they characterize the whole sweep of creaturely alienation from the Creator'. . . .[55] Moo also argues that physical and spiritual death are intended:

> He may refer to physical death only since 'death' in v. 14 seems to have this meaning. But the passage goes on to contrast death with eternal life (v. 21). Moreover, in vv. 16 and 18 Paul uses 'condemnation; in the same way that he uses death here. These points suggest that Paul may refer here to 'spiritual' death: the estrangement from God that is a result of sin and that, if not healed through Christ, will lead to 'eternal' death. In fact, however, we are not forced to make a choice between these options. Paul frequently uses 'death' and related words to designate a 'physico-spiritual entity' — 'total death', the penalty incurred for sin. Here, then, Paul may focus on physical death as the evidence, the outward manifestation of this total death; or, better, he may simply have in mind this death in both its physical and spiritual aspects.[56]

5:13-14   After writing the first half of his comparison of the effects of Adam's action and Christ's action, in which he stresses that 'sin entered the world through one man, and death through sin, and in this way death came to all people' (5:12), Paul breaks off to counter a possible objection: 'How can one say sin entered the world through Adam's disobedience, when sin cannot be known unless there is a law to define it?' Paul responds to such an objection by saying, *To be sure, sin was in the world before the law was given, but sin is not charged against anyone's account where there is no law.* That sin was in the world[57] is evident in that the penalty for sin, death, continued to affect humanity, but the apostle states that it is not 'charged to anyone's account'[58] when there is no law. This implies that the law's role is to make people accountable for sin (something also implied in 4:15: 'be-

---

55. Dunn, *Romans 1–8*, 273.

56. Moo, *Romans*, 320.

57. Meredith G. Kline, 'Gospel until the Law: Rom 5:13-14 and the Old Covenant', *JETS* 34 (1991) 445, argues that in 5:13-14 Paul is not talking generally about sin being in the world, but particularly about sin in the covenant community between Adam and Moses. He says: 'The pre-law period is selected . . . because covenant administration in that epoch clearly exemplified the principle of justifying grace (vv. 13b and 14b), whereas with the coming of the law the situation was complicated by the introduction of the principle of works into the covenant at the level of the typological kingdom, as reflected in Paul's identification of law as antithetical to grace/promise/faith'. However, it seems that in 5:12-21 as a whole Paul is talking about the humanity-wide effects of sin (cf. esp. 5:12: 'death came to *all men*', italics added), and this militates against Kline's view.

58. 'Taken into account' translates *ellogeitai*, a word the apostle also uses in Philem 18: 'If he [Onesimus] has done you any wrong, or owes you anything, charge it to me' *(touto emoi elloga)'*.

cause the law brings wrath. And where there is no law, there is no transgression'). That Paul will go on immediately to say that death (the penalty for sin) still reigned indicates that what he says about sin not being taken into account must have a relative sense only — perhaps something like sin is not recorded in detail in God's ledgers,[59] or people have lesser responsibility for their sin before they have been made fully aware of its nature by the law.[60]

Paul is adamant that, even if sin was not charged to people's account when there was no law, nevertheless sin 'was in the world'. He states the evidence for this as follows: *Nevertheless, death reigned from the time of Adam to the time of Moses.* For Paul it was self-evident that 'sin was in the world' even before the law that defined sin explicitly was given, because the penalty for sin continued to be applied: death reigned from the time of Adam (whose action unleashed sin in the world) to the time of Moses (through whom the law was given).[61] People continued to die throughout the period between Adam and Moses. The apostle then explains that this was the case *even over those who did not sin by breaking a command, as did Adam* (lit. 'even over those who did not sin after the likeness of the transgression of Adam'). Adam sinned by disobeying a specific command: 'You must not eat from the tree of the knowledge of good and evil' (Gen 2:17). Paul knows that although it cannot be said that people coming after Adam and before Moses sinned in the same way as Adam did, nevertheless sin still dominated them; otherwise, the penalty for sin, death, would not continue to have been applied.

Some have seen in Paul's treatment in 5:13-14 a plain contradiction. Bultmann put forward what he regarded as two 'unanswerable questions': (i) 'What sort of sin was it if it did not originate as a contradiction of the Law?' (ii) 'And how can it have brought death after it if it was not "counted"?'[62] Others speak of an inconsistency in Paul's thought at this

---

59. Cf. Fitzmyer, *Romans*, 417; Cranfield, *Romans*, I, 282. Tobin, 'The Jewish Context of Rom 5:12-14', 174-75, says: 'In offering this explanation, Paul draws on an image common in Jewish literature that human actions [cf. Ps 106:31; 1 Macc 2:52; Dan 7:10; 2 *Apoc. Bar.* 24.1; *Test. Benj.* 11:4; *Jub.* 30:17; 1 *Enoch* 104:7], both good and bad, are recorded in heavenly ledgers that would be opened at the time of God's final judgment. But he revises the image so as to distinguish between sins being committed and sins being both committed and 'accounted' in the heavenly ledgers, a distinction not originally part of the image in Jewish literature. One purpose of the distinction was to corroborate Paul's view in Romans that the purpose of the Mosaic Law was the recognition of what was sinful (Rom 3:20) and so the increase of the trespass (Rom 5:20). A second purpose was to insinuate that the ethical character of human actions, either good or evil, does not depend exclusively on the existence of the Mosaic Law as such and so is possible apart from the Law (as he argued in Rom 1:18-32 and especially in Rom 2:12-16)'.

60. Cf. Moo, *Romans*, 332-33, n. 78.

61. Later in this passage Paul will speak again and again of death reigning because of sin, only to stress that where sin reigned in death, grace will reign through righteousness leading to eternal life through Jesus Christ (cf. 5:17, 21).

62. Bultmann, *Theology of the New Testament*, I, 252.

point.[63] However, to deal with this matter by simply arguing that Paul contradicts himself is too easy — an evasion of the challenge to wrestle with the apostle's teaching.

Poirier offers an interpretation of 5:13-14 that avoids the charge of contradiction brought against the apostle. He identifies a major premise: 'Death prerequires sin (5:12, cf. 6:23), and sin prerequires law (5:13, cf. 4:15; 7:8; 1 Cor 15:56)'; a minor premise: 'Death reigned from the time of Adam to the time of Moses'; and a conclusion: 'the people living between Adam and Moses were under law just as surely as the Jews now are'. He argues that there was 'another law preceding the Mosaic law: the universal law that had made its entrance in 2:14 [the Gentiles are a law to themselves, showing the requirements of the law written on their hearts]. In short, the usual interpretation of Rom. 5:13-14 should be turned on its head. We should no longer think in terms of a "qualifying parenthesis". The point of 5:13-14 is not to qualify Paul's economy of law, sin, and death, but to reinvoke it'.[64] While this view has some attraction, it founders on the fact that when law is spoken of in 5:12-21 it seems to refer consistently to the Mosaic law, which Paul notes, 'was added so that the trespass might increase' (5:20). It is probably better, therefore, to stay with the view that 'sin is not charged to anyone's account when there is no law' should be regarded as a relative statement, as suggested above.

After alluding to Adam and his transgression, Paul says of him: *who is a pattern of the one to come* (lit. 'who is a type of the coming one'). Normally Paul uses the word 'type' to denote an example of behavior (Phil 3:17; 1 Thess 1:7; 2 Thess 3:9; 2 Tim 4:12; Tit 2:7). In one place he uses it rather strangely to mean a 'form' of teaching (1 Cor 10:6). However, there is one other place where he uses it in a way similar to his use of it here in 5:14, that is, as a 'type' in the form of a person or an action of God that foreshadows the future. Thus in 1 Corinthians 10:6, where the apostle says, having spoken of Israel's sins and God's punishment: 'These things occurred as examples [lit. 'types'] to keep us from setting our hearts on evil things as they did'. God's *action* in bringing judgment upon Israel because of her sins is a 'type' of the judgment the Corinthians may expect if they do not heed Paul's warning and persist in their sins. Here in 5:14 he identifies a *person* who functions as a type of another person yet to come. Thus he indicates that Adam is a type of the coming one, that is, Christ. Considering the stark contrast between the effect of Adam's action and Christ's action that Paul will highlight in 5:15-17, it is surprising that he should refer to Adam as the type of Christ. In one respect alone is Adam the type of the coming one: The action of Adam affected all people in him just as the action of Christ af-

---

63. Hübner, *Law in Paul's Thought*, 81; Stowers, *A Re-reading of Romans*, 112; Sanders, *Paul, the Law, and the Jewish People*, 35-36.

64. John C. Poirier, 'Romans 5:13-14 and the Universality of Law', *NovT* 38 (1996) 352-53.

fects all those in him. So that there will be no misunderstanding Paul spends the next three verses (5:15-17) highlighting the differences, before completing his comparison of the effects of the acts of Adam and Christ (5:18-19).

5:15 Contrasting the effects of Adam's action and Christ's action, Paul says: *But the gift is not like the trespass.*[65] Immediately noteworthy is the fact that Paul describes the work of Christ as a gift, something freely and graciously given, while describing what Adam did as a trespass (an offense or wrongdoing). To further highlight the difference between the gift and the trespass, Paul exclaims: *For if the many died by the trespass of the one man, how much more did God's grace and the gift that came by the grace of the one man, Jesus Christ, overflow to the many!* The 'trespass' is Adam's disobedience to the divine command, resulting in death for the many. The gift is the result of God's grace, a gift that came through Jesus Christ, a gift that overflowed to the many. What this gift of God's grace is, and how it came through the grace of Christ, remains to be explained.

'God's grace and the gift that came by the grace of one man' could also be translated 'the grace of God and the gift by grace in the one man', that is, interpreting the 'gift' as God's gift in giving his Son rather than the gift of Christ in giving himself.[66] What the apostle is saying here, then, is that the grace of God expressed in the gift of his Son more than compensates for the effects of Adam's transgression. The trespass of Adam meant that 'many' died, while the grace of God in the gift of his Son meant that grace overflowed (lit. 'abounded') to the 'many'. What is meant by this overflow of grace will be spelled out in the following verses.

Paul says that 'the many' were affected by both Adam's transgression and God's grace gift, but 'the many' affected by Adam's trespass must be distinguished from 'the many' affected by the grace gift. In the first case 'the many' refers to all humanity, but in the second case it refers to those 'who *receive* God's abundant provision of grace and of the gift of righteousness' (5:17, italics added), that is, believers.

5:16 The explanation of the contrast continues: *Nor can the gift of God be compared with the result of one man's sin.* The Greek behind this translation is very truncated. Literally rendered, it would read something like:

---

65. Jewett, *Romans,* 379, commenting on the opening words, says: 'Since *all' ouch* ("but not") is a typical opening for a rhetorical question in a diatribe, I understand the question "But [is] not the grace-gift just like the trespass?" as aiming to show that "the free gift affects all men in the same way as [Adam's] sin did'. This is a possible rendering of the phrase, and the point that Jewett sees it making, that Christ's gift affected all people in the same way as Adam's trespass did, is true in the limited sense that all descendants of Adam are affected by his sin just as all those who believe in Christ are the beneficiaries of his free gift.

66. Cranfield, *Romans,* I, 285-86, identifies the gift as the gift of righteousness. However, in the light of 5:16 where the apostle says the 'gift' *brought* justification (*dikaiōma,* lit. 'righteousness'), the gift is not righteousness, but rather that through which righteousness came, that is, the grace of God expressed in giving his Son.

'and the gift [is] not like [what occurred] through the one who sinned'. It will be noticed that the NIV's 'of God' is an addition to the text and, therefore, to construe 'the gift' as 'the gift of God' is interpretive but nevertheless appropriate.

The difference between 'the result of one man's sin' and the 'gift' is highlighted once again. In the first case, *judgment followed one sin and brought condemnation* (lit. 'for the judgment of one man [sinning led] to condemnation'). In the second case *the gift followed many trespasses and brought justification.* The word translated 'judgment' as used by Paul can denote either a judicial verdict or the punishment following such a verdict.[67] In the context of 5:16 it denotes the judicial verdict,[68] pronounced by God upon Adam for his sin. This verdict, Paul says, then led to 'condemnation', a word Paul uses only three times in his letters — here in 5:16, in 5:18, and in 8:1. It denotes 'not merely a pronouncement of guilt . . . but an adjudication of punishment'; thus it may be translated as a 'judicial pronouncement upon a guilty person leading to, *punishment*'.[69] As has already been foreshadowed (5:12), the punishment was death, something spelled out in 5:17.

In contrast to the judgment on 'one sin' that led to condemnation, 'the gift followed many trespasses and brought justification'. The 'gift' was God's gift in providing his Son as the atoning sacrifice for sins (cf. 3:25), and this gift made justification possible.[70] Bringing out the real significance of Paul's statement here in 5:16, Cranfield remarks: 'That one single misdeed should be answered by judgment, this is perfectly understandable: that the accumulated sins and guilt of all the ages should be an-

67. *Krima* means verdict in 2:2-3; 5:16; 11:33 and punishment in 3:8; 13:2; 1 Cor 11:29, 34; Gal 5:10; 1 Tim 3:6; 5:12. In 1 Cor 6:7 it is used to mean a 'lawsuit'.

68. Cf. BAGD, *ad loc.*

69. BAGD, *ad loc.*

70. The word translated 'justification' here is *dikaiōma*, not the normal word the apostle uses for 'justification' *(dikaiōsis)*. In fact, *dikaiōma* is found in only four other places in Paul's letters, all of them in Romans. In 1:32 it means God's 'decree'; in 2:26 it denotes the 'requirements' of the law; in 5:18 it is usually translated 'justification'; and in 8:4 it again means the 'requirement' of the law. Thus only in 5:16, 18 has it been translated 'justification', a meaning that would seem to be demanded by the context in both these verses. This view is challenged by J. R. Daniel Kirk, 'Reconsidering *Dikaiōma* in Romans 5:16', *JBL* 126 (2007) 791-92, who says: 'In Rom 5:16b *dikaiōma* denotes the reparation demanded by God in the face of transgression and further connotes a demanded death — a demand met in the cross of Christ. The clause in question is thus better translated something along these lines: "but the gift came through many transgressions leading to reparation". Or, if one prefers to keep the terminology of righteousness visible, a more periphrastic rendering might go something like this: "but the gift came through many transgressions leading to the righteous requirement [of death] being met". Romans 5:16b refers not to justification but rather to what leads to justification, and our translations will be more accurate and helpful as they find ways to reflect this'. Jewett, *Romans,* 382, offers another suggestion: 'The translation "righteous decree" is preferable. Condemnation is therefore juxtaposed with God's righteous decree of salvation in Christ; a new regimen of salvation, a new "law of the spirit of life in Christ Jesus", which Paul will clarify in 8:2, had been enacted that overcomes the legacy "of the trespasses of many"'.

swered by God's free gift, this is the miracle of miracles, utterly beyond human comprehension'.[71]

5:17 In this verse Paul continues to highlight the difference between the actions of Adam and Christ. He begins: *For if, by the trespass of the one man, death reigned through that one man. . . .* The trespass of Adam attracted God's judgment that led to punishment that took the form of death. But it was not only Adam who was subject to death, but death 'reigned' through him over all people, as Paul put it in 5:12: 'death came to all people'. If this was the baleful result of the trespass of one man, Paul says, *how much more will those who receive God's abundant provision of grace and of the gift of righteousness reign in life through the one man, Jesus Christ!* The contrast between the effect of the actions of Adam and Christ could not be more stark. Adam's action meant that people were subject to the reign of death, but Christ's action means that people can 'reign in life' because they receive 'the abundant provision of grace and the gift of righteousness'. Paul makes a statement along similar lines in 1 Corinthians 15:21-22: 'For since death came through a man, the resurrection of the dead comes also through a man. For as in Adam all die, so in Christ all will be made alive'.

A number of things call for further comment. First, in relation to 'the abundance of grace', it is worth noting that in 3:24 Paul spoke of believers being 'justified freely by his grace through the redemption that came by Christ Jesus', in 5:15 of 'God's grace and the gift that came by the grace of the one man, Jesus Christ', overflowing to the many, and in 5:20-21 he shortly will say that 'where sin increased, grace increased all the more, so that, just as sin reigned in death, so also grace might reign through righteousness to bring eternal life through Jesus Christ our Lord'. All that comes to believers through Jesus Christ originates in the abundant grace of God.

Second, in relation to 'the gift of righteousness', Paul has already emphasized that 'God's grace and the gift that came by the grace of the one man, Jesus Christ' has overflowed to many (5:15) and that 'the gift followed many trespasses and brought justification' (5:16). Paul puts it in other words in Ephesians 2:8: 'For it is by grace you have been saved, through faith — and this not is from yourselves, it is the gift of God'. Believers' standing before God, their acceptance by him as his people, their salvation, is a gift. It is not earned, only received.

Third, having said that as a result of 'the trespass of the one man, death reigned through that one man [Adam]', we might expect Paul to say that through the provision of grace and the gift of righteousness, life reigned through the one man, Jesus Christ, thus balancing his former statement. However, Paul says instead that 'those who receive God's abundant provision of grace and of the gift of righteousness [will] reign in life through the one man, Jesus Christ'. While 'death reigned' (aorist tense) as a result of

71. Cranfield, *Romans*, I, 286.

Adam's sin, those who receive the gift of righteousness 'will reign (future tense) in life'. Cranfield comments: 'The effectiveness and the unspeakable generosity of the divine grace are such that it will not merely bring about the replacement of the reign of death by the reign of life, but it will actually make those who receive its riches to become kings themselves'.[72]

For the apostle the reign of believers is still in the future. He himself makes no claim to be reigning now, and in 1 Corinthians he sarcastically admonishes those who think they do: 'Already you have all you want! Already you have become rich! You have begun to reign [lit. 'you reign'] — and that without us! How I wish that you really had already begun to reign [lit. 'you reigned'] so that we might reign with you [lit. 'so that we also may reign with you']' (1 Cor 4:8). That the reign of believers is still in the future is also implied in 2 Timothy 2:12: 'If we endure, we will also reign with him. If we disown him, he will also disown us'. On the last day believers will receive the crown that lasts forever (1 Cor 9:25), the crown of righteousness (1 Tim 4:8).[73]

Collins draws attention to the similarity existing between Paul's statement here in 5:17 and that of Rabbi Hanina in the Mishnah (*m. Makk.* 3:15):

m. Makkot 3.15	Romans 5:17
If a sin of one sinner	If the sin of one man
causes his death ['he forfeits his life'],	caused death,
is it not logical to assume that	all the more so
a meritorious deed of one man	one meritorious deed [of Jesus Christ]
causes his life to be given!	causes life!

Collins says: 'Paul has of course adapted the mishnaic statement to serve his own cause. Thus, whereas in the Mishnah, the sinner and the practitioner of the meritorious deed are both anonymous ciphers for any man, Paul, on the other hand, identifies them both, alluding to the sinner as Adam, while the man who performs a meritorious deed is clearly identified as Jesus Christ'.[74]

5:18   In this verse Paul completes the comparison of the effects of the actions of Adam and Christ that he began in 5:12. As he does so, he states the dire consequences of Adam's action for all humanity and the blessed results of Christ's action for all (believers). He begins: *Consequently, just as*

---

72. Cranfield, *Romans*, I, 288.

73. There are passages in Ephesians and Colossians that speak of believers having been raised and seated with Christ in heaven: Eph 2:6: 'And God raised us up with Christ and seated us with him in the heavenly realms in Christ Jesus'; Col 3:1: 'Since, then, you have been raised with Christ, set your hearts on things above, where Christ is seated at the right hand of God'. Whatever the apostle means by these statements, they do not appear to be saying that death reigns over them no longer and that they already reign in life.

74. Nina L. Collins, 'The Jewish Source of Rom 5:17, 16, 10, and 9: The Verses of Paul in Relation to a Comment in the Mishnah at *m. Makk* 3.15', *RB* 112 (2005) 36.

the one trespass resulted in condemnation for all people. . . . Paul has already asserted that the judgment following Adam's sin brought condemnation (5:16), and here in 5:18 he adds that this condemnation extended to all people. Then, completing the comparison, Paul says, *so also one righteous act resulted in justification and life for all people* (lit. 'so also through one act of righteousness for all men [leads] to justification of life). The 'one righteous act' is Christ's obedience to his Father in offering himself as the atoning sacrifice for sins, the act that made it possible for God to justify freely those who believe in his Son (cf. 3:21-26). Paul asserts that this 'one righteous act' resulted in 'justification and life' (lit. 'justification of life'), repeating in different words the point made in 5:17 that those who received 'the gift of righteousness reign in life through the one man, Jesus Christ', and anticipating what he will say in 5:21, that 'grace might reign through righteousness to bring eternal life through Jesus Christ our Lord'.[75]

Paul statement that 'just as one trespass resulted in condemnation for all people, so also one righteous act resulted in justification and life for all people' would appear on first reading to imply that just as Adam's trespass affected all people without exception, so also Christ's righteous act likewise affects all people without exception, and in fact there are those who argue that this is what Paul intends.[76] But this would be a misreading of the apostle, for already he has said that it is 'those who *receive* God's abundant provision of grace and of the gift of righteousness' who will 'reign in life' (5:17, italics added). The 'all people' of the latter part of the phrase is best understood to mean all who receive the gift of grace, whether they are Jews or Gentiles.[77]

5:19 In this verse Paul restates in different terms the completed comparison contrasting the effects of the actions of Adam and Christ made in 5:18. He says: *For just as through the disobedience of the one man the many were made sinners, so also through the obedience of the one man the many will be made righteous.* This time the contrast is expressed, not in terms of Adam's 'trespass' and Christ's 'righteous act', but in terms of Adam's 'disobedience' and Christ's 'obedience'. Adam disobeyed God by ignoring the command given him not to eat of the tree of the knowledge of good and evil (Gen 2:16-17; 3:1-6, 11). Christ obeyed God by submitting to death on the cross to effect salvation (cf. Phil 2:8: 'And being found in appearance as a man, he hum-

---

75. The same belief underlies Tit 3:7: 'so that, having been justified by his grace, we might become heirs having the hope of eternal life'.

76. So, e.g., Richard H. Bell, 'Rom 5.18-19 and Universal Salvation', *NTS* 48 (2002) 425-32.

77. So also Mark Rapinchuk, 'Universal Sin and Salvation in Romans 5:12-21', *JETS* 42 (1999) 433-41. Jewett, *Romans*, 385, says: 'This verse strongly suggests that Adamic damnation has been overturned by Christ's righteous act and that the scope of righteousness in Christ includes all believers without exception, both now and at the parousia. This has a powerful bearing on the issues of mutual condemnation between Christian groups that surface in 14:1–15:6'.

bled himself by becoming obedient to death — even death on a cross!'). The
result of Adam's disobedience here is not condemnation for all (as in 5:18),
but that the many were made sinners. Paul is saying that because of Adam's
action all people were born with a sinful tendency, one that manifests itself
in their subsequent sinful actions.[78] The result of Christ's obedience was that
'the many will be made righteous'. Here Paul uses the future tense of the
verb, probably indicating that the justification of those who believe in Christ
properly takes place in the future. While Adam's disobedience has constituted all people sinners, Christ's obedience will lead to God's declaration
'righteous' in respect to believers on the last day.

5:20-21 In 5:19 Paul argued that the effect of Adam's disobedience
upon humanity is more than counteracted by the effect of Christ's obedience upon those in him. This sweeping comparison leaves little place in salvation history for the giving of the law. It is perhaps with this in mind that
the apostle offers an explanation of the role of the law: *The law was brought
in so that the trespass might increase.* 'Was brought in' is a translation of a verb
that means 'to enter' or 'slip in'.[79] Paul may have chosen this word to describe the entry of the law in this context to portray it as something that
came in 'as a side issue, having no primary place in the divine plan',[80]
something whose effect was negative. If this is the case, what follows describes that negative effect: 'The law was brought in *so that the trespass might
increase*' (italics added). A number of suggestions have been made concerning the way the entry of the law might have increased the trespass: (i) It increased the number of commandments, and this made possible an increase
in the number of trespasses. It is unlikely that anything as banal as this is
intended. (ii) It increased the number of trespasses by causing the Jews to
take pride in the law so that they identified righteousness with distinc-
tively Jewish actions.[81] This suggestion does not fit well with a passage
where trespassing is conceived of as disobedience to God's commands (cf.
5:14), not Jewish pride. (iii) It led to an increase in the number of trespasses
in the sense that what were not known to be trespasses before the giving of
the law were clearly recognized as such thereafter (cf. 4:15: 'where there is
no law there is no transgression').[82] (iv) The law actually incited rebellion

---

78. Fitzmyer, *Romans,* 421, notes: 'Yet so astute a commentator as Taylor has re-
marked, "No one can be made a sinner or made righteous" (*Romans,* 41). But that is exactly
what Paul says, and he is not speaking of personal sinful acts alone. Adam's disobedience
placed the mass of humanity in a condition of sin and estrangement from God; the text does
not imply that they became sinners merely by imitating Adam's transgression; rather, they
were constituted sinners by him and his act of disobedience'.

79. In its only other occurrence in Paul's letters it has the negative connotation of
'sneaked in' or 'infiltrated': '[This matter arose] because some false brothers had *infiltrated*
our ranks to spy on the freedom we have in Christ Jesus and to make us slaves' (Gal. 2:4,
italics added).

80. Cf. BAGD, *pareiserchomai.*

81. Cf. Dunn, *Romans 1–8,* 299-300.

82. Cf. Moo, *Romans,* 348.

against its own demands, thereby promoting more transgressions (cf. 7:8: 'But sin, seizing the opportunity afforded by the commandment, produced in me every kind of coveting'). (v) The entry of the law made possible the human competition for honor and thereby increased the trespass.[83] (vi) Paul may have seen the entry of the law bring about a number of the above.[84] The third suggestion (the law led to an increase in the number of trespasses in the sense that what were not known to be trespasses before the giving of the law were clearly recognized as such thereafter) receives some support from Paul's statement in 7:7: 'I would not have known what sin was had it not been for the law. For I would not have known what coveting really was if the law had not said, "You shall not covet"', and for that reason would seem to be the preferable interpretation. Wright offers the following comment and striking illustration: 'To sin outside the law is still to sin; Paul has made that clear in 5:13-14; but to sin under the law — in other words, to transgress, to break a known commandment — is to make the problem worse. Think of sin as a small color transparency; the law puts a bright light behind it and a large screen in front of it. That is what Paul means by "increase the trespass"'.[85] One thing is clear: Paul sees the law as part of the human predicament, not its solution.[86]

Paul continues: *But where sin increased, grace increased all the more.* The place 'where sin increased' is where the law entered, that is, in the nation Israel, who were the recipients of the law. It increased in the sense that actions that had always been sinful were now clearly defined by the law as such. It is important to note that when Paul says that with the entry of the law 'sin increased', his main purpose is to highlight the effects of grace: 'where sin increased, grace increased all the more'.[87] If sin *abounded,* God's

---

83. So Jewett, *Romans,* 387-88.

84. So, e.g., Witherington, *Romans,* 151; Cranfield, *Romans,* I, 292-93.

85. Wright, 'Romans', 530.

86. The early church fathers made various comments on this verse. Ambrose wrote: 'Sin abounded by the law because through the law came knowledge of sin, and it became harmful for me to know what through my weakness I could not avoid. It is good to know beforehand what one is to avoid, but if I cannot avoid something, it is harmful to have known about it. Thus the law changed to its opposite, yet it became useful to me by the very increase of sin, for I was humbled' ('Letters to Laymen 83' [*ACCSR,* 149]). Diodore wrote: 'Paul does not mean that the law increased the incidence of sin but rather that once it was given it uncovered sin and showed that it was more widespread than people had thought' ('Pauline Commentary from the Greek Church' [*ACCSR,* 149]). Ambrosiaster adds: 'An objector might say: If the law merely served to increase sin, it should never have been given. If there was less sin before the law came, there was no need of the law. Obviously the law was necessary to show that sins, which many thought they could get away with, actually counted before God and so that people might know what they ought to avoid. How could the law have increased sin, when it warns people not to sin? . . . The law began to show an abundance of sins, and the more it forbade them the more people committed them. That is why it is said that the law was given so that sin might increase . . .' ('Commentary on Paul's Epistles' [*ACCSR,* 149-50]).

87. The verb translated 'to increase all the more' *(hyperperisseuō)* used by Paul when

grace has *superabounded!* Harrison has argued that Paul's reference to the superabounding beneficence of Christ would have 'registered' with his Roman audience, who recalled the Augustan period and the imperial propaganda that extolled the remarkable beneficence of Caesar Augustus. For them, he says, Paul's words about the superabounding grace of Christ would be understood as an implicit claim that the beneficence of Christ outshone that of Caesar.[88]

In 5:21 Paul explains further the effect of this superabounding grace of God: *so that, just as sin reigned in death, so also grace might reign through righteousness to bring eternal life through Jesus Christ our Lord.* The contrast between the effects of sin increasing and grace superabounding could not be greater: Sin 'reigned in death', grace reigned 'through righteousness to bring eternal life'. The agencies through which grace reigned are twofold: 'through righteousness' on the one hand, and 'through Jesus Christ our Lord' on the other. 'Through Jesus Christ our Lord' is a reference to the fact that the gift of eternal life comes to believers only through Jesus Christ, through his atoning sacrifice that effected salvation, an action so different from the death-delivering action of Adam. 'Through righteousness' could be a reference to either the righteousness of God, in this case his saving action to redeem humanity, the very essence of the gospel message (cf. 1:16-17) or the gift of righteousness he bestows upon believers (cf. 5:16-17), or a combination of the two: God's saving action in Christ that makes possible the bestowal of the gift of righteousness upon those who believe in his Son. When God bestows the gift of righteousness, this in turn brings eternal life to believers. In the writings of Paul (unlike, e.g., the Gospel and Letters of John) 'eternal life' appears to denote the future reward in store for believers.[89]

---

speaking of God's grace is peculiar to him in the NT, and used elsewhere only in 2 Cor 7:4 ('I take great pride in you. I am greatly encouraged; in all our troubles *my joy knows no bounds*' [*hyperperisseuomai tē chara*], italics added).

88. J. R. Harrison, 'Paul, Eschatology and the Augustan Age of Grace', *TynBul* 50 (1999) 83-91.

89. Cf. 2:7: 'To those who by persistence in doing good seek glory, honor and immortality, he will give eternal life'; 5:21: 'just as sin reigned in death, so also grace might reign through righteousness to bring eternal life through Jesus Christ our Lord; 6:22: 'But now that you have been set free from sin and have become slaves of God, the benefit you reap leads to holiness, and the result is eternal life'; 6:23: 'the wages of sin is death, but the gift of God is eternal life in Christ Jesus our Lord'; Gal 6:8: 'Whoever sows to please their flesh, from the flesh will reap destruction; whoever sows to please the Spirit, from the Spirit will reap eternal life'; 1 Tim 1:16: 'But for that very reason I was shown mercy so that in me, the worst of sinners, Christ Jesus might display his immense patience as an example for those who would believe in him and receive eternal life'; 1 Tim 6:12: 'Fight the good fight of the faith. Take hold of the eternal life to which you were called when you made your good confession in the presence of many witnesses'; Tit 1:1-2: 'the faith of God's elect and their knowledge of the truth that leads to godliness — in the hope of eternal life, which God, who does not lie, promised before the beginning of time'; Tit 3:7: 'so that, having been justified by his grace, we might become heirs having the hope of eternal life'.

ADDITIONAL NOTE: ADAM'S SIN IN JEWISH LITERATURE

The following texts represent Jewish reflections on the entrance of sin and death into the world through the sin of Adam (or Eve or the devil) in the garden. The texts themselves date from the period 200 B.C. to A.D. 200. Approximate dates for each of the texts are shown below.[90] The texts are arranged chronologically. The similarities and differences between these texts and Paul's views as seen in Romans will be obvious.

Sirach 25:24 (early second century B.C.)
From a woman sin had its beginning, and because of her we all die.

1QS 3:21-22 (c. 100 B.C.):
The Angel of Darkness leads all the children of righteousness astray, and until his end, all their sin, iniquities, wickedness, and all their unlawful deeds are caused by his dominion in accordance with the mysteries of God.

Wisdom of Solomon 2:23-24 (first or second century B.C.):
For God created us for incorruption, and made us in the image of his own eternity, but through the devil's envy death entered the world, and those who belong to his company experience it.

Apocalypse of Moses 28 (= Greek Life of Adam and Eve, first century A.D.):
And the Lord turned and said to Adam, 'From now on I will not allow you to be in Paradise'. And Adam answered and said, 'Lord, give me from the tree of life that I might eat before I am cast out'. The Lord spoke to Adam, 'You shall not now take from it; for it was appointed to the cherubim and the flaming sword which turns to guard it because of you, that you might not taste of it and be immortal forever, but that you might have the strife which the enemy has placed in you. But when you come out of Paradise, if you guard yourself from all evil, preferring death to it, at the time of the resurrection I will raise you again, and then there shall be given to you from the tree of life, and you shall be immortal forever'.

Life of Adam and Eve 3:1-2 (first century A.D.):
And Eve said to Adam, 'My Lord, would you kill me? O that I would die! Then perhaps the Lord God will bring you again into Paradise, for it is because of me that the Lord God is angry with you'. Adam an-

90. The sources of the texts themselves are the NRSV for those from the Apocrypha; Vermes, *Dead Sea Scrolls,* for those from the Qumran Literature; Charlesworth, ed., *The Old Testament and Pseudepigrapha,* Volumes 1 and 2, for those from the Pseudepigrapha; and LCL for those from Philo.

swered, 'Do not wish to speak such words lest the Lord God bring on us some further curse. How is it possible that I should let loose my hand against my flesh? But rather let us rise and search for ourselves, how we might live, and not weaken'.

4 Ezra 3:7 (late first century A.D.):
And you laid upon him one commandment of yours; but he transgressed it, and immediately you appointed death for him and for his descendants.

2 Baruch (early second century A.D.):
For what did it profit Adam that he lived nine hundred and thirty years and transgressed that which he was commanded? Therefore, the multitude of time that he lived did not profit him, but it brought death and cut off the years of those who were born from him. (17:2-3)

For when Adam sinned and death was decreed against those who were to be born, the multitude of those who would be born was numbered. And for that number a place was prepared where the living ones might live and where the dead might be preserved. (23:4)

For, although Adam sinned first and has brought death upon all who were not in his own time, yet each of them who has been born from him has prepared for himself the coming torment. . . . Adam is, therefore, not the cause, except only for himself, but each of us has become our own Adam. (54:15-19)

And as you first saw the black waters on the top of the cloud which first came down upon the earth; this is the transgression which Adam, the first man, committed. For when he transgressed, untimely death came into being, mourning was mentioned, affliction was prepared, illness was created, labor accomplished, pride began to come into existence, the realm of death began to ask to be renewed with blood, the conception of children came about, the passion of the parents was produced, the loftiness of men was humiliated, and goodness vanished. (56:5-6)

For a grain of evil seed was sown in Adam's heart from the beginning, and how much ungodliness it has produced until now, and will produce until the time of threshing comes. Consider now for yourself how much fruit of ungodliness a grain of evil seed had produced. When heads of grain without number are sown, how great a threshing floor they will fill! (4:30-32)

O Adam, what have you done? For though it was you who sinned, the fall was not yours alone, but ours also who are your descendants.

For what good is it to us, if an eternal age has been promised to us, but we have done deeds that bring death? (7:118-19)[91]

---

3. *Freedom from Sin's Dominion, 6:1-23*

Towards the end of chapter 5 Paul said: 'The law was brought in so that the trespass might increase. But where sin increased, grace increased all the more' (5:20). Such teaching led Paul's opponents to claim that he was encouraging sinful behavior. This is reflected in his strong reaction to such a suggestion in 3:7-8: 'Someone might argue, "If my falsehood enhances God's truthfulness and so increases his glory, why am I still condemned as a sinner?" Why not say — as some slanderously claim that we say — "Let us do evil that good may result"? Their condemnation is just!' The apostle's purpose in chapter 6 is twofold: to refute such objections, thus rejecting the charge that acceptance of his gospel leads to moral anarchy, while at the same time exhorting his audience to offer themselves to God as instruments of righteousness and not offer their bodies as instruments of sin. He does this in two stages: (i) In 6:1-14 he argues that believers cannot continue in sin because they died to sin with Christ and in him they are now alive to God, and (ii) in 6:15-23 he argues that they have been set free from slavery to sin so as become slaves of God.

a. *Dying and Rising with Christ, 6:1-14*

[1]What shall we say, then? Shall we go on sinning so that grace may increase? [2]By no means! We are those who have died to sin; how can we live in it any longer? [3]Or don't you know that all of us who were baptized into Christ Jesus were baptized into his death? [4]We were therefore buried with him through baptism into death in order that, just as Christ was raised from the dead through the glory of the Father, we too may live a new life.

[5]For if we have been united with him in a death like his, we will certainly also be united with him in a resurrection like his. [6]For we know that our old self was crucified with him so that the body ruled by sin might be done away with, that we should no longer be slaves to sin — [7]because anyone who has died has been set free from sin.

[8]Now if we died with Christ, we believe that we will also live with him. [9]For we know that since Christ was raised from the dead, he cannot die again; death no longer has mastery over him. [10]The death he died, he died to sin once for all; but the life he lives, he lives to God.

---

91. Cf. Tobin, 'The Jewish Context of Rom 5:12-14', 160-69, who holds that there are three ways in which Adam's sin was interpreted in texts such as these: (i) as *examples* of the human condition; (ii) as interpretations of Genesis 1–3 *illustrative* of the human condition; and (iii) as *explanations* of the human condition.

> [11]*In the same way, count yourselves dead to sin but alive to God in Christ Jesus.* [12]*Therefore do not let sin reign in your mortal body so that you obey its evil desires.* [13]*Do not offer any part of yourself to sin as an instrument of wickedness, but rather offer yourselves to God as those who have been brought from death to life; and offer every part of yourself to him as an instrument of righteousness.* [14]*For sin shall no longer be your master, because you are not under the law, but under grace.*

The first passage, 6:1-14, has been seen as crucial in the quest to discover Paul's understanding of Christian baptism, for here more than anywhere else in his letters, and for that matter anywhere else in the NT as a whole, hints as to the meaning of baptism are to be found. However, it is important to recognize that the apostle's purpose in writing 6:1-14 was not to provide information about the meaning of baptism, but to demonstrate that acceptance of his gospel does not lead to moral anarchy. By the grace of God those who accept this gospel have died to sin with Christ and now live for God. The reference to the audience's baptism is introduced to reinforce this gospel fact.[92] The structure of this important passage has been variously analyzed.[93] The following analysis will serve our exegesis:

6:1-2   The question posed: 'Shall we go on sinning so that grace may increase?' and the short answer given: 'By no means! We are those who have died to sin; how can we live in it any longer?'

6:3-4   Elaboration of the answer based upon union with Christ in his death and resurrection, reinforced with references to baptism

6:5-11   Further elaboration of the answer based upon union with Christ in his death and resurrection (without references to baptism)

6:12-13 Exhortation not to allow sin to reign in our bodies

6:14   Sin will not reign over believers precisely because they live under the grace of God.

This passage, and in particular 6:1-11, is marked by the repeated use of 'with' *(syn-)* formulae to denote believers' death and new life 'with' Christ.

---

92. A fact noted by many recent interpreters. Cf., e.g., Hendrikus Boers, 'The Structure and Meaning of Romans 6:1-14', *CBQ* 63 (2001) 664-71; A. J. M. Wedderburn, *Baptism and Resurrection: Studies in Pauline Theology against Its Graeco-Roman Background* (WUNT 44; Tübingen: Mohr Siebeck, 1987), 49-50.

93. Simon Légasse, 'Être baptisé dans la mort du Christ: Étude de Romains 6,1-14', *RB* 98 (1991) 546, offers the following analysis of 6:1-14: 'Rom 6:1-14 consists of three essential parts: the first consists of a question (objection) and a response that is the 'thesis' (6:1-2). This thesis is defended in the second part (vv. 3-10) with an argument. Finally, in vv. 11-14, comes the application of what has been said for the conduct of Christians, v. 11 serving as a transition and v. 14 the conclusion'.

In 6:4 they were 'buried with him' at baptism into death; in 6:5 they have been 'united with him' in a death like his; in 6:6 they have been 'crucified with him'; in 6:8 they have died 'with Christ' and 'will also live with him'. Because believers have been identified with Christ in these ways, Paul exhorts them to count themselves to be 'dead to sin but alive to God in Christ Jesus' (6:11).

6:1-2 Paul begins by putting the question that his statement in 5:20 ('where sin increased, grace increased all the more') would invite: *What shall we say, then? Shall we go on sinning so that grace may increase?* This question introduces an 'internal debate', whereby Paul provides both sides of an argument for the benefit of this audience. However, the question is not merely hypothetical, for 3:7-8 indicates that when the apostle wrote Romans he was aware there were people who slandered him and opposed his gospel, claiming it encouraged sinful behavior. Paul's response is unequivocal: *By no means!* This translates an expression found fourteen times in Paul's letters, and, though variously rendered, in every case but one it functions as a strong rejection of the preceding proposition.[94] The apostle explains the basis of his response: *We are those who have died to sin; how can we live in it any longer?* The basic assumption is that believers have 'died to sin', and therefore any suggestion that they should continue to 'live [lit. 'remain'] in sin' is unthinkable.[95] Wright comments: 'Of course, to "remain in sin", in English and for that matter in Greek, will mean to go on committing sin, but Paul is interested here in where one is first and foremost; it is like saying "shall we remain in France", with the assumption that if one does one will continue to speak French'.[96]

Paul does not explain here just what he means by saying 'we died to sin',[97] but in 6:3-4 he speaks of being buried with Christ in baptism, indicat-

94. *mē genoito* is variously translated as 'Not at all!' (3:4, 31; 9:14; 11:11), 'Certainly not!' (3:6; 7:7), 'By no means!' (6:2, 15; 7:13; 11:1), 'Never!' (1 Cor 6:15), 'Absolutely not!' (Gal 2:17; 3:21). The one exception is Gal 6:14: 'May I never boast *(emoi de mē genoito kauchasthai)* except in the cross of our Lord Jesus Christ', but even this involves a strong rejection — of the temptation to boast in anything but the cross of Christ.

95. Commenting on the meaning of dying to sin, Origen says: 'To live to sin, therefore, means to obey the desires of sin. . . . To die to sins is the opposite of this; it means refusing to obey the desires of sin. . . . If someone dies to sin, it is through repentance that he dies' ('Commentary on the Epistle to the Romans' [*ACCSR*, 153]). Chrysostom comments in similar vein: 'This is what dying to sin means: to be set free from sin and to become a servant of God' ('Commentary on Paul's Epistles' [*ACCSR*, 153]).

96. Wright, 'Romans', 537.

97. Cranfield, *Romans*, I, 299-300, identifies four different senses in which Christians die to sin and four in which they are raised up: '(i) They die to sin in God's sight, when Christ died on the cross for them. This is a matter of God's decision. . . . We may call this first sense the *juridical sense*. . . . (ii) They died to sin, and were raised up, in their baptism. . . . This we may call the *baptismal sense*. . . . (iii) They are called, and have been given the freedom, to die daily and hourly to sin by the mortification of their sinful natures, and to rise daily and hourly to newness of life in obedience to God. . . . This we may call the *moral sense*. . . . (iv) They will die to sin finally and irreversibly when they actually die, and will —

ing that it is at the time of conversion that believers die to sin — baptism being a shorthand way of referring to the whole conversion experience. Further clues to what it means to die to sin are found in the following verses.

6:3-4 To reinforce his point Paul links his audience's death to sin with their baptism by asking them: *Or don't you know that all of us who were baptized into Christ Jesus were baptized into his death?*[98] Paul begins his question with the words, 'don't you know' (lit. 'are you ignorant'), an expression he uses again in 7:1 when he says, 'Do you not know, brothers and sisters — for I am speaking to those who know the law — that the law has authority over someone only as long as that person lives?' In both cases, it would appear, he is referring to something he expects his audience to know already.

Within Romans it is only here in 6:3-4 that Paul refers to baptism. It is a baptism 'into Christ Jesus'.[99] An examination of the references made to baptism across the letters of Paul indicates that he saw it as an initiatory rite undergone by people as a means by which they confessed Christ as their Lord. It is a part of the full conversion-initiation experience that involves repentance and faith in Christ expressed in submission to baptism on the part of the convert, when God for his part grants forgiveness and the gift of his Spirit.

What it means to be 'baptized into Christ Jesus' and to be 'baptized into his death' is difficult to understand and has been variously interpreted. Jewett is content to describe it as 'some form of incorporation', claiming that Paul's audience would be familiar with such a concept, knowing about 'initiation in the cult of Isis and Osiris [that] also involved baptism, in which the believer identified with the god Osiris, whose death in the Nile was one of the central myths of the Isis cult'.[100] There are those who interpret it spatially, involving union with Christ, participation in the redemptive events of his career,[101] or being drawn into his sphere of influence, the milieu of salvation.[102] Others interpret it as coming under Christ's lordship so that the bap-

---

equally finally and irreversibly — at Christ's coming be raised up to the resurrection life. This is the *eschatological sense*'.

98. William B. Badke, 'Baptised into Moses — Baptised into Christ: A Study in Doctrinal Development', *EvQ* 60 (1988) 24-29, shows that in Paul's letters prior to the writing of Romans there is, in the nine references where baptism is mentioned, no connection with the idea of dying and rising with Christ (cf. 1 Cor 1:13, 14, 15, 16, 17; 10:2; 12:13; 15:29; Gal 3:27). Furthermore, he argues that in 1 Corinthians, the letter in which most of the pre-Romans references to baptism are found, the first reference implies that Christian baptism is 'a declaration of allegiance to Christ' (24-25).

99. Elian Cuvillier, 'Evangile et traditions chez Paul: Lecture de Romains 6,1-14', *Hokhma* 45 (1990) 7, suggests that this an abbreviation of the traditional formula; 'Baptised in the name of Jesus Christ'.

100. Jewett, *Romans*, 396-97.

101. Moo, *Romans*, 355, 359-60.

102. Byrne, *Romans*, 190.

tized become Christ's people.[103] Another view is that Christ's death was vicarious (2 Cor 5:14: 'one died for all, and therefore all died'), and baptism is a reception of this fact and participation in Christ's fate.[104] Of these possible interpretations of baptism into Christ and his death the easiest to comprehend are those that explain it as coming under Christ's sphere of influence or lordship on the one hand, and reception of what Christ did for us vicariously when 'one died for all, and therefore all died', on the other. (See 'Additional Note: Baptism in the Pauline Corpus', 270-72, and 'Additional Note: Dying and Rising with Christ', 272-79.)

In 6:4 Paul spells out for his audience the implications of being baptized into Christ: *We were therefore buried with him through baptism into death in order that, just as Christ was raised from the dead through the glory of the Father, we too may live a new life.* This could be simply a metaphorical way of saying that just as Christ died and was raised by the glory of the Father, so when believers are baptized they 'died' to their old life and began a new life as Christians (turning over a new leaf). However, more seems to be intended. The apostle says that the purpose of our being 'buried with him through baptism into death' was 'in order that . . . we may live a new life'. Our death to sin at baptism makes it possible for us to live a new life. It seems to be implied that our death and burial with Christ in baptism must be as real as the newness of life that it makes possible. Perhaps this is best understood as our benefiting from Christ's vicarious death and as a result being transferred from the realm of darkness and sin into the realm of Christ's influence and power so that we experience new life (mediated to us by the Holy Spirit).

6:5-7 In these verses the apostle ties believers' union with Christ in his death with their union with him in his resurrection: *For if we have been united with him in a death like his, we will certainly also be united with him in a resurrection like his.* The conjunction 'for' at the beginning of 6:5 indicates that 6:5-6 constitutes the basis upon which Paul can say that 'we too may live a new life'. Rendered literally, the Greek underlying the clause, 'if we have been united with him[105] in a death like his', would read: 'if we have been grown together with [him] in the likeness of his death'. Wright offers

---

103. Fitzmyer, *Romans*, 433; Barrett, *Romans*, 122; Cranfield, *Romans*, I, 304; Badke, 'Baptised into Moses — Baptised into Christ', 29.

104. Käsemann, *Romans*, 165-66.

105. Here 'united with [him]' translates an adjective *(symphytos)* found only here in the NT. While its literal meaning is 'grown together', figuratively it can mean 'associated in a related experience' or 'identified or united with something or someone'. Cf. BAGD, *ad loc.* Jewett, *Romans*, 400, says: 'The adjective *symphytos* . . . is used in a wide variety of secular contexts, including horticultural references to grafting or growing together, biological references to knitting together the edges of a wound or the ends of broken bones, and social references to citizens clustering around their leader or sharing a particular ethos. In view of these wide-ranging references, I prefer a generic translation such as "joined together" or "united together", which implies that believers share an indivisible, organic unity with Christ'.

the following explanation of this clause: 'the existence of the Christian is, as it were, intertwined with that of the Messiah, like two young trees whose trunks grow around one another'.[106]

Paul does *not* say here that believers are united with Christ in his death, but 'in the likeness of his death'. This probably means that Paul has in mind people being identified with Christ's death at baptism.[107] The apostle has already said that to be baptized into Christ is to be baptized into his death (6:3-4).

Paul says that if we have been united with Christ in the likeness of his death, we *'will* certainly also *be* united with him in a resurrection like his' (italics added). To express this, the apostle uses the future tense of the verb 'to be', leaving open the possibility of two interpretations: (i) it can be construed as a logical future: those who have allowed themselves to be identified with Christ's death in baptism will certainly also share his resurrection life now, or (ii) it can be construed as an eschatological future: those who have allowed themselves to be identified with Christ's death in baptism now will be united with him in resurrection life on the last day.[108] In the context of 6:1-14, where the apostle, as well as exhorting his audience to offer themselves to God as instruments of righteousness, is also combating charges that his gospel promotes moral anarchy in the present time, the former appears more appropriate.[109]

In 6:6-7 Paul continues to explain the basis upon which 'we too may live a new life': *For we know that our old self was crucified with him.*[110] Here Paul links the death of our 'old self' with Christ's crucifixion and without any reference to baptism. While this is difficult to understand, it is not the only place where the apostle speaks in this way. In Galatians 2:20 he says: 'I have been crucified with Christ and I no longer live, but Christ lives in me'. However, while Paul's reference to the crucifixion of our 'old self' here is unique, there are references to the believer's 'old self' in two other places. In both cases the imagery is not that of crucifixion but of discarding clothing. In Ephesians 4:22 the audience is urged 'to put off your old self, which

---

106. Wright, 'Romans', 539.

107. Sorin Sabou, 'A Note on Romans 6:5: The Representation *(homoiōma)* of His Death', *TynBul* 55 (2004) 229, says: 'the proclamation of the gospel ("the disclosure" of God's salvation in Christ's death) is a "representation" *[homoiōmati]* of Christ's death and resurrection'. While it is true that people are united with Christ through (their reception of) the proclamation of the gospel, the emphasis upon being united with Christ through baptism in the previous verses (6:3-4) makes it more likely that *homoiōma* here is a reference to baptism.

108. So, e.g., Moo, *Romans*, 371.

109. Cf. Légasse, 'Être baptisé dans la mort du Christ', 556-57. Cranfield, *Romans*, I, 308, contends: 'The verse [6:5] as a whole may then be given an interpretation which perfectly suits the context . . . : "For if (in baptism) we have become conformed to His death, we shall certainly also (or "we are certainly also to") be conformed (in our moral life) to His resurrection"'.

110. The NIV adds 'for' to the beginning of 6:6 where there is no corresponding word in the original.

is being corrupted by its deceitful desires', and in Colossians 3:9 they are exhorted, 'do not lie to each other, since you have taken off your old self with its practices'. In these two places the 'old self' denotes believers' former way of life that they are to be done with.

What Paul means by 'our old self' in 6:6 is not part of, but the whole of what we were prior to conversion, what we were in solidarity with Adam.[111] It is this 'old self' that was co-crucified with Christ. Clearly we were not actually involved in the historic crucifixion of Christ. Rather, as Cranfield says, we came 'under God's condemnation' and 'died *in God's sight* in Christ's death'.[112] As Paul says in 2 Corinthians 5:14, 'one died for all, and therefore all died'.[113] If our 'old self' died in God's sight, at what point does this become effective in us as believers? By his references to baptism in 6:3-4 Paul indicates that it is at the time of our conversion-initiation/baptism that God's decision in our favor becomes effective, we receive a new status,[114] and, as the apostle will explain later (cf. 8:3-4), we are actually renewed by the Holy Spirit.

Paul adds that the purpose of our old self being crucified with him is *so that the body ruled by sin might be done away with, that we should no longer be slaves to sin.* The expression, 'the body ruled by sin' (lit. 'the body of sin'), is an unusual one. When speaking of the sinful impulses in human beings Paul normally employs the term 'flesh', not 'body'. However, there are a couple of other places where Paul links the body with sin. In 6:12 he urges his audience: 'do not let sin reign in your mortal body so that you obey its evil desires', and in 8:10 he assures them that 'if Christ is in you, then even though your body is subject to death because of sin, the Spirit gives life because of righteousness'. In the present context 'the body of sin' appears to be synonymous with 'flesh', and denotes human nature under sin's sway.

When speaking of the body ruled by sin being 'done away with', Paul employs a verb with a range of meanings.[115] Here its meaning is to cause the body ruled by sin 'to lose its power' over us, with the result 'that we should no longer be slaves to sin'. It would appear that Paul is asserting

---

111. Cf. Barrett, *Romans*, 125; Wright, 'Romans', 539.

112. Cranfield, *Romans*, I, 309. Moo, *Romans*, 373, adopts a similar interpretation: 'Paul's language throughout is forensic, or positional; by God's act, we have been placed in a new position. This position is real, for what exists *in God's sight* is surely (ultimately) real, and it carries definite consequences for day-to-day living. But it is a status, or power structure, that Paul is talking about here' (italics added).

113. It is perhaps significant that Paul employs the first person plural ('our old self') throughout — he may be thinking of a collective entity that died in God's sight rather than of individuals (cf. Jewett, *Romans*, 403).

114. Cf. Cranfield, *Romans*, I, 309; Moo, *Romans*, 373; Jewett, *Romans*, 403.

115. In Paul's letters the verb *katargeō* is variously translated by the NIV as 'nullify' (3:3; 3:31; 1 Cor 1:28); 'is worthless' (4:14); 'do away with' (6:6; Gal 3:17); 'release' (7:2, 6); 'come to nothing' (1 Cor 2:6); 'disappear' (1 Cor 13:10); 'put behind' (1 Cor 13:11); 'be transitory/pass away' (2 Cor 3:7, 11, 13); 'take away' (2 Cor 3:14); 'alienate' (Gal 5:4); 'abolish' (Gal 5:11); and 'set aside' (Eph 2:15). Cf. BAGD, *ad loc.*

that we are no longer bound to sin, as if we were sin's slaves, but are now free not to sin, though the possibility of doing so is ever present.[116]

In 6:7 Paul explains why believers are no longer 'slaves to sin': *because anyone who has died has been set free from sin.* Attention has sometimes been drawn to the rabbinic principle that a man's death pays all debts,[117] but Paul is unlikely to think that this principle, applicable in a human court, would apply to a person's relationship to God. In context Paul is thinking not of a person's own death, but the believer's death to sin by being united with Christ in his death at baptism.

A related issue is how the verb rendered 'set free' is to be understood here. In one form or another it is found twenty-seven times in Paul's letters, and is almost always rendered correctly in English translations as 'justify' or 'declare righteous'.[118] In the light of its overwhelming use to mean 'justify' elsewhere in Paul's letters, it could be understood in the same way here, thus producing the translation: 'he who has died is *justified* from sin', rather than 'he who has died is set free from sin'. Scholars are divided in their opinions regarding this matter. Some say that the context of chapter 6, which speaks of believers being no longer slaves to sin, and the real transformation occurring through conversion/baptism, suggest a translation, 'has been *set free* from sin'.[119] Most scholars argue that the word should be given its normal meaning and so opt for the translation, 'justified from sin'.[120] Wright asks: 'Why, then, "justified", rather than "freed"? The answer must be that . . . Paul is able to keep the law-court metaphor still running in his mind even while expounding baptism and the Christian's solidarity in Christ. The Christian's freedom from sin comes through God's judicial decision. And this judicial decision is embodied in baptism'.[121] Dunn claims: 'A better rendering would be "declared free from (responsibility in relation to) sin", "no longer has to answer for sin" (NJB, similarly NEB'),[122] which is not that different from rendering it 'justified from sin'.

116. Witherington, *Romans*, 160, quotes Talbert: 'The implication is that prior to our dying with Christ to sin we had no freedom to choose whom we should serve. The only freedom we had was a freedom to sin. After dying with Christ to sin, our freedom from sin is not automatic but must be chosen. With the power of sin broken, we have the freedom to make a choice for righteousness'.

117. Cf. Str-B 3:232.

118. The verb *dikaioō* is correctly rendered 'justify' or 'declare righteous' in 2:13; 3:20, 24, 26, 28, 30; 4:2, 5; 5:1, 9; 8:30, 33; 1 Cor 6:11; Gal 2:16, 17; 3:8, 11, 24; 5:4; Tit 3:7. The only exceptions to this normal use are in 3:4: 'So that you may be *proved right* when you speak and prevail when you judge'; 1 Cor 4:4: 'My conscience is clear, but that does not *make* me *innocent*. It is the Lord who judges me'; 1 Tim 3:16: 'He appeared in the flesh, was *vindicated* by the Spirit, was seen by angels, was preached among the nations, was believed on in the world, was taken up in glory': and possibly here in 6:7 where Paul says, 'he who has died has been *set free* from sin'.

119. E.g., Witherington, *Romans*, 161.

120. E.g., Cranfield, *Romans*, I, 310-11; Fitzmyer, *Romans*, 437.

121. Wright, 'Romans', 540.

122. Dunn, *Romans 1–8*, 320.

6:8 Applying all this to his audience, in 6:8-14 Paul argues that just as Christ died to sin and now lives to God, so we who have died to sin with him must likewise live to God. He begins: *Now if we died with Christ, we believe that we will also live with him.* Paul has already argued that believers have died with Christ (6:4, 6), and now he makes this the premise ('if we died with Christ') for the belief that 'we will also live with him'. Noteworthy is Paul's stress upon the fact that both these things occur because believers are united with Christ. There is a difference of opinion among scholars whether the future tense ('we will live with him') is to be understood as a logical future denoting the believers' experience of life with Christ in the present or as a normal future expressing believers' hope — their being raised with Christ on the last day. In favor of the first option is the whole thrust of the paragraph, and especially 6:11, which is exhortatory in character.[123] In favor of the second option is that Paul says that 'we *believe* that we will also live with him (Christian hope)'. This suggests that at this point Paul is thinking not so much about new life for believers in the here and now but of their belief that they will be raised with him on the last day.[124]

6:9-10 In these two verses Paul focuses upon Christ's death and resurrection and what that involved for Christ himself. He begins by focusing upon the significance of his resurrection: *For we know that since Christ was raised from the dead, he cannot die again; death no longer has mastery over him.* There are accounts in the Gospels and Acts of those who were restored to life by Jesus and his apostles, for example, Jairus's daughter (Mark 5:21-24, 35-43; Luke 8:40-42, 49-56), the widow of Nain's son (Luke 7:11-17), Lazarus (John 11:1-44), and Dorcas (Acts 9:36-42), but all these would subsequently die again. However, the resurrection of Christ was of a different order altogether — being raised from the dead, 'he cannot die again', and therefore it may be said that death no longer rules over him.

In respect to Christ's own death, Paul says: *The death he died, he died to sin once for all.* In 6:2 Paul said of believers, 'we died to sin', and here in 6:10 he says of Christ, 'he died to sin once for all'.[125] While the statements appear similar, there is a marked difference in their significance. Believers died to sin through their union with Christ. Christ died to sin when he was crucified. Believers' death to sin means freedom from sin's dominion, but this is not the case with Christ, for he was never dominated by sin. Elsewhere when Paul speaks about Christ's death and its relation to sin, he speaks of it as the atoning sacrifice for our sins: 'For what the law was powerless to do in that it was weakened by the flesh, God did by sending his

123. Cf. Cranfield, *Romans,* I, 313; Fitzmyer, *Romans,* 437.

124. So Dunn, *Romans 1–8,* 322.

125. Jacques Winandy, 'La mort de Jésus: Une morte au péché?' *ETL* 76 (2000) 434, argues that 6:10a refers not to Christ but is an abstract statement that should be rendered, 'But the one (whoever he may be) who has died, it is to sin that he has died once and for all'. However, the context militates against this view because it is Christ's death and resurrection that is to the fore.

own Son in the likeness of sinful flesh to be a sin offering' (8:3); 'For what I received I passed on to you as of first importance: that Christ died for our sins according to the Scriptures' (1 Cor 15:3); 'God made him who had no sin to be sin for us, so that in him we might become the righteousness of God' (2 Cor 5:21); '[Christ] who gave himself for our sins to rescue us from the present evil age' (Gal 1:4). To assert, then, that Christ 'died to sin once for all' should be understood to mean that he died to deal with the problem of human sin, and he did so 'once for all', that is, once and for all in the sense of once and never again.[126] His death 'once' was sufficient to deal fully and for all time with the problem of human sin.

Paul balances his statement that 'the death he [Christ] died, he died to sin once for all' by adding, *but the life he lives, he lives to God.* It is easier to discover what it means for human beings to 'live to God' — something the apostle urges his audience to do in the very next verse, and something upon which other Pauline texts shed some light. We can only surmise what Paul means by saying that Christ, following his death, now 'lives to God'. Perhaps we should understand it in this way: Following that horrendous break in relationship within the Godhead ('My God, my God, why have you forsaken me?') by which human sin was dealt with 'once and for all', that relationship was restored so that Christ lives again to God, as he did beforehand.

6:11 Having spoken of Christ's own death to sin and that he now lives to God, Paul exhorts his audience: *In the same way, count yourselves dead to sin but alive to God in Christ Jesus.* There is strong emphasis on the fact that we must count ourselves to be dead to sin.[127] On first reading it would appear that believers must 'count'[128] themselves dead to sin in the same way as Christ died to sin. However, Paul would be the first to say that the way Christ died to sin is unique (being himself without sin, he became an atoning sacrifice for the sins of humanity). Paul's meaning, then, ap-

---

126. 'Once for all' translates *ephapax*, which is found in only four other places in the NT: Once in Paul's First Letter to the Corinthians: 'After that, he appeared to more than five hundred of the brothers and sisters at the same time *(ephapax)*, most of whom are still living, though some have fallen asleep' (1 Cor 15:6), and three times in the letter to the Hebrews, and in each case to denote the 'once and never again' character of Christ's sacrifice for sins: 'Unlike the other high priests, he does not need to offer sacrifices day after day, first for his own sins, and then for the sins of the people. He sacrificed for their sins once for all *(ephapax)* when he offered himself' (Heb 7:27); 'He did not enter by means of the blood of goats and calves; but he entered the Most Holy Place once for all *(ephapax)* by his own blood, thus obtaining eternal redemption' (Heb 9:12); 'And by that will, we have been made holy through the sacrifice of the body of Jesus Christ once for all *(ephapax)*' (Heb 10:10).

127. 'You' *(hymeis)* is added for emphasis, and 'count' *(logizesthe)* is imperative.

128. The verb translated here as 'to count' is *logizomai*, one used predominantly by Paul in the NT. It is found a total of 40 times in the NT, and 34 of these are found in the Pauline letters, 19 of them in Romans. *Logizomai* means essentially to calculate or reckon, and may used to denote taking something into account, crediting something to someone, and looking upon or considering something to be the case. It is in this last sense that it is used here in 6:11; cf. BAGD, *ad loc.*

pears to be something like this: As Christ died for our sins once for all, so we ought now to count ourselves dead to sin in the sense that we are released from its tyranny as a result of what Christ has done (cf. 6:14); and as Christ now lives in a restored relationship with God following his death on the cross, so we are to count ourselves 'alive' (lit. 'living') to God in Christ. In 6:13 Paul will refer to believers as those 'who have been brought from death to life'. In Galatians 5:25 he says: 'Since we live by the Spirit, let us keep in step with the Spirit'. In Ephesians 2:4-5 we read, 'God, who is rich in mercy, made us alive with Christ even when we were dead in transgressions' (cf. also Col 2:13). All this suggests that when Paul calls upon his audience to consider themselves to be 'alive to God', it is in recognition of the fact that they are no longer dead in transgressions, they have been made alive with Christ, and they now live by the Spirit. This counting/reckoning oneself dead to sin and alive to God is not just pretending. Wright's comment is apposite:

> The key word here is 'reckon', the same root as in 4:3 and elsewhere, and with the same bookkeeping metaphor in mind. Do the sum, he says; add it up and see what it comes to. The Messiah has died, once for all, and has been raised; you are, by baptism, in the Messiah; therefore, you, too, have died, once for all, and been raised. The 'reckoning' in question is to take place in the believing thought processes of the Christian. . . . The point is not, as in some schemes of piety, that the 'reckoning' *achieves* the result of dying to sin and coming alive to God, any more than someone adding up a column of figures creates the result out of nothing; it opens the eyes of mind and heart to recognize what is in fact true. It is here that one might almost say that Paul appeals for faith on the basis of baptism. Those who have received the sign of the new exodus in the Messiah are urged to think through, and to believe, what has in fact happened to them.[129]

What Wright says happens to people at baptism is reasonable so long as the term 'baptism' functions as shorthand for the whole conversion-initiation experience: repentance and faith focused in their submission to baptism on the part of human beings and the concomitant forgiveness and bestowal of the Spirit by God.

6:12-13 In 6:11 Paul exhorted his audience: 'count yourselves dead to sin but alive to God in Christ Jesus'. In 6:12-13 he spells out in detail how this is to express itself in practical terms. As a consequence of their having died to sin and now being alive to God, Paul exhorts his audience: *Therefore do not let sin reign in your mortal body so that you obey its evil desires.*[130] This ex-

---

129. Wright, 'Romans', 541.

130. Joel Marcus, '"Let God Arise and End the Reign of Sin!" A Contribution to the Study of Pauline Parenesis', *Bib* 69 (1988) 387-89, argues for a different translation of this text. He notes that the imperative 'let not sin reign' *(mē basileuetō)* is in the third, not the sec-

hortation makes it clear that believers' death to sin does not mean that they are immune to temptation or incapable of falling into sin. It means that sin's tyranny has been broken so they are free to choose not to sin, but they must continue to choose not to do so. In the apostle's words, they must 'not let sin reign' in their mortal bodies; they must not yield to evil desires. Paul's reference to our 'mortal bodies' is, of course, to believers' present bodies that are subject to death.[131] In this context, 'our mortal bodies' are also the locus in which the evil desires that we must refuse to obey manifest themselves.

Paul spells out in more detail what this involves when he adds: *Do not offer any part of yourself to sin as an instrument of wickedness.* This further underlines the active choice believers must make not to yield to temptations to sin. 'Any part of yourself' [lit. 'your members'] here denotes the body in all its parts in which evil desires can manifest themselves (cf. 6:19; 7:5, 23; Col 3:5).[132] In his reference to offering any part of their bodies as 'instruments' of wickedness the apostle employs a word used to denote either 'armor' (13:12) or 'weapons' (2 Cor 6:7; 10:4) or, as here, 'instruments',[133] that is, a tool used to accomplish something, in this case wickedness. Yielding to sin is not merely passive but active.

Alongside the negative exhortation not to offer any part of themselves to sin, Paul includes the positive alternative: *but rather offer yourselves to God, as those who have been brought from death to life; and offer every part of yourself to him as an instrument of righteousness.*[134] Not only do believers need

---

ond person, and as such could be construed as a prayer request (similar to that in the Lord's Prayer, 'Let your kingdom come'). He offers the following paraphrase to express this: 'Let Sin be dethroned in your mortal body! May God vanquish it! And you, for your part, remove your bodily members from the battle line where they serve Sin as weapons of its unrighteousness, and present them for duty to God as weapons of his righteousness! For Sin will no longer be your master . . .' (394).

131. These same 'mortal bodies' are also to be redeemed and raised to immortality (cf. 8:11; 1 Cor 15:53-54; 2 Cor 5:4; Phil 3:21).

132. More frequently Paul uses the word 'parts' *(melē)* in quite a different way in relation to believers being members of Christ's body, the church (12:4-5; 1 Cor 6:15; 12:12, 14, 18-20, 22, 25-27; Eph 4:25; 5:30),

133. This word, *hoplon*, is not common in the NT, being found in only five places (John 18:3; Rom 6:13; 13:12; 2 Cor 6:7; 10:4). In 13:12 it denotes 'armor', and elsewhere it denotes either weapons or instruments usually understood metaphorically, except in John 18:3, where it refers to actual military weapons.

134. In 6:12-13 the two negative imperatives/prohibitions are expressed using the present imperative form of the verbs *(mē basileuetō and mēde paristanete)*, which has traditionally been regarded as a command to stop doing something already in progress, and the positive imperative/command is expressed with the aorist imperative *(parastēsate)*, which has traditionally been regarded as a command to start doing something. However, this approach to the significance of present and aorist imperatives has been called into question by the supporters of verbal aspect theory (cf., e.g., Dave Mathewson, 'Verbal Aspect in Imperative Constructions in Pauline Ethical Injunctions', *FilolNT* 9 [1996] 27). We should not, therefore, simply assume that Paul was exhorting the Roman believers to stop doing something they were already doing (offering the members of their body to sin to be instru-

to refuse to employ their bodies as instruments of wickedness, but they are positively to offer themselves to God, and yield their members as instruments of righteousness.[135] The verb 'to offer' is used here to mean 'to place at someone's disposal', and because this 'offering' of themselves is to be as 'instruments' or 'weapons' of righteousness to God, it is possible that Paul is employing a military allusion here.[136]

6:14 In this verse Paul sums up why his audience need not be dominated by sin: *For sin shall not be your master, because you are not under law, but under grace.* First, Paul maintains that sin will not be their master (lit. 'for sin will not rule over you') because they are 'under grace'. Under God's grace they have been buried with Christ at baptism into death so that they may live a new life (6:4), and their old selves have been crucified with Christ in order that the body of sin might be done away so that they should no longer be slaves to sin (6:6). Second, Paul contends that sin will not rule over them because they are not 'under law'. This statement is unexpected here as 'law' has not been part of the discussion prior to this in 6:1-14. However, it paves the way for Paul's discussion in the next section, introduced in 6:15a: 'Shall we sin because we are not under law but under grace?' Such a notion he vigorously refutes in 6:15b-23. Furthermore, by saying that they 'are not under law, but under grace' the apostle foreshadows his discussion of new life in the Spirit that makes possible what the law could not achieve because of the weakness of sinful flesh (8:1-17). It is noteworthy that 6:14 and 6:1 bracket the whole passage 6:1-14 insofar as 6:14 insists that precisely because believers are under grace they will not serve sin as their master, something that is the very opposite of what Paul's detractors were asking: 'Shall we go on sinning so that grace may increase?' (6:1; cf. 3:8).

To be 'under law' means to live under the regime of the Mosaic law, under the old covenant where the law was something written on tables of stone, and to be 'under grace' is to live under the new covenant, where the law is written on the human heart (cf. 2 Cor 3:3). What was impossible under the regime of the Mosaic law (the fulfillment of the law's own demands) because of humanity's weakness is made possible under the new covenant because of the renewing and transforming power of the Spirit (cf. 8:3-4; Gal 3:23-25; 4:1-7; 5:18). While believers who live under the new cov-

---

ments of wickedness) and to start doing something they had not yet been doing (offering the parts of their body to God as instruments of righteousness).

135. In 2 Cor 5:15 Paul makes a similar point: 'And he [Christ] died for all, that those who live should no longer live for themselves but for him who died for them and was raised again'.

136. Both Fitzmyer, *Romans*, 447, and Jewett, *Romans*, 410-11, see in the use of the word here a military allusion. Jewett says that 'believers are to view themselves not as the helpless tools of evil powers but as weapons in the hands of the living God'. Paul uses the same verb, *paristēmi*, in 12:1, this time embodying a sacrificial allusion: 'Therefore, I urge you, brothers and sisters, in view of God's mercy, to offer *(parastēsai)* your bodies as a living sacrifice, holy and pleasing to God — this is true and proper worship'.

enant of grace no longer live under the Mosaic law as a regime, this does not mean that they are free to flout the moral imperatives found in the law, for these are the moral standards required of humankind by God himself.[137] In fact, in those who walk by the Spirit the 'just requirement' of the law is fulfilled (8:4), for, as Paul says in 13:9, 'the commandments, "You shall not commit adultery", "You shall not murder", "You shall not steal", "You shall not covet", and whatever other command there may be, are summed up in this one command: "Love your neighbor as yourself"' (cf. Gal 5:14), and, of course, love is included in the fruit of the Spirit (Gal 5:22).

ADDITIONAL NOTE: BAPTISM IN THE PAULINE CORPUS

References to baptism in the Pauline corpus are restricted to just five letters. Prior to the writing of Romans Paul referred to baptism only in Galatians and 1 Corinthians.

In Galatians Paul tells his audience, 'all of you who were baptized into Christ have clothed yourselves with Christ' (Gal 3:27). It is noteworthy that in this text Paul connects people being baptized (passive) with their clothing themselves with Christ (active). In Romans 13:14 he uses the clothing metaphor in a similar way when he urges his audience: 'clothe yourselves with the Lord Jesus Christ'. Paul uses the putting on/clothing metaphor in a number of other ways as well. He speaks of putting on 'the armor of light' (13:12), 'the new self' (Eph 4:24; Col 3:10), 'the full armor of God' (Eph 6:11), 'the breastplate of righteousness' (Eph 6:14), 'compassion, kindness, humility, gentleness and patience' (Col 3:12), 'faith and love as a breastplate, and the hope of salvation as a helmet' (1 Thess 5:8). These other ways the apostle uses the idea of 'putting on' or 'clothing oneself' with something indicate that it is to be understood metaphorically, and thus his reference to those who were baptized as having put on Christ is best taken metaphorically also, not realistically. Paul's meaning seems to be that those who have been baptized have taken upon themselves the obligation to live like Christ.

In 1 Corinthians 1:13-17 Paul responds to unhealthy preferences for one apostle over another on the part of members of his audience. This apparently had some connection with who baptized them, Paul or Apollos. So he asks whether they were baptized 'in the name of Paul', and says that he is glad he baptized only Crispus and Gaius so that none of them could claim to be baptized 'in my name' (presumably Crispus and Gaius would have more sense than to say this, and so would Stephanas whom Paul mentions as an afterthought as another person whom he baptized). The unexpressed implication is that the Corinthian believers had not been baptized

---

137. Cf. Moo, *Romans*, 390; Fitzmyer, *Romans*, 447-48.

in Paul's name but rather in the name of Christ. By being baptized they had expressed their allegiance, not to Paul, but to Christ. Baptism here, then, is to be understood as an expression of allegiance to Christ. Paul concludes with a surprising statement: 'Christ did not send me to baptize, but to preach the gospel'. This is not something he would say if baptism was essential even if it was the normal rite people underwent in order to experience the power of the gospel and be incorporated into Christ.

In 1 Corinthians 10 Paul refers to the experience of the Israelites in the wilderness when warning his audience against compromise with idolatry. He reminds them that 'our forefathers were all under the cloud and that they all passed through the sea. They were all baptized into Moses in the cloud and in the sea'; nevertheless, 'God was not pleased with most of them; their bodies were scattered in the wilderness' (1 Cor 10:1-5). This is a strange use of baptismal imagery, implying, it would seem, that the Israelites' 'baptismal' experience with Moses in the cloud and the sea involved their identification with and obedience to him so that together they experienced God's salvation.[138]

In 1 Corinthians 12:12-13, to counteract the divisive effects of his audience's unhelpful attitudes towards *charismata*, Paul emphasizes the unity of believers in Christ: 'For just as the body is one and has many members, and all the members of the body, though many, are one body, so it is with Christ. For in the one Spirit we were all baptized into one body — Jews or Greeks, slaves or free — and we were all made to drink of one Spirit' (NRSV). Believers are those who have been baptized in the one Spirit into one body, those who have been made to drink of the one Spirit. Paul is speaking here primarily of baptism 'in the Spirit', though this may be coincidental with baptism in water.

In 1 Corinthians 15:29, to correct his audience's defective understanding of resurrection, the apostle, who thought of an afterlife essentially as resurrection to immortality, asked them: 'Now if there is no resurrection, what will those do who are baptized for the dead? If the dead are not raised at all, why are people baptized for them?' This refers to a practice adopted by some of the Corinthians, one that Paul would not approve, but to which he appealed to show the inconsistency in their thinking. This being the case, his reference to it reveals nothing of his own understanding of baptism.

It is only when we come to Romans 6:1-14 that we find Paul's first reference to the baptism of believers linked to the idea of dying and rising with Christ. Within this passage the connection is made in just two verses: 'Or don't you know that all of us who were baptized into Christ Jesus were baptized into his death? We were therefore buried with him through bap-

---

138. Badke, 'Baptised into Moses — Baptised into Christ', 25-26, commenting upon the phrase 'baptized into Moses', says: 'The point of baptism in this context is the adherence of the people to Moses and thus to God, along with the benefits which should have resulted from such a union'.

tism into death in order that, just as Christ was raised from the dead through the glory of the Father, we too may live a new life' (6:3-4). His reference to baptism is probably a shorthand way of referring to their whole conversion-initiation experience by which he understood that they were buried with Christ to rise to new life in him.

Colossians 2:8-15 is the one other passage where Paul connects baptism and dying and rising with Christ. In it he exhorts his audience not to be taken in by sub-Christian philosophy, reminding them that in Christ they have already come to fullness of life. In this context he tells them that they have 'been buried with him in baptism, in which you were also raised with him through your faith in the working of God' (Col 2:12). It is significant that here Paul states explicitly what is only implied in Romans 6:3-4, that is, that they were not only buried with Christ in baptism but in it they 'were also raised with him through faith in the working of God'. It is also significant that Paul makes plain that this is effected 'through faith', suggesting that baptism is a shorthand way of referring to the whole conversion-initiation experience that involves essentially, on the human side, (repentance and) faith.

The final reference to baptism in the Pauline corpus is found in Ephesians 4:4-6, where the apostle asks his audience to maintain the unity of the Spirit, and reminds them of seven important matters that unify them: 'there is one body and one Spirit, just as you were called to one hope when you were called; one Lord, one faith, one baptism; one God and Father of all, who is over all and through all and in all'. The one Lord is Jesus Christ, the one faith is probably the confession of Jesus as Lord, and the one baptism is that initiatory rite to which they all submitted when they made that confession, and so became disciples of Christ.[139]

Summing up, for Paul baptism in the name of Christ appears to have been an initiatory rite undergone by people as a means by which they confessed Christ as their Lord, a part of the full conversion-initiation experience that involved repentance and faith in Christ expressed in submission to baptism when God for his part granted forgiveness and the gift of his Spirit (cf. Acts 2:37). In only two texts is baptism connected with the idea of dying and rising with Christ. It remains to be considered what the apostle meant by this (see 'Additional Note: Dying and Rising with Christ', below).

ADDITIONAL NOTE: DYING AND RISING WITH CHRIST

The idea of dying (and rising) with Christ is found in three of Paul's letters: 2 Corinthians, Romans, and Colossians. Of these, 2 Corinthians is

---

139. Cf. Fitzmyer, *Romans*, 430-31.

probably the most important because it is the earliest of the three and because in it Paul explains directly the significance of the death of Christ and how believers are involved in it, whereas in the relevant passages in the other letters the death of believers with Christ is simply assumed and used to support an exhortation to godly living. We will look at each passage in turn.

2 Corinthians

The relevant passage in 2 Corinthians is 5:14-21. The key text is verse 14, which reads as follows: 'For Christ's love compels us, because we are convinced that one died for all, and therefore all died'. The apostle makes it plain here that it is because 'one [Christ] died for all' that 'all died'. In the same passage Paul explains 'that God was reconciling the world to himself in Christ, not counting people's sins against them' (v. 19), and that 'God made him who had no sin to be sin for us, so that in him we might become the righteousness of God' (v. 21). Putting these things together, we may say that God himself was the one who initiated reconciliation, and he did so by 'not counting men's sins against them'. He acted justly in this respect because 'God made him [Christ] who had no sin to be sin for us, so that in him we might become the righteousness of God'. Two main interpretations have been suggested for the profound statement that God made him to be sin for us: (a) Christ was made a sin offering, and (b) Christ was made to bear the consequences of our sins.

The first interpretation can be supported by appeal to Paul's use of sacrificial terminology elsewhere to bring out the significance of Christ's death (e.g., 3:25; 1 Cor 5:7). It has also been pointed out that in Leviticus 4:24; 5:12 (LXX) the same word translated 'sin' is used to mean 'sin offering'. However, with only one possible exception (8:3), the word is never used in this way in the NT, and it is doubtful that it carries this meaning there.

The second interpretation is supported by the fact that in Galatians 3:13 Paul interprets the work of Christ in terms of his bearing the consequences of our sins: 'Christ redeemed us from the curse of the law by becoming a curse for us, for it is written: "Cursed is everyone who is hung on a pole"'. This interpretation is further supported by the fact that the statement, 'he made him to be sin, who knew no sin' (5:21a), is balanced in antithetical parallelism by the words, 'so that in him we might become the righteousness of God' (5:21b). We must construe the former in such a way that the latter is understood as its antithetical counterpart. In seeking to understand what it means to be the righteousness of God, we receive assistance from certain other passages where Paul touches upon the same subject (3:21-26; Phil 3:7-9). In these passages the righteousness of God, understood as that which believers have or become, is the gift of a right status be-

fore God based upon the fact that he has adjudicated in their favor by refusing to take account of their sins because of the death of Christ in their place.
If becoming the righteousness of God means that God has adjudicated in
our favor and with all the attendant blessings, then to become sin, being the
antithetical counterpart of this, will mean that God has adjudicated against
Christ because he took upon himself the burden of our sins (cf. Isa 53:4-6,
12), bearing all the consequences in our place. The upshot of all this is that
when Paul said, 'he died for all', it means that he died in the place of all,
bearing the consequences of their sins, and in this respect we may say, 'all
died'.

Romans

The second of the letters in which Paul speaks about our dying and rising
with Christ is his letter to the Romans. The key passage is 6:1-14. There
are several elements in this passage that call for comment. First, believers
are said to have died and been raised to new life *with Christ.* For his part
Christ is said to have been raised from the dead by the glory of the Father,
and, having been raised from the dead, he dies no more and death no longer rules over him; he has died to sin once and for all time, and now he
lives to God. The believers' dying and rising is intimately connected to
Christ's own dying and rising. Paul uses the word 'with' *(syn),* mostly as
a prefix in compound verbs and once standing on its own as a preposition. He does so no fewer than five times in 6:1-14 to underline the believers' union with Christ in his death and resurrection. Thus believers are
said to have been 'buried with him' *(synetaphēmen autō)* (6:4); to have been
'united with him'. *(symphytoi)* in a death like his (6:5); to have had their
old self 'crucified with him' *(synestaurōthē)* (6:6); to have died 'with
Christ' *(syn Christō)* (6:8); and to 'live with him' *(syzēsomen)* in the future
(6:8). In whatever way believers' dying and rising is understood, clearly
it must be interpreted in relation to Christ's own historic death, burial,
and resurrection.

Second, believers' death to sin and resurrection to new life with
Christ is *linked with baptism.* Those who have been baptized into Christ are
said to have to have been baptized into his death and to have been buried
with him at baptism into death. Paul may also be referring to baptism
when he speaks of our having been 'united with him in a death like his'.
Believers' share in Christ's death and resurrection is linked with their baptism. How this is to be understood is discussed below.

Third, believers' death with Christ means that they have died *to sin.*
Paul asks, 'We are those who have died to sin; how can we live in it any longer?' He reminds his audience that 'our old self was crucified with him so
that the body ruled by sin might be done away with, that we should no longer be slaves to sin — because anyone who has died has been freed from

sin'. What Paul means by dying to sin is an end to one's slavery to sin — freedom from sin's dominion.[140]

Fourth, believers, having being raised with Christ, now live *to God.* Paul insists that we were buried with him at baptism into death 'in order that, just as Christ was raised from the dead through the glory of the Father, we too may live a new life'. He tells his audience to 'count yourselves dead to sin but alive to God in Christ Jesus', and to 'offer yourselves to God, as those who have been brought from death to life'. This new life is mediated to believers by the Spirit.

Colossians

The third of the letters in which Paul speaks about our dying and rising with Christ is his letter to the Colossians. There are two relevant passages. The first is Colossians 2:8-15 in which he exhorts his audience not to be taken in by sub-Christian philosophy, because they have already come to fullness of life in Christ. In the key text (Col 2:12) he reminds them that they have 'been buried with him in baptism' in which they 'were also raised with him through your faith in the working of God'. It is by faith in the working of God and through their submission to baptism that they have been buried and raised with Christ. The mention here of both faith and baptism suggests that Paul had in mind the conversion-initiation experience of his audience in which they expressed their repentance and faith in Christ, acknowledging his lordship by submission to baptism, whereupon God forgave their sins and bestowed upon them the gift of the Holy Spirit.

The other relevant passage is Colossians 3:1-3, in which Paul, assuming that his audience have both died and been raised with Christ, says to them: 'Since, then, you have been raised with Christ, set your hearts on things above, where Christ is seated at the right hand of God. Set your minds on things above, not on earthly things. For you died, and your life is now hidden with Christ in God'. The apostle does not explain how this dying and rising with Christ took place. We can explain this only in the light of 2 Corinthians 5:14, 21 and Colossians 2:12.

It remains to mention now some of the ways in which believers' dying and rising with Christ and its connection with baptism have been interpreted in recent times. Tannehill argues that when Paul speaks of the dying and rising of Christ, he is speaking of eschatological events which relate to the old and new aeons. He asserts that 'through this death and resurrection the believers are free from the old aeon and the new aeon is founded'.

---

140. That dying to sin means release from sin's bondage is confirmed when we examine what Paul says about dying to other powers — in each case he implies that the dominion of those powers has been brought to an end. So, e.g., believers are said to be dead to the law (Rom 7:4; Gal 2:19) and to the basic principles *(stoicheia)* of the world (Col 2:20).

These aeons, he says, are spheres of dominion ruled by specific powers. 'Christ as inclusive man is the aeon-man of the new aeon, just as Adam was of the old. He is the one who represents and embodies the whole of the new aeon because he determines the nature of existence there'.[141] Explaining how this affects the believer, Tannehill says: 'The individual is baptised "into Christ" and "into his death", that is, through baptism he enters the new dominion which is determined by Christ and his saving acts. This means that he has been "buried with" Christ, that is, through baptism into Christ's death he has been fully and finally separated from the old life'.[142] Tannehill emphasizes that dying and rising with Christ is not effected by baptism itself, and that baptism has no independent significance. 'What takes place in baptism is a manifestation of the power of the cross. The individual can enter into Christ and be separated from the old dominion of sin through baptism only because of the eschatological significance of the cross. It is only because it is the effect of Christ's cross to bring the old dominion to an end and establish a new dominion that baptism can mean the realization of this eschatological change in the life of the individual'.[143]

Others see in Paul's statements about baptism allusions to initiatory rites of the mystery religions. Bligh, for example, suggests that Paul was assimilating, either consciously or unconsciously, Christian baptism to the mystery religions, in particular the mysteries of Demeter at Eleusis.[144] Bligh, while acknowledging the differences between Christian baptism and the initiatory rites of the mystery religions, also sees certain similarities: 'Initiation at Eleusis did not incorporate the initiated into a group which would meet and act as a group. It was a once-only rite, the memory of which an initiate could keep as a secret in his or her own breast and could speak of, cautiously, to other initiates. . . . Christian Baptism could be regarded in the same way, and probably was so regarded by many Jewish Christians'. . . .[145] Bligh adds: 'Paul clarifies the connection between faith, baptism, the death of Christ, the gift of the Spirit, and the fulfillment of the moral teaching of Christ: those who believe in Christ express their faith by submitting to Baptism; through Baptism they are *mystically united to Christ's obedient death;* Christ's death wins for them the gift of the Spirit, a share in the life of the risen Christ; the Spirit strengthens them to resist temptation and live a life of charity' (italics added).[146] The weakness of Bligh's statement is that it still leaves the way believers are united with Christ in his death unexplained. To say people are *mystically united to Christ's obedient death* does nothing to explain how this occurs.

141. Robert C. Tannehill, *Dying and Rising with Christ: A Study in Pauline Theology* (Berlin: Töpelmann, 1966), 39.

142. Tannehill, *Dying and Rising with Christ*, 41.

143. Tannehill, *Dying and Rising with Christ*, 42.

144. John Bligh, 'Baptismal Transformation of the Gentile World', *HeyJ* 37 (1996) 373.

145. Bligh, 'Baptismal Transformation of the Gentile World', 379.

146. Bligh, 'Baptismal Transformation of the Gentile World', 376.

Commenting on 6:3-4, Taylor argues that Paul's reference to believers being buried with Christ at baptism should be interpreted not as burial with him, but as undergoing 'funeral rites' with him. He points out that it should not be 'assumed that *synthaptō* ['to bury'] denotes the lowering of a body vertically into a hole in the ground and covered with earth which is symbolised by submersion into a tank of water'. He says that 'word *thaptō* ['to bury'] . . . had a wide semantic range and can refer to 'the performance of or participation in all manner of funeral rites, from processions to cremation and embalming, as well as interment in tombs. . . . In Gen 50.26, LXX *ethapsan* . . . [denotes] the embalming of Joseph, but quite explicitly not the deposition of his body in a tomb. . . . What is clear is that the word refers to the performance of funeral rites in all their complexity and diversity. . . . Moreover, *thaptein* does not refer specifically or exclusively to the act of deposition in a grave, of any kind. . . . The ritual form is incidental; of consequence is that the funeral commits the deceased to the next stage in his/her existence, and expedites progress towards the fulfillment of that life beyond the grave.[147] He adds: 'Interpreting *eis ton thanaton* ['into death'] in Rom 6.4 as meaning "into Hades" or "into the netherworld" would make sense not merely of the logic of the metaphor in this verse, but also of Paul's association of baptism with death and resurrection, and of the identification of the Christian, in baptism, with the death and resurrection of Jesus. I would therefore suggest that the first clause in Rom 6.4 be rendered into English as follows: "We underwent funeral rites with him through baptism into the netherworld". . . . Understood together with the sense of the "funeral" as expediting the journey into the afterlife, baptism denotes death, not so much in terms of the termination of vital functions, as of being committed to the journey from the present world to that existence which pertains beyond the grave. Baptism, in other words, transports the new Christian symbolically to that state of existence which Jesus Christ entered through his death on the cross'.[148]

Commenting on *ek nekrōn* ('from [the] dead'), Taylor says: 'In the LXX . . . *ek nekrōn* refers not to an abstract state of being, but to people who have died. . . . Christ, having died on the cross, is understood to be not an isolated individual denuded of meaningful existence, but a "shade" who has entered the same place and state of being (*eis ton thanaton* ['into death']) as other deceased humans, and shares in their collective identity and aspirations for continued meaningful existence. . . . From Hades, Jesus was raised *ek nekrōn*, from among the dead, i.e., the shades of the dead. This I would propose . . . provides a key to understanding how dying with Christ in baptism could be conceived as establishing union with him in his resurrection. By entering through baptism into Christ's death, Christians symbolically join him in

---

147. N. H. Taylor, 'Dying with Christ in Baptism: Issues in the Translation and Interpretation of Romans 6.3-4', *BibTrans* 59 (2008) 40-44.

148. Taylor, 'Dying with Christ in Baptism', 45-47.

Hades, from where Christ Jesus was raised. From there, Christians too would be raised *en kainotēti zōēs* [in newness of life]'.[149] The weakness of Taylor's suggestion is twofold: (i) Paul's only other use of the verb *thaptō* ('to bury') in 1 Corinthians 15:4 clearly refers to burial, not funeral rites, and (ii) to reduce dying and rising with Christ to mere symbolism does not do justice to the reality of the believers' death to sin and their newness of life.

Petersen advocates a 'ritual-theoretical' approach. He says: 'It is evident . . . that the death of Christ is identified as the event which has brought about the new order of being, but it is by virtue of baptism that the Christian's death to sin has occurred as a "Projektion der Aonwende in unser persönliches Dasein" ['a projection of the change of aeons in our personal existence']',[150] and again: 'Participation in the death and resurrection of Christ through baptism incorporates the individual in the new order of being. In this sense baptism into Christ Jesus is a transference to a new lord and an incorporation into a new covenant'.[151] Petersen likens baptism to engagement for marriage. The engagement represents the 'liminal' stage' during which the betrothed person's status has certainly changed but is still not what it will be when the engagement is consummated in marriage. In similar fashion baptism marks a change in the status experienced by believers — one in which 'the death of Christ is existentially actualised for the believer'. As in the case of an engagement in which the state of those concerned is 'characterised by "betwixt and between", the premarital phase has already come to an end, whereas the phase of marriage has not yet occurred to full extent', so also 'the order of being into which the baptised is incorporated is also characterised by the dialectic tension of an "already" and a "not yet"'.[152] Petersen's ritual-theoretical approach is helpful, but it must be added that the ritual of baptism itself does not effect the Christian's death to sin. Baptism itself is important only insofar as it is the focal point of the whole conversion-initiation experience in which a person expresses his or her repentance and faith in Christ and receives from God the forgiveness of sins and the gift of the Spirit. As such, baptism is, on the one hand, more than a ritual and theoretical, but, on the other hand, it alone does not bring about the Christian's death to sin.

What appears to be the best approach to what it means to die with Christ is to recognize that behind it lies what Paul says in 2 Corinthians 5:14: 'we are convinced that one died for all, and therefore all died'. Cranfield describes the significance of this text: 'God's decision to take our sin upon himself in the person of his own dear Son involved the decision to see Christ's death as died "for us" and to see us as having died in his death. So this having died with Christ of ours is a matter of God's gracious deci-

---

149. Taylor, 'Dying with Christ in Baptism', 47-48.
150. Anders Klostergaard Petersen, 'Shedding New Light on Paul's Understanding of Baptism: A Ritual-Theoretical Approach to Romans 6', *ST* 52 (1998) 13.
151. Petersen, 'Shedding New Light on Paul's Understanding of Baptism', 14.
152. Petersen, 'Shedding New Light on Paul's Understanding of Baptism', 15-16.

sion about us'.[153] This avoids the necessity of invoking either 'mystical' or 'symbolic' interpretations of baptism. We are regarded by God as having died to sin because his Son died *for* us. We receive the benefits of this decision through conversion, one element of which is baptism, and another element of which is God's gift of the Spirit so that we experience newness of life now and look forward to a resurrection like Christ's at his return.

---

b. Slaves of Christ 6:15-23

[15]What then? Shall we sin because we are not under the law but under grace? By no means! [16]Don't you know that when you offer yourselves to someone as obedient slaves, you are slaves of the one you obey — whether you are slaves to sin, which leads to death, or to obedience, which leads to righteousness? [17]But thanks be to God that, though you used to be slaves to sin, you have come to obey from your heart the pattern of teaching that has now claimed your allegiance. [18]You have been set free from sin and have become slaves to righteousness

[19]I am using an example from everyday life because of your human limitations. Just as you used to offer yourselves as slaves to impurity and to ever-increasing wickedness, so now offer yourselves as slaves to righteousness leading to holiness. [20]When you were slaves to sin, you were free from the control of righteousness. [21]What benefit did you reap at that time from the things you are now ashamed of? Those things result in death! [22]But now that you have been set free from sin and have become slaves of God, the benefit you reap leads to holiness, and the result is eternal life. [23]For the wages of sin is death, but the gift of God is eternal life in Christ Jesus our Lord.

In 6:1-14 Paul responded to the charge that his gospel promoted moral anarchy while exhorting his audience not to offer their bodies as instruments of sin but rather to offer themselves to God as instruments of righteousness. This he did by arguing that believers cannot continue in sin because they died to it and are now alive to God in Jesus Christ. That passage concluded with the affirmation, 'For sin shall not be your master, because you are not under law, but under grace'. This paves the way for Paul to respond to another charge brought against his gospel: because he teaches that believers are not under the law, he is again encouraging moral anarchy. It also paves the way for the apostle to explain to his audience the true nature of Christian freedom and the choice that faces them — either to be slaves to sin or slaves to righteousness. As far as Paul is concerned, there is no intermediate position. The concept of slavery would have been well known to the Roman believers, for it is estimated that 70 percent of them

---

153. C. E. B. Cranfield, 'Romans 6:1-14 Revisited', *ExpTim* 106 (1994-95) 41. Cf. Jewett, *Romans*, 395.

were from the slave class (see Introduction, 3). What Paul emphasizes in this passage is that life under grace is still a life of obedience.

6:15-16 Setting up an internal dialogue, Paul puts the question those who charged him with promoting sin and those who were afraid his law-free gospel would undermine godliness would ask: *What then? Shall we sin because we are not under law but under grace?* It is noteworthy that at the beginning of this passage Paul uses the first person plural ('we'), including himself among those for whom this is a live question (6:15), before addressing his audience directly using the second person plural ('you') in the rest of the passage. Paul's detractors, as well as believers with a background in the synagogue, would have seen the law as the primary deterrent to sin. They would have regarded Paul's claim that believers are not under the law as the removal of this deterrent and an encouragement to sin.[154]

Paul's response to the question is unequivocal: *By no means!* As noted above (see commentary on 3:4; 6:2), this expression functions as a strong rejection of a preceding proposition. Addressing his audience directly now, the apostle explains the basis of his rebuttal: *Don't you know that when you offer yourselves to someone as obedient slaves, you are slaves of the one you obey?* The expression, 'Don't you know', is one Paul uses repeatedly when reminding people of what they ought to know (6:16; 11:2; 1 Cor 3:16; 5:6; 6:2, 3, 9, 15, 16, 19; 9:13, 24). In this case he asks whether they are unaware of the obvious fact that to offer oneself as a slave to obey someone means becoming the slave of that person. Here Paul begins a lengthy exploitation of the language of slavery/control that runs throughout 6:15-23, alluding to matters well known in first-century Mediterranean culture. Being a slave involved both status (someone wholly owned by another) and control (subservience to another). Among Paul's audience there could well have been those who had offered themselves as slaves because of economic necessity. There would also have been freedmen — those who had once been slaves but had been granted or purchased their freedom. The former would know what it was like to be someone's slave; the latter might have found the idea of believers being slaves unpalatable.[155]

Applying the general principle that people are obliged to obey those to whom they offer themselves as slaves, Paul spells out the options: *whether you are slaves to sin, which leads to death, or to obedience, which leads to righteousness* (lit. 'whether of sin to death or of obedience to righteousness'). The apostle's reference to being a slave to sin is reminiscent of the

---

154. Wright, 'Romans', 544, comments: 'This question, like that of 6:1, is not confined to committing actual acts of sin. As the parallel in Gal 2:17 demonstrates, part of the point is that to come out from the sphere of Torah, for a Jew, meant that one was joining the "sinners", the *hamartōloi* ..., the lesser breeds without the law. "Shall we then be 'sinners?'"'

155. Cf. Dunn, *Romans 1–8*, 341: 'For Paul to call freemen "slaves" could therefore be regarded as insulting, and this may explain the rather labored and tautologous way in which Paul makes his point: if you show by your conduct that you are obeying the mandates of a certain power, then you belong to that power, you are in effect and in reality its slave'.

teaching of Jesus in John 8:34: 'Very truly I tell you, everyone who sins is a slave to sin'. Paul is saying that the idea that a believer can continue in sin because they are not under the law is tantamount to offering oneself as a slave to sin, and the outcome of that is death. Later the apostle will speak in a similar vein when he says, 'the wages of sin is death' (6:23), and 'when we were in the realm of the flesh . . . we bore fruit for death' (7:5). Whereas yielding oneself to sin leads to death, yielding oneself to obedience 'leads to righteousness'. As will be made clear in the next verse, the obedience Paul has in mind is obedience to the gospel, and this leads to righteousness in the sense of being declared righteous by God on the last day.[156] While this is the case, as the passage unfolds it becomes clear that Paul's main concern is with actual ethical righteousness in the here and now.[157]

6:17-18 Continuing to address his audience directly, Paul says, *But thanks be to God that, though you used to be slaves to sin, you have come to obey from the heart the pattern of teaching that has now claimed your allegiance.* The apostle uses the expression, 'but thanks be to God', to introduce the wonderful contrast in the state of affairs brought about by God in the lives of his audience (cf. the similar use of the same expression in 7:25). Prior to their conversion they were 'slaves to sin', but all that changed, Paul points out, when you came 'to obey from the heart the pattern of teaching that has now claimed your allegiance'. 'From the heart' is an expression found only here in the NT. What Paul appears to be emphasizing is that their obedience was not merely outward conformity but really 'from the heart', perhaps alluding to the promise of Jeremiah 31:33: '"This is the covenant I will make with the house of Israel after that time", declares the LORD. "I will put my law in their minds and write it on their hearts"'.

There are other unusual features in the way Paul speaks of conversion here. To talk about obedience to the gospel is common enough (1:5; 6:16; 10:16; 15:18; 16:19, 26; 2 Cor 10:5, 6; 2 Thess 1:8), but to refer to the gospel as 'the pattern of teaching' that claimed their allegiance is unusual. Paul's reference to the gospel as 'a pattern of teaching' *(typos didachēs)* is unique. He once uses *typos* to denote an example of behavior to be avoided (1 Cor 10:6) and frequently to denote examples of behavior to be followed (Phil 3:17; 1 Thess 1:17; 2 Thess 3:9; 1 Tim 4:12; Tit 2:7). On another occasion he uses it to denote a 'type' given by God foreshadowing the future (Adam as a type of Christ, 5:14), but only here does he use it in the expression 'a pattern of teaching' to denote the gospel message, though he does refer to the gospel as 'teaching' in a couple of other places (16:17; Tit 1:9). Witherington suggests that the pattern of teaching 'probably involved the imitation of the faithful and obedient Christ, though Paul does not say so here. Nonetheless, *typos* in Paul's letters almost always has a personal refer-

---

156. Dunn, *Romans 1–8*, 342, says: 'Paul here has no misgivings about representing "righteousness" as an "end product", a condition or state or relationship yet to be realized'.
157. Cf. Moo, *Romans*, 400.

ence to a particular individual who provides a pattern of conduct (cf. Rom. 5.14; Phil. 3.17; 1 Thess. 1.7; 2 Thess. 3.9; and especially Col. 2.6 for the idea)'.[158] Gagnon draws attention to the basic meaning of *typos*, an 'imprint', and suggests that there is a 'strong link between teaching and the imprint *(typos)* left by such teaching on the inner person', and that 'the "imprint of teaching" in Rom 6:17b is of one piece with the eschatological promise of a heart engraved with the law (Jer 31:33), of the new heart (Ezek 11:19-20; 36:26-27), and of a circumcised heart (Deut 30:6; *Jub.* 1:23) made possible by the gift of the Spirit'.[159] He offers the following translation of 6:17b: 'you obeyed from the heart the imprint stamped by teaching, to which (imprint) you were handed over'.[160]

Only here does Paul speak of believers as those whose allegiance has been claimed by a pattern of teaching, that is, the gospel. Literally rendered, this expression says that the Corinthians were obedient from the heart 'to the pattern of teaching to which you were handed over'. Elsewhere the apostle uses the verb 'hand over' as a technical term for passing on the gospel and gospel traditions (1 Cor 11:2, 23; 15:3). A number of suggestions have been made concerning what it means for people to be handed over to a pattern of teaching. Fitzmyer thinks that it reflects converts' experience at baptism. By submitting to baptism they entrusted themselves to a summary of the gospel message, the 'pattern of teaching', making their confession that 'Jesus is Lord'.[161] Moo believes that 'becoming a Christian means being placed under the authority of Christian "teaching", that expression of God's will for NT believers. The new convert's "obedience" to this teaching is the outgrowth of God's action in "handing us over" to that teaching when we were converted'.[162] It is difficult to know which of these suggestions best describes what the apostle had in mind. The context is one that reflects conversion, whereby people cease to be slaves of sin and become slaves of righteousness, and this in turn suggests that the handing over to the pattern of teaching is part of the conversion experience, and in fact all of the suggestions above can be seen as part of the conversion-initiation experience.

Having obeyed from the heart the gospel, Paul informs his audience, *You have been set free from sin and have become slaves to righteousness.* This is a paradoxical statement — set free to become slaves! To be a slave of righteousness clearly has an ethical sense, being the opposite of being a slave to sin, but people can become slaves to righteousness only if they have already become slaves of God. Slavery to God, paradoxically, is genuine freedom. Once more, anyone who thinks that Paul's gospel is a license to sin is shown to be mistaken.

158. Witherington, *Romans*, 171.

159. Robert A. J. Gagnon, 'Heart of Wax and a Teaching That Stamps: *Typos Didachēs* (Rom 6:17b) Once More', *JBL* 112 (1993) 685.

160. 'Heart of Wax and a Teaching That Stamps', 687.

161. Fitzmyer, *Romans*, 449-50. Cf. Käsemann, *Romans*, 181; Wright, 'Romans', 545.

162. Moo, *Romans*, 401.

6:19 Paul now says of his teaching about freedom from sin and becoming slaves of righteousness, *I am using an example from everyday life.* The apostle speaks in everyday language when using the analogy of actual slavery as an illustration of slavery to either sin or righteousness.[163] He tells his audience that he speaks in this way *because of your human limitations.* The apostle thinks he must offer some explanation for comparing Christian 'slavery' to God with the human institution of slavery as it was known in the ancient world, and which often involved fear and degradation. He makes this artificial comparison 'because of your human limitations' (lit. 'on account of the weakness of your flesh'). Paul apparently had doubts about his audience's ability to understand what he was saying without some such analogy.

Paul reminds his audience of their lives prior to conversion: *Just as you used to offer yourselves as slaves to impurity and to ever-increasing wickedness,* and follows this up with an exhortation: *so now offer yourselves as slaves to righteousness leading to holiness.* Paul virtually repeats here the exhortation he gave in 6:13 ('Do not offer any part of yourself to sin as an instrument of wickedness, but rather offer yourselves to God as those who have been brought from death to life; and offer every part of yourself to him as an instrument of righteousness'). There the basis of the appeal was that as believers they are people who have been 'brought from death to life', whereas here the basis is that they have been 'set free from sin and become slaves to righteousness' (6:18). This reflects the apostle's dual argument in 6:1-14 and 6:15-23 respectively against any suggestion that his gospel condones or encourages sinful behavior. The exhortation to avoid yielding one's members in slavery to sin here in 6:19 is more specific than the earlier exhortation. They are to avoid 'impurity' and 'ever-increasing wickedness'. In Romans 'impurity' denotes sexual immorality (1:24; 6:19), as it does mostly elsewhere in Paul's letters (2 Cor 12:21; Gal 5:19; Eph 4:19; 5:3; Col 3:5; 1 Thess 4:7).[164] Paul's reference to 'ever-increasing wickedness', linked as it is here with 'impurity', probably denotes ever-increasing immorality.

Instead of offering their bodies in slavery to sexual impurity leading to ever-increasing immorality, Paul exhorts his audience to offer themselves as slaves to righteousness leading to holiness. 'Righteousness' in this

163. Chrysostom comments: 'Paul says that he is speaking in human terms in order to show that he is not making any exorbitant demand, nor even as much as might be expected from someone who enjoyed so great a gift, but rather a moderate and light request' ('Homilies on Romans' [*ACCSR*, 171]). Witherington, *Romans*, 172, says: 'In rhetorical terms the introductory phrase (whether *kata anthrōpon* or, as here, *anthrōpinon legō*) signals an artificial proof, as opposed to an inartificial proof like the earlier appeals to experience or Scriptures. It is a weaker form of argument than the inartificial proof, in part because it is an argument from human analogy or human example (see Quintilian, *Instit. Or.* 5.11.1ff)'.

164. In 1:24, describing the judgment of God upon those who suppress the truth, Paul, employing the word 'impurity' *(akatharsia)* again, says: 'Therefore God gave them over in the sinful desires of their hearts to sexual impurity *(akatharsian)* for the degrading of their bodies with one another'. There is an unusual usage of *akatharsia* in 1 Thess 2:3 where Paul uses it to denote impure motives for ministry.

case denotes righteous behavior. Origen offers the following exposition of what this means: 'Once your feet ran to the temples of demons; now they run to the church of God. Once they ran to spill blood; now they run to set it free. Once your hands were stretched out to steal what belonged to others; now they are stretched out for you to be generous with what is your own. Once your eyes looked at women or at something which was not yours with lust in them; but now they look at the poor, the weak and the helpless with pity in them. Your ears used to delight in hearing empty talk or in attacking good people; now they have turned to hearing the Word of God, to the exposition of the law and to the learning of the knowledge of wisdom. Your tongue, which was accustomed to bad language, cursing and swearing, has now turned to praising the Lord at all times; it produces healthy and honest speech, in order to give grace to the hearers and speak the truth to its neighbor'.[165]

Offering themselves as slaves to righteousness, Paul says, will lead to holiness. 'Holiness' may be understood here as a *state* to which yielding one's members to righteousness leads, a state acceptable to God and making one fit for his presence.[166] Alternatively it could be understood as a *process*, so that yielding one's members to righteousness, itself a process, finds expression in another process, sanctification.[167] This may be one of those occasions where Paul implies both aspects: yielding one's members to righteousness not only leads to the process of sanctification but also results in a state of fitness for God's presence. Jewett puts it this way: 'Although it [holiness] is ordinarily interpreted as an individual virtue, the second person plural imperatives throughout this pericope point to a new form of social life as the primary embodiment of holiness'.[168]

6:20-21   In these verses Paul reminds his audience once more of their pre-Christian past: *[For] when you were slaves to sin, you were free from the control of righteousness.* The NIV omits any translation of *gar* ('for') which links these verses somehow to what precedes, probably by indicating that what follows in 6:20-23 provides the basis upon which the command in 6:19b, to offer themselves 'as slaves to righteousness', rests.

Slavery to one master means freedom from control by another master. Before their conversion they were sin's slaves, in bondage to 'impurity and ever-increasing wickedness', and outside the control of righteousness. Both 'sin' and 'righteousness' are here personified as controlling powers. To be subservient to the one meant being free from the other. To remind his audience of the effects of their previous subservience to sin, Paul asks: *What benefit did you reap at that time from the things you are now ashamed of?*[169] *Those*

---

165. 'Commentary on the Epistle to the Romans' (*ACCSR*, 170).
166. So, e.g., Wright, 'Romans', 546. Cf. Dunn, *Romans 1-8*, 347.
167. So, e.g., Moo, *Romans*, 405; Fitzmyer, *Romans*, 451; Cranfield, *Romans*, I, 327.
168. Jewett, *Romans*, 421.
169. What Paul means by the things of which they were now ashamed would include such things as those listed in 1 Cor 6:9-11: 'Do not be deceived: Neither the sexually im-

things result in death! The expected answer to the question is that they reaped no real benefits from their subservience to sin. And looking back, they are only ashamed of their former way of life under sin's mastery.

Sinful living, Paul declares, is not only profitless and makes people feel ashamed; it also calls down God's judgment — death, something Paul speaks of repeatedly (1:32; 5:12, 14, 17, 21; 6:16, 23; 7:5, 10, 13; 1 Cor 15:21, 56; 2 Cor 7:10). In these texts, 'death' most often means physical death, though the fact that sometimes its opposite is eternal life (6:22, 23) suggests that eternal death is also involved.[170]

6:22 If 6:20-21 reminds the audience of their pre-Christian past and the outcome of lives lived in subservience to sin, 6:22 reminds them of what they experience now and may look forward to in the future: *But now that you have been set free from sin and have become slaves to God, the benefit you reap leads to holiness, and the result is eternal life.* Paul here says something quite similar to what he said in 6:18: 'You have been set free from sin and have become slaves to righteousness'. The difference is that here in 6:22 he says that, having been set free from sin, they 'have become slaves to God' rather than 'slaves to righteousness', although there is obviously a close connection between the two. In stark contrast to the effects of subservience to sin, the benefit reaped by those who become slaves of God is holiness in the here and now, and the final 'result' (lit, 'end') is eternal life (see 'Additional Note: Eternal Life in the Pauline Corpus', 287-88). The holiness that is the benefit (lit. 'fruit') of being slaves of God will have communal as well as individual implications.[171] Godly living is worked out primarily in the life of the Christian community.[172]

---

moral nor idolaters nor adulterers nor men who have sex with men nor thieves nor the greedy nor drunkards nor slanderers nor swindlers will inherit the kingdom of God. And that is what some of you were. But you were washed, you were sanctified, you were justified in the name of the Lord Jesus Christ and by the Spirit of our God'. Jewett, *Romans,* 422-23, comments: 'This is not a threatening question for this congregation of first-generation converts, who knew full well the dismal shape of their former lives and, if they were similar to contemporary converts, would have been happy to admit the sordid details because of their tremendous sense of liberation therefrom'.

170. Byrne, *Romans,* 203, comments: 'It was all ultimately leading to death — not simply to that physical death which remains for all the legacy of Adam's sin, but to the abiding separation from God which makes physical death eternal death, the complete ruin of human existence'.

171. Jewett, *Romans,* 424-25, says: 'Holiness defines the group identity of the new movement, ensures it boundaries against outsiders, and explains the vitality that the community experiences. In view of the OT precedents, this vitality includes a sense of wholeness, material and spiritual well-being, moral uprightness, harmonious relationships, and some form of fecundity. As members contribute to the community's common life — economically and spiritually — the fruit of their labor is holiness in this broader sense of the term. Holiness is certainly not to be reduced, as in modern thought forms, to moralistic strictures'.

172. Jeffrey T. Reed, 'Indicative and Imperative in Rom 6,21-22: The Rhetoric of Punctuation', *Bib* 74 (1993) 244-47, argues on grammatical and rhetorical grounds that 6:21-22 should be read, not as an interrogative-indicative as it is rendered in the NIV and inter-

6:23   Paul concludes his contrast between a life of slavery to sin and slavery to God with the statement: *For the wages of sin is death, but the gift of God is eternal life.* The apostle uses the term 'wages' in just two other places in his letters: in 1 Corinthians 9:7, where it denotes the 'wages'/'expenses' of the serving soldier, and in 2 Corinthians 11:8, where it denotes the 'wages'/'support' Paul himself received from other churches, enabling him to carry out his ministry in Corinth. Here in 6:23 he maintains that those who serve sin will receive the 'wages' they deserve — death. That sin leads to death is something the apostle stresses again and again in his letters, most frequently in Romans (1:32; 5:12, 14, 17, 21; 6:16, 21, 23; 7:5) but elsewhere as well (1 Cor 15:21, 56; 2 Cor 7:10). The word Paul uses for 'wages' *(opsōnion)* is seen by many commentators as an allusion to the wages paid by a general to his soldiers (as it is in 1 Cor 9:7);[173] however, as Jewett points out, the word was used more broadly of wages in general. He says, 'While the *opsōnion* in ordinary usage provided sustenance for life, this wage provides its opposite — death. Since wages are paid in increments as well as at the end of a task, the death that Paul has in mind is a present reality that will extend into the future'.[174]

However, those who serve God do not receive the wages they deserve; rather, they receive the free 'gift' of eternal life (see 'Additional Note: Eternal Life in the Pauline Corpus', 287-88). Witherington's comment is apposite: 'Eternal life is a grace gift. Even if Christian persons managed to live an entirely sanctified life, this would not oblige God to reward them with eternal life, for they will have done no more than what was required of them. Thus Paul does not see eternal life as some sort of quid pro quo for holy living in this lifetime. Salvation is indeed a matter of grace received through faith, from start to finish'.[175] The gift of eternal life is both provided by God and received by believers *in Christ Jesus our Lord.* While the wages of sin is death for all who sin, the gift of eternal life is only for those who are 'in Christ', that is, those who are united with him through faith and by the Spirit.

---

preted as such by most commentators, but rather as an indicative-imperative. He offers the following translation encapsulating his view: 'For when you were slaves of sin, you were free with respect to righteousness, i.e., you did not have to serve it. Consequently, you produced a certain kind of fruit then of which you are now ashamed because such things end in death [indicative]. Now that you have been freed from sin but enslaved to God, produce (your) fruit which results in holiness [imperative]. This will, in addition, result in eternal life. For indeed, the wages of sin is death, but the gift of God is eternal life in Christ Jesus our Lord [text within square brackets added]'.

173. So, e.g., Fitzmyer, *Romans,* 452; Cranfield, *Romans,* I, 329; Käsemann, *Romans,* 185.

174. Jewett, *Romans,* 426.

175. Witherington, *Romans,* 174.

ADDITIONAL NOTE:
ETERNAL LIFE IN THE PAULINE CORPUS

Paul never speaks of 'eternal life' as the present possession of believers, as does the Fourth Evangelist (cf., e.g., John 5:24: 'Very truly I tell you, whoever hears my word and believes him who sent me has eternal life and will not be judged but has crossed over from death to life'). In Paul's letters eternal life is always the final reward bestowed upon the righteous on the last day:

Rom 2:7	To those who by persistence in doing good seek glory, honor and immortality, he will give eternal life.
Rom 5:21	so that, just as sin reigned in death, so also grace might reign through righteousness to bring eternal life through Jesus Christ our Lord.
Rom 6:22	But now that you have been set free from sin and have become slaves to God, the benefit you reap leads to holiness, and the result is eternal life.
Rom 6:23	For the wages of sin is death, but the gift of God is eternal life in Christ Jesus our Lord.
Gal 6:8	Whoever sows to please their sinful nature, from the flesh will reap destruction; whoever sows to please the Spirit, from the Spirit will reap eternal life.
1 Tim 1:16	But for that very reason I was shown mercy so that in me, the worst of sinners, Christ Jesus might display his immense patience as an example for those who would believe in him and receive eternal life.
1 Tim 6:12	Fight the good fight of the faith. Take hold of the eternal life to which you were called when you made your good confession in the presence of many witnesses.
Tit 1:2	in the hope of eternal life, which God, who does not lie, promised before the beginning of time,
Tit 3:7	so that, having been justified by his grace, we might become heirs having the hope of eternal life.

Paul does not explain just what eternal life entails, but clearly it includes a glorious resurrection body — the present mortal body will die, sown, as it were, in dishonor to be raised in glory (1 Cor 15:43; Rom 8:23), for when Christ appears he will 'transform our lowly bodies so that they will be like his glorious body' (Phil 3:21). At this time creation itself will be released from its bondage to decay and be brought into the freedom of the glory of the children of God (Rom 8:21). While Paul never speaks of 'eternal life' as the present possession of believers, he does, of course, refer often to the 'new life' believers experience in the here and now:

Rom 6:4   We were therefore buried with him through baptism
             into death in order that, just as Christ was raised from
             the dead through the glory of the Father, we too may
             live a new life.
Rom 8:6   The mind governed by the flesh is death, but the mind
             governed by the Spirit gives life and peace.
Rom 8:10   But if Christ is in you, even though your body is sub-
             ject to death because of sin, the Spirit gives life because
             of righteousness.
2 Cor 4:10   We always carry around in our body the death of Je-
             sus, so that the life of Jesus may also be revealed in
             our body.
2 Cor 4:11   For we who are alive are always being given over to
             death for Jesus' sake, so that his life may also be re-
             vealed in our mortal body.
Col 3:4   When Christ, who is your life, appears, then you also
             will appear with him in glory.

---

4. Freedom from the Law, 7:1-25

In Romans 7 Paul turns his attention to the believer's freedom from the law
(7:1-6) and to a historic and experiential exposition of what life is like for
those under the law (7:7-25). The nature of Paul's understanding of freedom from the law has been variously understood. Some argue that it is limited to freedom from the law's condemnation,[176] others that it is freedom
from the law's jurisdiction, arguing that Paul would not have distinguished between the cultic and ethical demands of the law.[177] Paul's purpose in writing Romans 7 has likewise been variously explained. On the
hand, it has been seen as a necessary vindication of the law itself in the light
of his claim that believers are not under the law.[178] On the other hand, it has
been claimed that it is not essentially a defense of the law but rather a portrayal of life under the law that provides a negative foil for the apostle's
presentation of Christian freedom in the Spirit that follows in Romans 8.[179]
Paul's overarching purpose in the chapter is to answer objections that his
gospel involves a denigration of the law.

a. Freed from the Law to Bear Fruit for God, 7:1-6

*¹Do you not know, brothers and sisters — for I am speaking to those who
know the law — that the law has authority over someone only as long as that*

176. So, e.g., Cranfield, *Romans*, I, 330-31.
177. So, e.g., Käsemann, *Romans*, 186-87.
178. So, e.g., Wright, 'Romans', 550.
179. So, e.g., Byrne, *Romans*, 209.

person lives? ²For example, by law a married woman is bound to her hus-
band as long as he is alive, but if her husband dies, she is released from the
law that binds her to him. ³So then, if she has sexual relations with another
man while her husband is still alive, she is called an adulteress. But if her
husband dies, she is released from that law and is not an adulteress if she
marries another man.

⁴So, my brothers and sisters, you also died to the law through the body of
Christ, that you might belong to another, to him who was raised from the
dead, in order that we might bear fruit for God. ⁵For when we were in the
realm of the flesh, the sinful passions aroused by the law were at work in us,
so that we bore fruit for death. ⁶But now, by dying to what once bound us, we
have been released from the law so that we serve in the new way of the Spirit,
and not in the old way of the written code.

Paul's rejection of any suggestion that believers are encouraged to sin
because they are not under law but under grace leaves little place for the
law as a deterrent to sin. Paul does not resile from this conclusion. In fact,
in 7:1-6 he strongly upholds the view that believers are free from the law,
but shows that, contrary to expectations, this does not lead to an immoral
life, but one that 'bears fruit for God' (7:4).[180] Only after doing this will he
go on to explain in 7:7-25 that sin, not the law, is the real problem.

7:1 Upholding his teaching that believers are not under the law but
under grace, Paul asks his audience, [Or] *do you not know, brothers and sisters*
— for I am speaking to those who know the law — that the law has authority over
someone only as long as that person lives? The NIV and NRSV omit the particle
'or', which is a pity because it clearly connects 7:1ff. with what precedes it
in chapter 6. The expression 'do you not know' is used by the apostle both
here and in 6:3 to remind his audience of something he expects them to
know already. What Paul implies his audience might be ignorant of is the
statement of 6:14: 'you are not under the law, but under grace'.

Those to whom he addresses his question are 'those who know the
law'. This has been variously interpreted. Noting that the recipients of this
letter are predominantly Gentile believers, it has been suggested that those
'who know the law' are: (i) Gentiles believers who are cognizant of the Roman marriage laws,[181] (ii) Gentile believers who prior to their conversion to
Christ were God fearers or proselytes and had become acquainted with the
Jewish law through their involvement in the synagogue,[182] (iii) Jewish be-

---

180. Cf. Andrzej Gieniusz, 'Rom 7,1-6: Lack of Imagination? Function of the Passage
in the Argumentation of Rom 6,1–7,6', *Bib* 74 (1993) 392-95, who argues correctly that the
main point of 7:1-6 is not to establish the believers' freedom from the law, but to show that
freedom from the law does not lead to immoral living, but to the very opposite. He sums up
Paul's point in 7:1-6: '*freedom from* (the law) cannot be seen except as *freedom for*, i.e., for a
new obedience' (395).

181. So, e.g., Käsemann, *Romans*, 187.

182. So, e.g., Byrne, *Romans*, 210; Wright, 'Romans', 558.

lievers, a minority group in the Roman Christian community, whom Paul is addressing directly and specifically, as he elsewhere addresses Gentile believers specifically and directly (11:13). As the context is related to freedom from the Mosaic law, either (ii) or (iii) is preferable, or even a combination of (ii) and (iii), that is, Paul is addressing all who know the law, whether they be Jews or Gentiles, with some background in the synagogue.

The law his audience know about, Paul says, 'has authority over someone only as long as that person lives'. The word the NIV translates as 'someone' is *anthrōpos*, and it clearly does not mean just a 'man/male' here, because in the verses that follow immediately (7:2-3) the principle is applied to a 'woman' whose husband has died. The principle is a simple one: a law can apply to people only while they are alive.

7:2-3 Illustrating the principle enunciated in 7:1b, Paul continues: *For example, by law a married woman is bound to her husband as long as he is alive, but if her husband dies, she is released from the law that binds her to him.* A similar statement is found in 1 Corinthians 7:39: 'A woman is bound to her husband as long as he lives. But if her husband dies, she is free to marry anyone she wishes, but he must belong to the Lord'. The words 'for example' in 7:2 bring out the fact that what the apostle says functions as an illustration of the principle enunciated in 7:1b ('the law has authority over someone only as long as that person lives'). When he argues, 'by law a married woman is bound to her husband as long as he is alive', he is not citing the Mosaic law explicitly, for it allows a divorced woman to remarry while her first husband is still living if he has divorced her. Nor does Paul's statement correspond explicitly to Roman law. For under Roman law a woman was not irrevocably bound to her husband for life.[183] The best way to handle this problem is to recognize that in OT law there was provision for a man to divorce his wife (Deut 24:1-4) but none for a woman to divorce her husband. In this sense, then, a woman was bound to her husband as long as he was alive because she had no right to divorce him.[184] It may be with this

---

183. Jewett, *Romans*, 431, comments: 'This description of male rights certainly does not match Roman divorce law, which allowed either partner to divorce the other'. Cf. Witherington, *Romans*, 175. Dunn, *Romans 1-8*, 360, says: 'Moreover, in Roman law a woman was *not* freed from the law of her husband by his death, since she was obliged to mourn his death and to remain unmarried for twelve months; otherwise she would forfeit everything which had come to her from her first husband'.

184. Peter J. Tomson, 'What Did Paul Mean by "Those Who Know the Law"? (Rom 7.1)', *NTS* 49 (2003) 575-77, 579, offers a different interpretation of the law to which Paul appeals. He argues: 'in the light of Paul's teaching about marriage and divorce in 1 Corinthians 7:10-11, 39-40 where the apostle cites the command of Christ, that the law Paul expects his Roman audience to know is not the Mosaic Law *per se* but Christ's teaching about marriage regarded as law for all believers. This law Paul applies literally in 1 Corinthians and metaphorically in 7:2-3. Noting allusions to Deuteronomy 24:1-4 and the Mishnah (*m. Gittin* 9:3) in what Paul writes about marriage, Tomson concludes that the 'law' the apostle refers to in 7:1 is 'apostolic, Jewish-Christian law tradition', something 'confirmed by the observation that the word *moichalis* (adulteress) (Rom 7:3) is uniquely Jewish and Christian'.

in mind that Paul says, 'a married woman is bound to her husband as long as he is alive',[185] and that only after he dies is she released from 'the law that binds her to him' (lit. 'the law of the husband').[186] The corollary is, then, that *if she has sexual relations with another man while her husband is still alive, she is called an adulteress.* The essential point of Paul's illustration is expressed in 7:3b: *But if her husband dies, she is released from that law and is not an adulteress, even though she marries another man.* That the death of her husband frees a woman from the law that previously bound her to him so that she is now free to marry another man is in accordance with both the Mosaic law and 'apostolic Jewish-Christian law tradition'.

    7:4 In this verse Paul brings to a conclusion his argument in 7:1-3 that believers are no longer under the authority of the Mosaic law: *So, my brothers and sisters, you also died to the law through the body of Christ, that you might belong to another, to him who was raised from the dead, in order that we might bear fruit to God.*[187] The conclusion he draws here raises some difficulties because of its lack of exact correspondence with the illustration he employs in 7:2-3 to support it. In 7:1 he asserted 'that the law has authority over someone only as long as that person lives', and in 7:4a he makes the same point: believers who have died (in Christ) are discharged from their obligation to the law. However, in the illustration (7:2-3) it is not the death of the wife that releases her from the law binding her to her husband (what we might expect and something Paul could have said to make his point), but it is the death of

---

185. Cf. Byrne, *Romans*, 210.

186. Luzia Sutter Rehmann, 'The Doorway into Freedom: The Case of the "Suspected Wife" in Romans 7.1-6', *JSNT* 79 (2000) 97-99, 102, argues that 'the law of the husband' is a reference to the Jewish 'law of jealousy' (Num 5:12-31) according to which a husband suspecting his wife of adultery could bring her before the priest, who would require her to undergo the *sotah* ordeal. The woman under suspicion (the *sotah*) is given a drink that inflicts a curse. If she is taken ill, she is regarded as guilty; if not, she is declared innocent. Should the husband die before his wife is subjected to the *sotah* test, she is then free from the law of jealousy, or what Paul refers to as 'the law of the husband', something Rehmann equates with 'the law of sin' from which the 'wretched man' cries for deliverance in 7:23. However, there appears to be little in the Romans context to suggest that Paul is alluding to the law of jealousy, for it speaks of a woman's freedom to remarry once the husband dies, not her freedom from the curse.

187. Cranfield, *Romans*, I, 335, comments: 'But the decisive clue to the right interpretation of these verses [7:2-3] is the recognition that they were not intended to be connected directly with v. 4 but with v. 1. They are not an allegory (nor yet a parable), the interpretation of which is to be found in v. 4, but an illustration designed to elucidate v. 1. Verse 4 is the conclusion drawn from vv. 1-3 as a whole, that is, from v. 1 as clarified by vv. 2-3: it is not an interpretation or application of vv. 2-3. The rightness of this view of the matter is confirmed by the fact that v. 4 is introduced by *hōste*, and not by *houtōs*; for, had Paul thought of v. 4 as interpreting vv. 2-3, it would have been much more natural to introduce it by a word expressive of similarity or correspondence than by a word which (as used here) can only mark a conclusion drawn from what has been said. We take it then that these two verses are simply intended as an illustration of the principle stated in the *hoti*-clause of v. 1 or — rather more accurately — of its corollary, namely, that the occurrence of a death effects a decisive change in respect of relationship to the law'.

the husband that releases her. Perhaps, the reason why Paul's illustration lacks the sort of exact correspondence that we might expect is that he wanted to use it to make an additional point. Not only did he want to show that the death of believers in Christ frees them from obligation to the law, but also that it frees them to belong to Christ and to 'bear fruit to God' (7:4b). For the analogy to be able to be used to make this additional point the wife must remain alive in order to be able to marry another man, and so it must be the death of the husband that discharges her from the marriage law. Paul does not seem to have been concerned about the lack of exact correspondence (as we, his modern audience, might be), being satisfied with an analogy in which death (albeit the husband's and not the wife's) frees from the law[188] so that the one freed can then belong to another.[189]

Apart from the problem of lack of formal correspondence, there is the further problem of the actual meaning of Paul's statement, 'you also died to the law through the body of Christ'. A number of matters in this statement call for clarification. First is the fact that the apostle does not actually say that 'you . . . died', but, when literally translated, 'you were put to death' to the law. This emphasizes that, unlike the death of the husband by natural causes in the illustration, the death of believers to the law is the result of divine initiative — they were 'put to death'. This is best understood as a mat-

---

188. Käsemann, *Romans*, 187, says: 'The only point of comparison is that death dissolves obligations valid throughout life'.

189. Ziesler, *Romans*, 174-75, notes that the analogy makes one straightforward point ('legal obligations are removed by death'), and that attempts to work out the illustration in detail run into confusion. Joyce A. Little, 'Paul's Use of Analogy: A Structural Analysis of Romans 7:1-6', *CBQ* 46 (1984) 90, disagrees with Dodd's conclusion that 'he [Paul] lacks the gift for sustained illustration of ideas through concrete images (though he is capable of a brief illuminatory metaphor). It is probably a defect of imagination'. Little argues instead that 'the defect Paul suffers from in the writing of this passage is, if anything, an excess of imagination which propels him through the above-noted succession of ideas so rapidly that he has neither the time nor the opportunity to bring his images to completion'. She adds that it is not certain that Paul could have brought his images to completion, even if he had been so inclined. But cf. John D. Earnshaw, 'Reconsidering Paul's Marriage Analogy in Romans 7.1-4', *NTS* 40 (1994) 72, who holds that 'Paul's marriage analogy is properly understood only when *the wife's first marriage is viewed as illustrating the believer's union with Christ in his death and her second marriage is viewed as illustrating the believer's union with Christ in his resurrection*'. Gieniusz, 'Rom 7,1-6: Lack of Imagination?', 400, argues: 'The incompatibility of the example with the announcement of v. 1 is to be understood as follows: the Apostle can permit this incongruity because freedom from the law is not the point of his demonstration and he cannot avoid it because of the absolute and paradoxical novelty of the Christian experience, which contradicts any comparison and escapes any illustration'. Jean-Sébastien Viard, 'Loi, chair et liberation: Une solution structurelle au problème de Romains 7,1-6', *Théoforum* 36 (2005) 170-71, contends that in the analogy of 7:2-3 the woman symbolizes the believer and the man/husband symbolizes the flesh. If the flesh (symbolized by the husband) has been put to death (by believers' participation in the death of Christ), then the believers (symbolized by the woman) are now free from the domination of sinful flesh and the way it uses the law to manipulate the believer. Thus believers are now free from the law's condemnation and free to serve God under the inspiration of the Spirit.

ter of God's decision to regard Christ's death for all as the death of all, something that becomes effective for believers at the time of their baptism/conversion.

Second, to 'die to the law' means living no longer under its authority, something made clear by Paul's marriage law illustration. Just as a married woman is freed from the marriage law that binds her to her husband when her husband dies, so believers have been freed from the Mosaic law, having died to it 'through the body of Christ'.

Third, what does Paul mean by the unusual statement that believers died to the law 'through the body of Christ'? In other letters the apostle does speak of, or allude to, salvation being effected through the body or flesh of Christ. Thus in 1 Corinthians 10:16 he refers to the cup and the bread of the Lord's Supper as 'a participation in the blood of Christ' and 'a participation in the body of Christ' respectively. Recalling the institution of the Lord's Supper in 1 Corinthians 11:24, Paul quotes Jesus' words, 'This is my body, which is for you'. In Ephesians 2:13-15, which is especially pertinent, Paul says, 'But now in Christ Jesus you who once were far away have been brought near by the blood of Christ. For he himself is our peace, who has made the two groups one and has destroyed the barrier, the dividing wall of hostility, by setting aside in his flesh the law with its commands and regulations'. This clearly implies that Christ abolished the law through his death on the cross. In Colossians 1:22 he tells his audience: 'But now he [God] has reconciled you by Christ's physical body [lit. 'in the body of his flesh'] through death to present you holy in his sight, without blemish and free from accusation'. Finally, in Colossians 2:14, though without actual reference to Jesus' body or flesh, Paul speaks of Christ 'having cancelled the charge of our written indebtedness, which stood against us and condemned us; he has taken it away, nailing it to the cross'. This text, like Ephesians 2:13-15, implies that it was through his crucifixion that Christ freed his people from the law and the written indebtedness that stood against them.[190] Allowing all these to guide our interpretation of 7:4, we may conclude that Paul's statement, 'you also died to the law through the body of Christ', is a shorthand way of saying that believers have been freed from the law because Christ offered his body as a sacrifice for our sins and by so doing freed us from the law's condemnation. More than this, however, Christ's death and resurrection brought the period of the Mosaic law as the regulatory norm to an end for the people of God and inaugurated the new covenant under which the Mosaic law is replaced by the work of the Spirit in believers' lives. In this sense also believers have died to the law 'through the body of Christ'.[191]

190. Outside the Pauline corpus two texts in particular connect salvation with the sacrifice of the body of Christ: Heb 10:10: 'We have been made holy through the sacrifice of the body of Jesus Christ once for all'; 1 Pet 2:24: 'He himself bore our sins in his body on the tree, so that we might die to sins and live for righteousness; by his wounds you have been healed'.

191. Wright, 'Romans', 559, says: 'The whole clause [you also died to the law through

In 7:4 Paul also makes the point that believers are freed from the law so that they might belong to another. As in the marriage illustration the woman is freed from the law binding her to her former husband so that she may become the wife of another man, so believers are freed from the law, Paul says, that they 'might belong to another, to him who was raised from the dead'. Christian freedom from the law does not mean that people are free to sin (as Paul's critics accused him of teaching; cf. 3:7-8; 6:15) but to live for Jesus Christ by the power of the Spirit without submitting to the Mosaic law as a regulatory norm.

What Paul affirms in 7:4 is that his law-free gospel, far from promoting immorality, actually enables people to 'bear fruit for God'. At first reading it seems odd that Paul should introduce a fruit-bearing metaphor when talking about marriage, but perhaps this fruit-bearing image may not carry an agricultural connotation, but rather that of fruitfulness in childbearing, which is appropriate when talking about marriage. What the fruit-bearing metaphor denotes in 7:4 is a life of righteousness that is pleasing to God.[192] What is particularly striking about 7:4 is Paul's assertion that believers need to be released from the law in order that they may 'bear fruit for God'. Paul's marriage analogy and its application in 7:4 constitute the clearest expressions of his conviction that believers (Jews as well as Gentiles) are freed from obligations to the Mosaic law as a regulatory norm.[193]

7:5-6 These verses foreshadow what will be argued in more detail in 7:7–8:13, and accordingly their programmatic nature has been noted by a number of scholars.[194] In particular, 7:5 foreshadows 7:7-25, where the life of the unconverted person in the flesh and under the law is depicted,[195] and 7:6 foreshadows 8:1-13, where the life of the converted person freed for service in the new life of the Spirit is explained.[196] In these verses Paul contrasts the lives of believers before they were converted (7:5)[197] with their lives after conversion (7:6).

---

the body of Christ] appears to be a shorthand way of saying three things simultaneously: (a) the bodily death of Jesus the Messiah is the representative event through which the Messiah's people die "with him" (6:4-11); (b) you are in the Messiah by baptism, and therefore shared that death; (c) your solidarity with the Messiah can be expressed in terms of your membership in his "body"'.

192. The apostle uses the verb 'bear fruit' *(karpophoreō)* four times in his letters (7:4, 5; Col 1:6, 10). Similar to its usage here in 7:4 is what is found in Col 1:10, where bearing fruit involves performing good works and growing in the knowledge of God.

193. Cf. Kruse, *Paul, the Law and Justification,* 206-8.

194. Cf., e.g., Bruce Morrison and John Woodhouse, 'The Coherence of Romans 7:1–8:8', *RTR* 47 (1988) 14; S. Voorwinde, 'Who Is the "Wretched Man" in Romans 7:24?' *VoxRef* 54 (1990) 21.

195. Not all scholars agree that 7:7-25 depicts the life of the unconverted person, preferring to see in this passage a depiction of the struggle with sin experienced by all believers. See the discussion of this important matter in 'Additional Note: The Identity of the "I" in 7:7-25', 314-21.

196. So, e.g., Voorwinde, 'Who Is the "Wretched Man"?' 21; Wright, 'Romans', 559-60.

197. Heinz Giesen, 'Das heilige Gesetz — missbraucht durch die Sünde (Röm 7)',

Depicting believers' lives prior to conversion Paul says: *For when we were in the realm of the flesh, the sinful passions aroused by the law were at work in us.* Here, to be 'in the realm of the flesh' describes the situation of the unbeliever. It is a situation in which Paul and his audience were found prior to their conversion, but one in which they are no longer. Wright describes 'flesh' as 'physicality seen on the one hand as corruptible and on the other as rebellious; it is another way of saying "in Adam"'.[198] Moo describes it as the '"power" of the old age, set in opposition to the Spirit'.[199]

The NIV's 'the sinful passions aroused by the law were at work in us', when translated literally, is 'the sinful passions that were at work through the law in our members'. What Paul is saying is not that the sinful passions were *aroused by the law* but that they were *at work through the law*. He is not blaming the law but showing that it was, as it were, the unwilling means through which sinful passions were at work. This is something that Paul will spell out in 7:7ff. (see the commentary below). Suffice it to say here that for Paul the law, far from being an effective deterrent to sin, was actually laid under tribute by sinful passions prior to our conversion to bring us into greater bondage.

Paul describes the baleful outcome of lives dominated by sinful passions with the words: *so that we bore fruit for death.*[200] Lives dominated by sinful passions draw down God's judgment — death, something Paul has emphasized again and again already in this letter, as the following texts (with italics added) illustrate:

Although they know God's righteous decree that those who do such things deserve *death,* they not only continue to do these very things but also approve of those who practice them. (1:32)

Don't you know that when you offer yourselves to someone as obedient slaves, you are slaves of the one you obey — whether you are slaves to sin, which leads to *death,* or to obedience, which leads to righteousness? (6:16)

What benefit did you reap at that time from the things you are now ashamed of? Those things result in *death!* (6:21)

For the wages of sin is *death,* but the gift of God is eternal life in Christ Jesus our Lord. (6:23)

TTZ 114 (2005) 204-5, says that in v. 5 Paul looks back to the unsaved situation when Christians were still in the flesh and declares that they were sinners.

198. Wright, 'Romans', 560.

199. Moo, *Romans,* 418.

200. Austin Busch, 'The Figure of Eve in Romans 7:5-25', *BibInt* 12 (2004) 13, sees in the reference to 'fruit for death' an allusion to 'the primeval transgression, in which Adam and Eve taste the fruit of the knowledge of good and evil that God commanded them not to eat lest they die (Gen. 2:16–3:24)'.

For Paul, death as the outcome of a life given over to sinful passions is not only physical death, to which all people are subject (itself the result of human sin; cf. 5:12-21), but exposure to the wrath of God (5:9; 1 Thess 1:10), the very opposite of the eternal life promised to believers (cf. 6:23).

7:6 Building upon what he said in 7:4 about believers having died to the law 'through the body of Christ', and in contrast to what he has said in 7:5 about life in the realm of the flesh, Paul now describes the life of believers following their conversion: *But now, by dying to what once bound us, we have been released from the law so that we serve in the new way of the Spirit, and not in the old way of the written code.* Again he uses the first person plural, 'we', and includes himself with his audience as one of those who have been released from the law. As 7:4 implied, they have been freed from the law because Christ offered his body as a sacrifice for their sins and by so doing freed them from the law's condemnation *and* the obligation to submit to it as a regulatory norm. Like the woman whose husband has died and therefore is free from the marriage law binding her to him so that she is free to marry another man, so Paul declares that believers have been released from the Mosaic law 'so that we serve in the new way of the Spirit, and not in the old way of the written code' (lit. 'so that[201] we serve in [the] newness of [the] Spirit and not in [the] oldness of [the] letter').

The contrast between serving 'in the newness of the Spirit' and serving 'in the oldness of the letter' is a contrast between life under the old covenant and life under the new covenant. In 2 Corinthians 3:6 Paul speaks in similar terms when he says: 'He has made us competent as ministers of a new covenant — not of the letter but of the Spirit; for the letter kills, but the Spirit gives life'. That believers are enabled to do this is in fulfillment of the prophecies of Ezekiel and Jeremiah:

> I will give you a new heart and put a new spirit in you; I will remove from you your heart of stone and give you a heart of flesh. And I will put my Spirit in you and move you to follow my decrees and be careful to keep my laws. (Ezek 36:26-27)

> 'The days are coming', declares the LORD, 'when I will make a new covenant with the people of Israel and with the people of Judah. It will not be like the covenant I made with their ancestors when I took them by the hand to lead them out of Egypt, because they broke my covenant, though I was a husband to them', declares the LORD. 'This is the covenant I will make with the people of Israel after that time', declares the LORD. 'I will put my law in their minds and write it on their hearts. I will be their God, and they will be my people. No longer will they teach their neighbor, or say to one another, "Know the LORD", because they will all know me, from the least of them to the greatest', declares the

---

201. By employing the expression 'so that' (*hōste* plus the infinitive) Paul shows that believers' freedom from the law *results in* service 'in the newness of the Spirit'.

LORD. 'For I will forgive their wickedness and will remember their sins no more'. (Jer 31:31-34)

The apostle will explain this in more detail in 8:1-13 (see the commentary below). What he makes clear at this point is that 'the new way of the Spirit' replaces 'the old way of the written code'. 'The old way of the written code', relating to God through the Mosaic law as the regulatory norm, is now replaced by 'the new way of the Spirit'[202] in which believers, having been made alive through the Spirit, now walk in the Spirit (cf. Gal 5:25).[203]

b. Sin, Not the Law, Is to Blame for the Human Predicament, 7:7-25

Having argued in 7:1-6 that people need to be freed from the law to bear fruit for God, in 7:7-25 Paul shows that he is not suggesting that the law itself is to blame for human moral failure. The law is holy, righteous, and good (7:12). It is only because it has become the unwilling ally of sin that it is part of the problem rather than part of the solution to the human predicament.[204] Paul's purpose in 7:7-25 is not to defend the law per se, as, for example, Kümmel argues,[205] but to reject allegations that his gospel involves a denigration of the

202. In several other places Paul contrasts those things that are of the written code/the letter with those of the Spirit. In 2:29 Paul speaks of the 'true' circumcision as something 'of the heart, by the Spirit, not by the written code' (*en pneumati ou grammati*, lit. 'by [the] Spirit, not by [the] letter'). In 2 Cor 3:6, when contrasting his ministry under the new covenant with the ministry of Moses under the old covenant, he says: 'He has made us competent as ministers of a new covenant — not of the letter but of the Spirit *(ou grammatos alla pneumatos)*; for the letter kills, but the Spirit gives life *(to gar gramma apoktennei, to de pneuma zōopoiei)'*.

203. Both Cranfield and Dunn deny that it is 'the law as such' that Paul has in mind in 7:6. Thus Cranfield, *Romans*, I, 339-40, alleges: 'That Paul is not opposing the law as such and in itself to the Spirit is clear, since only a few verses later he affirms that he law is "spiritual" (v. 14). He does not use "letter" as a simple equivalent of "the law". "Letter" is rather what the legalist is left with as a result of his misunderstanding and misuse of the law. It is the letter of the law in separation from the Spirit. But since "the law is spiritual" (v. 14), the letter of the law in isolation from the Spirit is not the law in its true character, but the law as it were denatured'. Dunn, *Romans 1–8*, 373 asserts: ' "The oldness of the letter" is clearly a reference to the law. . . . But not the law as such. It is not the law as such which Paul sees as characterizing the old epoch before Christ, but the law as "letter" (cf. 2 Cor 3:6). As in 2:27-29, Paul presumably means by this the law observed at what he sees as a superficial level, at indeed the level of the flesh (2:28), with obedience to the law understood in terms of the ritual and cultic acts which mark out the chosen people, the law as the "works" done by devout Jews'. However, in the light of both 2 Cor 3 and Gal 3:23-25, it is clear that life in the Spirit under the new covenant replaces life under the law under the old covenant, and it seems that it is life under 'the law as such' that Paul opposes to life in the Spirit. Cf. Käsemann, *Romans*, 189-91.

204. Cf. Giesen, 'Das heilige Gesetz — missbraucht durch die Sünde (Röm 7)', 220, who says that as any good thing can be misused, so the power of sin misused the holy law.

205. Werner G. Kümmel, *Römer 7 und die Bekehrung des Paulus* (Munich: Kaiser, 1974), 9. Cf. Dunn, *Romans 1–8*, 377. Stefano Romanello, 'Rom 7,7-25 and the Impotence of the Law: A Fresh Look at a Much Debated Topic Using Literary-Rhetorical Analysis', *Bib* 84 (2003) 522, rightly points out that 'naming this pericope an "apology for the Law" is . . . highly questionable, because it does not take into account the statements about the impotence of the Law'.

law. Sin is the basic problem, not the law (whose only deficiency is its ineffectiveness when countering the power of sin).[206] In order to demonstrate this, Paul describes the interaction of sin and the law in the life of the human person, in fact in the life of Israel, something he foreshadowed in 7:5. He does so in such a way as to place the blame for the human dilemma firmly upon sin, not the law. To achieve his purpose the apostle uses the rhetorical technique of impersonation *(prosopopoeia)* or 'speech-in-character', and in the case of 7:7-25 this takes the form of a first person narrative.[207]

In this passage Paul employs the technique of speech-in-character using the first person singular, 'I' *(egō)*, to show how sin makes the good law of God its unwilling ally for evil. Paul's use of the first person singular in 7:7-25 has attracted many different interpretations. In the commentary on 7:7-25 below the rhetorical *egō* is understood in 7:7-12 to refer primarily to Israel's experience before and after the Mosaic law was given to them, and in 7:13-25 to refer to the ongoing experience of the unbelieving Jewish person under the law, one with whom the apostle himself could readily identify when considering his own pre-Christian experience (for an extended discussion of the ways in which the *egō* in has been interpreted, see 'Additional Note: The Identity of the "I" in 7:7-25', 314-21). The apostle's purpose in dealing with the matter here is both to answer criticisms of his gospel that may be circulating among the members of his audience, and to make clear to them that the law, though good in itself, is unable to counter the effects of sin — that can be achieved only through God's action in Christ and their walking in the Spirit, something the apostle will spell out in chapter 8.

Formally, 7:7-25 falls into three parts. The first, 7:7-12, is introduced with a question (7:7a: 'What shall we say, then? Is the law sin?'), followed by a firm denial employing the rhetorical 'I' (7:7b-12). The second part, 7:13-20, is likewise introduced with a question (7:13a: 'Did that which is good, then, become death to me?') and is followed by another strong denial employing the rhetorical 'I' (7:13b-20). In the third part, 7:21-25, Paul draws conclusions from what he said in the former parts.

---

206. Cf. Käsemann, *Romans*, 192. So too Mark A. Seifrid, 'The Subject of Rom 7:14-25', *NovT* 34 (1992) 324. Romanello, 'Rom 7,7-25 and the Impotence of the Law', 525, describes the argument of 7:7-25: 'If I am right in interpreting this argument as *concessio*, in which the main thrust is to reaffirm the impotence of the Law, then the different depictions of the relationship between Law and sin, in vv. 7-13 and 14-25 respectively, cease to be a problem. It is true that in the first part of the chapter a direct instrumentality of the Law in the prevalence of sin is stated, while from v. 14 onwards sin is an active subject quite apart from the Law, merely remaining ineffective in counteracting it. But these different statements may be reconciled when regarded as different examples pointing to the same reality: the powerless character of the Law with respect to sin. If this is the main thrust of the argumentation, then it may well be depicted by means of one case in which the Law itself serves as a direct weapon in the hand of sin personified, and through another case in which it simply proves to be too feeble to face this inauspicious actor at this stage of human history. In each case the Law is powerless, absolutely and dramatically powerless, which is the factor underlined by this pericope'.

207. Cf. Witherington, *Romans*, 179-80.

(i) Israel's historical encounter with the law, 7:7-13

> [7]*What shall we say, then? Is the law sinful? Certainly not! Nevertheless, I would not have known what sin was had it not been for the law. For I would not have known what coveting really was if the law had not said, 'You shall not covet'.* [8]*But sin, seizing the opportunity afforded by the commandment, produced in me every kind of coveting. For apart from the law, sin was dead.* [9]*Once I was alive apart from the law; but when the commandment came, sin sprang to life and I died.* [10]*I found that the very commandment that was intended to bring life actually brought death.* [11]*For sin, seizing the opportunity afforded by the commandment, deceived me, and through the commandment put me to death.* [12]*So then, the law is holy, and the commandment is holy, righteous and good.*
>
> [13]*Did that which is good, then, become death to me? By no means! Nevertheless, in order that sin might be recognized as sin, it used what is good to bring about my death, so that through the commandment sin might become utterly sinful.*

This passage is marked by the extensive use of the aorist tense in its depiction of the experience of the 'I' that is appropriate if Paul is employing the rhetorical 'I' to depict Israel's historical encounter with the law, her experience before and after receiving the law at Sinai. The way Paul portrays this encounter is in terms reminiscent of Adam's encounter with God's commandment to him in the Garden of Eden.

7:7 To respond to criticisms that his gospel involves a denigration of the law, Paul is at pains to show that he rejects any suggestion that he implies that the law is evil — a conclusion that his audience might reach from comments the apostle made earlier (cf. 3:20; 4:15; 5:20; 6:14). Adopting first of all the style of the diatribe, he begins by asking: *What shall we say, then? Is the law sinful?* 'What shall we say, then?' is an expression the apostle uses six times in Romans, either when introducing a proposition he will immediately refute as he does here cf. (6:1; 7:7; 9:14), or one that will stretch the thinking of his audience (cf. 4:1; 8:31; 9:30). To suggest that the law God gave his people Israel is 'sinful' is for Paul, as well as those who reject his gospel, utterly preposterous.[208] Hence he responds to the question with his characteristic retort: *Certainly not!*[209]

Having rejected out of hand any idea that the law is sinful, Paul proceeds to explain its true function. He does so adopting the rhetorical device

---

208. Dunn, *Romans 1–8*, 378, says: 'the phrase reads literally "the law, sin?!" and can only be given effect by inflection of the voice. The fact that Paul can pose the question quite so sharply (the law = sin!) is a clear indication and measure of the extent to which vv 1-6 seem to consign the law solely to the old epoch, equally abhorrent as its partners, sin and death'.

209. This translates *mē genoito*, which is employed fourteen times in his letters, ten of which are found in Romans: 3:4, 6, 31; 6:2, 15; 7:7, 13; 9:14; 11:1, 11; 1 Cor 6:15; Gal 2:17; 3:21; 6:14.

of speech-in-character employing the rhetorical 'I': *Nevertheless, I would not have known what sin was had it not been for the law.* Paul rejects the notion that the law is sin and points out that the law's role is to expose sin. Far from the law being sin, Paul argues that the 'I' would not know what sin was unless the law had exposed it.[210] Here Paul introduces for the first time the rhetorical 'I'[211] to depict Israel's encounter with the law at Sinai. Sin, of course, was in the world before the law was given, as the apostle explains in 5:13-14, but with the coming of the law it was explicitly defined as transgression. As Napier points out, all transgression is sin, but not all sin is transgression. This is why Paul could say, 'death reigned from the time of Adam to the time of Moses, even over those who did not sin by breaking a command, as did Adam' (5:14). However, with the coming of the law, what was previously sin was then defined also as transgression, and in transgressing the law Israel recapitulated Adam's transgression — by breaking actual commandments.[212]

To illustrate the point Paul shows how the tenth commandment of the Decalogue exposes sin: *For I would not have known what coveting really was if the law had not said, 'You shall not covet'.* Christopher Wright draws attention to the radical nature of the tenth commandment, going, as it does, to the root of human wickedness. It involves not just external conformity to statute law, but touches upon people's desires and affections.[213] In Jewish tradition, covetousness is 'the root of all sin',[214] 'the core and sum of the

210. J. A. Ziesler, 'The Role of the Tenth Commandment in Romans 7', *JSNT* 33 (1988) 48-49, argues that while Paul's point holds in respect to the tenth commandment of the Decalogue ('You shall not covet'), it does not apply generally to all the demands of the Mosaic law. For example, one could not say, 'I would not have known what it is to murder if the law had not said, "You shall not murder"'. However, for Paul's purposes it is not necessary to show that every single commandment functions in this way. It is enough to show that one of the functions of the law, operating through some of its commandments, is to make sin known.

211. Witherington, *Romans*, 186, argues: 'Those who claim that there is no signal in the text that we are going into impersonation at v. 7 are simply wrong. "The section begins in v. 7 with an abrupt change in voice following a rhetorical question, [which] serves as a transition from Paul's authorial voice, which has previously addressed the audience explicitly . . . in 6.1-7.6. This constitutes what the grammarians and rhetoricians described as change of voice *(enallagē* or *metabolē).* These ancient readers would next look for *diaphonia,* a difference in characterization from the authorial voice. The speaker in 7.7-25 speaks with great personal pathos of coming under the Law at some point, learning about desire and sin, and being unable to do what he wants to do because of enslavement to sin or flesh"'.

212. Daniel Napier, 'Paul's Analysis of Sin and Torah in Romans 7:7-25', *ResQ* 44 (2002) 20-22.

213. Christopher J. H. Wright, *Deuteronomy* (NIBC; Peabody, Mass.: Hendrickson, 1996), 85.

214. Cf. Dunn, *Romans 1–8,* 380: 'That wrong desire, lust, or covetousness was the root of all sin was an already established theologoumenon in Jewish thought. The point is already clear in Philo *(Opif.* 152; *Decal.* 142, 150, 153, 173; *Spec. Leg.* 4.84-85). According to the *Apocalypse of Moses* (middle first century A.D.?), Eve attributes her failure to "lust the root and beginning of every sin" (19:3). . . . And James makes precisely the same affirmation: "desire/lust *(epithymia)* conceives and gives birth to sin" (1:15)'.

law'.[215] Paul is not saying that there was no covetousness before the law was given, but that it was not defined as such until the law came in (cf. 5:13-14). Perhaps even more is intended. To know what coveting is could mean, not just information about its nature, but knowing in the sense of experiencing it. If this is the case, the law not only defines sin but is also involved in bringing it about,[216] and this is what the apostle sets forth in the next verse.

7:8 Paul now explains how the law was used to produce sin. Continuing to employ the rhetorical 'I' (in this case referring to 'me'), he depicts Israel's encounter with the law: *But sin, seizing the opportunity afforded by the commandment, produced in me every kind of coveting. For apart from the law, sin was dead.* It is important to note what Paul does *not* say here. He does not say that the law produced in him the desire to covet, but rather that sin, seizing the opportunity afforded by the commandment, produced in him all kinds of covetousness. As far as the apostle is concerned, the law is good (7:13, 16) and spiritual (7:14). However, the very existence of the prohibition of covetousness provided 'sin' with the opportunity to bring to life in the 'I' what previously lay 'dead'. Sin was not absolutely dead prior to the giving of the law (cf. 5:13-14), but it was not as active as it was after the law was given. Cranfield offers the following explanation:

> We shall not do justice to Paul's thought here, if we settle for a merely psychological explanation along the lines of . . . the proverbial wisdom that speaks of forbidden fruits as sweetest. It is rather that the merciful limitation imposed on man by the commandment and intended to preserve his true freedom and dignity can be misinterpreted and misrepresented as a taking away of his freedom and an attack on his dignity, and so can be made an occasion of resentment and rebellion against the divine Creator, man's true Lord. In this way sin can make use of the commandment not to covet as a means of arousing all manner of covetousness.[217]

Moo offers an illustration:

> It was only after the Israelites had heard the commandment not to make any idols for themselves (Exod 20:4) that they had Aaron fashion a golden calf for them to worship (Exod 32). In just this way the law,

---

215. Cf. Käsemann, *Romans,* 194: 'In understanding the commandment against covetousness as the core and sum of the law the apostle follows a Jewish tradition. . . . In *Apoc. Mos.* 19:3 and also in Philo *De Decalogo* 142, 150, 173 covetousness is described as the beginning of all sin, and Jas 1:15 develops this psychologically. . . . The Talmud takes the same view. . . . This does not mean merely that all other sins stem from covetousness, and sexuality is certainly not meant. . . . The point is that it is absolutely the basic sin . . . against which the whole law is directed and which the law in fact provokes'. . . .

216. Cf. Wright, 'Romans', 562.

217. Cranfield, *Romans,* I, 350.

abused by the sinful tendency already resident in every person, has been instrumental in stimulating all kinds of sinful tendencies.[218]

7:9 Continuing to explain the way the law became the unwilling ally of sin, Paul refers to the experience of the 'I'/Israel before and after the giving of the law: *Once I was alive apart from law; but when the commandment came, sin sprang to life and I died.* There is a clear reversal here. Before the coming of the commandment, 'I' was alive and 'sin' was dead; after the coming of the commandment, 'I' was dead and 'sin' was alive'. We may say that before the giving of the law Israel was 'alive' and 'sin' was 'dead'. However, when Israel was given the law, 'sin sprang to life' and Israel 'died'. It is likely that Paul saw Israel's encounter with the law as a recapitulation of Adam's encounter with the commandment in the Garden. It may be said that Adam was 'alive' before the commandment was given and then, when the commandment came, the serpent took the opportunity it provided to provoke him to sin, which in turn brought about the entry of death (cf. 5:12).[219] In similar fashion, Israel was 'alive' prior to the giving of the law, but once the law came in, sin 'sprang to life', provoking her to transgress the law, and drew down upon her the sanction of the law, death. The apostle explains this further in 7:10-11.

7:10-11 Paul explains: *I found that the very commandment that was intended to bring life actually brought death.* The idea of the law promising life is based on Leviticus 18:5, a text cited by the apostle in 10:5: 'Moses writes this about the righteousness that is by the law: "The person who does these things will live by them"'. Although the law did hold out a promise of life (cf. also Deuteronomy 27–28), as far as Paul is concerned, no one could access what the law promised. His whole argument in 1:18–3:20 leads to the following conclusions: 'Therefore no one will be declared righteous in God's sight by the works of the law; rather, through the law we become conscious of our sin' (3:20); and 'for all have sinned and fall short of the glory of God' (3:23). In 7:10, then, Paul is saying that while the law given at Sinai promised life to Israel if she continued to obey it, in fact it brought death when she failed to do so.

Next the apostle explains how the 'commandment that was intended to bring life actually brought death': *For sin, seizing the opportunity afforded by the*

---

218. Moo, *Romans*, 436.

219. Cf. Wright, 'Romans', 563; Dunn, *Romans 1–8*, 381, interprets it in terms of Adam's encounter with the commandment which he regards as typical of everyman: 'Paul is almost certainly speaking in typical terms, using the Adam narrative to characterize what is true of man (*'adam*) in general, *every*man — somewhat as 2 *Apoc. Bar.* 54.19, "Each of us has been the Adam of his own soul". . . . The stages marked by *ezōn pote* and *apethanon* (v 10) clearly reflect the stages of Adam's fall: Gen 2:7, 16-17, "man became a *living* being (*psychēn zōsan*). . . . And the Lord *commanded* Adam, 'You may certainly eat of every tree which is in the garden/paradise, but of the tree of the knowledge of good and evil you shall not eat; for in the day you eat of it you shall certainly die [*thanatō apothaneisthe*]'"'. Cf. Käsemann, *Romans*, 196-97.

commandment, deceived me, and through the commandment put me to death. Paul probably saw in Israel's encounter with the law a recapitulation of Adam's encounter with God's command to him in Eden, as many scholars have observed.[220] Verses 8-11 make sense when read in terms of the serpent's temptation of Adam and Eve in the Garden: Of the first couple it is singularly true that they were once 'alive apart from the law' but that 'when the commandment came, sin sprang to life' and they died. For them especially the words, 'sin, seizing the opportunity afforded by the commandment, deceived me, and through the commandment put me to death', are true. The Mosaic law and the commandment of God given in Eden were already associated in Jewish thinking in Paul's day.[221] Paul's purpose here is clear: he is asserting that sin is to blame for Israel's predicament, not the law, and no one should assume that in his preaching of the gospel he intends any criticism of the law. These things are spelled out clearly in the verses that follow.

7:12 Paul concludes that the law is not to blame, for in fact the law is good: *So then, the law is holy, and the commandment is holy, righteous and good.* Paul's statement here echoes the words of Deuteronomy 4:8 ('And what other nation is so great as to have such righteous decrees and laws as this body of laws I am setting before you today?') and also of Nehemiah 9:13 ('You came down on Mount Sinai; you spoke to them from heaven. You gave them regulations and laws that are just and right, and decrees and commands that are good'). However, the form of the sentence here in 7:12 (lit. 'So then, on the one hand, the law is holy, and the commandment is holy and righteous and good . . .') indicates the existence of an anacoluthon, the audience expecting the apostle to complete it with something like: 'but on the other hand sin is evil and the real culprit'.[222]

The significance of the three epithets Paul applies to the law have been described as follows: 'holy' — its origin is God himself whose nature is holy;[223] 'just' — it cannot in any way be said to promote anything that is wrong;[224] 'good' — its provisions are universally positive and desirable.[225]

220. Cf. Dunn, *Romans 1–8*, 384; Byrne, *Romans*, 223; Barrett, *Romans*, 144; Cranfield, *Romans*, I, 352-53. Moo, *Romans*, 436, however, restricts the allusion to Israel's encounter with the law at Sinai.

221. Wright, 'Romans', 563, says: 'Paul seems here to be referring also to the "fall" of Genesis 3 (particularly with v. 11: sin "deceived me . . . and killed me", alluding to Gen 3:13; cf. 2 Cor 11:3). We should not attempt to decide between these two (Sinai and Eden): Paul's point is precisely that what happened on Sinai recapitulated what had happened in Eden. Other Jewish exegetes linked the two moments; Paul's view falls well within recognizable Second Temple understandings of the meaning both of covetousness and of the primal sin [n. 243; see *b. Sanh.* 38b; 102a; *Exod. Rab.* 21:1; 30:7; 32:1, 7, 11]'. Cf. Dunn, *Romans 1–8*, 400.

222. Cf. Jan Lambrecht, 'Grammar and Reasoning in Romans 7,12 and 7,13-14', *ETL* 80 (2004) 470-74, who argues on this basis that 7:12 functions as the conclusion to the passage 7:7-12, and 7:13 is part of the next long section, 7:13-25.

223. Dunn, *Romans 1–8*, 385; Moo, *Romans*, 440.

224. Moo, *Romans*, 441.

225. Dunn, *Romans 1–8*, 386.

Paul's purpose in stressing these characteristics of the law is to rule out any false conclusions that people might draw from his assertions that the law, having become the unwilling ally of sin, is part of the human dilemma, not its solution.[226]

7:13 In 7:12, to ensure that people do not draw wrong conclusions concerning what he says about the law, Paul stresses that 'the law is holy, and the commandment is holy, righteous and good'. The question thrown up by 7:13 is: *Did that which is good, then, become death to me?* Paul's immediate response is an emphatic denial: *By no means!* his characteristic response to preposterous suggestions.[227] Once again he insists that sin is the culprit, not the law: *Nevertheless, in order that sin might be recognized as sin, it used what is good to bring about my death, so that through the commandment sin might become utterly sinful.* In what way does 'sin' bring about the death of the 'I' through the law? The answer would appear to be that the very existence of the commandments of the law provides 'sin' with the opportunity to entice the 'I' to violate those commandments. This violation in turn invokes the sanctions of the law — the judgment of God. By showing how utterly sinful sin is, and how it lays even the law of God under tribute to achieve its purposes, Paul makes clear that he has no criticism of the law per se, and that his gospel does not involve any denigration of the law.

Two purpose clauses are included in Paul's response. Together they form a part, but certainly not all, of God's purpose in giving the law: (i) 'in order that sin might be recognized as sin'; (ii) 'so that through the commandment sin might become utterly sinful'. 'Sin', by bringing about death through the holy, righteous, and good law of God, is revealed in its true colors — 'utterly sinful'. Paul could hardly have emphasized more that sin is the real culprit. By bringing about the death of the 'I' the full 'sinfulness' of sin is revealed. At this point, where Paul stresses the devastating effects of sin, it is important to remember what he says earlier in the letter: 'where sin increased, grace increased all the more' (5:20).

(ii) Israel's ongoing experience of living under the law, 7:14-20

[14]*We know that the law is spiritual; but I am unspiritual, sold as a slave to sin.* [15]*I do not understand what I do. For what I want to do I do not do, but what I hate I do.* [16]*And if I do what I do not want to do, I agree that the law is good.* [17]*As it is, it is no longer I myself who do it, but it is sin living in me.* [18]*For I know that good itself does not dwell in me, that is, in my sinful na-*

---

226. Wright, 'Romans', 564, says: 'At the present stage of the argument, it is vital that they do not react against the Torah itself (as so many of Paul's subsequent audience, since at least the second century, have been tempted to do), but that they see instead the strange but vital role it has played within the saving purpose of the one God'.

227. As already noted above, *mē genoito* (which underlies the expression, 'By no means!') occurs fourteen times in Paul's letters, ten of which are found in Romans — 3:4, 6, 31; 6:2, 15; 7:7, 13; 9:14; 11:1, 11 — and the others in 1 Cor 6:15; Gal 2:17; 3:21; 6:14.

ture. For I have the desire to do what is good, but I cannot carry it out. ¹⁹For I do not do the good I want to do, but the evil I do not want to do — this I keep on doing. ²⁰Now if I do what I do not want to do, it is no longer I who do it, but it is sin living in me that does it.

In this passage again Paul adopts the 'speech-in-character' mode of address employing the rhetorical 'I'. Whereas this was employed in 7:7-13 to refer to Israel's historical encounter with the law given at Sinai, in 7:14-20 it is used to depict Israel's ongoing experience, the experience of non-Christian Jews under the law. The apostle Paul could identify to a certain extent with both of these — he is a member of the people of Israel and her history is his history, and he was prior to his conversion a Jew living under the law — but neither represents his present experience as a Christian.

Unlike the previous passage (7:7-13), which employs the aorist tense of the verb almost exclusively, 7:14-25 is marked by the complete absence of the aorist and uses the present tense extensively (36 times), a tense that more vividly expresses the dire situation of the 'I' than does the aorist tense. It is a situation in which the 'I' struggles with an inner conflict between what it wills on the one hand and what it does on the other. Whereas the rhetorical 'I' was used in 7:1-13 to depict Israel's historical encounter with the law, in 7:14-21 it is used to depict vividly the ongoing struggle of the Jewish person still living under the law.[228]

It must not be imagined that this portrayal of a conflict of will and action represents the day-to-day experience of all people who live under the law. As Witherington says: 'We have here a Christian analysis of the general malaise of fallen humanity when it comes to sin, death, and Law, and the truth is that only by coming to the point of being convicted, convinced, and converted is it likely for fallen persons to see themselves as described here'.[229]

7:14 Paul departs briefly from his use of the first person singular 'I' in this verse, adopting instead the first person plural 'we' to include himself with members of his audience in what he is about to say. At least he includes those among them who are Jews or Gentiles who have a background in the synagogue or Gentiles who since their conversion have been instructed in the law: *We know that the law is spiritual; but I am unspiritual, sold as a slave to sin.* This is something "we know" — Paul is assuming they know this as well as he does.

Having described the law as holy, good, and righteous (7:12), the apostle now describes it as 'spiritual'. This is the only place in his writings where Paul contrasts the law that is 'spiritual' with the 'I' that is 'unspiri-

228. Bray, *ACCSR*, 189-90, points out: 'Most of the Fathers believed that here Paul was adopting the persona of an unregenerate man, not describing his own struggles as a Christian. As far as they were concerned, becoming a Christian would deliver a person from the kind of dilemma the apostle is outlining here'.

229. Witherington, *Romans*, 198.

tual'. Paul uses the adjective 'spiritual' *(pneumatikos)* a total of twenty four times in his letters. In all cases but one things are spiritual because they are God given and inspired: spiritual gifts (1:11; 1 Cor 12:1; 14:1), spiritual blessings (15:27; Eph 1:3), spiritual truths (1 Cor 2:13), spiritual people (1 Cor 2:13, 15; 3:1; 14:37; Gal 6:1), spiritual seed, that is, the gospel (1 Cor 9:11), spiritual food or drink (1 Cor 10:4), the spiritual rock, that is, Christ (1 Cor 10:4), the spiritual body (1 Cor 15:44, 46), spiritual songs (Eph 5:19; Col 3:16), and spiritual understanding (Col 3:16). The one exception is the spiritual forces of evil (Eph 6:12). Allowing the predominant usage of 'spiritual' in Paul's letters to guide us, we may say that the law is spiritual because it is God given. If it is spiritual in this sense, it can in no way be the fundamental cause of the death of the 'I'.

While the law is spiritual, the 'I', Paul says, is unspiritual. The word 'unspiritual' is used by Paul in 1 Corinthians 3:1, where he says that he can speak to Corinthian believers only as those who are unspiritual (NIV: 'worldly'), where the implication is that they are motivated not by the Holy Spirit, but instead by their own unspiritual/worldly desires. In 7:14 'unspiritual' is used with a similar meaning. When the apostle asserts that the 'I' is unspiritual, he means that it, unlike the law which is God given, is 'sold as a slave to sin' (lit. 'sold under sin'). The verb 'to sell' is found only here in Paul's letters but is used elsewhere in the NT usually to mean simply 'to sell' one's possessions (Matt 13:46; 26:9; Mark 14:5; John 12:5; Acts 2:45; 4:34; 5:4). However, in Matthew 18:25 the context indicates that selling people into slavery is intended, and it is used in this sense frequently in the OT (cf., e.g., Exod 22:3; Lev 25:39, 42, 47-48; Deut 15:12; 21:4; 28:68; Ps 105:17; Isa 50:1; 52:3; Jer 34:14 — particularly relevant are those texts which speak of people selling themselves 'to do evil': 1 Kgs 21:20, 25; 2 Kgs 17:17).[230] As far as Paul is concerned, the 'I', apart from Christ, is in the state of having been sold as a slave to sin.[231] Clearly the cause of the human predicament is not the law but humanity's slavery to sin.

7:15-16 In these verses Paul depicts the slavery of the 'I' to sin by highlighting its moral weakness. As he depicts it, this moral weakness is something that perplexes, even distresses the 'I', for he prefaces the actual depiction with the words, *[For] I do not understand what I do*. The word 'for'

---

230. Gary S. Shogren, 'The "Wretched Man" of Romans 7:14-25 as *Reductio ad absurdum*', *EvQ* 72 (2000) 125, notes: 'in the LXX, the four appearances of *eimi pepramenos* that relate to the covenant do not denote conflict or temptation, but a full-blown descent into idolatry or other gross sin. . . . Consistently, "being sold to do evil" denotes calamitous apostasy which leads straight to judgment. Paul's phrase "sold under sin" (*eimi pepramenos hypo tēn hamartian*) is altered slightly from the LXX because of Paul's personification of sin as slave-driver'.

231. That the apostle describes the 'I' as 'sold under sin' militates against the view that the apostle is using the 'I' to depict Christian existence (cf. 6:17-18: 'though you used to be slaves to sin . . . you have been set free from sin and have become slaves to righteousness'). So, e.g., Moo, *Romans*, 454; Käsemann, *Romans*, 200, *contra* Dunn, *Romans 1–8*, 388-89; Cranfield, *Romans*, I, 356.

(omitted in the NIV translation) indicates that what Paul is about to say is in explanation of his statement, 'I am unspiritual, sold as a slave to sin'. The evidence for the 'I' being 'sold as a slave to sin' is, he says, that 'I do not understand what I do'. He explains: *For what I want to do I do not do, but what I hate I do.* The bondage of the 'I' to sin is seen in its inability to carry out the good it wants to do and its inability to desist from doing the evil it despises. This echoes similar sentiments in classical authors, though there are also significant differences between what they say and Paul's depiction of human moral weakness here (see 'Additional Note: Classical Parallels regarding Moral Weakness', 312-14).

This experience of the 'I' enables Paul to conclude: *And if I do what I do not want to do, I agree that the law is good.* By depicting Israel's ongoing experience under the law in this way, Paul seems to speak in a way that is at odds with the account of his own preconversion experience under the law when he says that he was in respect to 'righteousness based on the law, faultless' (Phil 3:6). The apparent contradiction may be resolved as follows: In 7:15-16 Paul is speaking from a Christian perspective of the way he now sees Israel's life under the law, whereas in Philippians 3:6 he is dealing with what we might call his Jewish credentials. He claims to have been a Jew whose pedigree and piety could not be called into question. It is very unlikely that he is claiming never to have fallen short of what the law demanded, or never to have suffered the qualms of conscience because he had done so.[232]

Two things are implied by what Paul says in 7:15-16: first, what the 'I' does not want to do is to transgress the law, and this underlines the fact that the law is good. Second, Paul, far from denigrating the law itself, locates the cause for the human dilemma in human bondage to sin, not in the law.

7:17 The apostle lays the blame for Israel's predicament squarely upon sin: *As it is, it is no longer I myself who do it, but it is sin living in me.* The 'I', Israel as Paul perceives her living under the law,[233] wants to keep the law, but indwelling sin causes it to transgress the law. Attention has been drawn to possible similarities between what Paul says here and the Jewish idea of the two impulses, the 'evil impulse' and the 'good impulse'. In Jewish thought a person's observance of Torah enabled him/her to follow the good impulse and overcome the evil impulse. For Paul, however, deliverance came, not through observance of the law enabling the good impulse to

---

232. Cf. Peter T. O'Brien, *The Epistle to the Philippians: A Commentary on the Greek Text* (NIGTC; Grand Rapids: Eerdmans, 1991), 379-81; Moo, *Romans*, 456.

233. *Contra* Cranfield, *Romans*, I, 359, who argues that the experience of the 'I' here denotes the experience of the Christian: 'For in the Christian there is a continual growth in understanding of the will of God and therefore also an ever-deepening perception of the extent to which he falls short of it: and this growing knowledge and the deepening hatred of sin which accompanies it are not merely phenomena of the Christian's human psychology but the work of the Spirit of God. The Holy Spirit Himself is active in him in opposition to the continuing power of his egotism'.

triumph, but rather through what God has done in Christ.[234] By laying the blame on 'sin' Paul is not denying human responsibility for sinful actions, but recognizing 'sin' as a power operating within humanity.

7:18 Recognizing the ongoing baleful effects of indwelling sin, Paul continues: *For I know that good itself does not dwell in me, that is, in my sinful nature. For I have the desire to do what is good, but I cannot carry it out.* Paul qualifies his statement that 'nothing good lives in me' by adding 'that is, in my sinful nature'. The 'I' can desire 'to do what is good', but because of the 'sinful nature' it is unable to carry it out. By so saying, Paul continues to depict the ongoing experience of Jewish people under the law. Like the rest of humanity they are not altogether evil, for the desire to do good is present, but the capacity to do so is lacking because of the sinful nature.[235] The contrast with the more optimistic view of Sirach 15:14-15 is stark: 'It was he who created humankind in the beginning, and he left them in the power of their own free choice. If you choose, you can keep the commandments, and to act faithfully is a matter of your own choice'. This is not how Paul saw things.

7:19-20 Repeating what he said in 7:15, Paul spells out again the predicament of the 'I': *For I do not do the good I want to do, but the evil I do not want to do — this I keep on doing. Now if I do what I do not want to do, it is no longer I who do it, but it is sin living in me that does it.* By arguing that the 'I' is unable to carry out the good it wants to do because of the power of indwelling sin, Paul shows that sin is responsible for the predicament of the 'I'/Israel (as is the case with the rest of humanity) and not the law. The significance of this statement is that it reinforces Paul's rebuttal of claims that his gospel involves a denigration of the law. Paul lays the blame for Israel's predicament upon sin, not upon the law.

(iii) Paul's conclusions about Israel, sin, and the law, 7:21-25

[21]*So I find this law at work: Although I want to do good, evil is right there with me.* [22]*For in my inner being I delight in God's law;* [23]*but I see another law at work in me, waging war against the law of my mind and making me a prisoner of the law of sin at work within me.* [24]*What a wretched man I am!*

---

234. Shogren, 'The "Wretched Man" of Romans 7:14-25', 133, contends that in Rom 7:14-25 Paul does not depict 'the doctrine of the Two Impulses, but its parody. In a moment of panicked awareness the Man exclaims: "I am . . . sold into slavery under sin. I'm an apostate in God's eyes and the accepted path of deliverance only underscores my bondage! The Wretched Man is a reductio ad absurdum of any system that hinges on a good impulse as a way of escape'. Wright, 'Romans', 567, adds: 'Contrary to much popular opinion, this small section does not portray what is usually meant by the "cloven ego" (this increases the probability that Paul is not here dependent of the rabbinic idea of two "inclinations". . . . The "I", though frustrated, is actually, like Torah, exonerated, with the blame going (of course) to sin. Paul, having moved the problem off Torah on to the "I", now moves it one stage further, on to sin itself'.

235. Käsemann, *Romans*, 205, describes the flesh [sinful nature] as 'the workshop of sin, the whole person in his fallenness to the world and alienation from God'.

Who will rescue me from this body that is subject to death? 25Thanks be to God, who delivers me through Jesus Christ our Lord!

So then, I myself in my mind am a slave to God's law, but in my sinful nature a slave to the law of sin.

In these verses Paul continues to make use of the rhetorical 'I' as he draws conclusions based upon his treatment of Israel's ongoing frustration living under the law, a treatment that is colored by his postconversion experience as a Christian.

7:21-23 He begins: *So I find this law at work: Although I want to do good, evil is right there with me.* The frustrating experience of the 'I' points to a principle operating within it; one that expresses itself in the fact that when the 'I' wants to do good, 'evil is right there with me' (lit. 'evil is present [and ready to exercise its power] with me').[236] The apostle then describes more explicitly what this means: *For in my inner being I delight in God's law; but I see another law at work in me, waging war against the law of my mind and making me a prisoner of the law of sin at work within me.* 'My inner being' (lit. 'the inner man'),[237] in this context, is virtually synonymous with 'the law of my mind'. On the one hand 'the inner being' delights in God's law yet on the other hand 'the law of my mind' is under attack by that other law, the law of sin.

Paul uses the word 'law' four times in 7:22-23 as he speaks of three distinct 'laws' or 'principles' in relation to the 'I': (i) There is 'God's law', in which the 'I' delights, which in this context refers to the law of Moses. (ii) There is 'another law', also referred to as 'the law of sin', which is to be understood as the 'sin principle' at work 'in me'. This law of sin wages war against (iii) 'the law of my mind' (here virtually synonymous with 'my inner being' that delights in God's law) and makes the 'I' its prisoner. Once again the root cause of the human predicament is identified as sin (the law of sin) and not the law of Moses. All this highlights the predicament in which the 'I' finds itself. This is in line with Paul's overall purpose in 7:7-25 to show that his gospel involves no denigration of the law.

Not all commentators agree with the explanation of the various nuances of meaning given the word 'law' above. In particular, Wright and Dunn argue that it should be understood to mean the Jewish Torah throughout. Thus it is 'the law of God' because it is given by God, it is 'the law of my mind' because it is the law which the mind approves, and it is 'the law of

---

236. Cf. BAGD, *ad loc.*

237. The expression 'the inner man' is found in two other places in Paul's letters but with slightly different connotations: In 2 Cor 4:16 the apostle contrasts what is happening to him 'outwardly' (in the 'outer man' [*exō anthrōpos*]) as a result of persecution with the renewal he experiences 'inwardly' (in the 'inner man' [*esō anthrōpos*]) as a result of the power of the life of Christ at work in him. In Eph 3:16 Paul prays that God will strengthen his audience 'with power through his Spirit in your inner being (*ton esō anthrōpon,* lit. 'the inner man').

sin' because it functions (unwillingly) as a 'base of operations' for sin.[238] Commenting on this view, Moo says: 'Paul, it is argued, has throughout this context been detailing the "duality" of the law: "good", "holy", "just", "spiritual", and "for life", yet the stimulator of sin, an "imprisoning" force, and an instrument of death. . . . The distinction, on this view, is not between two different laws but between the different operations and effects of the same law. . . . However, there are serious objections to this view, both exegetical and theological. The greatest exegetical difficulty is Paul's qualification of the *nomos* in v. 23a as "another": if Paul had intended to refer in v. 23a to the same law as in v. 22, even if viewed from a different perspective, or with a different function, or even as "renewed and transformed", he would not have called it "another" or "different" law'.[239] The majority view among commentators is that Paul does use the word 'law' with different shades of meaning in 7:22-23 and that, in particular, when the apostle refers to 'another law' and the 'law of sin', he is referring to a principle of sin, a power, or a controlling force operating within humanity.[240]

7:24 Paul's depiction of the war being waged between the law of the mind and the law of sin within the members of the 'I' leads him add: *What a wretched man I am!* To be 'wretched' is the opposite of being 'blessed'. It means to be miserable, in mental or emotional turmoil.[241] It is found in two places in the Wisdom of Solomon with similar connotations:

> For those who despise wisdom and instruction are *miserable*. Their hope is vain, their labors are unprofitable, and their works are useless. (Wis. 3:11, italics added)

> But *miserable*, with their hopes set on dead things, are those who give the name 'gods' to the works of human hands, gold and silver fashioned with skill, and likenesses of animals, or a useless stone, the work of an ancient hand. (Wis. 13:10, italics added)

The 'wretchedness' of the 'I' here consists in its being in slavery to sin, a slavery from which it is unable to rescue itself.[242] Hence the cry: *Who will*

---

238. Cf. Wright, 'Romans', 569-70; Dunn, *Romans 1–8*, 377, 392, 395.

239. Moo, *Romans*, 463.

240. Cf., e.g., Witherington, *Romans*, 201; Byrne, *Romans*, 228; Cranfield, *Romans*, I, 361-62, 364; Moo, *Romans*, 464.

241. The word 'wretched' *(talaipōros)* is used with similar connotation by Epictetus: *ti gar eimi? talaipōron anthrōparion*, 'What am I? Just a miserable particle of humanity' (Epict 1, 3, 5, cited in BAGD, *ad loc.*). Cf. Shogren, 'The "Wretched Man" of Romans 7:14-25', 128.

242. Shogren, 'The "Wretched Man" of Romans 7:14-25', 127, says: 'It is time to make clear that the Wretched Man's experience is quite different from Martin Luther's dismay as a monk, popularly thought to parallel Romans 7. The Wretched Man is in despair because he cannot perform the works of the Torah, no matter how he sets his mind to it. Luther, by contrast, testified that "however irreproachable my life as a monk, I felt myself, in the presence of God, to be a sinner with a most unquiet conscience" (cited in Moo, 450, n. 22) Luther was no moral failure! His torment grew alongside the realization that God's holiness far transcended any performance. The Wretched Man never reached even that level of religious success'.

rescue me from this body that is subject to death?[243] The expression, 'this body that is subject to death' (lit. 'this body of death'), is an unusual one, found only here in Paul's letters (and only here in the NT), although elsewhere in Romans the apostle speaks of the entailment of the body with sin; for example, in 6:6 he speaks of 'the body ruled by sin', and in 8:10 he says that the 'body is subject to death because of sin'.[244]

The longing of the 'I' depicted by Paul here in 7:24 is not a desire for release from the body per se (as if an incorporeal existence is desired), but rather deliverance from slavery to sin even while, for the present, continuing in bodily existence.[245] The cry of 'I' is the cry of Jewish people under the law,[246] here depicted by a Jew who was once under the law but is so no longer.

7:25 In answer to the question, 'Who will rescue me from this body of death?' Paul says: *[But] thanks be to God, who delivers me through Jesus Christ our Lord!* The NIV omits the adversative 'but' *(de)* by which the apostle highlights the difference between the plight of the 'I' and his own Christian hope. Even in the present time deliverance from slavery to sin is available; deliverance made available by God himself by what he has done 'through Jesus Christ our Lord'. Here (7:25a) Paul anticipates what he will spell out in detail in 8:1-13 (see esp. 8:2) before adding the summarizing conclusion that follows (7:25b).[247]

---

243. Christian Grappe, 'Qui me délivera de ce corps de mort? L'esprit de vie! Romains 7,24 et 8,2 comme éléments de typologie adamique', *Bib* 83 (2002) 473-74, argues that there is in 7:24 and 8:2 a twofold allusion to *4 Ezra* 3:4-5, where Adam is said to have been created with a dead body that is brought to life by the Spirit: 'O sovereign Lord, did you not speak at the beginning when you formed the earth — and that without help — and commanded the dust and it gave you Adam, a lifeless body? Yet he was the workmanship of your hands, and you breathed into him the breath of life, and he was made alive in your presence'.

244. Wright, 'Romans', 571, says: 'Like Cain, bearing about the mark of his brother's death, the "I" finds itself unable to escape from "this body of death", referring perhaps both to its own "fleshly" state but also to the solidarity of sin, of Adamic humanity, with which it is unavoidably bound up (cf. 6:6)'.

245. So Jewett, *Romans*, 471: 'Paul's exclamation cannot refer to the tension between the two aeons or to a yearning for resurrection, which reflect the experience of believers rather than the pre-Christian Paul. The sense of hopeless misery resonates with Paul's admission in 1 Cor 15:9, "For I am . . . unfit to be called an Apostle, because I persecuted the church of Christ"'. Ultimately Paul does look forward to 'the redemption of the body' (8:23), and the transformation of his lowly body to be like Christ's glorious body (Phil 3:21), but this is not what he has in mind here. *Contra* James I. Packer, 'Le "malheureux" de Romains 7', *Hokhma* 55 (1994) 24, who holds that the cry for deliverance is a cry to be released from this mortal body through resurrection. Similarly Dunn, *Romans 1–8*, 397: 'The deliverance in view here therefore is . . . final deliverance, which is the completion of the good work already begun (Phil 1:6). That is to say, it is not for a deliverance which can be experienced *within* the fleshly constraints of this life, but for deliverance *from* the fleshly constraints of this life'.

246. *Contra* Cranfield, *Romans*, I, 365-66, who argues that it is the cry of Christian people who are conscious of the disparity between what God requires of them yet and are painfully aware of their shortcomings.

247. Cf. Stephen W. Frary, 'Who Will Deliver Me? An Exegesis of Rom. 7:24–8:11',

In 7:25b, then, Paul provides a summarizing conclusion emphasizing that apart from the grace of God in Christ, the situation of the 'I' remains bleak: *So then, I myself in my mind am a slave to God's law, but in my sinful nature a slave to the law of sin.*[248] The 'I' still denotes Jewish people under the law. In their minds they might be slaves to the law of God, but in their sinful natures they remain slaves to sin (cf. 7:23).

Some see in 7:25 evidence for the view that Paul is depicting Christian experience in 7:14-25. On the one hand Christians are thankful to God for the hope of final deliverance, but on the other they acknowledge the actuality of their situation — desiring with the mind to be a slave to God's law, but still struggling with a propensity to yield themselves as slaves to sin, this being the eschatological tension in which believers live.[249] However, it is unlikely that the apostle, who declares that 'sin shall not be your master, because you are not under law, but under grace' (6:14) and adds in 7:5-6 that believers who were once controlled by the sinful nature are now released from the law to serve in the new way of the Spirit, would then speak of them as slaves 'to the law of sin'.

Yet once more in this chapter Paul firmly locates the root cause of the human dilemma with sin, not the law, and by so doing rejects all suggestions that his gospel involves a denigration of the law. At the same time he provides a negative foil for his presentation of Christian freedom that is to follow in chapter 8.

ADDITIONAL NOTE:
CLASSICAL PARALLELS REGARDING MORAL WEAKNESS

Attention has been drawn to statements by classical authors that appear similar to Paul's depiction of humanity's inability to perform the good they

---

Faith & Mission 17 (2000) 19, who cites Charles D. Myer Jr., 'Chiastic Inversion in the Argument of Romans 3–8', *NovT* 35 (1993) 35, who in turn cites Bassler, *Divine Impartiality,* 156: 'Paul occasionally employs the stylistic device of the postponed conclusion in which the summarizing conclusion of an argument is delayed until after the next argumentative unit has begun'.

248. Hermann Lichtenberger, 'Der Beginn der Auslegungsgeschichte von Römer 7: Röm 7,25b', *ZNW* 88 (1997) 294-95, argues that 7:25b is a non-Pauline gloss, and as such represents the beginning of the history of interpretation of Romans 7. The 'Glossator', a nameless exegete and theologian, has misunderstood Paul and is responsible for subsequent mistaken readings of Paul, e.g., Luther's *simul iustus et peccator,* the Lutheran two kingdoms teaching, Pietism, as well as present-day theological reflection and practice. If the gloss is removed, then 8:1 follows seamlessly on after 7:25a. However, there is no indication in the textual tradition that 7:25 is a gloss. And to treat it as such is to overcome an exegetical challenge just too easily.

249. So, e.g., Cranfield, *Romans,* I, 367-69; Dunn, *Romans 1–8,* 397; D. B. Garlington, 'Romans 7:14-25 and the Creation Theology of Paul', *TrinJ* 11 N.S. (1990) 199-200.

want to do and to desist from the evil they do not want to do. Huggins lists the following as examples:

> Euripides (c. 480-406 B.C.): 'That which is good we learn and recognise, yet practice not the lesson, some from sloth, and some preferring pleasure in the stead of duty'. (*Hippolytus* 379-83)
>
> Plato (427-347 B.C.): '. . . most people . . . say that many, while knowing what is best, refuse to perform it'. (*Protagoras* 352d)
>
> Aristotle (384-322 B.C.): 'The man . . . does not think the action right before he comes under the influence of passion'. (*Ethica Nicomachea* 7.2)
>
> Plautus (c. 254-184 B.C.): 'I know what sort I ought to be, but I couldn't be it, poor fool'. (*Trinummas* 657-58)
>
> Ovid (43 B.C.–A.D. 17): 'I see the better and approve it; but I follow the worse'. (*Metamorphosis* 7.21)[250]

To these may be added:

> Epictetus (A.D. 55-135): 'What I will I do not do and what I do not will I do'. (*Dissertations* 2.26.4)

In addition to the passages cited above, Napier draws attention to Euripides' drama, *Medea* (c. 455 B.C.):

> The myth of Medea contains a scene that is the fount of a discussion in Greco-Roman moral philosophy that partially parallels the sentiment of 7:15. The tradition looks back to Euripides' *Medea* (ca. 455 B.C.) as its source. As the scene opens Medea has been told that Jason is going to send her away and marry Creon's daughter. Both Medea and her sons by Jason will be banished from the land. In rage she deliberates with herself how to take revenge on Jason; she will kill their sons to injure him. As she moves toward this decision, she argues furiously with herself. At one point (1056-58) she talks herself out of the deed, but in the end Medea follows through with her plot. The decision is sealed (1078-79): 'Though indeed I learn what sort of evil I am about to commit, still wrath is greater than my resolutions'.[251]

Huggins argues that in the case of Plato's Socrates '(1) evil conduct stems from ignorance rather than the overwhelming of better judgment by the passions, and (2) right knowledge inevitably leads to right conduct'.[252] This is clearly different from Paul's depiction of human inability to do the

---

250. Ronald V. Huggins, 'Alleged Classical Parallels to Paul's "What I want to do I do not do, but what I hate, that I do" (Rom 7:15)', *WTJ* 54 (1992) 153-54.

251. Napier, 'Paul's Analysis of Sin and Torah', 28.

252. 'Alleged Classical Parallels', 154.

good they know. As for Aristotle, Huggins says, 'the appellation he assigns
to the problem of knowing the right but failing to carry it out is *akrasia* (in-
continence), which stands in opposition of *enkrateia* (continence) . . . the in-
continent man does so against his better judgment: "mastered by passion
sufficiently for him not to act in accordance with right principle, but not so
completely as to be of such a character as to believe that the reckless pursuit
of pleasure is right"'.[253] What is 'right' for Aristotle is what is regarded as
normal behavior for most people, something quite different from the standard adopted by Paul, that is, the divine will expressed in the law. In the
cases of Ovid (usually cited as the closest parallel to Paul) and Euripides,
Huggins argues that what is involved is not a general condition — a propensity to yield to passion, but rather people making 'a single disastrous
response to extraordinary trying circumstances'.[254]

Dunn comments: 'It is not difficult to parallel such complaints. The
most frequently quoted are Epictetus 2.26.4 . . . and Ovid, *Metamorphoses*
7.20-21. . . . But there are significant differences. Epictetus finds the answer
in the "rational soul" *(psychē logikē)*: "Point out to the rational governing
faculty a contradiction and it will desist" (2.26.7). And Ovid lacks the
sharpness of existential frustration which comes to increasingly anguished
expression as the passage here continues. This indicates the difference'.[255]

ADDITIONAL NOTE: THE IDENTITY OF THE 'I' IN 7:7-25

The significance of Paul's use of the first person singular in 7:7-25 has been
interpreted in many different ways, including appeals to Hellenistic psychology, identification with various aspects of Paul's own experience (autobiographical approaches), identification with humanity in general or with
Israel the nation and/or Jewish people (rhetorical approaches). A number
of these interpretations are described briefly below followed by brief
evaluative comments.

The 'I' Understood in the Light of Hellenistic Moral Psychology

Wasserman argues 'that an appreciation for certain Platonic assumptions,
images, and metaphors allows for a more coherent reading of Romans 7 as
depicting reason's defeat at the hands of passions and desires'.[256] She says:

253. 'Alleged Classical Parallels', 155.
254. 'Alleged Classical Parallels', 161.
255. Dunn, *Romans 1–8*, 389.
256. Emma Wasserman, 'The Death of the Soul in Romans 7: Revisiting Paul's Anthropology in Light of Hellenistic Moral Psychology', *JBL* 126 (2007) 816.

'This makes sense of why the narrator in Romans 7 speaks, reflects on its own disempowerment, understands God's just law, and knows the difference between good and evil despite being powerless to put these judgments into action. Thus, the speaker states in v. 12 that the law is "holy, just, and good", and its grasp of good and evil becomes painfully clear in vv. 14-25, as the speaker complains some eleven times that it understands the good but is unable to put this into action. . . . This plight makes sense when understood as the reasoning part of the soul powerless to put its judgments into action because of the domination of the passions. Like Plato's tyrannical man, Galen's undisciplined man, and Philo's mind in the prison house of the passions, Paul depicts reason as fundamentally good and rational but completely ineffectual. The restatement of this plight in vv. 22-23 also supports the identification of the speaker as mind. Here the speaker seems to stand outside itself and reflect on the nature of the struggle within the body as a whole, as the mind *(nous)*, the inner person *(esō anthrōpos)*, and God's law have lost a war against sin that is allied with the members and the flesh. The *nous* designates the reasoning part of the soul, as does *ho esō anthrōpos*, which is an analogy for the reasoning faculty that comes from the *Republic* (9.588c-591b). The speaker is the *ho esō anthrōpos* and the *nous* that reflects here on its relation to the flesh and members. This interpretation requires that reason stand outside itself and reflect on itself, but this, too, is consistent with the literary use of the self-in-dialogue, where the mind often speaks about itself in the third person'.[257]

While some superficial parallels are evident between the way Paul expresses himself in 7:14-25 and the plight of the human person whose reason is overcome by his or her passions, this approach to the interpretation of the 'I' fails to take proper cognizance of the fact that Paul is treating the issue of the interaction between the 'I' and the Mosaic law.

The 'I' Denotes Humankind in General

Morrison and Woodhouse suggest that Paul employs the 'I' rhetorically to depict the experience of humankind in general.[258] Strelan adopts a similar view: 'Either in solidarity with Adam, or in solidarity with Israel, or both, all people — Jew and Greek together, and "I" — stand guilty as charged: all have sinned (Rm. 3:23a)'.[259] Aletti likewise argues that the rhetorical 'I' represents not only the Jew under the law but also the Greek, in fact humanity without Christ in general.[260]

257. Wasserman, 'The Death of the Soul in Romans 7', 812-13.

258. 'The Coherence of Romans 7:1–8:8', 14.

259. G. Strelan, 'A Note on the Old Testament Background of Romans 7:7', *LTJ* 15 (1981) 24.

260. Jean-Noël Aletti, 'Rm 7.7-25 encore une fois: Enjeux et propositions', *NTS* 48 (2002) 375.

While it may be possible to depict the human dilemma in general in terms of a failure to carry out in practice what one knows to be right, to identify the 'I' in 7:7-25 as humankind in general fails to take full account of the specific emphasis Paul places upon the interaction of the 'I' with the Mosaic law.

The 'I' Denotes Paul's Experience as a Jewish Boy

When Paul says, 'once I was alive apart from law; but when the commandment came, sin sprang to life and I died' (7:9), he is referring, first, to his experience as a young Jewish boy when he did not have to obey the Torah, and then to his experience following his bar Mitzvah when he became a son of the commandment and was obliged to do so. It was then that 'the commandment came, sin sprang to life and I died'.[261] Gundry suggests that it was at puberty, which coincided with the apostle's taking upon himself the full obligation to obey the law, that he found the law's prohibition of sexual desire only further aroused such desires.[262]

While it is true that Jewish boys were not required to keep all the commandments of the law prior to their Bar Mitzvah (when they became sons of the commandment), they were encouraged to do so. They could not be described even then as being 'alive apart from the law'.

The 'I' Denotes Paul's Pre-Christian Experience

The apostle refers to his (adult) experience as a Jew prior to his conversion,[263] representing either how he felt then about his moral failures,[264] or how he feels about it in the light of his later Christian experience.[265]

261. Cf. Jewett, *Romans*, 451; Manson, *On Paul and John*, 40.

262. Robert H. Gundry, 'The Moral Frustration of Paul before His Conversion: Sexual Lust in Romans 7:7-25', in *Pauline Studies*, Festschrift for F. F. Bruce, ed. Donald A. Hagner and Murray J. Harris (Exeter: Paternoster, 1980), 232-33.

263. So, e.g., Brice L. Martin, 'Some Reflections on the Identity of *egō* in Rom. 7:14-25', *SJT* 34 (1981) 39-47.

264. So, e.g., D. J. W. Milne, 'Romans 7:7-12, Paul's Pre-conversion Experience', *RTR* 43 (1984) 12; Jan Lambrecht, *The Wretched "I" and Its Liberation: Paul in Romans 7 and 8* (Louvain Theological and Pastoral Monographs 14; Louvain: Peeters, 1992), 90-91. Many modern scholars reject this position out of hand in the light of Phil 3:6, where Paul describes his pre-conversion life in respect to righteousness under the law as 'faultless'. This, it is claimed, proves that Paul had a 'robust conscience' and felt no such sense of failure in his encounter with the law as that depicted in 7:7-25. However, this pushes the evidence of Phil 3:6 further than is warranted. In context, Paul is matching the boasting of those who have confidence in the flesh and boasting of outward things. He is speaking there of outward observance of the law rather than claiming to be exempt from the sort of experience depicted in 7:7-25.

265. So, e.g., Käsemann, *Romans*, 192.

Lambrecht says: 'The picture of Paul's pre-Christian situation appears to be more Jewish than many interpretations which accentuate a universal human application suggest. The certainly rhetorical quality of the "I" should not disguise the pre-eminently personal character of this Pauline chapter. Once sufficient attention is given to the inner dimensions of the cited commandment in Romans 7:7e ("you shall not covet"), the autobiographical understanding does not contradict, I think, Paul's utterances elsewhere about his faultless Jewish past. It may be true that in Romans 7 Paul is depicting himself as a wretched man in order to warn his fellow Christians not to fall back into the former unregenerate state'.[266] Jewett agrees with Lambrecht and suggests further that the use of the 'I' points to 'Paul the zealot prior to his conversion'.[267]

Of the autobiographical approaches to the identification of the 'I' this is probably the best. It overcomes the problems of the identification of the 'I' as the Paul the Christian, in particular the problem raised for that view by 6:14 (see the discussion of this latter view below). If the view that the 'I' denotes Paul's pre-Christian experience is combined with the view that the 'I' denotes Israel and her encounter with the law, it is more attractive.

The 'I' Denotes Paul's Pre-Christian and Post-Christian Experiences

In 7:7-12 the apostle refers to his life as prior to conversion (employing the aorist tense), and then in 7:13-25 (employing the present tense) he refers to his life as a Christian with its struggles with sin. Banks believes that the argument for the autobiographical interpretation along these lines is clinched by the presence of the additional reflexive pronoun 'I myself' in 7:25b. Parallel uses of this expression elsewhere in Paul's writings, he says, always refer to the apostle himself, being synonymous with the expression 'I Paul'.[268]

To identify the 'I' of 7:73 as the pre-Christian Paul and to combine it with its identification with Israel's encounter with the law is feasible. However, to interpret the 'I' of 7:14-26 as the Christian Paul runs into the same difficulties described below in relation to the view that identifies the 'I' of the whole passage, 7:7-25, as Paul the Christian.

The 'I' Denotes Paul's Experience as a Christian

Commenting on 7:14-25, Cranfield concludes: 'But again, as with regard to vv. 7-13, we may assume that Paul's use of the first person singular

---

266. Lambrecht, *The Wretched "I" and Its Liberation*, 90-91.
267. Jewett, *Romans*, 443-45.
268. Robert Banks, 'Romans 7.25a: An Eschatological Thanksgiving?', *ABR* 26 (1978) 41.

throughout vv. 14-25 reflects not only his desire to state in a forceful and vivid manner what is generally true — in this case, of Christians — but also his sense of his own deep personal involvement in what he is saying'.[269] Segal offers another interpretation of the 'I' denoting Paul's experience as a Christian. He suggests that 7:9 depicts Paul's personal experience after giving up his allegiance to the ceremonial Torah and then having to observe it in part again for pragmatic reasons (cf. 1 Cor 9:19-20). It was then that 'sin' again entered his actions, and he came under the condemnation of the law (cf. Gal 2:17). Segal concludes that Romans 7 'is the *apologia* of a reasonable man who formulated a radical solution to the problem of food laws in Christianity, but who, as an apostle, was willing to compromise when his solution was not accepted by the more conservative members of the Christian community.[270]

While this view has received significant support from influential commentators, it seems to run afoul of other telling statements Paul makes about the Christian's experience, in particular 6:14 ('For sin shall no longer be your master, because you are not under law, but under grace'); 6:18 ('You have been set free from sin and have become slaves to righteousness'); and 8:8-9 ('Those who are in the realm of the flesh cannot please God. You, however, are not in the realm of the flesh but are in the realm of the Spirit, if indeed the Spirit of God lives in you. And if anyone does not have the Spirit of Christ, they do not belong to Christ').

The 'I' Denotes Paul's Situation Intrinsically Considered

Seifrid draws attention to the parallels between Paul's statements about the 'I' and Jewish penitential confessions and suggests, in the light of these, that the 'I' refers, not to what Paul once was, but to what he still is 'intrinsically considered', that is, a fallen human being confronting the law apart from the resources now available through the saving work of Christ.[271] Seifrid argues that the confessing 'I' of the Jewish penitential prayers (in particular those found, e.g. in the Qumran *Hodayoth*) provide the best background for understanding 7:14-25. He says, 'such passages represent the penitent(s) from a limited perspective determined by group or personal guilt, while acknowledging that a broader framework exists, which is dependent upon divine mercies'.[272] Seifrid adds: 'Although he is a believer in Christ who has died to the Law (7:4), in 7:14-25 Paul portrays his present person as one in the flesh and under the Law in the same manner that other early Jewish confessions focus on the inherent capacities of the individual

269. Cranfield, *Romans*, I, 347.

270. Alan F. Segal, 'Romans 7 and Jewish Dietary Law', *SR* 15 (1986) 365, 371.

271. Mark A. Seifrid, *Justification by Faith: The Origin and Development of a Central Pauline Theme* (Leiden: Brill, 1992), 234-37.

272. Seifrid, 'The Subject of Rom 7:14-25', 322-23.

despite the awareness of a broader context. The fundamental distinction between the believing Paul and the "I" is not temporal, i.e., the "I" is not what Paul once was: it is what he still is, intrinsically considered'.[273]

This is an interesting suggestion; however, while the employment of 'the confessing 'I' of the Jewish penitential prayers' found in the Qumran *Hodayoth* is appropriate in the context of prayers addressed to God, it would be most unusual to employ this in the letter genre without explanation.

The 'I' Denotes the Experience of Israel as a Nation

Trudinger holds that in 7:7-25 Paul is not speaking of himself personally but 'as a representative Jew tracing his nation's history. The Hebrew nation was "once alive apart from the law", as Paul so clearly and specifically points out in Gal 3:17, where he states that the law came 430 years after the promise made to Abraham. Again he says in Rom 5:14, "Death reigned from Adam to Moses". Then came the law, which had the effect of highlighting the presence of sin, the universal experience of breaking the law'.[274]

Russell also argues that 'Paul is speaking as a representative of his people Israel's reception of the Law at Sinai (7:7-13) and as a representative of their struggle under its diagnostic and condemning function throughout their history (7:14-25)'.[275] Wright adopts a similar position: 'Paul appears to be speaking of Israel: of Israel under Torah; of Israel at the time when Torah arrived (7:7-12); of Israel continuing to live under Torah thereafter (7:13-25). But he is not thereby speaking of how Israel under Torah would itself analyze the problem. Though in a sense that is Paul's own story, as a Jew who had lived under Torah himself, it is not a transcript of "how it felt at the time". . . . The present passage seems, then, to be Christian theological analysis of what was in fact the case, and indeed what is still the case for those who live "under the law", not a description of how it felt or feels. It is a vivid, rhetorically sharpened way of saying something very similar to what Paul said in 2:17-9: those who embrace Torah find that Torah turns and condemns them. . . . The change of tense has to do, rather, with the change from the description of what happened when Torah first arrived in Israel, the time when Israel recapitulated the sin of Adam (5:20a; 7:9-11), to the description of the ongoing state of those who live under the law, who find themselves caught between the one exodus and the other, freed from Egypt and yet not freed from the "Egypt" of sin and death'.[276]

Byrne, adopting a similar position, says that 7:7-13 'described the en-

---

273. Seifrid, 'The Subject of Rom 7:14-25', 326.

274. Paul Trudinger, 'An Autobiographical Digression? A Note on Romans 7:7-25', *ExpTim* 107 (1996) 173.

275. Walt Russell, 'Insights from Postmodernism's Emphasis on Interpretive Communities in the Interpretation of Romans 7', *JETS* 37 (1994) 523.

276. Wright, 'Romans', 552-53.

counter with the law as a quasi-historical narrative about the past. It contrasted life before or apart from the law with what happened when the "commandment" arrived on the scene and sin sprang to life in full virulence, bringing death in its train. Now, changing to the present tense, the "I" describes "from the inside", as it were, the enduring consequences of that fatal encounter: the situation of "ethical impossibility" that results from having been "sold into slavery under sin" (v 14)'.[277]

This view, which is receiving increasingly wider support, has the advantage not only of recognizing that Paul is adopting the rhetorical device of speech-in-character *(prosopopoeia)*, something recognized by the early church fathers in connection with their exposition of Romans 7, but also of recognizing the fact that it is the encounter of the 'I' with the Mosaic law that is described in this passage. It has the added advantage of being able to take into account the Adamic allusions in the passage, seeing in Israel's encounter with the law a recapitulation of Adam's encounter with the commandment in Eden. Also, this view is able to account for the shift from the use of the aorist tense in 7:7-13 to the use of the present tense in 7:14-25 by explaining the former in terms of Israel's historical encounter with the law at Sinai and the latter in terms of Israel's ongoing experience of life under the law. This approach can also take into account the autobiographical overtones of the whole passage by recognizing that Paul himself could identify his own pre-Christian experience with that of Israel the nation of which he himself is a member.

The 'I' Denotes the Experience of the Religious Jew

Édart argues that Paul employs the rhetorical 'I' to 'show that Man under the Law remains a slave of sin, and so, that he cannot save himself. A Jew, wishing to fulfill the Law, discovers his basic incapacity to implement his wish.[278] This view may be combined with the view that the 'I' denotes Israel's encounter with the law. What is true of the nation is true of its individual members.

The 'I' Denotes the Jewish Believer in Christ

Jervis argues that the 'I' is the Jewish believer in Christ. 'Paul, as a representative Jewish believer, is speaking to other Jewish believers (7:1) who are on the way to a free identity'.[279] In respect to 7:8b-9 Jervis argues 'not only that

277. Byrne, *Romans*, 225.

278. Jean-Baptiste Édart, 'De la nécessité d'un sauveur: Rhétorique et théologie de Rm 7,7-25', *RB* 105 (1998) 359.

279. L. Anne Jervis, 'Reading Romans 7 in Conversation with Post-Colonial Theory: Paul's Struggle toward a Christian Identity of Hybridity', *Theoforum* 35 (2004) 181.

Paul is referring to believers' lives but also that in 7:9b he is referring to the commandment *(entolē)* not of the Torah, but of the Christian life',[280] adding: 'I propose, then, that the "commandment" that comes (7:9b), and that is focused on life (7:10), and that is holy, just, and good (7:12), and that is used by sin with the result that sin's character might be revealed (7:13) is not a commandment of Torah, but the commandment inherent to faith in Christ'.[281]

This interpretation of the 'I' is susceptible to the same objections as those to which the view that the 'I' denotes the experience of Paul the Christian is susceptible. It runs afoul of those texts in which Paul emphasizes that the believer has been set free from sin and is no longer controlled by the sinful nature (see the comment on *The 'I' Denotes Paul's Experience as a Christian;* above, 317).

Summary Evaluation

It will have become evident from a reading of the brief evaluative comments following the descriptions of the various views above, that the approach adopted in this commentary is that the 'I' denotes Israel's historical encounter with the law and her ongoing experience of life under the law. To this some aspects of the autobiographical view that the 'I' represents Paul's pre-Christian experience could be added because he could identify with the predicament of Israel since, prior to his conversion to Christ, he would have experienced what it was like to live under the law.

---

5. *Life in the Spirit, 8:1-13*

> [1]*Therefore, there is now no condemnation for those who are in Christ Jesus,* [2]*because through Christ Jesus the law of the Spirit who gives life has set you free from the law of sin and death.* [3]*For what the law was powerless to do because it was weakened by the flesh, God did by sending his own Son in the likeness of sinful flesh to be a sin offering. And so he condemned sin in the flesh,* [4]*in order that the righteous requirement of the law might be fully met in us, who do not live according to the flesh but according to the Spirit.*
>
> [5]*Those who live according to the flesh have their minds set on what the flesh desires; but those who live in accordance with the Spirit have their minds set on what the Spirit desires.* [6]*The mind governed by the flesh is death, but the mind governed by the Spirit is life and peace.* [7]*The mind governed by the flesh is hostile to God; it does not submit to God's law, nor can it do so.* [8]*Those who are in the realm of the flesh cannot please God.*

280. Jervis, 'Reading Romans 7', 183.
281. Jervis, 'Reading Romans 7', 186.

> [9]You, however, are not in the realm of the flesh but are in the realm of the Spirit, if indeed the Spirit of God lives in you. And if anyone does not have the Spirit of Christ, they do not belong to Christ. [10]But if Christ is in you, then even though your body is subject to death because of sin, the Spirit gives life because of righteousness. [11]And if the Spirit of him who raised Jesus from the dead is living in you, he who raised Christ from the dead will also give life to your mortal bodies because of his Spirit who lives in you.
>
> [12]Therefore, brothers and sisters, we have an obligation — but it is not to the flesh, to live according to it. [13]For if you live according to the flesh, you will die; but if by the Spirit you put to death the misdeeds of the body, you will live.

In 7:5 Paul spoke of life in the realm of the flesh, foreshadowing what he would expound in 7:7-25, where he insisted that the essential problem was not the law itself but sin. In 7:6 he spoke of life in the new way of the Spirit now made possible for believers because they have been released from the law. This foreshadows what the apostle expounds here in 8:1-13. It stands as a 'negative counterpart' to 7:7-25.[282] All of this Paul does in order to defend his gospel against accusations that it involves a denigration of God's law, while providing encouragement for his audience and incentives for them to live godly lives.[283]

In 7:7-25 Paul departed from the use of the first and second person plural employed in 6:1–7:6 and adopted the first person singular, the rhetorical 'I', to depict Israel's encounter with the law at Sinai and her ongoing experience of living under the law. In 8:1ff. he returns to the use of the first and second person plural to speak again of the experience of those who are 'in Christ Jesus'.

8:1   Paul begins his exposition of life in the Spirit with the statement: *Therefore, there is now no condemnation for those who are in Christ Jesus.*[284] In the immediate context 'therefore' refers back to the rescue of believers from their bondage to sin under the law (7:25a). This bondage to sin, Paul explained, was exacerbated by the law. Their rescue from sin's bondage also involved release from the law's jurisdiction (7:6), and as a result Paul can say, 'there is now no condemnation [by the law] for those who are in Christ Jesus'. The 'now' relates back to 7:6, foreshadowed by 5:9; 6:22, and refers

---

282. Cf. Byrne, *Romans*, 235.

283. Dillon, The Spirit as Taskmaster', 690, says: 'Romans 8 should be read . . . as a continuation of the dialogue between the apostle and his critics — or more accurately, between him and a community in which his critics were on one side of a polarizing dispute about him. . . . In Romans 8 Paul has to deliver the final *coup de grâce* to that hurtful accusation of 3:7-8 which has remained on his mind over the three chapters that have built up to this one as to a climax'.

284. This is the text of the early, more reliable manuscripts. Later manuscripts add, 'who do not walk according to the flesh' or 'who do not walk according to the flesh but according to the Spirit'. Both of these variants appear to have arisen by assimilation to the similar statement in 8:4.

to the new time in salvation history inaugurated by Christ's death and resurrection and the coming of the Spirit, the blessings of which time those 'who are in Christ Jesus' now enjoy.

'Condemnation' is a word the apostle employs only three times in his letters — here in 8:1 and in 5:16, 18. It denotes 'not merely a pronouncement of guilt . . . but an adjudication of punishment'; thus, it may be translated as 'judicial pronouncement upon a guilty person, *condemnation, punishment, penalty*'.[285] In 5:16, 18 Paul explains that condemnation for all people followed Adam's transgression, something he contrasts with justification for all those who believe because of Christ's obedience.[286] However, condemnation is not only the result of Adam's transgression but also of each person's own sins.[287] God's wrath, Paul warns, is 'being revealed from heaven against all the godlessness and wickedness of people, who suppress the truth by their wickedness' (1:18), and is stored up against those who are stubborn and unrepentant (2:5).

However, what the apostle emphasizes here in 8:1 is that this condemnation *now* no longer applies to those who are in Christ. To be 'in Christ' means to belong to Christ and to live in the realm where his power and lordship are experienced. Here, as 8:2-4 explains, being in Christ means being recipients of the redeeming and transforming grace of God made available to humanity through the saving work of his Son Jesus Christ.[288] What it means in practice for believers that there is no condemnation is spelled out in 8:28-39: God has adjudicated in our favor and no charge against us can stand; no one can condemn us (see the commentary on these verses below).

8:2 Here Paul provides a further reason why there is no condemnation for those in Christ Jesus: *because through Christ Jesus the law of the Spirit who gives life has set you*[289] *free from the law of sin and death*. It is evident that

285. BAGD, *ad loc.*

286. Cf. 5:16: 'Nor can the gift of God be compared with the result of one man's sin: The judgment followed one sin and brought condemnation, but the gift followed many trespasses and brought justification'; 5:18: 'Consequently, just as one trespass resulted in condemnation for all people, so also one righteous act resulted in justification and life for all people'.

287. In 3:20-23 the apostle concluded: 'Therefore no one will be declared righteous in God's sight by the works of the law; rather, through the law we become conscious of sin. . . . for all have sinned and fall short of the glory of God'.

288. Chuck Lowe, '"There Is No Condemnation" (Romans 8:1): But Why Not?' *JETS* 42 (1999) 231, 246, argues that here 'the basis is not the substitutionary death of Christ but the righteous life of believers made possible when the law of the Spirit of life frees them from the law of sin and death'. He concludes: 'Theologically, the absolute contrast between grace and works (common in populist evangelicalism) is an exaggeration of their opposition. Romans 6–8, no less than 8:1-2, indicate that good works are a precondition for — albeit not the meritorious cause of — eschatological salvation'.

289. Both the readings 'you' *(se)* and 'me' *(me)* are well supported in the manuscript evidence (but not the other alternative 'us' [*hēmas*]). 'You' *(se)* has the strongest support. The meaning of the text is not substantially altered by the adoption of either variant.

8:2, introduced with the word 'because', provides further explanation of the basis for the declaration in 8:1 that 'there is now no condemnation for those who are in Christ Jesus'. The further explanation is 'because through Christ Jesus the law of the Spirit who gives life has set you free from the law of sin and death'.

The two 'laws' here have been interpreted in two different ways. First, it is argued that 'law' should be construed consistently, as it has been claimed is the case in the preceding chapter, as the law of Moses. Dunn, for example, says: 'Paul is able to think of the law in two different ways: the law caught in the nexus of sin and death, where it is met only by *sarx* ['flesh'], is the law as *gramma* ['letter'], caught in the old epoch, abused and destructive . . . ; but the law rightly understood, and responded to *en pneumati ou grammati* ['by Spirit, not by letter'] is pleasing to God (2:29)'.[290] Second, 'law' is construed as a rule or principle.[291] Paul is saying that the principle of life in the Spirit sets people free from the principle of sin and death that would otherwise reign in their lives.[292] The first interpretation, that 'law' refers consistently to the Mosaic law, is problematic because it creates a contradiction: on the one hand, in 8:2 it liberates the believer from sin and death but, on the other hand, in 8:3 God had to send his Son to effect what it could not do. The second interpretation is to be preferred for two reasons: (i) It enables 8:1-2 to be read as a continuation of the argument brought to a climax in 7:22-25 in which the apostle laments the bondage humanity experiences because of the law of sin operating within them (something that prevents them from keeping the Mosaic law) (7:22-24), and where he foreshadows the deliverance from this bondage effected for them by Jesus Christ (7:25). (ii) It enables 8:1-2 to be read as an introduction to what follows in 8:3-17 where Paul explains, not the function of the Mosaic law, but the role of the Spirit in overcoming the sinful impulses operating in humanity (8:5-14).[293] Before explaining this, however, in 8:3-4 Paul

290. Dunn, *Romans 1-8*, 417. Cf. Wright, 'Romans', 577. Dillon, 'The Spirit as Taskmaster', 692, while not supporting this view, lists the following arguments adduced to support it: '(1) the Law was declared to be *pneumatikos* in 7:14, despite the fallen condition of its subjects; (2) in 8:4 the finality of Christ's mission is determined as the fulfillment of the just demand of the Law among his new Spirit people (the historic torah is surely meant here); (3) it is difficult, as Wilckens has said, to find comparable uses of the word *nomos* in the transferred sense of competing "norms" or "orders" which exegetes usually find in 7:23 (and 3:27)'.

291. So, e.g., Witherington, *Romans*, 211-12; Fitzmyer, *Romans*, 482-83; Byrne, *Romans*, 235-36; Moo, *Romans*, 474-76; Jewett, *Romans*, 481.

292. So, too, John A. Bertone, 'The Function of the Spirit in the Dialectic between God's Soteriological Plan Enacted but Not Yet Culminated: Romans 8.1-27', *JPT* 15 (1999) 79-80.

293. Dillon, 'The Spirit as Taskmaster', 692, asks: 'can we really understand the Torah as the subject of *ēleutherōsen* in 8:2 after the analogy of the freed wife has been applied in 7:4 to all who have "died to the Law through the body of Christ", and after "dying to that which held us captive" has been added in 7:6? Without some expedient like the distinction between the historic and the eschatological Torah, it hardly seems possible to avoid the

shows why it was necessary for 'the law of the Spirit who gives life' to set people free from 'the law of sin and death', that is, why this liberation could not be effected by the law of Moses.

8:3-4 While these verses comprise one long, complex sentence in the original language, the NIV translation that follows presents it as two separate sentences: *For what the law was powerless to do because it was weakened by the flesh, God did by sending his own Son in the likeness of sinful flesh to be a sin offering. And so he condemned sin in the flesh, in order that the righteous requirement of the law might be fully met in us, who do not live according to the flesh but according to the Spirit.* Several things here need clarification. First, as Jewett notes: 'The sentence in vv. 3-4 begins with "for", indicating that the Christological content sustains the claim in v. 2 concerning being set free from sin and death'.[294]

Second, what the law was powerless to do (8:3a) was to set people free from the power of sin and so bring about the fulfillment of its own demands, as 8:4 implies. Paul had already established the powerlessness of the law in this respect in 7:7-25 when he argued that, far from being the solution to the human dilemma, it had become the unwilling ally of sin, bringing people into deeper bondage. There was nothing wrong with the law's demands, the problem being, as Paul says, that 'it was weakened by the flesh'.[295] It was necessary for the problem of the flesh, that is, sinful human nature, to be dealt with before the requirements of the law could be fulfilled.

Third, what the law was unable to do, Paul says, 'God did by sending his *own* Son' (italics added), thus emphasizing the close relationship between God the Father and his Son Jesus Christ. The sending of his own Son also implies, as most,[296] but not all,[297] scholars recognize, the preincarnational existence of the Son (cf. 1:3; Phil 2:5; and Gal 4:4).

Fourth, Paul says that to achieve this, God sent his own Son 'in the likeness of sinful flesh'. On first reading it seems Paul intends to highlight Christ's identification with humanity in his incarnation while stopping short of saying that he shared their 'sinful' flesh. He was sent only 'in the

---

thought that within a single chapter in Romans Paul openly contradicted himself on the relationship of Law and Spirit'.

294. Jewett, *Romans*, 482.

295. J. F. Bayes, 'The Translation of Romans 8:3', *ExpTim* 111 (1999) 14-16, offers a different translation of 8:3: 'For this being the law's disability while it used to be weak in the sphere of the flesh, God sent His own Son . . . and condemned sin in the flesh'. This is based on seven grammatical points Bayes makes and enables him to argue that 'this disablement characterizes the law only in the sphere of the flesh. . . . Romans 8:3a implies that there is another sphere, that which Paul denominates "the Spirit", where the law is weak no longer, and that, for the Christian, the weakness of the law is a thing of the past. The believing life is not one in which the law has no place. In the power of the Spirit the law has become a mighty instrument for the sanctification of the believer'.

296. E.g., Fitzmyer, *Romans*, 484-85; Käsemann, *Romans*, 216.

297. Cf. Dunn, *Romans 1–8*, 420-21.

likeness of sinful flesh', not 'in sinful flesh'. However, the matter is more complicated. Elsewhere in Romans Paul does use the word 'likeness' to suggest similarity while recognizing distinctions. He speaks in 1:23 of humanity exchanging the glory of God for the 'likeness' of images made of mortal man and birds and animals and reptiles; in 5:14 of death reigning over those who did not sin after the 'likeness' of Adam's transgression; and in 6:14 of believers having been planted in the 'likeness' of Christ's death — a reference to baptism. However, in Philippians 2:7 he uses the word 'likeness' to denote Christ's real identification with humanity: 'he made himself nothing, by taking the very nature of a servant, being made in human likeness'. Therefore, Paul's usage of 'likeness' indicates that it may denote either similarity with certain distinctions, or real identity.

It is not surprising, then, that two main interpretations of Paul's expression, 'in the likeness of sinful flesh', have been put forward: (i) it denotes similarity while recognizing distinctions — Christ identified with humanity in his incarnation but did not share their sinful flesh;[298] (ii) it denotes real identification — Christ identified fully with humanity in his incarnation even to the extent of sharing their sinful flesh, but he did not succumb to the temptations of the flesh and was not guilty of sinful thoughts or acts.[299] It is clear that whichever interpretation is preferred, all agree that Christ remained personally sinless in that he never succumbed to temptation like other human beings. This is strongly attested elsewhere in the NT (John 8:46; Matt 27:4, 24; Luke 23:47; 2 Cor 5:21; Heb 4:15; 1 Pet 1:19; 2:22). What is hard to determine is whether Christ could have been 'tempted in every way, just as we are' (Heb 4:15), if he did not have to struggle with 'sinful flesh' as we do. However, even prior to the fall, Adam and Eve appear to have been tempted 'as we are'. Perhaps we should think of Christ (by virtue of his virgin birth and having been conceived by the Holy Spirit) being like the primeval couple in their original state, and so take 'in the likeness of sinful flesh' to imply that Christ identified with humanity in his incarnation but did not share their sinful flesh.

---

298. Käsemann, *Romans*, 217 says: 'the term *homoiōma* ['likeness'] denotes a limit (J. Schneider, *TDNT*, V, 195f.). Jesus came in the likeness of sinful flesh. He was passively exposed to sin, but in distinction from us he did not actively open himself to it'. Cf. Witherington, *Romans*, 213. Wright, 'Romans', 578, says: 'To debate whether Jesus' humanity was therefore "sinful humanity" or "sinless humanity", whether "fallen" or "unfallen" seems to me beside the point. What matters is that it was genuine humanity, not a sham (cf. Phil 2:7, where *en homoiōmati anthrōpōn* . . . does not mean "like a human being, but not actually one", but rather, "a true human being, bearing the true likeness"'.

299. So, e.g., Florence Morgan Gillman, 'Another Look at Romans 8:3: "In the Likeness of Sinful Flesh"', *CBQ* 49 (1987) 597-604; Cranfield, *Romans*, I, 381-82; Barrett, *Romans*, 156; Byrne, *Romans*, 236; Dunn, *Romans 1–8*, 421; Vincent P. Branick, 'The Sinful Flesh of the Son of God (Rom 8:3): A Key Image of Pauline Theology', *CBQ* 47 (1985) 250. Jewett, *Romans*, 484, offers an unusual interpretation: 'If "sinful flesh" is understood as the perverse quest for honor that poisons every human endeavor, it is clear that Christ entered fully and without reservation into that social arena with all its evil consequences, at the cost of his own life'.

Fifth, the NIV's 'to be a sin offering' translates an expression whose literal translation, 'for sin', is also susceptible to a number of interpretations. It could be construed, as it is in the NIV, to mean 'to be a sin offering';[300] or as in the NRSV, where it is rendered simply as 'to deal with sin'; or with the more general meaning 'in relation to sin'[301] that it has in John 8:46; 16:8, 9. In the light of Paul's statement in 3:25 that God presented Christ Jesus as 'a sacrifice of atonement' to effect redemption for sinners, it is preferable to interpret it here in 8:3 as 'a sin offering'.[302]

Sixth, by sending his Son in the likeness of sinful flesh and as a sin offering, Paul says, God 'condemned sin in the flesh' (lit. 'he condemned sin in the flesh'). This is an unusual expression, for normally the object of the verb 'to condemn' is a person and not, as in this case, 'sin'. It is also difficult to explain what it means to 'condemn sin in the flesh'. It is unlikely that sin 'in the flesh' designates the type of sin condemned, that is, human sin, because there is no other type of sin in view. Therefore, 'in the flesh' is better taken to designate the place where sin was condemned. And because the apostle has just said that God sent his Son 'in the likeness of sinful flesh and as a sin offering', it is best to think of sin being condemned in the 'flesh' of Jesus Christ, that is, when God presented his Son as a sin offering, the condemnation that humanity's sin deserved was absorbed by the incarnate Christ when he died on the cross (cf. 2 Cor 5:21; Col 2:14-15).[303]

An alternative view is that the condemning of sin in the flesh of Christ

---

300. The expression *peri hamartias* is used extensively to mean 'a sin offering' in the LXX (66 times), predominantly but not exclusively in Leviticus and Numbers, and it carries this meaning also in Heb 10:6, 8, 18; 14:11.

301. So, e.g., Cranfield, *Romans*, I, 382.

302. So, e.g., Dunn, *Romans, 1–8*, 422. M. Dwaine Greene, 'A Note on Romans 8:3', *BZ* 35 (1991) 105, deals with some of the objections to this view, namely (i) that such a reference to Christ's death as an atoning sacrifice at this point would be a rather abrupt insertion in the context; (ii) a reference to a sin offering dealing with actual sins is theologically out of place in a context where the apostle is speaking of sin as an evil power. In response Greene argues: (i) 'When Paul speaks of Jesus' death using sacrificial concepts, the references are invariably brief, and receive little if any elaboration (e.g., 1 Cor. 5:7; 10:16; 11:23-35; Rom. 5:8-11; 8:32). Even Paul's most detailed statement about Jesus' death as a sacrifice, Rom. 3:24-26, is not a thoroughly-developed argument about the sacrificial nature of Christ's death, but is instead a statement used to develop his notion of justification by faith. Actually, then, the relative abruptness of the phrase *kai peri hamartias* in Rom. 8:3 is generally consistent with Paul's manner of alluding to the sacrificial nature of Jesus death'. (ii) 'A wedge cannot be driven between the different aspects of Paul's view of sin, for the apostle himself holds them together; quite clearly in places such as Rom. 3:21-26 and 5:12-21. . . . To press the theological considerations further, one notices that if *kai peri hamartias* in 8:3 is a reference to the sin-offering, then there is present an obvious conjunction of sacrificial and cosmic notions: God sent his Son *as a sin-offering to condemn sin* in the flesh, i.e., Jesus is sent as a sin-offering to overcome the power of sin. This conjunction of ideas is hardly unusual for Paul. It can be seen, for example, in Gal. 1:3-4: "Grace to you and peace from God our Father and our Lord Jesus Christ, who *gave himself for our sins* in order that he might *deliver us from the present evil age,* according to the will of our God and Father"'.

303. So too Cranfield, *Romans*, I, 382-83; Witherington, *Romans*, 214.

means the breaking of sin's power over humanity. Wright contends that 'God's purpose in and through all this — in giving the Torah with this strange intention — was that sin might be drawn together, heaped up, not just in Israel in general, but upon Israel's true representative, the Messiah, in order that it might there be dealt with, be condemned, once and for all'.[304] But what exactly these fine words mean is difficult to comprehend — just how is sin drawn together and heaped up in Israel's Messiah there to be condemned? Byrne's somewhat similar interpretation is equally difficult to comprehend: '"Condemnation" . . . is a passing of judgment upon sin which, while not destroying it absolutely, has radically exposed it for what it is (7:13), reversed its deceptive power (7:11) and broken its *necessary* grip upon human life; for those "in Christ Jesus" sin no longer "reigns" (cf. 5:21)'.[305] In just what way this exposure, reversal, and breaking of sin's deceptive power was achieved when God condemned sin in the flesh is not explained. It is better, then, to think of sin being condemned in the 'flesh' of Jesus Christ when the condemnation that humanity's sin deserved was absorbed by the incarnate Christ when he died on the cross, as suggested above.

Seventh, God's purpose in doing this, Paul says, was 'in order that the righteous requirement of the law might be fully met in us, who do not live according to the flesh but according to the Spirit'. 'Righteous requirement' is singular in number. This is significant because the plural form is used frequently in the LXX (99 times) and usually denotes the sum of the law's demands, and Paul himself uses it in this way in 2:26. However, the singular form found here in 8:4 is not used in the LXX to mean the totality of the law's demands. Paul's choice of the singular form indicates that he is not saying that the sum total of the law's demands are fulfilled in believers who live according to the Spirit.[306] If this is the case, then it needs to be explained what he did mean by 'the righteous requirement [singular] of the law'.

One suggestion is that the 'righteous requirement' of the law here in 8:4 refers to the law as a unity expressing the fatherly will of God for his people.[307] Also, a good case can be made for interpreting this phrase in terms of the love commandment, especially in the light of the parallels between 8:4 and Galatians 5:13-16. It is precisely at these points in Romans and Galatians respectively that (i) the notion of the Spirit first comes to the

---

304. Wright, 'Romans', 578-79.

305. Byrne, *Romans*, 243.

306. J. A. Ziesler, 'The Just Requirement of the Law (Romans 8.4)', *ABR* 35 (1987) 79, taking note of the singular *dikaiōma*, suggests that when Paul speaks of the just requirement of the law in 8:4 he means the tenth commandment, which he claims the apostle had in mind throughout 7:7-25. Because, on this view, 8:4 refers only to the command not to covet, it cannot be taken to refer to the sum of the law's demands. While it is important to note Paul's use of the singular *dikaiōma* in 8:4, it is not at all certain that it should be interpreted as narrowly as Ziesler suggests. Even interpreting it in the light of the Paul's reference to the tenth commandment in 7:7-25, we need to remember that Paul used the tenth commandment there as a paradigm for the whole law, as Ziesler himself acknowledges.

307. Cf. Cranfield, *Romans*, I, 384-85; Jewett, *Romans*, 485.

fore, (ii) the Spirit/flesh antithesis is mentioned for the first time, and (iii) there is a striking convergence of the concepts of freedom, fulfillment, walking in the Spirit, and the negative aspects of the flesh.[308] In the light of these striking similarities between 8:4 and Galatians 5:13-16, it is desirable to interpret the former in the light of the latter, and to say that the fulfillment of the just requirement of the law (in the Romans text) is best understood in terms of the love of neighbor (in the Galatians text). This conclusion is strengthened by the fact that, in Romans 13:8-10, Paul says that all the other commandments are summed up in the commandment, 'Love your neighbor as yourself', and concludes: 'therefore, love is the fulfillment of the law'.[309] Clearly believers were not required to obey all the law's requirements. So, for example, Gentile believers were certainly not required to be circumcised in accordance with the law.[310]

Eighth, it is significant that 8:4 speaks about 'the just requirement of the law' *being fully met* (passive) in those who live according to the Spirit, not about believers *fulfilling* (active) this requirement. The fulfillment of the law's requirement in believers is therefore not achieved because they are continuously careful to observe its many stipulations. Rather, it is fulfilled in them as they live, not according to the flesh but according to the Spirit — something the apostle teases out in the flowing verses. The word translated 'live' in the clause, '[those] who do not *live* according to the flesh but according to the Spirit', is *peripateō*, whose literal meaning is 'to walk'. Paul uses it extensively as a metaphor for the way people should live and behave.[311] When the apostle says that the just requirement of the law is fulfilled 'in us'

308. Cf. Richard W. Thompson, 'How Is the Law Fulfilled in Us? An Interpretation of Rom 8:4', *LS* 11 (1986) 32-33, who cites the observations of H. W. M. van de Sandt, 'Research into Rom. 8:4a: The Legal Claim of the Law', *Bijdr* 37 (1976) 252-69.

309. This is the view of a majority of commentators. Cf., e.g., Byrne, *Romans,* 237; Moo, *Romans,* 482. *Contra* N. T. Wright, *The Climax of the Covenant: Christ and the Law in Pauline Theology* (Edinburgh: T&T Clark, 1991), 211-12, who rejects this view, arguing that *to dikaiōma tou nomou* means 'the just decree of the law', i.e., 'the decree that gives life in accordance with the covenant'.

310. An alternative interpretation of the just requirement of the law being fulfilled in us relates it, not to the law being fulfilled in believers as they walk according to the Spirit, but to the fulfillment of the law by Christ himself. He perfectly fulfilled the law, and by absorbing in himself the law's condemnation he made it possible for God to transfer his righteousness to us. There would then be an 'interchange'. Christ, as it were, became what we are so that we might become what he is. Cf. M. D. Hooker, 'Interchange in Christ', *JTS* n.s. 22 (1971) 349-361. Moo, *Romans,* 482-85. To support this view the reference to 'those who do not walk according to the flesh but according to the Spirit' has to be construed as descriptive of those to whom God transfers Christ's righteousness, rather than explaining how the righteous requirement of the law is fulfilled in them, i.e., when they walk according to the Spirit. The latter is preferable, especially in the light of the parallel in Gal 5:13-16 referred to above. Cf. Kevin W. McFadden, 'The Fulfillment of the Law's *Dikaiōma:* Another Look at Romans 8:1-4', *JETS* 52 (2009) 483-97, who provides cogent arguments against the view that Paul had in mind fulfillment of the law in believers by virtue of Christ's righteousness being transferred to them, and for the view that it is fulfilled in believers as they walk in the Spirit.

311. It is used in this way, and only in this way, thirty-two times in Paul's letters.

(or 'among us'), he is probably thinking of corporate as well as individual fulfillment. Trocmé thinks that it relates to members of a community gathered together,[312] and Jewett believes that the apostle has the house and tenement churches in mind.[313]

8:5 In this verse Paul provides a general description of two types of people: *[For] those who live according to the flesh have their minds set on what that nature desires; but those who live in accordance with the Spirit have their minds set on what the Spirit desires* (lit. 'for those who are according to [the] flesh set their minds on the things of the flesh; but those who [are] according to [the] Spirit [set their minds on] the things of the Spirit'). The NIV omits the conjunction 'for' that indicates that 8:5 provides a basis for the statement in 8:4 that the righteous requirement of the law is fulfilled in us who walk according to the Spirit. It is because believers *are* not 'according to the flesh' but 'according to the Spirit' that they are able to fulfill the righteous requirement of the law. What Paul says in 8:5, then, constitutes *descriptions* of two types of people, those who are 'according to the flesh' and those who are 'according to the Spirit'. His intention in 8:5 is to *describe*, not *exhort*.[314]

Galatians 5:16-25 provides the best explanation of what it means to have one's mind set on what the sinful nature desires and to have one's mind set on what the Spirit desires. A mind set on what the sinful nature desires gives place to 'sexual immorality, impurity and debauchery; idolatry and witchcraft; hatred, discord, jealousy, fits of rage, selfish ambition, dissensions, factions and envy; drunkenness, orgies, and the like' (Gal 5:19-21). A mind set on the things of the Spirit gives place to the fruit of the Spirit: 'love, joy, peace, forbearance, kindness, goodness, faithfulness, gentleness and self-control' (Gal 5:22-23).

8:6-8 Having described those of the flesh and those of the Spirit as those whose minds are set on the flesh and on the Spirit respectively, Paul spells out in 8:6 the final outcome in each case: *[For] the mind governed by the flesh is death, but the mind governed by the Spirit is life and peace* (lit. 'for the mind of [the] flesh [is] death, but the mind of the Spirit [is] life and peace'). In general terms Paul is saying that death is the ultimate outcome for those whose minds are of the flesh, whereas life and peace are the ultimate outcome for those whose minds are of the Spirit. The apostle has already indicated that the outcome of living according to the flesh is death (7:5; cf. 6:16, 21, 23), and he speaks repeatedly of peace as one of the blessings of those who submit to God (2:10; 5:1; 15:13).[315]

---

312. Etienne Trocmé, 'From "I" to "We": Christian Life according to Romans, Chapters 7 and 8', *ABR* 35 (1987) 74-75.

313. Jewett, *Romans*, 485-86.

314. Cf. Moo, *Romans*, 486; Jewett, *Romans*, 486; Byrne, *Romans*, 238.

315. Jewett, *Romans*, 487, comments: 'the addition of "peace" is rather puzzling, because it muddles the neat contrast between death and life required by the antithetical parallelism in this verse'. . . . He suggests, however, that 'it does serve to emphasize the social, relational quality of mind of the Spirit, erecting a barrier against individualistic, proto-

Paul explains why the outcome for those whose minds are of the flesh is death: [*Because*] *the mind governed by the flesh is hostile to God. It does not submit to God's law, nor can it do so* (lit. 'because the mind of the flesh [is] hostile to God, for it does not submit to God's law, and it is not able [to do so]'). By its very nature the mind of the flesh is hostile to God and therefore will not submit to his law. And because of this Paul adds, *those who are in the realm of the flesh cannot please God* (lit. 'but those who are in [the] flesh are not able to please God'). Several matters call for special comment. First, in 8:7 Paul describes the relationship of those whose minds are of the flesh as one of hostility towards God.[316] For Paul sin is not only something that has adverse effects on humanity itself, but it also constitutes enmity with God. For this reason, not only does human sin need expiation, but God's wrath needs propitiation as well.

Second, Paul's statement that 'the sinful mind is hostile to God, [for] it does not submit to God's law, nor can it do so', implies that the mind controlled by the Spirit does submit to God's law. However, this should not be interpreted to mean that believers, despite all that the apostle has said concerning believers being no longer under the law but under grace, must still obey all its demands. It is best understood in terms of the fulfillment of the 'righteous requirement of the law' of which the apostle spoke in 8:4. This is in turn best understood as fulfillment of the love commandment that sums up the whole thrust of the law, but such fulfillment does not mean obedience to all of its demands (see the commentary on 8:3-4).

Third, Paul concludes his general statement in these verses by saying: 'Those who are in the realm of the flesh cannot please God'. Already, in 7:5, describing life outside Christ, Paul said: 'For when we were in the realm of the flesh, the sinful passions aroused by the law were at work in us, so that we bore fruit for death'. To be 'in the realm of the flesh' means to be controlled by sinful passions.[317]

Gnostic understandings of life in the Spirit. Even more significant is the bearing of this detail on the congregation, which stands in need of peace (Rom 14:17, 19; 15:13)'.

316. Elsewhere Paul uses *echthros* ('hostile', substantive: 'enemy') to make a similar statement in 5:10: 'For if, while we were God's enemies *(echthroi)*, we were reconciled to him through the death of his Son, how much more, having been reconciled, shall we be saved through his life!'; 11:28: 'As far as the gospel is concerned, they are enemies *(echthroi)* for your sake; but as far as election is concerned, they are loved on account of the patriarchs'; Phil 3:18: 'For, as I have often told you before and now tell you again even with tears, many live as enemies *(echthrous)* of the cross of Christ'; and Col 1:21: 'Once you were alienated from God and were enemies *(echthrous)* in your minds because of your evil behavior'. In Jas 4:4 the word *echthra* ('enmity') and its cognate, *echthros* ('hostile', substantive: 'enemy'), are used of those who choose friendship with the world and become enemies of God: 'You adulterous people, don't you know that friendship with the world means enmity *(echthra)* against God? Therefore, anyone who chooses to be a friend of the world becomes an enemy *(echthros)* of God'.

317. Paul uses the expression *en sarki* in a number of ways: (i) to mean outward and physical as contrasted with what is inward and spiritual (2:28-29; Phil 3:3-4); (ii) to mean in a worldly fashion (2 Cor 10:3; Gal 6:12); (iii) to denote life in the body (Gal 2:20; Phil 1:22;

In this commentary 8:5-8 has been treated as a general description of two types of people. On the one hand there are unbelievers — walking according to the flesh that leads to death. On the other hand there are believers — walking according to the Spirit that leads to life and peace.[318]

8:9 Turning from his general third person statements in 8:6-8, the apostle now begins to address his audience directly: *You, however, are not in the realm of the flesh but are in the realm of the Spirit, if indeed the Spirit of God lives in you.* Paul is assuring his audience that they are not included among those who are in the flesh; they are not like those described in 7:5: 'For when we were in the realm of the flesh, the sinful passions aroused by the law were at work in us'. On the contrary, they are in the Spirit, and in this respect they are like those described in 7:6: 'we have been released from the law so that we serve in the new way of the Spirit, and not in the old way of the written code'. To make it abundantly clear that this is the true state of believers, the apostle makes another general statement: *And if anyone does not have the Spirit of Christ, they do not belong to Christ.* In Galatians 4:6 Paul wrote: 'Because you are his sons, God sent the Spirit of his Son into our hearts, the Spirit who calls out, "*Abba*, Father"', and here in 8:9 he makes the possession of 'the Spirit of Christ'[319] the *sine qua non* of Christian existence. Paul's overall purpose in 8:9 is positive, to assure his audience that because they are in the Spirit they do belong to Christ, though it is implied that those who do not have the Spirit do not belong to him, even though this is not what the apostle is emphasizing here.[320]

---

1 Tim 3:16); (iv) to mean 'by nature' (Eph 2:11); (v) to denote personal acquaintance (Col 2:1); (vi) to mean as a human being (Phlm 16); and (vii), as here in 8:8-9, to mean under the control of sinful passions.

318. Jan Lambrecht, 'The Implied Exhortation in Romans 8,5-8', *Greg* 81 (2000) 449-50, argues that 8:5-8 is not only descriptive but includes an implied caution to believers. In support of this view, among other things, he draws attention to the similarities between 8:4-8 and Galatians 5:16-18. He concludes: 'In Romans 8 Paul most probably thinks of the behavioral life of his addressees. His language is not just the description of the two contrasting ages. In a hidden way his admittedly positional language in 8,1-11 is intensively paraenetic. He has in mind the concrete and endangered existence of the community as well as that of the individual believer'.

319. It is worth noting that in 8:1-17 the Spirit is variously called 'the Spirit of life' (8:2), simply 'the Spirit' (8:4, 5, 6, 9, 13, 16), 'the Spirit of God' (8:9, 14), 'the Spirit of Christ' (8:9), 'the Spirit of him who raised Jesus from the dead' (8:10), and 'the Spirit of adoption' (8:15).

320. Cf. Cranfield, *Romans*, I, 388; Moo, *Romans*, 490. Dunn, *Romans 1–8*, 429-30, points out that 'Paul's definition of "Christian" . . . is not a verbal profession or ritual act (from which possession of the Spirit may be deduced, even if not evident . . .) . . . but evidence of the Spirit active in a life as the Spirit of Christ. . . . That evidence could include a variety of manifestations (e.g., love — 5:5; joy — 1 Thess 1:5; charisms — 1 Cor 1:4-7, Gal 3:3, 5; moral transformation — 1 Cor 6:9-11; illumination — 2 Cor 3:14-17), as well as a particular, verbal profession (1 Cor 12:3; Rom 10:9-10) and the baptismal act (Rom 6:4)'. Jewett, *Romans*, 489-91, suggests that Paul's use of the second person plural when giving assurance to his audience ('you are . . . in [the] Spirit, since the Spirit of God dwells in you') indicates that the experience of the Spirit that is evidence of his audience's belonging to Christ

8:10 Following the last general statement (8:9b), Paul addresses his audience directly once more: *But if Christ is in you, then even though your body is subject to death because of sin, the Spirit gives life because of righteousness.* What Paul has to say here is conditional: 'But if Christ is in you'. . . . In the case of his audience he is sure this condition is fulfilled, for in the previous verse he makes clear that they 'have the Spirit of Christ'. In the statement, 'your body is subject to death because of sin, the Spirit gives life because of righteousness', the first clause is best understood as concessive: '[though] your body is dead because of sin', so that the main point is expressed in the second clause: 'The Spirit gives life because of righteousness'.

Paul's statement, 'the Spirit gives life because of righteousness', is rendered differently as 'the spirit is alive because of righteousness' in some translations (e.g., NASB). This means that a number of decisions need to be made: (i) Should 'spirit' here be understood as the human spirit, or as the Spirit of God? (ii) Are those translations that speak of the spirit being 'alive' justified? (iii) What does Paul mean by saying the spirit/Spirit is alive/life 'because of righteousness'?

The decision concerning whether (human) spirit or (the Holy) Spirit is intended in the statement 'the spirit/Spirit is alive/life' depends in turn upon whether or not it is justified to render the noun 'life' that the apostle employs here as 'alive', and so this matter needs to be addressed first. The noun 'life' occurs thirty-seven times in Paul's letters, and on every occasion the NIV translates it as 'life'.[321] Elsewhere when the apostle wants to speak of people being 'alive', he does not use the noun 'life' but one form or another of either the verb 'to be alive' or the verb 'to make alive'.[322] It is preferable, therefore, to stay with the literal translation, 'the Spirit is life', in 8:10 (as does the NRSV) or as 'the Spirit gives life' (as here in the NIV).

If this translation is adopted, 'the Spirit gives life because of righteousness' must be understood as a statement about the Holy Spirit. This is also supported by the fact that in a couple of places earlier in this chapter the apostle connects the Holy Spirit with the concept of life. He says that 'the law of the Spirit of life set you free from the law of sin and death' (8:2), and reminds his audience that 'the mind governed by the Spirit is life and

---

is corporate. On the other hand, his use of the third person singular ('if anyone does not have the Spirit of Christ . . .') suggests that he is thinking individualistically when implying that one who does not have the Spirit does not belong to Christ. While Paul does elsewhere speak of the experience of the Spirit in corporate terms, it is doubtful that he does so here, because in the very next verse, still using the second person plural, he is plainly thinking in individualistic terms ('if Christ is in you, your body is dead because of sin, yet your spirit is alive because of righteousness').

321. 2:7; 5:10, 17, 18, 21; 6:4, 22, 23; 7:10; 8:2, 6, 10, 38; 11:15; 1 Cor 3:22; 15:19; 2 Cor 2:16; 4:10, 11, 12; 5:4; Gal 6:8; Eph 4:18; Phil 1:20; 2:16; 4:3; Col 3:3, 4; 1 Tim 1:16; 4:8; 6:12, 19; 2 Tim 1:1, 10; Tit 1:2; 3:7.

322. 6:11; 7:2, 3, 9; 8:10; 1 Cor 15:22; 2 Cor 4:11; Eph 2:5; Col 2:13; 1 Thess 4:15, 17.

peace' (8:6). So it is not strange that Paul should say here that 'the Spirit gives life'. By this he appears to mean that the Spirit is the source of life. His point in 8:10, then, would be that while humanity is subject to physical death because of sin, the Spirit gives them life because of righteousness.

If the interpretations offered for 'Spirit' and 'life' above are accepted, it remains to seek an understanding of what the apostle means by saying that 'the Spirit gives life *because of righteousness*'. There is only one other place in Paul's letters where he joins the Spirit with the concept of righteousness (14:17: 'For the kingdom of God is not a matter of eating and drinking, but of righteousness, peace and joy in the Holy Spirit'), but this throws little light on the matter. One way to understand the statement 'the Spirit gives life *because of righteousness*' is in terms of the righteousness of God revealed in the gospel (1:17). Because of the saving righteousness of God revealed in the gospel believers will become the recipients of resurrection life effected by the Spirit.[323]

8:11 In 8:9 Paul insisted that possession of the Spirit is the *sine qua non* of Christian existence, and he employs this fact in the protasis of the conditional sentence here in 8:11: *And if the Spirit of him who raised Jesus from the dead is living in you, he who raised Christ from the dead will also give life to your mortal bodies because of his Spirit who lives in you.* Paul speaks frequently of God as the one who raised Christ from the dead (4:24; 6:4; 8:11; 10:9; 1 Cor 6:14; 15:15; 2 Cor 4:14; Gal 1:1; Eph 1:20; Col 2:12; 1 Thess 1:10), but only here is the Spirit referred to as the one who raised him from the dead. Paul's assurance to his audience is that the Spirit who lives in them and who raised Christ himself from the dead will do the same for them — he will give life to their mortal bodies also (a reference to believers' resurrection on the last day).[324]

8:12-13 Addressing his audience now as those in whom the Spirit lives, Paul continues: *Therefore, brothers and sisters, we have an obligation — but it is not to the flesh, to live according to it.* Seeing that the law of the Spirit of life has set us free from the law of sin and death, Paul says, we are no longer, like slaves subject to their masters, required to live according to the flesh. The apostle then explains that there are two ways of living: *For if you live according to the flesh, you will die; but if by the Spirit you put to death the misdeeds of the body, you will live.* These words are reminiscent of Deuteron-

---

323. It is noteworthy that 8:9 variously refers to the Holy Spirit as 'the Spirit', 'the Spirit of God', and 'the Spirit of Christ', and 8:10 implies that the indwelling of the Spirit (of God) is the same as the indwelling of Christ.

324. Moo, *Romans*, 493, says: 'Since the reference to resurrection is so plain in the first part of the sentence, "will make alive" must also refer to future bodily transformation — through resurrection for dead believers — rather than, for instance, to spiritual vivification in justification, or to the "mortification" of sin in the Christian life'. Jewett, *Romans*, 492, adopts a both-and approach: 'The verb *zōopoieō* ['to make alive'], which appeared earlier in 4:17, alludes in other Pauline letters to enlivening activity with regard *both* to restoring the dead *and* to enhancing the quality of life for those currently in Christ' (italics added).

omy 30:15, 19: 'See, I set before you today life and prosperity, death and destruction. . . . This day I call the heavens and the earth as witnesses against you that I have set before you life and death, blessings and curses. Now choose life, so that you and your children may live'. In Deuteronomy, however, the alternatives are blessing and life in the promised land or destruction, which means that they will enjoy no more that life in the promised land. However, the alternatives of 'life' and 'death' that Paul has in mind are eschatological, expressed by the use of the future tenses ('will die' and 'will live'). The alternatives are eternal life in the presence of God or death without any prospect of a life with God.

Unusually in 8:13, when explaining the way to life, Paul says that it involves putting to death the misdeeds of the *body* rather than the misdeeds of the *flesh*. For Paul, the 'body' when conceived of as the locus of sin's power is virtually synonymous with the 'flesh'. In a couple of other places Paul juxtaposes the flesh and the body:

> In him you were also circumcised with a circumcision not performed by human hands. Your whole self ruled by the flesh [lit. 'the body of flesh'] was put off when you were circumcised by Christ. (Col 2:11)

> Such regulations indeed have an appearance of wisdom, with their self-imposed worship, their false humility and their harsh treatment of the body, but they lack any value in restraining sensual indulgence [lit. 'the indulgence of the flesh']. (Col 2:23)

In 8:13 Paul expresses the different ways of living in two conditional sentences: (i) 'For if you live according to the flesh, you will die'; (ii) 'but if by the Spirit you put to death the misdeeds of the body, you will live'.[325] What the apostle affirms in the first conditional clause he foreshadowed in 7:5: 'For when we were in the realm of the flesh, the sinful passions aroused by the law were at work in us'. Similarly, what he affirms in the second conditional clause he foreshadowed in 7:6: 'But now, by dying to what once bound us, we have been released from the law so that we serve in the new way of the Spirit'. As those who have been made alive by the saving righteousness of God, Paul's audience belongs to the latter group. What they are by grace must be expressed now in the way they live, and must be expressed in their corporate as well as individual lives.[326]

Similar teaching to that in 8:12-13 is found in Galatians 6:8: 'Whoever sows to please their flesh, from the flesh will reap destruction; the one who sows to please the Spirit, from the Spirit will reap eternal life'. In Colossians 3:3, 5 the apostle puts it this way: 'For you died, and your life is now hidden with Christ in God. . . . Put to death, therefore, whatever belongs to

---

325. Dunn, *Romans 1–8*, 448-49, points out that here 'death' is eschatological death and 'life is eschatological life beyond physical death'.

326. Cf. Jewett, *Romans,* 494-95.

your earthly nature: sexual immorality, impurity, lust, evil desires and greed, which is idolatry'.

Unfortunately, Paul does not spell out *how* people are to put to death the misdeeds of the body (8:13) and serve in the new way of the Spirit (7:6), or *how* they may crucify the flesh (Gal 5:24) and sow to please the Spirit (Gal 6:8). Perhaps we could say that it involves calling upon God to produce the fruit of his Spirit in us when we are faced with temptations of the flesh, so that we may live in ways pleasing to God.

6. The Spirit of Adoption, 8:14-17

> [14]*For those who are led by the Spirit of God are the children of God.* [15]*The Spirit you received does not make you slaves, so that you live in fear again; rather, the Spirit you received brought about your adoption to sonship. And by him we cry, 'Abba, Father'.* [16]*The Spirit himself testifies with our spirit that we are God's children.* [17]*Now if we are children, then we are heirs — heirs of God and co-heirs with Christ, if indeed we share in his sufferings in order that we may also share in his glory.*

In this brief section Paul focuses upon the privilege believers enjoy being children of God. They enjoy an intimacy with God that is facilitated by the Spirit's witness, and they have become heirs of God, joint heirs with Christ.

8:14 The apostle further explains why believers are able to be free from bondage to the flesh and free to live by the Spirit by adding: *For those who are led by the Spirit of God are the children of God.* Earlier Paul said that the *sine qua non* of the Christian life was possession of the Spirit and assured his audience that they were of the Spirit and not of the flesh (8:9). Here in 8:14 believers are described as children of God who are 'led' by the Spirit. There may be an allusion here to the many Jewish scriptures that speak of Israel being led by God out of slavery in Egypt and through the wilderness.[327]

Being led by the Spirit of God here is juxtaposed with a reminder in the previous verse (8:13) of the need to put to death the misdeeds of the body by the Spirit. This suggests that the sort of 'leading' the apostle has in mind involves the call and empowering to live a godly life. The only other place where Paul speaks about the leading of the Spirit is in Galatians 5:18 ('if you are led by the Spirit, you are not under law'), a statement that is part of an extended exhortation (5:13-23) to live by the Spirit and not gratify the desires of the flesh. In this context also the leading of the Spirit is re-

---

327. Exod 6:6; 13:3, 14, 21-22; 14:19, 24; 15:13; 20:2; 40:28; Num 9:15-23; 10:34; 14:14; Deut 1:33; 6:12; 7:8; 8:14; 13:5, 10; 32:12; Judg 6:8; 1 Kgs 9:9; Neh 9:12; Pss 78:14; 104:42-43; 105:39; Isa 63:14; Jer 34:13; 38:8-9; Mic 6:4; Tob 13:4-5; Bar 5:6). Cf. Sylvia C. Keesmaat, 'Exodus and the Intertextual Transformation of Tradition in Romans 8.14-30', *JSNT* 54 (1994) 37-43, 49.

lated to the call and empowerment not to gratify the sinful desires of the flesh.[328] The leading of the Spirit in both contexts then is moral, not vocational. It is significant that Paul describes believers as those who are 'led' (passive) by the Spirit, indicating that even their moral transformation is fundamentally the Spirit's work, though, as Paul has already shown, believers have a part to play — by the Spirit they are to put to death the deeds of the body (8:13).

Paul designates believers as 'children of God' (lit. 'sons of God'), a term that in the OT is applied to various figures: Israel's king (2 Sam 7:14; Ps 2:7); Israel the nation (Exod 4:22-23; Jer 31:9); and angels (Gen 6:2; Job 1:6; 38:7; Dan 3:25). Paul uses the word 'son' to designate both Jesus Christ as the unique Son of God and believers as 'sons' of God, something avoided in John's Gospel and Letters. There the word 'son' is reserved for Jesus Christ, and believers are described as 'children' of God. Paul emphasizes two privileges experienced by believers because they are sons of God: (i) 'Because you are his sons, God sent the Spirit of his Son into our hearts, the Spirit who calls out, "*Abba*, Father"' (Gal 4:6), and (ii) they are 'led by the Spirit of God' 8:14).[329]

8:15 In this verse Paul continues to speak about the role of the Spirit in the lives of believers, but in this case he speaks, not of the Spirit empowering believers to resist the sinful desires of the flesh, but rather of the Spirit creating in believers a sense of intimacy with God. He begins: *The Spirit you received does not make you slaves, so that you live in fear again* (lit. 'for you did not receive a spirit of slavery again [leading] to fear'). There is a healthy 'fear of God' that the apostle speaks of elsewhere (3:8; 2 Cor 5:11; 7:1; Eph 5:21; Phil 2:12), but this is quite different from the fear he speaks of here — the fear slaves might have of harsh masters.[330]

The Spirit does not produce that sort of fear. Paul says, *rather, the Spirit you received brought about your adoption to sonship* (lit. 'you received [the] Spirit of adoption'). The word translated 'adoption' does not occur in the LXX, and the practice of adoption, though common in the Greco-Roman world (where it involved conferring upon the adopted child all the rights and privileges of a natural child), was rare among the Jewish people.[331] However, the concept of Israel becoming God's son is found often in

---

328. So also Trevor J. Burke, 'Adoption and the Spirit in Romans 8', *EvQ* 70 (1998) 319.

329. Jewett, *Romans*, 496-97, says that the designation of believers as 'sons of God' (*huioi to theou*) would have a twofold resonance for Paul's audience. On the one hand, it would recall the designation of heroes and rulers in the Roman world as 'sons of God', and on the other, for those who were familiar with the OT, it would recall Israel's designation as God's son (cf. Exod 4:22; Hos 2:1; 11:1).

330. Fitzmyer, *Romans*, 500, comments: 'because of faith baptized Christians have been taken into the family of God, have come under the *patria potestas*, "paternal authority", of God himself, and have a legitimate status in that family, not simply that of slaves (who belonged, indeed, to the ancient *familia*), but as sons'.

331. Cf. Byrne, *Romans*, 249-50.

the OT. The exodus from Egypt seems to have been regarded as the adoption of Israel by God as his son (Hos 11:1). In 9:4 Paul speaks of Israel's 'adoption' by God as one of a number of advantages enjoyed by the Jewish people. All these things form the background to Paul's statement to his Roman audience here in 8:15 that 'the Spirit brought about your adoption'.[332] In 8:23 he speaks again of believers' adoption when he equates it with the 'redemption' of their bodies, something they look forward to experiencing (at the *parousia*). It is clear from the context that the expressions 'spirit of fear' and 'Spirit of adoption' do not both denote human attitudes. The former does, but the latter certainly does not since in the very next verse Paul says, 'The Spirit himself testifies with our spirit that we are God's children' (cf. Gal 4:6). Believers relate to God, not as slaves afraid of harsh masters, but as those graciously adopted into his family.[333]

The Spirit whom believers received when they gave their allegiance to Christ creates within them a sense of intimacy with God, and this leads Paul to add, *And by him we cry, 'Abba, Father'.* The apostle makes a similar point in Galatians 4:6: 'Because you are his sons, God sent the Spirit of his Son into our hearts, the Spirit who calls out, "*Abba*, Father"'.[334] As is well known, *Abba* was the term of address Jesus himself used when praying to his Father (cf. Mark 14:36). Some commentators suggest that when Paul speaks about believers crying, 'Abba, Father', by the Spirit, he has in mind the work of the Spirit in the context of prayer or proclamation within congregational worship.[335] If this is the case, it is not to the exclusion of the work of the Spirit in the individual.

332. Burke, 'Adoption and the Spirit', 315, notes that 'in the intertestamental period the twin aspects of the Spirit and adoption are brought together in the promise "He will pour down upon us the spirit of grace. And you shall be his true children by adoption. And you shall walk in his commandments first and last" (T. Judah 24:3-4)'. Burke suggests that Paul understood these things, and it is reflected in his use of the expression *pneuma huiothesias* ('spirit of adoption'). For Paul, however, what was only an eschatological hope for the Jews is fulfilled already, in part at least, for believers, even though its consummation still lies in the future.

333. Trevor Burke, 'Pauline Adoption: A Sociological Approach', *EvQ* 73 (2001) 119-34, describes the socio-legal practice of adoption in the Roman world; 'From a social perspective, adoption primarily and fundamentally constituted, on the one hand, a break with the old family ties and, on the other, a commitment to a new one with all its attending privileges and responsibilities. In short, it involved a whole new way of life' (124). He writes: 'For these early Christians, and the Pauline communities in particular, their adoption/conversion was perceived as belonging to the divine family where a new loyalty had replaced all others, one in which "*God* acts as a proper, well-to-do *paterfamilias*"' (125). 'Paul's *huiothesia* ['adoption'] term also underscores the sense of community and, as such, has a corporate dimension — "the adopted child is not an only child" — where *relatedness* itself is valued' (130-31). Burke asserts: 'In sociological terms, if the conversion is going to continue it will do so in an environment and atmosphere which *resembles* that of "a family-like fellowship"' (129). 'This is a family in which God functions as the "Divine Parent"' (130).

334. These are the only places where Paul uses the Aramaic expression, *Abba*. In both cases he immediately provides a translation ('Father') for his audience.

335. Cf. Fitzmyer, *Romans*, 501; Käsemann, *Romans*, 228. E. A. Obeng, 'Abba, Father:

8:16 The apostle further explains what it means to receive the Spirit of adoption when he says: *The Spirit himself testifies with our spirit that we are God's children.* The verb translated 'testifies' is found only three times in the NT, and in every case in Romans (in 2:15, 8:16, and 9:1). While it might be argued etymologically that this verb *(symmartyreō)* means 'to bear witness with, or alongside of',[336] the way Paul uses it elsewhere suggests that it should be construed more generally to mean simply 'to confirm' or 'bear witness', as the following quotations (where the relevant verbs are in italics) show: In 2:15 Paul writes, 'They [Gentiles] show that the requirements of the law are written on their hearts, their consciences also *bearing witness,* and their thoughts sometimes accusing them, and at other times even defending them'. Here the consciences of the Gentiles bear witness, confirming the 'the effects of the law' in their hearts. In 9:1 Paul says, 'I speak the truth in Christ — I am not lying, my conscience *confirms* it through the Holy Spirit'. In this case Paul's conscience confirms to him that he is speaking the truth in Christ. Here in 8:16 where Paul says, 'the Spirit himself *testifies* with/to our spirit that we are God's children', he is affirming that the Holy Spirit bears witness to the spirit of believers, confirming that they are children of God.[337] This is better than saying that the Spirit bears witness alongside [the witness of] our own spirits that we are children of God. It is 'by the Spirit' that we cry *'Abba,* Father' — we are reliant upon the Spirit alone for confirmation that we are children of God.[338]

The Prayer of the Sons of God', *ExpTim* 99 (1988) 364-65, argues that, despite its brief form, *'Abba,* Father' is a prayer, something he believes is confirmed by the use of the verb 'to cry' *(krazein)* in relation to it. *Krazein* is used in the LXX predominantly in situations where people cry out to God for help in dire circumstances (Gen 18:20; Exod 2:23; 3:7; 22:23; 1 Sam 5:12; Job 34:28; Ps 34:15). In the NT the verb is used when describing people crying out to Jesus to help them or their relatives who are sick (Matt 9:27; 20:31; 15:22-23; Mark 9:23-24). *Krazein* is also used of Jesus' final utterance, possibly a prayer, on the cross (Matt 27:50). While 'Abba, Father' is a prayer, it is not, as some have suggested, an ecstatic utterance, an instance of glossolalia because clearly it is understandable, and generally glossolalia is not.

336. Obeng, 'Abba, Father', 365, contends that, while the verb *symmartyreō* can mean either 'bear witness alongside of' or 'bear witness to', in 8:16 it is best understood to mean 'bear witness alongside of'. He offers three pieces of evidence in support of this view: (i) Paul was aware of the need for multiple witnesses (cf. 2 Cor 13:1; 1 Tim 5:19), so the notion of the Spirit bearing witness alongside of our spirit would not be alien to Paul. (ii) The apostle speaks of the Spirit praying in us and we praying in the Spirit, indicating that the apostle believed the Spirit worked with our spirit. (iii) In the power of the Spirit Christians declare their sonship to the world, in which case it is the world that is the recipient of the 'Abba, Father' cry, not our spirit. However, Paul's own use of the word, as described above, militates against this view.

337. Cf. BAGD, *ad loc.*

338. Burke, 'Adoption and the Spirit in Romans 8', 320, notes: ' "Abba, Father" could either be linked with the preceding clause, giving the sense "we have received the Spirit of adoption enabling us to cry 'Abba, Father' ", or it could be attached to the next phrase, giving the meaning "When we cry 'Abba, Father', it is the Spirit bearing witness with our spirit that we are the children of God". Probably the second is to be preferred since Paul's thinking has progressed from the Christian's relationship and attitude to God (i.e., no longer

8:17 To be children of God, Paul explains, brings additional blessings: *Now if we are children, then we are heirs — heirs of God and co-heirs with Christ.*[339] It is perhaps significant that here, where the apostle speaks about believers being heirs of God, he no longer refers to them as 'sons' as he has done (in the original language) heretofore, but as 'children'. Watson claims that this is due to the fact that the apostle was conscious that he was writing to a Christian community he did not know, and one that resided in Rome. According to Roman legal practice, daughters as well as sons could be designated as heirs of their father's estate, hence his reference to 'children' and not 'sons'.[340]

To be adopted as God's children means to become God's heirs. To be 'heirs of God' means to be those to whom God will give an inheritance. To be 'co-heirs with Christ' means to be those who share the inheritance God gives to Christ. The inheritance was first promised to Abraham and his seed (Gal 3:16, 18). Those who belong to Christ are now Abraham's seed (cf. Gal 3:29) because Christ himself is the true and ultimate seed of Abraham (Gal 3:16). The inheritance promised to Abraham, Paul says, consists of 'the world' (4:13). When the apostle speaks specifically of the inheritance promised to believers and forfeited by the ungodly, it consists of 'the kingdom of God' (1 Cor 6:9-10; 15:50; Gal 5:21; Eph 5:5; cf. Jas 2:5) and 'eternal life' (Tit 3:7; cf. 1 Pet 3:7).[341]

Those who are to be co-heirs with Christ in the future must identify with him in a hostile world now. Hence Paul goes on to say, *if indeed we share in his sufferings in order that we may also share in his glory* (lit. 'if we suffer together in order that we may also be glorified together'). For the apos-

---

slaves but sons) to the expression of that filial relationship through the witness of the Spirit. The Spirit brings home to the Christian the awareness of his new filial disposition'.

339. In Gal 4:7 Paul makes a similar point: 'So you are no longer a slave, but God's child; and since you are his child, God has made you also an heir'.

340. Nigel Watson, ' "And if children, then heirs" (Rom 8:17) — Why Not Sons?' *ABR* 49 (2001) 53-56, comments: 'It is true that in 169 B.C. a tribune called Voconius, with the support of the notoriously conservative elder Cato, introduced a bill which forbade anyone in the first census class to nominate a woman — even an only daughter — as his or her heir. But, in the next century, Cicero in one speech described the *Lex Voconia* as vile and inhumane [*In Verrem* 2.1.105], and in another as a measure "passed for the benefit of men but utterly unjust to women" [*De Republica* 3.17]. In any case, there were various ways in which people could, and did, evade this law. Anyone in the top census class was still free to leave half of his property to his wife or daughter in the form of a legacy. Alternatively, the testator could contrive not to be registered in the first class. Cicero notes that in 75 B.C. a wealthy Sicilian named Annius bequeathed the whole of his considerable estate to his only daughter. This action was in strict conformity with the *Lex Voconia,* simply because he had not registered'.

341. To enter upon their inheritance, Paul says, believers will have to be transformed because 'flesh and blood cannot inherit the kingdom of God, nor does the perishable inherit the imperishable' (1 Cor 15:50). Thus Paul adds: 'Listen, I tell you a mystery: We will not all sleep, but we will all be changed — in a flash, in the twinkling of an eye, at the last trumpet. For the trumpet will sound, the dead will be raised imperishable, and we will be changed' (1 Cor 15:51-52).

tle there was a necessary link between suffering and glory. He wrote to the Corinthians: 'For our light and momentary troubles are achieving for us an eternal glory that far outweighs them all' (2 Cor 4:17). According to the Acts of the Apostles, after being stoned in Lystra and left for dead, Paul recovered, and he and Barnabas retraced their steps through Iconium, Lystra, and Derbe, 'strengthening the disciples and encouraging them to remain true to the faith. "We must go through many hardships to enter the kingdom of God", they said' (Acts 14:22). It important to note that 8:17 functions as a transition verse preparing the reader for the extended treatment of suffering and the Spirit in 8:18-27.

7. Present Suffering and Future Glory, 8:18-30

The previous section, 8:1-17, concluded with Paul's reminder to his audience that we did not receive a spirit that made us slaves again to fear, but 'the Spirit of sonship' who confirms that we are God's children. Being children, we are also 'heirs of God and co-heirs with Christ'. To this the apostle added the reminder that as co-heirs with Christ we are to 'share in his sufferings in order that we may also share in his glory' (8:15-17). In the section that follows (8:18-30) Paul describes the situation of believers and the creation itself during the present age. The creation *groans* with frustration while it awaits liberation along with believers (8:19-22), believers *groan* while they await their final redemption (8:23-25), and the Holy Spirit intercedes for believers 'with wordless *groans*' (8:26-27). Paul explains that even in this age God ensures that all things work together for good for those who love him, those who are called according to his purpose (8:28-30). The whole section is bracketed by the theme of glory. Thus in 8:18 Paul says that 'our present sufferings are not worth comparing with the glory that will be revealed in us', and in 8:30 he closes the section assuring his audience that God will glorify those whom he has called and justified.[342]

8:18 Having introduced the notion of sharing in Christ's sufferings in 8:17, the apostle immediately downplays the severity of the sufferings experienced by believers: *I consider that our present sufferings are not worth comparing with the glory that will be revealed in us* (NRSV, 'to us').[343] Our fu-

---

342. Olle Christoffersson, *The Earnest Expectation of the Creature: The Flood-Tradition as Matrix of Romans 8:18-27*, ConBNT 23 (Stockholm: Almqvist & Wiksell, 1990), 18-19, says: 'It is evident that vv. 18-27 separate themselves from the preceding and the following text. They are marked by a strange set of words [hapax legomena: *mataiotēs, systenazein, synantilambanesthai, stenagmos, alalētos, katho dei*] and thoughts [revelation of the sons of God, the concept of creation, *doxa* contrasted with *phthora*]. All these strange thoughts can, taken together with the peculiarities of the vocabulary, strengthen the suspicion that Paul alludes to some background which is so particular that we do not immediately recognize it'.

343. Wright, 'Romans', 595, asserts that this text implies 'not merely that we are to be shown a vision of glory (as the NRSV implies), nor simply that a glory will appear within us

ture glory will include a glorious resurrection body: the present mortal body will die, sown, as it were, in dishonor to be raised in glory (1 Cor 15:43), for when Christ appears he will 'transform our lowly bodies so that they will be like his glorious body' (Phil 3:21). See 'Additional Note: The Glory in Store for Believers', 228-29.

In 2 Corinthians 4:17 also Paul speaks of the connection between suffering and glory. There he says that our own present 'light and momentary troubles' (in fact, his were heavy and ongoing) are achieving (lit. 'producing/working') for us an eternal glory that far outweighs them all'. In this case Paul has in mind his apostolic sufferings, those endured as a consequence of his mission. But, as Moo observes, in the case of 8:18: 'These "sufferings of the present time" are not only those "trials" that are endured directly because of confession of Christ — for instance, persecution — but encompass the whole gamut of suffering, including things such as illness, bereavement, hunger, financial reverses, and death itself. . . . The word Paul uses here refers to "sufferings" in any form; and certainly the "travail" of creation, with which the sufferings of Christians are compared (vv. 19-22), cannot be restricted to sufferings "on behalf of Christ"'.[344]

a. The Groaning and Renewal of Creation, 8:19-22

19For the creation waits in eager expectation for the children of God to be revealed. 20For the creation was subjected to frustration, not by its own choice, but by the will of the one who subjected it, in hope 21that the creation itself will be liberated from its bondage to decay and brought into the freedom and glory of the children of God. 22We know that the whole creation has been groaning as in the pains of childbirth right up to the present time.

In these verses Paul makes it clear that God's redemptive work not only restores the lost glory of human beings (cf. 3:23) but also involves the renewal of the whole creation.

8:19-21 The apostle says: *For the creation waits in eager expectation for the children of God to be revealed.* Introduced with the conjunction 'for', this verse provides some explanation of the reason why the apostle considers the sufferings of believers in the present time not worth comparing with the glory they will experience in the future. How it does so can perhaps be explained in this way: By saying that even the creation is eagerly awaiting the revelation of the sons of God in their glory, Paul underlines the greatness of their future glory, which will far outweigh their present sufferings.

Paul depicts creation itself eagerly awaiting the time of the revelation

---

(as the NIV implies), but that the future revelation will bestow glory upon us, from above, as a gift'.

344. Moo, *Romans*, 511.

of the sons of God,[345] for until then creation will continue in the state to which it was reduced when it *was subjected to frustration, not by its own choice, but by the will of the one who subjected it.* The word translated 'frustration' is one found frequently (54x) in the LXX, in the Psalms (14x), Proverbs (1x) and particularly in Ecclesiastes (39x), where it denotes futility and meaninglessness. It is found in only two other places in the NT: in Ephesians 4:17 to denote the 'futility' in the thinking of unbelieving Gentiles, and in 2 Peter 2:18 to speak of the 'empty', boastful words of the ungodly. Here in 8:20 it is used in an allusion to Genesis 3:17-19 in which God cursed the earth following the sin of the primeval couple, subjecting it to 'futility' — something creation personified neither sought nor deserved: it was 'not by its own choice, but by the will of the one [God] who subjected it'. A similar idea is found in 4 *Ezra* 7:11-12: 'And when Adam transgressed my statutes, what has been made was judged. And so the entrances of this world were made narrow and sorrowful and toilsome; they are few and evil, full of dangers and involved in great hardships'. A similar idea is found in the rabbinic literature: 'Although things were created in their fullness, when the first man sinned they were corrupted, and they will not come back to their order before Ben Perez (the Messiah) comes' (*Gen. Rab.* 12.6).[346]

The question, Who is responsible for creation being 'subjected to frustration'? has been answered in two ways. First, it has been suggested that Adam is responsible because when he fell into sin, it affected not only himself but the created order also. Adam had been charged to subdue the creation, and when as the subduer he lapsed into futility, the creation was forced to lapse into futility as well.[347] Second, and more likely, is the view that God himself is the one who subdued the creation to futility when, because of the fall of the primeval couple, he pronounced a curse upon the earth (Gen 3:17-19).[348] Rimbach says: 'In Deuteronomic theology, the blessing and/or curse involving the natural environment is attendant upon covenant fidelity or infidelity as the case may be (see Deut. 28)'. He points out that this is picked up and given impetus in the prophetic tradition, a case in point being Isaiah 24:4-6:

---

345. Susan Eastman, 'Whose Apocalypse? The Identity of the Sons of God in Romans 8:19', *JBL* 121 (2002) 266-72, argues that the meaning of 'the sons of God' here in 8:19 is different from its meaning in 8:14 (where they are identified as 'those who are led by the Spirit of God', i.e., those who are currently believers). She claims that in 8:19 Paul is referring to a future revelation of the sons of God that will include those who are not yet Christians, in particular Jewish people, for they are the ones who must be included in the adoption, for in Rom 9:4 Paul says that the 'adoption' belongs to the Jews. However, in the context where Paul is speaking about the glory that will be revealed in/to *us*, a glory that even the creation eagerly awaits to see and so share in the liberation it will bring, the meaning of 'the sons of God' should not be limited to Jewish people who are not yet believers.

346. Cited by Jewett, *Romans*, 514.

347. Cf. Byrne, *Romans*, 258.

348. Cf. Dunn, *Romans 1-8*, 471.

The earth dries up and withers, the world languishes and withers, the heavens languish with the earth. The earth is defiled by its people; they have disobeyed the laws, violated the statutes and broken the everlasting covenant. Therefore a curse consumes the earth.[349]

Cranfield describes the futility endured by creation: 'We may think of the whole magnificent theatre of the universe together with all its splendid properties and all the chorus of sub-human life, created to glorify God but unable to do so fully, so long as man the chief actor in the drama of God's praise fails to contribute his rational part'.[350]

This subjection of creation, Paul says, was done *in hope that the creation itself will be liberated from its bondage to decay and brought into the freedom and glory of the children of God.* Here the apostle indicates the nature of creation's frustration: it was subjected 'to bondage and decay'. The creation itself is in slavery to decay because of God's curse following humanity's fall into sin. From this it eagerly awaits its liberation, when it shares in the 'freedom and glory of the children of God'. Paul does not explain what creation's liberation will look like. Cranfield points out: 'We may, however, assume that the liberty proper to the creation is indeed the possession of its own proper glory — that is, of the freedom fully and perfectly to fulfill its Creator's purpose for it, that freedom which it does not have, so long as man, its lord (Gen 1.26, 28; Ps 8.6), is in disgrace'.[351] What is clear from all this is that Paul's understanding of salvation is not restricted to humanity but encompasses the whole cosmos. Believers will enter their glorious freedom as children of God, and the cosmos too will be renewed. See 'Additional Note: Creation's Bondage to Corruption and Liberation', 346-49.

8:22 Paul continues: *[For] we know that the whole creation has been groaning as in the pains of childbirth right up to the present time.* The conjunction 'for', found in the original (but omitted in the NIV translation), connects this verse with the previous verses (8:19-21). It is as if Paul is saying that 'we' who are the cause of creation's groaning 'right up to the present time' recognize this fact, and look forward to its relief[352] when the children of God are brought into their freedom and glory.

---

349. James A. Rimbach, '"All Creation Groans": Theology/Ecology in St. Paul', *Asia Journal of Theology* 1 (1987) 383. Cf. Jonathan Moo, 'Romans 8.19-22 and Isaiah's Cosmic Covenant', *NTS* 54 (2008) 74-89.

350. Cranfield, *Romans*, I, 414.

351. Cranfield, *Romans*, I, 416.

352. There is, perhaps, in Paul's reference to creation's 'groaning as in the pains of childbirth' some allusion to Gen 3:16 where, as the result of her sin, God says to Eve: 'I will make your pains in childbearing very severe; with painful labor you will give birth to children'. Cf. D. T. Tsumura, 'An OT Background to Rom 8.22', *NTS* 40 (1994) 621, who argues that 'the literary and theological background of Rom 8.22 is not only Gen 3.17, which refers to the cursed earth, but also v. 16a, which refers to both the "trembling pain" and "pain of childbirth" that Eve was destined to go through. Hence the origin of the term *synōdinei* ['suffers pain together'] in Rom 8.22 is to be seen also in this Genesis passage. As Lange

There has been some debate concerning what Paul is saying about the creation and its redemption. Some argue that by the creation the apostle means the whole of creation, including humanity, but that his interest is primarily focused upon the redemption of human beings — the redemption of the rest of creation being only the 'backdrop' for human redemption. Others argue that cosmic redemption and human redemption are separate and independent, thus bestowing upon creation a worth of its own independent of the worth of humanity. Paul's reference to 'the whole creation' and his use in the original language of the verbs meaning 'groans together' and 'suffers pain together' have been interpreted to mean that humanity and the subhuman creation share together in this groaning and suffering as they await liberation. Jewett notes that this was the view of both Origen and Athanasius, and he himself and a few other modern commentators adopt it.[353] The more generally adopted view is that 'the whole creation' here in 8:22 denotes the subhuman creation only, which, because of the sin of the primeval couple, has been subjected to futility and in that state groans and suffers pain.[354] The fact that in the next verse (8:23) Paul distinguishes believers from the subhuman creation supports this view. Wright's comment on the prospect of the liberation of creation along with the liberation of believers is helpful:

> The basis of Paul's belief here must be a combination of two things: the biblical promise of new heavens and new earth (Isa 65:17; 66:22), and the creation story in which human beings, made in God's image, are appointed as God's stewards over creation. Putting the picture together, in the light of the observable way in which the created order is out of joint, and the clear biblical and experiential belief that the human race as a whole is in rebellion against God, Paul, in company with many other Jews, saw the two as intimately related. After the fall, the earth produced thorns and thistles, humans continued to abuse their environment, so that one of the reasons why God sent Israel into exile, according the Scriptures, was so that the land could at last enjoy its sabbaths (Lev 26:34-43 [cf. 25:2-5]; 2 Chr 36:21). But the answer to the problem was not (as in some New Age theories) that humans should keep their hands off creation. . . . The answer, if the creator is to be true to the original purpose, is for humans to be redeemed, to take their place at last as God's imagebearers, the wise stewards they were always meant to be. Paul sees that this purpose has already been accomplished in principle in the resurrection of Jesus, and that it will be accomplished fully when all those in Christ are raised and together set in saving au-

---

noted more than a century ago, this figure "reflects in travailing Eve the fate of the travailing earth, and *vice versa*"'.

353. Jewett, *Romans*, 517.

354. Cf., e.g., John Bolt, 'The Relation between Creation and Redemption in Romans 8:18-27', *CalvTheolJourn* 30 (1995) 35, 44; Dunn, *Romans 1–8*, 472; Cranfield, *Romans*, I, 411-12.

thority over the world (see 1 Cor 15:20-28). That is why, Paul says, creation is now waiting with eager longing.[355]

What the apostle says here about the liberation of creation is brief and tantalizing, and there's not much more about it to be found in his letters. There is a possible allusion in Ephesians 1:9-10: 'He made known to us the mystery of his will according to his good pleasure, which he purposed in Christ, to be put into effect when the times will have reached their fulfillment — *to bring unity to all things in heaven and on earth under Christ*' (italics added). Elsewhere in the NT there are a couple of references to a new heaven and a new earth, and these may reflect belief in the renewal of creation: 'But in keeping with his promise we are looking forward to a new heaven and a new earth, where righteousness dwells' (2 Pet 3:13); 'Then I saw "a new heaven and a new earth", for the first heaven and the first earth had passed away' (Rev 21:1).

ADDITIONAL NOTE: CREATION'S BONDAGE TO CORRUPTION AND LIBERATION

Romans 8:19-22 with its references to the creation's present bondage to corruption and its future liberation is virtually unique in Paul's letters. To understand the apostle's teaching about this matter a number of issues need clarification: (i) Do the OT and other Jewish literature contain references to creation's subjection to bondage? (ii) What does Paul mean by 'the creation'? (iii) Who is responsible for subjecting the creation to bondage? (iv) What is the nature of its bondage to corruption? (v) Do the OT and other Jewish literature contain references to the liberation of creation? (vi) When will the creation experience its liberation and what will be the nature of that liberation? (vii) What do other NT documents say about the matter? These issues are discussed in turn below.

Do the OT and Other Jewish Literature Refer to the Creation's Subjection to Bondage?

A possible reference to the creation's subjection to bondage is found in Genesis 3:17-18, where, because of Adam's transgression, God curses the earth: 'To Adam he said, "Because you listened to your wife and ate from the tree about which I commanded you, 'You must not eat of it', "Cursed is the ground because of you. . . . It will produce thorns and thistles for you"'. (Cf. Gen 5:29: 'He named him Noah and said, "He will comfort us in the la-

---

bor and painful toil of our hands caused by the ground the LORD has cursed"'.) There are other traditions in Jewish literature of which Paul may have known, in particular *4 Ezra* 7:11-12: 'And when Adam transgressed my statutes, what has been made was judged. And so the entrances of this world were made narrow and sorrowful and toilsome; they are few and evil, full of dangers and involved in great hardships'.[356]

What Does Paul Mean by 'the Creation'?

A variety of interpretations of 'the creation' have been offered, including the human and subhuman creation as well as angels and the stars; the subhuman creation and the angels; the subhuman creation alone; humans alone, and angels alone.[357] Of these, the main alternatives are the subhuman creation, and the human as well as the subhuman creation. Of these two the former is to be preferred in the light of 8:21, where the creation itself is distinguished from humanity and where it is said that creation itself is going to be brought into the glorious freedom of the children of God.

Who Is Responsible for Subjecting the Creation to Bondage?

If, as seems most likely, Paul is alluding to Genesis 3:17-18 when he speaks of creation being subjected to the bondage of corruption, then the one who subjected it is God himself when he pronounced the curse upon it following the primeval couple's disobedience.[358] It is very unlikely that evil angels are responsible, as Christoffersson has suggested.[359]

What Is the Nature of the Creation's Bondage to Corruption?

As Hahne correctly observes, creation's fallen state is not the same as that of humanity, which is the result of disobedience to God's command. The natural world is a victim of humanity's disobedience, now subject to futility and unable to fulfill the purpose for which it was created. It brings forth weeds more easily than useful crops.[360] Fitzmyer says: 'The world, created

356. Cf. Christoffersson, *The Earnest Expectation of the Creature,* 136-37, finds parallels between what Paul says about the bondage of creation to corruption and the flood traditions of Genesis, but his arguments are less than compelling.

357. Christoffersson, *The Earnest Expectation of the Creature,* 19-21.

358. Cf. Harry Alan Hahne, *The Corruption and Redemption of Creation: Nature in Romans 8.19-22 and Jewish Apocalyptic Literature* (LBS 336; London/New York: T&T Clark, 2006), 207.

359. Christoffersson, *The Earnest Expectation of the Creature,* 136-37.

360. Hahne, *The Corruption and Redemption of Creation,* 207.

for humanity and the service of it, was drawn into Adam's ruin; the blessing given to him (fertility of the soil, fecundity of trees, brilliance of stars,
friendliness of animals, limitation of insects) were all lost, because Eve gave
Adam (= humanity) to eat of the forbidden fruit. Paul is tributary to such
Jewish thinking. He realizes that through Adam come not only sin and
death (5:12-14), but "bondage to decay" and the "slavery of corruption",
which affect all material creation, even apart from humanity (8:19-23)'.[361]

Do the OT and Other Jewish Literature Contain References to the Liberation of the Creation?

There are such references in this literature. Fitzmyer draws attention to the
promises in the OT about a new heaven and a new earth and to the apocalyptic promises in Trito-Isaiah (Isa 65:17; 66:22). He notes also that 'in the
intertestamental literature such promises were transferred to the messianic
age: 1 *Enoch* 45:4-5 (the earth will be transformed for the upright along with
the Chosen One); *Jub.* 4:26; 2 *Apoc. Bar.* 31:5–32:6; 4 *Ezra* 7:11, 30-32, 75'.[362]

When Will the Creation Experience Its Liberation and What Will Be the Nature of That Liberation?

Paul makes clear that the creation's liberation from corruption is tied to the
destiny of redeemed humanity. As its submission to corruption and futility
resulted from humanity's fall, so its liberation is tied to the final redemption of the children of God — when they enter upon their glorious freedom.
Paul does not explain the nature of the creation's liberation. Cranfield offers the following suggestion: 'We may, however, assume that the liberty
proper to the creation is indeed the possession of its own proper glory —
that is, of the freedom fully and perfectly to fulfil its Creator's purpose for
it, that freedom which it does not have, so long as man, its lord (Gen 1.26,
28; Ps 8.6), is in disgrace'.[363]

What Do Other NT Documents Say about the Matter?

Outside the Pauline corpus there are two brief references to a new heaven
and a new earth. In 2 Peter 3:13 we find: 'In keeping with his [God's] promise we are looking forward to a new heaven and a new earth, where righteousness dwells', and in Revelation 21:1-2 we read: 'Then I saw "a new

---

361. Fitzmyer, *Romans*, 505.
362. Fitzmyer, *Romans*, 505.
363. Cranfield, *Romans*, I, 416.

heaven and a new earth", for the first heaven and the first earth had passed away, and there was no longer any sea. I saw the Holy City, the new Jerusalem, coming down out of heaven from God, prepared as a bride beautifully dressed for her husband'.

---

b. The Groaning and Redemption of Believers, 8:23-25

[23]*Not only so, but we ourselves, who have the firstfruits of the Spirit, groan inwardly as we wait eagerly for our adoption to sonship, the redemption of our bodies.* [24]*For in this hope we were saved. But hope that is seen is no hope at all. Who hopes for what they already have?* [25]*But if we hope for what we do not yet have, we wait for it patiently.*

In these verses Paul makes it clear that it is not only the subhuman creation that groans in the present time. This, too, is the lot of believers as they long for their redemption.

Paul writes: *Not only so, but we ourselves, who have the firstfruits of the Spirit, groan inwardly as we wait eagerly for our adoption to sonship, the redemption of our bodies.* The way Paul begins here, 'not only so, but we ourselves', distinguishes believers from the subhuman creation of the previous verse, confirming the interpretation of the creation adopted above.

Paul describes believers as those who have the 'firstfruits of the Spirit'. He employs the expression 'firstfruits', an agricultural image, in a number of ways in his letters. He uses it to refer to the first converts in a particular area (16:5; 1 Cor 16:15; 2 Thess 2:13), and to refer Christ's resurrection as the 'firstfruits' of those who have died and will likewise be raised (1 Cor 15:20, 23). Here in 8:23 he likens the firstfruits of the crop and the subsequent full harvest to believers' present experience of the Spirit and their subsequent adoption as God's children, including the redemption of their bodies respectively.[364] The expression, 'firstfruits of the Spirit', has been read in two different ways: (i) construing the genitive 'of the Spirit' as epexegetical, yielding a translation, 'firstfruits which is the Spirit';[365] (ii) construing the genitive 'of the Spirit' as appositional, referring to the Spirit's work in us.[366] The first option is preferable in the light of Paul's references to the Spirit himself being given to believers and living in them (5:5; 8:9, 11) and particularly his parallel depiction of the Spirit himself

---

364. The apostle uses 'firstfruits' *(aparchē)* also in 11:16, where he likens the believing remnant of Israel to part of a dough offering which is sanctified — the whole batch of dough then referring to 'all Israel': 'If the part of the dough offered as firstfruits is holy, then the whole batch is holy'. Elsewhere Paul uses the word 'deposit, down payment' *(arrabōn)* to make a similar point, depicting the gift of the Holy Spirit to believers as his 'down payment' guaranteeing their future full inheritance (2 Cor 1:22; 5:5; Eph 1:13-14).

365. Dunn, *Romans 1–8*, 473.

366. Fitzmyer, *Romans*, 510; Cranfield, *Romans*, I, 418.

given to believers as the 'down payment' or 'deposit' guaranteeing their future inheritance (cf. 2 Cor 1:22; 5:5; Eph 1:13-14).

As those who have the firstfruits of the Spirit, Paul says, 'we . . . groan inwardly as we wait eagerly for our adoption to sonship'. This inward groaning is probably to be understood as the nonverbal sighs of believers as they experience the tensions of the present time, what Dunn describes as 'the inward sense of frustration of individual believers (as a whole) at the eschatological tension of living in the overlap of the ages'.[367] The groaning of believers here in 8:23 recalls the groaning of creation in 8:22.

The 'adoption'[368] for which believers eagerly await is their final salvation, standing in juxtaposition as it does with the 'redemption' of their bodies, that is, their resurrection. While they eagerly wait for this, they groan inwardly. The apostle expresses himself in similar vein in 2 Corinthians 5:2-4 when he speaks of groaning as we long 'to be clothed instead . . . with our heavenly dwelling . . . so that what is mortal may be swallowed up by life', that is, our final redemption, including the resurrection of our bodies.

Continuing this line of thought, Paul says: *For in this hope we were saved*, that is, in hope of our adoption, the redemption of the body. This is a hope for something yet to be realized. The very nature of hope is anticipation of the yet unseen but nevertheless certain realities (see 'Additional Note: Hope in the Pauline Corpus', 365). So the apostle explains: *But hope that is seen is no hope at all. Who hopes for what they already have?* (cf. 2 Cor 5:7: 'We live by faith, not by sight'). Hope in the NT is always future oriented, and unseen in the sense that the object of hope is yet to be revealed. Yet hope is not wishful thinking, but what the writer to the Hebrews describes as both 'sure' and 'certain' (Heb 11:1). This being the case, Paul adds: *But if we hope for what we do not yet have, we wait for it patiently*. The NIV's 'patiently' translates an expression that denotes, not a passive waiting — killing time, as it were — until what is hoped for arrives, but rather a strenuous holding onto hope and doing good despite suffering and difficulties (cf. 2:7; 5:3-4; 15:4-5; 2 Cor 1:6; 6:4; Col 1:11; 1 Thess 1:3-4; 1 Tim 6:11; 2 Tim 3:10; Tit 2:2).[369] Wright notes that here again we encounter the characteristic 'now and not yet' that is so pervasive in Paul's letters: we have already received 'the spirit of adoption' (8:15); we are already 'children of God' (8:16-17); and 'yet there is a form of this "sonship/adoption" for which we still eagerly long. The link between present and future is made, again as usual, by the Spirit, who is the "first fruits"'.[370]

---

367. Dunn, *Romans 1-8*, 474.

368. Cf. the comments on the OT background to Paul's use of 'adoption *(huiothesia)* in the commentary on 8:15 above.

369. Cf. BAGD, *hypomonē*.

370. Wright, 'Romans', 597.

c. The Groaning of the Holy Spirit as He Intercedes for Believers, 8:26-27

26In the same way, the Spirit helps us in our weakness. We do not know what we ought to pray for, but the Spirit himself intercedes for us through wordless groans. 27And he who searches our hearts knows the mind of the Spirit, because the Spirit intercedes for God's people in accordance with the will of God.

Caught in the tension of living in the overlap of the ages, the period of the 'now and not yet', believers experience weakness, but in the midst of this weakness the Holy Spirit helps them through his intercession on their behalf, particularly when they do not know how to pray.

8:26 While believers hold on in hope, enduring the sufferings of this present age, they are not left alone. Paul goes on: *In the same way, the Spirit helps us in our weakness. We do not know what we ought to pray for, but the Spirit himself intercedes for us through wordless groans.* 'In the same way' seems on first reading to connect the groaning of the Spirit's intercession for believers with their own experience of groaning as they hold on in hope, awaiting their final redemption. However, what the text says is that likewise the Spirit 'helps', not likewise the Spirit 'groans'. 'Likewise' then refers back to some antecedent activity of the Spirit, not to the groaning of believers. Smith argues that 'likewise' is best understood to link the active work of the Spirit in intercession here in 8:26 right back to the active work of the Spirit confirming believers' sonship in 8:16 despite the amount of material separating the two statements. He sums up his view: 'Paul is saying: "Just as the Spirit is at work within our hearts to confirm to us our adoption (8:16), so in the same way also the Spirit is at work within our hearts to bear up our weakness (8:26)"'.[371]

The verb 'to help' used here[372] is found only twice in the NT, here and in Luke 10:40 ('But Martha was distracted by all the preparations that had to be made. She came to him and asked, "Lord, don't you care that my sister has left me to do the work by myself? Tell her to *help* me!"' — italics added), where it clearly means to 'lend assistance'.[373] Here in 8:26 Paul maintains that the Holy Spirit 'helps us in our weakness'. While the Spirit undoubtedly helps believers generally in their weakness, the particular weakness in which the Spirit helps them is their not knowing 'what we ought to pray for'. This is surprising, for elsewhere Paul gives many instances of what people ought to pray for and the things for which he him-

---

371. Geoffrey Smith, 'The Function of "Likewise" *(hōsautōs)* in Romans 8:26', *TynBul* 49 (1998) 32.

372. *Synantilambanomai.*

373. Cranfield, *Romans,* I, 421, comments: 'The *syn-* does not here mean "together with", but is simply intensive: the meaning is not that the Spirit joins our weakness in helping the creation by intercession for it or by adding further groanings (ours and His) to its groaning, but simply that the Spirit helps our weakness'.

self prays.[374] Nevertheless, it is clear that the apostle is aware that there are times when he and others just do not know what to pray for — perhaps in times of suffering and persecution. When this is the case, he assures his audience that the Spirit lends us assistance.

The assistance the Spirit gives is that he himself 'intercedes for us'.[375] The idea of the Spirit interceding for people is found only here in the NT, and is not found in the OT or pre-Christian Jewish literature.[376] Some have suggested that Paul is referring to believers' prayers in tongues inspired by the Spirit,[377] but this seems unlikely because: (i) the apostle is speaking of the Spirit's intercession *for us*,[378] not his inspiration of prayer in tongues *by us*; (ii) Paul says that the Spirit's intercession is 'through wordless groans' (lit. 'unspoken groans'),[379] which suggests that the intercession is silent and not oral as is speaking in tongues.[380]

While there is clearly a verbal connection between the groaning of creation, the groaning of believers, and the groaning of the Spirit, the Spirit's groaning is clearly of a different order. In the former cases groaning emanates from frustration or suffering, whereas in the case of the Spirit this is certainly not so — his groaning is associated with intercession for believers.

8:27 In this verse Paul explains further the Spirit's intercession, in particular the basis of its efficacy: *And he who searches our hearts knows what*

374. He urges people to pray for the ability to interpret when they speak in tongues (1 Cor 14:13), to offer 'all kinds of prayers and requests' for all the saints, and to pray that he may proclaim the mystery of Christ (Col 4:3; 1 Thess 5:25; 2 Thess 3:1). He himself prays that his converts may abound in love and knowledge (Phil 1:9) and be filled with the knowledge of God's will through spiritual wisdom and understanding (Col 1:9), and that God may count them worthy of their calling, and by his power fulfill every good purpose of theirs and every act prompted by faith (2 Thess 1:11).

375. Some manuscripts add *hyper hēmōn* after *hyperentynchanei*, making explicit what is already implicit in the verb *hyperentynchanei*, i.e., that the Spirit intercedes 'for us'.

376. Fitzmyer, *Romans*, 518, comments: 'The idea of "intercession" attributed by Paul to the Spirit (only here in the NT) is based on OT ideas: intercession is ascribed to Abraham (Gen 18:23-33), Moses (Exod 8:8, 12, 28-30), priests (Lev 16:21-22; Num 6:23-27), kings (2 Sam 12:16), prophets (1 Kgs 18:22-40), angels (Tob 12:12; cf. *T. Lev.* 3:5, 6), upright persons in the afterlife (2 Macc 15:12-16; cf. *As. Mos.* 11:14-17). But nowhere in the OT or in pre-Christian Jewish writings does one find the idea of the Holy Spirit as an intercessor. It is, then, a Pauline novelty'.

377. So, e.g., Käsemann, *Romans*, 241; Bertone, 'The Function of the Spirit', 88-89, 92-93.

378. The words 'for us', added in the NIV translation, have no counterpart in the Greek text, but they are a legitimate addition seeing that intercession involves praying for others. In any case, this is made clear in the next verse where Paul says, 'the Spirit intercedes *for the saints* in accordance with God's will' (italics added).

379. Cf. BAGD, *ad loc.*: 'sighs too deep for words'.

380. Cf. Cranfield, *Romans*, I, 423-24; Dunn, *Romans 1-8*, 478; Byrne, *Romans*, 271. Wright, 'Romans', 599, puts it this way: 'Many writers from various standpoints, have suggested that Paul here refers to the gift of *glossolalia*, "speaking in tongues". . . . The present writer certainly has no prejudice against such a reference here. . . . Yet I find it strange that Paul, if he wished to refer to speaking in tongues, for which words of the *laleō . . .* root would be used . . . should here use the word *alalētos . . .* to describe the practice'.

is the mind of the Spirit, because the Spirit intercedes for God's people in accordance with the will of God. In the OT God is regularly depicted as the one who knows or searches the hearts of human beings (1 Sam 16:7; 1 Kgs 8:39; 1 Chr 28:9; 29:17; 2 Chr 6:30; Pss 44:21; 139:23; Prov 24:12; Jer 12:3; 17:9-10). In Revelation 2:23 the risen Christ says: 'I am he who searches hearts and minds, and I will repay each of you according to your deeds'.

Only here does Paul speak about God knowing the mind of the Spirit, but in 1 Corinthians 2:10-11 he discloses that the Spirit knows the mind of God: 'The Spirit searches all things, even the deep things of God. For who knows a person's thoughts except their own spirit within them? In the same way no one knows the thoughts of God except the Spirit of God'. Clearly there is a deep mutual understanding between 'God' and 'the Spirit of God'. Two things inherent in this mutual understanding guarantee the efficacy of the Spirit's intercession for believers: (i) God knows what is the mind of the Spirit, and (ii) the Spirit intercedes for believers 'in accordance with the will of God'.[381]

d. God Works All Things Together for Good for Those Who Love Him, 8:28-30

> [28]*And we know that in all things God works for the good of those who love him, who have been called according to his purpose. [29]For those God foreknew he also predestined to be conformed to the image of his Son, that he might be the firstborn among many brothers and sisters. [30]And those he predestined, he also called; those he called, he also justified; those he justified, he also glorified.*

Here the apostle encourages his audience by reminding them of another of those things 'we' know; in this case 'we know' that God works all things together for the good of believers whom he has called according to his purpose, those whom he has predestined to be conformed to the image of his Son.

8:28 Having encouraged his audience with the fact that the Spirit intercedes on their behalf, and that *God* knows the mind of the Spirit, Paul now encourages them with something that *we* know: *And we know that in all things*

---

381. Julie L. Wu, 'The Spirit's Intercession in Romans 8:26-27: An Exegetical Note', *ExpTim* 105 (1993-94) 13, comments: 'Since in the Garden of Gethsemane, Jesus's address to God as "Abba, Father" is followed by his prayer of conforming to God's will despite sufferings (Mk 14:36), believers, as children of God, are to follow Jesus's example by living according to God's will in the midst of a suffering world (vv. 18-25). Now that believers cannot do this owing to their not knowing what to pray for as they ought (v. 26), the Spirit, who searches God's mind (cf. 1 Cor 2:10), makes up the deficit by interceding for them according to God's will to the effect that they will be able to live *kata theon,* or *kata pneuma* ["according to God" or "according to (the) Spirit"] (8:4). This explains why the Spirit's intercession is described as "according to God's will" in this context'.

God works for the good of those who love him, who have been called according to his purpose.[382] This is one of five occasions in Romans where the apostle says that 'we know' something.[383] What 'we know' in 8:28 is that 'in all things God works for the good of those who love him'. This text could also be translated: 'for those who love God all things work together for good' (construing 'all things' as the subject of the verb 'work') or possibly, 'for those who love God he works all things together for good' (construing 'he' as the implied subject of the verb 'works'), yielding the same sense as that provided by the NIV. There is a textual variant that makes this latter sense explicit: 'for those who love God, God works all things for good').[384] While this variant reading is generally regarded by scholars as the result of scribal emendation to make explicit what the scribe thought was implicit, Rodgers has argued that, for the sake of stylistic improvement, a scribe may have omitted an original second reference to God.[385] In addition, he suggests that there may be an echo here of Genesis 50:20, which reads: 'You intended to harm me, but God intended it for good to accomplish what is now being done, the saving of many lives'.[386] Gignilliat, noting that *synergei* ('work with') denotes a collaboration, argues that this rules out 'all things' as the subject of this verb, and this is further supported by the fact that the verb 'work' in Paul's letters 'takes a personal subject, not an impersonal one' such as 'all things'.[387]

If God is the implied subject of the verb 'to work' here, with whom or what does he work together? As Gignilliat notes, Paul has already suggested a synergistic collaboration between God and the Spirit in the matter of intercession for believers in 8:26-27. This idea of synergistic collaboration is then carried forward into 8:28, where God and the Spirit work together for the good of believers.[388] The context suggests that the 'all things' that God works together with the Spirit to promote the good of believers includes their suffering (8:18) and weakness (8:26), though the 'all things' here should probably not be restricted to sufferings but include all the circumstances of their lives.[389] In 8:35-39 the apostle insists that nothing that believers encounter will be able to separate them from the love of God.

---

382. Hilderbrecht Hommel, 'Denen, die Gott lieben . . . Erwägungen zu Römer 8,28', *ZNW* 80 (1989) 126-29, argues that Paul was using a well-known quotation from Plato here in 8:28 (*Politeia* 10).

383. The others are 2:2 ('we know that God's judgment against those who do such things is based on truth'); 3:19 ('we know that whatever the law says, it says to those who are under the law'); 7:14 ('We know that the law is spiritual'); 8:22 ('We know that the whole creation has been groaning as in the pains of childbirth right up to the present time').

384. *tois agapōsin ton theon panta synergei ho theos eis agathon.*

385. Peter R. Rodgers, 'The Text of Romans 8:28', *JTS* 46 (1995) 548-49.

386. Rodgers, 'The Text of Romans 8:28', 550.

387. Mark S. Gignilliat, 'Working Together with Whom? Text-Critical, Contextual, and Theological Analysis of *synergei* in Romans 8,28', *Bib* 87 (2006) 513.

388. Gignilliat, 'Working Together with Whom?', 514.

389. Cf. Cranfield, *Romans*, I, 428; Witherington, *Romans*, 226. Wright, 'Romans', 600, says: '"All things" — not just the groanings of the previous verses, but the entire range of

Paul describes the people for whom God works all things together for good as 'those who love him [God]'. Many times Paul speaks of God's love for believers, but much less frequently of believers' love for God, as he does here.[390] Nevertheless, it is an important mark of true believers. The expression is a common designation for the faithful in Israel (cf., e.g., Exod 20:6; Deut 5:10; 7:9; Ps 145:20 [LXX 144:20]; Neh 1:5; Dan 9:4; Sir 1:10; 2:15, 16; *Pss. Sol.* 4:25; 10:3; 14:1), one that the apostle now applies to believers, both Jews and Gentiles.

Paul further describes those for whom God works all things together for good as people 'who have been called according to his purpose' (lit. 'those who are called ones according to [his] purpose'). He uses the substantive 'called ones' several times elsewhere to describe believers,[391] as he does here. This calling is according to his (God's) 'purpose'. When the apostle uses the word 'purpose', he does so usually to emphasize that things occur by the sovereign will of God, for example, his choice of Jacob rather than Esau (9:11), his choice before the foundation of the world of those to be adopted as his children and to receive the promised inheritance (Eph 1:11), and his eternal purpose hidden for ages to make known the rich variety of his wisdom to rulers and authorities through the church (Eph 3:9-11). In the following verses (8:29-30) it becomes clear that the aspect of God's purpose Paul has in mind is conforming believers to the likeness of his Son, and having called and justified them to bring them to glory.[392]

8:29 What Paul has in mind regarding the good towards which God makes all things work is then made clear: *For those God foreknew he also predestined to be conformed to the image of his Son, that he might be the firstborn among many brothers and sisters.* In this world where believers groan inwardly as they await their adoption they may experience suffering and

experiences and events that may face God's people — are taken care of by the creator God who is planning to renew the whole creation, and us along with it'.

390. The only other instances are 1 Cor 2:9: '"What no eye has seen, what no ear has heard, and what no human mind has conceived" — the things God has prepared for those who love him'; 1 Cor 16:22: 'If anyone does not love the Lord — a curse be on him'; Eph 6:24: 'Grace to all who love our Lord Jesus Christ with an undying love'; 2 Tim 4:8: 'Now there is in store for me the crown of righteousness, which the Lord, the righteous Judge, will award to me on that day — and not only to me, but also to all who have longed for [lit. 'all who have loved'] his appearing'. To these some would add Rom 5:5: 'And hope does not put us to shame, because God's love has been poured out into our hearts through the Holy Spirit, who has been given to us'.

391. Cf. Paul's use of the substantive adjective 'called one' *(klētos)* in 1:1, 6, 7; 1 Cor 1:1, 2, 24. More frequently he uses the verb *kaleō* to describe believers as those whom God has called (cf. 8:30; 9:24; 1 Cor 1:9; 7:15, 18, 20, 21, 22, 24; Gal 1:6; 5:8; Eph 4:1, 4; Col 3:15; 1 Thess 2:12; 5:24; 2 Thess 2:14; 1 Tim 6:12; 2 Tim 1:9).

392. Wright, 'Romans', 601, paints the broader picture of God's purpose: 'That purpose — namely, that God would sum up all things in Christ (Col 1:15-20; Eph 1:10); that God would be all in all (1 Cor 15:28); that the whole creation would be liberated into the freedom that goes with the glorification of God's children — this whole purpose was always designed to be fulfilled through the agency of God's image-bearing children, the human race'.

persecution, but God in his sovereign power makes even these things serve the end of their conformity to Christ. This is what God has 'predestined' for those whom he 'foreknew', each and every individual believer.[393] Paul uses the verb 'to predestine' when speaking of matters that God has predetermined. In Ephesians he says that God predestined believers to be adopted as his children (Eph 1:5) and to live for his praise and glory (Eph 1:11-12).[394] Here in 8:29 Paul points out that God predestined believers 'to be conformed to the image of his Son'.

For believers to be conformed to the image of Christ will involve transformation. When Paul speaks of transformation elsewhere, it can involve moral transformation that takes place in the present: 'And we . . . are being transformed into his image with ever-increasing glory, which comes from the Lord, who is the Spirit' (2 Cor 3:18); 'you have taken off your old self with its practices and have put on the new self, which is being renewed in knowledge in the image of its Creator' (Col 3:9-10). In other places he speaks of an eschatological transformation: 'And just as we have borne the image of the earthly man, so shall we bear the image of the heavenly man' (1 Cor 15:49); 'the Lord Jesus Christ . . . will transform our lowly bodies so that they will be like his glorious body' (Phil 3:20-21). We may say, then, that God has predestined believers to be conformed to the image of his Son, both through moral transformation in the present and finally by resurrection on the last day.[395] In the present context, where those who are predestined, called, and justified are also to be glorified, Paul probably has in mind the final eschatological conforming of believers to the image of Christ through resurrection (cf. 1 Cor 15:49; Phil 3:21; 1 John 3:2).

God's purpose in conforming believers to the image of his Son is 'that he [Christ] might be the firstborn among many brothers and sisters'. The word 'firstborn' itself can be understood either literally as the firstborn child in a family (Luke 2:7; Heb 11:28), or metaphorically to denote preeminent status (Col 1:15; Heb 1:6), or to denote the first to experience resurrection from the dead (Col 1:18; Rev 1:5).[396] The concept of Christ being the

393. Moo, *Romans*, 533, asks: 'What, or whom, precisely, has God "foreknown" in this way? The answer of many contemporary exegetes and theologians is "the church". What is "foreknown", or "elected", is not the individual but Christ, and the church as "in Christ". But whatever might be said about this interpretation elsewhere, it does not fit these verses very well. Not only is nothing said here about "in Christ" or the church, but the purpose of Paul is to assure individual believers — not the church as a whole — that God is working for *their* "good" and will glorify *them*'.

394. Acts 4:28 uses the same word to speak of the way God predestines the events of history, in this instance the crucifixion of Christ at the hands of sinful human beings: 'They did what your power and will had decided beforehand should happen'.

395. Cf. D. Edmond Hiebert, 'Romans 8:28-29 and the Assurance of the Believer', *BSac* 148 (1991) 180-82.

396. 'Firstborn' (*prōtotokos*) is used somewhat unusually in Heb 12:23 in plural form where it denotes 'the church of the firstborn', who are further described as those 'whose names are written in heaven'.

firstborn among many brothers and sisters here in 8:29 probably refers to his preeminence among his 'many brothers and sisters', those who bear the family likeness through transformation and will share his glory. It is noteworthy that the writer to the Hebrews says that to bring his brothers and sisters to glory Christ had to be made perfect through suffering to become the author of their salvation:

> In bringing *many* sons and daughters to glory, it was fitting that God, for whom and through whom everything exists, should make the pioneer of their salvation perfect through what he suffered. Both the one who makes people holy and those who are made holy are of the same family. So Jesus is not ashamed to call them *brothers and sisters.* He says, 'I will declare your name to my *brothers and sisters;* in the assembly I will sing your praises'. (Heb 2-10-12, italics added)

8:30 Concluding his thought in this section (8:28-30), Paul says: *And those he predestined, he also called; those he called, he also justified; those he justified, he also glorified.* In this verse the apostle describes succinctly the broad sweep of God's gracious dealings with believers, aspects of which are found scattered throughout his letters. They were 'predestined' before the world began 'for adoption to sonship through Jesus Christ' (Eph 1:4-5). Then they were 'called' by God according to his purpose (8:28) through the preaching of the gospel (2 Thess 2:14) to belong to and be in fellowship with Jesus Christ (1:6; 1 Cor 1:9) and to enter his kingdom and glory (1 Thess 2:12). Being predestined and called, they were justified through faith in Jesus Christ (5:1; Gal 2:16) and by the blood of Christ (5:9) (see 'Additional Note: Justification for the Doers', 142-44). Finally, those whom God predestined, called, and justified, Paul says, he also glorified'. This is an unusual statement, for he uses the aorist tense as he does when speaking of their predestination, calling, and justification, suggesting that their glorification may also be understood as something that has already occurred. Clearly this is not the apostle's understanding, for it runs counter to everything else he says about believers' glorification. Normally he speaks of it as a hope for the future. Just a few verses earlier in 8:18 he asserts that 'our present sufferings are not worth comparing with *the glory that will be revealed in us*' (italics added).

Three ways of handling this problem have been suggested. One is to say that Paul uses the aorist tense in respect to believers' glorification because he wants to depict it as something that is absolutely certain, as certain as their predestination, calling, and justification that have already occurred.[397] A second way is to recognize that in 2 Corinthians 3:18 Paul

---

397. Cf. Moo, *Romans,* 536. Cranfield, *Romans,* I, 433, comments: 'The use of the aorist here is significant and suggestive. In a real sense, of course, their glory is still in the future. . . . But their glorification has already been foreordained by God (cf. v. 29); the divine decision has been taken, though its working out has not been consummated. Moreover,

speaks of glorification as a process already begun ('we . . . are being trans-formed into his image with ever-increasing glory, which comes from the Lord, who is the Spirit'), and this process is to be consummated at the Lord's return (see 'Additional Note: The Glory in Store for Believers', 228-29.).[398] A third way is to note that the aorist tense does not necessarily refer to past events, but may be used to describe a complete action, whether in the past, present, or future — in this case the future.[399] Each of these three suggestions has value, but to decide which of them the apostle had in mind when he wrote is impossible to say with any certainty.

While what Paul says in 8:28-30 has implications for an understand-ing of the doctrine of predestination, it was not the apostle's intention to formulate such a doctrine in these verses. His primary purpose was to pro-vide comfort and encouragement for vulnerable believers caught in the overlap of the ages and exposed to suffering and persecution (cf. 8:18, 31-39). They are to know that the Holy Spirit comes to their assistance by his intercession on their behalf, and that God works with the Spirit to make all things work for their ultimate good. They are to know also that, as those whom God foreknew and predestined to be conformed to the image of his Son, having been called and justified, they will also certainly be glorified.[400]

8. The Emotive Climax — If God Be for Us, Who Can Be against Us? 8:31-39

> [31]What, then, shall we say in response to these things? If God is for us, who can be against us? [32]He who did not spare his own Son, but gave him up for us all — how will he not also, along with him, graciously give us all things? [33]Who will bring any charge against those whom God has chosen? It is God who justifies. [34]Who then is the one who condemns? No one. Christ Jesus who died — more than that, who was raised to life — is at the right hand of God and is also interceding for us. [35]Who shall separate us from the love of Christ? Shall trouble or hardship or persecution or famine or naked-ness or danger or sword? [36]As it is written: 'For your sake we face death all day long; we are considered as sheep to be slaughtered'. [37]No, in all these things we are more than conquerors through him who loved us. [38]For I am

---

Christ, in whose destiny their destiny is included, has already been glorified, so that in Him their glorification has already been accomplished. So it can be spoken of as something con-cealed which has yet to be revealed (cf. v. 18 — *mellousin doxan apokalyphthēnai*)'. Lambrecht, *The Wretched "I" and Its Liberation 8*, 109, adds: 'We may perhaps understand the verb "glori-fied" as follows: in principle God has already glorified Christians. Future end-time glorifi-cation determines their present existence; it is anticipated in an already present Christian glory'.

398. Cf. Byrne, *Romans*, 269-70; Jewett, *Romans*, 530.
399. Cf. Porter, *Verbal Aspect in the Greek of the New Testament*, 37.
400. Cf. Barrett, *Romans*, 171; Witherington, *Romans*, 229.

convinced that neither death nor life, neither angels nor demons, neither the present nor the future, nor any powers, 39neither height nor depth, nor anything else in all creation, will be able to separate us from the love of God that is in Christ Jesus our Lord.

In the previous section (8:18-30) Paul described the predicament in which believers and the creation find themselves during the overlap of the ages. He showed how the creation groans with frustration while it awaits its liberation along with that of believers (8:19-22) and how believers groan while they await their final redemption (8:23-25). He also revealed how the Holy Spirit intercedes for them 'with groans that words cannot express' (8:26-27), and how God works all things for the good of those who love him, those who are called according to his purpose (8:28-30). The following section, 8:31-39, constitutes an emotive climax to Paul's exposition and defense of his gospel so far. In it he makes extensive use of the first person plural and by so doing associates himself with his audience in affirming what they together hold to be true: that God is for us (8:31), that having given up his own Son for us, he will freely give us all things with him (8:32), that God justifies us (8:33), that Christ died for us and, being now raised from the dead, intercedes for us (8:34), and that nothing whatever can separate us from the love of God which is in Christ Jesus our Lord (8:35-39).

This passage constitutes a peroration, the function of which, according to classical rhetorical theory, was to move the audience to accept the case made already in the speech, of which the peroration formed the climax. If, as seems likely, this is what Paul is seeking to achieve in 8:31-39, the passage forms an important transition between his response to objections that his gospel undermines moral standards and the status of the law on the one hand (6:1–8:13), and to charges that his gospel does away with Israel's special place in the purposes of God on the other (9:1–11:36). In other words, Paul is seeking to gain his audience's agreement to what he has argued so far, and to carry them along with him into the argument he is about to mount in 9:1–11:36.[401]

The peroration, containing seven questions, is reminiscent of the style of the diatribe, but it is employed here not to confront but to encourage the audience. Four of the questions provide the basic structure of the passage (8:31: 'What, then, shall we say in response to these things?'; 8:33: 'Who will bring any charge against those whom God has chosen?'; 8:34: 'Who is the one who condemns?'; 8:35: 'Who shall separate us from the love of Christ?'); each of which provides a cue for positive statements about God's love and grace that follow.

8:31-32 Paul commences his peroration with the first of the basic questions: *What, then, shall we say in response to these things?* 'These things'

---

401. Cf. A. H. Snyman, 'Style and Rhetorical Situation of Romans 8.31-39', *NTS* 34 (1988) 227-28.

refers back to Paul's exposition and defense of the gospel so far in 1:18–8:30. What 'we' have to say is expressed in the first instance with another question: *If God is for us, who can be against us?* The expected answer is, of course, 'No one!' Paul then adds: *He who did not spare his own Son, but gave him up for us all — how will he not also, along with him, graciously give us all things?* In the reference to God as the one 'who did not spare his own Son' there is, very probably, an allusion to Abraham's 'sacrifice' of Isaac. When Abraham was tested by God, he was willing to sacrifice his own son, but in the end Isaac was spared. However, when God acted for the salvation of sinful human beings, he 'did not spare his own Son but gave him up for us all'.[402] When Paul says that he 'gave him up' for us, he means that God 'handed him over to death' for us (cf. 4:25),[403] so that Christ became the atoning sacrifice for our sins (3:25). While there may be an allusion here to Abraham's son being spared (whereas God did not spare his own Son), it is doubtful that notions of vicarious sacrifice were ever associated with the 'sacrifice' of Isaac, or that he was regarded as a prototype of the Messiah.[404]

The expected response to the question, 'how will he not also, along with him, graciously give us all things?' is that, having given the greatest thing of all, his beloved Son, he will indeed graciously give us all things along with him.[405] The 'all things' to which Paul refers in 8:32 refers probably to the blessings of salvation and includes the inheritance promised to

---

402. Cf., e.g., Ziesler, *Romans*, 228. Dunn, *Romans 1–8*, 501, comments: 'The point being made rather comes out in the contrast between chap. 4 and 8:32; Paul has excluded or ignored any reference to the offering of Isaac in chap. 4, where his Jewish interlocutor would have expected it; and instead he has introduced this allusion at the climax of his argument, and referred it to God. In what must be accounted a very neat turning of the tables, Paul indicates that Abraham's offering of his son serves as a type not of the faithfulness of the devout Jew, but rather of the faithfulness of God'.

403. Paul also speaks of Christ handing himself over to death for our sakes (Gal 2:20; Eph 5:2, 25).

404. Cf. Jewett, *Romans*, 537. Fitzmyer, *Romans*, 531-32, remarks: 'There is, indeed, reference to the sacrifice of Abraham (Genesis 22) in 4 Macc 7:14, but there is no mention of the vicarious, soteriological, or expiatory understanding of that sacrifice. The same has to be said about 4 Macc 13:12; 16:20; 18:11; *Jub.* 17:15–18:19. . . . Moreover, even Josephus's recasting of the Genesis story (*Ant.* 1.13.1-4 . . .) includes no such understanding. . . . Nor do we find it in Philo . . . nor in Pseudo-Philo. . . . These texts do present Abraham's willingness to offer his son in sacrifice, at times even to admit that he was "to be sacrificed for piety's sake" (4 Macc 13:12); and that God rewarded Abraham. But the vicarious aspect of it, that Isaac was to be sacrificed on behalf of Israel or on behalf of someone else, is never mentioned. . . . The vicarious soteriological understanding of the *'Aqēdāh* emerged in rabbinical writings of later centuries. . . . Hence Abraham's willingness to sacrifice vicariously his only son is hardly an idea that Paul might have known in his Jewish past and thus alluded to. As the Pauline allusion is not clear, there can be no certainty about it'.

405. This is something about which the apostle had to remind his Corinthian converts, who were guilty of inappropriate boasting about their preferred leaders: 'So then, no more boasting about human leaders! *All things* are yours, whether Paul or Apollos or Cephas or the world or life or death or the present or the future — all are yours, and you are of Christ, and Christ is of God' (1 Cor 3:21-23, italics added).

believers (cf. 4:13; 8:17). We might add that God will also supply all believers' other needs so that they will be able to be generous in their support of those who, like Paul, labor in the preaching of the gospel (cf. Phil 4:14-19).

8:33-34 In these verses,[406] where Paul introduces his second basic question, he picks up again the theme of God as judge, and humanity appearing before him in his law court. In 2:1-16 he spoke of God's impartial judgment and said he '[would] give to each person according to what he [had] done'. In 3:19-20 he spoke of the whole world being held accountable to God, and insisted that no human being would be justified in his sight by deeds prescribed by the law. Here in 8:33-34 he again speaks of God as judge. This time it is believers who stand in his law court, but in their case, Paul says, God will entertain no accusations brought against them, for he has already justified them (5:1). Already Christ has died for them, and he now intercedes on their behalf.[407]

8:33 The second basic question is: *Who will bring any charge against those whom God has chosen?* The verb translated 'bring a charge' is found only here in Paul's letters, but used frequently in Acts where Luke speaks of Paul's opponents pressing charges against him (Acts 19:38, 40; 23:28-29; 26:2, 7). The charges that Paul has in mind in 8:33 are accusations that could be brought against believers before God the judge of all. Though not stated, Paul probably has in mind the charges brought against God's people by Satan, the accuser of the brethren, charges that would have substance, for they are all guilty of sin against God.[408] In Revelation 12:10 we read: 'Then I heard a loud voice in heaven say: "Now have come the salvation and the power and the kingdom of our God, and the authority of his Messiah. For the accuser of our brothers and sisters, who accuses them before our God day and night, has been hurled down"'.

Believers are described as 'those whom God has chosen' (lit. 'God's elect ones'), a term found frequently in the OT. In its singular form it can re-

406. As translated by the NIV (and the NRSV), these verses consist of two questions, each with corresponding responses. Barrett says that these verses, if punctuated differently, may be seen simply as a series of questions that may be translated as: 'Who can bring a charge against God's elect? God — who justifies us? Who condemns us? Christ Jesus — who died, or rather was raised, who is at the right hand of God, who actually is interceding on our behalf?' (Barrett, *Romans*, 172; cf. Jewett, *Romans*, 540-41). This is a legitimate way of construing the Greek text. Either way, the purpose of the verses is to highlight the fact that God entertains no charges against his elect. The commentary below is based on the NIV translation.

407. Wright, 'Romans', 613, points out: 'We should note that at this point Paul is once again speaking of the *final* day of judgment, as in 2:1-16 and 8:1. As he looks ahead to that future moment, he puts his confidence in the *past event* of justification and hence the *present standing* of God's people that results from it, knowing that "those God justified, God also glorified". The logic of justification comes full circle'.

408. Isabelle Parlier, 'La folle justice de Dieu: Romains 8,31-39', *FoiVie* 91 (1992) 105-6, argues that God himself is both accuser and justifier, but this is unlikely, seeing that this whole section is introduced with a question which demands the most positive answer about the attitude of God towards believers: 'If God is for us, who can be against us?'

fer to an individual (Ps 89:3; Sir 47:22) or to the nation Israel (Isa 42:1; 43:20; 45:4), while in its plural form it can refer to the nation of Israel (1 Chr 16:13; Ps 105:6; Isa 65:9; Sir 46:1) or to a number of individual Israelites (Wis 3:9; 4:15). Here in 8:33 in its plural form it refers to believers.

The expected answer to Paul's second basic question is that no one will be able to bring charges against God's elect because *it is God who justifies*. When responding to the question in this way, the apostle may have in mind Isaiah 50:8: 'He who vindicates me is near. Who then will bring charges against me? Let us face each other! Who is my accuser? Let him confront me!' When God himself vindicates his people, no charges against them can stand.

8:34 The third basic question is: *Who then is the one who that condemns?* The verb 'to condemn' that Paul uses here means to pronounce a sentence upon a person after determination of guilt.[409] The answer to the question is *No one*, and for this very important reason: *Christ Jesus who died — more than that, who was raised to life — is at the right hand of God and is also interceding for us*.[410] In 8:26 we are told that the Spirit intercedes for us because of our weakness and not knowing what to pray for. Here we are told that the crucified and now risen Christ intercedes for us in the light of our possible condemnation. He acts as our advocate with God, at whose right hand he sits and pleads the efficacy of his atoning sacrifice so that there is now no condemnation for those who believe in him.[411]

8:35 This verse opens with the fourth basic question: *Who shall separate us from the love of Christ?* The expected answer is 'no one'. However, Paul is aware that this does not mean that believers will be exempt from suffering, so he continues: *Shall trouble or hardship or persecution or famine or nakedness or danger or sword?* 'Trouble' in Paul's case was the ongoing and nearly ever-present reality of his life, this was often the case also in the lives of his converts, and he mentions these things no fewer than twenty-one times.[412] 'Hardship' also features several times in Paul's characterization of the life and ministry of both himself and other servants of God (2:9; 8:35; 2 Cor 6:4; 12:10), as do 'persecution' (8:35; 2 Cor 12:10; 1 Thess 1:4; 2 Tim 3:11), and less often 'famine' and 'nakedness' (8:35; 2 Cor 11:27), 'danger' (8:35; 1 Cor 11:26), and the 'sword', that is, death by execution (8:35).

---

409. Cf. BAGD, *ad loc.*

410. Parlier, 'La folle justice de Dieu', 105-6, contends that Christ is both the judge who condemns and the advocate for the defense, interceding for believers before God, but this is as unlikely as her suggestion that God is both accuser and justifier, and for the same reason — it is inconsistent with the positive attitude of God towards believers depicted in this passage.

411. A similar point is made in 1 John 2:1-2: 'My dear children, I write this to you so that you will not sin. But if anybody does sin, we have one who speaks to the Father in our defense — Jesus Christ, the Righteous One. He is the atoning sacrifice for our sins, and not only for ours but also for the sins of the whole world'.

412. Cf. 5:3; 8:35; 12:12; 1 Cor 7:28; 2 Cor 1:4, 8; 2:4; 4:17; 6:4; 7:4; 8:2, 13; Eph 3:13; Phil 1:17; 4:14; Col 1:24; 1 Thess 1:6; 3:3, 7; 2 Thess 1:4, 6.

8:36 All of these trials, Paul believes, are foreshadowed in Scripture: *As it is written: 'For your sake we face death all day long; we are considered as sheep to be slaughtered'.* The quotation is from Psalm 44, where the psalmist laments the fact that God has apparently rejected and humbled his people, something he could understand if they had not been faithful. Because the psalmist believes they had been faithful, he thinks their suffering has been for God's sake, and so calls upon God to rise up and redeem them:

> ¹⁷All this came upon us,
>   though we had not forgotten you;
>   we had not been false to your covenant.
> ¹⁸Our hearts had not turned back;
>   our feet had not strayed from your path.
> ¹⁹But you crushed us and made us a haunt for jackals;
>   you covered us over with deep darkness.
> ²⁰If we had forgotten the name of our God
>   or spread out our hands to a foreign god,
> ²¹would not God have discovered it,
>   since he knows the secrets of the heart?
> ²²*Yet for your sake we face death all day long;*
>   *we are considered as sheep to be slaughtered.*
> ²³Awake, O Lord! Why do you sleep?
>   Rouse yourself! Do not reject us forever.
> ²⁴Why do you hide your face
>   and forget our misery and oppression?
> ²⁵We are brought down to the dust;
>   our bodies cling to the ground.
> ²⁶Rise up and help us;
>   redeem us because of your unfailing love.
>
>   (Ps 44:17-26, italics added).

Parlier argues that it is not by chance that Paul quotes a passage from Psalm 44 in which the psalmist complains that God's people are suffering though they remain faithful to the covenant, and calls upon God to redeem them in his 'unfailing love'. It is as if Paul is responding to the psalmist's complaint by asserting that no suffering is able to separate believers from the love of God in Christ.[413] Jewett, on the other hand, suggests that Paul incorporated the quotation to adduce scriptural support to show that suffering is not a disqualifying mark for those claiming to be true disciples. He had to do this to silence criticisms of his apostleship along these lines.[414] The apostle certainly had to defend himself in this way in 2 Corinthians 11:22-33, but whether this is the case here in Romans 8 is debatable.

8:37 The followers of Christ may be 'considered as sheep to be

---

413. Parlier, 'La folle justice de Dieu', 108-9.
414. Jewett, *Romans*, 548.

slaughtered', but even this cannot separate them from the love of Christ. On the contrary, he says: *No, in all these things we are more than conquerors through him who loved us.* 'We are more than conquerors' (lit. 'we are completely victorious') translates a verb found only here in the NT, and is a heightened form of the more common verb 'to overcome', which is found twenty-eight times in the NT.[415] The two predominant NT uses of 'to overcome' are (i) in relation to believers being victorious over pressure from those who would lead them astray doctrinally (1 John 2:13, 14; 4:4; 5:4, 5), and (ii) in relation to believers being victorious in face of trouble and persecution by not denying their faith in Christ even in the face of death (Rev 2:7, 11, 17; 3:12; 12:11). The latter seems to be the meaning of being 'more than conquerors' in 8:37. Believers are 'more than conquerors' when they refuse to deny their Lord even when they are 'considered as sheep to be slaughtered'. Their victory is achieved 'through him who loved us', that is, through the Lord Jesus Christ, who stands beside his followers and strengthens them when they face persecution for his name's sake (cf. Acts 18:9-11; 2 Tim 4:16-18).[416]

8:38-39 These verses constitute the triumphant conclusion to Paul's response to the fifth question, 'Who shall separate us from the love of Christ?' (8:35a), and in fact to the whole emotive climax to his gospel presentation and defense so far. In 8:35b Paul listed earthly trials as those things that conceivably separate us from the love of Christ, while here in 8:38-39 he lists supernatural powers that may conceivably do so. However, he insists that neither earthly trials nor the hostility of supernatural powers 'will be able to separate us from the love of God that is in Christ Jesus our Lord'.[417]

Paul declares: *For I am convinced that neither death nor life, neither angels nor demons, neither the present nor the future, nor any powers, neither height nor depth, nor anything else in all creation, will be able to separate us from the love of God that is in Christ Jesus our Lord.* The apostle's list includes the pairs death and life (cf. 1 Cor 3:22; Phil 1:20), angels and demons (lit. 'angels nor authorities'), the present and the future (cf. 1 Cor 3:22), and height and depth. Each of these represents some power or reality that, together with other 'powers' and 'anything else in all creation' (lit. 'any creature'), could conceivably separate believers from the love of Christ. He lists all these things only to deny emphatically that any or all of them could possibly separate believers from 'the love of God that is in Christ Jesus our Lord'. It is signifi-

---

415. Apart from one occurrence in Luke 11:22 and two in Rom 3:4; 12:21, all the others are in the Gospel of John, the Letters of John, and Revelation (John 16:33; 1 John 2:13, 14; 4:4; 5:4, 5; Rev 2:7, 11, 17, 26; 3:5, 12, 21; 5:5; 6:2; 11:7; 12:11; 13:7; 15:2; 17:14; 21:7).

416. Fitzmyer, *Romans*, 534, offers a different perspective on the significance of 'we are more than conquerors' (*hypernikaō*), suggesting that it means '"we are supervictors", i.e., victors in court, because we have been vindicated and justified in a superabundant way by what Christ has done for sinful humanity'.

417. Cf. F. J. Leenhardt, *L'épître de St Paul aux Romains* (Commentaire du Nouveau Testament VI; Neuchâtel: Delachaux et Niestlé, 1957), 137.

cant that the fifth question was, 'Who shall separate us from the love of Christ?' and the final triumphant declaration is that nothing 'will be able to separate us from the love of God that is in Christ Jesus our Lord'. The love of Christ is none other than the love of God that is in Christ, something Paul makes clear in 5:8: 'But God demonstrates his own love for us in this: While we were still sinners, Christ died for us', and 2 Corinthians 5:19: 'God was reconciling the world to himself in Christ, not counting men's sins against them'.

Commenting on the fact that nothing can separate believers from the love of God in Christ, Barrett says: 'Of course not; for Christ Jesus is — the Lord. He is Lord over all spiritual powers, for he has triumphed over them in the Cross (Col. ii.15); he is Lord over life and death, for he was crucified, and raised from the dead; he is Lord over things present and things to come, for it was in him that God elected us in love, and it is with him that we shall enter into God's glory beyond history. In Christ Jesus, God is *for us*; and it is in Christ Jesus that we know him and trust him'.[418]

ADDITIONAL NOTE: HOPE IN THE PAULINE CORPUS

The concept of the believer's hope is both important and pervasive in Paul's letters. In Romans Abraham looks forward in hope to the fulfillment of God's promise of offspring even though humanly speaking there was no hope (4:18); believers rejoice in their hope of sharing in the glory of God, a hope that is strengthened through suffering and that will not be disappointed (5:2-5); they are said to be saved in this hope (8:24); exhorted to be joyful in hope (12:12); they are reminded that through endurance and the encouragement of the Scriptures they have hope (15:4); and that by the power of the Holy Spirit they may overflow with hope (15:13).

Elsewhere the apostle speaks of the great triad of faith, hope, and love (1 Cor 13:13); hope in the unfading glory of the new covenant (2 Cor 3:12); the righteousness for which believers hope (Gal 5:5); and hope for the glorious inheritance God has in store for them (Eph 1:18; 4:4; Col 1:5, 23). He speaks of Christ in believers as their hope of glory (Col 1:27) and of endurance inspired by hope in the Lord Jesus Christ (1 Thess 1:3). He regards his converts as his hope, joy, and crown at the coming of the Lord Jesus (1 Thess 2:19). He speaks of the hope of salvation as a helmet (1 Thess 5:8); hope for a share in the glory of the Lord Jesus (2 Thess 2:14-16); Christ Jesus himself as our hope (1 Tim 1:1); the hope of eternal life (Tit 1:2; 3:7); and the blessed hope of 'the glorious appearing of our great God and Savior, Jesus Christ' (Tit 2:13).

---

418. Barrett, *Romans*, 174.

D. Israel and the Purposes of God, 9:1–11:36

Romans 9–11 constitutes the next major section of Paul's exposition and defense of his gospel. Already he has shown that Jews and Gentiles are alike
in the matters of sin, judgment, and salvation (1:18–5:21). He has answered
objections to his gospel by showing that it is not, as some have said, an invi-
tation to moral anarchy (3:8; 6:1-23), nor does it involve a denigration of the
law (7:1-25); on the contrary, it does what the law could not do, that is,
bring about the fulfillment of the 'just requirement of the law' in those who
walk according to the Spirit (8:1-13). Paul then explained that if believers
share now in Christ's sufferings, they will share also in his glory, even
though in the meantime they, along with creation itself, groan while they
await the revelation of their glory. In this they are sustained by the Holy
Spirit's intercession and by God himself, who works all things together for
good for his people (8:14-30). There followed the great emotive climax of
8:31-39 in which Paul argued that, if God is for us and gave up his own Son
for us, he will freely give us all things with him. He declared that because
God justifies us, and Christ died for us and now, being raised from death,
intercedes for us, nothing whatever can separate us from the love of God
that is in Christ Jesus our Lord (8:31-39). This emotive climax prepares the
way for what the apostle has to say in chapters 9–11, where he deals with
the fact that many of his Jewish contemporaries rejected his gospel and the
inferences that some of them might draw from this fact, that is, his gospel
denies God's faithfulness to Israel, does away with her special place in the
purposes of God, and therefore implies that God's word has failed.

According to the Acts of the Apostles, Paul carried out his mission by
preaching first in the local Jewish community in each town he visited.
However, this ministry was generally greeted with minimal response and
was often followed by outright opposition and persecution. This picture
emerging from the Acts of the Apostles is confirmed by references in Paul's
own letters to the opposition he faced from his Jewish kinsfolk and the bitter persecution he experienced at their hands (1 Thess 2:14-16; 2 Cor 11:24,
26). However, when Paul turned to the Gentiles, he often found a ready response among them. It appears that it was this experience, as well as objections that his gospel implies that the promises of God had failed, that
prompted Paul to write Romans 9–11.

The exact way in which Paul approaches the problem in Romans 9–11
has been variously defined. For example, Getty says that Paul tries to rec-
oncile two fundamental ideas: (i) that Israel is God's people, and (ii) that
the Gentiles have been included in the plan of God for universal salvation.[1]
Longenecker sees Paul dealing with the question, 'How can God, whose
people are presently marked out by their faith in Jesus Christ, be a faithful

---

1. Mary Ann Getty, 'Paul and the Salvation of Israel: A Perspective on Romans 9–11',
CBQ 50 (1988) 468.

God if, in the past, he promised Israel a unique place as his covenant people?'[2] However, it would be a mistake to regard Romans 9–11 merely as
Paul's endeavor to answer a theological objection to his gospel by stating
his views about the place of Israel in God's purposes. The apostle had a
deep personal involvement in this issue. It distressed him that Israel had
rejected her messiah. This is nowhere more poignantly expressed than in
Romans 9:1-5.

As chapters 9–11 unfold, it becomes clear that Paul is also counteracting a tendency on the part of Gentile believers to look down on Jews and
Jewish believers. This suggests that the Gentile believers in his audience
are primarily in view here. However, the apostle's theological explanation
of the rejection of his gospel by many Jews would be relevant to Jewish believers in Paul's audience also, just as it was a matter of great concern to
Paul himself.

Paul's treatment of the problem of Jewish rejection of the gospel, and
the consequent suggestion that God's word, his promises to the Jews, had
failed comprises three main parts: (i) 9:1-29, in which he argues that the
present exclusion of many Jews from the blessings of salvation is the result
of God's own sovereign choice, the exercise of his prerogative as Creator;
(ii) 9:30–10:21, where the apostle demonstrates that the Jews themselves are
also responsible for their failure to enjoy these blessings because they rejected the God who held out his hands to them all day long; (iii) 11:1-36, in
which Paul shows that despite the fact that many of the Jews were rejecting
God's call, God has not rejected the Jewish people as a whole. He has maintained a faithful remnant among them, as he has always done. More than
that, when the full number of the Gentile elect has come in, it will be seen
that the full number of the Jewish elect also will have been brought in, and
so 'all Israel' will be saved.

1. Paul's Concern for Israel and Her Privileges, 9:1-5

> [1]*I speak the truth in Christ — I am not lying, my conscience confirms it
> through the Holy Spirit —* [2]*I have great sorrow and unceasing anguish in
> my heart.* [3]*For I could wish that I myself were cursed and cut off from Christ
> for the sake of my people, those of my own race,* [4]*the people of Israel. Theirs is*

2. Bruce W. Longenecker, 'Different Answers to Different Issues: Israel, the Gentiles
and Salvation History in Romans 9–11', *JSNT* 36 (1989) 95. Longenecker suggests that Paul
emphasizes different things concerning Israel, depending on the issues he is addressing.
When the apostle is thinking of the present stage of salvation history, he strongly defends
the freedom of the Gentiles from Jewish ethnic constraints. But when he has the grand plan
of salvation history in mind, he argues that the Gentiles cannot exist as believers except as
participants in the promises first made to Israel. Put more briefly, the Gentiles do not have
to adopt the ethnic symbols of the Jewish people, but, nevertheless, God brings about the
salvation of the Gentiles through an ethnic people, Israel (113).

the adoption to sonship; theirs the divine glory, the covenants, the receiving of the law, the temple worship and the promises. ⁵Theirs are the patriarchs, and from them is traced the human ancestry of the Messiah, who is God over all, forever praised! Amen.

The matter of Israel's failure as a whole to embrace the gospel was for Paul not merely a theological issue demanding an explanation, but it was something that caused him great personal anguish.

9:1 He begins his response to Israel's rejection of the gospel with the words: *I speak the truth in Christ — I am not lying, my conscience confirms it through the Holy Spirit.* This remarkably strong affirmation of the veracity of what he is about to say about his deep concern for his own people probably reflects an awareness that some of his fellow Jews doubted his devotion to Israel, probably in the light of his commitment to a Gentile mission.

Elsewhere Paul prefaces important statements with oath formulae, calling upon God as witness to what he says (cf. 1:9; 2 Cor 1:23; 13:1; Phil 1:8; 1 Thess 2:5, 10). Here he asserts positively that he is speaking the truth 'in Christ' (i.e., as someone united by faith with Jesus Christ), and reinforces this by asserting negatively, 'I am not lying'. Paul adds, alongside his claim that he speaks the truth and is not lying, that his conscience confirms the truth of what he is about to say. In 2 Corinthians 1:12 also Paul appeals to the testimony of his conscience in support of the truthfulness of what he says: 'Now this is our boast: Our conscience testifies that we have conducted ourselves in the world, and especially in our relations with you, with integrity and godly sincerity'. It may be with an awareness that the human conscience is not infallible (see 'Additional Note: Conscience', 141) that Paul says here that his conscience confirms the truth of his affirmation 'through the Holy Spirit'. It is an implied claim that the Holy Spirit confirms the testimony of his conscience. We might say that for Paul the Spirit not only bears witness with our spirits that we are children of God (8:16), but he also bears witness alongside our consciences when we speak the truth.

9:2-4a What Paul wants to affirm with such solemnity is: *I have great sorrow and unceasing anguish in my heart.* He explains the reason for this sorrow and anguish: *For I could wish that I myself were cursed and cut off from Christ for the sake of my people.* The NIV construes the imperfect form of the verb 'to wish' here as 'I could wish', so as to denote a contemplated action, but one that was not actually brought about (so too most other English translations, including NRSV, NASB, ASV). An alternative translation that brings out the force of the imperfect tense of the verb is 'I used to pray' or 'I was praying'.[3] Either way, whether contemplated or actual, the prayer was

---

3. Jewett, *Romans*, 560, comments: 'Paul provides the reason for his anguish by a complex construction introduced by the imperfect verb ēuchomēn ("I was praying, wishing"), which has "the force of throwing this wish into the past, and into a past that remains always unfinished, so that this expression takes away from the wish all possibility of realization"'. . . . It is better in this context to translate, "I used to pray that I myself be banned . . . ," implying

that he might be 'cursed and cut off from Christ' for the sake of his Jewish kinsfolk. This sort of prayer finds a parallel in the intercession of Moses for Israel following her worship of the golden calf:

> The next day Moses said to the people, 'You have committed a great sin. But now I will go up to the LORD; perhaps I can make atonement for your sin'. So Moses went back to the LORD and said, 'Oh, what a great sin these people have committed! They have made themselves gods of gold. But now, please forgive their sin — *but if not, then blot me out of the book you have written*'. (Exod 32:30-32, italics added)[4]

Moses asked the Lord to forgive the people, and, if he would not do so, that he blot him out of the book he has written. However, the Lord replied: 'Whoever has sinned against me I will blot out of my book' (Exod 32:33). Paul would certainly know of Moses' request and that it had been rejected. Perhaps it was this knowledge that led him not to pray along those lines (any longer). Alternatively he may have come to realize that the Lord would not accept such a request. Even so, the fact that he had once contemplated praying or had once actually prayed in this way underlines the greatness of the anguish he felt in the light of his kinsfolk's rejection of their messiah. Why Paul felt so strongly will become apparent as his argument unfolds in chapters 9–11, but implied here already is his belief that in their present state the majority of his 'brothers' were 'accursed and cut off from Christ',[5] a fate he would have accepted in their place if it would bring about their salvation.[6]

When Paul says that he wished that he could be 'cursed' in place of his unbelieving kinsfolk, he employs the noun *anathema* (lit. 'accursed'). Barrett notes: 'The word *anathema* is found in the LXX as the equivalent of *ḥerem*, "thing or person devoted (to destruction or sacred use and therefore secluded from profane use)". Here, of course, destruction is in mind; to be separated from Christ is to be consigned to damnation'.[7] Paul uses *anathema*/accursed elsewhere in various connections. He does so when express-

---

actual prayer requests made sometime before the moment of writing, requests that God had thus far chosen not to fulfill'.

4. Paul would have also known of the belief that the death of the Maccabean martyrs was thought to atone for the sins of Israel (cf. 4 Macc 17:22), but it is doubtful that his prayer would have been motivated by that sort of thinking.

5. Paul speaks, albeit in different terms, of being cut off from Christ when he warned the Galatians against embracing the teaching of the Judaizers: 'Again I declare to every man who lets himself be circumcised that he is obligated to obey the whole law. You who are trying to be justified by the law have been alienated from Christ; you have fallen away from grace' (Gal 5:3-4).

6. Michael Cranford, 'Election and Ethnicity: Paul's View of Israel in Romans 9.1-13', *JSNT* 50 (1993) 30, notes that 'the implication . . . is that Paul sees his people as anathema, as excluded from the covenant and therefore the object of God's wrath, and he therefore would desire to assume their place vicariously, that they might enjoy the covenant blessings resulting from union with Christ, as Paul himself did'.

7. Barrett, *Romans*, 176.

ing his strong disapproval of those who do not love the Lord (1 Cor 16:22: 'If anyone does not love the Lord, let that person be cursed'), and of those who preach another gospel (Gal 1:8-9: 'But even if we or an angel from heaven should preach a gospel other than the one we preached to you, let them be under God's curse! As we have already said, so now I say again: If anybody is preaching to you a gospel other than what you accepted, let them be under God's curse!').

Paul identifies the 'people' on whose behalf he could pray in this way as *those of my own race, the people of Israel* (lit. 'my kinsfolk according to [the] flesh, who are Israelites'). Paul employs the term 'Israelites' rather than the more common ethnic or political designation, 'Jews'. He uses the term 'Israelite' in only three places, and in each case it signifies something of the sacredness of being a member of God's chosen people (9:4; 11:1; 2 Cor 11:22).[8] It is significant that he still applies this sacred term to those who were currently rejecting their Messiah. As Israelites, his kinsfolk have been blessed with many advantages, eight of which he enumerates in 9:4b-5.

9:4b-5 These verses contain a unique list of the privileges of Israel as God's people, one without parallel in Jewish literature, and therefore probably of Paul's own compilation.[9] It may be, as Moo suggests, that Paul's intention in providing this list of privileges is to explain why he was willing to sacrifice himself for them: 'We are justified in suggesting a causal relationship between vv. 4-5 and v. 3: "I have great sorrow for my fellow Jews and could even pray that I might be condemned so that they could be saved *because* they are"'. . . .[10]

Listing the privileges, Paul says first: *Theirs is the adoption to sonship.* In the Old Testament the people of Israel are called God's sons (cf., e.g., Isa 63:8; Jer 3:19), and the nation of Israel his son (cf., e.g., Exod 4:22). The exodus from Egypt seems to have been regarded as the adoption of Israel by God as his son (Hos 11:1).[11]

Secondly, he says: *theirs [is] the divine glory.* There is no counterpart for

---

8. Richard H. Bell, *The Irrevocable Call of God: An Inquiry into Paul's Theology of Israel* (WUNT 184; Tübingen: Mohr Siebeck, 2005), 199-200, comments: 'In early times (e.g., in the Song of Deborah, Judg. 5.2, 7), "Israel" was a sacred term denoting the chosen community of God. Later it became the designation of the Northern Kingdom (1 Kgs 12ff.), but after the Assyrian attack on the North and subsequent deportation the term was applied to Judah. After the exile "it became the self-designation of the Jewish people aware of its status as the holy and chosen people of God". . . . In later Palestinian Judaism, "Israel" was the self-designation of the Jews expressing their consciousness of being the people of God, and in the New Testament, 'Israel' and 'Israelite' continue to have a salvation-historical significance. Therefore, in using the word 'Israelites' in Rom. 9.4, Paul would seem to be asserting that the Jews are the chosen people of God'.

9. Cf. Bell, *The Irrevocable Call of God,* 201.

10. Moo, *Romans,* 560.

11. Paul uses the expression 'adoption' *(huiothesia)* five times in his writings, but only here in relation to the nation Israel. Elsewhere he applies it to believers (8:15, 23; Gal 4:5; Eph 1:5).

the NIV's 'divine' in the Greek text, but its addition clarifies things because the glory belonging to Israel was the glory of God that filled the tabernacle (Exod 16:10; 24:15-17; 40:34-35; Lev 9:6, 23; Num 14:10; 16:19, 42; 20:6; Deut 5:24), Solomon's temple (1 Kgs 8:11; 2 Chr 5:13-14; 7:1-3), and that will fill 'Jerusalem' and its 'temple' in the coming age (Zech 2:5; Isa 60:19; Ezek 43:2, 4-5; 44:4; 11QT 29:8).

Thirdly, Paul says: [*theirs are*] *the covenants*. There is a variant reading at this point with the singular 'covenant' instead of the plural 'covenants'. The textual evidence is adjudged by most scholars to favor the plural form.[12] If we adopt the plural 'covenants', what Paul had in mind could include God's covenant with Abraham in which he promised to bless him and make him a blessing, to provide him with a vast progeny, and to give them the land of his sojourning, a covenant repeated with Isaac and Jacob. The covenants could also include the one made by God with Israel at Sinai in the time of Moses when, having redeemed them from Egyptian slavery, he brought them to himself and gave them his law by which they were to regulate their lives in relationship with him. Also included may be God's covenant with David in which he promised to establish his throne forever, a promise ultimately fulfilled with the coming of the Lord Jesus Christ, the great Son of David.[13]

Fourthly, he says: [*theirs is*] *the receiving of the law.* The word translated 'the receiving of the law' (lit. 'lawgiving') can mean either the 'giving of the law' or the 'law' itself, that is, 'the law given'. In the three places it is found in the LXX it means the 'law' itself.[14] This suggests that Paul has in mind the possession of the law itself, rather than the giving of the law,[15] or even

---

12. Cf. Metzger, ed., *A Textual Commentary, ad loc.* Bell, *The Irrevocable Call of God,* 205, argues: 'In Rom. 9.4, the plural form is most likely the original reading since it is the *lectio difficilior.* The singular *diathēkē,* despite its early attestation (P[46] B D F G vg[cl]), may have been written in order to make clear a reference to the covenant of Moses. Ironically, though, such a covenant was probably not uppermost in Paul's mind. If any covenant stood out for Paul, it was the one made with Abraham'. Barrett, *Romans,* 177-78, comments: 'If the singular "covenant" . . . is read, the reference is evidently to the covenant made at Mount Sinai. This makes excellent sense, for this covenant was of course the basis of Israel's national and religious life. The plural, however, also makes good sense. There were several covenants — with Adam, with Noah, and with Abraham, as well as with Moses — and it is possible that Paul refers to these; but it is more likely (like other Jewish writers; see S.B. iii.262) he distinguished three covenants within the great covenant of the Exodus — a covenant at Horeb, a second in the plains of Moab, and a third at Mounts Gerizim and Ebal'.

13. Abasciano, *Paul's Use of the Old Testament in Romans 9.1-9,* 145, argues that the covenants refer to the Sinaitic/Mosaic covenant with its renewals as an extension of the Abrahamic covenant and looking forward to the new covenant.

14. The word 'lawgiving/legislation' (*nomothesia*) is found only here in the NT. It occurs three times in the LXX (2 Macc 6:23; 4 Macc 5:35; 17:16) as well as in the writings of classical authors and early church fathers.

15. James D. G. Dunn, *Romans 9–16* (WBC 38B; Dallas: Word Books, 1988), 527, holds: 'It is doubtful if the distinction [giving of the law, or the law given] would have been seen to make any difference'.

less likely the receiving of the law. Having the law was one of Israel's most outstanding privileges, something that Moses said distinguished her from all other nations:

> See, I have taught you decrees and laws as the LORD my God commanded me, so that you may follow them in the land you are entering to take possession of it. Observe them carefully, for this will show your wisdom and understanding to the nations, who will hear about all these decrees and say, "Surely this great nation is a wise and understanding people". What other nation is so great as to have their gods near them the way the LORD our God is near us whenever we pray to him? And what other nation is so great as to have such righteous decrees and laws as this body of laws I am setting before you today? (Deut 4:5-8)

Fifthly, he says: [*theirs is*] *the temple worship* (lit. 'and [theirs] the worship'). The word 'temple' is not found in the original, being added by the translators of the NIV. The fifth great privilege of Israel was the service/worship (of God). God provided Israel with a sacrificial system by which they could approach him and through which their sins could be forgiven. This was practiced first in the tabernacle and then in Solomon's temple. This system foreshadowed the sacrifice of Christ on the cross, by which alone sins could be truly removed. Paul's reference to the 'worship' here would have the sacrificial system in mind primarily, but may also include non-sacrificial elements such as prayer, Sabbath observance, and the recitation of the Shema as well.[16] Paul uses the word translated 'worship' in only one other place (12:1) to refer to the spiritual or rational worship of believers.

Sixthly, he says: *and* [*theirs are*] *the promises.* When Paul speaks of 'the promises', he has in mind the promises God made when he established his covenants with his people Israel. In one place he speaks of the promises made to the patriarchs (15:8), but most often he has in mind the promises God made to Abraham when he established his covenant with him, promises regarding progeny, the land, and blessing for the nations (cf. Gen 12:2-3; 18:18; 22:18; 26:14; Sir 44:21; Acts 3:25).

Seventhly, he says: *theirs are the patriarchs.* In a number of places the apostle refers generally to the patriarchs of Israel (11:28; 15:28), meaning Abraham, Isaac, and Jacob. However, for Paul Abraham above all was the patriarch (father) of Israel, and indeed the father of many nations — all those who believe as Abraham did (4:11-12, 16-18). In one place only does he refer explicitly to anyone else as a father of Israel, in this case to 'our father Isaac' (9:10).

Finally, Paul says: *and from them is traced the human ancestry of the Messiah* (lit. 'and from whom [is] the Christ according to the flesh'). It is no

---

16. Cf. Cranfield, *Romans*, II, 463; Bell, *The Irrevocable Call of God*, 206-7; Jewett, *Romans*, 564-65.

doubt significant that this last and most important privilege accorded Israel is introduced differently from all the preceding ones. They were said to belong to Israel ('theirs is . . .'), but this cannot be said of the Christ. He does not 'belong' to Israel. However, according to the flesh he is 'from' Israel. As the NIV has it, his human ancestry is traced from Israel. In a couple of other places Paul refers to the Christ being from the stock of Israel: in 1:3 he refers to him as the one 'who as to his earthly life was a descendant of David', and in Galatians 4:4-5 he speaks of him being 'born of a woman, born under law, to redeem those under law'. Byrne comments: 'There is great poignancy and irony in this final member . . . since it is precisely Israel's failure to recognize the Messiah to whom she gave birth that puts in question all the other privileges and gives rise to this entire discussion'.[17]

To his reference to the human ancestry of the Christ Paul adds: *who is God over all, forever praised! Amen.* In the way the NIV construes this text it describes Christ as 'God over all', a remarkable statement involving the closest possible identification of Jesus Christ with God the Father. Another legitimate way of construing this text is followed by the NRSV: '[Christ], who is over all, God blessed forever. Amen'. Christ is described as the one who rules over all, and is blessed by God forever. This does not involve so close an identification of Christ with God. A third option is to render the text: '[Christ], who is over all. God be praised forever! Amen'. In this case the description of the final advantage of Israel, that through her is traced the human ancestry of the Christ, concludes with the affirmation that Christ is over all. What follows is an ascription of praise to God: 'God be praised forever'. A fourth way of construing the text is: '[Christ]. God who is over all be forever praised! Amen'. In this case the final advantage of the Jews is simply that 'from them is traced the human ancestry of Christ'; the words 'who is over all' then refer to God to whom the ascription of praise is made.

All four options are possible interpretations of Paul's words as they stand in this text. Scholars are divided in their opinions concerning whether 9:5b should be read as an ascription of divinity to Christ or not.[18] However, similar ascriptions of praise by Paul always have God the Father as their object. In 1:25 he refers to the Creator, 'who is forever praised'; in 2 Corinthians 11:31 he refers to 'the God and Father of the Lord Jesus, who is to be praised forever', and in Ephesians 1:3 he exults, 'Praise be to the God and Father of our Lord Jesus Christ'. This being the case, either the

---

17. Byrne, *Romans*, 286.

18. Those supporting an ascription of divinity to Christ here include Abasciano, *Paul's Use of the Old Testament in Romans 9.1-9*, 145; Wright, 'Romans', 630-31; Cranfield, *Romans*, II, 468; Jewett, *Romans*, 568; Moo, *Romans*, 566-67; Witherington, *Romans*, 251-52; Hans-Christian Kammler, 'Die Prädikation Jesu Christi als "Gott" und die paulinische Christologie: Erwägungen zur Exegese von Röm 9,5b', *ZNW* 94 (2003) 164-80; Fitzmyer, *Romans*, 549. Those reading 9:5b as an ascription of praise to God include Byrne, *Romans*, 288; Dunn, *Romans 9–16*, 529.

third or the fourth of the options above is probably to be preferred, and
thus the text should be rendered either as: 'from whom [is] the Christ according to the flesh, who is over all. God be praised forever. Amen', or
'from whom is the Christ. God who is over all be forever praised! Amen'.

In 9:1-5, then, Paul has emphasized both his own deep concern for the
people of Israel and their many God-given privileges. This would undercut
any suggestion that he undervalues his own people, and paves the way for
answering objections that his gospel is flawed because Israel as a whole has
rejected it, or because it involves a denial of Israel's special place in the purposes of God, or, most important of all, that it implies that God's word has
failed.

2. Israel and God's Election, 9:6-29

In this section Paul begins his explanation of the reasons for Israel's failure
to embrace the gospel and experience its blessings. He insists that her failure is in no way the result of any failure of God's word. God by his own
sovereign choice determines to whom he will show mercy. But this does
not mean that there is any injustice on his part. As Creator he has the right
to do whatever he wills with what he has made. However, this is not the
whole story, for as 9:30–10:21 will show, Israel herself bears responsibility
for the rejection of the gospel.

a. God's Word Has Not Failed, 9:6-13

*6It is not as though God's word had failed. For not all who are descended
from Israel are Israel. 7Nor because they are his descendants are they all
Abraham's children. On the contrary, 'It is through Isaac that your offspring
will be reckoned'. 8In other words, it is not the children by physical descent
who are God's children, but it is the children of the promise who are regarded
as Abraham's offspring. 9For this was how the promise was stated: 'At the
appointed time I will return, and Sarah will have a son'.*

*10Not only that, but Rebekah's children were conceived at the same time
by our father Isaac. 11Yet, before the twins were born or had done anything
good or bad — in order that God's purpose in election might stand: 12not by
works but by him who calls — she was told, 'The older will serve the younger'. 13Just as it is written: 'Jacob I loved, but Esau I hated'.*

Paul writes this section to deal with the problem raised in relation to
his gospel by the fact that the majority of the Jews of his day were rejecting
it. If the gospel is God's word to Israel, then it would appear that God's
word has failed. Paul responds by reminding those in the Roman churches
that the fact that some Jews had responded negatively while others had responded positively is in accord with the way God has always exercised his

sovereign choice. In this passage he illustrates the point by appeal to the case of Abraham and his descendants, Isaac and Ishmael, Jacob and Esau.

9:6-7 To begin his response Paul asserts: *It is not as though God's word had failed.* Paul's use of the expression 'the word of God' elsewhere regularly denotes the gospel message (cf. 1 Cor 2:1; 14:36; 2 Cor 2:17; 4:2; Col 1:25;1 Thess 2:13; 2 Tim 2:9), and it is best to read it this way here also.[19] One of the recurring themes of the OT is the absolute certainty that God's word never fails. His word always achieves the purpose for which it was spoken. The clearest example is Isaiah 55:10-11:

> As the rain and the snow come down from heaven, and do not return to it without watering the earth and making it bud and flourish, so that it yields seed for the sower and bread for the eater, so is my word that goes out from my mouth: It will not return to me empty, but will accomplish what I desire and achieve the purpose for which I sent it.

Having asserted that God's word has not failed, even though many Jews reject the gospel and therefore fail to experience its blessings, Paul offers an explanation for this state of affairs: *For not all who are descended from Israel are Israel.* He said something similar earlier in the letter when he addressed a hypothetical Jewish dialogue partner and accused him of failing to live in a way consistent with the great privileges he enjoyed as a Jew:

> A person is not a Jew who is one only outwardly, nor is circumcision merely outward and physical. No, a person is a Jew who is one inwardly; and circumcision is circumcision of the heart, by the Spirit, not by the written code. Such a person's praise is not from other people, but from God. (2:28-29)

In 9:6 Paul makes a similar point to explain that, even if many Jews do not accept the gospel and enjoy its benefits, this does not mean God's word has failed to achieve its purpose. By rejecting the gospel, Jews show they are not 'true Jews'. In their case it is evident that, as Paul puts it, 'not all who are descended from Israel are Israel'.[20] To drive this home the apostle

---

19. Jewett, *Romans,* 573-74, comments: 'In contrast to the plural forms of "promises" given to Israel in 9:4 and of the "oracles" and "words" of God in 3:2, 4, Paul uses here the singular, which implies that the issue is broader than the status of Israel's advantages. It seems more likely that "the word of God" in this context is roughly synonymous with "gospel"'. *Contra* Fitzmyer, *Romans,* 559; Byrne, *Romans,* 293, who take it to mean the promises of God made to Israel.

20. Cranford, 'Election and Ethnicity', 33, points out that in this way Paul shows that 'the failure of Israel does not imply there is none to whom the covenant promises apply; rather, the boundaries constituting covenant membership have been misunderstood. This is seen in a redefinition of who is marked out by the name Israel'. Klaus Haacker, 'Die Geschichtstheologie von Röm 9–11 im Lichte philonischer Schriftauslegung', *NTS* 43 (1991) 211-16, notes that Philo also relativizes the importance of physical descent from Israel

speaks not only of those who are true descendants of Israel, but also of those who are the true descendants of Abraham: *Nor because they are his descendants are they all Abraham's children.* Here the term 'descendants' (lit. 'seed') is the broader category to which all Abraham's offspring belong, and the term 'children' is the narrower term that denotes the children of promise.[21] The point Paul makes is that not all physical descendants of Abraham can be regarded as his 'children'. To support his point Paul cites Genesis 21:12: *On the contrary, 'It is through Isaac that your offspring will be reckoned'.* This was the word of God to Abraham when he was distressed by Sarah's demand that he send away the slave woman, Hagar, and her son, Ishmael, because Ishmael was mocking her son Isaac. Genesis 21:12 reads: 'But God said to him, "Do not be so distressed about the boy and your slave woman. Listen to whatever Sarah tells you, because *it is through Isaac that your offspring will be reckoned* (italics added)"'. Right at the beginning, as every Jew would know, God exercised his sovereign choice and selected Isaac's offspring as those through whom his promises to Abraham would be fulfilled. The statement by Nils Dahl is apposite:

> As Isaac, not Ishmael, as Jacob, not Esau, as the seven thousand at the time of Elijah, not the many who bowed the knee to Baal, so the Jews who believe in Christ, not the rest, are the children of promise, chosen by grace. The remnant that remains proves to Paul that God has not rejected his people and that his word stands firm.[22]

In chapter 9 Paul's concern is for the salvation of Israel. He explains the rejection of the gospel by many of them as the result of God's choice. Only the believing Israelites are chosen for salvation; only believing Israelites are Abraham's true children, not ethnic Israel as a whole.[23]

9:8-9 From the Genesis 21:12 text Paul inferred that not all those who are descended physically from Abraham are his 'true' children. To drive home this point he adds: *In other words, it is not the children by physical descent who are God's children, but it is the children of the promise who are re-*

---

and from Abraham, but stresses ethical behavior; Abraham's descendants were all sinners except one (213).

21. So Jewett, *Romans,* 575; Byrne, *Romans,* 293. *Contra* Dunn, *Romans 9–16,* 540; Barrett, *Romans,* 180-81.

22. N. A. Dahl, 'The Future of Israel', in *Studies in Paul: Theology for the Early Christian Mission* (Minneapolis: Augsburg, 1977), 149.

23. Günther H. Junker, '"Children of Promise": Spiritual Paternity and Patriarch Typology in Galatians and Romans', *BBR* 17 (2007) 147-48, says, 'not all members of *national* or *empirical* Israel are members of *true* Israel'. However, he adds, 'And the cross-reference to Romans 4 in particular shows how unwise it is to imagine that the true "seed" of Abraham in 9.7 is simply a subset of ethnic Israel. In 4.16 it is already clearly a worldwide family. . . . The *church* thus stands as the final proof that God's word has not fallen. The salvation of a believing Jewish remnant, important as it is, affords no such proof. It affords no such proof simply because God had promised Abraham *a multitude of nations* and *seed as innumerable as the stars in the heavens* (Gen 15:5, 22:17; cf. Rom 4:13-14)'.

garded as Abraham's offspring. To support this assertion he appeals once again to the Scripture: *For this was how the promise was stated: 'At the appointed time I will return, and Sarah will have a son'*. This time the quotation is from Genesis 18, which recounts the appearance of 'three men' to Abraham at Mamre and the word of the Lord they conveyed to him: 'Then the one of them said, "I will surely return to you about this time next year, and Sarah your wife will have a son"' (Gen 18:10). Sarah overheard the Lord's word to Abraham and laughed to herself thinking it was impossible that she and Abraham could have children of their own, seeing that they were so advanced in years (Gen 18:12). In response the Lord said to Abraham: 'Is anything too hard for the LORD?' then repeated his promise: 'I will return to you at the appointed time next year, and Sarah will have a son' (Gen 18:14). Paul's point is that God did indeed exercise his sovereign choice in determining who would be his children — it was to be the children born in accordance with his promise to Abraham and by divine intervention, not just those born by natural means as in the case of Ishmael.[24] The corollary is that people should not think the word of God has failed if only some Jews enjoy the blessings of the gospel while others do not. This is in accordance with the way God has always operated.[25]

9:10-13   In these verses Paul illustrates the principle of God's sovereign choice once more, this time in relation to Isaac and Rebekah's children, Jacob and Esau. So he begins: *Not only that, but Rebekah's children were conceived at the same time by our father Isaac* (lit. 'and not only [that], but also Rebekah having sexual relations with/conceiving children by, one man, Isaac our Father'). Paul's point seems to be that there was nothing to distinguish the children one from the other apart from God's sovereign choice, as the apostle proceeds to explain: *Yet, before the twins were born* [lit. 'for before they were born' — the NIV has added the reference to 'the twins'] *or had done anything good or bad*[26] — *in order that God's purpose in election might*

---

24. Ambrosiaster remarks: 'It is not because Jacob is praised that all those descended from him are worthy to be called his children. Nor is it because Esau was rejected that all those descended from him are condemned, for we see that Jacob the deceiver had unbelieving children, and Esau had children who were faithful and dear to God. There is no doubt that there are many unbelieving children of Jacob, for all the Jews, whether they are believers or unbelievers, have their origin in him. And that there are good and faithful children of Esau is proved by the example of Job, who was a descendant of Esau, five generations from Abraham and therefore Esau's grandson' ('Commentary on Paul's Epistles' [*ACCSR*, 249-50]).

25. Abasciano, *Paul's Use of the Old Testament in Romans 9.1-9*, 214 asserts: 'Provoked to overwhelming grief at the accursed state of Israel and faced with a challenge to the faithfulness of God's word, Paul has gone to the Scriptures and found there the pattern for his own response and the content of his own teaching. Indeed, the road contours of Paul's argument in Romans 9–11 are anticipated by the story of Abraham in Genesis 18–21'.

26. Jewett, *Romans*, 578, says: 'The wording of the antithesis "anything good or worthless" is perhaps an allusion to the rather trashy quality of their later behavior, with Jacob cheating his brother and Esau selling his birthright for a bowl of soup'.

stand: not by works but by him who calls — she was told, 'The older will serve the younger'. The quotation comes from Genesis 25:21-23:

> Isaac prayed to the LORD on behalf of his wife, because she was child-
> less. The LORD answered his prayer, and his wife Rebekah became
> pregnant. The babies jostled each other within her, and she said, 'Why
> is this happening to me?' So she went to inquire of the LORD. The LORD
> said to her, 'Two nations are in your womb, and two peoples from
> within you will be separated; one people will be stronger than the
> other, and *the older will serve the younger'.* (italics added)

The older was Esau, and the younger Jacob. There was nothing to distinguish the one from the other apart from God's sovereign choice — they had
the same father, and neither had yet done anything either good or bad.[27]
Had it been the younger that would serve the older, it would be in accordance with the natural order of things in the ancient Near East.[28] By reversing this order, God was indicating that it was his choice, not ancient Near
Eastern custom, that was the determining factor as far as the outworking of
his purpose is concerned. This is expressed in the clause, 'in order that
God's purpose in election might stand'.[29]

27. Haacker, 'Die Geschichtstheologie von Röm 9–11', 211-16, draws attention to certain parallels found in the works of Philo, namely, *Virt.* 207–10; *Praem.* 58–60. However,
Philo, unlike Paul, attributes the choice of Jacob rather than Esau to their personal qualities,
to the obedience of Jacob on the one hand, and the disobedience and indulgence of Esau on
the other.

28. Frank Thielman, 'Unexpected Mercy: Echoes of a Biblical Motif in Romans 9–11',
SJT 47 (1994) 177, says: 'For the ancient reader familiar both with Genesis and with social
custom, this statement would link Paul's argument to one of the most shocking and enter-
taining features of Genesis. In the words of Robert Alter, Genesis "is about the reversal of
the iron law of primogeniture, about the election through some devious twist of destiny of a
younger son to carry on the line". Hence, not only does God choose Isaac over Ishmael and
Jacob over Esau, but for no clear reason, he prefers the sacrifice of Abel, the younger of
Adam's two sons, to that of Cain, the elder (4:5). Again, for no clear reason, he preserves
Abraham's seed through Joseph (45:4-7; cf. 49:4), for many years the youngest of Jacob's
children and born to the younger of the two daughters of Laban, rather than through Reu-
ben, the legitimate heir. Similarly, Zerah is mistakenly thought to be the oldest of Tamar's
twins through a blunder of the attending midwife (38:27-30), and Jacob, at the end of his
life, blesses Ephraim the second born rather than the first born, Manasseh, despite the protests of their father Joseph (47:17-22)'. Further, Thielman points out that the author of *Jubi-
lees* goes to great lengths 'to show that the choice of Jacob over Esau was a proper but highly
unusual violation of this principle. Esau's sale of his birthright to Jacob, he contends, actually transformed Jacob into the elder brother (*Jub* 24.7). Moreover, Esau was hopelessly
wicked, as even Isaac was forced to admit in his old age. "At one time", says the Isaac of *Ju-
bilees*, "I loved Esau more than Jacob, because he was the firstborn; but now I love Jacob
more that Esau, for Esau has done all kinds of evil and there is no righteousness in him at
all" (35.13; cf. 35.9)'.

29. Jewett, *Romans*, 578, points out: 'Although the word *eklogē* ['election'] was a technical term in Pharisaism for freedom of choice, the phrase *kat' eklogēn* ['according to elec-
tion/selection'] was so well established in military and governmental contexts to depict se-

It is important to note that God's choice of Jacob through whom to effect his purposes and not Esau was made before they were born, and before they 'had done anything good or bad'. It was determined, Paul emphasizes, 'not by works but by him who calls'. The indications are that the 'works' the apostle denies had any effect upon God's choice are the 'good' or the 'bad' that people do. Clearly, such works are not the performance of, or the failure to perform, 'works of the law', that is, those things that are prescribed by the Mosaic law and understood by some as Jewish sociological markers, because Paul is speaking of the patriarchal period prior to the giving of the law.[30] Nevertheless, Paul may have used the expression 'works' here to prepare the ground for his later contention that Israel, in spite of her pursuit of righteousness (by works of the law), failed to achieve it (9:30-33).[31]

All this, Paul says, is in accordance with Scripture: *Just as it is written: 'Jacob I loved, but Esau I hated'*. This time Paul's Scripture quotation is drawn from Malachi, where, through his prophet, the Lord makes a complaint against Israel — they fail to honor him, their priests show contempt for his name by offering defiled food and blind, crippled, and diseased animals on his altar, offerings they would not dare offer their governor (Mal 1:6-8). The passage from which Paul draws his quotation precedes these verses, and refers to God's love for Israel, something she was calling into question: '"I have loved you", says the LORD. But you ask, "How have you loved us?"' The Lord responds: '"Was not Esau Jacob's brother?" declares the LORD. "Yet I have loved Jacob but Esau I have hated"' (Mal 1:2-3; cf. 2 Esdr 3:16). What distinguishes Jacob from Esau, Israel from Edom, Paul asserts, is God's choice to 'love' the one and 'hate' the other, just as it was his sovereign choice that the elder would serve the younger. If this was the case in respect to Jacob and Esau, something Paul's Jewish contemporaries would affirm, then it should come as no surprise to them that God's choice is the determining factor in the present time as well. He decides who will experience the blessings promised in the gospel preached by his apostle. That some Jews did not enjoy these blessings is no more a failure of God's word than was the fact that Esau/Edom was not chosen while Jacob/Israel was.

Paul's language, 'Jacob have I loved, but Esau I hated', has caused consternation, as if God capriciously shows love to one and regards the

---

lections for special roles that it is likely to be understood in that sense here by a Roman audience'.

30. *Contra* Bell, 'Election and Ethnicity', 39-40, who argues in the opposite direction, saying: 'The expression *ouk ex ergōn* in v. 11 is a connection with the context of Romans 2–3 (esp. 3.20). The expression appears in contexts of justification and election, justification being the consequence of election (as in 8.30), and in both cases the expression must refer to the point at hand; namely that the children of God — God's privileged elect — are not to be distinguished by ethnic boundary markers. "Works" refers to the law kept not as a means of meriting salvation, but as an external identifier of covenant membership'.

31. Cf. Byrne, *Romans*, 292.

other with hatred. However, as has often been pointed out, what is involved here is a Semitic way of expressing the exercise of choice.[32] Another question raised in regard to this statement is whether it should be taken to apply to individuals (Jacob and Esau) or to the nations emanating from them (Israel and Edom). Fitzmyer, for example, contends, 'There is no hint here of predestination to "grace" or "glory" of an individual; it is an expression of the choice of corporate Israel over corporate Edom'.[33] However, those who opt for the individual interpretation have the stronger case for two reasons: (i) in context the statement is part of the apostle's response to the failure of some Jews (individuals) to accept God's word, the gospel, and (ii) even though in both Genesis 25:23 and Malachi 1:2 reference is made to nations, Paul applies the passages to individuals. Bell observes: 'God's oracle to Rebecca in Gen. 25.23 is: "Two nations are in your womb, and two peoples from within you will be separated: one people shall be stronger than the other, the older will serve the younger". Paul has chosen to quote just the final clause and has probably deliberately omitted Gen. 25.23a precisely because it points to "two nations". . . . Paul in Rom. 9.6b-13 is not therefore proving that God freely elected the nation of Israel (although that may be true); rather he is establishing a principle by which he could explain how individual Israelites were accursed, and yet God's word has not failed'.[34]

b. Is God Unjust? 9:14-18

[14]*What then shall we say? Is God unjust? Not at all!* [15]*For he says to Moses, 'I will have mercy on whom I have mercy, and I will have compassion on whom I have compassion'.* [16]*It does not, therefore, depend on human desire or effort, but on God's mercy.* [17]*For Scripture says to Pharaoh: 'I raised you up for this very purpose, that I might display my power in you and that my name might be proclaimed in all the earth'.* [18]*Therefore God has mercy on whom he wants to have mercy, and he hardens whom he wants to harden.*

In this passage Paul deals with an objection he anticipates because of his insistence in 9:10-13 that God's election of some people and not others is a matter of God's choice and not their works, whether good or bad. He anticipates the objection that his gospel implies injustice on God's part. It is part of his response to the wider objection that God's word has failed if the majority of Paul's Jewish kinsfolk have rejected his gospel. To answer the objection Paul reverts to the diatribe style, using questions and answers that he himself formulates. He reminds his audience of God's words to Mo-

---

32. Cf. Byrne, *Romans*, 295; Moo, *Romans*, 587; Fitzmyer, *Romans*, 563. Cranfield, *Romans*, II, 480, prefers not to identify the expression as Semitic idiom, but nevertheless says that it denotes election on the one hand and rejection on the other.

33. Fitzmyer, *Romans*, 563.

34. Bell, *The Irrevocable Call of God*, 211-12. Cf. Moo, *Romans*, 585.

ses and Pharaoh, both of which emphasize the priority of God's sovereign choice. These reminders would be telling for Jewish members of his audience and for all with a background in the synagogue. Paul vigorously defends the justice of God. Moo comments helpfully on this matter:

> Many commentators are troubled by Paul's apparent disregard for human choice and responsibility. Dodd criticizes the argument here as 'a false step'. O'Neill goes further, claiming the teaching is 'thoroughly immoral', and follows a number of the church fathers in ascribing the offending verses to someone other than Paul. These criticisms are sometimes the product of a false assumption: that Paul's justification of the ways of God in his treatment of human beings (his 'theodicy') must meet the standard set by our own assumptions and standards of logic. Paul's approach is quite different. He considers his theodicy to be successful if it justifies God's acts against the standards of his revelation in Scripture (vv. 15-18) and his character as Creator (vv. 20-23). In other words, the standard by which God must be judged is nothing less and nothing more than God himself. Judged by this standard, Paul contends, God is indeed 'just'.[35]

9:14   Paul begins by asking, *What then shall we say? Is God unjust?* 'What shall we say then?' is an expression the apostle uses six times in Romans (and only in Romans), either to introduce a proposition he will immediately refute as he does here (6:1; 7:7; 9:14) or to stretch the thinking of his audience (4:1; 8:31; 9:30). Implicit in the question, 'Is God unjust?' (lit. 'Is there unrighteousness with God?'), is a notion that runs counter to everything said about God in the OT. He is righteous, all his ways are just, and he does no wrong (Deut 32:4; Dan 9:14); he is righteous and loves justice (Ps 11:7; cf. Pss 61:8; 116:5; 119:137; 129:4; [Ps 145:17]; Jer 12:1; Lam 1:18). The idea that God is 'unjust is unthinkable. Paul's immediate response to the question, "Is God unjust?' therefore is: *Not at all!* an expression he uses frequently in Romans (3:6, 31; 6:2, 15; 7:7, 13; 9:14; 11:1, 11) and in other letters (1 Cor 6:15; Gal 2:17; 3:21; 6:14) to express strong denial, as he does here. He proceeds to back up this denial with appeals to God's word to Moses and Pharaoh in the verses that follow.

9:15-16   To back up this emphatic denial Paul reminds his audience: *For he [the LORD] says to Moses, 'I will have mercy on whom I have mercy, and I will have compassion on whom I have compassion'.* The text he quotes is taken from Exodus 33:19. Moses had asked the Lord to show him his glory. The Lord responded: 'I will cause all my goodness to pass in front of you, and I will proclaim my name, the LORD, in your presence. I will have mercy on whom I will have mercy, and I will have compassion on whom I will have compassion'. Intimately connected to the promise of divine disclosure is

---

35. Moo, *Romans*, 590-91.

the Lord's insistence upon his right to have mercy on whom he will have mercy and to have compassion on whom he will have compassion. Paul establishes God's justice in the light, not of human standards, but of God's own revelation of himself. There is no higher standard to which the apostle could appeal.

The conclusion Paul draws from this is: *It does not, therefore, depend on human desire or effort, but on God's mercy* (lit. 'So therefore it is not [a matter] of the one who wills or the one who runs but of God who shows mercy').[36] Once again Paul stresses the divine prerogative in dealing with human beings — showing mercy to whomever he will. There is no injustice involved if God chooses to bestow the blessings of the gospel on some Jews and not on others.

9:17-18   Having spoken of God's word to Moses, Paul now recounts his word to Pharaoh: *For Scripture says to Pharaoh: 'I raised you up for this very purpose, that I might display my power in you and that my name might be proclaimed in all the earth'.* It is noteworthy that here Paul equates what Scripture says with what God said. This scriptural quotation is taken from Exodus 9:16, which constitutes the conclusion to the message God gave Moses for Pharaoh prior to the plague of hail that was to devastate Egypt:

> Then the LORD said to Moses, 'Get up early in the morning, confront Pharaoh and say to him, "This is what the LORD, the God of the Hebrews, says: Let my people go, so that they may worship me, or this time I will send the full force of my plagues against you and against your officials and your people, so you may know that there is no one like me in all the earth. For by now I could have stretched out my hand and struck you and your people with a plague that would have wiped you off the earth. *But I have raised you up for this very purpose, that I might show you my power and that my name might be proclaimed in all the earth"'*. (Exod 9:13-16, italics added)

The Lord's message for Pharaoh was that on this occasion he has spared him because he raised him up in order to show his power in dealing with him so that God's name might be proclaimed throughout the world. Paul implies that just as God hardened Pharaoh in the time of the exodus, so now the failure of his Jewish kinsfolk to experience the blessings of the gospel may be explained by God's sovereign choice to show mercy on some and harden others.[37]

---

36. Dunn, *Romans 9–16*, 553, says discerningly: 'Paul does not disparage "willing" and "running"; willing and running are, of course, part of the human response to God. . . . But they are not factors in election, neither in the initial choice nor in its maintenance'.

37. Witherington, *Romans*, 256, comments: 'Pharaoh was raised up to demonstrate God's saving power on behalf of Israel and thus to show the glory of God throughout the earth. That he was judged or hardened is a by-product, but God acted to redeem his people. It is a regular feature of God's work that redemption of one person may require or involve

Paul quotes Exodus 9:16 once more in response to the questioning of God's justice to emphasize that God's sovereignty is determinative in the affairs of humankind: *Therefore God has mercy on whom he wants to have mercy, and he hardens whom he wants to harden.* This was the case with Israel and Pharaoh respectively in the time of the exodus, and, Paul implies, it was still the case in his own day in respect to the Jewish people. God shows mercy to some and as a result they accept the gospel, while he hardens others and as a result they reject it. There is no injustice with God. He has the right to have mercy on whomever he wants to have mercy, and to harden whomever he wants to harden in order to achieve his own purpose.[38] This, of course, is not the whole story — human responsibility in the matter will be expounded in 9:30–10:21 — but it is an important part, one might even say the most important part, of the story.[39]

c. Why Does God Still Blame Us? 9:19-21

[19]*One of you will say to me: 'Then why does God still blame us? For who is able to resist his will?'* [20]*But who are you, a human being, to talk back to God? 'Shall what is formed say to the one who formed it, "Why did you make me like this?"'* [21]*Does not the potter have the right to make out of the same lump of clay some pottery for special purposes and some for common use?*

Paul recognizes that defending his gospel by insisting upon God's sovereign will as determinative in human affairs is susceptible to the objection that there is 'unfairness' on God's part. Why does God blame people for their lack of response if it is determined by his will? The apostle confronts this objection head-on. He in no way resiles from what he has said; in fact, he emphasizes even more God's right to carry out his will and purpose in this regard.

9:19 Recognizing such an objection, Paul asserts: *One of you will say to me: 'Then why does God still blame us? For who is able to resist his will?'* To the

---

judgment on another person. Liberation of the oppressed requires judgment of the oppressor. Nothing is said about Pharaoh's eternal state, but rather only how he was used by God during the exodus'.

38. Jewett, *Romans*, 585-86, is correct when he observes: 'There was no scandal in reiterating this theme for Paul's audience, and its avoidance would hardly have done justice to the citation from Exod 9:16. . . . Paul applies the widely shared teaching about Pharaoh's hardening in order to make the much more controversial case that God's mercy is sovereign. Paul was convinced that the refusal of this sovereign grace revealed in the gospel placed his Jewish compatriots in "the position of Pharaoh", incredibly reversing their status before God'.

39. Moo, *Romans*, 599-600, stresses: 'It is imperative that we maintain side-by-side the complementary truths that (1) God hardens whomever he chooses; (2) human beings, because of sin, are responsible for their ultimate condemnation. Thus, God's bestowing of mercy and his hardening are not equivalent acts. God's mercy is given to those who do not deserve it; his hardening affects those who have already by their sin deserved condemnation'.

introductory statement, 'One of you will say to me' (lit. 'you [sing.] will say to me'), the NIV has added 'one of (you)', thus treating it as if it was addressed directly to one of the members of the Roman churches. It is better to recognize that this is not direct address but that Paul is using the rhetoric of the diatribe. He is addressing a hypothetical dialogue partner in order to counteract an objection to his assertion about God's sovereign freedom on the grounds that his gospel implies that there is 'unfairness' in God: surely God is unfair to blame those whose hearts are hardened if God himself hardened them, for no one is able to resist his will. Similar thoughts are expressed in Wisdom 12:12a: 'For who will say, "What have you done?" or will resist your judgment?'

9:20-21 Paul's response is as robust as the objection. Continuing to speak in the style of the diatribe, he asks: *But who are you, a human being, to talk back to God?* Paul highlights the impudence of the objector, who is a mere human being, in talking back to God by placing 'O man' right at the beginning of the question (in the original language it reads: 'O man, who are you . . . ?'). He continues by asking: *Shall what is formed say to the one who formed it, 'Why did you make me like this?' Does not the potter have the right to make out of the same lump of clay some pottery for noble purposes and some for common use?* Paul's rejoinder echoes statements in Isaiah, Jeremiah, the Wisdom of Solomon, and Sirach:

> You turn things upside down, as if the potter were thought to be like the clay! Shall what is formed say to the one who formed it, 'He did not make me'? Can the pot say of the potter, 'You know nothing'? (Isa 29:16)

> Woe to those who quarrel with their Maker, those who are but potsherds among the potsherds on the ground. Does the clay say to the potter, 'What are you making?' Does your work say, 'The potter has no hands'? (Isa 45:9)

> So I went down to the potter's house, and I saw him working at the wheel. But the pot he was shaping from the clay was marred in his hands; so the potter formed it into another pot, shaping it as seemed best to him. Then the word of the LORD came to me: He said, 'Can I not do with you, Israel, as this potter does?' declares the LORD. "Like clay in the hand of the potter, so are you in my hand, Israel'. (Jer 18:3-6)

> A potter kneads the soft earth and laboriously molds each vessel for our service, fashioning out of the same clay both the vessels that serve clean uses and those for contrary uses, making all alike; but which shall be the use of each of them the worker in clay decides. (Wis 15:7)

> All human beings come from the ground, and humankind was created out of the dust. In the fullness of his knowledge the Lord distinguished

them and appointed their different ways. Some he blessed and exalted, and some he made holy and brought near to himself; but some he cursed and brought low, and turned them out of their place. Like clay in the hand of the potter, to be molded as he pleases, so all are in the hand of their Maker, to be given whatever he decides. (Sir 33:10-13)

What is clear from these passages is that Paul's insistence upon God's right to do whatever he will with his own creation would be nothing new to Jewish people and others with a background in the synagogue. They would recognize it as part of their scriptural tradition. It is noteworthy that in the wider context of Jeremiah 18 and Wisdom 12 the possibility that God will change his mind when people repent is stressed (Jer 18:5-10), as is the fact that God's exercise of power is always just (Wis 12:12-18).[40] Jewett is correct when he says: 'The rhetorical effectiveness of this verse, supported by so broad a tradition of using the language of molding for divine sovereignty in creation, renders it unlikely that the original audience would have retorted with Dodd, "But the trouble is that a man is not a pot; he *will* ask, 'Why did you make me like this?' and he will not be bludgeoned into silence". The deft hand that reformulated the question . . . is not swinging a blackjack but stating the obvious absurdity of "talking back" to the Creator in this manner, a point on which his audience is sure to agree'.[41]

Paul's question, 'Does not the potter have the right to make out of the same lump of clay some pottery for special purposes and some for common use?' may be seen to apply in the first instance to God's actions in respect to Israel and Pharaoh respectively, but Paul's purpose in asking it is to reinforce his point that the rejection of his gospel by some Jews is a reflection of the fact that God is free to show mercy to some and harden others. Byrne puts it this way: 'The force of the image as Paul employs it . . . stems from the fact that the potter has to make vessels for a wide variety of uses, some noble (the banquet cup), some homely (the chamber pot); he will turn the same lump of clay in either direction as he sees fit. Like the potter, the Creator has a perfect right to turn the creature in whatsoever direction he chooses'.[42]

d. God Has the Right to Exercise His Prerogative, 9:22-29

²²What if God, although choosing to show his wrath and make his power known, bore with great patience the objects of his wrath — prepared for de-

---

40. Cranfield, *Romans*, II, 492, says: 'It cannot be emphasized too strongly that there is naturally not the slightest suggestion that the potter's freedom is the freedom of caprice, and that it is, therefore, perverse to suppose that what Paul wanted to assert was a freedom of the Creator to deal with His creatures according to some indeterminate, capricious, absolute will'.

41. Jewett, *Romans*, 593.

42. Byrne, *Romans*, 297-98.

struction? ²³*What if he did this to make the riches of his glory known to the objects of his mercy, whom he prepared in advance for glory —* ²⁴*even us, whom he also called, not only from the Jews but also from the Gentiles?* ²⁵*As he says in Hosea: 'I will call them "my people" who are not my people; and I will call her "my loved one" who is not my loved one',* ²⁶*and, 'In the very place where it was said to them, "You are not my people", there they will be called "children of the living God."'.* ²⁷*Isaiah cries out concerning Israel: 'Though the number of the Israelites be like the sand by the sea, only the remnant will be saved.* ²⁸*For the Lord will carry out his sentence on earth with speed and finality'.* ²⁹*It is just as Isaiah said previously: 'Unless the Lord Almighty had left us descendants, we would have become like Sodom, we would have been like Gomorrah'.*

In this passage Paul continues to insist upon God's right to exercise his prerogative in determining human destiny in respect to those prepared for destruction and those prepared for glory. But in so doing the apostle argues that those prepared for glory are drawn from both Jews and Gentiles, something that is in accordance with the prophecy of Hosea, and that a Jewish remnant will be included among those who are saved, is in accordance with the prophecy of Isaiah.

9:22 This verse presents some problems, beginning as it does with what appears to be the protasis of a conditional sentence: *What if God, although choosing to show his wrath and make his power known, bore with great patience the objects of his wrath — prepared for destruction?*[43] The problem is that there is no corresponding apodosis. The NIV and a number of other translations overcome the problem by construing the whole verse adversatively, implying that Paul is challenging a hypothetical objector to show cause for rejecting his assertion that it is God's prerogative to show his wrath towards those prepared for destruction, while expecting him to concede God's right to do so.

The participle 'choosing' may be construed either as causal ('because God chose') or concessive ('although God chose'). The meaning, if it is construed as causal, would be: 'But what if God bore with great patience the objects of his wrath, prepared for destruction, *because* he chose to show his wrath and to make known his power'. . . . If it is construed as concessive, the meaning would be: 'What if God, *although* he chose to show his wrath and make his power known, (nevertheless) bore with great patience the objects of his wrath prepared for destruction'. . . . Cranfield prefers the causal option, noting then the parallelism between 9:22 ('God bore with great patience the objects of his wrath, prepared for destruction, *because* he wanted to show his wrath and to make known his power' . . .) and 9:17 ('For Scrip-

---

43. This appears to echo the words of Wis 12:12 ('For who will say, "What have you done?" Or will resist your judgment? Who will accuse you for the destruction of nations that you made? Or who will come before you to plead as an advocate for the unrighteous?').

ture says to Pharaoh, "I have raised you up for the very *purpose* of showing my power in you, so that my name may be proclaimed in all the earth"").[44] Fitzmyer chooses the concessive option 'because of the phrase "with much long-suffering" in the next clause, i.e., though wrath might have led God to make known his power, his loving-kindness restrained him'.[45] It is difficult to decide between these two options, because support for both ideas involved can be found elsewhere in Paul's letters (for the causal in 9:17, and for the concessive in 2:4). In the present context, where the emphasis is upon the fact that God acts justly when making known his wrath (and mercy), the scales tip slightly in favor of the causal option.

Paul does not explicitly identify 'the objects of his wrath'. In the following verses (9:23-24) he identifies 'the objects of his mercy' as 'even us, whom he also called, not only from the Jews but also from the Gentiles', that is, those who have been called and have responded positively to the gospel. We may, therefore, confidently infer that the objects of his wrath are those who reject the gospel call, and, in this context, those of Israel whose hearts were hardened.

Paul recognizes that God shows 'great patience' towards those who attract his wrath. Back in 2:4 Paul asked his hypothetical morally superior dialogue partner, 'Do you show contempt for the riches of his kindness, forbearance and patience, not realizing that God's kindness is intended to lead you to repentance?' And in 1 Timothy 1:13 he refers to the great patience shown to him personally when he was, prior to his conversion, a 'blasphemer and a persecutor, and a violent man'. He says: 'I was shown mercy, so that in me, the worst of sinners, Jesus Christ might display his immense patience as an example for those who would believe in and receive eternal life' (1 Tim 1:16). Guided by these texts, we may say that God's patience towards the objects of his wrath is intended to bring them to repentance (cf. 2 Pet 3:9: 'He is patient . . . not wanting anyone to perish, but everyone to come to repentance').

Paul's description of the objects of God's wrath as those who have been 'prepared for destruction' has been variously interpreted. If the verb 'prepared' is construed as a perfect middle participle, it would mean that people have prepared themselves for destruction by their own impenitence (cf. 2:5). If it is construed as a perfect passive participle, it could be understood as a divine passive, in which case the agent of their preparation for destruction is God.[46] The latter is more likely in this context where Paul in the previous two verses (9:20-21) has just employed the image of the potter and the clay to stress God's prerogative to do with his creatures as he will.

9:23-24 Having spoken of God's patience towards those 'prepared for destruction', Paul speaks next of those God 'prepared for glory'. *What if*

---

44. Cranfield, *Romans,* II, 494. Cf. Moo, *Romans,* 605-6; Barrett, *Romans,* 190.
45. Fitzmyer, *Romans,* 569. Cf. Witherington, *Romans,* 258.
46. Dunn, *Romans 9–16,* 559-60.

he did this to make the riches of his glory known to the objects of his mercy, whom he prepared in advance for glory (lit. 'and in order that he might make known the riches of his glory upon vessels that he prepared for glory?'). In the original language this is a continuation of what appears to be the protasis of the conditional sentence begun in 9:22. Because there is no corresponding apodosis, the NIV renders the question here in 9:23 adversatively: In this case the apostle would be now challenging the hypothetical objector to show cause for rejecting his assertion that it is God's prerogative to make known the riches of his glory towards those prepared for glory, while expecting him to concede his right to do so. For what this 'glory' involves, see 'Additional Note: The Glory in Store for Believers', 228-29.

Those whom God has prepared for glory Paul further describes as *even us, whom he also called, not only from the Jews but also from the Gentiles.* Those whom God has prepared for glory he has 'called', that is, called out of the unbelieving world for salvation through belief in his Son (cf. 1 Cor 1:9). What Paul emphasizes here is that those whom God called are 'not only from the Jews but also from the Gentiles'. This is in line with his description of the gospel in 1:16 as 'the power of God for the salvation of everyone who believes: first for the Jew, then for the Gentile', and this functions as a controlling theme throughout the letter.

9:25-26 Paul finds in the prophecy of Hosea scriptural support for the inclusion of the Gentiles among those God has prepared for glory. He quotes from two places, first from Hosea 2:23: *As he says in Hosea: 'I will call them "my people" who are not my people; and I will call her "my loved one" who is not my loved one'*, and then Hosea 1:10: *'In the very place where it was said to them, "You are not my people", there they will be called "children of the living God"'*. In their original contexts these two quotations refer to northern kingdom of Israel, not the Gentiles. Because of her sins the northern kingdom was disowned by God — 'it was said to them, "you are not my people"' — but in his mercy God promised to reinstate them: 'I will call them "my people" who are not my people'. Paul sees in these texts a typological pattern revealing the way God deals with people — something he applies to the inclusion of the Gentiles. They had never been 'my people', and were therefore, like the disowned northern kingdom, 'not my people'. Just as she was to be reinstated to become God's people, so too Gentiles who were previously 'not my people' have now become 'my people', called by God through the gospel.[47] Moo thinks that something more than an analogy is involved here. He explains: 'Paul requires more than an analogy to establish from Scripture justification for God's calling of Gentiles to be his people. Therefore, we must conclude that this text reflects a hermeneutical supposition of which we find evidence elsewhere in Paul and in the NT; that OT predictions of a renewed Israel find their fulfillment in the

47. Cf. J. Paul Tanner, 'The New Covenant and Paul's Quotations from Hosea in Romans 9:25-26', *BSac* 162 (2005) 102-3; Wright, 'Romans', 642-43.

church'.[48] In 1 Peter 2:9-10 a similar point is made, also alluding to Hosea 2:23 and applying it to a Gentile audience: 'But you are a chosen people, a royal priesthood, a holy nation, God's special possession, that you may declare the praises of him who called you out of darkness into his wonderful light. Once you were not a people, but now you are the people of God; once you had not received mercy, but now you have received mercy'.[49]

9:27-28 Just as Paul saw the inclusion of the Gentiles in the new covenant people as something foreshadowed in Scripture, so too he saw the minimal response he found among the Jews to be foreshadowed there: *Isaiah cries out concerning Israel: 'Though the number of the Israelites[50] be like the sand by the sea, only[51] the remnant will be saved. For the Lord will carry out his sentence on earth with speed and finality'.[52]* Paul's quotation is taken from Isaiah 10:22-23 (LXX), the English translation of which reads as follows:

> Though your people be like the sand by the sea, Israel, only a remnant will return. Destruction has been decreed, overwhelming and righteous. The Lord, the LORD Almighty, will carry out the destruction decreed upon the whole land.[53]

Contextually, Isaiah 10:22-23 is part of a prophecy about the judgment of God upon an arrogant Assyria, and the salvation of a remnant of Israel. The prophecy says also that though the number of the Israelites taken into captivity was 'as the sand of the sea',[54] it is a remnant that will saved when the

---

48. Moo, *Romans*, 613. W. Edward Glenny, 'The "People of God" in Romans 9:25-26', *BSac* 152 (1995) 55, writing as a dispensationalist, argues that Hos 2:23 and 1:10 find fulfillment not only in the church (made up of believing Jews and Gentiles) but also in a future salvation of ethnic Israel. *Contra* Moo, he argues that the church does not take the place of ethnic Israel in the program of God.

49. Theodoret of Cyrrhus says: 'This passage originally applied to Jews, not to Gentiles. . . . It meant that God's people would lose their status and be called "Not my people" and "Not beloved". But then God promised that the rejected Jews would be called back again. Thus from having been God's people and then rejected they would return. . . . The Gentiles, on the other hand, would become God's people for the first time, having never been his people before' ('Interpretation of the Letter to the Romans' [*ACCSR*, 266]).

50. The opening words of Paul's quotation, 'though the number of the Israelites . . .' (lit. 'the number of the sons of Israel . . .'), differ from Isa 10:22 ('your people, O Israel'), and appear to have been taken from Hos 2:1 LXX (= Hos 1:10 ET) ('the number of the sons of Israel').

51. The NIV has added the word 'only' to the phrase 'only the remnant' — it is found neither in the original of 9:27 or Isa 10:22.

52. 'With speed and finality' translates: *syntelōn kai syntemnōn,* an expression found only here in the NT and only in the text that Paul cites in the LXX (Isa 10:22). Alternative translations that have been suggested are: (i) *'closing the account and shortening (the time),* i.e., God will not prolong indefinitely the period of divine patience'; (ii) *'cutting off;* in this case the shortening is thought of as referring either to God's promise to Israel, which will be fulfilled only to a limited degree . . . or to the Israelite nation, which is to enter into salvation trimmed and cut down' (cf. BAGD, *syntemnō*).

53. From the translation by Sir Lancelot C. L. Brenton (1851).

54. The reference to the number of the sons of Israel being as the sand of the sea recalls God's promise to Abraham that his descendants would be as numerous as the sand on

Lord will make short work of his judgment of the world.[55] Paul quotes this prophecy to explain that the minimal response to the gospel he found among the Jews was foreshadowed in Scripture — a remnant will be saved — and therefore the rejection of the gospel by the majority of his contemporary kinsfolk cannot be claimed as evidence that 'the word of God has failed'. And by implication it cannot be claimed that Paul's gospel is not true because many of his own people failed to embrace it.[56]

9:29   Next Paul cites Isaiah 1:9: *It is just as Isaiah said previously: 'Unless the Lord Almighty* [lit. 'the Lord of hosts'] *had left us descendants, we would have become like Sodom, we would have been like Gomorrah'*. Through Isaiah the Lord pronounced imminent judgment upon the nation Israel, to be carried out by the Assyrians. Isaiah says that when this judgment fell, unless the Lord had spared some descendants, the nation would have fared like Sodom and Gomorrah. These were the cities of the plain that God wiped out completely in the time of Abraham and Lot because of the wickedness of their inhabitants (Gen 19:24-25). Both texts from Isaiah (10:2-3 and 1:9) speak of a remnant of Israel that was spared when the Lord judged the nation. In like fashion the apostle Paul regarded the relatively small number of Jews who had responded to his gospel as a remnant preserved by God. The word of God had not failed. But the apostle still agonized over the rest of Israel. The question of their ultimate destiny Paul will address in chapter 11.

---

the seashore (Gen 22:17: 'I will surely bless you and make your descendants as numerous as the stars in the sky and as the sand on the seashore'), a promise fulfilled by the time of Solomon (1 Kgs 4:20: 'The people of Judah and Israel were as numerous as the sand on the seashore; they ate, they drank and they were happy').

55. Cf. Erich Seitz, '*Logon syntemnōn* — Eine Gerichtsankündigung? (Zu Römer 9,27/28)', *BN* 109 (2001) 56-82.

56. John Paul Heil, 'From Remnant to Seed of Hope for Israel: Romans 9:27-29', *CBQ* 64 (2002) 703-20, 705-18, argues for a different interpretation of 9:27-28. He claims that (i) the word *hyper* should be translated as 'on behalf of' and not 'concerning', so that the Isaiah text should read, 'Isaiah calls out on behalf of Israel'; (ii) the word 'only' added by the NIV should be omitted, so that the text should read: 'If the number of the sons of Israel be as the sand of the sea (surely, at least) a remnant will be saved; (iii) 'a close consideration of both the grammar and context of both the MT and the LXX in Isa 10:22a reveals that this verse expresses not a destructive judgment on Israel but a promising hope represented by a remnant'; (iv) 'the Patriarchal allusion reinforces the certainty of the hope that, surely, at least a remnant of presently unbelieving Israel will be saved if God has long ago and repeatedly promised that the descendants of Israel will be as the sand of the sea'; (v) the expression *syntelōn kai syntemnōn* means 'what has been determined and decided' (not 'finishing and cutting short' nor 'only to a limited degree' nor 'a shortening of time'). Accordingly he argues that 'Rom 9:28 should be understood to confirm 9:27 as follows: [The Lord will act by] definitively deciding a word *(logon)* — namely, God's word of promise that the descendants of Israel will be as numerous as the sand of the sea — which God has repeatedly stated and thus "definitively decided" (Gen 16:13; 17:22; 28:14; 32:12; Isa 10:22; Hos 2:1; Dan 3:35-36 [LXX]), and God will accomplish this decided word of promise on the earth. That God will fully accomplish this definitively decided word of promise thus makes even more certain the further hopeful promise based on it, namely, that at least a remnant of presently unbelieving Israel will surely be saved'.

ADDITIONAL NOTE: PREDESTINATION IN ROMANS — CORPORATE OR INDIVIDUAL?

One of the issues thrown up by Romans 9 is the nature of election that Paul's argument in this chapter implies. The chapter opens with Paul lamenting the fact that many of his kinsfolk are not saved, and he goes on to insist that this is not because the word of God, his gospel, has failed. Instead, he says that it is in line with the way God has always exercised his prerogative to choose one and not another in order to fulfill his purposes. One of the important issues debated in this connection is whether election to salvation applies to individuals or only to corporate entities.

According to the view that sees election in terms of corporate entities, God chooses certain groups/entities for salvation. Whether or not individuals are saved is dependent upon their decision to join the group God has elected to save. Thus it is argued that God has elected to save all those 'in Christ', but inclusion in Christ is a matter of free choice on the part of individuals. There is on this view no election of individuals to salvation (and accordingly no election of individuals to damnation either). Several arguments have been advanced in favor of the view that election applies only to corporate entities and not to individuals. Abasciano, for example, supports this view with the following arguments: (i) in the OT election is corporate; (ii) in the NT explicit language of election is always corporate, though it can be applied to individuals; (iii) Mediterranean culture is corporate (and presumably therefore Paul and his audience would have understood election corporately); (iv) election focuses upon the community, while individuals are elect only as they are members of the elect community; (v) The 'remnant' to which Paul refers is a corporate entity, though this does not exclude individuals; (vi) group identity (in the ancient world) always transcends individual identity.[57] Witherington contends: 'Paul's views on predestination, election, the remnant, apostasy and salvation fall within the parameters of such discussions in early Judaism, rather than within the framework of later Augustinian, Lutheran, and Calvinist discussions of the matter. Those early Jewish discussions make full allowance for both corporate election and the meaningful choices of individuals who may commit apostasy and opt out of the people of God'.[58]

Schreiner argues against the corporate view of election and in favor of the view that election does indeed entail the election of individuals, on the following grounds: (i) In Paul's quotation of Exodus 33:19 in Romans 9:15, which reads: 'For he says to Moses, "I will have mercy on whom I have mercy, and I will have compassion on whom I have compassion"', the pronoun 'whom' is singular, indicating that the OT does speak of the election of

---

57. Brian J. Abasciano, 'Corporate Election in Romans 9: A Reply to Thomas Schreiner', *JETS* 49 (2006) 353-61.

58. Witherington, *Romans*, 246.

individuals; (ii) the election of a remnant does involve the choice of some individuals and not others; (iii) election of individuals, which is criticized as an arbitrary choice on God's part, is in fact no more arbitrary than the election of communities; (iv) on the corporate view election is the choice of the individual to belong to the elect community, and therefore the real initiative lies with the individual, not with God — God's choice of a group saves no one; (v) individual election is found in the NT (e.g., John 6:44: 'No one can come to me unless the Father who sent me draws him, and I will raise him up at the last day'); (vi) While corporate election is prominent in the OT, individuals are also elected (e.g., Abraham, Isaac, and Jacob).[59] Moo, who also champions the individual view of election, argues that: (i) Paul's explanation of why some of his fellow Israelites and not others are saved requires that it apply to individuals; (ii) key words in 9:9-12 such as 'children of God', 'descendants', 'counted', 'children of promise', 'name' or 'call', and 'not of works' are used regularly by Paul elsewhere in relation to the salvation of individuals; (iii) individuals are involved when Paul says that God has called people from among both Jews and Gentiles to be his people.[60]

The argument that there is no such thing as the election of individuals, only communities, is to be rejected primarily because it fails exegetically. Such a notion of election does not support an explanation of why some Jewish individuals accept the gospel while others do not, which is the reason Paul introduces it in chapter 9.

---

3. Jewish Responsibility for Failure to Embrace the Gospel, 9:30–10:21

Having argued that the failure of the Jews to embrace the gospel and its blessings was not due to a failure of God's word, but reflects God's election and the exercise of his rightful prerogative to show mercy to whomsoever he will (9:6-29), here in 9:30–10:21 Paul shows that Israel herself must also bear responsibility for this failure. The passage consists of three sections: (i) in 9:30–10:4 Paul states that what Israel pursued and did not find (righteousness) was found by Gentiles who did not pursue it, and then explains the reason for Israel's failure; (ii) in 10:5-13 he provides scriptural support for the righteousness of faith; (iii) in 10:14-21 he asserts that Israel's failure is to be attributed neither to ignorance on her part nor failure on God's part, but rather to Israel's intransigence. It is noteworthy that the whole passage is bracketed by reference to inclusion of the Gentiles among the people of God, something promised to Abraham when God established his

---

59. Thomas R. Schreiner, 'Does Romans 9 Teach Individual Election unto Salvation? Some Exegetical and Theological Reflections', *JETS* 36 (1993) 35-40; Schreiner, 'Corporate and Individual Election in Romans 9: A Response to Brian Abasciano', *JETS* 49 (2006) 377-84.

60. Moo, *Romans*, 571-72.

covenant with him, and a major theme introduced in Paul's thematic statement in 1:16-17.

a. Why Israel Did Not Attain the Righteousness She Pursued, 9:30–10:4

[30]What then shall we say? That the Gentiles, who did not pursue righteousness, have obtained it, a righteousness that is by faith; [31]but the people of Israel, who pursued the law as the way of righteousness, have not attained their goal. [32]Why not? Because they pursued it not by faith but as if it were by works. They stumbled over the stumbling stone. [33]As it is written: 'See, I lay in Zion a stone that causes people to stumble and a rock that makes them fall, and the one who believes in him will never be put to shame'.

[10:1]Brothers and sisters, my heart's desire and prayer to God for the Israelites is that they may be saved. [2]For I can testify about them that they are zealous for God, but their zeal is not based on knowledge. [3]Since they did not know the righteousness of God and sought to establish their own, they did not submit to God's righteousness. [4]Christ is the culmination of the law so that there may be righteousness for everyone who believes.

In these verses Paul explains the reason why Israel did not attain the righteousness that she sought while Gentiles attained the righteousness they were not seeking. He then expresses again his heartfelt concern for his own people and acknowledges their zeal for God before explaining why, nevertheless, they failed to attain what they zealously sought.[61]

9:30-31 Paul begins by noting a striking historical paradox. He introduces it with a question: *What then shall we say?* This expression, peculiar to Paul in the NT and found only in Romans (6x), is used by the apostle to introduce either an important matter that he wants to explore (4:1; 8:31; 9:30) or one that he will emphatically deny (6:1; 7:7; 9:14). He wants to explore an important matter here in 9:30-31, and he states it as follows: *That the Gentiles, who did not pursue righteousness, have obtained it, a righteousness that is by faith; but the people of Israel, who pursued the law as a way of righteousness, have not attained their goal.* The NIV has added the definite article in the expression 'the Gentiles', which is not found in the original. Paul may well have omitted the article so as not to imply that Gentiles as a class have obtained righteousness, but rather to say that some Gentiles have obtained it.[62]

The apostle's statement, 'Gentiles . . . did not pursue righteousness',

---

61. *Contra* Jan Lambrecht, 'The Caesura between Romans 9.30-3 and 10.1-4', *NTS* 45 (1999) 141-47, who argues that 9:30-33 constitutes the conclusion to the section 9:6-33, and that 10:1 'marks a caesura, just before the beginning of the second major section' (144). He argues that, despite the apparent continuity between 9:30-33 and 10:1-4, there is in fact 'a significant break in the argument; in chapter 10 there is no longer diatribe-style, no longer theodicy; the focus lies on human responsibility and culpability' (147).

62. Cf. Dunn, *Romans 9–16*, 580.

should not be understood to mean that there were no Gentiles who were serious about seeking moral rectitude (which is clearly not the case) but that they were not pursuing the righteousness that comes from God, that is, a right standing before him. To pursue righteousness is, as Jewett notes, an idiom of Hebrew piety (cf. Sir 27:8: 'If you pursue righteousness, you shall attain it and put it on as a glorious garment').[63]

Paul appears to be utilizing a metaphor of the race to express this paradox: Gentiles and Jews are, as it were, both straining to reach the finishing line (cf. Phil 3:12-16; 1 Cor 9:24-27),[64] which in this case stands for the righteousness from God. Before trying to comprehend just what is being expressed in this paradoxical statement, it is important to note the imbalance in the paradox itself: Paul says that the Gentiles *did* get what they *did not* pursue (namely, righteousness by faith), while the Jews *did not* get what they *did* pursue (namely, the law as a way of righteousness).[65] It is also important to note that the righteousness obtained by the Gentiles but not by Israel is forensic righteousness, God's adjudication in their favor resulting in a right standing before him. Essentially this is an eschatological righteousness to be declared by God on the last day, but applied in the present for those who believe.

When Paul says that the Gentiles *did* obtain 'a righteousness that is by faith', he means that righteousness was credited to them because they believed the gospel message when they heard it and as a consequence obtained righteousness, even though they were not seeking it as the Jews were. To 'obtain righteousness' means to be the recipients of God's favorable adjudication, confirming that their sins are forgiven and are, therefore, no longer counted against them. This is what the apostle refers to when he says, 'this righteousness from God comes through faith in Jesus Christ' (3:22; cf. Phil 3:9), and describes it as 'the gift of righteousness' (5:17).

However, the experience of the majority of the Jews in Paul's day was quite different: 'Israel, who pursued the law as a way of righteousness, have not attained their goal'. Unfortunately, the NIV translation obscures some of the nuances in this verse, which, when translated literally, reads: 'but Israel, pursuing a law of righteousness, did not attain [the] law'. Rendering the latter part of this verse as 'Israel . . . has not attained *their goal*', instead of 'Israel . . . did not attain [*the*] *law*', implies that what Israel did not attain was *righteousness*, whereas Paul says what they did not attain is [*the*] *law*. The corollary is: because Israel did not succeed in carrying out what the law prescribed, she did not obtain what she pursued — a righteousness based on observance of the law.[66]

63. Jewett, *Romans*, 609.

64. So, e.g., Steven Richard Bechtler, 'Christ, the *Telos* of the Law: The Goal of Romans 10:4', *CBQ* 56 (1994) 292.

65. Cf. T. David Gordon, 'Why Israel Did Not Obtain Torah-Righteousness: A Translation Note on Rom 9:32', *WTJ* 54 (1992) 165.

66. Cf. John Paul Heil, 'Christ, the Termination of the Law (Romans 9:30–10:8)', *CBQ* 63 (2001) 487.

What the apostle means by referring to Israel as pursuing 'the law as a way of righteousness' can best be understood in the light of his description of the righteousness he sought prior to his conversion to Christ: 'a righteousness of my own that comes from the law' (Phil 3:9). Similarly, Paul says that the problem with many Jews in his day was that 'they did not know the righteousness of God and sought to establish their own', and as a result 'they did not submit to God's righteousness' (10:3).

9:32a In this verse Paul asks why the Jews failed to attain what they sought, and provides his own explanation of the reason for this: *Why not? Because they pursued it not by faith but as if it were by works.* Literally translated, this text would read: 'Why? Because not of faith but as of works'. Clearly a verb and subject have to be provided to bring out the sense of this elliptical statement. But what verb and what subject should be supplied? There are two options.

Most modern commentators say that the verb 'to pursue' is to be supplied, carried over from 9:31, and that its implied subject is 'the Jews'. This yields the translation, 'because they [the Jews] pursued it [the law of righteousness] not by faith but as it were by works'. When the text is construed in this way, the failure of the people of Israel is due, not to *what* they pursued ('a law for righteousness'), but rather to the *manner* of their pursuit ('not by faith but by works').[67]

However, if the verb 'to be' is provided and the implied subject is understood to be the law, we end up with the translation: 'because it [the law] is not of faith, but of works'. When the text is construed in this way, the reason for the failure of the people of Israel is not the *manner* of their pursuit, but *what* they pursued ('a law for righteousness'). In this case, the people of Israel pursued the law for righteousness, and because the law is not of faith but of works, they were not able to attain righteousness.[68] The difficulty with this option is the stubborn fact of Paul's inclusion of 'as if it were', which suggests that it is Israel's attitude to the law that is in view. Instead of pursuing righteousness on the basis of faith they did so *as if it were* based on the law. Of course, to obey the law was not only legitimate but praiseworthy, but to pursue righteousness as if it were based on that obedience is

---

67. So, e.g., Dunn, *Romans 9–16*, 582; Ziesler, *Romans*, 254; Thomas Schreiner, 'Israel's Failure to Attain Righteousness in Romans 9:30–10:3', *TrinJ* 12 (1991) 214; Davies, *Faith and Obedience in Romans*, 123-24, 180-85; Heil, 'Christ, the Termination of the Law', 488; Bechtler, 'Christ, the *Telos* of the Law', 294-95; Cranfield, *Romans*, II, 508-10; Jewett, *Romans*, 610-11.

68. Gordon, 'Why Israel Did Not Obtain Torah-Righteousness', 166, offers the following reasons in support of this option: (i) Gal 3:12 attaches precisely the negated prepositional phrase *(ouk ek pisteōs)* of Rom 9:32 to the Torah; (ii) Rom 10:5-6 refers to Torah's righteousness by citing the same OT 'doing' *(poiēsas)* text cited by Paul in Gal 3:12; and (iii) the paradox of Rom 9:30-31 has the Gentiles pursuing nothing, rendering unlikely a translation of 9:32 which distinguishes correct pursuit from incorrect pursuit, and supporting the notion that whereas the Gentiles pursued nothing, the Jews pursued something but it was the wrong thing. Each of these considerations suggests that it is more likely that the negated prepositional phrase *(ouk ek pisteōs)* qualifies *nomos* itself, and not some mispursuit thereof.

mistaken, as Paul will shortly make abundantly clear (10:3). The first option adopted by the majority of commentators is therefore preferable.

To say that the Jews (and Paul himself prior to his conversion to Christ; cf. Phil 3:8-9) made the mistake of pursuing the law for righteousness is not to say that first-century Judaism in its entirety was *in principle* a religion in which acceptance before God depended upon amassing merit by keeping the law. Rather, even if it is acknowledged that first-century Judaism was essentially covenantal and nomistic as many do, it has to be acknowledged also that there was a tendency for the nomistic obligations of the covenant to be emphasized at the expense of God's saving grace. A nomistic religion often degenerated, in practice, into a legalistic one. Paul believed that many of his Jewish kinsfolk, being proud of their exclusive possession of the law, fell into the trap of believing that it was their observance of the law, rather than God's saving grace, that guaranteed their acceptance by him. This is not an uncommon phenomenon. Wherever people take their commitment to biblical religion seriously, there is a tendency to end up in one form of legalism or another. This is a complicated issue. For further discussion see 'The Influence of the "New Perspective"', in the Introduction, 14-23.

9:32b-33   For Paul it was inevitable that those Jews who were pursuing the law for righteousness would stumble at the preaching of Christ, an outcome which he saw foreshadowed in Scripture: *They stumbled over the stumbling stone. As it is written: 'See, I lay in Zion a stone that causes people to stumble and a rock that makes them fall, and the one who believes in him will never be put to shame'.* Those who pursued the law for righteousness were in no frame of mind to seek righteousness through faith, especially faith in a crucified (and risen) Messiah, so 'they stumbled over the "stumbling stone"'. The apostle's scriptural 'quotation' is drawn from two passages in Isaiah:

> So this is what the Sovereign LORD says: 'See, I lay a stone in Zion, a tested stone, a precious cornerstone for a sure foundation; the one who relies on it will never be stricken with panic'. (Isa 28:16)

> And he will be a holy place; for both Israel and Judah he will be a stone that causes people to stumble and a rock that makes them fall. And for the people of Jerusalem he will be a trap and a snare. (Isa 8:14)

Paul's 'quotation' is an amalgamation of parts of these two texts, and corresponds exactly with neither of them. The merging of the two passages such as Paul does here was not uncommon, being found also in the Qumran literature.[69] Capes says that 'Isaiah 8 clearly — and Isaiah 28 somewhat less

---

69. Cf. Douglas A. Oss, 'The Interpretation of the "Stone" Passages by Peter and Paul: A Comparative Study', *JETS* 32 (1989) 183, who cites E. E. Ellis, 'Midrash, Targum and New Testament Quotation', in *Neotestamentica et Semitica* (ed. E. E. Ellis and M. Wilcox; Edinburgh: T&T Clark, 1969), 68-69, who provides examples from 1QIs^a of the merging of texts.

clearly — names YHWH as the "stone of stumbling". If Paul is cognizant of this connection, as he seems to be of other contextual factors in these texts, his application of the "stone" passage to Jesus carries significant christological implications. At the level of exegesis he brings Christ into intimate relation to YHWH and posits Christ in an eschatological role which scripture reserves for God'.[70] Paul's use of the 'stone' passages Christologically reflects a tradition that may be traced back to Jesus himself (cf. Mark 12:10-11 par.). When the apostle says, 'the one who trusts in him will never be put to shame', he probably has in mind, as Witherington suggests, 'the eschatological shame of appearing at final judgment naked — that is, in the wrong condition'.[71] This fits the context in which obtaining righteousness, which is essentially an eschatological concept, is under discussion.[72] The apostle Peter uses Isaiah 28:16 in a similar fashion: 'For in Scripture it says: "See, I lay a stone in Zion, a chosen and precious cornerstone, and the one who believes in him will never be put to shame". Now to you who believe, this stone is precious. But to those who do not believe, "The stone the builders rejected has become the capstone"', and, '"A stone that causes people to stumble and a rock that makes them fall". They stumble because they disobey the message — which is also what they were destined for' (1 Pet 2:6-8).[73]

Paul's point in all this is to show that the reason for the Jews' failure to embrace the gospel was in part an unwillingness to set aside their attempt to use 'a law for righteousness' (that is to pursue a righteousness of their own that comes from the law) and in part also due to their stumbling over the stumbling stone that God placed in Zion, and proclaimed by Paul as Christ crucified.[74]

---

70. David B. Capes, 'YHWH and His Messiah: Pauline Exegesis and the Divine Christ', *HorBibTheol* 16 (1994) 124.

71. Witherington, *Romans,* 259.

72. Heil, 'Christ, the Termination of the Law', 489, commenting on the last clause in 9:33, 'and the one who trusts in him will never be put to shame', says that here Paul makes a final appeal to his Jewish kinsfolk: 'although the way to attain righteousness by doing the works of the Law is a dead end, the way of attaining righteousness by faith in Christ, even though Israel at this point has stumbled over him, is still available to Israel as it is to anyone who believes'. There is no doubt that Paul would want to make such a final appeal to his unbelieving Jewish kinsfolk, but the place to do it would not be in a letter to the Christians in Rome.

73. Oss, 'The Interpretation of the "Stone" Passages', 192-93, points out that there is a significant difference in the way Peter uses the Isaiah text — he does so to bring out the election of the church. Nevertheless, he argues, there are striking similarities also: 'For although Paul uses the quotation in Rom 9:33 to explain the rejection of the Jews (9:32–10:3), a feature not explicitly present in the Petrine passage, on the basis of those same texts he goes on to support the election of all who have faith in Christ (10:4-13), just as Peter does in 1 Pet 2:4-10'.

74. Cf. Wolfgang Reinbold, 'Paulus und das Gesetz: Zur Exegese von Röm 9,30-33', *BZ* 38 (1994) 257-64, who argues that the reason the Jews did not attain the righteousness they sought was that they stumbled over the preaching of Christ crucified, not because they sought righteousness through law observance (legalism). He argues that *ouk ek pisteōs all' hōs ex ergōn* should be regarded as a parenthesis and then 9:32 should be translated as: 'Why [not]? Because they (not from faith [in Christ] but engrossed in works) stumbled over the

10:1 Before spelling out the reasons why many of his fellow Jews did not 'attain righteousness', Paul reiterates his longing for their salvation. Back in 9:1-4a he said: 'I speak the truth in Christ — I am not lying, my conscience confirms it in the Holy Spirit — I have great sorrow and unceasing anguish in my heart. For I could wish that I myself were cursed and cut off from Christ for the sake of my people, those of my own race, the people of Israel'. Now here in 10:1 he reiterates that deep concern: *Brothers and sisters, my heart's desire and prayer to God for the Israelites is that they may be saved.* He reminds his Roman audience of how much he longs and prays for the salvation of his unbelieving fellow Jews so that they will know that his criticisms of his own people do not arise out of any lack of concern for their well-being. That Paul maintained such concern indicates that he did not regard their present unbelieving state as necessarily final.

10:2 There is one other thing Paul wants to emphasize before voicing his criticisms: *For I can testify about them that they are zealous for God.* Unlike the Gentile world that Paul condemned for their failure to honor God or give him thanks, indulging rather in idolatry and immorality (1:18-32), Paul testifies that his fellow Israelites do have a zeal for God. 'Zeal for God' was an important aspect of Jewish piety with its roots in the OT. It denoted passionate concern for God's honor and his law, often involving violence. It is exemplified in people like Phinehas, Elijah, Simeon, Levi, and Mattathias (see 'Additional Note: Zeal in Israel and in Paul', below). Prior to his conversion the apostle himself was 'zealous for God'. Describing this in Philippians 3:5-6, he says that he was: 'in regard to the law, a Pharisee; *as for zeal, persecuting the church;* as for righteousness based on the law, faultless' (italics added). Paul's zeal led him to engage in violent opposition to Christians. While zeal for God could lead to violence, the aspect of Jewish zeal Paul has in mind here in 10:2-3 is an earnest desire to be accounted righteous by God. But, he says, it was misdirected: *their zeal is not based on knowledge.*[75] What this means is explained in the following verse.

ADDITIONAL NOTE: ZEAL IN ISRAEL AND IN PAUL

There is a long tradition of zeal in Israel. It begins with Simeon and Levi, who killed the Shechemites for raping their sister Dinah (Genesis 34; cf. Jdt

---

stumbling stone'. Jewett, *Romans*, 613, adds: 'If it is God who has "laid" the messianic stone "in Zion", there is a "divine purpose" in Israel's current stumbling that will become fully apparent in the revelation of the mystery of the inclusion of the Gentiles in 11:7-12, 25-32. Meanwhile the "twofold meaning of the stone" remains, in that the one "who is placed there for faith Himself becomes an 'obstacle to faith'"'.

75. Paul connects his own former misplaced zeal also with ignorance: 'Even though I was once a blasphemer and a persecutor and a violent man, I was shown mercy because I *acted in ignorance* and unbelief' (1 Tim 1:13, italics added).

9:2-4; *Jub.* 30:1-6, 18-20; *T. Levi* 5:3–7:3). There follows the action of Phinehas, who killed the Israelite man and the Midianite woman whom he brought into the camp of Israel at the very time Israel was seeking to turn away the anger of the Lord towards them for their sexual liaisons with Moabite women and sacrificing to their gods (Num 25:7-11; cf. Ps 106:28-31). Then there are the actions of Elijah, who slaughtered the prophets of Baal (1 Kgs 19:16-18), and Jehu, who slaughtered Jezebel and the descendants of the apostate king Ahab (2 Kings 9–10). Elijah's zeal became the basis of an exhortation by Mattathias to the faithful in Israel to maintain their obedience to the commandments of God in the face of the persecutions of Antiochus Epiphanes (1 Macc 2:49-69, esp. 58). Mattathias himself burned with zeal for the law when he saw a renegade Jew offering sacrifice on a pagan altar in Modein. He slew the renegade Jew and the officer of King Antiochus who was presiding over the sacrifices. He called upon everyone who was 'zealous for the law and supports the covenant' to come out with him into the wilderness from whence they engaged in guerrilla warfare against the armies of Antiochus (1 Macc 2:23-28).

There were zealots in Israel in NT times as well, people who resisted the Roman occupation. More relevant for our present concerns, there were zealots who opposed, often violently, fellow Jews suspected of disobedience to, or speaking against, the law. It was fear of this persecution that led some of the Jerusalem Christians to insist that Gentile believers be circumcised so that they themselves would escape persecution (Gal 6:12). Paul, prior to his conversion to Christ, zealously persecuted Jewish Christians (1 Cor 15:9; Gal 1:13; Acts 8:2-3; 9:1-2), and was present at the martyrdom of Stephen (Acts 7:57–8:1). Paul regarded his pre-Christian violent opposition to Christians as evidence of his zeal for the law (Phil 3:5-6). Following his conversion, Paul himself became the object of persecution by other zealous Jews (1 Thess 2:14-16; 2 Cor 11:24, 26, 30-33; Rom 15:31) because they believed he was advocating disregard for the law (Gal 5:11; Rom 3:7-8).[76]

Dunn argues that the main motivation for Jewish zeal was to maintain the national identity of Israel. After reviewing the actions of the heroes of Jewish zeal in the OT and Intertestamental periods he says:

> There are three striking features of 'zeal' thus understood. First, in each case the zeal was an unconditional commitment to maintain Israel's distinctiveness, to prevent the purity of its covenant set-apartness to God from being adulterated or defiled, to defend its religious and national boundaries. Second, a readiness to do this by force. In each case it is the thoroughgoing commitment expressed precisely in the slaughter of those who threatened Israel's distinctive covenant status which merited the description 'zeal' or 'zealot'. And third, the fact that this zeal

---

76. Cf. Kruse, 'The Price Paid for a Ministry among Gentiles', 260-72.

was directed not only against Gentiles who threatened Israel's boundaries, but against fellow Jews too.[77]

However, a close reading of accounts of the actions of OT and Intertestamental zealots indicates that the essential motivation for their zeal was a sense of obligation to observe the law for its own sake. Smiles puts it well:

> That zeal was not primarily characterized by nationalism, a desire to keep Gentiles at a distance or to maintain Israel's distinctiveness. Its essential character was an impassioned defense of the law for its own sake as the basis of Israel's obligation under the covenant. Gentiles and their encroachments certainly provoked outbursts of zeal, and the actions of zealots can properly be seen as defense of Israel's integrity and identity. But the latter was extraneous to the primary issue of the sacred obligation to keep the covenant by obeying the Law. Gentiles or not, that obligation remained paramount.[78]

10:3 Paul explains the nature of his fellow Jews' ignorance and its outcome: *Since they did not know the righteousness of God and sought to establish their own, they did not submit to God's righteousness.* The verse is chiastic in structure, built around the motif of righteousness:

They did not know the righteousness of God	A
They sought to establish their own righteousness	B
They did not submit to God's righteousness	A[79]

'The righteousness of God' is contrasted with what they sought to establish instead: 'their own righteousness'. 'The righteousness of God' may be understood as declaratory on God's side (he adjudicates in favor of those who put their faith in Christ), and denoting status on the human side (the status of those who are beneficiaries of that adjudication). What Paul describes as 'their own [righteousness]' may be understood as a righteousness based on the law. Instructive here is the similar contrast Paul makes in Philippians 3:8-9 when describing his own change of attitude in respect to righteousness as a result of his conversion to Christ:

> What is more, I consider everything a loss compared to the surpassing greatness of knowing Christ Jesus my Lord, for whose sake I have lost all things. I consider them rubbish, that I may gain Christ and be found in him, *not having a righteousness of my own that comes from the law*, but

---

77. James D. G. Dunn, *The Theology of Paul the Apostle* (Edinburgh: T&T Clark, 1998), 351. Bechtler, 'Christ, the *Telos* of the Law', 296, reaches a similar conclusion.

78. Vincent M. Smiles, 'The Concept of "Zeal" in Second-Temple Judaism and Paul's Critique of It in Romans 10:2', *CBQ* 64 (2002) 291.

79. Cf. Byrne, *Romans*, 311.

that which is through faith in Christ — *the righteousness that comes from God on the basis of faith.* (italics added)

In this passage also Paul contrasts two types of righteousness: 'not having a righteousness of my own that comes from the law' on the one hand and 'the righteousness of God on the basis of faith' on the other. It is reasonable to say that 'their own righteousness' (10:3) is equivalent to 'a righteousness of my own that comes from the law' (Phil 3:9).[80] Prior to his conversion Paul had been proud of his careful observance of the law, describing himself as one who was 'as to righteousness based on the law, faultless' (Phil 3:6). But such a basis of confidence he now counted as 'rubbish' in comparison with knowing Christ (Phil 3:8).

Some, however, have argued that 'their own [righteousness]' in 10:3 is not a standing before God that some Jewish people sought to establish by observing the law, but the righteousness that belongs to Israel as the people of the law; their exclusive covenant status that distinguished them from the Gentiles.[81] While it is certainly true that some Jews relied upon their national privileges as people of the covenant (cf. 2:17-29), and this might well be called 'a righteousness of their own', there are reasons to believe that this is not what Paul intended by the expression in 10:3. Here, as Moo notes, the 'immediate contrast to "their own righteousness" is "God's righteousness". This suggests that "their own", like the contrasting term, "God's", is not simply possessive, but has the nuance of source. And this, in turn, favors an individualizing rather than a corporate interpretation: a righteousness that comes from one's own efforts'.[82]

What Paul describes as 'the righteousness of God' is God's freely given adjudication in favor of believers, confirming that their sins are not counted against them so that they enjoy a restored relationship with God. This is the same thing to which Paul referred in Philippians 3:9 when he expressed his desire to be 'found in him, not having a righteousness of my own that comes from the law, but that which is through faith in Christ — the righteousness that comes from God and is based on faith'. Whereas the righteousness of one's own to which Paul refers is based on observance of the law, the righteousness of God is based on God's grace and is received by faith.

80. Jewett, *Romans,* 618, identifies 'their own [righteousness]' as 'a reference to the sense of ethnic or sectarian righteousness claimed by Jewish groups. . . . The zealot movement sought to achieve righteousness by violent warfare. . . . The Pharisees taught that perfect obedience to the written and oral law would usher in the righteous messianic era. . . . The Essenes argued that adherence to their calendar and cultic regulations for the temple would satisfy the conditions of righteousness. . . . The Sadducees believed that maintaining the purity of the temple and following the laws of the Pentateuch would achieve righteousness. . . . In their sectarian competition with each other, and their sense of superiority over the corrupt Gentile world, each of these groups sought to "validate their own righteousness"'.
81. So, e.g., Dunn, *Romans 9–16,* 587; Bechtler, 'Christ, the *Telos* of the Law', 297-98.
82. Moo, *Romans,* 634-35. Cf. Byrne, *Romans,* 314; Thomas R. Schreiner, 'Paul's View of the Law in Romans 10:4-5', *WTJ* 55 (1993) 121-22.

There are, Paul implies here, two reasons why many of his Jewish kinsfolk did not attain the righteousness they so zealously sought. The first was that they were determined to seek a righteousness of their own. The second was they 'they did not submit to God's righteousness'.[83] In practice this expressed itself in a refusal to accept the way God provided whereby human beings could become acceptable in his sight, that is, by submission and obedience to the gospel's call to repent and believe in his Son.

10:4 Concluding his explanation of the reason why many of his fellow Jews failed to attain the righteousness they zealously sought, Paul says: *[For] Christ is the culmination of the law so that there may be righteousness for everyone who believes*. The NIV omits the conjunction, 'for', thus obscuring somewhat the causal connection between this verse and those preceding it. What Paul is actually doing in 10:4 is explaining further the nature of the Jewish ignorance which underlay their misdirected zeal. Their refusal to submit to God's righteousness is evidence of ignorance, not only of the righteousness of God, but also of the fact that 'Christ is the culmination [lit. 'end' or 'goal'] of the law'. It is important not to lose sight of the essential point Paul is making here: Christ is the end of the law 'so that there may be righteousness for everyone who believes'.[84] His purpose in 10:4 is a modest one. He is not here discussing whether the law has any role at all now that Christ has come, but rather asserting that the coming of Christ has brought the era of the law to an end with the result that there may be (or with the purpose of making available) righteousness for everyone who believes, that is, Gentiles as well as Jews. Righteousness before God is now offered on the same basis to Jews and Gentiles alike — through faith in Christ, and the Jews who failed to attain this did so because they would not believe in him. This interpretation assumes that 'Christ is the culmination/end of the law' means that Christ has brought to an end the era of the law. However, not all scholars accept this view. The precise meaning of this statement has been much debated; see 'Additional Note: *telos nomou*', below.

ADDITIONAL NOTE: *TELOS NOMOU*

When Paul declares, 'For Christ is the culmination/end *(telos)* of the law so that there may be righteousness for everyone who believes' (10:4), is he im-

---

83. Paul uses the verb 'to submit' *(hypotassō)* 23 times in 18 verses, but this is the only place he uses it in relation to righteousness. As a rule he uses it to denote submission to one sort of authority or another.

84. 'So that there may be righteousness for everyone who believes' translates *eis dikaiosynēn panti tō pisteuonti,* construed correctly by the NIV and NRSV as indicating the result/purpose of Christ's coming, i.e., to bring an end to the era of the law, thereby removing it as an obstacle preventing Gentiles from obtaining righteousness. Cf. Barrett, *Romans,* 197-98; Moo, *Romans,* 637-38.

plying that the era of the law has come to an end now that Christ has come,[85] or that the goal of the law has been reached in Christ?[86] The question cannot be answered on the grounds of lexicography, because *telos* can mean either 'end' or 'goal'. The issue can be resolved only if one or other of its meanings can be shown to make better sense in the context.

Some scholars who support the view that *telos* here means 'end' do so assuming that Paul is saying that Christ has put an end to the law as the way to obtain righteousness.[87] However, Paul would deny that the law was ever intended to provide the way to obtain righteousness, and therefore such a view trivializes the relationship between Christ and the law.[88] It is much better to interpret Christ as having brought the law to an end in terms of bringing to an end the era of the law's jurisdiction. This is consistent with Paul's use of the 'disciplinarian' and 'guardian' imagery in Galatians 3:23–4:7, imagery he used to illustrate the freedom of believers from the law's jurisdiction that, like the role of the disciplinarian or guardian, came to an end at a specified time. It is also consistent with Paul's teaching in 2 Corinthians 3:7-11, where he contrasts the transitory nature of the ministry of Moses (associated with the 'letter' which kills) that has been set aside with the permanent ministry (associated with the Spirit) entrusted to Paul (and the other apostles).[89] It also has a parallel in 2 Corinthians 3:13-14, where Paul speaks of Moses veiling his face so that the people of Israel might not see the end of the glory of the old covenant which was being set aside.[90]

However, significant objections have been raised against this view, and in favor of construing *telos* as goal: (i) If Paul were to admit that, according to his gospel, the law had been annulled by Christ, he would placing at risk his credibility with the Jerusalem and Roman churches[91] — something he was seeking to establish by writing Romans. However, it appears that Paul is prepared to take this risk, because in Romans 7:1-6 he says quite straightforwardly that believers have been released from the jurisdiction of the law so that they 'serve in the new way of the Spirit, and not in the old way of the written code' (v. 6). (ii) Because Paul argues (in 10:5-8) that the law itself testifies to the righteousness by faith in Christ, he must

85. So, e.g., François Refoulé, 'Note sur Romains IX, 30-33', *RB* 92 (1985) 161-86; Werner Führer, '"Herr ist Jesus": Die Rezeption der urchristlichen Kyrios-Akklamation durch Paulus Römer 10,9', *KD* 33 (1987) 137-49; Räisänen, *Paul and the Law*, 53-56; Heil, 'Christ, the Termination of the Law', 498.

86. So, e.g., C. Thomas Rhyne, '*Nomos Dikaiosynēs* and the Meaning of Romans 10:4', *CBQ* 47 (1985) 498; Getty, 'Paul and the Salvation of Israel', 466-67; Robert Jewett, 'The Law and the Co-existence of Jews and Gentiles in Romans', *Int* 39 (1985) 349.

87. Cf. Wilhelm C. Linss, 'Exegesis of *telos* in Romans 10:4', *BR* 33 (1988) 9-10; Witherington, *Romans*, 261.

88. Cf. Davies, *Faith and Obedience in Romans*, 188.

89. Cf. Räisänen, *Paul and the Law*, 56.

90. Cf. Dunn, *Romans 9–16*, 590-91.

91. Getty, 'Paul and the Salvation of Israel', 466.

have believed that there was a positive relationship between Christ and the law, which in turn suggests that Christ is the goal of the law, not its end.[92] There is a positive relationship between Christ and the law insofar as the law testifies to the salvation effected through Christ. However, it is quite another matter to say that, because the law testifies to Christ in this way, he did not bring the era of the law to an end so that righteousness may be made available to everyone who believes. Further, if it is admitted that 10:5-8 actually contrasts the righteousness of the law with the righteousness through faith in Christ, it is unlikely that Paul saw Christ as the goal of the law as far as righteousness is concerned. It is also worth noting that the author of Hebrews bases his whole argument on the OT, and yet regards the old covenant as superseded. (iii) In the light of the many positive statements Paul makes about the law in Romans (7:12, 14a; 8:4; 13:8-10) and the categorical statement in 3:31 ('Do we then nullify the law by this faith? Not at all! Rather, we uphold the law'), and his appeals to the Pentateuch in 10:5-8 in support of his arguments, it is highly improbable that Paul would want to say that Christ is the termination of the law.[93] It is, of course, true that Paul makes many positive statements about the law. As far as the apostle is concerned, sin is the real culprit, not the law. However, in order that people may be delivered from sin's dominion they must be freed from the law's jurisdiction, so as to 'bear fruit for God' (7:4-6). The era of the law has come to an end so that Gentiles as well as Jews may obtain righteousness. (iv) Hills argues that the copula to be provided for the statement, *telos gar nomou Christos*, is not *estin* ('is') as usually assumed, but *ēn* ('was'), yielding the translation, 'Christ was the goal of the law'. He says: 'It is hard to see how the proposed reading of 10:4b could be compatible with the still popular interpretation of *telos* as 'end' or 'termination' in some absolute sense. If Christ was the law's termination, then the law lingers on only as a venerable but otiose religious monument — an unlikely conclusion for Paul (see, e.g., Rom. 3:31; 7:12).[94] However, to say that Christ is the end of the law, meaning that he brought to an end the era of the law in the sense that obedience to the law was required of all who are numbered among God's new people, does not mean there is no further role for the law as a witness to Christ or in providing guidelines for living when applied paradigmatically.

Moo argues for a both/and approach. He affirms the temporal sense (*telos* denotes 'end') because discontinuity between the law and Christ is implied in 10:3-4, but he also acknowledges a teleological sense (*telos* denotes 'goal'). Appealing to the athletic imagery, he says: 'The analogy of a race course (which many scholars think *telos* is meant to convey) is helpful: the finish line is both the "termination" of the race (the race is over when it

---

92. Rhyne, 'Nomos Dikaiosynēs', 498.

93. Cranfield, *Romans*, II, 518-19. Cf. Bechtler, 'Christ, the *Telos* of the Law', 298-301.

94. Julian V. Hills, '"Christ Was the Goal of the Law . . ." (Romans 10:4)', *JTS* 44 (1993) 585-90.

is reached) and the "goal" of the race (the race is run for the sake of reaching the finish line). Likewise, we suggest, Paul is implying that Christ is the "end" of the law (he brings its era to a close) and its "goal" (he is what the law anticipated and pointed toward)'.[95] This is helpful, highlighting the fact that Christ brings to an end the era of the law's jurisdiction, while at the same time recognizing that Christ is the goal of the law insofar as he is the one to whom it testifies, and the one who through his death and resurrection and the sending of the Spirit makes it possible for the 'righteous requirement' of the law to be fulfilled in believers.

b. The Testimony of the Law to Faith, 10:5-13

5Moses writes this about the righteousness that is by the law: 'The person who does these things will live by them'. 6But the righteousness that is by faith says: 'Do not say in your heart, "Who will ascend into heaven?"' (that is, to bring Christ down) 7or "Who will descend into the deep?"' (that is, to bring Christ up from the dead). 8But what does it say? 'The word is near you; it is in your mouth and in your heart', that is, the message concerning faith that we proclaim: 9If you declare with your mouth, 'Jesus is Lord', and believe in your heart that God raised him from the dead, you will be saved. 10For it is with your heart that you believe and are justified, and it is with your mouth that you profess your faith and are saved. 11As Scripture says, 'Anyone who believes in him will never be put to shame'. 12For there is no difference between Jew and Gentile — the same Lord is Lord of all and richly blesses all who call on him, 13for, 'Everyone who calls on the name of the Lord will be saved'.

In this passage Paul provides further support for his claim in 10:4 that the coming of Christ marks the end of the law so that there may be righteousness for everyone who believes. He does so by using the law itself to make his point, contrasting 'the righteousness that is by the law' with 'the righteousness that is by faith'.

10:5 Paul introduces his explanation with the word 'for' (omitted in the NIV translation) to indicate that in this and the following verses he is going to provide a basis for the claim he made in 10:4, that Christ is the end of the law so that there may be righteousness for everyone who believes. The apostle begins: [For] Moses writes this about the righteousness that is by the law: 'The person who does these things will live by them'. It is most unusual for Paul to introduce a quotation from Scripture as he does here with 'Moses writes'.[96] Almost always Paul introduces his scriptural quotations with the

---

95. Moo, *Romans*, 641.

96. Käsemann, *Romans*, 284, comments: 'The lawgiver Moses stands over against the personified righteousness of faith. . . . Whereas he characteristically writes, she speaks with the living voice of the gospel, with which there is doubtless an allusion to the relation of

words, 'as it is written'. The quotation itself is taken from Leviticus 18:5. In its original context, this text forms part of an introductory exhortation to a list of sexual prohibitions. By obeying these laws the Israelites would distinguish themselves from both the Egyptians (from whom they had recently escaped) and the Canaanites (among whom they were soon to live). Those who failed to observe these laws would be cut off from the people (Lev 18:24-30), while those who kept them would continue to enjoy life within the promised land, that is, 'the person who does these things will live by them'.[97] The promise did not relate to life in the new age (eternal life) but life within the covenant community in the promised land.[98] This interpretation was adopted by the early church fathers Origen,[99] Jerome,[100] and Diodore.[101] To continue to experience this life, then, depended upon obedience.

There have been various interpretations of Paul's use of Leviticus 18:5. Some scholars argue that the reference to Leviticus 18:5 in 10:5 is not to be taken negatively, but positively, either as an allusion to the perfect obedience of Christ[102] or the obedience to the law that springs from faith.[103] In such cases the connection between 10:5 and 10:6-8 is not adversative, depicting two different ways achieving righteousness; rather, Leviticus 18:5 describes obedience that springs from faith. Schreiner correctly rejects this view on the grounds that 'the doing of the commandments of the law in Rom 10:5 is equivalent to establishing one's own righteousness in 10:3', and because 'the antithesis between doing and believing which permeates the text in Rom 9:30–10:13' supports an adversative relationship between 10:5 and 10:6-8.[104] It would appear, then, that in 10:5 Paul uses Leviticus 18:5 to depict a righteousness which is based on law observance,[105] one that

---

pneuma and *gramma* in 2:27ff.; 7:6; 2 Cor 3:6ff. This already brings out the antithesis . . . and secures the meaning "end of the law" in v. 4'.

97. Deut 5:32–6:3 contains a similar promise of life in the promised land for Israelites if they were careful to do what the Lord commanded them. And as Westerholm, *Israel's Law and the Church's Faith*, 146-47, points out, there are dozens of similar texts in the OT.

98. Commenting on Lev 18:1-5, Philo says: 'So then the true life is the life of him who walks in the judgements and ordinances of God' (*The Preliminary Studies* 87).

99. 'Commentary on the Epistle to the Romans' (*ACCSR*, 273).

100. 'Sermons' (*ACCSR*, 274).

101. 'Commentary from the Greek Church' (*ACCSR*, 274).

102. Cranfield, *Romans*, II, 521-22; W. S. Campbell, 'Christ the End of the Law: Romans 10:4', in *StudBib1978: III. Papers on Paul and Other New Testament Authors. Sixth International Congress on Biblical Studies*, ed. E. A. Livingstone (JSNTSup 3; Sheffield: JSOT Press, 1980), 77-78.

103. Daniel P. Fuller, *Gospel and Law: Contrast or Continuum?* (Grand Rapids: Eerdmans, 1980), 85-86; Davies, *Faith and Obedience in Romans*, 189-200; Robert Badenas, *Christ the End of the Law: Romans 10.4 in Pauline Perspective* (Sheffield: JSOT, 1985), 118-25.

104. Schreiner, 'Paul's View of the Law in Romans 10:4-5', 128-29.

105. Paul uses Lev 18:5 in the same way in Gal 3:12. Cf. Ziesler, *Romans*, 259. Mark A. Seifrid, 'Paul's Approach to the Old Testament in Rom 10:6-8', *TrinJ* 6 n.s. (1985) 16, argues that the essential point Paul makes by citing Lev 18:5 is that obedience is the prerequisite for a righteous status, and in this he reflects the concerns of the original text well.

allows continuance in the promised land, and then in 10:6 contrasts that with the righteousness based on faith that brings life in the new age.[106]

10:6-8 The next step in Paul's explanation of the basis for his claim that Christ is the end of the law for righteousness is to quote Moses again, this time to depict the righteousness that is by faith. He introduces his quotation with the statement: *But the righteousness that is by faith says. . . .* This differs from the way he introduced his quotation describing 'the righteousness that is by the law'. In the first case Moses *writes*, and in the second 'righteousness by faith' personified *says* (Paul is employing the rhetorical device of speech-in-character).[107]

The 'quotation' Paul provides to depict what 'the righteousness by faith says' is: *Do not say in your heart, 'Who will ascend into heaven?' (that is, to bring Christ down) or 'Who will descend into the deep?' (that is, to bring Christ up from the dead). But what does it say? 'The word is near you; it is in your mouth and in your heart', that is, the message concerning faith that we proclaim.* The introductory exhortation, 'Do not say in your heart . . .', is taken from Deuteronomy 9:4. The remainder of the quotation is drawn from Deuteronomy 30:11-14, which reads as follows:

> Now what I am commanding you today is not too difficult for you or beyond your reach. It is not up in heaven, so that you have to ask, 'Who will ascend into heaven to get it and proclaim it to us so we may obey it?' Nor is it beyond the sea, so that you have to ask, 'Who will cross the sea to get it and proclaim it to us so we may obey it?' No, the word is very near you; it is in your mouth and in your heart so you may obey it.

Paul's 'quotation' diverges from the original in that he has replaced 'Who will cross the sea?' with 'Who will descend into the deep?' Lindars notes

---

106. Jewett, *Romans*, 625, comments: 'At this point Paul is no longer concerned with the question of whether Jews in fact had complied with the law. He simply reiterates the traditional Jewish premise that Israel was obligated to live by the law. This sets the stage for the *pesher*, which reinterprets the subsequent texts in the light of the "by faith" principle. He thereby shows that the law itself points to faith in Christ and provides no foundation for justification by works. This is one more instance of Paul's skill in becoming "one under the law" in order to win over "those under the law" (1 Cor 9:20)'.

107. Some suggest that there is an intended distinction between what Moses *writes* about the righteousness that comes from the law on the one hand, and what the righteousness that is by faith *says* on the other. What Moses writes *(graphō)* relates to the letter of the law, and what righteousness says *(legō)* relates to the Spirit. However, this is to build too much upon the distinction between *writing* and *saying* in respect to Paul's citations from Scripture. He often uses *legō* when speaking of what Scripture says in quite straightforward ways without any implied reference to the Spirit (cf. 4:3; 9:17; 10:11; 11:2; Gal 4:30; 1 Tim 5:18) even though he uses *graphō* far more often in this connection (38x). Akio Ito, 'The Written Torah and the Oral Gospel: Romans 10:5-13 in the Dynamic Tension between Orality and Literacy', *NovT* 48 (2006) 234, 238, 248, 251-52, says that there is an implied contrast between 'the orality of the Gospel' and 'the literacy of the Torah' — something Paul stresses because he sees himself as 'working in the tradition of the "herald" of Isaiah 52'.

that 'this change appears in the Targum, and indicates that Paul is at this point taking advantage of a contemporary Jewish exegesis'.[108] Paul has also added to the quoted material his own interpretive comments (introduced in each case by 'that is') by which he makes it speak of the gospel that he proclaims.[109] This seems to the modern reader to be an arbitrary use of the OT, but this is not the case when read in the light of first-century Jewish exegetical practice and Paul's recognition of the pattern of salvation history.[110] See 'Additional Note: Paul's Use of the OT in 10:6-8', 413-14.

Paul's main point in 10:6-8 is clear enough. He uses Deuteronomy 30:12-14 to emphasize that, just as the law was not something hidden and distant from the Israelites, so likewise the gospel of faith-righteousness is not something hidden or distant from Paul's contemporaries — it is freely available to both Jews and Gentiles through the gospel he proclaims. What that gospel is he defines in 10:9-10. Fitzmyer's comment is apposite:

> Just as Moses tried to convince the Israelites that the observance of the law did not demand that one scale the heights or cross the seas, so Paul plays on Moses' words, applying them in an accommodated sense to Christ himself. The heights have been scaled and the depths have been plumbed, for Christ has come down to the world of humanity and has been raised from the dead. To attain the status of uprightness before God, no one is being asked to bring about an incarnation or a resurrection, one is asked only to accept in faith what has already been done for humanity and to associate oneself with Christ incarnate and raised from the dead.[111]

To what Paul refers when he speaks of bringing Christ down and bringing Christ up from the dead has been variously interpreted. Dunn argues that

---

108. Barnabas Lindars, 'The Old Testament and Universalism in Paul', *BJRL* 69 (1987) 519.

109. Hans-Joachim Eckstein, '"Nahe ist dir das Wort": Exegetische Erwägungen zu Röm 10 8', *ZNW* 79 (1988) 215-19, argues that when Paul interpreted Deut 30:11-14 in terms of the gospel, he was influenced by his reading of such texts as Jer 38:31-34 LXX; Ezek 11:19; 36:26-27 which speak of the heart, Isa 46:13; 51:5: 56:1 which speak of the revelation of God's righteousness as salvation, Isa 53:1 with its emphasis on faith, and Isa 52:7 with its reference to the good tidings.

110. Cf. J. S. Vos, 'Die hermeneutische Antinome bei Paulus (Galater 3.11-12; Römer 10.5-10)', *NTS* 38 (1992) 254-70, who suggests that the hermeneutical oppositions discernible in Rom 10:5-10 follow the principles laid down in Graeco-Roman rhetorical handbooks concerning *leges contrariae*, principles also adopted by Hillel and Philo.

111. Fitzmyer, *Romans*, 590. Jewett, *Romans*, 626-27, explains: 'The reference to ascending to heaven "to bring Christ down" is neither a "fanciful" allusion to "looking high and low for Christ", nor a warning against spiritual journeys to master heaven's secrets or to gain access even to the inaccessible Wisdom revealed in Christ. It is instead a historically apt depiction of the goals of some of the Jewish parties in Paul's time. They sought to hasten the coming of the divinely appointed *Christos* . . . by religious programs associated with the law. . . . For example, Rabbi Levi taught that "[i]f Israel kept the Sabbath properly even for a single day, the son of David would come"'.

bringing Christ down cannot be a reference to his incarnation (he believes such teaching emerged only later) but instead is to be understood as bringing down the exalted Christ. The objection that this has Paul referring to Christ's exaltation before his resurrection from the dead Dunn dismisses by saying the apostle was not speaking chronologically.[112] However, there are good reasons to believe that Paul did speak of Christ's incarnation, and, if so, there is no reason to reject an allusion to Christ's incarnation and resurrection here.[113]

It is significant that in 10:8 Paul describes the gospel he proclaims as 'the message concerning faith'. It highlights a crucial aspect of the gospel, that is, its promise of salvation is for those who respond to its message with faith. The crucial importance of faith is reflected in the frequency of Paul's use of the noun 'faith' (40x) and the verb 'to believe' (21x) in Romans.[114]

10:9-10 In these verses Paul explains further what he means by 'the word of faith which we preach': *If you declare with your mouth, 'Jesus is Lord', and believe in your heart that God raised him from the dead, you will be saved.*[115] It should be noted that what is declared with the mouth is 'Jesus is Lord'. This was both the fundamental aspect of Paul's preaching of the gospel and the

---

112. Dunn, *Romans 9–16*, 605.

113. Cf. Capes, 'YHWH and His Messiah', 130-31, who offers the following reasons for his belief that 10:6 does contain an allusion to Christ's incarnation: (i) 'the analogy between Christ and the commandments is obvious. Just as God brings the commandments near for Israel, so at the proper time (Gal 4:4) he brings the Messiah down and makes him available to all of faith'. (ii) 'By identifying Christ as Torah-Wisdom which comes from heaven, Paul appears to be attributing to him pre-existence. Pre-existence, of course, is a prerequisite for incarnational thinking'. (iii) 'By interpreting 10:6 as incarnation, the order of the clauses (a) bringing Christ down and (b) bringing Christ up corresponds to both the narrative order of Deuteronomy and the chronological order of Jesus' life, namely, (a) incarnation and (b) resurrection'. (iv) 'Other passages in Paul offer similar motifs and clarify his use of these texts. . . . 2 Cor 8:9 . . . the description of Jesus as "rich" before he became "poor", parallels the movement bringing down (to earth) Christ who was in heaven. . . . The Philippian hymn (2:6-11) may also be interpreted in a descent/ascent (incarnation/resurrection) framework. . . . Paul contrasts Adam as the man "from earth" with the Second Adam as the "man from heaven" (1 Cor 15:47)'.

114. Paul uses the noun 'faith' when speaking of the preaching of the gospel that is intended to bring about the obedience of faith (1:5; 16:26), righteousness that is received by faith (1:17; 3:22; 4:5, 9, 11, 13; 9:30, 32; 10:6), people who are justified by faith (3:28, 30; 5:1, 2), Abraham who received the promises by faith (4:16), became the father of those who have faith (4:12), and did not waver in his faith (4:19-20), believers who stand by faith (11:20), receive gifts, and are to use them according to the measure of faith (12:3, 6), and who are to accept those who are weak in faith (14:1). The apostle uses the verb 'to believe' when speaking of the salvation of those who believe (1:16; 10:9-10), the righteousness that is credited to those who believe (3:22; 4:3, 5, 24; 10:4), Abraham who believed God (4:3, 11, 17, 18), and when quoting Scripture to emphasize that those who believe will never be put to shame (9:33; 10:11). In the following verses, 10:9-10, Paul explains what he means by 'the word of faith'.

115. The strange order, 'declare with your mouth' before 'believe in your heart', matches the order of Deut 30:14: 'the word is very near you; it is in your mouth and in your heart so you may obey it'.

fundamental expression of faith required of people responding to its message (cf. 1 Cor 12:3; 2 Cor 4:5; Phil 2:11; Col 2:6). Cranfield, who notes that 'Lord' *(kyrios)* is used more than 600 times in the LXX to translate YHWH, comments that 'for Paul, the confession that Jesus is Lord meant the acknowledgment that Jesus shares the name and the nature, the holiness, the authority, power, majesty and eternity of the one and only true God'.[116]

Confession of Jesus as Lord meant that one belonged to him and submitted to him. This confession was a public matter in Paul's day, and some believe that it would have been seen as a challenge to Caesar's claim to be Lord with all the attendant dangers of doing so.[117] Dunn, however, questions this: 'How much more of Christological significance would be seen in the confession in Greco-Roman circles is less clear, since there were many "lords" (1 Cor 8:5), and since different lordships could be acknowledged in different spheres without necessarily involving conflict between them'.[118]

Underlying the public confession 'Jesus is Lord' there was to be a personal belief ('in your heart') that God raised Jesus from the dead. The death and resurrection of Christ are fundamental tenets of the Christian gospel (cf. 1 Cor 15:1-5).[119] Genuine faith involves both confession with the mouth and belief in the heart. This is the only place in his letters where Paul speaks of believing 'in the heart', and also the only place where he speaks of confessing 'with the mouth'. These are not separate activities but two aspects of the one expression of faith in Jesus as Lord. Believing with the heart without confession with the mouth is not true faith.[120] Confession with the mouth without belief in the heart would be hypocrisy. Those who believe in their hearts and confess with their mouths are saved. In Romans salvation is *from* the wrath of God and *for* a share in the glory that is to come.

Paul explains the importance of belief and confession when he adds: *For it is with your heart that you believe and are justified, and it is with your mouth that you profess your faith and are saved.* The order here in 10:10 (with the heart that you believe — with the mouth you confess) is the reverse of what is found in 10:9 (confess with the mouth — believe in the heart), indicating that there is no theological significance to the order — it is simply rhetorically determined. Just as belief in the heart and confession with the mouth are so closely related that they cannot be separated, so too are justification and salvation.[121]

---

116. Cranfield, *Romans*, II, 529.

117. Cf. Jewett, *Romans*, 639-30.

118. Dunn, *Romans 9–16*, 608.

119. In 4:24 Paul affirms that God credits righteousness to those 'who believe in him who raised Jesus our Lord from the dead'.

120. Jesus himself said, 'I tell you, whoever publicly acknowledges me before others, the Son of Man will also acknowledge before the angels of God. But whoever disowns me before others will be disowned before the angels of God' (Luke 12:8-9; cf. Matt 10:32-33).

121. Fitzmyer, *Romans*, 592, comments: 'The chiastic balance [of 10:9-10] stresses the different aspects of the one basic act of personal adherence to Christ and its effect. The differ-

10:11-13 In these verses Paul appeals to the testimony of Scripture to support what he has just asserted. He begins: *As the Scripture says, 'Anyone who trusts in him will never be put to shame'.* He begins: 'as the Scripture says' (lit. 'for the Scripture says'), indicating that he is providing scriptural support for the assertion that those who believe in their hearts and confess with their mouths will be saved. Paul's quotation is drawn from Isaiah 28:16 (quoted previously in 9:33). The full text of Isaiah 28:16 reads: 'So this is what the Sovereign LORD says: "See, I lay a stone in Zion, a tested stone, a precious cornerstone for a sure foundation; the one who relies on it will never be stricken with panic"', Paul modifies slightly that part of the text he cites.[122]

Paul's change of the LXX's 'he who believes' to 'anyone who believes' implies a universal application (consistent with the theme of Romans that the gospel is for Gentiles as well as Jews). This is reinforced when he adds: *For there is no difference between Jew and Gentile — the same Lord is Lord of all and richly blesses all who call on him.* That there is no difference between Jews and Gentiles is something Paul stressed in 3:22-24, where he argued that there is no difference because both Jews and Gentiles have sinned and fallen short of the glory of God, and both are justified freely by God's grace through the redemption that came through Christ. Here in 10:12 there is no difference, he says, because 'the same Lord is Lord of all', something affirmed previously in 3:29-30 when he asks: 'Is God the God of Jews only? Is he not the God of Gentiles too?' and gives the answer, 'Yes, of Gentiles too, since there is only one God, who will justify the circumcised by faith and the uncircumcised through that same faith'. What Paul emphasizes here in 10:12 is not only that 'the same Lord is Lord of all' but also that he 'richly blesses all who call on him'. The verb translated 'to call upon' is frequently (but not exclusively) used in both the LXX and the NT in relation to invoking God in prayer, and it is used in this way also here in 10:12. The richness of the blessing Paul spells out in 10:13 by including another OT quotation: *for, 'Everyone who calls on the name of the Lord will be saved'.* Paul's quotation

ence between justification and salvation should not be stressed. The verse formulates rhetorically the relation of human uprightness and salvation to faith and the profession of it'.

122. The LXX text is *kai ho pisteuōn ep' autō ou mē kataischynthē* ('and he who believes in him will never be put to shame'). The LXX uses the double negative *(ou mē)* with the aorist passive subjunctive *(kataischynthē)* to emphatically deny the possibility of a person's trust in the Lord ever being betrayed. Paul modifies this to become *pas ho pisteuōn ep' autō ou kataschynthēsetai* ('anyone who believes in him will never be put to shame'). He adds *pas* (better translated 'all' than 'anyone' as in the NIV, for in context Paul probably has Gentiles as well as Jews in mind, rather than any individual). He also substitutes a simple negative *(ou)* for the emphatic double negative *(ou mē)* and the future indicative passive *(kataschynthēsetai)* for the aorist subjunctive passive *(kataischynthē)*. This lessens the emphatic nature of the Isa 28:16 text, and also implies a future reference in the text, affirming that on the last day those who put their trust in the Lord will never be put to shame; their trust in him will be fully honored. Cf. C. Kavin Rowe, 'Romans 10:13: What Is the Name of the Lord?' *HorBibTheol* 22 (2000) 144-45.

reproduces exactly the LXX version of Joel 3:5 (E.T. Joel 2:32). This is part of a prophecy of the last days (E.T. Joel 2:28-32, LXX 3:1-5, also quoted in Acts 2:17-21) promising that the Lord would pour out his Spirit on all people and that, in those days, 'all who call upon the name of the Lord will be saved'. The richness of the blessing is none other than salvation itself.

In the context of Joel 2:32 'the name of the Lord' is the name of Yahweh. However, as Rowe argues, throughout 10:9-13 Paul intends his audience to understand 'the Lord' to be understood as 'the Lord Jesus Christ', for this is what the flow of the apostle's thought in these verses demands: in 10:9 people confess with their mouths, *Jesus is Lord,* and in 10:11 'all who trust in *him* will never be put to shame', because (10:12) 'there is no difference between Jew and Gentile — the same *Lord* is *Lord* of all and richly blesses all who call on *him,* because (10:13): 'all who call on the name of *the Lord* will be saved'.[123] In addition, it may be noted that for Paul 'the name' is almost without exception used in connection with the Lord Jesus Christ. Thus in 1 Corinthians 1:2 the apostle describes his audience as those 'who call on the name of our Lord Jesus Christ'. Elsewhere he appeals to people to be of one mind 'in the name of our Lord Jesus Christ' (1 Cor 1:10); speaks of people being 'assembled in the name of our Lord Jesus' (1 Cor 5:4 NRSV); refers to those who 'were justified in the name of the Lord Jesus Christ' (1 Cor 6:11); encourages people to give thanks to God 'in the name of the Lord Jesus Christ' (Eph 5:20); urges people to do whatever they do 'in the name of the Lord Jesus' (Col 3:17); prays that 'the name of our Lord Jesus may be glorified' (2 Thess 1:12); and issues commands 'in the name of the Lord Jesus Christ' (2 Thess 3:6). Striking in this respect is Paul's statement in Philippians 2:9-11:

> Therefore God exalted him to the highest place and gave him the name that is above every name, that at the name of Jesus every knee should bow, in heaven and on earth and under the earth, and every tongue acknowledge that Jesus Christ is Lord, to the glory of God the Father.

In this text Paul alludes to Isaiah 45:23, in which God declares that to him every knee will bow and every tongue confess. He quotes Isaiah 45:23 in 14:11 with the same sense. It is therefore all the more significant that in Philippians 2:9-11 the apostle says that *at the name of Jesus* every knee will bow and every tongue confess that he is Lord to the glory of God the Father. There would seem to be little doubt, therefore, that when Paul quotes Joel 2:32, 'Everyone who calls on the name of the LORD will be saved', he would have his audience understand that to mean 'Everyone who calls on the name of the Lord [Jesus Christ] will be saved'. This implies a striking identification of Jesus Christ with Yahweh. Rowe makes the following statement:

---

123. Rowe, 'Romans 10:13: What Is the Name of the Lord?' 146-47.

It is quite astonishing, then, that Paul explicitly uses *to onoma kyriou* ('the name of the Lord') of Joel 3:5 to refer to Jesus. In this way he makes an unreserved identification of Jesus with YHWH, the unique and only God of Israel. However, since Paul is not foremost a propositional theologian, he does not simply say, 'Jesus is YHWH'. His theological medium is instead that of overlap and resonance, such that he creates the overlapping conceptual space wherein this resonating identification occurs. The identification within this unquestionable resonance and 'conceptual overlap' is one of dialectical *identity*. The name which *is* the God of Israel alone, is now the name which *is* Jesus. The saving name in its original context was YHWH, now the saving name is Christ's. In Joel the Israelites would have called out 'YHWH' to be saved, and now in Romans, all would call out 'Jesus'. 'The name of the Lord' = YHWH has become, through Paul's OT citation, 'the name of the Lord' = Jesus.[124]

ADDITIONAL NOTE:
PAUL'S USE OF THE OLD TESTAMENT IN 10:6-8

Paul cites from Deuteronomy 30:12-14 in 10:6-8, and adds his own comments (introduced in each case by 'that is') by which he relates it to the gospel he proclaims. In its original context Deuteronomy 30:12-14 refers to the law (all the commandments of God conveyed to the Israelites at the time of the covenant renewal). This law, Moses told the Israelites, was not difficult to find, nor was it beyond their reach. They did not have to ascend to heaven to get it, nor go beyond the sea to obtain it. On the contrary, he said, 'the word is very near you; it is in your mouth and in your heart so you may obey it' (Deut 30:14). What Deuteronomy says about the law Paul applies to the gospel. By applying Scripture in this way, Paul is employing Jewish exegetical practices current in his day, as the following examples illustrate.

Baruch 3:29-30 (dating probably from the second century B.C.) interprets Deuteronomy 30:12-14 in terms of the pursuit of Wisdom: 'Who has gone up into heaven, and taken her, and brought her down from the clouds? Who has gone over the sea, and found her, and will buy her for pure gold?' Capes, drawing attention to Baruch 3:29-30 and several other Wisdom texts and comparing them with Paul's application of Deuteronomy 30:12-14 to the gospel, says: 'The apostle's comments expand these quotations beyond their original and developed referents of Torah and Wisdom to include Christ as well. He reads these texts to suggest that what humankind needs ultimately to establish righteousness is the Messiah, whom God has brought

---

124. Rowe, 'Romans 10:13: What Is the Name of the Lord?' 160.

near. This righteousness is not attained through human effort; but it has been brought near by God's gracious act'.[125]

The way Paul adds his comments to the text he cites from Deuteronomy 30:12-14 is also similar to the *pesher* exegesis practiced at Qumran in which the texts cited were interpreted and seen as fulfilled in the time of the interpreter. For example, the commentary on Habakkuk 2:4b ('the righteous will live by his faith') in 1QpHab 8:1-3 reads: 'Interpreted, this concerns all those who observe the Law in the House of Judah, whom God will deliver from the House of Judgement because of their suffering and because of their faith in the Teacher of Righteousness' (cf. also 1QpHab 5:6-8; 6:2-8; 7:3-5; 10:2-4; 12:2-10).

However, Paul's interpretation of Deuteronomy 30:12-14 in terms of his gospel not only employs the model found in Jewish texts. It is, more importantly, determined by his understanding of the significance of the revelation of God in Jesus Christ. Ziesler asserts: 'If Paul believes (v. 4) that Christ is the fulfilment of the Law, then he may also see him as the fulfilment of what the OT says about the Law, so that it is proper to make Deut. 30:12-14 refer to him'.[126] Seifrid also sees in Paul's treatment of Deuteronomy 30:12-14 a Christologically determined exegesis, one which identifies a correspondence between what Moses says about the law and the way the apostle understands the gospel, a correspondence informed by salvation history.[127]

Coxhead concludes: 'We should say that the text of Deut 30:11-14 *both* contextually *and* grammatically looks forward to a future fulfilment, and that Paul saw Jesus as the fulfilment of this important text. Thus, there is no impediment from the perspective of the Hebrew text of Deut 30:11-14 to the view that Paul is interpreting Deut 30:11-14 in Rom 10:6-8 in a way that is consistent with the grammatical meaning of the text. Paul is simply employing a christologically informed method of Jewish midrash, which is consistent with the grammatical meaning of Deut 30:11-14, to defend the Christian gospel from particular Jewish opposition by showing how Jesus Christ and the Christian gospel are the fulfilment of the (eschatological) torah spoken of in this passage of Scripture'.[128]

---

125. Capes, 'YHWH and His Messiah', 129.

126. Ziesler, *Romans*, 260. Somewhat similarly, Cranfield, *Romans*, II, 524.

127. Cf. Seifrid, 'Paul's Approach to the Old Testament in Rom 10:6-8', 27; J. W. Aageson, 'Typology, Correspondence, and the Application of Scripture in Romans 9–11', *JSNT* 31 (1987) 51-72; Moo, *Romans*, 653; G. K. Beale and D. A. Carson, eds., *Commentary on the New Testament Use of the Old Testament* (Grand Rapids: Baker, 2007), 658-59.

128. Steven R. Coxhead, 'Deuteronomy 30:11-14 as a Prophecy of the New Covenant in Christ', *WTJ* 68 (2006) 312-13.

ADDITIONAL NOTE:
THE MEANING OF SALVATION IN ROMANS

Salvation is a fundamental theme in Paul's letter to the Romans. His articulation of the theme includes the affirmation: 'I am not ashamed of the gospel, because it is the power of God that brings salvation to everyone who believes' (1:16). He says that believers will be saved by the blood of Christ from the wrath of God (5:9), wrath that is (to be) revealed from heaven against all human wickedness (1:18) and that is being stored up for those who are stubborn and refuse to be led to repentance by God's kindness, tolerance, and patience (2:3-4).

Paul's concept of salvation is multifaceted. As has often been observed, the apostle can speak of people *having been saved* in the past (Rom 8:24; 11:11; Eph 2:5, 8; 2 Tim 1:9; Tit 3:5), *being saved* in the present (1 Cor 1:18; 15:2; 2 Cor 2:15), and *going to be saved* in the future (Rom 5:9-10; 13:11; 1 Cor 3:15; 5:5; Phil 1:28; 2 Tim 2:10; 4:18).[129] Salvation as a past event relates in the first instance to what God achieved for humankind by his grace and mercy through the death of his Son, and, based on that, the restoration of a right relationship between God and the believer (Eph 2:8, 12-16; 2 Tim 1:9; Tit 3:5). As a present reality salvation relates to God's ongoing work in the lives of believers,[130] and has corporate as well as individual expression in the formation and sanctification of Christian 'faith communities'.[131] As a future blessing it relates negatively to deliverance from wrath on the Day of Judgment, and positively to a share in eternal glory. But even more is involved. For Paul the scope of salvation is not restricted to humanity but, as the apostle makes clear in 8:19-22, extends to the renewal of creation itself.

In 5:10 the apostle stresses that believers, who have been reconciled to God through the death of Christ, shall 'be saved by his life', possibly referring to the intercessory work of the risen Christ on behalf of believers (cf. 8:34). He emphasizes that salvation is received through faith (10:9-10), by calling upon the name of the Lord (10:13). Believers may be said to have already been saved by the blood of Christ (5:9), but they still await their full salvation to be experienced in the future. Accordingly, Paul says that believers are saved in hope, adding, 'But hope that is seen is no hope at all. Who hopes for what they already have?' (8:24). What they hope for, as 'heirs of God and co-heirs with Christ', is that, as they share in his sufferings now, they will share in his glory then (8:17). Paul insists that our present sufferings 'are not worth comparing with the glory that will be revealed

---

129. Cf. Cranfield, *Romans*, I, 89.

130. Witherington, *Romans*, 51, adds: 'Thus one can say "I have been saved, I am being saved, and I will be saved", but not "I am saved", if by that one means that the process of salvation is already complete. There is always the working out of salvation with fear and trembling to be done while one lives in the flesh (Phil. 2.12)'.

131. Cf. Jewett, *Romans*, 143.

in us' (8:18), and he reminds his audience: 'our salvation is nearer now than when we first believed' (13:11).

More than anywhere else, Paul's references to salvation in Romans are found in chapters 9–11, where his agonizes over the fate of his unbelieving kinsfolk. He repeatedly expresses his deep concern for them. In 9:1-4 he says, 'I speak the truth in Christ — I am not lying, my conscience confirms it through the Holy Spirit — I have great sorrow and unceasing anguish in my heart. For I could wish that I myself were cursed and cut off from Christ for the sake of my people, those of my own race, the people of Israel'. And in 10:1 he reminds his audience of how much he longs and prays for the salvation of his still unbelieving fellow Jews so that they will know that his criticisms of his own people do not arise out of a lack of true concern for their well-being: 'Brothers and sisters, my heart's desire and prayer to God for the Israelites is that they may be saved'. Wrestling with the fact that so many of his fellow Jews had not responded to the gospel, Paul found an explanation in the scriptural doctrine of the remnant: 'Isaiah cries out concerning Israel: "Though the number of the Israelites be like the sand by the sea, only the remnant will be saved' (9:27). Nevertheless, Paul hoped that the rejection of the gospel by Jews that meant that salvation came to the Gentiles would in turn provoke the Jews to jealousy, leading them to seek salvation in Christ and thus leading to the salvation of 'all Israel' (11:11, 14, 26).

---

c. Has Israel Not Heard? 10:14-21

14How, then, can they call on the one they have not believed in? And how can they believe in the one of whom they have not heard? And how can they hear without someone preaching to them? 15And how can anyone preach unless they are sent? As it is written: 'How beautiful are the feet of those who bring good news!'

16But not all the Israelites accepted the good news. For Isaiah says, 'Lord, who has believed our message?' 17Consequently, faith comes from hearing the message, and the message is heard through the word about Christ. 18But I ask: Did they not hear? Of course they did: 'Their voice has gone out into all the earth, their words to the ends of the world'. 19Again I ask: Did Israel not understand? First, Moses says, 'I will make you envious by those who are not a nation; I will make you angry by a nation that has no understanding'. 20And Isaiah boldly says, 'I was found by those who did not seek me; I revealed myself to those who did not ask for me'. 21But concerning Israel he says, 'All day long I have held out my hands to a disobedient and obstinate people'.

Paul's overriding concern in chapters 9–11 is for his own people the Jews, a concern prompted by the failure of the majority of them to respond positively to the gospel. In 10:2-4 he acknowledged their zeal for God but said that it was not based on knowledge. Being ignorant of the righteousness that comes from God, they set about trying to establish their own righteousness and did not submit to God's righteousness — the righteousness of faith. In 10:5-10 he argued that the message of righteousness by faith is not something far away and difficult to find but close at hand, found in the very message he preaches. It may be summed up in the words of Joel 2:32 that he quotes in 10:13: 'Everyone who calls on the name of the Lord will be saved'. This leads the apostle to ask in 10:14-21 how people can call upon one of whom they have not heard, and then to ask whether the failure of his own people to respond is due to their having not heard.

10:14-15a Paul begins this section with four rhetorical questions, each of which anticipates a negative answer: *How, then, can they call on the one they have not believed in? And how can they believe in the one of whom they have not heard? And how can they hear without someone preaching to them? And how can they preach unless they are sent?* When he asks these questions, Paul is speaking in general terms but has his Jewish kinsfolk in the back of his mind. Paul's questions clearly imply that people cannot call on one in whom they have not believed, cannot believe in one of whom they have not heard, cannot hear unless someone preaches to them, and cannot preach unless they are sent. To be 'sent' here denotes being sent with a commission. Paul himself was sent and commissioned by Christ (1:4-5), and here he implies that all preachers of the gospel should be sent by Christ.

10:15b-16 To underline the importance of the preachers, Paul cites the Scripture: *As it is written: 'How beautiful are the feet of those who bring good news!'* The quotation is from Isaiah 52:7, part of a prophecy declaring the end of the Babylonian exile and the return to Zion: 'How beautiful on the mountains are the feet of those who bring good news, who proclaim peace, who bring good tidings, who proclaim salvation, who say to Zion, "Your God reigns!"' If the 'feet' of those who brought the message of the return from the exile were beautiful, how much more beautiful, Paul implies, are the 'feet' of those who proclaim the gospel of Christ.

Continuing to wrestle with the problem of Jewish resistance to the gospel, the apostle notes what happened in Isaiah's day: *But not all the Israelites accepted the good news* (lit. 'but not all obeyed the good news'). If this happened in Isaiah's day, it is not surprising that it should recur in Paul's day, the corollary being that there is nothing wrong with the gospel message or its messenger. The problem lies with the hearers. The failure of many Jews of his own day to accept the gospel is something Paul finds foreshadowed in the words of the prophet himself: *For Isaiah says, 'Lord, who has believed our message?'* The quotation is from Isaiah 53:1, part of a passage (Isa 52:13–53:12) depicting the suffering and glory of the Servant of the Lord. Included is Isaiah's lament that his message was not believed. Paul's experience was similar.

10:17 This verse, *Consequently, faith comes from hearing the message, and the message is heard through the word about Christ,* sits awkwardly in its context, so much so that some scholars suggest that rearrangement would improve the logic of the text,[132] and others regard it as a gloss.[133] If 10:15b-16 were omitted, 10:17 would flow naturally on from 10:15a, summing up the main point of 10:14-15a, that is, the indispensability of hearing the message for the production of faith. It is awkward in its present context because, being introduced by 'consequently', it appears to draw a conclusion from what immediately precedes in 10:15b-16, and that is hard to understand. Possibly Paul intended 10:17 to connect back to 10:14-15a, and 10:15b-16 is interspersed to highlight both the importance of the preachers who bring the good news and the sad fact that often their message is not believed. This was the reaction of many of Paul's kinsfolk to his preaching, and it caused him great anguish (cf. 9:1-4a).

It is important to note what Paul says about the way faith is generated: 'faith comes from hearing the message', that is, 'the word of Christ', which in this context is the gospel of Christ.[134] Faith, then, is generated through the preaching of the gospel (and, we may add, through the ministry of the Holy Spirit).

10:18 Paul, believing that faith is generated through the preaching of the gospel of Christ and confronted with Jewish intransigence, goes on: *But I ask: Did they not hear?*[135] Paul answers the question with an emphatic particle[136] translated here as: *Of course they did.* Indeed, the Israelites have heard. Paul supports this assertion with a quotation from Scripture: *'Their voice has gone out into all the earth, their words*[137] *to the ends of the world'.* The quotation is an exact citation of Psalm 18:5 (LXX; E.T. Ps 19:4). It is from that part of the psalm that speaks of the revelation of God through the created order (Ps 19:1-4, LXX 18:2-5):

The heavens declare the glory of God; the skies proclaim the work of his hands. Day after day they pour forth speech; night after night they

132. Cf. Barrett, *Romans*, 205.

133. Cf. Rudolf Bultmann, 'Glossen in Römerbrief', in *Exegetica: Aufsätze zur Erforschung des Neuen Testaments* (Tübingen: Mohr Siebeck, 1967), 280.

134. When Paul refers to the 'word about Christ', he employs the Greek word *rhēma*, and by it he means the 'gospel' of Christ. This is confirmed by the fact that he has already used *rhēma* in this way in 10:8, where he says, ' "The word *(rhēma)* is near you; it is in your mouth and in your heart", that is, the message *(rhēma)* concerning faith we proclaim'.

135. Dunn, *Romans 9–16*, 623-24, comments: 'The *ēkousan* picks up the *ex akoēs* of v 17 (Wilckens). It is regrettable that English cannot reproduce the cognate link between *hypakouō* ("obey"), *akoē* ("hearing, report"), and *akouō* ("hear"), which is an obvious feature of vv 16-18 and which would of course be evident to the first hearers — all the more so where they were familiar with the Hebrew usage, since all three were used in the LXX to represent *shāmah*'. . . .

136. Paul employs the emphatic particle *menounge* to correct the mistaken suggestion implied in the question.

137. Jewett, *Romans*, 643, observes that 'their words' translates *ta rhēmata autōn*, which 'resonates nicely with *rhēma Christou* ("word of Christ") in 10:17 and *to rhēma tēs pisteōs ho kēryssomen* ("the word of faith that we preach") in 10:8'.

reveal knowledge. They have no speech, they use no words; no sound is heard from them. Yet *their voice goes out into all the earth, their words to the ends of the world.* (italics added)

Paul appears to be saying that, just as God's revelation through creation has gone out into all the world, so too through his ministry the message of the gospel has been proclaimed to the ends of the earth. The implication is that ignorance is not the reason many of his kinsfolk fail to embrace the gospel. What Paul means when he implies that his gospel has gone into all the world,[138] and how his audience would have understood it are not easy to determine. Suggestions include that the world should be understood as the Roman Empire (Paul had already preached from Jerusalem all around to Illyricum [15:19] and intended to go on to Spain [15:23-24]); that Paul was thinking of nations, not individuals, especially of Jews and Gentiles; and that we should recognize here the use of hyperbole, the apostle employing 'the language of the Psalm to assert that very many people by the time he writes Romans have had opportunity to hear'.[139] This last option may be closer to the mark.

10:19-21 If the reason for Jewish failure to respond to the gospel is not that they have not heard, then a further question arises: *Again I ask: Did Israel not understand?* Did they not understand what they heard? To answer to this question Paul draws upon the prophetic words of Moses and Isaiah. He begins: *First, Moses says, 'I will make you envious by those who are not a nation; I will make you angry by a nation that has no understanding'.* Paul's quotation is from Deuteronomy 32:21, and reproduces exactly the LXX text except that Paul substitutes 'you' for 'them'.[140] The full text of Deuteronomy 32:21 is:

> They made me jealous by what is no god
>   and angered me with their worthless idols.
> I will make them envious by those who are not a people;
>   I will make them angry by a nation that has no understanding.

The quotation is from the Song of Moses (Deut 32:1-43) in which Moses recounts the many blessings the Lord bestowed upon the people of Israel and rebukes them for turning to foreign gods. The people of Israel made the Lord jealous by turning to what was *no god,* and angered him with their idols; therefore, when the Lord brings judgment upon them, he will make

---

138. In Col 1:23 we find a similar statement: 'This is the gospel that you heard and that has been proclaimed to every creature under heaven, and of which I, Paul, have become a servant'.

139. Cf. Moo, *Romans,* 667.

140. Wolfgang Reinbold, 'Israel und das Evangelium: Zur Exegese von Römer 10,19-21', *ZNW* 86 (1995) 122-29, advances the unlikely thesis that by substituting *hymas* ('you') for *autous* ('them') Paul is using the quotation to address Gentile Christians in Rome and is not concerned with Israel's guilt.

them jealous by those who are *not a people* and make them angry by 'a people that have no understanding'.[141] Those who are 'no people' and 'a people without understanding' are the Gentiles through whom the Lord will punish Israel. Then, languishing under foreign domination, the people of Israel will become envious as they remember the blessings they have lost, and become angry towards those who have vanquished them.[142] By citing this text Paul seems to be implying that the failure of the Jewish people of his own day to understand the gospel they have heard is evidence of God's judgment upon them.

Paul next quotes the prophet Isaiah to further explain why Israel 'did not understand': *And Isaiah boldly says, 'I was found by those who did not seek me; I revealed myself to those who did not ask for me'. But concerning Israel he says, 'All day long I have held out my hands to a disobedient and obstinate people'.* Paul is citing Isaiah 65:1-2 (with some minor emendations):

> I revealed myself to those who did not ask for me; I was found by those who did not seek me. To a nation that did not call on my name, I said, 'Here am I, here am I'. All day long I have held out my hands to an obstinate people, who walk in ways not good, pursuing their own imaginations.[143]

In the text Paul quotes, Isaiah makes two points: (i) God has revealed himself to those who did not seek him nor ask for him, that is, Gentiles — a point made already by the apostle in 9:30-31. (ii) God has continually 'held out his hands' to Israel, but they have proved disobedient and obstinate. To hold out the hands is a gesture of welcome and friendship. To do so 'all day long' expresses the steadfastness of God's mercy. Paul implies that the

---

141. Wright, *Deuteronomy*, 301, commenting on the text of Deut 32:21, says: 'The pain turns to bitter irony in the sarcastic wordplay of verse 21: "They have made me jealous by *no-god (lō'-'ēl)*; I will make them jealous by a *no-people (lō'-'ām)*". Israel would suffer at the hands of a nation as worthless in their eyes as their gods were worthless in God's eyes. In this context, the verse simply reinforces the tragedy of Israel's pathetic idolatry and the historical sovereignty of God over the nations as agents of judgment. The idea, however, of God making Israel jealous by the nations kindles a flame of hope beyond the fire of judgment in the thinking of the Apostle Paul. For God is in the business of turning "no-peoples" into God's people (cf. Rom. 9:24f., quoting Hosea 2:23 and 1:10). And if that should succeed in fanning Israel to jealousy, and thereby to repentance, faith, and salvation, then Paul's personal mission strategy would be vindicated (Rom 10:19; 11:11-14)'.

142. Pelagius explains: 'It is just as if someone has a disobedient son and in order to reform him gives half his inheritance to his slave, so that when he finally repents he may be glad if he deserves to receive even that much' ('Commentary on Romans' [*ACCSR*, 282]).

143. He reverses the order of the two clauses found in Isa 65:1, substituting the verb 'seek' for the verb 'ask for', and relocates the words 'all day long' before the words, 'I held out my hands', none of which alters the sense of the text. Origen comments: 'The Hebrew text does not contain the words *and contrary*, but here the apostle has followed the Septuagint and quoted the passage as they understood it' ('Commentary on the Epistle to the Romans' [*ACCSR*, 282-83]).

problem with many of the Jews in his own day was not a failure to understand the gospel but an obstinate refusal to obey it. In 10:3 he said that, being ignorant of the righteousness that comes from God and seeking to establish their own, they did not submit to the righteousness of God. Here in 10:21 he implies that their ignorance was culpable — they were 'a disobedient and obstinate people'. Here it is certainly not a case of God rejecting his people — he held out his hands to them all day long — but of God's people rejecting him.[144]

4. Has God Rejected Israel? 11:1-36

In chapter 10 Paul, wrestling still with the problem of Israel's failure to embrace the gospel, concluded that one major reason for this was their obstinacy and disobedience to the God who held out his hands to them 'all day long'. This inevitably raises the question: If Israel has rejected God's overtures, has God also rejected Israel? In chapter 11 Paul addresses this question. The chapter consists of two major parts each being introduced with a question. The first part (11:1-10) is introduced with the question: 'I ask then: Did God reject his people?' to which the short answer is, 'By no means!' The second part (11:11-36) is introduced with the question: 'Again I ask: Did they stumble so as to fall beyond recovery?' to which the short answer is: 'Not at all!'

a. The Significance of the Remnant, 11:1-10

[1]*I ask then: Did God reject his people? By no means! I am an Israelite myself, a descendant of Abraham, from the tribe of Benjamin.* [2]*God did not reject his people, whom he foreknew. Don't you know what Scripture says in the passage about Elijah — how he appealed to God against Israel:* [3]*'Lord, they have killed your prophets and torn down your altars; I am the only one left, and they are trying to kill me?'* [4]*And what was God's answer to him? 'I have reserved for myself seven thousand who have not bowed the knee to Baal'.* [5] *So too, at the present time there is a remnant chosen by grace.* [6]*And if by grace, then it cannot be based on works; if it were, grace would no longer be grace.*

[7]*What then? What the people of Israel sought so earnestly they did not obtain. The elect among them did, but the others were hardened,* [8]*as it is written: 'God gave them a spirit of stupor, eyes that could not see and ears that could not hear, to this very day'.* [9]*And David says:* [10]*'May their table become a snare and a trap, a stumbling block and a retribution for them. May their eyes be darkened so they cannot see, and their backs be bent forever'.*

---

144. Fitzmyer, *Romans,* 600, comments: 'So ends Paul's scathing indictment of Israel. It is surpassed in his letters only by what he says in 1 Thess 2:14-15. Cf. Acts 13:45; 28:22'.

In this part of the chapter Paul deals with the question, 'Did God reject his people?' This suggestion he emphatically rejects. He explains that God has always preserved a faithful remnant, among whom he himself is numbered, as were the seven thousand who did not bow the knee to Baal in the time of Elijah. This remnant Paul describes as a remnant chosen by grace, not on the basis of their works. The reason why the remnant obtained the blessing of God and the others did not Paul attributes to God's action in choosing the former and hardening the latter.

11:1 Following on from his conclusion in chapter 10 that a major reason why Israel as a whole has not obeyed the gospel was her own obstinacy, Paul says: *I ask*[145] *then: Did God reject his people?*[146] If Israel rejected the gospel of God, the question is: Has God in turn rejected Israel? To this question the apostle responds with an emphatic, *By no means!* an expression denoting strong denial used here for the ninth time in Romans and found frequently elsewhere in this letter and other letters where the apostle expresses strong disagreement (cf. 3:4, 6, 31; 6:2, 15; 7:7, 13; 9:14; 11:11; 1 Cor 6:15; Gal 2:17; 3:21; 6:14). In her previous history Israel had to face the possibility that God had rejected his people, but in 2 Maccabees 6:16 at least it is asserted: 'He never withdraws his mercy from us. Although he disciplines us with calamities, he does not forsake his own people' (cf. 1 Sam 12:22; Jer 31:37, LXX 38:35).

In support of his denial that God has rejected his people, Paul stresses: *I am an Israelite myself, a descendant of Abraham, from the tribe of Benjamin.* This is one of three places in his letters where Paul describes himself along these lines. In 2 Corinthians 11:22, when asserting that he is in no way inferior to the false apostles troubling his converts, he says, 'Are they Hebrews? So am I. Are they Israelites? So am I. Are they Abraham's descendants? So am I'. In Philippians 3:4-5, when comparing himself with rivals, he adds: 'If someone else thinks they have reasons to put confidence in the flesh, I have more: circumcised on the eighth day, of the people of Israel, of the tribe of Benjamin, a Hebrew of Hebrews'. If Paul is an Israelite,

---

145. The NIV's 'I ask' translates *legō* (lit. 'I say'), which Jewett, *Romans*, 653, regards as an indication that the letter was intended to be read (by 'a trained scribe employed by Phoebe').

146. 'People' *(laos)* is preferred to the alternate textual variant, 'inheritance' *(klēronomia)*, in 11:1. However, Mark D. Given, 'Restoring the Inheritance in Romans 11:1', *JBL* 118 (1999) 91-96, argues in favor of *klēronomia* on the grounds that: (i) it is the earliest attested reading (P[46]), (ii) and that as the more obscure reading it cannot be explained in terms of transcriptional probabilities. Furthermore, he notes that (iii) *laos* and *klēronomia* are twin designations of Israel in Deuteronomy and in Deuteronomic history (Deut 9:26-29; 32:8-9), (iv) that Israel as both God's people *(laos)* and inheritance *(klēronomia)* is 'a pervasive and comforting reminder of the permanence' of the relationship between Israel and her God, and (v) that 'the very vocabulary of the fully restored echo of Ps 93(94):14 in Rom 11:1-2 is a reminder that though God frequently rejects his people, he will never *finally* reject them, not even the majority in favour of a remnant' — all of which, we might add, serves Paul's purpose in Romans 11.

and if he has experienced the blessing of God through acceptance of the gospel, then clearly God has not rejected his people.[147]

Paul introduces himself not only as a descendant of Abraham but also as one 'from the tribe of Benjamin' (cf. Phil 3:4-5). Various suggestions have been made concerning the significance of Paul's inclusion of the information that he is 'from the tribe of Benjamin'. It has been noted that Benjamin was 'one of the few tribes left in his day that could trace their ancestry all the way back, being from the southern tribes, who returned after the Babylonian exile'.[148] Alternatively this may simply be part of a traditional self-introduction in which a person would provide not only his father's name but also that of his tribe.[149]

11:2-6 In these verses Paul reinforces the assertion made in 11:1 by adding: *God did not reject his people, whom he foreknew.* The reference to God's not rejecting his people appears to be a quotation from 1 Samuel 12:22 ('For the sake of his great name the LORD will not reject his people'; cf. Ps 94:14, LXX 93:14). The reference to 'his people, whom he foreknew' in this context refers to the nation Israel. Contrary to what the present situation in which the majority in Israel had rejected the gospel might indicate, God has not rejected his people. In this context God's foreknowledge relates to the nation, not to individuals.[150] To 'foreknow' can mean simply 'know someone or something beforehand' (as, e.g., in Wis 8:8; 18:6; Acts 26:5; and 2 Pet 3:17) or 'choose beforehand' (as in 8:29; 1 Pet 1:20), and it is used in latter sense here in 11:2.

Paul reinforces the assertion that God has not rejected his people by appeal to Scripture (1 Kgs 19:10, 14, 18). First he recalls Elijah's complaint to God about the rebellious character of Israel: *Don't you know what the Scripture says in the passage about Elijah — how he appealed to God against Israel?* The reference is to 1 Kings 19, which recounts Elijah's flight from Jezebel, who threatened the prophet's life following his successful contest with the prophets of Baal on Mount Carmel. Elijah made his way to 'the mountain of God', where 'the word of the LORD came to him: "What are you doing here, Elijah?"' (1 Kgs 19:9). Paul then quotes Elijah's reply to this question: *'Lord, they have killed your prophets and torn down your altars; I am the only one left, and they are trying to kill me'?* (1 Kgs 19:10, 14). It would appear that Paul saw in Elijah's response something analogous to the erroneous conclusion some of his Jewish contemporaries might draw from his gospel, that is, that God had rejected Israel. To reinforce his assertion that this was certainly not true, Paul cites the Lord's response to Elijah. He introduces it with the

---

147. Theodoret of Cyrrhus points out: 'Paul could have supported his statement by referring to the 3,000 who believed at Jerusalem and to the many thousands spoken of by St. James, not to mention all those Jews of the diaspora who believed the message. But instead he uses himself as an example' ('Interpretation of the Letter to the Romans' [*ACCSR*, 285]).

148. Wright, 'Romans', 675.

149. Cf. Dunn, *Romans 9–16*, 635.

150. Cf. Cranfield, *Romans*, II, 545; Witherington, *Romans*, 264-65.

question: *And what was God's answer to him?* (lit. 'but what says the oracle to him?'). The word 'oracle' is found only here in the NT, where it clearly denotes a divine oracle.[151] Then he reproduces the oracle: *'I have reserved for myself seven thousand who have not bowed the knee to Baal'* (1 Kgs 19:18).[152] Although Elijah thought that the whole nation of Israel had turned away from God and that he was the only faithful Israelite left, this was not the case. The Lord had preserved for himself a faithful remnant numbering seven thousand.

Finally in 11:5, to apply the Scripture to the matter at hand, Paul says: *So too, at the present time there is a remnant chosen by grace* (lit. 'So also in this way in the present time there is a remnant according to election of grace'). The word 'remnant' is found only here in the NT,[153] and only twice in the LXX, where it means 'survivors'.[154] Paul says that just as there was a remnant in Elijah's time because God reserved them for himself (11:4), so 'at the present time' there was a remnant because they were chosen by the grace of God (11:5). The expression 'at the present time' used here and in 3:26 ('he did it to demonstrate his justice at the present time, so as to be just and the one who justifies those who have faith in Jesus') carries overtones of the 'eschatological now'; the time when God acts in history to effect salvation.[155]

The remnant, Paul notes, is 'chosen by grace'. He has already spoken of God's 'election' in relation to his choice of Jacob and not Esau 'before the twins were born or had done anything good or bad — in order that God's purpose in election might stand: not by works but by him who calls' (9:11-

---

151. Cf. 2 Macc 2:4: 'the prophet, having received an oracle [*chrēmatismou*], ordered that the tent and the ark should follow with him'.

152. Paul's quotations correspond exactly to no known text, neither the LXX codices nor the Lucianic tradition, nor even the MT. Christopher D. Stanley, 'The Significance of Romans 11:3-4 for the Text History of the LXX Book of Kingdoms', *JBL* 112 (1993) 52-54, following a discussion of the textual tradition, concludes: 'The evidence seems strong that the Greek text quoted by Paul in Rom 11:3-4 reflects an earlier stage in the textual history of 3 Kingdoms than the version that appears in the codices (the so-called "LXX" text). The majority tradition of 3 Kingdoms 19 would then represent a later "Hebraizing" revision of a rather loose Greek translation of the type used by Paul in Rom 11:3-4'. He further concludes: 'The line of development thus runs from the Pauline text through the "Lucianic" tradition to the version that appears in the great codices of the fourth and fifth centuries' (54).

153. The word translated 'remnant' here is *leimma*. Paul uses a different, albeit a cognate word *(hypoleimma)* when speaking of a remnant in 9:27 ('Isaiah cries out concerning Israel: "Though the number of the Israelites be like the sand by the sea, only the remnant will be saved"'). It is noteworthy that Paul refers to the remnant in 9:27 to explain the diminished number of the faithful in Israel, whereas in 11:5 he employs it to emphasize God's faithfulness and grace (cf. Byrne, *Romans*, 330).

154. Cf. 2 Sam 21:2: 'Now the Gibeonites were not a part of Israel but were survivors *(leimmatos)* of the Amorites; the Israelites had sworn to [spare] them, but Saul in his zeal for Israel and Judah had tried to annihilate them'; 2 Kgs 19:4: 'It may be that the LORD your God will hear all the words of the field commander, whom his master, the king of Assyria, has sent to ridicule the living God, and that he will rebuke him for the words the LORD your God has heard. Therefore pray for the remnant *(leimmatos)* that still survives'.

155. Cf. Jewett, *Romans*, 658.

12). That text made it clear that election is independent of the good or bad done by the one chosen; God's sovereign choice is determinative. Paul says something similar here in 11:6: *And if by grace, then it cannot be based on works; if it were, grace would no longer be grace.* He emphasizes that God's choice is determined by God's grace, and is independent of people's works. 'Works' here probably refers to Jewish attempts to establish righteousness by observance of the law — something Paul says they were doing instead of submitting to God's righteousness (cf. 9:30–10:4).

11:7-10   In these verses Paul turns his attention from the remnant chosen by grace (those who have responded to the gospel) to explain why Israel as a whole failed to obtain what they sought when the elect did. In 9:30–10:4 the apostle said one reason why this was so was that 'they did not know the righteousness of God and sought to establish their own; they did not submit to God's righteousness'. Here in 11:7-10 he gives another reason: *What then? What the people of Israel sought so earnestly they did not obtain. The elect among them did, but others were hardened.* Paul mentions three entities: the people of Israel, the elect within Israel, and those who are hardened. As he did in 10:2, Paul acknowledges Israel's earnest seeking, but says that what they earnestly sought they did not obtain (cf. 9:31). However, here he says that while 'the elect' (i.e., the [Jewish] remnant chosen by grace) did obtain it, 'the others' were hardened.

In 9:17-18 Paul spoke of God raising up Pharaoh to display his power in him so that God's name might be proclaimed in all the earth, adding that 'God has mercy on whom he wants to have mercy, and he hardens whom he wants to harden'. From this hardening it would seem Pharaoh did not escape. But this may not be entirely the case when Paul speaks of the hardening of the 'rest' in 11:8. Later in the chapter he speaks of a 'hardening' experienced in part (or for a while) by Israel 'until the full number of the Gentiles has come in. And so all Israel will be saved' (11:25-26). Paul's hope was that, though Israel as a national entity was hardened, some of his kinsfolk who were presently in that hardened state would repent and find salvation.[156]

When Paul says that 'the others' did not obtain it because they 'were hardened', he uses the passive voice, suggesting that they were hardened by God. This the apostle makes explicit when he provides scriptural support for it: *as it is written: 'God gave them a spirit of stupor, eyes that could not see and ears that could not hear, to this very day'.* Paul's 'quotation' draws in part upon Isaiah 29:10 — the reference to 'a spirit of deep sleep' — but

---

156. Wright, 'Romans', 677, argues that hardening 'is what happens during a temporary suspension of the judgment that would otherwise have fallen, to allow time for some to escape. In the case of Pharaoh, the result was the exodus from Egypt, seen as a sign of God's glorious power and the reputation of the divine name (9:17) In the present case, the result is that there is time not only for the Gentiles to come in (11:11-15), but also for more Jews, like Paul himself, to recognize that the risen Jesus is indeed Israel's Messiah and to serve him in "the obedience of faith"'.

mainly upon Deuteronomy 29:4 NRSV (LXX 29:3) — the reference to Israel not being given 'eyes to see or ears to hear'.

In Deuteronomy 29:2-8 Moses recalls God's care for the Israelites during their sojourn in the wilderness, reminding them: 'With your own eyes you saw those great trials, those signs and great wonders' (Deut 29:3). However, Moses indicates that, despite these things, the Israelites still lacked understanding, when he adds, 'But to this day the LORD has not given you a mind that understands or eyes that see or ears that hear' (Deut 29:4). It is this text that Paul picks up, adding to it words drawn from Isaiah 29:10, to explain the resistance of Jewish people to the gospel in his own day — God gave them a spirit of stupor, and eyes that could not see and ears that could not hear. Moses said of the Israelites that this state of affairs persisted 'to this day', and Paul, confronted by the intransigence of his contemporary kinsfolk, saw a similar state of affairs persisting in his day.[157]

To further support his explanation of his Jewish contemporaries' failure to obtain what they sought, Paul adds to his quotation from Isaiah 29:10/Deuteronomy 29:4 one from the Psalms (thus making use of the three sections of the OT, the law, the prophets, and the writings):[158] *And David says: 'May their table become a snare and a trap, a stumbling block and a retribution for them. May their eyes be darkened so they cannot see, and their backs be bent forever'.* Paul's quotation follows fairly closely, but not exactly, Psalm 69:22-23 (LXX 68:23-24),[159] a psalm in which David calls upon God to punish those who have persecuted him. It is not easy to see how Paul wanted this quotation to function here. 'Their table' in Psalm 69:22 and its significance for Paul has been variously interpreted: (i) as a tablecloth spread on the ground over which one might trip;[160] (ii) as the Jewish cultus representing Jewish piety that causes the blinding of Israel;[161] (iii) a reference to

---

157. Paul makes a similar point using similar expressions in 2 Cor 3:14-15 when speaking of the dullness of mind and the veil that covers the heart of many of his fellow Jews when they hear the Scriptures read: 'But their minds were made dull, for to this day the same veil remains when the old covenant is read. It has not been removed, because only in Christ is it taken away. Even to this day when Moses is read, a veil covers their hearts'.

158. Mary Ann Getty, 'Paul on the Covenants and the Future of Israel', *BTB* 17 (1987) 98, noting that Paul quotes from the three major divisions of the Hebrew Bible, remarks: 'The law (cf. Deut 29:3 in Rom 11:8a), the Prophets (Isa 29:10 in Rom 11:8b) and the writings (Ps 69:22-23 in Rom 11:9-10) all conspire to call Israel to repentance. Far from giving up on Israel, God through the Jewish scriptures as well as the mission of Paul and the conversion of the Gentiles, is still acting in fidelity to the covenants. The individual and concerted meaning of these quotations is the constancy of God'.

159. Origen comments: 'The trap is not mentioned either in the Hebrew or in the Septuagint. We have recorded these things about the order of the words and the quality of the witnesses consulted in order to show by these details that the authority of the apostle does not rely on the texts of the Hebrew nor does it always retain the words of the translators, but rather it expounds the meaning of the Scriptures in whatever words are most suitable' ('Commentary on the Epistle to the Romans' [*ACCSR*, 288]).

160. Fitzmyer, *Romans,* 606.

161. Käsemann, *Romans,* 302.

Pharisaic rules for table fellowship — their attempt to maintain purity by such works proved to be a stumbling block preventing them from accepting the gospel.[162] The latter two suggestions read too much into Paul's use of this quotation, and we should probably recognize that he simply intends his audience to see a parallel between what God himself does (gives people a spirit of stupor, eyes that cannot see and ears that cannot hear) and what David asks God to do to his enemies (to use the good thing they enjoy to put a stumbling block in their path).

b. Israel Stumbled, but Her Fall Is Not Irrevocable, 11:11-36

This second part of the chapter may be subdivided into four sections: 11:11-15, in which an assurance is given that Israel's present situation is not final; 11:16-24, in which two metaphors are employed to illustrate the fact that God has not rejected Israel; 11:25-32, in which Paul spells out the mystery — Israel's hardening will give way to 'all Israel' being saved; and 11:33-36, the concluding section, in which the apostle expresses praise for God's wisdom. Paul will show that Israel's failure is part of God's plan, arguing that it allows salvation to come to the Gentiles, and that he hopes this will make Israel jealous, and will in turn lead her to repentance and salvation. Moo is correct when he says that 'the issue in vv. 11ff. is therefore not "Can the hardened within Israel still be saved?" but "Can Israel as a whole still be saved?" As the contrast with the Gentiles throughout vv. 11-32 suggests, Paul is thinking mainly in terms of corporate bodies, not in terms of individuals within those bodies'.[163]

(i) Israel's transgression means salvation for the Gentiles, 11:11-15

[11]*Again I ask: Did they stumble so as to fall beyond recovery? Not at all! Rather, because of their transgression, salvation has come to the Gentiles to make Israel envious.* [12]*But if their transgression means riches for the world, and their loss means riches for the Gentiles, how much greater riches will their full inclusion bring!* [13]*I am talking to you Gentiles. Inasmuch as I am the apostle to the Gentiles, I take pride in my ministry* [14]*in the hope that I may somehow arouse my own people to envy and save some of them.* [15]*For if their rejection brought reconciliation to the world, what will their acceptance be but life from the dead?*

David's request that God place a stumbling block in the path of his enemies in the psalm that Paul quoted in 11:9-10 provides the link to what follows in 11:11-15. Here the apostle explains that the stumbling of Israel provided the occasion for carrying the message of salvation to the Gentiles.

---

162. Dunn, *Romans 9–16*, 643.
163. Moo, *Romans*, 686.

If their stumbling had this beneficial effect, Paul says their restoration will signal even greater blessing.

11:11-12   Picking up the reference to stumbling in 11:9-10, Paul raises the question about the results of Israel's stumbling: *Again I ask: Did they stumble[164] so as to fall beyond recovery?[165]* Paul asks if God's action in giving Israel eyes that cannot see, and ears that cannot hear, and causing them to stumble was intended to cause them to fall 'beyond recovery'. When Israel rejected the gospel, she 'stumbled over the stumbling stone' placed in Zion (9:32-33). Paul's question is whether this stumbling will result in a fall from which there is no recovery, a rejection by God and therefore spiritual ruin.[166] To this question Paul replies: *Not at all!* (an expression he uses for emphatic denial and found here for the tenth time in Romans; see the commentary on 11:1).

Paul insists that this is not the case and that God has a wider and more positive purpose to achieve through Israel's stumbling: *Rather, because of their transgression, salvation has come to the Gentiles to make Israel envious.* This is reflected in Paul's missionary experience as described in the Acts of the Apostles. When Jewish people in a particular location 'transgressed' by rejecting the gospel message, Paul felt that, having discharged his responsibility to preach 'first to the Jews', he could then turn his attention to the Gentiles (cf. Acts 13:42-49). However, for Paul salvation coming to the Gentiles was not simply an end in itself but was also intended 'to make Israel envious'. Paul's point is that Jews, when they see Gentiles experiencing the blessing of God as they accept the gospel, might become jealous and then hopefully repent and become recipients of the gospel blessings themselves.

Paul then explains what he hopes will be the upshot of all this: *But if their transgression means riches for the world, and their loss means riches for the Gentiles, how much greater riches will their fullness bring!*[167] Israel's 'transgression' in refusing to obey the gospel call meant loss for them but great riches for the world as Gentiles accepted the gospel and enjoyed its blessings. Being sure that God has not rejected his people, Paul anticipates a time when Israel will attain her 'fullness'. In 11:25 the apostle speaks of the time when 'the full number of the Gentiles has come in', by which he means clearly the totality of those Gentiles who believe. In the light of this use of 'fullness' in

---

164. The verb translated 'stumble' is *ptaiō,* used only here in Paul's letters but found elsewhere in the NT in contexts where stumbling into sin is involved (Jas 2:10; 3:2; 2 Pet 1:10).

165. The NIV's 'so as to fall beyond recovery' translates *hina pesōsin* (lit. 'in order that they may fall').

166. Moo, *Romans,* 686-87.

167. Haacker, 'Die Geschichtstheologie von Röm 9–11', 220-21, notes certain parallels in the writings of Philo, namely, *Vit. Mos.* 2.43-44: 'It is but natural that when people are not flourishing their belongings to some degree are under a cloud. But, if a fresh start should be made to brighter prospects, how great a change for the better might we expect to see!'

respect to Gentiles in 11:25 we are justified in concluding that Israel's 'full inclusion' means the full number of believing Jews, which will be made up when those yet to believe are added to the remnant that already believe.[168]

When the full number of the elect of Israel will have repented and believed in their Messiah, their 'fullness' will signal even greater riches.[169] The nature of these greater riches remains to be explained. Some hints of what these riches will comprise emerge as this chapter unfolds.

11:13-14 In these verses Paul addresses those members of the Roman church who are Gentiles (just as earlier in the letter he had addressed those 'who know the law'; cf. 7:1): *I am talking to you Gentiles.*[170] The reason for addressing them directly may be that he realized that they might be resistant to what he has to say about Israel. Shortly he will warn them not to adopt a boastful attitude towards unbelieving Jews (11:17-24), but before doing so he tells of his hope that his ministry among the Gentiles will bring benefits to Jews: *Inasmuch as I am the apostle to the Gentiles, I take pride in my ministry in the hope that I may somehow arouse my own people to envy and save some of them.* When he says that he is the apostle to the Gentiles, he is recalling both his commission by the risen Christ (1:1-6; Gal 1:1, 15-16; Acts 9:15-17; 22:14-15, 21) and its recognition by the pillar apostles of Jerusalem (Gal 2:6-9). By so saying, Paul informs the Gentile members of the Roman church of one of the important strategies he has in prosecuting a mission in the Gentile world, that is, to arouse his own people, the Jews, to jealousy with a view to saving some of them. The idea of provoking Jews to jealousy is one Paul has already employed in 10:19, where he cites Moses' words in Deuteronomy 32:21 to show that God is going to make Israel envious by blessing Gentiles while he brings judgment upon the Jews. It is possible that Paul was encouraged by the divine strategy of Deuteronomy 32:21 to vigorously pursue his Gentile mission in the hope of making his fellow Jews jealous as they saw Gentiles enjoying the blessings of God through acceptance of the gospel.[171]

---

168. So too, Moo, *Romans*, 689; Witherington, *Romans*, 267-68; Wright, 'Romans', 680-81.

169. Terence L. Donaldson, '"Riches for the Gentiles" (Rom 11:12): Israel's Rejection and Paul's Gentile Mission', *JBL* 112 (1993) 94, suggests that 'the logic at work in Paul's statements here is not the spatial logic of displacement but the temporal logic of delay. Israel's failure to respond to the gospel makes possible the "riches for the Gentiles" by opening up not some space but some *time*. If Israel had responded to the gospel immediately, if God had not been prepared to harden all but the remnant, the Gentiles would have remained branches of the wild olive tree and vessels fitted for destruction'.

170. 'To you' (*hymin*) is in the emphatic position, making it very clear that the apostle is addressing these remarks only to the Gentile members of his audience.

171. Wright, *Deuteronomy* 16 (cf. 301), comments on Paul's mission strategy: 'Paul picks up a rhetorical pun in Deuteronomy 32:21, on God making Israel "jealous", and develops it into a theology of history and mission: the ingathering of the Gentiles will arouse jealousy among the Jews, so that ultimately "all Israel", extended and inclusive of believing Jews and Gentiles, will share in salvation (Rom. 10:19–11:26). Clearly Paul reflected deeply on Deuteronomy 32 especially (it has been called "Romans in a nutshell") and quotes its fi-

He hoped that they would become envious, would repent and accept the gospel, and some of them would be saved.

Several interpreters have commented on Paul's realism when he says that he hopes his ministry among the Gentiles will result in the salvation of 'some of them'.[172] It has also been noted that Paul says 'I am *an* apostle to the Gentiles' (NRSV, italics added)', not 'I am *the* apostle to the Gentiles' (NIV, italics added)'. He did not regard himself as the only apostle to the Gentiles.[173]

11:15 That Israel, currently resistant to the gospel, should ultimately be saved is a glorious prospect for Paul. This is what lies behind his question: *For if their rejection brought reconciliation of the world, what will their acceptance be but life from the dead?* On first reading the apostle's reference here to the 'rejection' of Israel appears to contradict what he said back in 11:1-2: 'I ask then: Did God reject his people? By no means! I am an Israelite myself, a descendant of Abraham, from the tribe of Benjamin. God did not reject his people, whom he foreknew'. However, the overall context in Romans 11 makes it clear that the issue addressed in 11:1-2 is that of ultimate rejection, whereas in 11:15 Paul has in mind a temporary rejection.[174] Thus the apostle's question in this verse could be paraphrased as follows: 'If Israel's (temporary) rejection (by God) has led to the reconciliation of the world, that is, the reconciliation of Gentiles, what will Israel's reacceptance (by God)[175] be but life from the dead?'

The 'reconciliation of the world' has been interpreted in different ways. Cranfield believes that it is better to take it 'to refer to the objective reconciliation of the world to God through the death of Christ than to either the subjective reconciliation of conversion (cf. 2 Cor 5.18-20) or the reconciliation of Jews and Gentiles (cf. Eph 2.16)'.[176] Dunn agrees in part: 'Paul no doubt has in mind the death of Christ (5:10), though here once again we should avoid either-or exegesis . . . since it is unlikely that if the point was

---

nal doxology (32:34) in his exposition of the multinational nature of the gospel and its implications for the need for cross-cultural acceptance and sensitivity between Jewish and Gentile Christians (Rom. 15:7-10)'.

172. So, e.g., Moo, *Romans*, 692; Dunn, *Romans 9–16*, 657; Witherington, *Romans*, 268; John Murray, *The Epistle to the Romans: The English Text with Introduction, Exposition and Notes* (Grand Rapids: Eerdmans, 1965), 80.

173. Cf. Dunn, *Romans 9–16*, 656.

174. Verena Jegher-Bucher, 'Erwählung und Verwerfung im Römerbrief? Eine Untersuchung von Röm 11,11-15', *TZ* 47 (1991) 329-34, argues that *apobolē* in 11:15 should not be translated as 'rejection', but rather as 'loss', and that this enables one to understand 11:11-15 in terms, not of Israel's rejection by God, but the loss of Israel as Paul's co-worker in the mission of God vis-à-vis the world. Thus, if the loss of Israel as co-worker has meant gain for the Gentiles, Paul asks, what will their reinstatement as co-workers in God's redemption of the world mean but life from the dead? There seems to be little in the context to support this view.

175. BAGD, *ad loc.*, interprets *proslēmpsis* here as 'acceptance into a relationship, acceptance (by God)'.

176. Cranfield, *Romans*, II, 562.

put to him Paul would want to exclude the idea of reconciliation accepted . . . or of a world reconciled as including the reconciliation of Jew and Gentile . . . ; in Paul's gospel and theology these strands are too closely interwoven to be easily separated (here not least)'. . . .[177] However, in the context of 11:13-15 where Paul has in mind the stumbling of Israel making possible the salvation of Gentiles, it is probably the salvation of the Gentiles that Paul has in mind primarily when he refers to the 'reconciliation of the world'.

As already noted above, in Paul's mission it was the rejection of the gospel by the Jews that led him to preach to the Gentiles, resulting in their salvation. If Jewish rejection of the gospel and their (temporary) rejection by God had this positive result for the Gentiles, Paul asks, what will be the result of their acceptance (of the gospel) and their ultimate acceptance by God? The result, Paul says, will be 'life from the dead', a reference, it would seem, to the general resurrection.[178] When the full number of the elect of Israel is accepted by God, then will have arrived the time of 'life from the dead', that is, the resurrection of all believers, both Jews and Gentiles (see the commentary on 11:25-27).

ADDITIONAL NOTE: ISRAEL'S JEALOUSY

The predominant view of Israel's jealousy as Paul depicts it in 11:11-14, and the view adopted above, is a positive one: Israel, seeing the Gentiles responding to the gospel and enjoying the blessings first promised to her, will become envious, and this will lead some of her people to repentance and a share in those blessings. As Munck put it long ago, the 'no' of the Jews to the message of the gospel will lead to the 'yes' of the Gentiles, and this in turn will lead to the ultimate 'yes' of the Jews.[179] Paul's hope was that his mission to the Gentiles would have the effect of provoking Israel to jealousy, and this in turn would lead to her repentance and a share in the blessings of the gospel.

In recent times this approach has been called into question, and the jealousy of Israel is seen not as a positive thing leading to her salvation, but a negative thing leading to the salvation of the Gentiles. As in the case of Deuteronomy 32:21 quoted by Paul in 10:19 (see the commentary on that text), Israel's jealousy is a sign of God's judgment. Baker offers the following explanation of this view. He notes first the close connection between the

---

177. Dunn, *Romans 9–16*, 657.

178. So, too, Byrne, *Romans*, 339-40; Moo, *Romans*, 694-96; Witherington, *Romans*, 269; Barrett, *Romans*, 215; Jewett, *Romans*, 681. Bell, *The Irrevocable Call of God*, 254-256, holds that 'Life from the dead' means 'the general resurrection of the dead and the everlasting life in fellowship with God and Christ'.

179. Johannes Munck, *Paul and the Salvation of Mankind* (London: SCM, 1959), 275-78.

verb 'to provoke to jealousy' used by Paul in 11:14 and the noun 'zeal' employed by the apostle in 10:2 when he spoke of the Jews' zeal for God that was not according to knowledge, and suggests that Paul saw a connection between Israel's jealousy and their misplaced zeal. Baker concludes: 'For Paul, then, in both Rom 10:19 and 11:11, 14, Israel's jealousy and zeal may coalesce: when Israel sees the community of salvation extended to the Gentiles and the place of Christ in defining that community, Paul envisions Israel being provoked to angry jealousy in which it zealously upholds Torah'.[180] The problem with this view is that it does not account satisfactorily for Paul's statement, 'I take pride in my ministry in the hope that I may somehow arouse my own people to envy and save some of them'. He does not envisage them being provoked to jealousy to uphold Torah.

(ii) The lump of dough and the olive tree, 11:16-24

> [16]*If the part of the dough offered as firstfruits is holy, then the whole batch is holy; if the root is holy, so are the branches.* [17]*If some of the branches have been broken off, and you, though a wild olive shoot, have been grafted in among the others and now share in the nourishing sap from the olive root,* [18]*do not consider yourself to be superior to those other branches. If you do, consider this: You do not support the root, but the root supports you.* [19]*You will say then, 'Branches were broken off so that I could be grafted in'.* [20]*Granted. But they were broken off because of unbelief, and you stand by faith. Do not be arrogant, but tremble.* [21]*For if God did not spare the natural branches, he will not spare you either.*
>
> [22]*Consider therefore the kindness and sternness of God: sternness to those who fell, but kindness to you, provided that you continue in his kindness. Otherwise, you also will be cut off.* [23]*And if they do not persist in unbelief, they will be grafted in, for God is able to graft them in again.* [24]*After all, if you were cut out of an olive tree that is wild by nature, and contrary to nature were grafted into a cultivated olive tree, how much more readily will these, the natural branches, be grafted into their own olive tree!*

In these verses Paul employs two metaphors to illustrate the fact that God has not rejected Israel: a lump from the whole batch of dough, and the root of an olive tree and its branches.

11:16 Employing the first of the metaphors, he says: *If the part of the dough offered as firstfruits is holy, then the whole batch is holy.* The allusion appears to be to the offering of the first of the ground meal required of Israelites under the law of Moses: 'The LORD said to Moses, "Speak to the Israelites and say to them: 'When you enter the land to which I am taking you and

---

180. Murray Baker, 'Paul and the Salvation of Israel: Paul's Ministry, the Motif of Jealousy, and Israel's Yes', *CBQ* 67 (2005) 474-75.

you eat the food of the land, present a portion as an offering to the LORD. Present a loaf from the first of your ground meal and present it as an offering from the threshing floor. Throughout the generations to come you are to give this offering to the LORD from the first of your ground meal'"" (Num 15:17-21).[181] At a metaphorical level, then, Paul is saying that if the first part of a lump of dough is yeast-free, the rest of the lump will be yeast-free also.

Paul carries over the notion of the holiness of part of the dough guaranteeing the holiness of the whole lump into his second metaphor, that of a tree:[182] *if the root is holy, so are the branches.* This is the first of five references to the root/branches metaphor in this chapter (11:16, 17, 18, 19, 21; cf. 11:24; 15:12). At a metaphorical level Paul is saying that if the root of a tree is sound, its branches will be sound also. In one of the subsequent uses of the metaphor (11:17) Paul makes it clear that he is thinking of the root and branches of an *olive tree,* a symbol used to denote Israel (cf. Jer 11:16-17).

The significance of the various elements of these two metaphors has been variously interpreted. In the case of the first part of the lump and the whole lump the following interpretations have been suggested: (a) 'the first part' has been identified as the remnant (i.e., Jewish believers);[183] all early converts (both Jews and Gentiles; cf. 16:5; 1 Cor 16:5; 2 Thess 2:13);[184] the patriarchs;[185] and Christ (cf. 1 Cor 15:23),[186] and (b) the whole lump has been interpreted as the entire seed of Abraham (Jewish and Gentile believers);[187] and Israel according to the flesh as a whole.[188]

In the case of the root and the branches interpretations that have been suggested include: (a) 'the root' has been understood to denote the patriarchs,[189] Abraham in particular;[190] the remnant;[191] and Christ him-

---

181. Paul uses the image of 'the lump of dough' *(phyrama)* in two other places, but in each case with a different purpose: the lump is said to be defiled by the presence of yeast, illustrating people being defiled by sin (1 Cor 5:6-7; Gal 5:7-8).

182. Cf. Matthias Hartung, 'Die kultische bzw. Agrartechnisch-biologische Logik der Gleichnisse von der Teighebe und vom Ölbaum in Röm 11.16-24 und die sich daraus ergebenden theologischen Konsequenzen', *NTS* 45 (1999) 129-30.

183. Wright, 'Romans', 683; Cranfield, *Romans,* II, 564; Barrett, *Romans,* 216.

184. Dunn, *Romans 9–16,* 659.

185. Moo, *Romans,* 699.

186. So, e.g., [Pseudo] Constantius, 'The Holy Letter of St Paul to the Romans'; Theodore of Mopsuestia, 'Commentary from the Greek Church'; Theodoret of Cyrrhus, 'Interpretation of the Letter to the Romans' *(ACCSR,* 293).

187. Dunn, *Romans 9–16,* 659.

188. Barrett, *Romans,* 216; Wright, 'Romans', 683; Moo, *Romans,* 700; Cranfield, *Romans,* II, 564.

189. Moo, *Romans,* 699; Cranfield, *Romans,* II, 565.

190. So, e.g., [Pseudo] Constantius, 'The Holy Letter of St Paul to the Romans'; Theodore of Mopsuestia, 'Commentary from the Greek Church'; Theodoret of Cyrrhus, 'Interpretation of the Letter to the Romans' *(ACCSR,* 293); Moo, *Romans,* 700; Käsemann, *Romans,* 308.

191. Barrett, *Romans,* 216; Alan F. Segal, 'Paul's Experience and Romans 9–11', *PSB* Sup. 1 (1990) 65.

self,[192] and (b) 'the branches' have been interpreted as Israel as a whole;[193] the full number of the Jewish elect; and the totality of the Gentile and Jewish elect.[194]

It is obvious that with so many views concerning the meaning of the various elements of these metaphors, the metaphors themselves are susceptible to multiple interpretations. The two major approaches to their interpretation are: (i) Just as the first part of a lump of dough offered yeast free guarantees that the rest of the lump will be yeast free also, and as the root of a tree being sound guarantees that its branches will be sound also, so too the present existence of a believing remnant of Jews who are holy guarantees the future existence of their full number who will be holy also.[195] This interpretation is problematic because in the following verses (11:17-18), where the apostle speaks of believing Gentiles along with believing Jews (the faithful remnant) being fellow participants in the richness of the 'root', the 'root' must mean something other than the remnant, because the Jewish remnant along with believing Gentiles are fellow participants in what is a third entity, the 'root'. This has led to the second major interpretation. (ii) The 'first part of the lump of dough' and the 'root' refer to the patriarchs (cf. 11:28-29), in particular Abraham, and as the 'the first part of the lump' and 'the root' was holy, so too are those Jews who are joined to him in a similar faith.[196] These are the 'true' Jews whom Paul describes as those 'who not only are circumcised but who also walk in the footsteps of the faith that our father Abraham had before he was circumcised' (4:12), those who will make up the full number of the elect of Israel. This is the view adopted in this commentary.

11:17-18 In these verses Paul continues to address directly Gentile members of his audience, an address that began in 11:13 and continues down to 11:32. He does so essentially to warn them against adopting an arrogant attitude towards unbelieving Jews. He begins: *If some of the branches have been broken off, and you, though a wild olive shoot, have been grafted in among the others and now share in the nourishing sap from the olive root. . . .* 'Some of the branches' that have been broken off are unbelieving Jews removed from 'the olive tree' of 'true Israel' because of unbelief. Then, using the second person singular ('you'), Paul depicts a representative Gentile member of the Roman churches as 'a wild olive shoot' grafted in 'among the others', that is, among the other branches of the (cultivated) olive tree that have not been broken off (i.e., Jewish believers). With them the wild ol-

---

192. Wright, 'Romans', 684.

193. Wright, 'Romans', 683; Moo, *Romans*, 700; Cranfield, *Romans*, II, 564; Barrett, *Romans*, 216.

194. Dunn, *Romans 9-16*, 659.

195. Bell, *The Irrevocable Call of God*, 273-77, argues that the 'first Jewish converts are the first of the harvest; they are an offering to God and they serve to sanctify the whole harvest' (275), and that 'the 'root is the patriarchs, especially Abraham' (277).

196. So, e.g., Byrne, *Romans*, 340.

ive shoots will 'share in the nourishing sap from the olive root'. Gentile believers have become, with Jewish believers, fellow participants in the richness of the 'root of the olive tree', a reference to the patriarchs/Abraham and the blessings promised to them by God, brought to fulfillment in Christ, and now enjoyed by all who put their trust in him (cf. Gal 3:14: 'He [Christ] redeemed us in order that the blessing given to Abraham might come to the Gentiles through Christ Jesus, so that by faith we might receive the promise of the Spirit').

The idea of grafting a wild olive shoot into a cultivated olive tree is contrary to normal arboricultural practice (despite suggestions that there is evidence which supports the practice; see 'Additional Note: Paul's Olive Tree Analogy', 439-41). That Paul's analogy runs counter to normal practice is most likely a result, not of Paul being an urban dweller and ignorant of arboricultural practice as some have suggested, but rather a deliberate manipulation of the image to make a point. The point is that he wants to prick the bubble of Gentile pride by depicting them as shoots cut from a wild, unproductive olive tree, and by so doing to stress the undeserved privilege they have been given of sharing in the blessings first promised to Israel.[197] The grafting in of Gentiles is, as Wright calls it, 'a miracle of grace'.[198]

To believing Gentiles, who now find themselves enjoying the blessings first promised to Israel, Paul says, *do not consider yourself to be superior to those other branches.* This exhortation reflects Paul's belief that there existed some negative attitudes on the part of Gentile believers in Rome towards unbelieving Jews. It has been suggested that this arose when, due to the edict of Claudius (A.D. 49), Jews were expelled from Rome and so for a few years Gentile believers had little contact with either believing or unbelieving Jews. As a result, they were tempted to think that God had rejected his people in favor of them. This is the very issue raised by the apostle in 11:1-2 and is the essential subject of Romans 11. To those who might be tempted to adopt such an attitude, Paul warns: *If you do, consider this: You do not support the root, but the root supports you.* If the 'root' here still refers to the patriarchs/Abraham, then the apostle is reminding his Gentile audience that they are dependent upon them, and they enjoy the blessings first promised to them and now fulfilled in Christ. They are indebted to them, and they should remember this (cf. 15:26-27).

11:19-21 Paul anticipates another unhealthy attitude on the part of Gentiles in his audience. They might agree that they are indebted to the patriarchs/Abraham and the promises God made to them, but still adopt a superior attitude towards unbelieving Jews: *You will say then, 'Branches were broken off so that I could be grafted in'.* They believe that God has rejected unbelieving Jews and that they, believing Gentiles, have replaced them — 'branches were broken off so that I could be grafted in'. Once again the im-

---

197. Cf. Moo, *Romans*, 703; Cranfield, *Romans*, II, 565-66.
198. Wright, 'Romans', 684.

plication is that has God rejected his people. Paul's response to such an attitude is twofold. First he says: *Granted.*[199] *But they were broken off because of unbelief, and you stand by faith.* While unbelieving Jews have been removed from the number of 'true' Jews because of their unbelief, Gentiles are included among the people of God only because of their belief. Second, the apostle issues a salutary warning: *Do not be arrogant, but tremble. For if God did not spare the natural branches, he will not spare you either.* If Jewish people have been removed because of unbelief, the last attitude Gentiles can afford to adopt towards them is one of arrogance. Instead they should be afraid because if God did not spare the 'natural branches' (Jewish people) because of their unbelief, he will not spare 'unnatural branches' (Gentile people) either if they fall into unbelief.

11:22   Paul's note of warning continues into this verse. He says to his audience: *Consider therefore the kindness and sternness of God: sternness to those who fell, but kindness to you, provided that you continue in his kindness. Otherwise, you also will be cut off.* Two key attributes of God's character are referred to in Paul's warning. The first is his 'kindness', an attribute the apostle predicates of God in three other places in his letters. In 2:4 he warns that those who take the high moral ground, condemning others for their actions while doing the same things themselves, 'show contempt for the riches of his *kindness,* tolerance and patience'. In Ephesians 2:6-7 he reminds his audience that 'God raised us up with Christ and seated us with him in the heavenly realms in Christ Jesus, in order that in the coming ages he might show the incomparable riches of his grace, expressed in his *kindness* to us in Christ Jesus'. In Titus 3:3-5 he reminds his colleague: 'At one time we too were foolish, disobedient, deceived and enslaved by all kinds of passions and pleasures. We lived in malice and envy, being hated and hating one another. But when the *kindness* and love of God our Savior appeared, he saved us, not because of righteous things we had done, but because of his mercy'. In Paul's letters, then, wherever the kindness of God is mentioned it is related, not merely to a benevolent disposition, but always to his kindness in leading people towards or bestowing upon them his salvation.

The second attribute of God's character that Paul refers to is his 'sternness' or 'severity'.[200] It is not surprising that Paul speaks more of God's kindness than he does of his severity, for the expression of kindness

---

199. Jewett, *Romans,* 687, comments: 'Paul answers the witty objection that he has placed in the mouth of the Gentile interlocutor with a single adverb *kalōs,* which could be taken as a flat rejection ("No, thank you!"), an ironic concession ("Well, well!"), a qualified acceptance ("All right, but!"), or an acceptance of the point ("Well said!"). The latter is most likely in this context because it preserves the wit of this discourse, in that Paul accepts the transparently arrogant comment that he himself has invented for the interlocutor from the words of his own previous argument. The audience would enjoy Paul's admission that a sharp riposte was made at his own expense by such an undiscerning Christian blockhead'.

200. 'Sternness' *(apotomia)* is found only here in the NT, and not at all in the LXX. The cognate adverb is used in Tit 1:13 when Paul urges his colleague to rebuke sharply *(apotomōs)* deceivers of the circumcision group who were disturbing Christian households,

and compassion is God's primary work (cf. 1 Tim 2:3-4) and something he delights to do, whereas the expression of severity is his strange work and something he is reluctant to carry out (cf. 2 Pet 3:9). The psalmists put it this way: 'For his anger lasts only a moment, but his favor lasts a lifetime' (Ps 30:5); 'Yet he was merciful; he forgave their iniquities and did not destroy them. Time after time he restrained his anger and did not stir up his full wrath' (Ps 78:38).

Here in 11:22 Paul asks his audience to 'consider the kindness and sternness of God'. His sternness has been shown to those who fell, in this case to Jewish people who have rejected the gospel, and his kindness has been shown to Paul's Gentile audience who have accepted it. However, the apostle informs them that they must 'continue [lit. 'remain'] in his kindness'. This involves, as Paul puts it in Colossians 1:23, continuing 'in your faith, established and firm, and do not move from the hope held out in the gospel'. Paul warns them that if they do not continue in God's kindness, 'they will be cut off also'. As he warned them in the previous verse: 'For if God did not spare the natural branches, he will not spare you either'.

For modern readers, all this raises questions of perseverance, eternal security, and the possibility of apostasy. There have been various responses to this issue. On the one hand, it has been recognized that Paul's statements elsewhere, not least in Romans 6–8, suggest that it would be unwise to rule out the possibility of individual believers falling away. In 8:13, for example, Paul warns his audience, 'if you live according to the flesh, you will die'. Dunn cautions: 'A doctrine of "perseverance of the saints" which does not include the lessons of salvation-history has lost its biblical perspective. Even more than in 8:13 the personal singular address *(sou)* [in 11:22] gives the warning more pressing point'.[201] Moo points out: 'In issuing this warning, Paul echoes a consistent NT theme: ultimate salvation is dependent on continuing faith; therefore, the person who ceases to believe forfeits any hope of salvation (cf. also Rom. 8:13; Col. 1:23; Heb. 3:6, 14)'.[202]

On the other hand, Wright finds it 'highly unlikely that Paul would envisage individual Christians being justified by faith at one moment, assured of "sharing the glory of God" (5:2; 8:30), and at another moment losing both faith and salvation. On the contrary, his regular view is that when God begins a good work, through the gospel and the Spirit, that good work will come to completion (Phil 1:6). What is more likely is that this is a warning to an entire church (as, for instance, in the messages to the churches of Asia in Revelation 2–3). Individual Christians may be muddled or sinful, but they will be saved, even if only, in some cases, "as through fire" (1 Cor

---

and in 2 Cor 13:10 where he tells his audience that he has written this letter while away from them so he won't have to be severe *(apotomōs)* in the use of the authority when present with them.

201. Dunn, *Romans 9–16*, 664.
202. Moo, *Romans*, 707.

3:15). A church, however, that begins to boast in the way Paul is warning against may not last another generation'.[203]

11:23-24 In these verses Paul changes his tack somewhat to inform his audience that just as unbelief leads to people being cut off, belief will mean their being grafted back in. With his unbelieving Jewish kinsfolk in mind, then, he says: *And if they do not persist in unbelief, they will be grafted in, for God is able to graft them in again.* Here again Paul stretches the metaphor so that it goes beyond what could be expected in arboriculture. Those branches cut off from an olive tree, if left for any length of time, could not possibly be grafted back in again. But Paul's thinking is not circumscribed by what is possible in arboriculture; no, he is thinking about what God can do with people, the miracles of God's grace. If his unbelieving kinsfolk do not persist in unbelief, God is well able to graft them back into the olive tree of true Israel. Unbelief need not be terminal, only persistence in unbelief.[204]

Paul tells his audience that this is not a difficult thing for God to do — certainly less difficult than 'grafting' in Gentiles: *After all, if you were cut out of an olive tree that is wild by nature, and contrary to nature were grafted into a cultivated olive tree, how much more readily will these, the natural branches, be grafted into their own olive tree!* 'The olive tree that is, wild by nature' denotes the unbelieving Gentile world from which Paul's Gentile audience were 'cut'. Then, contrary to their nature as Gentiles, they were grafted into 'a cultivated olive tree', that is, they were joined to 'true' Israel. The result is, as the apostle has already said, that the Gentiles, 'though a wild olive shoot, have been grafted in among the others and now share in the nourishing sap from the olive root' (11:17). Paul's point is that the fact that God has grafted Gentiles as unnatural branches cut from a wild olive tree into the cultivated olive tree of the 'true' Israel demonstrates that he can 'much more readily' graft presently unbelieving Jews back into their own olive tree, back into the 'true' Israel, 'if they do not persist in unbelief'.[205] These verses contain something of a put-down for arrogant Gentiles; they are depicted as branches from a 'wild olive tree', while Jews are depicted as branches from the 'cultivated olive tree' (see 'Additional Note: Paul's Olive Tree Analogy', 439-41).[206] It should be noted that Paul's olive tree analogy

203. Wright, 'Romans', 686.

204. Byrne, *Romans*, 343.

205. Moo, *Romans*, 708, says: 'We must allow for Paul's hortatory purpose in evaluating this "how much more" argument. . . . Paul does not mean that it is easier to save a Jew than a Gentile or that the Jew, by reason of being a Jew, can make any claim on God; for this would be to give the Jew an "advantage" in salvation that Paul has plainly denied (see chap. 2). . . . Their quality as "natural branches" does not itself qualify them for grafting onto the tree. But, as branches that trace their origin to a "holy" root (v. 16), their regrafting is easier to understand than the grafting in of those alien, wild olive branches'.

206. Hartung, 'Die kultische bzw. Agrartechnisch', 138-40, suggests that Paul has used the olive tree analogy to make two points — (i) to show that God is free to act however he will (in cutting off and grafting in), and (ii) to counteract tendencies among Gentile believers to lose interest in a church made up of both Jews and Gentiles — and reminds them

suggests that the apostle believed in only one true olive tree, one true people of God, made up of both Jewish and Gentile believers, but that he still distinguished between its natural branches, believing Jews, and unnatural branches, believing Gentiles.

ADDITIONAL NOTE: PAUL'S OLIVE TREE ANALOGY

Paul's use of the olive tree analogy in 11:17-24 raises some problems for interpreters. First the idea of grafting a wild olive shoot into a good olive tree seems to be contrary to normal oleicultural practice that did the opposite, that is, grafted shoots from a good olive tree into a stock of a stronger wild olive tree in order to increase the production of good-quality olives. To graft a wild olive shoot into a good olive tree would result in the production of poor-quality wild olives.[207] It has been suggested that Paul, as an urban dweller, was ignorant of oleiculture and so did not realize the inappropriateness of his analogy. But this is unlikely, and certainly there would be those among his audience who would recognize that what he was saying was contrary to normal practice. There have been a couple of attempts to account for this.

Baxter and Ziesler, citing works of the ancient author Columbella *(De re rustica* and *De arboribus)*, argue that Paul was aware of the practice of grafting scions of a wild olive onto an aged or diseased olive tree, to restore the latter to health and fruit bearing.[208] The apostle used this practice to illustrate the way God would restore Israel. He would incorporate believing Gentiles into the people of God, and the people of Israel would then recognize that God was gathering the elect and that they themselves were not being included. 'This would make them repent, be forgiven, and return to being true Israel'. Baxter and Ziesler argue that it is the ingrafting of the Gentiles, rather than the Gentiles themselves, that will bring about the restoration of Israel: 'In the overall divine strategy, the ingrafting of Gentile

---

that they are only partakers of the privileges first promised to the Jews, and that there is no such thing as a purely Gentile church — it would not be a true church.

207. Philip F. Esler, 'Ancient Oleiculture and Ethnic Differentiation: The Meaning of the Olive-Tree Image in Romans 11', *JSNT* 26 (2003) 114, cites Theophrastus's work *De causis plantarum* 1.6.10 and provides this translation: 'It is also reasonable that grafted trees are richer in fine fruit, especially when a scion from a cultivated tree is grafted onto a stock of a wild tree of the same bark, since the scion receives more nourishment from the strength of the stock. This is why people recommend that one should first plant wild olive trees and graft in buds or branches later, for the grafts hold better to the stronger stock and by attracting more nourishment the tree bears rich fruit. If, on the other hand, someone were to graft a wild scion into a cultivated stock, there will be some difference, but there will be no fine fruit'.

208. A. G. Baxter and J. A. Ziesler, 'Paul and Arboriculture: Romans 11.17-24', *JSNT* 24 (1985) 25-32.

scions is a crucial and necessary intermediate stage' leading to the salvation of 'all Israel'.[209]

Esler questions the validity of Baxter and Ziesler's appeal to Columbella's writings to explain Paul's use of the olive tree analogy. He argues the reversal of the usual practice is so blatant that the apostle's audience would assume that Paul was deliberately subverting it to make a point about the position of Jews and Gentiles in the Christian movement.[210] Esler also contends that the process described by Columbella is a recuperative measure for an *unproductive tree,* hardly consistent with the grafting of Gentiles into the *productive olive tree of Israel* from which they draw nutrients.[211] He goes on: 'In opting for the wild olive, when he and his audience well knew that its branches did not bear edible fruit, Paul was consciously crafting an image most unflattering to the non-Judeans. This was exactly the result he wished to achieve and accords closely with his statements that the stock was the source of support and fertility, not the ingrafted branches (11.17-18), as well as with his admonitions to them not to make honour claims for themselves at the expense of the branches (that had been cut off) in v. 18 and not to entertain haughty thoughts in v. 20. Paul is virtually describing the "barbarianization" of the olive tree'.[212]

Grindheim offers the following observations about Paul's use of the olive tree analogy: 'The usual method of grafting in involves taking cultivated branches and grafting them into a wild tree. That way the cultivated branches may bear more fruit. Grafting wild branches into a cultivated tree will not produce good fruit. In other words, the reason for God's inclusion of the Gentiles does not lie in their desirability but can only be explained as a manifestation of God's tendency in his election to do the opposite. Paul's imagery of the olive thus emphasizes his exhortation to the Gentiles that they not become arrogant (v. 18). With regard to the Jews that were cut off, Paul announces that yet another reversal is forthcoming. They will be grafted back in. God in his goodness is capable of reuniting them with the tree from which they were cut off. . . . Despite the fundamental difference in origins, these two types of branches share the very same predicament: they are off and they need to be grafted in. This is the only way to God that Paul knows: from death to life by God's mercy. In the olive metaphor the concepts of Israel's privilege and the Gentiles being at no disadvantage come together'.[213]

---

209. Baxter and Ziesler, 'Paul and Arboriculture', 28. Cf. Mark Harding, 'The Salvation of Israel and the Logic of Romans 11:11-36', *ABR* 46 (1998) 62. Haacker, 'Die Geschichtstheologie von Röm 9–11', 216-19, notes certain parallels to Paul's use of the analogy of the olive tree in the works of Philo, namely, *Praem.* 152.

210. Esler, 'Ancient Oleiculture and Ethnic Differentiation', 115.

211. Esler, 'Ancient Oleiculture and Ethnic Differentiation', 120-21.

212. Esler, 'Ancient Oleiculture and Ethnic Differentiation', 122.

213. Sigurd Grindheim, *The Crux of Election: Paul's Critique of the Jewish Confidence in the Election of Israel* (WUNT 2/202; Tübingen: Mohr Siebeck, 2005), 164-65.

To provide some background to Paul's use of the grafting metaphor Rastoin[214] draws attention to the following passage in the Talmud: 'R. Eleazar further stated: What is meant by the text, *And in thee shall the families of the earth be blessed?* The Holy One, blessed be He, said to Abraham, "I have two goodly shoots to engraft on you: Ruth the Moabitess and Maamah the Ammonitess" (*b. Yebamoth* 63a)'.[215] Rastoin stresses that the use of the grafting metaphor enables Paul to connect the tree of the holy people (vine or olive tree) with that of the salvation of the nations. It reconciles the election of the one with the source of salvation of all.[216]

(iii) The mystery: The final salvation of 'all Israel', 11:25-32

[25]*I do not want you to be ignorant of this mystery, brothers and sisters, so that you may not be conceited: Israel has experienced a hardening in part until the full number of the Gentiles has come in,* [26]*and in this way all Israel will be saved. As it is written: 'The deliverer will come from Zion; he will turn godlessness away from Jacob.* [27]*And this is my covenant with them when I take away their sins'.* [28]*As far as the gospel is concerned, they are enemies for your sake; but as far as election is concerned, they are loved on account of the patriarchs,* [29]*for God's gifts and his call are irrevocable.* [30]*Just as you who were at one time disobedient to God have now received mercy as a result of their disobedience,* [31]*so they too have now become disobedient in order that they too may now receive mercy as a result of God's mercy to you.* [32]*For God has bound everyone over to disobedience so that he may have mercy on them all.*

In this section Paul continues to address the Gentiles among his audience, explaining the mystery of God's dealings with Israel. He does so to prevent them from becoming conceited and thinking that God has chosen them instead of Israel. He reminds them that they were at one time as disobedient to God as the majority in Israel is now, and that just as they received mercy, so Israel will also experience God's mercy.

11:25-26a Continuing to address the Gentiles in his audience, Paul says: *I do not want you to be ignorant of this mystery, brothers and sisters, so that you may not be conceited: Israel has experienced a hardening in part until the full number of the Gentiles has come in, and in this way all Israel will be saved.* He begins with the formula, '[For] I do not want you to be ignorant', one he employs frequently when about to provide information his audience needs to know (cf. 1:13; 11:25; 1 Cor 10:1; 12:1; 2 Cor 1:8; 1 Thess 4:13). In this case,

214. Marc Rastoin, 'Une bien étrange greffe (Rm 11,17): Correspondances rabbiniques d'une expression paulinienne', *RB* 114 (2007) 74-75.

215. *The Babylonian Talmud: Seder Nashim* 1, trans. I. Epstein (London: Soncino, 1936), 420.

216. Rastoin, 'Une bien étrange greffe (Rm 11,17)', 79.

the Gentiles in his audience need to know about the 'mystery' of the hardening in part of Israel. This is an unusual use of the word 'mystery', for normally Paul employs it to refer to the mystery of the gospel 'hidden for long ages past, but now revealed and made known' (16:25-26; cf. 1 Cor 2:1, 7; 4:1; Eph 1:9; 3:3, 4, 9; 6:19; Col 1:26, 27; 2:2; 4:3; 1 Tim 3:9, 16). However, he sometimes uses it to denote something mysterious or hard to understand too (1 Cor 13:2; 14:2; 15:51; Eph 5:32; 2 Thess 2:7). It is in this latter sense that he uses it here in 11:25, where he speaks of the 'mystery' of the hardening that has come upon Israel.[217]

The reason Paul wants Gentiles in his audience to understand this mystery, he says, is 'so that you may not be conceited'. Already he has warned them about being arrogant — thinking that unbelieving Jews were removed from the olive tree of 'true' Israel to make room for them (11:17-21). In 11:25-27 he informs that there is still a place for Israel in God's plans so as to remove any basis for Gentile hubris vis-à-vis Jews.

There are three aspects to Paul's description of this mystery: (i) 'Israel has experienced a hardening', (ii) 'until the full number of the Gentiles has come in', and (iii) 'and in this way all Israel will be saved'. The essential point of the mystery is not found in any one of the three aspects, but rather in the whole sequence of these interdependent events.[218] What is surprising about this mystery is that it constitutes a reversal of Jewish expectations — the entry of the Gentiles into salvation would *precede* that of Israel, and not vice versa. For the Jewish expectation see Isaiah 2:2-3; 56:6-7; 60:3-14; Micah 4:1-2; Zechariah 14:16-17; Tobit 14:6-7.[219]

Integral to the mystery Paul wants the Gentiles in his audience to understand is that 'Israel has experienced a hardening in part'. The expression translated here as 'in part' is used later by Paul to mean both 'in part' (15:15: 'I have written you quite boldly on some points [lit. 'in part']') and 'for a while' (15:24: 'I plan to do so when I go to Spain . . . after I have enjoyed your company for a while'; cf. 2 Cor 1:14). It may be better to translate it here in 11:25 as 'for a while', that is, Paul is saying that Israel's hardening is temporary rather than partial.[220] This would be consistent with the fact that Paul says straightaway that this hardening will persist 'until the full number of the Gentiles has come in'.

In the context of chapter 11 the hardening that has happened to Israel refers to many of Paul's fellow Jews whose hearts were hardened to the gospel.[221] They are, as the apostle said previously, quoting Isaiah, 'a disobe-

---

217. Jewett, *Romans*, 699, comments: 'It is best to acknowledge that Paul's use of the word "mystery" in this context reflects the perspective of a mystic whose "revelation experiences" remain partially beyond analysis. Even though it can be publicly disclosed, its origin and content remain partially "unfathomable and incomprehensible"'.

218. Cf. Getty, 'Paul and the Salvation of Israel', 458, 460.

219. Byrne, *Romans*, 349-50.

220. Cf. Wright, 'Romans', 688.

221. That *pōrōsis* is to be understood here as a 'hardening of *the heart*' is supported by

dient and contrary people' (10:21). Included in the mystery that Paul wants the Gentiles in his audience to understand is that this hardening of Israel is not permanent; it will persist only 'until the full number of the Gentiles has come in'. The full number of the Gentiles refers to the full number of the elect from among the Gentiles called by God (cf. 9:22-24). Their full number will be made up as the gospel is proclaimed throughout the world and will be completed by the time Christ appears for the second time. Paul insists that the hardening of Israel will persist only until this time. The expression 'in this way' refers to what precedes.[222] In this case it is used to indicate the way 'all Israel will be saved', that is, in the same way as the full number of the Gentiles come in.[223] Paul's meaning is that a hardening of Israel will persist until the full number of Gentiles has come in, and as the Gentiles are coming in, many Jews will be coming in also and in this way, and by the time Christ appears the second time, the hardness will have disappeared and all Israel will be saved. By 'all Israel' Paul means the Jewish elect of all ages (see, 'Additional Note: "All Israel Will Be Saved"', 448-51).[224] At that

---

the fact that the word is found only twice elsewhere in the NT, and in both cases in connection with this meaning: Mark 3:5: 'He looked around at them in anger and, deeply distressed at their stubborn hearts *(pōrōsei tēs kardias)*, said to the man, "Stretch out your hand". He stretched it out, and his hand was completely restored'; Eph 4:18: 'They are darkened in their understanding and separated from the life of God because of the ignorance that is in them due to the hardening of their hearts *(pōrōsin tēs kardias)*. But cf. Maria-Irma Seewann, 'Semantische Untersuchung zu *pōrōsis*, veranlasst durch Röm 11,25', *FilolNT* 10, nos. 19-20 (1997) 156, who argues that *pōrōsis* should rather be translated as 'ignorance' on the grounds, she argues, that in Greek usage *pōrōsis* generally functions as the opposite of 'knowing'.

222. Bell, *The Irrevocable Call of God*, 259-60, notes four different ways in which *kai houtōs* has been interpreted, concluding that only two deserve serious consideration: (i) *kai houtōs* has been understood as modal, referring to that which precedes, i.e., referring back to the first two lines of the *mystērion* in 11:25b. Thus *kai houtōs* is translated as 'and in this way' or 'and in such a way'; (ii) it is possible that *kai houtōs* could be understood 'in a logical sense following on from *achri hou to plērōma tōn ethnōn eiselthē*. Although *kai houtōs* is here understood as logical, it will also inevitably carry a temporal sense. This use of *kai houtōs* is attested in the 'intertestamental literature'. It is generally agreed that *houtōs* never means 'at that time' or 'then', and so to construe 11:25-26 as to mean that once the full number of the Gentiles has come in, *then* God will act so that all Israel will be saved is not tenable. However, Peter W. van der Horst, '"Only Then Will All Israel Be Saved": A Short Note on the Meaning of *kai houtōs* in Romans 11:26', *JBL* 119 (2000) 521-25, has shown there are instances where *kai houtōs* is used with a temporal sense by classical writers (e.g., Theophrastus, *Characteres* 18), postclassical writers (e.g., Epictetus 2.15.8), in Judeo-Greek literature (e.g., *Life of Jeremiah* 6), elsewhere in the NT (e.g., Acts 7:8; 1 Thess 4:16-17), and in early Christian literature (e.g., Irenaeus, *Haer.* 1.30.14). He states that the purpose of his essay is not 'to exclude the possibility that Paul used *kai houtōs* in the modal sense in Rom 11:26. What I do want to exclude, however, is the use of the false argument that it is impossible to take *houtōs* in the temporal sense because this is "not found otherwise in Greek" (Fitzmyer)' (524-25).

223. Cf. Dunn, *Romans 9–16*, 681.

224. It is unlikely that Paul means that there will be a last minute national turning to Christ on the part of the last generation, something that would have no significance for those many generations of Jews who had come and gone in the meantime.

time the 'fullness of the Gentiles' (11:25) will stand alongside the 'fullness' of the Jews (11:12). Paul was contributing *directly* to bringing in the 'fullness of the Gentiles' by his mission to the Gentiles. He hoped to contribute *indirectly* to bringing about the 'fullness' of the Jews by provoking Jewish people to jealousy as they saw Gentiles enjoying the blessings first promised by God to them. This is the thrust of the apostle's statement in 11:13-14: 'Inasmuch as I am the apostle to the Gentiles, I take pride in my ministry in the hope that I may somehow arouse my own people to envy and save some of them'.

11:26b-27   In support of his hope for the salvation of 'all Israel' Paul appeals to Scripture: *As it is written: 'The deliverer will come from Zion; he will turn godlessness away from Jacob. And this is my covenant with them when I take away their sins'*. The greater part of the quotation is drawn from Isaiah 59:20-21 (LXX), the last few words ('when I take away their sins') being drawn from Isaiah 27:9 (LXX). The main text that Paul cites, Isaiah 59:20 (LXX), predicts the coming of the redeemer *for* Zion, and Paul may have substituted 'from Zion'.[225]

Paul, with his citation from Isaiah, says that the redeemer will come from Zion to turn away ungodliness from Jacob. This prophetic prediction was given in the context of a declaration of the deep depravity of Israel (Isa 59:2-15).[226] Because there was none other to save, God himself declared that he would turn away godlessness from Jacob (Isa 59:16-21).[227] This text is appropriate for Paul's purposes. He is faced with the intransigence of the majority of his fellow Jews who will not accept the gospel, but his hope is that the God who promised to turn away ungodliness from Jacob will do so by taking away their sins in accordance with his covenant.

When the apostle adds, 'And this is my covenant with them when I take away their sins', he probably has in mind the promise of the new covenant spoken of by the prophet Jeremiah:

> 'The days are coming', declares the LORD, 'when I will make a new covenant with the people of Israel and with the people of Judah. It will not be like the covenant I made with their ancestors when I took them by

---

225. Alternatively the text Paul cites may be a corruption of 'to Zion' (based on the MT's 'to Zion'), as Dunn, *Romans 9–16*, 682, says: '*EIS* ['to'] being easily misread as *EK* ['from']'.

226. Paul drew on this same passage in 3:15-17 to depict universal guilt.

227. While the Isaiah text speaks of God as the Deliverer, there is some evidence in rabbinic literature that the deliverer was understood to be the Messiah. Cranfield, *Romans*, II, 578, says: 'So in *Sanh.* 98ª Rabbi Johanan (about A.D. 250) is reported as saying: "When thou seest a generation over which many oppressions break like a torrent, then expect him [i.e., the Messiah]; for it is said (Isa 59:19), 'When the oppressor shall come like a torrent which the tempest of the LORD driveth' [so the Midrash], and thereupon follows (v. 20), 'He comes for Zion as redeemer'". See SB 4, p. 981)'. Cf. Dunn, *Romans 9–16*, 682. However, Getty, 'Paul and the Salvation of Israel', 461, argues that Paul is not making a Christological statement but, as is the case in Isa 59:20-21 (LXX), God himself is the subject.

the hand to lead them out of Egypt, because they broke my covenant, though I was a husband to them', declares the LORD. 'This is the covenant I will make with the people of Israel after that time', declares the LORD. 'I will put my law in their minds and write it on their hearts. I will be their God, and they will be my people. No longer will they teach their neighbor, or say to one another, "Know the LORD", because they will all know me, from the least of them to the greatest', declares the LORD. 'For I will forgive their wickedness and will remember their sins no more'. (Jer 31:31-34)[228]

11:28-29 Referring to many of his Jewish kinsfolk, Paul says: *As far as the gospel is concerned, they are enemies for your sake.* They showed themselves to be enemies of God when they rejected his gospel, and Paul indicates that this happened 'on your account', that is, for the benefit of the Gentiles in his audience. However, that is not the end of the matter because the apostle goes on to say, *but as far as election is concerned, they are loved on account of the patriarchs, for God's gifts and his call are irrevocable.* To be loved as far as election is concerned clearly means to be loved by God, suggesting that being enemies means to be regarded as enemies by God (but only 'as far as the gospel is concerned'). To be enemies of God could have an active sense meaning 'those who hate God' or a passive sense meaning 'those who are hated by God'. In this context where being enemies of God is contrasted with being loved by God, Paul probably has in mind 'one who is hated by God', but it must be added, only insofar 'as the gospel is concerned'.[229] When Paul says, 'they are enemies for your sake' (i.e., for the sake of Paul's Gentile audience), he may be alluding to the fact that when the Jews became 'enemies' by rejecting the gospel, he took it to the Gentiles. By so saying Paul repeats points he made in 11:12, 15, where he argued that the transgression of the Jews meant riches for the world, and their rejection is the reconciliation of the world.

When Paul writes, 'as far as election is concerned, they are loved on account of the patriarchs', he is speaking of the election of Israel as a nation,

---

228. Jan Lambrecht, 'Grammar and Reasoning in Romans 11,27', *ETL* 79 (2003) 183, has a different view. He thinks that the reference to covenant here 'most probably refers to the past covenant with Abraham (and the other patriarchs; cf. vv. 28-29). Through ungodliness and sin Israel has often broken the covenant, but on God's side there remains a continuing relationship (cf. v. 29: the call is irrevocable). "God has not rejected his people whom he foreknew" (11,2). God or Christ will restore the covenant through the forgiveness of sins. This restored covenant is not a new and different covenant; yet as such it is also a future reality. In that covenant Israel's past, present and future are firmly joined together'.

229. Moo, *Romans*, 730-31, suggests that 'it is best to give the word both an active and passive sense, captured adequately in the English word "enemies". This meaning effectively captures the dual note Paul has sounded throughout Rom 9-11 when speaking of Israel's failure: "hated", "hardened", and "rejected" by God (cf. 9:13, 17-23; 11:7b-10, 15, 25); for their part, disobedient, unbelieving, and stubborn (9:31-32; 10:3, 14-21; 11:11, 12, 20, 23, 30-31)'.

the only place he does so in his letters.[230] However, there are frequent references to the election of the nation in the OT, predominantly in Deuteronomy, Psalms, and Isaiah.[231] The election of the nation did not mean that every individual Israelite would enjoy God's blessings irrespective of their response to his word, something dramatically illustrated by the fact that virtually an entire generation was refused entry to the promised land (Numbers 14).

Paul affirms that God's gifts and calling 'are irrevocable'. The basic meaning of the word so translated is 'without regret'. Thus God's gifts and call to Israel are made 'without regret', and will therefore not be revoked.[232] That God's gifts are 'irrevocable' does not mean that all Israelites will automatically be included among the elect. What it does mean is that God has not forgotten his promises to the patriarchs, his promise to bless their seed. Israel is still loved on account of the patriarchs, and this means that God has not rejected Israel in his preference for the Gentiles. It also means that he will fulfill his promises to the patriarchs.[233] Paul is encouraged by this that many of his kinsfolk, though currently 'enemies' of God, will yet experience God's blessing as God makes up the full number of the Jewish elect. How this will be brought about, Paul explains in the following verses.

11:30-31　In these verses Paul explains to the Gentiles in his audience how God will fulfill his irrevocable (but not unconditional) promises to the patriarchs. He begins by saying: *Just as you who were at one time disobedient to God have now received mercy as a result of their disobedience. . . .* Paul, concerned about his fellow Jews who were currently disobedient to the gospel, reminds his Gentile audience that they were once in the same boat. They were 'at one time disobedient to God', but they have now received his mercy as a result of the disobedience of the Jews (which prompted Paul to offer the gospel to the Gentiles). The real point Paul wants to make here, however, concerns the currently disobedient Jews, and it is one of hope: *so they too have now become disobedient in order that they too may now receive mercy as a result of God's mercy to you.*

---

230. Elsewhere Paul speaks of the election of Jacob not Esau (9:11), the remnant (11:5, 7), and believers (8:33; 16:3; Eph 1:4; Col 3:12; 1 Thess 1:4; 2 Tim 2:10; Tit 1:1).

231. Deut 4:37; 7:7; 10:15; 14:2; 1 Kgs 3:8; Pss 33:12; 47:4; 65:4; 105:5; 106:5; 135:4; Isa 14:1; 41:8, 9; 42:1; 43:10, 20; 44:1, 2; 45:4; 49:7; 65:9.

232. Jewett, *Romans*, 708-9, says: 'The adjective *ametameletos* is usually translated "irrevocable", which implies a legal axiom that cannot be repealed, but the basic meaning is "without regret", as in 2 Cor 7:10, the only other use of this term in the OT or NT: "repentance that leads to salvation and brings no regret". . . . That the God of biblical faith was in fact frequently depicted as changing his mind provides the background for this denial that she [sic] had done so with regard to Israel's distinctive gifts and calling. Although God was free to withdraw such privileges, while humans often come to regret and then to renege on their gifts and commitments, God's faithfulness remains firm. In the end, despite the current rejection of their divinely designated Messiah by a large portion of Israel, the divine gifts and calling will achieve their intended purpose of salvation'.

233. Cf. Wright, 'Romans', 693.

The choice between textual variants in 11:31 influences the way this verse is understood. The NIV and NRSV adopt the variant that includes a second 'now' ('so they too have *now* become disobedient in order that they too may *now* receive mercy'). Two other variants involve either omitting the second 'now' or replacing it with 'later'. The textual evidence supporting both the inclusion and the omission of the second 'now' is 'evenly balanced'.[234] If the second 'now' is omitted, Paul could be implying that the time when Israel receives mercy is still in the future. If the second 'now' is retained, he could be implying that, just as the Gentiles are 'now' receiving mercy through Israel's disobedience, so too Israel is also 'now' receiving mercy as a result of God's mercy to the Gentiles. Paul then would be seeing the effects of his ministry among the Gentiles, provoking Israel to jealousy and motivating them to repent and believe in the Messiah and so experience God's mercy in the present time.[235] Some who retain the second 'now' still interpret Paul's statement in terms of a future reception of mercy by the Jews. In this case, as Moo suggests, Paul's 'now' is 'an expression of imminence, expressing his conviction that this final manifestation of God's mercy to Israel could take place "now, at any time"'.[236] If the second 'now' is replaced by 'later', clearly Paul would be envisaging a future experience of God's mercy by the currently unbelieving Israel, and therefore the passage would have an eschatological sense.

11:32 In this verse Paul makes clear that the salvation of God is the same in respect to both Jews and Gentiles: *For God has bound everyone over to disobedience so that he may have mercy on them all.* Speaking of God 'binding' people over to disobedience, the apostle employs a verb that means 'to con-

---

234. Cf. Metzger, ed., *A Textual Commentary*, 465. Robert W. Miller, 'The Text of Rom 11:31', *Faith & Mission* 23 (2006) 47, sums up his discussion of the variants: 'It has been argued on the basis of external and internal evidence that the original text in Rom. 11:31 did not contain the second *nyn*. Because the omission is both geographically widespread and ancient, it is believed to be the original reading. The internal evidence then supports the omission by showing that it is probable in light of both intentional and unintentional errors. Finally, the context, Paul's style, and his theology confirm that He [sic] did not pen either the *nyn* or the *hysteron* but used an aorist subjunctive with a future meaning to speak of the future plan God has for His chosen people'.

235. Wright, 'Romans', 694, comments: 'The mercy that is shown to Israel according to the flesh is not something for which they will have to wait until some putative final day. . . . It is available "now"; and Paul's kinsfolk can, he hopes and believes, be provoked into seeking it by being "jealous" of the way in which Israel's privileges are being enjoyed by Gentiles'.

236. Moo, *Romans*, 735. Similarly Käsemann, *Romans*, 316, who says: 'The second and apparently inadequate *nyn* in v. 31b has always caused trouble, and for this reason it is already left out in P[46] . . . and replaced by *hysteron* in other MSS. But it is understandable in the light of the apocalyptic view of the context. The end-time is so far advanced that the *plērōma tōn ethnōn* ['the fullness of the Gentiles'] will soon be completed and the parousia is at hand . . . Paul expects the parousia, probably in his own lifetime'. So too Bell, *The Irrevocable Call of God*, 284-85.

fine' or 'to imprison'. He uses the same word in two other places: in Galatians 3:22 to denote imprisonment under sin, and in Galatians 3:23 to denote imprisonment under the law. Here in 11:32 he speaks of God imprisoning people in their disobedience. People choose to disobey God, and God consigns them to the prison of disobedience from which they cannot escape. Paul's emphasis here is that God had bound 'everyone' over to disobedience. There are no exceptions — Jews and Gentiles are both in the same prison. But that is not the end of the matter, for the apostle says that God has bound both Jews and Gentiles over to disobedience 'so that he may have mercy on them all'. The emphasis is on 'them all'. God will have mercy on all alike. What Paul is saying in this verse is no different in essence from what he said back in 3:22-24: 'This righteousness is given through faith in Jesus Christ to all who believe. There is no difference between Jew and Gentile, for all have sinned and fall short of the glory of God, and all are justified freely by his grace through the redemption that came by Christ Jesus'.

ADDITIONAL NOTE: 'ALL ISRAEL WILL BE SAVED'

There are, essentially, six interpretations of the expression 'all Israel' in Paul's statement that 'all Israel will be saved': (i) all Israelites from every age; (ii) all the elect of Israel of all time; (iii) all Israelites alive at the end of the age; (iv) Israel as a whole alive at the end of the age, but not including every individual Israelite; (v) a large number of Israelites at the end of the age; (vi) Israel redefined to include all Jews and Gentiles who believe in Jesus Christ.

Few have supported the first interpretation that 'all Israel' means all Israelites from every age. Bell is one who does support this view, arguing that at the parousia they will hear the gospel from Christ himself, their hardness of heart will be removed, and they will come to faith in a way similar to that of the apostle Paul when confronted by the risen Christ on the Damascus Road.[237]

Merkle, among others, supports the second interpretation, that 'all Israel' means all the elect of Israel of all time. He takes 'all Israel' to refer to the elect of ethnic Israel who throughout history 'repent, believe and share in the promises made originally to them' (he thinks that it is unlikely that Paul has in mind 'a future mass conversion of Israel at a future time').[238]

---

237. Bell, *The Irrevocable Call of God*, 264-70. So too, it seems, Winfrid Keller, *Gottes Treue — Israels Heil, Röm 11,25-27: Die These vom "Sonderweg" in der Diskussion* (SBB 40; Stuttgart: Katholisches Bibelwerk, 1998), 229; Otfried Hofius, '"All Israel Will Be Saved": Divine Salvation and Israel's Deliverance in Romans 9–11', *PSB* Sup 1 (1990) 19-39.

238. Ben L. Merkle, 'Romans 11 and the Future of Ethnic Israel', *JETS* 43 (2000) 717, 721. So, too, François Refoulé, 'Cohérence ou incohérence de Paul en Romains 9–11?' *RB* 98 (1991) 78-79.

There is also some support for the third view, that 'all Israel' means all Israelites alive at the end of the age. Witherington claims that Paul is speaking about 'a mass conversion of non-Christian Jews at the end of salvation history'.[239]

The majority of interpreters adopt the fourth view, that 'all Israel' denotes Israel as a whole at the end of the age, but that this does not include every individual Israelite. This position is supported by the church father, Diodore, who argues: 'Just as we say that the whole world and all the nations are being saved because everywhere and among all nations there are those who are coming to faith, so also *all Israel will be saved* does not mean that every one of them will be but that either those who were understood by Elijah or those who are scattered all over the world will one day come to faith'.[240] Moo contends that 'Paul writes "all Israel", not "every Israelite" — and the difference is an important one. "All Israel", as the OT and Jewish sources demonstrate, has a corporate significance, referring to the nation as a whole and not to every single individual who is a part of that nation'.[241] Barrett cites the belief articulated in *Sanhedrin* 10:1: 'All Israelites have a share in the world to come', noting that this does not mean every individual Israelite, for 'it proceeds to enumerate a long list of exceptions: from "all Israel" must be subtracted all Sadducees, heretics, magicians, the licentious, and many more. It means that Israel as a whole is destined for eternal life in the Age to Come. This, of course, does not prove that Paul's meaning was the same; but when his two statements, about Gentiles and Jews, are taken together, it seems probable that the is thinking in representative terms . . . ; first the remnant of Israel, then the Gentiles, finally Israel as a whole'.[242]

The fifth view, that 'all Israel' signifies a large number of Israelites who will be saved at the end of the age, is supported by Vasholz, who says: 'While the meaning of "all" is debated . . . it has to mean, at the least, that a noticeable number of ethnic Israelites will become ardent followers of the Messiah'.[243] Voorwinde also adopts this view. He holds: 'Once this majority of Gentiles has come in, "all Israel will be saved" (v. 26). Again this would appear to be a reference to a majority of Israel, to the Jews as a whole, rather than to every single Jew'.[244] He adds: 'This anticipated salvation of the majority of the Jews has been made possible through Christ's first coming. It was then that he came as the Deliverer from Zion and made a cov-

---

239. Witherington, *Romans*, 275. Similarly, Jewett, *Romans*, 702, 704.

240. 'Pauline Commentary from the Greek Church' (*ACCSR*, 298).

241. Moo, *Romans*, 722.

242. Barrett, *Romans*, 223-24. So, too, Cranfield, *Romans*, II, 576, 577; F. David Satran, 'Paul among the Rabbis and the Fathers: Exegetical Reflections', *PSB* Sup 1 (1990) 105.

243. Robert Vasholz, 'The Character of Israel's Future in Light of the Abrahamic and Mosaic Covenants', *TrinJ* 25 (2004) 57.

244. Stephen Voorwinde, 'Rethinking Israel: An Exposition of Romans 11:25-27', *VoxRef* 68 (2003) 38-40.

enant with them to take away their sins. Up till now he has turned godless-ness (unbelief) away from only a remnant or minority in Jacob. The time will come when that number is dramatically increased. The trickle will be-come a torrent!'[245] Romerowski also looks for a massive conversion of Isra-elites to Christ at the end of the present era. Because Jesus Christ is the only way of salvation, the Israelites of the last generation will be saved by faith.[246] Grindheim says: 'The most natural way to understand the expres-sion "all Israel" is in relation to v. 25, where a part of Israel has been hard-ened, reflecting the partition of Israel into the remnant and the rest ex-plained in v. 7. Verse 26 describes the situation when this internal division will be overcome. Israel is no longer made up by the remnant and the rest but is referred to as "all Israel". This would be in keeping with the use of the term "Israel" throughout chapter 11 as referring to ethnic Israel (vv. 2, 7, 25) and the direction in which Paul's argument has been going, especially since 11:11'.[247] Dunn also supports this position: 'There is now a strong con-sensus that *pas Israēl* ['all Israel'] must mean Israel as a whole, as a people whose corporate identity and wholeness would not be lost even if in the event there were some (or indeed many) individual exceptions. . . . For Paul, who has stressed the power of his gospel to *all* who believe (1:16), that his apostleship was for the obedience of faith among *all* the Gentiles (1:5), and that the promise to Abraham was to *all* the seed (4:16), it was clearly important to be able to say *all* Israel'.[248]

The sixth interpretation of 'all Israel', that it refers to all believers, both Jews and Gentiles who believe in Jesus Christ, was espoused by some early church fathers. Augustine wrote: 'Not all the Jews were blind; some of them recognized Christ. But the fullness of the Gentiles comes in among those who have been called according to the plan, and there arises a truer Israel of God . . . the elect from both the Jews and the Gentiles,[249] Theodoret of Cyrrhus says, '*All Israel* means all those who believe, whether they are Jews, who have a natural relationship to Israel, or Gentiles, who are related to Israel by faith'.[250] Wright adopts a similar position, emphasizing how-ever, that the process of the salvation of 'all Israel' takes place in the course of history, not at the end of the age. He writes: 'I remain convinced that . . . God will save "all Israel" — that is the whole family of Abraham, Jew and Gentile alike; this will take place during the course of present history; it will happen through their coming to Christian faith. . . . The phrase "all Is-rael", then, is best taken as a polemical redefinition, in line with Paul's redefinitions of "Jew" in 2:29, of "circumcision" in 2:29 and Phil 3:3, and of "seed of Abraham" in Romans 4, Galatians 3, and Rom 9:6-9. It belongs

---

245. Voorwinde, 'Rethinking Israel', 48.
246. Sylvain Romerowski, 'Israël dans le plan de Dieu', *La revue réformée* 51 (2000) 66.
247. Grindheim, *The Crux of Election*, 165-68.
248. Dunn, *Romans 9–16*, 681.
249. 'Letters 149' (*ACCSR*, 298).
250. 'Interpretation of the Letter to the Romans' (*ACCSR*, 299).

with what seems indubitably the correct reading of "the Israel of God" in Gal 6:16'.[251]

Of the six different interpretations described above, four (1, 3, 4, 5) have the salvation of 'all Israel' taking place at the end of the age when all Israelites of all time (1), or all Israelites alive then (3), or Israel as a whole, but not every individual Israelite (4), or a large number of Israelites (5) will be saved. According to the other two interpretations (2, 6), the salvation of 'all Israel' takes place during the course of history, during which all the elect of ethnic Israel (2), or Israel redefined as all believing Jews and Gentiles (6), are saved. Impressive arguments for most of these six interpretations have been mounted, and in the light of this caution is needed in reaching a conclusion. I am reluctant to embrace any of the interpretations placing the salvation of 'all Israel' at the end of the age because that involves a special provision for the salvation of Jews different from that provided for Gentiles. This flies in the face of the overall argument of Romans that Jews and Gentiles are treated alike in the matters of sin, judgment, and salvation. For this reason it seems that one or other of the interpretations that locates the salvation of 'all Israel' in the course of history is preferable. Of these two, the one that interprets 'all Israel' as the elect of Israel of all time, rather than 'all Israel' redefined as all Jews and Gentiles who believe in Christ, seems preferable for two reasons: (i) in chapters 9–11 Paul is concerned about his *kinspeople* according to the flesh; (ii) it encompasses all faithful Israelites of all time.

ADDITIONAL NOTE:
A CONTRADICTION BETWEEN 9:6-13 AND 11:25-32?

Thielman describes the apparent contradiction between 9:6-13 and 11:25-32 noticed by a number of scholars: 'In 9:6-13 Paul denies the charge [that God's promises have failed] by defining Israel on the basis of God's choice rather than on the basis of national affiliation. In 11:25-32, however, he denies the charge by pointing forward to a time in which God will fulfill his promises and secure the salvation of all Israel. The problem is that these two defenses of God's faithfulness seem to contradict one another, and the defense in chapter 11 seems not only to contradict the one in chapter 9 but to oppose Paul's frequent and emphatic denial in several letters, and especially in Romans, that national Israel has any soteriological advantage over the Gentiles'.[252]

Contrary to the tendency of some to draw contrasts between what

251. Wright, 'Romans', 689-90.
252. 'Unexpected Mercy, 169.

Paul says in chapter 9 and chapter 11, Kyrychenko draws attention to the parallels existing between what Paul says in these two chapters. He does so in the following tabular form:[253]

Romans 9	Romans 11
The issue of ethnic Israel's salvation — Paul's grief (vv. 1-3)	The issue of ethnic Israel's salvation — has Israel been rejected? (vv. 1a, 11a)
God's gifts and promises to the Jews; the word of God has not failed (vv. 4-6a)	God's gifts and promises to the Jews are irrevocable (vv. 28-29)
The election of ethnic Israel and the inclusion of the Gentiles (vv. 6b-10, 24-26)	The inclusion of the Gentiles and salvation of ethnic Israel (vv. 25-26)
The call, election, and faith vs. works (vv. 11-13, 32)	Grace vs. works (v. 6)
What shall we say then: the human effort vs. mercy of God (vv. 14-16)	What then: The Jews made an effort, but did not win the race (v. 7a)
What shall we say then: the human effort vs. faith — the Jews did not win the race; the Gentiles did (vv. 30-31)	
God has hardened the Gentiles to save the Jews (vv. 17-18)	God has hardened the Jews to save the Gentiles (vv. 7b-10, 11b-12; 15:25)
Paul's dialogue with an interlocutor (vv. 19-24)	Paul's dialogue with an interlocutor (vv. 16-24)
The remnant is a guarantee of the salvation of the nation of Israel (vv. 27-29)	The remnant is a guarantee of the salvation of the nation of Israel (vv. 1b-5)
The stumbling stone is put in Zion (v. 33)	The Deliverer will come from Zion (v. 27)

Thielman offers the following explanation of the apparent contradiction: 'Packed within Paul's use of scripture in Rom 9:6-13, then, is not only a redefinition of Israel in terms of divine choice rather than human ethnicity, but an allusion to the unusual pattern of God's choices in the past. The traditional scriptures of Israel, Paul hints in 9:6-13, show that God often communicates his blessing through precisely the candidate whom cultural norms would exclude. For Jews this meant recognizing that their own scriptures allowed for the possibility that God would include Gentiles within his people, and this is Paul's primary point not only in Rom. 9:6-13 but in the whole section from 9:1 to 11:10'.[254]

We might add that the contradiction is more apparent than real, especially when Paul's purposes in chapters 9 and 11 respectively are taken into account. In chapter 9 the apostle responds to the question whether God's

253. Alexander Kyrychenko, 'The Consistency of Romans 9–11', *ResQ* 45 (2003) 224.
254. Thielman, 'Unexpected Mercy', 180.

word has failed insofar as the majority of Jews were not experiencing the blessings of the gospel. This represents no failure of God's word, for 'not all who are descended from Israel are Israel'. His word is being fulfilled in 'true' Israel, evident in the fact that now, as always, he is preserving a remnant (9:27-29). In chapter 11 the issue is a quite different one. It is not whether God's word has failed but rather whether, in the light of Israel's rejection of the gospel, has God rejected his people (11:1). Paul answers the question by insisting that God has always preserved a remnant of believing Jews, and in due course the full number of the elect of Israel will be brought in. (He reminds the Gentiles in his audience of this to counteract any tendency to dismiss or despise Jewish people.) A contradiction would be involved only if, contrary to the approach adopted in this commentary, Paul's reference to 'all Israel will be saved' is interpreted in terms of a special way of salvation for the Jews distinct from the way Gentiles are saved, something that would be in opposition to the overall thrust of the letter (cf. 2:28-29; 3:21-24; 4:11b-12; 9:6-8; 10:16-21; 11:22-24).

ADDITIONAL NOTE:
A SPECIAL WAY OF SALVATION FOR ISRAEL (11:1-32)?

The Scripture cited in 10:13 ('Everyone who calls on the name of the Lord will be saved') led Paul to highlight the need for preaching the gospel so that people might hear the good news and then call on the Lord (10:14-15). This in turn led him to ask why Israel did not respond to the good news. Was it because they had not heard it? No, says the apostle, they have heard, but they were obstinate and disobedient (10:16-21). This raises the question whether, in the light of Israel's rejection of God's word, God has rejected Israel. In 11:1b-32 Paul answers the question by denying that God has rejected his people. Instead, he argues that God has preserved a remnant among them. As in the days of Elijah when God preserved a remnant of faithful Jews who would not bow the knee to Baal, so in the present, Paul says, God has preserved a remnant of believing Jews, among whom he himself is included (11:1b-5).

Paul's primary concern in chapter 11, however, is not with the *remnant* of believing Jews, but with the *rest* of Israel; with those who persist in unbelief. It is in this connection that the apostle speaks of the mystery of the salvation of 'all Israel' in 11:25-27:

> I do not want you to be ignorant of this mystery, brothers and sisters, so that you may not be conceited: Israel has experienced a hardening in part until the full number of the Gentiles has come in, and in this way all Israel will be saved. As it is written: 'The deliverer will come from

Zion; he will turn godlessness away from Jacob. And this is my covenant with them when I take away their sins'.

A crucial question raised by the promise of eventual salvation for 'all Israel' is whether there is *Sonderweg* (a special way of salvation) for Israel which is different from that provided in the gospel for Gentiles. Put another way: Has God one way of justifying the Gentiles, and another for the Jews? Hvalvik provides a succinct description of the view that there is a *Sonderweg* for the Jews when he summarizes the views of Stendahl and Mussner:

> We can summarize the views of Stendahl and Mussner in three points: The Jews will be saved (1) without acceptance of Jesus as the Messiah (Stendahl), (2) without conversion to the gospel (Mussner) and (3) through the parousia of Christ (Mussner). . . . It should be clear that Stendahl and Mussner do not hold identical views. Nevertheless, they have two things in common: (1) they both tie their view to Rom 11.26f. and (2) they both hold that the Jews have a special way of salvation, a 'Sonderweg'.[255]

However, there are other ways of explaining what Paul means by 'all Israel will be saved' that do not involve asserting that there is a special way of salvation for Israel. For example, Johnson, who sees the metaphor of 'the remnant and the whole' as the dominating theme of Romans 11, argues that the way 'all Israel' is saved at the end of history must be the same as the way the remnant was saved within history, that is, through faith in Jesus Christ. Otherwise Paul's whole argument would fall to the ground.[256]

Hvalvik argues that what is special about Israel's salvation is that she will be saved *as a people*, not that she will be saved *at once* (either at a particular moment in history or at the parousia). He too argues that 11:25-27 cannot be used as a basis for belief in a *Sonderweg* for Israel.[257]

To elucidate what Paul means by the expression 'all Israel', Osborne draws attention to the repeated use of the term in 1–2 Chronicles.[258] He argues that, at the beginning of David's reign, 'all Israel' consisted of military leaders, but after David's consolidation of power, other leaders such as judges, priests, and Levites (but not elders) were included in 'all Israel'. In the period of the divided kingdom the term was used of all those who were loyal to the king and the cult of Yahweh, including those of the northern kingdom who met these criteria. In the books of Chronicles, then, the term

---

255. Reidar Hvalvik, 'A "Sonderweg" for Israel: A Critical Examination of a Current Interpretation of Romans 11.25-27', *JSNT* 38 (1990) 88.

256. Dan G. Johnson, 'The Structure and Meaning of Romans 11', *CBQ* 46 (1984) 98-99, 102-3.

257. Hvalvik, 'A "Sonderweg" for Israel', 87-107.

258. William L. Osborne, 'The Old Testament Background of Paul's "All Israel" in Romans 11:26a', *AsiaJT* 2 (1988) 282-93.

'all Israel' usually means those who attach themselves to the Davidic house and to Yahweh. It is used only in connection with those kings who are loyal to Yahweh, and in theological terms it comes to mean 'the people of God'. This suggests that in Romans 11:26a 'all Israel' is a collective term denoting a majority of the people of Israel who give their loyalty to the Davidic Messiah.[259] In the context of Romans, faith in the Davidic Messiah can only mean faith in Jesus Christ. In this case also, there is no *Sonderweg* for Israel.

However, it must be asked whether the time and means by which Israel will be brought to faith in Jesus Christ constitutes something of a *Sonderweg* for Israel. Mussner, for example, argues that Israel will be saved at the parousia of Christ (11:26-27), but even then it will be by grace, through faith and apart from the law, in a way fully consistent with Paul's teaching on justification.[260] According to this approach, the way Israel is saved is special insofar as it is brought about by the appearance of Christ on the last day, but it is no different from the way in which the Gentiles are saved insofar as it still takes place by grace and through faith, apart from the law.

Others argue that Paul saw the mission to the Jews proceeding alongside the mission to the Gentiles, and the success of the latter would provoke the Jews to jealousy, and so cause them to repent. These things would occur concurrently and in the present time,[261] so that by the time the full number of the Gentiles had been brought in, it would be discovered that all the elect of Israel would also have been gathered into the people of God, and in this manner all Israel will be saved.[262] According to this approach, there is, clearly, no *Sonderweg* for Israel.

Baxter and Ziesler seek to shed some light on the matter by appealing to the ancient practice of arboriculture. They argue that Paul was aware of the practice of grafting scions of a wild olive onto an aged or diseased olive tree, to restore the latter to health and fruit bearing.[263] The apostle used this practice to illustrate the way God would restore Israel. He would incorporate believing Gentiles into the people of God, and the people of Israel would then recognize that God was gathering the elect and that they themselves were not being included. 'This would make them repent, be forgiven, and return to being true Israel'. Baxter and Ziesler argue that it is the

259. Osborne, 'The Old Testament Background of Paul's "All Israel"', 287.

260. Franz Mussner, 'Heil für alle: Der Grundgedanke des Römerbriefs', *Kairos* 23 (1981) 207-14.

261. D. Judant, 'A propos de la destinée d'Israel: Remarques concernant un verset de l'épître aux Romains XI,31', *Divinitas* 23 (1979) 108-125, claims that no text-critical or theological argument can justify the removal of the word 'now' (*nyn*) from the phrase, 'in order that they too may now receive mercy' (*hina kai autoi nyn eleēthōsin*) in 11:31. He argues that the mercy of God in 11:30-31 refers to faith in Christ; so the entrance of the Jews into the church should take place now.

262. So, e.g., D. W. B. Robinson, 'The Salvation of Israel in Romans 9–11', *RTR* 26 (1967) 94-96; Wright, *The Climax of the Covenant*, 249-50.

263. Baxter and Ziesler, 'Paul and Arboriculture', 25-32.

ingrafting of the Gentiles, rather than the Gentiles themselves, that will bring about the restoration of Israel: 'In the overall divine strategy, the ingrafting of Gentile scions is a crucial and necessary intermediate stage' leading to the salvation of 'all Israel'.[264] Such a view implies that there is no *Sonderweg* for Israel. She will be brought to repentance by seeing the Gentiles repent, and from this we may infer that 'all Israel' must come to salvation in the same way.

The one thing common to most of these various approaches to the salvation of 'all Israel' is their denial that God has provided a *Sonderweg* for Israel, a means of salvation different from that provided in the gospel for Gentiles (i.e., a salvation by grace through faith in Christ apart from the works of the law). That this common conviction is true to Paul's own views is confirmed by the way he concludes his argument in 11:28-32. He acknowledges that as far as the gospel is concerned the Jews are the enemies of God, but asserts that as far as election is concerned they are beloved on account of the patriarchs, God's gifts and calling being irrevocable. And because of their election, those who are the enemies of the gospel will, through the mercy shown to the Gentiles, themselves receive mercy. As Paul has previously indicated, this will occur as the Jews, seeing the Gentiles repenting and being gathered into the elect while they themselves are presently excluded, will also be brought to repentance and faith in Jesus Christ. In this way God, having bound both Jew and Gentile over to disobedience, will have mercy on Jew and Gentile alike.

While there are no distinctions between Jews and Gentiles in the matter of salvation (no *Sonderweg* for Israel), that does not negate Israel's special place in the purposes of God. In 11:17-24 Paul reminds Gentile believers that the blessings they enjoy are derived from the root of Israel (the patriarchs/Abraham) to which they have been joined. He also reminds them that God is able to graft Israelites back in 'if they do not persist in unbelief' (11:23). There is, therefore, no place for Gentile Christian hubris.

(iv) Doxology, 11:33-36

[33]*Oh, the depth of the riches of the wisdom and knowledge of God! How unsearchable his judgments, and his paths beyond tracing out!* [34]*'Who has known the mind of the Lord? Or who has been his counselor?'* [35]*'Who has ever given to God, that God should repay them?'* [36]*For from him and through him and for him are all things. To him be the glory forever! Amen.*

Paul brings the exposition and defense of his gospel, including his treatment of the place of Israel in the purposes of God, to a grand conclusion with an ascription of praise to God. He has shown that God treats Jews

---

264. Baxter and Ziesler, 'Paul and Arboriculture', 28.

and Gentiles alike in the matters of sin and judgment (1:18–3:20), and that he offers salvation freely to them both and without reference to the law. God does this on the basis of what he did for them through Jesus Christ, whom he set forward as the atoning sacrifice for their sins, thus showing not only his great love for humanity but also his justice in justifying sinners who put their faith in his Son (3:21–5:21). Paul has shown that this law-free gospel does not lead to moral anarchy, as some have suggested (3:8; 6:1-23), nor does it imply that the law itself is the problem; in fact, the law-free gospel actually enables people to fulfill the 'just requirement of the law' (7:1–8:17). He has also shown that his gospel does not negate the place of Israel in the purposes of God, nor does it imply that God's word has failed or that he has rejected the Jewish people. In so doing, he spells out the scope of God's dealings with Israel and the Gentiles, bringing blessing to the Gentiles out of the disobedience of the Jews, and in turn bringing blessing to the Jews by blessing the Gentiles (9:1–11:36). Paul's response to all this is a great doxology in which he celebrates the depth of the wisdom and knowledge of God, the one from whom, through whom, and to whom are all things, the one who is worthy of eternal praise and glory.

11:33 Paul's doxology begins: *Oh, the depth of the riches of the wisdom and knowledge of God!* (lit. 'O [the] depth of [the] riches and wisdom and knowledge of God'). Paul celebrates three (not two, as implied by the NIV translation) characteristics of God revealed in his saving action in Christ for all people. The first is the depth of his 'riches'. This is one of only two instances in which Paul speaks of divine riches in an absolute sense.[265] The other is found in Ephesians 3:8, where he refers to the grace given to him to preach 'the boundless riches of Christ'. In that context the 'boundless riches' he preaches is the mystery, hidden for ages past and now made known — 'that through the gospel the Gentiles are heirs together with Israel, members together of one body, and sharers together in the promise in Christ Jesus' (Eph 3:6). It is noteworthy that Paul's references to the 'riches . . . of God' in 11:33 and to the 'boundless riches of Christ' in Ephesians 3:8 denote the riches of divine grace in bringing salvation to both Jews and Gentiles.

The second characteristic of God that Paul celebrates is his 'wisdom'. When Paul speaks of the wisdom of God elsewhere, he says that it is found in Jesus Christ: he is the wisdom of God (1 Cor 1:24, 30), and in him are hidden the treasures of God's wisdom (Col 2:3). He also affirms that the wisdom of God is seen in his plan to bring salvation through the cross of Christ (1 Cor 2:6-7), and that this wisdom will be made known through the church 'to rulers and authorities in the heavenly realms' (Eph 3:10). This wisdom of God is expressed in the great mystery revealed — God is making

---

265. Elsewhere he uses 'riches' *(ploutos)* to qualify another attribute of God, as in 'the riches of his kindness' (2:4), 'the riches of his glory' (9:23; Eph 3:16; Phil 4:19), and 'the riches of his grace' (Eph 1:7; 2:7).

Gentiles fellow heirs with the Jews of the promises of God fulfilled in Christ Jesus (Eph 3:4-6).

The third characteristic of God celebrated by Paul is his 'knowledge'. Like the wisdom of God, the knowledge of God, Paul says, is hidden in Christ (Col 2:3). In Colossians 2:3 the expression 'wisdom and knowledge', is a hendiadys, one idea expressed by using two different words. We may say that for Paul the riches, wisdom, and knowledge of God are all seen in his plan to bring salvation to Jews and Gentiles alike through the work of Christ.

Continuing to extol God's riches, wisdom, and knowledge, Paul exclaims: *How unsearchable his judgments, and his paths beyond tracing out!* The two words translated 'unsearchable' and 'beyond tracing out' are virtual synonyms, the first found only here in the NT and not at all in the LXX, the second found also in Ephesians 3:8 ('the *boundless* riches of Christ'), Job 5:9; 9:10 ('He performs wonders that *cannot be fathomed*'), and the Prayer of Manasseh 6 ('immeasurable and *unsearchable* is your promised mercy'). God's great plan of salvation is something that no one could have conceived. No one would have anticipated that God would effect salvation through the death of his Son on a cross. No one would have anticipated that God would bring salvation to Gentiles through the disobedience of Israel, or that the blessings enjoyed by Gentiles would lead to salvation for Israel.[266]

11:34-35   To underline the unsearchable nature of God's wisdom Paul cites two texts from the OT. The first is taken from Isaiah 40:13 LXX, which it follows closely but not exactly: '[For] *who has known the mind of the Lord? Or who has been his counselor?'* Isaiah 40 announces the good tidings of the return of the exiles from Babylon to Jerusalem (Isa 40:1-11), then declares the power and greatness of the Lord (Isa 40:12-31). To underline this the prophet asks:

> Who has measured the waters in the hollow of his hand, or with the breadth of his hand marked off the heavens? Who has held the dust of the earth in a basket, or weighed the mountains on the scales and the hills in a balance? *Who can fathom the Spirit of the* LORD, *or instruct the* LORD *as his counselor?* Whom did the LORD consult to enlighten him, and who taught him the right way? Who was it that taught him knowledge, or showed him the path of understanding? (Isa 40:12-14, italics added)

Paul has taken his first scriptural quotation from this passage to emphasize the peerless nature of the wisdom of God, the wisdom the apostle sees revealed supremely in God's plan of salvation for both Jews and Gentiles and effected through Christ. God needed no counselor when he determined how he would bring salvation to a fallen humanity.

---

266. Cf. Jewett, *Romans*, 718.

The second text Paul cites is Job 41:11: *'Who has ever given to God, that God should repay them?'*[267] This is part of the Lord's response to Job's complaints (Job 38–41) in which he questions Job and demonstrates the smallness of Job's wisdom compared to the vastness of the Lord's wisdom. In this context the Lord asks Job: 'Who has a claim against me that I must pay? Everything under heaven belongs to me' (Job 41:11). It would seem that Paul cites this text to show that God's great salvation plan is implemented, not because he is under any obligation towards humanity, as if he has to repay them. Rather, he implements it, as Paul has insisted, as a matter of sheer grace (cf. 3:24; 4:4-8; 11:6; Eph 2:8).

11:36 In this verse Paul highlights the fact that God is the primary cause and sole source of all things: *For from him and through him and to him are all things.* The apostle makes similar statements in two other places. In the first, 1 Corinthians 8:6, he says: 'Yet for us there is but one God, the Father, from whom all things came and for whom we live; and there is but one Lord, Jesus Christ, through whom all things came and through whom we live'. In the second place, Colossians 1:16, he adds: 'For in him [Christ] all things were created: things in heaven and on earth, visible and invisible, whether thrones or powers or rulers or authorities; all things have been created through him and for him'. While 11:36 bears strong similarities to both these texts, it is clear from the context that Paul has in mind the fact that God is the sole and ultimate source of the blessings of salvation made available through Christ to Jews and Gentiles.

In 11:36b we come to the doxology proper: *To him be the glory forever! Amen.* This is one of seven similar doxologies in Paul's letters, each of which expresses the desire that glory be given to God forever and ever (11:36b; 16:27; Gal 1:5; Eph 3:21; Phil 4:20; 1 Tim 1:17; 2 Tim 4:18). It is interesting to note how Paul believes human beings can bring glory to God: Abraham gave glory to God by his unwavering faith in the promise of God (4:20). Believers bring glory to God by accepting one another as Christ accepted them (15:7); by praising God 'with one heart and mouth' (15:6); by praising God for his mercy (15:9); by sexual purity (1 Cor 6:20); by abstaining from actions that will cause offense to others (1 Cor 10:31); by giving thanks to God for his blessings (2 Cor 4:15); by contributing to fellow believers in need (2 Cor 8:19); by praising God for the generosity of his people (2 Cor 9:13); by being 'filled with the fruit of righteousness' (Phil 1:11); by praising God for the conversion of Paul the persecutor of the churches (Gal 1:24); and by confessing that Jesus Christ is Lord (Phil 2:11). From all this it is evident that one of the driving concerns of the apostle was to bring glory to God.

---

267. Atypically, Paul's quotation (*ē tis proedōken autō, kai antapodothēsetai autō*, lit. 'or who has given to him, and he will repay him?') is not derived from the LXX (*ē tis antistēsetai moi kai hypomenei*, 'or who has opposed me, and he will remain?'), but follows, though not exactly, the Hebrew text ('Who has a claim against me that I must pay?' Job 41:3, E.T. 41:11).

III. THE ETHICAL OUTWORKING
OF THE GOSPEL, 12:1–15:13

After the extended theological exposition and defense of his gospel (1:18–11:36) with its secondary purpose of providing a basis for the resolution of problems between Jewish and Gentile believers in Rome, Paul appeals to his audience to live in the light of this gospel, and spells out its ethical implications in 12:1–15:13. He begins by setting down the basis of his ethical appeal (12:1-2), then applies this to the way the Roman believers relate to one another and the proper employment of the gifts God has given (12:3-13); their relations with one another and with outsiders (12:14-21); their relation to the state (13:1-7); their fulfillment of the law by love (13:8-14); and relationships between the 'weak' and the 'strong' (14:1–15:13).[1]

This ethical section includes the sort of exhortations Paul gave to all his churches, but it also includes some that are specific to the Roman audience. Among the latter are his instructions about civil obedience required of believers as citizens of the empire, and exhortations for both those who eat and those who refrain from eating meat. Moiser believes that these issues arose following the separation of church and synagogue, and needed to be resolved so that Paul's mission to Spain would not be jeopardized.[2] Smiga argues that just as 1:18–11:36 is an epistolary presentation of the gospel, so 12:1–15:13 is epistolary encouragement, and these fulfill in part the apostle's desire to preach the gospel in Rome and provide encouragement for the believers there (cf. 1:12, 15).[3] There is an important connection between the long theological presentation of the gospel in 1:18–11:36 and the ethical section that follows in 12:1–15:13: the ethical section expounds important aspects of the obedience of faith required by the gospel. This obedience, as Cranfield points out, is not general and abstract, but is concrete and must be expressed in both thought and action.[4]

A. The Basis of Paul's Ethical Appeal, 12:1-2

> [1]*Therefore, I urge you, brothers and sisters, in view of God's mercy, to offer your bodies as a living sacrifice, holy and pleasing to God — this is your*

1. Kuo-Wei Peng, *Hate the Evil, Hold Fast to the Good: Structuring Romans 12:1–15:1* (LNTS 300; London/New York: T&T Clark, 2006), 196-98, offers an analysis of the structure of 12:1–15:13, the broad outline of which is as follows: 12:1-8: two prerequisites for the discernment of the will of God (12:1-2: unity in devotion; 12:3-8: diversity in function); 12:9–13:10: the will of God to be discerned as genuine love; 13:11-14: eschatological motivation: discerning the time; 14:1–15:13: the will of God to be discerned as genuine love (continued): hate what is evil in the community life among Christians.

2. Jeremy Moiser, 'Rethinking Romans 12-15', *NTS* 36 (1990) 575-79, 582.

3. George Smiga, 'Romans 12:1-2 and 15:30-32 and the Occasion of the Letter to the Romans', *CBQ* 53 (1991) 266.

4. Cf. Cranfield, *Romans*, II, 594.

true and proper worship. [2]*Do not conform to the pattern of this world, but be transformed by the renewing of your mind. Then you will be able to test and approve what God's will is — his good, pleasing and perfect will.*

Paul begins by setting down the basis of his ethical appeal: God's mercy. The appeal itself has two parts. The first is a call that his audience offer themselves to God (12:1), and the second is an appeal that they not be conformed to the world (12:2).

12:1 The apostle commences to spell out the ethical implications of the gospel with the exhortation: *Therefore, I urge you, brothers and sisters, in view of God's mercy, to offer your bodies as a living sacrifice, holy and pleasing to God.* Paul's 'therefore' signals that his appeal is based on what has preceded, that is, the exposition and defense of his gospel in 1:18–11:36. In 11:32 the apostle said that 'God has bound everyone over to disobedience so that he may have mercy on them all', and his appeal is made 'in view of God's mercy', mercy encapsulated in the gospel. The number of times Paul refers to God's mercy in his letters reveals how important a theme it was for him. In Romans Paul's references to God's mercy relate to God's sovereign right to show mercy to whomever he will (9:15-16, 18, 23), and God's plan that Israel should receive mercy as a result of his mercy shown to Gentiles (11:30-32; cf. 15:9). Elsewhere in his writings Paul speaks of the mercy of God by which he himself has been made a minister of the gospel (1 Cor 7:25; 2 Cor 4:1; 1 Tim 1:13, 16), the mercy of God shown to those who believe in Christ (12:1; 15:9; Gal 6:16; Phil 2:27), the mercy of God bringing salvation (Eph 2:4-5; Tit 3:5), the mercy of God he invokes upon those who have helped him (2 Tim 1:16, 18) and upon those to whom he addressed letters (1 Tim 1:2; 2 Tim 1:2), and finally of God as 'the Father of compassion/mercy' (2 Cor 1:3).

The appeal Paul makes to his audience in the light of God's mercy is 'to offer your bodies as a living sacrifice, holy and pleasing to God'. The verb 'to offer' has already been used by Paul in 6:13, 16, and 19 when urging his audience not to 'offer' the parts of their bodies to sin, as instruments of unrighteousness, but rather to 'offer' them as instruments of righteousness to God. When Paul exhorts his audience to offer their 'bodies' as living sacrifices, the term is to be understood as their whole selves, as Wright describes it, 'the complete person seen from one point of view: the point of view in which the human being lives as a physical object within space and time'.[1]

When Paul refers to the offering of believers as 'a living sacrifice, holy

---

1. Wright, 'Romans', 704. Cf. Cranfield, *Romans,* II, 598-99, who cites Calvin: 'By *bodies* he means not only our skin and bones, but the totality of which we are composed'. . . . Cf. also Käsemann, *Romans,* 327: '*sōma* ['body'] should not be flattened to a cipher for the person. . . . Nor is it merely the organ of moral self-confirmation. . . . It is our being in relation to the world. . . .' Similarly Barrett, *Romans,* 231; Byrne, *Romans,* 362-63. Jewett, *Romans,* 729, comments: 'In contrast to 8:23 where the singular *sōma* refers to the collective body of believers, here the plural *ta sōmata hymōn* clearly refers to "your bodies", each of which is to be sacrificed individually'.

and pleasing to God', he appears to be alluding to instructions concerning sacrifices in the OT. When the animals were presented at the tabernacle/ temple, they were still living,[2] and had to be 'holy' (Lev 6:25; 7:1; 22:3, 15) and 'acceptable to God' (Lev 1:3; 22:19, 20). We might add that Paul employs the idea of a 'living sacrifice' deliberately because the sacrifice he has in mind is not martyrdom, but rather lives that are pleasing to God.

The offering of believers to God, Paul says, is to be 'holy and pleasing to God'. In this context 'holy and pleasing' functions as a hendiadys, a figure of speech expressing one idea with two related words. To be holy is to be pleasing to God. Holiness and acceptability to God are matters the apostle refers to repeatedly elsewhere. In 15:16 he says that his ministry of the gospel is intended to make the offering of the Gentiles 'acceptable to God, sanctified [i.e., made holy] by the Holy Spirit'. In 1 Corinthians 7:34 he depicts single female believers as those who are 'anxious about the affairs of the Lord, so that they may be holy in body and spirit' (NRSV).[3]

Paul says of the offering of believers' bodies a living sacrifice, holy and pleasing to God: *this is your true and proper worship* (NRSV: 'which is your spiritual worship'). The word translated here as 'worship' is found in only one other place in Paul's letters, in 9:4, where he lists [temple] worship as one of the great privileges enjoyed by Israel. It is found three times elsewhere in the NT and several times in the LXX.[4] In virtually all of these

---

2. Cf. Cranfield, *Romans*, II, 600. Nobuyoshi Kiuchi, 'Living like the Azazel-Goat in Romans 12:1b', *TynBul* 57 (2006) 258-59, argues that the counterpart to Paul's 'living sacrifice' is to be found in the *Azazel*-goat of Lev 16:10 ('But the goat chosen by lot as the scapegoat [*Azazel*] shall be presented alive before the LORD to be used for making atonement by sending it into the desert as a scapegoat [*Azazel*]'). In this case the scapegoat *(Azazel)* is presented 'alive' and carries the people's guilt away from the presence of the Lord. Kiuchi adds: 'While in the burnt offering the offerer dedicates himself completely but not for other people, the *Azazel*-goat is sent away into the wilderness, bearing the guilt of *others*. It is unclear how far this thought was in Paul's mind when he wrote Romans 12:1. But in view of the relationship between the two sacrifices in Leviticus, he may well be saying that the believer is encouraged to dedicate himself not just for himself, but for others too'.

3. Paul mentions a number of actions that are 'pleasing' *(euarestos)* to God: limiting one's freedom in relation to what is eaten out of consideration for fellow believers who might be distressed by an insensitive insistence upon one's freedom in Christ (14:14-18); providing financial support for those (in this instance Paul) who are engaged in the ministry of the gospel (Phil 4:15-18); and, if children, obeying one's parents (Col 3:20).

4. Elsewhere in the NT the word translated 'worship' *(latreia)* is found John 16:2, where Jesus warns his disciples that those who kill them will think they are offering worship to God; in Heb 9:1 in connection with regulations for worship, and in Heb 9:6 in connection with the ministry *(latreia)* of the priests in the tabernacle. It occurs several times in the LXX, where it denotes the ceremony *(latreia)* that the Israelites had to observe when they entered the promised land (Exod 12:25-26; 13:5), the worship to be carried out in the tabernacle/temple (Josh 22:27; 1 Chron 28:13), the idolatrous worship demanded of Israelites during the reign of the Seleucid king, Antiochus IV (1 Macc 1:43), the religion *(latreia)* of the ancestors abandoned by many of other nations when obeying Antiochus IV (1 Macc 2:19), and the religion *(latreia)* Mattathias and his followers refused to abandon despite Antiochus IV's command (1 Macc 2:22).

places it is used in connection with religious worship,[5] and so we should understand Paul to be saying here that believers' offering of their bodies as living sacrifices constitutes their worship of God. It is noteworthy that while the apostle uses the terminology of cultic worship, what he means by worship has to do with the way people live rather than their activities in a cultic setting.

Paul describes the self-offering of believers as their 'true and proper worship' (NRSV: 'spiritual act of worship'), in which 'spiritual' translates a word *(logikos)* that is relatively rare in the NT. It is found only here and in 1 Peter 2:2, and not at all in the LXX.[6] However, it was a favorite expression of ancient philosophers from the time of Aristotle, and is found often in the writings of Philo, Justin, Tatian, and Athenagoras, where it carries the idea of 'being carefully thought through' or 'thoughtful'.[7] Epictetus's famous statement is often quoted: 'If, indeed, I were a nightingale, I should be singing as a nightingale; if a swan, as a swan: But as it is, I am a rational [*logikos*] being, therefore I must be singing hymns of praise to God . . . and I exhort you to join me in this same song' *(Diatr.* 1.16.20-21). If we were to allow these things to guide us, we would say that 'spiritual' worship in 12:1 means 'thoughtful' service. Such a view is supported by the fact that in the next verse Paul goes on to speak of the renewing of the *mind* so as to 'test and approve what God's will is'.[8]

Byrne notes correctly that such worship is not to be thought of 'in the sense of being opposed to the physical, but in the sense . . . of proceeding from that which is distinctive of human beings as rational, reflective creatures whose highest powers are engaged in the homage they bring to their Creator'. . . .[9] Cranfield describes this worship as 'intelligent understanding worship, that is, worship which is consonant with the truth of the gospel, . . . indeed nothing less than the offering of one's whole self in the course of one's concrete living, in one's inward thought, feelings and aspirations, but also in one's words and deeds'.[10]

12:2 After urging his audience to offer their bodies to God as a 'spiritual act of worship', Paul adds, [*and*] *do not conform to the pattern of this*

---

5. There is one other occurrence of *latreia* in the LXX — the only instance of it carrying a different meaning: 'The entire race was to be registered individually, not for the hard labour *(latreian)* that has been briefly mentioned before' (3 Macc 4:14).

6. In 1 Pet 2:2 the NIV also translates *logikos* as 'spiritual' — 'Like newborn babies, crave pure spiritual [*logikon*] milk' — where 'it is to be borne in mind that *logikos* means *spiritual* not only in the sense of *pneumatikos,* but also in contrast to "literal", w. the mng. "metaphorical"' (BAGD, *ad loc.*).

7. BAGD, *ad loc.*

8. Barrett, *Romans,* 231, says: 'The Hellenistic parallels do not prove that Paul's thought was based on Stoic material. The Old Testament itself knows inward as well as material sacrifice (e.g. Ps. li.17)'.

9. Byrne, *Romans,* 363. Similarly, Fitzmyer, *Romans,* 640; Moo, *Romans,* 753.

10. Cranfield, *Romans,* II, 605. Similarly, David Peterson, 'Worship and Ethics in Romans 12', *TynBul* 44 (1993) 275.

world (lit. 'and do not be conformed to this age'). The NIV omits 'and', adds 'the pattern of', and substitutes 'this world' for the more literal sense, 'this age'. By omitting 'and' the NIV construes 12:2 as a new sentence, thus obscuring the fact that 12:2 is a continuation of the sentence in 12:1 and that as such it provides the clue to the sort of worship the apostle had in mind.

Stated negatively, then, spiritual worship involves a refusal to be conformed to this age.[11] The verb translated 'conform' means 'to be conformed to' or 'guided by'.[12] It is found elsewhere in the NT only in 1 Peter 1:14 ('As obedient children, do not conform to the evil desires you had when you lived in ignorance'), where it carries a meaning similar to that in 12:2. In the case of 12:2 conformity to the values of this (evil) age is meant, while in the case of 1 Peter 1:14 conformity to the sort of evil desires that predominated prior to conversion is intended. Those who render spiritual worship to God resist all such pressures to conform.

Stated positively, spiritual worship of God involves transformation. Paul urges his audience: *be transformed by the renewing of your*[13] *mind*. The use of the passive imperative, 'be transformed',[14] suggests both that the transformation is effected by God, and that believers must cooperate in order that it take place.[15] The verb 'to transform' is found only four times in the NT, twice in the Gospels referring to Jesus' transfiguration (Matt 17:2; Mark 9:2) and twice in Paul's letters, and on both latter occasions it refers to the transformation of believers (12:2; 2 Cor 3:18). In the case of 2 Corinthians 3:18 believers are progressively transformed into the likeness of Christ because the veil over their minds has been removed, enabling them to see the glory of Christ in the Scriptures (cf. 2 Cor 4:3-4).

---

11. J. B. Phillips's famous paraphrase of this expression is: 'don't let the world around you squeeze you into its own mould' (*The New Testament in Modern English* [London: Geoffrey Bles, 1960], 332).

12. BAGD, *ad loc.*

13. The word 'your' *(hymōn)* is missing from the earlier and better manuscripts, but included in the Textus Receptus.

14. Daniel B. Wallace, *Greek Grammar beyond the Basics: An Exegetical Syntax of the New Testament* (Grand Rapids: Zondervan, 1996), 440-41, classifies *metamorphousthe* ('be transformed') as a causative/permissive passive that implies consent, permission, or cause of the action. Peterson, 'Worship and Ethics in Romans 12', 282, comments: 'There is now a strong consensus of opinion that the two verbs *syschēmatizesthe* ('be conformed') and *metamorphousthe* ('be transformed') are more or less synonymous in Koine Greek. However, there is a difference of emphasis in the relevant clauses of Rom 12:2. The first warns against transformation according to the pattern of 'this world/age' *(tō aiōni toutō)* . . . the second verb *(metamorphousthe)* suggests the transforming work of God, through his Spirit in the life of believers (cf. Rom 8:4; 8:13-14; 2 Cor 3:18)'.

15. Cranfield, *Romans*, II, 607, comments: 'The use of the passive imperative *metamorphousthe* is consonant with the truth that, while this transformation is not the Christian's own doing but the work of the Holy Spirit, they nevertheless have a real responsibility in the matter — to let themselves be transformed, to respond to the leading and pressure of God's Spirit. We may bring out the force of the tense by translating: "stop allowing yourselves to be conformed . . . continue to let yourselves to be transformed"' . . . .

The word translated 'mind' in 12:2 is capable of conveying various nuances of meaning: the faculty of intellectual perception (intellect), the way of thinking (attitude), or the result of thinking (thought, opinion, decree).[16] Paul's exhortation in 12:2 is that his audience's way of thinking (and the thoughts they have as a result) ought not to be influenced by the world's way of thinking but rather be transformed by the renewal of their minds. The word translated 'renewal' is found here for the first time in Greek literature.[17] Elsewhere in the NT it is found only in Titus 3:5b: 'He saved us through the washing of rebirth and renewal by the Holy Spirit'. Paul's meaning here in 12:2 would appear to be that believers are to allow their way of thinking to be renewed by the Spirit of God in the light of the gospel. This will mean the reversal of the effects of the fall that resulted in humanity being handed over by God to a 'depraved mind' (1:28).

In this context Paul does not explain how the renewal of the mind takes place. However, in Ephesians 4:21-24 he urges his audience: 'be made new in the attitude of your minds' in accordance with 'the truth that is in Jesus'. Linking this with what the apostle says in 2 Corinthians 3:18 and 4:3-4 about believers being transformed as the veil is lifted from their minds to see the glory of Christ in the Scriptures, we may conclude that Paul understood the renewal of the mind to take place as people encountered and embraced the teaching of Scripture. Cranfield correctly notes that what Paul says implies that the mind, 'so far from being an unfallen element of human nature, needs to be renewed, if it is to be able to recognize and embrace the will of God'.[18]

Paul describes the purpose of transformation by the renewing of the mind in 12:2b: *Then you will be able to test and approve what God's will is*. The NIV renders this as the beginning of a new sentence, but in fact it is a dependent purpose clause, correctly rendered by the NRSV as follows: '(be transformed by the renewing of your minds) so that you may discern what is the will of God'. . . . The NIV's translation, 'test and approve', brings out well the meaning of the original Greek verb. It is one that the apostle uses many times — occasionally where it is said that God tests/approves the works of men and women (1 Cor 3:13; 1 Thess 2:4), but more often where believers are told to exercise their discretion in testing and approving people and behavior (2:18; 14:22; 1 Cor 11:28; 16:3; 2 Cor 8:8, 22; 13:5; Gal 6:4; Phil 1:10; 1 Tim 3:10), and to test/approve the validity or otherwise of prophecies (1 Thess 5:21). Jewett suggests that when Paul speaks of testing and approving what is the will of God, the apostle has in mind 'group decision making' rather than individual discernment. He states, 'it is clear that Paul understands the early Christian community in Rome as needing to weigh alternatives in the light of the "renewed mind" given by Christ —

16. BAGD, *nous*.
17. Cf. Jewett, *Romans*, 733.
18. Cranfield, *Romans*, II, 609.

and also in the light of this letter, which sets forth an agenda of the divine will to resolve disputes and cooperate in a missionary venture of great significance'.[19]

It is only in 12:2 that Paul speaks of testing and approving 'what God's will is'. Paul speaks often about God's will. In his letters he often introduces himself as an apostle by the will of God (1 Cor 1:1; 2 Cor 1:1; Eph 1:1; Col 1:1; 2 Tim 1:1). He understands that it is only by the will of God that he is able to fulfill his plans (1:10; 15:32). He also specifies certain actions of believers that are according to the will of God: generous giving (2 Cor 8:5); the obedience of slaves to their masters (Eph 6:6); the avoidance of sexual immorality (1 Thess 4:3); and giving thanks to God in all circumstances (1 Thess 5:18). Paul's point here in 12:2 appears to be that the renewing of the mind (by being exposed to and embracing the teaching of the Scriptures) will enable believers to test for themselves and approve what God expects of them. Wright comments: 'The Christian is not meant to rely simply on lists of ethical commands, but to be able to discern (NRSV), to test and approve (NIV), what God's will is — God's will, it seems, primarily for general ethical conduct but also, perhaps, for specific decisions and occasions; Paul's vision of living sacrifice, and mind renewed, generates a picture of Christian behavior in which rules matter but are not the driving force, in which thought and reflection matter but without reducing ethics to purely situational decisions'.[20]

Paul describes the will of God as *his good, pleasing and perfect will.* It is axiomatic that the will of God is both 'good' and 'perfect', but in what sense and to whom is it 'pleasing'? Paul employs the word 'pleasing' regularly in his letters (12:1, 2; 14:18; 2 Cor 5:9; Eph 5:10; Phil 4:18; Col 3:20; Tit 2:9) to refer to what is pleasing to God;[21] therefore, we conclude that he is using it in this sense here also. He is exhorting his audience, then, to be transformed by the renewing of their minds so that they may practice what is good, perfect, and pleasing to God. Paul certainly made it the aim of his life to be pleasing to God (2 Cor 5:9).

B. The Believers' Relationships with Others, 12:3-21

This passage comprises prescriptions for Christian living. They may be generic in nature, the sort of obligations Paul believed were applicable to all believers, but they may also include some exhortations particularly applicable to the Roman churches, for example, the emphasis on personal rela-

---

19. Jewett, *Romans,* 734. Byrne, *Romans,* 364, also says that 'the casting of the appeal in the second person plural suggests that communal rather than individual discernment is principally in view'.

20. Wright, 'Romans', 705-6.

21. The one exception is Tit 2:9, where the apostle speaks of the obligation of slaves to try to be pleasing to their masters.

tionships (Jew-Gentile relationships were an issue in the Roman churches); and the need to abstain from returning evil for evil (believers in Rome could well be subject to hostility from outsiders). The passage may be analyzed as follows: using different gifts for the benefit of the Christian community (12:3-8); enhancing relationships within the Christian community (12:9-13); strengthening relationships without and within the Christian community (12:14-16); and responding to hostile people and their hostile acts (12:17-21).

1. Using Different Gifts for the Benefit of the Christian Community, 12:3-8

> [3]*For by the grace given me I say to every one of you: Do not think of yourself more highly than you ought, but rather think of yourself with sober judgment, in accordance with the faith God has distributed to each of you.* [4]*For just as each of us has one body with many members, and these members do not all have the same function,* [5]*so in Christ we, though many, form one body, and each member belongs to all the others.* [6]*We have different gifts, according to the grace given to each of us. If your gift is prophesying, then prophesy in accordance with your faith;* [7]*if it is serving, then serve; if it is teaching, then teach;* [8]*if it is to encourage, then give encouragement; if it is giving, then give generously; if it is to lead, do it diligently; if it is to show mercy, do it cheerfully.*

Having set down the basis of his ethical appeal in 12:1-2, Paul begins to spell out what this means in practice (the connection of 12:3-8 with 12:1-2 is indicated by the preposition 'for' with which 12:3 opens). In 12:3-8 he explains how this applies to the way members of his audience should relate to one another and employ the gifts God gives (12:3-13). Similar instructions are found in 1 Corinthians 12.

12:3 Paul prefaces his practical instructions with the words: *For by the grace given me I say to every one of you.* . . . Again and again the apostle refers to the grace of God given to him for the exercise of his ministry (cf. 1:5; 15:15; 1 Cor 3:10; Gal 2:9; Eph 3:2, 7, 8), and here, in particular, to the grace given to him to instruct fellow believers. In this case what he says to 'every one' of the members of the Roman churches (perhaps reflecting an awareness of tensions among them) is: *Do not think of yourself more highly than you ought, but rather think of yourself with sober judgment.* Paul engages in a play on words here by employing the verb 'to think' and its cognates.[1] Jewett notes: 'There are frequent examples of this particular wordplay in Greek lit-

---

1. Translated literally, it reads: 'Do not think more highly *(mē hyperphronein)* than what it is necessary to think *(phronein)* but think *(phronein)* in order to think soberly *(eis to sōphronein)*'.

erature, so that Paul's formulation would have evoked delight and immediate comprehension in his hearers'.[2]

While the actual word translated 'to think too highly of oneself' is found only here in Paul's writings (and in fact only here in the NT), the apostle does elsewhere warn against this sort of attitude. In 11:20-21 he told his Gentile Christian audience not to look down upon unbelieving Jews: 'They were broken off because of unbelief, and you stand by faith. Do not be arrogant, but tremble. For if God did not spare the natural branches, he will not spare you either', and in 12:16 he says to them, 'Live in harmony with one another. Do not be proud, but be willing to associate with people of low position. Do not be conceited'. Rather than thinking too highly of themselves, Paul tells his audience: 'think of yourself with sober judgment'. In other contexts 'to think with sober judgment' carries the idea of being in one's right mind (2 Cor 5:13; Mark 5:15; Luke 8:35) or self-controlled (Tit 2:6; 1 Pet 4:7). Here in 12:3, where it stands in contrast to 'thinking too highly of oneself', it means, as the NIV translation suggests, to exercise sober judgment in relation to oneself. This, Paul goes on to say, will mean thinking of oneself *in accordance with the faith God has distributed to each of you* (lit. 'as God has distributed a measure of faith to each of you'). Exactly what the apostle means by 'a measure of faith' has been interpreted in different ways.

One view is that it is to be related to the different gifts of ministry believers receive from God and their faith in exercising these. This view is consistent with the way Paul uses the word 'measure' elsewhere in connection with what God assigns to particular people. Thus in 2 Corinthians 10:13 Paul speaks of the 'measure' of the field for missionary endeavor God assigned (lit. 'measured') to him (cf. Gal 2:7-9), and in Ephesians 4:7 he speaks of the grace given to each believer 'according to the measure of Christ's gift' (NRSV), which he then interprets in terms of gifts of ministry (Eph 4:8-13). When, here in 12:3, Paul speaks of the 'measure of faith' God has given to believers, he is probably also thinking in terms of gifts for ministry, for this is what the apostle speaks of in the following verses (12:4-8).[3]

Another view is that 'the measure of faith' refers not to some special form of faith given to different individuals, but to basic Christian faith which all believers have in the same 'measure'. Moo, for example, asserts: '"Measure of faith", then, should be compared in this paragraph not to the many different "gifts" that God distributes to believers, but to the one com-

---

2. Jewett, *Romans*, 739.

3. So, e.g., Witherington, *Romans*, 288. Byrne, *Romans*, 371, says: 'It is preferable, on the basis esp. of 1 Cor 7:17 (*ei mē hekastō hos emerisen ho kyrios*), to see an allusion here to Paul's conviction that God gives a particular gift (lit. "allots a measure" [*emerisen metron*]) to each person who comes to faith at the moment of their coming to faith. . . . This gift — and, notably, the effectiveness or not, with which the person exercises the gift — is the true basis for self-judgment'.

mon grace from which they stem (v. 6). It is that faith which believers have in common as fellow members of the body of Christ that Paul here highlights as the standard against which each of us is to estimate himself'.[4] Dunn comments on 'faith' in a way that preserves both the commonality of the basic faith of all believers and the differing gifts they exercise: 'This trust, which is the common denominator of all Christians (= believers), Paul clearly sees as variable in different believers. . . . Here there is no sharp distinction in fact between "saving faith" and "miracle-working faith" (as in 1 Cor 12:9). Both indicate that measure of reliance on God which enables *charis* ['grace'] to come to expression in *charisma* ['gift']'.[5]

There are good arguments in favor of both views, and each can be related to Paul's purpose in writing. The view that 'the measure of faith' is to be interpreted as the basic faith of all believers has the advantage of reinforcing Paul's aim of minimizing division and promoting unity among Jewish and Gentile believers. The view that it should be interpreted in connection with the various gifts of ministry of different believers has the advantage of relevance to the immediate context, and is therefore probably preferable.

12:4-5 In the original these verses, together with verses 6-8, may be construed as one long sentence, even though they are translated as three sentences in the NIV.[6] Before mentioning different gifts with which believers are endowed by God, Paul explains that while believers do not all have the same function, they nevertheless form one body. He begins: *For just as each of us has one body with many members, and these members do not all have the same function. . . .* The word 'for' at the beginning of this verse connects it with what precedes, that is, it explains one of the reasons why believers should think soberly about themselves in line with their 'measure of faith' and the gifts God has given to each of them.

The NIV's 'Just as each of us has one body with many members' departs a little from the original (lit. 'for just as in one body we have many members'); however, the overall sense remains the same. Making use of an image he employs at much greater length in 1 Corinthians 12:4-31, the apostle draws out a lesson from the fact that the human body, though one entity, has many different members, and the various members all have different functions: *so in Christ we, though many, form one body,*[7] *and each member*

---

4. Moo, *Romans*, 761. Cf. Fitzmyer, *Romans*, 646. Wright, 'Romans', 709 argues, 'there is more to be said for the rival view: that the "measure of faith" is the same for all. Throughout the letter so far, "faith" is the same for everybody (3:27-30); belief that Jesus is Lord and that God raised him from the dead. . . . Paul's point here is not that some should give themselves airs and that others should feel inferior, but that all should exercise their varied gifts on a level one with another'.

5. Dunn, *Romans 9–16*, 722.

6. Kenneth Berding, 'Romans 12.4-8: One Sentence of Two?' *NTS* 52 (2006) 433-39, argues that seven different factors suggest that not only 12:6-8 but the whole of 12:4-8 should be read as one long sentence.

7. Fitzmyer, *Romans*, 646, argues: 'As in 1 Cor 12:31, the phrase "one body" probably

belongs to all the others. Again the NIV translation departs somewhat from
the original (lit. 'in this [same] manner we, the many, are one body in
Christ, and individually members of one another'). Paul's point is that
while members of the church, like the parts of the human body, have different functions, they belong to one another and therefore are to serve and
promote the well-being of one another.[8] The apostle gives instructions
about how this should be put into practice in relation to seven different
gifts *(charismata)* in the next few verses.

12:6-8 Paul begins his treatment of *charismata: We have different gifts,
according to the grace given to each of us.* It is according to the grace given by
God (cf. 12:3) that believers receive gifts. In Ephesians 4:7, making a similar
point, the apostle speaks of the gifts given to each one 'as *Christ* apportioned it' (lit. 'according to the measure of the gift of Christ'). In 1 Corinthians 12:7-11 Paul makes the same point but says there that it is the *Spirit*
who gives the various gifts to believers. The apostle clearly functions with
a Trinitarian concept of God.

Paul now gives instruction concerning the way the first of the different gifts given to believers is to be exercised: *If your gift is prophesying, then
prophesy in accordance with your faith.* This has been interpreted in two different ways. First, prophecy must be in accordance with 'the faith', that is,
Christian belief. Fitzmyer, for example, says: 'The best interpretation is to
understand it as *fides quae creditur,* the body of Christian belief, the
believed-in object, as in 12:3; Gal 1:23; 3:23. This sense would mean, then,
that inspired preaching must not contradict Christian faith, for there can
also be false prophecy (1 Thess 5:20-21)'.[9]

Second, it has been interpreted to mean that people should use the
gift of prophecy in accordance with their faith', that is, with the gift of
prophecy comes the gift of faith needed to exercise it, and in proportion to
this faith people should prophesy. This is the interpretation adopted in the
NIV translation. It is supported, as Dunn points out, by the fact that 'in proportion to his faith' stands in parallel to and as an elaboration of 'according
to the grace given us' — and this implies 'that the faith is the faith exercised
by the one who prophesies'. He concludes that 'in proportion to his faith',
then, describes how the prophet functions, or, more precisely, how the act
of prophecy comes about — that is, by the prophet speaking forth in pro-

---

does not suggest anything more than a moral union of the members who work together for
the common good of the whole, as in the body politic'.

8. Dunn, *Romans 9–16,* 723, says that what influences Paul's use of the metaphor of
the body 'is the actual *experience* of the community, of common participation *(koinōnia).* He
adds, 'it fits fully into the strongly charismatic emphasis of the immediate context: the simple fact is that Paul uses the body of Christ as an ecclesiological concept only in connection
with charisms (Rom 12; 1 Cor 12; also Eph 4); the Christian community as the body of Christ
exists for him only as the charismatic community'. . . . Similarly, Jewett, *Romans,* 744.

9. Fitzmyer, *Romans,* 647. So, too, Jewett, *Romans,* 747; Käsemann, *Romans,* 341-42;
Wright, 'Romans', 711; Moo, *Romans,* 765.

portion to his faith = in dependence on God'.[10] This second interpretation fits the context better and is therefore to be preferred.[11]

Paul refers to the second of the gifts when he says: *If it is serving, then serve.* There are clues concerning what Paul means by service here in references to it found in his other letters. He uses the term translated 'service' to denote general assistance given to believers (1 Cor 16:15), the financial support provided by Gentile believers to the 'saints' in Jerusalem (15:31; 2 Cor 8:4; 9:1, 12-13), and the 'work of service' for the building up of the body of Christ for which believers are prepared by the ministry of apostles, prophets, evangelists, pastors, and teachers (Eph 4:11-12). Jewett prefers to define its meaning more closely as 'the diaconal role in early Christianity developed from functions related to the common meal. . . . The Eucharistic celebration, probably celebrated as a daily, common meal by many of the congregations, was the center of their common life . . . the remarkably rich development of *diakon-* [service] terminology in Pauline thought rests on this vital foundation in the experience of "love feasts" in early churches'.[12]

The apostle refers to the third of the gifts when he says: *if it is teaching, then teach* (NRSV: 'the teacher, in teaching'). It is noteworthy that at this point Paul ceases to speak about functions (prophecy, service), and instead begins to speak about the persons who exercise these functions (those who teach, the one who exhorts, he who shares, etc.). In a number of other places Paul uses the word 'teacher' to refer to those whom God/Christ appointed as teachers (1 Cor 12:28, 29; Eph 4:11), and to his own calling as a 'teacher' (1 Tim 2:7; 2 Tim 1:11).[13] The role of the teacher and the importance of good teaching/sound doctrine were fundamental in Paul's understanding of Christian ministry. For him, the source of good teaching is to be found the gospel tradition (1 Tim 4:6; Tit 2:10) and in the Scriptures that promote endurance and encouragement in believers, as well as providing the basis for rebuke, correction, and training in righteousness (15:4; 1 Tim 4:13; 2 Tim 3:16; Tit 1:9). Good teaching, backed up by the integrity of the teachers, saves both the teachers themselves and those who hear them (1 Tim 4:16; 2 Tim 3:10; Tit 2:7). References to the teaching function (1 Cor 4:17; Col 1:28; 2:7; 3:16; 2 Thess 2:15) and exhortations to teach (1 Tim 4:11;

10. Dunn, *Romans 9–16*, 727-28.

11. Dunn, *Romans 9–16*, 727, says that the distinctiveness of Christian prophecy is to be found 'in its spontaneous and unstructured immediacy of inspiration (cf. 1 Cor 14:30), as over against the more formalized prophetic ritual and procedures of the recognized shrines [of the hellenized world]; and distinct in the Pauline emphasis on rationality (1 Cor 14:12-19), as over against the ecstatic experiences prized in manticism, in the frenzy of the Dionysiac festivals and also evidently within the church at Corinth (1 Cor 12:2; 14:12)'.

12. Jewett, *Romans*, 748.

13. This militates against the suggestion made by Jewett, *Romans*, 749: 'Paul's formulation entails an avoidance of the technical term *didaskalos*, used frequently in the gospels for Jesus and others playing the role of "teacher". . . . Rengstorf hinted that the reluctance to use *didaskalos* for early Christian teachers expresses the sense that there could be no real successors to Jesus the teacher'.

6:2; 2 Tim 2:2) are fairly pervasive in Paul's letters. Jewett describes the content of early Christian teaching as 'general parenesis (1 Cor 4:17; Col 1:28; 2:6f.; 3:16), theological instruction derived from early Christian tradition (Gal 1:12; 2 Thess 2:15; Col 2:7; Rom 6:17), as well as exposition of Scripture (Rom 2:21)'.[14] Dunn makes the important observation: 'The fact that Paul thinks of teaching also as a charism should indicate sufficiently that Paul did not think of teaching merely as a conveying and passing on of established tradition (cf. 6:17 and 16:17). The implication is that he recognized an interpretative role for the teacher, in which the teacher must depend (equally as the prophet) on the Spirit for insight into the traditional formulae and for the significance he draws from them for his own context and congregation. Consequently the line between teaching and prophecy becomes very thin — the latter characterized more as new insight into God's will . . . the former more as new insight into old revelation'.[15]

Paul refers to the fourth of the gifts when he says: *if it is to encourage, then give encouragement* (lit. 'he who encourages, in encouragement'). The verb translated 'encourage' is employed extensively by the apostle in his letters, means either 'to exhort'[16] or 'to encourage'.[17] It is difficult to decide the particular nuance of meaning the apostle intended here in 12:8 — whether we should follow the NIV ('if it is to encourage, then give encouragement') or the NRSV ('the exhorter, in exhortation'). Perhaps it is better to adopt a 'both and' approach. Encouragement and positive exhortation are closely related. Cranfield distinguishes exhortation and encouragement from the gift of teaching mentioned in the previous verse: 'While the immediate purpose of teaching was to instruct, to impart information, to explain, the immediate purpose of exhortation was to help Christians to live out their obedience to the gospel. It was the pastoral application of the gospel to a particular congregation, both the congregation as a whole and also to the members of it severally. So the eyes of the exhorter had to be firmly fixed not only on the gospel but also on the concrete situation of his hearers'.[18]

Speaking about the fifth of the gifts, Paul says: *if it is giving, then give generously* (lit. 'the one who shares, with generosity'). The apostle employs the verb 'to share' in three other places: 1:11: 'For I am longing to see you so that I may *share* with you some spiritual gift to strengthen you'; Eph 4:28: 'Thieves must give up stealing; rather let them labor and work honestly with their own hands, so as to have something to *share* with the needy'; 1 Thess 2:8: 'So deeply do we care for you that we are determined to *share*

14. Jewett, *Romans*, 750.
15. Dunn, *Romans 9–16*, 729.
16. Cf. 12:1; 15:30; 16:7; 1 Cor 1:10; 4:16; 16:12, 15; 2 Cor 2:8; 5:20; 6:1; 8:6; 9:5; 10:1; 12:8, 18; 13:11; Eph 4:1; Phil 4:2; 1 Thess 4:1, 10; 5:14; 2 Thess 3:12; 1 Tim 1:3; 2:1; 5:1; 6:2; Tit 2:6, 15; Phlm 9, 10.
17. Cf. 1 Cor 4:13; 14:31; 2 Cor 1:4, 6; 2:7; 7:6-7, 13; Eph 6:22; Col 2:2; 4:8; 1 Thess 2:12; 3:2, 7; 4:18; 5:11; 2 Thess 2:17; 2 Tim 4:2; Tit 1:9.
18. Cranfield, *Romans*, II, 624.

with you not only the gospel of God but also our own selves'. The noun 'generosity' may also be translated as 'sincerity' (as in 2 Cor 1:12; 2 Cor 11:3; Eph 6:5; Col 3:22), but in this context, where it is used in relation to sharing one's possessions, it clearly means generosity — something the apostle commended and encouraged when urging the believers in Corinth to participate in the collection for the poor saints in Jerusalem (cf. 2 Cor 8:2; 9:11, 13).

Speaking of the sixth of these gifts, Paul says: *if it is to lead, do it diligently* (lit. 'he who leads, with zeal'). The verb translated 'to lead' can be used to mean either 'to lead/rule over' or 'to care for/give aid'.[19] Elsewhere Paul uses it to mean 'to lead' in the congregation (1 Thess 5:12; 1 Tim 5:17) or in the family (1 Tim 3:4-5, 12), and to devote oneself to good works (Tit 3:8, 14). There is a difference of opinion concerning the way it is to be interpreted here in 12:8. Some suggest that it should be rendered 'give aid', seeing that Paul's exhortation regarding this gift comes between two other exhortations concerning social service: giving generously and showing mercy.[20] Others argue that it should be rendered 'lead/rule over', whether in the Christian community or the home, and this would appear to be preferable seeing that it is used by Paul elsewhere predominantly in this way.[21] Whether Paul has in mind specifically those who are appointed as elders and overseers in the congregations is not clear.[22] Paul's point is that those who lead should do so with 'zeal', an attribute Paul saw as vital for Christians (cf. 12:11; 2 Cor 7:11, 12; 8:7, 8, 16).

Finally, speaking of the seventh gift, Paul says: *if it is to show mercy, do it cheerfully* (lit. 'he who shows mercy, with cheerfulness').[23] In other places Paul refers to God as the one who shows mercy (9:23; 11:31; 15:9; Gal 6:16; Eph 2:4; 1 Tim 1:2; 2 Tim 1:2, 16, 18; Tit 3:5). For believers to show mercy, then, is to imitate God himself. Paul stresses here that those who show mercy must do it 'cheerfully' (cf. 2 Cor. 9:7: 'God loves a cheerful giver'). For Paul, mercy must be shown cheerfully, not grudgingly, for only when shown in this way will it be truly a ministry of grace to the recipient.[24]

19. BAGD, *ad loc.*

20. So, e.g., Dunn, *Romans 9–16*, 731; Byrne, *Romans*, 373-74. Similarly, Cranfield, *Romans*, II, 626-27.

21. So, e.g., Fitzmyer, *Romans*, 649; Moo, *Romans*, 769; Jewett, *Romans*, 753.

22. Cf. Fitzmyer, *Romans*, 649. Moo, *Romans*, 768-769, thinks that it does probably refer to elders/overseers, but Jewett, *Romans*, 752-53, leaves it more open: 'The expression probably implies appointment to a leadership role in an early house or tenement church, whether as presider, administrator of charitable work, or pastoral supervision'.

23. There is only one other place in his letters (9:16) where Paul uses the verb *eleaō* ('to show mercy'). He uses the synonym *eleeō* more often (9:15, 18; 11:30, 31, 32; 1 Cor 7:25; 2 Cor 4:1; Phil 2:27; 1 Tim 1:13, 16).

24. Jewett, *Romans*, 754, comments: 'There is a clear scriptural echo when Paul connects mercy with "cheer", as the parallel in the LXX version of Prov 22:8 suggests: *andra hilaron kai dotēn eulogei ho theos* ("God blesses a cheerful and generous man"). Whether directly derived from the LXX or from a Greco-Roman proverb, the same association between *hilaro-* and acts of charity is found in 2 Cor 9:7'.

Cranfield suggests that when Paul speaks of the one who shows mercy he has in mind 'the person whose special function is, on behalf of the congregation, to tend the sick, relieve the poor, or care for the aged and disabled'.[25] He adds: 'It is instructive to notice that out of the seven *charismata* referred to in vv. 6-8 not less than four . . . most probably have to do with the practical assistance of those who are in one way or another specially in need of help and sympathy. This fact by itself is a clear and eloquent indication of the importance of the place of *diakonia* ['service'] in the life of the church as Paul understood it'.[26]

2. Enhancing Relationships within the Christian Community, 12:9-13

> [9]*Love must be sincere. Hate what is evil; cling to what is good.* [10]*Be devoted to one another in love. Honor one another above yourselves.* [11]*Never be lacking in zeal, but keep your spiritual fervor, serving the Lord.* [12]*Be joyful in hope, patient in affliction, faithful in prayer.* [13]*Share with the Lord's people who are in need. Practice hospitality.*

This passage contains a general principle (12:9), followed by a series of short practical examples of how the principle should be expressed in the Christian community (12:10-13).[27] It is noteworthy that these verses comprise a series of clauses employing only participles (rather than finite verbs). These participles are generally regarded as equivalent to imperatives (so, e.g., NIV, NRSV), a usage that is thought to reflect a Semitic origin.[28] It is possible to construe the whole passage as descriptive rather than prescriptive — as a statement about love followed by examples of how this love expresses itself. The passage would then read: 'love is genuine, abhorring the evil, clinging to the good, devoted to one another with brotherly love, outdoing one another showing honor, not lacking in zeal, being fer-

25. Cranfield, *Romans*, II, 627.

26. Cranfield, *Romans*, II, 628.

27. John N. Day, '"Coals of Fire" in Romans 12:19-20', *BSac* 160 (2003) 414-15, comments on the whole section, 12:9-21: 'Rather than being a haphazard collection of ethical injunctions, verses 9-21 evidence a highly stylized structure whose content is summed up in and subsumed under the introductory heading of *hē agapē anypokritos*, "genuine love" — a love that includes abhorrence of what is evil and adherence to what is good (v. 9). The verses that follow serve to explicate what that sincere or un-hypocritical love looks like in several concrete examples'.

28. Cf. Barrett, *Romans*, 239-40. However, Byrne, *Romans*, 375, notes that 'the content suggests that the passage taps a considerable variety of source material: the prophetic and wisdom traditions of the Old Testament, the "Jesus" tradition preserved in the early communities, ethical reflection and maxims of popular Greco-Roman philosophy. In any case, the close parallels with similar sequences in 1 Thess 5:12-22 and 1 Pet 3:8-12 suggest that the immediate source of the present sequence is the early Christian parenetical tradition, which had already associated and absorbed more remote material'.

vent in spirit, serving the Lord, rejoicing in hope, being patient in affliction, persevering in prayer, contributing to the needs of the saints, practicing hospitality'.[29] The commentary on this passage below is based on the NIV translation, which treats the participles as imperatives.

12:9 This verse contains three short exhortations. The first is: *Love must be sincere.* The word Paul uses here for love *(agapē)* is relatively rare in nonbiblical Greek literature, and occurs only nineteen times in the entire LXX. Therefore, its prolific use in the Pauline corpus is remarkable (75x). Early Christians very possibly took up this otherwise rare word to express the distinctive nature of the love they had come to experience as the recipients of God's grace, and then the quality of love they were to show to one another. The particular nature of this love may account for Paul's including the article before the noun 'love' (lit. 'the love'). Love is to be 'sincere' in the sense of 'genuine' or 'without pretense'. Paul speaks of love that is 'genuine' in 2 Corinthians 6:6, and faith that is 'genuine' in 1 Timothy 1:5 and 2 Timothy 1:5. In the exhortations that follow in 12:9b-13 Paul provides examples of the way love is to be expressed in the Christian community, and by doing so illustrates the nature of love that is sincere/genuine.

The next exhortation is: *Hate what is evil.* The verb 'to hate' that Paul uses is found only here in the NT. It expresses very strong emotions, meaning 'to have a vehement dislike' for something or 'strongly abhor'.[30] Evil, Paul implies, must be anathema for believers. Moo comments: 'Love is not genuine when it leads a person to do something evil or to avoid doing what is right — as defined by God in his Word'.[31]

The third short exhortation is the opposite of the second: *cling to what is good.* Paul uses the same verb, 'to cling' ('be joined'), in 1 Corinthians 6:16-17, where he exhorts his audience to flee from sexual immorality and contrasts being 'joined' to a prostitute to being 'joined' to the Lord. In Matthew 19:5 the Lord Jesus uses it in relation to a man's leaving his father and mother and being joined to his wife. Paul's exhortation to hate what is evil and cling to what is good has a parallel in 1 Thessalonians 5:21-22: 'Hold on to the good. Avoid every kind of evil'. For Paul, the 'good' is essentially what is pleasing to God (cf. 12:2) but includes doing what is right in the in the eyes of the authorities (13:3; Tit 3:1), doing good to one's neighbors and to all people (15:2; Gal 6:10; 1 Thess 5:15), and returning good for evil (12:21). Believers, he says also, are to be given to good works (2 Cor 9:8; Eph 2:10; Col 1:10; 1 Tim 2:10; 5:10).

12:10 The two exhortations in this verse concern how believers should relate to one another. The first is: *Be devoted to one another in love.* 'Love' here translates *philadelphia*, which means 'brotherly love'. To love one another was something expected of early believers (cf. 1 Thess 4:9; Heb

---

29. Cf. Jewett, *Romans*, 755, 758.
30. BAGD, *ad loc.*
31. Moo, *Romans*, 776.

13:1; 1 Pet 1:22; 2 Pet 1:7), and was especially important when they were exposed to persecution from unbelievers. The second exhortation, *Honor one another above yourselves*, may be interpreted to mean 'as far as honor is concerned, let each one esteem the other more highly (than oneself)'.[32] The NRSV renders this text as 'outdo one another in showing honor', meaning 'try to outdo one another in showing respect'. This interpretation is adopted by most recent commentators.[33]

12:11-13 These verses are introduced with a general warning against lacking in zeal, followed by seven positive exhortations. Each of these exhortations features a participle functioning as an imperative. Paul's general warning is: *Never be lacking in zeal* (lit. '[be] not lazy in zeal').[34] As noted in the commentary on 12:8, zeal was an important character attribute in Paul's mind, one he saw as vital for Christians (12:11; 2 Cor 7:11, 12; 8:7, 8, 16).

The first positive exhortation is: *but keep your spiritual fervor* (lit. 'be on the boil in spirit'). A similar expression is found is in Acts 18:25, in which Apollos is described as one who 'spoke with great fervor', indicating that the alterative rendition, 'Be aglow with the [Holy] Spirit', is unlikely.[35] Some see the mention of 'the spirit' here as a reference, not to the human spirit, but the Holy Spirit. In this case Paul's exhortation would be 'to allow the Holy Spirit to "set us on fire"; to open ourselves to the Spirit as he seeks to excite us about the "rational worship" to which the Lord has called us'.[36] However, as the other exhortations in the series relate to the attitude of believers as they serve the Lord, it is probably best to stay with the view that Paul is speaking about the need for believers to maintain fervor in their own spirits.[37]

The second of the exhortations is: *serving the Lord*. Paul describes the Thessalonian believers as those who 'turned to God from idols to serve the living and true God' (1 Thess 1:9). He reminds his Roman audience that, having been released from the law, believers are now enabled to serve God 'in the new way of the Spirit' (7:6). Believers, he indicates, are to 'serve one another humbly in love' (Gal 5:13). Even when Christian slaves serve

32. So, e.g., Cranfield, *Romans*, II, 633.

33. So, e.g., Moo, *Romans*, 777-78; Dunn, *Romans 9–16*, 741; Jewett, *Romans*, 761-62, who asserts: '"Taking the lead in honouring one another" fits the basic meaning of the verb and meets the requirement of the accusative *allēlous* in the context of *timē* ("honor"). It takes account of the social context of honor that marked the ancient Mediterranean world, in which public recognition was the essential basis of personal identity. . . . This translation matches the congregation situation in Rome, in that members of competing groups were refusing to accept each other in their love feasts'.

34. The adjective *oknēros* ('lazy') is used in Jesus' parable of the Talents where the master addresses one of his servants as, 'You wicked, lazy servant!' (Matt 25:26).

35. Cf..Kim Paffenroth, 'Romans 12:9-21 — A Brief Summary of the Problems of Translation and Interpretation', *IBS* 14 (1992) 91. *Contra* Dunn, *Romans 9–16*, 742.

36. Moo, *Romans*, 778.

37. Cf. Fitzmyer, *Romans*, 654. Early church fathers appear divided in their opinions. Some read it as referring to the human spirit (e.g., Ambrosiaster, 'Commentary on Paul's Epistles' [*ACCSR*, 315]), others to the Holy Spirit (e.g., Origen, 'On First Principles 2.8.3' [*ACCSR*, 315]).

earthly masters, they are serving the Lord (Eph 6:7; Col 3:24; 1 Tim 6:2). Believers' 'service to the Lord' was not restricted to such things as preaching and teaching but was also performed when they acted lovingly towards one another and when they carried out their everyday obligations faithfully.

The third brief exhortation is: *Be joyful in hope*. In 5:2 also Paul speaks of rejoicing in hope: 'And we boast in the hope of the glory of God'. Together with faith and love, hope for Paul is one of the three major Christian attributes (1 Cor 13:13). References to hope abound in Paul's letters (the word occurring some 36 times). Believers rejoice in their hope of salvation (1 Thess 5:8), their justification (Gal 5:5), their glorious inheritance (Eph 1:18; Col 1:5), and their share in the glory of God (5:2; Col 1:27). See 'Additional Note: Hope in the Pauline Corpus', 365.

The fourth exhortation is: [*be*] *patient in affliction*. As far as Paul was concerned, affliction was par for the course for believers. In fact, he reminded the Thessalonian Christians: 'You know quite well that we are destined for them [afflictions]' (1 Thess 3:3). In Philippians 1:29, in a similar vein, he reminds his audience: 'For it has been granted to you on behalf of Christ not only to believe on him, but also to suffer for him'. The apostle makes some twenty-four references to affliction in his letters. He could say that 'we also glory in our sufferings' because he knew that God uses them to produce perseverance, which in turn develops character (5:3-4). He was convinced that afflictions could not separate believers from the love of Christ (8:35), and that God himself comforts us in all our afflictions (2 Cor 1:4). He knew that, compared with the glory to be revealed in them, the afflictions of God's people are but light and momentary (2 Cor 4:17). He also knew that God will pay back those who afflict his people (2 Thess 1:6). While elsewhere Paul could speak of rejoicing in afflictions, here in 12:12 he urges his audience to be 'patient in affliction'. The word translated 'be patient' means to maintain one's belief or course of action in the face of opposition, that is, to stand one's ground, to hold out, or to endure.[38]

Paul's fifth exhortation is: [*be*] *faithful in prayer* (lit. 'persevere in prayer'). Prayer was extremely important to him. He prayed that God would open the way for him to visit the Roman believers (1:10), he prayed for his converts (Eph 1:16; Phil 1:9; Col 1:3, 9; 1 Thess 1:2; 2 Thess 1:11; 2 Thess 3:1; Philem 4), and he prayed with his spirit in tongues (1 Cor 14:14-15). He urged his converts to pray for him (15:30; Col 4:3; 1 Thess 5:25; 2 Thess 3:1) and for all the saints (Eph 6:18; 1 Tim 2:1), and that they be constant in their prayers (12:12; 1 Cor 7:5; Phil 4:6; Col 4:2; 1 Thess 5:17; 1 Tim 2:8; cf. Col 4:12; 1 Tim 5:5). Paul taught that the Holy Spirit helps believers in their weakness when they do not know what they ought to pray for (8:26). Here in 12:12 Paul's exhortation to his audience is that they 'be faithful' in prayer. In Colossians 4:2 there is a similar exhortation: 'Devote yourselves to prayer, being watchful and thankful'. Commenting on the need

38. BAGD, *ad loc.*

for persistence in prayer, Cranfield says: 'But it is precisely this thing, which is altogether vital and necessary if he [the Christian] is to endure, which he is specially tempted whether through sloth or discouragement or self-confidence to give up: hence the special frequency with which the verb *proskarterein* ['to persevere'] is used in the NT in connexion with prayer'.[39]

The sixth exhortation is: *Share with the Lord's people who are in need.* Every use of the verb 'to share' in Paul's letters relates to the sharing of financial/material resources. In Ephesians 4:28 Paul encourages his audience to work with their hands so that they may have something to share with those in need. He also thanked God for those who provided for his needs, and reminded them that God will meet their needs as they do so (Phil 4:16, 19; cf. Phil 2:25). The apostle believed that it was incumbent upon Gentile believers to share material blessings with Jewish believers in need because they have shared in the spiritual blessings of the Jews (15:27). He also taught that those who receive instruction from teachers 'should share all good things' with them (Gal 6:6). The apostle was especially grateful to the Philippian believers for sharing with him in the matter of giving and receiving (Phil 4:15). Jewett points out how applicable this exhortation may have been, especially to the Gentile majority in the Roman churches: 'Those who escaped the deportation under Claudius are thus to participate fully in the plight of the returnees, which in this context would imply the actual sharing of economic resources'.[40]

Paul's seventh and final exhortation in these verses is: *Practice hospitality.* To practice hospitality and to be hospitable was very important among believers in Paul's day (see 'Additional Note: Hospitality', below). It was one of the requirements for those who would exercise leadership in the church (1 Tim 3:2; Tit 1:8), and believers generally were to be generous in hospitality (Heb 13:2; 1 Pet 4:9). Jewett sees this exhortation, like the previous one, as specially appropriate to Gentile believers in Rome: 'With a large number of Jewish Christians and other leaders returning to Rome after the lapse of the Edict of Claudius, evoking conflicts and hostilities, there was a concrete need for the kind of hospitality that marked the Jesus movement and subsequent Christianity'.[41]

ADDITIONAL NOTE: HOSPITALITY

Hospitality may be defined as 'the process by means of which an outsider's status is changed from stranger to guest'. It is not something a person provides for family or friends but for strangers. Strangers need hospitality, for

39. Cranfield, *Romans*, II, 637.
40. Jewett, *Romans*, 764.
41. Jewett, *Romans*, 765.

otherwise they will be treated as non-human because they are potentially a threat to the community. Strangers had no standing in law or custom, and therefore needed a patron in the community they were visiting. There was no universal brotherhood in the ancient Mediterranean world.

Certain 'rules' of hospitality had to be observed by guests and hosts. Guests must not (i) insult their host or show any kind of hostility or rivalry; (ii) usurp the role of their host in any way, for example, making themselves at home when not invited to do so, ordering the dependents of the host about, and making demands of their host; (iii) refuse what is offered, especially food. Hosts, for their part, must not (i) insult their guests or make any show of hostility or rivalry; (ii) neglect to protect their guests' honor; (iii) fail to show concern for the needs of their guests.

Hospitality was not reciprocated between individuals (because once people became guests they were no longer strangers), but it was reciprocated between communities. And it was to the strangers' own community that they were obliged to sing the praises of their hosts if they had been treated well (cf. 3 John 5-8) and to which they would report adversely if they had not been welcomed properly (cf. 3 John 9-10). Communities would repay hospitality to strangers from another community if that community had treated their own people well.

Letters of recommendation were important in the matter of hospitality. Their function was 'to help divest the stranger of his strangeness, to make him at least only a partial stranger, if not an immediate guest'. To refuse to accept those recommended was to dishonor the one who recommended them, and in the Mediterranean culture of the first century the one dishonored had to seek satisfaction or bear the shame heaped upon him by the refusal of his commendation.[42]

---

3. Relationships without and within the Christian Community, 12:14-16

> [14]*Bless those who persecute you; bless and do not curse.* [15]*Rejoice with those who rejoice; mourn with those who mourn.* [16]*Live in harmony with one another. Do not be proud, but be willing to associate with people of low position. Do not be conceited.*

In this passage Paul no longer employs imperatival participles as he did in 12:9-13, using instead simple imperatives. Relationships among believers are still in view (12:15-16), but the difficulties believers experience in their relationships with hostile outsiders is introduced (12:14) and spelled out in more detail in 12:17-21.

---

42. Cf. Bruce J. Malina, 'The Received View and What It Cannot Do: III John and Hospitality', *Semeia* 35 (1986) 181-87.

Paul's exhortation in 12:14, *Bless those who persecute you;*[43] *bless and do not curse,* relates to believers' response to a hostile world.[44] While there is no evidence for specific persecution in Rome around the time of the writing of Romans (though Jewish believers had been expelled from Rome in A.D. 49 and recently returned), believers in the capital would have been exposed to ostracism just as believers were elsewhere in the empire. It was part of Paul's teaching to new believers that they should expect persecution (cf. 1 Thess 2:14-15; Phil 1:29). Jesus himself forewarned his disciples of the persecution they would encounter (cf. Mark 13:9; Luke 21:12; John 16:2) and gave them a command that is similar to Paul's exhortation: 'Love your enemies and pray for those who persecute you' (Matt 5:44); 'Love your enemies, do good to those who hate you' (Luke 6:27). Wright comments: 'It is hard to imagine this teaching becoming the norm in the church, as it clearly did from the very start, unless it was firmly rooted in the words and example of Jesus himself'.[45]

The apostle continues with two further brief exhortations. The first is: *Rejoice with those who rejoice; mourn with those who mourn.* Paul makes a similar point in 1 Corinthians 12:25-26: 'There should be no division in the body, but . . . its parts should have equal concern for each other. If one part suffers, every part suffers with it; if one part is honored, every part rejoices with it'. (Cf. Sir 7:34: 'Do not avoid those who weep, but mourn with those who mourn' [NRSV].) Fitzmyer comments: 'Since John Chrysostom (*In ep. ad Romanos* hom. 22.1 . . .) commentators have noted that it is easier to "sympathize" with those who mourn than to "congratulate" those who succeed and rejoice over their success, because the latter usually excites envy and jealousy. For that reason Paul puts rejoicing in the first place'.[46]

The second is: *Live in harmony with one another.* The expression, 'live in harmony', is characteristically Pauline and is found only in his letters in the NT. The apostle prays for this harmony/like-mindedness/unity among the Roman believers in 15:5 (NRSV): 'May the God of steadfastness and encouragement grant you to live in harmony with one another, in accordance with Christ Jesus'. In Philippians he urges his audience to 'make my joy complete by being like-minded, having the same love, being one in spirit

---

43. The word 'you' *(hymas)* is missing in some manuscripts but retained in others. It is difficult to decide whether it should be included or not.

44. Kent L. Yinger, 'Romans 12:14-21 and Nonretaliation in Second Temple Judaism: Addressing Persecution within the Community', *CBQ* 60 (1998) 75-94, argues that the exhortation relates, not to believers' response to a hostile world, but to relations within the Christian community, noting that 12:14 is sandwiched between verses containing exhortations related to life within the Christian community. Cf. David A. Black, 'The Pauline Love Command: Structure, Style, and Ethics in Romans 12:9-21', *FilolNT* 2 (1989) 10. This view has real problems because every other reference the apostle makes to persecution is to that of believers from without, not within, the Christian community (1 Cor 4:12; 15:9; 2 Cor 4:9; Gal 1:13, 23; 4:29; 5:11; 6:12; Phil 3:6; 2 Tim 3:12).

45. Wright, 'Romans', 713.

46. Fitzmyer, *Romans*, 655.

and of one mind' (Phil 2:2), and also pleads with his fellow workers, Euodia and Syntyche, 'be of the same mind in the Lord' (Phil 4:2). The sense of these instructions is not that believers should hold exactly the same opinions but that they should think and act in ways that promote harmony and agreement.

The third of these instructions is: *Do not be proud, but be willing to associate with people of low position. Do not be conceited.* Paul, who wants his audience to live in harmony and be of the same mind, knows that to do this they must 'not be proud' (lit. 'not think about high things', or possibly, 'don't be a social climber').[47] To live in harmony they will also need to be willing to 'associate with people of low position' and 'not be conceited'.[48] When issuing this instruction Paul may have had in mind Proverbs 3:7, where a similar instruction is found: 'Do not be wise in your own eyes'.

4. Responding to Hostile People and Their Hostile Acts, 12:17-21

> [17]*Do not repay anyone evil for evil. Be careful to do what is right in the eyes of everyone.* [18]*If it is possible, as far as it depends on you, live at peace with everyone.* [19]*Do not take revenge, my dear friends, but leave room for God's wrath, for it is written: 'It is mine to avenge; I will repay', says the Lord.* [20]*On the contrary: 'If your enemy is hungry, feed him; if he is thirsty, give him something to drink. In doing this, you will heap burning coals on his head'.* [21]*Do not be overcome by evil, but overcome evil with good.*

These verses, like verse 14, provide instructions about how believers should respond to those who may harm them. In brief they are to 'overcome evil with good' (12:21).

12:17-18 First, Paul says, *Do not repay anyone evil for evil.* This reiterates the teaching of Jesus (Luke 6:28: 'bless those who curse you, pray for those who mistreat you'; cf. Matt 5:44). It also echoes statements in Proverbs (17:13: 'Evil will never leave the house of one who pays back evil for good'; 20:22: 'Do not say, "I'll pay you back for this wrong!" Wait for the LORD, and he will avenge you'). It is an exhortation that Paul repeats, in substance at least, in 1 Thessalonians 5:15: 'Make sure that nobody pays back wrong for wrong, but always strive to do what is good for each other and for everyone else', and is teaching the apostle himself to put into prac-

---

47. Cf. BAGD, *ad loc.*
48. Moo, *The Romans*, 783-84, remarks: 'It is not certain what Paul means by this positive exhortation. The adjective "lowly" could be neuter, in which case Paul might be urging Christians, in contrast to being haughty, to devote themselves to humble tasks. But "lowly" could also refer to persons, in which case Paul would be exhorting believers to associate with "lowly people", that is, the outcasts, the poor, and the needy. A decision between these two options is impossible to make; both fit the context well and both are paralleled in the NT'.

tice (1 Cor 4:12: 'When we are cursed, we bless; when we are persecuted, we endure it'). He saw persecution as par for the course for believers (Phil 1:29: 'For it has been granted to you on behalf of Christ not only to believe on him, but also to suffer for him'; 2 Tim 3:12: 'In fact, everyone who wants to live a godly life in Christ Jesus will be persecuted'). Prior to his conversion Paul himself had been a persecutor of the church of God (1 Cor 15:9; Gal 1:13, 23; Phil 3:6), and afterwards he became the object of persecution himself (2 Cor 4:9; Gal 5:11). The persecutions Paul suffered were for the most part inflicted upon him by unbelieving Jews, and were precipitated by his mission among the Gentiles and his proclamation of a law-free gospel.[49] What Paul makes clear in this verse is that the Christian response to persecution must never be to curse those who inflict it; rather, it should be to bless them.

While believers must 'not repay anyone evil for evil', they should also be careful not to provoke opposition. They should *be careful to do what is right in the eyes of everyone,* an instruction that appears to draw upon Proverbs 3:4 LXX ('take thought for/try [to do] good before [the] Lord and men'), and which Paul draws upon also in 2 Corinthians 8:21: 'For we are taking pains to do what is right, not only in the eyes of the Lord but also in the eyes of man'. Similar instructions are found in 1 Peter as well:

> Live such good lives among the pagans that, though they accuse you of doing wrong, they may see your good deeds and glorify God on the day he visits us'. (1 Pet 2:12)

> For it is God's will that by doing good you should silence the ignorant talk of foolish people. (1 Pet 2:15)

> Keeping a clear conscience, so that those who speak maliciously against your good behavior in Christ may be ashamed of their slander. (1 Pet 3:16)

Such instructions not only draw upon Proverbs 3:4 (LXX) but also reflect the teaching of Jesus himself: 'In the same way, let your light shine before others, that they may see your good deeds and glorify your Father in heaven' (Matt 5:16). All this suggests that when Paul speaks about doing 'what is right in the eyes of everyone', he is not suggesting that believers should simply let their behavior be determined by public opinion, but that under God they should be careful not to offend outsiders unnecessarily.[50]

Paul adds to his advice to 'be careful to do what is right in the eyes of

---

49. Kruse, 'The Price Paid for a Ministry among Gentiles', 260-72.

50. Cf. Cranfield, *Romans*, II, 645-46. Moo, *Romans*, 785, maintains: 'We should . . . take Paul's words at face value: he wants us to commend ourselves before non-Christians by seeking to do those "good things" that non-Christians approve and recognize. There is, of course, an unstated limitation to this command, one that resides in the word "good" itself'.

everyone' the exhortation: *If it is possible, as far as it depends on you, live at peace with everyone.*[51] Elsewhere Paul urges believers to live at peace with one another (2 Cor 13:11; 1 Thess 5:13), but it is only here that he applies this instruction to those outside the Christian community as well ('everyone'). Recognizing that despite believers' best efforts to live at peace others may make it impossible, the apostle prefaces his instruction with the double qualification: 'If it is possible, as far as it depends on you'. . . . Beyond that it is no longer the believers' responsibility if peace does not prevail. Dunn comments: 'Paul neither presses an unrealistic ideal upon them nor expects them to compromise their faith for the sake of a quiet life'. . . .[52]

12:19 Jesus (Matt 5:10-11; John 16:2-3) and Paul (12:14; 2 Tim 3:12) warned believers that they would be the objects of unjust persecution. When this occurs, Paul says: *Do not take revenge, my dear friends* (lit. 'do not avenge yourselves, beloved').[53] Paul makes a similar point in 1 Thessalonians 5:15: 'Make sure that nobody pays back wrong for wrong, but always strive to do what is good for each other and for everyone else', and in so doing he reiterates the commands of Jesus (Matt 5:39; Luke 6:28). It is hard to imagine in what circumstances the politically powerless Christian minority in Rome might be tempted to take revenge against their persecutors, but as Dunn points out, 'the growing and increasingly desperate activity of the Zealots in Palestine was warning enough of how an oppressed people or persecuted minority might turn to acts of revenge, and the Christian congregations would not need reminding of how vulnerable they were to hostile pressures'.[54]

Instead of taking personal revenge, Paul warns they should *leave room for God's wrath* (lit. 'give place to wrath').[55] The NIV adds the word 'God's'. In this case the addition is helpful because it is clearly God's wrath (not human wrath) that the apostle has in mind, as the quotation that follows immediately makes clear: *for it is written: 'It is mine to avenge; I will repay', says the Lord.* Paul's quotation is based upon but not identical with Deuteronomy 32:35 LXX ('in the day of vengeance I will repay').[56] Rather than taking vengeance themselves, believers are to leave it to God to do so. The idea of vengeance is widespread in the OT. The noun 'vengeance' occurs seventy-nine times and the verb 'to take vengeance' eighty-nine times in the LXX. In

---

51. Cf. Heb 12:14, 'Make every effort to live in peace with all men and to be holy; without holiness no one will see the Lord'.

52. Dunn, *Romans 9–16*, 748. Cf. Paffenroth, 'Romans 12:9-21', 94.

53. Dunn, *Romans 9–16*, 750, says: 'The taking of vengeance, that is, acting independently of or beyond the law, is denounced in the OT (Lev 19:18; Prov 20:22; 24:29; Sir 28:1-7), with the specific thought sometimes added in postbiblical Judaism that vengeance can be left to the Lord (*T. Gad* 6.7; 1QS 10.17-18; CD 9.2-5; *Ps. Phoc.* 77; *2 Enoch* 50:4)'.

54. Dunn, *Romans 9–16*, 749.

55. The expression 'to give place' *(didōmi topon)* is used elsewhere in the NT of giving up one's seat to another (Luke 14:9), and giving opportunity to the devil (Eph 4:27).

56. The writer to the Hebrews also quotes from Deut 32:35: 'For we know him who said, "It is mine to avenge; I will repay"' (Heb 10:30).

many cases these words are used in relation to God's vengeance. Paul sought to comfort the Thessalonians who were being troubled by persecution by reminding them that God will avenge them: 'God is just: He will pay back trouble to those who trouble you. . . . He will punish those who do not know God and do not obey the gospel of our Lord Jesus' (2 Thess 1:6-8). Cranfield's comment is apt: 'When we recall what God has done for us "when we were enemies" (5.10), we cannot but hope that His mercy will finally embrace those who now are our enemies. "We give place to wrath", says Calvin, ". . . only when we wait patiently for the proper time for our deliverance, praying in the meantime that those who now trouble us may repent and become our friends". It certainly does not mean hoping and praying for God to punish our enemies'.[57]

12:20 Having just told them not to take revenge, Paul goes on: *On the contrary: 'If your enemy is hungry, feed him; if he is thirsty, give him something to drink. In doing this, you will heap burning coals on his head'*. Paul here quotes virtually word for word Proverbs 25:21-22 (while omitting the final clause found in Prov 25:22, 'and the LORD will reward you'). What Paul says here is consistent with his earlier advice in 12:14, and reiterates for a second time the teaching given by the Lord Jesus (Matt 5:43-44: 'You have heard that it was said, "Love your neighbor and hate your enemy". But I tell you, love your enemies and pray for those who persecute you'; cf. Luke 6:27, 35).

What it means to heap burning coals on someone's head has been variously interpreted. The expression 'coals of fire' is found nine times in the OT, and in five cases it is related to judgment (2 Sam 22:9, 13; Pss 18:8, 12; 140:10). This has led some of the early church fathers and recent commentators to interpret Paul's statement, 'you will heap burning coals on his head', as a reference to God's judgment upon those who persecute his people.[58] The problem with this interpretation is that it requires an understanding of heaping coals of fire on one's enemy's head that is in conflict with the kindness of feeding him if he is hungry and giving him something to drink if he is thirsty. To do this with a view to bringing judgment upon him renders the acts of kindness hypocritical.

A second interpretation of what it means to heap coals of fire upon the head of one's enemy relates it to ancient Egyptian reconciliation rituals. Isaak describes the ritual as follows: 'Apparently, by giving coals of fire to the one you have wronged, you show that you are sorry for hurting them (fire is a valuable commodity for desert people where wood for cooking and heating is not in abundance). Paul takes this ancient figure (Prov 25:21-22) and modifies it for his purpose here — such life-giving demonstrations of restored relationships are regularly used to characterize the hope the

---

57. Cranfield, *Romans*, II, 648.
58. So, e.g., Chrysostom; cf. Paffenroth, 'Romans 12:9-21', 95-96; Day, '"Coals of Fire" in Romans 12:19-20', 418-20.

Christian community brings to all interactions. . . . "Heaping burning coals on the head" is not manipulative. It is a significant life-giving act to heap fire-starting coals into the neighbor's — and even enemy's — pot so that they may carry them on their heads back to their campsites to use and enjoy. In this way, the community is not "overcome with evil, but overcomes evil with good" '.[59] There are two problems with this interpretation. First, it is questionable that Paul would have been familiar with Egyptian reconciliation rituals, and second, in Paul's exhortation it is the one who is wronged who does the act of kindness, not the one who did the wrong as in the Egyptian ritual.

The third interpretation, adopted by several early church fathers[60] and the majority of recent commentators,[61] is that heaping coals of fire upon the head of one's enemy means to cause the enemy to blush with shame and remorse, and this might lead to his conversion. Acts of kindness are to be carried out, not with a view to causing shame and remorse, though they may well have that effect, but because it is the godly thing to do.[62] Of the three suggested interpretations this third one fits best in the context where Paul exhorts his audience to adopt a positive response to persecution, one that does not return evil for evil but overcomes evil with good.

12:21 Paul concludes the section 12:17-21 containing his advice about how believers should respond to hostile people and their hostile acts with the instruction: *Do not be overcome by evil, but overcome evil with good.* As already noted, this was what Jesus demanded of his disciples, even though, unlike Paul, he expressed it in terms of 'loving' one's enemies, not only doing them good: 'But to you who are listening I say: Love your enemies, do good to those who hate you, bless those who curse you, pray for those who mistreat you. . . . But love your enemies, do good to them' (Luke 6:27-28, 35). Jesus himself provided the supreme example of such behavior when,

59. Jon Isaak, 'The Christian Community and Political Responsibility: Romans 13:1-7', *Direction* 32 (2003) 37. Similarly, S. Hre Kio, 'What does "YOU WILL HEAP BURNING COALS UPON HIS HEAD" mean in Romans 12.20?' *BibTrans* 51 (2000) 423-24.

60. So, e.g., Origen: 'Perhaps here also these coals of fire which are heaped on the head of an enemy are heaped for his benefit. For it may be that a savage and barbarous mind, if it feels our good will, our kindness, our love and our godliness, may be struck by it and repent, and he will swear that as his conscience torments him for the wrong which he has done, it is as if a fire were enveloping him' ('Commentary on the Epistle to the Romans' [*ACCSR*, 321]).

61. Cf. Byrne, *Romans*, 383-84; Wright, 'Romans', 715; Moo, *Romans*, 788-89; Dunn, *Romans 9–16*, 751; Barrett, *Romans*, 242-43; Cranfield, *Romans*, II, 648-49.

62. Jewett, *Romans*, 777-78, says: 'Given the context of the house and tenement churches in Rome, and the fact that hospitality and benevolence were expressed through the system of love feasts that each of these small communities sponsored, this admonition should not be understood in terms of "contributing to your local charity" in which care for the needy is accomplished with a minimal level of personal involvement. If Paul's social context is kept in mind, the implication for the Roman believers can be understood in a straightforward way: they are to invite hostile neighbours and other enemies to their communal meals'.

being crucified unjustly, he prayed for those responsible: 'Father, forgive them, for they do not know what they are doing' (Luke 23:34). His faithful witness, Stephen, stoned to death by his enemies, prayed in similar vein: 'Lord, do not hold this sin against them' (Acts 7:60). Similar sentiments are expressed in the *Testaments of the Twelve Patriarchs* (*T. Gad* 6:1-3; *T. Joseph* 18:2; *T. Benj.* 4:2-3).

ADDITIONAL NOTE: THE RELATIONSHIP BETWEEN PAULINE ETHICS AND STOIC TEACHING

In recent times there has been renewed scholarly interest in the study of Greek ethics from the classical, Hellenistic, and Roman periods.[63] Several scholars have studied the connections between the NT, in particular Paul's ethical instructions, and Stoic teaching.[64] This interest is understandable since these coexisted in the first-century Greco-Roman world. Particularly important is Engberg-Pedersen's work[65] that highlights the similarities of Paul's ethics with the ethical teaching of Stoicism. The recent debate between Esler and Thorsteinsson described briefly below highlights important issues in recent discussion,

Esler acknowledges the importance of Engberg-Pedersen's work, which focused upon the similarities between Pauline ethics and Stoicism, but questions the approach he adopted. He argues that it is more profitable to note the dissimilarities existing between Pauline ethics and Stoic teaching than the similarities. He studies Romans 12 as a test case for his proposal. He notes that Paul's reference to 'rational worship' in 12:1-2 has clear parallels in Stoic philosophy, but then points out that Paul immediately proceeds in 12:3 to warn his audience against thinking arrogantly, something that introduces a social element, which is lacking in Stoic ethics.[66] Turning to 'the collection of some 30 general statements' in 12:9-21, Esler notes that Paul shares with the Stoics an emphasis on moral development (cf. 12:3, 6; 14–15; 1 Cor 9:25; Phil 1:25; 3:12-16), but again notes the dissimilarities, for example, in

---

63. Philip F. Esler, 'Paul and Stoicism: Romans 12 as a Test Case', *NTS* 50 (2004) 106, notes the works of G. E. Anscombe, 'Modern Moral Philosophy', *Philosophy* 33 (1958) 1-19; Alasdair McIntyre, *After Virtue: A Study in Moral Theory* (London: Duckworth, 1981); Julia Annas, *The Morality of Happiness* (New York/Oxford: Oxford University Press, 1993).

64. Esler, 'Paul and Stoicism', 106-7, lists the following: Abraham J. Malherbe, ed., *The Cynic Epistles: A Study Edition* (Missoula, Mont.: Scholars Press, 1977); *Moral Exhortation: A Greco-Roman Sourcebook* (Philadelphia: Westminster, 1986); *Paul and the Thessalonians: The Philosophic Tradition of Pastoral Care* (Philadelphia: Fortress, 1987); *Paul and the Popular Philosophers* (Minneapolis: Fortress, 1989); Wayne A. Meeks, *The Moral World of the First Christians* (Philadelphia: Westminster, 1986); *The Origins of Christian Morality: The First Two Centuries* (New Haven, Conn.: Yale University Press, 1993).

65. Troels Engberg-Pedersen, *Paul and the Stoics* (Edinburgh: T&T Clark, 2000).

66. 'Paul and Stoicism', 114-17.

respect of the common good, love expressed in 'being on fire with the Spirit', 'serving the Lord', and 'persisting in prayer', all of which reflect the charismatic nature of early Christianity, something virtually absent in Stoicism. Similarly, Paul's exhortation to bless those who persecute you is radically different from anything in Stoicism.[67] Esler sums up his approach to Romans 12 as follows: 'Throughout the course of Rom 12 Paul works closely with ideas and language that have parallels in Stoicism and yet thoroughly subverts them as he paints his own very different picture'.[68]

Thorsteinsson argues against Esler's view concerning the radical differences between Pauline ethics and Stoicism on the grounds that he did not take proper notice of the Roman Stoic philosophers, Seneca, Musonius, and Epictetus.[69] By extensive references to and quotations from these three Stoic thinkers, Thorsteinsson argues that Esler's claims do not stand up. Commenting on 12:1-2, he contends that Epictetus, like Paul, associates reason with worship: 'If, indeed, I were a nightingale, I should be singing as a nightingale; if a swan, as a swan. But as it is, I am a rational being, therefore I must be singing hymns of praise to God . . . and I exhort you to joint *(sic)* me in this same song *(Diatr.* 1.16.20-21)'.[70]

Further, Thorsteinsson says that when Paul exhorts his audience to be transformed by the renewal of the mind (12:2), he comes very close to Seneca's observation: 'Philosophy is divided into knowledge and state of mind. For one who has learned and understood what he should do and avoid, is not a wise man until his mind *(animus)* is metamorphosed *(transfiguratus est)* into the shape of that which he has learned *(Ep.* 94.47-48; cf. Epictetus, *Diatr.* 3.21.1-3)'.[71]

Commenting on 12:3, Thorsteinsson lists the four traditional Stoic virtues: prudence, moderation, justice, and courage, and notes that 'to most Stoics prudence was the pre-eminent virtue on the basis of which the other three were determined', and then observes: 'All the virtues were thus viewed by them as consequences of inner intellectual judgments. . . . Paul's allusions to two of the four cardinal virtues [prudence and moderation] suggest that he was familiar with current Graeco-Roman moralistic discussions. Moreover, it is unlikely that the Roman audience would have missed his playing on the root *(phron-)* of the Stoic primary virtue [prudence], especially as such linking had already been established in the verses immediately preceding. Paul's usage of the verb *phronein* in 12.3 thus maintains the attention drawn to the intellect in v. 2, and reinforces the Stoic associations in 12.1-2 (cf. repetition in v. 16)'.[72]

---

67. 'Paul and Stoicism', 117-23.
68. 'Paul and Stoicism', 124.
69. Runar M. Thorsteinsson, 'Paul and Roman Stoicism: Romans 12 and Contemporary Stoic Ethics', *JSNT* 29 (2006) 139-61.
70. Thorsteinsson, 'Paul and Roman Stoicism', 147.
71. Thorsteinsson, 'Paul and Roman Stoicism', 147-48.
72. Thorsteinsson, 'Paul and Roman Stoicism', 149-50.

Thorsteinsson also argues that the body-metaphor employed by Paul in 12:4 was frequently used with similar application by Seneca, a fact over-looked by Esler.[73] Thorsteinsson points out the emphasis upon humankind as social creatures with obligations to promote the common good. Thus, for example, Seneca says: 'Nature bids me do good to all mankind . . . whether slaves or freemen, freeborn or freed-men, whether the laws gave them free-dom or a grant in the presence of friends — what difference does it make? Wherever there is a human being there is the opportunity for a kindness (*benedici*) (*Vit. Beat.* 24.3)'.[74] Thorsteinsson also asserts: 'There is no good reason to assume that the Stoics would have differed from Paul in this re-spect to the effect that for them the social aspect would only have been a theoretical, not an actual, reality (so Esler 2004: 121). On the contrary, one characteristic of Roman Stoicism is the very weight put on the practical ap-plication of its ethics'.[75]

Rejecting Esler's comment that Paul's exhortation not to curse but to bless is radically different from anything in Stoicism, Thorsteinsson cites passages from Musonius and Seneca. So, for example, Seneca: 'It is not right to correct wrong-doing by doing wrong . . .' (*Ira* 1.16.1); 'How much more human to manifest toward wrong-doers a kind and fatherly spirit, not hunting them down but calling them back' (*Ira* 1.14.3). Instead of de-feating it with its match, 'unkindness must be treated with kindness . . .' (*Ira* 3.27.3).[76]

Thorsteinsson does acknowledge some specific differences between Pauline ethics and Stoicism. When the apostle exhorts his audience to 'weep with those who weep' (12:15), 'this', Thorsteinsson says, 'would probably have sounded rather un-Stoic to contemporary audiences who were (fairly) well acquainted with Stoic perspectives on *pathē* ("passions") such as grief. According to Seneca, the Stoic sage, who is "born to be of help to all and to serve the common good", will certainly aid those in need, those who suffer, and those who weep, but he will lend his hand with a tranquil mind. Thus, "he will bring relief to another's tears, but will not add his own" (*Clem* 2.6.2-3)'.[77] Another difference Thorsteinsson notes is that of ethical scope: 'Whereas the ethics of the Roman Stoics is universal in its scope, Paul's "love ethic" is not. His primary concern is the community of Christ-believers and morality within that particular community'.[78]

The recent debate between Esler and Thorsteinsson serves to high-light both the dissimilarities (Esler) and the similarities (Thorsteinsson) be-tween Pauline and Stoic ethics such that neither of these facts should be overlooked. There are certainly aspects of Paul's ethical teaching that

73. Thorsteinsson, 'Paul and Roman Stoicism', 150-52.
74. Thorsteinsson, 'Paul and Roman Stoicism', 152-53.
75. Thorsteinsson, 'Paul and Roman Stoicism', 154.
76. Thorsteinsson, 'Paul and Roman Stoicism', 156-58.
77. Thorsteinsson, 'Paul and Roman Stoicism', 156.
78. Thorsteinsson, 'Paul and Roman Stoicism', 159.

would resonate with those acquainted with Stoic moral philosophy, but equally there are significant differences between them, the most obvious being the impact of Christian tradition and the experience of the Spirit reflected in Paul's ethical teaching.

C. Christians and the Roman Authorities, 13:1-7

[1]Let everyone be subject to the governing authorities, for there is no authority except that which God has established. The authorities that exist have been established by God. [2]Consequently, whoever rebels against the authority is rebelling against what God has instituted, and those who do so will bring judgment on themselves. [3]For rulers hold no terror for those who do right, but for those who do wrong. Do you want to be free from fear of the one in authority? Then do what is right and you will be commended. [4]For the one in authority is God's servant for your good. But if you do wrong, be afraid, for rulers do not bear the sword for no reason. They are God's servants, agents of wrath to bring punishment on the wrongdoer. [5]Therefore, it is necessary to submit to the authorities, not only because of possible punishment but also as a matter of conscience.

[6]This is also why you pay taxes, for the authorities are God's servants, who give their full time to governing. [7]Give to everyone what you owe them: If you owe taxes, pay taxes; if revenue, then revenue; if respect, then respect; if honor, then honor.

The last section of the previous chapter, 12:17-21, in which Paul gave instructions to his audience concerning the way they should conduct themselves towards outsiders, concluded with the exhortation, 'Do not be overcome by evil, but overcome evil with good'. In 13:1-7 the apostle continues to give instructions concerning believers' relationships with outsiders, in particular their relationship to the governing authorities, reminding them that rulers are not a terror to [those who do] good but to [those who do] wrong (13:3). In fact, he says, the governing authorities are God's servants to you for good and also agents of God's wrath to the one who does evil (13:4). The theme of doing good or evil in relation to outsiders connects 13:1-7 and 12:17-21.[1] It is noteworthy that Paul, when speaking about believers' relations with outsiders, employs the category of the 'good', and

---

1. This fact negates the view held by some scholars that 13:1-7 is a later interpolation into the main body of Romans, a view held, e.g., by James Kallas, 'Romans 13:1-7: An Interpolation', *NTS* 11 (1965) 365-66. Wright, 'Romans', 718, notes another connection: 'The point he stresses throughout 12:14-21 dovetails exactly into what he says in 13:1-7. One must not call down curses on persecutors, nor repay evil with evil, nor seek private retribution; punishment is God's business. . . . But he now articulates, as a central point in 13:1-7, a standard Jewish and then Christian belief: that ruling authorities are what they are because God wants order in the present world'.

when speaking about their relations within the Christian community, he uses the category of 'love'.[2]

Various attempts have been made to determine what influenced Paul to exhort his audience to submit to the ruling authorities. Fitzmyer observes: 'What Paul teaches in this passage has to be understood against the background of the OT itself, in which Israel was instructed, especially in the time of the exile, to respect governing authorities, even to pray for them: Jer 29:7 ("Seek the welfare of the city to which I have exiled you, and pray to the Lord on behalf of it, for in its welfare will be your welfare"); Bar 1:11 ("Pray for the life of Nebuchadnezzar king of Babylon")'.[3] Others suggest that Paul's advice is best understood against the background of nationalistic tendencies in Palestine that led some Jews to regard payment of Roman taxes as a betrayal of their commitment to God,[4] and the likelihood that this attitude was adopted by some Jewish believers in the Roman churches. Paul urged them to pay the taxes and avoid unnecessary conflict with Rome.[5]

Another view is that Paul was responding to the possible effects upon Roman believers of the widespread dissatisfaction among Roman citizens towards Nero's taxation policies.[6] The Roman historians Suetonius and Tacitus document the popular outcry against these policies that caused Nero to implement some reforms. In this situation Paul would advise his audience not to be caught up into the popular revolt, and in the light of the reforms in the early part of Nero's reign to pay the taxes and respect Roman authority.[7]

Others have argued that it was the relatively peaceful situation in the empire in the early years of Nero's reign that prompted Paul to encourage his audience to respect authority and pay their taxes. Witherington notes that Seneca in *De clementia* said 'that Nero could boast of having ruled the state at a time when no blood had been shed (11.3), and the arms he wore were for adornment alone (13.5). Without question, Paul will have heard of the imperial rhetoric. . . . He could in good faith exhort his audience to pay their taxes and do their civic duties and live at peace with their neighbors

2. Cf. Troels Engberg-Pedersen, 'Paul's Stoicizing Politics in Romans 12-13: The Role of 13:1-10 in the Argument', *JSNT* 29 (2006) 166.

3. Fitzmyer, *Romans*, 665.

4. Cf. the question addressed to Jesus about taxation in Matt 22:17: 'Tell us then, what is your opinion? Is it right to pay the imperial tax to Caesar or not?'

5. Daniel Kroger, 'Paul and the Civil Authorities: An Exegesis of Romans 13:1-7', *AsiaJT* 7 (1993) 352-54, 357-58. Similarly, Elian Cuvillier, 'Soumission aux autorités et liberté chrétienne: Exégèse de Romains 13,1-7', *Hokhma* 50 (1992) 46-47; Matthew G. Neufeld, 'Submission to Governing Authorities: A Study of Romans 13:1-7', *Direction* 23 (1994) 93-96.

6. Cf. Thomas M. Coleman, 'Binding Obligations in Romans 13:7: A Semantic Field and Social Context', *TynBul* 48 (1997) 326-27. Cf. Dunn, *Romans 9–16*, 768; Byrne, *Romans*, 386.

7. Cf. J. I. H. McDonald, 'Romans 13.1-7: A Test Case for New Testament Interpretation', *NTS* 35 (1989) 546-47.

because there was great and widespread hope, and not only in Rome, that Nero would keep the peace and govern wisely, fairly, and justly'.[8] This situation, of course, changed radically in the later period of Nero's reign.

Carter adopts a very different approach to 13:1-7. He argues that, while the surface meaning of the text may be read to promote submissive obedience to Roman authority, if the passage is read as a piece of ironic rhetoric, it in fact subverts that very notion. He says: 'The lack of correspondence between his [Paul's] words and the reality to which they referred was too great. This points in the direction of the rhetorical use of verbal irony, where the tension between the words and the reality they denote can be enough to reverse the plain meaning of the text. In Rom. 13:1-7, Paul's commendation of the authorities is sufficiently overstated for his audience to understand it as a covert exposure of the shortcomings of Roman rule: the apostle adopts the ironic policy of "blaming through apparent praise". The governing authorities may have been appointed by God, but they were not fulfilling their divinely allotted function. The reasons given for the required submission to the authorities are thus seen to be spurious'. . . .[9]

Others suggest that it was Paul's own experience with sensible Roman magistrates that influenced him to portray the authorities in such a positive way in 13:1-7. This would accord with his view that the authorities are God's provision for the good order of society, even though particular rulers may from time to time fail in the carrying out of their God-given duties (something of which the apostle was well aware, as what he says about persecution and overcoming evil with good indicates). On this view, Paul's instructions would provide guidelines for all believers, not only those living in Rome but also for those living in places outside Rome. As always, caution is necessary when applying Scripture to situations different from those of the original audience.[10] One obviously different situation is that of modern democracies in which governments are ultimately answerable to the people rather than people being answerable to the government.

It is impossible to be dogmatic about the exact *Sitz im Leben* of Paul's exhortations in 13:1-7,[11] whether one or other of the suggestions mentioned

---

8. Cf. Witherington, *Romans*, 306.

9. T. L. Carter, 'The Irony of Romans 13', *NovT* 46, no. 3 (2004) 226.

10. Cf. Jewett, *Romans*, 786-87: 'My approach is to interpret the verbal details in view of their rhetorical significance. Romans 13:1-7 was not intended to create the foundation of a political ethic for all times and places in succeeding generations — a task for which it has proven to be singularly ill-suited. Believing himself to be a member of the end-time generation, Paul had no interest in the concerns that would later burden Christian ethics, and which continue to dominate the exegetical discussion. His goal was to appeal to the Roman audience as he conceived it, addressing their concerns in a manner that fit the occasion of his forthcoming visit'.

11. Stein, 'The Argument of Romans 13:1-7', 327-28, notes that the various attempts to define the *Sitz im Leben* of Paul's advice regarding taxation, 'while interesting, always suffer from their hypothetical nature' and cannot be reconstructed with any degree of certainty. Therefore we should be content to discuss what he said rather than why he said it.

above is to be preferred, or a combination of two or more of them. Carter's view that Paul is speaking ironically, and even subverting the need for submission, is doubtful for two reasons: (i) Jesus' own response to those who asked whether it was right to pay taxes to Caesar ('Give to Caesar what is Caesar's and to God what is God's' [Mark 12:17 par. Matt 22:21; Luke 20:25]) would probably have been known to Paul and influenced him; (ii) it is consistent with the straightforward advice given in Titus 3:1: 'Remind the people to be subject to rulers and authorities, to be obedient, to be ready to do whatever is good'.

13:1   The apostle begins: *Let everyone be subject to the governing authorities*.[12] 'Everyone' (lit. 'every soul', denoting, of course, the whole person) is emphatic, implying that none in Paul's audience should regard themselves as exceptions as far as obedience to this rule is concerned.[13] When exhorting believers to 'submit' to the governing authorities appointed by God, the apostle employs the same verb he uses when pointing out the failure of many of his kinspeople to 'submit' to God's righteousness (10:3), when he insists that the spirits of the prophets 'are subject' to the control of the prophets (1 Cor 14:32), when he urges the Corinthian believers to 'submit' to Christian workers who labor in the service of the saints (1 Cor 16:15-16), and when he instructs believers to 'submit' to one another (Eph 5:21), namely, that wives should 'submit' to their husbands (Eph 5:24; cf. Col 3:18; Tit 2:5) and slaves should 'submit' to their masters (cf. Tit 2:9).[14] Submission to the ruling authorities is to be given willingly, but not uncritically, for there will be occasions when what the authorities demand is contrary to 'what God's will is' (cf. 12:2).[15]

Believers are to submit to human governing authorities, Paul says, *for*

---

12. Paul uses the word *exousia* here when referring to the 'authorities' to which believers should submit, and does so in only one other place (Tit 3:1: 'Remind the people to be subject to rulers and authorities *(exousiais)*, to be obedient, to be ready to do whatever is good'). However, he frequently uses *exousia* when referring to Christ's dominion over the authorities, including both those in heaven and those on earth (1 Cor 15:24; Eph 1:21; Col 1:16; 2:15). In the present context there is little to suggest that the apostle has anything other than civil authorities in mind. Cf. Cranfield, *Romans*, II, 659; Dunn, *Romans 9–16*, 760

13. Paul refers to the 'authorities' as 'governing' authorities using a participial form of *hyperechō*, a verb used in this connection in only one other place in the NT (1 Pet 2:13: 'Submit yourselves for the Lord's sake to every human authority: whether to the emperor, as the supreme authority *(hōs hyperechonti)*'. Jewett, *Romans*, 788, argues: 'Since the participle *hoi hyperechontes*, as well as the noun *exousiai*, can be used to refer to governmental officials, their somewhat redundant combination here has a cumulative sense that encompasses a range of officials placed in superior positions of political authority, duly appointed to their tasks and currently exercising their power . . . that is, the local magistrates in Rome'.

14. Paul gives similar instructions using the verb 'to obey' *(hypakouō)* rather than 'submit' *(hypotassō)* when he instructs children to obey their parents (Eph 6:1; Col 3:20) and slaves to obey their masters (Eph 6:5-6; Col 3:22).

15. Cf. Isaak, 'The Christian Community and Political Responsibility', 41; Cranfield, *Romans*, II, 662; Jewett, *Romans*, 789; Moo, *Romans*, 797.

there is no authority except that which God has established.[16] *The authorities that exist have been established by God.* In so saying, Paul is drawing upon teaching in Jewish literature about God's sovereignty over the rise and fall of earthly rulers.[17] This literature recognizes that there are both good and bad rulers, but affirms that ultimately God rules over them all. The following texts illustrate this:

> By me kings reign and rulers issue decrees that are just; by me princes govern, and nobles — all who rule on earth. (Prov 8:15-16)

> In the LORD's hand the king's heart is a stream of water that he channels toward all who please him. (Prov 21:1)

> With my great power and outstretched arm I made the earth and its people and the animals that are on it, and I give it to anyone I please. Now I will give all your countries into the hands of my servant Nebuchadnezzar king of Babylon; I will make even the wild animals subject to him. All nations will serve him and his son and his grandson until the time for his land comes; then many nations and great kings will subjugate him. (Jer 27:5-7)

> He changes times and seasons; he deposes kings and raises up others. (Dan 2:21)

> The Most High is sovereign over the kingdoms on earth and gives them to anyone he wishes. (Dan 4:17, 25, 32)

> For your dominion was given you from the Lord, and your sovereignty from the Most High; he will search out your works and inquire into your plans. (Wis 6:3)

> The government of the earth is in the hand of the Lord, and over it he will raise up the right leader for the time. (Sir 10:4)

> He will for ever keep faith with all men, especially with the powers that be, since no ruler attains his office save by the will of God. (Josephus, *Jewish Wars* 2.140)

Most importantly, Paul's statement here echoes what the Lord Jesus said to Pilate at his trial: 'You would have no power over me if it were not given to you from above' (John 19:11).

16. 'For there is no authority except that which God has established' translates *ou gar estin exousia ei mē hypo theou* (lit. 'for there is no authority except from God').

17. Jon Nelson Bailey, 'Paul's Political Paraenesis in Romans 13:1-7', *ResQ* 46 (2004) 15, 16-18, after detailing the teaching of Cicero, Seneca, Epictetus, and Marcus Aurelius, shows that Paul's teaching about the need for believers to submit to governing authorities was consistent not only with Jewish but also with Hellenistic traditions.

The way the early church fathers explained Paul's teaching and applied it is very instructive, for they knew from experience that individual rulers could abuse their God-given authority. So Origen asks: 'Is an authority which persecutes the children of God, which attacks the faith and which undermines our religion, from God? We shall answer this briefly. Nobody will deny that our senses — sight, sound and thought — are given to us by God. But although we get them from God, what we do with them is up to us. . . . God's judgment against the authorities will be just, if they have used the powers they have received according to their own ungodliness and not according to the law of God.'[18]

Apollinaris of Laodicea, citing the case of Judas the Galilean (who 'in the days of the census . . . led a band of people in revolt' [Acts 5:37]), says, 'as Judas's decision was the cause of domestic murders and of a rebellion against the authorities which did much harm to the people, it seems to me that here the apostle is condemning any attempt to imitate him based on the illusion that it is a godly thing to disobey rulers. He has a good deal to say about this, condemning it as a mistaken way of thinking'.[19] Chrysostom adds: 'He does not speak about individual rulers but about the principle of authority itself. For that there should be rulers and ruled and that things should not just lapse into anarchy, with the people swaying like waves from one extreme to the other, is the work of God's wisdom'.[20]

Augustine points out: 'If anyone thinks that because he is a Christian he does not have to pay taxes or tribute nor show proper respect to the authorities who take care of these things, he is in very great error. Likewise, if anyone thinks that he ought to submit to the point where he accepts that someone who is his superior in temporal affairs should have authority even over his faith, he falls into an even greater error. But the balance which the Lord himself prescribed is to be maintained: *Render unto Caesar the things which are Caesar's but unto God the things which are God's.* For although we are called into that kingdom where there will be no power of this world, nevertheless, while we are on the way there and until we have reached that state where every principality and power will be destroyed, let us put up with our condition for the sake of human affairs, doing nothing falsely and in this very thing obeying God who commands us to do it, rather than men'.[21]

Theodoret of Cyrrhus comments: 'The holy apostle teaches us that both authorities and obedience depend entirely on God's providence, but he does not say that God has specifically appointed one person or another to exercise authority. For it is not the wickedness of individual rulers which comes from God but the establishment of the ruling power it-

---

18. 'Commentary on the Epistle to the Romans' (*ACCSR*, 324).
19. 'Commentary from the Greek Church' (*ACCSR*, 324).
20. 'Homilies on Romans 23' (*ACCSR*, 325).
21. 'Augustine on Romans' (*ACCSR*, 325).

self. . . . Since God wants sinners to be punished, he is prepared to tolerate even bad rulers'.[22]

13:2 In the light of the fact that 'the authorities that exist have been established by God', Paul says: *Consequently, whoever rebels against the authority is rebelling against what God has instituted.* To rebel against the authority is a serious matter because it means to rebel against what God has instituted,[23] and Paul adds: *those who do so will bring judgment on themselves.* The judgment is God's judgment, but, as Paul explains in the following verses, it is carried out by the authorities that he has appointed. Jewett, however, cautions: 'In view of the earlier references in Romans to divine judgment (2:2, 3; 3:8; 5:16), it seems likely that Paul had in mind the threat of facing God's tribunal, as well as governmental verdicts'.[24]

13:3-4 In these verses Paul speaks of the role of the authorities as God's agents to reward those who do good and punish those who do evil. He begins with a word of assurance to those who do good: *For rulers hold no terror for those who do right, but for those who do wrong.*[25] Following on from what he said in 12:17-21 about the way believers should conduct themselves in the world — overcoming evil with good — Paul now assures his audience that those who do right (lit. 'the good') have nothing to fear from Roman rulers. They 'hold no terror for those who do right, but for those who do wrong' (lit. 'they are not a terror to good work but to evil'). Dunn explains that Paul's good/evil antithesis signals that he 'is expressing himself in terms which would gain the widest approbation from men and women of good will. . . . Whatever the abuses perpetrated on the system by corrupt rulers, this statement of principle would be widely accepted'. . . .[26]

If it is granted that rulers 'hold no terror for those who do right', Paul asks: *Do you want to be free from fear of the one in authority?* He follows up this rhetorical question with the exhortation: *Then do what is right and you will be commended* (lit. 'do what is good and you will have approval from it [the au-

---

22. 'Interpretation of the Letter to the Romans' (*ACCSR*, 325-26).

23. Origen says: 'This injunction does not apply in the case of authorities who persecute the faith. It only applies to those who are going about their proper business' ('Commentary on the Epistle to the Romans' [*ACCSR*, 326]). It is not certain that Paul would recommend opposition to those who persecute Christians, except when their demands explicitly involved a denial of the faith.

24. Jewett, *Romans*, 791-92. Similarly, Dunn, *Romans 9–16*, 762-63. Cf. Stein, 'The Argument of Romans 13:1-7', 331-32, who holds, in the light of the fact that 9 or perhaps 10 of the other uses of *krima* in Paul refer to God's judgment, that 'the judgment referred to in 13:2b is the final judgment of God at the end of history'.

25. Here those in authority are referred to as *hoi archontes* ('rulers'). The word *archōn* used here is found in only three other places in Paul's letters — to denote earthly rulers in 1 Cor 2:6, 8, and to denote 'the ruler of the kingdom of the air, the spirit who is now at work in those who are disobedient' in Eph 2:2. Here in 13:3 it functions as a synonym for *exousia* ('authority').

26. Dunn, *Romans 9–16*, 763.

thority]'.[27] When Paul says that those who do 'good' may expect commendation from the governing authority, he is using the terminology of Hellenistic civic life.[28] Winter argues that 'there is a considerable body of evidence from inscriptions which shows that Paul's assurance, and also that of the parallel statement in 1 Pet. 2.15, was fully justified. This epigraphic evidence clearly demonstrates along with literary evidence that not only did rulers praise and honor those who undertook good works which benefited the city, but at the same time they promised likewise to publicly honor others who would undertake similar benefactions in the future'.[29] To do 'good' was understood to mean doing things that were useful for society, things of worth and social significance.[30] Jewett stresses, 'the fact that Romans was drafted during a period of exemplary Roman administration led by Seneca and Burrus augments the likelihood that Paul's formulation would have resonated positively in Rome. However, before and after that period, Paul's unqualified formulation that officials punish the bad and praise the good seems far from accurate. . . . Paul's wording clearly implies that within the Roman churches "there must have been Christians of very considerable means" who could play the role of public benefactors and gain such recognition'.[31]

When believers do 'good' they may expect the approval of the Roman authority, Paul says, *For the one in authority is God's servant for your good.* However, Paul adds, *But if you do wrong, be afraid, for rulers do not bear the sword for no reason.* Those who do good have no reason to fear the authority, but those who do wrong (lit. 'evil') should fear the consequences ('be afraid' is imperative), for the authorities 'bear the sword'.

What Paul means by 'bearing the sword' has been variously interpreted. Isaak argues that the 'sword' here refers to a small dagger used by police to ensure that people complied with their orders, but does not imply the right to inflict capital punishment.[32] Jewett identifies it as the military sword carried by law enforcement officers who were specially trained soldiers. He claims that there is evidence in the papyri from the period of Paul's Letter to the Romans that refers to police officers as 'sword bearers', adding that many in Paul's audience, who had little protection from the power of the state, would have no illusions about the fate of evildoers.[33] Engberg-Pedersen supports the view that Paul's reference to 'bearing the sword' implies that the authorities have the right to inflict capital punishment. Nero was the sovereign arbiter of life and death for all his subjects.[34]

---

27. The pronoun *autēs* is feminine, agreeing with the feminine noun *exousia* (authority)
28. Cf. Bailey, 'Paul's Political Paraenesis', 20.
29. Winter, 'The Public Honouring of Christian Benefactors', 87.
30. BAGD, *ad loc.*
31. Jewett, *Romans*, 793.
32. Isaak, 'The Christian Community and Political Responsibility', 42.
33. Jewett, *Romans*, 795.
34. Engberg-Pedersen, 'Paul's Stoicizing Politics in Romans 12-13', 167. Similarly, Cranfield, *Romans*, II, 667; Dunn, *Romans 9–16*, 764.

The fact that references to the 'sword' in the NT frequently imply violent death (cf. 8:35; Acts 12:2; 16:27; Heb 11:34, 37) supports the view that 'bearing the sword' in 13:4 means having the power to inflict capital punishment. Because the rulers 'do not bear the sword for no reason', those who do evil should be afraid.

When Paul says, [*For*] *they are God's servants, agents of wrath to bring punishment on the wrongdoer,* he is making clear that in inflicting punishment upon evildoers the authority is acting as God's agent. In practice the Roman authority inflicted punishment upon evildoers without any regard for the God and Father of our Lord Jesus Christ. Nevertheless, it still functioned under the sovereign will of God by whom 'kings reign and rulers issue decrees that are just' and by whom 'princes govern' (Prov 8:15-16). Stein's comment is apposite:

> Paul, of course, was not naïve about the rule of Rome. He had himself been mistreated and beaten by Roman officials (2 Cor 6:5; 11:23-25, 32-33; cf. also Acts 16:22-24). He knew full well that 'Christ suffered under Pontius Pilate' and that the rulers of this age had crucified the Lord of glory (1 Cor 2:8). Furthermore, earlier in Romans he had already spoken of the tribulation, distress, persecution, and sword (Rom 8:35) which Christians faced, and he knew full well that this could come from the State. Yet at the time when Paul wrote, the Roman government could be seen as a positive force for good. Governments, even oppressive governments, by their very nature seek to prevent the evils of indiscriminate murder, riot, thievery, as well as general instability and chaos, and good acts do at times meet with their approval and praise. As a result Paul asserts that the state '. . . is God's servant for your good'.[35]

13:5-6 In 13:5 Paul reiterates what he said at the beginning of this section, introducing again the verb 'to submit' and summarizing what he has said on the subject to this point. In the light of the fact that the governing authority is God's servant, Paul says: *Therefore, it is necessary to submit to the authorities, not only because of possible punishment but also as a matter of conscience.* Paul has already urged his audience to submit on account of the wrath they would experience at the hands of the authority if they refused to do so (13:4), and now he says that it is necessary for them to submit on account of conscience. Conscience is a human faculty that adjudicates upon human action in the light of the highest standard a person perceives. It passes judgment upon past actions and also upon future intentions, as 13:5 implies (see 'Additional Note: Conscience', 141). In the case of believers, conscience demands submission to the authority because that is God's will. Paul's call for submission to the authorities should be understood in

---

35. Stein, 'The Argument of Romans 13:1-7', 334.

terms of the historical situation of the Roman believers to whom Paul
wrote before attempts are made to apply it to different socio-political situations today.

Paul continues: *This is also why you pay taxes, for the authorities are God's servants, who give their full time to governing.* The reason ('because of conscience') just explained is one reason why Christians pay taxes. Another is the recognition of the role of the authorities as 'God's servants'. The word translated 'servant' is frequently used with cultic connotations in the LXX. Paul uses it in 15:16 to describe himself as 'a *minister* of Christ Jesus to the Gentiles in the priestly service of the gospel of God, so that the offering of the Gentiles may be acceptable, sanctified by the Holy Spirit' (italics added), where the cultic allusions are obvious. It would be an appropriate term for the apostle to use in respect to the Roman authorities, whom he describes as 'God's servants'. However, the term was also widely used in Hellenistic society to denote those who perform public service. Dunn is of the opinion that 'in the present context, where the obligations of good citizenship are at the heart of Paul's parenesis, this is most naturally the sense which stands at the forefront of Paul's mind'.[36]

The NIV's 'who give their full time to governing' is better translated as '[who are] devoted to this very thing'.[37] The verb translated 'devoted to' is used by the apostle in 12:12 and Colossians 4:2 to denote perseverance in or devotion to prayer, and it is best understood to bear a similar meaning here in 13:6, where Paul speaks of the authorities as God's servants 'devoted to this very thing'. In context, 'the very thing' to which the authorities are devoted is the collection of taxes.[38]

Dunn remarks: 'Paul must have been aware that the subject [of paying taxes] was a particularly sensitive matter in Rome itself. We know from Tacitus (*Ann.* 13) that the year A.D. 58 saw persistent complaints against the companies farming indirect taxes and the acquisitiveness of tax collectors . . . so that some reform became essential. Presumably these complaints had been building up, or at least the occasion for them, in the years preceding 58, during the period when Romans was written'.[39] This being the case, Paul's exhortation was all the more applicable. It has been suggested that Paul advocates civil obedience precisely because his gospel contained an implicit polemic against imperial power and this could lead some in his audience to withhold taxes.[40]

---

36. Dunn, *Romans 9-16*, 767.

37. NRSV: 'busy with this very thing'.

38. Stein, 'The Argument of Romans 13:1-7', 342, notes three possible interpretations of 'this very thing' *(eis auto touto)*: (i) appointment to minister wrath upon evildoers; (ii) appointment to receive taxes; (iii) appointment to be ministers of God, of which he believes the third is to be preferred because of its agreement with *dia touto*. Cf. Dunn, *Romans 9–16*, 767; Cranfield, *Romans*, II, 669.

39. Dunn, *Romans 9-16*, 766.

40. Cf. Wright, 'A Fresh Perspective on Paul?' 37-39.

13:7 Paul concludes his instructions concerning believers' relationship with the Roman authorities with the general exhortation: *Give to everyone what you owe them: If you owe taxes, pay taxes; if revenue, then revenue; if respect, then respect; if honor, then honor.* The 'everyone' here refers to those Roman officials who can demand the payment of taxes and who can collect revenue,[41] and to whom honor and respect should be accorded.[42]

The terms 'taxes' and 'revenue' represent tangible obligations to be met by citizens, and denote direct taxes and indirect taxes respectively. Coleman describes 'taxes' as the direct poll tax that carried overtones of subjugation imposed upon all imperial subjects, except those granted exemption (e.g., citizens of Rome and Italy). 'Revenue' he describes as an indirect tax levied on goods and services, such as sales of land, houses, oil, and grass.[43] 'Respect' and 'honor' represent intangible obligations required of citizens. Commenting on these obligations, Coleman says: 'Failure to give due reverence and honor for benefactions attracted legal penalties. Claudius, for instance, "reduced to slavery again any such (freedmen) as were ungrateful and a cause of complaint to their patrons (i.e., their former masters)". Nero went even further, making into law a practice which Gaius had initiated and Claudius had continued: punishment of the ungrateful. Nero legislated that the estates of the "ungrateful" — those who failed to make monetary provision for him in their wills — would be confiscated'.[44]

Porter points out that there are two 'prongs' to Paul's arguments concerning the Roman authorities. First, believers are to willingly submit to the authorities on the assumption that they are just. Second, if rulers' authority derives from God, they must rule in a way that is consistent with God's justice. He draws the following conclusion: 'The important implication is that unjust authorities are not due the obedience of which Paul speaks, but rather are outside these boundaries of necessary obedience. Rather than being a text which calls for submissive obedience, Rom 13:1-7 is a text which only demands obedience to what is right, never to what is wrong'.[45]

41. 'Revenue' here translates *telos*, which usually denotes the end, completion, or goal of something. However, it does on occasion denote revenue, as here and in Matt 17:24-26: 'After Jesus and his disciples arrived in Capernaum, the collectors of the two-drachma tax came to Peter and asked, "Doesn't your teacher pay the temple tax *(telei [ta] didrachma)?*" "Yes, he does", he replied. When Peter came into the house, Jesus was the first to speak. "What do you think, Simon?" he asked. "From whom do the kings of the earth collect duty *(telē)* and taxes — from their own sons or from others?" "From others", Peter answered. "Then the children are exempt", Jesus said to him'. Cf. BAGD, *ad loc.*

42. Paul's instruction to his audience that they fulfill their obligations in the matter of taxes and revenue, respect and honor, echoes Jesus' response to the question about paying taxes to Caesar: 'Give back to Caesar what is Caesar's and to God what is God's' (Mark 12:17 par. Matt 22:21; Luke 20:25).

43. Thomas M. Coleman, 'Binding Obligations in Romans 13:7: A Semantic Field and Social Context', *TynBul* 48 (1997) 309-15.

44. Coleman, 'Binding Obligations in Romans 13:7', 326-27.

45. Stanley E. Porter, 'Romans 13:1-7 as Pauline Political Rhetoric', *FilolNT* 3 (1990) 117-18.

D. Love Fulfills the Law, 13:8-10

> [8]*Let no debt remain outstanding, except the continuing debt to love one another, for whoever loves others has fulfilled the law.* [9]*The commandments, 'You shall not commit adultery', 'You shall not murder', 'You shall not steal', 'You shall not covet', and whatever other command there may be, are summed up in this one command: 'Love your neighbor as yourself'.* [10]*Love does no harm to a neighbor. Therefore love is the fulfillment of the law.*

If Engberg-Pedersen is correct and Paul's politics can be summed up as acting with 'love' in the in-group (among fellow believers) and doing 'good' in relationship with the out-group (nonbelievers), then here in 13:8-10 the apostle returns to the politics of the in-group, that is, the way believers should act in their relationships with one another. There is a verbal connection between 13:7 and 13:8-10. In 13:7 Paul exhorts his audience to give everyone 'what you *owe* them', and in the opening exhortation of 13:8-10 he says: 'Let no debt remain outstanding' (lit. '*owe* no one anything').

Paul begins this new section with the exhortation that in relationships with one another believers should 'owe' no one anything with only one exception: *Let no debt remain outstanding, except the continuing debt to love one another* (lit. 'owe no man anything except to love one another'). That Paul speaks of the obligation to love 'one another' confirms that he has in mind specifically relationships between fellow members of the Christian community, not all and sundry.[1] This does not mean that believers are not to show love to others. Paul makes that plain in 1 Thessalonians 5:15: 'Make sure that nobody pays back wrong for wrong, but always strive to do what is good for each other *and for everyone else*' (italics added).[2]

Paul speaks of many different obligations that believers ought to fulfill so that they 'let no debt remain outstanding'. All debts must be paid.[3]

---

1. Paul's predominant use of *allēlōn* suggests that it refers to relationships between believers here. Cf. Jewett, *Romans*, 807. *Contra* Dunn, *Romans 9–16*, 776. Of the 40 occurrences of the expression 'one another' *(allēlōn)* in Paul's letters, 36 concern relationships between believers, two concern the behavior of pagan Gentiles, one concerns the flesh and the Spirit being in conflict with one another, and one relates to believers' pre-conversion relationships.

2. Paul often urges his audiences to fulfill their obligations to one another: 'We who are strong ought *(opheilomen)* to bear with the failings of the weak' (15:1); 'They were pleased to do it, and indeed they owe it *(opheiletai)* to them. For if the Gentiles have shared in the Jews' spiritual blessings, they owe it *(opheilousin)* to the Jews to share with them their material blessings' (15:27); 'The husband should fulfill his marital duty *(opeilēn)* to his wife, and likewise the wife to her husband' (1 Cor 7:3); 'If anyone is worried that he might not be acting honorably toward the virgin he is engaged to, and if his passions are too strong and he feels he ought *(opheilei)* to marry, he should do as he wants. He is not sinning. They should get married' (1 Cor 7:36); 'I will not be a burden to you, because what I want is not your possessions but you. After all, children should not have *(opheilei)* to save up for their parents, but parents for their children' (2 Cor 12:14); 'Husbands ought *(opheilousin)* to love their wives as their own bodies' (Eph 5:28).

3. Moo, *Romans*, 812-13, comments: 'This command does not forbid a Christian from

There is, however, one debt that is ongoing, the debt 'to love one another'. Sanday and Headlam cite Origen: 'Let your only debt that is unpaid be that of love — a debt which you should always be attempting to discharge in full, but will never succeed in discharging'.[4]

By continuing to pay their debt of love to one another, believers will give expression in their lives and behavior to what the law of Moses sought to inculcate. So Paul adds, *for whoever loves others has fulfilled the law.* The NIV's 'others' in 13:8b is to be interpreted in the light of 'one another' in 13:8a, that is, a fellow believer. When a person loves his fellow believer, Paul says, he has 'fulfilled the law'. The apostle then explains how this is so: *The commandments, 'You shall not commit adultery', 'You shall not murder', 'You shall not steal', 'You shall not covet', and whatever other command there may be, are summed up in this one command: 'Love your neighbor as yourself'.* The reference to 'whatever other commandment there may be' probably refers to the other commandments of the Decalogue, rather than being a generalizing reference to other legal systems.[5] This is implied by the fact that all these commandments are summed up in the one rule, 'Love your neighbor as yourself', and that such love fulfills the law, clearly a reference to the law of God, in particular the Decalogue.

The command to 'love your neighbor as yourself' derives from Leviticus 19:18: 'Do not seek revenge or bear a grudge against one of your people, but love your neighbor as yourself. I am the LORD'. This passage is cited or alluded to frequently in the NT (Matt 5:43; 19:19; 22:39; Mark 12:31, 33; Luke 10:27; Gal 5:14; Jas 2:8). In its context the command of Leviticus 19:18 to love one's neighbor as oneself refers to love of one's fellow Israelite. However, when Jesus answered the expert in the law who asked him, 'Who is my neighbor?' he responded with the parable of the Good Samaritan, showing that our neighbor is the person we encounter in need (Luke 10:25-37). While elsewhere Paul taught that believers should do good to all (Gal 6:10), here in 13:8-10 he has in mind love for 'one another', that is, for one's fellow believers.

Paul makes a similar point about the entire law being summed up in this single command in Galatians 5:14. Both that text and 13:9 echo not only Leviticus 19:18 but also, and more importantly, the teaching of Jesus himself: '"Love the Lord your God with all your heart and with all your soul and with all your mind". This is the first and greatest commandment. And the second is like it: "Love your neighbor as yourself". All the Law and the Prophets hang on these two commandments' (Matt 22:37-40).

Paul adds: *Love does no harm to a neighbor. Therefore love is the fulfillment of the law.* By so doing he explains how he understands love to be the fulfill-

---

ever incurring a debt (e.g., to buy a house or a car); it rather demands that Christians repay any debts they do incur promptly and in accordance with the terms of the contract'.

4. Sanday and Headlam, *Romans*, 373.

5. *Contra* Fitzmyer, *Romans*, 679.

ment of the law, that is, if believers love one another, they will certainly not want to harm one another. In this way they will fulfill the law, in particular the laws of the second table of the Decalogue. It is important to note that Paul is not saying that love will lead believers to carry out all that the law demands (which would include, e.g., the practice of circumcision, obedience to calendrical rules, and the observance of food taboos; things which Paul taught were not obligatory for believers [cf. 2:26; 14:2-6]). What he says is that love *fulfills* the law, and that is clearly something different. When Paul claims that love is the fulfillment of the law, he has in mind particularly those laws that relate to the neighbor's well-being. Thus he cites four commandments from the second table of the Decalogue (only the commandments to honor one's father and mother and not to bear false witness are omitted from Paul's list), and says that these, 'and whatever other commandment there may be, are summed up in this one command: "Love your neighbor as yourself"' (13:9). It is clear that what Paul is asserting here is of limited application: love is the fulfillment of the law insofar as the law is concerned to ensure that no harm is done to a neighbor (13:10); he is not saying that love leads believers to observe all the demands of the Mosaic law. This text has important implications for our understanding of the relationship of Paul's gospel to the Mosaic law. It indicates again that his gospel is not antinomian, for it results in the fulfillment of the law. However, this does not mean a reinstatement of the law. Rather, the effect of Paul's gospel is that believers, by walking in the Spirit, are enabled to love one another, so that what the law sought, but was unable to produce, is fulfilled in them (cf. 8:3-4). Understood in this way, Paul's teaching does not involve inner contradictions. It is not a matter of the apostle, having argued that believers have died to the law in 7:1-6, reinstating it again as a regulatory norm for them in 13:8-10.[6]

Wright makes two important comments about these verses. First he says, 'It should not be supposed that the full achievement of "love" consists simply in doing no evil; as Dr Johnson said, "to do no harm is the praise of a stone, not a man. Rather, love, on its way to higher and more positive goals, takes in this negative one in a single stride". If love seeks the highest good of the neighbor, it will certainly do no wrong to him or her'. Second, he insists: 'We should notice that Paul leaves no room for the slippery argument whereby sexual malpractice has been routinely justified in the modern world; "love", as the summary of the law, includes the command not to commit adultery, and could never be confused with the "love" that is frequently held to excuse it. One only has to ask the question whether adultery routinely builds up or breaks down human communities and families to see the point'.[7]

6. Cf. Kruse, *Paul, the Law and Justification*, 237-38, 248.
7. Wright, 'Romans', 725.

E. Living in the Light of the Coming of the Day, 13:11-14

> *11And do this, understanding the present time: The hour has already come for you to wake up from your slumber, because our salvation is nearer now than when we first believed. 12The night is nearly over; the day is almost here. So let us put aside the deeds of darkness and put on the armor of light. 13Let us behave decently, as in the daytime, not in carousing and drunkenness, not in sexual immorality and debauchery, not in dissension and jealousy. 14Rather, clothe yourselves with the Lord Jesus Christ, and do not think about how to gratify the desires of the flesh.*

In these verses Paul urges his audience to live and behave in ways that are consistent with the 'present time', the time when their salvation is 'nearer than when they first believed'. This will mean putting aside the 'deeds of darkness', such things as carousing and drunkenness, dissension and jealousy, and putting on the Lord Jesus Christ instead. The passage, 13:11-14, falls into two parts. The first, 13:11-12a, relates to the nature of the time in which Paul's audience lives, and the second, 13:12b-14, gives exhortations about how they should live in these circumstances.

13:11-12a   Having called upon them to go on discharging their debt of love to one another, the apostle says: *And do this, understanding the present time* (lit. 'and this, knowing the time'). The NIV supplies, probably correctly, the verb 'to do' to function as the main verb of this clause. 'To do this', then, would mean to fulfill the law by loving one another. The NIV also provides the word 'present' to define the 'time'. The 'present time' for Paul is the time ushered in by the first advent of Jesus Christ. So in 3:25-26, speaking of God presenting Christ as the sacrifice of atonement, he declares, 'he did it to demonstrate his righteousness at *the present time,* so as to be just and the one who justifies those who have faith in Jesus'. Similarly, in 5:6 he asserts, 'You see, *at just the right time,* when we were still powerless, Christ died for the ungodly'. In 2 Corinthians 6:2 he adds that the present time is the day of salvation: 'For he says, "In the time of my favor I heard you, and in the day of salvation I helped you". I tell you, now is the time of God's favor, *now is the day of salvation'.* And in 1 Corinthians 7:29-31 he concludes: 'What I mean, brothers and sisters, is that *the time is short.* From now on those who have wives should live as if they did not; those who mourn, as if they did not; those who are happy, as if they were not; those who buy something, as if it were not theirs to keep; those who use the things of the world, as if not engrossed in them. For this world in its present form is passing away' (italics added).

On the basis of the shortness of the 'present time', Paul exhorts his audience to 'wake up': *The hour has already come for you to wake up from your slumber, because our salvation is nearer now than when we first believed. The night is nearly over; the day is almost here.*[1] The 'night' that is 'nearly over' is

---

1. This is one of just four places where Paul speaks of the coming day. Two of these

this present evil age (cf. Gal 1:4), which will finally pass when the 'day' dawns, that is, when the new age is ushered in with the second coming of Christ. At that time believers will experience final salvation.[2] Those who 'slumber' do not understand the nature of the interim time in which they live. Believers, however, should be 'awake', knowing the present time is drawing to a close, and therefore their salvation is nearer that when they first believed.

Augustine, who lived from A.D. 354-430, being aware of the long time that had already elapsed since Paul wrote Romans, comments: 'Paul said this, yet look at how many years have passed since then! Yet what he said was not untrue. How much more probable it is that the coming of the Lord is near now, when there has been such an increase of time toward the end!'[3] We who live now, on this reasoning, must be that much nearer to the time. This long delay has led some to argue that Paul was mistaken. Here Wright's comment is apposite: 'Paul does not say, as many of his interpreters have supposed that he said, that the final end of which he speaks in Romans 8, 1 Corinthians 15, 1 Thessalonians 4–5, and elsewhere, will certainly come within a generation; but he knows that it might well do so, and insists that it is the more urgent that Christians behave already in the manner that will then be appropriate'.[4]

As the next verse indicates, waking up from slumber involves putting away those things that belong to the night, that belong to the darkness.

13:12b Believers, then, even though for the present they still live in the 'night', must live as people of the 'day'. So Paul says: *So let us put aside the deeds of darkness and put on the armor of light.* He speaks of laying aside one thing to take up another. The imagery is a military one, perhaps that of a soldier putting aside nightwear to put on his armor.[5] Paul uses this imagery to exhort his audience to put off the 'deeds of darkness' and to put on the 'armor of light'.[6] (What is involved in putting off the 'deeds of dark-

---

relate to end-time judgment (2:5-11; 14:10-12a), and the other two relate to the day of salvation and glory (8:18-25; 13:11-12).

2. While believers for the present live in the night, they are not children of the night, but children of the coming day (cf. 1 Thess 5:5: 'You are all children of the light and children of the day. We do not belong to the night or to the darkness'). As children of the day, believers must wake up from sleep. They must not be like those whom the apostle describes in 1 Thess 5:7: 'For those who sleep, sleep at night, and those who get drunk, get drunk at night'.

3. 'Letters 77' (ACCSR, 334).

4. Wright, 'Romans', 728. Similarly, Cranfield, *Romans*, II, 681-82. Moo, *Romans*, 82, comments: 'Paul certainly betrays a strong sense of expectation about the return of Christ (e.g., Phil. 4:5) and can even speak at times as if he will be alive at that time (e.g., 1 Thess. 4:15). But nowhere does he predict a near return; and, more importantly, he does not ground his exhortations on the conviction that the parousia would take place very soon but on the conviction that the parousia was always imminent — its coming certain, its timing incalculable'.

5. Fitzmyer, *Romans*, 683, says: 'Christians cannot afford to remain in the unprotected condition of scantily clothed sleepers at a time when the situation calls for "armor"'.

6. Paul uses the word 'darkness' *(skotos)* in a similar way in the following texts: 2 Cor 6:14: 'Do not be yoked together with unbelievers. For what do righteousness and wicked-

ness' and putting on the 'armor of light' Paul will describe in 13:13 and 13:14 respectively.) Paul uses the word translated here as 'armor' in other contexts where it is rendered as 'instruments' or 'weapons',[7] but it is here correctly translated as 'armor', something one *puts on*, rather than something one *wields*. As 13:14 makes clear, the 'armor' that is to be put on is 'the Lord Jesus Christ'.[8]

13:13 Before explaining what it means to 'put aside the deeds of darkness', Paul says: *Let us behave decently, as in the daytime.* To behave 'decently' is to act honorably, or in a fitting and proper way (cf. 1 Cor 14:40; 1 Thess 4:12). In this context to behave fittingly is to behave as children of the day, to behave as if they were already living 'in the daytime'. Eschatologically speaking, even though believers are still living in the 'night' that is 'nearly over', there is also a sense in which they already live in the light of the 'day' that is 'almost here'. As people of the day, they must have nothing more to do with the deeds of darkness.

Explaining now to his audience what it means to 'put aside the deeds of darkness', Paul emphasizes that they are to behave decently, *not in carousing and drunkenness, not in sexual immorality and debauchery, not in dissension and jealousy.* The word translated 'carousing' means excessive feasting or revelry in a bad sense. 'Drunkenness', when associated with 'carousing', denotes 'a drinking bout'.[9] 'Sexual immorality' translates a word which by

---

ness have in common? Or what fellowship can light have with darkness?' Eph 5:8: 'For you were once darkness, but now you are light in the Lord. Live as children of light'; Eph 5:11: 'Have nothing to do with the fruitless deeds of darkness, but rather expose them'; Col 1:13: 'For he has rescued us from the dominion of darkness and brought us into the kingdom of the Son he loves'; 1 Thess 5:4: 'But you, brothers and sisters, are not in darkness so that this day should surprise you like a thief'; 1 Thess 5:5: 'You are all children of the light and children of the day. We do not belong to the night or to the darkness'.

7. In 6:13 he writes: 'Do not offer any part of yourself to sin, as an instrument *(hoplon)* of wickedness, but rather offer yourselves to God, as those who have been brought from death to life; and offer every part of yourself to him as an instrument *(hoplon)* of righteousness'; in 2 Cor 6:7 he speaks of the way he commends himself as a servant of Christ 'in truthful speech and· in the power of God; with weapons of righteousness *(tōn hoplōn tēs dikaiosynēs)* in the right hand and in the left'; and in 2 Cor 10:4: 'The weapons *(hopla)* we fight with are not the weapons of the world. On the contrary, they have divine power to demolish strongholds'.

8. In Eph 6:11-17 Paul uses the same imagery, but does so with a somewhat different application: 'Put on the full *armor* of God so that you can take your stand against the devil's schemes. For our struggle is not against flesh and blood, but against the rulers, against the authorities, against the powers of this dark world and against the spiritual forces of evil in the heavenly realms. Therefore put on the full *armor* of God, so that when the day of evil comes, you may be able to stand your ground, and after you have done everything, to stand. Stand firm then, with the belt of truth buckled around your waist, with the breastplate of righteousness in place, and with your feet fitted with the readiness that comes from the gospel of peace. In addition to all this, take up the shield of faith, with which you can extinguish all the flaming arrows of the evil one. Take the helmet of salvation and the sword of the Spirit, which is the word of God' (italics added).

9. Cf. BAGD, *ad loc.*

itself denotes sexual intercourse, but together with 'debauchery'[10] denotes 'gross sexual excesses'. 'Dissension' denotes strife, discord, and contention, and 'jealousy' denotes 'intense negative feelings over another's achievements or success'.[11] Jewett notes that 'carousing remained typical for Roman dinners, as Bruce Winter reports: tables were reserved for drinking bouts and activities with prostitutes. Cicero describes how young men behaved in the parties celebrating their coming-of-age *(toga virilis)*: "If there is anyone who thinks that youth should be forbidden affairs even with courtesans, he is doubtless eminently austere but his view is not only contrary to the license of this age, but also to the custom and concessions of our ancestors"'.[12] Paul exhorts his Ephesian converts in terms similar to those in 13:13:

> Have nothing to do with the fruitless deeds of darkness, but rather expose them. For it is shameful even to mention what the disobedient do in secret. But everything exposed by the light becomes visible, and everything that is illuminated becomes a light. This is why it is said: 'Wake up, O sleeper, rise from the dead, and Christ will shine on you'. (Eph 5:11-14)

13:14 Using the same metaphor employed when he urged his audience to 'put on the armor of light' (13:12), the apostle says here that, instead of being involved in carousing, drunkenness, and the like, you should *rather, clothe yourselves with the Lord Jesus Christ*. Only here and in Galatians 3:27 does Paul speak of clothing oneself 'with the Lord Jesus Christ'. How are we to understand this? As the 'Additional Note: Paul's Uses of the Clothing Metaphor' (507-8) reveals, many of Paul's uses of the metaphor are related to Christian character and virtues. It would appear that to clothe oneself with the Lord Jesus Christ in 13:14 has similar connotations, because what follows immediately is an exhortation to avoid the opposite: *and do not think about how to gratify the desires of the flesh*. In Galatians 5:19-21 Paul lists a number of 'the acts of the flesh': 'sexual immorality, impurity and debauchery; idolatry and witchcraft; hatred, discord, jealousy, fits of rage, selfish ambition, dissensions, factions and envy; drunkenness, orgies, and the like', a list not unlike that found in 13:13. It is significant that in Galatians 5:16-17 Paul tells his audience: 'Walk by the Spirit, and you will not gratify the desires of the flesh. For the flesh desires what is contrary to

10. The word translated as 'debauchery', *aselgeia*, by itself denotes 'lack of self-constraint which involves one in conduct that violates all bounds of what is socially acceptable, *self-abandonment*'. Cf. BAGD, *ad loc.*

11. BAGD *ad loc.* Ambrosiaster comments: 'Crimes are hatched in large supplies of wine, and many kinds of lust are stirred up. Therefore banquets of this kind are to be avoided. . . . Debauchery is another result of this sort of thing. Paul was right to warn them against quarrelling and jealousy, because both of these things lead to enmity' ('Commentary on Paul's Epistles' [*ACCSR*, 33]).

12. Jewett, *Romans*, 826.

the Spirit, and the Spirit what is contrary to the flesh. They are in conflict with each other, so that you are not to do whatever you want'. When people live by the Spirit, they are enabled to resist the desires of the sinful nature (cf. Gal 5:22-24). When we compare 13:13-14 with Galatians 5:16-24, it seems clear that to clothe oneself with the Lord Jesus Christ is equivalent to living by the Spirit. Both lead to overcoming the desires of the sinful nature and promoting Christian character and virtues.

There has been some discussion regarding the possible background to Paul's image of clothing oneself with the Lord Jesus Christ. Byrne suggests that what lies behind the image could be the Greek drama in which actors put on garments to portray various characters.[13] Others relate it to Christian baptism in which believers are 'incorporated into Christ'. This is a relationship established at conversion and that has to be reappropriated and lived out day by day 'in such a way that his character is manifested in all that we do and say'.[14] Dunn argues that 'the closest parallels come in talk of the final "putting on" of the incorruptibility and immortality (1 Cor 15:53-54) which is "the image of the heavenly", "the last Adam" (15:45-49), and of "putting on the new man" (Col 3:9-10; Eph 4:24). So it is part of the important Pauline understanding of the process of salvation as a becoming conformed to the image of Christ . . . and it speaks of the believers' responsibility within that process, the determined cooperation with the outworking of grace in this time of eschatological tension'.[15]

ADDITIONAL NOTE:
PAUL'S USES OF THE CLOTHING METAPHOR

The clothing metaphor is one Paul uses in several connections. These may be grouped into three categories. First, there are those uses that relate to the resurrection body: In 1 Corinthians 15:53-54 he says regarding the resurrection of the dead and the transformation of the living: 'For the perishable must *clothe itself* with the imperishable, and the mortal [must clothe itself] with immortality. When the perishable has been *clothed* with the imperishable, and the mortal [has been clothed] with immortality, then the saying that is written will come true: "Death has been swallowed up in victory"'. In 2 Corinthians 5:2 he brings out that 'we groan, longing to be *clothed* instead with our heavenly dwelling', in 2 Corinthians 5:3 he notes that 'when we are *clothed*,[16] we will not be found naked', and in 2 Corinthians 5:4 he

---

13. Byrne, *Romans*, 400.

14. Moo, *Romans*, 825-26. Cf. Fitzmyer, *Romans*, 683-84; Cranfield, *Romans*, II, 688-89.

15. Dunn, *Romans 9–16*, 790.

16. Some manuscripts have 'unclothed' (*ekdysamenoi*) rather than 'clothed' (*endysamenoi*) in 2 Cor 5:3.

adds, 'we do not wish to be *unclothed* but to be *clothed* instead with our heavenly dwelling' (italics added).

Second, there are those uses related to putting on 'armor': In 13:12 Paul urges, 'let us put aside the deeds of darkness and *put on* the armor of light'. In Ephesians 6:11 he exhorts his audience: '*put on* the full armor of God', and in Ephesians 6:14-17 he lists the elements of the armor (for the most part, Christian virtues or blessings of the gospel): 'the belt of truth', 'the breastplate of righteousness', 'feet fitted with the readiness that comes from the gospel of peace', 'the shield of faith', and 'the helmet of salvation'. Similarly, in 1 Thessalonians 5:8 Paul tells his audience that they are to 'be sober, *putting on* faith and love as a breastplate, and the hope of salvation as a helmet' (italics added).

Third, there are those references in which the audience is told to put on Christ or the new self: In Galatians 3:27, as in 13:14, Paul speaks of being clothed with Christ: 'for all of you who were baptized into Christ have *clothed yourselves* with Christ'. In Ephesians 4:24 he tells his audience 'to *put on* the new self, created to be like God in true righteousness and holiness'. In Colossians 3:10 he urges his audience to '*put on* the new self, which is being renewed in knowledge in the image of its Creator' (italics added). To clothe oneself with the Lord Jesus Christ appears to be equivalent to living by the Spirit, both of which lead to overcoming the desires of the sinful nature and the promotion of Christian character and virtues.

F. Instructions for the 'Weak' and the 'Strong': Accept One Another, 14:1–15:13

The exhortations of 12:1–13:14 were general in nature with the exception of 13:1-7, which dealt with believers' attitude to Roman authorities. What we find in 14:1–15:13 is by contrast quite specific and relates to a concrete and difficult situation in the Roman churches. It involved disagreements between the 'weak' and the 'strong' concerning what people may or may not eat and drink and whether or not certain days should be regarded as sacred.[1] The precise identity of the 'weak' and the 'strong' and the nature of their controversy have been the subject of some debate. Some of the contributions to this debate are described in 'Additional Note: The "Weak" and the "Strong"', 509-10.

---

1. Witherington, *Romans*, 327, suggests that Paul is employing a rhetorical technique when he treats this contentious ethical issue of the 'weak' and the 'strong' last in the ethical section of the letter, just as he treats the contentious theological issue of Israel last in the theological section (9–11). It allows Paul to gain concurrence from his audience about less contentious matters before confronting them with more contentious matters.

ADDITIONAL NOTE: THE 'WEAK' AND THE 'STRONG'

Cranfield lists six approaches to understanding the differences between the 'weak' and the 'strong' (i) the 'weak' are legalists who think they are accounted righteous by their works; (ii) the 'weak' and the 'strong' disagree over the matter of eating things sacrificed to idols; (iii) abstaining from meat and wine was a type of fast expressing sorrow at the unbelief of the majority of the Jews, a fast that the Jewish, but not Gentile Christians observed; (iv) abstention from meat and wine was a fast but practiced for the disciplining of the body; (v) abstinence from meat and wine was a carry-over of practices from various religious-philosophical movements; and (vi) the 'weak' were those who continued to practice literal observance of the ceremonial laws of the OT. Cranfield's own view is that the 'weak' were those who continued to observe the ceremonial parts of the OT law, whereas the 'strong' recognized that with the coming of Christ the ceremonial law no longer applied.[2]

Reasoner offers a different list of interpretations: (i) the 'weak' are a literary construct based on the situation in Corinth; (ii) the 'weak' are Jewish believers; (iii) the 'weak' are Gentile believers; (iv) the 'weak' include both Jewish and Gentile believers; (v) the 'weak' are practicing Jews outside the church; and (vi) the difference relates to agnosticism towards a historical situation in Rome.[3] Reasoner's own view is that the difference between the 'weak' and the 'strong' is related to status in first-century Roman society. He contends that 'most of the "strong" were Roman citizens, and identified positively with Roman culture', whereas 'the "weak" were a group of believers with low status in the Roman churches. Some of them were convinced that Jewish dietary laws must be observed'. He adds, 'it is also likely that the difference over day observance (14.5-6) was an actual difference in the Roman churches. The "weak" were probably observing the Sabbath and perhaps other fast days. Some of the "weak" may also have been observing Sunday. . . . The "strong" considered the "weak" to be superstitious. We have seen that it was around the time when this letter was written that Christianity was called a superstition in Rome. With their abstinence from certain foods and observance of days, the "weak" were prime candidates for the charge of being superstitious'.[4]

McCruden argues that there was no actual conflict between the 'weak' and the 'strong' in Rome. Instead he suggests that 'the one who eats vegetables and observes one day more than another functions as a literary theological model for both ethnic Jewish Christians and conservative Gentile Christians, while the one who eats all things and makes no distinction

---

2. Cranfield, *Romans*, II, 690-97.

3. Mark Reasoner, *The Strong and the Weak: Romans 14.1–15.13 in Context* (SNTSMS 103; Cambridge: Cambridge University Press, 1999), 5-22.

4. Reasoner, *The Strong and the Weak*, 218-20.

with respect to days functions as a literary model for both Gentile Christians and more liberal Jews like Paul (Rom 14,1-5). When the strong and the weak are viewed in this way, as literary theological models for Jews and Gentiles conceived as a whole, then Rom 14,1–15,13 emerges as the concrete theological explication of the theme of God's gracious and impartial call of salvation for Jew and Gentile alike (Rom 9,24)'.[5] This view is unsatisfactory in that it fails to take proper account of the explicit exhortations contained in 14:1–15:13. There are exhortations to the 'strong' not to despise the 'weak' (14:3a, 10, 13), nor to cause distress to the 'weak' by what they eat (14:15), and to bear with the failings of the 'weak' (15:1). There are also exhortations to the 'weak' not to condemn the 'strong' (14:3b-4), and to both the 'strong' and the 'weak' to accept one another as Christ has accepted them (15:7).

The most widely accepted view, and that adopted in this commentary, is that the 'weak' are Jewish Christians (including possibly proselytes) who practiced essentially Jewish customs, and the 'strong' were mainly Gentile Christians (including some Jewish believers who were liberated like Paul himself) who felt no obligation to practice these customs.[6]

---

1. Accept Those Who Are Weak in Faith, 14:1-12

What emerges as a controlling factor in the way the apostle Paul addresses this issue is believers' accountability to the Lord. All must do what they do 'for the Lord' (14:6, 8), seeking to please God (14:18) and remembering that all must stand before God's judgment seat and give an account of themselves to God (14:10-12). In the light of this fact Paul calls upon all members of his audience to accept one another (cf. 15:7).

a. The Matter of Eating All Foods, 14:1-4

¹Accept the one whose faith is weak, without quarreling over disputable matters. ²One person's faith allows them to eat anything, but another, whose faith is weak, eats only vegetables. ³The one who eats everything must not treat with contempt the one who does not, and the one who does not eat everything must not judge the one who does, for God has accepted them. ⁴Who are you to judge someone else's servant? To their own master, servants stand or fall. And they will stand, for the Lord is able to make them stand.

14:1 Paul begins to address the question of what people's consciences allow or do not allow them to eat with an exhortation to the

5. Kevin B. McCruden, 'Judgment and Life for the Lord: Occasion and Theology of Romans 14,1–15,13', *Bib* 86 (2005) 243.

6. Cf. Dunn, *Romans 9–16*, 795; Wright, 'Romans', 731-32; Moo, *Romans*, 831; Fitzmyer, *Romans*, 686-88.

'strong': *Accept the one whose faith is weak, without quarreling over disputable matters* (lit. 'not for conflict about opinions' or 'not for the purpose of getting into quarrels about opinions').[7] When the apostle exhorts his audience to accept one whose faith is weak[8] 'without quarreling over disputable matters', he has in mind those who welcome people only to set them right in accordance with their own opinions. The exhortation is clearly directed to those who, like Paul, are strong in faith. They are predominantly (but not necessarily exclusively) Gentile believers who make up the majority of the Roman Christian community. To be 'weak in faith' in this context does not denote some lack in fundamental Christian belief, but is equivalent to being troubled in conscience. These are people whose grasp of the implications of the gospel is limited, so that their consciences do not allow them to do certain things that are permissible under the new covenant (cf. 1 Cor 8:7-13).

Augustine comments on Paul's exhortation not to pass judgment on disputable matters: 'Paul says this so that, when something might be done with either good or bad motives, we should leave the judgment to God and not presume to judge the heart of someone else, which we do not see. But when it comes to things which obviously could not have been done with good and innocent intentions, it is not wrong if we pass judgment. So in the matter of food, where it is not known what the motive in eating it is, Paul does not want us to be judges, but God. But in the case of that abominable immorality where a man has taken his stepmother, Paul taught us to judge [1 Cor 5:1-13]. For that man could not possibly claim that he committed such a gross act of indecency with good intentions. So we must pass judgment on things which are obviously wrong'.[9]

14:2 Explaining the nature of the difference of opinion existing between the 'strong' and the 'weak', Paul says: *One person's faith allows them to eat anything, but another, whose faith is weak, eats only vegetables.* Faith that allows a person to eat anything is a faith based upon a proper understanding of the gospel. Such faith is strong and frees the conscience from scruples. Faith that allows a person to eat only vegetables is a faith based upon an inadequate understanding of the gospel. Such a faith is weak and leaves the conscience bound to scruples (see 'Additional Note: Faith and Conscience', 514). [Pseudo-] Constantius remarks: 'Paul calls weak in faith those who thought that meats which were being sold in the markets of that time had been sacrificed to idols, and for that reason they ate only vegetables, thinking that that way they would not be polluted'.[10] Similarly Augustine: 'At that time many people who were strong in their faith and who knew the Lord's teaching, that it is what comes out of the mouth which defiles a man,

7. BAGD, *diakrisis*.

8. Jewett, *Romans*, 835, argues that what it means to 'accept' those who are weak in faith is to welcome them into fellowship, in particular to the common meal.

9. 'Augustine on Romans 79' (*ACCSR*, 340).

10. 'The Holy Letter of St. Paul to the Romans' (*ACCSR*, 337).

not what goes into it, were eating whatever they liked with a clear conscience. But some weaker ones abstained from meat and wine, so as to
avoid unknowingly eating foods which had been sacrificed to idols. At that
time the Gentiles sold all sacrificed meat in the butcher shops, poured out
the first fruits of the wine as a libation to their idols and even made some
offerings in the wine presses'.[11] Bruce Winter claims that 'when Claudius
banned the Jews from Rome in A.D. 49 the officials who controlled the meat
market would have withdrawn the provision of "suitable food". There may
have been some in Rome who were no longer eating meat because kosher
meat was not available in the markets'.[12] This could account for the vege-
tarianism of the 'weak'.

14:3   Those of strong faith and those of weak faith both have a tendency to act in uncharitable ways. Thus, concerning those of strong faith
Paul says: *The one who eats everything must not treat with contempt the one who
does not.* The apostle has in mind for the most part Gentile believers who
made up the greater part of Roman Christian congregations and who continued to be part of those congregations when Jews and Jewish believers
were expelled from Rome under the edict of Claudius. When that edict
lapsed and Jews returned to the capital, Jewish believers again became a
part of the Christian congregations. Very likely, at that time, Gentile believers, strong in their faith, looked down on Jewish believers whom they regarded as still in bondage to a scrupulous conscience. This, Paul contends,
they must not do.

To those of weak faith the apostle says: *and the one who does not eat everything must not judge the one who does, for God has accepted them.* He has in
mind, for the most part, Jewish believers who formed a minority in the Roman congregations following their return to the capital when the edict of
Claudius lapsed. These believers Paul regarded as weak in faith because
they were still conscience-bound to observe Jewish food laws and, if
[Pseudo-] Constantius is right, would eat only vegetables, fearing that meat
sold in the markets had been offered to idols. Their tendency was to condemn other believers because they did not observe these food taboos. Paul
seems to imply that they even questioned the acceptability to God of such
Gentile believers.[13] Hence Paul tells them not to condemn those who eat ev-

---

11. 'Augustine on Romans 78' (*ACCSR*, 338-39).

12. Bruce Winter, 'Roman Law and Society in Romans 12–15', in *Rome in the Bible and
the Early Church*, ed. P. Oakes (Grand Rapids: Baker, 2002), 90. Cf. Witherington, *Romans*,
334-35.

13. In fact these Gentile believers understood better the implications of the gospel
that undergirded Paul's advice to the Corinthians in respect to food offered to idols (1 Cor
8:7-8; 10:23-30). Their stance on eating all sorts of food also reflects the teaching of the Lord
Jesus. Cf. Mark 7:14-19: 'Again Jesus called the crowd to him and said, "Listen to me, everyone, and understand this. Nothing outside a person can defile them by going into them.
Rather, it is what comes out of a person that defiles them". After he had left the crowd and
entered the house, his disciples asked him about this parable. "Are you so dull?" he asked.
"Don't you see that nothing that enters a person from the outside can defile them? For it

erything, 'for God has accepted them'; and God had accepted them without their having to observe food taboos. Just as Paul exhorted the 'strong' to accept the 'weak' without passing judgment in 14:1, so here he exhorts the 'weak' not to pass judgment upon the 'strong' because God has 'accepted' them. The verb translated 'accepted' here (also used in 14:1; 14:3; 15:7 [2x]) is one that carries, in these sorts of contexts, the basic meaning 'to extend a welcome, receive into one's home or circle of acquaintances'.[14] Acceptance of one believer by another is mandatory in the light of the fact that God himself has accepted them both. This point the apostle reiterates a little later: 'Accept one another, then, just as Christ accepted you' (15:7)

14:4 Continuing to address those of weak faith, Paul asks: *Who are you to judge someone else's servant? To their own master, servants stand or fall.* The tendency of the 'weak' is to stand in judgment over the 'strong', criticizing them for not sharing the same scruples in relation to foods. This is tantamount to criticizing 'someone else's servant'. Paul uses an unusual word for 'servant' here,[15] the basic meaning of which is 'a member of the household', and then, specifically, a 'domestic slave'.[16] To criticize someone else's servant was inadmissible, and in the case of a guest, a violation of hospitality rules in the ancient world (see 'Additional Note: Hospitality', 478-79).

Servants are responsible to their own masters and to no one else, and it is before their own masters that they stand or fall. When the 'weak' judge the 'strong', they are not simply judging a fellow believer, but one who is the Lord's servant. *And,* Paul reminds them, *they will stand, for the Lord is able to make them stand.* What Paul means is that the Lord is able to make his servants stand firm in their faith,[17] that is, God is able to preserve them blameless before him in the freedom of Christ even though they do not submit to the scruples of the 'weak'.[18] The error of the 'weak' when they pass judgment on the 'strong' is that they presume that when the 'strong' live in

---

doesn't go into their heart but into their stomach, and then out of the body". (In saying this, Jesus declared all foods clean.)'

14. BAGD, *ad loc.* Jewett, *Romans,* 840-41, explains: 'Welcome to the banquet is the crucial issue here, and Paul probably relies on the widely shared tradition of Christ as the host of the Lord's Supper, the master of the love feast, acting in behalf of God to welcome the faithful into the messianic banquet in fulfillment of the ancient prophecies'.

15. The word he uses is *oiketēs,* found only here and in three other places in the NT (Luke 16:13; Acts 10:7; 1 Pet 2:18).

16. BAGD, *ad loc.* Cf. Jewett, *Romans,* 841-42.

17. In 11:20 the apostle reminds the Gentile members of his audience that they 'stand by faith', and should not therefore be arrogant. In 1 Cor 15:1 he reminds his audience of the gospel he preached to them, 'which you received and on which you have taken your stand'. In 2 Cor 1:24 he says: 'it is by faith you stand firm'. In Eph 6:11 Paul urges his audience to 'put on the full armor of God' so they can take their 'stand against the devil's schemes'.

18. When in 1 Cor 10:12 Paul warned his audience about abusing their freedom by eating in idol temples ('if you think you are standing firm [*estanai*], be careful that you don't fall [*pesē*]!), he used the same verbs, 'to stand' and 'to fall' (*histēmi* and *piptō*), that he employs here in 14:4. In both cases to stand and not fall means to stand firm in faith and not fall into sin.

the freedom the gospel provides, they will to fall into sin. They fail to recognize that the Lord who establishes his servants in this freedom is able to make them stand.[19] Cranfield puts it this way: 'The metaphor of standing or falling . . . is much more naturally understood as denoting perseverance in, or falling away from, faith and obedience. Christ (or God) Himself is concerned, His interest is at stake, in the question whether the strong Christian continues in faith or falls away from it'.[20]

ADDITIONAL NOTE: FAITH AND CONSCIENCE

It is noteworthy that in 14:1-2 Paul says that it is people's 'faith' that allows or disallows them to eat anything. However, in 1 Corinthians 8:7, 10, 12; 10:25, 27-29 he indicates that it is people's 'conscience' that comes into play in the matter of eating or not eating meat offered to idols. For Paul, conscience is a human faculty whereby a person either approves or disapproves his or her actions (whether already performed or only intended) and those of others. It is not to be equated with the voice of God or the moral law; rather, it is a human faculty which adjudicates upon human action in the light of the highest standard a person perceives. People cannot reject the voice of conscience with impunity, but they can modify the highest standard to which it relates by gaining a greater understanding of the truth (see 'Additional Note: Conscience', 141). With this in mind we can explain the relationship between faith and conscience: strong faith, based upon a proper understanding of the gospel and the liberty it brings, frees the conscience to allow a person to eat anything. However, weak faith, based on an inadequate understanding of the gospel and the liberty it brings, will render the conscience unable to allow a person to eat anything — he or she will be unnecessarily in bondage to scruples.

---

b. The Matter of Observing Special Days, 14:5-8

> [5]_One person considers one day more sacred than another; another considers every day alike. Each of them should be fully convinced in their own mind._ [6]_Whoever regards one day as special does so to the Lord. Whoever eats meat does so to the Lord, for they give thanks to God; and whoever abstains does so to the Lord and gives thanks to God._ [7]_For none of us lives for ourselves alone, and none of us dies for ourselves alone._ [8]_If we live, we live for the Lord; and if we die, we die for the Lord. So, whether we live or die, we belong to the Lord._

19. Some, e.g., Wright, 'Romans', 736; Jewett, _Romans_, 843, see in the reference to 'standing' a possible reference to resurrection and/or vindication in the last judgment, but in context the primary reference is to standing firm in one's freedom and not stumbling into sin.
20. Cranfield, _Romans_, II, 703.

Whereas in 14:1-4 Paul dealt with issues between the 'weak' and the 'strong' in relation to eating all sorts of food, in 14:5-8 he deals with the issues between them in relation to the observance of special days, though without losing sight altogether of the matter of foods.

14:5 Summarizing this next issue, Paul says: *One person considers one day more sacred than another; another considers every day alike* (lit. 'for one man judges a day distinct from [another] day; one man judges every day'). It is generally believed that those who considered one day more sacred than another were Jewish believers (and Gentile believers who were influenced by Jewish traditions) who felt obliged to observe Jewish calendrical rules, including the observance of the Sabbath and festival days. They would have done so not necessarily believing such observance determined their acceptability to God, but because they were convinced that it was the appropriate way to express their allegiance to him. Their tendency would have been to pass judgment upon those who neglected to observe sacred days. Those who considered 'every day alike' have generally been regarded as Gentile and liberated Jewish believers for whom sacred days were irrelevant and who therefore treated all days alike. Their tendency would have been to despise the scruples of those who felt obliged to observe sacred days.[21]

Literally translated, Paul says that it is 'a day' that some judged distinct from another day, and in 14:6 this day is described as 'the day'. Weiss argues that 'the day' was the Sabbath, and that while some judged the Sabbath as more sacred than other days, there were others who judged all days, that is, they treated all days as Sabbaths, and not as profane.[22] This is unlikely, for if the 'strong' regarded all days as Sabbaths, they would hardly invite judgment from the weak for doing so. It is better to understand Paul to mean that the 'strong' regarded all days the same, that is, they treated none of them as particularly sacred.

Paul's exhortation to those of each persuasion is: *Each of them should be fully convinced in their own mind.*[23] Paul's exhortation is that members of his audience 'be fully convinced in their own minds' even when they differ from one another concerning the significance of special days. In matters of

---

21. Early church fathers, including Augustine ('Letter 36'), Chrysostom ('Homilies on Romans 25'), and [Pseudo-] Constantius ('The Holy Letter of St. Paul to the Romans'), interpret these special days that Paul says some observe and some do not as fasting days (*ACCSR*, 340-41).

22. Herold Weiss, 'Paul and the Judging of Days', *ZNW* 86 (1995) 142-44.

23. The apostle had some important things to say about the Christian mind *(nous)*. In 12:2 he urged his audience not to be conformed 'to the pattern of this world, but be transformed by the renewing of your mind *(noos)'*. In 2 Thess 2:2 (NRSV) he urged people 'not to be quickly shaken in mind *(noos)* or alarmed, either by spirit or by word or by letter, as though from us, to the effect that the day of the Lord is already here', and in Tit 1:15, a text which has some relevance for the present context, he said: 'To the pure, all things are pure, but to those who are corrupted and do not believe, nothing is pure. In fact, both their minds *(nous)* and consciences are corrupted'. The renewing of the mind in accordance with the truth and the steadiness of the mind in face of false teaching were both crucial for the apostle.

ultimate indifference — in this case the days one holds or does not hold as sacred — he encourages people to hold to their own convictions and act accordingly (as long as they don't try to impose their views upon others). But when it concerns matters of gospel fact as, for example, the resurrection of Christ from the dead (1 Cor 15:12-14), or flagrant immorality as, for example, in the matter of incest in the congregation (1 Cor 5:1-13), there is no room for some people to hold one view while others hold another.

Paul responded to the Galatian believers' observance of days quite differently because in their case it was not a matter of indifference. He despaired of them when they were 'observing special days and months and seasons and years' (Gal 4:10) because they regarded it as a necessary addition to their faith in Christ if they were to be acceptable to God. The issue in 14:5-6 is quite different. Here it is not a salvation issue. Paul regards it essentially as a matter of indifference and therefore does not try to correct them. He is content to let the Roman believers adopt different attitudes to the observance of sacred days.

14:6   In this verse Paul reminds the 'weak' and the 'strong' that their different observances are both expressions of devotion to the Lord. Thus, he says to the 'strong': *Whoever regards one day as special does so to the Lord.* While the 'strong' may believe that observance of sacred days is not necessary, they need to know that when the 'weak' observe special days, they do so with a desire to honor the Lord. For that reason, they should be respected, not despised. The apostle tells the 'weak': *Whoever eats meat does so to the Lord, for they give thanks to God.* While the 'weak' may abstain from eating meat out of fear of contamination, they should not condemn the 'strong' for their consumption of meat but instead recognize that they 'eat to the Lord' in the sense that they do so in the freedom of Christ, giving thanks to God. *And* Paul reminds the 'strong': *whoever abstains does so to the Lord and gives thanks to God.* The 'weak' practice abstinence in the matter of eating meat as an expression of their devotion, while giving thanks for what they do eat. Therefore they should be respected and not despised for doing so.

14:7-8   In these verses Paul provides a general reason why the 'weak' and the 'strong' should show mutual respect. He begins: *For none of us lives for ourselves alone, and none of us dies for ourselves alone.* On first reading we might assume Paul is saying that what we do affects not only ourselves but others also, and therefore we should act in ways considerate of them (he makes a point like this in 1 Cor 8:4-13; 10:23-33). We might think that Paul is anticipating the famous saying of John Donne (1572-1631): 'No man is an island, entire of itself . . . any man's death diminishes me, because I am involved in mankind; and therefore never send to know for whom the bell tolls; it tolls for thee'. Taken from Meditation XVII, this saying expresses the fact that humankind does not consist of isolated individuals but of people who are interconnected. This is, of course, an important truth, but not what the apostle Paul is emphasizing here. His point is that people do not live or die to themselves but for the Lord. This becomes plain when Paul adds: *If we live, we live for the Lord; and if we die, we die for the Lord. So, whether we live or die, we belong to the Lord.* He is not interested here in our interconnectedness as human beings but rather in our accountability to the Lord. The apostle makes a similar point in 2 Corinthians 5:15: 'And he [Christ] died for all, that those who live should no longer live for themselves but for him who died for them and was raised again' (cf. Gal 2:19-20). In 1 Corinthians 6:20 he explains why believers 'belong to the Lord': 'You are not your own; you were bought at a price. Therefore honor God with your bodies'.

c. We Will All Stand before God's Judgment Seat, 14:9-12

⁹*For this very reason, Christ died and returned to life so that he might be the Lord of both the dead and the living.* ¹⁰*You, then, why do you judge your brother or sister? Or why do you treat them with contempt? For we will all stand before God's judgment seat.* ¹¹*It is written: ' "As surely as I live", says the Lord, "every knee will bow before me; every tongue will acknowledge God" '.* ¹²*So then, each of us will give an account of ourselves to God.*

14:9 Paul reinforces his point that all believers live and die for the Lord and that they all belong to the Lord by adding: *For this very reason, Christ died and returned to life so that he might be the Lord of both the dead and the living.* 'For this very reason' places heavy stress upon the 'reason' for which Christ died and rose, namely, 'that he might be the Lord of both the dead and the living'. Following his death and subsequent resurrection Christ was confirmed as Lord of all (cf. 1:4; Phil 2:8-11), and this includes 'both the dead and the living'. As Moo correctly points out: 'This is not to say, however, that Paul intends Christ's death to have particular relationship to his lordship over the dead and his "coming to life" over the living. It is Christ's death and resurrection *together* that establish his lordship over all people, including especially here Christians, whether they are living or dead'.[24] Shogren believes that Paul's statement that Christ is 'the Lord of both the dead and the living' relates to 'a present reign in this age, for in the age to come the categories of 'living and dead' will be no longer meaningful.[25]

14:10 Applying the fact of the lordship of Christ to the matters of observing food taboos and special days, Paul asks his audience: *You, then, why do you judge your brother or sister? Or why do you treat them with contempt?* Those who judge their brothers or sisters are the 'weak'. Those they judge are the 'strong', and they judge them because they do not practice abstinence as they do. Those who look down on their brothers or sisters are

---

24. Moo, *Romans,* 845-46.
25. Cf. Gary Steven Shogren, ' "Is the Kingdom of God about Eating and Drinking or Isn't It?" (Romans 14:17)', *NovT* 42 (2000) 253.

the 'strong'. Those they look down upon are the 'weak', and they look down on them because of their scruples in the matter of foods and special days. Implied in Paul's questions is a criticism of both those who judge and those who look down upon their fellow believers.[26] That Paul describes both those who are judged and those who are looked down upon as 'brothers and sisters', as Cranfield notes, 'is yet one more reminder that the member of the other group, in spite of his different ideas and different practice, is in the fullest sense a fellow-believer, one who belongs altogether to the same Lord'.[27]

Paul points out that those who judge or look down on their fellow believers will have to answer to God: *For we will all stand before God's judgment seat.* Paul refers to God's 'judgment seat' also in 2 Corinthians 5:10 : 'For we must all appear before the judgment seat of Christ, that each one may receive what is due us for the things done while in the body, whether good or bad'. It may be significant that he refers to it both in 2 Corinthians and here in Romans, a letter written from Corinth, for according to Acts 18:12 it was in Corinth in the time when Gallio was proconsul of Achaia that Paul was brought before his judgment seat. The experience of having to do so may have provided Paul with a strong reminder that one day all believers must stand before the 'judgment seat' of Christ.

14:11-12   Paul reinforces this reminder with a scriptural quotation: *It is written: 'As surely as I live', says the Lord, 'every knee will bow before me; every tongue will acknowledge God'.*[28] The quotation follows closely the LXX text of Isaiah 45:23,[29] to which Paul has added the opening words, '"As surely as I live"', says the Lord', an oft-used introductory formula in the prophetic writings.[30] From this quotation Paul draws the conclusion: *So then, each of us will give an account of ourselves to God.* This solemn truth undergirds Paul's exhortation to both the 'weak' and the 'strong' in this passage. Both parties should heed his warnings not to judge or look down upon the other

---

26. Theodore of Mopsuestia observes: '*Why do you pass judgment on your brother?* was said to the Jews. *Why do you despise your brother?* was said to the Gentiles. Neither of you should do either, says Paul, because you are under obligation to maintain Christ's standards of behavior in your life' ('Pauline Commentary from the Greek Church' [*ACCSR*, 345]).

27. Cranfield, *Romans*, II, 709.

28. In its original Isaian context, as here in 14:11, it is to *God* that every knee will bow and every tongue confess. It is very significant, therefore, that when Paul alludes to this same text in Phil 2:9-11, he applies it to Christ: 'Therefore God exalted him to the highest place and gave him the name that is above every name, that at the name of Jesus every knee should bow, in heaven and on earth and under the earth, and every tongue acknowledge that Jesus Christ is Lord, to the glory of God the Father'.

29. Paul's quotation reproduces the LXX text word for word apart from a slight rearranging of words: 14:11: *hoti emoi kampsei pan gony kai pasa glōssa exomologēsetai tō theō*; LXX: *hoti emoi kampsei pan gony kai exomologēsetai pasa glōssa tō theō*.

30. Dunn, *Romans 9–16*, 809, notes that the formula 'occurs quite frequently in the prophets (Num 14:28; Isa 49:18; Jer 22:24; 46 [LXX 26]:18; Ezek 5:11; 14:16; 16:48; 17:16; 18:3; 20:31, 33; Zeph 2:9), though not in Isa 45:23. However, since it is such a regular introductory formula, no violence is done to either text when Paul thus uses it in its regular function'.

because they will both have to give account of themselves to God himself for their actions in this regard.

Some see in Paul's stress on the fact that every knee will bow before God and every tongue will acknowledge him as Lord an implied assertion that God (and his Christ), not Caesar, is the master of the world, and that this constitutes an implied antiimperial rhetoric.[31] It is true that sometime later believers would be asked to acknowledge Caesar as Lord and so deny Christ. If they would not do so, they would have to pay with their lives. However, it is questionable whether Paul, who had just described the Roman authorities as God's servants (13:1-7), would so soon afterwards indulge in antiimperial rhetoric.

2. No Passing Judgment and No Placing Stumbling Blocks, 14:13-23

13Therefore let us stop passing judgment on one another. Instead, make up your mind not to put any stumbling block or obstacle in the way of a brother or sister. 14I am convinced, being fully persuaded in the Lord Jesus, that nothing is unclean in itself. But if anyone regards something as unclean, then for that person it is unclean. 15If your brother or sister is distressed because of what you eat, you are no longer acting in love. Do not by your eating destroy someone for whom Christ died. 16Therefore do not let what you know is good be spoken of as evil. 17For the kingdom of God is not a matter of eating and drinking, but of righteousness, peace and joy in the Holy Spirit, 18because anyone who serves Christ in this way is pleasing to God and receives human approval.

19Let us therefore make every effort to do what leads to peace and to mutual edification. 20Do not destroy the work of God for the sake of food. All food is clean, but it is wrong for a person to eat anything that causes someone else to stumble. 21It is better not to eat meat or drink wine or to do anything else that will cause your brother or sister to fall.

22So whatever you believe about these things keep between yourself and God. Blessed is the one who does not condemn himself by what he approves. 23But whoever has doubts is condemned if they eat, because their eating is not from faith; and everything that does not come from faith is sin.

In this section Paul makes quite specific his exhortation to his Roman audience regarding food taboos. On the one hand he says that they should stop passing judgment upon others, and on the other that they should avoid putting any stumbling block before others. He himself adheres to the fundamental position held by the 'strong', that 'no food is unclean in itself', and urges them not to allow what they consider good to be spoken of as evil, but implying, nevertheless, that if their eating distresses others, they

---

31. Cf., e.g., Wright, 'Romans', 738-39; Witherington, *Romans*, 337-38.

should abstain, 'For the kingdom of God is not a matter of eating and drinking, but of righteousness, peace and joy in the Holy Spirit'.

14:13   In the light of the fact that all people must give an account of themselves to God, Paul says: *Therefore let us stop passing judgment on one another.* The apostle, including himself with the 'strong' in his audience, exhorts them not to judge one another, that is, the 'weak' among them, implying that such judging has been going on and that it should cease. He adds: *Instead, make up your mind not to put any stumbling block or obstacle in the way of a brother or sister* (lit. 'but rather judge in this way, not to put a stumbling stone or cause of sin in the brother['s way]'). The judgment he exhorts them to make is a determination 'not to put any stumbling block or obstacle in your brother's way'. Shortly Paul will say that 'all food is clean, but it is wrong for a person to eat anything that causes someone else to stumble' (14:20). Clearly he has in mind those who, like him, may be called the 'strong' and who, if they are not considerate in the exercise of their freedom, may cause those who are weak in faith to stumble. Paul gave similar teaching and at much greater length in 1 Corinthians 8 (cf. esp. 8:7-13).[32]

The words 'stumbling block' and 'obstacle' function here as virtual synonyms meaning something that causes people to stumble (into sin) by causing them to act contrary to their consciences, for to act contrary to one's conscience/faith is to fall into sin (cf. 14:23). Paul uses these words elsewhere (cf. 14:20; 16:17; 1 Cor 8:9) in the same way to mean something that causes people to fall (into sin).

14:14-16   Identifying himself as one of the 'strong', Paul says: *I am convinced, being fully persuaded in the Lord Jesus, that nothing is unclean in itself.* Paul wants his audience to know that this is something about which he is fully persuaded. He may be alluding to Jesus' teaching about foods — that what people eat is not what defiles them but what comes out of their hearts, and he may also have been aware of the tradition found in Mark's Gospel that by saying this Jesus 'declared all foods clean' (Mark 7:19). Paul reiterates the point in 14:20: 'All food is clean, but it is wrong for a person to eat anything that causes someone else to stumble'.

Then, speaking of the position of the 'weak', Paul adds: *But if anyone regards something as unclean, then for that person it is unclean.* The 'strong', understanding their freedom in Christ, regard no foods as unclean, but the 'weak' still regard some foods as unclean, and Paul says, 'for that person it is unclean'. The 'weak' cannot eat such foods without violating their consciences, and so while the food itself is clean, for them it is unclean.

---

32. But cf. Jewett, *Romans*, 856-58, who explains: 'The argumentative function of v. 13 is to provide a thematic admonition to both the weak and the strong, which is elaborated and explained through the rest of the pericope. This leads me to modify the current consensus that while v. 13a refers both to the "weak" and the "strong", v. 13b is directed only to the latter. . . . Käsemann and Barrett are correct in applying this inclusive reference to both sides: "We should avoid putting stumbling blocks in each other's way"'.

Addressing the 'strong' directly now, the apostle goes on: *If your brother or sister is distressed because of what you eat, you are no longer acting in love.* The 'strong' know that all foods are 'clean' and that they may therefore eat of them with impunity. Paul's point is that if this distresses (rather than attracts the judgment of) the 'weak', to insist on doing so in their presence is to fail to act in love towards them. Accordingly, he instructs the 'strong': *Do not by your eating destroy someone for whom Christ died.* Paul's point is that the 'strong' should not insist on eating (unclean) food in the presence of the 'weak' lest they embolden them to do the same against their consciences, and so bring about their destruction by encouraging them to contravene the dictates of their consciences. In similar teaching in 1 Corinthians 8 Paul asserts that when the 'strong' act in this way, they 'sin against Christ' (1 Cor 8:12). Jewett argues that the assumed context in which this exhortation must be put into practice is the Christian love feast. He says, 'it is clear that what a Roman Christian consumed in his or her private lodging would not be expected to give offense to a "brother"'.[33]

Paul further addresses the 'strong' when he adds: *Therefore do not let what you know is good be spoken of as evil.* While the 'strong' must not, by the exercise of their freedom in matters of food, grieve the 'weak', they must not allow the freedom they know is good to be spoken evil of by the 'weak' when the latter become judgmental.[34] It is one thing for the 'strong' to limit their freedom for the sake of the tender consciences of the 'weak', but it is quite another thing for the 'strong' to sacrifice their freedom in face of their judgmental attitudes.

Some object to the view that 'what you know is good' refers to Christian freedom. They do so because the verb used in the expression 'spoken evil of' is used elsewhere in relation to things far more fundamental than the freedom of the 'strong' to eat all things, for example, blaspheming the name of God, slandering Paul and the gospel he preaches, and maligning the word of God (cf. 2:24; 3:8; 1 Tim 1:20; 6:1; Tit 2:5). Accordingly, it is argued, what is 'blasphemed' in 14:16 must be something far more important than the freedom of the 'strong'. However, the close parallel to what Paul says in 14:16 found in 1 Corinthians 10:28-30 is decisive in favor of the view that the 'good' spoken of here is Christian freedom:

> But if someone says to you, 'This has been offered in sacrifice', then do not eat it, both for the sake of the one who told you and for the sake of conscience. I am referring to the other person's conscience, not yours. For why is my freedom being judged by another's conscience? If I take

33. Jewett, *Romans*, 860.

34. That the 'good' that Paul says the strong should not allow to be spoken of as evil is the Christian freedom of the strong is recognized by the majority of interpreters. So, e.g., Barrett, *Romans*, 264; Byrne, *Romans*, 417; Moo, *Romans*, 855; Fitzmyer, *Romans*, 697; Jewett, *Romans*, 862; Robert A. J. Gagnon, 'The Meaning of *hymōn to agathon* in Romans 14:16', *JBL* 117 (1998) 676-77.

part in the meal with thankfulness, why am I denounced because of something I thank God for?

In this parallel text the verb meaning 'to denounce' is used in exactly the same way as in 14:16 and in reference to exactly the same behavior, that is, exercising one's freedom in Christ to eat food regarded by others as unclean.

14:17 For the apostle Paul, whether people ate particular foods or abstained from eating them is a matter of indifference, and is ultimately irrelevant in terms of God's kingdom. Accordingly he adds: *For the kingdom of God is not a matter of eating and drinking, but of righteousness, peace and joy in the Holy Spirit.*[35] Paul's reference to the kingdom of God here in 14:17 is one of the very few places where he depicts the kingdom as something experienced in the present — most other references are future related.[36] His one other clear reference to the kingdom as a present reality also depicts it as not one thing but another: 'For the kingdom of God is not a matter of talk but of power' (1 Cor 4:20).[37] In both cases what Paul says the kingdom of God is and is not relates to the issues he is treating. In 1 Corinthians 4:20 he is dealing with those who are puffed up in pride about their knowledge and speaking ability, and so he says that the kingdom of God is not a matter of talk but of power. In Romans 14 he is dealing with positions taken regarding what may or may not be eaten, so in 14:17 he says that 'the kingdom of God is not a matter of eating and drinking, but of righteousness, peace and joy in the Holy Spirit'. To define the kingdom of God, as he does here, in terms of righteousness, peace and joy in the Holy Spirit is striking. Within Romans the only other place where these four concepts (though not the same words in the original language) come together is in 5:1-5:

---

35. Dunn, *Romans 9–16*, 823, argues: 'At first sight Jesus' likening the kingdom to a banquet seems to be at odds with Paul's denial that the kingdom should be understood in terms of eating and drinking. Not so! Jesus' parable of the banquet was a protest against the sort of restrictions on table fellowship which Pharisees, and in that case particularly the Essenes, practiced (cf. Luke 14:13, 21 with 1QSa 2.3-9). Paul is making precisely the same sort of protest against a measuring of what is acceptable in God's presence in terms of rules governing eating and drinking. It is very likely therefore that Paul's language here is a further example of the influence of the Jesus tradition on Paul's teaching, but at the level of shaping his thought rather than as a formal yardstick'.

36. Cf. 1 Cor 6:9-10; 15:24, 50; Gal 5:21; Eph 5:5; 1 Thess 2:12; 2 Thess 1:5; 2 Tim 4:1.

37. The formula, 'not one thing . . . but another' *(ouk estin . . . alla)* is one the apostle Paul uses elsewhere in several different connections: 'You, however, are not in the realm of the flesh but are in the realm of the Spirit' (Rom 8:9); 'man did not come from woman, but woman from man' (1 Cor 11:8); 'the body is not made up of one part but of many' (1 Cor 12:14); 'God is not a God of disorder but of peace' (1 Cor 14:33); 'our struggle is not against flesh and blood, but against the rulers, against the authorities, against the powers of this dark world and against the spiritual forces of evil in the heavenly realms' (Eph 6:12); 'In a large house there are articles not only of gold and silver, but also of wood and clay' (2 Tim 2:20).

Therefore, since we have been justified ['declared *righteous*'] through
faith, we have *peace* with God through our Lord Jesus Christ, through
whom we have gained access by faith into this grace in which we now
stand. And we boast [*rejoice*] in the hope of the glory of God. Not only
so, but we also *glory* [*rejoice*] in our sufferings, because we know that
suffering produces perseverance; perseverance, character; and character, hope. And hope does not put us to shame, because God's love has
been poured out into our hearts through *the Holy Spirit*, who has been
given to us. (italics added)

Allowing this passage to guide us, we may say that Paul thinks of the present experience of the kingdom of God in terms of righteousness/justifica-
tion and its fruits: peace, joy, and the presence of the Holy Spirit, and that
these all must find expression in the way believers relate to one another,
and especially in the way the 'strong' willingly limit the exercise of their
freedom if it becomes an occasion of stumbling to the 'weak'. That is, one's
righteous standing before God must express itself in righteous behavior towards one's fellow believers; the peace the believer enjoys with God must
express itself in peaceful relations with other believers; and joy in the Holy
Spirit should promote joyful interaction between believers.[38] Paul's depiction of the kingdom of God in these terms serves to highlight the absurdity
of 'the strong Christian's readiness to bring about his weak brother's spiritual ruin for the sake of such a triviality as the use of a particular food'.[39]

Smit appeals to the rules of the symposium (formal dinner) to help interpret Paul's words here in 14:17. Righteousness (proper order), peace
(harmony), and joy (not somberness or sadness) ought to be the characteristics of a good symposium. Disputes about what may and may not be
eaten at the common meal in Roman communities destroy the righteousness, peace, and joy without which the fellowship of the meal became a
mere eating and drinking, thus destroying the symposium ideal. This is
what Paul is stressing in 14:17, that the kingdom of God, as reflected in the
communal meal, is not just a matter of eating and drinking, something one
could do on one's own, but right order, peace, and joy in the Holy Spirit.[40]

14:18 Having stressed that the kingdom of God is not a matter of
eating and drinking but of righteousness, peace, and joy in the Holy Spirit,
Paul adds: *because anyone who serves Christ in this way is pleasing to God and
receives human approval*.[41] To serve Christ 'in this way' in this context ap-

38. Cf. Barrett, *Romans,* 264-65; Dunn, *Romans 9–16,* 823; Byrne, *Romans,* 417.

39. So Cranfield, *Romans,* II, 717. The early church fathers, Origen ('Commentary on
the Epistle to the Romans'), [Pseudo-] Constantius ('The Holy Letter of St. Paul to the
Romans'), and Theodore of Mopsuestia ('Pauline Commentary from the Greek Church') all
declare that there is no physical eating or drinking in the kingdom of God, for people will
live in a 'spiritual' way (*ACCSR,* 348).

40. Peter-Ben Smit, 'A Symposium in Rom. 14:17? A Note on Paul's Terminology',
NovT 49 (2007) 40-53.

41. To be pleasing *(euarestos)* to God is an important theme in Paul's letters. Believers

pears to mean serving him without being focused upon issues of eating and drinking (or abstaining from these things). In the case of the 'strong' it means being prepared to limit their freedom for the sake of the 'weak'.

'Human approval' is not something Paul speaks about elsewhere. Usually, when speaking about people being 'approved', it is God's approval he has in mind (16:10; 1 Cor 11:19; 2 Cor 13:7; 2 Tim 2:15). However, in 12:17-18 Paul does urge believers to live in a way that is acceptable in the eyes of all: 'Be careful to do what is right in the eyes of everyone. If it is possible, as far as it depends on you, live at peace with everyone'.

14:19-21   Having said that 'the kingdom of God is not a matter of eating and drinking, but of righteousness, peace and joy in the Holy Spirit', and having added that 'anyone who serves Christ in this way is pleasing to God and receives human approval', Paul gives two exhortations. The first is: *Let us therefore make every effort to do what leads to peace and to mutual edification.* While the kingdom of God is experienced, in part, as peace with God, it does not end there. It must lead on to peace among the people of God as well. Thus Paul's exhortation to both the 'weak' and the 'strong' is to make every effort to do what leads to peace (lit. 'to pursue peace') with one another instead of judging or despising one another. For rhetorical reasons Paul includes himself in the exhortation: 'let *us* pursue the things of peace'.[42] In this context what leads to 'mutual edification' will be the respect shown by both the 'weak' and the 'strong' as they avoid judging and despising the other respectively, thereby promoting genuine peace.

The second exhortation is: *Do not destroy the work of God for the sake of food.* This exhortation applies to the 'strong' who, by inconsiderate exercise of their freedom in 'eating everything', distress the 'weak' and embolden them to act against their consciences, thus causing shipwreck of their faith. In this way the 'strong' would destroy the work of God in the lives of the 'weak', and that merely for the sake of food. Paul gave similar advice at greater length, albeit in a different context, in 1 Corinthians 8:9-12:

> Be careful, however, that the exercise of your freedom does not become a stumbling block to the weak. For if someone with a weak conscience sees you, with all your knowledge, eating in an idol's temple, won't

---

please the Lord when they offer themselves to God as living sacrifices and are transformed by the renewing of their minds (12:1-2). Whether he lived or died, it was Paul's great aim to please the Lord (2 Cor 5:9). To be pleasing to God believers need to live as children of light, producing the fruit of goodness, righteousness, and truth, and eschewing the deeds of darkness (Eph 5:8-11). It is also pleasing to the Lord when believers support those who proclaim the gospel (Phil 4:18), when children obey their parents (Col 3:20), and when slaves obey their masters (Tit 2:9).

42. There are only two other places in the Pauline corpus where the verb 'to pursue' (*diōkō*) is used to denote the pursuance of Christian virtues: 1 Tim 6:11: 'But you, man of God, flee from all this, and pursue righteousness, godliness, faith, love, endurance and gentleness'; 2 Tim 2:22: 'Flee the evil desires of youth, and pursue righteousness, faith, love and peace, along with those who call on the Lord out of a pure heart'.

that person be emboldened to eat what is sacrificed to idols? So this weak brother or sister, for whom Christ died, is destroyed by your knowledge. When you sin against them in this way and wound their weak conscience, you sin against Christ.

Paul acknowledges the freedom of the 'strong' to eat everything when he says, *All food is clean.* Thus he reiterates what he said in 14:14, alludes again to Jesus' teaching about foods, and echoes the tradition found in Mark's Gospel that by this teaching Jesus 'declared all foods clean' (Mark 7:19). However, he adds two important qualifications. The first is negative: *it is wrong for a man to eat anything that causes someone else to stumble.* The best commentary on this is the text from 1 Corinthians 8:9-12 cited above. The second qualification is the positive counterpart to the first: *It is better not to eat meat or drink wine or to do anything else that will cause your brother or sister to fall.* Paul goes even further in 1 Corinthians 8:13: 'Therefore, if what I eat causes my brother or sister to fall into sin, I will never eat meat again, so that I will not cause them to fall'.[43]

14:22-23 In these two verses Paul gives advice to both the 'strong' and the 'weak' respectively. First he says: *So whatever you believe about these things keep between yourself and God.* This rather difficult text is generally interpreted as an instruction to the 'strong' not to brag about their freedom, for that would cause distress in the 'weak'. Instead they should be content to hold the knowledge of their freedom as a secret between themselves and God if to do otherwise would cause distress.[44] However, there is another way of interpreting this text so that it applies to both the 'weak' and the 'strong'.

The text underlying the NIV's 'So whatever you believe about these things keep between yourself and God', when rendered literally, reads: 'Have the faith that you have in accordance with yourself in the presence of God'. Jewett argues: 'The issue is integrity, not privacy or discreet silence, as in the ordinary translation, "keep your faith to yourself"'.[45] The apostle's exhortation may then be understood to mean that both the 'weak' and the 'strong' should act with integrity before God in accordance with their faith, that is, in accordance with their understanding of the faith and its implications for behavior. In the case of the 'strong' this would mean that they do not need to be secretive about their faith, but act with integrity in the way

43. Jewett, *Romans,* 868, comments: 'Given the restricted circumstances of space and resources available to early Christian love feasts, some of which met in the poorest slums of Rome, there was no possibility of envisioning the permanent joining of groups of weak and strong churches. Nevertheless, when a member of an abstaining group was invited, the host group is here encouraged to view their "conscious self-limitation of personal liberty for the sake of the 'weak'" as "good", that is, matching the high standards of the Christian ethic (12:2; 16:16)'.

44. Cf. Moo, *Romans,* 861-62; Cranfield, *Romans,* II, 726.

45. Jewett, *Romans,* 870.

they express it, whether that means enjoying their Christian freedom or limiting it for the sake of the 'weak'. In the case of the 'weak' it would mean that they too should act with integrity and abstain from doing things they believe are wrong and, we might add, to do so without adopting a judgmental attitude towards those who think differently.

Over the 'strong' Paul pronounces this blessing: *Blessed is the one who does not condemn himself by what he approves* (NRSV: 'Blessed are those who have no reason to condemn themselves because of what they approve').[46] Those whose minds are informed by the truth of the gospel enjoy the blessing of no condemnation when they practice freedom in the matter of foods. But things are different with the 'weak'. Concerning them Paul says: *But whoever has doubts is condemned if they eat, because their eating is not from faith.* When the 'weak' eat food being unsure whether what they are doing is permissible, they are not acting 'from faith', and therefore their consciences condemn them for their actions. To act 'not from faith' is to stifle conscience, and to do so is sin. Hence Paul adds: *and everything that does not come from faith is sin.* It is sin because in doing so believers act contrary to what they believe God requires of them, and in that sense they sin against God.[47] Ambrosiaster puts it this way: 'It is true that if someone thinks it wrong to eat but does so anyway, he is condemned. For he makes himself guilty when he does what he thinks he ought not to. If someone acts against his better judgment in a matter of conscience, then Paul says that is a sin'.[48]

Paul's statement, 'everything that does not come from faith is sin', is his clinching argument to emphasize that any eating of food that one has scruples about, and, therefore, acting in a way that is not based upon faith, is sin. The general nature of Paul's statement that 'everything that does not come from faith is sin' suggests that it could apply to other matters in which believers might act contrary to what they believe is true.

At this point in the letter some manuscripts add the closing blessing, which we know as 16:25-27 (see the commentary on 15:33).

3. The 'Strong' to Bear the Failings of the 'Weak', 15:1-6

> [1]*We who are strong ought to bear with the failings of the weak and not to please ourselves.* [2]*Each of us should please our neighbors for their good, to build them up.* [3]*For even Christ did not please himself but, as it is written:*

---

46. This is the only place in Paul's letters where he coins his own beatitude. As part of his address to the Ephesian elders recorded in Acts 20:35, the apostle cites an otherwise unknown beatitude of Jesus: 'In everything I did, I showed you that by this kind of hard work we must help the weak, remembering the words the Lord Jesus himself said: "It is more blessed to give than to receive"'.

47. Cf. Byrne, *Romans*, 419.

48. 'Commentary on Paul's Epistles' (*ACCSR*, 352).

'The insults of those who insult you have fallen on me'. ⁴For everything that was written in the past was written to teach us, so that through the endurance taught in the Scriptures and the encouragement they provide we might have hope.

⁵May the God who gives endurance and encouragement give you the same attitude of mind toward each other that Christ Jesus had, ⁶so that with one mind and one voice you may glorify the God and Father of our Lord Jesus Christ.

Here Paul urges those who, like him, may be numbered among the 'strong' to bear the failings of the 'weak', putting aside the right to please themselves so as to please their neighbors and thus build them up. By so doing they will follow the example of Christ, who did not please himself. He concludes this section by invoking God to give them a spirit of unity so that together they may glorify God.

15:1-2 Focusing further upon the way the 'strong' should conduct themselves, Paul says: *We who are strong ought*[49] *to bear with the failings of the weak and not to please ourselves.* By prefacing his exhortation with 'we who are strong' Paul associates himself with those who are strong in faith, thereby endorsing their understanding of Christian freedom. 'To bear with the failings of the weak' in this context could be construed either to mean bearing a burden or tolerating something. In this context, where it is a matter of the 'strong' not pleasing themselves but seeking to please their neighbors, to bear a burden in the sense of helping and supporting is more appropriate than merely tolerating the failings of the 'weak' (cf. Gal 6:2: 'Carry each other's burdens, and in this way you will fulfill the law of Christ').[50]

The obligation resting upon the 'strong' to bear with the failings of the 'weak' in this context means to respect their scruples concerning food. This, Paul implies, will mean that the 'strong' will not insist upon pleasing themselves in what they eat when dining with the 'weak'. Instead they will limit themselves so as not to cause them distress. Jewett notes that placing the onus upon the 'strong' to carry the weaknesses of the powerless is countercultural, as it was typical of Greco-Roman culture that the 'weak' should submit to the 'strong'.[51]

Reinforcing the point, and stating positively what he just stated negatively, Paul says, *Each of us should please our neighbors for their good, to build them up.* This will mean acting considerately and in love towards our neigh-

49. Scott Hafemann, 'Eschatology and Ethics: The Future of Israel and the Nations in Romans 15:1-13', *TynBul* 51 (2000) 164, notes that 'since social "obligation" was the basis of the Roman patronage system and, as such, one of the most powerful of the Roman cultural values, this reference to fulfilling one's "obligation" was one of the strongest "cultural bullets" Paul could fire against the Romans'.

50. Cf. Wright, 'Romans', 745.

51. Jewett, *Romans*, 877.

bors (i.e., towards fellow believers who are weak in faith). This will be 'for their good', that is, 'to build them up' in the sense that no stumbling stone will be put in their way causing them to act contrary to their conscience. Rather, being allowed to act according to their conscience in the matter of eating food, the 'weak' will be built up. Pleasing our neighbors does not mean making them happy at all costs, but acting, as Paul teaches, 'for their good' and 'to build them up'.[52]

15:3-4   To support his exhortation to the 'strong' not to please themselves, Paul appeals to the example of Christ: *For even Christ did not please himself.* Did the apostle know of the Synoptic saying of Jesus: 'For even the Son of Man did not come to be served, but to serve, and to give his life as a ransom for many' (Mark 10:45)? Even if he did not know this saying, he certainly knew of Christ's self-giving love. In 2 Corinthians 8:9 he wrote: 'For you know the grace of our Lord Jesus Christ, that though he was rich, yet for your sake he became poor, so that you through his poverty might become rich'. In Galatians 2:20 he expresses this more personally: 'The life I live in the body, I live by faith in the Son of God, who loved me and gave himself for me'. In Philippians 2:6-8, more perhaps than in any other passage in his letters, Paul makes this plain when he says that Christ, though 'being in very nature God, did not consider equality with God something to be used to his own advantage; rather, he made himself nothing by taking the very nature of a servant, being made in human likeness. And being found in appearance as a man, he humbled himself and became obedient to death — even death on a cross!' It was primarily in his sufferings and in his death upon the cross for us that 'Christ did not please himself', a 'remarkable understatement'.[53]

To support his statement that Christ did not please himself, Paul adds, *but, as it is written: 'The insults of those who insult you have fallen on me'.* The quotation is taken from Psalm 69:9, and the original follows the LXX text (Ps 68:10) exactly. The noun 'insult' and the verb 'to insult' connote finding fault and shaming. In its context this quotation is part of the psalmist's lament over the scorn and shame heaped upon him because of his zeal for God:

---

52. The concept of 'building up'/'edification' is pervasive in Paul's letters and is effected in several different ways. In 14:19; 15:2 the 'strong' build up the 'weak' by considerate behavior. In 1 Cor 14:3, 5, 12, 26 believers build one another up through the exercise of spiritual gifts for the common good. In 2 Cor 10:8; 12:19; 13:10 Paul claims that when he defends his ministry against the criticism of his opponents, when he defends his integrity in financial matters, and when he writes in a stern fashion, he is acting only to build up (and not tear down) his audience. In Eph 4:12, 16 Paul says that Christ's gifts of ministry are for building up the body of Christ, and in Eph 4:29 he exhorts his audience to let come out of their mouths only things that build others up, that benefit those who hear. It is noteworthy that Paul always uses the word 'edification' (*oikodomē*) in relationship to the church, the Christian community, not individuals.

53. Wright, 'Romans', 745.

> For I endure scorn for your sake,
>   and shame covers my face.
> I am a foreigner to my family,
>   a stranger to my own mother's children;
> for zeal for your house consumes me,
>   and *the insults of those who insult you fall on me.*
>
> (Ps 69:7-9, italics added)

The quotation suits well Paul's purpose to reinforce the statement that Christ did not please himself. There is a clear correspondence between the psalmist's experience of suffering for the sake of God and because of his zeal for the house of God, and Christ's experience of suffering as the insults of those who insulted God fell on him and culminated in his death upon the cross. All this Christ bore, not only for the sake of God but also for the sake of human beings. Paul implies that the 'strong' in the Roman Christian community ought to be willing to act like Christ did and not seek just to please themselves, but to please others by limiting the exercise of their freedom for the sake of the 'weak'.

Paul follows up his quotation from the psalm with the statement: *For everything that was written in the past was written to teach us.* Introduced as it is with the word 'for', Paul's statement functions as justification for his use of Psalm 69 in this context and reflects his attitude to the OT as a whole. Similar statements are found in 4:23-24 ('The words "it was credited to him" were written not for him alone, but also for us, to whom God will credit righteousness — for us who believe in him who raised Jesus our Lord from the dead'); 1 Corinthians 10:11 ('These things happened to them as examples and were written down as warnings for us, on whom the culmination of the ages has come'), and in 2 Timothy 3:16-17 ('All Scripture is God-breathed and is useful for teaching, rebuking, correcting and training in righteousness, so that the servant of God may be thoroughly equipped for every good work').

For Paul instruction from the Scriptures was not an end in itself. He points out that it was written for our instruction *so that through the endurance taught in the Scriptures and the encouragement they provide we might have hope.* He speaks here of the role of the Scriptures providing encouragement so that people might have hope. But he adds that it is also 'through endurance . . . we might have hope'. Paul makes a connection between 'endurance' and 'hope' in two other places. He makes the connection, albeit indirectly, in 5:3-4: 'we also glory in our sufferings, because we know that suffering produces perseverance; perseverance, character; and character, hope'. In 1 Thessalonians 1:3 the apostle tells his converts that he remembers continually their 'endurance inspired by hope', but this reverses the equation of 15:4, where it is through endurance that people have hope.

This is the only place in his letters where Paul says that it is through the encouragement of the Scriptures that believers have hope. 'Encouragement' and 'hope' are brought together in 2 Thessalonians 2:16-17: 'May our Lord Jesus Christ himself and God our Father, who loved us and by his grace gave us eternal encouragement and good hope, encourage your hearts'. Ultimately, of course, it is God who by his grace provides encouragement that produces hope (cf. 15:5). What Paul affirms in 15:4 is that one way God does so is through the Scriptures. Barrett offers the following paraphrase of this verse: 'In a situation marked by reproaches (v. 3) we have hope (a) because we practice that endurance which looks to God for the meaning of its present lot, and (b) because Scripture, by foretelling our situation, encourages us to pass through it in hope'.[54]

15:5-6   Aware of the tensions in the Roman Christian communities, Paul invokes divine assistance for them: *May the God who gives endurance and encouragement give you the same attitude of mind toward each other that Christ Jesus had*. Paul's invocation to God that he may give the Roman believers 'the same attitude of mind', literally translated, would be an invocation that they 'think the same thing'.[55] What Paul has in mind is that people should reach agreement in their thinking. This does not mean that they will necessarily agree about every disputed matter (Paul did not expect that to be the case, cf. 14:2-8), but rather that they will seek to maintain unity in the Spirit when they must agree to differ. This agreement will be one that is similar to what Jesus Christ had, the one of whom Paul said he did not please himself. The apostle hopes that those who differ will refrain from pleasing themselves and seek to please others, and perhaps that those who are able to do so might be willing to compromise a little so that they can share food at the common meals.

The purpose for which Paul invokes God to help the Roman believers in this matter is *so that with one mind and one voice you may glorify the God and Father of our Lord Jesus Christ*. The adverb translated here as 'with one mind' is found only here in Paul's letters, and elsewhere in the NT only in Acts, where it occurs ten times (Acts 1:14; 2:46; 4:24; 5:12; 7:57; 8:6; 12:20; 15:25; 18:12; 19:29). Its basic meaning is 'of one accord' or 'unanimously', or with the weakened meaning 'together'.[56] Paul wants the Roman believers to be of one accord in following Christ, seeking not to please themselves but to please one another. This will not be easy, for, as Paul acknowledges in 14:1-6, different ones among them had very different ideas about what should and should not be eaten at the common meals. Therefore Paul asks that God would enable them to think in the same way about these matters (probably involving the 'strong' not looking down on the 'weak', and the 'weak' not judging the 'strong'), so that unanimously they will be able to glorify God when they come together.

54. Barrett, *Romans*, 270.

55. The apostle uses the same expression in Phil 4:2, where he says: 'I plead with Euodia and I plead with Syntyche to be of the same mind (*to auto phronein*, lit. 'to think the same thing') in the Lord'.

56. Cf. BAGD, *ad loc*.

It is noteworthy that Paul describes God as 'the God and Father of our Lord Jesus Christ'. This appears to be a peculiarly Pauline designation for God, one he uses in several places (2 Cor 1:3; 11:31; Eph 1:3, 17; Col 1:3).[57] God, who was known previously as the God of Abraham, Isaac, and Jacob (cf. Gen 31:53; 32:9; Exod 3:6, 15, 16; 4:5; Matt 22:32; Mark 12:26; Luke 20:37; Acts 3:13; 7:32), is, following the coming of Christ, now better known as 'the God and Father of our Lord Jesus Christ'.

4. Accept One Another, 15:7-13

> [7]*Accept one another, then, just as Christ accepted you, in order to bring praise to God.* [8]*For I tell you that Christ has become a servant of the Jews on behalf of God's truth, so that the promises made to the patriarchs might be confirmed* [9]*and, moreover, that the Gentiles might glorify God for his mercy. As it is written: 'Therefore I will praise you among the Gentiles; I will sing the praises of your name'.* [10]*Again, it says, 'Rejoice, you Gentiles, with his people'.* [11]*And again, 'Praise the Lord, all you Gentiles; let all the peoples extol him'.* [12]*And again, Isaiah says, 'The Root of Jesse will spring up, one who will arise to rule over the nations; in him the Gentiles will hope'.*
>
> [13]*May the God of hope fill you with all joy and peace as you trust in him, so that you may overflow with hope by the power of the Holy Spirit.*

In these verses Paul brings to a conclusion his instructions to the 'weak' and the 'strong'. He concludes where he began. In 14:1 he said: 'Accept the one whose faith is weak, without quarreling over disputable matters', and his conclusion begins in similar fashion: 'Accept one another, then, just as Christ accepted you (15:7)'.[58]

15:7 Bringing his instructions to the 'weak' and the 'strong' to a conclusion, Paul begins with this exhortation: [*Therefore*] *accept one another, then, just as Christ accepted you.* This encapsulates his advice and constitutes the main point of the whole passage. The NIV omits 'therefore' in its translation of this verse, thus obscuring the connection with what precedes. It is in the light of the fact that Paul has invoked God's blessing to bring about unanimity of mind in his audience so they might glorify God (15:5-6) that he now exhorts them to accept one another as Christ has accepted them. This acceptance of one another will find expression not least in their communal meals. The call to do so is predicated upon the fact that Christ has accepted all of them. Not to accept one another when Christ has accepted them all is unthinkable. The apostle's exhortation to members of his audi-

---

57. Elsewhere in the NT it is found only in 1 Pet 1:3.

58. Cf. Gerhard Sass, 'Röm 15,7-13 — als Summe des Römerbriefs gelesen', *Evangelische Theologie* 53 (1993) 510-27, esp. 512-15, 515-23, 523-26; J. Ross Wagner, 'The Christ, Servant of Jew and Gentile: A Fresh Approach to Romans 15:8-9', *JBL* 116 (1997) 473.

ence to accept one another *just as* Christ accepted them indicates that in doing so they will be following Christ's example.[59]

They need to accept one another *in order to bring praise to God.* The
context is probably still that of the communal meal. In that setting, if the believers were not accepting one another, they could hardly bring praise to
God. It is implied that for Paul glorifying God and bringing praise to him is
not just an individual but also a communal thing.

15:8-9 To reinforce the call to accept one another so as to bring
praise to God, Paul starts by saying: *For I tell you that Christ has become a servant of the Jews on behalf of God's truth, so that the promises made to the patriarchs might be confirmed.* Paul's first step in reinforcing his call is to emphasize that Christ became 'a servant of the Jews', and thereby to affirm the
importance of the Jewish believers in the Roman Christian communities. In
9:4-5 Paul highlighted the many privileges of the Jewish people, chief
among which was the fact the 'from them is traced the human ancestry of
the Messiah' (9:5).

That Christ became a servant of the Jews is something reflected in Peter's speech to the 'men of Israel' following the healing of the lame man at
the Gate Beautiful in which he says: 'He [God] said to Abraham, "Through
your offspring all peoples on earth will be blessed". *When God raised up his
servant, he sent him first to you to bless you by turning each of you from your
wicked ways'* (Acts 3:25-26, italics added). It also reflected in Jesus' own
statement about being sent only to 'the lost sheep of Israel' (Matt 15:24).
Paul's purpose in telling his audience that 'Christ has become a servant of
the Jews' is probably to emphasize, by the example of Christ, the need for
Gentile believers to likewise serve their Jewish Christian brothers and sisters, and also possibly to counteract any anti-Semitic attitudes on their part
(cf. 11:17-21).[60]

Paul is quick to show that Christ became a servant of the Jews not
only to confirm the promises made to the patriarchs, but also so *that the
Gentiles may glorify God for his mercy.* This was, of course, foreshadowed by
the apostle in 1:16, where he described the gospel as 'the power of God that
brings salvation to everyone who believes: first to the Jew, then to the Gentile'. In 11:30 he said that the Gentiles were receiving mercy as a result of
the Jews' disobedience. But from the time of the call of Abraham God's
dealings with his chosen people were intended to bring his blessing to all
the peoples of the earth:

> The LORD had said to Abram, 'Go from your country, your people and
> your father's household to the land I will show you. I will make you

59. In this case *kathōs* is treated as an adverb of comparison. It is also possible to construe Paul's exhortation as a call for members of his audience to accept one another *because*
Christ has accepted them, in which case *kathōs* is treated as a conjunction indicating the reason why they should accept one another. Cf. Käsemann, *Romans,* 385.

60. Cf. Witherington, *Romans,* 343.

into a great nation, and I will bless you; I will make your name great, and you will be a blessing. I will bless those who bless you, and whoever curses you I will curse; and all peoples on earth will be blessed through you'. (Gen 12:1-3)

The promises of God to the patriarchs were fulfilled when Christ came as a servant of the Jews and made possible the extension of the blessings of God to 'all peoples on earth', with the result that 'the Gentiles may glorify God for his mercy'. This is the second step Paul takes to reinforce his call to the Roman believers to accept one another so as to bring praise to God, that is, having affirmed the importance of the Jewish believers in the Roman Christian communities, he now does the same for the Gentile believers. Paul affirms the place of the Gentiles in the purposes of God with a series of OT quotations that, as Reichrath notes, all have a common theme: the call of the Gentiles and their inclusion among the people of God.[61] That the four quotations which follow all make essentially the same point is indicated by the threefold 'and again' which connects them.

Paul begins: *As it is written: 'Therefore I will praise you among the Gentiles; I will sing the praises of your name'*. This quotation is drawn from Psalm 18:49 (LXX Ps 17:50), of which it is virtually an exact citation.[62] The superscription of the psalm reads as follows: 'For the director of music. Of David the servant of the LORD. He sang to the LORD the words of this song when the LORD delivered him from the hand of all his enemies and from the hand of Saul'. In its original context the verse Paul cites is David's grateful response to God for deliverance and victory over his enemies. It appears that in the reference to David's praise of God *among* the *Gentiles* Paul saw some anticipation of the Gentiles themselves glorifying God for his mercy.

15:10 The second of Paul's OT quotations affirming the place of the Gentiles in the purposes of God is drawn from Deuteronomy 32:43: *Again, it says, 'Rejoice, you Gentiles, with his people'*. In the original, the quotation corresponds exactly with the text of the LXX. Deuteronomy 32:43 is the last verse in the extended Song of Moses (Deut 32:1-43) in which, having described the early blessings heaped upon Israel and their subsequent rebellion, Moses depicts the Lord calling upon the Gentile nations to rejoice with Israel that he had acted to 'avenge the blood of his servants . . . and make atonement for his land and people'. It appears that in this call of God to the Gentiles to rejoice with Israel over his salvation Paul sees foreshadowed the time of fulfillment when Gentiles and Jews together will rejoice in the salvation effected by Christ.

---

61. Hans L. Reichrath, 'Juden und Christen — Eine Frage von "Ökumene?"/ Was uns Römer 15,7-13 dazu lehrt', *Judaica* 47 (1991) 26.

62. The only difference being that Paul has omitted the vocative *kyrie*: Ps 17:50: *dia touto exomologēsomai soi en ethnesin kyrie kai tō onomati sou psalō*; Rom 15:9: *dia touto exomologēsomai soi en ethnesin kai tō onomati sou psalō*.

15:11   The third of Paul's quotations to make his point about the place of the Gentiles comes from Psalm 117:1 (LXX Ps 116:1): *And again, 'Praise the Lord, all you Gentiles; let all the peoples extol him'.*[63] Psalm 117 is very short, consisting of only two verses: 'Praise the Lord, all you nations; extol him, all you peoples. For great is his love toward us, and the faithfulness of the Lord endures forever. Praise the Lord' (Ps 117:1-2). The psalmist calls upon the nations to praise the Lord because of his great love and faithfulness towards Israel. Apparently Paul sees in this exhortation to the nations to praise the Lord a foreshadowing of the time when people of all nations would glorify the God and Father of our Lord Jesus Christ.

15:12   The fourth and final quotation from the OT is drawn from Isaiah 11:10: *And again, Isaiah says, 'The Root of Jesse will spring up, one who will arise to rule over the nations; in him the Gentiles will hope'.*[64] In its Isaianic context this text forms part of a prophecy of the rule of God in the hands of a king of the Davidic dynasty. It is a text recognized as messianic both within Judaism[65] and the early church. The Messiah's beneficent rule will extend not only over Israel but over the nations as well, and 'in him the Gentiles will hope'. This text speaks of the place of the Gentiles among God's people and serves well Paul's purpose of affirming the status of Gentile believers in the Roman communities.

15:13   Paul concludes this long section dealing with the 'weak' and the 'strong' in the Roman Christian communities (14:1–15:13) by invoking God's blessing upon them all: *May the God of hope fill you with all joy and peace as you trust in him, so that you may overflow with hope by the power of the Holy Spirit.* In 14:17 Paul had reminded his audience that what was important in their common meals was not the eating and drinking but 'righteousness, peace and joy in the Holy Spirit', as these are the marks of the kingdom of God as it is experienced in the present time. Now he asks God to bestow such things upon his audience as he concludes this section, things which are so important if their lives together are to reflect the values of the kingdom of God.[66]

The apostle invokes God as 'the God of hope'. This is an unusual description of God found nowhere else in the NT or the LXX. Seeing that Paul in this verse prays that the believers may 'overflow with hope', the expression 'the God of hope' probably means the God who inspires hope in his

---

63. The original Greek form of Paul's quotation follows closely, but not exactly, the LXX: Ps 116:1: *aineite ton kyrion panta ta ethnē epainesate auton pantes hoi laoi*; Rom 15:11: *aineite, panta ta ethnē, ton kyrion, kai epainesatōsan auton pantes hoi laoi*, i.e., Paul relocates *panta ta ethnē*, thereby placing the reference to the Gentiles in the emphatic position, and adds the conjunction *kai*.

64. In the original Paul's quotation follows the LXX apart from one omission: Isa 11:10: *estai en tē hēmera ekeinē hē riza tou Iessai kai ho anistamenos archein ethnōn, ep' autō ethnē elpiousin*; Rom 15:12: *estai hē riza tou Iessai kai ho anistamenos archein ethnōn, ep' autō ethnē elpiousin*, i.e., Paul omits the reference to 'in that day' (*en tē hēmera ekeinē*).

65. Cf. 1Q28b 5:20-29; 4Q161 frag. 9-14; 4Q285 frag. 5.

66. Cf. Sass, 'Röm 15,7-13 — als Summe des Römerbriefs gelesen', 527.

people. This he does 'by the power of the Holy Spirit'. Paul implies that if God blesses his people with 'all joy and peace' as they 'trust in him', this will bring about in them an overflow of hope produced 'by the power of the Holy Spirit'. This is clearly an experience he wants the diverse members of the Roman Christian communities to share so that their common meals are not marked by judgmentalism and derision, but by righteousness, peace, and joy in the Holy Spirit.

IV. PAUL'S MINISTRY AND FUTURE PLANS, 15:14-33

Paul concluded the long section (14:1–15:13) dealing with the 'weak' and the 'strong' by invoking God's blessing upon his audience: 'May the God of hope fill you with all joy and peace as you trust in him, so that you may overflow with hope by the power of the Holy Spirit'. In this next major section, 15:14-33, the apostle affirms his audience, explains the grounds upon which he has written to them 'quite boldly', and describes his 'priestly' ministry of the gospel intended to ensure that the self-offering of Gentile believers will be acceptable to God (15:14-16). He also speaks of his pride in what Christ has effected through his ministry and his ambition to preach where Christ has not been named (15:17-21). Paul concludes this section by sharing his long-held desire as well as his present plan to visit Rome on his way to Spain (15:22-33).

A. Paul Affirms the Roman Believers and Explains the Nature of His Ministry, 15:14-16

> [14] I myself am convinced, my brothers and sisters, that you yourselves are full of goodness, filled with knowledge and competent to instruct one another. [15] Yet I have written you quite boldly on some points to remind you of them again, because of the grace God gave me [16] to be a minister of Christ Jesus to the Gentiles. He gave me the priestly duty of proclaiming the gospel of God, so that the Gentiles might become an offering acceptable to God, sanctified by the Holy Spirit.

Here in 15:14-16 Paul affirms his confidence in his audience before saying that he has taken it upon himself to be bold in reminding them of things they need to remember. This he does in the light of the grace given to him to be a minister of the gospel to the Gentiles — among whom, of course, the majority of the Roman believers were numbered.

15:14 To affirm his audience, Paul begins: *I myself am convinced, my brothers and sisters. . . .* Paul's introduction is affectionate ('my brothers and sisters') and emphatic. Its emphatic nature is obvious in the original, which, literally translated, would read: 'And I am convinced, my brothers and sisters, even I myself'. . . . Paul uses the verb 'to be convinced' frequently in his letters, as he does here, to speak of the things about which he is confident.[1] The apostle spells out now what he is convinced about as far as his audience are concerned: *that you yourselves are full of goodness, filled with knowledge and competent to instruct one another*.[2] 'Goodness' may be described as a 'positive moral quality characterized esp. by interest in the welfare of others',[3] and is something, the apostle says, that is produced in believers' lives by the Spirit (Gal 5:22). 'Knowledge', as far as Paul is concerned, is something embodied in the law (2:20) but found supremely in Christ, in whom, he says, 'are hidden all the treasures of wisdom and knowledge' (Col 2:3). Competence to 'instruct' carries not so much the idea of the ability to convey information as to provide counsel about proper behavior, and thus often the notion of admonition or warning (cf. 1 Cor 4:14; Col 1:28; 3:16; 1 Thess 5:12, 14; 2 Thess 3:15).[4]

It is striking, in the light of what Paul wrote in chapters 9–11 and 12–15, that he describes his audience here as being 'full of goodness, filled with knowledge and competent to instruct one another'. 'Goodness' seems to have been lacking when the Gentile believers were arrogant in their attitudes towards unbelieving Jews (11:17-20), when the 'weak' adopted judgmental attitudes towards the 'strong', and when the 'strong' despised the 'weak' (14:3). They do not appear to have been 'filled with knowledge' because, Paul implies, they were ignorant of the mystery of God's plans for the salvation of Jews and Gentiles (11:25). Their 'competency to instruct one another' also appears to have been rather limited, especially when it came to dealing with the question of what foods could and could not be eaten at their communal meals (14:2-6). Does all this mean that we should read Paul's glowing description of his Roman audience as an epistolary device, as an endeavor to create a good ethos — one by which his audience would be well disposed to receive what he wanted to say to them as this passage unfolds?[5] Pelagius comments on this text: 'As a good teacher Paul

1. These include his conviction that nothing can separate him from the love of Christ (8:38); no food is unclean of itself (14:14); the Corinthians would share his joy (2 Cor 2:3); the Galatian believers would adopt no other view than his own (Gal 5:10); the one who began a good work in the Philippians would continue it until the day of Christ (Phil 1:6); his confidence 'in the Lord' that he would be able to visit the Philippian believers in the near future (Phil 2:24); that the Thessalonian believers will continue to follow his instructions (2 Thess 3:4); that the faith that first lived in Timothy's mother and grandmother now lives in Timothy (2 Tim 1:5), and finally his conviction that the one in whom he has believed is able to guard what he has entrusted to him for that day (2 Tim 1:12).

2. This is reminiscent of what Paul wrote in 1:8: 'I thank my God through Jesus Christ for all of you, because your faith is being reported all over the world'. In passing it is worth noting that the apostle's conviction concerning his audience stated here puts paid to any notions that what he wrote, e.g., in chap. 2, refers to them and indicates rather that the chapter needs to be read as an example of the rhetoric of the diatribe.

3. BAGD, *ad loc.*

4. BAGD, *ad loc.*

5. Cf. Byrne, *Romans*, 435.

rouses the people to further progress by praising them, so that they might blush for not being the sort of people the apostle thought they were'.[6] Cranfield comments: 'Paul recognized — something which the clergy have too often been apt to forget — that it is courteous to assume that one's fellow-Christians are moderately mature until they have given positive evidence of their immaturity. What we have here is Christian courtesy, not flattery, though there is no doubt an element of hyperbole in the use of the words *mestoi, peplērōmenoi* and *pasēs* ['full', 'complete', and 'all']'.[7]

15:15-16 Having affirmed his audience, Paul states one of the reasons for writing this letter to them. He begins: *Yet I have written you quite boldly on some points.* Coming straight after the two long sections dealing in turn with God's salvation plans for both Jews and Gentiles (1:18–11:36) and the issue of the 'weak' and the 'strong' (14:1–15:13), Paul's reference to speaking quite boldly 'on some points' probably relates to the rather straight words he had to say to them in these sections.[8]

Paul's purpose in writing 'quite boldly', he says, was *to remind you of them again,* which suggests that much of what he wrote he expects them to have known already, but now believes needs reinforcing. The word translated 'to remind' is a rare one found only here in the NT and not at all in the LXX. Jewett stresses that this word 'accents the formal politeness of Paul's discourse and coordinates well with the qualification: "in part as a mere reminder"'.[9]

The apostle explains the basis on which he believes he has the right to write 'quite boldly' to the Roman believers: *because of the grace God gave me to be a minister of Christ Jesus to the Gentiles.* Paul introduced himself at the beginning of the letter as one who had 'received grace and apostleship' (see the commentary on 1:5), and now he says that it is because of this grace that he is in a position to write boldly as he does. But he writes in this way also because of his calling to be a minister 'to the Gentiles', among whom the majority of his audience are numbered (cf. 1:6). The word he employs when describing himself as a 'minister' of Christ can be used with just secular connotations,[10] but is more generally employed with a cultic meaning, denoting someone who offers service to God (or the gods). As Paul continues, it becomes evident that this is how he is employing the term here.

Paul describes the ministry he has been entrusted with by the grace of God as *the priestly duty of proclaiming the gospel of God* (lit. 'serving as a priest

---

6. 'Commentary on Romans' (*ACCSR,* 360).

7. Cranfield, *Romans,* II, 752.

8. Byrne, '"Rather Boldly" (Rom 15,15)', 93, 95-96, suggests that Paul was speaking boldly when he informed those who were still clinging to the law in order to obtain eschatological righteousness that this was futile, and that only faith in what God has done in Christ makes salvation possible.

9. Jewett, *Romans,* 905.

10. Paul uses the same word *(leitourgos)* in 13:6 to describe the Roman authorities as 'God's servants'.

of the gospel of God').[11] By so saying he implies that his function is, as it were, that of a priest presiding over offerings presented to God. Accordingly, he says, the purpose of his ministry is *so that the Gentiles might become an offering acceptable to God*. Rendered literally, this would read: 'so that the offering of the Gentiles might be acceptable'. The 'offering' is susceptible of two interpretations: (i) the offering consists of the Gentiles themselves, and (ii) the offering consists of donations made by the Gentiles, that is, their contributions to the collection.[12] The former interpretation, which is adopted by the NIV, is preferable in the light of three facts: (i) that the apostle has already urged the audience to offer their bodies (i.e., themselves) as living sacrifices, holy and pleasing to God (12:1); (ii) that he speaks immediately of this offering being 'sanctified by the Holy Spirit', not something that Paul would say about contributions to a collection; and (iii) that Paul was heading for Jerusalem with the collection before his planned visit to Rome and therefore the Roman believers would not have opportunity to donate to the collection to which he refers in 15:25-32.

When, here in 15:16, Paul speaks of the 'offering' of the Gentiles, he uses a word found in only one other place in his letters, in Ephesians 5:2, where he says: 'Christ loved us and gave himself up for us as a *fragrant offering* and sacrifice to God' (italics added). In this text the word also denotes self-offering (the self-offering of Christ to God) and not something that Christ offers. This provides extra support for the view that 'the offering of the Gentiles' here in 15:16 is correctly portrayed by the NIV translation as the self-offering of the Gentiles. Over this offering Paul presides as a priest to ensure that it is acceptable to God.

The means by which Paul seeks to ensure the acceptability of the self-offering of the Gentiles is his priestly ministry of 'the gospel of God'. It is as he proclaims the gospel and it is heard and embraced that people are *sanctified by the Holy Spirit* and thus become acceptable to God (cf. 1 Cor 6:11; Eph 5:26; Tit 3:5). Gentiles who were once regarded as 'unclean' are now 'clean' through their faith in the gospel and sanctification by the Holy Spirit. Putting it all together, Paul depicts himself as a 'priest' presiding over the self-offering of the Gentiles, who by his preaching and teaching of the gospel seeks to ensure that they are acceptable to God, sanctified by the Holy Spirit as they embrace his message.[13]

11. The verb, 'to serve as a priest' (*hierourgeō*), is found only here in the NT, and in the LXX only in one manuscript of 4 Maccabees where it means to minister (to the law) (4 Macc 7:8). It is used by Josephus and Philo without an object to mean 'to offer sacrifice' (*Ant.* 14.4.3 §65; 17.6.4 §166; *Cherub.* 28 §96). Cf. Fitzmyer, *Romans*, 711.

12. So, e.g., David J. Downs, '"The Offering of the Gentiles" in Romans 15.16', *JSNT* 29 (2006) 173-86, argues that the phrase *hē prosphora tōn ethnōn* in Rom 15:16 should be taken as a subjective genitive and therefore as a reference to an offering given by the Gentiles, namely, the collection for the saints that Paul discusses in Rom 15:25-32.

13. Witherington, *Romans*, 355, draws attention to the 'Trinitarian progression here — Paul is a minister of Christ, serving the gospel of God, offering the Gentiles who have been consecrated by the Spirit'.

B. Paul's Pride in What Christ Has Wrought through Him, 15:17-21

17Therefore I glory in Christ Jesus in my service to God. 18I will not ven-
ture to speak of anything except what Christ has accomplished through me in
leading the Gentiles to obey God by what I have said and done — 19by the
power of signs and wonders, through the power of the Spirit of God. So from
Jerusalem all the way around to Illyricum, I have fully proclaimed the gospel
of Christ. 20It has always been my ambition to preach the gospel where Christ
was not known, so that I would not be building on someone else's founda-
tion. 21Rather, as it is written: 'Those who were not told about him will see,
and those who have not heard will understand'.

While this passage is presented as several separate sentences in the
NIV, it is in fact one long and complex sentence in the original. In it Paul
speaks of his legitimate pride in what Christ has effected through his ministry, as he has carried out his commission to preach the gospel to the
Gentiles and implemented his ambition to preach where Christ has not previously been named. The passage appears to have an apologetic note — the
apostle explaining that he does not boast in his own achievements in ministry, but only in what the Lord has done through him, and that he studiously
avoids building upon another person's foundation, that is, working in an
area pioneered by another missionary. All this is possibly to head off criticisms of the way he carries out his ministry.

15:17-19   Referring to the fact that it is on account of the grace of God
given to him that he is a minister of the gospel (15:15-16), Paul says: *There-*
fore I glory in Christ Jesus in my service to God (lit. 'therefore in Christ Jesus I
have pride in the things related to God').[1] In this context 'the things related
to God' appear to be what Christ has wrought through his apostolic ministry. Chrysostom suggests that 'after humbling himself, Paul here raises the
tone, so as not to become an object of contempt in the eyes of his readers'.[2]

Paul continues: *I will not venture to speak of anything except what Christ*
has accomplished through me in leading the Gentiles to obey God. It is worth noting that in 15:15 Paul was prepared to say, 'on some points I have written
you quite boldly', when it was a matter of speaking about the truth of God
and its implications for Christian living, but when it comes to speaking of
his own ministry he was not bold enough to say anything, except about
what Christ had accomplished through him. What Christ accomplished
through him was 'leading the Gentiles to obey God' (NRSV: 'to win obedience from the Gentiles'). It was for this very purpose that he had received
the grace of apostleship (see the commentary on 1:5). Paul was very aware
that the power for his successful ministry among the Gentiles came from

---

1. BAGD, *kauchēsis*, offers the following translation of 15:17: 'I may boast in Christ of
my relation to God'.
2. 'Homilies on Romans 29' (*ACCSR*, 361).

540 *Romans 15:17-19*

Christ, though this did not mean that he was not himself involved in a mighty struggle to carry out that ministry. He brings these two things together in Colossians 1:28-29: 'He [Christ] is the one we proclaim, admonishing and teaching everyone with all wisdom, so that we may present everyone fully mature in Christ. To this end I strenuously contend with all the energy Christ so powerfully works in me'.

Paul next explains the means by which Christ has led the Gentiles to the obedience of faith through his ministry. It was, he says, *by what I have said and done* (lit. 'by word and deed'). What he means by this is then spelled out in more detail: *by the power of signs and wonders, through the power of the Spirit of God.* What is effected 'by deed', he points out, is effected by the power of 'signs and wonders', an expression used in the Acts of the Apostles in reference to the earthly ministry of Jesus (Acts 2:22) and the ministry of the apostles after him (Acts 2:43; 4:30; 5:12; 6:8; 14:3; 15:12). Paul himself believed that signs and wonders were among the marks of a true apostle (2 Cor 12:12).[3] Paul also says that what Christ wrought through him was effected 'through the power of the Spirit'. Luke-Acts describes the earthly ministry of Jesus as one carried out in the power of the Spirit (Luke 4:14; Acts 10:38) and records the promise of Jesus to his disciples prior to his ascension: 'you will receive power when the Holy Spirit comes upon you; and you will be my witnesses' (Acts 1:8). Paul himself was very conscious that it was the power of the Spirit that made his own ministry effective (cf. 15:19; 1 Cor 2:4; 1 Thess 1:5).

It is significant that Paul's reference to Christ working through his ministry to win the obedience of the Gentiles recalls the descriptions of Jesus' own earthly ministry — effected by signs and wonders and through the power of the Spirit. One might say that Paul believed that what Christ began to do in his own ministry he has continued to do through the ministry of his apostles, including himself (cf. Acts 1:1-2).

To further explain the effect of what Christ wrought through his ministry, Paul adds: *So from Jerusalem all the way around to Illyricum, I have fully proclaimed the gospel of Christ.* When Paul says he has preached the gospel from Jerusalem 'all the way around' to Illyricum, he employs an adverb whose essential meaning is 'in a circle'. Its use here indicates that Paul thought of his ministry up until the time of writing Romans as having followed a wide arc beginning in Jerusalem and reaching as far as Illyricum. Jewett claims that 'world maps from the Roman period placed the circle of the Mediterranean at the center of the four quarters of the world', adding that 'with this geographic framework, it is not at all mysterious that Paul

---

3. Origen says: 'Signs differ from wonders in that signs are miracles which point to some future happening, whereas wonders are just miracles' ('Commentary on the Epistle to the Romans' [*ACCSR*, 362]). Steve Strauss, 'Missions Theology in Romans 15:14-33', *BSac* 160 (2003) 461-62, notes that 'the phrase "signs and wonders" was the standard Old Testament way of referring to the miracles of the Exodus, and "the expression regularly designates events surrounding the great redemptive acts of God"'.

would have thought of Illyricum as lying on a circle from Jerusalem, and that Illyricum was the closest point he had reached on the route to Rome'.[4] The extent of the Roman province of Illyricum is difficult to define as its outer limits changed over time. In terms of present-day geography Illyricum lay along the Adriatic coast and took in present-day Croatia, Montenegro, and Albania.

It is somewhat strange that Paul describes his mission as beginning 'from Jerusalem' rather than from Antioch (cf. Acts 13:1-3). However, Acts 9:28 does record that, following his introduction to the Jerusalem church, Paul 'moved about freely in Jerusalem, speaking boldly in the name of the Lord'. This may be enough to justify a beginning in Jerusalem. Alternatively, it may be noted that the NIV's 'I have fully proclaimed the gospel of Christ', when translated literally, would read, 'I have brought to completion the gospel', in which case Paul might mean that the preaching of the gospel begun by other apostles in Jerusalem has been brought to completion by him, that is, by carrying it all the way to Illyricum. Of course, fully preaching the gospel in this whole region does not mean that he had proclaimed it to every person, only that he had done so in major centers along the way.

15:20 As already noted, 15:17-21 constitutes one long sentence in the original. Nevertheless, for ease of reading in English, the NIV translation renders 15:20 as an independent sentence, beginning: *It has always been my ambition to preach the gospel where Christ was not known* (lit. 'in this way making it my ambition to proclaim the gospel not where Christ has been named'). The connection with what the apostle said in previous verses is difficult to express in English. The following abbreviated paraphrase might help: 'I will not dare to speak of anything that Christ has not effected through me to win obedience from the Gentiles, by word and deed . . . so that I have brought to completion the [preaching of the] gospel begun in Jerusalem [through other apostles] by carrying it as far as Illyricum, and in this way making it my ambition to preach the gospel not where Christ has been named'. . . . The phrase, 'to make it one's ambition', appears to be a characteristic Pauline expression, being found in the NT only in Paul's letters.[5]

The reason Paul wanted to preach where Christ was not known, he says, was *so that I would not be building on someone else's foundation.* He was very conscious of being one who laid new foundations, one who planted new churches. In 1 Corinthians 3:10 he speaks of himself as the one who 'laid a foundation as a wise builder, and someone else is building on it'. In 2 Corinthians 10:13-16 Paul speaks about confining 'our boasting to the

---

4. Jewett, *Romans,* 912-13.

5. Apart from its use here, the apostle employs it in 2 Cor 5:9, where he says that, in the light of the fact that we must all appear before the judgment seat of Christ, 'we make it our goal *(philotimoumetha)* to please him'. He uses it again in 1 Thess 4:11 when urging his converts to 'make it your ambition *(philotimeisthai)* to lead a quiet life'.

sphere of service God himself has assigned to us, a sphere that also includes you', says that he was the one who 'did get as far as you with the gospel of Christ', and tells of his ambition to 'preach the gospel in the regions beyond you', adding, 'for we do not want to boast about work already done in someone else's territory'. The early church fathers seem to have been quite interested in Paul's policy in this respect and sought to explain why he adopted it. Ambrosiaster comments: 'It was not without reason that Paul says that he tried to preach in places where Christ had not been named. For he knew that false apostles went about sharing Christ in ways which were wrong in order to ensnare the people by some other teaching under the name of Christ, which was then very difficult to put right afterward. Therefore he wanted to get there first, in order to preach the right message'.[6] Diodore explains: 'Paul was not trying to avoid the other apostles, but he thought it was wrong and unfair to steal the credit from what someone else had done'.[7] Modern commentators correctly observe that Paul's ambition to preach where Christ was not known was not for him an absolute rule. Rather, it is what he says it was, his 'ambition'. There were clearly times when he ministered in churches planted by others (e.g., the church in Antioch in Syria).[8]

15:21   Paul saw his ambition to preach Christ in places where he had not been named as a fulfillment of prophecy. Thus he adds: *Rather, as it is written: 'Those who were not told about him will see, and those who have not heard will understand'.* In the original language Paul's quotation reproduces exactly the LXX text of Isaiah 52:15.[9] The passage from which it is taken constitutes the opening verses of the last of the Servant Songs (Isa 52:13–53:12), which read as follows:

> See, my servant will act wisely;
>   he will be raised and lifted up and highly exalted.
> Just as there were many who were appalled at him —
>   his appearance was so disfigured beyond that of any human being
>   and his form marred beyond human likeness —
> so will he sprinkle many nations,
>   and kings will shut their mouths because of him.
> *For what they were not told, they will see,*
>   *and what they have not heard, they will understand.*
>   (Isa 52:13-15, italics added)

Jesus Christ was identified with the Suffering Servant by several other NT authors (Matt 8:17; Luke 22:37; John 12:38; Acts 8:26-35; 1 Pet 2:22), as he is by Paul here in 15:20. The kings of whom Isaiah spoke will see things they

---

6. 'Commentary on Paul's Epistles' (*ACCSR*, 362).
7. 'Pauline Commentary from the Greek Church' (*ACCSR*, 362).
8. Cf. Moo, *Romans*, 897; Cranfield, *Romans*, II, 765; Fitzmyer, *Romans*, 715-16.
9. *Hois ouk anēngelē peri autou opsontai kai hoi ouk akēkoasin synēsousin.*

have not been told about and will understand things they have not heard, things about the Suffering Servant. Paul implies that, as a result of his preaching where Christ had not previously been named, his hearers will see him (Christ) of whom they had not previously been told, and understand things that they had not previously heard. The text from the Servant Song that Paul chose to cite in this connection is very appropriate, for the content of Paul's preaching was Jesus Christ crucified, the one whom Paul and other NT writers identified with the Suffering Servant.

C. Paul's Long-Held Desire and Present Plan to Visit Rome en Route to Spain, 15:22-33

In this passage the apostle speaks of his desire and current plans to visit the Roman believers on his way to Spain. This he will do once he has delivered the collection received from the churches of Macedonia and Achaia to the poor believers in Jerusalem.

1. Paul's Plan to Visit Rome en Route to Spain, 15:22-24

> [22]*This is why I have often been hindered from coming to you.* [23]*But now that there is no more place for me to work in these regions, and since I have been longing for many years to visit you,* [24]*I plan to do so when I go to Spain. I hope to see you while passing through and to have you assist me on my journey there, after I have enjoyed your company for a while.*

15:22 In these verses Paul explains to his audience why it was taking him so long to come to Rome and visit them. Earlier he had emphasized his calling to be the apostle to the Gentiles, among whom the majority of the Roman believers were numbered (1:5-6; 11:13), and yet he had still not made personal contact with them. Explaining why he had not done so earlier, he says: *This is why I have often been hindered from coming to you* (lit. 'for this reason also I was being hindered for many [years][1] from coming to you'). Jewett describes the many factors that hindered Paul:

> When we reconstruct the events of the two to three years immediately preceding the writing of Romans, the hindrances to his advancing further along the arc from Jerusalem to Illyricum are obvious. In my sketch of Paul's career, I count several imprisonments (1 Cor 15:32; 2 Cor 1:8; Phlm 1; Phil 1:14); congregational problems in Colossae (Col 2:8-23), Laodicea (Col 2:1), Philippi (Phil 3:1-21), and Corinth (all of 1 and 2 Corinthians); postponed plans to deliver the Jerusalem offering because of

---

1. Interpreting *ta polla* as 'many years' in the light of Paul's reference in the next verse (15:23) to having desired to visit the Romans believers 'for many years' *(apo pollōn etōn)*.

congregational conflicts and threats from zealots (2 Cor 8–9; Acts 20:3); and extensive travels such as the abortive trip to Corinth (2 Cor 2:1; 12:14; 13:1) and the anxious trip to Troas in search of Titus bearing news about his alienated congregation (2 Cor 2:12-13; 7:5-16).[2]

15:23-24 In addition to all the problems that Jewett mentions, there was of course the mammoth task of pioneer evangelization in the eastern Mediterranean. Paul believed that he had now completed this work, and so he says: *But now that there is no more place for me to work in these regions, and since I have been longing for many years to visit you, I plan to do so when I go to Spain.* Paul uses the word 'region' in two other places, in one to denote the Roman provinces of Syria and Cilicia (Gal 1:21) and in the other to denote regions within the Roman province of Achaia (2 Cor 11:10). 'These regions' here in 15:23 probably denote the Roman provinces in which Paul had been evangelizing prior to the writing of Romans, that is, Syria, Cilicia, Galatia, Asia, Macedonia, Achaia, and even Illyricum.

Paul's statement, 'I have been longing for many years to see you', reflects the fact that this was something that had weighed heavily upon his mind for some time, something he emphasized at the beginning of his letter (1:9-13). By so saying Paul probably sought to ensure that the Roman believers did not interpret his failure to visit them previously as lack of interest on his part. So now he states explicitly: 'I plan to do so when I go to Spain'. Here and 15:28 are the only places in the NT where Spain is mentioned. Whether Paul's ambition to evangelize Spain was ever fulfilled remains a matter of debate among scholars. Clement, writing some thirty years after Paul's death, says:

> After that he had been seven times in bonds, had been driven into exile, had been stoned, had preached in the East and in the West, he won the noble renown which was the reward of his faith, having taught righteousness unto the whole world *and having reached the farthest bounds of the West;* and when he had borne his testimony before the rulers, so he departed from the world and went unto the holy place, having been found a notable pattern of patient endurance. (*1 Clem.* 5:5-7, italics added)

The *Anchor Bible Dictionary* entry has the following comment:

> Whether he [Paul] actually traveled to Spain remains in doubt. Although Clement, writing approximately thirty years after Paul's death, records that the apostle reached "the boundary of the West" (*1 Clem.* 5:7), an expression that probably refers to Spain, and the *Acts of Peter* and the *Muratorian Fragment* concur explicitly, this evidence has not removed the uncertainty from the minds of most scholars.[3]

2. Jewett, *Romans*, 922-23.
3. Warren J. Heard Jr., 'Spain', *ABD*, VI, 176.

It is possible, as various scholars have speculated, that Paul's aim was to complete his mission around the northern side of the Mediterranean by preaching in Spain, and then to complete the circle of the Mediterranean by preaching along its southern side, passing through the Roman provinces of Africa, Cyrenaica, and Egypt.[4]

Having stated that he planned to visit the believers in Rome en route to Spain, Paul now adds: *I hope to see you while passing through*. To visit the Roman believers was evidently not his primary motivation. He intended to do so only 'while passing through' on his way to Spain. Such a statement might have undermined the declarations about how much he longed to see the Roman Christians. And what he says next may have added to that effect: *and to have you assist me on my journey there*.[5] It would appear from this that Paul's primary motive in 'passing through' Rome was to gain practical assistance from the believers there for his projected mission in Spain. In light of the fact that recent studies have shown that Spain lacked any Jewish settlements in this period, Jewett suggests that Paul would have been looking for 'resources such as translators, letters to local contacts, and including perhaps escorts . . . needed to mount this expedition'.[6]

Paul's intimation that he would be looking for assistance for his mission to Spain is qualified somewhat by adding: *after I have enjoyed your company for a while*.[7] He did not want it to appear that he was just 'using' them. He was looking forward to enjoying the time spent with them. What he envisaged in this respect may be derived from comments made at the beginning of the letter: 'I long to see you so that I may impart to you some spiritual gift to make you strong — that is, that you and I may be mutually encouraged by each other's faith' (1:11-12, see the commentary on these verses).

2. Paul's Collection Visit to Jerusalem prior to His Trip to Rome, 15:25-29

> [25]*Now, however, I am on my way to Jerusalem in the service of the Lord's people there.* [26]*For Macedonia and Achaia were pleased to make a contribution for the poor among the Lord's people in Jerusalem.* [27]*They were pleased to do it, and indeed they owe it to them. For if the Gentiles have shared in the Jews' spiritual blessings, they owe it to the Jews to share with them their ma-*

4. Cf., e.g., Wright, 'Romans', 755; Witherington, *Romans*, 363

5. 'To have you assist me on my journey' translates *propemphthēnai* ('to be sent on one's way), an expression used in relation to assisting a person making a journey by providing food and money, by arranging companions and means of travel, etc.' BAGD, *ad loc*. Cf. Strauss, 'Missions Theology in Romans 15:14-33', 465-66.

6. Jewett, *Romans*, 926.

7. The verb *empiplēmi*, whose fundamental meaning is 'to fill up', is appropriately translated here as 'enjoy [your] company', in a context where it is used in relation to people.

terial blessings. ²⁸So after I have completed this task and have made sure that they have received this contribution, I will go to Spain and visit you on the way. ²⁹I know that when I come to you, I will come in the full measure of the blessing of Christ.

15:25 Before the planned trip via Rome to Spain, Paul had to make a visit to Jerusalem. So he informs his audience: *Now, however, I am on my way to Jerusalem in the service of the Lord's people there.* He is referring to the delivery of a collection taken up among the Gentile churches to meet the needs of poor believers in Jerusalem. Paul refers to this collection a number of times as a 'service' to the saints (15:31; 2 Cor 8:4; 9:1, 12, 13; cf. 15:25; 2 Cor 8:19, 20). It may have come as a surprise to Paul's Roman audience to hear he was heading to Jerusalem before making his way to Rome. To go to Jerusalem from Corinth would be heading in the opposite direction he would need to take in order to reach Rome. He explains that he needed to do this 'in the service of the Lord's people' in Jerusalem. Paul had been asked by the leaders of the church in Jerusalem to assist the poor believers there (Gal 2:10). This he had proceeded to do. He wrote about the matter twice to the believers in Corinth (1 Cor 16:1-4; 2 Corinthians 8–9). He took up the matter, not only with the churches of Achaia including Corinth (15:26; 2 Cor 9:2) but also with those in Galatia (1 Cor 16:1) and Macedonia (15:16; 2 Cor 8:1-5).

The significance of the collection for Paul and his mission has been the subject of some debate.[8] Was it (i) simply a compassionate response to the pressing needs of Judean Christians; (ii) an important expression of the unity of the Jewish and Gentile sections of the church (2 Cor 8:14, 15; cf. Rom 15:25-27); (iii) similar to the collection of the Jewish temple tax (though with some differences);[9] or, (iv) more conjecturally, a fulfillment of the OT prophecies of the latter days when the nations and their wealth would flow into Zion (Isa 2:2, 3; 60:5-7; Mic 4:1, 2)?[10] The way Paul promotes the collection for the saints in 2 Corinthians 8–9 shows clearly that he wanted it to be an expression of love and generosity, one that would enhance the relationship between the Corinthian believers and those in Jerusalem. As Wright makes clear: 'For Gentiles to give money for Jewish Christians was a sign that the Gentiles regarded them as members of the same family; for Jewish Christians to accept it would be a sign that they in turn accepted the Gentiles as part of their family'.[11] As there is no hint in either Paul's letters to the Corinthians or in Romans that he regarded the collection as a counterpart to the Jewish temple tax, or that it would be in fulfillment of the OT

8. Keith F. Nickle, *The Collection: A Study in Paul's Strategy* (SBT 48; London: SCM, 1966), provides a readable coverage of the main issues involved. See also Munck, *Paul and the Salvation of Mankind*, 287-305.

9. Nickle, *The Collection*, 74-93.

10. Cf. Nickle, *The Collection*, 129-42.

11. Wright, 'Romans', 756.

prophecies of the wealth of the Gentiles flowing into Jerusalem, these suggestions must remain speculations.[12]

15:26 The fact that the believers in Achaia and Macedonia had responded positively to Paul's request on behalf of the poor in the Jerusalem church is confirmed by what he tells the Roman Christians in 15:26: *For Macedonia and Achaia were pleased to make a contribution for the poor among the Lord's people in Jerusalem.* The churches of the Roman province of Macedonia would have included those in Philippi and Thessalonica. Paul speaks glowingly of the sacrificial giving of the Macedonian churches generally in 2 Corinthians 8:1-4:

> And now, brothers and sisters, we want you to know about the grace that God has given the Macedonian churches. In the midst of a very severe trial, their overflowing joy and their extreme poverty welled up in rich generosity. For I testify that they gave as much as they were able, and even beyond their ability. Entirely on their own, they urgently pleaded with us for the privilege of sharing in this service to the Lord's people. And they exceeded our expectations: They gave themselves first of all to the Lord, and then by the will of God also to us.

The churches of the Roman province of Achaia would have included believers in Athens, Corinth, and Cenchreae. We have no information that those in Athens or Cenchreae contributed to the collection. However, after much cajoling by Paul (1 Cor 16:1-4; 2 Corinthians 8–9) the believers in Corinth did follow through with their promised contribution, as 15:26 confirms.

The NIV's 'to make a contribution' and the NRSV's 'to share their resources' represent similar interpretations of the underlying expression in the original language. Peterman argues such translations are mistaken, and that the expression is better translated more literally as 'to establish fellowship', so that what Paul is saying here is that Macedonia and Achaia were pleased to establish fellowship with the poor by means of material gifts in return for spiritual blessings.[13] Whether this is in fact what the expression means, it was certainly an outcome that the apostle wanted to see brought about.

Paul indicates that the collection was made for 'the poor among the

---

12. According to the fourth view, Paul hoped that the collection would convince Jewish Christians that God was fulfilling his ancient prophecies, that as this realization dawned upon unbelieving Jews they would become jealous as they saw Gentiles enjoying the blessings of God, and that this would trigger the repentance for which Paul longed (11:11-13, 25-32). If this was the case, it did not work out as Paul hoped. His journey to Jerusalem with those bearing the collection (Acts 24:17) resulted in a tumult, his arrest, and a further hardening of the Jews against the gospel. This fourth suggestion has not been found convincing by the majority of recent commentators. In fact, it constitutes a rather large superstructure built upon a foundation made up of inferences from rather limited evidence.

13. G. W. Peterman, 'Romans 15.26: Make a Contribution or Establish Fellowship?' *NTS* 40 (1994) 457-63, provides six reasons in support of the view that *koinōnian tina poiēsasthai* is better translated more literally as 'to establish fellowship'.

Lord's people in Jerusalem', and this seems to imply that not all the believers in Jerusalem were poor and in need. Presumably there were more who were poor than could be provided for by those who were not, thus necessitating a collection among the churches of the Gentiles.

15:27 Speaking of the believers in Macedonia and Achaia who were giving material gifts for the poor in Jerusalem, Paul emphasizes: *They were pleased to do it, and indeed they owe it to them.* For their part, Paul says, 'they were *pleased* to do it'. This was certainly the case with the Macedonians (cf. 2 Cor 8:1-2), and in the end it proved to be the case with the Achaians also, but in the case of the Corinthians this was only after the apostle stressed to them the importance of a generous and voluntary gift (2 Cor 9:5-7). In Paul's mind, if not in the mind of the Macedonians and the Achaians, it was a matter of obligation: 'they owe it to them' (lit. 'they are their debtors'). Paul describes the nature of their indebtedness: *For if the Gentiles have shared in the Jews' spiritual blessings, they owe it to the Jews to share with them their material blessings* (lit. 'For if the Gentiles have shared in their spiritual things, they are obligated also to serve them with material things'). Their obligation was moral, not legal, for all contributions to the collection had to be made generously and cheerfully (2 Cor 9:5-7).[14]

The 'spiritual blessings' of the Jewish believers in which the Gentiles have shared are the blessings of the gospel, promised first to the Jewish people. The 'material blessings' with which the Gentiles are to serve the Jewish believers are their financial contributions. It is perhaps significant that when Paul speaks of the Gentiles 'serving' the Jewish believers in this way, he employs a verb used only here by Paul but belonging to a word group that has cultic connotations,[15] suggesting that the Gentiles' contributions constitute a sacrifice well pleasing to God as well as a helpful gift to the poor in Jerusalem (cf. Phil 4:18).

15:28 Having explained his immediate plan to take the collection to Jerusalem, Paul speaks again of his longer-term plans: *So after I have completed this task and have made sure that they have received this contribution, I will go to Spain and visit you on the way.* The task to be completed is, of course, the delivery of the collection to the poor believers in Jerusalem. In this connection Paul speaks of the time when he has 'made sure that they have received this contribution' (lit. 'and having *sealed* to them this fruit'). Two things here call for comment. First, the verb Paul uses here has the basic meaning 'to put a seal upon' something to ensure its safe delivery (e.g., sacks of grain). It appears to be used with this general meaning here in

14. Jewett, *Romans*, 930, argues that the reference to the Macedonians and Achaians being 'well pleased' (*eudokēsan*) to share their resources 'lifts up the element of an uncoerced decision that derives from grateful hearts, transformed by divine righteousness, rather than from any form of social or political pressure.'

15. The verb is *leitourgeō*, which can denote the service rendered, e.g., by 'priests and Levites in God's temple (cp. Ex 28:35, 43; 29:30; Num 18:2; Sir 4:14; 45:15; Jdth 4:14; 1 Macc 10:42)' (BAGD, *ad loc*).

15:28 where Paul is to make his journey to Jerusalem and ensure the safe delivery of the collection. Second, if this is the general idea behind the use of the verb here, it is strange that it is used in connection with the imagery of 'fruit'. However, in this context 'fruit' would represent the results of Paul's ministry among the Gentiles (cf. 1:13), expressed concretely in their contributions for the poor among the Jewish believers in Jerusalem.[16] So the overall thrust of Paul's statement could be paraphrased: 'when I have placed the sum that was collected safely (sealed) in their hands'.[17]

Having completed the safe delivery of the collection monies, Paul says, 'I will go to Spain and visit you on the way' (lit. 'I will depart via you to Spain'). It would appear that the thing uppermost in the apostle's mind at this point was to complete his business in Jerusalem and then depart for Spain. To visit the Roman believers seems, at this point, to be only a means to an end and somewhat at variance with what he said earlier about his great desire to see them (1:8-13). However, Paul has already qualified a similar statement of his plans to show that his visit with the Roman believers is not just a means to an end: 'I hope to see you while passing through and to have you assist me on my journey there, after *I have enjoyed your company for a while*' (15:24, italics added).

15:29 Contemplating his visit to Rome, Paul says: *I know that when I come to you, I will come in the full measure of the blessing of Christ.* Before Paul could set out for Rome, he had to travel to Jerusalem with the collection. He was fully aware of the dangers that could be awaiting him there and was unsure about how 'the saints in Jerusalem' would respond to offerings of the Gentiles (cf. 15:31). Despite what the outcome of his visit to Jerusalem might be, he asserts that he is still confident that when he arrives in Rome it would be 'in the full measure of the blessing of Christ'. What he looked forward to upon his arrival included both fruitful ministry among the believers there and the enjoyment of mutual encouragement (1:11-12).

3. Paul's Appeal for the Roman Believers' Support in Prayer, 15:30-33

> [30]*I urge you, brothers and sisters, by our Lord Jesus Christ and by the love of the Spirit, to join me in my struggle by praying to God for me.* [31]*Pray that I may be kept safe from the unbelievers in Judea and that the contribution I take to Jerusalem may be favorably received by the Lord's people there,* [32]*so*

---

16. Byrne, *Romans*, 442, says: 'Paul speaks in terms of "this fruit" probably to convey the sense that the collection will be a token of how richly the "spiritual seed" of the gospel, originating in Israel, has borne "fruit" among the Gentiles'.

17. BAGD, *ad loc.* Jewett, *Romans*, 932, comments: 'To seal the fruit of the Jerusalem offering is . . . to guarantee its delivery against theft and embezzlement, which conforms to the arrangements Paul made in 2 Cor 8:20-23 to ensure that the Corinthian contribution would be securely delivered'.

that I may come to you with joy, by God's will, and in your company be re-freshed. ³³The God of peace be with you all. Amen.

15:30 Paul faced his upcoming trip to Jerusalem with a mixture of apprehension and fear, neither of which proved to be without foundation. In these verses he appeals to his audience for their prayers: *I urge you, brothers and sisters, by our Lord Jesus Christ and by the love of the Spirit, to join me in my struggle by praying to God for me.* This is a most unusual way for Paul to make an appeal. Elsewhere he appeals to people 'in the name of our Lord Jesus Christ' (1 Cor 1:10) and 'by the humility and gentleness of Christ' (2 Cor 10:1). But here he makes his appeal 'by our Lord Jesus Christ and by the love of the Spirit'. It would appear that he is making his appeal to his audience on the basis of the lordship of Christ that both he and they acknowledge on the one hand, and in the light of the love of the Spirit they both experience on the other. Paul appeals to the Roman believers 'to join me in my struggle by praying to God for me'.[18] It is noteworthy that Paul speaks about 'struggling' in prayer. It was evidently something he found very demanding, and it was a demanding task in which he urged his audience to share with him.

15:31 Paul solicited his audience's prayers for two specific things. First, he asked: *Pray that I may be kept safe from the unbelievers in Judea.* Paul was about to set sail for Jerusalem, and he anticipated violent opposition from unbelieving elements among his own kinsfolk in Judea. He knew what that opposition could be like because prior to his conversion he himself had perpetrated it against Jewish Christians. As it turned out, his fears were not without foundation, for, according to the Acts of the Apostles, on his way to Jerusalem he was given repeated prophetic warnings of trouble in Jerusalem (Acts 20:22-24), and when he arrived there he became the object of an assassination plot made by unbelieving Jews, a plot that was foiled only when the Roman authorities were told of it and removed him from Jerusalem and took him to Caesarea secretly by night (cf. Acts 23:12-23). Prayers that Paul be rescued from the unbelievers were answered, but in an unusual way, 'only by being locked up by the Romans for two years'.[19]

Second, he asked his audience to pray *that the contribution I take to Jerusalem may be favorably received by the Lord's people there.* The 'Lord's people' here are the Jewish believers of Jerusalem. The 'contribution' Paul was taking to Jerusalem was the collection taken up in the Gentile churches he had founded. His request that this service would be 'favorably received' by the Lord's people reflects some apprehension on his part as to whether the Jewish believers in Jerusalem would accept the offerings of the Gentile churches

---

18. The verb *synagōnizomai* ('to struggle with') is found only here in the NT; however, the unaugmented form of the verb, *agōnizomai*, is found eight times, six of which are in Paul's letters. In each of these six cases the verb denotes the struggle involved in Christian life and ministry (1 Cor 9:25; Col 1:29; 4:12; 1 Tim 4:10; 6:12; 2 Tim 4:7).

19. Moo, *Romans*, 911.

in the spirit in which they were given. For the Jewish believers to do so would involve a *de facto* recognition of the *bona fides* of Gentile believers as true members of the people of God, and this was something that some of them had previously called into question (cf. Gal 5:6-10; 6:12-15; Acts 15:1-2, 4-5). According to the Acts of the Apostles, when Paul arrived in Jerusalem, 'the brothers and sisters' received him warmly (Acts 21:17), and later, when appearing before Felix the Roman governor in Caesarea and referring to his recent visit to Jerusalem and the collection, Paul said, 'After an absence of several years, I came to Jerusalem to bring my people gifts for the poor and to present offerings' (Acts 24:17). The indications are, then, that the offering of the Gentile believers was accepted, and his prayers and those of the Roman believers had been answered. Dunn, citing Minear, says: 'Nothing more fully proves the significance of the fund in Paul's eyes than the fact that he judged its safe delivery to be worth the risk of his life'.[20]

15:32 Paul asked members of the Roman churches to join him in praying for these two specific things *so that I may come to you with joy, by God's will, and in your company be refreshed.*[21] The verb translated 'be refreshed' (found only here in the NT)[22] has the fundamental meaning of 'relaxing in someone's company'.[23] By being rescued from attacks from Jewish opposition, by receiving a warm welcome from the Jewish believers, and by their gracious acceptance of the collection monies, Paul hoped that he would be greatly relieved and that the memory of it would be an ongoing source of joy to him as he made his projected trip west to Rome and then on to Spain. In this state of mind he hoped to relax in the company of the Roman believers before the planned trip to Spain.

15:33 The apostle completes this part of this letter by invoking God's blessing upon his audience: *The God of peace be with you all. Amen.* The blessing he invokes is nothing less than the presence of 'the God of peace'. The description of God as 'the God of peace' is one Paul employs a total of six times in his letters (15:33; 16:20; 1 Cor 14:33; 2 Cor 13:11; Phil 4:9; 1 Thess 5:23; cf. Heb 13:20).[24] He is the God of peace supremely because through

---

20. Dunn, *Romans 9–16*, 878.

21. There are a number of textual variants for 15:32, none of which alter materially the meaning of the text (see Metzger, ed., *A Textual Commentary*, 474).

22. The verb is *synanapauomai* ('to rest with'). The cognate verb *anapauō* ('to give rest, refresh') is found twelve times in the NT, and of these four are found in Paul's letters (1 Cor 16:18; 2 Cor 7:13; Philem 7, 20).

23. BAGD, *synanapauomai.*

24. Jewett, *Romans,* 939, notes: 'Outside of the NT, the only occurrence of this expression "the God of peace" is in *T. Dan* 5:1-2, where it deals with conflicts within the faith community. . . . ("Observe the Lord's commandments, then, my children. . . . Each of you speak truth clearly to his neighbor, and do not fall into pleasure and troublemaking, but be at peace, holding to the God of peace. Thus no conflict will overwhelm you".) In contrast to the suggestion of *T. Dan* that conflicts should be resolved by following the law more carefully, Paul understands peace as the activity of God through the gospel, which transforms antagonists and makes cooperation possible'.

Christ he made peace by the blood of the cross (Col 1:20), or as Paul says elsewhere: 'God was reconciling the world to himself in Christ, not counting people's sins against them' (2 Cor 5:19). On the basis of the fact that God is the God of peace, and that he has made peace with humanity through the death of his Son, Paul repeatedly invokes God's peace upon the audiences of his letters (1:7; 15:13, 33; 1 Cor 1:3; 2 Cor 1:2; Gal 1:3; 6:16; Eph 1:2; 6:23; Phil 1:2; Col 1:2; 1 Thess 1:2; 1 Tim 1:2; 2 Tim 1:2; Tit 1:4; Philem 3).

V. CONCLUSION, 16:1-27

While the majority texts include this chapter as an integral part of Romans, there are variations in the textual tradition that have caused questions to be raised about its place in the letter. In particular there is evidence for the placement of the doxology (located traditionally at 16:25-27) in six different locations listed by Metzger as: (a) 1:11–16:23 + doxology; (b) 1:1–14:23 + doxology + 15:1–16:23 + doxology; (c) 1:1–14:23 + doxology + 15:1–16:24; (d) 1:1–16:24; (e) 1:1–15:23 + doxology + 16:1-23; (f) 1:1–14:23 + 16:24 + doxology. Summarizing the conclusions reached by those who prepared the text of the United Bible Societies' *The Greek New Testament*, Metzger says: 'In evaluating the complicated evidence, the Committee was prepared to allow (1) for the probability that Marcion, or his followers, circulated a shortened form of the epistle, lacking chapters 15 and 16, and (2) for the possibility that Paul himself had dispatched a longer and shorter form of the epistle (one form with, and one without, chapter 16). . . . On the basis of good and diversified evidence supporting sequence (a) [1:11–16:23 + doxology], it was decided to include the doxology at its traditional place at the close of the epistle, but enclosed within square brackets to indicate a degree of uncertainty that it belongs there'.[1] Lampe provides five detailed and well-argued reasons why chapter 16 should be regarded as an original part of Romans.[2]

Chapter 16 comprises five discernible sections: a commendation of Phoebe (16:1-2); greetings for twenty-six individuals (16:3-16); warnings about troublemakers (16:17-20); greetings from eight individuals (16:21-23); and the concluding doxology (16:25-27).

A. Commendation of Phoebe, 16:1-2

> [1] *I commend to you our sister Phoebe, a deacon of the church in Cenchreae.* [2] *I ask you to receive her in the Lord in a way worthy of his people and to give*

---

1. Metzger, ed., *A Textual Commentary*, 470-73.
2. Lampe, 'The Roman Christians', 217-21.

her any help she may need from you, for she has been the benefactor of many people, including me.

16:1   Paul commences this closing chapter with a commendation for Phoebe: *I commend to you our sister Phoebe, a deacon of the church in Cenchreae.* Paul wrote Romans from Corinth (see the commentary on 16:23), and one of that city's ports was Cenchreae, which was located about ten kilometers to the southeast on the Saronic Gulf. There would have been contact between the churches of Corinth and Cenchreae, Phoebe was well known to Paul, and as he says in 16:2, she was one of his benefactors. Seeing that Paul's commendation of Phoebe comes at the beginning of this closing part of the letter, and precedes the greetings to twenty-six named individuals belonging to the Roman churches, it would appear that she acted as the courier who conveyed Paul's letter to Rome.[1]

Paul describes Phoebe as 'our sister', a designation that Dunn says 'seems to have been particularly characteristic of Christianity (1 Cor 7:15; 9:5; Philem 2; James 2:15; Ign. *Pol.* 5:1; 2 *Clem.* 12:5; 19:1; 20:2; Herm. *Vis.* 2.2.3; 2.3.1)'.[2] He also describes Phoebe as 'a deacon' [= 'servant'] of the church in Cenchreae'. Doing so, he uses the same word he employs regularly to describe both himself and others as servants of God (2 Cor 6:4), servants of the gospel (Eph 3:7; Col 1:23), servants of a new covenant (2 Cor 3:6), servants in the Lord (Eph 6:21; Col 4:7), and servants of Christ (Phil 1:1; Col 1:7; 1 Tim 4:6). Only here in 16:1 do we find anyone described as 'a deacon of the church', and this appears to be the earliest historical reference to such a ministry in 'the church'. In Colossians 1:24-25 Paul does speak of the body of Christ, the church, of which he became a 'servant'. All this suggests that the apostle recognized Phoebe as a servant of the church similar to his other colleagues and himself.

There has been debate about the exact nature of Phoebe's role as a 'deacon of the church in Cenchreae'. Some early church fathers believed that she fulfilled an official role. Origen said: 'This passage teaches that there were women ordained in the church's ministry by the apostle's authority. . . . Not only that — they ought to be ordained into the ministry, because they helped in many ways and by their good services deserved the praise even of the apostle'.[3] Pelagius said, 'Even today, women deaconesses in the East are known to minister to their own sex in baptism or even in the ministry of the Word, for we find that women taught privately, e.g.,

---

1. [Pseudo-] Constantius observes: 'Here the apostle demonstrates that no discrimination or preference between male and female is to be tolerated, because he sends his letter to Rome by the hand of a woman' ('The Holy Letter of St. Paul to the Romans' [*ACCSR*, 369]). Jewett, *Romans*, 943, explains, 'Ancient epistolary practice would therefore assume that the recommendation of Phoebe was related to her task of conveying and interpreting the letter in Rome as well as in carrying out the business entailed in the letter'.

2. Dunn, *Romans 9–16*, 886.

3. 'Commentary on the Epistle to the Romans' (*ACCSR*, 369).

Priscilla, whose husband was called Aquila'.[4] Some recent commentators agree. Wright thinks that she occupied a position of leadership in the Cenchrean church.[5] Jewett argues that 'servant' (*diakonos*) was 'an official title of leadership' and that Phoebe's role cannot be restricted to philanthropic activity; rather, she functioned as an official teacher in the church in Cenchreae.[6] Arichea contends that '*diakonos* should be understood not simply as a generic word describing Phoebe as a useful and active member of the church in Cenchreae, but as a word which somewhat depicts Phoebe's role as a leader within the Christian community. And while we can grant that *diakonos* in Romans does not yet refer to an ecclesiastical office with a set place within the hierarchy of the church and with specific qualifications of the office bearers, yet it does describe a person with a special function in the pastoral and administrative life of the church; and such functions would most probably include pastoral care, teaching, and even missionary work'.[7] However, Dunn, while acknowledging that 'Phoebe is the first recorded "deacon" in the history of Christianity', says that 'it would be premature to speak of an established office of diaconate, as though a role of responsibility and authority, with properly appointed succession, had already been agreed upon in the Pauline churches'.[8]

Others deny that Paul's reference to Phoebe as a 'deacon of the church in Cenchreae' implies that she held an official leadership position. Romaniuk argues that Paul's designation of Phoebe as a deacon is a 'courteous exaggeration'. He contends: Paul knowingly magnifies the role of Phoebe when he likens her role in the community to that of an official deacon. . . . The term *diakonos* is emphasized in such a general way as regards Phoebe that we should deny that in the early church Phoebe was something more than an ordinary lay-woman'.[9] However, if Phoebe was no more than 'an ordinary lay-woman', it is strange that Paul adds to his description of her as a 'sister' that she was also a 'deacon of the church in Cenchreae', although he leaves unstated and unspecified the nature or the service she rendered in the church.

References to the role of deacons in the church in Paul's letters provide no evidence for his understanding of their actual function. His address to the church in Philippi includes reference to deacons along with overseers (Phil 1:1) but provides no clues as to their function. His advice to Timothy concerning the qualifications required of those aspiring to the office of deacon includes matters relating to marital status (1 Tim 3:12), and

---

4. 'Commentary on Romans' (*ACCSR*, 369).

5. Wright, 'Romans', 761-62.

6. Jewett, *Romans*, 944-45.

7. Daniel C. Arichea Jr., 'Who Was Phoebe? Translating *Diakonos* in Romans 16.1', *BibTrans* 39 (1988) 409.

8. Dunn, *Romans 9-16*, 887.

9. Kazimierz Romaniuk, 'Was Phoebe in Romans 16,1 a Deaconess?' *ZNW* 81 (1990) 133-34.

he says that 'those who have served well gain an excellent standing and great assurance in their faith in Christ Jesus' (1 Tim 3:13), but again he provides no information concerning the nature of their service.[10]

16:2 Having commended Phoebe, Paul adds: *I ask you to receive her in the Lord in a way worthy of his people. . . .* While the NIV construes this as the beginning of a new sentence, it is in fact a continuation of what is found in 16:1. The connection can be indicated by the literal translation: 'I commend to you our sister Phoebe . . . in order that you may receive her in the Lord in a way that is worthy of his people'. . . .[11] The need for travelers to be received by people in the places they visited was crucial in the ancient world.[12] Unless they were accorded hospitality they would have no standing in either law or custom. There was no such thing as universal brotherhood in the ancient world (see 'Additional Note: Hospitality', 478-79).[13] Paul commends Phoebe to the believers in Rome knowing that she needs to be afforded hospitality, and with the expectation that they will receive her in a way worthy of God's people. This is an unusual expression for Paul. He normally speaks of acting in a way that is worthy of one's calling, or the gospel, or the Lord, or God (cf. Eph 4:1; Phil 1:27; Col 1:10; 1 Thess 2:12). Only here in 16:2 does he speak of acting in a way that is worthy of God's people. By this, presumably, he means to receive her in a way that is commensurate with their standing as people of God, that is, according to the love, generosity, and hospitable traits that should mark God's people.

Having asked the believers in Rome to receive Phoebe in this way, Paul continues: *and to give her any help she may need from you.* Like the previous clause, this one is dependent upon the opening commendation. The connection can be indicated in a literal translation: 'I commend to you our sister Phoebe . . . [in order that] you help her in whatever things she may need from you'. A courier like Phoebe would need food and lodging and people to guarantee her *bona fides* in a strange city, and these 'things' the Roman believers could provide for her. It has been suggested that the 'help she may need' could also relate to church matters she was acting on in behalf of the Cenchrean church, preparations for Paul's visit to Rome, or

---

10. Cranfield, *Romans*, II, 781, thinks that it is inherently probable that 'a specialized use of *diakonos* in NT times will have corresponded to the clearly attested specialized use of *diakonein* and *diakonia* with reference to the practical service of the needy, and there are some features, for example, what is said about Phoebe in v. 2b, which would provide plenty of scope, for the practical expression of Christian compassion and helpfulness is hardly to be doubted'.

11. Paul made a similar request of the Philippian believers using the same verb when he asked them to 'welcome/receive' *(prosdechesthe)* Epaphroditus, whom he was sending back to them (Phil 2:29).

12. Jewett, *Romans*, 945, notes: 'The fact that *prosdechesthai* often appears in secular letters of recommendation with the connotation of hospitality for the bearer of a letter indicates that Käsemann was on the right track ["welcoming and offering lodging and help"]'.

13. Cf. Bruce J. Malina, 'The Received View and What It Cannot Do, III: John and Hospitality', *Semeia* 35 (1986) 182-83.

some business matters of her own, though it is impossible to be definite about this because of lack of evidence.[14]

Paul says that there is a good reason why the Roman believers should welcome and assist Phoebe in this way: *for she has been the benefactor of many people, including me.* That she was able to act as a benefactor for many people, including Paul, indicates that she was a person of substantial means, and therefore able to travel, and as a servant of the church in Cenchreae she was an appropriate person to act as a courier for Paul's crucial letter to the churches of Rome.

The word Paul uses when describing Phoebe as a benefactor is *prostatis*. His use of the term here has prompted extensive research into its significance.[15] On the one hand, there are those who argue that it means little more than 'helper', while acknowledging that Phoebe was a helper of significant social status and independence.[16] Ng, for example, rejects the view that Phoebe occupied any position of leadership in the church. She holds that 'the text does not say she was *prostatis* of the church in Cenchreae but of individuals, and that if there is some correspondence between the service Paul asks the Roman believers to provide for her and the service she provided as *prostatis* of many, this would rule out the notion of church leader or president.[17] She also rejects the view 'that *prostatis* means patron or benefactor, either in a juridical and technical sense (Paul would not have needed that sort of help, being a Roman citizen and well able to speak for himself), or in a financial sense (Paul refused all financial support from the Corinthians and it is unlikely that doing so he would then accept it from a Cenchrean)'.[18] Ng's view is that Phoebe was a *prostatis* simply in the sense that she provided practical assistance and hospitality.[19]

On the other hand, there are those who ascribe great significance to Paul's use of *prostatis* in relation to Phoebe, arguing that it denotes one who is a patron and benefactor of others in a legal or financial sense. Contrary to earlier belief that only the masculine form of the word (*prostatēs*) was used in this way,[20] recent studies have shown that the feminine form (*prostatis*) was used of women fulfilling a patronage role. Kearsley, for example, having investigated inscriptional evidence related to two women of importance in the Roman east around the middle of the first century, Iunia Theodora and Claudia Metrodora, who acted as benefactors, concludes that some women

14. Cf. Witherington, *Romans*, 383; Byrne, *Romans*, 447.

15. BAGD, *ad loc.*, defines the word *prostatis* as 'a woman in a supportive role, patron, benefactor', but adds: 'the relationship suggested by the term *pr[ostatis]* is not to be confused w[ith] the Rom[an] patron-client system, which was of a different order and alien to Gk. Tradition'. It translates 16:2b as follows: 'she has proved to be of great assistance to many, including myself'.

16. So, e.g., Cranfield, *Romans*, II, 782-83.

17. Esther Yue L. Ng, 'Phoebe as *Prostatis*', *TrinJ* 25 (2004) 4-6.

18. Ng, 'Phoebe as *Prostatis*', 6-9.

19. Ng, 'Phoebe as *Prostatis*', 9-10.

20. So, e.g., Käsemann, *Romans*, 411.

did have prominent public roles, and that in relation to Phoebe 'there appears to be no reason on grounds of sex alone to deny her the role of the benefactor of Paul and the Christians living in Kenchreai'.[21] Jewett cites the work of E. A. Judge, Theissen, Holmberg, Funk, Murphy-O'Connor, Meeks, Kearsley, Trebilco, and Garrison, all of whom document the role played by both male and female benefactors in early Christians communities which provides the social background to Paul's description of Phoebe as a benefactor.[22] Jewett goes further and argues that Phoebe, being a woman of substantial means and with a house large enough to accommodate the gathering of church members, was the host of the house church in Cenchreae. As such she 'presided over the Eucharistic celebrations and was responsible for the ordering of the congregation'.[23] This builds too much on the meaning of the term 'benefactor' and its use in 16:2. However, it is reasonable to say that recent studies of the word, and the fact that Paul's description of Phoebe both as a deacon of the church and a benefactor of himself and many others, is sufficient to show that she exercised a significant ministry in the church at Cenchreae in addition to being a patron of Paul's ministry.[24]

B. Greetings for Twenty-Six Named Individuals, 16:3-16

[3]Greet Priscilla and Aquila, my co-workers in Christ Jesus. [4]They risked their lives for me. Not only I but all the churches of the Gentiles are grateful to them. [5]Greet also the church that meets at their house. Greet my dear friend Epenetus, who was the first convert to Christ in the province of Asia. [6]Greet Mary, who worked very hard for you. [7]Greet Andronicus and Junia, my fellow Jews who have been in prison with me. They are outstanding among the apostles, and they were in Christ before I was. [8]Greet Ampliatus, my dear friend in the Lord. [9]Greet Urbanus, our co-worker in Christ, and my dear friend Stachys. [10]Greet Apelles, whose fidelity to Christ has stood the test. Greet those who belong to the household of Aristobulus. [11]Greet Herodion, my fellow Jew. Greet those in the household of Narcissus who are in the Lord. [12]Greet Tryphena and Tryphosa, those women who work hard in the Lord. Greet my dear friend Persis, another woman who has worked very hard in the Lord. [13]Greet Rufus, chosen in the Lord, and his mother, who has

---

21. R. A. Kearsley, 'Women in Public Life in the Roman East: Iunia Theodora, Claudia Metrodora and Phoebe, Benefactress of Paul', *TynBul* 50 (1999) 202.

22. Jewett, *Romans*, 946-47. Cf. Dunn, *Romans 9–16*, 888-89; Witherington, *Romans*, 384-85.

23. Jewett, *Romans*, 946-47.

24. Cf. Dunn, *Romans 9–16*, 888-89; Witherington, *Romans*, 384-85. Caroline F. Whelan, 'Amica Pauli: The Role of Phoebe in the Early Church', *JSNT* 49 (1993) 72-73, adopts a rather unique view of the matter. She argues that Romans 16 is a fragment of another letter intended not for the Roman churches but for the church in *Ephesus*, and that Paul expected her to play some role in supporting his efforts in that city.

been a mother to me, too. [14]*Greet Asyncritus, Phlegon, Hermes, Patrobas, Hermas and the other brothers and sisters with them.* [15]*Greet Philologus, Julia, Nereus and his sister, and Olympas and all the Lord's people who are with them.* [16]*Greet one another with a holy kiss. All the churches of Christ send greetings.*

In this second section of chapter 16 Paul asks those of his audience to greet (on his behalf) twenty-six named individuals in the Roman churches, together with a number of unnamed people associated with them. Apart from Priscilla and Aquila, and possibly Mary and Rufus, these named individuals are not mentioned elsewhere in the NT. The inclusion of so many personal greetings makes Romans unique among Paul's letters. It also provides us with some important clues concerning the nature of the Christian churches in Rome and the roles of individuals within the churches. Investigations have been carried out on the personal names mentioned to discover possible clues to their background and social status (see 'Additional Note: The Twenty-Six Named Individuals in Romans 16:3-15', 574-75).

There are a number of possible reasons why Paul should have included so many personal greetings in Romans: (i) Wright notes that in five cases Paul greets certain couples along with other Christians in their household. It appears that he is greeting various household churches to show that he does not favor one against another, especially if some could be identified with 'the weak' and others with 'the strong' mentioned in 14:1–15:13. He does so to ensure that when he comes to Rome he will not find that he has further fueled divisions already existing in the Christian community there.[1] (ii) Witherington, noting that Paul does not greet the twenty-six named individuals directly but asks the dominantly Gentile audience to do so on his behalf, suggests that this is a strategy to promote reconciliation among the various individuals and groups. In particular Paul's purpose is to ensure that the Jewish Christians returning to Rome are embraced by the believers, who are predominantly Gentile.[2] (iii) Croft sees in the inclusion of these formal greetings 'a kind of internal commendation' of those mentioned. He says: 'The majority of people in the list are singled out for some kind of praise or other comment. As the letter is read out in its original context, each person is, as it were, lifted up within the receiving congregation and their ministry is commended to the whole community'.[3] While it is impossible to be sure about Paul's motivation in this matter, one or even all of these suggestions could well represent what he had in mind.

16:3-5a Paul opens this section with: *Greet Priscilla and Aquila, my co-workers in Christ Jesus.* Priscilla and Aquila, probably husband and wife (or

---

1. Wright, 'Romans', 761.

2. Witherington, *Romans,* 379.

3. Steve Croft, 'Text Messages: The Ministry of Women and Romans 16', *Anvil* 21 (2004) 88.

possibly brother and sister), are mentioned as a pair six times in the NT. They are mentioned three times by Paul, who always refers to her as Prisca[4] and mentions her before Aquila twice (16:3; 2 Tim 4:19) and after him once (1 Cor 16:9).[5] They are referred to three times in the Acts of the Apostles, where the diminutive 'Priscilla' is used and where she is mentioned before Aquila on two occasions (Acts 18:18, 26) and after him on the other occasion (Acts 18:2).

The reason why Priscilla's name appears before that of Aquila has been variously explained. Cranfield believes that it is 'to be explained as due either to her having been converted before him (and perhaps having led her husband to faith in Christ) or to her having played an even more prominent part in the life and work of the Church than Aquila had, and to her having been socially superior to him'.[6] Jewett suggests that the fact that her name is mentioned first indicates that she was of a higher social status.[7]

Paul refers to Priscilla and Aquila as his 'co-workers in Christ Jesus'. 'Co-worker' appears to be a favorite term of Paul's to describe those who labor alongside him in the gospel, and not one he uses in general of Christians. Those whom he describes as co-workers include, besides Priscilla and Aquila, Urbanus (16:9), Timothy (16:21), Apollos (1 Cor 3:9), Titus (2 Cor 8:23), Epaphroditus (Phil 2:25), Clement (Phil 4:3), Jesus and Justus (Col 4:11), Philemon (Philem 1), Mark, Aristarchus, Demas, and Luke (Philem 24).

According to the Acts of the Apostles, Paul met Priscilla and Aquila in Corinth, when, following Claudius's edict in A.D. 49, they, along with other Jews, were expelled from Rome. Because Paul and this couple shared the same trade as tentmakers, Paul stayed with them and worked with them (Acts 18:1-3). When Paul left Corinth en route to Syria, he was accompanied as far as Ephesus by Priscilla and Aquila (Acts 18:18-19). While they were in Ephesus, the Alexandrian Jew, Apollos, arrived there and began teaching fervently about Jesus, even though 'he knew only the baptism of John'. Priscilla and Aquila invited him into their home and 'explained to him the way of God more adequately' (Acts 18:24-26).

---

4. The NIV substitutes for the strongly attested 'Prisca' the less-well-attested diminutive 'Priscilla'. The latter is the reading adopted by the Textus Receptus. Paul mentions her in two other places (1 Cor 16:19; 2 Tim 4:19), where he refers to her as 'Prisca', not 'Priscilla', though in both cases the NIV has 'Priscilla'.

5. Jerome Murphy-O'Connor, 'The Pauline Network', *BibToday* 42 (2004) 220, points out: 'Typically he underlines the superiority of the woman by calling her Prisca, as opposed to Priscilla, the "little girl" version of the name that Luke uses consistently (Acts 18:2, 18, 26), and by mentioning her before her husband Aquila (see 2 Tim 4:19)'.

6. Cranfield, *Romans*, II, 784.

7. Jewett, *Romans*, 955, adds: 'The inference that Prisca came from a noble background is consistent with the ancient naming of the Santa Prisca parish in the Aventine district of Rome, probably on the site of the original house church that was named after her rather than Aquila. The *Titulus Priscae* address strongly suggests that this expensive property was originally registered in Prisca's name, reverting to church ownership centuries later'.

Paul's references to Priscilla and Aquila are quite brief. He mentions them in 1 Corinthians 16:19, where he passes on their warm greetings to the Corinthians and refers to 'the church that meets at their house'. There is an even briefer reference in 2 Timothy 4:19 in which he urges his colleague, Timothy, to greet Priscilla and Aquila (and Onesiphorus), who were then still in Ephesus (cf. 2 Tim 1:15-18). Most important is how Paul portrays them here in 16:3-5. He not only describes them as his 'co-workers in Christ Jesus' (see above) but also says: *They risked their lives for me* (lit. 'they risked their own necks for my life'). The expression 'to risk one's neck' was a colloquialism for risking execution.[8] We do not know when they did this. It may have been on the occasion of the 'great disturbance' in Ephesus when a riot broke out following Paul's preaching. He appears to refer to this in 2 Corinthians 1:8-11 when he speaks of despairing even of life, and of feeling within himself, as it were, the sentence of death — from which on that occasion he was delivered. One can only wonder what part Priscilla and Aquila might have played in this deliverance, and whether it was at this time that they risked their necks for Paul. If it was the intervention of Priscilla and Aquila that saved Paul on this occasion, it would reveal, as Jewett points out, 'a patronal capacity that derived from high social status'.[9]

The other comment Paul makes about Priscilla and Aquila is that *not only I but all the churches of the Gentiles are grateful to them.* For what reason were all the Gentile churches grateful to them? Perhaps it was because this couple of Jewish believers had opened their homes in Ephesus (1 Cor 16:9) and Rome (16:5a) to Gentile believers?[10]

Paul's final reference to Priscilla and Aquila is contained in his request to his Roman audience not only to greet them but also to *greet . . . the church that meets at their house.* In whatever circumstance they found themselves, whether in Corinth, Ephesus, or Rome, they were active as Paul's 'co-workers in Christ Jesus', not least in allowing their premises to be used for the meeting of Christian congregations.

16:5b   Paul next asks his audience: *Greet my dear friend Epenetus, who was the first convert to Christ in the province of Asia.* This is the only place in the NT that Epenetus is mentioned, so apart from what the apostle says in 16:5b we know nothing about him. Paul describes him first as 'my dear friend' (lit. 'my beloved'). This is not unusual, for Paul uses the adjective 'beloved' to describe individuals and churches twenty-four times in his let-

---

8. Cf. Jewett, *Romans,* 957.

9. Jewett, *Romans,* 957.

10. Richard E. Oster Jr., '"Congregations of the Gentiles" (Rom 16:4): A Culture-based Ecclesiology in the Letters of Paul', *ResQ* 40 (1998) 48-51, argues that Paul's reference to 'the churches of the Gentiles' *(ekklēsiai ethnōn)* should be understood culturally and religiously and not racially to denote those congregations made of people who were once pagans. They were culturally and religiously quite different from the churches of the Jews. On these grounds Oster argues that early Christian congregations were 'separate but equal' — there were the churches of the Gentiles and churches of the Jews.

ters. However, Paul's affection for Epenetus may be special seeing that he depicts him next as 'the first convert to Christ in the province of Asia' (lit. 'who is [the] firstfruits of Asia for Christ'). Whether Epenetus was one of Paul's converts is not certain. Paul wanted to preach in the province of Asia at the beginning of his second missionary journey but was 'kept by the Holy Spirit' from doing so (Acts 16:6). On his way back to Antioch at the close of his second missionary journey he spent just a brief time in Ephesus, where he reasoned with Jews in the synagogue, but then departed, promising to return to Ephesus if it was God's will (Acts 18:19-21). It was only on his third missionary journey that Paul spent an extended period of time in Ephesus, during which 'all the Jews and Greeks who lived in the province of Asia heard the word of the Lord' (Acts 19:10, 22). Whether Epenetus was one of these we do not know.[11]

16:6 Next Paul asks his audience: *Greet Mary, who worked very hard for you.* This is the only mention of a Mary by Paul. Six other women are identified as Mary elsewhere in the NT,[12] but the one to whom Paul refers and who lived in Rome cannot be identified with any of the other six. Paul describes her as one 'who worked very hard for you'. Paul employs the verb 'to work hard' fourteen times in his letters, and on every occasion except two he uses it to denote hard work done in the service of the Lord, and mostly explicitly related to the task of preaching the gospel, teaching, and nurturing believers. It is significant that Paul tells his audience that Mary worked hard 'for you', suggesting work done for the congregations.

16:7 Paul asks his audience next: *Greet Andronicus and Junia, my fellow Jews who have been in prison with me.* 'Junia' translates *Iouniān,* which, when accented with an acute on the '*i*' as *Iounían,* is feminine in form and would refer to a woman, 'Junia'. If it is accented with a circumflex on the '*a*', it is masculine in form, hence denoting a man, 'Junias'. Ancient Greek manuscripts were written in uncial script (capital letters) without accents. The choice of accents was made much later. There is now an emerging consensus that it should have been accented as a feminine name; in other words, Paul was referring to Junia (a woman), not Junias (a man).[13] See 'Additional Note: Junia or Junias?' 563-65.

11. Jewett, *Romans,* 960, conjectures: 'Epainetos was probably associated with Prisca and Aquila's house church on the basis of his conversion during the period of their Ephesian residence. Since he is in Rome at the time of Paul's letter, it also seems likely that he "may have moved from Ephesus to Rome together with Prisca and Aquila"'.

12. Mary the mother of Jesus; Mary Magdalene; the 'other' Mary — mother of James and Joses; Mary the wife of Clopas; Mary the sister of Martha; and Mary the mother of John Mark.

13. Origen assumed that Paul was speaking of a woman when he wrote: 'Think how great the devotion of this woman Junia must have been, that she should be worthy to be called and apostle!' ('Homilies on Romans 31' [*ACCSR,* 372]). Theodoret of Cyrrhus made the same assumption when he said: 'These people [Andronicus and Junia] were companions of Paul in his sufferings and even shared imprisonment with him. Hence he says that they are men and women of note, not among the pupils but among the teachers, and not

Andronicus and Junia are mentioned only here in the NT, so all we know of them is what can be gleaned from this brief reference. However, in just this one verse Paul provides several pieces of information concerning this couple. First he describes them as 'my fellow Jews', that is, his compatriots or kinspeople.[14] We cannot say whether Andronicus and Junia were simply fellow countrymen (KJV, NASB, ASV, TNIV) or if they were his relatives (NRSV).

Second, Paul indicates that they 'have been in prison with me' (lit. 'and my fellow prisoners'). This imprisonment cannot be identified. Prior to the writing of Romans, Paul had been imprisoned briefly in Philippi (cf. Acts 16:16-40), but there is no mention of Andronicus and Junia being involved then. Paul may have been imprisoned in Ephesus (cf. 2 Cor 1:8-11). If so, it is possible that Andronicus and Junia were his fellow prisoners at that time.

Third, Paul says of Andronicus and Junia: *They are outstanding among the apostles.* The interpretation of this statement has been the subject of extensive debate. The adjective translated here as 'outstanding' has the literal meaning of 'well known', which can have a positive meaning as here, or a negative one ('notorious') as it does in the only other place where it is found in the NT (Matt 27:16). What is controversial is Paul's meaning when he said that Andronicus and Junia were 'well known among the apostles'. Did he mean they were well known as those who were themselves numbered among the apostles, or that they were well known to the apostles? The NRSV appears to opt for the former when it translates the text as they are 'prominent among the apostles'; similarly the NASB and TNIV ('outstanding among the apostles'). The KJV, KJVS, and the ASV preserve the ambiguity ('of note among the apostles'). If it were not for the fact that the text should read Junia (feminine), not Junias (masculine), it would not have given rise to such sustained debate. However, the possibility that Andronicus and Junia were not just well-known *to* the apostles, but were themselves prominent *among* the apostles has fueled an ongoing debate. The real issue has become: Was Junia a female apostle in the early church? Those who answer this question in the affirmative appear to have made the strongest case for their point of view. See 'Additional Note: "Well Known among", or "Well Known to", the Apostles?' 565-67.

The final piece of information Paul provides in 16:7 concerning Andronicus and Junia is: *and they were in Christ before I was,* that is, they had become followers of Jesus Christ before Paul had his encounter with him on the Damascus Road. In the list of greetings in 16:3-16 Paul repeatedly describes those he greets as being 'in Christ' or 'in the Lord' (16:3, 7, 9, 10, 11, 12 [2x], 13), an expression which in this context appears to mean simply being a Christian.

---

among the ordinary teachers but among the apostles. He even praises them for having been Christians before him' ('Interpretation of the Letter to the Romans' [*ACCSR*, 372]).

14. Cf. BAGD, *ad loc.*

ADDITIONAL NOTE: JUNIA OR JUNIAS?

Cervin draws attention to the fact that Iunia is a Latin name. He notes:

> The typical Latin name consisted of three parts in the following order: the *praenomen* (personal name), the *nomen* (the name of the *gens*, or clan), and the *cognomen* (family name). . . . Nearly all Latin *nomina* (clan names) bear the adjectival suffixes *-ius* (masc.) and *-ia* (fem.). Women generally did not have *praenomen*, but were named after their *gens*. Thus, Gaius Iulius (Julius) Caesar is masculine while his daughters were named Iulia Maior and Iulia Minor (Julia I and II), 'Iulius' being the *nomen*. There are a large number of Latin *nomina*, e.g., Aelius, Cassius, Claudius, Cornelius, Licinius, Octavius, etc. all bearing the suffix *-ius*, and all with corresponding feminine forms in *-ia*. . . .[15]

Cervin then asks:

> How were Latin names transcribed into Greek? They were generally transferred to the appropriate grammatical paradigm, e.g., Latin names ending in *-us* are rendered as Greek names in *-os* (e.g., Paulus → *Paulos*); Latin masculine names in *-o* are rendered as Greek names in *-ōn* (e.g., Piso → *Peisōn*); Latin feminine names in *-a* are rendered as Greek names in *-a* or *-ē* (e.g., Drusilla → *Drousilla*; Roma → *Rōmē*); but Latin masculine names in *-a* are rendered as Greek names in *-as* (e.g., Agrippa → *Agrippas*). Other names are rendered appropriately. These principles of transcribing Latin names into Greek can be seen consistently throughout the NT, and indeed throughout Greek literature of the Roman period. What is important for this paper is the fact that all of the Latin *nomina* ending in *-ius* are regularly transcribed into Greek as names in *-ios* (e.g., Afrinius → *Aphranios*; Antonius → *Antonios*; Caecilius → *Kekilios*; Cassius → *Kassios*; Domitius → *Domitios*; Favonius → *Phaōnios*; Iulius → *Ioulios*; Lucius → *Leukios*; Publius → *Poplios*; Tiberius → *Tiberios*; and so forth). Likewise the feminine forms of the *nomina* (*-ia*) are rendered into Greek as names in *-ia* (e.g., Aemilia → *Aimylia*; Calpurnia → *Kalpournia*; Cornelia → *Kornēlia*; Fulvia → *Phoulbia*; Iulia → *Ioulia*; Marcia → *Markia*; Octavia → *Octaouia*; Poppaea → *Poppaia*; and so on.

Thus, according to the standard method of transcribing Latin names into Greek, the *nomen Iunius/Iunia* is rendered as *Iounios/Iounia*. The accusative form (which is the necessary form in Romans 16) of this name in Latin is *Iunium/Iuniam* and the gender is readily discernible. Similarly with the accusative form in Greek, *Iounion/Iounian*, where there is again no ambiguity in the form of the gender.[16]

---

15. Richard S. Cervin, 'A Note regarding the Name "Junia(s)" in Romans 16.7', *NTS* 40 (1994) 467.

16. Cervin, 'A Note regarding the Name "Junia(s)"', 468-69.

Thorley, after discussing in detail the evidence of the Greek manuscripts and ancient translations in relation to Junia(s) in 16:7, summarises it
as follows:

(i)   The earliest translations into Latin and Coptic (Syriac is of little help)
      do occasionally transcribe the accusative of male names in -*ās* in a
      form which could morphologically be either masculine or feminine.
      However, this ambiguity is statistically uncommon and offers at best
      only a tenuous possibility that the Greek text *IOUNIAN* was ever
      taken as a masculine name; it is far more likely that it was taken quite
      universally as the accusative of the common Roman female name
      'Junia';
(ii) the linguistic possibility of a masculine name *Iounías* or of a
      hypocoristic name *Iouniās* is doubtful in the extreme;
(iii) There is no manuscript evidence for the perispomenon accentuation
      Iouniān;
(iv) The context of Rom. 16:7 in no way implies, and certainly does not re-
      quire, *IOUNIAN* to be taken as a masculine name;
(v)   Chrysostom extols Junia as an apostle,[17] and neither he nor any other
      of the patristic writers ever suggests that the text here refers to a man.
      So is it not time that Junia was restored to her rightful place in the text
      and translations?[18]

Jewett comments: 'The modern scholarly controversy over this name
rests on the presumption that no woman could rank as an apostle, and thus
that the accusative form must refer to a male by the name of Junias or
Junianus. However, the evidence in favor of the feminine name "Junia" is
overwhelming. Not a single example of a masculine name "Junias" has
been found. The patristic evidence investigated by Fàbrega and Fitzmyer
indicates that commentators down through the twelfth century refer to
Junia as a woman, often commenting on the extraordinary gifts that ranked
her among the apostles'.[19]

Dunn observes: '*Iounian* has usually been taken in the modern period
as *Iounian* = Junias, a contraction of Junianus (so RSV, NEB, NIV, NJB). But
the simple fact is that the masculine form has been found nowhere else, and
the name is more naturally taken as *Iounian* = Junia (Lampe, 139-40, 147, indicates over 250 examples of "Junia", none of Junias), as was taken for

17. Earlier in his article, Thorley quotes Chrysostom: 'Why, what a great love of
learning this woman possessed! Great enough indeed to be considered worthy of inclusion
amongst the apostles' (John Thorley, 'Junia, A Woman Apostle', *NovT* 38 [1996] 28).
18. Thorley, 'Junia, A Woman Apostle', 28-29. Cf. also U.-K. Plisch, 'Die Apostelin
Junia: Das exegetische Problem in Röm 16.7 im Licht von Nestle-Aland[27] und der
sahidischen Überlieferung', *NTS* 42 (1996) 477-78; Eldon J. Epp, *Junia: The First Woman Apostle* (Minneapolis: Fortress, 2005).
19. Jewett, *Romans*, 961.

granted by the patristic commentators, and indeed up to the Middle Ages. The assumption that it must be male is a striking indictment of male presumption regarding the character and structure of earliest Christianity. . . . The most natural way to read the two names within the phrase is as husband and wife (cf. v 3)'.[20]

ADDITIONAL NOTE: 'WELL KNOWN AMONG', OR 'WELL KNOWN TO', THE APOSTLES?

Burer and Wallace, in their reexamination of 16:7, happily concede that IOUNIAN should be regarded as feminine and therefore Paul was referring to Junia, a woman.[21] However, they reject the view that *episēmoi en tois apostolois* is to be taken inclusively ('well known among the apostles'), arguing rather that it is to be taken exclusively ('well known to the apostles'). They base their case on evidence from ancient texts in which instances of *episēmos* plus *en* with a dative personal adjunct are found. They sum up their conclusions as follows:

> In sum, our examination of *episēmos* with both genitive modifiers and *en* plus dative adjuncts has revealed some surprising results — surprising, that is, from the perspective of the scholarly consensus. Repeatedly in biblical Greek, patristic Greek, papyri, inscriptions, classical and Hellenistic texts, our working hypothesis was born out. The genitive personal modifier was consistently used for an inclusive idea, whilst the (*en* plus) dative personal adjunct was almost never so used. Yet to read the literature, one would get a decidedly different picture. To say that *episēmoi en tois apostolois* 'can *only* mean "noteworthy among the apostles"' is simply not true. It would be more accurate to say that *episēmoi en tois apostolois* almost certainly means "well known to the apostles."' Thus Junia, along with Andronicus, is recognized by Paul as well known to the apostles, not as an outstanding member of the apostolic band.[22]

Belleville conducted similar investigations to those of Burer and Wallace, casting her net so as to include evidence from the TLG, papyri, and inscriptions. She argues: 'Indeed, an examination of primary usage in the available databases confirms the feminine Junia and the traditional attribution "of note among the apostles". It also shows that the masculine Junias and

---

20. Dunn, *Romans 9–16*, 894. So too, Moo, *Romans*, 921-22.
21. Michael H. Burer and Daniel B. Wallace, 'Was Junia Really an Apostle? A Reexamination of Rom 16.7', *NTS* 47 (2001) 76-78.
22. Burer and Wallace, 'Was Junia Really an Apostle?' 90.

the attribution "well known to the apostles" are without linguistic or grammatical foundation'.[23] Stated more fully, her conclusions are as follows:

> An examination of primary usage in Greek and Latin databases confirms the traditional feminine *Junia* (or possibly *Julia*) and the time-honored attribution 'esteemed among the apostles'. It also demonstrates that the masculine *Junias* and the attribution 'well known to the apostles' lack grammatical and lexical support. Indeed, not even one first-century parallel can be adduced. Over against this is the uniform inclusive use of *episēmoi en* plus the dative plural usage and the unbroken tradition among Greek and Latin fathers from Origen in the third century and Ambrose in the fourth through Lombard in the twelfth century of a woman who was not only 'notable among the apostles' (*insignes* or *nobiles in apostolis*) but lauded as such and situated in the group of 72 that Jesus commissioned and sent out (*quod fortassis ex illis septuaginta duobus apostolis fuerint et ipsi nobiles*; Haymo, Rabanus Maurus, Hatto of Vercelli, Bruno of Querfurt). Although Burer and Wallace argue for an *exclusive* rendering of *episēmoi en tois apostolois* ('well known to the apostles'), all patristic commentators attest to an inclusive understanding ('prominent among the apostles'). The simple fact is that if native, educated speakers of Greek understood the phrase to be inclusive and *Iounian* to be feminine, the burden of proof lies with those who could claim otherwise. Indeed, the burden of proof has not been met. Not even reasonable doubt has been established, for all the extra-biblical parallels adduced support an inclusive understanding. The sole basis is a theological and functional disposition against the naming of a woman among the first-century cadre of apostles.[24]

Witherington comments: 'The conclusion then follows that Paul has no problem with women as teachers (Priscilla) or leaders, proclaimers, or missionaries of the Good News. Indeed, it is hardly likely that a woman would be incarcerated in Paul's world without having made some significant public remark or action. Junia said or did something that led to a judicial action. Chrysostom recognizes that Paul is referring to a woman apostle and says that she had a keen interest in *philosophia*; indeed, "the supposition that Paul was addressing a female apostle Junia dominated among the patristic exegetes and the early Translations (Old Latin, Vulgate, Sahidic, and Bohairic)'.[25]

Cranfield comments: 'That Paul should not only include a woman (on the view taken above) among the apostles but actually describe her, to-

---

23. Linda Belleville, '*Iounian . . . episēmoi en tois apostolois*: A Re-examination of Romans 16.7 in Light of Primary Source Materials', *NTS* 51 (2005) 232.

24. Belleville, '*Iounian . . . episēmoi en tois apostolois*', 248. Cf. Epp, *Junia: The First Woman Apostle*, 79-81.

25. Witherington, *Romans*, 390.

gether with Andronicus, as outstanding among them, is highly significant evidence (along with the importance he accords in this chapter to Phoebe, Prisca, Mary, Tryphaena, Tryphosa, Persis, the mother of Rufus, Julia and the sister of Nereus) of the falsity of the widespread and stubbornly persistent notion that Paul had a low view of women and something to which the Church as a whole has not yet paid sufficient attention'.[26]

Jewett comments: 'The honorific expression *episēmoi en tois apostolois* should be translated "outstanding among the apostles" . . . because the adjective *episēmos* lifts up a person or thing as distinguished or marked in comparison with other representatives of the same class, in this instance with other apostles'.[27]

Moo comments: 'Many scholars on both sides of this issue are guilty of accepting too readily a key supposition in this line of reasoning: "apostle" here refers to an authoritative leadership position such as that held by the "Twelve" and by Paul. In fact, Paul often uses the title "apostle" in a "looser" sense: sometimes simply to denote a "messenger" or "emissary" and sometimes to denote a "commissioned missionary". When Paul uses the word in the former sense, he makes clear the source and purpose of the "emissary's" commission. So "apostle" here probably means "travelling missionary". Since Paul, in the second relative clause, acknowledges that they were "in Christ" before him, we might infer that Andronicus and Junia were among those early "Hellenistic" Jews in Jerusalem and that, like Peter and his wife (cf. 1 Cor 9:5), they moved about in the eastern Mediterranean (where they encountered and perhaps were imprisoned with Paul), seeking to bring men and women to faith in Christ'.[28]

16:8-15 There follow here a series of brief greeting requests: *Greet Ampliatus, my dear friend in the Lord* (lit. 'Greet Ampliatus, my beloved in the Lord'). Ampliatus is mentioned only here in the NT and is otherwise unknown — apart from the fact Paul refers to him as 'my beloved in the Lord'. Jewett remarks: 'The name "Ampliatus" was coined as a slave name with the meaning "ample" during the Augustan period, and it is highly likely that he was a slave or freedman'.[29]

Greet Urbanus, our co-worker in Christ, and my dear friend Stachys. Only here in the NT are Urbanus and Stachys mentioned, so our knowledge of them is limited to the fact that Urbanus is called 'our fellow worker in Christ (see the comment on 16:3) and Stachys is described as 'my dear friend' (lit. 'my beloved'). Jewett says: 'The facts that this [Urbanus] is a "wish-name" with the meaning "refined, cultivated, ingenious" that usu-

26. Cranfield, *Romans*, II, 789.
27. Jewett, *Romans*, 963.
28. Moo, *Romans*, 923-24.
29. Jewett, *Romans*, 964.

ally was given to slaves, and that twenty-five of the Roman references are definitely to slaves while all of the feminine form, Urbana, are slaves, lead me to believe that this particular Urbanus was likely a freedman of Roman origin'.[30]

Greet Apelles, whose fidelity to Christ has stood the test. Apelles is another contact of Paul's mentioned only here in the NT. He describes him as one 'whose fidelity to Christ has stood the test' (lit. 'the one approved in Christ'). 'Approved' is a characteristic expression of Paul's, one that he uses six times in his letters (the only other use in the NT is in Jas 1:12). He uses it to refer to those who have human approval (14:18; 16:10; 2 Cor 13:7) or God's approval (1 Cor 11:19; 2 Tim 2:15). To describe Apelles as one approved 'in Christ' appears to mean that his status as a Christian has been tested and approved. Paul does not say how this occurred.

Greet those who belong to the household of Aristobulus. Aristobulus's name appears only here in the NT. 'Those of his household' could refer to only members of his family or, more likely, include his servants as well. Jewett, opting for the latter, comments: 'Paul's request that greetings be extended to "those from among the [slaves] of Aristoboulos" is a probable reference to a congregation among the slaves of his household. It is significant that Aristoboulos is not greeted by Paul, indicating that it is not he but the members of his household who were believers'.[31]

Greet Herodion, my fellow Jew. Herodian is another person mentioned only here in the NT. All we know about him is that he, like Andronicus and Junia, is called Paul's 'fellow Jew'. Jewett notes: 'The name is otherwise unattested in Rome and was likely given to a slave or freedman who had been in the service of a member of the Herodian family'.[32]

Greet those in the household of Narcissus who are in the Lord. Narcissus is yet another person whose name appears only here in the NT. Paul wants his greeting conveyed to those of Narcissus's family or extended household who are 'in the Lord', that is, who are believers. This may imply that there were members of his household who were not 'in the Lord'.

---

30. Jewett, *Romans*, 965.

31. Jewett, *Romans*, 966. Dunn, *Romans 9–16*, 896, says: 'Although Aristobolus was a common name (MM, BGD), there is certainly a strong plausibility in the suggestion that the Aristobolus here mentioned was the grandson of Herod the Great and brother of Agrippa I. According to Josephus (*War* 2.221) he died . . . as "a private person", that is, as opposed to one who held a public office or took part in public affairs (LSJ). Since his brother Agrippa had lived long in Rome and had been on friendly terms with Claudius (e.g., *Ant.* 20.12), it is quite probable that he was kept out of the way (and under surveillance) in Rome till his death (in the second half of the 40's [Agrippa died in A.D. 44]). Even if he had died some years before the occasion of this letter, his household staff could well have retained their identity when merged with another (the imperial?) household (Lightfoot, SH, Cranfield). His household slaves and freemen would then still be known as *hoi Aristoboulou*, and the Christians among them therefore as *hoi ek tōn Aristoboulou*. Presumably some at least of them would have been Jews'. Cf. du Toit, '"God's beloved in Rome" (Rm 1:7)', 377-82.

32. Jewett, *Romans*, 967.

Greet Tryphena and Tryphosa, those women who work hard in the Lord. These two women are mentioned only here in the NT. All we know of them is that Paul describes them as women 'who work hard in the Lord'. Paul employs the verb 'to work hard' fourteen times in his letters, and on every occasion but two he uses it to denote hard work done in the service of the Lord, and mostly explicitly related to the task of preaching the gospel, teaching, and nurturing believers. We may assume that Tryphena and Tryphosa, like Mary (16:6), worked hard in this sort of ministry as well. Jewett remarks: 'The feminine name Tryphaina is a Greek slave name derived from the masculine name, Tryphon, with the meaning "dainty". . . . The name Tryphosa means "luscious". . . . On the basis of thirty-two examples of Tryphosa and sixty examples of Traiphena found in Roman inscriptions and papyri, Peter Lampe concludes that they were probably Gentile Christians from slave background, but cannot say whether they were sisters, which seems likely to other scholars because of the similarity in their names and because the *kai* ['and'] . . . indicates that they belonged together'.[33]

Greet my dear friend Persis, another woman who has worked very hard in the Lord (lit. 'Greet Persis, the beloved, who worked very hard in [the] Lord'). Once again this is a person unknown in the NT apart from the mention of her name here. Paul describes her as 'my dear friend', indicating the affection in which she was held by him as well as by others. She is another woman Paul describes as one 'who has worked hard in the Lord', and, as suggested above, this probably included the task of preaching the gospel, teaching, and nurturing believers.[34] Jewett says: 'The name "Persis" is a typical name for a feminine slave originating in Persia, a name occurring six times in Roman epigraphic and literary sources. She may be a Gentile believer of ethnic Persian origin, or perhaps a believer of Jewish background whose family had lived in the larger Persian-Babylonian Diaspora'.[35]

Paul continues: *Greet Rufus, chosen in the Lord, and his mother, who has been a mother to me, too* (lit. 'Greet Rufus, the chosen one in [the] Lord, and his mother and mine'). There is one other NT mention of a person named Rufus, in Mark 15:21: 'A certain man from Cyrene, Simon, the father of Alexander and Rufus, was passing by on his way in from the country, and they forced him to carry the cross'. Whether the two mentions of Rufus refer to the same person can be neither confirmed nor denied.[36] When Paul

33. Jewett, *Romans*, 968.

34. Stefan Schreiber, 'Arbeit mit der Gemeinde (Röm 16.6, 12): Zur versunkenen Möglichkeit der Gemeindeleitung durch Frauen', *NTS* 46 (2000) 224, after an examination of the use of the verb *kopiaō* in Romans 16 and Paul's other letters, argues that 'hard work' in these contexts points to an increasingly technical meaning of a concept in the sense of charismatic leadership'.

35. Jewett, *Romans*, 968.

36. Murphy-O'Connor, 'The Pauline Network', 221, thinks that he is 'probably to be identified as one of the sons of Simon of Cyrene, who carried the cross of Jesus'. So, too, J. B. Lightfoot, 'Excursus on "Caesar's Household"', in *Saint Paul's Epistle to the Philippians* (New York: Macmillan, 1903), 176.

describes Rufus as one 'chosen one in the Lord', he is not saying any more than he could say about other believers. The apostle uses the word 'chosen' five times elsewhere in his letters, and, with just one exception (1 Tim 5:21, where it refers to the 'elect angels'), it always refers to believers in general (8:33; Col 3:12; 2 Tim 2:10; Tit 1:1). Paul sends greetings also to Rufus's mother, whom he calls 'his mother and mine'. In what way she acted as Paul's mother may only be surmised — perhaps as one who had cared for his physical needs, perhaps even as a mother 'in the Lord' who ministered to his spiritual needs (cf. 2 Tim 1:5). Theodoret of Cyrrhus says: 'The mother of Rufus by nature had become Paul's mother by grace'.[37] Jewett observes: 'To refer to Rufus's mother as "mine" indicates that she had provided hospitality and patronage in such a manner that Paul has at some point in his career became virtually a member of their family'.[38]

Greet Asyncritus, Phlegon, Hermes, Patrobas, Hermas and the brothers and sisters with them. The names of the five 'men' greeted here occur nowhere else in the NT,[39] and therefore little is known of them. The reference to 'the brothers and sisters with them' suggests that Paul is also greeting a group of believers who met with these men in (one of) their house(s). Origen writes: 'I think this Hermas was the author of the book called *The Shepherd of Hermas*, which seems to me to be a useful book and one which was inspired by God. I think the reason Paul does not praise him is that he himself tells us in his book that he was converted only after many sins. Scripture tells us not to rush to honor someone who has just repented from sin nor to give him praise as long as the angel of repentance is still over him'.[40]

Jewett comments: 'The name [Asynkritos] is Greek with the meaning "incomparable", which one would expect to have been used for slaves or freedmen. . . . "Phlegon" appears nine times in Roman records, of which seven come from the first century. Three of these references are to persons of slave background. The name is Greek, and was used in earlier times as a dog's name, which likewise indicates servile status. . . . The name "Hermes" is very frequently found at Rome, being often used for slaves or freedmen. Named after the god, Hermes was, in Lampe's words, "the Roman name for slaves". A strikingly large number of persons with this name are found among Claudian freedmen. . . . "Patrobas" is not found at all in Rome, but a similar name, Patrobius, occurs eight times, of which four are in the NT period. Lampe identifies Patrobas as a Greek name; the Latinized ending "ius" on associated names may indicate an effort to avoid the social status of slaves and freedmen. . . . "Hermas" is found six times in Roman records, of which three are from the NT period. This particular Hermas is not to be confused with the author of the Shepherd of Hermas from the

---

37. 'Interpretation of the Letter to the Romans' (*ACCSR*, 374).

38. Jewett, *Romans*, 969.

39. The name 'Hermes' is found in Acts 14:12, but there it refers to the Hellenic deity, Hermes.

40. 'Commentary on the Epistle to the Romans' (*ACCSR*, 374).

mid-second century C.E. The name is Greek, derived from the god Hermes, and probably borne by eastern immigrants to Rome. One of the three references from the NT period is to a slave, and in view of his association with others from slave background in this list of five congregational leaders, it is best to assume a menial social status of Hermas. The reference to "the brothers with them" indicates that the five persons named are the leaders of this group'.[41]

Greet Philologus, Julia, Nereus and his sister, and Olympas and all the Lord's people who are with them. Once again all the names mentioned occur only here in the NT. All those mentioned are men except for Julia and the sister of Nereus. The fact that Paul mentions 'all the saints with them' suggests again the existence of another house church. Jewett provides the following background information for the names listed here:

> 'Philologos', a Greek name, is found twenty-three times in Roman materials, of which eighteen references are from the NT period. Half of the references are explicitly to slaves or freedmen. 'Julia' is the most frequently used of any of the names in Rom 16, being found more than 1,400 times in Roman records, mostly for persons of unfree background. The name was given to slaves and other members of the Julian households who usually received Roman citizenship. It is a Latin rather than a Greek name, but of course could be given to a noble member of the Julian house or to a Greek or Jewish slave belonging to a Julian family. If she were part of the nobility, it seems incredible that she is not listed as the patron of the church, rather than, as in v. 14, part of a group of five leaders. She is likely a slave or freedwoman. The fact that Julia is connected with Philologos with *kai* ['and'] . . . probably indicates that they were a married couple, or possibly brother and sister. . . . 'Nereus' was a name typically given to slaves, named after the god of the ocean, and carried by thirty-six persons in Roman materials, of which twenty-eight are of the NT period. A majority of those so named are clearly identified as slaves or freedmen. It is a Greek name, which ordinarily indicates an origin outside of Rome. . . . 'Olympas' is found only twice in Roman records, of which no examples are from the NT period. This masculine name is a short form of a name like Olympiodorus, Olympianus, and so on. The origin of the word and the menial status of associated names in the empire point to the likelihood of unfree background. . . . This congregation, like that mentioned in the preceding verse, fits the profile of a tenement church. Instead of a patron there is a collective leadership by five persons. This group probably meets for its love feast somewhere in an insula building where the majority of Rome's underclass lived.[42]

41. Jewett, *Romans*, 970.
42. Jewett, *Romans*, 971-72.

As one looks back over the twenty-six individuals to whom Paul wants greetings extended, a couple of matters are noteworthy: (i) nine of these are women, and five of them are commended for their labor 'in the Lord', indicating that they shared with men in Christian ministry;[43] (ii) Paul had numerous colleagues in ministry, reflecting the fact that he was 'not a "lone ranger" kind of missionary'.[44]

16:16   Paul concludes his request to his audience that greetings be extended to these people with the exhortation: *Greet one another with a holy kiss*. The word 'kiss' is found seven times in the NT. Luke uses it twice in his gospel, once in reference to Simon, who failed to give Christ a kiss when he entered his house (Luke 7:45), and the other time referring to Judas betraying Christ with a kiss (Luke 22:48). It is also found in 1 Peter 5:14: 'Greet one another with a kiss of love'. The other four uses of the word 'kiss' are in Paul's letters, each in the exhortation, 'Greet one another with a holy kiss', which forms part of the conclusion of his letters (16:16; 1 Cor 16:20; 2 Cor 13:12; 1 Thess 5:26).[45] Paul's repeated exhortations to Christian communities in three major cities to 'greet one another with a holy kiss' suggests that this had become a common way for believers to welcome one another in the mid–first century. Paul's reference to 'a holy kiss' rules out any erotic overtones.[46] See 'Additional Note: Kissing', 573-74.

After exhorting his audience to greet one another with a holy kiss, Paul adds: *All the churches of Christ send greetings*. Those churches whose greetings Paul conveys to the Roman believers by this letter would include, obviously, the Corinthian church, for it was in Corinth that Paul wrote this letter. The reference to 'all the churches of Christ' suggests, perhaps, that on his missionary travels numbers of Christian communities asked him to convey greetings to the Roman Christians, knowing that he intended to visit Rome. Dunn comments: 'Paul has the churches of his own mission in mind ("all the churches" is not an unfair abbreviation for "all the churches with which I am associated" = "all the churches of the Gentiles" — v 4)'.[47]

---

43. Cf. Byrne, *Romans*, 450-51; Moo, *Romans*, 927.

44. Moo, *Romans*, 927.

45. The cognate verb 'to kiss' is found nine times in the NT, four of which relate to Judas's kiss of betrayal (Matt 26:48-49; Mark 14:44-45; Luke 22:47), two more relate to the woman who kissed the feet of Christ (Luke 7:38; 7:45), one is in reference to the prodigal's father who welcomed his son home by throwing his arms around him and kissing him (Luke 15:20), and the last relates to the reaction of the Ephesian believers to the news they would not see Paul again: 'They all wept as they embraced him and kissed him' (Acts 20:37). All NT references to kissing appear to be public acts, and, apart from the references to the woman kissing Jesus' feet, appear to refer to men kissing men.

46. Jewett, *Romans*, 973, notes: 'In the post-NT period, when the church was attempting to conform to the society, "the men kissed the men and the women the women", thus avoiding the appearance of promiscuity. It is therefore likely that the adjective "holy" was attached to this inclusive greeting in response to sexual promiscuity encouraged by such kissing. As Murray observes, "Paul characterizes the kiss as 'holy' and thus distinguishes it from all that is erotic or sensual"'.

47. Dunn, *Romans 9–16*, 899.

ADDITIONAL NOTE: KISSING

In the OT there are numerous references to people kissing one another. Jacob kissed his father Isaac (Gen 27:26-27), Jacob kissed Rachel when he first met her (Gen 29:11), Laban kissed Jacob when he first met him (Gen 29:13), and later rebuked him for leaving without allowing him to kiss his daughters and grandchildren good-bye (Gen 31:28), a rebuke that Jacob heeded (Gen 31:55). Esau kissed Jacob when he returned to Canaan (Gen 33:4). Joseph kissed his brothers when he made himself known to them in Egypt (Gen 45:15). In his frail old age Israel/Jacob kissed Joseph's sons (Gen 48:10), and Joseph kissed his father Jacob/Israel (Gen 50:1). Moses kissed Aaron when he met him at the mountain of God (Exod 4:27), and also kissed his father-in-law (Exod 18:7). Naomi kissed her daughters-in-law, Ruth and Orpah (Ruth 1:9), and Orpah kissed Naomi good-bye (Ruth 1:14). Samuel kissed Saul when he anointed him king (1 Sam 10:1). David and Jonathan kissed each other and wept at their parting (1 Sam 20:41). David kissed Absalom (2 Sam 14:33), Absalom kissed those who entered the city of Jerusalem in order to gain their allegiance (2 Sam 15:5). David kissed Barzillai, telling him to return to Jerusalem when he himself was fleeing from the city (2 Sam 19:39), Joab kissed Amasa to put him off guard before murdering him (2 Sam 20:9), and Elisha asked Elijah to allow him to kiss his father and mother good-bye before becoming his follower (1 Kgs 19:18). Proverbs speaks of the prostitute who kisses with brazen face (Prov 7:13), the honest answer that is like a kiss on the lips (Prov 24:26), and the enemy who multiplies kisses (Prov 27:6). The Song of Songs alone speaks of passionate kisses (Song 1:2; 8:1). There are places where kisses are associated with idolatry: 1 Kings 19:18 speaks of the 7,000 in Israel whose mouths have not kissed Baal, and Hosea 13:2 speaks of those who kiss 'the calf idols'. There are those references in which to kiss is to pay homage (Job 31:27; Ps 2:12) and where 'righteousness and peace kiss each other' (Ps 85:10). Summing up, apart from the two references in the Song of Songs, kissing in the OT is not related to erotic love. It was a way of greeting or saying good-bye to a person, expressing reconciliation, acknowledging a familial relationship, paying homage, and acknowledging God's anointed. Sometimes kissing is a smoke screen for enmity or murder, or a means to curry favor. Sometimes kissing is associated with idolatry, and with the allurements of the prostitute. Kissing can be used metaphorically, for example, when an honest answer is likened to a kiss on the lips, and when righteousness and peace are said to kiss each other.

The story of Joseph and Asenath, thought to be a first-century-B.C. or first-century-A.D. Jewish writing (though some have argued that it is a fourth- or fifth-century Christian work) refers to kissing more than most ancient writings. Asenath is the beautiful Egyptian virgin given by Pharaoh to Joseph as his wife (cf. Gen 41:45, 50-52; 46:20). Included among its many references to kissing is Asenath welcoming her father with a kiss (*Joseph and Asenath* 4), the aged Jacob, upon meeting his daughter-in-law Asenath, 'blessed her and kissed her', and Asenath 'took hold of Jacob's neck and hung on to his neck and kissed him' (*Joseph and Asenath* 22). The most striking passage records how, following angelic visits to both Asenath and Joseph saying they were to become husband and wife, '[Joseph says] "for that man came from heaven to me today and said these words to me concerning thee. And now come hither to me, thou virgin and pure, and wherefore standest thou afar off?" Then Joseph stretched out his hands and embraced Asenath, and Asenath Joseph, and they kissed one another for a long time, and both lived again in their spirit. And Joseph kissed Asenath and gave her the spirit of life, then a second time he gave her the spirit of wisdom, and the third time he kissed her tenderly and gave her the spirit of truth' (*Joseph and Asenath* 19).[48]

In Greco-Roman society public kissing tended to be treated with some reticence. It seems that as a form of welcome it was becoming more common in the imperial period, and, if that was the case, 'it may have been easier for the church to make the public kiss into a group rule and provide it with a deeper motivation'.[49]

ADDITIONAL NOTE: THE TWENTY-SIX NAMED INDIVIDUALS IN ROMANS 16:3-15

Lampe made a thorough study of the twenty-six named individuals to whom Paul asks members of the Roman churches to convey his greetings.[50] He notes that two of them, Aristobulus and Narcissus, are non-Christians, and that Paul asks that greetings be conveyed to those who are Christians in their households.[51] Of the twenty-six named individuals he notes that nine are women and seventeen are men, and that more women than men are commended for being specially active in the church (6 or 7 women, and 3 or 5 men).[52] He also argues that only three of the twenty-six can be positively identified as Jews (those designated Paul's kinspeople). He says, 'even "Maria" cannot be considered especially Jewish' since the epigraphical data suggest that Maria 'represents the pagan name of a Roman *gens*. . . . This Latin-pagan "Maria" occurs approximately 108 times in the city of Rome inscriptions of CIL VI. The Semitic "Maria" cannot be counted even 20 times

---

48. Quotations from E. W. Brooks, *Joseph and Asenath: The Confession and Prayer of Asenath Daughter of Pentephres the Priest* (London: SPCK, 1918).

49. William Klassen, 'Kiss (NT)', *ABD*, IV, 91.

50. Lampe, 'The Roman Christians', 212-30.

51. Lampe, 'The Roman Christians', 222.

52. Lampe, 'The Roman Christians', 222-24.

in Rome'.[53] Lampe argues further that 'about 14 people out of 26 were presumably not born in Rome itself' — they were immigrants — and that 'an oriental origin of the remaining 12 cannot be excluded — but neither can it be indicated. We do not even get a clue about Prisca: Did Aquila meet and start seeing her in Pontus — or in Rome?'[54] Lampe's investigations reveal that 'more than two thirds of the people for whom we can make a probability statement have an affinity to slave origins', and that this proportion corresponds with the proportion of slaves (30%) and freed [wo]men (30%) over against freeborn (40%) in the Roman population as a whole. He argues that this same proportion is likely to be reflected in the social profile of the churches of Rome as well.[55] Finally, Lampe argues that the Roman Christians did not meet in a single place of worship but that there were at least seven and possibly eight groups that worshipped separately, functioning as 'house congregations'.[56]

C. Warning, Exhortation, and Affirmation, 16:17-20

> [17]*I urge you, brothers and sisters, to watch out for those who cause divisions and put obstacles in your way that are contrary to the teaching you have learned. Keep away from them.* [18]*For such people are not serving our Lord Christ, but their own appetites. By smooth talk and flattery they deceive the minds of naive people.* [19]*Everyone has heard about your obedience, so I rejoice because of you; but I want you to be wise about what is good, and innocent about what is evil.*
> [20]*The God of peace will soon crush Satan under your feet.*
> *The grace of our Lord Jesus be with you.*

Paul's warning in this section is a surprise, coming as it does after his request that greetings be extended to twenty-six members of the Roman churches in 16:3-16 and before the greetings he conveys from his associates in 16:21-23. The abrupt transitions, from greetings to be extended to warnings about those who cause divisions and then to greetings to be conveyed, have raised questions about the authenticity of 16:17-20 and its place in this letter. Some regard it as authentically Pauline, but because of the rough transitions argue that it belongs in another letter. Boismard argues that it should be located in the Epistle to the Ephesians after 6:10-17, which includes a reference to 'the evil one' and so would connect with Paul's reference to Satan in 16:20.[1]

---

53. Lampe, 'The Roman Christians', 224-25.
54. Lampe, 'The Roman Christians', 226-27.
55. Lampe, 'The Roman Christians', 227-29.
56. Lampe, 'The Roman Christians', 229-30.
1. Marie-Émile Boismard, 'Rm 16,17-20: Vocabulaire et style', *RB* 107 (2000) 556. Cf. also M.-É. Boismard, *L'énigme de la lettre aux Éphésiens* (Études bibliques N.S. 39; Paris: Gabalda, 1999).

Fitzmyer thinks that its similarity to Philippians 3:17-19 'makes one think that these verses could have come from another fragment of Pauline epistolary correspondence such as that used to make up the composite letter to the Philippians'.[2]

Others regard 16:17-20 as a non-Pauline (or deutero-Pauline) passage that has been interpolated into the text of Romans.[3] Mora claims that 16:17-20 contains too many stylistic features that are contrary to the apostle's style for it to be regarded as authentic. Because he regards Ephesians as authentically Pauline, he also holds that it cannot be regarded as originally part of Paul's letter to the Ephesians.[4]

Yet others argue that the significance of the rough transitions has been exaggerated, and that 16:17-20 may be regarded both as authentically Pauline and appropriate in its present context. Hassold says: 'Though seemingly abrupt, Paul's warning may have been triggered in his mind by the directive, *Greet one another with a holy kiss* (v. 16), with which he brings his greetings to his acquaintances in Rome to a conclusion. The holy kiss was an action that served as a mark of fellowship in the early church (cf. 1 Cor 16:20; 2 Cor 13:12; 1 Thess 5:16; 1 Pet 5:14). As he thought of the Christians greeting one another, Paul may have recognized the possibility that peace and harmony in the church might be shattered by the activities of people who cause dissension in the life of the congregation'.[5] Moo notes that there is no textual evidence supporting the omission of 16:17-20, and draws attention to the fact that it is not unusual for Paul to include exhortations and warnings in the final sections of his letters (cf. 1 Cor 16:13-14; 2 Cor 13:11b; Col 4:17; cf. also Gal 6:12-15; Eph 6:10-17).[6] In the commentary that follows, 16:17-20 is treated as an original part of Paul's letter.

16:17   Paul begins the section: *I urge you, brothers and sisters, to watch out for those who cause divisions and put obstacles in your way that are contrary to the teaching you have learned. Keep away from them.* Had the apostle been made aware of such troublemakers operating in the Roman Christian communities? If so, in what way did they cause division, and what sort of obstacle did they place in the way of the believers there? The way Paul words his warning indicates that the divisions caused and the stumbling block placed before the believers involved teaching contrary to what they had learned, that is, by false teaching.[7]

It is not certain whether Paul had in mind specific individuals causing trouble in Rome (as others had done in churches he founded elsewhere), or whether he was giving a general warning about the sort of thing the believers

---

2. Fitzmyer, *Romans*, 745.

3. So, e.g., Byrne, *Romans*, 456; Jewett, *Romans*, 986.

4. Vincent Mora, 'Romains 16,17-20 et la lettre aux Éphesiens', *RB* 107 (2000) 541-47.

5. William J. Hassold, '"Avoid Them": Another Look at Romans 16:17-20', *CurrTheolMiss* 27 (2000) 198. So, too, Cranfield, *Romans*, II, 797-98.

6. Moo, *Romans*, 928.

7. Cf. Hassold, 'Avoid Them', 200.

might encounter, based, for example, upon his knowledge of the divisions that had arisen in Corinth (1 Cor 1:10-12; 11:18) and the stumbling blocks put in the way of the Galatian believers by the Judaizers (Gal 6:12; cf. Acts 15:1).[8]

Whatever may have been the case, the apostle's exhortation stands: the Roman believers should watch out for any who might influence them in a way that was 'contrary to the teaching you have learned'. In 6:17 Paul gave thanks to God that the Roman believers had obeyed from the heart 'the pattern of teaching' that had claimed their allegiance. Now he warns them about listening to those who might influence them otherwise, and tells them to 'keep away from them'. Cranfield softens this exhortation by saying: 'one can avoid subjecting oneself to a person's evil influence without hardening one's heart against him and refusing him kindly help, should he be in distress'.[9] Hassold likewise tones down Paul's words by saying that they 'should not be taken to mean that Christians should have no dealings with such people, but rather that they should not involve themselves in divisive activities, because of the harm that divisiveness produces in the life and work of the congregation'.[10] But the verb 'to keep away' is used elsewhere to mean to stay away from or avoid people (e.g., 1 Macc 6:47), to turn away from God (3:12; Pss 13:3; 52:4), and to turn away from evil (1 Pet 3:11; 1 Clem. 22:4, citing Ps 34:15). In the light of this usage, it would seem that Paul is counseling definite avoidance of these troublemakers.

16:18 The apostle then gives his opinion of those who cause divisions: *For such people are not serving our Lord Christ, but their own appetites* (lit. 'For such people do not serve our Lord Christ but their own stomachs'). These people presented themselves as believers, and in their own minds were probably true believers, but in Paul's eyes they were 'not serving our Lord Christ'. In other letters and on other occasions Paul denigrated those who presented themselves as Christian teachers but who caused havoc in the churches. In Galatians he exposed the activity and motivation of the Judaizers (Gal 5:7-12; 6:12-13), in 2 Corinthians he branded those who were seeking to win over his converts as false apostles, deceitful workmen who were masquerading as apostles of Christ (2 Cor 11:13-15), and in Philippians he said of the Judaizers that 'their God is their stomach, and their glory is in their shame' (Phil 3:19). His attack on false teachers both here in

---

8. Hassold, 'Avoid Them', 201, opts for the view that 'Paul is not singling out particular individuals or groups, but rather his reference is to any who foment dissension in the congregation and thus threaten the faith of Christians'. Ambrosiaster states: 'Now Paul goes on to mention the false apostles, whom he warns against throughout the epistle just as he does here as well. But he attacks their teaching without saying what it is. They were forcing believers to become Jews and thereby making the benefits of God worthless. . . . They compiled long genealogies and used them to support their teaching, by which they were deceiving the hearts of the simple' ('Commentary on Paul's Epistles' [*ACCSR*, 376]). Theodoret of Cyrrhus says: 'The people Paul is referring to here were men who defended the law' ('Interpretation of the Letter to the Romans' [*ACCSR*, 377]).

9. Cranfield, *Romans*, II, 799, n. 4.

10. Hassold, 'Avoid Them', 208.

16:18 and in Philippians 3:19 includes the charge that they were concerned about filling their own stomachs, probably through payment received for their teaching. This they did, Paul says, when *by smooth talk and flattery they deceive the minds of naive people.* The word translated as 'smooth talk'[11] is found only here in the NT. 'Flattery' translates a word used nine times by Paul, but usually with its normal meaning, 'blessing'. The word is sometimes used in an extended sense to mean 'fine speaking', and sometimes in a pejorative sense, as here, to mean 'words that are well chosen but untrue', hence 'flattery'.[12]

By 'smooth talk and flattery', the apostle stresses, false teachers 'deceive the minds of naïve people'.[13] The deception of believers was something the apostle contended with continuously. The Corinthian believers were susceptible to deception by false apostles (2 Cor 11:3-4), and the Thessalonian Christians by those who taught that the Day of the Lord had already come (2 Thess 2:1-3). Paul warned his converts about those who deceive 'with empty words' (Eph 5:6) and 'fine-sounding arguments' (Col 2:4), and alerted his colleagues to the work of impostors who deceive and are being deceived (2 Tim 3:13) and to 'rebellious people, full of meaningless talk and deception, especially those of the circumcision group' (Tit 1:10). It has been suggested that those Paul had in mind here in 16:17-18 were a few of the 'strong' who were causing trouble for the 'weak',[14] but this is unlikely since what he says here is quite different from the way he handled that matter in 14:1–15:13. It is difficult if not impossible to identify those about whom Paul warns his audience here, and probably we should be content not to try to do so.[15]

16:19 From warnings in 16:17-18 Paul turns to affirmation: *Everyone has heard about your obedience.* This is the third time in this letter that Paul has affirmed the Christian standing of the Roman believers (cf. 1:8: 'I thank my God through Jesus Christ for all of you, because your faith is being reported all over the world'; 15:14: 'I myself am convinced, my brothers and sisters, that you yourselves are full of goodness, filled with knowledge and competent to instruct one another'). In the light of the report of the Roman believers' obedience about which 'everyone has heard', Paul exults, *so I rejoice because of you.* Thereby he expresses again the emotion he always feels when there is evidence of true Christian character in his converts (cf. 1 Cor

---

11. *Chrēstologia.* BAGD, *ad loc.*, gives the meaning of the cognate noun *chrēstologos* as 'a bad person who makes a fine speech'.

12. BAGD, *ad loc.* Jewett, *Romans,* 992, observes: 'Taken together, the expression "sweet talk and well-chosen words" is a rhetorical hendiadys that reinforces the idea of misusing rhetorical gifts to mislead and corrupt others'.

13. The word translated 'naïve' *(akakos)* in the NIV is found only here in Paul's letters, but occurs once more in the NT in Heb 7:26, where it is used to describe Jesus as our high priest, 'one who is holy, blameless *(akakos)*, pure, set apart from sinners, exalted above the heavens'.

14. So, e.g., Witherington, *Romans,* 397-98.

15. Cf. Cranfield, *Romans,* II, 802.

16:17; 2 Cor 7:7, 9, 13, 16; Phil 4:10; Col 2:5; 1 Thess 3:9) and when he sees the cause of the gospel advancing (Phil 1:18; 2:17-18; Col 1:24).

Paul's affirmation here in 16:19a, while genuine, is also intended to prepare his audience to accept the exhortation that follows: *but I want you to be wise about what is good, and innocent about what is evil.* Paul says something similar in 1 Corinthians 14:20: 'Brothers and sisters, stop thinking like children. In regard to evil be infants, but in your thinking be adults'.[16] There may be an allusion here to Jesus' charge to his disciples: 'be as shrewd as snakes and as innocent as doves' (Matt 10:16).

To understand and to do the good is a surprisingly pervasive theme in Paul's letters. In Romans he urges his audience to be transformed by the renewing of their minds so as to approve God's good, pleasing, and perfect will (12:2); to cling to what is good (12:9), to overcome evil with good (12:21), to please one's neighbors for their good (15:2), and to be wise about what is good (16:19). In 2 Corinthians he indicates that believers will receive what is due to them at the judgment seat of Christ for the things done in the body, whether good or bad (2 Cor 5:10), and that God is able to make grace abound so that believers may abound in every good work (2 Cor 9:8). In Galatians believers are exhorted to 'do good to all people, especially to those who belong to the family of believers' (Gal 6:10). Ephesians speaks of believers being 'created in Christ Jesus to do good works' (Eph 2:10), doing something useful (good) with their hands (Eph 4:28), allowing only what is helpful (good) for building up to come out of their mouths (Eph 4:29), and of the Lord's rewarding believers for whatever good they do (Eph 6:8). In Colossians Paul speaks of believers 'bearing fruit in every good work' (Col 1:10). In 1 Thessalonians Paul exhorts his audience 'to do what is good for each other and for everyone else' (1 Thess 5:15), and in 2 Thessalonians he prays that God will strengthen his audience in every good deed and word (2 Thess 2:16-17). In 1 Timothy women are to encouraged to do good deeds (1 Tim 2:10; 5:10). In 2 Timothy people are urged to cleanse themselves from what is ignoble so as to be prepared for 'any good work' (2 Tim 2:21) and reminded that Scripture, being inspired by God, is useful for equipping them 'for every good work' (2 Tim 3:16-17). Finally, in his letter to Titus Paul exhorts the older women to be good managers of households (Tit 2:5), and believers are told to be subject to the authorities and 'ready to do whatever is good' (Tit 3:1). It is no wonder, then, that in 16:19b Paul says, 'I want you to be wise about what is good'.

In addition to being wise about what is good, Paul wants his audience to be 'innocent about what is evil'. The innocence of believers is an important though not pervasive theme in the NT. Jesus told the disciples he sent out on mission to be 'as shrewd as snakes and as innocent as doves' (Matt 10:16), and in Philippians 2:14-15 Paul exhorted his audience to 'do every-

---

16. Ambrosiaster comments on this verse: 'Being *wise to what is good* means doing good works, while being *guileless as to what is evil* means avoiding unrighteous deeds' ('Commentary on Paul's Epistles' [*ACCSR*, 377]).

thing without grumbling or arguing, so that you may become blameless [innocent] and pure, children of God without fault in a warped and crooked generation'. Paul wants his Roman audience to be wise in regard to good, but innocent, that is, blameless, in respect to evil. They will know what is evil, but they must avoid it and be blameless. In this context Paul does not spell out what evils they are to avoid, but one does not need to look far in his letters to see what he means (cf., e.g., Gal 5:19-21).

16:20 Paul concludes this section of chapter 16 with an assurance and an invocation. The assurance is: *The God of peace will soon crush Satan under your feet*. This description of God as 'the God of peace' is one Paul employs several times in his letters. It reflects the saving activity of God, making peace through the death of his Son (see the commentary on 15:33).

Paul assures his audience that this God 'will soon crush Satan under your feet'.[17] In the OT Satan functions as an accuser of God's people (cf. Job 1–2; Zech 3:1-2). In the Intertestamental literature and the Dead Sea Scrolls the role of the accuser 'crystallized into that of outright adversary to God, leader of the angelic armies opposed to God'.[18] Paul mentions Satan frequently elsewhere in his letters. The Corinthian believers were told to hand the incestuous person over to Satan for the destruction of the flesh (1 Cor 5:5), that husbands and wives should not deprive one another sexually lest Satan tempt them because of their lack of self-control (1 Cor 7:7), that they should reinstate the presumably repentant offender so that Satan might not outwit us (2 Cor 2:11), that Satan masquerades as angel of light (2 Cor 11:14), and that the apostle himself was given a thorn in the flesh, a messenger of Satan, to torment him so as to prevent him from becoming conceited (2 Cor 12:7). He informed the Thessalonian believers that Satan prevented him from revisiting them (1 Thess 2:18) and that 'the coming of the lawless one will be in accordance with how Satan works. He will use all sorts of displays of power through signs and wonders that serve the lie, and all the ways that wickedness deceives those who are perishing' (2 Thess 2:9-10). He informed his colleague, Timothy, that he had handed over Hymenaeus and Alexander to Satan to be taught not to blaspheme (1 Tim 1:20) and that some others had 'already turned away to follow Satan' (1 Tim 5:15). In addition to these references to 'Satan', we find in Paul's letters several references to the devil, referring of course to the same adversary of God's people. In Ephesians believers are warned about giving the devil a foothold (Eph 4:27) and urged to put on the full armor of God so that they can stand against the devil's schemes (Eph 6:11). He informs Timothy that an overseer in the church must 'have a good reputation with outsiders, so that he will not fall into disgrace and into the devil's trap' (1 Tim 3:7), and that the

---

17. Origen writes: 'It seems to me that *Satan* here refers to any spirit which is opposed to God. For in our language, *Satan* means *adversary*' ('Commentary on the Epistle to the Romans' [*ACCSR*, 377]).

18. Dunn, *Romans 9–16*, 905.

Lord's servant must be able to gently instruct those who oppose him in the hope that God will grant them repentance so that they come to their senses and escape the trap of the devil (2 Tim 2:24-26). Paul's point here is that, despite his awareness of Satan's activity in all sorts of ways to wreak havoc among God's people, God will most certainly crush him under their feet.

Putting one's enemies under one's feet is a military metaphor expressing a resounding victory over one's foe (cf. Josh 10:22-26). The hope of Satan being crushed underfoot is found often in Jewish apocalyptic writings (*Jub.* 5:6; 10:7-11; 23:29; *1 Enoch* 10:4; 13:1-2; 1QM 17:5-6; 18:1). Paul speaks of all things being put under *Christ's* feet (1 Cor 15:24-28; Eph 1:20-22), alluding to Psalm 110:1, as do other NT writers (Matt 22:44; Mark 12:36; Luke 20:43; Acts 2:35; Heb 1:13; cf. Heb 2:8; 10:13), but it is only here in 16:20 in the NT that we read that God will soon crush Satan under the feet of *believers*. Paul probably means that if the Roman believers watch out for and keep away from those who cause divisions (16:17), then God will crush Satan under their feet, that is, confound Satan's designs to lead them astray.[19]

After giving them the assurance that the God of peace will soon crush Satan under their feet, Paul invokes a blessing upon his audience: *The grace of our Lord Jesus be with you.* Paul brings all his letters to a close with an invocation like this (cf. 1 Cor 16:23; 2 Cor 13:14; Gal 6:18; Eph 6:24; Phil 4:23; Col 4:18; 1 Thess 5:28; 2 Thess 3:18; 1 Tim 6:21; 2 Tim 4:22; Tit 3:15; Philem 25). To stand in the grace of God is of the essence of salvation — something believers experience in the here and now as a result of their having been justified by faith (see the commentary on 5:1-2).

D. Greetings from Eight of Paul's Associates, 16:21-23

> [21]*Timothy, my co-worker, sends his greetings to you, as do Lucius, Jason and Sosipater, my fellow Jews.*
>
> [22]*I, Tertius, who wrote down this letter, greet you in the Lord.*
>
> [23]*Gaius, whose hospitality I and the whole church here enjoy, sends you his greetings.*
>
> *Erastus, who is the city's director of public works, and our brother Quartus send you their greetings.*

The greetings conveyed here in 16:21-23 appear to be from eight of Paul's associates present when the apostle was completing the dictation of his letter.

---

19. Jewett, *Romans*, 995, remarks: 'The shift from the traditional wording of "placing enemies under his [Christ's] feet" to *hypo tous podos hymōn* ("under your feet") makes it clear that the author of this formula has the action of the current church in mind which will quickly result in a defeat of demonic heresy'. An alternative view is that when Paul speaks of God crushing Satan under the feet of believers, he has in mind the fact they will reign with Christ (2 Tim 2:12) and, associated with Christ, they will judge evil angels (cf. 1 Cor 6:1-3).

16:21 The first of these is from Timothy: *Timothy, my co-worker, sends his greetings to you.* According to the Acts of the Apostles, Timothy was from Lystra.[1] His 'mother was Jewish and a believer, but [his] father was a Greek'. Seeing that he was a Jew, Paul circumcised him before taking him along on his missionary journey so as to avoid problems from Jewish people living in the area (Acts 16:1-3).

Paul calls Timothy here his 'co-worker', a designation he uses for many other colleagues (Priscilla and Aquila, Urbanus, Apollos, Titus, Epaphroditus, Jesus called Justus, Philemon, Mark, Aristarchus, Demas, Luke, as well as many unnamed colleagues; cf. 16:3, 9; 1 Cor 3:6-9; 2 Cor 8:23; Phil 2:25; Col 4:11; Philem 1, 24). Timothy was a companion of Paul during much of his missionary activity. The apostle associates Timothy with himself in the addresses of a number of his letters (2 Cor 1:1; Phil 1:1; Col 1:1; 1 Thess 1:1; 2 Thess 1:1; Philem 1), indicating that he was with him when he wrote those letters, but possibly not when he began Romans.[2] Paul used Timothy as his envoy in relations with the churches of Corinth, Ephesus, Philippi, and Thessalonica (1 Cor 4:17; 16:10; Eph 1:3; Phil 2:19; 1 Thess 3:2, 6), and he was active alongside Paul in preaching the gospel of Christ (2 Cor 1:19). Paul regarded Timothy as his 'true son in the faith' and put him in charge of the church in Ephesus when he himself left for Macedonia (1 Tim 1:2-3).

The second of those sending greetings is *Lucius.* There is a Lucius of Cyrene mentioned in Acts 13:1-3 as one of the prophets and teachers in Antioch whom the Holy Spirit told to set Paul and Barnabas apart for the work to which God was calling them, and who laid hands on them and sent them off (released them). Both Dunn and Jewett think that this is an unlikely identification because someone associated with Paul from the beginning of his mission would have warranted a fuller commendation.[3] Origen says: 'Lucius may have been the same person as Luke the Evangelist, because names are sometimes given in the native form and sometimes in the Greek or Roman one'.[4] Murphy-O'Connor, in similar fashion, notes that '"Lucius" is a variant form of "Luke", the beloved physician who had been with Paul in Ephesus (Col 4:14) and would appear at his side much later during Paul's second visit to Rome (2 Tim 4:11)'.[5] While we cannot be certain about this identification, it is by no means impossible.

1. Strangely, Origen, 'Commentary on the Epistle to the Romans' (*ACCSR*, 378), says that Timothy was from Derbe.
2. Dunn, *Romans 9–16*, 909, comments: 'Conceivably he could have been absent when Paul began to write the letter to Rome (it would take some time to compose such a lengthy and closely argued letter). But the difference from his usual practice is probably sufficiently explained by the fact that Timothy was well enough known as Paul's aide-de-camp in other cases but less known in Rome (Schmidt); in writing to introduce himself, Paul presumably thought it more appropriate to do so only in his own name'. . . .
3. Dunn, *Romans 9–16*, 909; Jewett, *Romans*, 977.
4. 'Commentary on the Epistle to the Romans' (*ACCSR*, 378).
5. Murphy-O'Connor, 'The Pauline Network', 223. Cf. Dunn, *Romans 9–16*, 909.

The third of those whose greetings are conveyed is *Jason*. This is the only mention of Jason in Paul's letters. However, a Jason appears in the Acts 17 account of Paul's brief mission in Thessalonica. He apparently provided Paul with hospitality (Acts 17:5) and was forced to post a bond (Acts 17:9), presumably to guarantee that he would not provide Paul with hospitality again, thus making it virtually impossible for the apostle to return to Thessalonica (cf. 1 Thess 2:18).[6]

The fourth person to send greetings is *Sosipater*. This is the only mention of someone by this name in the NT, though a Sopater from Berea is mentioned in Acts 20:4. It is linguistically possible that these two names refer to the same person.[7] Sopater of Berea was one of those who accompanied Paul when he set out from Ephesus to Macedonia following the riot in that city (Acts 20:1-4). Paul describes Lucius, Jason, and Sosipater as *my fellow Jews* (lit. 'relatives, kinspeople'). Ambrosiaster says: 'Paul calls these people his kinsmen, partly by blood and partly by faith'.[8]

16:22 The fifth of Paul's associates adds his own greeting: *I, Tertius, who wrote down this letter, greet you in the Lord.* Tertius is mentioned as Paul's scribe only in the Letter to the Romans. Paul probably used different scribes in other places. The content of Tertius's greeting suggests that he was also a follower of 'the Lord', and that he adds his greeting here indicates that he had some acquaintance with the believers in Rome. Jewett suggests that Tertius was a member of Phoebe's staff and as such had traveled with her on previous trips to Rome, and that Phoebe placed him at Paul's disposal in Corinth when he was composing his letter to the Romans,[9] though all this is hard to substantiate. The indications are that Paul dictated most of his letters to professional scribes, adding a greeting in his own hand to authenticate his letters (cf. 1 Cor 16:21; Gal 6:11; Col 4:18; 2 Thess 3:17).

Elmer suggests that Tertius may have been much more than a scribe, and that he was partly responsible for giving the letter its present shape. He says: 'Much of the final editing and incorporation of these materials must have even been left to him. Given the length and complexity of Romans, it is inconceivable that Paul could have directly dictated the letter. On another level, Tertius' previous association with the recipients would have been utilized at various stages in drafting the letter so as to make the content both germane and personal to the Roman congregations'.[10] This latter point accords with Jewett's suggestion that Tertius had accompanied

---

6. So, too, Jewett, *Romans*, 977-78, who claims that this identification is supported by 'the listing of Jason's name next to the name of Sosipatros, who is identified in Acts 20:4 as representing the neighboring church at Beroea in traveling with Paul to deliver the Jerusalem offering'.

7. BAGD, *ad loc.*

8. Ambrosiaster, 'Commentary on Paul's Epistles' (*ACCSR*, 378).

9. Jewett, *Romans*, 979.

10. Ian J. Elmer, 'I, Tertius: Secretary or Co-author of Romans', *ABR* 56 (2008) 59.

Phoebe on previous trips to Rome. However, Jewett's suggestion and Elmer's proposal cannot be regarded as any more than interesting speculations. There is no hard evidence that Tertius's knowledge of the Roman churches was any greater than Paul's.

16:23   The sixth of those sending greetings is Gaius: *Gaius, whose hospitality I and the whole church here enjoy, sends you his greetings*. A Gaius is mentioned as one of Paul's traveling companions in Acts 19:29, and a Gaius from Derbe, possibly the same person, is mentioned as his traveling companion in Acts 20:4. Another Gaius is mentioned in 1 Corinthians 1:14 as one of the few people actually baptized by Paul in Corinth. It is most likely that this is the Gaius who sends greetings here in 16:23.[11] Paul describes Gaius as the one 'whose hospitality I and the whole church here enjoy' (lit. 'my host and [host] of the whole church').[12] It would appear that this Gaius was a person of some wealth, having a home of sufficient size to provide hospitality not only to Paul but also to 'the whole church', presumably meaning that he provided the venue for the meeting of the various house churches of Corinth when they all came together.[13]

The seventh and eighth of Paul's associates to send greetings are Erastus and Quartus: *Erastus, who is the city's director of public works, and our brother Quartus send you their greetings*. An Erastus is mentioned in Acts 19:22 as one of Paul's two 'helpers' sent by the apostle to Macedonia when he himself remained in Asia, just prior to the riot that broke out in Ephesus. An Erastus is mentioned again in 2 Timothy 4:20 as the one Paul left in Corinth prior to his second journey to Rome, and it is likely that he is the same person mentioned in Acts 19:22. Whether Paul's traveling companion, Erastus, is the same person whom he describes as 'the city's [Corinth's] director of public works' and whose greetings are sent here in 16:23 to the Roman believers is difficult to say.

The NIV calls Erastus 'the city's director of public works' (lit. 'the

---

11. The Elder addressed 3 John 'to my dear friend Gaius, whom I love in the truth' (3 John 1), but there are no indications that this Gaius is to be identified with either of Paul's associates with that name.

12. The word translated 'host' in this more literal rendering is *xenos*, which as an adjective means 'strange', as a substantive means a 'stranger' or a 'foreign country', and much less frequently, as here, means 'the host', i.e., 'one who extends hospitality and thus treats the stranger as a guest'. Cf. BAGD, *ad loc.*

13. However, Jewett, *Romans*, 980-81, contends: 'That it ['the whole church'] refers to all of the believers in Corinth is also unlikely because of the presence of other house churches and groupings mentioned in the Corinthian correspondence that were too numerous to be accommodated in a single house, and also because the Corinthians would hardly qualify as strangers needing hospitality. The more likely interpretation is that Gaius had the reputation of extending hospitality to Christian travelers from all over the world, an inference supported by most commentaries'. Dunn, *Romans 9–16*, 910-11, disagrees: 'The objection that Gaius' house could hardly have accommodated all the Christians in Corinth (Michel) makes unsubstantiated assumptions about the size of the church in Corinth. A typical well-to-do home of the time could accommodate meetings of 30-40, at best 50 . . . and there is no good reason to suppose that "the whole church" in Corinth was by this time any larger'.

manager of the city'). The word 'manager' *(oikonomos)* is used elsewhere in the NT to denote the manager of a household or an estate (cf. Luke 12:42; 16:1, 3, 8; Gal 4:2). An inscription with the name Erastus was discovered in 1929 east of the stage building of the theatre in Corinth. This inscription reads: 'Erastus for his aedileship laid (the pavement) at his own expense'.[14] It has been argued that the 'aedile' of the inscription is equivalent to 'the manager of the city' in 16:23, and that therefore the Erastus of the inscription and the Erastus of 16:23 are the same person. If this is the case, we have firm evidence that a person of wealth and high standing in Corinthian society was a member of the church. However, this conclusion has been the subject of recent debate (see 'Additional Note: Erastus of 16:23 and the Erastus of the Inscription', below).

'Our brother Quartus', the eighth of those sending greetings, is mentioned only here in the NT and, apart from his association with Paul implied here in 16:23, we know nothing of him. Why Paul should designate only Quartus as 'our brother', meaning a fellow believer, when all the others could be similarly described is not known. Perhaps, because each of the other seven whose greetings are conveyed have some description added to their name, Paul felt it necessary to add something to Quartus's name as well, choosing to describe him simply as 'our brother'.[15]

It will be noted that the NIV, and other English translations as well as Greek editions of the NT, omit verse 24 ('May the grace of our Lord Jesus Christ be with all of you. Amen'). This is so because it is omitted by earlier and better Greek manuscripts. Origen comments: 'Marcion, who interpolated both the Gospels and the epistles, deleted this passage [16:24] from the text, and not only this but everything [after 14:25] as well. In other manuscripts not edited by Marcion we find this passage in different places. Some have it immediately after [14:25], and others have it here, at the end of the epistle'.[16]

ADDITIONAL NOTE: THE ERASTUS OF 16:23 AND THE ERASTUS OF THE INSCRIPTION

Gill holds that there were two aediles in Corinth who were 'responsible for the maintenance of public streets and buildings, which included the market places they managed the revenues derived from such places, and served as

---

14. *Erastus pro aedilit[at]e s(ua) p(ecunia) stravit* ([ ] indicates lost text; ( ) indicates an expansion of Latin abbreviations). Cf. David W. J. Gill, 'Erastus the Aedile', *TynBul* 40 (1989) 293-94.

15. Jewett, *Romans,* 984, suggests that '"and his brother Quartus [sends greetings]", referring to Quartus as the brother of Erastus, eliminates this impression of an afterthought, because it was natural to mention the office held by Erastus before referring to his sibling'.

16. 'Commentary on the Epistle to the Romans' *(ACCSR,* 380).

judges'.[17] If Erastus is to be identified with the aedile of the inscription, he would have been a wealthy person of high standing in Corinthian society. Murphy-O'Connor, who assumes this identification, observes: 'In order to hold municipal office, Erastus (Rom 16:3) must have been a Roman citizen. How high he ranked in the city hierarchy at this point in his career is impossible to say, but an inscription shows that he went on to become an aedile, which was just one step below the two ruling magistrates. He must have rationalized his presence at the obligatory pagan sacrifices associated with municipal meetings by reminding himself that an idol has no real existence (1 Cor 8:4)'.[18] Gill is more cautious in identifying Erastus of 16:13 with the aedile of the inscription. He sums up his examination of the evidence as follows:

> How are we to interpret this epigraphic evidence? Some . . . have taken the view that an *oikonomos* was a slave, which would not allow a link with Erastus the aedile. However, this does not explain why Paul draws attention to this man's standing in society, something he rarely does. The context of the epistle to the Romans may be of help here. In it Paul commanded: 'Do the good (deed) and you shall have praise from the (civil) authority'. Does Paul emphasise the status of Erastus because here is a Christian official who has indeed become a benefactor of his city, possibly in his capacity as aedile? . . . The evidence does not allow us to be certain about the link between the two Erasti, but at the very least it is clear that Paul is here reminding Christians to take an active role in the running of the city just like Erastus the *oikonomos*.[19]

Meggitt raises a number of objections to the identification of Erastus the manager of the city of 16:23 with Erastus the aedile of the inscription: (i) the dating of the inscription to the middle of the first century A.D. is more problematic than often maintained; (ii) while the expression *oikonomos tēs poleōs* ('manager of the city') may denote an official of high standing like an aedile, it can also refer to low-ranking public slaves, those carrying out menial tasks; (iii) the name Erastus itself is far less rare than has been assumed. Meggitt claims to have 'discovered 55 examples of the use of the Latin cognomen Erastus and 23 of the Greek *Erastos*, making it, in fact, a relatively common name for our period'.[20] Meggitt's conclusion is as follows:

> We can conclude therefore that, despite the current fashion to the contrary, Erastus' socio-economic situation was most likely indistinguishable from that of his fellow believers. He cannot be used as evidence of the spread of the new faith amongst the socially powerful of the

17. David W. J. Gill, 'Erastus the Aedile', *TynBul* 40 (1989) 294.
18. Murphy-O'Connor, 'The Pauline Network', 223.
19. Gill, 'Erastus the Aedile', 300.
20. Justin J. Meggitt, 'The Social Status of Erastus (Rom. 16:23)', *NovT* 38 (1996) 220-22.

Principate. He is incapable of bearing the weight of the speculative reconstructions that have been placed upon his shoulders by "new Consensus" scholars.[21]

Clarke notes the discovery in 1960 of another Erastus inscription immediately north of the ancient city centre of Corinth, and thought to date from the second century A.D., thus excluding any identification of this Erastus with the Erastus of 16:23.[22] However, Clarke, citing Hemer, draws attention to how infrequently the cognomen Erastus is found in Hellenistic Greek, and comments in regard to the possible identification of the Erastus the *oikonomos* of 16:23 with the Erasti of the later and earlier inscriptions as follows: 'There are significant grounds for exclusion in the case of the later inscription. With regard to the first century Corinthian aedile, however, the grounds for exclusion are not certain, and identification should remain therefore a significant possibility. It may indeed be the case that in the Corinthian Pauline community there was a prominent civic leader and wealthy benefactor'.[23]

E. Concluding Doxology, 16:25-27

> [25]*Now to him who is able to establish you in accordance with my gospel, the message I proclaim about Jesus Christ, in keeping with the revelation of the mystery hidden for long ages past,* [26]*but now revealed and made known through the prophetic writings by the command of the eternal God, so that all the Gentiles might come to the obedience that comes from faith —* [27]*to the only wise God be glory forever through Jesus Christ! Amen.*

While the manuscript evidence for the location of this doxology in its traditional position at the end of chapter 16 is quite strong, in a few manuscripts it is found sometimes at the end of chapter 14 or chapter 15, or at the end of both chapters 14 and 16, while others omit it altogether. Because of this some scholars regard the doxology as an interpolation,[1] reminiscent of post-Pauline development, and therefore not an original part of Paul's letter to the Romans.[2] In the commentary below the doxology is treated as an original part of Paul's letter to the Romans and as appropriate in its present location because of the impressive textual support in favor of this location.[3]

---

21. Meggitt, 'The Social Status of Erastus (Rom. 16:23)', 223.
22. Andrew D. Clarke, 'Another Corinthian Erastus Inscription', *TynBul* 42 (1991) 146-48, 150-151.
23. Clarke, 'Another Corinthian Erastus Inscription', 151.
1. E.g., Jewett, *Romans*, 998-1002.
2. So, e.g., Byrne, *Romans*, 461-62.
3. For a full discussion of the textual evidence see Metzger, ed., *A Textual Commentary*, 470-73, 476-77.

Paul's doxology begins: *Now to him who is able to establish you in accordance with my gospel, the message I proclaim about Jesus Christ.* God is described as the one who is able to establish (NRSV: 'to strengthen') believers,
and this he does, Paul says, 'in accordance with my gospel'. At the beginning of his letter Paul said he longed to see the Roman believers in order to
share some spiritual gift with them 'to make you strong' (1:11) and that he
was eager to preach the gospel to them (1:15). The spiritual gift he wanted
to share was most likely an explanation of the gospel, and through this he
hoped to be an agent through whom God would strengthen the believers in
Rome.[4]

Paul says that his gospel and the proclamation of Jesus Christ are *in
keeping with the revelation of the mystery hidden for long ages past, but now revealed and made known through the prophetic writings by the command of the
eternal God.*[5] Paul speaks often of the gospel as a mystery 'hidden for long
ages past but now revealed', which is revealed to him and made known
through the proclamation of the gospel (cf. 1 Cor 2:1, 7; Eph 1:9; 3:3-4, 9;
6:19; Col 1:26; 4:3). But here he adds that it is revealed 'and *made known
through the prophetic writings* by the command of the eternal God' (italics
added). Some scholars who see the doxology as a later post- or non-Pauline
addition regard 'the prophetic writings' as a reference to Christian Scriptures, perhaps including Paul's own letters.[6] However, if the doxology is regarded as an authentic part of Romans, the reference to the prophetic writings will be to the OT Scriptures. In 1:1-2 Paul describes the gospel as
something God 'promised beforehand through his prophets in the Holy
Scriptures'. Perhaps we could say that as the gospel is preached God opens
people's eyes, especially Jewish eyes, to see that the OT Scriptures testify to
Christ (cf. 2 Cor 3:14-18; Luke 24:25-27, 44-47).

The purpose of the revelation of the mystery of the gospel, Paul
states, was *so that all the Gentiles might come to the obedience that comes from
faith.* When Paul began this letter, he explained that he had received grace
and apostleship 'to call people from among all the Gentiles to the obedi-

---

4. Here Paul says that God strengthens believers by the proclamation of the gospel of
Jesus Christ, whereas in Eph 3:16 he prays that God may 'strengthen' (*krataiōthēnai*) his audience 'with power through his Spirit'. Putting these things together, we may say that it is
both by the gospel of Christ and through his Spirit that God effects the strengthening of
those who believe.

5. Chrysostom remarks: 'This secret was contained in the law. Indeed, it is what the
law was all about. We cannot ask why it should be disclosed now. For to do this would be to
call God to account. We ought not to behave like busybodies but instead be content with
what we have been given' ('Homilies on Romans 27' [*ACCSR*, 381]).

6. Byrne, *Romans*, 463, who believes that the doxology is inauthentic, offers a different interpretation of the prophetic writings through which the mystery has been revealed:
'Taking into account the time when the doxology is likely to have been written, the more
likely reference is to later writings, considered "prophetic" in the sense of being filled with
revelatory power. These could include New Testament texts such as the letters of Paul (cf.
2 Pet 3:1b-16) and, specifically, Romans itself'.

ence that comes from faith' (1:5). Towards the end of the letter he says that
he won't boast except of what Christ has accomplished through him 'in
leading the Gentiles to obey God' (15:18), and in 16:19 he tells his audience
that he rejoices because 'everyone has heard about your obedience'. The
mystery that has been revealed clearly now is that Gentiles as well as Jews
should come to 'the obedience that comes from faith'. What Paul means by
'the obedience that comes from faith' is primarily the obedience that consists in faith in the gospel (see the discussion in the commentary on 1:5).

The doxology concludes: *to the only wise God be glory forever through Jesus Christ! Amen.* Paul's doxology is addressed to 'the only wise God'.[7] The
apostle extols God's wisdom in 11:33: 'O the depth of the riches and wisdom and knowledge of God! How unsearchable his judgments, and his
paths beyond tracing out!' The wisdom of God, Paul says, was once secret
and hidden but is now being made known in its rich variety through the
church (1 Cor 2:7; Eph 3:10). To believers, Paul adds, Christ is the wisdom
of God (1 Cor 1:24, 30), for in him 'are hidden all the treasures of wisdom
and knowledge' (Col 2:3). For Paul the wisdom of God determines the way
people will come to know him — not through human wisdom but through
the preaching of the cross of Christ (1 Cor 1:21-24; 2:6-7). Also, it is God's
intention that 'through the church, the manifold wisdom of God should be
made known to the rulers and authorities in the heavenly realms' (Eph
3:10), that is, the manifold wisdom of God in the mystery of the gospel now
revealed.

In his doxology, Paul ascribes glory to God. To glorify God, Paul believed, should be the aim of every believer. We can gain some understanding of what he understands is involved in giving glory to God from the following: He speaks of Abraham giving glory to God by his unwavering
faith (4:20). He urges his Roman audience to bring praise to God by accepting one another (15:7). He encourages the Corinthian believers to glorify
God in whatever they do (1 Cor 10:31), and reminds them that when they
add their 'Amen' to the promises of God it brings glory to God (2 Cor 1:20).
Paul endures the hardships and suffering of his ministry for the Corinthian
believers' benefit so that, as God's grace reaches more and more people,
'thanksgiving will overflow to the glory of God' (2 Cor 4:15). The apostle
prays that the love of his Philippian converts may abound in knowledge
and insight and be filled with righteousness to the glory of God (Phil 1:9-
11). In Philippians 4:20 and 1 Timothy 1:17 Paul ascribes glory to God, as he
does here in 16:27.

---

7. Chrysostom comments: 'Do not think that Paul said this in disparagement of the
Son. For if all the things whereby his wisdom was made apparent were done by Christ and
nothing was done without him, it is quite plain that the Son is equal to the Father in wisdom
also. The word *only* is used in order to contrast God with every created being' ('Homilies on
Romans 27' [*ACCSR*, 381]). Theodoret of Cyrrhus says: 'If the heretics try to use this [verse]
to prove that Christ is not God, it should be remembered that Christ not only is called wise,
he is even called *Wisdom*' ('Interpretation of the Letter to the Romans' [*ACCSR*, 381]).

Index of Subjects

Index of Modern Authors

Index of Scriptural References

6:7	133	24:25-27	588	2:37	272
6:22	40	24:36	55	2:43	540
6:27	480, 484	24:44-47	588	2:45	306
6:27-28	484	24:46-48	53	2:46	530
6:28	481, 483			3:13	99, 531
6:35	484	**John**		3:25	372
7:11-17	265	1:18	92	3:25-26	532
7:38	572	3:36	90, 127	4:10	89
7:45	572	5:21	216	4:16	89
8:35	468	5:28-29	124	4:24	530
8:40-42	265	5:45	133	4:28	356
8:49-56	265	6:44	392	4:30	540
10:25-37	501	6:46	92	5:4	306
10:27	501	6:63	216	5:12	530, 540
10:40	351	7:42	43	5:37	494
11:22	364	8:6	133	6:8	540
11:42	192	8:34	281	7:7	60
12:8-9	410	8:46	326, 327	7:8	443
12:11	133	10:16	53	7:32	531
12:21	122	11:1-44	265	7:33	241
12:42	585	12:5	306	7:38	160
14:9	483	12:38	542	7:42	60
14:13	522	12:42-43	157	7:46	203
14:21	522	13:17	129	7:57	530
15:20	572	16:2	480	7:57–8:1	399
16:1	585	16:2-3	483	7:60	486
16:3	585	16:8	327	8:2-3	399
16:8	585	16:9	327	8:6	530
18:13	189	16:33	364	8:26-35	542
18:38-39	43	18:3	268	9:1-2	399
20:20	99	18:14	234	9:15-17	429
20:25	492, 499	18:15	89	9:36-42	265
20:37	531	18:16	89	9:42	89
20:41-42	43	19:11	493	10:34	128
20:44	43	20:19	55	10:38	540
20:43	581	20:19-23	44	10:42	45
20:46	157	20:21	55	11:29	45
21:12	480	20:26	55	12:2	497
21:14	133			12:20	530
21:23	90	**Acts**		12:23	219
21:28	183	1:1-2	540	13:1-3	541, 582
22:22	45	1:6-8	53	13:2	40
22:31-32	230	1:8	540	13:4-5	68
22:37	542	1:14	530	13:14-44	68
22:47	572	1:19	89	13:14-46	52
22:48	572	1:25	147	13:34	43
23:2	133	2:14	89	13:38	89, 171
23:10	133	2:17-18	231	13:42-49	428
23:14	133	2:22	540	13:45	421
23:15	107	2:23	45	13:46-47	69
23:34	486	2:32-36	47	13:47	148
23:47	326	2:35	581	14:1	52, 68
23:49	89	2:36	47	14:2	127

Index of Extrabiblical Literature